SIGLA AND SYMBOLS

The sigla on the facing page are here arrang̶e̶d̶

ALEX: Alexander, 1951

ARD: ARD1 & ARD2

ARD1: Moorman, 1912

ARD2: Pafford, 1963

(AYS): AYS1 & AYS2

(AYS1, 2): Ayscough, 1784, 1790

BEV: BEV3 & BEV4

BEV3, 4: Bevington, 1980, 1988

(BLAIR): Blair, 1753

BUL: Bullen, 1905

CAM: CAM1 & CAM3

CAM1: Clark, Glover, & Wright, 1863

(CAM2): Wright, 1891

CAM3: Wilson, 1931

CAP: Capell, 1768

(CAPN): Capell, *Notes*, 1783

CLN2: Bethell, 1956

COL: COL1, COL2, COL3, & COL4

COL1, 2, 3, 4: Collier, 1842, 1853, 1858, 1875

(COLNE): Collier, *Notes*, 1853

DEL: DEL2 & DEL4

DEL2, 4: Delius, 1860, 1872

(DODD): Dodd, *Beauties*, 1780

DYCE: DYCE1 & DYCE2

DYCE1, 2, (3): Dyce, 1857, 1864, 1875

EVNS: Evans, 1974

Ff: F1, F2, F3, & F4

F1, 2, 3, 4: Folios 1623, 1632, 1663-4, 1685

(GENT): Gentleman, 1774

GLO: Clark & Wright, 1864

HAL: Halliwell, 1859

HAN: HAN1 & HAN2

HAN1, 2, (3): Hanmer, 1743, 1745, 1770

(HARN): Harness, 1825

HUD: HUD1 & HUD2

HUD1, 2: Hudson, 1852, 1880

IRV: Irving & Marshall, 1890

JOHN: JOHN1 & JOHN2

JOHN1, 2: Johnson, 1765, 1765

(K&R): Kittredge-Rib̶m̶... 1967

(KEM): KEM1 & KEM2

(KEM1, 2): Kemble, 1802, 1811

KIT1: Kittredge, 1936

KNT: KNT1, KNT2, & KNT3

KNT1, 2, 3: Knight, 1841, 1842, 1867

KTLY: Keightley, 1864

(m1733FL4): Anon., 1733?-

(m1768FL): Anon., c. 1790

(m1773FL3): Anon., 1778?-

(m1778BL): Anon., -1785

(m1790aFL): Anon., 1790-

(m1790bFL): Anon., 1790-

(m1793BOD): Steevens et al., 1793-1803?

(m1793FL): Anon., 1793-

MAL: Malone, 1790

(mBRAE): Brae, 1877

(mCAL): Caldecott, 1813-33

(mCAP2): Capell, 1754

(mCOL1, 2, 3): Collier, c. 1840, c. 1850, 1858-78?

(mCOLE): Coleridge, c. 1834

(mF1H): Anon., -1650?

(mFLV.a.80): Evans, 1655-9

(mF1FL10): Anon., 1700-

(mF2FL21): Anon., 1754-65

(mF2FL27): Anon., c. 1750

(mF2FL48): Anon., -1747

(mF4TCC): Anon., 1733?-

(mGREY): Grey, 1747-66

(mHAN): Hanmer, 1735-9

(mLET): Lettsom, 1840-65

(mLONG): Long, -1733?

(mLUSH): Lushington, c. 1754

(mMAL1): Malone, 1773-90

(mMAL2): Malone, 1777-80

(mPER): Perring, 1885-1920?

(mPOPE): Pope, -1723

(mSING): Anon., 1632-1856

(mSTAU): Staunton, 1864-74

(mTAY): Taylor, c. 1850

(mTBY1, 2, 3, 4): Thirlby, 1709-25, 1725-33?, 1733-47?, 1747-53

...): Theobald, -1729?

(mTOL): Tollet, 1740-79

(mTOOK): Tooke, 1790-1812

(mTYR): Tyrwhitt, -1767

(MUN): Munro, 1957

(mWARB): Warburton, 1747-79

(mWRAY): Wray, 1891-3?

(N&H): Neilson-Hill, 1942

NLSN: Neilson, 1906

OXF: OXF1 & OXF2

OXF1: Craig, [1891]

OXF2: Wells, 1986

PEL1: Maxwell, 1956

(PEL2): Maxwell, 1969

(PEN1): Harrison, 1947

PEN2: Schanzer, 1969

POPE: POPE1 & POPE2

POPE1, 2: Pope, 1725, 1728

RANN: Rann, 1787

(RID): Ridley, 1935

(RLTR): Chambers, [1907]

ROWE: ROWE1, ROWE2, & ROWE3

ROWE1, 2, 3: Rowe, 1709, 1709, 1714

SIG: Kermode, 1963

SING: SING1 & SING2

SING1, 2: Singer, 1826, 1856

SIS: Sisson, 1954

STAU: Staunton, 1859

THEO: THEO1, THEO2, & THEO4

THEO1, 2, (3), 4: Theobald, 1733, 1740, 1752, 1757

v1773, v1778: Johnson & Steevens

v1785: Johnson, Steevens, & Reed

v1793: Steevens & Reed

v1803, v1813: Reed

v1821: Boswell

(v1898): Furness

(VALPY): Valpy, 1833

WARB: Warburton, 1747

WH: WH1 & WH2

WH1, 2: White, 1857, 1883

A New Variorum Edition of Shakespeare

Founded by Horace Howard Furness (1833–1912),
continued by Horace Howard Furness, Jr. (1865–1930),
and now issued under the sponsorship of
The Modern Language Association of America

Richard Knowles and Paul Werstine
General Editors

A New Variorum Edition of Shakespeare

THE WINTER'S TALE

Edited by

ROBERT KEAN TURNER
VIRGINIA WESTLING HAAS

with

ROBERT A. JONES
ANDREW J. SABOL
PATRICIA E. TATSPAUGH

The Modern Language Association of America

For information about obtaining permission to reprint material from MLA book
publications, send your request by mail (see address below),
e-mail (permissions@mla.org), or fax (646-458-0030).

Library of Congress Cataloging-in-Publication Data

Shakespeare, William, 1564–1616.
    The winter's tale / edited by Robert Kean Turner, Virginia Westling Haas; with
Robert A. Jones, Andrew J. Sabol, Patricia E. Tatspaugh.
        p.   cm. — (A new variorum edition of Shakespeare)
    Includes bibliographical references and index.
    ISBN 0-87352-294-X (alk. paper)
    1. Fathers and daughters — Drama. 2. Kings and rulers — Drama. 3. Married
people — Drama. 4. Sicily (Italy) — Drama. 5. Castaways — Drama. I. Turner, Robert
Kean, 1926 – II. Haas, Virginia Westling, 1935 – III. Jones, Robert A. IV. Sabol,
Andrew J. V. Tatspaugh, Patricia Elizabeth, 1938 – VI. Modern Language Association
of America. VII. Title.
    PR2839.A2T87 2004
    822.3'3 — dc22   2003021749

Published by The Modern Language Association of America
26 Broadway, New York, New York 10004-1789
www.mla.org

CONTENTS

Contents

PREFACE

The first New Variorum edition of *The Winter's Tale*, the work of Horace Howard Furness, appeared in 1898. The present edition retraces Furness's but does not replace it, for often the more recent scholarship and criticism reported here could be accommodated only by reducing Furness's ampler treatment of the early material. The reader who finds this book useful is urged to consult Furness's as well to obtain a fuller account of many subjects.

Patricia Tatspaugh wrote the section of this edition on performances and Andrew Sabol that on music. Robert Jones handled criticism in German. Although Virginia Haas worked primarily on the sections on criticism and the text on the stage, she had a hand throughout. Except for specific contributions acknowledged in their place, Robert Turner did the rest. Much of the work was done at the University of Wisconsin – Milwaukee, having been underwritten by its College of Letters and Science (William F. Halloran, dean, and Jessica R. Wirth, associate dean). The Research Committee of the university's Graduate School provided generous support, as did its Golda Meir Library (William F. Roselle and Peter Watson-Boone, library directors), which created and fostered a Shakespeare collection rivaled by few universities in the United States and by hardly any recently established ones. The Memorial Library of the University of Wisconsin – Madison (Kenneth L. Frazier, director of libraries) maintains a similarly distinguished collection for the use of the general editors of the Variorum series. The support of both libraries has been invaluable.

Financial aid for this edition was provided by the National Endowment for the Humanities, the Folger Shakespeare Library, the John Simon Guggenheim Memorial Foundation, the American Philosophical Society, the American Council of Learned Societies, the Newberry Library Renaissance Consortium, and the Modern Language Association of America (Phyllis Franklin, executive director). Libraries at which research was done include the Folger Shakespeare Library; the Furness Memorial Library of the University of Pennsylvania; the New York Public Library; the British Library; the Bodleian Library; the Cambridge University Library; the Libraries of the Shakespeare Centre, Trinity College and Pembroke College, Cambridge; the University of

London; the Research Services Department of the Theatre Museum (Victoria and Albert Museum); the Library of the Garrick Club; and the Hampden Booth Theatre Library. Their hospitality is greatly appreciated. The Beinecke Library, Yale University Library, and the Henry E. Huntington Library supplied information, and among the individuals who helped in various ways are Walter S. Achtert, Stephen Booth, Fredson Bowers, Gerry Flynn, Philip Gaskell, Joseph Gibaldi, Charlton Hinman, Cyrus Hoy, Taro Kusanagi, James G. McManaway, Barbara A. Mowat, Marvin Spevack, Judith Cook Svenheim, Roy Swanson, John Velz, George Walton Williams, and George T. Wright. I especially want to thank Patricia Rieselbach and James P. Hammersmith for their excellent assistance. Richard Knowles, the general editor of the New Variorum Shakespeare, made innumerable improvements, caught many mistakes, contributed his own critical ideas and evaluations, and in general shaped this edition much for the better. More recently, Paul Werstine, his fellow general editor, began to do the same. Virginia Haas and I are grateful to them both. We are also obliged to Susan Joseph, our copy editor, whose sharp eye saved us from error and sharp mind gave rise to a number of changes for the better.

Robert Kean Turner

PLAN OF THE WORK

This edition of *The Winter's Tale* has four main parts: a text of the play reprinted with little change from that of the first edition in *Mr. William Shakespeares Comedies, Histories, & Tragedies*, the Folio of 1623 (F1); textual notes of significant departures from the F1 text in eighty-six editions of the play ranging in date from 1632 to 1988; commentary on the meaning or the artistry of the text drawn from editions, dictionaries, and critical works; and a collection of more general textual, historical, critical, and theatrical information about the play.

The text printed here derives from photocopies of one of the copies of F1 in the Folger Shakespeare Library. The transcript of these prints was compared with the *WT* texts of several other Folger copies, Sidney Lee's *Shakespeares Comedies, Histories, & Tragedies being a Reproduction in Facsimile of the First Folio Edition* (Oxford, 1902), and Charlton Hinman's *The Norton Facsimile: The First Folio of Shakespeare* (New York, 1968), the object being to make the Variorum text as accurate as possible. No F1 press variants affecting *WT* readings have as yet been found (see p. 601). Silent alterations of the F1 text include the representation of roman long *s* by *s*; the printing of logotypes (at lines 1672 and 2146) and ligatures (e.g., roman *ss* and *st*) as two letters; the suppression or reduction of framing rules, display types, ornaments, printing space types, quads, and packing; the alignment of irregular letters and normalization of spacing (except in some instances noted below); the positioning of marginal stage directions to the right regardless of their placement in the F1 line; and the correction of wrong-font types, including alteration of italic punctuation marks to roman in a roman context and vice versa. Other errors are corrected when there is no doubt what the true reading should be. In a few instances missing punctuation is supplied, words turned up or down by F1 because the full line of text exceeded the measure of the column are printed in one line, and conventional closing punctuation is substituted for other marks at the end of completed speeches where no suspension seems intended. A list of these changes appears on pages 567–9. Also listed there are spellings probably adopted by F1 for justification. The line numbers of the text are the Through Line Numbers introduced by Charlton Hinman in *The Norton Facsimile: The First Folio of Shakespeare* (New York, 1968), but the headlines include, as well, the act-scene-line numbers of the 1974 Riverside *WT*, edited by G. Blakemore Evans. Riverside act and scene divisions are indicated by boldface numerals in the right margin. Also in the right margins, signature and column indicators of the beginning of each Folio column appear in parentheses.

The textual notes record alterations in the meaning or meter of the F1 text found in the editions collated; alteration of meaning was decided by the variant's receiving separate listing in the *Oxford English Dictionary* and a different definition. Modernizations of form are ignored. So are misprints unless the misprint creates an English word or was taken for a word. Conjectural emendations are included in the textual notes if the reading has been adopted by one of the editions collated; others are in the list of unadopted conjectures (pp. 569–85). Alterations in punctuation and capitalization are ignored unless the alteration creates a different meaning. Stage directions added or altered in later editions appear only if the action implied by F1 is affected in a major way.

Variant lining affecting meter — verse as prose, prose as verse, verse as different verse — is noted. The elision or expansion of syllables is recorded only if the alteration shifts the word's accent or alters the number of feet in a verse line. When words that may be elided must be elided to make regular verse (e.g., *in the* to one-syllable *i'th*) it is assumed that elision was intended and no note is provided. The expression *one verse line* indicates that part lines of verse shared by speakers have been arranged to indicate that taken together they constitute a pentameter. If the subject of the note is variant punctuation only, a word in the lemma that is repeated in the variant is represented there by a swung dash ($\sim$), and the absence of punctuation is indicated by an inferior caret ($_\wedge$). Editions are represented by the sigla listed on pages xiii–xviii and on the endpapers of this book.

The basic form of the textual note may be illustrated by

647 ha's] hath ROWE1-JOHN2, v1773-MAL

which records the fact that in line 647 — "He ha's discouer'd my Designe, and I" — Rowe's editions of 1709 and editions following through Johnson's second edition of 1765 for "ha's" in the Variorum text read "hath." Capell's edition of 1768 reads "has," the equivalent of "ha's," and so is represented by an honorable absence, but the variorum edition of 1773 and those editions following through Malone's of 1790 revert to "hath." The variorum edition of 1793 restores the F1 reading and is followed by all other collated editions.

Another type of textual note employs the formula *etc.* For example:

30 hath been] F1, BUL, NLSN, SIS, CLN2, PEN2+; have been so COL2, COL3, KTLY; have been F2 *etc.*

Here the editions that read with the Variorum text (F1, BUL, NLSN, SIS, CLN2, PEN2, and all later editions collated) appear first, then those that read "have been so," then those that read "have been," F2 being the first to do so, and *etc.* means "and all other editions collated but not already accounted for."

Still another type of note makes use of family sigla:

32 Vast] Vast Sea F2-POPE2, HAN, CAP

HAN here represents both of Hanmer's editions (1743 and 1745) that were collated, but not Hanmer's edition of 1770, which was only quoted from occasionally. CAP also looks like a family siglum and it is, but the family has but a single member, Capell's 1768 edition. Occasionally the family siglum will not be based on the editor's name; CAM, for example, indicates the Cambridge editions of 1863 (CAM1) and 1931 (CAM3). In this note the hyphen, as one might expect, represents "through." Elsewhere a minus sign is used to indicate exclusion:

32 Vast] Vast Sea F2-POPE2 (−F4), HAN, CAP

means that F4 reads not "Vast Sea" but "Vast," as does the lemma. Had F4 read "Huge Sea" the note would have been

32 Vast] Vast Sea F2, F3, POPE, HAN, CAP; Huge Sea F4

Although most variant readings originate in editions, some are found in other sources:

34 Loues] love mTBY3 *conj.*, HAN, DYCE2, HUD2, KIT1

Here the variant originates in Styan Thirlby's manuscript notes in a volume of Theobald's edition of 1733 (see p. xvi), where it is considered a conjecture because it does not appear in a published edition. The reading does appear in Hanmer's edition of 1743 (and it also occurs in his second edition of 1745 and in three later editions). The note does not mean, however, that Hanmer necessarily found the reading in Thirlby's notes or that Dyce found it there or in one of Hanmer's editions. Here and in similar notes the variant is given in the form in which it was first printed rather than in the sometimes eccentric form of its manuscript source.

Added stage directions calling for action clearly implied by the text are not recorded, nor are those calling in different words for essentially the same action as the stage direction of the text. The abbreviation *subst.* indicates that although their language differs, the collated stage directions have the same significance. For example:

198 *Wipes the boy's face.* HAN, CAP, CAM3 (*subst.*)

There is no equivalent of Hanmer's stage direction in F1; it is derived from Leontes's

> Why that's my Bawcock: what? has't smutch'd thy Nose?
> They say it is a Coppy out of mine. Come Captaine,
> We must be neat; not neat, but cleanly, Captaine:

Capell's version of the stage direction is *pulling the Boy to him, and wiping him*; Wilson's (CAM3) is nearly identical to Hanmer's. The note has no lemma because no direction appears in F1.

Beneath the textual notes is commentary on specific words or passages in the text. The glosses and explanatory notes of many editions of *WT* are quoted there, and definitions are drawn from works of reference and dictionaries, especially the *Oxford English Dictionary* but also dictionaries nearer Shakespeare's time such as John Minsheu's *Ductor in Linguas, The Guide into Tongues* (1617) and Henry Cockeram's *English Dictionarie* (1623), as well as Samuel Johnson's *Dictionary of the English Language* (1755). Foreign language dictionaries — John Florio's English-Italian *Queen Anna's New World of Words* (1611), for example — are sometimes used, as are specialized glossaries such as Henry Manwayring's *Sea-mans Dictionary* (1644), B. E.'s *Dictionary of the Terms . . . of the Canting Crew* (1699), and Edward Sugden's *Topographical Dictionary* (1925). Alexander Schmidt's *Shakespeare-Lexicon* and C. T. Onions's *Shakespeare Glossary* are the sources of many definitions, and E. A. Abbott's *Shakespearian Grammar* and Wilhelm Franz's *Die Sprache Shakespeares* are frequently alluded to. In general, the first comment to be made is quoted, but if a later one is clearer, more accurate, or more explicit, it appears instead. In these notes and elsewhere square brackets within quotations enclose corrections or comments made by the editors of this volume; the square brackets of the quotations themselves have been transformed to angle brackets (< >). The spelling and punctuation of the works cited are retained except that if the beginning or the end of a sentence has been omitted but a complete sentence remains, it is provided with a beginning capital or a final period. Initial capitals are also supplied for direct discourse. No notes are printed entirely in italics even though the source may have done so.

The remainder of the edition begins with a list of the F1 readings emended in the present text. Following that is another collection, a listing of proposed substantive emendations never adopted in the editions of *WT* collated. The subsequent sections are more general. Included are an essay on the text of the play — its authenticity, the printing of the F1 version, the scribal copy from which the compositors worked, and the copy from which the scribe worked and his fidelity to it. A second essay considers the date of the play's composition; a third examines the play's sources, primarily Robert Greene's *Pandosto* but also minor sources and analogues. Imitations are also mentioned. Following is a selection of the literary criticism of the play and then a stage history that includes a record of how the text has been altered for the theater, an account of important performances, and a discussion of the actors who have taken major roles, as well as of directors responsible for significant interpretations. Finally, there is an account of the songs and dances that embellish the play's dialogue and action.

The versions of *WT* published in the following editions were collated for substantive differences from F1. Each title is preceded by the siglum that identifies the edition in the textual notes and other textual apparatus. The place of publication of these and all other books mentioned throughout the edition is London unless otherwise specified.

F2	*Mr. William Shakespeares Comedies, Histories, and Tragedies. . . . The second Impression.*	1632
F3	*Mr. William Shakespear's Comedies, Histories, and Tragedies. . . . The third Impression.*	1663–4
F4	*Mr. William Shakespear's Comedies, Histories, and Tragedies. . . . The Fourth Edition.*	1685
ROWE1	NICHOLAS ROWE. *Works.* 6 vols. 1709. Vol. 2.	1709
ROWE2	NICHOLAS ROWE. *Works.* 6 vols. 1709. Vol. 2.	1709
ROWE3	NICHOLAS ROWE. *Works.* 8 vols. 1714. Vol. 3.	1714
POPE1	ALEXANDER POPE. *Works.* 6 vols. 1725. Vol. 2.	1725
POPE2	ALEXANDER POPE. *Works.* 8 vols. 1728. Vol. 3.	1728
THEO1	LEWIS THEOBALD. *Works.* 7 vols. 1733. Vol. 3.	1733
THEO2	LEWIS THEOBALD. *Works.* 8 vols. 1740. Vol. 3.	1740
HAN1	THOMAS HANMER. *Works.* 6 vols. Oxford, 1743–4. Vol. 2.	1743
HAN2	THOMAS HANMER. *Works.* 6 vols. 1745. Vol. 2.	1745
WARB	WILLIAM WARBURTON. *Works.* 8 vols. 1747. Vol. 3.	1747
THEO4	LEWIS THEOBALD. *Works.* 8 vols. 1757. Vol. 3.	1757
JOHN1	SAMUEL JOHNSON. *Plays.* 8 vols. Printed for J. and R. Tonson, C. Corbet . . . , 1765. Vol. 2.	1765
JOHN2	SAMUEL JOHNSON. *Plays.* 8 vols. Printed for J. and R. Tonson, H. Woodfall . . . , 1765. Vol. 2.	1765
CAP	EDWARD CAPELL. *Comedies, Histories, & Tragedies.* 10 vols. [1768.] Vol. 4.	1768
v1773	SAMUEL JOHNSON & GEORGE STEEVENS. *Plays.* 10 vols. 1773. Vol. 4.	1773
v1778	SAMUEL JOHNSON & GEORGE STEEVENS. *Plays.* 10 vols. 1778. Vol. 4.	1778
v1785	SAMUEL JOHNSON, GEORGE STEEVENS, & ISAAC REED. *Plays.* 10 vols. 1785. Vol. 4.	1785
RANN	JOSEPH RANN. *Dramatic Works.* 6 vols. Oxford, 1786– [94]. Vol. 2.	1787
MAL	EDMOND MALONE. *Plays & Poems.* 10 vols. 1790. Vol. 4.	1790

v1793	GEORGE STEEVENS & ISAAC REED. *Plays*. 15 vols. 1793. Vol. 7.	1793
v1803	ISAAC REED. *Plays*. 21 vols. 1803. Vol. 9.	1803
v1813	ISAAC REED. *Plays*. 21 vols. 1813. Vol. 9.	1813
v1821	JAMES BOSWELL. *Plays & Poems*. 21 vols. 1821. Vol. 14.	1821
SING1	SAMUEL W. SINGER. *Dramatic Works*. 10 vols. Chiswick, 1826. Vol. 4.	1826
KNT1	CHARLES KNIGHT. *Comedies, Histories, Tragedies, & Poems*. Pictorial Ed. 55 pts. [1838–43.] Reissued in 8 vols. Pt. 30 (Comedies, vol. 2).	1841
KNT2	CHARLES KNIGHT. *Comedies, Histories, Tragedies, & Poems*. 2nd ed. 12 vols. 1842–4. Vol. 4.	1842
COL1	JOHN PAYNE COLLIER. *Works*. 8 vols. 1842–4. Vol. 3.	1842
HUD1	HENRY N. HUDSON. *Works*. 11 vols. Boston & Cambridge, Mass., 1851–6. Vol. 4.	1852
COL2	JOHN PAYNE COLLIER. *Plays*.	1853
SING2	SAMUEL W. SINGER. *Dramatic Works*. 10 vols. Vol. 4.	1856
DYCE1	ALEXANDER DYCE. *Works*. 6 vols. 1857. Vol. 3.	1857
WH1	RICHARD GRANT WHITE. *Works*. 12 vols. Boston, 1857–66. Vol. 5.	1857
COL3	JOHN PAYNE COLLIER. *Comedies, Histories, Tragedies, & Poems*. "The Second Edition." 6 vols. 1858. Vol. 3.	1858
HAL	JAMES O. HALLIWELL. *Works*. 16 vols. 1853–65. Vol. 8.	1859
STAU	HOWARD STAUNTON. *Plays*. 50 pts. 1856–60. Reissued in 3 vols. 1858–60. Pts. 37–8 (Vol. 3).	1859
DEL2	NICOLAUS DELIUS. *Werke*. 7 vols. Elberfeld, 1854–[61]. Vol. 6.	1860
CAM1	WILLIAM GEORGE CLARK, JOHN GLOVER, & WILLIAM ALDIS WRIGHT. *Works*. Cambridge Sh. 9 vols. Cambridge & London, 1863–6. Vol. 3.	1863
GLO	WILLIAM GEORGE CLARK & WILLIAM ALDIS WRIGHT. *Works*. Globe Ed. Cambridge & London.	1864
KTLY	THOMAS KEIGHTLEY. *Plays*. 6 vols. 1864. Vol. 2.	1864
DYCE2	ALEXANDER DYCE. *Works*. 2nd ed. 9 vols. 1864–7. Vol. 3.	1864
KNT3	CHARLES KNIGHT. *Works*. Pictorial Ed. "The Second Edition, Revised." 8 vols. 1867. Comedies, vol. 2.	1867
DEL4	NICOLAUS DELIUS. *Werke*. "Dritte, Revidirte Auflage." 2 vols. Elberfeld, 1872. Vol. 1.	1872
COL4	JOHN PAYNE COLLIER. *Plays & Poems*. 43 pts. in 8 vols. 1875–8. Vol. 3.	1875
HUD2	HENRY N. HUDSON. *Works*. Harvard Ed. 20 vols. Boston, 1880–1. Vol. 7.	1880

WH2	RICHARD GRANT WHITE. *Comedies, Histories, Tragedies, & Poems*. Riverside Sh. 6 vols. Boston, 1883. Vol. 2.	1883
IRV	HENRY IRVING & FRANK MARSHALL. *Works*. Henry Irving Sh. 8 vols. N.Y., 1888–90. Vol. 7. Notes and Introd. by Arthur Symons.	1890
OXF1	W. J. CRAIG. *Works*. Oxford Sh.	[1891]
BUL	A. H. BULLEN. *Works*. Stratford Town Ed. 10 vols. Stratford-on-Avon, 1904–7. Vol. 4.	1905
NLSN	WILLIAM ALLAN NEILSON. *Works*. Cambridge Ed. Boston & N.Y.	1906
ARD1	F. W. MOORMAN. *WT*. Arden Sh.	1912
CAM3	ARTHUR QUILLER-COUCH & JOHN DOVER WILSON. *WT*. New [Cambridge] Sh. 1931; rev. 1950.	1931
KIT1	GEORGE LYMAN KITTREDGE. *Works*. Boston.	1936
ALEX	PETER ALEXANDER. *Works*.	1951
SIS	CHARLES JASPER SISSON. *Works*.	1954
PEL1	BALDWIN MAXWELL. *WT*. Pelican Sh. Baltimore.	1956
CLN2	S. L. BETHELL. *WT*. New Clarendon Sh.	1956
ARD2	J. H. P. PAFFORD. *WT*. New Arden Sh.	1963
SIG	FRANK KERMODE. *WT*. Signet Classic Sh.	1963
PEN2	ERNEST SCHANZER. *WT*. New Penguin Sh.	1969
EVNS	G. BLAKEMORE EVANS et al. *Works*. Riverside Sh. Boston.	1974
BEV3	DAVID BEVINGTON. *Works*. 3rd ed. Glenville, Ill.	1980
OXF2	STANLEY WELLS & GARY TAYLOR. *Works*. Oxford Sh. (Modern Sp.) Oxford.	1986
BEV4	DAVID BEVINGTON. *The Late Romances*. Bantam Books. Toronto.	1988

The editions, books, and manuscripts listed below are also referred to. Although all editions mentioned in the textual notes have been fully collated, only readings that they first print or, in a few instances, revive after long disuse are reported. Readings from revised editions (N&H, K&R, and PEL2) appear only when those editions differ from their predecessors.

mSING	MS notes in F2, S. W. Singer copy, quoted in SING2.	1632–1856
mF1H	MS notes in F1, Honeyman copy. See HOOK (1959).	–1650?
mFLV.a.80	[Evans, John. "Hesperides, or The Muses Garden."] Commonplace book. Folger Library. See SORELIUS (1973).	1655–9
mF1FL10	MS notes in F1. Folger Library, Copy 10.	1700–

mPOPE	ALEXANDER POPE. MS notes in F3. Folger Library, Copy 20.	–1723
mTBY1	STYAN THIRLBY. MS notes in one of Rowe's 1709 eds., now lost but quoted in mTBY2.	1709–25
mTBY2	STYAN THIRLBY. MS notes in Pope's 1725 ed. Beinecke Library, Yale. Vol. 5.	1725–33?
mTHEO1	LEWIS THEOBALD. MS notes in F2. Folger Library, Copy 20.	–1729?
mLONG	ROGER LONG. MS notes in F2. Pembroke College Library, Cambridge.	–1733?
mTBY3	STYAN THIRLBY. MS notes in Theobald's 1733 ed. Folger Library, Copy 2.	1733–47?
mF4TCC	MS notes in F4. Trinity College Library, Cambridge, H.18.12.	1733?–
m1733FL4	MS notes in Theobald's 1733 ed. Folger Library, Copy 4.	1733?–
mHAN	THOMAS HANMER. Letters to William Warburton. British Library.	1735–9
mTOL	GEORGE TOLLET. MS notes in Theobald's 1740 ed. Folger Library, Copy 4.	1740–79
mF2FL48	MS notes in F2. Folger Library, Copy 48.	–1747
mTBY4	STYAN THIRLBY. MS notes in Warburton's 1747 ed. Folger Library, Copy 2.	1747–53
mGREY	ZACHARY GREY. Notes and Extracts from Mr. Warburton's Shakespear. Cambridge University Library.	1747–66
mWARB	WILLIAM WARBURTON. MS notes in his 1747 ed. Folger Library, Copy 5.	1747–79
mF2FL27	MS notes in F2. Folger Library, Copy 27.	c. 1750
THEO3	LEWIS THEOBALD. *Works*. 8 vols. 1752. Vol. 3.	1752
BLAIR	[HUGH BLAIR.] *Works*. 8 vols. Edinburgh, 1753. Vol. 3.	1753
mLUSH	HENRY LUSHINGTON. MS notes in Theobald's 1733 ed. Folger Library, Copy 5.	c. 1754
mCAP2	EDWARD CAPELL. MS text of *WT*. Trinity College Library, Cambridge.	1754
mF2FL21	MS notes in F2. Folger Library, Copy 21.	1754–65
mTYR	THOMAS TYRWHITT. MS notes in F2. (c.39.i.13) British Library.	–1767
HAN3	THOMAS HANMER. *Works*. 6 vols. Oxford, 1770–1. Vol. 2.	1770
mMAL1	EDMOND MALONE. Notebook. British Library.	1773–90

GENT	FRANCIS GENTLEMAN & SAMUEL DERRICK. *WT: A Tragedy, . . . As Performed at the Theatre-Royal, Covent-Garden.* Bell's Sh. 1773. Issued in 9 vols. [1773–4.] Vol. 5. 2nd ed. 1775.	1774
mMAL2	EDMOND MALONE. Notebook. Furness Collection, Univ. of Pennsylvania Library.	1777–80
m1773FL3	MS notes in Johnson & Steevens's 1773 ed. Folger Library, Copy 3.	1778?–
DODD	WILLIAM DODD. *The Beauties of Shakespear.* 3rd ed. 2 vols. (1st ed. 1752.)	1780
CAPN	EDWARD CAPELL. *Notes and Various Readings to Shakespeare.* 3 vols.	1783
m1778BL	ISAAC REED and others (Edmond Malone? Samuel Henley? John? Henderson?). MS notes in Johnson & Steevens's 1778 ed. British Library.	–1785
AYS1	[SAMUEL AYSCOUGH.] *Works.* John Stockdale, [etc.].	1784
AYS2	SAMUEL AYSCOUGH. *Dramatic Works.* 3 vols. 1790. Vol. 1.	1790
m1768FL	MS notes in Capell's 1768 ed. Folger Library, Copy 6.	c. 1790
mTOOK	JOHN HORNE TOOKE. MS notes in Malone's 1790 ed. Folger Library.	1790–1812
m1790aFL	Anon. MS notes in Ayscough's 1790 ed. Folger Library, Copy 8.	1790–
m1790bFL	Anon. MS notes in Malone's 1790 ed. Folger Library, Copy 4.	1790–
m1793BOD	GEORGE STEEVENS, ISAAC REED, et al. MS notes in Johnson & Steevens's 1793 ed. Bodleian Library.	1793–1803?
m1793FL	Anon. MS notes. Folger Library S.a.113	1793–
KEM1	JOHN PHILIP KEMBLE. *WT.* As acted at the Theatre Royal.	1802
KEM2	JOHN PHILIP KEMBLE. *WT.* As acted at the Theatre Royal.	1811
mCAL	THOMAS CALDECOTT (d. 1833). MS notes in v1813. British Library.	1813–33
HARN	WILLIAM HARNESS. *Dramatic Works.* 8 vols. Vol. 3.	1825
VALPY	A. J. VALPY. *Plays and Poems.* 15 vols. 1832–4. Vol. 5.	1833
mCOLE	SAMUEL TAYLOR COLERIDGE. MS notes in Theobald's 1733 ed. British Library.	c. 1834

mLET	W. NANSON LETTSOM. MS notes in a facsimile F1, 1807? Dyce Collection, Victoria and Albert Museum.	1840–65
mCOL1	JOHN PAYNE COLLIER. MS notes in F1, Bridgewater Copy. Huntington Library.	c. 1840
mCOL2	JOHN PAYNE COLLIER. MS notes in F2, Perkins Copy. Huntington Library.	c. 1850
mTAY	JOHN TAYLOR. MS notes in Reed's 1813 ed. Trinity College Library, Cambridge.	c. 1850
COLNE	JOHN PAYNE COLLIER. *Notes and Emendations.* 2nd ed., rev. & enl. 1853. (1st ed. 1852.)	1853
mCOL3	JOHN PAYNE COLLIER. MS notes in his 1853 ed., vol. 3. Bodleian Library.	1858–78?
mSTAU	HOWARD STAUNTON. MS notes, copied by P. A. Daniel, in Staunton's 1864 ed., vol. 3. Folger Library.	1864–74
DYCE3	ALEXANDER DYCE. *Works.* 3rd ed. 9 vols. 1875-6. Vol. 3.	1875
mBRAE	ANDREW E. BRAE. Letter to Joseph Parker Norris, 24 Dec. 1877. Folger Library.	1877
mPER	PHILIP PERRING. MS notes on *WT.* Trinity College Library, Cambridge.	1885–1920?
CAM2	WILLIAM ALDIS WRIGHT. *Works.* Cambridge Sh. 2nd ed. 9 vols. 1891-3. Vol. 3.	1891
mWRAY	G. O. WRAY. Corrections and suggestions from the revd. Dr. Wray. Trinity College Library, Cambridge.	1891–3?
v1898	HORACE HOWARD FURNESS. *WT.* New Variorum Sh. Philadelphia.	1898
RLTR	E. K. CHAMBERS. *WT.* Red Letter Sh.	[1907]
RID	MAURICE R. RIDLEY. *WT.* New Temple Sh.	1935
N&H	WILLIAM A. NEILSON & CHARLES J. HILL. *Plays and Poems.* Cambridge, Mass.	1942
PEN1	G. B. HARRISON. *WT.* Penguin Sh.	1947
MUN	JOHN MUNRO. *Works.* London Sh. 6 vols. 1957. Vol. 2.	1957
K&R	GEORGE LYMAN KITTREDGE & IRVING RIBNER. *WT.* Waltham, Mass.	1967
PEL2	BALDWIN MAXWELL. *WT.* In *Works.* Pelican Sh., rev. Baltimore.	1969

The following sources are occasionally quoted in the commentary or critical discussion:

DAVID GARRICK. *Florizel and Perdita*. . . . As it is performed   1758
at the Theatre Royal in Drury Lane.

DAVID GARRICK. *The Winter's Tale, or Florizel and Perdita*. A   1785
dramatic pastoral altered from Shakspeare.

JOHANN JOACHIM ESCHENBURG. *Schauspiele*. 12 vols. Zürich,   1801
1798-1806. Vol. 5. (1st ed. 1775-6.)

[ELIZABETH] INCHBALD. *WT*. British Theatre. 25 vols. Vol. 3.   1808

ALEXANDER CHALMERS. *Plays*. 8 vols. Vol. 3.   1823

JOHANN WILHELM OTTO BENDA. *Werke*. 19 vols. Leipzig,   1825
1825-6. Vol. 8.

JOHANN HEINRICH & ABRAHAM VOSS. *Schauspiele*. 9 vols.   1829
Leipzig & Stuttgart, 1818-29. Vol. 9.

D[ANIEL], G[EORGE]. *WT*. Cumberland's Sh. 5.   [1830?]

LUDWIG TIECK. *Dramatische Werke*. Tr. A. W. von Schlegel.   1832
9 vols. Berlin, 1825-33. Vol. 8.

J. R. PITMAN. *The School-Shakspeare*. 2nd ed.   1834

WILLIAM CHARLES MACREADY. *WT*. Ed. Elizabeth Inchbald.   1837
Annotated by J. R. Anderson.

BARRY CORNWALL (i.e., Bryan Waller Procter). *Works*. 3 vols.   1844
Vol. 1.

SAMUEL PHELPS. *WT*. Cumberland's British Theatre 6.   1845-
Annotated by Phelps and William C. Williams.

GULIAN VERPLANCK. *Plays*. 138 pts. [N.Y., 1844-7.] Reissued   1845
in 3 vols. Vol. 2.

CHARLES KNIGHT. *WT*. The Stratford Shakespeare. 4 vols.   1854
Vol. 4.

WILLIAM BURTON. *WT*. Ed. Elizabeth Inchbald. Annotated by   1856
John Moore.

CHARLES KEAN. *WT*. Extracted from *Works*. Ed. Charles Knight.   1856
[1841]. MS alterations.

CHARLES KEAN. *WT*. As performed 28 Apr. 1856.   1856

J. B. WRIGHT. *WT*. French's Standard Drama, no. 317.   [1860?]

R. CARRUTHERS & W. CHAMBERS. *Dramatic Works*.   1862
Chambers's Household Ed. 10 vols. in 5. 1861-3. Vol. 4.

CHARLES & MARY COWDEN CLARKE. *Plays*. Cassell's Illustrated   1865
Sh. 270 pts., 1864-9. Reissued in 3 vols. Vol. 1.

CHARLES CALVERT. *WT*. Manchester.   [1869]

OTTO GILDEMEISTER (tr.). *Das Wintermärchen*. Leipzig.   1870

ALEXANDER SCHMIDT. *Das Wintermärchen*. In *Dramatische*   1870
Werke. Tr. August Wilhelm von Schlegel & Ludwig Tieck.
Ed. H. Ulrici. 12 vols. Berlin, 1867-71. Vol. 9.

S. C. BOORMAN. *WT*. London English Literature Ser.   1964
R. R. YOUNG & C. W. R. D. MOSELEY. *WT*. South Bank Sh.   1965
LOUIS B. WRIGHT & VIRGINIA A. LAMAR. *WT*. Folger Library   1966
 General Reader's Sh.
TREVOR NUNN. *WT*. Promptbook based on Kermode, ed. 1963.   1969
JOHN BARTON. *WT*. Promptbook based on Wilson, ed. 1931   1976
 (rpt. 1959).
RONALD EYRE. *WT*. Promptbook based on Schanzer, ed. 1969.   1981
CHRISTOPHER PARRY. *WT*. Macmillan Sh.   1982
INGEBORG BOLTZ. *WT. Das Wintermärchen*. Englisch-deutsche   1986
 Studienausgabe.
TERRY HANDS. *WT*. Promptbook based on Schanzer, ed. 1969.   1987
DAVID BEVINGTON. *Works*. 4th ed. N.Y.   1992
STEPHEN ORGEL. *WT*. Oxford Sh.   1996
RICHARD KNOWLES. *Lr*. New Variorum Sh.   forthcoming

Unless otherwise specified, quotations of authors other than Shakespeare are drawn from these editions:

The Dramatic Works in the Beaumont & Fletcher Canon. Gen. ed. Fredson
 Bowers. 10 vols. Cambridge, 1966–96.
The Life & Complete Works in Verse & Prose of Robert Greene, M.A. Ed.
 Alexander B. Grosart. 15 vols. 1881–6. (Rpt. N.Y.: Russell & Russell, 1964.)
Ben Jonson. Ed. C. H. Herford & Percy & Evelyn Simpson. 11 vols. 1925–
 52.
The Works of Thomas Kyd. Ed. Frederick S. Boas. Oxford, 1901.
The Complete Works of John Lyly. Ed. R. Warwick Bond. 3 vols. Oxford,
 1902.
The Complete Works of Christopher Marlowe. Ed. Fredson Bowers. 2nd ed.
 2 vols. Cambridge, 1979.
The Life & Works of George Peele. Gen. ed. Charles Tyler Prouty. 3 vols.
 New Haven, 1952–70.
The Dramatic Works and Poems of James Shirley. Ed. William Gifford; rev.
 Alexander Dyce. 6 vols. 1833.

In addition to others commonly employed, the following abbreviations occur:

a	in a signature, left-hand column
a.	adjective
ad.	added, additionally
Ado	*Much Ado about Nothing*
AEB	*Analytical and Enumerative Bibliography*
AI	*American Imago*

ALitASH	*Acta Litteraria Academiae Scientiarum Hungaricae*
Anon.	Anonymous
Ant.	*Antony and Cleopatra*
app.	appendix
Archiv	*Archiv für das Studium der Neueren Sprachen und Literaturen*
Assn.	Association
attrib.	attributed to
aug.	augmented
AWW	*All's Well That Ends Well*
AYL	*As You Like It*
b	in a signature, right-hand column
BJRL	*Bulletin of the John Rylands University Library of Manchester*
BL	British Library
BLC	*British Library General Catalogue of Printed Books*
BSUF	*Ball State University Forum*
Bull.	Bulletin
BuR	*Bucknell Review*
c.	circa, century
CahiersE	*Cahiers Elisabéthains*
C&L	*Christianity and Literature*
CE	*College English*
CentR	*Centennial Review*
cf.	compare
ch.	chapter
CLAJ	*College Language Association Journal*
CLS	*Comparative Literature Studies*
CML	*Classical and Modern Literature: A Quarterly*
CompD	*Comparative Drama*
Comp. Lit.	Comparative Literature
comp(s).	compiler(s)
conj.	conjecture, conjectural
ConR	*Contemporary Review*
CritQ	*Critical Quarterly*
Cym.	*Cymbeline*
degr.	degraded (usually to a note)
diff.	different
diss.	dissertation
DNB	*Dictionary of National Biography*
DR	*Dalhousie Review*
DUJ	*Durham University Journal*
EA	*Etudes Anglaises*
EAA	*Estudos Anglo-Americanos* (São Paulo)

E&S	*Essays and Studies* (London)
ed(s).	edited by, editor(s), edition(s)
EDD	*The English Dialect Dictionary*, ed. Joseph Wright, 6 vols. 1898–1905
EIC	*Essays in Criticism*
EIE	*English Institute Essays*
EigoS	*Eigo Seinen*
EIRC	*Explorations in Renaissance Culture*
EiT	*Essays in Theatre*
ELH	the title per se; formerly *Journal of English Literary History*
ELN	*English Language Notes*
ELR	*English Literary Renaissance*
EM	*English Miscellany*
Eng.	English
enl.	enlarged
Err.	*The Comedy of Errors*
ES	*English Studies* (Netherlands)
ESC	*English Studies in Canada*
ESn	*Englische Studien*
et al.	and others
etc.	(in a textual note) and all other collated editions
Expl	*Explicator*
f.	folio (leaf or page number)
F, F1	First Folio (1623)
F2, F3, F4	Second (1632), Third (1663–4), Fourth (1685) Folios
Ff.	Folios
FQ	*Faerie Queene*
Fr.	French
Gen.	Genesis
Gent.	Gentleman
Gent. Mag.	*Gentleman's Magazine*
Ger.	German
1H4	*The First Part of Henry the Fourth*
2H4	*The Second Part of Henry the Fourth*
H5	*Henry the Fifth*
1H6	*The First Part of Henry the Sixth*
2H6	*The Second Part of Henry the Sixth*
3H6	*The Third Part of Henry the Sixth*
H8	*King Henry the Eighth*
HAB	*Humanities Association Bulletin* (Canada)
Ham.	*Hamlet*
HLB	*Harvard Library Bulletin*
HLQ	*Huntington Library Quarterly*
IDEM	the same commentator

IJPP	*Interpretation: A Journal of Political Philosophy*
ISJR	*Iowa State Journal of Research*
JAMS	*Journal of the American Musicological Society*
JC	*Julius Caesar*
JEGP	*Journal of English and Germanic Philology*
JHI	*Journal of the History of Ideas*
Jn.	*King John*
Jour.	*Journal*
l(l).	line(s)
L&P	*Literature and Psychology*
LanM	*Les Langues Modernes*
LC	*A Lover's Complaint*
Libr.	Library
LLL	*Love's Labour's Lost*
Lr.	*King Lear*
m	with a siglum, a manuscript source
Mac.	*Macbeth*
Mag.	*Magazine*
M&L	*Music and Letters*
MdF	*Mercure de France*
Met.	*Metamorphoses*
MLN	the title per se; formerly *Modern Language Notes*
MLQ	*Modern Language Quarterly*
MLR	*Modern Language Review*
MLS	*Modern Language Studies*
MM	*Measure for Measure*
MND	*A Midsummer Night's Dream*
MP	*Modern Philology*
MQ	*Midwest Quarterly*
MS(S)	manuscript(s)
MSE	*Massachusetts Studies in English*
MSpr	*Moderna Språk*
MSR	Malone Society Reprint
MV	*The Merchant of Venice*
n(n).	note(s)
N&Q	*Notes and Queries*
NCCH	*New Century Classical Handbook*
n.d.	not dated
n.p.	place of publication unspecified
NS	new series
NUC	*National Union Catalogue*
OCD	*Oxford Classical Dictionary*
OED	*Oxford English Dictionary*
om.	omitted by

Oth.	*Othello*
OUP	Oxford University Press
p(p).	page(s)
PBA	*Proceedings of the British Academy*
PBSA	*Papers of the Bibliographical Society of America*
PCLS	*Proceedings of the Comparative Literature Symposium* (Lubbock, Texas)
PCP	*Pacific Coast Philology*
Per.	*Pericles*
PhT	*The Phoenix and Turtle*
pl.	plural
PMLA	*Publications of the Modern Language Association of America*
PQ	*Philological Quarterly*
prep.	preposition
Preuss.	*Preussische* (Prussian)
pseud.	pseudonym
PsyR	*Psychoanalytic Review*
pt(s).	part(s)
pub., publ.	published, publication
Q	quarto
QQ	*Queen's Quarterly*
R2	*King Richard the Second*
R3	*King Richard the Third*
RAA	*Revue Anglo-Américaine*
REL	*Review of English Literature*
RenD	*Renaissance Drama*
RenQ	*Renaissance Quarterly*
RES	*Review of English Studies*
Rev.	*Review*
rev.	revised
RMR	*Rocky Mountain Review of Language and Literature*
Rom.	*Romeo and Juliet*
rpt.	reprint, reprinted
RSC	Royal Shakespeare Company
RSTC	Revised ed. (1986–91) of *STC*
SAB	*South Atlantic Bulletin*
sb.	substantive (noun)
SB	*Studies in Bibliography*
SCL	Shakespeare Centre Library, Stratford-upon-Avon
SD(s)	stage direction(s)
SEL	*Studies in English Literature, 1500–1900*
ser.	series
ShAB	*Shakespeare Association Bulletin*

ShakB	*Shakespeare Bulletin* (New York Sh. Soc.)
ShakS	*Shakespeare Studies*
Sh(n).	Shakespeare(an) (any spelling)
ShN	*Shakespeare Newsletter*
Shr.	*The Taming of the Shrew*
ShS	*Shakespeare Survey*
sig(s).	signature(s)
SJ	*Shakespeare-Jahrbuch*
SJH	*Shakespeare-Jahrbuch* (Heidelberg)
SJW	*Shakespeare-Jahrbuch* (Weimar)
SN	*Studia Neophilologica*
SoAR	*South Atlantic Review*
Soc.	Society
Son.	Shakespeare's *Sonnets*
SoRA	*Southern Review* (Adelaide)
SP	*Studies in Philology*
SP(s)	speech prefix(es)
SPWVSRA	*Selected Papers from the West Virginia Shakespeare and Renaissance Association*
SQ	*Shakespeare Quarterly*
SR	*Sewanee Review*
Sr.	Sister
SSEng	*Sydney Studies in English*
STC	*A Short-Title Catalogue of Books Printed in England, Scotland, and Ireland . . . 1475–1640.* (by A. W. Pollard and G. R. Redgrave; 2nd ed., rev. and enl. Ed. W. A. Jackson, F. S. Ferguson, & Katherine F. Pantzer. 3 vols. 1986–91)
Stud.	Studies
subst.	substantially
supp.	supplement
s.v.	*sub verba*
TGV	*Two Gentlemen of Verona*
Th.	Theater, Theatre
ThS	*Theatre Survey*
THSt	*Theatre History Studies*
Tim.	*Timon of Athens*
Tit.	*Titus Andronicus*
TLN	Through Line Number(s)
TLS	[London] *Times Literary Supplement*
TM	Theatre Museum, London
Tmp.	*The Tempest*
TN	*Twelfth Night* or *Theatre Notebook*
TNK	*The Two Noble Kinsmen*

TPB	*Tennessee Philological Bulletin*
tr.	translation, translated by
Tro.	*Troilus and Cressida*
TSLL	*Texas Studies in Literature and Language*
UCrow	*The Upstart Crow*
UES	*Unisa English Studies*
UMSE	*University of Mississippi Studies in English*
Univ.	University
UTQ	*University of Toronto Quarterly*
v	(in a signature, superscript) verso; (with a siglum) variorum edition
v.	verb
Var.	variorum edition
vol(s).	volume(s)
Wiv.	*Merry Wives of Windsor*
WS	*Women's Studies*
WT	*The Winter's Tale*
WVUPP	*West Virginia University Philological Papers*
YES	*Yearbook of English Studies*

Symbols used in the textual apparatus include

^	punctuation absent
~	corresponding word of the lemma is repeated
-	all collated editions between the two specified
+	all succeeding collated editions
(−)	except the editions specified, which read with the lemma (i.e., with F1)

THE WINTER'S TALE

The Winters Tale.

0 The Winters Tale.] FELPERIN (1972, p. 215): "If you believe that the representation of character, the ability to touch all the stops of human passion, is Shakespeare's greatest gift as a dramatist, then *The Winter's Tale*, as Inspector Bucket would say, is the play for you."

The title means "an idle tale" (*OED*, Winter, *sb.*[1] 5); for its proverbial status, see DENT (W513.1). The expression occurs frequently in Elizabethan literature — e.g., in Peele's nearly synonymous *Old Wives Tale* (ed. Binnie, 1980, lines 85-6, 98-9) and in Marlowe's *Dido, Queen of Carthage* (3.3.59). Sh. himself had approximated it in *3H6* 5.5.25 (2999): "Let *Æsop* fable in a Winters Night." HALLIWELL (ed. 1859, 8:45) finds other occurrences, in Richard Robinson, *The Rewarde of Wickednesse* (1574, sig. B1ᵛ) and Michael Drayton, *Heroical Epistles* (1597; *Works*, ed. Hebel, 2:292). PAFFORD (ed. 1963, p. liii) adds more: "Although the phrase was common it may not be altogether a coincidence that it appears in print at least twice in 1610 — in *A Mirror for Magistrates* (which Shakespeare may have been rereading at that time [in preparation for *Cym.*]) and in Campion" (*Two Bookes of Ayres*, ed. c. 1613, Cantus xix). In Marlowe's *The Jew of Malta*, "winters tales" are linked with "spirits and ghosts that glide by night" (2.1.25-6), as they are in *WT* at 618-19. SCHANZER (ed. 1969, p. 7) compares Lady Macbeth's "woman's story at a winter's fire, Authoriz'd by her grandam" (3.4.64-5 [1334-5]). STEEVENS (ed. 1785) notes the seasonal opposite, "summers story," in *Son.* 98, and DANIEL (ed. 1830?, p. 6) finds the tone of some winter's tales conveyed by *R2* 5.1.40-2 (2301-3): "In Winters tedious Nights sit by the Fire With good old folkes, and let them tell thee Tales Of wofull Ages, long agoe betide." This connotation, not to mention the events of the plot, evidently inspired Jonson in the Induction to *Bartholomew Fair* (128-32) to disclaim including "a nest of *Antiques*" and making "Nature afraid in his *Playes*, like those that beget *Tales*, *Tempests*, and such like *Drolleries*, to mixe his head with other mens heeles, let the concupisence of *Iigges* and *Dances*, raigne as strong as it will amongst you." Although ESTRIN (1977, p. 29) takes the tempest to be the blusters of 3.3 that sink Antigonus's ship, Jonson refers to Sh.'s play. Jonson's *Tale* is *WT*; the "nest of *Antiques*" is a group of grotesques (cf. *OED*, Antic, *sb.* 4), said by MALONE (in STEEVENS, ed. 1778) to be the satyrs who dance at 2164; and the "*Iigges* and *Dances*" are other performances at the sheepshearing festival, such as the dance at 1988-9. There is some disagreement about what else Jonson is getting at. HERFORD & SIMPSON (10:177) think he objects mainly to "the masque-like incidents" in *Tmp.* and *WT*; E. M. WAITH (ed. *Ben Jonson*: Bartholomew Fair, New Haven, 1963, p. 32 n.) says Jonson is displeased by the "fantasy and romance as well as spectacular production" of these comedies, although, as FREY (*Vast Romance*, 1980, p. 15) remarks, "there is no indication . . . that spectacle . . . was actually employed."

GENTLEMAN (1774, 5:151): Sh. is "particularly right in his choice of a title for this piece . . . for it has all the improbabilities and jumble of incidents, some merry,

1

and some sad, that constitute Christmas stories." DRAKE (1817, 2:498-9 n.): "That Shakspeare considered the romantic incidents of this play as properly designated by the appellation of *an old tale*, is evident from his own application of the phrase to several parts of the plot." He cites 3038, 3070, and 3328. Similarly, SCHLEGEL (1808; 1846, p. 396): *WT* is appropriately named because it is "peculiarly calculated to beguile the dreary leisure of a long winter evening" and is "attractive and intelligible even to childhood." WHITE (ed. 1857, 5:272): "Shakespeare sought only to put a very popular story into dramatic form; and of this he advertised his hearers by calling this play a Tale, just as before he had called a play similarly wanting in dramatic interest a Dream." HALLIWELL (ed. 1859, 8:45): "The longer appellation, the Winter Night's Tale . . . confirms the suggestion that it was considered in the light of a history appropriate to the long nights of winter; but the observation of Mamillius . . . can scarcely be imagined to have any intimate connection with the selection of the title of the comedy." He does not say why not. GERVINUS (1877, p. 803): "[Five] times in the play, and once for all in the title, he dwelt as emphatically as possible on the fictitious character of the play, which is wholly founded on the incredible and improbable." A consequence, GERVINUS thinks, is a deliberate flaunting of probability, so that the play's famous mistakes—Bohemia's seashore (see n. 1440), the island of Delphos (n. 1147), the costume crux (n. 2557-8), the Shepherd's intuition that Antigonus was an old man (n. 1548-9)—"may well have been purposed by the poet." Robert Louis Stevenson may have had similar ideas of the improbable when he subtitled *The Master of Ballantrae* (1889), "which extends over many years and travels into many countries" (p. v), "A Winter's Tale"; one of its many incidents is the strange return to life of the frozen James Durie. QUILLER-COUCH (ed. 1931, p. xiii): "The sort of tale . . . concerning the gentry and their mysteries, that a child, escaping from his nursery, may gather from hints of gossip in servants' hall or housekeeper's room . . . something eerie, concerning *his* forbears, keeping him awake, to piece it fearfully in his little mind." HERFORD (ed. 1916-, p. xv) believes that Sh. chose the title to forestall "rationalist cavil at the outset by a frank disclaimer of actuality and even coherence." COOK (1940, p. 156), evidently a rationalist: "The titles of some of the plays are misleading, for *The Winter's Tale* [uses] midsummer flowers and spring-blooming flowers." BOOTH (1977, p. 320), however: "'Winter's tale' seems to have had two not-quite-compatible connotations . . . : a solemn one appropriate to the season when it is told; the other shares some of the probable attributes of a *summer's story*: . . . an old wives' tale credited only by the gullible."

The earliest critic to notice a connection between the title and 618 is TYRWHITT (in STEEVENS, ed. 1773, 10:Mm2). SCHANZER (ed. 1969, pp. 8-9) finds the resemblance powerful: "By the end of the third Act we have come to realize that the winter's tale Mamillius begins to tell mirrors that of the play. Leontes has become the man who dwelt by a churchyard, and even of the sprites and goblins we have had a glimpse in the vision of Antigonus [3.3.15-36 (1457-78)]. . . . It [*WT*] is also a tale which is principally *about* winter, the winter which Leontes creates within him and around him." COLERIDGE (1813; 1960, 1:206) finds implied in the titles of *MND*, *AYL*, and *WT* "the one idea which gives the tone to each play." In 1818, contrasting these plays and *TN* with those named after dominant characters (e.g., *Lr.*, *Ham.*), he finds their "total effect . . . produced by a co-ordination of the characters, by a wreath of flowers" (ed. Foakes, 1989, p. 58). For a more elaborate comparison of *WT* with *MND*, see PYLE (1969, pp. 2-3). The CLARKES (ed. 1865) interpret Time's "so shall I . . . make stale The glistering of this present, as my Tale Now seems to it" (1591-4) as follows: "'as the tale I have previously told seems "stale" (old, or gone by) to "this present" time and its incidents.'" *The Winter's Tale*, therefore, "refers especially to the first three acts." The events of "the latter portion of the play, poetically consist with the ripeness of summer." Only to HALLIWELL (ed. 1859, 8:45) is the title "perhaps

a reason for supposing that [*WT*] originally appeared at the Blackfriars, a theatre . . . which restricted its season to the winter months." For the efforts of modern
directors to reinforce the seasonal allusions in the two parts of the play, see p. 806.
  STEEVENS (ed. 1778): "At Stationers' Hall, May 22. 1594, Edward White entered
'[a] booke entit[u]led *a* [*Wynters nightes pastime*]'" (see ARBER, 1875–94, 2:650). If
ever published, this book has not survived, and its relation to *WT*, if any, is indeter-
minable (see p. 602). WARD (1875, 1:437) entertains the idea that "the title was
suggested . . . by that of *A Winter Night's Vision*, an addition to the *Mirror for
Magistrates* published by Niccols in 1610." Quite early, however, the play may have
had a similar variant title, for the Accounts of the Revels at Court note that on 5 Nov.
1611 the King's Men performed a play "called yᵉ winters nightes Tayle" (see p. 602).
Coincidentally, probably, the play is identified as "The WINTER-NIGHT's TALE" on
the title page of BLAIR (ed. 1753), and perhaps in consequence WALPOLE (1768, 2:
173) calls it "The Winter Evening's Tale." In STEEVENS (ed. 1778) the play's head title
and running titles are "WINTER's TALE," although the head title is keyed to a note
the lemma of which is "*The Winter's Tale.*" The article may have been dropped for
typographical convenience when the head title was set. Later eds. followed, however,
and the play was sans article until "A" was adopted by KNIGHT (ed. 1842) and "The"
was restored by COLLIER (ed. 1842). HUNTER (1845, 1:412): "There is perhaps no
very strong reason for preferring one to the other, but on the whole the indefinite
article appears to me to express more exactly the meaning of the author than the
definite"; he also implausibly believes (p. 413) that "the title *Twelfth Night* may have
suggested the title *A Winter's Tale.*" The preference for *A* was generally diminished
by the authority of CLARK & WRIGHT (ed. 1863)—the first Cambridge ed.—and its
offspring The Globe ed. (1864), though once in a while *A* reappears—e.g., in SMEA-
TON (1911, pp. 500–3), COLIE (1974, p. 291), and STONE (1977, p. 376). CHAMBERS
(1923; 1945) uses *The* on one page (2:215) and *A* on the next two; and WILSON (1929),
in his facsimile of F1, follows a title page to *The Winter's Tale* with an introduction
to *A Winter's Tale*. Because the article is omitted in Sir Henry Herbert's 1623 memorandum concerning the play and because a performance took place on 5 Nov. 1611
(see p. 602), HOTINE (1967) argues that *Winter's Tale*, the true title, alludes to Thomas
Winter, a conspirator in the Gunpowder Plot. Despite Winter and the Plot, however,
Simon Forman, who saw the play on 15 May 1611, called it *the* (see p. 798). PYLE
(1969, p. 1) wonders whether "some quality of uniqueness [is] suggested by *The*,"
and perhaps a hint of ostentation; he compares (p. 2) *MND*, "a parallel case, its title
ostensibly implying a 'weak and idle theme, / No more yielding but a dream' [5.1.427–
8 (2211–12)]," which, like *WT*, combines "courtly and popular elements in a setting
of courtly or pastoral romance." TREWIN (1978, p. 259), who regards *A* as a misquo-
tation, believes *WT* is "a play that demands its definite article."
  Considering puns on the titles of plays as a form of derogatory comment on the
plays themselves, RICHARDS (1994) asks, "Was 'The Winter's Tale' ever referred to in
alehouse circles as 'The Winter's Stale'?"

(2C

Leontes, King of Sicillia.
Mamillus, yong Prince of Sicillia.
Camillo.
Antigonus. ⎫ *Foure*
Cleomines. ⎬ *Lords of Sicillia.*   3375
Dion. ⎭
Hermione, Queene to Leontes.
Perdita, Daughter to Leontes and Hermione.
Paulina, wife to Antigonus.
Emilia, a Lady.   3380 (2C
Polixenes, King of Bohemia.
Florizell, Prince of Bohemia.
Old Shepheard, reputed Father of Perdita.
Clowne, his Sonne.
Autolicus, a Rogue.
Archidamus, a Lord of Bohemia.   3386
[Mariner.]   +1
[Gaoler.]   +2
Other Lords, [Ladies,] and Gentlemen, [Officers,] and Seruants.   3387
Shepheards, and [Mopsa, Dorcas, and other] Shephearddesses.

3372 *Mamillus*] *Mamilius* F3+ (−ROWE3, POPE, HAN)
3383 *Old . . . Perdita.*] *Om.* OXF2
3384 *his*] *his* (i.e., Autolycus's) OXF2
3385 *Ad.* Time, *as* Chorus. THEO1+
3388 SCENE *partly in* Sicilia, *and partly in* Bohemia. ROWE1+ (−PEN2, OXF2)
(*subst.*). HAN *reads* Bithynia *for* Bohemia *throughout*.

3370 **The . . . Actors.**] As the line numbers indicate, in F1 this list follows the play (sig. Cc2). Among the plays in F1, *Tmp.*, *TGV*, and *MM* are similarly equipped, and all are believed to derive from transcripts by Ralph Crane (see p. 587). So are *2H4*, *Tim.*, and *Oth.*, but because these lists fill pages that otherwise would have been blank (in the case of *Oth.* nearly blank), they may have been made up in the printing

4

house. Regarding the names generally, HALES (1876; 1884, p. 109) observes that *WT* is "remarkable for its Greek nomenclature . . . remarkable because there is little in the original [Greene's *Pandosto*; see p. 618] to suggest or encourage such Hellenism." LEIMBERG (1988, p. 138): "The acoustic affinity of the names Apollo-Polixenes-Paulina, let alone the near-identity of Flora/Florizel, shows clearly enough that . . . baroque sound-patterns play a part in the constellation of the *dramatis personae* and their names." F1 includes no formal indication of the scene, but the major locations, except perhaps that of 3.1, are made clear by the dialogue. PETERSON (*Time*, 1973, p. 153), however: "The characters . . . exist in a fiction which . . . deliberately avoids particularizations of place and time, and exploits the license of romance to focus upon a reality beyond the level of physical and psychological verisimilitude."

In the following notes on major characters, the number of spoken lines is from SPEVACK (1968–80, 1:1264 ff.); the count was made by EVANS (ed. 1974).

3371 *Leontes* (682 lines)] Sh. formed the names of several other characters on the root *Leo-*, including Leonardo (*MV*), Leonato (the governor of Sicilian Messina in *Ado*), and Leonine (*Per.*); as PAFFORD (ed. 1963) notes, none of them is heroic. RANDALL (1988, p. 123): "A lion is a model not only of nobility but also of danger," although Leonardo and Leonine, a murderer, are servants. The father of Posthumus in *Cym.* was Sicilius Leonatus (1.1.29 [38]). Many of the characters' names in *WT* derive from Plutarch (see p. 697), but *Leontes* is found in the *Lives* not as a personal name but only as the name of a tribe, the Leontines, and their city, Leontium. COOPER (1565) likewise lists the Leontini, "People of Sicilie." PETTET (1949, p. 162, n. 1) observes that four characters' names — Leontes, Antigonus, Archidamus, and Mopsa — occur in Sidney's *Arcadia*, "probably a significant pointer to Shakespeare's reading." His reading definitely introduced him to Mopsa, the wife of the shepherd in Greene's *Pandosto*. In Sir Thomas North's translation of Plutarch's *Lives*, Sh. found *Cleomenes* (see n. 3375–6), so spelled by North and *OCD*, although in *WT* he is always *Cleomines*. The resemblance between Leontes and Posthumus Leonatus has often been observed — PAFFORD (ed. 1963), for example: "Each is overcome by jealousy, each wills the death of his wife and actually thinks that he has caused it, each is shown his criminal folly, becomes remorseful, and is reunited to and reconciled with his wife." KNIGHT (1958, p. 196): "The name hints a leonine nobility, underlined also by Paulina's 'he is touch'd to the noble heart' [1412–13]." He is further leonine in that "the Lion so abhorreth this crime [adultrie], as he killeth the Liones for commiting this fact" (Robert Greene, *The Myrrour of Modestie*, 1584, 3:39; the statement is repeated in *Francescos Fortunes*, 1590, 8:141, and virtually repeated in *Greenes Farewell to Folly*, 1591, 9:310). To GRIFFIN (1936) the name suggests "the lion of England," King James, who is supposed to have suspected his wife of infidelity; RANDALL (1988, p. 123) points out that James's "crest bore no less than thirteen" lions. BERGERON (1985, p. 9) also thinks that Sh., "at least on the edge of his consciousness," linked Leontes (and Pericles, Prospero, and Henry VIII) with King James, "a father of similar age."

Sicillia] STOKES (1924): "The Roman name for Sicily." Because ancient Sicily had once been a Greek colony, Kean set the Sicilian scene of his production in Syracuse "when at the summit of her political prosperity" (see n. 3370, above, and pp. 802, 822). Following COOPER (see above), RANDALL (1988, pp. 126–8) associates Leontes with Leontini, another Greek colony in Sicily, where coins bore the head of Apollo on one side and a lion on the other. LEES (1976): In Plutarch's Life of Dion, Sh. found not only Dion himself but also an Archidamus and a Polyxenus; he was thus led to make the "capricious, cruel and tyrannical" Leontes a Sicilian, for "Plutarch's Sicilia is the Sicily of the notorious tyrants Dionysius the Elder and Dionysius the Younger." Although the historical Dion's widow does give birth to a child while imprisoned, Sh.'s audiences are unlikely to have made the connection, since the tyrants are unmentioned in the play.

Sh.'s Sicilia corresponds to Bohemia in Greene's *Pandosto*, the source of *WT*, and the exchange of names has caused much speculation. GRIFFIN (1936): "England was frequently referred to in literature and drama under the pseudonym of Sicily (cf. e.g. Lyly's *Sapho* and Massinger's *Maid of Honor* . . .). Can it be that here we have the key to Shakespeare's assignment of the jealous king of [i.e., to] Sicily [because King James was supposed to be jealous of Queen Anne]?" KNIGHT (1947; 1965, p. 128): "It was Sicily, at first sight ill-suited to the sombre scenes [there] staged, that gave us the myths of Proserpine or Persephone"; KNIGHT perhaps associates these mythical figures with Perdita and springtime or with Hermione's return to life.

Finding, in George Sandys's commentary on Ovid's *Met.*, that Ceres, angry because Proserpina was abducted from Sicily, struck the island with barrenness, KUHL (1952) thinks Sh. gave jealous Leontes a barren land to suggest England's "lean years under a jealous king," James I. Yet the scene of *Ado* is Messina in Sicily, and few signs of penury are found there. MAHOOD (1957, p. 157 n.): "Shakespeare may have changed round the Sicily and Bohemia of his source in order to avoid the literary associations of Sicilian shepherds," which would be inappropriate to the shepherds he created. SCHANZER (ed. 1969, p. 18) amplifies: "It may well have been the thought that the seacoast of Bohemia seems a more suitable habitat for a bear than that of Sicilia. . . . [For more on the seacoast of Bohemia, see n. 1440.] Another consideration may have been the wish to locate his sheep-shearing feast in Bohemia in order to keep it free from the intrusion of misleading or irrelevant conceptions of Sicilian pastoral life, with which the more educated part of his audience were familiar from their reading of the classics. The transposition may also have been unconsciously aided by the fact that [*Ado*], which [because of the resurrection of Hero] was much in Shakespeare's mind while reshaping the plot of *Pandosto*, is his only other play with a Sicilian setting."

SCOTT (1963, pp. 412-13 n.) suggests that Bohemia's reputation for herbs and spices (e.g., the rosemary and rue distributed by Perdita at 1880) may be a part of the reason for the exchange; for Bohemia's production of "hearbes without number" he quotes *Batman vppon Bartholome* (1582, f. 219ᵛ). BURTON (1970, p. 218): "One country was a setting for the dark wintry realities of courtly life, the other for the bright spring of youth and love in an idealized countryside. . . . Sicily, well-known to Elizabethan travelers and seamen, was too real a place for this magical atmosphere; Bohemia was much more mysterious and evocative, and is so still." COLIE (1974, pp. 270-1): In *WT* the "court bears the name of the never-never locale preeminently pastoral—Leontes rules in Sicily, is himself called 'Sicilia', is king and center of that pastoral island . . . [where] all is utterly antipastoral. We never hear of shepherding or poetry, and even courtliness is denied in Leontes' frenzy. . . . There is no hint in his country of the greening Sicilian muse, who has, in a highly unliterary way, migrated to Bohemia. . . . Shakespeare has turned the pattern around, both from his source and from the larger tradition." BULLOUGH (1975, 8:125): "The most probable explanation is that Sicily was well known for crimes of jealousy and revenge, while Bohemia with its fabled sea-coast was currently a frequent centre for romantic adventure." COHEN (1982, p. 125): In *WT* "this reversal at once calls into question the standard opposition between court and country and, paradoxically, permits the entire sequence of events, regardless of locale, to be seen as part of a pastoral world." With the possible exception of 3.1, however, all the Sicilian scenes appear to be set indoors.

In other plays, Sh. shows next to no imaginative affinity for Bohemia; in *MM*, Barnardine, imprisoned for nine years, is Bohemian born (4.2.134 [1996]), a detail that seems to derive from Sh.'s reading of *2 Promos and Cassandra*, and "Bohemian-Tartar" is a piece of the Host's fustian in *Wiv.* (4.5.21 [2238]). The word *Sicily* and its forms do not appear very often either, but two Sicilian provinces do: Syracuse in *Err.* is the home of one Antipholus and one Dromio, and Messina, as mentioned above, is the location of *Ado*. In *WT* ten scenes are set in Sicilia, only four in Bohemia. A similar disparity is found in other contemporary plays. Excluding *MM* and *WT*, BERGER & BRADFORD (1975) list Bohemia eight times but Sicily thirty-three.

3372 **Mamillus** (22 lines)] I.e., Mamillius. Three public figures of this name are listed by *OCD*, but none is in any way connected with *WT*. PAFFORD (ed. 1963): "May be taken from Greene's two romances entitled *Mamillia* [1580? and 1583?]." The author of *Pandosto* may have made this further contribution to *WT*, but, except for the names, there is no correspondence between the *Mamillia*s and Sh.'s play, since Mamillia was a lady of fair face, golden locks, and coral cheeks. ADAMS (1989, p. 94): "It compounds a diminutive *-lillus* with the word for mother, *mama*, or perhaps breast, *mamma*. . . . A gentleman of supreme promise [40–2] not far removed from the nipple." NEELY (1985, p. 173): "His name connotes the intimate physical bond between mother and child, which extends beyond birth and makes the loss of a child a kind of death. Hermione . . . 'dies' at the announcement of Mamillius's death." Mamillius is indirectly or directly mentioned in the play's second part (e.g., 2759, 2869 ff., 2886–9), but never by his mother. WATSON (1984, p. 242): His "name . . . and nicknames ('egg' [206 presumably, but the word is not a nickname] and 'calf' [201]) mark him as a creature of regenerative nature." He has other nicknames as well, including *captain* (197–8) and *villain* (212), which do not suggest regeneration.

3373 **Camillo** (301 lines)] STOKES (1924): "May have been suggested by Camillus, the subject of one of Plutarch's *Lives*. It is also the name of a character in Webster's *The White Devil* [1611?]." PAFFORD (ed. 1963): "Shakespeare was possibly indebted to the Lives for rather more than the names: Camillus, for example, is a kind and noble man in Plutarch as Camillo is in the play. . . . The name was well known in Shakespeare's day. The Patrician name continued as a surname and Christian name in Italy and several books by authors named Camillus were published before 1611." Before *WT, Camillo*s appear in Thomas Dekker (?), *Blurt Master-Constable* (1601–2) and Ben Jonson, *The Case is Altered* (1597–8). LEVITH (1978, p. 109) derives the name from *camilla*, "attendant." H. SMITH (1974, p. 1565): "A stock type—the courtier who is loyal to the better side of his sovereign's character rather than to his . . . passionate rage." These qualities influence MERRIAM (1982) to think that Sh., a contributor to *Sir Thomas More*, modeled Camillo on the historical person. HIBBARD (1964, p. 104): "In some shape or form, this figure appears in the other three romances also, as Helicanus in *Pericles*, . . . as Bellarius, Cornelius and Pisanio in *Cymbeline*, though in this play the pattern is less clear and evident, [and as Gonzalo in *Tmp.*]." Paulina, he points out, is similarly a counselor, and (p. 110) both she and Camillo also exemplify another type, "servants . . . who disobey their superiors and act according to the dictates of their consciences."

For the possible doubling of this part, see n. 3388, and for speculation about Camillo's age, n. 1885.

3374 **Antigonus** (110 lines)] MALONE (ed. 1790): From North's Plutarch. The name occurs in several lives (but see n. 3375–6). For Josephus as a possible source, see n. 1437, and for *Arcadia*, n. 3371. COOPER (1565) lists three figures so named: Alexander's brother, king of Macedonia; a king of Asia; and "an other of Jury." LEVITH (1978, p. 109): The name "stems from the Greek words for 'born against', and foreshadows the ill-luck of Shakespeare's character." FOWLER (1978, p. 43) makes it "against offspring," with the same implication. KNIGHT (1958, p. 196), more sympathetically: "Antigonus' kindly soul opposes tyranny like that of his namesake Antigone in Sophocles."

3375–6 **Cleomines** (23 lines) . . . **Dion** (27 lines)] HALES (1876, p. 210): Found in Plutarch's *Lives*. Plutarch's figures resemble Sh.'s in name only, although, as LAW (1951, p. 61) notes, both Archidamus and Antigonus appear in the Life of Cleomenes. For another possible source of Cleomines's name, see n. 3371.

3377 **Hermione** (211 lines)] She was the beautiful daughter of Menelaus and

Helen, by various authors associated in various ways with Neoptolemus and with
Orestes. Although she appears in Plutarch's *Lives*, DUNCAN-JONES (1966) believes Sh.
drew the name from Ovid's *Heroides*, in which Hermione is the fictional author of
the eighth epistle. She is mentioned in Pickeryng's *Horestes* (1567) at line 1017, and
she appears at line 1122. There was also a male Hermione, a grandson of Phoroneus,
who, some say, founded a city in the Peloponnesus bearing his name. FOWLER (1978,
p. 38 n.): This town had "a famous cult of Ceres and Proserpina. . . . The statue
[was] of special importance in Ceres' cult." He notes (p. 38) that in Renaissance
mythology Hermione was "identified with Harmonia, daughter of Jupiter and Electra
(or of Mars and Venus). . . . If Hermione signifies the soul's harmony, her loss would
aptly symbolize Leontes' sinful state of psychological discord." BATESON (1978, p. 70
n.): "Pronounced HARMIONE. . . . Her role is to bring harmony into the play."

COLLIER (ed. 1842, 3:427): "The name . . . had been employed as that of a male
character: in 'The rare Triumphs of Love and Fortune', acted at court [on 30 Dec.
1582], and printed in 1589, Hermione is the lover of the heroine." BULLOUGH (1975,
8:21–6) considers this play a probable source of *Cym.* SALINGAR (1974, p. 38) believes
that Sh. "recalled the general style of a whole group of similar old plays," including
Rare Triumphs. RUSKIN (1882; 1906, 25:418) associates Hermione with classical virtues: "Fortitude and Justice personified, with unwearying affection. She is Penelope,
tried by her husband's fault as well as error." Elsewhere (1863; 1905, 17:258) RUSKIN
connects her name with ἔρμα, "pillar-like," which is appropriately statuesque, and
with ἡ εἶδος ἔχε χρυσέης Ἀφροδίτης, "who has the form of golden Aphrodite"
(*Odyssey* 4.14). Although he had been associated with Autolycus by ANON. ("Notes,"
1891, p. 225), MELDRUM (1968, p. 59) suggests "Hermes, the messenger of the Olympian gods"; GASPER & WILLIAMS (1986) extend this idea to the herm, the square
column surmounted by a head, usually of Hermes; *herm* was first documented by
OED in North's Plutarch. From *herm*, which "by the seventeenth century . . . was
also used to mean a statue of a saint in a church," Sh. reached *Hermione*. Or, GASPER
& WILLIAMS suggest, the name came from a book of memorial verse, *Hermae* (1596),
"the idea of a memorial constructed from words instead of stone [being] very close
to Hermione's situation in Act V, since she is not 'really' a statue at all." LEIMBERG
(1988, p. 139): "In the comedies the name . . . is foreshadowed several times, for
instance in Hermia [*MND*] or in the various Helenas [who appear or are mentioned
in *AWW*, *MND*, *Rom.*, and *Tro.*] (since Helena in Homer is Hermione's mother) and
in Hero [*Ado*] and the story of her being slain by slander but finally revived by love
and trust—a telling example of Shakespeare's latent interest in the theme of death
and redemption." KAMACHI (1991, pp. 22 ff.): "The multiple and sometimes contradictory aspects of Hermes can be of great help in understanding the complex nature
of Hermione." He discusses seven attributes—e.g., Hermes as "the guardian of shepherds and the herald of Spring . . . the guardian of petty thieves and swindlers [and]
the magician who works the Hermetic magic [including] the feat of making a statue
move." According to DRAPER (1945, pp. 37–9), Hermione's astral sign is Venus and
her dominant humor is phlegm, traits she shares with Ophelia (*Ham.*), Desdemona
(*Oth.*), and Imogen (*Cym.*).

MATTHEWS (1913, p. 325) speculates that the part was taken by the same boy actor
who had impersonated Regan in *Lr.* and Lady Macbeth. See n. 3378 for a similar guess.
SPENCER (1940, p. 369): One reason why the play is seldom produced "is the reluctance of a leading actress to play a part which contains only seven lines after Act III
[3333–40]."

3378 **Perdita** (128 lines)] HUNTER (ed. 1872): "Either the Italian word which
means *loss*, or the feminine Latin participle meaning *lost*." The Latin sense is usually
understood and translated "the lost one" or, in the style of RUSKIN (1863; 1905, 17:
223), "lost lady." Hermione names her at 1474–6, "for the babe Is counted lost for
euer," and Sh. draws this idea from *Pandosto* (p. 631). The Oracle also names her at

1315-16—*that which is lost*. DASH (1976, p. 105) attempts to connect her name with *perdit* or *perdite*, "lost to virtue; abandoned, wicked" (*OED*, a rare word, first citation 1632), the connotation of which "is certainly attached [by Leontes] to Hermione."

GREENLAW (1916, p. 145): "Perdita resembles Pastorella [in Spenser's *The Faerie Queene*, bk. 6] in that ignorant of her high station she is brought up by an old shepherd as his daughter." And like Pastorella she is very beautiful. HEILBRUN (1973, p. 33): "The appealing boy child [Mamillius] dies with the expulsion of his mother, the feminine quality in his world. But the lost girl child reappears as redeemer: dressed as Flora in the early scenes in which she appears, Perdita is literally the savior of the world to which she returns." BARTON (1990, pp. 150-1): "'Perdita' ceases to be appropriate once Leontes' daughter sets foot in her own kingdom of Sicily. At this point, it vanishes from the play. She is addressed and referred to as 'Princess', the 'daughter of a king', from that time forward. . . . Spoken only once again in the play, by Paulina [3331-2], the name reappears briefly only in order to be cancelled out ['Our *Perdita* is found']."

MATTHEWS (1913, p. 325): The part may have been taken by the same boy who had previously played Cordelia in *Lr.* and would play Miranda in *Tmp.* (cf. n. 3377). PARTRIDGE (1982, p. 4): "On Shakespeare's stage the parts of Hermione and Perdita were probably doubled, which explains why Perdita is given so little to say in the final scene [3234-8 and 3287-8]." He alone thinks so, although the parts have been doubled on the modern stage (see p. 804).

In the Prologue to *Every Man in his Humour*, Jonson censures the ill customs of the stage, including making "a child, now swadled, to proceede Man, and then shoote vp, in one beard and weede, Past threescore yeeres." HUNTER (1845, 1:138) finds that Sh. stands "exposed [not only] to the general censure of the prologue" but also to this point, the depiction in the same play of "infancy and maturity in the same character." INGLEBY (1879, p. 118) asserts that the allusion is to *WT*, but beardless Perdita is the only character who appears as an infant and as an adult, though hardly one of threescore.

3379 **Paulina** (329 lines)] PAFFORD (ed. 1963, p. 163): Maybe from Paulinus in North's Plutarch. LENNOX (1753, 2:72): "An old Lady," which some find reasonably accurate by the end of the play (see nn. 819 and 3355-7). SKOTTOWE (1824, 2:300): "Paulina is not one of Shakspeare's happiest female portraits: however good her heart and her intentions, her manners are not well adapted for a court; her candour is ill-bred bluntness, and her vehemence vulgar passion." BENDA (ed. 1825, 8:168), in contrast, is unreserved in his praise of her; she is like a god who works throughout the play. DOBREÉ (1960, p. 144): "At once virago and priestess."

GREENE (1982, p. 10): Paulina "is given extraordinary power to protect her mistress, to exact repentance from an erring Leontes, and to regenerate a sterile, self-destructive patriarchy." SMITH (1972, p. 112): "She is made into the second most important character in the play, measured by the number of lines spoken. And if Shakespeare had first intended to have Hermione really die and not brought back to life [see JAMIESON (1964, p. 81)], it is difficult to see why he would have invented Paulina at all." Her part is half again as long as Hermione's. She is Sh.'s invention; there is no corresponding character in *Pandosto*. PEARSON (1979) alone believes that Sh.'s depiction of her was influenced by the traditional figure of the bawd, procuress, and matchmaker found in *La Celestina*, among many other Renaissance works.

DAVIES (1986, p. 167), following KNIGHT (1958, p. 196) and BATTENHOUSE (1980, p. 137): "The name . . . , so intimately associated with Grace . . . , inevitably alludes to that of St. Paul," an inevitability less compelling after Christian interpretations of the play ran their course. ENGLAND (1982, p. 75): Her "name is not only intentionally Christian but may even suggest her role as a healer in the Pauline tradition. . . . She immediately identifies the King's 'dangerous, unsafe lunes' [856] and presents herself to him as 'your physician' [965]." ORNSTEIN (1986, p. 223): "If . . . Paulina's name has momentous significance, it is curious that she is not identified by name before the fifth act [the 3rd actually (1478)]." IRVINE (1945) gives her a short *i* (as in *machine*); KÖKERITZ (1959), a long *i* (as in *lime*).

3380 **Emilia** (20 lines)] According to Plutarch's Life of Romulus, some say that Mars sired Romulus upon Æmilia, the daughter of Æneas and Lavinia. Emilia, one of the women accompanying Hermione to prison because the queen's "plight requires it" (726), has four speeches in 2.2. MAHOOD (1992, p. 45) identifies her with the Second Lady of 2.1; see n. 594. PORTER & CLARKE (ed. 1908): "It is perhaps a reminder of the Æmilia attendant upon another cruelly maligned wife that this intimate attendant is named . . . *Emilia*. Æmilia is the Paulina of 'Othello.'" Sh. would have found the name *Æmilia* elsewhere in Plutarch, as well as in Chaucer's Knight's Tale, the Æmilii being an ancient Roman patrician family. MELDRUM (1968, p. 59): The name means "follows the good."

3381 **Polixenes . . . Bohemia** (271 lines)] STOKES (1924): "No attempt is made to identify it [Bohemia] with the European country so named, which is nowhere mentioned by Sh." For its seacoast, see n. 1440. SUGDEN (1925): "There is no King of Bohemia whose name even distantly resembles either Pandosto [see p. 618] or Polixenes." For the Polyxenus in Plutarch's Life of Dion, see n. 3371. LEVITH (1978, p. 109), improbably: The "name suggests 'an entertainer', from *polyxenos* for 'hospitable and much visited.'" KNIGHT (1958, p. 196) had groped along the same root. MARTZ (1980, p. 114 n.) suggests a connection with Polyxena, Hecuba's daughter. "Such a name, of course, is significant only for evoking a legendary or tragic atmosphere, not for specific relation."

3382 **Florizell** (205 lines)] Following SOUTHEY (1807, 1:xliv–xlv), BROWNE (1876, p. 147) believes that Sh. drew the name from *Amadis de Grecia* (see p. 680); Florisel is the hero of the ninth book: "Florisel, in the guise of a shepherd, woos a princess, who is disguised as a shepherdess." In *Amadis* he is "the prettiest prince in the world." Originally published in Burgos in 1535, book 9 was soon translated into French and Italian, though not into English. That it was known in England, however, is indicated by the probability that Greene drew the name *Garinter* from it (see p. 681). Yet *Florizel* was also the name adopted by Antonio disguised as an Amazon in John Marston's *1 Antonio and Mellida* (1599; ed. 1602, sig. C1), a possible source closer to home than *Amadis*, from which Marston may have borrowed. As FRYE (1962, p. 244) says, Sh. wanted a name appropriate to the masculine counterpart of Perdita as the goddess Flora (see lines 1799–1800); LEVIN (1965, p. 70), following KNIGHT (1958, p. 196), speaks of Florizel as a flowery prince. WALKER (1860, 2:33) discovers *Doricles*, Florizel's assumed name, in the *Aeneid* 5.620; a Doryklos appears in the *Iliad*; Doricus is Plutarch's closest approach. Rather than in a classical source, however, Sh. may have found the name in George Chapman's *Blind Beggar of Alexandria* (1596), in which a Prince Doricles of Arcadia appears. Since this play survives only in a truncated form, the extent of Sh.'s debt to it, if any, cannot be ascertained. Chapman's Doricles, however, and perhaps Sh.'s, too, probably derives from Sidney's *Arcadia*; the "name combining elements of Musidorus (himself called 'Dorus' in his [disguise as a shepherd]) and Pyrocles" (ANDREWS, 1972, p. 200 n.). ORGEL (ed. 1996): "Doric, from Doris, in Greece, was used to mean rustic, as the Doric order was the simplest of the Greek architectural orders." STOPES (1916, p. 35 n.): "'Florizel' was the Christian name of a man in Stratford, in Shakespeare's time." This was Florisell Bovey of Alcester (see ECCLES, 1961, p. 107).

3383 **Old Shepheard** (139 lines)] HOLME (1688, 3.72) describes a typical one: He is "*clothed* in a *loose Coat*, and round or *close kneed Breeches*." He carries a crook and wears a wide-brimmed hat. "A Shepherd is, and ever was esteemed a Noble Employ, it being the business of the Patriarchs *Abraham* and *Jacob*, Gen. 47.3, and

who knoweth not, that *David* from following his Ewes, was made King of *Judah*."
The age of the Old Shepheard is fourscore three (2300). For more, see n. 1501.

   3384 **Clowne** (194 lines)] HOLME (1688, 3.72): "A Country unbred fellow, which
the *Dutch term the Boors* of the Countrey, such as have neither Learning, Wit, nor
Manners." For more on boors, see n. 3168. LEGOUIS (1916, p. 406): Just at the end
of his career Shakespeare restored the clown exactly to his original condition, before
he had become a professional entertainer. He identified him with the silly peasant
whose name the clown bore but whom he hardly remembered any more to have
been. . . . [This clown] is a true country boy, stupid and artless. The clown had
deserted the fields for the stage; he is returned at last to the sheepfold (in Fr.). CA-
ZAMIAN (1945, p. 39), similarly: Only at the end of his career . . . did Sh. bring the
clown back to his origins to make anew of him a figure with overtones of the dullest
(de la plus épaisse) rusticity (in Fr.). BALDWIN (1927, p. 241), describing the "lines," or
specialties, of the actors in Sh.'s company: "Near akin to the fool is the rustic or clown,
so labelled in *Antony, All's Well*, and *Winter's Tale*. To this foolish, philosophical crew
would belong the First Gravedigger [*Ham.*], the Clown of Othello, the Porter [*Mac.*],
and the First Citizen in *Coriolanus*. Of more dignified position, but of equally comic
characteristics, are the very Welsh parson Evans [*Wiv.*], and the clownish gull Cloten
[*Cym.*]." To the clowns CLARK (1936, p. 47) adds Costard (*LLL*) and the rural fellow
who brings the asps to Cleopatra (*Ant.*). BERGERON (1985, p. 164): "The Shepherd and
Clown become a parody of Leontes and Mamillius or Polixenes and Florizel," but he
does not discuss how this parody works. See n. 3147–53, however.

   3385 **Autolicus** (295 lines)] "My Father nam'd me *Autolicus*, who being (as I am)
lytter'd vnder Mercurie, was likewise a snapper-vp of vnconsidered trifles" (1692–
4). THEOBALD (ed. 1733): The allusion is to *alipedis de stirpe dei versuta propago
nascitur Autolycus furtum ingeniosus ad omne* "a son was born to the wing-footed
god [Mercury], Autolycus, of crafty nature, well versed in cunning wiles" (Ovid, *Met.*
11.312–13, trans. Miller). Sh. could have read the passage in Latin or in GOLDING's
1567 translation, in which Chione bears Mercury "A sonne that hyght *Awtolychus*,
who provde a wyly pye [magpie, a thieving bird], And such a fellow as in theft and
filching had no peere. He was his fathers owne sonne right: he could mennes eyes
so bleere, As for to make the black things whyght, and whyght things black appeere"
(11.360–4). THEOBALD continues, "The true *Autolycus* was the Son of *Mercury*; our
fictitious one, born under his Planet: the first a Copy of his Father; the other, suppos'd
to derive his Qualities from natal Predominance [the planet ascendant at the time of
his birth]," one of these qualities being thievishness. Hermes, with whom Mercury
was identified, was also a trickster; according to Homer, his gift to Autolycus was a
stealthy disposition (*Iliad* 24.334–5). ANON. ("Notes," 1891, p. 225) is struck by the
resemblance of Autolycus "to the great master-thief of antiquity, Hermes, as he is
described in the so-called 'Homeric Hymn.' . . . They are uncommon thieves, who
do their stealing in such a clever, taking way that we are completely captivated by
their artfulness." The Autolycus of the *Iliad* in his turn gave rich gifts to his grandson
Odysseus when Odysseus visited him. According to WARBURTON (ed. 1747), "the
whole speech is taken from *Lucian*['s] . . . *discourse on judicial Astrology*, where
Autolicus talks much in the same manner." DOUCE (1807, 1:354): Autolycus does not
speak in Lucian's *Astrology*; as FIELD (in HALLIWELL, ed. 1859) remarks, WARBURTON
"must have been dreaming." BROWNE (1876, p. 147), more diplomatically: "The Renaissance attributed several things to Lucian which modern criticism has rejected, and
it is possible that, in the course of his multifarious reading, Warburton had come
across some French or Italian Autolycus." HOLLAND (1970, p. 36): Among the characters in *WT*, only he "is merely adaptable, protean, a shape-changer who belongs
everywhere and nowhere, like his patron [Hermes] who freely travels as an intermediary among the gods and the living and the dead." WILSON (ed. 1931, p. xxi)

unnecessarily suggests that Sh. saw Chapman's translation of the *Odyssey* before its publication in 1614–15(?) and drew from the description there of Homer's Autolycus some inspiration for his own. In Chapman, "Autolycus, who th'Art Of Theft and swearing (not out of the hart, But by equivocation) first adorn'd Your witty man withall, and was suborn'd By Jove's descent, ingenious Mercurie" (ed. Nicoll, 1956, 19.545–9). Following HUGHES (1940, p. 222), THOMSON (1952, p. 131): "Autolycus appears first in the *Odyssey* . . . , but it was in Ovid that Shakespeare found him." For the possible contributions of commentators on Ovid to Autolycus's character, see LAMB (1989).

Other speculators on Autolycus's ancestry include BURNEY (1776–89; 1935, 2: 272): "This Autolychus is the true ancient minstrel, as described in the old Fabliaux." DOUCE (1807, 1:351–2) says this "observation is inaccurate. Autolycus has nothing in common with the character of a minstrel but the singing of a song or two." MOORE (1922, p. 164) shows that, in Autolycus, "Shakespeare has combined the attributes of the singing vagabonds of the later moralities and interludes." FURNIVALL (ed. 1877?, p. xci, n. 4): "He [Sh.] may have recollected the amusing pedlar in the curious *Book of Dives Pragmaticus*, 1563 . . . , who sold everything then known under the sun." This book is "very preaty for children to rede: wherby they may the better, and the more readyer, rede and wryte wares and Implements" (sig. A1). Dives is a spirited fellow ("What lacke you good people? come hether fayre mayde, What bye you what seeke you? speake, be not affrayde" [sig. A3ᵛ]), but being short on turpitude, he bears only a professional similarity to Autolycus ("Also this shall be now, my next exhortation, That you forsake Dice, Cardes, and fornication" [sig. B3ᵛ]). Equally unlikely is the suggestion of PEROTT (1910) that Autolycus is based on a horse thief named Fraudador in Feliciano de Silva's *Don Florisel de Niquea* (1532–67), 4.2.20. HASTINGS (1940) asserts that Sh. remembered Simplicity, the Vice in Robert Wilson's *The Three Ladies of London* and *The Three Lords and the Three Ladies of London*, but the resemblance is remote. ELTON (1947, p. 115) adds another parallel, the Pedlar in John Heywood's *The Four P's* (c. 1520–2). SPEIRS (1957, p. 341 n.) finds Autolycus "to have descended from a tradition other than the Greek or Roman, most probably the Celtic or Norse. Among the Norse gods, Loki was not only a shape-shifter . . . but dishonest, a ne'er-do-well and a thief." ANON. (1957), however: "We know for a fact that Shakespeare knew a great deal of classical mythology. . . . We know for as near a fact as makes no matter that he knew no Celtic or Norse mythology at all." He did know Plutarch, though, in which one Autolycus appears in the Life of Lysander and another in the Life of Lucullus, as LAW (1951, p. 62) points out. BOWERS (1960, pp. 88–9): Yet another Autolycus, "a bland replica of Shakespeare's," appears in George Wilde's [i.e., John Speed's] *The Converted Robber* (BL Add. MS 14047 dated 1637), a play possibly to be identified with Speed's *Stonehenge* of 1635 (see Harbage et al., *Annals*, 3rd ed., 1989). An Autolycus with whom Sh. was probably entirely unacquainted was a fourth-century B.C. astronomer and mathematician.

SPENCE (1920, p. 46) on the astrological significance of Mercurial birth: "If ill dignified [of low station], then the native is a mean, unprincipled character, pretending to knowledge, but an imposter and a slanderer, boastful, malicious, and addicted to theft." STEEVENS (ed. 1778) quotes *Non fuit Autolyci tam [piperata] manus*— "Autolycus' hand was not so sharp" (Martial, *Epigrams* 8.59, trans. Walter C. A. Ker). The CLARKES (1879, p. 479) call him "mercurial-natured and Mercury-propensitied." Speaking generally of the ancient Autolycus, HALES (1876; 1884, pp. 109, 111): "His name probably is significant of his nature. It should mean All-wolf, Very-wolf, Wolf's-self"; and he, like Sh., had "a ready gift for self-transformation. . . . [Sh.'s Autolycus] appears as a shabby, *ci-devant* valet—which he is, as the denuded victim of thieves, as a most successful pedlar, as a courtier, and lastly as a fawning and servile dependent." For more on Autolycus's social station, see n. 3009. Regarding All-wolf, etc.,

NUTTALL (1966, p. 39): "The suggestion of voracity makes good sense." NICHOLS (1981, p. 179): "The wolf is the antithesis of the good shepherd." BROWN (1947, p. 45 n.) adds that the classical Autolycus "lives on Mount Parnassus; like other outlaws, he is credited with magical powers." SCHANZER (ed. 1969, p. 11): His Greek name "is in violation of Shakespeare's practice of bestowing English names upon his comic low-life characters, whatever country they belong to." SALINGAR (1966, p. 32 n.): "Is there an autobiographical joke in Autolycus, the shape-changer, the ballad-singer, the 'snapper-up of unconsidered trifles' [1694]?" KNIGHT (1958, p. 196) associates the snapping up with *lukos*, wolf; to him, "'auto' suggests an individualist, one who thinks only of himself."

GRANTLEY (1986), arguing for "the clearly religious and didactic nature of Shakespeare's conception" of *WT* (p. 18), asserts that Sh.'s model was early Tudor religious drama—Leontes, for example, is Mankind, specifically exemplifying Anger; Hermione, patient Griselda; Paulina, Conscience; Autolycus, the Vice—but on a similar level of abstraction Sh. probably could be made indebted to the No play. For an attempt to identify Autolycus with Leontes and to connect Autolycus with various themes in the play, see ROCKAS (1975, pp. 10-13). DRAPER (1985, p. 29): "He and Florizel become curiously connected: their common experience of 'transformations' [cf. 1832, with Autolycus as tinker, traveller, snapper-up, peddler, courtier] hints at a transforming power at work in the play." JAMES (1937, pp. 227, 238) admires him more than most: "Autolycus . . . is enough to reconcile the hardest heart to thieving, if thieves be such as he. . . . Autolycus is a desirable member of any right-minded community." CAZAMIAN (1945, p. 204), also an admirer: The humor of Autolycus is truly what liberates him from all the obstacles that hinder the play of his desire (in Fr.).

FELVER (1961, p. 62): "Of all the fool's parts [in Sh.'s plays], Autolycus is third in size." For the possible doubling of this part, see n. 3388 below.

3386 **Archidamus** (21 lines)] The name of several Spartan kings. Sh., who, according to BERGER & BRADFORD (1975), was first to have used it for a dramatic character, could have found it in Plutarch's Life of Agesilaus, though nothing but the name connects Plutarch's king with Polixenes's courtier. For names in *Arcadia*, see n. 3371; and for the possible doubling of this part, see n. 3388 below.

3387-8 **Other . . . Shephearddesses**] F. W. CLARKE (in FURNIVALL, ed. 1908) analyzes this collective listing. The first lines of speeches are indicated, and (*) marks the entrances of mutes:

```
1st Lord to Leontes 630, 929, 1296
Other Lords to Leontes 628*, 1074
1st Servant to Leontes 909, 1323
2nd Servant to Leontes 935
Servant to the Shepherd of Bohemia 2006
Servants to Leontes 2725*; one speaks 2831
A Lord of Polixenes's court 2941
Lords of Leontes's court 3185*
Shepherds and Shepherdesses 1988-9*
1st Lady to Hermione 588
2nd Lady to Hermione 594
Sicilian Guards 585*
Sicilian Gaoler 826
Attendants on Paulina 820*
Officer of Leontes's court of justice 1184
A Mariner 1441
A Bear 1499 (growls)
```

Time, the Chorus 1580 (see n. 1579)
Mopsa, a Bohemian Shepherdess 1985 (for a possible source of her name,
    see n. 3371)
Dorcas, a Bohemian Shepherdess 1983 (her name is found in Acts 9:36)
Three Carters, three Shepherds, three Neatherds, three Swineherds of
    Bohemia as twelve Satyrs 2164*
A small Train to Florizel and Perdita 2878*
1st Gentleman of Leontes's court 3013
2nd Gentleman of Leontes's court (Rogero) 3032
3rd Gentleman, Paulina's Steward 3040; he may also be the Gentleman
    at 820*

3388 *Shephearddesses*] ROWE (ed. 1709) first lists Mopsa and Dorcas, identifying them as Shepherdesses. They may be, but their milking and tattling at the kiln-
hole (2068–9) suggest that they work in the barnyard and about the house. FURNESS
(ed. 1898): "Dorcas is Biblical [Acts 9:36–9], and, in *Dorastus and Fawnia* [*Pandosto*] Mopsa is the name of the old shepherd's wife." Hers is the only name that Sh.
brings over from *Pandosto* (see p. 635). Dorcas had previously appeared in Sidney's
Arcadia and *The Merry Devil of Edmonton* (1602), and Mopsa had appeared in *Arcadia* and Day's *Isle of Gulls* (1606). COOPER (1565) gives *Mopsus* as a shepherd's
name. MOUNT ("Sidney," 1893): Since no *Mopsa* is found in classical verse (though
Mopsus often), Sh. must have taken the name from *Arcadia. Pandosto*, however, is
the more probable source. See n. 1951–62. BARBER (1964, p. 238) finds Mopsa and
Dorcas to be foils for Perdita; "her refined and delicate behaviour toward Florizel is
contrasted with the behaviour of the comic rustic girls . . . towards the Clown."

    Regarding the casting of women, JAMIESON (1964, p. 27): "Mamillius and the ladies
of the court could be doubled with Mopsa, Dorcas, and other shepherdesses; it is
possible that Mamillius and Perdita, in the interest of family likeness, were played by
one boy, and that the boys who play Hermione and Paulina 'walked on' as shepherdesses in the sheepshearing interlude [4.4]. Thus the play met the basic requirements
of the King's Men—it did not tax the numerical strength of their boy actresses [three
to five according to CHAMBERS (1930, 1:82)]." MAHOOD (1992, p. 14), who agrees
that the parts of Mamillius and Perdita would have been doubled, notices (p. 225, n.
30) that Trilby James "played both parts in the English Shakespeare Company's 1990
production." As for men, BOOTH (1979, p. 130 n.): "The case for one actor playing
the phonetic triplets Archidamus, Antigonus, and Autolycus is at least as good as the
one for doubling Antigonus and Camillo."

Actus Primus. Scœna Prima. 1.1 (2A1)

Enter Camillo and Archidamus. (2A1ᵃ)

1 *Scœna Prima.*] THEO *om. scene numbers throughout.*
SCENE *A Palace.* ROWE, POPE, HAN, CAM3-SIS, SIG+ (−PEN2, OXF2); SCENE, *an Antichamber in* Leontes's PALACE. THEO, WARB, JOHN1-NLSN, ARD1; *Before Leontes' palace.* RLTR (*and so for* 1.2, 2.1, 2.3, 3.1, 5.1, *and* 5.2); in or near Leontes' palace. ARD2. PEL1, CLN2, PEN2, and OXF2 *om. exact locales throughout.*

---

1 ***Actus . . . Prima.***] For the location of the scene and its relation to 1.2, see n. 48. CLAPP (1885, p. 402): It is "introductory, and of no particular position in time." ARCHER (1912; 1960, p. 58): "The situation would be entirely comprehensible if the scene . . . were omitted." LAWLOR (1962, p. 106), however, supplies a good reason for retaining it: So "that Leontes' passion shall break with full force on the audience, the play opens with a dialogue . . . which tells of peace and amity." HERFORD (ed. 1916–): "The conversation serves to initiate us into the general situation: the visit of the Bohemian king to Sicily, the old friendship of the two kings, and the elaborate politeness, touched with a prophetic suggestion of hollowness, which prevails between the two courts." LAWLOR continues: "Here are assembled and inter-acting the ideas of natural growth (in affection), the promise of a new generation, and the desire of the old to outlive time, if necessary, to see its fulfilment. The scene that follows is to reverse these expectations." PURDOM (1963, p. 180): "He [Sh.] let the play open in happiness. . . . Leontes usually comes on the stage [in 1.2] glowering, but Shakespeare did not intend that he should." ARTHOS (1964, p. 172) has a different impression: "The happiness of [1.1] has within it the note of those outside a place happily looking on something within — they themselves are not at the heart of the perfection they speak of." Some critics, anticipating what is to come, find ominous hints. EWBANK (1964, p. 85): The scene "proceeds via a series of references to time seen as a natural growth; it places the play in a perspective of naturally ripening time, opening backwards as well as forwards. Camillo . . . introduces the whole span of human life by way of talking about the little Prince Mamillius . . . and this subject is expanded to provide . . . an ironically foreboding note [46–7]." NEELY (1985, p. 192): *WT* "begins in a static, barren masculine world that appears determinedly self-sufficient, capable of sustaining itself without the violent trauma of birth. . . . Women are strikingly absent from the idyllic picture." The barren world contains imaginary vegetation (25–7), however, and the two kings' imaginary embrace (33) does not suggest complete self-sufficiency. See also HOLBROOK in n. 24–34 and n. 25–6.

DELIUS (1870, p. 250): The euphuistical coloring of the prose corresponds to the somewhat ceremonious tone in which the two courtiers exchange compliments. BARBER (1964, pp. 241-3), however, discovers a rather sinister affectation: The speeches "tend to be just a little bit too stilted, too mannered. . . . The opening speech . . . is a single complex sentence in which the main verb is held back a long time—which gives a sense of contrivance . . . and is neatly rounded off with the balance of 'our Bohemia, and your Sicilia'. . . . [At 14 ff.] the very sense of incoherence is contrived . . . a deliberate rhetorical device." He compares 3090-3100, "contrived to the point of preciosity." The courtiers' style emphasizes the artificiality of the court, where the king's tyranny is spinelessly accepted by all but Paulina. PYLE (1969, p. 12) disagrees: "Archidamus the guest [is] extravagant and profuse in gratitude[;] Camillo . . . , playing the deprecating host, can be much blunter [as at 20-1]."

FELPERIN (1972, p. 223): "Given the courtly setting, the idiom . . . with its mildly euphuistic balance, witty turns of phrase, and frequent figures of speech, is perfectly colloquial. But to the extent that their figures of speech play on the impossible and conjure up the miraculous, their language is simultaneously an oracular language, reflective of the romantic nature of the play as a whole." HATTORI (1982, p. 90): "What idyllic voidness of matter there is in this wordy conversation." PARTRIDGE (1982, p. 1): The "scene . . . deliberately inflates the style in order to present the luxury and artificiality of court life in Sicilia, and to contrast it with the rural simplicity of Bohemia." MAHOOD (1992, p. 35): "The difficulty with all such dialogues is that they are palpable contrivances which lack the plain-dealing of a prologue or chorus. Shakespeare sensibly exploits their artificiality rather than attempting to conceal it: . . . there is mild mockery of courtly elaborations of language as the Bohemian visitor struggles to emulate the Sicilian's verbal airs and graces." BETHELL (ed. 1956) disagrees: "The scene is highly ironic: the friendship which 'must branch' [27] is to be broken, the young prince's death is to disappoint people's hopes. [See nn. 24-34, 35-6.] . . . The *wit* [of the courtiers, presumably] which treats serious matters lightly [is] a mark of sophistication." See n. 16-19. SUMMERS (1984, p. 25): "The language . . . becomes extravagantly in excess of what seems proper for the occasion or matter described, until each of the speakers in turn is interrupted [12 and 13] and his extravagance gently rebuked [43 and 44-5]."

2 *Archidamus*] THEOBALD (ed. 1733): "This is a Character of that Sort [protactic] . . . introduc'd only to open Something, necessary to be known, previous to the Action of the *Fable*." SPRAGUE (1935, p. 112): Archidamus "is never addressed by name, and disappears as soon as the conversation is over." ROCKAS (1975, pp. 4-5), noting that the gentlemen of 5.2 are unnamed (Rogero, 3031, excepted), speculates that Sh. "intended a further role for Archidamus . . . as Polixenes' courtier and Camillo as Leontes', but later found that the plot required Camillo for both." HARRISON (ed. 1947): "In *Lear* and in *Antony and Cleopatra* Shakespeare also introduces the action with a short conversation between two characters of secondary rank to lead up to the entrance of the principals. There is a faintly topical significance in the situation [here] as it would have reminded courtly spectators of the notable state visit paid to King James I by his brother-in-law, the King of Denmark, in 1606," for which see n. 50-1. BOOTH (1979, p. 128, n. 4): A trick used by masters of ceremonies is to show the superstar for a moment at the beginning of a performance, to let the audience know that he is really there. "Shakespeare may have created Francisco [*Ham.*], Archidamus, and Philo [*Ant.*], characters who speak the opening lines of their plays and never appear after Scene One, for the specific purpose of allowing Burbage or an actor of similar stature to quiet the audience by his talent and, perhaps, reassure them by his presence."

Arch.
If you shall chance (*Camillo*) to visit *Bohemia*, on
the like occasion whereon my seruices are now   5
on-foot, you shall see (as I haue said) great difference betwixt our *Bohemia*, and your *Sicilia.*
    Cam. I thinke, this comming Summer, the King of
Sicilia meanes to pay *Bohemia* the Visitation, which hee
iustly owes him.   10

---

8 comming] common F2-ROWE2

---

4 **shall**] BRADLEY (1916, 2:555): Corresponding to modern *should*. See ABBOTT
§348, FRANZ §644.
    4-6 **on . . . on-foot**] DEIGHTON (ed. 1889): "On an occasion like to that in
which I am now employed" (*OED*, Foot, *sb.* 32c). ADAMS (1989, p. 91): Archidamus
"defines that occasion and those services no further," but ADAMS (p. 92) suggests
that "he has just arrived from Bohemia, bringing news that all is well in Polixenes'
kingdom" (see 87-8). RANN (ed. 1787) interprets the passage differently: "As an
attendant on your soveraign." WHITE (ed. 1883) objects to the repetition in *on*
. . . *whereon* . . . *on-foot*, calling it "heedlessness in regard to nicety of style";
FURNESS (ed. 1898) terms it "careless, colloquial ease," appropriate to the chitchat
noticed by COLERIDGE (see n. 48). KITTREDGE & RIBNER (ed. 1967), however: "Both
Camillo and Archidamus use a highly elaborate and formal kind of speech."
    6 **as . . . said**] FURNESS (ed. 1898): "Quite needless, but . . . it conveys the
idea of a conversation of which we hear only the closing portion."
    6-7 **great difference**] MAHOOD (1957, p. 147): As it develops, "'contention' as
well as 'dissimilarity.'" PYLE (1969, p. 11 n.) considers such a "search for double
meanings . . . the extreme of literary as distinct from dramatic interpretation. . . . It would be a poor playwright who would start his play with double meanings before even a single meaning had been imparted."
    7 ***Bohemia*** . . . ***Sicilia***] PORTER & CLARKE (ed. 1908): "Shakespeare, in placing
his opening in Sicily, draws here a contrast between the greater elegance and culture
of its older maritime civilization and that of the ruder continental country of Bohemia,
and that his change was intentional this contrast indicates." HOLBROOK (1964, p.
134): The difference to which Archidamus alludes is that "to some extent Bohemia
represents the simple, more natural, intuitive bodily life: Sicilia the life of the civilized—or cultivated—mind." Regarding Bohemia, he perhaps has in mind the pastoral scenes and the love story; the cultivation of Sicilia may be implied by the magnificence of the entertainments Archidamus has enjoyed and perhaps of Paulina's
gallery in 5.3. On the other hand, the two countries were so remote from Sh.'s London
that such implications are as irrelevant as locating *AYL*'s Forest of Arden in France.
    9 ***Bohemia***] I.e., Polixenes. HARDINGE (1818, 3:48): "Calling the Sovereign by the
name of his *kingdom personified*" is a habit peculiar to Sh. The CLARKES (1879, p.
755) give examples from *Ham.* (Denmark, Norway), *Ant.* (Egypt), and other Shn.
plays. *The Masque of Blackness*, however, mentions "*Albion* the faire; So call'd of
Neptunes son, who ruleth here" (lines 206-7); Jonson notes, "Alluding to the *rite* of
stiling princes, after the names of their princedoms."
    Visitation] *OED*'s earliest instance of *visit* as a noun is 1621; as SCHMIDT (1875)
notes, Sh. uses that word only as a verb. Other visitations, which also happen to be
visits of state, occur at 2421 and 2838. BOORMAN (ed. 1964): "'A friendly visit' [*OED*

Arch. Wherein our Entertainment shall shame vs: we
will be iustified in our Loues: for indeed —
   Cam. 'Beseech you —
   Arch. Verely I speake it in the freedome of my knowledge: we cannot with such magnificence — in so rare —   15
I know not what to say — Wee will giue you sleepie
Drinkes, that your Sences (vn-intelligent of our insufficience) may, though they cannot prayse vs, as little accuse vs.
   Cam. You pay a great deale to deare, for what's giuen   20
freely.

---

11 vs:] ~ , THEO1-NLSN (−SING2), KIT1, ALEX, PEL1, SIG, OXF2, BEV4
12 Loues] love JOHN2

5], but also 'an unwelcome visit, an affliction' [6c].'' In the light of the kings' imminent
separation, everything said here about their friendship becomes ironical (see nn. 24–
34, 25–6, 27, 35–6), though how much irony is intentional, not to mention perceptible to an audience, is open to question. Several critics believe that the irony of 34,
for instance, is plain and memorable. The present instance is questionable, as are 27
and 33.
   10 **iustly owes him**] DEIGHTON (ed. 1889): "He having a right to expect a return
of the compliment.''
   11–12 **Wherein . . . Loues**] Eds. retaining F's colon after *vs* make
"Wherein . . . vs" Archidamus's continuation of Camillo's speech, a clause modifying *Visitation.* MOORMAN (ed. 1912) paraphrases this construction as "on the occasion of your visit our entertainment of you, compared with your entertainment of
us, may put us to shame; but the cordiality of our welcome shall make amends.''
HERFORD (ed. 1916–), however: Such "harsh concision is not Archidamus's foible.''
Those reducing the colon to a comma (or omitting it, as do CLARK & WRIGHT, ed.
1863) make the clause modify "will be iustified.'' Thus RANN (ed. 1787), somewhat
inaccurately: "Our good will must atone for the deficiencies of our entertainment.''
JOHNSON (ed. 1765): "Though we cannot give you equal entertainment, yet the consciousness of our good-will shall justify us.'' The CLARKES (ed. 1865), similarly: "In
whatsoever the entertainment we then give you will do us discredit in comparison
with that which you now give us, our love shall make up for the deficiency.'' MAXWELL
(ed. 1956) compares "the broken sentences [14–19].'' ORGEL (ed. 1996): "This
[THEOBALD's comma] gives an undeniably easier sense, but Archidamus' next speech,
emphasizing the absolute insufficiency of Bohemian entertainment, suggests that F's
syntax is correct.'' PAFFORD (ed. 1963): "This courtly language is similar to that of
[5.2].'' CUTTS (1968, p. 55): "The overwhelming entertainment Leontes has put
on . . . is not unlike Timon's need to create an *embarras de richesses* to make
visitors incapable of repaying him in kind—an attempt to assert dominance over the
visitor.'' REID (1970, p. 264), similarly: "Archidamus is aware that there is something
amiss, something strained and overdone in Leontes' show of hospitality to his friend
Polixenes. It is a neurotic show of affection which Polixenes will have no need to
display when visited by Leontes.'' ERICKSON (1982, p. 819) also finds a sober side:

"Tension stems from the disparity in the two kings' munificence; mutuality is threatened because the two cannot give equally."

11 **Entertainment**] JOHNSON (1755): "Hospitable reception."

12 **iustified**] SCHANZER (ed. 1969): "Acquitted, absolved (of the sin of entertaining you unworthily—a glance at the doctrine of salvation by faith rather than by good works)." As n. 11–12 indicates, however, other eds. are less theological. SCHMIDT (1874, Justify): "To vindicate."

13 **'Beseech you**] DEIGHTON (ed. 1889): "*I.e.* pray continue what you were saying." KNOWLES (privately): "Oh, please, don't depreciate yourself to flatter us." For the omission of the nominative, see ABBOTT §399.

14–16 **Verely . . . say**] DELIUS (ed. 1860): Archidamus cannot find words to describe the magnificent hospitality of Leontes's court. PORTER & CLARKE (ed. 1908): "Shakespeare's way of making use of Greene's mention of the reception of the royal guest in Bohemia." See *Pandosto*, p. 622. MOWAT (1969, p. 41) argues that the "magnificent entertainment . . . is explained by Camillo as being rather a duty of Leontes to his childhood friend" (see lines 25–7).

14 **Verely**] A limber vow, according to Hermione (106).

14–15 **in . . . knowledge**] CALDECOTT (MS 1813–33), inaccurately: "As frankly, plainly, as assuredly." ROLFE (ed. 1879): "As my knowledge makes me free to do, or gives me the right to do." PARRY (ed. 1982): "And not because I want to flatter you." TAYLOR (1972, p. 49): "Imprisoned in his compulsive jealousy, yet continually affirming the fictions of objectivity and truth, his [Leontes's] situation makes a mockery of Archidamus' words." Yet the courtiers' words, "more than counters in a game of courtlier-than-thou . . . inform and sustain a necessary and delightful mutual esteem."

16–19 **Wee . . . vs**] HERFORD (ed. 1916–): "The euphuistic balance of the sentence [*prayse vs . . . accuse vs*], as well as its pretentiously learned words [*vn-intelligent . . . insufficience*], are proper to a speech of courtly compliment." BETHELL (ed. 1956): "This is *wit*: . . . the speaker wishes to convey a polite depreciation of his own country." TINKLER (1937, p. 359), however, believes that because sleepy drinks "lull the intelligence," the words "hint at a basic uneasiness," although a drugged Sicilian should not alarm an alert Bohemian. Drinks "take on a more sinister meaning" (p. 360) when they become the bespiced cup that gives a lasting wink (413–14), although that cup is to be administered to a Bohemian.

16–17 **sleepie Drinkes**] DEIGHTON (ed. 1889): "Soporifics." ADAMS (1989, p. 93) thinks the visiting Sicilians will be got drunk so "they won't recognize the inadequacy of their entertainment," Bohemia being a Germanic country.

17 **that**] I.e., so that (ABBOTT §283). Cf. 31, 1962, and 2804.

Sences] *OED* (Sense, *sb.* 6. *pl.*): "A general term for the faculties of perception (including the 'five senses' . . .) which are in abeyance when their owner is asleep or otherwise unconscious."

17–18 **vn-intelligent . . . insufficience**] JOHNSON (1755) defines these words as "not knowing [or] not having any consciousness" and "inadequateness." HARRISON (ed. 1947): "Unable to perceive our shortcomings." DEIGHTON (ed. 1889): Regarding their rarity, these words are used nowhere else in Sh., though, as KNOWLES (privately) points out, *insufficiency* is found in *MND* 2.2.128 (783) and *Son.* 150.2, and Dogberry comes fairly close with *suffigance* (*Ado* 3.5.52 [1643]).

20–1 **You . . . freely**] CALDECOTT (MS 1813–33): "You are at too great a waste & expense in apology, when your dealings are so liberal & generous." DEIGHTON (ed. 1889), more accurately: "You thank us too lavishly for our hospitality which is so readily given." BROWN (1962, p. 210): "A reminder of love's wealth [a theme in *MV*], of mutual, unprompted giving in friendship." BOORMAN (ed. 1964), without explanation: "More ironic ambiguity."

Arch. 'Beleeue me, I speake as my vnderstanding instructs me, and as mine honestie puts it to vtterance.

Cam. *Sicilia* cannot shew himselfe ouer-kind to *Bohe-*
mia: They were trayn'd together in their Child-hoods;   25
and there rooted betwixt them then such an affection,
which cannot chuse but braunch now. Since their more
mature Dignities, and Royall Necessities, made seperation of their Societie, their Encounters (though not Personall) hath been Royally attornyed with enter-change of   30

---

25 Child-hoods] childhood DODD, IRV
26 then] *Om.* DODD, BUL
30 hath been] F1, BUL, NLSN, SIS, CLN2, PEN2+; have been so COL2, COL3, KTLY;
have been F2 *etc.*

---

23 **honestie**] This noun is found eight times later; *honest* is used 16 times. At
first these words imply truthfulness and uprightness; after Leontes's fit of jealousy and
suspicion, they usually signify chastity. For the latter use, see n. 381.

   puts . . . vtterance] HAPPÉ (1969, p. 30): "Forces me to say." BOORMAN (ed.
1964): "'To the utterance' was associated with fighting to the death." It was (*OED*,
Utterance[2] 2a), but the relevance is too remote to matter.

   24-34 *Sicilia . . . Loues*] HERFORD (ed. 1916-): "Camillo's description of the
lifelong and intimate friendship . . . has, in retrospect, the effect of unconscious
irony. It heightens our sense of the shallowness of Leontes, who can imagine himself
betrayed by such a friend." TRAVERSI (1955, p. 108): "As a mere exposition of fact,
this would be elaborate to a fault. It is, however, more than that. The force of the
passage lies in the combination under one set of images of two processes apparently
contradictory—that of natural unified development existing side by side with that of
widening division. The word 'branch' can imply either the unity of living growth or
a spreading division within that growth [see n. 27]. If the affection of the royal friends
is such that it 'cannot choose but branch', this may mean either that it will continue
to grow and bear fruit, or that it must inevitably separate and break down as it grows.
In other words, though rooted and deeply natural, it bears within itself the causes of
future disunion [see n. 25-7]. The concluding words return to the same idea, and
the reference to 'opposed winds' further anticipates not only the emotional storm in
which the present unity is shortly to be tested but also the actual tempest in
which . . . Perdita is lost and found, and which is to play . . . a decisive part in
the whole construction."

   The style of this and the following speeches is analyzed in detail by LUDWIG (1974,
pp. 382-5). HOLBROOK (1964, p. 134), more simply, finds a "preponderance of the
imagery of nature [used] to express the quality of the affection between Leontes and
Polixenes" (see 25-7, for example), and PYLE (1969, p. 10) believes that TRAVERSI's
"suggestion is quite out of keeping with Camillo's cheerful mood." ENRIGHT (1970,
p. 155) calls TRAVERSI's interpretation "an instance of commentator's tic, for there is
no doubt . . . that Shakespeare means anything other than what Camillo means: the
good word 'root' does not lend itself readily to a bad interpretation of its associated
word and derivative, 'branch.'" SCHWARTZ (1973, pp. 254-5), undeterred: "This

speech becomes a metaphor of the whole. . . . The hands, for example, will shortly become the sign of the bond between Leontes and Hermione [175]. Then, as Leontes becomes immersed in a fantasy of betrayal, the hands become a symbol of boundary violation [188, 200–1]. The image of 'a vast' . . . suggests, in its temporal dimension, the 'wide gap of time' [3368]." Also rising above training and rooting, NEVO (1987, p. 100): "The image, rebuslike, conceals (or does not conceal) the ubiquitous Elizabethan cuckold's horns." On the speech as a whole, WELLS (1994, p. 340): "Any experienced playgoer knows that this cannot last."

24 **Sicilia**] See n. 9 for kings called by the names of their countries.

ouer-kind] HERFORD (ed. 1916–): "Too kind. An excess of kindness is, between them, impossible." Cf. "ouer-fond" (3125).

25–7 **They . . . now**] BROOKE (1905; 1913, p. 255): "The breaking up of it [the kings' friendship] is half suggested by the reiterated insistence of Camillo and Archidamus on its constancy. Their confidence appears to fly in the face of the known mutability of the course of the world." FARRELL (1975, p. 47): "Ambiguity undermines his words with opposite, unwanted meanings. Expecting his understanding and not his heart to 'instruct' his speech [22–3], Archidamus confutes himself."

25–6 **trayn'd . . . rooted**] MINSHEU (1617, to Traine vp): "To Instruct, or to bringe vp." FURNESS (ed. 1898): "The *training* of vines and young trees suggested *rooted*." Cf. *braunch* (27). MAHOOD (1957, pp. 147–8): "Anticipates [1903–6], which is symbolic both of the union of court and country in Perdita's upbringing as a Shepherd's daughter and of the reunion of the two kings through the marriage of Perdita and Florizel." ORGEL (ed. 1996): "The plant that roots is their affection for each other, not the two stocks."

26 **affection**] Used in *WT* in several senses, it means here "Good disposition towards, goodwill, kind feeling, love, fondness, loving attachment" (*OED, sb.* 6). Cf. nn. 214, 2206, 2332–3, 3046, and 3110. PAFFORD (ed. 1963): "This friendship is of a deeply emotional kind. Cf. [n. 3247–50]."

27 **which**] SEYMOUR (1805, 1:156): "As." ABBOTT (§278), however: "*Such* [26] . . . was by derivation the natural antecedent to *which*; *such* meaning 'so-like', 'so-in-kind'; *which* meaning 'what-like', 'what-in-kind?' . . . So *W.T.* [2638–9]." Cf. FRANZ §340.

cannot chuse] HUNTER (ed. 1872): "Cannot help; naturally or necessarily cannot."

braunch] *OED* (*v.* 1, citing this line): "To . . . put forth branches." MAXWELL (ed. 1956): "Flourish." KITTREDGE & RIBNER (ed. 1967): "Grow to maturity." See n. 24–34 for *braunch* as "divide."

28 **mature . . . Necessities**] GILDEMEISTER (ed. 1870): In Sh.'s usual laconic fashion, the royal rank to which they both have grown in their maturity. DEIGHTON (ed. 1889): "And the duties attendant upon that position." For further uses of *dignity*, see nn. 2326, 2946, and 3088.

28–9 **made seperation**] *OED* (Separation 1, citing this line): "To make a severance or division."

29 **Societie**] SCHMIDT (1875): "Company." ONIONS (1986): "Companionship."

Encounters] HUNTER (ed. 1872): "Intercommunications." SCHMIDT (1874): "Meeting[s]." See n. 1222–4 for the word in other, but uncertain, senses.

29–30 **Personall**] PIERCE (ed. 1918): "Performed in person."

30 **hath**] ABBOTT §334 gives examples of other verbs inflected in *-th* in the 3rd-person plural, as in line 50. SMITH (1902, p. 8), however, finds that by the year 1632, the construction was considered a failure of concord, which F2 rectified here, at 1055, and at 2344. "There are two hundred and thirty-five passages in the First Folio containing a plural subject of one member followed by a singular predicate; of

Gifts, Letters, louing Embassies, that they haue seem'd to
be together, though absent: shooke hands, as ouer a Vast;
and embrac'd as it were from the ends of opposed Winds.
The Heauens continue their Loues.

   Arch. I thinke there is not in the World, either Malice   35
or Matter, to alter it. You haue an vnspeakable comfort
of your young Prince *Mamillius*: it is a Gentleman of the
greatest Promise, that euer came into my Note.

---

  31 Gifts] Gift F2
     that] though v1785
  32 Vast] Vast Sea F2-POPE2, HAN, CAP
  34 Loues] love mTBY3 *conj.*, HAN, DYCE2, HUD2, KIT1
  37 *Mamillius*] *Mamillus* ROWE2-POPE2, HAN (*all throughout, except* ROWE2 Mamillus *at* 584 *only*)

---

these . . . the Second Folio changes fifty-nine to the singular" (p. 14). F2's handling
of compound subjects followed by a singular predicate, as at 870, is different. Of F1's
188 constructions of this kind, F2 changes only two (pp. 14-16).
    Royally attornyed] CAPELL (1783 [1774], 1:glos., Attorney'd): "Performed
by . . . Deputy." JOHNSON (ed. 1765): "Nobly supplied by substitution of embassies,
&c." *OED*'s citation of this as the only use of the word as a verb is inexact; it appears
as such in *MM* 5.1.390 (2769), written in 1604. See *MM* (ed. Mark Eccles, 1980), n.
2769.
   31 **Embassies**] SCHMIDT (1874, Embassy 2): "Message."
     that] So that. See n. 17.
   31-3 they . . . Winds] REYHER (1947, p. 592): Commonplace artfulness, which
Reyher compares unfavorably with *Cym.* 5.2.51-6 (2312-17). BROWN (1962, p. 210):
"The description . . . speaks of more than tempests; it is also a reminder that love
has its own order and that 'true' hearts never know separation." NEVO (1987, p. 101):
The passage "is totally reversible, indeterminately an affirmation of their togetherness
when apart, or their estrangement even when together." Camillo is not describing
their time together, however.
   32 shooke . . . Vast] JOHNSON (1755, Vast): "An empty waste" (*OED, sb.* 1).
STEEVENS (ed. 1778): "At a great and vacant distance"; he adds, citing *Per.* 3.1.1,
"*Vast* . . . may be used for the *sea*" (*OED, sb.* 1b).
   HENLEY (in MALONE, 1780, 2:702): The image derives from "a device common in
the title-page[s] of old books, of two hands extended from opposite clouds, and joined
as in token of friendship." Several cloudy hands are illustrated by McKERROW (1949;
e.g., nos. 119, 402), but all clasp some such object as an anchor or caduceus as well
as each other. BETHELL (ed. 1956), more to the point: "'Hands across the
sea' . . . applies more aptly to the situation of Leontes and Polixenes and the symbolic use of the sea . . . (see [n. 1525-51])."
   33 ends . . . Winds] The CLARKES (ed. 1865): "The quarters from which the
four winds blow . . . as figurative of opposite regions." PAFFORD (ed. 1963): "In
contemporary maps and emblem books it is common to find faces of cherubs representing winds blowing from the four corners." YOUNG & MOSELEY (ed. 1965) find
irony in the juxtaposition of *embrac'd* and *opposed*, but see nn. 9 *Visitation*, 24-34,
27 *braunch*.

34 **The . . . Loues**] PAFFORD (ed. 1963): "The irony is marked." LANGMAN (1976, p. 200), taking this line together with the ten preceding it, finds it "unmistakably portentous. In the opening scene of a play, assurances so strong are immediately recognizable as covert signals of storms ahead." TOLIVER (1989, p. 159), on the other hand: "An acknowledgement of providence that hints of Apollo's directorial function." COLLINS (ed. 1904–24?, Continue): "Subjunctive of wish" (i.e., "may the heavens"); see ABBOTT §365. HOLBROOK (1964, pp. 134–5): "Or it may be a statement of an inevitable development . . . (*thus*) the Heavens continue their loves."

34–6 **Loues . . . it**] Because "the final *s* [is] frequently interpolated and frequently omitted in the first folio" and because of the singular pronoun, WALKER (1860, 1:233, 1:252), like THIRLBY, would read "Love." Cf. n. 237. WILSON (ed. 1931), however: "But he could hardly have said 'them' and the singular 'it' is quite natural in conversation." For similar plurals, see 717, 720, and 750 and ABBOTT §333.

35–6 **I . . . it**] DELIUS (ed. 1860): "It" refers inaccurately to "their Loues" (34). DEIGHTON (ed. 1889): "I believe that neither malicious suggestions of designing persons, nor any cause however important, would be able to interrupt the continuance of their love for each other." SCHMIDT (1875, Matter): "Cause." CARRINGTON (1956): "Real reason, as opposed to 'malice' — unworthy reason." But BETHELL (ed. 1956): "Leontes will soon have the malice, and the matter will be the innocent friendship of Hermione and Polixenes." MOORMAN (ed. 1912): "This speech . . . , and to a less degree the whole of this first scene . . . is intensely ironic. Equally ironic are the hopes expressed [in 36–41] that Mamillius may grow to man's estate and succeed his father on the throne. So marked an employment of dramatic irony in the opening scene of a play is unusual in Shakespeare." It actually is not — witness *Mac.* and *Lr.* ENRIGHT (1970, pp. 155–6): "This is a stock device for heralding in a sudden reversal of a situation apparently firm and immutable, and its economy may excuse its obviousness." GIRARD (1987, p. 40) agrees: "As we hear this, we realize, of course, that the friendship is doomed." HERFORD (ed. 1916-), however: "Those who surround Leontes are completely unprepared for the affair which wrecks 'their loves', notwithstanding that Polixenes has been for nine months a guest."

Malice or Matter] GIRARD (1987, p. 40): *Malice* is "what a villain can do" and *Matter* is "all seemingly rational grounds for quarreling that two close friends may have. . . . The words . . . cover everything that the traditional critics would regard as appropriate 'motivation.'"

36 **vnspeakable**] HAPPÉ (1969): "Inexpressible."

37 **of your**] CHARLTON (ed. 1916): "'In [your]', in a local or even instrumental sense." See ABBOTT §172.

37–47 **Mamillius . . . one**] PAFFORD (ed. 1963): "From [here] to the end of the scene the hyperbole is no longer expressed in courtly idiom but in simple and direct speech." Although the style seems simple, the matter has seemed complicated; see n. 40–1.

37 **it**] SEYMOUR (1805, 1:156): The neuter for the personal pronoun "seems to be employed where signal pre-eminence is meant," as in *Mac.* 1.4.58 (346) — "It is a peerelesse Kinsman." OED (*pron.* 1d), however, is less specific: "*It* . . . occurs where *he, she*, or *that* would now be preferred," and ROLFE (ed. 1879) finds instances of contemptuousness — *Rom.* 4.2.14 (2437) and *Ant.* 3.2.6 (1545). That usage is obviously inappropriate here. BETHELL (ed. 1956): "Perhaps because referring to a child." See FRANZ §297. MAHOOD (1957, p. 148), looking ahead, finds the praise of Mamillius threatening, and NICHOLS (1981, p. 170) remembers "that Polixenes also has a son, with whom Archidamus must also be familiar."

38 **Note**] SCHMIDT (1875): "Knowledge." HENLEY (ed. 1902): "Observation." For other instances of noting, see nn. 50–1 and 298.

Cam. I very well agree with you, in the hopes of him:
it is a gallant Child; one, that (indeed) Physicks the Sub-   40
iect, makes old hearts fresh: they that went on Crutches
ere he was borne, desire yet their life, to see him a Man.
Arch. Would they else be content to die?
Cam. Yes; if there were no other excuse, why they should
desire to liue.   45

39-42 **I . . . Man**] NELSON (1973, p. 59): "The idea is . . . that one older generation gains some form of immortality through the hopes and abiding new life of a
younger generation."

40-3 **it . . . die?**] HOLLAND (1964, p. 292): "A nice compliment, but
. . . Archidamus breaks in to show, laughingly, that it's really just words, formality."
Rather than preparation for the sense of loss following Mamillius's death, ADAMS
(1989, pp. 94-5) believes the words to be "fatuous praise. . . . The hyperbole is
piled a little too high for the common sense of Archidamus: he turns on his host
[43] . . . and, brushing aside Camillo's silly evasion [44-5], concludes with [the]
blunt realism [of 46-7]." ENRIGHT (1970, p. 156) discovers in 46-7 not realism but
"an irony of a finer kind," for "it is the king himself who is going to live on crutches
till he recovers his daughter." That would seem an irony of an opaquer kind. CUTTS
(1968, p. 56) alone: A "hint that Leontes showed remarkable promise in childhood
which did not come to fruition. . . . The visit of Polixenes is . . . a harking back
to his [Leontes's] childhood when he stood heir to men's great expectations of him
to see him a man."

40 **gallant**] KERSEY (1708): "Fine." JOHNSON (1755): "Noble." *OED* (*a.* 4):
"*Loosely*, as a general epithet of admiration or praise."

40-1 **Physicks the Subiect**] MINSHEU (1617, Physicke): "Curing by Medicines."
JOHNSON (ed. 1765): "Affords a cordial [see n. 3278] to the state; has the power of
assuaging the sense of misery." Cf. *Mac.* 2.3.50 (796) and *Cym.* 3.2.34 (1503). SEY-
MOUR (1805, 1:156): "Conciliates, keeps in wholesome political temperament, the
people." COLLIER (ed. 1842): *Subiect* "is used in a plural sense for 'subjects'"; *OED*
(*sb.* 1b) finds this usage only in Sh. Thus NEILSON & HILL (ed. 1942): "Does the people
good." STAUNTON (ed. 1859) wrongly thinks the meaning is particular — "the afflicted." BETHELL (ed. 1956): "The aged and infirm want to go on living in order to
see Mamillius grow up. [Camillo] intends to praise Mamillius but has chosen a poor
means of doing so as Archidamus hints by asking if they would otherwise be content
to die. This quibbling movement from courtly praise to experienced moralizing on
the human tendency to cling to life aptly closes a short scene which sets the tone of
Sicilian sophistication."

41-2 **they . . . Man**] KNIGHT (1947; 1966, p. 77): "Youth is conceived as a
power; as a renewer of life and antagonist to death. Thus early is the central theme
of *The Winter's Tale* set before us."

44-7 **if . . . one**] PYLE (1969, p. 11): "An exchange of jests [sets] off the regal
stateliness of the principal characters' entrance" at 49.

44 **excuse**] SCHMIDT (1874): "Plea offered in extenuation." Or "ground for excuse" (*OED, sb.* 3).

46-7 **If . . . one**] GOLDMAN (1972, p. 137): "They are making fun of the artificiality of the extremer tropes of their courteous and courtier-like speech. Yet the little
joke they make in doing so has its own related resonance. Its point is that people are
not content to die — they will find some reason to live." PARRY (ed. 1982), similarly:
Archidamus "implies that a motive for living rather than dying can always be found,

Arch. If the King had no Sonne, they would desire to
liue on Crutches till he had one.   *Exeunt.*

Scœna Secunda.   1.2

---

47 *Exeunt.*] *Om.* THEO, WARB, JOHN; *they pass out of hearing* CAM3
48 Located at the palace by ROWE, POPE, HAN, CAM3, SIS, K&R, EVNS, BEV; SCENE
opens to the Presence. THEO, WARB, JOHN, CAP-NLSN, ARD1, KIT1, ALEX, ARD2, SIG
(*subst.*)

---

whether the future looks secure or not." For the next prose passage and the significance of the medium, see n. 1521–77.
    46 **If . . . Sonne**] HAPPÉ (1969, p. 31): "A hint of things to come; it is a note of
foreboding against the apparent unanimity of the two kings." HAPPÉ must detect hints
of the death of Mamillius as well as Leontes's plot to kill Polixenes in lines that seem
intended to provoke mild amusement.
    48 *Scœna Secunda*] Both DANIEL (1879, p. 177) and CLAPP (1885, p. 402) con-
sider that the first day of the action concludes at the end of this scene. Beginning
with THEOBALD (ed. 1733), eds. usually locate 1.1 in an antechamber in the palace,
1.2 in the presence chamber or a room of state, although Sh. is specific about neither.
SCHANZER (ed. 1969): "A precise location [of such scenes as 1.1] is often impossible,
as well as undesirable." A consideration is the law of reentry formulated by Robert
Prölss in *Von den ältesten Drucken der Dramen Shakespeares und dem Einfluss*
(Leipzig, 1905); it holds that a character exiting at the end of one scene will not enter
at the beginning of the next, as Camillo does here. TANNENBAUM (1928, p. 358): "If
there is anything in the so-called 'law of re-entry', . . . in Shakspere's mind these
two scenes were regarded as one. Archidamus and Camillo stand aside as the King
and his train enter. . . . That Shakspere did not intend a change of scene is sufficiently indicated by his failure to put into the mouth of either . . . words signifying
an intention to depart." TANNENBAUM's conclusion is inconsistent with the presence
of Camillo's name in the SD, yet the SD may be a massed entry, for which see n. 49.
    PYLE (1969, p. 12 n.): "They remain apart: even Camillo is quite unaware of Leon-
tes' jealousy when he is called forward at [292] (or is called upon to re-enter, having
exited with the other lords at [266 approximately]?)." No ed. takes Camillo off there,
however. To RINGLER (1968, p. 114 n.), "it is clear that he does not reenter until
Leontes exclaims [at 292]," yet, as the textual notes indicate, this has by no means
been clear to eds. THEOBALD, WARBURTON, and JOHNSON omit Camillo here, but by
having the scene open to the presence at 48, they have left him on stage but in the
background. WILSON (ed. 1931) essentially does the same. STEEVENS (ed. 1773) concludes 1.1 with *exeunt* and then ignores Camillo until he speaks at 293. As WELLS (in
WELLS & TAYLOR, 1987, p. 601) says, "The . . . conversation [following 293] requires
Camillo to have observed part, at least, of the earlier action. As Shakespeare has not
involved him earlier, he may not have originally intended Camillo to reenter at [49];
there is no other obvious point for him to do so, but, as Leontes' [i.e., Polixenes's] cup-
bearer he could come and go." He is Leontes's chief courtier, but the audience

has no idea at this point that he enjoys special privileges. Regarding THEOBALD's Attendant, WELLS observes, "This is a domestic, not a formal scene." As to the atmosphere of both 1.1 and 1.2, VAN DOREN (1939, p. 314): "The Sicilian court is a brilliantly and frankly sensual place, the heavy richness of whose life and the animal leisureliness of whose pleasures we gather at once from the first scene and from the luxury of the second. Both are baroque, and it cannot be said of the two kings that they . . . have grown into ascetics, or that Hermione . . . longs delicately for compliment [quotes 161-6]." WATSON (1984, p. 240) disagrees: "The Sicilians' elegantly sensual display deceives both them and us, by suggesting that sensuality has been safely sublimated into something more refined."

COLERIDGE (1813; ed. Foakes, 1989, pp. 173-4) notices the "difference of style of the first scene, between two chit-chatters [Camillo and Archidamus] and the rise of diction on the introduction of the kings and Hermione." BETHELL (ed. 1956): "Religious images and references throughout draw our attention to the prevailing theme of sin, which is exemplified in Leontes' jealousy." PARTRIDGE (1982, p. 2): "The blank verse of [this scene] is free in the use of redundant syllables. . . . It was probably the dramatist's notion that iambic pentameters would appear less artificial as a stage language, if not readily distinguishable from prose. This scene contains over sixty visual contractions [e.g., *to't* (68), *'t may* (187), *communicat'st* (216)]; it is not possible for an actor to observe such elisions in pronunciation. They were orthographic conventions of . . . Ralph Crane, who . . . wanted to ensure that there were not more than ten or eleven syllables in a verse line" (see p. 594). PARRY (ed. 1982): "The poise, refinement and wit of this verse . . . are rudely shattered — and given alarmingly different intensity — in the mouth of Leontes in the course of the scene."

As for structure, HERFORD (ed. 1916-): Scene 1.2 is "a striking example of the swift and slightly motivated changes characteristic of the plots of the 'Romances'. It consists of three sub-scenes, with links of subordinate dialogue. The first [50-282] carries us through the whole gamut of moods from Leontes's urgent but vain entreaties to his guest to stay, successfully reinforced with exquisite charm by his wife, to the first indication of his mad suspicion [181] and its violent explosion [268] after their departure. In the second sub-scene, Camillo hears it with incredulous amazement, but finally consents unwillingly to 'remove' Polixenes by poison. In the third, confronted by Polixenes himself, Camillo is overcome by his palpable innocence, resolves to throw in his lot with him, discloses the king's plot, and arranges for the instant departure of both. The demeanour of Polixenes and Camillo, in the face of the king's charge, like that of Hermione herself, convinces us of Leontes's moral isolation, and that he could do nothing but for his royal power."

COGHILL (1958, pp. 32-3), comparing 1.1 with the opening scenes of two Shn. tragedies: "Now whereas Kent and Gloucester [*Lr.*], Philo and Demetrius [*Ant.*], prepare the audience for what it is about to see . . . , Camillo and Archidamus prepare it for what it is about *not* to see . . . ; directed to expect a pair of happy and affectionate friends, the audience is startled by seeing exactly the opposite: the two monarchs enter separately, and one [Leontes] . . . wears a look of barely controlled hostility. . . . The proof of this is in the dialogue, which contains all the stage directions necessary." An example of such a tacit SD is that Polixenes, who mentions "nine changes of the watery star," which would be understood as "the inconstant moon," and who stands next to the pregnant Hermione, would be suspected to be the father. "These things do not happen by accident." For the pregnant Hermione, see n. 49. COGHILL's opinion has had some effect (e.g., MATCHETT in n. 49), but most critics disagree. BARTON (1980, p. 132), for instance: *WT* "begins where many of Shakespeare's earlier comedies had ended. Friendship, no longer love's rival, has found a

Enter Leontes, Hermione, Mamillius, Polixenes, Camillo. 49

---

49 *Camillo*] Ff, ROWE, POPE, CLN2, OXF2, BEV4; *and Attendants* THEO, WARB, JOHN, v1773, CAM3; Camillo, and *Attendants* HAN1 *etc.*

---

spacious if subordinate place for itself within the domain of marriage. . . . The story is, or should be, over." For the sudden onset of jealousy, see n. 181–92. BROWN (1962, p. 213) finds oddities in the pungency of Leontes's speech, in Polixenes's failure to argue that he must return home to see Florizel, and in the way Hermione is ready to make Polixenes her "Prisoner" (111); they convey "something incomplete or constrained in the image of life shown." See further in n. 49.

49 *Enter* . . . *Camillo*] KATO (1983, p. 138, n. 9): "The order . . . probably represents the family and the status, not the visual grouping." Eds. add "Attendants" because at 302 ff., Leontes seems to refer to people who are present. Although THEO-BALD (ed. 1733) and his followers seem to omit Camillo here, they evidently include him among the Attendants, because he is present in the editions' *manent* at 266. WILSON (ed. 1931) may be an exception. RINGLER (1968, pp. 114–15 n.), however: "Camillo and Archidamus exeunt at the end of I, 1 . . . where Camillo is named as immediately reentering [at 49]; but he is not addressed until [292] and it is clear that he does not reenter until [292] — therefore the massed stage direction needs emending."

Hermione] BROWN (1962, p. 212): She "is in an advanced stage of pregnancy but no reference is made to this obvious visual fact; while this is normal behaviour off-stage, it is peculiar as dramatic exposition, a reminder that words do not express all thoughts and feelings." MATCHETT (1969, pp. 95–7): 2.1 follows 1.2 "after a supposed lapse of not more than a few hours"; hence, "the visible pregnancy of Hermione [here] can be confirmed" by 607, 611–12, 661–2, and 726. Thus, the "diction of conception, fertility and gratitude in Polixenes' speech"— "Nine" months (50), "Burthen" (52), "fill'd vp" (53), "Goe hence in debt" (55), "standing in rich place" (56)— causes us to "see the pregnant woman and . . . hear the apparent allusions to adultery." The suggestive language continues, so that, by 181, "far from feeling that Leontes is too rapidly jealous, we should feel that he has been very slow about it." THOMPSON (1971, p. 155) is typical of later critics who take this tack: "To Leontes and to Shakespeare's audience Polixenes' opening words seem an extraordinarily significant way of drawing attention to the queen's advanced pregnancy. . . . The evident fruits of love and the presence of the guest king, thus strongly associated, give Leontes something to notice." LEGOUIS (ed. 1936, p. xv): In specifying the length of this stay, he [Sh.] makes the jealousy of Leontes more absurd. On this reckoning, Polixenes and Hermione would have committed adultery on almost the very day of the king of Bohemia's arrival. But, LEGOUIS continues, Sh. never intended such an exact computation [in Fr.]. Perdita is, of course, born prematurely (849). Moreover, PYLE (1969, pp. 16–17): "A dramatic fact becomes a dramatic fact only when the audience learns of it, not before. . . . Hermione's pregnancy is first mentioned in the second act. It is not a factor in the present situation." DRAPER (1985, p. 15): "Such an interpretation [as MATCHETT's] implies the injection of meaning into Polixenes' words of which he himself is unconscious, and it requires the audience to grasp that Leontes is already distorting what he hears— which, as a matter of practical theatre, is absurd."

Pol. Nine Changes of the Watry-Starre hath been   50
The Shepheards Note, since we haue left our Throne   (2A1ᵇ)

---

50 hath] have CAP, MAL-DEL2, DYCE2-HUD2, OXF1
51 ∧The Shepheards Note,∧] (~ ~ ~ ,) WARB
   Shepheards] Shepherd's ROWE1+

50-8 **Nine . . . it**] HARRISON (ed. 1947): "Polixenes makes his formal farewell
in slightly stilted language." KITTREDGE & RIBNER (ed. 1967) call it "elaborately
courtly"; ADAMS (1989, p. 96), comparing the inversion of 1236-8, labels it "syntactical high-jinx." HUNT ("Standing," 1984, p. 15): "Polixenes labors in his speech
because the usual expression of gratitude cannot ideally convey his profound affection."

ENRIGHT (1970, p. 156): "Polixenes should not have stayed away from his own
country for too [so?] long, since he is to profess fears 'of what may chance or breed
upon our absence' [62-3]." COOPER (1977, p. 173) also finds "an implied comment
by Polixenes on his own negligence." FRENCH (1972, p. 137): "The suave, fluent
rhetoric may momentarily blind us to the fantastic nature of what Polixenes is saying—the exaggeration of his claim that nine months of saying 'thank you' would be
insufficient, that he owes [Leontes] 'thousands' of thanks. A man who talks like this
either means less than he says (in effect, nothing at all), or else a good deal
more. . . . The idiom of this court is such that he cannot come right out with his
(perfectly understandable) reasons for wanting to go home. . . . There is a real contest of real feelings going on, and there are signs of a jarring antagonism between the
two kings." Another interpretation would be that friendship and courtesy forbid
Polixenes's bluntly saying, "I have stayed too long and want to be at home."

KNIGHT (1947; 1965, p. 88): "Nature rules our play. Despite the court-setting,
nature-suggestion has been, from the start, vivid, introduced by [these lines]. The
following dialogue is sprinkled with natural imagery in close association with youth—
[130, *vnfledg'd* (143), 199, *kernell, squash* (238-9)]. A general pastoralism rings in
[191 'The Mort o'th'Deere']. . . . Seasons, to be so important in the general design,
are suggested in [64] and twice actually mentioned [at 249 and 618]." BETHELL (ed.
1956, p. 167): "A shepherd figures in the King of Bohemia's opening words, distinguishing him and his kingdom from urbanized Sicilia and pointing forward to the
partly symbolic shepherd who becomes Perdita's foster-father. More immediately the
reference relates to the religious imagery of the lambs in [130]." Nothing indicates
that Sicilia is urbanized.

50 **Nine . . . Watry-Starre**] HEATH (1765, p. 202) identifies the star as the
moon; so does TOLLET (MS 1740-79), who refers to 542. *OED* (Watery, *a.* 6c, citing
this line): "An epithet of heavenly bodies . . . thought to bring rain." DYER (1884,
p. 74): "The moisture of the moon is invariably noticed by Shakespeare." He cites
"moist starre," in *Ham.* 1.1.118 (124 + 11); "gouernesse of floods," in *MND* 2.1.103
(478); and other instances. In addition to governing the tides, the moon was believed
to produce a moisture that benefited plants; see KNOBEL (1916, 1:454). MAHOOD
(1957, p. 147), far-fetchedly: "The leading theme of [the] scenes in Bohemia [3.3-
4.4], the summer harmony of heaven and earth, is prepared here by mention of the
'watery star' that draws the tides." HARDINGE (1818, 3:49): "The word *nine*, has
genius in it; for it just enables *Polyxenes* to have been the father of *Perdita*: NINE
wat'ry stars means a period of *nine months*." HUNTER (ed. 1872), missing the point:

"Nine quarters of the moon; nine weeks." BROOKE (1905; 1913, p. 256), who understands that nine months is meant: "No wise man would expose his friend [i.e., Leontes] to so severe a trial. Polixenes must have been something of a good-natured fool; and his conversation confirms that judgment." PAFFORD (ed. 1963): The period is "a maximum for reasonable holiday absence from a throne and family," an idea that CUTTS (1968, p. 58) finds inconsistent with "Polixenes' statement of extreme fondness for his son" (245 ff.). SHERMAN (1902, p. 111): The reason for the "extraordinary attachment" of Polixenes and Leontes described in 1.1 is to "meet the improbability of the former's prolonged visit." PYLE (1969, p. 12) amplifies: "If Sicilia is brief in comparison with Bohemia's elaborate courtesy, that is rather to be expected in the circumstances, and has been adumbrated [in 1.1] by the contrasting attitudes of Archidamus . . . and Camillo." See n. 1. ROWSE (1963, p. 429) wonders "if the theme of King Polixenes' overstaying his welcome at his friend Leontes' Court may not bear a touch of Christian IV's [of Denmark] visit to his brother-in-law [King James] in 1606." The visit in *WT* derives from *Pandosto* (see p. 621). King Christian spent the first two weeks of his stay in England quietly with his sister and the second two weeks (if Sir John Harington is to be believed) drunk (see G. P. V. Akrigg, *Jacobean Pageant*, 1962, pp. 79–83). It is by no means certain, moreover, that Polixenes has overstayed his welcome.

Some critics speculate on why Sh. here connects time's passage with the moon. MAHOOD (1957, p. 147): "The moon's nine changes imply the themes of pregnancy (helped perhaps by 'Burthen' [52]), of sudden changes of fortune, and of madness, which are all to become explicit in the course of [this] scene." PAFFORD (ed. 1963): "Although associated with Diana and therefore with chastity, the moon is also associated with fertility and with growth and decay." He cites Sir James G. Frazer, *The Golden Bough* (1935, 6:129–39).

Watry-Starre] The hyphen is probably Crane's (see p. 594); his reason for inserting it may be clarified by opinion formed when it was still thought to be Sh.'s. SIMPSON (1911, p. 86): "The hyphen sometimes has a metrical function in indicating where the accent falls on a compound word." Pointing out (p. 87) that the hyphenated word may be in prose or verse, he refers to Jonson's *English Grammar*: "All Nounes compounded [are accented] in the first, of how many *Syllabes* soever they be: as *Ténnis-court-keeper*. *Chímney-sweeper*" (8:503). *Watry-Starre* could be a simple compound or a comparison (with *Fiery Star*); the hyphen suggests the former, but in either case the stress would be on the first word.

50–1 hath . . . Note] THIRLBY (MS 1725–33?): "Have been noted or observed by the shepherds," which is what WARBURTON's (ed. 1747) parenthesis signifies— "I use the shepherd's reckoning." HUNTER (1845, 1:418): "Because there was an opinion abroad that the shepherds feeding their flocks by night were great observers of the heavenly bodies." FURNESS (ed. 1898): *Hath* "may be the singular by attraction after 'Starre'; it may be a 3rd pers. plu. in *th* [see ABBOTT §334 and n. 30]; and, lastly, its nominative [subject] may be 'Note.'" ADAMS (1989, pp. 95–6) is more decisive: "What looks like the subject of the sentence [*changes*] turns out . . . to be a predicate noun and in its force not far from a direct object; . . . 'The shepherd has celebrated nine times the cycle of the moon'. 'Hath' . . . goes more naturally with 'note' than with 'changes'; though Shakespeare is not always meticulous about this sort of numerical agreement, still Polixenes' sentence floats between two grammars. . . . The king of Bohemia actually speaks of an inanimate object, the throne, lacking a dead weight, himself—not of royal duties to be performed, a family needing its father, or anything else involving people. This is courtly deference with a vengeance."

51 Note] SCHMIDT (1875) distinguishes between the meaning here—"a mark, a sign by which something may be perceived or known"—and that in 38—"knowledge." By "the shepherd has recorded the passage of nine months," PAFFORD (ed.

Without a Burthen: Time as long againe
Would be fill'd vp (my Brother) with our Thanks,
And yet we should, for perpetuitie,
Goe hence in debt: And therefore, like a Cypher   55

1963) means that he has kept a written record; see n. 1715. For other instances of noting, see n. 298.

51-2 since . . . Burthen] SEYMOUR (1805, 1:157): "Either, since we . . . disburthen'd ourself of regal care; or, since we left the throne empty; without our weight upon it."

51 we] Royal we (ABBOTT §222).

52 Burthen] MARTZ (1980, pp. 120-1), who thinks "Leontes has been in the grip of jealousy before the play has opened," believes the word *burthen* would have an "impact . . . upon the jealous Leontes," for Hermione bears a nine-months' *burden. . . .* And there are innuendoes that a jealous man might find in 'filled up' [53], 'standing in rich place' [56], and 'multiply' [56]." Other critics place the inception of Leontes's jealousy later; see n. 59-60.

52-8 Time . . . it] Some critics find the elaborate politeness ominous. TRAVERSI (1954, p. 109): "Polixenes' words suggest a relation between 'perpetuity' and the inadequacy imposed by the speaker's temporal condition, between the infinite 'debt' of gratitude and the limited possibility of expressing it, between the 'cipher' of conceivable utterance and the 'rich place' in which it stands as a symbol of emotional value." There is "an implied suggestion of impermanence" that, with the following dialogue, "points obscurely to the coming break-down." ERICKSON (1982, p. 820): "Polixenes, echoing Archidamus [at 11-12], announces his inability to repay. . . . Both giving and accepting become obligatory as Leontes' insistence on his liberality grows into an imposition. The barely suppressed tension in the situation comes out in the odd language [of 67-8 and 79-81]."

52-5 Time . . . debt] BETHELL (ed. 1956): "A further nine months of saying thank you would not repay his host."

54 for perpetuitie] RANN (ed. 1787): "Considering the length of our visit." Polixenes means "forever in debt." BOORMAN (ed. 1964) makes it "(Even if we thanked you) forever."

55-8 like . . . it] *OED* (Cipher 1, citing line 56): "An arithmetical symbol or character (0) of no value by itself, but which increases or decreases the value of other figures according to its position." DEIGHTON (ed. 1889): Cf. "A crooked Figure may Attest in little place a Million" (*H5* Prol. 15-16 [16-17]). The idea is proverbial; see WILSON (1970) and HULME (1962, p. 79). CALDECOTT (MS 1813-33): "This poor and single acknowledgement, if added in arithmetical character to my just account, would shew the weight or immensity of my debt of obligation." Following DELIUS (ed. 1860), HERFORD (ed. 1916-): Polixenes's "one we thanke you" implies "all the thanks unsaid, as a 'nought' added to a figure multiplies all that precedes." The rich place, to the extent that it is at all exact, would be in the company of his brother, Leontes. BALDWIN (1943, pp. 164-5): "The cipher was suggested by the opening 'nine' [50]. . . . The whole figure was thus naturally suggested by the [arithmetical] doctrine of place. . . . The idea of place was itself evoked by the rich place or position in which Polixenes as king stood." CAVELL (1987, p. 210): "A latent picture of sexual intercourse." Cf. n. 56. BETHELL (ed. 1956): "This *conceit* [Polixenes's, not CAVELL's]

(Yet standing in rich place) I multiply
With one we thanke you, many thousands moe,
That goe before it.
   Leo. Stay your Thanks a while,
And pay them when you part.   60

---

is typical of 'metaphysical wit.'" COGHILL (1958, p. 33): "To a visiting King there can
be no richer place than next to the Queen. . . . she is *visibly pregnant.* . . . The
visiting King has been there nine months [50]; who can fail to wonder whether the
man so amicably addressing this expectant mother may not be the father of her child?"
The answer is, several critics; cf. n. 49, *Hermione.* Others, however, find nothing to
account for the sudden onset of Leontes's jealousy; see n. 181-92. BOORMAN (ed.
1964) even thinks Polixenes may pun "in compliment to Leontes' palace."

   56 **Yet standing in**] COLLINS (ed. 1904-24?): "Yet one which stands" in. FEL-
PERIN ("Deconstruction," 1985, p. 9) on possible sexual innuendo: "A sniggering allusion to his 'standing in' for Leontes?" *Stand-in* = "substitute" is American movie
slang, but FELPERIN may have a more anatomical sense in mind.

   multiply] *OED* cites this line for the first figurative use of the word in its
mathematical sense.

   57 **moe**] WILSON (ed. 1931): "More (in number) [thus 'moe Ballads' (2095-6)
and 'moe Children' (3135)]. Formerly 'more' = more (in quantity) only ['more rags'
(1722)]." See FRANZ §221 and BROOK (1976, p. 119).

   59-60 **Stay . . . part**] HARDINGE (1818, 3:50): "We are to read all the affection
of *Leontes* here set forth as a *part acted,* and a counterfeit; *as a net* for the two
delinquents *whom he had suspected before.* . . . The *change,* if produced by the
accident of *Hermione's galanteries* in [1.2], would be against *nature and character.*"
WILSON (ed. 1931) agrees: "The actor who plays him [Leontes] should display signs
of jealousy from the very outset and make clear . . . that the business of asking
Polixenes to stay longer is merely the device of jealousy seeking proof." Hence, WIL-
SON finds these words "though very gracious on the surface, . . . ominous." He has
Leontes draw apart after 101, "observing Hermione and Polixenes unobserved." After
148, "Leontes comes softly foward . . . unseen," so that he seems to overhear 149-
52 (see the n.). YOUNG & MOSELEY (ed. 1965): "Leontes is very curt in his speech in
contrast to the polished thanks of Polixenes." SHERMAN (1902, p. 112): Leontes "implies that Polyxenes, for all his saying, does not mean to go." PYLE (1969, p. 13),
following MOULTON (1903, p. 67): It is "dramatically essential that we should see
Leontes in his true likeness before he is distorted. . . . If he is to be saved, he must
be seen to be worth saving." Following ESCHENBURG (ed. 1801, 5:212), SCHLEGEL
(1808; 1846, p. 397): Sh. "might perhaps have wished slightly to indicate that Hermione, though virtuous, was too warm in her efforts to please Polyxenes; and it
appears as if this germ of inclination first attained its proper maturity in their children": in other words, Florizel and Perdita make manifest the unconscious attraction
to each other now felt by Hermione and Polixenes. His perceiving this attraction
enrages Leontes. If so, he would speak these words with an edge. BENDA (ed. 1825,
8:206), however, believes that no trace of coquetry would be appropriate in
Hermione.

   59 **Stay**] SCHMIDT (1875): "Restrain." PIERCE (ed. 1918): "Postpone."

   60 **part**] HUNTER (ed. 1872): "Depart."

Pol. Sir, that's to morrow: 61
I am question'd by my feares, of what may chance,
Or breed vpon our absence, that may blow
No sneaping Winds at home, to make vs say,

---

62 feares] fear HUD2
63 absence, that may] F1-THEO2, THEO4-JOHN2, SING2, KTLY, CAM3, ALEX+; absence: there may HAN, CAP; absence, may there WARB, COL2, COL4, HUD2; absence; that may v1773 *etc.*
     blow∧] ~ . JOHN2
64 ∧No . . . home,] (~ . . . ~) RID
     No] Some HAN, CAP

---

61 **to morrow**] KATO (1983, p. 134): "Polixenes talks about his return 'tomorrow' . . . after nine months' stay. This is unrealistic in our life but not unnatural in the theater."
     62-5 **I . . . truly**] WARBURTON (ed. 1747): "This is nonsense." RALEIGH (1907, p. 221): "No grammatical analysis of this sentence is possible, yet its meaning is hardly doubtful. The fears [62] are made to imply hopes in [63-4], and in [65] are alluded to in the singular number as a feeling of apprehension." WILSON (ed. 1931): "Surely Hanmer was right in seeing a connexion between 'breed' and 'sneaping' and 'put forth'. [WILSON seems to refer to HANMER's repunctuation, though it is unclear how that makes the connection.] What Polixenes fears is conspiracy or faction at home, the breeding of which every fresh day's absence encourages; and it is 'absence' which 'may (= can) blow no sneaping winds' to nip breeding conspiracy in the bud and tell it that it puts forth shoots too like itself." RIDLEY (ed. 1935) accepts this general idea but adds, confusingly: "On this interpretation the key is that *blow* is used as of a flower, not as of a wind. I should feel more happy about it if it were more natural to use *sneaping* in a semi-complimentary sense." SISSON (1956, 1:195): "that . . . Winds" is an inversion of *that no sneaping winds may blow*. MUNRO (ed. 1957) offers, "My fears ask me what may happen or be hatched in consequence of my absence, which may give rise to no <merely> nipping winds <of trouble> at home <but hurricanes of it> and so make me say This <trouble> has too truly arisen <as the result of my long absence>." A recent paraphrase is PAFFORD's (ed. 1963): "I am tormented by my fears concerning what may happen by chance or develop because of my absence. <I am tormented in this way in order> that no biting winds may <indeed> blast <affairs> at home, and make me say that there were only too good grounds for this <anxiety>." PAFFORD comments: "Polixenes is merely saying here and at [78-80] that because of affairs of state he must go home. This was perfectly understood by Camillo who remembers Polixenes' reason and cites it at [299-300]." KERMODE's (ed. 1963) version becomes more unintelligible than the original: "I'm worried about what may happen at home, perhaps as a result of my absence—worried in case blighting influences may not be at work which we shall regret, saying 'We went away only too well.'" SCHANZER (ed. 1969): "*That* . . . is probably a wish: 'O, that no sneaping winds may blow at home, to make me say 'my fears were only

too well grounded!'" BEVINGTON (ed. 1992) makes this: "I am anxious about what may happen in my absence, especially a stirring up of envy and backbiting that would cause me to say my fears were all too plausible." KNOWLES (privately): "Polixenes gives three reasons why he must part tomorrow: (1) I am apprehensive of what may be developing at home; (2) I should be there to prevent troubles; (3) I've been here too long anyway. All three clauses are elliptical: '[I must part tomorrow because] I am questioned; [I must part tomorrow so] that may blow; [I must part tomorrow because] I have stay'd.'" ORGEL (ed. 1996): Polixenes's "metaphor changes in mid-sentence. The kingdom is conceived as a garden; with the gardener absent, the plants have no protection against the 'sneaping winds', whatever these may be. Attempts to make 'This is put forth too truly' part of the same metaphor have resulted in outright revision or paraphrases that wander very far from the text."

If they do not try to make sense by emending words or, more often, punctuation, other eds. attack F piecemeal, as follows.

62 question'd] SCHMIDT (1875): "To ask . . . the thing asked after with *of*," a construction also found in 121-2. NEILSON & HILL (ed. 1942) extend this to "i.e., motivated," which may be what Polixenes means but, according to *OED*, not what he says. CARRINGTON (1956): "Given anxiety," possibly *OED, v.* 5b. HAPPÉ (1969): "Troubled, badgered." Probably *OED* (*v.* 3. *intr.*): "To ask or put questions."

63 breed vpon] SCHMIDT (1874): "Be produced," by design presumably, since the word is contrasted with *chance*, "by accident." Cf. n. 480. HAPPÉ (1969): "Develop because of."

that may blow] JOHNSON (ed. 1765, 8:Ii3): "May there blow." FARMER (in STEEVENS, ed. 1773, 10:Pp4ᵛ): "*That*, for *Oh! That*." DYCE (ed. 1857) greatly doubts this interpretation, but some later eds.—e.g., SCHANZER (ed. 1969)—accept it. Following JOHNSON, HUDSON (ed. 1852): "Expressive of a wish . . . *would that*." The CLARKES (ed. 1865): If *that* means "O that," the interpretation is "I am questioned by my fears of what may chance from or be occasioned by my absence"; if it means "whether," the meaning is "I am questioned by my fears of what may chance or grow out of my absence, and whether no nipping winds may blow [&c.]." For the unusual sense of *that*, the CLARKES compare *AWW* 1.3.244 (579). ABBOTT §425 thinks that because *there* is omitted—"that (there) *may blow*"—*No sneaping Winds* and *may blow* are transposed for emphasis. KINNEAR (1883, pp. 175-6) holds that *fears* in the sense of "misgivings, doubts" (*OED* 3c) "is followed by *the subjunctive* with a negative. . . . The construction and meaning . . . is,—I am questioned by my fears [doubts] that sneaping winds may *not* blow at home. There is an inversion of '*sneaping winds*,' and '*may blow*.'" FURNESS (ed. 1898) favors the explanation of DEIGHTON (ed. 1889): "The expression may be elliptical, and as 'fears' that a thing may happen necessarily involve 'hopes' that it may not, the full expression would be, 'I am questioned by my fears as to what may happen, and only hope that no sneaping winds, etc.'" HERFORD (ed. 1904): "*That may blow*, etc. . . . is somewhat loosely dependent upon ['I . . . absence']—'fears of what may chance' being mentally replaced by the equivalent 'wish that they may not,'—that no sneaping winds, etc."

64 sneaping Winds] RAY (1691, p. 65): "*Snape* or *Sneap*; to check: . . . Herbs and Fruits *sneapt* with cold weather." JOHNSON (1755): "Nip," as in "sneaping Frost" (*LLL* 1.1.100 [109]). THORNE (1968, p. 35): They "symbolize evil forces, winter ill winds." KNIGHT's (ed. 1841) "ruffling" is unsupported by *OED*. HUNTER's (ed. 1872) "No rebuking rumours may be in circulation" seems simply wrong.

This is put forth too truly: besides, I haue stay'd   65
To tyre your Royaltie.
   Leo. We are tougher (Brother)
Then you can put vs to't.
   Pol. No longer stay.

---

65 truly] early mTBY3 *conj.*, HAN, COL2, COL4; tardily CAP
68 Then] That DYCE1

---

65 **This . . . truly**] RANN (ed. 1787): "These fears are just." KNOWLES (privately): "*This* refers to the Wind, whose buffeting is the opposite of courtly flattery, and instructs one of his human weaknesses. The idea occurs repeatedly, e.g., *AYL* 2.1.6-11 (612-17), *Lr.* 4.6.96-105 (2543-51)." CAPELL (1783, 2.4:161): *Put forth* should not be confined "to the gard'ning sense of it"; Polixenes means "he had . . . put forth towards home at too late an hour for his charge's [i.e., kingdom's] proper security." SCHMIDT (1875, Put forth), however: "Shoot out, . . . bud." HENLEY (ed. 1902): "Advanced." PIERCE (ed. 1918): "Resulted." BOORMAN (ed. 1964): "This can mean both 'sprouted' and 'uttered'"; the first meaning may be justified by *sneaping* as "nipping," the association being with buds killed by a late frost. MALONE (ed. 1790), for the expression: "To make me say, *I had too good reason for my fears* concerning what might happen in my absence from home."
65-6 **besides . . . Royaltie**] CAVELL (1987, pp. 212-13): "Taken as pro forma, civilized excuses these [this and 80-2] must receive pro forma, civilized denials. . . . He is [actually] departing because Hermione's filling up and approaching term seems to him to leave no more room and time for him in Sicilia." Or for the reasons given in 62-5.
66 **To**] HUNTER (ed. 1872): "Long enough to." DEIGHTON (ed. 1889): "So as to."
  Royaltie] SCHMIDT (1875): "A title of kings, = majesty." DEIGHTON (ed. 1889) disagrees: "Your royal hospitality." FURNESS (ed. 1898): "The royal dignity or state, as in 'Royalties repayre' [2763]" (*OED* 1b, citing this line).
67-73 **We . . . gaine-saying**] ORNSTEIN (1986, pp. 216-17): "When he importunes Polixenes to stay longer, it is not because he cannot bear to part with his company; it is because he wants to prevail in this contest of wills."
67-8 **We . . . to't**] RANN (ed. 1787): "We are not so soon tired of our friends, as you will find on experiment." DEIGHTON (ed. 1889), more accurately: "We are made of better stuff than to have our hospitality taxed beyond its strength by any visit . . . from one so dear to us," or, as EVANS (ed. 1974) puts it, "You couldn't stay long enough to tire me." For *put to it*, SCHMIDT (1875): "To drive to straits." NEILSON & HILL (ed. 1942): "Lay upon." Cf. n. 1969-71. COLLINS (ed. 1904-24?) compares "He puts transgression to't" (*MM* 3.2.94-5 [1582-3]). SHERMAN (1902, p. 112), who thinks the king of Sicily is sick of his visitor: Leontes "grimly declares that he has an indeterminate capacity to be bored." YOUNG & MOSELEY (ed. 1965): "Yet Leontes does not really go out of his way to persuade Polixenes to stay—he does no more than form demands," an opinion confuted by the speeches immediately following. STEWART (1983, p. 255): "The host appears to be entirely insensitive to his guest's needs and desires, and even determined to obstruct them," an interpretation that disregards the ceremonies of courtesy and friendship.
69-71 **No . . . morrow**] KNOWLES (privately): "The dialogue is staccato, elliptical. The whole scene is remarkable for this kind of compression."

Leo. One Seue'night longer.   70
Pol. Very sooth, to morrow.
Leo. Wee'le part the time betweene's then: and in that
Ile no gaine-saying.
Pol. Presse me not ('beseech you) so:
There is no Tongue that moues; none, none i'th'World   75
So soone as yours, could win me: so it should now,
Were there necessitie in your request, although

72–3 *Prose* (I'll | no) ROWE1, ROWE2, (that | I'll) ROWE3
72–4 72–3 *prose* (I'll | no), 74 *indented as if to make verse line with* no gain-saying HAL
73–4 *One verse line* MCAP2, V1793-COL3, DEL2, CAM1+
74 ('beseech you) so] so, 'beseech you CAP
     so] *Om.* HAN, COL2, COL3, COL4
76–7 *Verse lines ending* there . . . although CAP

---

71 **Very sooth**] BAILEY (1721): "*In sooth, for sooth,* In deed, verily, truly." *OED* (Sooth, *sb.* 4): "In phrases used expletively or parenthetically to strengthen or emphasize an assertion." *OED* (*sb.* 4b) also recognizes *good* and *very sooth.*
     72 **part**] SCHMIDT (1875): "Divide into . . . shares." DEIGHTON (ed. 1889): "Halve [the week]."
     betweene's] The CLARKES (1879, p. 291) find *'s* for *us* also at 260, 288, 615, [1511], and 3352, as well as in *Tmp., 3H6, H8, Tim.,* and *Cym.*
     73 **Ile**] MOORMAN (ed. 1912): "I will have." For *will* without another verb, see ABBOTT §316.
     gaine-saying] MINSHEU (1617, to Gainsay): "To say gainst, or resist with words." *OED* (Gainsay, *sb.* b): "Contradiction."
     74 **'beseech**] VAN DAM (1900, p. 28): Sh. intended the aphetised form *seech,* a form that does not appear anywhere in Sh. Cf. n. 77. For the omission of the nominative, see ABBOTT §399.
     so] SCHMIDT (1875): "In such a manner, thus."
     75–6 **none, . . . yours**] FURNESS (ed. 1898): Parenthetical.
     75 **none, none i'th' World**] The CLARKES (ed. 1865): Sh. knew "the potent effect of an iterated word; but . . . used it but sparingly, and, of course, on that account, with redoubled force of impression. Here it has the effect of intense earnestness." The CLARKES (1879, p. 628) find other repetitions at 1323, 1387, 1958, and 2807, and there is yet another at 1545. They give examples from other plays on p. 423. MIRIAM JOSEPH (1947, p. 87): "Epizeuxis, the repetition of words with none between." KNOWLES (privately): Since the line is extrametrical, the repetition may result from dittography.
     76 **So soone**] HUNTER (ed. 1872): "That so soon."
     77–8 **Were . . . it**] CALDECOTT (MS 1813–33): "If it were necessary to your occasions, how strong soever the interference with mine." PYLE (1969, p. 19): "It is but common courtesy for Leontes to ask him to stay longer, but not for him to press his friend further when he refuses — except for a specific reason, which, as Polixenes observes [here], Leontes does not offer."
     77 **Were . . . although**] ABBOTT §499 considers *although* an isolated foot and

'Twere needfull I deny'd it. My Affaires
Doe euen drag me home-ward: which to hinder,
Were (in your Loue) a Whip to me; my stay,   80
To you a Charge, and Trouble: to saue both,
Farewell (our Brother.)
    Leo. Tongue-ty'd our Queene? speake you.

---

the line only apparently an alexandrine. See nn. 185, 190, 499, 1264-5, and 2187. VAN DAM (1900, p. 33): Sh. intended the aphetised forms *quest* and *necessity'in*. Not likely; cf. n. 74. KNOWLES (privately): *necessitie* may be elided to a trisyllable (ABBOTT §467.3).

79 **euen**] SCHMIDT (1874): "Quite." COLLINS (ed. 1904-24?): "Even now" or "at this moment." HERFORD (ed. 1916-): The word "does not contrast 'dragging' with a more moderate compulsion, but stamps 'dragging' as a literally true . . . description of his situation. 'Just drag me.'" For *even* in Elizabethan English, HERFORD refers to BRADLEY (1916, 2:559-60).

    which to hinder] DEIGHTON (ed. 1889): "To hinder which (*i.e.* my return home)."

80 **in . . . me**] RANN (ed. 1787): "Tho' meant in kindness, a pain to me." DEIGHTON (ed. 1889), similarly: "To make your love to me a punishment." FURNESS (ed. 1898): "I think it rather means: . . . a punishment to me, although you inflicted it out of love." PORTER & CLARKE (ed. 1908): "The sense of punishment . . . is not in point. The incentive to hurry, to tear away, is opposed to the dragging which implies both need to go and inner yielding to stay." PAFFORD (ed. 1963): "(If you will excuse me saying so) be grievous to me." WILSON (ed. 1931): "The F brackets convey the tone of deference."

81 **Charge**] SCHMIDT (1874): "Load, burden." PIERCE (ed. 1918), probably wrongly: "Expense."

    to saue both] DEIGHTON (ed. 1889): "Probably refers to the inconvenience to himself [the 'Whip' of line 80] as well as to 'the charge and trouble' to Leontes."

83 **Tongue-ty'd our Queene?**] For *tongue-tied* proverbially, see DENT (T416). ABBOTT §13: "The possessive Adjectives, when unemphatic, are sometimes transposed, being really combined with nouns." Here *our Queene* is a vocative (§222). Thus he thinks Leontes says, "Speak, our tongue-tied queen" rather than "Are you tongue-tied, our queen? Speak." MUIR (1957, pp. 240-1): "Partly to save time and partly to leave no doubt in the minds of the audience of Hermione's innocence, he [Sh.] begins the play with Leontes already jealous, and he makes Hermione press Polixenes to stay in order to test his suspicions. This, at least, seems to be the most satisfactory way of playing the first scene." There is considerable disagreement, however, over the onset of Leontes's jealousy; see especially nn. 59-60, 155, and 181-92. COGHILL (1958, p. 33): "'Our queen' are cold vocables for married love and 'tongue-tied' is a familiar epithet for guilt." The vocables, needed to identify Hermione, need not be coldly uttered (they certainly are not at 3197), and although the guilty may become tongue-tied when accused, it does not follow that all who are tongue-tied are guilty. None of *OED*'s citations connects *tongue-ty'd* with guilt; and Leontes's probable echo of *Tongue* in 75, STEWART (1983, p. 255) thinks, gives the king's words "terrific resonance." PYLE (1969, p. 18): "'Our queen' . . . can be seen

Her. I had thought (Sir) to haue held my peace, vntill
You had drawne Oathes from him, not to stay: you (Sir)   85
Charge him too coldly. Tell him, you are sure
All in *Bohemia's* well: this satisfaction,
The by-gone-day proclaym'd, say this to him,

---

84 to haue] to've POPE1-THEO2, WARB-JOHN2

---

to betoken respect and admiration not coldness." KEETON (1930; 1967, p. 147): Leontes's bidding Hermione to "join him in persuading Polixenes to stay . . . is entirely
in character, for Leontes . . . has already given us the impression of possessing an
impetuous nature, which will hardly brook contradiction." BELLETTE (1978, p. 66):
"Leontes is not at any point in the play revealed as being skilled in the arts of polite
discourse. . . . He turns naturally to his wife, who has the skill he lacks." ORNSTEIN
(1986, p. 217), however: His words "are somewhat petulant . . . , as if she were
remiss in not badgering Polixenes."

84-9 **I . . . ward**] PORTER & CLARKE (ed. 1908): "She tells Leontes, virtually,
that to meet his friend's good reasons for going, with good reasons against the need
to go, is better than teasing, for the need to go is his chief reason against staying."
CHARLTON (ed. 1916): "Hermione has been silent up to now: but her very first words
prevent our setting this down to weakness or ineffectual modesty." HERFORD (ed.
1916-): "Hermione's immense superiority to Leontes in brain as in heart is at once
evident. She is a fine strategist, and puts herself at once at Polixenes's point of view."

84-5 **vntill . . . stay**] DEIGHTON (ed. 1889): "Until he had bound himself in the
strongest possible way not to remain, and *then* to have attacked him." FURNESS (ed.
1898): "That is, so as to make her success the greater." BETHELL (ed. 1956): "Or
perhaps: 'I thought I should get no opportunity to speak until [he had sworn not to
stay]'— playful reproof of Leontes." BOORMAN (ed. 1964) finds "heavy irony, almost
reproof" in her words, and FRENCH (1972, p. 138) sees "implicit contempt," their
general idea being that, beneath the badinage, highly charged emotions are waiting
to erupt. STEWART (1983, p. 255), less insistently: "She introduces a competition
which is potentially dangerous."

86 **Charge**] SCHMIDT (1874): "Attack." DEIGHTON (ed. 1889): "Adjure," urge.
coldly] SCHMIDT (1874): "Without zeal or passion."

87-8 **this . . . proclaym'd**] THIRLBY (MS 1725-33?): "News or letters lately
rec[d]." STEEVENS (ed. 1773): "We had satisfactory accounts yesterday of the state of
Bohemia." JOHNSON (1755, Satisfaction): "Release from suspense, uncertainty, or uneasiness." PAFFORD (ed. 1963, Satisfaction), perhaps inexactly: "The pleasure of this
news." PARRY (ed. 1982): "So Polixenes' 'fears' do indeed seem groundless. Perhaps
they were his polite way of warding off the 'charge' [81] of Leontes' pressing hospitality."

88 **by-gone-day**] OED (Bygone, *ppl. a.* 1, citing this line): "Former." HERFORD
(ed. 1916-): I.e., "a long undefined period. . . . Hermione is arguing boldly from
the quiet that has prevailed there during Polixenes's visit." LEE (ed. 1907), however:
"Yesterday."

say] ORGEL (ed. 1996): "I.e. if you say."

He's beat from his best ward.
    Leo. Well said, *Hermione.*   90
    Her. To tell, he longs to see his Sonne, were strong:
But let him say so then, and let him goe;

---

90 *He walks apart.*] COL2, COL3, PEN2 (*after* 94)

---

89 **beat . . . ward**] ABBOTT (§343), regarding *beat*: "Owing to the tendency to drop the inflection *en*, the Elizabethan authors frequently used the curtailed forms of past participles." HUDSON (ed. 1852, Ward): "*Place* or *posture of defence*" (*OED, sb.*[2] 8). FURNESS (ed. 1898) thinks the word "a continuation of the figure of a 'charge' [86]." For the phrase, EVANS (ed. 1974): "Forced from his best defensive position," or LEE (ed. 1907), less literally: "Deprived of his best excuse for going."

90 *Hermione*] Regarding COLLIER's SD, FURNESS (ed. 1898): "When Hermione addresses Leontes personally, as she does at [99], it was at least awkward to have her speak to the empty air. That Leontes retires is certain; in no other way can we understand his question [at 153] except by supposing that he has not heard what Polixenes has said to Hermione. Just when he retires it is not easy to determine; most probably, I think, after ['Lord,' 101]." SCHANZER (ed. 1969) has Leontes withdraw after 94: "Up to this point Hermione has been addressing her words to him, speaking of Polixenes in the third person. . . . The remainder of the speech is addressed directly to Polixenes. Her *yet . . . Lord* [99–101] would then be spoken to herself, out of his hearing. This hypothesis is supported by the fact that, whenever elsewhere in the play she addresses her husband, Hermione calls him 'sir', 'my lord', 'your highness', but never 'Leontes.'" Cleopatra excepted, no queen in Sh. addresses her husband by his first name; and, for what the fact may be worth, Hermione never calls Polixenes by name either. PYLE (1969, p. 14 and n.): "It must be that he is intended to play with Mamillius . . . who if he were not drawn into the action at this point would be left unoccupied for more than half the time he is on the stage. . . . Hermione's mention of Polixenes' son [91] . . . looks like a cue, putting Leontes in mind of Mamillius. . . . Leontes is still near by at [99], where Hermione speaks or calls out her endearment." For theatrical solutions, see pp. 806, 809, 814.

91 **To . . . strong**] I.e., [for him] to tell [us that] he longs . . . were [a] strong [argument]. PARRY (ed. 1982): "As opposed to his weak general reason of pressing 'affairs.'"

    he . . . Sonne] MARTIN (1891; 1893, p. 341): "The mother, to whom her own son was inexpressibly dear, speaks [of Florizel], of whom no word has hitherto been said."

92-4 **But . . . Distaffes**] The CLARKES (1879, p. 26): A passage "where there is an effect given of an intended antithesis, but where there is no real antithesis existing." DEIGHTON (ed. 1889): "Let him *only* say so, and he is free to go; let him *only* swear it, and we will not merely let him go, but will not allow him to stay, we will forcibly drive him away: *distaffs*, because it is a woman who is speaking." *OED* (Distaff 1): "A cleft staff about 3 feet long, on which, in the female mode of spinning, wool or flax was wound. . . . [3b] Symbolically, for the female sex, female authority." HARRISON (ed. 1947): "We women <understanding that plea> will send him packing." BOORMAN (ed. 1964), questionably: "There may even be a suggestion that Polixenes is womanish in being so anxious." PARRY (ed. 1982): "With this light-hearted reference to scolding housewives, Hermione implies Polixenes ought to put family claims before affairs of state." She implies that women understand parental love; affairs of state do not seem to have been involved in the visit. PAFFORD (ed.

But let him sweare so, and he shall not stay,
Wee'l thwack him hence with Distaffes.
Yet of your Royall presence, Ile aduenture   95
The borrow of a Weeke. When at *Bohemia*
You take my Lord, Ile giue him my Commission,
To let him there a Moneth, behind the Gest

---

97 him] you mTBY2 *conj.*, HAN, WARB, JOHN1-v1793 (−MAL), DYCE2, HUD2, BUL, SIS

98 let] set KTLY

Gest] Guest F3, F4; gist CAP; *giste* mHAN *conj.* (12 July 1736 *and withdrawn*), CAP (*errata*); list mTBY3 *and* HEATH (1765, pp. 202–3) *conj.*, RANN; gest-day KTLY

1963): In 106–8, Hermione "appears to contradict the view expressed here." For further distinctions between saying and swearing, see 663–4 and 3166.

94 thwack . . . Distaffes] Imitated in *Tom a Lincoln* (c. 1611; MSR, ed. Richard Proudfoot, 341–2). See n. 1578 for another such imitation.

95 aduenture] MINSHEU (1617): "Hazard." *OED* (*v.* 5) adds "to venture." PAFFORD (ed. 1963): A risk is incurred, "since a loan must be repaid." EVANS (ed. 1974): "With interest." BEVINGTON (ed. 1992): "As she explains, she'll undertake to repay each week with a month." For one week now, she will concede one month then.

96 borrow] *OED* (*sb.* 4), citing this instance only: "A borrowing." For *of* in this construction, see ABBOTT §174.

at] For *at* as *in*, see Franz §461.

97 take] SEYMOUR (1805, 1:157): "Find . . . have possession of," which is probably the equivalent of ONIONS's (1986, *vb.* 4) "catch, meet, find," SCHMIDT's (1875) "to find at advantage," and perhaps SCHANZER's (ed. 1969) "receive" (*OED, v.* 34). KITTREDGE & RIBNER (ed. 1967): "Literally 'capture', the implication being that Leontes will be equally enthralled in Bohemia by the love of Polixenes." MOORMAN (ed. 1912), similarly: "Charm, delight," as in 1933 and, in an unfavorable context, 1211. SCHANZER believes that this meaning is probably wrong, but other good eds., such as PAFFORD (ed. 1963) and EVANS (ed. 1974), choose it.

Commission] MINSHEU (1617): "Mandate" (*OED, sb.*[1] 1). The CLARKES (ed. 1865), glossing 220: "Permission," but Hermione may be facetiously using an official term; COLLINS (ed. 1904–24?) says that she speaks "as if it were a written document." Hence, PAFFORD (ed. 1963) for "giue . . . Commission": "Authorize."

98 let him] GENTLEMAN (ed. 1774, Let): "Stay," and RANN (ed. 1787): "Detain." MALONE (ed. 1790): "I'll give him my permission to tarry [let or detain himself] for a month." For *him* as a reflexive, see ABBOTT §223. SCHMIDT (1874), followed by COLLINS (ed. 1904–24?) and MOORMAN (ed. 1912), however: "L[et] him remain," i.e., allow him to (*OED, v.*[1] 1, citing this line). Either interpretation is possible. As for the choice of the word, Hermione may artfully vary the sense of the three *let*s in 92–3.

behind] After. See nn. 100–1, 125. ORGEL (ed. 1996): "As is usual in the Renaissance, the future is not ahead but behind us, i.e. still to come: compare [line 125]."

Gest] PECK (1740, pp. 239–40): A place where the king of England "was to be received & lodged" while on progress. WARBURTON (ed. 1747): "A stage or journey." STEEVENS (ed. 1773): "Time of sojourning" (*OED, sb.*[4] b, citing this line). CAPELL's (ed. 1768) *giste* is (1779 [1774], 1:glos.) "a Roll or journal Book, made out by Heralds, for the Appointment of Days or Stages in royal Progresses" (from Fr. *giste*, according to COTGRAVE [1611], "a place . . . to rest in"). ROLFE (ed. 1879): "The *gests* were strictly stopping places, but the name came to be applied to the written list of them."

Prefix'd for's parting: yet (good-deed) *Leontes*,
I loue thee not a Iarre o'th' Clock, behind   100
What Lady she her Lord. You'le stay?   (2A1ᵛᵃ)

---

99 good-deed] good-heed F2-POPE2, HAN, WARB, JOHN
101-2 *One verse line* mCAP2, v1793+
101 Lady she] lady-she STAU
    she] should COLLIER (1841, p. 14) *conj.*, COL, HUD1, DYCE2; soe'er KTLY; e'er
HUD2; She CAM3

LOBBAN (ed. 1910): "Here . . . used of time and not of place." ORGEL (ed. 1996),
who finds the *OED* wrong, seems to agree: "Any of the stages of a royal progress;
hence, the predetermined date of the visit." STAUNTON (ed. 1859), improbably: "But
gest, or *jest*, also signified a show or revelry" (*OED*, Jest, *sb.* 8); hence, "he shall have
my permission to remain a month after the farewell entertainment."
    99-101 **yet . . . Lord**] COLERIDGE (1813; ed. Foakes, 1989, p. 174) admires the
"preparation in Polixen[es's] obstinate refusal to Leontes [at 75-6] and yet his after
yielding [at 116] to Hermione—which is at once perfectly natural from mere courtesy
of sex, and the exhaustion of the will by the former effort—and yet so well calculated
to set in nascent action the jealousy of Leontes—and this once excited increasedly
by Hermione [in these lines] accompanied (as a good witness [Leontes] ought to
represent it) by an expression and recoil of apprehension that she had gone too far."
COLERIDGE's point is that Hermione's assurance that she loves him only exacerbates
Leontes's suspicion. MOWAT (1969, p. 42), who believes "that not once in the 'tragic
phase' of [*WT*] does a character refer to Leontes' goodness, or praise a single of his
virtues," nevertheless allows for Hermione's (p. 39) "affection" to him in her "playful
words" here (see MOULTON in n. 181-92). One critic who seems to disagree that the
play even has a tragic phase is FIEDLER (1972, p. 150): In *Cym.* and *WT*, "that absurd
passion [jealousy] is entirely subdued to the mood and structure of comedy." Regarding Hermione's declaration, SANDERS (1987, p. 9): "You do not say such things
to a man who is secure in his own sufficiency." No one, however, is so self-sufficient
as not to need assurances of love; Hermione, moreover, is establishing that the reason
she grants her husband another month's leave is *not* that she wishes him away.
    99 **good-deed**] STEEVENS (ed. 1773): "Indeed, in very deed [truth]" (*OED*, Good
D.3, citing this line). HALLIWELL (ed. 1859) quotes Marston, *The Malcontent*
(1604): "Whither in good deed? [i.e., where are you actually going?]" (ed. Hunter,
2.2.27-8).
    100-1 **I . . . Lord**] The CLARKES (1879, p. 516): "Not so much as a tick of the
clock less than any lady loves her lord, however dearly she may love him." TILLYARD
(1938, p. 41), oddly: "There is nothing strained or hectic about her love for her
husband: it is rooted in habit."
    100 **Iarre**] STEEVENS (ed. 1778): Tick (*OED*, *sb.*¹ 2, quoting this line only). TOLLET
(in STEEVENS, ed. 1778): "Minute, for I do not suppose the ancient clocks ticked or
noticed the seconds"; he refers to HOLINSHED's (Harrison's) statement that only hours
are observed by clocks (1577; 1807, 1:405). WILSON (ed. 1931): *Iarre o'th' Clock*
"keeps up the notion of time begun in 'week' [96] and 'month' [98]."
    100-1 **behind . . . she**] Hermione may again be varying the meaning of a word
she has just used—*behind* as "after" in 98. CALDECOTT (MS 1813-33): "Less than
what lady soever she be," his equivalent of *what* being supported by *OED* (*a.* 9c,
citing this line). ABBOTT §255 gives other examples of *what* in elliptical expressions
meaning "any." CHARLTON (ed. 1916): "The expression is doubly elliptical: it would

Pol. No, Madame.
Her. Nay, but you will?
Pol. I may not verely.
Her. Verely? 105

103–4 *One verse line* mCAP2, v1793+ (−OXF2)
103 will?] ~ . ROWE1-THEO1, HAN, CAP

---

read in full, 'I love thee not one jar of the clock behind that love with which whatever lady she loves her lord'. The first ellipsis would give, 'I love thee not one jar o' the clock behind what whatever [sic] lady she her lord': and the second, after cutting down 'whatever' to 'what' . . . and then squeezing the two 'whats' so obtained into one, gives [F's reading]." HUNTER (ed. 1872) finds *she* for "woman" or "girl" in *H5* 2.1.78 (578) and *AYL* 3.2.10 (1210); it is also in 2171 below, *TN* 1.5.241 (532), and *Son.* 130.14. GOLLANCZ (ed. 1894) thinks the *she* a pleonasm introduced for meter, and DEIGHTON (ed. 1889), probably wrongly, finds a similarity in "The skipping king he ambled up and down" (*1H4* 3.2.60 [1879]). LEE (ed. 1907): The pronoun "adds emphasis to 'what lady'"; his parallel is "God he knowes" (*R3* 3.1.10 [1582] and 3.1.26 [1605]). Eds., like COLLIER (ed. 1842), who emend to *should* think that in the MS the word was abbreviated as "sh^d" and that this was misread, an explanation accepted by WALKER (1860, 2:128), because confusion of final -*d* and -*e* is frequent in Shn. texts. See n. 2262. In STAUNTON (ed. 1859), *lady-she* means "high-born woman," like SCHMIDT's (1875, She), "a woman that is a lady." CHARLTON (ed. 1916), ridiculously: "A woman of rank would have a nobler conception of her honour, and hence, of the love owing to her husband, than would a woman of no rank."
101–80 **You'le . . . Friend**] STYAN (1967, p. 81): "It is hard to guess with what effect Leontes . . . could draw apart and remain critically silent for the gap of [79] ironic lines. . . . Where did he stand to observe his wife and Polixenes? What was the nature of his mime? In what relationship was he with the audience? The Elizabethan player would solve such problems from tradition and instinct, using stage space to provoke the nice visual ironies of the scene."
101–14 **You'le . . . Guest?**] JAMESON (1833; 1889, p. 185): A "mixture of playful courtesy, queenly dignity, and lady-like sweetness."
101–3 **stay? . . . will?**] BLAKE (1983, pp. 127–8): "The use of the question mark also as an exclamation mark makes it difficult to decide how particular sentences should be understood. Hermione's questions, particularly the latter, could as easily be interpreted as statements verging on commands." So ROWE seems to have taken 103.
104 **may not**] ABBOTT §310: Must not.
104–5 **verely . . . Verely?**] NOBLE (1935, p. 247): "A notable phrase in *St. John's Gospel* [John 1:51] as an asseveration. 'Thus did our Saviour Christ swear divers times, saying, Verily, verily' (Homily against Swearing and Perjury)." Whatever its origin, the term is used here as a limber vow; it is also the asseveration of Bohemian noblemen (see 14). SHIRLEY (1979, p. 145) finds "a pattern of oaths" in *WT*, "starting with the somewhat humorous, going to the serious, and ending in formalized ritual. . . . Serious oaths follow at the palace or in pastoral Bohemia, then give way to some comic examples with the Clown-turned-gentleman."
105–15 **Verely? . . . be**] BETHELL (ed. 1956): "Hermione rallies [makes fun of] Polixenes. . . . We see her as she must have been before Leontes brought tragedy into her life, gay and witty, a great lady who is still a lively young woman." FRENCH

You put me off with limber Vowes: but I,
Though you would seek t'vnsphere the Stars with Oaths,
Should yet say, Sir, no going: Verely
You shall not goe; a Ladyes Verely' is
As potent as a Lords. Will you goe yet?   110

---

108 Sir, no going] *As quotation* CAP, v1778+ (−WH2, SIS)
108-9 Sir . . . goe] *As quotation* THEO, WARB, JOHN, v1773 (*not closed in* THEO1)

(1972, pp. 139-40): "Leontes' importunities have been pretty well as insistent, so what Hermione says cannot, in itself, be the reason why Polixenes changes his mind. Not what she says, but what she is, and Polixenes' feeling for what she is—those must be the decisive factors. She is a woman, and in her words to Polixenes she is very obviously using her sex. . . . We are reminded of Desdemona interceding for Cassio." J. SMITH (1974, p. 144): She indulges in "a sort of gambolling around Polixenes. . . . She calls down upon herself one of the most disagreeable of all adjectives that can be applied to an adult: she is *arch*."

106 **limber**] SKINNER (1671): "*Laxus*," which COOPER (1565) glosses as "softe, weake." SCHMIDT (1874): "Easily bent, strengthless" (*OED, a*. 2, citing this line). CHAMBERS (ed. 1907), oddly for this instance: "Agile." WILSON (ed. 1931): "The point is that 'verily' is a feeble sort of oath; cf. [84-5]."

107 **Though . . . Oaths**] HUNTER (ed. 1872) compares "whose phrase of sorrow Coniures the wandring starres" (*Ham*. 5.1.255-6 [3450-1]). TAVERA (1974, p. 23), citing this line, observes that there are in *WT* audacious images, sometimes very succinct, which may pass unnoticed.

t'vnsphere the Stars] *OED* cites this line as its first instance of *unsphere*. FURNESS (ed. 1898): "The moon and the stars were supposed to be fixed in hollow crystalline spheres." The power of the oaths would, ROLFE (ed. 1879) says, "remove them from their *spheres* (as the word was used in Ptolemaic astronomy) or their orbits." "Remove" seems generally right, but something more explosive is intended— "blow," perhaps; the maid in *LC* raises her eyes "as they did battry to the spheres intend" (23). DEIGHTON (ed. 1889): "An allusion to the belief that witches and sorcerers could by their oaths and incantations call down the moon from the sky," but that allusion seems unlikely.

108-15 **Verely . . . be**] STYAN (1967, p. 59): "Returning to the attack, she pursues him next with a verbal image: perhaps he must be made her 'prisoner' [114]? This sally proves to be her undoing. . . . The point must be stressed by gesture: she has taken him by the arm and holds him her prisoner in affection. This sign is enough to turn Leontes' head and start that jealous train of thought which provides the drive of the action." FARRELL (1983, p. 83): "She . . . matches wits with Polixenes on the subject of autonomy, asserting 'a . . . Lords'. . . . She detects the anxiety which would lead Polixenes to 'say Your queen and I are devils' as if he fears that women may be dangerously insubordinate and lead men into a sinful relaxation of self-control [147-52]."

109-10 **a . . . Lords**] ENRIGHT (1970, p. 157): "She means it is more potent." She says "as," however.

109 **Verely' is**] FURNESS (ed. 1898): The apostrophe indicates "that the *i* of the following 'is' is elided." This is the so-called Jonsonian elision, a characteristic of Ralph Crane (see p. 594).

110 **Will . . . yet?**] DEIGHTON (ed. 1889): "Are you still determined upon going?" RIDLEY (ed. 1935, Yet): "None the less."

Force me to keepe you as a Prisoner,
Not like a Guest: so you shall pay your Fees
When you depart, and saue your Thanks. How say you?
My Prisoner? or my Guest? by your dread Verely,
One of them you shall be. 115

Pol. Your Guest then, Madame:
To be your Prisoner, should import offending;
Which is for me, lesse easie to commit,
Then you to punish.

Her. Not your Gaoler then, 120
But your kind Hostesse. Come, Ile question you
Of my Lords Tricks, and yours, when you were Boyes:

---

112 Guest:] ~ ? ROWE1-THEO1, HAN, N&H; ~ , COL, HUD1, ARD1, PEL1, BEV3

---

111 **Force . . . Prisoner**] STEWART (1983, p. 256), alone: "The first hint of sexuality." See n. 105-15.

112 **Guest:**] FURNESS (ed. 1898): ROWE's question mark "adds a certain vivacity to the next sentence: Will you force me to keep you as a prisoner? Then all you will gain will be in saving your thanks." MOORMAN (ed. 1912): A comma after *guest* makes *force me* mean "If you can force me." CHARLTON (ed. 1916), reading "guest;": "The use of the imperative 'force' emphasizes her resolution: the interrogative would tend to throw the emphasis on the secondary question 'as a prisoner, not like a guest.'"

112-13 **so . . . Thanks**] COLLINS (ed. 1904-24?): "Hermione suggests humorously that if Polixenes chooses to stay as a prisoner, he will have no need to thank Leontes, as he will merely pay his fee."

112 **so**] DEIGHTON (ed. 1889): "In that case."

pay your Fees] CAMPBELL (1859, p. 59): "English law procedure [was] that, whether guilty or innocent, the prisoner was liable to pay a fee on his liberation." WILKES (1882, p. 168) vehemently objects: "Hermione, in her use of the word *fees*, doubtless alluded to the habitual *largess* distributed by parting guests, and especially by a king. It is absurd to suppose that she knew anything about *jail fees*." WILKES alone thinks so. For other legal allusions, see nn. 1304-10 and 2402.

113-19 **How . . . punish**] BATTENHOUSE (1980, p. 128): Hermione "offers him a mock-choice . . . thereby making it possible for him to abandon stubbornness without losing face, since he can handsomely reply that to be her prisoner would demean his own courtesy."

114 **by . . . Verely**] DEIGHTON (ed. 1889): "By that terrible asseveration of yours; said with merry scorn."

117 **should import offending**] FRANZ (Shall, 3): "*Should* [is] used to form the conditional tense." Hence HENLEY (ed. 1902): "Would mean that I were criminal," or, as PAFFORD (ed. 1963) puts it, would "imply that I had committed some offense."

118 **lesse easie**] DEIGHTON (ed. 1889): "More difficult; the negative form of phrase being somewhat more modest." It also fits the meter.

121-3 **Come . . . then?**] WALKER (1860, 3:91): "She sees Polixenes in a state of uneasiness, such as is natural to a person who has just given up his better reason (or what seems to him to be such) to importunity; and endeavours to divert his thoughts." PORTER & CLARKE (ed. 1908): From *Pandosto* (p. 622): "the two men when they met 'rode toward the Citie, deuising and recounting, howe being children they had passed their youth in friendly pastimes.' Nothing of the request to stay,

43

You were pretty Lordings then?
   Pol. We were (faire Queene)
Two Lads, that thought there was no more behind,   125
But such a day to morrow, as to day,
And to be Boy eternall.
   Her. Was not my Lord
The veryer Wag o'th' two?
   Pol. We were as twyn'd Lambs, that did frisk i'th' Sun,   130

---

123 Lordings] lordlings HARN, COL2
    then?] ~ . CAP, v1778-DEL2 (−DYCE1, STAU), KTLY, KNT3-COL4, OXF1, ALEX
124 (faire Queene)] ∧ ~ ~ . COL3
127-8 *One verse line* mCAP2, CAM1, GLO, WH2-OXF1, NLSN+ (−OXF2)
128-9 *One verse line* HAN, JOHN, v1773-HUD2 (−CAM1, GLO), OXF1, BUL

---

wherein Hermione, so innocently, proved her superior tact and incurred the suspicion of Leontes, appears in Greene." PARRY (ed. 1982): "Hermione . . . probably takes him by the hand here and leads him aside while she changes the subject (now that the 'struggle' between them is over)." For "question . . . Of," see n. 62. Interpreters may believe, as does Parry, that Leontes does not hear the following conversation (see, for further example, n. 153); some, however, to account for Leontes's unaccountable jealousy, believe that he hears and misunderstands all or a part of it—e.g., McCLOSKEY (1965): "Often her [Hermione's] words have two meanings: one on the surface intentional and of neutral suggestion; the other submerged and unintended, with the potential of suspicious suggestion and guilty image." The latter include "Tricks" (122); "Innocence" and "the Doctrine of ill-doing" (132-3); "weake Spirits," "stronger blood," and "not guilty" (135-7), "tript" (140); and Polixenes's association of temptation with the two wives (141-5). "Hermione's reply [146-52] intensifies the developing configuration of suggestive images, here assuming the shape of adultery, [and] her thought persists in seeking expression in the erotic image and the *double entendre* [e.g., 'You . . . Acre' (164-6)]. . . . The images of friendship are ironically images of guilty intimacy, and the ambiguity is resolved with an irresistible emotional logic, which presents Hermione as what she is not—an adulteress." Another dangerous word, according to NATHAN (1968, p. 21), is *Hostesse* (121), which "has two vastly different meanings in Shakespeare's plays, and the ambiguity of *kind bostess* would probably not be lost on the auditors of this bantering conversation." SCHMIDT (1874) gives the two meanings as "a woman who entertains guests" (*OED* 1) and "a woman who keeps an inn" (2), and Hermione obviously means (1). Since neither PARTRIDGE (1969) nor COLMAN (1974) lists *hostess* alone as bawdy, NATHAN perhaps alludes to the Hostess of the Boar's Head (*1H4* 3.3.112-13 [2120]).

   123 **You were**] WALKER (1860, 2:203-4): "One syllable"— *You're*, presumably.
   pretty] SCHMIDT (1875): "Neat, fine."
   Lordings] STEEVENS (ed. 1778): "Diminutive of *lord*" (*OED* 2, citing this line), though Sh. uses the word to mean "gentlemen" in *2H6* 1.1.145 (152), where the meter requires two syllables. *OED* adds "usually in a contemptuous sense," an indication that Hermione's tone is teasing; RUSHTON (1868, pp. 27-31) finds the word in PUTTENHAM (1589, p. 184) illustrating the figure *Meiosis* or the Disabler, "vsed . . . in derision."

124–38 **We . . . ours**] SCOTT (1920, p. 146): "Polixenes seems to be on the defensive, assuring Hermione of the innocence of this early friendship by an over-protestation. . . . Undertones of jealousy are first apparent in Hermione, revealing that the boyhood friendship of Leontes and Polixenes is the mainspring of the situation." SCOTT does not locate the undertones. QUENNELL (1963, p. 19): "Only writers who have themselves been happy in youth can afterwards recall the experiences of childhood . . . without some trace of lingering bitterness. . . . No such bitterness is discernible in the adult dramatist's [Sh.'s] pictures of childhood and boyhood; and he has left one tribute to the joys of early life [this one] . . . that appears to have been coloured by deep personal feeling." HARRIS (1966, pp. 203–4), however, finds these words, though not bitter, ominous: *WT* "offers us the initial terms for approaching this drama of intertwined family destiny through the appropriate device of personal human reminiscence charged with impersonal menace."

124–7 **We . . . eternall**] WILLIAMS (1967, p. 10): "Their youth was character-ized not only by innocence but by a relation to time that became impossible after the natural development to manhood." ALEXANDER (1979, p. 241), similarly: "Polixenes' nostalgia is not just for the innocence of youth, but for youth's confidence in an unending present." GARNER (1985, p. 348): "His lines subvert the very idea of time, for the words 'behind', 'tomorrow', and 'today' work upon each other in such a way that their distinctions . . . blend and dissolve . . . opening the moment into eternity." WILSON (ed. 1931): "A masterpiece of irony with the livid face of Leontes in the background." The moment at which Leontes's jealousy emerges is uncertain, however.

125 **behind**] SCHMIDT (1874): "Not yet happened, or not yet produced to view, future." Cf. n. 98.

127 **Boy eternall**] KAMACHI (1979, p. 21): The expression "suggests the timeless bliss in the Garden before the Fall."

eternall] BLAKE (1983, p. 105): "Can be understood as an adjective following the noun or as an adverb dependent upon *be*. The latter seems more likely, though the form of *eternall* [with no adverbial -*y*] may encourage modern readers to favour the former."

128–9 **Was . . . o'th' two?**] NICHOLS (1981, p. 171): "Something that she no-tices in Polixenes apparently leads her to think that he is different from her husband." The question more likely is an invitation to an amusing conversation.

129 **veryer**] JOHNSON (1755, Very, citing this line): "To note the things emphat-ically, or eminently." SCHMIDT (1875): "Full, complete, perfect."

Wag] WILSON (ed. 1931): "A merry or mischievous boy" (*OED, sb.*[2] 1). STEW-ART (1983, p. 257): "Suggesting . . . somebody sexually promiscuous." PARTRIDGE (1969), however, finds promiscuity in *wagtail*, not in *wag*.

130–8 **We . . . ours**] FARRELL (1975, p. 37): "Polixenes fancies children ab-solved of identity. . . . Life, he insists, was then pure play, unconscious of itself, natural even in its dreams. . . . Adult identity is a burden, defective yet inescapable." BETHELL (ed. 1956): "These lines introduce the general theme of innocence and sin. The lamb is a favorite symbol of innocence [TILLEY (1950) L33]. . . . Sin is associated with sexual maturity, the strengthening of the animal 'spirits' by the increase of 'blood'. . . . Polixenes' implication that sex is necessarily sinful (see lines [141–5]) is not truly Christian nor is it Shakespeare's belief, as we see from the treatment of Perdita later [e.g., 1916, presumably] and from the response, here, of the good Her-mione. It is, however, a dramatically fitting prelude to Leontes' jealousy." For further explicitly religious interpretation, see BETHELL (1947, pp. 76–104). ABARTIS (1977, p. 97): "Polixenes seems to remember his youth as a time of ideal innocence in a pastoral setting while he also mocks his own idealizing memory as he semi-jokingly com-plains . . . that their innocence was lost in sexual initiation." Insofar as it is lascivi-ous, sex is not Christian, however; ADAMSON (1986, p. 61) quotes the ninth Article

And bleat the one at th'other: what we chang'd,
Was Innocence, for Innocence: we knew not
The Doctrine of ill-doing, nor dream'd
That any did: Had we pursu'd that life,
And our weake Spirits ne're been higher rear'd   135

---

133 nor] no nor F2-v1813 (−MAL), COL3, HAL, DYCE2, COL4, HUD2, OXF1-NLSN
dream'd] dream'd even KTLY

---

of Religion: "This infection of nature doeth remaine, yea in them that are regenerated, whereby the lust of the fleshe . . . is not subiect to the lawe of GOD. . . . Concupiscence and lust hath of it selfe the nature of sinne" (ed. 1629). Conjugal love, of course, is sanctioned by the Form of Solemnization of Matrimony in the Book of Common Prayer (1559), which includes a prayer for fruitfulness in the procreation of children, yet, according to the order for Public Baptism, the child procreated is "conceived and born in sin." PAFFORD (ed. 1963): "If he [Polixenes] and Leontes had continued in their state of youthful innocence they would have been able, when called to their final account, to plead themselves guiltless . . . of all sin except original sin." To this, LINDENBAUM (1972, pp. 7–8 n.) objects that *clear'd* means "removed," not "excepted," as PAFFORD would have it. LINDENBAUM believes that the boys would plead "not guilty" to original sin, a theological error that causes Hermione to query Polixenes further, in 139 ff.

TAYLER (1964, p. 128): "The web of allusion . . . provides a frame of reference within which the main events of the play can receive meaning: the speech introduces the vision of the green world, the ideal of past harmony, and associates it with birth, innocence, spring, even with the Garden of Eden." WAIN (1964, p. 220): "This is to trust Nature further than is warranted by experience. The very title of the play is a reminder of the vulnerability of innocence. Mamillius . . . is exactly such a frisking lamb." IWASAKI (1984, pp. 61–2): The pastoral imagery exemplified here "in the second half of the play . . . is shifted to a more literal level and we meet real shepherds and real sheepshearing festivities."

130 **twyn'd Lambs**] PAFFORD (ed. 1963): "Lambs which were exactly alike." VOSS (ed. 1829) finds Juno's swans (*AYL* 1.3.75 [536]) a similar symbol for the friendship of Rosalind and Celia. For the resemblance between Polixenes and Leontes, see n. 3001–2.

131 **bleat**] Past tense, either because *did* is understood or because "in verbs in which the infinitive ends in -*t*, -*ed* is often omitted in the past indicative for euphony" (ABBOTT §341).

what we chang'd] LEE (ed. 1907): "The talk we exchanged." BETHELL (ed. 1956, Chang'd), more broadly: "Either in words or in deeds, going from one occupation to another." By *occupation*, BETHELL apparently means "activity," going from talking to playing or from one type of play to another. CHARLTON (ed. 1916): "Intense dramatic irony: just at this moment Leontes is exchanging not innocence, but guilt, for innocence! . . . As soon as the first step to tragedy is taken by Polixenes' surrender to Hermione, we have the alternating note of joy in the revival of remembered joy and the questionings of days of youth. Perhaps Hermione has already detected signs of moodiness in Leontes, and by her talking of youth is trying to draw him into conversation." CHARLTON alone thinks so.

132–3 **Was . . . ill-doing**] For the possible double meaning, see n. 121–3.

132-4 **we . . . did**] ALEXANDER (1979, p. 240): "Polixenes' comment prepares the audience for the moment, now imminent, when Leontes will definitively put behind him the innocence of youth." GRANTLEY (1986, p. 21): "Unknowingness implies weakness. . . . The assertion . . . is therefore in itself a preparation for the fall of Leontes: unknowingness offers no resistance to sin." Polixenes implies, however, that stronger blood has brought a knowledge of ill-doing to the innocence of childhood.

133 **The . . . dream'd**] ABBOTT (§505): "Lines with four accents are, unless there is a pause in the middle of the line, *very* rare." He accents *doc, of, do*, and *dream'd*. FURNESS (ed. 1898): "The missing syllable can be supplied by the pause after 'doing'. An omission, exactly similar to the present, occurs in [2291]," a line that few eds. emend. HERFORD (ed. 1904), who follows F2: F1's line, "however it be scanned, Shakespeare cannot have written." Most eds., though, apparently agree either with PORTER & CLARKE (ed. 1908) that "a single emphatic word, here long in quantity as well as taking special stress," fills the foot, or with MOORMAN (ed. 1912) that "the pause after 'ill-doing' may be looked upon as having metrical value." BETHELL (ed. 1956): "The time of half a foot." On the other hand, MALONE (ed. 1790) and some later commentators, such as SYMONS (in IRVING & MARSHALL, ed. 1890), consider *doctrine* a trisyllable, so that the stress falls on *ill* rather than on *doing*. In its six other appearances in Sh.'s verse, the word takes two syllables. Those who add F2's *no* to create a regular line often compare 2210.

The . . . ill-doing] SCHMIDT (1874, Doctrine): "Instruction" (*OED, sb.* 1). MARSH (1962; 1969, p. 127): This "revealing phrase . . . suggests that an awareness of evil is something that must be learned and taken account of." HAPPÉ (1969, Doctrine): "Notion," which *OED* does not support. KNOWLES (privately): "We still had no knowledge [*OED*, Doctrine 3 or 4] of doing ill; we hadn't learned to be bad."

135-6 **And . . . blood**] SCHMIDT (1875, Spirit): "Mind, soul" (*OED, sb.* 11). See nn. 917, 3230-3 for other meanings. SCHMIDT (1874) does not list this instance of *blood*, but the word here probably means "the supposed seat of animal or sensual appetite; hence the fleshly nature of man" (*OED, sb.* 6). See n. 182. Thus DEIGHTON (ed. 1889): "Had not our innocent disposition been stirred to a higher pitch by stronger animal passion. . . . *Rear'd* here seems to involve the idea not only of being *raised*, but also the secondary idea of being *brought-up*." A more likely secondary meaning would be "arouse . . . stimulate" (*OED, v.*[1] 6); KERMODE (ed. 1963) gives "fortified." MARSH (1962; 1969, p. 127): The contrast "suggests the passion of living, which makes up life, and also the way that it is both impossible and undesirable for anyone to remain in this state of innocence and immaturity." The word *blood* leads YOUNG & MOSELEY (ed. 1965) to the strange observation that "the first part of the play is a tragedy developed from the Jacobean Theatre of 'blood' — cp., for illustration of the genre, Tourneur's *Atheist's Tragedy*." BURTON (1988, p. 191): "'Higher reared' has an elevated ring to it, suggesting that the stronger state is more desirable than weak innocence. So strength, which is by implication the higher state, is only to be obtained by knowledge of sexual passion, or 'ill-doing.' There is no strength in innocence. . . . Ironically, Polixenes's relationship with a woman is the means by which he has sinned, but at the same time his knowledge of sin is the source of his strength and enoblement, and the index of his adult maturity." For *higher*, SCHMIDT (1874), however, gives "[more] violently, passionately," a meaning that does not seem very elevated. KNOWLES (privately) offers a physiological explanation: "The spirits (natural, animal, vital [*OED*, Spirit 16]) were fluids engendered in the blood, which gave rise both to one's mental powers (Spirit 18) and his emotions and passions, including anger (*OED*, Passion 12) and sexual desire (Passion 9). As the blood (the bodily fluid and the passions) grew stronger in maturity, so did the spirits contained in it, and the mental and emotional spirits animating the mind, leading to hostility and aggression and sin."

With stronger blood, we should haue answer'd Heauen
Boldly, not guilty; the Imposition clear'd,
Hereditarie ours.
    Her. By this we gather
You haue tript since.   140
    Pol. O my most sacred Lady,
Temptations haue since then been borne to's: for
In those vnfledg'd dayes, was my Wife a Girle;
Your precious selfe had then not cross'd the eyes
Of my young Play-fellow.   145

---

142 borne] born F3+
144 then not] not then WARB

135-7 **weake . . . guilty**] For a possible double meaning, see n. 121-3.
135 **rear'd**] SCHMIDT (1875, Rear): "Raise."
136 **should haue answer'd**] The conditional mood, *should* being equivalent to *would* (see FRANZ §612), and *haue*, as ABBOTT §327 says in connection with the use of these auxiliaries in the 2nd and 3rd persons, referring "to *a question about the past* which is to be *answered in the future.*" OED (Answer, *v.* 1b): "To answer charges."
137-8 **the . . . ours**] *OED* (Imposition 3), citing this as its only example: "Imputation, accusation, charge." THEOBALD (1729, in NICHOLS, 1817, 2:358): "Setting aside original sin, and the penalty denounced against the third and fourth generation, on the ancestor's transgressing." THEOBALD omits the second phrase from his ed. 1733. WARBURTON (ed. 1747) adds: "We might have boldly protested our innocence to heaven." HALLIWELL (ed. 1859), alternatively: "We should have even been so entirely innocent, the penalty to which we were subjected from the sins of our common ancestors was condoned," an interpretation preferred by FURNESS (ed. 1898), by COLLINS (ed. 1904-24?), and by BETHELL (ed. 1956), who takes Polixenes's statement to be "a witty hyperbole." MOORMAN (ed. 1912), too, allows that this "interpretation keeps nearer to the force of . . . 'clear'd,'" but CHARLTON (ed. 1916) thinks "'clear'd' implies the idea of the washing away of a stain, not merely the suspension of the consideration of it." PAFFORD (ed. 1963): "The construction seems to be a Latinism . . . : '<assuming> the penalty imposed on us, <original sin,> . . . to have been removed.'" BLAKE (1983, p. 126): "The last phrase need not actually be an example of ellipsis which implies something is missing grammatically." His paraphrase is similar to PAFFORD's, the same or equivalent words being supplied. Recent eds. differ as to whether the imposition is vacated or only temporarily or partially or not at all set aside. PAFFORD, for example: "Guiltless of all personally-committed sin, that is, of all sin except original sin." KERNAN (1975, 3:451), however: "They do not escape the imposed guilt. . . . [The] theological abstraction is dramatically translated into the existential fact of sex. . . . The court of Sicilia is intensely sexual, though the sexuality is submerged, often in puns, beneath the surface of civil life." A similar view is expressed by MACDONALD (1974, p. 1). ORGEL (ed. 1996): "The problem . . . is more doctrinal than syntactical: the ambiguity is solidly grounded in the nominative absolute of the text, and the question is how far one wants to allow Polixenes' Edenic fantasy to extend." On the apparent incongruity of the biblical concept, THIRLBY (MS 1725-33?): "Notwithstanding the mention of Apollo after-

wards [1136 etc.]." For *imposition* as charge or accusation, found only in Sh. (*OED* 3), cf. *MM* 1.2.94 (281-2).

138 **Hereditarie**] HOLBROOK (1964, p. 139), alone: "Heavenly hereditary—admission to Paradise. . . . 'Coming into one's own', into the birthright of gladly accepted adult reality."

139-48 **By . . . Deuils**] MILWARD (1964, p. 33): "The implication . . . is that women are the undoing of men by stirring temptations in their blood, and what took place in Paradise with the seduction of Adam by Eve is of universal application." EDWARDS (*Progress*, 1986, p. 145): "The jesting exchange . . . enforces what has already been clearly implied—that the marriages of the two men are part of the access of guilt and the departure of innocence. . . . The puritanical treatment of sex in the last plays . . . seems . . . closely related to Polixenes' nostalgia for childish innocence." FRENCH (1972, pp. 141-2): Hermione "turns Polixenes' assertion of childhood innocence into an admission of adult guilt. But most skilfully, he turns the 'tripping' into a matter of his and Leontes' relations to their wives, not to woman in general. . . . Polixenes' refutation of Hermione's insinuations has led him inexorably to saying that love, sexual and married love, is itself a temptation. . . . If marriage is but legalized 'ill-doing', then there is no question of 'tripping'. . . . If sexuality is sinful it doesn't matter whether it takes place within or outside marriage, and there is no distinction between the marital act and adultery. . . . Leontes . . . cannot be feeling very reassured about the way in which his wife regards her commitment to him." Critics are divided about whether Leontes overhears this conversation, and 153 may suggest he does not. See further in nn. 121-3 and 142-52.

140-5 **tript . . . Play-fellow**] For possible double meanings, see n. 121-3.

141 **O . . . Lady**] ERICKSON (1982, p. 820): "The automatic response to woman regarded as the source from whom it is blessed to receive." KNOWLES (privately): "Here *sacred* is used as prelude to teasing innuendo that Hermione is not entirely so."

sacred] MINSHEU (1617): "Holie." The CLARKES (ed. 1865): "Revered" (*OED* 4 *transf.* and *fig.*). HERFORD (ed. 1904), recognizing that, as in *Err.* 5.1.133 (1605), *sacred* may be used as a regal epithet: "Royal." The "sacred lady" becomes a "temptation" in 142 and nearly a "devil" in 148. See the next n.

142-52 **Temptations . . . vs**] HOLBROOK (1964, p. 139): "Polixenes speaks of 'temptations' in the shape of Hermione and his own Queen. But such 'temptations' and 'offences' are sanctified and sanctioned by marriage." That is the point; Polixenes's courtly wit treats the marital relationships as illicit, a premise for banter that Hermione accepts. This is clear to DEIGHTON (ed. 1889): "Hermione is humourously indignant at the inference, to be drawn from Polixenes' words, that his and Leontes' sins were due to their becoming acquainted with their wives." TAYLOR (1972, p. 50), slightly differently: "Polixenes suggests (perhaps playfully) . . . that their 'stronger blood', 'reared' by 'temptations' like Hermione, has since tripped them into the sin of sex and marriage. . . . Hermione continues to make gentle fun of the apparent seriousness with which Polixenes and Leontes hark back to their unsmudged pasts, enlivening the exchanges with frank sensuality [as in 164-6]. The slight tension between Hermione's jocularity and the men's self-reverence leads to the greater tension of Leontes' jealousy." Some critics, however, find nothing to joke about. LINDENBAUM (1972, pp. 8-10): Polixenes "is still not completely aware of some of the implications of his own statements. In effect, he is accusing Hermione of being the cause of Leontes' fall from grace. . . . The fear of sexual love that Polixenes . . . betrays in this scene amounts to an inadvertent confession that he and Leontes simply could not deal with sexual passion without disastrous results." Prior to 181, no disastrous results are on record. EGAN (1975, p. 66), however: "In terming sexual union a lapse from goodness, Polixenes has, by implication, denied the goodness of great nature's law and process no less than will Leontes in condemning Hermione's chaste vitality as

Her. Grace to boot: 146
Of this make no conclusion, least you say
Your Queene and I are Deuils: yet goe on,
Th'offences we haue made you doe, wee'le answere,

---

146 Grace] Oh! Grace HAN; Good grace KTLY; God's grace WALKER (1860, 1:214) *conj.*, HUD2
148 on] out PEN1

---

wanton lust and his own child as a bastard." GOURLAY (1975, p. 378), similarly: "Later we recognize that . . . Polixenes means what he says [in referring to women as 'temptations']: in [2278-85] he will denounce Perdita, blaming her as seducer of his son, in terms as bitter as Leontes' own." WRIGHT (1979, p. 153): "We are left with the impression of a vague sinfulness associated with sexual maturity. . . . Here and in the rest of the scene Hermione shows the assured self-confidence of the mature woman (as contrasted with Perdita's timidity)." Mark TAYLOR (1982, p. 37): The speech "is ill-mannered and boorish; even if Hermione were less gracious and hospitable than she is, Polixenes' rudeness in blaming her and his own wife for his and Leontes' fall from grace would be nearly inexcusable." TAYLOR also thinks that "vnfledg'd dayes" (143), "weake Spirits" (135), and "higher rear'd" (135) add up to "a distaste for height, flight, ascending—and by extension, possibly, for physical tumescence." Cf. n. 139-48.

142 **borne**] The past tense of "to give birth to" (see SCHMIDT [1874] Bear 5).

143 **vnfledg'd**] SCHMIDT (1875): "Young and unripe."

146-52 **Grace . . . vs**] CHARLTON (ed. 1916): Polixenes's words "serve to draw forth evidence of Hermione's gaiety and wit." HORWITZ (1988, p. 9): "Hermione . . . acknowledges [that] the subtext of Polixenes's courtly deference [in 141-5] . . . rests upon a profound mistrust of woman's sexuality." HORWITZ apparently does not recognize that a set of wit is being played; see n. 142-52.

146 **Grace to boot**] MILWARD (1964, p. 33): "This is by no means a stock exclamation, and it occurs nowhere else in the work of Shakespeare." WARBURTON (ed. 1747): "I.e. tho' temptations have grown up, yet I hope grace too has kept pace with them. . . . A proverbial expression" (but in neither TILLEY nor DENT). MINSHEU (1617) for *boot* gives "helpe, succour, aid and advantage"; see n. 2515 and *OED* (*sb.*[1] 7c, citing this line). Thus CAPELL (1783, 2.4:162): "Grace befriend us! Grace be merciful," which HUNTER (ed. 1872), a clergyman, amplifies to "And grace also to secure you against temptation has been born to you" (i.e., the grace of God in Christ). HAPPÉ (1969): "If she is a temptation, as Polixenes has just implied, she is in need of Grace." NEILSON & HILL (ed. 1942): "Heavenly grace help me," an interpretation that, KAMACHI (1983, p. 59) suggests, indicates "an unconscious attempt on the part of Hermione to suppress the power of 'devil' in herself."

PAFFORD (ed. 1963): "Grace in addition! i.e. 'What next indeed!'" LINDENBAUM (1972, p. 8): "Some thanks we get!" perhaps "pointing to the discrepancy in being addressed as 'sacred' while being called a . . . temptress." BATTENHOUSE (1980, p. 129): "Hermione may be questioning whether their behavior as boys had been as completely clear of hereditary sin as Polixenes supposes, and in reply she is saying that to trace sin's beginning to wives as its cause is to overlook the 'grace' a 'sacred' lady offers for overcoming temptation." BURTON (1988, pp. 191-2): "Hermione reminds Polixenes that only without the grace she brings as a woman does sexuality become base and a woman's inherent ability to tempt a man wicked. Female grace . . . elevates sexuality." BETHELL (ed. 1956): "The theme of sin [in 141–5] is followed by the theme of grace. Both are lightly introduced . . . but they will have their effect."

The word *grace* and its cognates *grac'd, graceful, graces* occur frequently in *WT* and in a wide range of meaning. CAPELL and HUNTER here no doubt mean God's grace, as some later eds. specify; SCHMIDT (1874), for this instance, gives "the headspring of mercy, God." MAHOOD (1957, p. 151): "In the dialogue which follows, the word *grace* is used three times [169, 177, 730] by Hermione, the implication being that she acts the role of regenerative grace to Leontes now he has exchanged innocence for experience." PORTER & CLARKE (ed. 1908) find a secular meaning: "Here is compliment in superfluity!" For other meanings of *grace*, see nn. 169, 355, 730, 1221, 1603, 1882, 2659, 3118, and 3216. For *gracious*, see n. 1639.

147–8 **Of . . . Deuils**] *This* = "this line of argument." WARBURTON (ed. 1747): I.e., "as for *our* tempting you . . . draw no conclusion from thence, for that would be making your Queen and me devils." MALONE (ed. 1790): "Do not draw any . . . inference from your . . . [becoming] acquainted with your queen and me; for, as . . . temptations have been born to you, . . . the . . . insinuation would be strong against us, as your corrupters." Recalling Polixenes's mention of the hereditary imposition (137–8), DEIGHTON (ed. 1889) finds here "a further reference to Eve tempting Adam after herself being tempted by the devil." WATSON (1984, p. 230): "Leontes, whether or not he overhears . . . , seems to reach in earnest the conclusion his wife reaches in jest."

149–52 **Th'offences . . . vs**] MACDONALD (1974, p. 1): Polixenes's "words [141 ff.] are both flattering to Hermione and playfully accusatory. Hermione's reply is based on the orthodox conception of marital chastity. . . . Sexual relations consummated within the sacrament of marriage are not sinful." Hermione uses the language of transgression to assert that no transgression occurred. PARRY (ed. 1982): "Hermione has in her mind . . . the Garden of Eden and the sin of carnal knowledge originally committed there." PARRY possibly means the "Loves disport" just after the Fall, of "mutual guilt the Seal" (*Paradise Lost* 9.1042–5); Milton makes it plain that before the Fall, carnal knowledge was bountiful and innocent. PARRY continues, "She means that she is counting on the fact that Leontes and Polixenes were virgins when they married, and that they have remained faithful to their wives ever since." KAMACHI (1979, p. 23): "'You' points to Polixenes and Leontes, and 'we' refers to Polixenes's wife and Hermione. Cut out from the context, however, 'you' may be taken as Polixenes only, and 'we' could suggest Hermione alone, for she is entitled to use the royal 'we.'" FRYE (1986, p. 162): "This is harmless badinage, but to a poisoned mind every syllable suggests a horrible leering innuendo." For *vs*, CARRINGTON (1956), alone: "Women folk."

WILSON (ed. 1931), supported by PAFFORD (ed. 1963): "Is it not more than probable that Leontes is intended by Shakespeare to overhear these equivocal words as he comes forward from behind, unseen by the speakers but in such a way that the audience can watch the play of his features?" Leontes has been out of earshot (see n. 90), and BETHELL (1947, p. 121) believes it is improbable that he would overhear and misunderstand Hermione's words without saying something indicative, aside if not openly. SCHANZER (ed. 1969, p. 23) agrees: "It is unbelievable that at this crucial point Shakespeare would not have given Leontes a word to utter which would have conveyed his misapprehension. . . . And when [at 181 ff.] he is made to vent for the first time his suspicions . . . there is no hint [there], or in anything he says later, that he has overheard what he takes to be a confession of adultery." The point seems well taken. Overhearing is represented in, for example, *MND* 2.1.188 ff. (566 ff.), *MM* 3.1.53 ff. (1261 ff.), *Ado* 3.3.95 ff. (1422 ff.), and *Rom.* 2.2.25 ff. (803 ff.), always with comment indicating that it has taken place. PYLE (1969, p. 15), however, thinks otherwise: "Surprise and mystification are all the actor need show ('What an odd

If you first sinn'd with vs: and that with vs 150
You did continue fault; and that you slipt not
With any, but with vs.
   Leo. Is he woon yet?
   Her. Hee'le stay (my Lord.)
   Leo. At my request, he would not: 155

---

153 *Coming forward.* COL2, COL3, PEN2
155 *Marked as aside* CAP, CAM3

---

thing to say. What can she be talking about?'). These together with resentment [155]
are enough in the shorthand of stage psychology to constitute the seeds of jealousy."
MACDONALD (1974, pp. 1-2), similarly: "The preceding dialogue, unheard yet observed by Leontes, has led Leontes to the unwarranted conclusion that he is a cuckold.
For Leontes' jealous reaction to appear motivated and at the same time unjustified,
the conversation should be staged with Leontes visibly reacting to a noticeably vivacious exchange." NATHAN (1968, p. 22) alone believes that Hermione's words "could
mean that she and Polixenes are lovers and that she is demanding that he remain
faithful to that illicit relationship." DRAPER (1985, p. 16): "From now on words that
have borne only one—and that an essentially innocent—meaning, take on a jealous
ambiguity." For more on Leontes's jealousy, see n. 181-92.
   149 **answere**] COLLINS (ed. 1904-24?): "Answer, be responsible for." Cf. n. 136.
   150-1 **that . . . that**] COLLINS (ed. 1904-24?): "'If', *if that* being equivalent to
if." ABBOTT (§285): "The purely conjunctional use of *that* is illustrated by the Elizabethan habit of omitting it at the beginning of a sentence [here after 'Th'offences'],
where the construction is obvious, and then inserting it to connect a more distant
clause with the conjunction on which the clause depends."
   151 **continue fault**] FURNESS (ed. 1898) compares the similar construction "made
fault" (1407). See also 2728.
   slipt] The CLARKES (1879, p. 591): "Err'd." See n. 365.
   153 **Is . . . yet?**] ROLFE (ed. 1879): "Leontes has been aside, playing with Mamillius, while Hermione has been pleading with Polixenes." The same comment is made
by the CLARKES (1879, p. 722). KEETON (1930; 1967, pp. 147-8): "This is not jealousy.
It is merely the impatience that a man could be so long in making up his mind."
Michael TAYLOR (1982, p. 229): An "impatient enquiry." But 156-7 seem amiable;
see the next n.
   155 **At . . . not**] COLERIDGE (1813; ed. Foakes, 1989, p. 174): The first working
of Leontes's jealousy. HUDSON (1855; 1872, 1:457): "There is a jealousy of friendship,
as well as of love. Accordingly, although Leontes invokes the Queen's influence to
induce a lengthening of the visit, yet he seems a little disturbed on seeing that her
influence has proved stronger than his own." ENRIGHT (1970, p. 158): It "commences
in a natural way and as a minor feeling of resentment." CHARLTON (ed. 1916): "This
is only intelligible as a working of jealousy if we assume that it has been simmering
for some time: . . . during the last fifty lines Leontes has been wrapped in jealous
broodings." But see n. 59-60. BETHELL (ed. 1956): "There is no textual support for
the notion that Leontes was already jealous; and a sudden, inexplicable jealousy is
quite acceptable both psychologically and in relation to the play's 'inner meaning'";
see pp. 775 ff. He is jealous now, however, and "the actor playing Leontes might
show bitterness behind the apparently loving dialogue that follows." GIRARD (1987,
p. 44) differs: "I detect no resentment in Leontes' congratulations, only admiration
and gratitude." SANDERS (1987, p. 10): "Editors have no warrant for marking this as

Hermione (my dearest) thou neuer spoak'st
To better purpose.
   Her. Neuer?
   Leo. Neuer, but once.
   Her. What? haue I twice said well? when was't before?   160

---

156 dearest . . . neuer] dearest . . . ne'er POPE1-JOHN2, v1773; dear'st . . .
never CAP, DYCE1 (*errata*), WH1, HAL, STAU, DYCE2, HUD2, BUL, SIS
  160 was't] 'twas v1778, v1785

---

an *Aside* [few do; see textual n.]: its awkward clumsiness is there for everyone to
hear." The tone, though, may be jocular; the remark is followed by congratulations
to Hermione on her success.
   156-7 *Hermione* . . . purpose] PYLE (1969, p. 19): "Leontes fights back his
disquiet with loving thoughts." MARTZ (1980, p. 119), quite differently: "Is this the
equivalent of saying that she has at last made clear her guilt?"
   156 dearest] WALKER (1854, p. 144): Pronounced *dear'st.* KÖKERITZ (1953, p.
266) and PAFFORD (ed. 1963) agree, but CERCIGNANI (1981, §109) evidently does not.
The elision of *neuer* (*ne'er*) seems preferable.
   157 to better purpose] SCHMIDT (1875): "Conformably to the subject or object
in view, well, rightly." BLUESTONE (1974, p. 33), believing Leontes already jealous:
"Leontes means to *his* purpose, which is to confirm his suspicion of their . . . illict
alliance."
   158 Neuer?] MARTIN (1891, p. 5): "In acting, how much should be indicated in
the tone of Hermione's 'Never'? Have you forgotten, it asks, your long wooing, and
the consent it at last won from me? Will not the words I then spoke rank for ever the
highest in your regard?" CHARLTON (ed. 1916): "Memories of happiness and joy are
called up—all of them to intensify what is to follow." LINDENBAUM (1972, p. 9),
however, thinks that a literal honesty is characteristic of Hermione; "she will not rest
until she hears the full and explicit truth [about the better purpose] from Leontes."
BLAKE (1983, p. 127): "Hermione's reply [may be] either a question or an exclamation." All eds. collated consider it a question, however, no doubt because the reply
makes no sense as an exclamation.
   159 Neuer, but once] BOORMAN (ed. 1964): "It is significant that Leontes is comparing Hermione's persuasion of Polixenes with . . . her decision to give Leontes
her love." Rather than making this comparison, Leontes may be responding to her
hint that her acceptance of his proposal of marriage was spoken to even better purpose, as MARTIN recognizes (n. 158).
   160-71 What? . . . long] This speech is a hunting ground for critics seeking
specific causes of Leontes's jealousy. TINKLER (1937, p. 359): "Such expressions [e.g.,
'cram's'] . . . have a suggestion of unpleasantness." BETHELL (ed. 1956): "The images used by the unsuspecting Hermione as well as the jealous Leontes have ominous
overtones. . . . The 'cramming' of domestic animals is for 'slaughter', and the latter
word is used, though in another connection, in [163]. Note also the sour crab-apples
of [173]." LIVINGSTON (1969, p. 342): "The extravagant language of court compliment
is potentially explosive. Hermione's use of elaborate metaphor for its own sake, separate from meaning, evokes the initial unpleasant suggestions in Leontes' imagination." WHITE (1981, p. 104): Leontes's later attack "leads us at least to recognise the
dangerousness and self-aware experience of the woman's amply relaxed sensuality of
language." NEVO (1987, p. 104): "This is spoken jestingly, of course, but it is not

I prethee tell me: cram's with prayse, and make's
As fat as tame things: One good deed, dying tonguelesse,
Slaughters a thousand, wayting vpon that.
Our prayses are our Wages. You may ride's
With one soft Kisse a thousand Furlongs, ere   165
With Spur we heat an Acre. But to th'Goale:

---

166 heat] clear COL2, COL3, COL4; heat us KTLY
      Acre.] ~ , WARB, JOHN, v1773
      Goale] good COL2, COL3, COL4

---

unknown for jests to be used to camouflage resentments. Neither [172-6] nor [235-7] do much to mitigate the impression we might receive of a couple in considerable marital stress, if not positive crisis." NEVO does not explain the mitigation of the muzzled dagger, nor why affectionate recollection of courtship and acceptance signifies marital stress. LINDENBAUM (1972, p. 10), differently: "The primary level of her [Hermione's] metaphor equates women with pets that one feeds. But she is eight months pregnant and plainly pleased with herself. . . . [This] and her later suggestion of being ridden by a man [164-5] are . . . openly and enthusiastically sexual." BERNARD (1979, p. 222): "In their permissible bawdry they [these lines] bring together the praise of generous doing and the act, cleared of the imposition of hereditary guilt, that has made the speaker herself as fat as tame things." The queen may or may not be at all fat; see nn. 49 and 607-12.

160 **when was't before?**] WILSON (ed. 1931): "She knows well enough, but thirsts to hear him say it."

161 **cram's . . . make's**] COLLIER (ed. 1842): I.e., "cram *us* . . . make *us.*" EVANS (ed. 1974): "Hermione speaks for herself [using the royal *we*] and all women." Regarding the contractions (and *ride's* in 164), CARRUTHERS & CHAMBERS (ed. 1862): "Shakespeare . . . never intended the verse to be read . . . in so harsh and unmusical a manner. The poet's verse often overflows into twelve feet [as in 162]." But 162 has five feet and an unaccented final syllable, if *dying* is slurred. For more on apostrophes in this text, see p. 594.

162 **tame things**] Following DELIUS (ed. 1860), DEIGHTON (ed. 1889): "Animals that are kept to be fattened for the table." PIERCE (ed. 1918): "Well-fed pets." HERFORD (ed. 1916-): "Hermione thinks of women's susceptibility to praise as making them . . . easily compliant; in [164-6], as stimulating them to effort." HOLBROOK (1964, p. 146): The expression "evokes a feeling of physical disturbance . . . touching on our fear of the vulnerability of the naked body in sexual love. But the wit of the phrase digests and assuages the fear and bravely comes to terms with it."

162-3 **One . . . that**] HUNTER (ed. 1872): "A good deed receiving no commendation, prevents the performance of a thousand which would have followed [had the first good deed been commended]." DEIGHTON (ed. 1889, Tonguelesse): "Not talked of. See Abb[ott] §3" (*OED, a.* 3, citing this line as its only example). For *that*, RIDLEY (ed. 1935): "*I.e.* its happening," but HAPPÉ (1969): "The good report which was deserved." C. G. SMITH (1963, nos. 59 and 237) finds parallels in Publilius Syrus, *Sententiae*, and Leonard Culman, *Sententiae Pueriles*.

162 **dying**] VAN DAM (1900, p. 50) notices the syncopation of *i* required for regular meter. For other syncopations of *i*, see nn. 313, 942, and 3369.

163 **wayting vpon**] SCHMIDT (1875): "Accompanying." Cf. 2898.

164-6 **You . . . Acre**] Substituting a comma for F's full stop after *Acre*, WARBURTON (ed. 1747): "Good usage will win us to any thing; but with ill, we stop short, even there where both our interest and our inclination would otherwise have carried us." For *heat*, CAPELL (1783, 2.4:162) gives "o'er-run." HARNESS (ed. 1825), more explicitly: "Run a heat, as in a race," with which SCHMIDT (1874) substantially agrees. So do the CLARKES (1879, p. 369), who list the expression as an idiom. *OED* is doubtful; citing this instance only, it gives HARNESS's meaning (*v.* 1c) but questions it, not only because no other examples of *heat* used in this sense as a verb exist but also perhaps because *heat* as a noun meaning "a single course in a race" (*sb.* 10) was not current until the late 17th c. Nevertheless, such recent eds. as SCHANZER (ed. 1969) accept this meaning. CALDECOTT (MS 1813-33) offers an unlikely alternative: "Accompany you with the glow . . . of cordiality the space of an acre: are induced to go freely, with spirit enough to warm us." As for *Acre*, *OED* states that the word may denote a lineal measure—"a furlong (*i.e.* furrow-length)." Following BETHELL (ed. 1956), KERMODE (ed. 1963) therefore glosses *heat an Acre* as "race over a single furlong." RIDLEY (ed. 1935) thinks the passage hopelessly corrupt, although eds. make pretty good sense of it, PARRY (ed. 1982), for example: "Affectionate treatment will get you a lot further in your relations with the female sex than harshness will." FURNIVALL (ed. 1877?, p. xcii n.): "Note the likeness of Hermione's how pretence of love will manage wives [sic], to that of Luciana in *Err.* [3.2.11-28 (797-814) presumably]." HOENIGER (1950, p. 16): This "rich image . . . fits the whole theme of the play, indeed contains in it its very words: the opposition of love and tyranny." For the possible double meaning, see n. 121-3, and for the contribution of what TAYLOR (1972, p. 50) calls Hermione's "frank sensuality," see n. 142-52. TAYLOR continues, "Hermione's equestrian metaphor is as remote in effect from gambolling lambs [130-1] as it is from beasts with two backs [*Oth.* 1.1.116-17 (129)]; it lacks the pristine ignorance of the one and the perverted 'knowledge' of the other. It represents a way of talking about married sex that remains chaste, while being sophisticated and free from illusion." DASH (1980, p. 277), along the same line: "The images are there: kiss, ride, spur, heat. And they suggest the sensuality of the speaker herself."

164 **ride's**] HOLBROOK (1964, p. 140) finds "overtones of the sadism inherent in the normal [sexual] relationship. . . . Shakespeare is himself seeking to tolerate the sexual reality, to take into account its disturbing elements, and to discover its place in human life as a whole." SANDERS (1987, p. 18): The words reach Leontes "as provocative femininity deliberately flaunting itself before another male." HENN (1972, pp. 73-4), more reasonably, associates the word with "disciplined control," as in "The third oth'world is yours, which with a Snaffle, You may pace easie, but not such a wife" (*Ant.* 2.2.63-4 [754-5]).

165 **Furlongs**] A furlong is one-eighth of a mile. The word occurs only one other time in Sh. (*Tmp.* 1.1.65 [76]), where, as SCHMIDT (1874) points out, a thousand furlongs are again opposed to an acre.

166 **But to th'Goale**] WARBURTON (ed. 1747) objects that eds. who retain the full stop after *Acre* imagine that this expression means "but to come to the purpose." Later commentators, however, think it means just that—for example, HEATH (1765, p. 204): "But to keep in view the point I was driving at" (at 154 ff.) and MALONE (ed. 1790): "Come to an end . . . of this matter." HERFORD (ed. 1916-): "Her phrase falls into the racing figure of the previous clause, but has nothing to do with it."

My last good deed, was to entreat his stay.   (2A)
What was my first? it ha's an elder Sister,
Or I mistake you: O, would her Name were *Grace*.
But once before I spoke to th' purpose? when?   170
Nay, let me haue't: I long.
    Leo. Why, that was when
Three crabbed Moneths had sowr'd themselues to death,
Ere I could make thee open thy white Hand:
A clap thy selfe, my Loue; then didst thou vtter,   175

---

167 deed] *Om.* v1803-v1821, SING1, HUD1, HAL
170 spoke] spake F3-JOHN2; speak v1773
175 A] And F2+
    clap] clepe ROWE3-v1773

---

168 it . . . Sister] DEIGHTON (ed. 1889): "I . . . did a deed that in goodness was akin to this." PAFFORD (ed. 1963) thinks that *elder Sister* is an appositive used in the sense of "fellow," but, as he remarks, *OED*'s first record of *sister* in this sense (10b) is dated 1641. KNOWLES (privately): "She considers a womanly good deed to be of the feminine gender."

169-77 O . . . indeed] KNOWLES (privately): "Cajoling Leontes, she hopes the deed was worth the grace [thanks, praise] that she has been inviting all through the speech. Leontes responds with mock reluctance, teasingly giving a speech more like complaint than praise, to which Hermione answers quibblingly: (a) 'Well, a marriage vow was a gracious (holy) speech,' and (b) (ironically), 'and you certainly make it sound praiseworthy.'"

169 O . . . Grace] SCHANZER (ed. 1969, *Grace*): "Probably . . . 'seemliness', 'becomingness', with an intentional pun on the female name." DEIGHTON (ed. 1889): "Having used the expression 'elder sister' in speaking of a former deed, she goes on to say how pleased she would be if Leontes would christen that deed 'Grace' . . . , *i.e.* would speak of it as being a gracious deed." Cf. 177. MELDRUM (1968, p. 55): "The context makes it clear that Hermione was thinking of matrimony when she spoke. . . . She hoped that her marriage to Leontes was a union blessed by grace." PAFFORD (ed. 1963): "She has playfully accused Polixenes of being about to say that there was devilry in her influence on Leontes [147-8], and in the same vein she now hopes that there will be something of the opposite . . . ; and at [178] she expresses relief to find that it is so." BETHELL (ed. 1956): "She hopes that her first good deed was inspired by divine grace (and so was truly good)." EVANS (ed. 1974): Spoken "with a backward glance at [141-52]." KAMACHI (1983, pp. 61-2) alone finds the possibility of double entendre. In Tourneur's (Middleton's) *Revenger's Tragedy* (1605-6) allusion is made to a bawd named Grace (ed. Foakes, 1966, 1.3.16); thus Hermione's "queer personification . . . might have reminded some audiences of a real bawd." Moreover, *sister* meaning "prostitute" in *The Revenger's Tragedy* 2.2.145 makes the "elder Sister" of Hermione's last good deed seem suspicious. For other meanings of *grace*, see n. 146.

170 But] Only.
    to th' purpose] *OED* (Purpose, *sb.* 12c, citing this line): "So as to secure the result or effect desired." DEIGHTON (ed. 1889): "*I.e.* well in your opinion."

171 haue't] DEIGHTON (ed. 1889): "Hear it, know it."

I long] BOORMAN (ed. 1964): "Hermione is pregnant, in which state women were supposed to have odd and sudden longings. (Cf. [2549])." This longing seems neither odd nor sudden; as CARRINGTON (1956) says, she means "I long to know." PAFFORD (ed. 1963) compares *LLL* 5.2.244 (2156), spoken by presumably unpregnant Katherine; in that scene "the ladies' speech and bantering tone are much like those of Hermione here."

172-201 **Why . . . Palme?]** LEIMBERG (1987, p. 132): "First Leontes recalls the hand-giving of boy and girl as the symbol of requited love. Hermione adds the religious as well as the legal sense of joining hands in holy matrimony and [alludes to] the triadic circle of the graces. Then . . . the hands of Hermione and Polixenes meet in friendship. And . . . for Leontes, all the rational meanings of handgiving become peripheral and only the magic of the age-old gesture remains in the centre of his emotional universe." As LEIMBERG notes, an explanation of the magic of the given hand is found in BULWER (1644, p. 101): "The gesture flowes from a secret and religious reverence to that comprehensive number *Ten*, for while each *Hand* doth extend five fingers . . . they premit [i.e., send forth] a resemblance of the *Decades* mystery." For other instances of hand giving, see nn. 564, 1971-3, and 3315, as well as lines 32, 1736-7, 2170, 2185, 2213, 2650, 3148-9, 3164, 3238, 3293, and 3358.

172-6 **Why . . . euer]** Critics read a dark significance into these lines in antic-ipation of the outburst of jealousy. HUDSON (1855; 1872, 1:457): "There is, I think, a relish of suppressed bitterness . . . , as if her long reluctance had planted in him a germ of doubt whether, after all, her heart was really in her words of consent." MORLEY (1887, p. 13): "Doubt of the 'for ever' was in the reminding of the promise, for here the paroxysm of insanity begins." CHARLTON (ed. 1916): "Otherwise the 'Too hot' immediately following [181] is an abrupt and inconsequential change." WILSON (ed. 1931) similarly thinks "Leontes puts much meaning into this recital of the troth-plight" (176). Rather than Hermione's reluctance, RAVENSCROFT (1971, p. 14) finds here a "hint that there is something youthfully impetuous in his [Leontes's] wooing." Michael TAYLOR (1982, p. 230), ominously: "He speaks in such a way as to alert us to the violence and corruption within him, as in this disturbing description of the ardor of his wooing." FURNESS (ed. 1898), however, does not find Leontes bitter. FOWLER (1978, p. 47): Her "having been stiff in courtship . . . is probably only Shakespeare's conventional sign of her virtue." Leontes later remembers that when he wooed her, she stood with "Life of Maiestie" (3226). DRAPER (1985, p. 17) thinks that the words *crabbed, sowr'd*, and *death* "give the natural anxiety of court-ship a bitterness that is obviously excessive," but Leontes may be responding to the humorous exaggeration of crammed praise, a thousand good deeds, and a thousand furlongs per soft kiss (161-5).

173 **Three crabbed Moneths]** FURNESS (ed. 1898): "This protracted wooing, extraordinarily long for Elizabethan days, is a noteworthy indication of Hermione's character." JOHNSON (1755, Crabbed, citing this line): "Harsh, unpleasing" (*OED, a.* 9). A few critics (e.g., LINDENBAUM, 1972, p. 10 n.) seem to think the crab a crusta-cean; BOORMAN (ed. 1964), who clearly never went crabbing, finds "possibly a sug-gestion of something slow and clumsy, like crabs." DEIGHTON (ed. 1889) and other eds., however, think the allusion is to the sourness of the crab apple; see n. 160-71. To SCHMIDT (1875) the expression means that the months "had gone by in bitter tediousness"; critics who wish to disparage Leontes in anticipation of his jealous outburst see the words as more ominous. SANDERS (1987, p. 16), for example: "Leon-tes . . . is exactly the man to feel this delay . . . a slur upon his sufficiency."

175 **A]** PAFFORD (ed. 1963): "Perhaps a manuscript ampersand was mistaken for an *A*." PORTER & CLARKE (ed. 1908), however, do not emend; to do so "rather spoils the colloquial touch of the happier mood recalling this fact which this careless *A* gives." They offer several examples of happy clapping but none illustrating the col-loquial touch.

clap] THIRLBY (MS 1733-47?): "Note clap hands." STEEVENS (ed. 1773) elab-

I am yours for euer.

   Her. 'Tis Grace indeed.

Why lo-you now; I haue spoke to th' purpose twice:

The one, for euer earn'd a Royall Husband;

Th'other, for some while a Friend.   180

   Leo. Too hot, too hot:

To mingle friendship farre, is mingling bloods.

I haue *Tremor Cordis* on me: my heart daunces,

But not for ioy; not ioy. This Entertainment

May a free face put on: deriue a Libertie   185

From Heartinesse, from Bountie, fertile Bosome,

And well become the Agent: 't may; I graunt:

But to be padling Palmes, and pinching Fingers,

As now they are, and making practis'd Smiles

As in a Looking-Glasse; and then to sigh, as 'twere   190

The Mort o'th'Deere: oh, that is entertainment

My Bosome likes not, nor my Browes. *Mamillius,*

---

   176 I am] I'm HUD2

   177 'Tis] This is HAN; It is mTBY3 *conj.,* CAP-DEL2 (−WH1, STAU), KTLY-HUD2 (−DEL4)

   180 *giving her Hand to* Pol. CAP, v1778-SIS (−CAM1, GLO, IRV, ARD1), CLN2, ARD2, PEN2+ (*subst.*); ad. *they rise and talk apart* CAM3, PEL1, OXF2 (*subst.*)

   180-1 *One verse line* mCAP2, v1793+ (−OXF1, PEN1, CLN2, ARD2)

   181-92 Too . . . Browes.] *Marked as an aside* ROWE1+

   181 Too hot, too hot:] Too hot— HAN

   182 farre] far F4+ (−OXF2)

   185 deriue] derives F2-POPE2

   186 Bountie,] bounty's mTBY2 *conj.,* HAN, COL2-COL3 (−DYCE1), KTLY-HUD2 (−DEL4), BUL, KIT1

   187 well] we'l F2-ROWE2

       become] becomes ROWE3-POPE2

       Agent:] ∼ ? POPE

---

orates: "She open'd her hand, to clap the palm of it into his, as people do when they confirm a bargain" (*OED, v.*[1] 7b, citing this line); as PAFFORD (ed. 1963) explains, when a bargain is made, "hands are struck together and then clasped." Thus HARRISON's (ed. 1947) "clasp hands" for *clap* is wrong. MALONE (ed. 1790): "A regular part of the ceremony of troth plighting." He compares *MM* 5.1.209-10 (2581-2) and *Jn.* 2.1.533 (853). Cf., as well, 2213. FARRELL (1975, p. 48): "Also prating or chatter [*OED, sb.*[1] 3, with no citations contemporaneous with Sh.]. In addition, it has theatrical connotations, and suggests applause for his 'performance' [*v.*[1] 5b, a significance that does not work with 'thy selfe.' Cf. n. 269-72.]." ORGEL (ed. 1996), citing *AYL* 5.3.11 (2541): "'To enter with alacrity and briskness upon anything' [*OED* 15b] also seems relevant."

   177 **'Tis Grace indeed**] RANN (ed. 1787), wrongly: I.e., "this indulgence of her wish for the stay of *Polixenes.*" CAPELL (1783, 2.4:162): Hermione refers to her wish in 169, signifying "that she now saw she had it." DELIUS (ed. 1860): *Grace* is also

used in its other sense as a proper name. DEIGHTON (ed. 1889), similarly: "Then the name of that deed of mine is really 'grace', as I hoped you would christen it." BETHELL (ed. 1956): *Grace* has "the theological meaning . . . (a free gift of divine power) and the social meaning (the *graciousness* of her consenting to marry)." YOUNG (1992, p. 183): "Graciousness and generosity, as well as virtue." For other meanings of *grace*, see n. 146. WRIGHT & LAMAR (ed. 1966), questionably: "Referring to the proverbial saying that 'Marriages are made in Heaven.'"

178 **lo-you now**] The CLARKES (1879, p. 465): "In playful surprise." DEIGHTON (ed. 1889): "An interjection, and nothing to do with 'look.'" *OED* (Lo, b): "Look!" PARRY (ed. 1982), however: "You see." There is a nearly identical expression at 960.

I . . . twice] HERFORD (ed. 1916-): "Hermione, by as it were 'bracketing' the two occasions on which she has 'spoken well', has innocently fomented Leontes's incipient suspicion; and the distinction she proceeds to draw between husband and friend, clear and final as it is, does not efface the fact that she *compares* them. Her ensuing demonstrations of her friendship seem to continue the dangerous comparison, and his morbid eye interprets the most innocent gestures for the worse." PETERSON (*Time*, 1973, p. 159): "The identification of present and past for Leontes is complete. In recalling that earlier occasion he re-experiences the feelings that Hermione's pledge . . . to return his love had awakened in him; and now in a moment of delirium . . . he attributes his own feelings to Polixenes and believes that he sees actual proof of his wife's infidelity."

179-80 **The . . . Friend**] SCHMIDT (1874, Friend): "One joined to another in benevolence and intimacy," which Hermione means, or "lover," which Hermione does not mean but to which Leontes alludes in 182. HARRISON (ed. 1947): "[Hermione] is attractive, vivacious, and demonstrative, and quite naturally takes Polixenes by the arm as she leads him away for their chat. Leontes is in a mood to think the worst. Polixenes has firmly resisted his embarrassing insistence. When Hermione so easily wins Polixenes over, the sudden awful thought strikes Leontes that there must be something between them." Hermione takes Polixenes by the hand, not the arm; see 188-9, from which CAPELL's SD derives. KEETON (1930; 1967, p. 148): She does so "to bind the compact she has made with him that he should stay. This jars on Leontes. It seems to force itself into contrast with the handfasting of their betrothal." BELLETTE (1978, p. 67): "Hermione distinguishes carefully between two kinds of love—love of a husband 'for ever' and of a friend 'for some while.' As if sensing the sudden delicacy of the situation she adopts a tone of greater seriousness." LENZ (1986, p. 95): "The parallel clauses encourage Leontes to equate the two purposes. Hermione's payment to the 'earned' (the correct verb to fill the ellipsis) friend is the same as her payment to the 'earned' husband: the marriage bed." See n. 149-52 for ambiguity in the preceding lines. PYLE (1969, p. 21): Hermione offers Polixenes her hand, "the white hand she opened to clap herself Leontes' love." A more recent version of this sequence is that of FREY (*Vast Romance*, 1980, p. 122): "Hermione, pregnant and charged with sensual energy, draws Polixenes into a discussion of sex, tells Leontes to praise her, speaks of being ridden with soft kisses, and asks for news of her first good deed . . . [171]. Leontes tells her that was when he 'made' her open her 'white hand' and vow to be his forever. So saying, he takes one of her hands in his. Hermione responds, 'Tis Grace indeed'. Turning then from Leontes, she extends her hand to Polixenes, saying [178-80]. And queen and 'friend' . . . draw off together, leaving Leontes to hiss his blistering aside [181]. In that single instance of handclasps transferred through Hermione, Camillo's image of kings who 'shook hands, as over a vast' [32] explodes into suspicion."

181-92 **Too . . . Browes**] TRAVERSI (1969, 2:301) on this and Leontes's following private speeches: "Shakespeare's rhythms were never more impressive, never more delicately adjusted to the breaks in an overwrought consciousness, never more vivid in their ultra-sensual repulsion from the physical." SELTZER (1971, p. 52) discusses this speech as a late example of the soliloquy: "In its physicalization it would perhaps not have varied greatly from many others, earlier in the period; but vocally and in terms of the actor's stance . . . it is entirely different. . . . As the speech progresses, its tempo and stress change suddenly, and the rhythm and diction mirror the chaos of Leontes' mind." KAMACHI (1979, p. 25): "Repetition of the monosyllabic words conveys the 'tremor cordis.'" GRIVELET (1980, p. 184): A bestiary lives in the soliloquy: the mort of the deer, cock, steer, heifer, calf; more briefly glimpsed, a beak, a snout. VICKERS (1985, 2:391): "Given the consistency with which the distinction between sanity and madness was observed in the linguistic medium, it may be significant that Leontes' mad jealousy never collapses into prose, as if to suggest that his mind is only temporarily 'infected.'" ABRAMS (1986, p. 156), however: The "seizure radically alters his manner of speaking. With their lightning free association, Leontes's mad speeches suggest glossolalia, 'language that I understand not' [1257], as Hermione confesses, speaking for most of the audience."

COLERIDGE (1813; ed. Foakes, 1989, p. 174) mentions among "the natural effects and concomitants" of jealousy: "1. Excitability by the most inadequate causes [as here]. 2. Eagerness to snatch at proofs <Leontes' trying to convince Camillo of Hermione's guilt [359 ff.]>. 3. Grossness of conception, and a disposition to degrade the object of it [188]. 4. Shame of his own feelings exhibited in moodiness and soliloquy." COLERIDGE later amplifies the first point: "The jealousy of [Leontes] proceeds from an evident trifle, and something like hatred is mingled with it" (1827; ed. Foakes, 1989, p. 116). FELPERIN (1972, p. 214 n.): "Coleridge may take his cue from the worldly wisdom of Emilia, who observes that 'jealous souls . . . are not ever jealous for the cause / But jealous for they're jealous' [*Oth.* 3.4.159-61 (2316-18)]."

Many critics find Leontes's jealousy an unexpected but credible aberration. MARTIN (1891, p. 6): "A sudden access of madness can alone account for the debasing change in the nature of Leontes. . . . Such inexplicable outbreaks of jealousy, I have been told, do occasionally occur in real life." BROOKE (1905; 1913, p. 260), however, is one of the many critics unable to accept that Leontes is struck with a jealousy as unaccountable as it is powerful: "Shakespeare intended us to understand that it [jealousy] had been brooding for a long time. Suspicions had arisen and been put aside. But at last they concentrated, and then the volcanic forces, long repressed, broke into full fury." Some support for this view is found in Pandosto's "melancholy passion" (see p. 622). MOULTON (1903, p. 66) also stresses the unanticipated onset of the emotion: "As to the general character of the Sicilian King, . . . three powerful witnesses speak for its depth and truth": his friendship with Polixenes, Hermione's love for him, and the "passionate attachment" of Camillo. "The outburst of jealousy . . . is not villa[i]ny, but moral disease; it is a fever fit." MOULTON refers to 390-1 and 491-4. WILSON (ed. 1931, p. 131): "The problem with this scene is to determine at what point Leontes first becomes jealous. . . . The actor who plays him should display signs of jealousy from the very outset and make it clear . . . that the business of asking Polixenes to stay longer is merely the device of jealousy seeking proof." DRAPER (1985, p. 17), however: "The difficulty [with jealousy as a donnée] is that the audience must appreciate that Leontes' opening remarks are ironical, without the help of any clear indication in the dialogue. Alternatively, the actor must speak with a bitterness sufficiently strong to make the point clear to the audience, but without the characters on the stage seeming to notice it."

FOAKES's (1971, p. 120) interpretation differs: "Shakespeare made Leontes blaze out unexpectedly in a concern precisely to leave aside or ignore questions of motive or possible explanations for his behaviour." GIRARD (1987, pp. 46-7) offers another view: "He was not suspicious in the slightest. His only problem was that he found Polixenes and Hermione too indifferent to one another, and he was doing his best to change that. . . . All of a sudden he thinks he has succeeded beyond his wildest dreams. . . . He thinks that his own love has exerted a perverse *mimetic* influence on the pair and that they love one another *after his own example*, but in the wrong manner." GIRARD cites 528-9 on Leontes's instrumentality; but that statement is conditional and there is no evidence of earlier indifference. HUNTER (1965, p. 188): Sh. depicts "a human mystery . . . *as* a mystery . . . the presence of hate within love, and the constant danger that love will succumb to the desire to hate. . . . He . . . emphasizes the complete irrationality of Leontes' suspicions through the reactions to them of other characters." LINDENBAUM (1972, p. 11): "With the definitions of innocence, sin, and the fall which Polixenes gives in [134-45], it is not surprising . . . that one or the other of the princes should be subject to an unaccountable outburst of sexual feeling. . . . There is every reason to believe that Polixenes' feelings about his youth and loss of innocence represent those of Leontes as well."

GODDARD (1951, p. 648) connects Leontes with Mamillius as the teller of a tale of "Sprights, and Goblins" (619); each has "the capacity to summon out of nothing things that both are and are not there," to create winters' tales. Cf. 615-18, 1593, 3038, 3070, and 3328. TILLYARD (1938, p. 41) compares "the god-sent lunacies of Greek drama." Leontes's lunacy "is as scantily motivated as these, and we should refrain from demanding any motive. . . . Its nature is that of an earthquake or the loss of the 'Titanic.'" BURTON (1970, p. 220): "He is jealous by nature before the play begins, and masochistically he arranges occasions on which his jealousy can feed." Other psychological explanations emphasize the child's separation from its mother. SCHWARTZ (1975, p. 156): "Leontes embodies the unsuccessful struggle to reconcile the desire for sacred, nurturant maternity with the violence associated with its loss." According to BEVINGTON (1985, 2:328), Leontes's outbreak "appears to derive from his idealization of childhood, a time of boyish innocence untroubled by the temptations of sex. Hermione's wholeness as a woman threatens Leontes." NEVO (1987, pp. 105-6): "Leontes has been (visibly) separated, isolated, by the *tête-à-tête* between Hermione and Polixenes . . . ; but he has already been separated or isolated by Hermione's new intimacy with her unborn child. . . . It is the ancient loss . . . that lies at the root of Leontes' seizure. . . . Hermione does betray Leontes, with her children." Polixenes, NEVO thinks, is similarly afflicted; see n. 246-51. WELLS (1994, p. 341): "However sketchy the motivation of Leontes' jealousy may be, once it has descended it is projected with vivid immediacy as a self-consuming, almost fanatical state of mind, impervious to suggestion, incapable of admitting the possibility of error."

Some critics find the motivation much too sketchy. CRAIG (1936, pp. 116-17) blames the application of the mechanistic psychological theory, which allowed for the total submersion of reason by passion. "Man and man under passion were different machines." He thus classifies Leontes with such other "monsters" of Jacobean tragedy as De Flores (Middleton, *The Changeling*), Vindici (Tourneur or Middleton, *The Revenger's Tragedy*), and Flamineo (Webster, *The White Devil*). Other investigators however, find that Sh. simply observed the conventions of the genre in which he was working. YOUNG (1972, p. 121): "Leontes' behavior, famous for its lack of motivation, is typical of the pastoral romance tradition of violent and inexplicable passions. He shares with Lear, with Duke Frederick [in *AYL*], and with a host of rulers in the novels of writers like Greene and Sidney, a kind of helpless impulse to tyranny, a combination, perhaps, of the pastoral criticism of court life and the romance tradition of arbitrary fortune." PETERSON (*Time*, 1973, p. 153): "To be troubled by Leontes' jealousy because its suddenness and lack of motivation detract from or violate the illusion of realism is no more to the point than objecting (on the grounds that such things just do not happen in the real world) to the scene in which Hermione is brought back into the play as a 'statue'. In each instance, our concern ought to be the 'matter' rehearsed in events that make no claim to verisimilitude. Shakespeare's indifference to the ways in which he might easily have made Leontes' jealousy probable is a clear indication that his concerns lay elsewhere." For the cause of jealousy in *Pandosto*, see p. 622.

PAFFORD (ed. 1963, pp. lvii–lviii n.) summarizes: "Briefly, the arguments for 'Jealousy from the start' are: (1) Until [181] Leo. is taciturn. This is true: his ten speeches occupy only nineteen lines in all. Subsequently he is rather verbose. (2) Herm. says that Leontes' persuasions are cold [85–6]. (3) Leo. notes pointedly that Herm. can persuade Polix. but he cannot [155]. (4) Leo. is preoccupied and apparently does not hear the talk between Polix. and Herm., for at [116] Polix. yields and agrees to stay, yet at [153] Leo. asks whether he is won yet. (5) There must be action between Herm. and Polix. that can be misinterpreted as indicated by [188–90, 200–1, 265–7, 377–89]. (6) Some conversation before [181] may be equivocal. [He also alludes to the opinion of COGHILL; see n. 55–8.] Answers are: (1) Leo. is obviously concluding a talk with Polix.; he has used up his arguments and his few speeches are little to go on. Furthermore, abruptness lies more in manner and tone than in length and Leontes' words could all be said in a warm and friendly way. . . . (2) and (3) Hermione's comment on Leontes' lack of warmth could be just the belittling of a husband in company which is the accepted privilege of a loving, confident wife. Leontes' speeches just before [181] are those of a devoted and appreciative husband: [155] itself could be just that—an echo of [90]. It could be an ominous half-aside, but it could also be the loving husband's admiration for his able wife's success. And that the latter is so is supported by Leontes' following lines, which are happy, loving memories of their early courting days. (4) Leo. may not be preoccupied. For a character not to hear is normal stage convention. Herm. and Polix. do not hear Leo. from [181] to [202]. In the happy passage [588–612] Herm. is out of earshot although she has no one but the speakers to engage her attention. (5) These passages after [181] are the forgeries of jealousy. *Oth*. [2.1.254 (1036)] speaks of 'paddling palms' and it is there clear that this can be normal behaviour to the normal mind. . . . (6) The conversation seems to be quite unambiguous. It must be made clear that Polix. has been there nine months to make it possible that he is the child's father. In 'like a cipher' [55] Polix. is referring to himself, not to Herm., and his meaning is clear" (see n. 55–8). PAFFORD adds (p. lviii): "The most we can assume from his [Leontes's] taciturnity is that although apparently happy he is a little uneasy, somewhat puzzled and hesitant." The difficulty of making up one's mind on the point is illustrated by MUIR (1957, pp. 240–1): "Partly to save time and partly to leave no doubt in the minds of the audience of Hermione's innocence, he [Sh.] begins the play with Leontes already jealous; and he makes Hermione press Polixenes in order to test his suspicions"; MUIR (1977, p. 266), similarly: "The scene can be played with Leontes jealous from the start, or becoming jealous [here]. The latter way, with its sudden destruction of love and friendship, is the one Shakespeare probably intended."

For Freudian explanations, see pp. 781 ff., and for solutions found in performance, pp. 803 ff. For the counterpart to this speech in *Pandosto*, see p. 622.

181 **hot . . . hot**] SCHMIDT (1874, Hot 4): "Amorous, lustful, lecherous." KATO (1983, p. 120): "'Hot' corresponds to Hermione's . . . 'coldly' [86]."

182 **To . . . farre**] KITTREDGE & RIBNER (ed. 1967): "To unite (mingle) excessively (far) in friendship," as KATO (1983, p. 120) notes, taking over "Friend" (180). PAFFORD (ed. 1963), for *farre*: "Perhaps the comparative. Cf. [n. 2275]."

mingling bloods] SCHMIDT (1874) believes that *blood* here is the red fluid, as it is in 2587, but it is also likely to be sensual passion, as in 135–6. Hence DEIGHTON (ed. 1889): "A reciprocity of passionate feeling." BOORMAN (ed. 1964): "Becoming too closely connected (with a sexual suggestion)." More than a suggestion, according to SCHANZER (ed. 1969): "In Aristotelian physiology sexual intercourse was thought of as a mingling of bloods." He cites Donne's *"Adam* and *Eve* had mingled bloods" (*Metempsychosis*, line 493, in *Complete Poetry*, ed. Shawcross, 1968). ORGEL (ed. 1996) adds Aristotle, *De Generatione Animalium* 1:18-19 and Aquinas, *Summa Theologia* IIIa (Supp.) 54.1 and 4.

183-4 **I . . . not ioy**] Following DELIUS (ed. 1860), YOUNG (1972, p. 122): "This recalls Lear's 'O, how this mother swells up toward my heart! / *Hysterica passio* — down, thou climbing sorrow' (2.4.56-7 [1328-9]), and the pain that disfigures Leontes' speech as he tries to amuse himself with his little boy is as real and moving as anything in *King Lear*."

183 ***Tremor Cordis***] GREY (1754, 1:244-5): "A palpitation of the heart. . . . It oft proceeds from an extraordinary contraction of the heart, or a thick and irritating matter that sticks in it." He cites John Quincy's trans. of Santorio Santorio's *Medicina Statica* (1712, etc.) and Stephen Blankaart's *A Physical Dictionary* (trans. of *Lexicon Medicum*, 1684, etc.). Cf. *OED* (2, citing this line). DELIUS (ed. 1860): This Latin term is [immediately] paraphrased by "my heart dances." DORAN (1916, 1:440): "Leontes's 'tremor cordis' . . . was 'psychical' and not due to heart disease." FRIPP (1938, 2: 736), however: "Leontes suffers from a *physical* malady. A muscle or bloodvessel breaks and he is no longer himself. Love turns to hate. . . . Lear had similar attacks, the third of which killed him; but Leontes recovers from the first by the shock of the second [word of Mamillius's death], and again has his senses." FRIPP alone believes this, and SIMPSON (1959, p. 164) seems to contradict the diagnosis by listing this line under "Palpitation."

183-4 **my . . . not ioy**] *OED* (Dance, *v.* 2, citing this line): "To leap, skip, spring . . . from excitement or strong emotion." ROLFE (ed. 1879): "*Dances* = throbs." ANON. (MS 1778?-): "A passage out of yᵉ Psalms," specifically 28.8, which in Coverdale's *Psalter* (1549) reads, "therfore my hearte daunceth for ioy." The Geneva Bible has "therefore mine heart shal reioyce." Yet PAFFORD (ed. 1963) points out that "Anon for joye his herte gan to daunce" is found in Chaucer's Franklin's Tale (ed. Robinson, 1957, line 1136), from which PAFFORD concludes that the expression was "common usage" and not necessarily derived from the Psalter. DENT (H331.1) compares "To have one's heart dance (leap) for joy." NOBLE (1935, p. 247): "The audience expected 'joy' and Leontes is at pains to dissipate the idea." BRISSENDEN (1981, p. 87): "A heart that is dancing, 'but not for joy', implies a savage lack of harmony at the centre of existence."

184-90 **This . . . Looking-Glasse**] GOURLAY (1975, p. 380): Leontes's "diction here and in the speeches that follow makes plain his disgust with all sex. . . . The sexuality he loathes in himself may be displaced to Hermione, but there it is out of his control. He cannot fully own her; neither can he trust her." No evidence that Leontes loathes his own sexuality is offered. NEELY (1975, p. 327): Leontes "depersonalizes Hermione and Polixenes from the moment jealousy emerges. . . . The referents of the speech are not clear until [189], and even then he refers to his guest and his wife only by the pronoun, 'they.'" This may be so rhetorically; dramatically the referents are perfectly plain, being present. McDONALD (1985, p. 320): An "anacoluthon, a statement that begins in one direction, shifts in the center, and concludes in the opposite direction."

184-7 **This . . . Agent**] HUNTER (ed. 1872, Entertainment): "The usage of welcoming guests" (*OED* 11), the meaning found by JOHNSON in line 11. Other senses may also apply, however— "Manner of social behaviour" (*OED* 4), "Treatment (of persons)" (5), "spending (of time)" (7), or "The action of occupying (a person's) attentions agreeably; . . . amusement" (8). HERFORD (ed. 1916-): "Simple unreserve." COLLINS (ed. 1904-24?) prefers "treatment (*i.e.*, of a man) as a mere friend." McIVER (1979, p. 343) follows HUNTER, but notes that, at 191, *entertainment* has become "sexual play" and that this sense leads to *entertainment* as "a play like the one we are watching." VAN LAAN (1978, pp. 227-8) analyzes the action in dramatic terms, as a playlet in which Leontes "is not just the director/spectator . . . but rather one of its principal actors." BLAKE (1983, pp. 119-20) on ambiguity arising from alterations in normal word order: "A free face may put on this entertainment or this entertainment may put on a free face. Since the sense is acceptable either way, it is not possible to decide which is right. . . . The following line [is] ambiguous as well. *Fertile bosome* may be . . . dependent upon a [missing] *from* . . . or it could be parallel to *Libertie* and thus a second object to *deriue* so that there was the rhetorical balance of object-prepositional group: prepositional group-object. Since these words are metaphorical abstracts either reading makes reasonable sense, though the former is that preferred by most editors." LOBBAN (ed. 1910), for example: "This kind treatment *may* be innocent; its freedom *may* result from mere hospitality and kindness and generosity of heart, and so honour the giver: it *may*, I grant." Or BETHELL (ed. 1956): Hermione has just offered her hand to Polixenes. "This behaviour . . . may have an appearance of candour (and) derive its freedom from good feeling, kindness, generosity, and so be quite correct in the person so acting." ERICKSON (1982, p. 819): "Hermione's visible pregnancy activates a maternal image that seems in and of itself to provoke male insecurity. Leontes' apposition, and thus connection, of 'bounty' with 'fertile bosom' suggests the maternal role in which he is casting his wife. . . . Once the 'free face' of nurturance appears to be a mask falsely 'put on', Leontes' belief collapses and his own facial composure disintegrates [474-5]." Hermione's pregnancy may be invisible (see n. 49); if it is not, Polixenes seems oblivious to the male insecurity it supposedly provokes. NOVY (1984, p. 165): "Leontes, at the beginning of his suspicions, experiences some uncertainty about his accusations but soon [at 188] abandons it." But *tremor cordis* does not suggest uncertainty.

185 **May . . . Libertie**] Rather than an alexandrine, ABBOTT (§503) thinks this line may be a pentameter, since *Libertie* has only two syllables. CHARLTON (ed. 1916): "A line with two extra unstressed syllables." NUTTALL (1966, p. 27) considers why it and 190 are hypermetrical. "Is it a deliberate device of metrical synaesthesia, designed to convey the feel of passion breaking free from restraint?" See nn. 77, 190, 499, 1264-5, and 2187.

free] SCHMIDT (1874, §10): "Guiltless, innocent" (see nn. 342 and 933), although LETTSOM (MS 1840-65) glosses oppositely—"immodest, unchaste." MOORMAN (ed. 1912): "Open, courteous, unreserved," which is SCHMIDT (1874, §7). For other adjectival senses of *free*, see nn. 342, 355, 812, 871, 933, 2413, and 2811.

face] SCHMIDT (1874): "Look, appearance" (though he does not cite this instance).

put on] SCHANZER (ed. 1969): "Wear (without any suggestion of deceit)."

deriue a Libertie] SCHMIDT (1874, Liberty): "Power of acting as one is inclined." RIDLEY (ed. 1935): "License," a sense SCHMIDT recognizes in other contexts but that is inappropriate here because *Libertie* reiterates *free*. CARRINGTON (1956), too narrowly: "Speak out freely."

186 **From . . . Bosome**] STEEVENS (ed. 1793): The bosom is "like that of the earth, which yields a spontaneous produce." HALLIWELL (ed. 1859): "The construction is, from a fertile bosom, in other words, from a bosom overflowing with kindness. Leontes says, this freedom may be justified by heartiness, hospitality, and excessive natural kindness." Objecting to THIRLBY's "bounty's," the CLARKES (ed. 1865): "It is . . . Shakespeare's style, when a speaker is arguing a question, to make him thus enumerate point by point, heaping up, as it were, successive motives. 'Fertile bosom' we take to mean here 'generous disposition', 'effusive nature'; he [Sh.] often uses 'bosom' in the sense of 'native disposition.'" LEE (ed. 1907), however, prefers "spon-

taneous exuberance, impulsiveness." DEIGHTON (ed. 1889): "This cordiality *may* (honestly) wear the look of innocence; its freedom *may* be the outcome of genuine friendship, of goodness of heart, that everteeming soil, and so be becoming to one who shows it." SCHANZER (ed. 1969), somewhat differently: "From cordiality, from generosity, from abundance of affection." ERICKSON (1982, p. 820) equates the bosom here with Hermione's breast (1278), the source of innocent milk, "that Leontes' delusory mistrust negates." ORGEL (ed. 1996, fertile Bosome): "Naturally generous affection." For more on *bosom*, see n. 327.

187 **And . . . Agent**] BEVINGTON (ed. 1992): "Do credit to the doer."

188–91 **But . . . o'th'Deere**] HARDINGE (1818, 3:51): "The act of giving the hand was in some degree *prompted* by himself, for he tells her *she opened her white hand to accept him* [174–5]. She turns it prettily and gracefully to her curtesies with her husband's dearest friend and sworn brother in affection, offering to him the hand she had given to her husband." SMITH (1953, p. 313): "To guarantee that spectators on all three sides of his platform stage simultaneously will perceive the by-play . . . as well as to call attention to the reaction of the jealous husband, Shakespeare has Leontes describe the action." Cf. 200–1, 265–7. SELTZER (1967, p. 138): "Leontes' description of some courtly manners . . . while grossly misinterpreted, of course, must nevertheless have been acted out in some way . . . and the description provides valuable evidence of this sort of action." HOLBROOK (1964, p. 146): "The texture [of the verse] enacts his loss of control, by the spitting alliteration and the nervous movement." Alliteration on *p* is also found in 2727–30, where it does not seem to spit.

188 **padling**] JOHNSON (1755) "To finger." *OED* (*v.*[1] 2b), citing this passage: "To finger idly, playfully, or fondly." HARRIS (1909, p. 281) compares Hamlet's "padling in your necke with his damn'd fingers" (3.4.185 [2561]) and *Oth.* 2.1.254 (1036). SCHANZER (ed. 1969): In *Oth.*, Desdemona's paddling of Cassio's palm, which Roderigo calls "but courtesie," is characterized by Iago as "Lechery, by this hand." HOLBROOK (1964, p. 147): "The word . . . has a flavour of revulsion from manual sex play." ANON. (MS 1778?–), curiously: "Playing with the fingers, as a rower with his oars."

pinching Fingers] A less familiar means of erotic communication than paddling palms, perhaps a substitute for Autolycus's placket pinching (2486). WEBB (1989, Fingers): "Covert fore-play (suspected)."

189–90 **practis'd . . . Looking-Glasse**] DELIUS (ed. 1860): As if one had rehearsed this smile in front of a mirror. SCHANZER (ed. 1969, Practis'd): "Studied" (*OED, ppl. a.* 2, citing this line). HAPPÉ (1969), however: "Scheming." PEYRÉ (1984, p. 144): As if, having found their mirror in each other (to Leontes's eyes, a mirror of vanity, lust, and hypocrisy), they would re-create a cell of monstrous twin pregnancy from which Leontes would be excluded, in which case the double mirror of love and friendship would break for him (in other words, risk breaking down his very self); that is why, in an effort to reconstitute his own identity, Leontes seeks desperately for another mirror, which he finds in Mamillius (in Fr.). PEYRÉ quotes 196–7, 205–6, and 232–8. FURNESS (ed. 1898) equates "For there was neuer yet faire woman, but shee made mouthes in a glasse" (*Lr.* 3.2.35–6 [1686–7]). FURNESS evidently thinks the fair woman is practicing attractive looks; others believe she is making ugly faces at herself. For the full range of interpretation, see Knowles, ed., *Lr.* (forthcoming), n. 1686–7.

190 **As . . . 'twere**] ABBOTT (§499) accents *As, Look, Glasse, then, sigh*, and *'twere*. He counts only five feet, *as 'twere* being what he calls an isolated foot. See nn. 77, 185, 499, 1264–5, and 2187. See also p. 570. A suggestion that *Looking* be omitted has gained no support, although DYCE (ed. 1875) points out that the word

for *mirror* is simply "glasse" at 1812 (and also 2475). KNOWLES (privately) would run *As in a* into one unaccented syllable.

191 **Mort o'th'Deere**] THEOBALD (ed. 1733): "A particular Air [on the horn] . . . to give notice that the Deer . . . is run down, and killing, or kill'd" (*OED*, Mort, *sb.*[1] 2, citing this line). FORTESCUE (1916, 2:343) says that the signal consisted of one short note and one long, and SINGER (ed. 1856) observes that it required "a deep-drawn breath." HALLIWELL (ed. 1859), however: The "prolonged note . . . is here compared to a lengthened sigh." COLLIER (ed. 1858), alternatively: "The heavy sighs of the animal while dying," with which SKEAT (1887) and LEE (ed. 1907) agree. LEE thinks it "unlikely that Leontes should liken the sighs of secret lovers to the blast of a horn," and BETHELL (ed. 1956) believes that *mort*, meaning "the deep, sobbing sighs of the dying animal," is being used literally, because "to give a literal significance to what is ordinarily understood figuratively is a form of wit." COLLINS (ed. 1904-24?), for his part, holds that the sighs are compared to the "notes of the horn, not . . . to the dying sighs of the deer, which would confuse the image." STAUNTON (ed. 1859) suggests "a latent play on the word 'deer', akin to that [in 198 and 200] on 'neet.'" If there is a pun on *Deere* as "dear," the mort would be sexual death as well as the mortal end, a sense preferred by, e.g., RIDLEY (ed. 1935) and MAHOOD (1957, p. 149). BETHELL (ed. 1956) concurs, and adds, "Hermione is the prey and has been won by Polixenes." Recalling that the deer or stag is "the beast with horns," HENLEY (ed. 1902) implies that the supposed lovers sigh for Leontes's death. To SCOTT (1920, p. 147), on the other hand, "the simile . . . symbolizes well the contest between two men for one woman, like stags fighting for mastery over the hind." GREEN (1870), even more questionably, although WRIGHT & LaMAR (ed. 1966) agree, finds an allusion to the emblem of "love incurable," a wounded stag. VOSS (ed. 1829) compares "What shall he have that killed the deer" (*AYL* 4.2.10-18 [2137-45]), a song about cuckoldom.

entertainment] HUSSEY (1992, p. 230): "Leontes takes up [the] word . . . savours it, and spits it out with quite another meaning." For various meanings, see n. 184-7.

192 **Bosome**] Probably *OED* (*sb.* 6 *fig.*): "The breast considered as the seat of thoughts and feelings." SCHMIDT (1874) does not list this occurrence of the word, but see n. 327. For *fertile Bosome*, see n. 184-7.

Browes] DELIUS (ed. 1860): Forehead, threatened by the horns of the cuckold to which Leontes again alludes at 204, 222, and 268. RIDLEY (1938, p. 15), alone: "We must see Leontes clutch his forehead as though he felt the horns, or the words . . . make no sense." LANGMAN (1976, p. 201): "He has allowed entry to the image that disarms his reason. . . . How fully this image of horns expresses his mortification, loathing, and shame, subsequent speeches will develop."

Mamillius] Observing that Crane's massed entries include characters that actually enter later (e.g., Leontes at 584, the Lords at 585), PARRY (1979, pp. 57-8) has *Mamillius* enter here. He imagines (p. 58) that the boy has been playing soldiers (see 197 and the dagger at 235) in the garden, where he has smutched his nose.

Art thou my Boy?

    Mam. I, my good Lord.

    Leo. I'fecks: 195

Why that's my Bawcock: what? has't smutch'd thy Nose?

---

195 I'fecks:] ~ ? CAP, v1778-SING2, WH1-DEL2, KNT3-COL4, OXF1, CLN2
196 has't] has HARN, HAL (*text*; has't *in notes*)

---

193 **Art . . . Boy?**] DEIGHTON (ed. 1889): "Are you really my son?" For possible emphasis on *my*, see n. 202. PETERSON (*Time*, 1973, p. 161): "He questions Hermione's honesty." But the question may be only an affectionate assertion — "You're my good boy, aren't you?" — for, in 206-11, Leontes concludes that Mamillius is his.

194 **I . . . Lord**] TERRY (1932, p. 30): "The child is puzzled by his father's attitude toward him, and rather scared. He does not chatter spontaneously, but answers [here and at 203] in a few mechanically dutiful words." Line 290 does not seem mechanically dutiful, however, and Elizabethan fathers and sons were more formal than their modern counterparts.

195-202 **I'fecks . . . Calfe?**] MORLEY (ed. 1887, p. 13): "Shakespeare not only represents a truth of life in the mingling of love for the child with a sudden outbreak of a mad aversion for the mother . . . , but he has dramatic purpose in strong indication . . . of the great affection of Leontes for the child, that we may know the force of the shock to him when tidings of the boy's death follow straight on his repudiation of the oracle [at 1325-7]."

195 **I'fecks**] CAPELL (1783 [1774], 1:glos.): "A clownish Corruption of—i'faith; or, in Faith." COLLIER (ed. 1842): "Of *in fact.*" CAPELL is right, according to *OED* (I'fegs). HUNTER (ed. 1872): "Really?"

196 **Bawcock**] HANMER (ed. 1743-4, 6:glos.): "A coaxing term," by which he means a pet name or blandishment (*OED*, Coax, *v.* 2). JOHNSON (1755): "Fine fellow." NARES (1876; 1905): "A burlesque word of endearment." *OED*: Fr. *beau coq.* Because in *H5* 3.2.25 (1141-2) and in *TN* 3.4.112 (1635) the word is joined with *chuck*, which was taken to be a corruption of *chick*, NARES and some eds. think the word means "*boycock* or young cock," but that is unlikely. DEIGHTON (ed. 1889): "Why . . . Bawcock" is "equivalent to 'well said, my fine fellow!'"

    smutch'd] MINSHEU (1617): See "Foule, & *to* Slubber." *OED* essentially agrees, citing this line as its first instance. CAPELL (1783 [1774], 1:glos.): "Dawb with Smut, *Mucus Narium* [of the nose]." The CLARKES (ed. 1865) think that "a flying particle of smut" is alluded to, and WILSON (ed. 1931) notes, mysteriously, that the "smutched nose is no doubt symbolical of the father's suspicions, and 'they . . . mine' [197] seems to confirm this." The CLARKES (1879, p. 336) consider the word one of Sh.'s "familiar and homely expressions," with a "peculiar fitness" that renders it, "in its way, poetical."

They say it is a Coppy out of mine. Come Captaine,
We must be neat; not neat, but cleanly, Captaine:
And yet the Steere, the Heycfer, and the Calfe,
Are all call'd Neat. Still Virginalling   200

---

197 *Two lines ending* mine.— . . . captain, CAP, COL, HUD1, WH1
198 not] nor POPE2
    but] *Om.* F2-F4
    Wipes the boy's face. HAN, CAP, CAM3 (*subst.*)
200 *Observing* Polixenes *and* Hermione. ROWE1-STAU (−CAP), KTLY-HUD2
(−DEL4)

---

197 **out of**] *OED* (*prep. phr.* 13, citing this line): "Taken from." FURNESS (ed. 1898), oddly, thinks that *out*, with *copy*, "forms one composite idea, and the two words might . . . be joined with a hyphen."

   Captaine] DEIGHTON (ed. 1889): "A humourous term of affection, see [248]." HOTSON (1952, p. 61): Because of "military resemblance." He supposes that Mamillius is clad in a child's long coat, "reminiscent of the cassock or gaberdine of the soldier," and carries a muzzled dagger (cf. 235). But the word also is a familiar term of address in *Tim.* 2.2.73 (740), where there is no military association. The CLARKES (1879, p. 761) list this and other facetious titles used by Sh.

198 **We . . . cleanly**] C. G. SMITH (1963, no. 28) finds parallels in Cato and in Leonard Culman, *Sententiae Pueriles*.

   not . . . Captaine] JOHNSON (ed. 1765): Leontes recollects "that *neat* is the term for *horned* cattle." CROSBY (1878; 1986, p. 277): Leontes adds "but cleanly" because the cattle, although termed *neat*, are anything but cleanly. An earlier effort by RUSHTON (1867, pp. 62-3) to make *neat* mean "dirty" is unsupported by *OED*.

199-200 **And . . . Neat**] DEIGHTON (ed. 1889): "The term is applicable to you, for it is given . . . also to the calf." MARSH (1962; 1980, p. 129): Leontes "sees the world around him as beastly, even the son he loves."

199 **Heycfer**] Among the dialectical forms of *heifer*, EDD lists *heckfor* (North Country) and *heifker* (East Anglia and Norfolk). *OED* gives *heicfar* for the 17th c., and PAFFORD (ed. 1963) points out that in the 1600 ed. of *2H4*, which, some say, derives from Sh.'s foul papers, the spelling is *heicfor* (MSR, 935-7).

   Calfe] *OED* (Calf[1] 1c, citing this line): "A term of endearment."

200 **Neat**] *OED* (*sb.* 2, citing this line): "Cattle."

   Still] MINSHEU (1617): "Always, continually."

   Virginalling] JOHNSON (1755): "To pat; to strike as on the virginal." SCHMIDT (1875): "Fingering." STEEVENS (ed. 1773): "A *virginal* . . . is a very small kind of spinnet" (*OED, sb.* 1). According to *OED*, "the reason for the name is obscure," but according to MINSHEU (1617), the instruments are "so called because Virgins and Maidens play on them," a derivation tentatively supported by Stanley Sadie (ed.), *The New Grove Dictionary of Musical Instruments* (1984). Leontes thus may be struck by the difference between the way a virgin virginals and the way Hermione seems to do so, as WEBB (1989) indicates by the gloss "as if playing the instrument/acting in a chaste manner (ironic)." KNIGHT (ed. 1841) compares *Son.* 128, and an off-color allusion to playing upon the virginals occurs in *TNK* 3.3.34, Fletcher's scene. BROOK (1976, p. 70) finds this word an example of "functional shift," the use of one part of speech (*virginal*, a noun) for another (a verb); according to *OED*, the verb (or verbal) is found only here. For more on the part of speech, see n. 2931.

Vpon his Palme? How now (you wanton Calfe)
Art thou my Calfe?
  Mam. Yes, if you will (my Lord.)
  Leo. Thou want'st a rough pash, & the shoots that I haue

---

201 **How now**] SCHMIDT (1875, Now): "Sometimes = how do you do? at other times = what is the matter? what are you doing here?" *OED* (*adv.* 4b): "Ellipt. for 'How is it now?' Often used interjectionally." According to the CLARKES (1879, p. 464), at 2167 the words are used "arousingly." Cf. 289, 1331, 1742, 2296, 2506, and 2597.

  wanton] JOHNSON (1755): "Frolicksome; gay; sportive." BETHELL (ed. 1956): "The sexual theme is punningly present in 'virginalling' (virgin) and 'wanton' (*frisky* but also a *loose woman*)." With "wanton Calfe," DENT compares "As Wanton as a whelp (calf, kid)" (W38.1).

  202 **my Calfe?**] *OED* (1c, citing this line): "A term of endearment," which MACKAY (1884, pp. 25-6) suggests is the antecedent of the "vulgar slang *kid*, a child." DEIGHTON (ed. 1889): Emphasizing *my*, as at 193. GODDARD (1951, p. 650): "He is so beside himself that he is actually questioning the paternity of his own boy." It is doubtful that Leontes ever seriously questions his paternity of Mamillius; see n. 193. The word, rather, arises from Leontes's bovine line of thought, and the question, like 193, may be jocular. BOORMAN (ed. 1964), improbably: "There is a suggestion of 'Are you going to grow up to have horns, like your father?'"

  204-22 **Thou . . . Browes**] SMITH (1968, p. 317): "The speech falls . . . into two parts, with the division at line [213]. Up until that point the vocabulary is colloquial, with a liberal number of slang words and low phrasing. . . . It is the language of 'blood'. In [214-22], however, a completely unique pattern exists. The language of 'grace' is invoked in an attempt to impose logic and a decorous cohesion on his thoughts." But the attempt fails. As SMITH says (p. 318), lines 214-22 "are very difficult to speak and to understand." See further, in n. 214-22. CRUTTWELL (1955, p. 62) notices "the series of starts and false starts, . . . parentheses and repetitions, which . . . conveys the quality of Leontes' hysterical jealousy."

  204 **want'st**] SCHMIDT (1875, Want): "To be without."

  pash] EDD (*sb.*²): "The head, *gen.* used in a ludicrous sense" (*OED*, *sb.*¹, citing this line as its first example). RANN (ed. 1787): "Pate, like a bull calf," which COLLIER (ed. 1842), anticipated by CALDECOTT (MS 1813-33), extends to "the hair on the forehead of a bull." Many similar glosses have been offered. RAY (1674, p. 37): "A mad *Pash*; a mad brain," a Cheshire word. WISE (1861, p. 155) lists *pash*, "a rough head," among the Warwickshire words used by Sh. DAVIES (1876) associates the word with *bash*, in Herefordshire "the front of the head of a bull or a pig" (*EDD*). SINGER's (ed. 1826) assertion that "*pash* in some places denot[es] a young bull calf whose horns are springing" is unsupported by *OED* or *EDD*. BENDA (ed. 1825) believes the word is a Scottish term for "head," and MACKAY (1884, p. 55) connects it with a Gaelic word "signifying the brow or forehead. . . . A 'rough *pash*' means a brow furrowed with care." HANMER (ed. 1743-4, 6:glos.), oddly, though followed by JOHNSON (1755 and 1773) and by STEEVENS (ed. 1778), who derives it from Sp. *paz*: "Kiss."

  shoots] STEEVENS (ed. 1778): "*Branches*, i.e. horns. . . . The ensigns of cuckoldom." HALLIWELL (ed. 1859): Or "beard." The association with horned cattle is probably dominant, though, since these animals are closely associated with marital infidelity. See NARES's (1876; 1905) article on the "*horn-fair*" at CHARLTON, s.v. Cuckold's Haven, and cf. n. 192. *OED* (*sb.*¹ 2d, citing this line), however: A transferred sense of "offshoot." CHARLTON (ed. 1916): "Leontes is coarsely and gruesomely revelling in his own imagined shame."

To be full, like me: yet they say we are   205
Almost as like as Egges; Women say so,
(That will say any thing.) But were they false
As o're-dy'd Blacks, as Wind, as Waters; false

205-11 yet . . . me.] *Marked as aside* HUD2
205 full,] ~ ∧ POPE1+
207 were they] they were BLAIR
208 o're-dy'd] our dead COL2, COL3, COL4
     Wind] Winds ROWE2-RANN (−CAP), DYCE2, HUD2

---

205 **full**] MALONE (ed. 1790): "Entirely."

205-7 **yet . . . thing**] KAHN (1980, p. 233): "While . . . this resemblance is the legitimate confirmation of Leontes' sexual union with Hermione, and the proof of her fidelity, Leontes finds Hermione's assertion of it another indication of female treachery." But no matter how false women may be, he continues, they are truthful in saying that "this Boy were like me" (211).

206 **as . . . Egges**] Proverbial (TILLEY E66).

207-8 **false . . . as Waters**] Because, strictly speaking, there is no such thing as a steady wind or current; both constantly vary in direction or velocity, if only by a little. Both are proverbially false; see TILLEY W86 and W412. With "false . . . as Waters," LEE (ed. 1907) compares *Oth.* 5.2.134 (3404).

208 **o're-dy'd Blacks**] HANMER (ed. 1743-4), who understands *o're* to mean "excessively": Too much black dye causes cloth to rot and "the colour it self to fade and grow rusty much the sooner," and thus be false. His explanation may be supported by ROBINSON (1969, p. 29): "It was a long time before indigo superseded woad as the most commonly used black/blue dye. This was in part due to the wrong use of the arsenic bath method which could rot fabric if improperly applied." Supporting this interpretation, PAFFORD (ed. 1963) quotes John Lyly, *Euphues. The Anatomy of Wit* (1:325): "the foolish Diar, who neuer thought his cloth blacke vntil it was burned." STEEVENS (ed. 1778), taking *o're* to mean "on top of": "*Black* . . . will receive no other hue without discovering itself through it. '*Lanarum nigrae nullum colorem bibunt*' [Black fleeces will not take dye of any colour—Pliny, *Natural History*, trans. H. Rackham, 8.73.193]." *O're-dy'd* consequently means "dyed over," the definition accepted by *OED*, which nevertheless cites this line as its only instance. MALONE (ed. 1790, 10:601-2): Thus "the *falsehood* will soon be discovered." He cites Lyly's *Euphues and his England* (ed. Bond, 2:169, lines 19-20): "Truly quoth *Cammila*, my Wooll was blacke, and therefore it would take no other colour" (cf. TILLEY B436). STEEVENS, however, also offers "Tradesmen . . . dye their faded or damaged stuffs, black . . . [and] it seems that *blacks* was the common term for mourning." In ed. 1785 he refers to Middleton & Rowley's *The Old Law* (ed. C. M. Shaw, 1982, 2.1.214-15): "For blacks are often such dissembling mourners There is no credit given to it," the blacks being false because worn in pretense of mourning. COLLIER (ed. 1842) prefers this explanation but not strongly enough to prevent his faking a different reading in his F2 and reporting it in *Notes and Emendations* (1853). HARBOTTLE (1853, p. 95) varies STEEVENS's idea without improving it: "False mourners, putting [on?] an *over* dark semblance of grief." GOLLANCZ (ed. 1894) quotes "the blacker the garb, the less sincere the mourning," which sounds proverbial but is not in WILSON (1970). WILSON (ed. 1931): "Leontes seems to have in mind the insincerity of widows who mourn a succession of husbands." CARRINGTON (1956): "Mourning clothes made by dyeing other garments (for the sake of economy)." BOORMAN (ed.

As Dice are to be wish'd, by one that fixes
No borne 'twixt his and mine; yet were it true,   210
To say this Boy were like me. Come (Sir Page)
Looke on me with your Welkin eye: sweet Villaine,

---

211 were] is HAN
212 Welkin] welking ROWE2-POPE2, HAN
     eye: sweet Villaine,] F1, WH1, SIS, SIG, OXF2; ~ , ~ ~ , BLAIR; ~ : ~ ~ . F2
etc.

1964) reverses this: "The metaphor suggests a widow's mourning soon after dyed another colour. Thus, it implies the briefness of the wife's love and of the unstable colour." But without bleaching, black cloth (or fleeces) cannot be dyed another color, as Pliny knew. ORGEL (ed. 1996): "Since the 15th century, protectionist legislation on behalf of the dyers' guilds required that all wool cloth be first dyed red or blue. Other colours were achieved by overdyeing (e.g. with yellow over blue to produce green); all black wool was overdyed, blue over red, red over blue, or black over either of these, and therefore 'false' by definition. Overdying in black was also frequently done to hide mistakes or accidents in dyeing." DELIUS (ed. 1860) asserts that *oft dyed* occurs in Webster's *Duchess of Malfi*, but it does not.

    208-9 **false As Dice**] STRUTT (1898, pp. 404-5) describes some of the "nefarious arts" by which dice are falsified, and Pistol alludes to two types of crooked dice in *Wiv.* 1.3.84-5 (376-7). SIEVEKING (1916, 2:469): "The falseness of dice . . . had become a proverb . . . , for cheating with false or loaded dice had been reduced to a fine art."

    209-10 **one . . . mine**] For *borne*, GILDON (1710, p. lxviii): "Limits, Bounds" (*OED*, Bourne, *sb.*[2] 2, citing this line). PORTER & CLARKE (ed. c. 1903): "Line of separation." For the expression, RANN (ed. 1787), inaccurately: One "that plays the deepest" (gambles the heaviest; see *OED*, Deep, *a.* 11.b). As YOU LIKE IT (1789, p. 711): "A man . . . who, by false dice, removes the boundary of property, and makes what was mine thus unjustly become his." HUDSON (ed. 1880): One who "makes no distinction" between his stake and mine.

    211 **were**] ABBOTT (§368): "The subjunctive in a subordinate sentence . . . is often used with or without 'that.'" Here *were* "is perhaps attracted to the mood of [*were* in 210]."

    Sir Page] KERSEY (1702, Page): "Young lad attending upon a person of quality." DEIGHTON (ed. 1889): "Like 'sweet villain!' 'my Collop!' [212, 213], a term of affection." PARRY (ed. 1982): With "the suggestion of a *command*." For *Sir* with a common noun as a term of address, see *OED* (*sb.* 6, citing this line).

    212 **Welkin eye**] COCKERAM (1623, Welkine): "The whole skie, the whole Heauens" (*OED* 2). JOHNSON (1755): "Blue . . . skycoloured," repeated by most eds. *OED* (5, citing this line): "Heavenly or blue," hence, clear and innocent. MAHOOD (1957, p. 154): "The adjective suggest[s] something providential and life-giving." As YOU LIKE IT (1789, p. 711) suggests that because of the expression "there is one above sees all," a welkin eye "may mean your discerning or overlooking eye." HOLLAND (1964, p. 289) alone finds the welkin's eye here to be the sun, with play upon *son* and allusion to Apollo, whose oracle reveals the truth. HANMER (ed. 1743-4, 6: glos.), perhaps incorrectly adapting *welked* = "withered": "Languishing, faint." Also wrongly, TOOKE (1805, 2:319): "Rolling or wandering" and MACKAY (1884, p. 67): "All-loving." For the eye's possible significance, see n. 214-22. For parts of speech "diversely used" in Sh., see n. 2931.

Most dear'st, my Collop: Can thy Dam, may't be
Affection? thy Intention stabs the Center.
Thou do'st make possible things not so held,   215
Communicat'st with Dreames (how can this be?)
With what's vnreall: thou coactiue art,
And fellow'st nothing. Then 'tis very credent,
Thou may'st co-ioyne with something, and thou do'st,
(And that beyond Commission) and I find it,   220
(And that to the infection of my Braines,
And hardning of my Browes.)

---

213 be∧] Ff, COL1, COL2, STAU, COL4; ~ — ROWE1-THEO2, WARB-JOHN2, SIS, OXF2
(*textual notes*); ~ ? HAN1 *etc.*
214 Affection? . . . Center.] Ff, COL1, COL2, COL4; Imagination! thou dost stab
to th' Center. ROWE1-JOHN2; Affection, thy intention stabs to the center: CAP, PEL1;
Affection thy intention stabs the centre? STAU; Affection! thy invention stabs the centre: MTBY4 *conj.*, WH2 (*withdrawn*, INGLEBY, 1885); Affection! thy intention stabs
the center. V1773 *etc.*
215 possible∧] ~ , MAL-V1821, SING, HUD, WH1, HAL
     not] not be F2-THEO2, WARB-JOHN2; not to be HAN
215-18 held . . . nothing.] held? | Communicat'st with dreams?—How! can this
be?— | With what's unreal thou coactive art, | And fellow'st nothing? STAU
216-17 be?) . . . vnreall:] ~ ?) . . . ~ , F3-ROWE3, THEO1-CAP, RANN+; ~ ∧ ∧
. . . ~ ? POPE
218 fellow'st] follow'st ROWE3
     nothing] nothings HAN
220 and] as HUD2
221 (And that] Ay, even HUD2

---

213 **Most dear'st,**] The CLARKEs (ed. 1865): A "double superlative." See ABBOTT
§11 and cf. line 1366. For *dear'st* and similar contractions—e.g., *fellow'st* (218),
sweet'st (1388)—see ABBOTT §473. BLAKE (1983, p. 118): "Most [all?] editors keep
the Folio's comma or even turn it into a heavier stop such as an exclamation mark.
Yet the phrase could be understood as if it were 'My most dear'st Collop', i.e., my
beloved child, which . . . parallels 'sweet Villaine' in the preceding line."
     Collop] KERSEY (1702): "Slice of meat." JOHNSON (1755): "In burlesque lan-
guage, a child" (*OED*, Collop[1] 2b and, "used of offspring," 3b, with this instance as
its last example). TILLEY C517: "It is a dear Collop that is taken (cut) out of the flesh."
Despite the word's proverbial status, NARES (1876; 1905) finds that "the metaphorical
use of it by a father to his child, as being part of his flesh, seems at present rather
harsh and coarse," and DELIUS (ed. 1860) discovers it used in *1H6* 5.4.18 (2658),
where a Shepherd speaks it. See MACKAY (1884, pp. 29–30) for a supposed Celtic
derivation. According to WILSON (ed. 1931), the expression makes Mamillius "'a cut
from the old bull', for Leontes' mind still runs on horned beasts; 'dam' (= cow) shows
this." More biblically, PARRY (ed. 1982): "Its sense here [is] 'flesh of my flesh,'" the
words being spoken as Leontes looks "into his son's eyes [and] is moved with tender
paternal love" (p. 22). MAXWELL's (ed. 1956) "small portion" is not exactly supported
by *OED*.
     213-22 **Can . . . Browes**] Several early critics attempt a close paraphrase of the

passage as a whole. CAPELL (1783, 2.4:163): Affection "hast fellowship with dreams, with what's unreal, nay, even with nothing, art that nothing's co-agent in working out thy own torment." Leontes has made "the passion ridiculous," yet "suddenly . . . matter is drawn by him to give his madness sanction. . . . Since nothings were the foundation for it, somethings might be, and were;— [quotes 'Then . . . Browes']." Unable to fit 220 into this explanation, CAPELL concludes that the line was an authorial first shot supposed to be replaced by 221–2. MASON (1785, p. 125): Leontes answers, "'If love can be co-active with what is unreal, and have communication with non-entities' . . . it may cojoin with something real in the case of Hermione, and having proved it possible, he concludes 'that it certainly must be so.'" MASON's idea, essentially right, is restated, augmented, and sometimes distorted by later critics. COLLIER (ed. 1842): "Is it possible she feels *love* for him? and then he [Leontes] goes on to observe that her intention [intentness, vehemence, ardour of mind] stabs him to the centre, and makes possible things considered impossible." DYCE (1844, p. 79) objects that COLLIER's explanation does not account for 216 ff. SINGER (ed. 1856): "The allusion is to the powers ascribed to sympathy between the human system and all nature, however remote or occult. Hence Leontes, like Othello, finds in his very agitation a proof that it corresponds not with fancy but with a reality." HUDSON (ed. 1880): "After referring to the potency of sexual desire [in 214–15], Leontes proceeds to descant on sundry workings of that potency: it achieves things that are deemed impossible; gives life to dreams; shapes imaginations; cooperates with unrealities; has commerce with things that are not; and is so like a planetary influence, that even what passes for angelic purity may not be proof against it. If it can do all these wonders, then he concludes that, in the person of his wife, it can certainly fellowship [sic] an actual object, and conspire with the answering motions of another person; and if this can be, then it is, and he is sure of it; and the *fact* is so working in his head as to cause a sprouting of horns."

HALLIWELL (ed. 1859), apparently misunderstanding "the infection of my Braines": "The mind of Leontes is rapidly descending into a state of ungovernable jealousy, but he is now disturbed by the reflection it is possible there may be a delusion." For *Affection*, STAUNTON (ed. 1859) accepts STEEVENS's "imagination" (see n. 214) and for *intention* "intensity" and does wonders with them: "The allusion . . . is plainly to that mysterious principle of nature by which a parent's features are transmitted to the offspring. Pursuing the train of thought induced by the acknowledged likeness between the boy and himself, Leontes asks, 'Can it be possible a mother's vehement imagination should penetrate even to the womb, and there imprint upon the embryo what stamp she chooses? Such apprehensive fantasy, then', he goes on to say, 'we may readily believe will readily co-join with something tangible, and it does.'" A recent interpretation of the passage is that of ORGEL (ed. 1996): "If F1's colon has its modern significance, 'what's unreal' is in apposition with 'dreams', and these are what 'thou communicat'st with'; and in that case the rest of the sentence means 'you are compulsive and consort with nothing.' . . . The problems with it [this reading] are that 'and fellow'st nothing' seems to paraphrase 'with what's unreal thou coactive art', and that *coactive* apparently means . . . not compulsory or acting under compulsion, its usual meaning in the period, but 'acting in concert', which makes better sense with 'and fellow'st nothing.'"

After STAUNTON, explanations become, not surprisingly, even more openly sexual. HUNTER (ed. 1872): "*Stabs the centre* means *penetrates to the womb*." At first, CROSBY (1876, p. 121) places the center geographically: "O, lust! thy intensity— the lengths thou wilt go to satiate thyself . . . —penetrates to, and permeates, every foot of the habitable globe." Later (1877; 1986, p. 246), however, he alludes to C. M. Ingleby's privately communicated opinion that *Center* "= *fem. pudendum*, very plainly. . . . Prof. Leo of Berlin . . . told him [Ingleby] that he and his German confrères had long ago so explained the passage. 'Stabs the centre' being a phrase of archery, the Dr [Ingleby] asks me what is the 'bull's eye' of *lust*, and the answer to that question solves the riddle of the passage. [Cf. n. 744-5.] The *'intention'* means (I presume) that the 'centre' need not necessarily be 'stabbed' *in reality*. It can be done in *imagination*." Regarding *center* as the *fem. pudendum*, WEBB (1989) agrees with Prof. Leo. Following CROSBY, HUDSON (ed. 1880) takes *Affection* as "lust," but *Intention* as "intenseness, energy, pervasive force" and *Center* as "the Earth . . . the centre of the visible Universe [cf. 708]"; hence, Leontes means "that the potency of sexual desire is universal; that it penetrates everywhere, and pervades the whole world." HUDSON compares 283-6. SCHMIDT (1874, Affection) calmly paraphrases: "Natural propensity [perhaps *OED, sb.* 4: 'State of mind generally, mental tendency; disposition'], thy power rules the inmost thoughts of men." For *Communicat'st with Dreames, coactiue art*, and *fellow'st nothing*, KINNEAR (1883, p. 177) gives "hast part in common *by* dreams," "act in unison," and "matest with." COLLINS (ed. 1904-24?): "Thou dost act together with (*i.e.* hast as object) what is unreal, and seek'st as thy companion what does not exist; and this being so, it is all the more to be believed that thou will associate thyself with some real object; as is the case now with Hermione's love." MOULTON (1903, p. 68): Leontes "can reason with his 'affection' ['With . . . nothing'] but this restraining thought suggests its opposite ['Then . . . do'st']."

HERFORD (ed. 1916-) follows earlier commentators but with somewhat different consequences: "Passion may lay hold of something of which there is no other warrant ('beyond commission'), but which is yet real, as the speaker's own mental and physical state bears witness. Leontes is confusedly wrestling with two opposed notions about passion: that it blinds and deludes reason, and that it discovers what cool reason fails to see. His infatuation pushes him toward the latter; but he still looks 'unsettled' and distraught." HERFORD glosses *center* as "the inmost mind." FURNESS (ed. 1898): "Leontes . . . reflects that . . . love carried to an extreme, or becoming to the last degree intense, pierces to the very soul. . . . If this intensest love can live in dreams and go hand in hand with what is actually nothing, *a fortiori*, it can mate with what is actually real." PIERCE (ed. 1918) shifts gender: "Love, thy intense passion masters the inmost hearts of women. Thou dost make possible on their part sins not believed to be possible. Thou dost make absent lovers communicate with each other through dreams (how can this be?). Thou dost cause the dreaming woman to make love to the unreal dream-image of her paramour, and to embrace nothingness. Then it is very believable that thou mayest bring her to the arms of a lover bodily present; and thou dost." For HENLEY (ed. 1902), *affection* = "suspicion, distempered fancy" and *intention* = "tortured and torturing purpose." According to STEWART (1914, pp. 96-122), Leontes's love for Mamillius makes it impossible for him to kill the boy's mother and thus (p. 98) "he must convince himself that, though he knows her to be his legitimate parent, she is *not* his parent in any deep essential way." Not surprisingly, this notion has won no support.

Recent eds. generally agree with WILSON's (ed. 1931) synthesis: "Desire! thy fancies penetrate the very soul of man: thou makest impossible things seem possible, partakest of the nature of dreams, cooperatest with unreality, and becomest fellow-worker with what does not exist. All the more then mayest thou combine with what *is* material, and thou dost and that beyond the pale of law as I have discovered to my cost." PAFFORD (ed. 1963, p. 166) differs slightly: "Can your mother (be faithless)? Is it possible? Lustful passions: your intensity penetrates to the very heart and soul of man. . . . Lust causes one to associate in the mind with persons who are purely imaginary, who do not exist at all, therefore it is very credible that the most unthinkable lustful association can take place between real people: and lust, you have brought it about in this case, going beyond what is lawful—and I am the sufferer to such an extent that I am losing my senses and grow cuckold's horns." KERMODE (ed. 1963): "Leontes recognizes that [jealousy] is sometimes baseless, but argues that it is not so in his case." EVANS (ed. 1974), however, following H. SMITH: *"Affectio*, a sudden, unexplained change in mind and body; here, jealousy." GARBER (1974, p. 166), differently: "According to this reasoning [Leontes's] 'affection', or passionate emotion, since it is known to ally itself with dreams and 'what's unreal', is even more likely to be provoked by a real stimulus, such as sexual infidelity. The logic is extremely dubious, itself affected by 'affection'. . . . [Leontes] has subconsciously . . . substituted the fictive for the real in order to give vent to a latent 'affection', a propensity for sexual jealousy." NEELY (1975, p. 325): "The motive force of the passage is a specific, ugly, free-floating image of intercourse, spewed forth by Leontes' subconscious: 'Lust, thy stretching and "tension in" penetrates the center.'" ABARTIS (1977, p. 99): "With 'Then . . . credent' . . . the tentative and questioning rhythms of his speech change to certainty, as if he has logically proved to himself what was being entertained in surmise before. His dreams have become his reality." HUNT (1983, pp. 50-1): "Leontes judges that love combines with dreams in lovers' minds and gives birth to fantasies—to nothing real. The wispy blending of affection and dream gives Leontes precedent for his belief that affection enters into something actual—his wife's and friend's scheming." BARTON (1986, pp. 34-5): "Leontes, commenting more acutely than he knows upon his predicament, observes that 'affection' communicates with 'dreams': 'With . . . nothing'; . . . upon [him] moral obtuseness descends like a disease."

PARRY (ed. 1982, pp. 22-4) joins the words to stage action, attempting to make Mamillius the subject of the soliloquy. Embarrassed by his father's show of feeling, Mamillius *"draws away and goes over to his mother,"* leaving Leontes isolated. The movement "directs his attention, and ours, back to Hermione. The full meaning of his clipped phrases may then be 'Can thy dam (attract you more than I can do)? May't be affection (for her that is drawing you away from me)?' For the rest of the speech he is watching *Mamillius*, to whom 'thou' and 'thy' apply throughout, in the company of Hermione and Polixenes. Now Leontes soliloquizes on what he sees." Along these lines PARRY continues to analyze the speech in detail, but he is alone in his interpretation. Having consulted Thomas Vicary, *The Anatomie of the Body of Man* (1st ed. 1546), "a very popular handbook," CUVELIER (1983, p. 37) finds that "Leontes' description closely follows the current [medical] doctrine: melancholy *stabs the centre* or middle ventricle of the brain, the seat of the *cogitative vertue*, and through the meatus between the ventricles, the infected spirits find their way into the front cell, so that the unsettling of reason has its simultaneous counterpart in the disturbance of the *fantasie* and the *imaginative vertue*. Thus the reception of the information conveyed by the senses becomes blurred and distorted, and sensations grow unreal: in other words, affection *communicates with dreams*." CUVELIER continues with an interesting discussion of how Leontes's distorted vision, "the optics of mad jealousy" (p. 40), causes reality to be perceived as though through a perspective glass (see p. 780 of this text). GIRARD (1987, pp. 59-61) analyzes the speech in terms of "mimetic desire," desire induced in another by one's own desire.

213 **Can . . . be**] ROLFE (ed. 1879): "Can thy mother be guilty of unfaithfulness? Is it possible?" For the use of *dam*, see n. 1385.

Dam] COTTRELL (1964, p. 75): The word suggests "the animal love he fancies in her actions."

214-22 **Affection? . . . Browes**] Most eds. agree that 213 should end with a stop or a suspension. VAN DOREN (1939, p. 316): "Leontes means in general that the impossible has become all too possible, but the particulars of his meaning are his own." HARRISON (ed. 1947): It "is deliberately obscure as Leontes' thick and incoherent mutterings take monstrous shape." KNIGHTS (1976, p. 602): "The general drift is clear. Whatever the precise meaning of 'affection' or 'intention', Leontes is trying to establish the validity of an emotional bias by claiming how very reasonable it is to accept it. After all, he says, a strong feeling that a thing is so can sometimes be more valid than common sense [quotes 215], and our intuitions can find truth in dreams. Dreams are 'unreal', are 'nothings', so if affection can work on such unsubstantial material, how much more likely that it can join what is actually there. In [218–19] his mind fairly pounces on his 'proof.'" WILLBERN (1980, p. 248), also citing 377–8 and 385–9: "'Nothing' gets obsessively repeated into thing-ness: an abstraction made concrete, which subsumes everything else. It becomes a self-reflexive, self-generating agent of its own creation, produced out of the mysterious, violent, sexual 'co-action', or coitus of 'dreams', the 'unreal', 'something', and 'nothing.'" DRAPER (1985, p. 19): "The obscurity . . . removes Leontes into a solipsistic world, which paradoxically makes the impossible seem possible and has its intercourse with dreams, yet forms relationship with nothing." WRIGHT (1989, pp. 226–30) objects to interpretations that ignore "the presence and dramatic value of the young Mamillius," whose "looks are the concrete eugenic evidence of Hermione's past faithfulness." The looks are the welkin eye, which earlier critics interpret as characterizing rather than as familial (see n. 212). WRIGHT thinks, however, that "the boy's manifestly innocent presence would . . . cast doubt on the validity of Leontes' own suspicions. . . . Such a reading becomes possible once 'Affection' is no longer taken to mean simply 'lustful passions.'" The word is usually, but not always, so taken; WRIGHT prefers H. SMITH's *affectio*, "mental seizure" (see n. 214). The heat alluded to in 181 thus may be a side effect of the perturbation, as is the *tremor cordis* (183). "Leontes is overcome . . . by a psychological aberration which overwhelms his rationality and has no evident moral significance at all—except, of course, in its consequences." HAPPÉ (1969): "Though he addresses Lust in the abstract, he is almost certainly addressing Hermione as well, particularly from *Thou* [219]."

The colon after "vnreall" in 217 suggests that Crane was as uncertain as most of the critics. WILSON (ed. 1931): "The F. brackets [in 220 and in 221–2] mark off the words which Leontes does not wish Hermione and Polixenes to hear," but the question at 223 is probably provoked by Leontes's agitation rather than anything Polixenes has or has not heard. See n. 223.

214 **Affection? . . . Center]** The first word is a nominative of address (Affection!) rather than a question, but, beyond that, critics find little to agree on. MINSHEU (1617, Affection): "A motion or passion of the mind" (*OED, sb.* 2), probably, as H. SMITH (1963, p. 163) argues, "the equivalent of the Latin *affectio*." This word, SMITH notes, COOPER (1565) glosses as "a disposition or mutacion happenyng to bodie or mynde: trouble of minde." HANKINS (1978, p. 98): "An emotional impulse that opposes the governance of reason." STEEVENS (ed. 1778), on the basis of *MV* 4.1.50–2 (1955–7), concludes that *affection* means "imagination." MASON (1785, p. 124), who says that the word "means the passion of love," may have in mind what TANNENBAUM is suggesting (see below). Among recent critics, BURTON (1970, p. 222) seems to be alone in thinking that Leontes's affection is his love for Hermione. BECKET's (1815, 1:351) "sensibility" for *affection* is not exactly borne out by *OED*, nor is SCHMIDT's (1874) "natural instinct, on which the disposition of the mind depends"; for other senses of the word, however, see nn. 26, 2206, 2332–3, 3046, and 3110.

Regarding *Intention*, CAPELL (1783, 2.4:163): *Affection* is told "that when full bent is given it, full *intentiveness* [*OED*: 'closeness of attention'], man often receives a stab in . . . his heart," that is, becomes jealous. CHEDWORTH (1805, p. 119), however: "Intenseness" (*OED*: "violence, intensity"). STEEVENS (ed. 1778): "*Intention* is . . . [the] vehemence of the mind . . . [that] affects Leontes so deeply, or . . . '*stabs him to the center*.'" SINGER (ed. 1856): "Sympathy between the human system and all nature . . . intenseness." KINNEAR (1883, p. 176) equates *intention* with *intent* in the sense of "illicit desire," as in *AWW* 4.3.27 (2133) and *Wiv.* 2.1.174 (707). PORTER & CLARKE (ed. 1908): "An intentness of mental forecast of the situation in the direction of a distrust so strong as to amount to an instinctive suspicion which is its own voucher." ORGEL (ed. 1996): "The relevant senses are 'meaning, significance, import' (*OED* 3) and 'purpose' (*OED* 4). . . . It is the direction, not the force [intensity], of the passion that is in question."

For the passage, MASON (1785, p. 125): "*Intention* . . . means eagerness of attention, or of desire," as in *Wiv*. 1.3.73 (357). "Thy" refers to Hermione, and as he speaks "thy . . . Center," the actor may strike his breast (his center). TANNENBAUM (1933, p. 100): "Lust can attain such a degree of intensity as to penetrate to the soul of even the best." His synonym for *affection* is supported and amply documented by PAFFORD (ed. 1963, pp. 166–7). CUNNINGHAM (1951, pp. 113–14): "*Affection* denotes the passions, emotions, and feelings which are associated with the will in the moving faculty of the soul, as distinguished from the rational faculty to which the will is attached as the rational appetite. *Intention* denotes the directed movement of a faculty of the soul toward realizing a possibility. . . . The passage means, then, that affection, directing its own movement, penetrates to the knowledge of the fact which gives the grounds for being jealous, and at the same time embraces the decision to be jealous. [In] modern terms: 'Feeling rather than reason hits the mark and furnishes the decision.'" HANKINS (1953, p. 153): "The 'affection' of jealousy presents to his imagination a picture which pierces him to the soul, figuratively speaking. This picture is based upon impressions brought by the senses to their 'centre', his soul [as in *Son*. 146]. These impressions were first received by the senses when he saw Polixenes kiss his wife," which Polixenes does not do. NEELY (1975, p. 325), in a thorough exploration of the entire speech: "Leontes is, in part, analyzing the effect which his own emotion has on him. . . . At the same time he is referring, perhaps only half consciously, to the imagined lustful intentions of Hermione and Polixenes: 'Lust (i.e. Hermione's and Polixenes'), your purpose (fulfillment) wounds my being.'"

SCOTT (1920, pp. 147–8), taking *affection* to mean "affect" in the psychological sense (i.e., feeling or emotion), finds the speech an "outpouring . . . from the unconscious mind of Leontes," an expression of paranoia. "It is not surprising that critics with no experience of psychiatry have found this passage difficult." Its writer, of course, had no experience of psychiatry. HUNT (1983, p. 51): In neo-Platonic doctrine, "'intention' was a synonym for 'image'—the product of an active phantasy. Leontes' exclamation thus concerns love's fantastic image . . . primarily a dreaming lover's fantasy. By means of this image . . . he 'stabs the center' (discovers the 'truth' about Hermione). If something romantically ideal and ephemeral exists, then something coarsely selfish and tangible must be an equal, or greater, possibility." WARD (1987, pp. 549–50), relying in part on Robert Burton's *Anatomy of Melancholy*: *Intention* is "'Intensification', . . . the word . . . used to describe the sudden onset and growth of unbalanced or diseased . . . mental states." A symptom of intention of the passions is palpitation of the heart, as in 183. "Can . . . Center" then becomes, according to WARD, "Could your mother <really commit adultery, or> may it be Affection? <which pushes me involuntarily towards this conclusion?—O Affection> the way in which you intensify <every passion, every bodily symptom of emotion> wounds and disables the centre <of my being, the soul>." If *affection* should refer to "Hermione's emotions in the moment of adultery," the meaning becomes "may it be Affection <which made *her* act in this way>?" For a possibly related passage, see n. 3225. STYAN (1967, p. 57): "Leontes feels the pang of jealousy as if it were a knife in his heart . . . , and for gesture his hand must fly to his breast." STYAN also links *affection* here with the word in a different sense in 26. ABRAMS (1986, p. 158): "Remarkable . . . is the degree to which Affection possesses originative power, figuring as a *malin genie* with which (or whom) Leontes shares his being. . . . He translates the war in his own psyche into confrontation with a pseudo-objective enemy." ORGEL (ed. 1996): "'Affection' . . . means passion or lust. . . . If 'thy' refers to 'affection' personified, then Leontes is saying that the purposes of Hermione's lust cut to his heart (or to the centre of the universe); if 'thy' indicates an address to himself, he is saying that his meaning has got to the heart—of the matter, as well as his own.

Whether it is then Hermione's passion that 'dost make possible things not so held, | Communicat'st with dreams', or Leontes' recognition of its significance, is indeterminable; but this is surely to the point: in talking about Hermione, Leontes is also talking about himself."

215-18 **Thou . . . nothing**] WARD (1987, pp. 551-2): "Leontes is debating the way in which affection (in itself neither good nor bad) by intention becomes like hallucinating fever . . . not just producing but *becoming* dreams." He agrees with JOHNSON's (ed. 1773) paraphrase of "Thou . . . held": "Thou dost make those things possible, which are conceived to be impossible"; but WARD (p. 552) continues: "<like a witch with her familiar> you merge your identity with dreams (how can this be?) with what is unreal: you are a coercive force <even over that which does not exist>, and consort with the non-existent'. Leontes . . . is exerting all the self-control in his power." ORGEL (ed. 1996): "(*a*) Lust facilitates what had been thought impossible, realizes fantasies and desires (or perhaps, does the impossible in dreams); (*b*) I can now believe things I had thought impossible, I am in touch with the world of fantasies and desires."

215 **possible**ₐ] Although not favored by recent eds., MALONE's (ed. 1790) comma prevents "Thou dost make things that are possible to be disbelieved."

216 **Communicat'st with Dreames**] CARRINGTON (1956): "Make dreams seem true." HANKINS (1978, p. 99): *Communicat'st* "is a formal term in psychology, used in its original sense of 'impart, share, hold in common.'"

how can this be?] DEIGHTON (ed. 1889): "Strange as this may seem." COLLINS (ed. 1904-24?), however: "A repetition of the question in line [213], and nothing to do with his present point." Later eds. divide over which interpretation is right.

217 **vnreall**] BARTON (1986, p. 32): "A word he [Sh.] may well have invented." *OED*'s first citation is of *Mac.* 3.4.106 (1384). (P. 34): "All the associations . . . are with ambiguous, riddling, intangible things," which is hardly surprising.

coactiue] JOHNSON (1755): "Acting in concurrence" (*OED, a.* 2, citing this line). HANKINS (1978, p. 99): The word "refers to the joint action of affection, through imagination, with the unreal things already mentioned." WARD (1987, p. 552) prefers "of the nature of force or compulsion; coercive, compulsory" (*a.* 1), though JOHNSON's definition shows that sense *a.* 2 was, as WARD argues, known before the 1840s.

218 **fellow'st**] JOHNSON (1755): "To suit with; to pair with; to match" (*OED, v.* 2a, citing this line, "to be a fellow to"). HENLEY (ed. 1902): "Art even as."

nothing] KNOWLES (privately): "I.e., a fantasy lover; cf. HUDSON (ed. 1880) in n. 213-22." KNIGHT (1947; 1965, p. 82 n.) finds Sh.'s use of this word "variously important. Repetitions . . . carry a weight of dramatic meaning" at *Ham.* 3.4.131-3 (2512-14), *AWW* 3.2.75-100 (1480-1509), and *Lr.* 1.1.87-90 (93-5) and 1.4.128-33 (658-62). KNIGHT compares *Lr.* 1.2.31 (365) with *Oth.* 3.3.36 (1629). "In *Macbeth* it [i.e., *nothing*] helps to characterize a nightmare state" at 1.3.141 (252) and "a general nihilism" at 5.5.28 (2349); and in *R2* the word "is used seven times to define a nameless fear" at 2.2.12-40 (964-92) "and twice for a peaceful Nirvana-like dissolution" at 5.5.38-41 (2704-7), this "pointing on to 'nothing brings me all things'" at *Tim.* 5.1.188 (2428). *Nothing*, KNIGHT says, "tends to occur at moments of crisis, or whenever what Nietzsche called the Dionysian element in tragedy is breaking into the rational and Apollonian: for the accompanying poetic implications," see *MND* 5.1.16 (1808). "A good apocalyptic use occurs later" in *WT* at 1158. For more on *nothing*, see n. 385-9.

credent] STEEVENS (ed. 1778): "Credible" (*OED* 2a, citing this line). The CLARKES (ed. 1865): "The active for the passive form." They also observe (1879, p. 55) that Sh. coined the word; it appears in *Ham.* 1.3.30 (493), *MM* 4.4.26 (2297), and *LC* 279. In *MM* its meaning is also "credible," in *Ham.* "trustful" (*OED* 1), and in *LC* both, according to John Roe (ed.), *Poems* (1992).

Pol. What meanes *Sicilia?*
Her. He something seemes vnsetled.
Pol. How? my Lord?   225

---

225 How? my lord?] Now, my lord? mTBY2 *conj.*, CAP; How now, my lord? mSING *conj.*, SING2; Ho, my Lord! DYCE1 *conj.*, HAL, DYCE2, KNT3, HUD2

---

219 **co-ioyne**] *OED*, citing this line: Obsolete variant of *conjoin*. HANKINS (1978, p. 100): The word "repeats the action of affection in imagining unreal images. Since affection can do this, it can certainly cojoin with a real image of a real thing, a 'some thing' as distinguished from the 'no thing' of phantasies and dreams. This 'some thing' is the physical presence of Hermione and Polixenes holding hands." KNOWLES (privately): "Holding hands does not harden brows. By the time he reaches 'beyond Commission,' Leontes is thinking of copulation."

220 **And . . . Commission**] MASON (1785, p. 125): "The commission he had given Hermione to prevail on Polixenes to defer his departure." STAUNTON (ed. 1859, Commission): "Warrant, permission, authority" (*OED, sb.* 3 and 8). For the phrase, SINGER (ed. 1856), probably wrongly: "Beyond the time of commission." Leontes means "illegally," perhaps "indecently."

find] Probably SCHMIDT (1874): "To perceive, to experience" (*OED, sb.* 5), although he does not cite this passage. The legal sense, "to determine and declare (an offense) to have been committed" (*sb.* 17b), is also appropriate.

221 **infection**] For jealousy as disease, see n. 390-1. HANKINS (1978, p. 100): "Leontes metaphorically speaks of his brain as being infected by his view of Hermione and Polixenes when he really means that his mind has been infected by the intention of 'guilty lovers' formed in his imagination."

222 **hardning**] HENLEY (ed. 1902): "Horning." VAN DAM (1900, p. 47) notices the syncopation of the *e* in *hardening*. For other syncopations of *e*, see nn. 313, 381, 692, 813, 1302, and 2953.

Browes] From which the horns of the cuckold spring. Cf. n. 192 and, for *brows* as "eyebrows" rather than "forehead," n. 596. CARRINGTON (1956): "'Brows' is in antithesis to 'brains'—Leontes' mind and body are affected by what he has seen." WARD (1987, p. 553) thinks the phrase "may have the more natural sense of 'producing a deep frown.'"

223 **What meanes *Sicilia?***] REESE (1953; 1980, p. 371): "A fair comment" on the speech. Following PORTER & CLARKE (ed. 1908), BOORMAN (ed. 1964): "A reference to Leontes' agitated manner, or perhaps Polixenes has overheard his last words." Probably the former, since the significance of "And . . . Browes" would be plain.

224 **something seemes vnsetled**] ROLFE (ed. 1879): Seems "somewhat disturbed." For *something* as "somewhat," see ABBOTT §68; and with this transposition of *something*, ROLFE compares "something a round bellie" (*2H4* 1.2.188 [445]). *OED* (Something, *adv.* 1b) cites 884.

vnsetled] WALKER (1854, p. 36) wants this word to have four syllables.

225 **How?**] DEY (1900) would give this line to Hermione, because Polixenes never addresses Leontes as "my lord." That is true, but Leontes calls Polixenes "my Lord" at 253. DYCE (ed. 1857): "Ho, . . . for Leontes is standing apart from Polixenes and Hermione; and 'how' . . . was frequently the old spelling of '*ho*.'" *OED* regards the words as separate though equivalent. The word may also be "*ellipt[ical]* for 'How is it?'" (*adv.* 4).

Leo. What cheere? how is't with you, best Brother?   226
Her. You look as if you held a Brow of much distraction:

226-7 *Verse lines ending* look, . . . Distraction. THEO1+ (−HAN, STAU, IRV)
226 *Leo.*] *Om.* mTBY2 *conj.*, HAN, CAP, RANN-SING1, DYCE1, WH1, STAU-GLO, DYCE2, DEL4, HUD2, WH2, OXF1, BUL, ARD1, KIT1-PEL1, ARD2, PEN2, BEV, OXF2
best] my best ROWE1-POPE2, HAN
Holding his forehead. COL2
227 look . . . held] seem to hold HAN

---

226 **What . . . Brother?**] Most eds. give this line to Polixenes. HARNESS (ed. 1825) accounts for F1's assignment of it to Leontes: "Leontes, startled from his moody abstraction by the sudden address of Polixenes, endeavours to conceal the disturbance of his mind by an assumed tone of cheerfulness and careless ease." Agreeing, CAL-DECOTT (MS 1813-33): "Conscious that he must have betrayed himself & that the workings of his passion and his perturbation of mind must have been visible (and in spite of the effort he makes to conceal it, his wife immediately afterwards notices and challenges it) Leontes makes a plunge & with an air & affection of ease & complacency & in a phrase of much candid courtesy, puts the most ordinary question as to the repose of his 'best brother's' mind, in the hope of doing away [with] the evidence he felt he had afforded of the conflict of passion & miserable agitation of his own." FURNESS (ed. 1898): "Shakespeare may have intended this line . . . as a flash of Leontes' old-time self,—a struggle to shake off the insane delusion which was beclouding his mind. There is certainly need of some words . . . from him, to span the gap from his turbulent soliloquy to the gay memories of his boyhood." SYMONS (in IRVING & MARSHALL, ed. 1890): Leontes calls Polixenes "brother" at 242 and 255 (but Polixenes does the same to him at 53, 82, and 1636). WILSON (ed. 1931), however: "'Best brother' is just the kind of exaggerated term of affection which a man would utter in [these] circumstances." The CLARKES (1879, p. 629): "As an epithet of affectionate esteem," *best* also occurs at 1666. WHITE (ed. 1857), for the continuation to Polixenes: In F "not only does *Leontes* express a solicitude not in keeping with his mood, but *Polixenes* does not put the very question which the situation required from him. It is clearly intended too that *Hermione* should continue the inquiry which her companion begins." PORTER & CLARKE (ed. 1908): Leontes's solicitude is dissembled. As the textual notes indicate, however, many, but not all, recent eds. side with WHITE. PAFFORD (ed. 1963), for example: "Polixenes asks [Leontes], with concern, how he is feeling, for the phrase 'how is't with you?' almost always carries the sense of 'are you feeling well?'" PAFFORD cites *TN* 3.4.88 (1611), *Oth.* 3.4.33 (2174), *Ham.* 3.4.116 (2497), and *Mac.* 2.2.55 (719).

227 **You . . . distraction**] Thinking this line should be taken literally, COLLIER (1852, p. 207) reports a faked SD meant to prove it. Although SCHMIDT (1874, Hold) agrees ("to support with the hand"), WHITE (1854, p. 289) had called this interpretation "tame and ridiculous literalism." ROLFE (ed. 1879) construes *held* as "have" (SCHMIDT, 1874, Hold, as at 2246), and he compares 3057 with "Brow . . . distraction." DEIGHTON (ed. 1889): "The look of your brow is that of a man much distracted, agitated." Hermione has inadvertently used a word painful to Leontes; see n. 222. PARRY (ed. 1982): "Hermione thinks at first that he is going to faint; then she realises from his expression that he is 'unsettled' for some other reason." Regarding lineation, SYMONS (in IRVING & MARSHALL, ed. 1890): "It is evident that the printers of the Folio set the line [as one, not partially joined with 226] for in the original copy the [speech prefix *Her.*] is moved back so as to get room for the whole line." He is right that the speech prefix was not indented as far as usual (the com-

Are you mou'd (my Lord?)
  Leo. No, in good earnest.
How sometimes Nature will betray it's folly?   230
It's tendernesse? and make it selfe a Pastime
To harder bosomes? Looking on the Lynes

---

228 you] not you THEO1-THEO2, WARB-JOHN2, v1773; you not THEOBALD (1729)
conj. in NICHOLS (1817, 2:359), HAN, HUD2
    229 earnest.] earnest, no. — CAP
    230-2 How . . . bosomes?] *Marked as aside* CAP, MAL, v1793, COL2, STAU

---

positor probably wished to avoid a turnover), and the line may have been undivided in the MS, but most eds. find the single line to be metrically hopeless.
    228 **mou'd**] CALDECOTT (MS 1813-33): "Disturbed." SCHMIDT (1874, Move): "To make angry, to exasperate." PYLE (1969, p. 22 n.): "It does not occur to her that he can be angry with her."
    230-2 **How . . . bosomes?**] Readers as early as ANON. (MS 1793-) see "no reason why the whole of the speech should not be heard by Hermione and Polixenes," and no recent ed. considers the passage an aside. Perhaps it should be. DEIGHTON (ed. 1889) paraphrases: "How sometimes natural affection will betray its weakness and make a man the laughing-stock of those less tender-hearted." If this is what Leontes means, his further explaining his distracted brow as a reflection of his love for his son seems as odd as his apparent assertion that his wife and friend have harder bosoms. Possibly "How . . . bosomes?" is a general observation spoken aside, Leontes having taken Polixenes's and Hermione's questions to be taunts. ENRIGHT (1970, p. 165): "A rather strange thing to say in this overtly soft-bosomed company; though of course it is by no means a strange thing for Leontes to say to himself, in the company of his new suspicions." PARRY (ed. 1982), however, glosses "make . . . bosomes" as "and so provide amusement for the less soft hearted"; this seemingly general observation is "a veiled jibe at Hermione and Polixenes." F1's question marks were transformed by ROWE to exclamation points, with which question marks were interchangable, and recent eds. reduce these to but one, following "bosomes."
    230-1 **it's . . . It's**] As a possessive pronoun, this word occurs five times in *WT*—here and at 236, 357, and 1488. The form was new in the early 17th c.; *OED*'s first citation is from 1598; see also BROOK (1976, p. 78). Elsewhere in Sh. the usage is found in *MM* 1.2.4 (100) and *Tmp.* 1.2.95 (192) and 1.2.394 (536), both from Crane transcripts; in *H8* 1.1.18 (62), also from a scribal transcript (WELLS & TAYLOR, 1987, p. 618); in *TNK* 1.1.154, from "a transcript of some sort" (Bowers ed., 7:156); and, unexpectedly, in the F text of *2H6* 3.2.393 (2110), possibly from revised foul papers (WELLS & TAYLOR, p. 176). In short, *it's* is unlikely to be Sh.'s. COLLINS (ed. 1904-24?) thinks "it is doubtful that Shakespeare ever wrote 'its'" and, doubtful himself, asserts that all the occurrences of the form "may be misprints." For more on the form, see ABBOTT §228 and FRANZ §320. Possessive *it* occurs at 1110 and 1279 and a dozen times in other plays.
    231 **Pastime**] MINSHEU (1617): "Sport." COLLINS (ed. 1904-24?): "Object of ridicule."
    232-7 **Looking . . . dangerous**] Some recent critics find these lines ominous. DEAN (1979, p. 290): "Leontes' character is marked by a melancholy awareness of time, which he feels especially when comparing himself to his son," but it is unclear how this awareness emerges here. SCHOTZ (1980, p. 51): "It is not mere coincidence that Leontes recalls himself unable to control his own 'weapon'. . . . Like all fathers

Of my Boyes face, me thoughts I did requoyle   (2A2
Twentie three yeeres, and saw my selfe vn-breech'd,
In my greene Veluet Coat; my Dagger muzzel'd,   235
Least it should bite it's Master, and so proue
(As Ornaments oft do's) too dangerous:
How like (me thought) I then was to this Kernell,
This Squash, this Gentleman. Mine honest Friend,

---

233 me thoughts] methought m1768FL *conj.*, SING1, HUD1, HAL, STAU, KTLY, DYCE2, HUD2, OXF2, BEV4; my thoughts mCOL1 *conj.*, COL, KNT2, SING2, WH
237 Ornaments . . . do's] Ff, KTLY, PEN1, CLN2, PEN2; ornament . . . does CAP-v1778, RANN, EVNS, OXF2; Ornaments . . . do ROWE1 *etc.*
239 Squash] quash KEM2, KNT

(before the advent of modern medicine), Leontes cannot authenticate his own pater-nal-generative role, and beside the power of the creating female, what is the power of a king? . . . The King of Sicily is flooded by barely suppressed feelings of the limits of masculine power." Regarding the role, Leontes's paternity is authenticated by Mamillius's resemblance to him (e.g., 196-7, 205-6). Michael TAYLOR (1982, p. 230): "Such dangerous-sounding nostalgia—the phallic dagger, the winsome 'green velvet coat'—is matched by the dangerous nonsense of his concurring with Polixenes that their sons cure in them thoughts that would make thick their blood. Nothing could be further from the truth. . . . Mamillius' presence intensifies Leontes' thick-ening thoughts." ERICKSON (1982, p. 821): "Leontes invokes the father-son identifi-cation enshrined in patriarchal succession and uses it to escape from the intolerable and genital present. . . . Instead of the son's becoming the father, the father be-comes the son, swallowing up Mamillius in the process." The present is genital be-cause Hermione and Polixenes are so equipped.

232 **Lynes**] JOHNSON (1755): "Lineaments, or marks in the hand or face" (*OED*, *sb.*[2] 14). JERVIS (1868): "Feature," unsupported by *OED*.

233 **me thoughts**] It seemed to me. COLLIER (ed. 1842) emends this reading because the expression recurs at 238 without the *s* and enclosed in parentheses. "Such would have been the case [here], if *methought* had been intended." Few eds. care for COLLIER's *my thoughts*. WALKER (1854, p. 284) accepts F's word as an alter-native form of *methought*, the *s* "perhaps by *contagion* from *methinks*." *OED* (Me-thinks) and ABBOTT §297 agree. *Me thoughts* is also found in *MV* 1.3.69 (395) and *R3* 1.4.9 (845) and 1.4.24 (860).

requoyle] KNIGHT (ed. 1842): "Put back [my thoughts]." *OED* (Recoil, *v.*[1] c, citing this line): "To go back in memory."

234 **Twentie three yeeres**] PAFFORD (ed. 1963, p. lxxxii and n.), whose estimate is based on the depiction of Mamillius in the play ("a child yet already something of a public figure, 'a gentleman of the greatest promise' [37-8], a page, kissed by ladies, who can yet offer to fight and who can argue with wit"): "A boy of about ten." Thus "this passage indicates that Leontes is about 33; the same age as Pandosto, who is about 50 when Fawnia is 16." PYLE (1969, p. 14 n.): "If mathematical computation is to be trusted, Mamillius is five years old. Sixteen years later Leontes judges Florizel, Mamillius's almost exact contemporary [see 2871-2], to be twenty-one [see 2881-3]." Since Leontes and Polixenes are coeval (130), they are now 28, and, in Acts 4 and 5, 44. BATESON (1978, p. 70) makes the same calculation with about the same result, the uncertainty arising because Mamillius may be six rather than five. He also

observes that "the 23 years are oddly, provocatively, precise. . . . 23 is also
. . . the number of days . . . that Cleomenes and Dion take to obtain the Delphic
oracle's pronouncement [1134]" and that the Shepherd wishes "there were no age
betweene ten and three and twenty (1501-2)." "There is no obvious connection
between the three passages," BATESON notes, "but they may help to keep its first use
fresh." FURNESS (ed. 1898): "An ingenious way of disclosing to us the present age of
Leontes, and incidentally of differentiating his jealousy from that of Othello, a much
older man. . . . The younger Leontes hopefully imagines that after Hermione's death
at least a moiety of the zest of life [his rest, actually] will return to him" (906-8).
BOORMAN (ed. 1964) finds the time reference "strangely exact," but it is not exact
enough for SMEATON (1911, p. 506), who discovers in Leontes "a capital portrait of
an impulsive, pragmatical old man, wedded to a wife doubtless a good deal younger
than himself." Moreover, by 1092 Leontes has a gray beard, a fact that causes some
critics to put him in his thirties (e.g., Mark TAYLOR, 1982, p. 28, thirty-five). JONES
(1971, pp. 50-1): "The number twenty-three [which] occurs . . . three times in *The
Winter's Tale* [here, 1134, and 1502] was possibly felt to have symbolic value: Being
one short of twenty-four it is expressive of a state of being *almost* complete and is
comparable to . . . 'the eleventh hour.'"

    vn-breech'd] HANMER (ed. 1743-4, 6:glos.): "Not yet in breeches, a boy in
coats [a skirt]" (*OED, a.*, citing this line as its first example). WRIGHT & LAMAR (ed.
1966): "Boys were dressed in gowns until about the age of six." PARRY (ed. 1982):
"The word means 'unsheathed' [*OED*, Unbreech, *v.*] also, which perhaps leads Leontes to speak [235-7] of the dagger (as a disguised warning to Hermione and Polixenes?)," an unlikely idea on both counts.

    235 **muzzel'd**] DEIGHTON (ed. 1889): "With its sheath carefully fastened." RIDLEY
(ed. 1935), less probably: "With the 'button' on, 'bated.'" Unable to confirm that
daggers were somehow locked into their sheaths, PAFFORD (ed. 1963) is dissatisfied
with DEIGHTON's sense. *OED* (*v.*¹ 3b, citing this line) finds the figurative meaning of
the word to be "to prevent by means of a muzzle from biting," which seems the
appropriate idea. MAVEETY (1963, p. 486): "A conscious echoing of a proverb recorded in English as early as Chaucer[:] 'A man may do no synne with his wyf, Ne
hurte hymselven with his owene knyf' [Merchant's Tale, line 1839]. In Chaucer the
speech is ironic since January [the cuckold] is unmistakably hurt by his own knife
[his young wife]. Leontes' use of the proverb is also ironic: Hermione proves a dangerous ornament but only because Leontes' irrational suspicion makes her one." Perhaps the same association leads BEVINGTON (ed. 1992) to find a phallic suggestion in
muzzel'd.

    236 **bite**] *OED* (*v.* 8, citing this line): "To cut into or penetrate."

    237 **As . . . dangerous**] STEEVENS (ed. 1793) compares "Thus ornament is but
the guilded shore To a most dangerous sea" (*MV* 3.2.98-9 [1443-4]), the ornament
in both instances being the beautiful appearance disguising a treacherous reality.
BOORMAN (ed. 1964) suggests that the parenthesis is "a threatening hint . . . at Hermione's politeness to Polixenes." Regarding the disagreement of *Ornaments* and *do's*,
WALKER (1860, 1:233, 252) and FURNESS (ed. 1898) believe that final -*s* was often
interpolated in F1; see n. 34-6. Eds. who emend to *ornament* no doubt believe that
a single terminal error is more probable than a double, the apostrophe and the *s*. *Do's*
occurs invariably in *WT*, 23 times. For other disagreements of subject and verb, see
nn. 870, 920-1, 1636-7, 1643, and 1724.

    238 **Kernell**] SCHMIDT (1874): "Any thing diminutive." MINSHEU (1617): "Prop-
erly in nuts."

    239 **Squash**] JOHNSON (1755): "Any thing unripe . . . soft." STEEVENS (ed.
1778), glossing *MND* 3.1.186 (1004): "An immature peascod" (*OED, sb.*¹ 1, citing this
line). He compares *TN* 1.5.166-7 (451). BURTON (1988, p. 193): "A seed, an unripe
fruit which suggests promise of future fruition."

    honest] See n. 294.

Will you take Egges for Money?   240
   Mam. No (my Lord) Ile fight.
   Leo. You will: why happy man be's dole. My Brother
Are you so fond of your young Prince, as we
Doe seeme to be of ours?
   Pol. If at home (Sir)   245
He's all my Exercise, my Mirth, my Matter;
Now my sworne Friend, and then mine Enemy;
My Parasite, my Souldier: States-man; all:
He makes a Iulyes day, short as December,
And with his varying child-nesse, cures in me   250

240-1 *One verse line* mCAP2, OXF1, PEL1, CLN2, OXF2
241 (my Lord)] *Om.* HAN
242 will:] ~ ? CAP, v1778-DEL2, DYCE2-BUL (−WH2), CAM3+
246 He's] Here's F3, F4
   all my Exercise] all Exercise ROWE1, ROWE2
248 my] mine STAU
249 December] December's mTBY4 *conj.*, KTLY, HUD2
250 his] this ROWE2
   child-nesse] childishness POPE, HAN

---

240 **Will . . . Money?**] The essential idea, as HUNTER (*AWW*, ed. 1962) says, is that "'eggs' is a synonym for something worthless" (*OED, sb.* 4, citing this line); annotating *AWW* 4.3.250 (2353), HUNTER quotes George Wilkins, *The Miseries of Enforced Marriage* (1607; MSR 1551): "they were indighted but for stealing of Egs." PAFFORD (ed. 1963) prefers "inferior value" to "worthless." TILLEY E90 quotes B. E. (1699): Will you "compound the matter with Loss"? or, as SMITH (in GREY, 1754, 1: 246) puts it, "will you put up affronts?" NEILSON & HILL (ed. 1942): Will you "let yourself be cheated"? CAPELL's (1783, 2.4:163-4) "stand and deliver" is a bad guess. JACKSON (1819, p. 132) believes that though Leontes "addresses his son, the dart is thrown at Hermione," which is improbable.
   for] MALONE (ed. 1790, 10:620): "In the place of."
   241 **No . . . fight**] VOSS (ed. 1829) compares Coriolanus's Boy: "A shall not tread on me: Ile run away Till I am bigger, but then Ile fight" (5.3.127-8 [3483-4]). PARRY's (ed. 1982) harks back to Mamillius as soldier (see n. 192).
   242 **happy . . . dole**] THIRLBY (MS 1733-47?) refers to RAY (1670, p. 12): "Happy man, happy dole." GREY (1754, 1:191): "*Dole* used for lot, or portion or division" (*OED, sb.*[1] 4). JOHNSON (ed. 1765): "May his *dole* or *share* in life be to be a *happy man*," which differs somewhat from the gloss of later eds.—e.g., PAFFORD (ed. 1963): "may his fortune be that of a happy man." HAPPÉ (1969) diverges slightly: "May it be his destiny (*dole*) to be called 'Happy man.'" KENRICK (1765, p. 85): "A common proverbial phrase, for wishing good luck to one's self or others" (TILLEY M158). The phrase also occurs in *1H4* 2.2.80-1 (809), *Shr.* 1.1.144 (442), and *Wiv.* 3.4.68 (1631-2). As YOU LIKE IT (1789, p. 711), connecting *dole* with funerals (*sb.*[1] 5 or *sb.*[2] 6, perhaps), thinks Sh. alludes to the idea that no man is happy until his death. RIDLEY (ed. 1935), at the other extreme: "Attaboy." PYLE (1969, p. 22): "Leon-

84

tes approves, for he also will not be content with something worthless—a worthless wife—and he too will fight back."

242-4 **My . . . ours?**] HATTORI (1982, p. 93), alone: "Leontes . . . suddenly hits upon the idea of trying (it's never too late) to suggest that Polixenes go home after all."

244 **Doe . . . be**] BOORMAN (ed. 1964), improbably: "Are seen to be."

245 **If at home**] SCHANZER (ed. 1969): "When I am at home."

246-51 **He's . . . blood**] CLARK (1935, p. 172): "This tender speech is in strong contrast to the uncompromising harshness of Polixenes towards the grown Florizel, when the young man desires to wed the shepherd's daughter" (2260 ff.). NEELY (1978, p. 183), however: "Their affection for their sons is as narcissistic and stifling as their affection for each other. . . . Polixenes' description, in which Leontes concurs, of the self-justifying use he makes of his son sums up the attitudes of both toward their children." NEVO (1987, pp. 107-8) finds even more sinister meanings: "Can we ignore the subversive connotations of 'enemy', of 'parasite', above all of the strange inversion of July and December? The game itself acts out subliminal hostilities. . . . The child is . . . a threat, a supplanter, a usurper." The kings' affection for their young sons, rather than undercutting the fathers, is more often understood as the backdrop for what is to follow, the death of Mamillius and Polixenes's bitter rejection of Florizel and his shepherdess. NEVO's comment on July and December is also odd; see n. 249. As the following notes show in more detail, Florizel's roles are drawn from real life and from fiction, chivalric romance and classical comedy—as KNOWLES (privately) points out, "a jocular summary of the different kinds of service surrounding a king."

246 **He's . . . Exercise**] SCHMIDT (1874, Exercise): "Occupation . . . habitual activity" (*OED, sb.* 2). PAFFORD (ed. 1963): I.e., "I spend all my time with him."

Mirth] *OED* (*sb.* 4c, citing this line): "Put for: The object of one's mirth."

Matter] THIRLBY (MS 1733-47?): "Business." SCHMIDT (1875): "Good sense . . . (quicum seria)." RIDLEY (ed. 1935): "Thoughts." BETHELL (ed. 1956): "Serious consideration (opposed to 'mirth')." Cf. *Wiv.* 4.6.14 (2358), *Ado* 2.1.344 (726).

247 **sworne Friend**] DEIGHTON (ed. 1889): "Probably an allusion to the *fratres jurati*, sworn brothers, who in the days of chivalry mutally bound themselves by oath to share each other's fortune." He compares the parodic sworn brothers in *H5* 2.1.12 (516) and 3.2.44 (1161). *OED* (Sworn, *ppl.a.* 1, citing this line), agrees. See also 2473.

248 **Parasite**] COTGRAVE (1611): "Flatterer, soother, smoother for good cheare sake." RIDLEY (ed. 1935): "Hanger-on." BOORMAN (ed. 1964): "(In a playful sense) wheedler, cajoler."

249 **He . . . December**] Although the expression has been differently interpreted (see n. 246-51), the idea here is familiar—boredom makes time long, diversion makes it short. At the summer solstice (22 June), the day in London is 16 hours 39 minutes long; at the winter solstice (22 December), it is 7 hours 50 minutes short.

Iulyes] COLLINS (ed. 1904-24?): "Accented on the first syllable."

December] SCHMIDT (1875, p. 1423a): "As a December's day," the whole for a part.

250-1 **with . . . blood**] QUINONES (1972, p. 434): "It is not simply the idea of continuity, but rather the gaiety and humor of the boy that take from his father's mind all brooding. He reminds his father of his own youth." NICHOLS (1981, p. 172): "In moving his viewer from sadness to mirth, the child prefigures the course of *The Winter's Tale*."

250 **varying child-nesse**] CAPELL (1783 [1774], 1:glos., Childness): "Childishness, childish Disposition." (*OED* cites only this instance until the 19th c.) The CLARKES (ed. 1865) are perhaps right that Sh. adopted the word for the meter. For the phrase, WRIGHT & LAMAR (ed. 1966): "Childish caprices."

Thoughts, that would thick my blood.
   Leo. So stands this Squire
Offic'd with me: We two will walke (my Lord)
And leaue you to your grauer steps. *Hermione,*
How thou lou'st vs, shew in our Brothers welcome;   255
Let what is deare in Sicily, be cheape:
Next to thy selfe, and my young Rouer, he's
Apparant to my heart.
   Her. If you would seeke vs,
We are yours i'th'Garden: shall's attend you there?   260

---

251 would] should F2-JOHN2, v1773
253 two] too ARD1
255 lou'st$_\wedge$] ~ , F2, F3
259 would] will THEO1, THEO2, WARB-JOHN2, v1773
260 Garden:] ~ ? HUD1
    there?] ~ . SING

---

251 **Thoughts . . . blood**] CAPELL (1783 [1774], 1:glos., Thick): "Thicken."
DEIGHTON (ed. 1889): "Curdle." Eds. disagree as to the effect. MAXWELL (ed. 1956):
"Make me melancholy." HAPPÉ (1969): "Make sluggish with care." BOORMAN (ed.
1964), however: "Terrify me," adding, "there is irony in the fact that Leontes (unlike
Polixenes) has just been using his son to increase his jealousy." Malign emotions are
associated with thick blood also in *Mac.* 1.5.43 (394) and *Jn.* 3.3.43 (1342). Regarding
Mac., Nicholas Brooke (ed. Oxford, 1990) notes that "healthy blood is clear, permitting the passage of 'natural spirits' (in this case pity and fear) to the brain; 'thick'
blood obstructs their passage." Regarding the latter, L. A. Beaurline (ed. New Cambridge *Jn.*, 1990) quotes Nashe, *Terrors of the Night* (1594; *Works*, ed. McKerrow,
1:354): "The grossest part of our blood is the melancholy humour, which . . . still
thickening as it stands still, engendreth many misshapen objects in our imaginations."
The melancholy humor itself is "cold and drie, thicke, blacke, and sowre" (Robert
Burton, *The Anatomy of Melancholy*, ed. Thomas C. Faulkner et al., 1.1.2.2). PARRY
(ed. 1982): "It is ironic that, unknowingly, Polixenes here 'prescribes' a possible
remedy for Leontes's distress."

    thick] RALEIGH (1907, pp. 219-20): Sh. obtains a "brilliant effect . . . by the
coinage of verbs"; RALEIGH offers this word as an example. *OED*, however, finds the
usage as far back as Ælfric (c. 1000).

    252-3 **So . . . me**] NEILSON & HILL (ed. 1942): "Such is the part this boy plays
in my life." LOBBAN (ed. 1910, p. xii): Sh. "confers on king Leontes the saving grace
of being the playfellow of his little son." PARRY (ed. 1982): "He *says* so: but it *is* not
so. The suggested 'cure' goes unheeded."

    252 **So stands**] SCHMIDT (1875) considers *stands* in this usage "almost equivalent
to the auxiliary verb to be" (*OED*, Stand, *v.* 15). MOORMAN (ed. 1912): "Such is the
function."

    Squire] ORGEL (ed. 1996): "Medieval chivalric language, literally a young man
of good birth attending on a knight." ROLFE (ed. 1879): "Used with half-sportive
tenderness." Cf. "Sir Page" (211). HOLDSWORTH (1986, p. 353), alone: Leontes's

"thoughts are smearing everything they touch including the birth and loyalty of Ma-millius [193-202]. . . . A play on [this word] would thus be characteristic and point-edly apt: Mamillius is performing a pander's [= 'squire' in bawdy slang] office in stilling Leontes' doubts about a liaison with a whore [Hermione]."

253 **Offic'd**] SCHMIDT (1875): "Having a place or function" (*OED, v.*, citing this line). PIERCE (ed. 1918) prefers "in relation to" as the definition for *offic'd with*. WILSON (ed. 1931, Stand officed): "Hold office, perform a function in a royal house-hold."

walke] SCHMIDT (1875): "Withdraw."

254 **grauer**] SCHMIDT (1874, Grave): "Worthy, sober, dignified." *OED* (*a.*[1] 3b): "Serious, solemn." PAFFORD (ed. 1963): "Used . . . in bitter irony."

Hermione] NEELY (1975, p. 327): Leontes "depersonalizes Hermione and Po-lixenes from the moment jealousy emerges. . . . He scarcely calls them by name again in the first act; even when exposing them to Camillo he refers to them as 'Bohemia' [e.g., 387] and 'my wife' [e.g., 365] — abstract categories of which such atrocities can be predicted, not the specific individuals whose natures would make them unthinkable. Leontes does not say his wife's name again until the fifth act [2784]." Because of meter, VAN DAM (1900, p. 92) thinks Sh. wrote *Hermion*, but this form never appears elsewhere.

255-6 **How . . . cheape**] WILSON (ed. 1931): With double meaning. PARRY (ed. 1982) makes the ambiguity explicit: "'Let your regard for our royal status be made clear in the way you entertain Polixenes' and (bitterly) 'Go ahead, show the same intimacy in love-making to Polixenes as you show to me,'" and "'Draw freely on the most valuable resources of our country (to make him welcome)' and (even more bitterly) 'All right, the most precious thing to me — you, yourself — is altogether de-graded (by this liaison with Polixenes); so be it.'" NUTTALL (1966, p. 28): The words "could be a private joke (of a bitter kind) between Leontes and himself, or the equiv-ocation could have arisen through a quite involuntary crossing of lines in his head."

256 **Sicily**] The CLARKES (1879, p. 777): Varied from *Sicil(l)ia* "for the sake of metre."

257-8 **Next . . . heart**] SANDERS (1987, pp. 26-9): Leontes, caught in the "con-fluence of many emotions," wishes to be rescued even as he indulges his growing jealousy. These words are genuine, "another grab at normality," although by 261-2 he is over the brink.

257 **Rouer**] HALLIWELL (ed. 1859): A "term . . . of familiarity applied to a frol-icsome child." *OED*, however, citing this line as its first instance: "One who roves or wanders," perhaps what CALDECOTT (MS 1813-33) means by "random boy." Mam-illius roves because he will run and play (294), but *young* may be secretly emphatic, for Leontes thinks Hermione ("thy selfe") a rover as well, as WILSON (ed. 1931) remarks. HENLEY (ed. 1902): "Ruffian (in endearment)." PORTER & CLARKE (ed. 1908) ask, "Does this possibly indicate that the play occupying Mamillius was a bow and a quiver full of arrows?" A *rover* in their sense, though, is not an archer but "a mark selected at will or at random" (*OED*, Rover[1] 1).

258 **Apparant**] THEOBALD (MS -1729?): "Next heire" (*OED*, B. *sb.*: "an heir-apparent," citing this line); DELIUS (ed. 1860) finds *apparent* (i.e., heir apparent) also in *3H6* 2.2.64 (936). RICHARDSON (in KNIGHT, ed. 1842) explains the phrase as "next to my heart." WILSON (ed. 1931): "Next . . . heart" "means at once 'dearest to me' and 'heir apparent' or 'claimant' to Hermione." MAHOOD (1957, p. 149) also detects a pun — "seen-through, obvious."

260 **We are yours**] DEIGHTON (ed. 1889): "You will find us."

shall's] SINGER (ed. 1856): "Shall we" (ABBOTT §215; FRANZ §285).

attend] THIRLBY (MS 1733-47?): "Wait for."

Leo. To your owne bents dispose you: you'le be found,
Be you beneath the Sky: I am angling now,
(Though you perceiue me not how I giue Lyne)
Goe too, goe too.
How she holds vp the Neb? the Byll to him?   265
And armes her with the boldnesse of a Wife
To her allowing Husband. Gone already,

---

261 you'le] you'd F3-ROWE2
262-8 I . . . one.] *Marked as aside* HARDINGE (1818, 3:52) *conj.*, KTLY
264 *Aside, observing* Her. ROWE1-THEO4; *the same, subst., marking aside from*
261 you: CAP; *the same, subst., or no SD, marking aside from* 262 Sky. JOHN, v1773+
266 *Exeunt* Polix. Her. *and Attendants. Manent* Leo. Mam. *and* Cam. ROWE1-
JOHN2, v1773-RANN, COL4 (*subst.*); *after* 268 CAP, MAL-KNT2, WH1, HAL, DEL2, KNT3
(*subst.*); *after* 267 COL1-DYCE1, STAU, KTLY (*subst.*); *after* 267 husband. COL3, CAM1,
GLO, DYCE2, DEL4, HUD2+ (*subst.*)

261-2 **To . . . Sky**] ROLFE (ed. 1879): "Dispose of yourselves according to your
inclination." DEIGHTON (ed. 1889): "In the concluding words there is the secondary
meaning, 'I shall detect your practices however secret you may be.'" Despite "I am
angling now," Michael TAYLOR (1982, p. 231) finds that "To . . . you" reveals Leontes's "own unconscious bent to be cuckolded."
    261 **bents**] THEOBALD (1726, p. 100): "Inclination, Purpose" (*OED, sb.*[2] b).
        you] COLLINS (ed. 1904-24?): "Reflexive, like *her* in line [266]."
        you'le] PAFFORD (ed. 1963) considers and rejects the possibility that the *e* may
be misprinted for *d* (representing *you'ld* = "you would," as at 1925), but insofar as
meaning is concerned, there is no need to think it might be.
        found] EVANS (ed. 1974): "With a pun on the sense 'found out.'"
    262 **Sky**] GILDEMEISTER (ed. 1870) puts the exit here rather than at 266 or later.
    262-3 **I . . . Lyne**] ENRIGHT (1970, p. 166): "This is the cunning of the suspi-
cious man, the self-congratulatory way in which, with conscious shrewdness, he sets
about confirming his suspicions." DEIGHTON (ed. 1889): "I am only 'playing' you as
a fisherman plays a fish, letting out plenty of line." Cf. DENT L304.1. SIEVEKING (1916,
2:373) finds Sh.'s references to angling generally commonplace, indicating neither
interest nor expertness in the sport (e.g., 1658 and 3091). This instance, "in which
the necessity of giving way to the rush of a large fish when first struck seems to be
alluded to," may be an exception. At 1658, Polixenes also uses an angling metaphor
to express enticement. CLEMEN (1951, p. 196): The image gives rise to 277. WATSON
(1984, p. 231), however: "Leontes has transformed himself from fisher-king to a diabolical version of Christ, the fisher of men. His bait is an apple of carnal knowledge."
For this speech as Leontes's attempt to persuade the audience of Hermione's infidelity,
see n. 272-89.
    263 **Though . . . Lyne**] With such other instances as "I know you what you
are" (*Lr.* 1.1.269 [294]) and "You heare the learnd *Bellario* what he writes" (*MV*
4.1.167 [2074]), WALKER (1860, 1:68-9) lists this line without comment but presumably as unusual syntax adopted for emphasis or as the reflection of an extraordinary
psychological state. See ABBOTT §414.

264 **Goe . . . too**] JOHNSON (1755): "Come, come. . . . A scornful exhortation." *OED* (Go 91b): "Used . . . to express disapprobation, remonstrance." Cf. n.
2575.

265-7 **How . . . Husband**] For the attention to stage business, see n. 188-91.
SLATER (1982, pp. 28-9) compares the scene in which "Othello watches Cassio laugh
with Iago about what he believes to be Cassio's affair with Desdemona.
. . . Othello's infuriated asides [e.g., 'Looke how he laughs already' (4.1.109 [2495])]
actually control the scene. . . . It is perhaps to be expected that the same technique
should be repeated in" *WT*.

265 **How . . . Neb**] MINSHEU (1617, Nebbe): "Bill, or beake." B. E. (1699): "*She
holds up her Neb*, she turns up her Snout to be Kist." HALLIWELL (ed. 1859) remembers that when lovers kiss, nose meets nose (378). But GROSE (1785) and most later
commentators extend the meaning to "mouth" (*OED, sb*. 1b, citing this line as its
first instance), which HENLEY (ed. 1902) makes "'kisser'" and MAXWELL (ed. 1956)
"face." ORGEL (ed. 1996): "The appositive that immediately follows, 'the bill', may
imply that the metaphor needed to be explained." COLES (1676) alone glosses as
"tooth," although in *AYL* 3.3.82 (1688), wedlock nibbles as pigeons bill. WILSON (ed.
1931): "No doubt Hermione glances smilingly up at Polixenes as they go out." KIT-
TREDGE & RIBNER (ed. 1967) agree: "Hermione appears to smile lovingly at Polixenes." HARRISON (ed. 1947) thinks "they bill and coo."

266 **armes her**] SCHMIDT (1874, Arm): "To fit up, to prepare, provide," a definition that DEIGHTON (ed. 1889) modifies to "behaves," *her* being reflexive, and
BEVINGTON (ed. 1992) to "assumes." Alternatively, RIDLEY (ed. 1935): "Links arms."
In *TNK* 5.3.135 (Sh.'s scene), "Arme your prize [i.e., Emily]" means "Take Emily by
the arm," but here, "her" indicates that Hermione takes Polixenes's arm.

267 **allowing**] Variously interpreted. MALONE (ed. 1790): "Approving" (*OED,
ppl.a.* 1). WILSON (ed. 1931): "Applauding" (also *ppl.a.* 1). SEYMOUR (1805, 1:158),
taking "Husband" specifically: "As Leontes cannot possibly be approving . . . , we
must [understand] '*enduring, suffering, restraining his just indignation*.'" CHED-
WORTH (1805, p. 119): The word "means the same as he before expresses by *giving
line* [263], permitting unrestrained conversation between *Polixenes* and *Hermione*."
STAUNTON (ed. 1859): "Allowed . . . lawful." STAUNTON probably means that Leontes thinks Hermione is as bold as the wife of a consenting cuckold. PORTER & CLARKE
(ed. 1908): "Complaisant." PARRY (ed. 1982), questionably: "Smugly proud of her."
See n. 1608-11 for a similar sense.

Husband] PARRY (ed. 1982, p. 24) follows earlier eds. in taking Hermione and
Polixenes off here, but to them he adds Camillo. "It would be strange if he were
present during Leontes' virulent soliloquy [268-89] without showing any reaction to
it. . . . Furthermore, [292] sounds . . . like a call to an off-stage servant." PARRY
brings Camillo back at 292. As for the exit, since Camillo's motivation for being
present seems to be to attend his lord, one wonders why he would silently leave.
Moreover, soliloquies represent thoughts, not spoken words.

Gone already] DEIGHTON (ed. 1889), literally: "*I.e.*, are they so eager to get
away from me and be alone together?" HERFORD (ed. 1916-), figuratively: "It is all
over with me; my wife is lost." PAFFORD (ed. 1963) finds a third sense: She is "departed from virtue and abandoned in sin." MATCHETT (1969, p. 98): "'Gone'—from
the scene; she has left the stage. 'Gone'—from me; my wife has left me. 'Gone'—
pregnant; she has conceived; 'Gone'—come to climax with Polixenes [cf. *Ant.* 1.2.64
(141)]."

267-72 **Gone . . . Knell**] HARRISON (ed. 1947): "The elaborate punctuation of
the Folio text . . . subtly conveys the insane jerkings of Leontes' mind." It is more
likely to be Crane's than Sh.'s, however.

Ynch-thick, knee-deepe; ore head and eares a fork'd one.   268
Goe play (Boy) play: thy Mother playes, and I

---

268 Ynch-thick, knee-deepe] DEIGHTON (ed. 1889): "Both expressive of excess, the idea in the former being of some substance usually thin [but thick like my lady's paint in *Ham.* 5.1.193 (3381)], . . . in the latter of sinking up to the knee in mud, etc." PAFFORD (ed. 1963): *Ynch-thick* "probably refers to the inch board, the thickest normal plank. To see or swear through an inch board was proverbial (Tilley, I61). The sense is 'solid, and so beyond all doubt.'" *OED*, however, gives this meaning under Inch, *sb.*[1] 4b, whereas *inch-thick*, for which this line is cited, is listed with other combinations under 4[a]. DEIGHTON and Hamlet appear to be right. On *knee-deep*, DEIGHTON is borne out by SCHMIDT (1874): "Very deep, thoroughly." PARRY's (ed. 1982) interpretation, "The imagery and movement of the line dramatise the sense of disgrace swiftly enveloping the whole person like a quicksand or mire that is at one moment 'inch-thick' and the next 'o'er head and ears,'" is probably mistaken; both terms, like *ore head and eares*, describe excess—"gone already." They are further discussed by THATCHER (1987).

ore . . . one] BETHELL (ed. 1956): "'O'er head and ears' at first [refers to the supposed love of Hermione and Polixenes], but the words suggest the growth of horns and so change their meaning as Leontes speaks." See PARRY in the n. preceding and TILLEY H268. JOHNSON (ed. 1765, Forked one): "A *horned* one; a *cuckold*." Cf. n. 192 and, as DELIUS (ed. 1860) points out, *Oth.* 3.3.276 (1907). WILSON (ed. 1931), however: "The cuckold's horns, but lately mere 'shoots' [204], have now grown 'o'er head and ears.'" PAFFORD (ed. 1963): "'Fork'd' may mean the cuckold's horns. But the whole line may refer to Hermione, . . . as deeply involved, deceitful, and double-dealing (fork'd)." Considering Hermione the subject, BOORMAN (ed. 1964) finds *fork'd one* "a crude physical reference to her," and HAPPÉ (1969) is reminded of "the forked tongue of a snake." ORGEL (ed. 1996): "Leontes begins by talking about Hermione, but the 'head and ears' inevitably bring to mind the cuckold's horns, and he concludes with himself, the 'forked one.'" YOUNG & MOSELEY (ed. 1965) note "the deliberate crudity of Leontes's imagery in this speech. It serves to heighten the impression of Leontes's self-inflicted suffering, and is indicative of the degradation of Leontes's feelings towards his family."

269-72 Goe . . . (Boy) play] For the probable origin of *play* in several senses, see p. 623. UPTON (1748, pp. 307-8): *Playes* "is used in the same sense as the Latins use *Ludere*, and the Greeks, Παιζειν [both mean 'to dally amorously']." He quotes Horace's *Odes* 4.13.4 and *Epistles* 2.2.214 and Propertius's *Elegies* 2.6.3-4, as well as Adam's intoxicated proposal to Eve after he has tasted the apple: "now let us play, As meet is, after such delicious Fare" (*Paradise Lost* 9.1027-8). For "hisse . . . Graue," HERFORD (ed. 1916-): Leontes imagines "not that he plays his part badly, but that his 'part' is one that is a disgrace to play." JONAS (1918, pp. 402-3): Other theatrical allusions may be found at 1210-11, 1764-5, 1948-9, 2467-9, 2533-4, 3088-9, and 3365-9.

MAHOOD (1951, pp. 206-7), transported by ambiguity: "Leontes is in that profoundly disturbed condition—the Elizabethans would have described it as demonic possession, we might call it a libidinous invasion—which finds its outlet in savage wordplay. . . . *Play* is saying 'Go and amuse yourself; your mother is pretending to play an innocent social game, but I know she is up to quite a different sport, and so making me act the contemptuous [sic] role of the deceived husband.' The notion of 'pretence' in each of these meanings of play reflects back upon Leontes; Shakespeare means to make it clear that *he* is playing too, in his confusion of appearance and reality. If the third *play* is thus ironic, the second is dramatic irony, because it is Hermione's play at being a statue, like his daughter's play of being a shepherdess, which is to restore Leontes to a sane discrimination of appearance from reality at the end of the play. [In MAHOOD (1957, p. 149) more puns are discovered, including *play* as 'playing her like a fish.'] *Disgrac'd* is also Leontes's pun—he means it in the double sense of 'ungraceful' and 'shameful'—which again Shakespeare counters with his meaning that Leontes is without the grace of heaven, in thus sinning against Hermione. And again, the irony is dramatic, because in the play Hermione acts the symbolic role of heavenly Grace which never deserts Leontes. *Issue* is used by Leontes for 'an actor's exit' and for 'result'. [In her 1957 work, p. 149, MAHOOD adds "perhaps also Polixenes' bastard child that Hermione now carries."] Shakespeare, however, uses it most frequently in the rest of the play to mean 'child', and here this meaning gives us a double dramatic irony. At first Leontes's play-acting has the effect of driving his child Mamillius to his grave, and himself to sixteen years of mortified existence; but ultimately his other issue, Perdita, will restore him to life. The dramatic irony of the puns here points to the reconciliation which is the theme of all these last plays." KNOWLES (privately): The bastard child may hiss Leontes because of the despicable role he has played, or *hiss* may "have figuratively a kind of passive meaning—cause to be hissed (by people in general)." ARONSON (1972, p. 195) discovers yet another frame of reference: "Leontes . . . addresses his little boy in the disillusioned language of Ulysses. Hermione, just as Cressida, is no better than any 'daughter of the game'" (*Tro.* 4.5.63 [2620]). BETHELL (ed. 1956): "The first of a series of theatrical metaphors." He repeats MAHOOD on *issue* and adds, "'Hiss', 'contempt and clamour', refer to the reaction of the people to Leontes' disgrace, but within the metaphor apply to a dissatisfied audience."

That *issue* is a theatrical word was originally the idea of WILSON (ed. 1931): "Refers to 'play . . . a part', and means the exit of a player on the conclusion of his speech." *OED* (*sb.* 1) does give "exit" as a definition, but no citation providing a theatrical association. Neither does SCHMIDT (1874). Rather than "actor's exit," the word here may mean merely "the outcome [*sb.* 10]," as MOORMAN (ed. 1912) and MAHOOD (1951, p. 207) indicate. UPHAUS (1981, p. 70): "Of the meanings of 'issue' recorded in the *OED*, the following play a significant role in *The Winter's Tale*: (1) the power of going, passing, or flowing out; egress, exit; (2) outgoing; termination, end, close; (3) a place or means of egress; way out; outlet; (4) progeny; a child or children; a descendant or descendants; (5) outcome of an action (the event or fortune befalling a person); (6) (Medicine) a discharge of blood or other matter from the body due to disease; (7) (Law) the point or question, at the conclusion of the pleadings between contending parties in an action, when one side affirms and the other denies." UPHAUS does not say where the various meanings occur. *Issue* is found 14 times in *WT* (*Issuelesse* once) and appears to mean either "outcome" or "progeny" only, the significances found in *WT* by SCHMIDT (1874). FARRELL (1975, p. 48): "The word's riddling complexity makes vivid for us Leontes' sense of bewildered entrapment in an evil drama. . . . To some extent he is aware of his own outrage as play-acting." FOAKES (1971, p. 121): Leontes is "aware of it [his passion] simultaneously as a role he is acting, and as a disease he thinks he can do nothing about." FREY (*Vast Romance*, 1980, p. 19): Leontes here, Hermione at 1210-11, Perdita at 1948-9, and Camillo at 2468-9 "conceive of their actions in terms of the stage and so invite the audience to keep in focus the theatricality of the whole." WEXLER (1988, p. 113): "The pun that connects a child's diversion to a wife's deception and a husband's shame suggests that every act is false." WEXLER connects these words as well with Perdita's playing the part of Flora in 4.4 and with "I see the Play so lyes, That I must beare a part" (2533-4), spoken as she escapes from Bohemia in disguise. "This pun also yokes the necessity of acting to the certainty of lying."

Play too; but so disgrac'd a part, whose issue   270
Will hisse me to my Graue: Contempt and Clamor
Will be my Knell. Goe play (Boy) play, there haue been
(Or I am much deceiu'd) Cuckolds ere now,
And many a man there is (euen at this present,

---

270 **disgrac'd**] In addition to the meanings given in n. 269-72, MAXWELL (in PAFFORD, ed. 1963), comparing *well-graced* in *R2* 5.2.24 (2391), suggests "unpopular"; and HAPPÉ (1969) offers "having lost honour and respect."

271 **Contempt and Clamor**] Following SCHMIDT (1874, And), DEIGHTON (ed. 1889): "Probably a hendiadys for 'contemptuous clamour,'" but not so considered by WRIGHT (1981). See n. 904-5. FURNESS (ed. 1898): "'Clamour' here is rather the derisive shouts of Leontes's subjects" (*OED* 1, citing this line).

272-89 **there . . . not**] BETHELL (ed. 1956): "A 'direct address' to the audience (see [275]: 'Now . . . this') and suggests the frequency of adultery *in the real world*. Coarse language is used to convey a sense of revulsion. 'Sir Smile' looks back to the 'practis'd smiles' of [189]. 'Gates' [see n. 279] are the floodgates opened for 'sluicing', in the fishing metaphor used for the sexual act. Leontes goes on to find a cause in astrology for the prevalence of adultery [see n. 283-4]. The second metaphor [285-8] is taken from siege operations, a frequent figure for sexual love." EGGERS (1977, p. 38): Leontes's "interpretation of the story has carried the authority of frequent solo speeches and asides, and at times [here and at 262-3 especially] he has even seemed cognizant of his audience [which is asked] to grant Leontes the authority he has demanded and to see things his way." At 262-3, however, the "you" is clearly Hermione and Polixenes, not the audience. Here "Now, while I speake this" makes EGGERS's assertion more persuasive. LAWLOR (1962, p. 109): "The tempo is rapid, the sense contorted as each fresh emphasis comes crowding parenthetically in; the speaker would enfold all men in his savage misery." "With Leontes' outburst here and elsewhere on the faithlessness of women," PAFFORD (ed. 1963) and others compare "the similarly mistaken Posthumus in *Cym.*, II.iv and v." The violation of the pond in 277 recurs in *Cym.* 1.4.89 (403). For more on the imagery, see n. 1362-89.

273 **Or . . . deceiu'd**] PARRY (ed. 1982): In a double sense.

274-8 **many . . . Neighbor**] WILSON (ed. 1931): *Euen . . . speake this* is a "side-glance at the audience followed up in [284-8] by 'think it . . . know't . . . many thousands on's.'" RIGHTER (1962, pp. 61-2) connects the notion of direct address with "traditional moralizings on the weakness of humanity" that allow "the dramatist to stress the intimacy of audience and actors while preserving inviolate the dramatic distance necessary to the life of the illusion." WAIN (1964, p. 12): "The insistent 'even . . . this' [274-5] is a finger pointed directly at the audience, reminding each of us that we are in a theatre, among a crowd of strangers, any one of whom might conceivably represent a threat to our emotional security." STYAN (1967, p. 144): F1 "is precise in punctuating for speech: the first parentheses abruptly cutting into the line of thought, its broken, staccato fling at the audience a little shrill, its triple repetition, 'even at this present' . . . 'now' . . . 'while I speak this', forcing a rising pitch by its urgency. Following upon this, the ugly jocularity embodies a sarcastic imagery which prompts the exact quality of feeling, jaundiced, defensive; while the sibilants, often stressing sexual bitterness elsewhere in Shakespeare ('sluiced in's absence' . . . 'fished' . . . 'Sir Smile') accumulate in a progression of increasing vocal emphasis. The repetition of 'neighbour' doubles the insinuation, and the second parenthetical phrase points the anger in the voice and suggests a quick turn upon the spectators, while the running-on accelerates the expression of

Now, while I speake this) holds his Wife by th'Arme,   275
That little thinkes she ha's been sluyc'd in's absence,
And his Pond fish'd by his next Neighbor (by
Sir *Smile*, his Neighbor:) nay, there's comfort in't,
Whiles other men haue Gates, and those Gates open'd
(As mine) against their will. Should all despaire   280
That haue reuolted Wiues, the tenth of Mankind
Would hang themselues. Physick for't, there's none:

---

276 ha's] hath AYS2, MAL

---

emotion." ORNSTEIN (1986, p. 220): "Leontes' fantasies of country matters are uniquely pastoral. . . . His rage at Polixenes is that of a petty freeholder who bites his lip when his aristocratic neighbor assumes the right to fish in his private pond."

276 **sluyc'd**] KERSEY (1702): "*To let in,* or *keep out water.*" HENN (1972, p. 62): "Either dragging the pond with a net, or opening a sluice of a particular pond so that it is drained, and the fish easily captured." CAPELL (1783 [1774], 1:glos., Open Sluices) recognizes, however, that Leontes is not thinking of drainage. So does COLMAN (1974): "As = to fuck." COLMAN is also explicit on *Pond* (277) and *Gates* (279). HAPPÉ (1969): "'Pour water over' (for sexual intercourse)."

277 **his Pond fish'd**] CLEMEN (1951, p. 196): For the origin of the image, see n. 262-3. MAHOOD (1957, p. 149), oddly, thinks *stews* may be suggested. MARSH (1962; 1969, p. 130): His wife "is a possession, who will betray her owner at the first opportunity, and one which it is impossible to guard." PAFFORD (ed. 1963) compares "strange Fowle light vpon neighbouring Ponds" (*Cym.* 1.4.89 [403]).

next] SCHMIDT (1875): "Nearest." Cf. n. 1563.

278 **Sir *Smile***] FURNESS (ed. 1898): "Possibly suggested by a smile on the face of Polixenes, whom Leontes is furtively watching," though most eds. take the couple off at 266 approximately. LEE (ed. 1907) compares "*Signior* Sooth" in *Per.* 1.2.44 (268), and PAFFORD (ed. 1963) finds several "satiric use[s] of *Sir* with a noun" — e.g., "Sir Prudence" (*Tmp.* 2.1.286 [985]) — as well as ten other linkings of smiling with villainy in Sh. ("the association goes back at least to Chaucer — 'The smyler with the knyf under the cloke' [Knight's Tale, 1141/1999]"). For more types "individualized by a courtesy title," see LEVIN (1965, pp. 81-2). Sir Smile's type is hypocrite. ARMSTRONG (1963, p. 207): Sh. "connected fishing with smiling because both were associated with lines. . . . Line = wrinkle = smile, but line also = fishing line, therefore 'smile' and fishing became associated."

comfort in't] PAFFORD (ed. 1963): "'I am not the first and shall not be the last.'" He compares "It is good to have Company in trouble (misery)" (TILLEY C571). C. G. SMITH (1963, no. 30) finds parallels in Leonhard Culmann, *Sententiae Pueriles,* Publilius Syrus, *Sententiae,* and elsewhere.

279 **Whiles**] ABBOTT (§137): "Genitive of *while* . . . 'of, or during, the time.'"

Gates] Recognizing the idea of a private fishing preserve violated, THIRLBY MS (1747-53): "Floodgates." FURNESS (ed. 1898): "Carrying out the simile of 'sluyc'd [276].'" WEBB (1989) gives other examples of *gate* as "vulva" and WILLIAMS (1994) as "vagina." For *pond* as "womb," cf. *Cym.* 1.4.89 (403).

281 **reuolted**] SCHMIDT (1875): "Faithless." *OED (ppl.a,* citing this line): "That has cast off allegiance; rebel, insurgent."

282 **Physick . . . none**] ENRIGHT (1970, p. 166): "No prevention, therefore no fault or defect implied in him [Leontes]."

Physick] KERSEY (1708): "A Remedy in general, a Purge."

It is a bawdy Planet, that will strike
Where 'tis predominant; and 'tis powrefull: thinke it:
From East, West, North, and South, be it concluded,   285
No Barricado for a Belly. Know't,
It will let in and out the Enemy,
With bag and baggage: many thousand on's
Haue the Disease, and feele't not. How now Boy?
    Mam. I am like you say.   290
    Leo. Why, that's some comfort.
What? *Camillo* there?
    Cam. I, my good Lord.

284-8 and . . . baggage:] *Degr.* HAN
    284-5 it: . . . South,] ~ . . . . ~ . JOHN; ~ , . . . ~ : mTBY2 *conj.*, CAP-CAM3, KIT1-ALEX, PEL1+ (−OXF2); ~ , . . . ~ , RID, SIS
    285-8 From . . . baggage:] *Om.* WARB (*lining* 288-9 Many . . . not. | How now, boy?)
    288 thousand on's] a thousand one's F4; a thousand of's ROWE1-v1773 (−CAP); a thousand of us v1778-SING1, HAL; thousand of us KNT; a thousand on's COL, HUD1, WH1, STAU, DEL, OXF1, CLN2
    290 you] you they F2+
    292-3 *One verse line* mCAP2, DYCE2, HUD2, IRV, BUL, CAM3(?), SIS, BEV, OXF2
    292 *Camillo*] is *Camillo* HAN, JOHN, CAP

283-4 **It . . . predominant**] BETHELL (ed. 1956, It): "Lust." CARRINGTON (1956): "Venus," the planet. DELIUS (ed. 1860) compares, for poetic creation rather than biological, "I was not born vnder a riming plannet" (*Ado* 5.2.40 [2459]) to make the point that, whereas other planets influence circumscribed actions, the bawdy one exerts its power everywhere. SCHMIDT (1875, Strike): "Applied to superhuman powers, especially to the influence of planets, = to blast, to destroy, to confound." For *predominant*, SCHMIDT (1875) gives "Prevalent, supreme in influence; used of planets." HAPPÉ (1969): "In the ascendant." DEIGHTON (ed. 1889): "The star [or planet] which rules these matters is a lustful one and will strike those under it, do what they may," and, according to CHARLTON (ed. 1916), those struck will be wives and the striking will make them unfaithful. PAFFORD (ed. 1963): "The unfaithfulness of wives is like a bawdy planet which will spread ruin wherever it is in the ascendant." ALLEN (1941, p. 158) compares Maquarelle's assertion, in Marston's *The Malcontent*, that if you "court any woman in the right [astrological] sign, you shall not miss. . . . as, when the sign is in Pisces, a fishmonger's wife is very sociable [etc.]" (ed. Hunter, 1975, 5.2.65 ff.).
    283 **strike**] GARDNER (1980, pp. 65-6): "The word seems to play a pivotal role, as it appears at each of the . . . climactic moments in Leontes' life." Here "he accuses Hermione of adultery"; at 1330-1, Apollo strikes at his injustice; at 2746-7, he is struck by the memory of Hermione's death and his responsibility for it; at 3306-8, music is struck to awaken the statue, the movement of which strikes all with wonder.
    284 **predominant**] VAN DAM (1900, p. 67): Pronounced *predom'nant.*

284-5 **'tis powrefull . . . South**] RANN (ed. 1787): "Acts powerfully all over the world."

284-8 **thinke . . . on's**] See n. 274-8.

284-6 **thinke it . . . Know't**] PAFFORD (ed. 1963): "Be assured . . . be certain of it."

285-8 **be . . . baggage**] MUIR (1957, p. 247): From *Pandosto* (B2ᵛ) Sh. "borrows a phrase describing the sudden flight of Egistus— 'for *Egistus* fearing that delay might breede daunger, and willing that the grasse should not be cut from vnder his feete, taking bagge and baggage with the helpe of *Franion*, conueyed himself and his men out of a posterne gate of the Citie.'" See p. 625.

285 **East . . . South**] YOUNG & MOSELEY (ed. 1965): Human beings are so lustful "that Venus has power whatever position it may have in the sky." For other astrological allusions, see n. 1278.

286 **Barricado**] The Elizabethan form, *OED*'s first citation of *barricade* being 1642. BULLOKAR (1616): "A warlike defence, of emptie Barrels . . . laide at the breach of a wall to keepe out the enemies." MINSHEU (1617) says the Fr. *barríques* "were filled with earth, to defend against shot," which might be the idea underlying Leontes's metaphor.

Belly] *OED* (*sb.* 7): "The womb, the uterus." This word is the antecedent of "It" (287).

288 **bag and baggage**] KNOWLES (privately): "Continuing the siege metaphor." WEBB (1989): "Leontes' grievous concerns are with both infidelity and bastardy; the individual words may therefore suggest both the male genitals and the unborn child." The idea of the unborn child is far-fetched. PARTRIDGE (1969, Let in) is more likely to be right that "bag = scrotum; baggage, probably = penis (? and testicles)." SMITH (1972, p. 113): Sh. seems to have remembered these words from *Pandosto* (see p. 625); Egistus's luggage was transformed because of Sh.'s "associations with the word *baggage*, which can be well illustrated from one of the brothel scenes in *Pericles* [i.e., 4.2.22-5]."

on's] SINGER (ed. 1856), objecting to *of us*: "*On* was frequently used for *of* and *of* for *on* [FRANZ §500], and it [*on*] is here characteristic of the tone of the speaker." *On* for possessive *of* was common idiom, however; see ABBOTT §182.

289 **Haue the Disease**] BETHELL (1947, pp. 80-1): I.e., "to be a cuckold." To be an adultress is also a disease (see 400-1), "and, more important, Leontes himself according to Camillo is diseased in 'opinion' [391]." Compare 1010-11. For jealousy as disease, see n. 390-1.

How now Boy?] For *how now*, see n. 201. PARRY (ed. 1982): "On the stage, as on the page, the speech has been a restless wandering in which Leontes has forgotten his son, with whom he now comes face to face."

290-1 **I . . . comfort**] PYLE (1969, p. 23): Leontes has kept Mamillius "at a distance [269, 272]; and when the boy insists on receiving attention by saying what he knows will please . . . , Leontes answers half-abstractedly, and kindly but firmly sends him away." Leontes's answer (291) might be bitter rather than abstracted and spoken to himself rather than to Mamillius. To us it is a reminder of Hermione's fidelity, which Leontes takes to be merely a former fidelity.

290 **say**] Instead of the universal emendation (for support of which, see 205), COLLIER (ed. 1842) suggests *like you*, you *say*, "the old printer having omitted the repetition of the pronoun."

292 **What? *Camillo* there?**] TRAVERSI (1954, p. 117): "In the following exchange with Camillo, his [Leontes's] concern is not so much to discover the truth as to confirm what he holds in his own mind to be certain."

Leo. Goe play (*Mamillius*) thou'rt an honest man:
Camillo, this great Sir will yet stay longer.   295

    Cam. You had much adoe to make his Anchor hold,
When you cast out, it still came home.

    Leo. Didst note it?

    Cam. He would not stay at your Petitions, made   (2A2

His Businesse more materiall.   300

    Leo. Didst perceiue it?
They're here with me already; whisp'ring, rounding:
Sicilia is a so-forth: 'tis farre gone,

---

294 *Exit* Mamillius. ROWE1+
295 SCENE III. POPE, HAN, WARB, JOHN
296 his] the HAN
299 Petitions, made∧] ~ ∧ ~ ; POPE1-JOHN2
302-3 *Marked as aside* HAN
302-4 They're . . . last.] *Marked as aside* CAP, MAL+
302 whisp'ring, rounding] whisp'ring round HAN
303 Sicilia . . . so-forth] F1-JOHN2 (−HAN), WH2, BEV, OXF2; *Sicilia* is a— so forth
HAN, SIS; Sicilia is a—*so forth* RANN; *Sicilia is a*—so forth MAL, COL, WH1; *Sicilia is
a—so forth* V1821, KNT, HUD, STAU, DEL, DYCE2, IRV, BUL, CAM3; Sicilia *is a so-forth*
CAP *etc.*

---

294 **thou'rt . . . man**] DEIGHTON (ed. 1889): "*I.e.* not disgraced as I am." Probably, however, a general term of approbation (*OED, a.* 1c). FURNESS (ed. 1898) suggests a comparison with Polixenes, *thou* being emphasized. WILSON (ed. 1931), comparing "Mine honest Friend" (239), thinks *honest* here means "legitimate." As
PAFFORD (ed. 1963) notes, the word may have that additional meaning at 239. WILSON,
further: "The usual Shakespearian form is 'th'art'; cf. [n. 622]." In *WT*, *thou'rt* also
occurs at 1496. By placing Mamillius's exit after this line, all eds. suggest that these
words are spoken to him. CARRINGTON (1956), however: "Spoken to Camillo."

    295 **Sir**] The CLARKES (ed. 1865): "Shakespeare, in several instances, uses 'sir' as
a noun-substantive [e.g., *TN* 3.4.73 (1596), *Cym.* 1.6.160 (778)]." See also 2184. *OED*
gives instances from other early writers.

    yet] DEIGHTON (ed. 1889): "In spite of his previous refusals."

    296-7 **You . . . home**] WILSON (ed. 1931): "Camillo is the perfect courtier and
amplifies his master's observations."

    297 **When . . . home**] When you dropped it, his anchor never held. MAN-
WAYRING (1644, p. 3): "The Anchor comes home, that is, when the Ship drives away
with the tyde or sea"; *home* is "towards or into the ship" (*OED, adv.* 3; see also
Anchor, *sb.* 6e). TANNENBAUM (1928, p. 361) regards these words as "a lapse in
Shakspere's artistry [that is] dramatically, not psychologically determined; unless we
take the view that . . . the relations between [Camillo] and the king were of such
an intimate nature that he took the liberty to tease his sovereign." Which is the view
we do take. According to WEBB (1989): "Camillo's choice of metaphor is unfortunate," for *cast anchor* is a euphemism for sexual intercourse. According to Camillo,
however, Leontes, not Polixenes, is doing the casting.

96

The Winters Tale 1.2.214-18

298 **Didst note it?**] BERNARD (1979, pp. 221-2): "Both halves of the play make much ado about noting." Leontes uses the word *note* here and at 311. "Other characters refer repeatedly to both the word and the act," at 38, 380, 1644, 1655, 1715, 2934, 3021, 3025, and 3359. "There even seems to be a deliberate pun on the word in Polixenes' speech at [51]." Perhaps BERNARD refers to the two meanings distinguished there by SCHMIDT and PAFFORD. See n. 51.

299 **stay**] HEATH (1765, p. 204): "Not . . . to tarry, but, to put off, or delay" (*OED, v.*¹ 3).

299-300 **made . . . materiall**] STEEVENS (ed. 1778): "The more you requested him to stay, the more urgent he represented that business to be that summoned him away." ROLFE (ed. 1879): Or made his business "more urgent than your *petitions.*" HUNT ("Standing," 1984, p. 20): "'Business' denotes 'private affairs'. But within the context of Leontes's jealousy, the term refers to adultery. Polixenes's imagined adultery was more important (more 'material') in detaining him than Leontes's pleas were." For *materiall,* SCHMIDT (1875) gives "important." HALLIWELL (ed. 1859): "The elision of the personal pronoun is common in this kind of construction"—i.e., where the subject is not in doubt. See ABBOTT §§399-401 and cf. 1992.

301 **Didst perceiue it?**] YOUNG & MOSELEY (ed. 1965): "Leontes assumes from Camillo's reply that his counsellor is aware of Hermione's infidelity." For the omission of *thou,* see ABBOTT §241.

302 **They're . . . already**] THIRLBY (MS 1747-53): "Not P[olixenes] & Hermione but people, the observers." COLLIER (ed. 1842): "They are aware of my condition." Citing *Cor.* 3.2.74 (2175), STAUNTON (ed. 1859) treats *here with me* as "a common form of speech" meaning "mock"; hence, "the King means,—the people are already mocking me with this opprobrious gesture (the cuckold's emblem with their fingers)." In *Cor.*, however, the expression means "do it (i.e., kneel) this way." Later, STAUNTON (1874, p. 462) adduces a more apposite parallel from Chapman's *May Day:* "as often as he turnes his backe to me, I shall be here [*makes* V] with him thats certaine" (ed. Welsh, 1970, 4.6.59-60), where the V "represents the actor's fingers in making horns." Leontes probably thinks of people deriding him as a cuckold, but, as FURNESS (ed. 1898) remarks, it is doubtful that he makes the gesture. See n. 303. As for the expression, SCHMIDT (1875, With): "They go so far with respect to me as to whisper." RIDLEY (ed. 1935): "They're on to it."

rounding] JOHNSON (ed. 1765): "*To round in the ear,* is to *whisper,* or *to tell secretly*" (*OED, v.*² 2, citing this line); STEEVENS (ed. 1785) compares Kyd, *The Spanish Tragedy* 1.1.81, where Boas and later eds. also gloss *rounded* as "whispered." To avoid the redundancy with *whisp'ring,* HARNESS (ed. 1825) guesses at "*hinting,* or *telling by circumlocution,*" a sense unsupported by *OED.* As COLLIER (ed. 1842, 1: cclxxxvi) mentions, Dyce in *The Poetical Works of John Skelton* (1843, 2:120)— noting that *whisper* and *round* are distinguished by Skelton, Lydgate, and Barclay as well as by Sh.—considers the latter to mean "mutter." *OED* includes "whisper" and "mutter" under Round (*v.*² 1), but the definition under Mutter *v.*¹ 1—"To speak in low tones, with the mouth nearly closed, so that one's words are barely audible"— may draw a fine distinction. Perhaps no distinction is necessary; Leontes could be repeating himself for emphasis; for similar repetitions, see 595, 634, 856, 890, 916, 1208, and 1214-16. Because the word is etymologically associated with *rune,* MOORMAN (ed. 1912) offers "Whispering with an air of mystery," but *rune* is not in Sh.'s vocabulary.

303 **so-forth**] EVANS (ed. 1974): "You-know-what." STEEVENS (ed. 1793): Used "when the speaker . . . wished to escape the utterance of an obnoxious term," here *cuckold. OED,* citing this instance only, refers to Forth (*adv.* 9b)— "And so forth"— "used . . . in breaking off an enumeration, quotation, etc." KNOWLES (privately): "Cf. *OED,* Et cetera, 2b." MAXWELL (ed. 1969): "Perhaps Leontes, unable to say 'cuckold', puts two fingers to his head to suggest horns." But see n. 302.

97

When I shall gust it last. How cam't (*Camillo*)
That he did stay?   305
    Cam. At the good Queenes entreatie.
    Leo. At the Queenes be't: Good should be pertinent,
But so it is, it is not. Was this taken
By any vnderstanding Pate but thine?
For thy Conceit is soaking, will draw in   310
More then the common Blocks. Not noted, is't,
But of the finer Natures? by some Seueralls
Of Head-peece extraordinarie? Lower Messes

---

310 thy] the F3-ROWE2
311 the] *Om.* HARN

303-4 **'tis . . . last**] THIRLBY (MS 1725-33?): "Dedecus ille domus sciet ulti-
mus"—loosely, "the cuckold is the last to know" (TILLEY C877, from Juvenal, *Satires*
10.342). COCKERAM (1623) glosses *gust* as "Taste" (*OED, v.*[1], which adds "relish");
JOHNSON (1755), as "love; liking"; RANN (ed. 1787), as "perceive"; and HENLEY (ed.
1902), oddly, as "nose," meaning the verb, no doubt. WARREN (1970) objects to
RANN's sort of extension of the meaning, as missing "the crucial tone of much of
Leontes's language in this scene and the next. . . . The physical implication of relishing taste in 'gust' . . . emphasizes how much Leontes is relishing, indulging in,
his jealousy." WARREN finds further evidence of "what Fitzroy Pyle calls the 'delighted
pain he causes himself'" in *cordial* (415), in the contrast between "How blest am
I . . . in my true Opinion" and "how accurs'd, In being so blest" (633-6), and in
the sight of the "Spider steep'd" (637-42), the last especially conveying "that mixture
of horror and satisfaction which characterizes his language." WARREN compares *Son.*
114.11, where *gust* also appears. Eds. nevertheless disagree somewhat on what Leontes means. HUDSON (ed. 1852): "The knowledge of my disgrace has spread far, since
all have it before myself." DEIGHTON (ed. 1889): "Matters . . . must be very bad
when they are *so* bad that no one dare speak of them to me." YOUNG & MOSELEY
(ed. 1965): "Since the cuckold was proverbially last to hear of his plight, Leontes
declares that the affair . . . must have been going on for a long time."
    303 **farre gone**] Polixenes's words at 2166. PAFFORD (ed. 1963): At 2275, *farre*
represents the comparative, but in nine other instances in *WT*, including this one, it
probably does not. See, however, nn. 182, 2275, and 3355.
    304-8 **How . . . not**] MIRIAM JOSEPH (1947, p. 175): "A conjunction of prop-
ositions is true only if all of its parts are true. It is false if any part is false. . . . Leontes
denies the conjunction asserted by Camillo, for in his jealous frenzy he will not allow
that Hermione is good." Cf. 2445-7, where "Perdita will not agree that both propositions are true."
    306 **At . . . entreatie**] *Good* here is "the conventional epithet prefixed to titles
of high rank" (*OED, a.* 2b, citing this line). HERFORD (ed. 1916-): "Camillo's innocently fatal words may be compared with Desdemona's equally innocent pleading for
Cassio at the moment when Othello's suspicion is awakened [3.3.45 ff. (1639 ff.)]."
    307 **pertinent**] SCHMIDT (1875): "Apposite." BETHELL (ed. 1956): "Applicable."
    308 **so . . . not**] For *so it is*, RANN (ed. 1787): "Being so applied." PORTER &
CLARKE (ed. 1908): "As it happens." HAPPÉ (1969): "Things being as they are." For

the expression, the CLARKES (ed. 1865): "But as the case exists, the word 'good' is not pertinent."

taken] HUNTER (ed. 1872): "Perceived." Cf. 577 and 817.

310-11 **For . . . Blocks**] JOHNSON (1755, Conceit): "Understanding; readiness of apprehension." WHITE (ed. 1857): "The omission of a pronoun or a conjunction here [before 'will draw in'], as [at 299-300] 'made . . . material', is a characteristic trait of the style of Elizabethan dramatic writers." The CLARKES (ed. 1865) associate "Blocks" with heads, blocks being molds for hats (*OED, sb.* 4a) and believe that Sh. punningly extends the word to mean "heads," though *blockhead(ed)* was current in the mid-16th c. (*OED*). Thus SCHMIDT (1874): "A stupid or insensible fellow." HERFORD (ed. 1916-): "Camillo's fine understanding, like a sponge, takes in matters that would make no impression on the common blocks" (cf. *OED, ppl.a.* 1, citing this line). SCHMIDT (1875), like HERFORD, takes *soaking* literally—"to draw in by the pores; to imbibe"—but MAXWELL (ed. 1956) glosses the word as "absorbing."

311-13 **Not . . . extraordinarie?**] For "But . . . Natures," SCHANZER (ed. 1969): "Except by the keener minds." For "by . . . extraordinarie," LEE (ed. 1907): "By some individuals [*OED*, Nature, *sb.* 3] of more than ordinary intellect." HUDSON (ed. 1852): "Leontes' fanatical passion . . . stuff[s] him with the conceit of a finer nature, a sharper insight, and a higher virtue than others had." BETHELL (ed. 1956), rather differently: "In his perversity [he] describes as 'finer natures' those who can detect adulteries." TURNER (1971, p. 155): "Shakespeare uses the extravagant language of 'wit.'"

311 **noted**] For other instances of noting, see n. 298.

312 **Seueralls**] JOHNSON (1755, citing this line): "Each particular singly taken." JERVIS (1868): "An individual" (*OED, sb.* 3c). CARRINGTON (1956): "Implying there were few." SCHMIDT (1875) finds this usage only here; for others, see nn. 554 and 2009. For adjectives used as nouns, see ABBOTT §5.

313 **Head-peece**] Although FURNESS (ed. 1898) thinks "the choice of the word was, possibly, still influenced by 'block,'" Leontes's line of thought has changed. For this word SCHMIDT (1874) offers "Helmet" generally and here "used of the skull as containing the brain and seat of thought."

extraordinarie] WHITE (ed. 1857) thinks the word "has its full original complement of six syllables," and DOBSON (1968, 2:466) supplies evidence of secondary stress on the penultimate syllable. The line thus seems to have six feet. VAN DAM (1900, p. 50) and CERCIGNANI (1981, p. 280), however, postulate the loss of the unaccented vowel before the *n*. For other syncopations of *i*, see nn. 162, 942, and 3369.

Lower Messes] STEEVENS (ed. 1773) corrects JOHNSON's (ed. 1765) "graduates of a lower form [grade in school]" to "the lowest degrees about the court," those given inferior food at table. He cites Beaumont & Fletcher, *The Woman Hater* 1.2.79. PERCY (in STEEVENS, ed. 1773, 10:Mm2) modifies this slightly to "courtiers of lower rank and less consideration," citing *The Regulations and Establishment of the Household of Henry Algernon Percy, the fifth Earl of Northumberland* (ed. *Thomas Percy*, 1905), in which, for example, service "for ij Mease of Gentilmen of Houshold at Suppers on Scamlynge Days in Lent" is specified (p. 83). A mess here could be specifically a group of four, a sense of the word known to Sh. (*LLL* 4.3.203 [1551] and cf. 1809 below). To MADDEN (1897, p. 92), the meaning is "somewhat akin to that of the masses, whom some are used to contrast with the classes who sit above the Salt." STEEVENS (ed. 1778), finding in *A Merye Jest of a Man That Was Called Howleglas* ([1528?], sigs. E2 f.) that public houses kept "ordinaries of different prices," connects the lower messes with "purblind" (314), because "inferiority of understanding is, on this occasion, comprehended in the idea of inferiority of rank." RITSON's (1783, p. 68) assertion that *mess* is "the Scottish pronunciation of *Mass*, and is only applied . . . to the *priest* or *minister*" and AYSCOUGH's (ed. 1790) that it "is

Perchance are to this Businesse purblind? say.

  Cam. Businesse, my Lord? I thinke most vnderstand   315
Bohemia stayes here longer.

  Leo. Ha?

  Cam. Stayes here longer.

  Leo. I, but why?

  Cam. To satisfie your Highnesse, and the Entreaties   320
Of our most gracious Mistresse.

  Leo. Satisfie?

Th'entreaties of your Mistresse? Satisfie?

Let that suffice. I haue trusted thee (*Camillo*)

With all the neerest things to my heart, as well   325

My Chamber-Councels, wherein (Priest-like) thou

Hast cleans'd my Bosome: I, from thee departed

316-19 316-18 *one verse line, then* 319 v1793-BEV3; 316, *then* 317-19 *one verse
line* BEV4

318 *Cam.*] *Om.* HAN

    Stayes] *Bohemia* stays CAP

322 Satisfie?] ∼ ∧ THEO1-HUD2 (−HAN, CAM1, GLO, DEL4), IRV, BUL, ALEX-PEL1, SIG

325 neerest . . . my] things nearest my POPE1-JOHN2; things nearest to my OXF1
as well] with all HAN; as well as CAPN *conj.*, KTLY

326 Chamber-Councels] chamber-counsels WH1, CAM3, ARD2-PEN2, K&R, OXF2

327 I,] I∧ POPE1-ARD1, KIT1, ALEX-ARD2, PEN2+; ay, FURNESS (ed. 1898) *conj.*,
CAM3, N&H, SIG

---

a contraction of *master*, an appellation used by Scots," are irrelevant. VAN DAM (1900,
p. 47): The *e* of *Lower* is syncopated; see also *extraordinarie* above. For other syncopations of *e*, see nn. 222, 381, 692, 813, 1302, and 2953.

    314 **purblind**] JOHNSON (1755, citing this line): "Nearsighted" (*OED, a.* 2b).
SCHMIDT (1875), however: "Quite blind" (*a.* 1).

    315 **Businesse, my Lord?**] DEIGHTON (ed. 1889): "Why do you use the term
'business'?" KNOWLES (privately): "What business do you mean?"

    315-16 **I . . . longer**] PARRY (ed. 1982): Nonplussed, Camillo "loses the thread
of the conversation for a moment."

    317-19 **Ha? . . . why?**] For metrical arrangements, see above. For attempts to
mend the meter by emendation, see p. 571.

    317 **Ha?**] FURNESS (ed. 1898): "Leontes evidently expected a different conclusion
to Camillo's sentence, after mentioning Bohemia." PAFFORD (ed. 1963): "Do they
think only that?" BOORMAN (ed. 1964): "Leontes' angry questioning tone is misunderstood by Camillo, who repeats his last words."

    321 **gracious**] See n. 1639.

    322-4 **Satisfie? . . . suffice**] HOLBROOK (1964, p. 150): "He imagines he has a
hint of calumny . . . and Leontes runs away with [the word's] physical sense, not
its courtesy value, meaning 'clear by proof.'" For *satisfie*, ORGEL (ed. 1996) compares
Rom. 2.2.125-6 (925-6). KNOWLES (privately): "Leontes sarcastically mocks the (he
thinks) pretended innocence of Camillo by repeating his words to show that he recognizes and to emphasize (if not sardonically savor) their bawdy meaning. 'Let that

suffice' means, this statement of yours shows you understand perfectly well what's going on; you need say no more—and so he proceeds to accuse Camillo of complicity." See the next n.

322–3 Satisfie? . . . Satisfie?] DEIGHTON (ed. 1889): "What do you mean by satisfying the entreaties of your mistress? do you mean satisfy her impure desires?" He notes "a similar repetition made by Othello in similar circumstances[:] . . . 'What committed?' [thrice]" (*Oth.* 4.2.72, 76, 80 [2768, 2772, 2776]). BETHELL (ed. 1956): "Leontes . . . thinks that by it [this word] the courtier Camillo intended to convey delicately that he knows of Hermione's (supposed) adultery."

323–4 your . . . thee] For the possible significance of the pronouns, see n. 359.

324–8 I . . . reform'd] MUTSCHMANN & WENTERSDORF (1950; 1952, p. 212) find that because Sh. repeatedly favors Catholic dogmas, ideas, and customs, and expresses "an aversion to Protestant preachers and teachings," his "personal views are quite clearly pro-Catholic and anti-Protestant." Into the pagan setting of *WT* Sh. interjects here a reference to the confession of sins; at 1397–1401, mortification of the flesh; at 1713, derision of psalm singing, a Protestant custom; at 2777–9, free will exercised in opposition to the will of heaven; and at 3235–6, the blessing of a child by its parent. All these are, of course, compatible with Anglican as well as with Roman Catholic opinion.

325 neerest things] HUNTER (ed. 1872): Things nearest. For other examples of this construction, see WALKER (1860, 2:160–79) or ABBOTT §419.

   as well] CALDECOTT (MS 1813–33): "Together with, as well as."

326 Chamber-Councels] CAPELL (1783, 2.4:164, Chamber): "Cabinet" or "the private room in which the confidential advisers of the sovereign . . . meet" (*OED* 7). Hence, for the compound, *OED* (Chamber, *sb.* 13, citing this line): "Private counsel or business." By "the neerest things to my heart," Leontes may mean only what SCHMIDT (1874) calls "private thought or care, as opposed to public business." BETHELL (ed. 1956), nevertheless: "Deliberations on state affairs." FURNESS (ed. 1898) supports SCHMIDT, in rather ominous terms: "The *private chamber-councils* involved no questions of state, or government, but were concerned with the private life of Leontes, with impure deeds from which the bosom of Leontes should be cleansed [327], and for which he should repent and depart a penitent. This reference to the past life of Leontes brings his character into harmony with what is known to experts in Mental Diseases, that those patients who are victims of sudden attacks of insane jealousy are, at times, not free from the reproach which they insanely ascribe to the objects of their suspicion." FURNESS is followed by STEWART (1949, p. 105): "Leontes's suppressed impulse to infidelity finds as it were excuse and license by projecting the infidelity upon another" (see n. 181–92). However, TANNENBAUM (1928, p. 360), who describes himself as "a professional psychotherapeutist," observes "that persons given to promiscuity do not suspect their mates to be guilty of illicit relationships just because they themselves are guilty." Be that as it may, the reason for Leontes's penitence is unstated, and lust is but one of the sins requiring absolution. Hence SCHANZER (ed. 1969): "It is unwarrantable to assume that this must refer to sexual transgressions." For another critic who does not think so, see n. 649–54. As for the reading, COLLINS (ed. 1904–24?) favors WHITE's (see textual n.), evidently because it means "a secret; a confidence" (*OED, sb.* 5b).

327 cleans'd my Bosome] SCHMIDT (1874) considers the meaning here to be "scarcely distinguishable from *heart*," as is also the case at 186 and 881. For another meaning, see n. 2430. DELIUS (ed. 1860) compares "Cleanse the stufft bosome" (*Mac.* 5.3.44 [2266]), where what is cleansed is perilous stuff that weighs on the heart. BOORMAN (ed. 1964), tamely: "Relieved my mind." PAFFORD (ed. 1963): "Camillo has clearly acted as a kind of father-confessor to Leontes," an apparently inappropriate role for a pagan Sicilian, but see n. 533.

I] FURNESS (ed. 1898): "'Ay', . . . the intensive affirmation of Leontes that not

Thy Penitent reform'd: but we haue been
Deceiu'd in thy Integritie, deceiu'd
In that which seemes so.   330
    Cam. Be it forbid (my Lord.)
    Leo. To bide vpon't: thou art not honest: or
If thou inclin'st that way, thou art a Coward,
Which hoxes honestie behind, restrayning
From Course requir'd: or else thou must be counted   335
A Seruant, grafted in my serious Trust,
And therein negligent: or else a Foole,
That seest a Game play'd home, the rich Stake drawne,
And tak'st it all for ieast.
    Cam. My gracious Lord,   340
I may be negligent, foolish, and fearefull,

---

334 hoxes] hockles HAN
335 counted] contented v1785

---

only had Camillo been his ghostly confessor, but had even reformed him." Few critics
agree.
    328-39 **we . . . ieast**] HOLBROOK (1945, p. 177): "One may gather from this
the sort of husband Leontes has been in the past: . . . petty in his outlook, unreasonable in his conclusions, lacking faith and dignity." She alone thinks so.
    328-9 **we . . . Integritie**] STAUFFER (1949, p. 294): "This is a drama that rings
changes on the theme of spiritual integrity." Among the other instances he finds are
1003-4 (Leontes); 1217-18 (Hermione); 1352-5 (Camillo); 1832-6, 1846-9, 2196-
2204, 2328-33, and 3004 (Florizel); and 1912-16 (Perdita).
    328 **we**] BETHELL (ed. 1956) notices a "change from the personal 'I' to the royal
'we', as Leontes stands upon his dignity."
    329-30 **in . . . In**] For both, PARRY (ed. 1982): "In relying upon." But both
could also mean "concerning."
    329 **Integritie**] WATSON (1984, p. 243), alone: "The word . . . seems to slip
from its common meaning, as honesty, back to its Renaissance theological meaning,
as the term for Adam's perfect capacity to resist evil through his unfallen will and
reason. Leontes merely means that Camillo . . . should have told him about Hermione's well-known adultery; but the transition in this speech seems to imply that
Camillo has negligently abdicated an ability to purge all sin from the court."
    330 **so**] FURNESS (ed. 1898): "That is, . . . like integrity." BETHELL (ed. 1956):
"He accuses Camillo of knowing the adultery of Hermione and concealing it." Thus
KNOWLES (privately): "In your integrity—no, rather in what only seems integrity,
since you have none."
    331 **Be it forbid**] DEIGHTON (ed. 1889): "*I.e.* that you should have been de-
ceived."
    332 **To . . . or**] SIMPSON (1955, pp. 80-1): "Ending [such verse lines as this] on
the lighter sounded syllables develops so much in the latest plays . .. . as almost to
become a mannerism."
    bide vpon't] RANN (ed. 1787), incorrectly: "Endure it." COLLIER's (ed. 1858,
6:glos.) "Rely upon it" is also unsupported by *OED.* HUNTER (ed. 1872), also incorrectly: Leontes chastises "Camillo for abiding, or giving no notice of, the supposed

dishonesty." CALDECOTT (MS 1813-33, Bide): "Dwell, persist in it" (*OED, v.* 2b, citing this line). DYCE (1853, p. 79): "My abiding opinion is." Citing "Captaine thou art a valiant Gentleman To abide upon't, a very valiant man" (Beaumont & Fletcher, *A King and No King* 4.3.145-6), MOORMAN (ed. 1912): "Insist upon." RIDLEY (ed. 1935), however: "Reiterate." KNOWLES (privately): "The ''t' is his seeming integrity, and Leontes 'bides,' or dwells, on the subject to prove by a series of particulars that Camillo has none." BOORMAN's (ed. 1964) idea that "there is a play on 'forbid'- 'bide'" is unlikely, because *abide* rhymes with *hide* and *pride* (CERCIGNANI, 1981, pp. 252-3) but *forbid* with *lid* and *did* (pp. 48-9, 53).

   333 **that way**] I.e., toward honesty.
   Coward] WILSON (ed. 1931): "It looks as if the metaphor here sprang from a quibble, or perhaps a false etymology which identified 'coward' with 'cowherd.'" Anon., *Gazophylacium Anglicanum* (1689) gives this etymology along with several others.
   334 **Which**] BEVINGTON (ed. 1992): "Which cowardice."
   hoxes] KERSEY (1702, To hough): "Hamstring," which is to cripple by cutting the tendons behind the knee. HERFORD (ed. 1916-): "A treacherous way of disabling instead of by a frontal attack." BETHELL (ed. 1956): Camillo's "cowardice maims his honesty, so that he does not do what he ought to do ('restraining . . . requir'd')."
   335 **From Course requir'd**] BEVINGTON (ed. 1992): "From the direction honest inquiry must take to find the truth."
   or else] CAPELL (1783, 2.4:164): "Either."
   counted] ORGEL (ed. 1996): "Accounted" (*OED, sb.*[1] 4).
   336 **Seruant**] Not only "the serving of the sovereign . . . in an official capacity" (*OED,* Service[1] 11) but a special relationship deriving from the feudal concept of fealty (8)—a bond that, because the king is divinely appointed, has religious as well as personal overtones.
   grafted . . . Trust] ROLFE (ed. 1879): "Thoroughly trusted by me." RIDLEY (ed. 1935, Grafted in): "Admitted to." PORTER & CLARKE (ed. c. 1903, Grafted): "Rooted." PAFFORD (ed. 1963), following SCHMIDT (1874): "Grown in, like a shoot to a tree."
   338 **home**] SCHMIDT (1874): "In good earnest" and ROLFE (ed. 1879): "Completely, to the end" (both *OED, adv.* 5).
   drawne] CARRINGTON (1956): "Won (at the end of the game)" (*OED,* Draw, *v.* 45). SCHANZER (ed. 1969) suggests "a bawdy quibble on *the rich stake drawn*," which seems improbable.
   339 **And . . . ieast**] BETHELL (ed. 1956): "Camillo may be foolish enough to regard . . . adultery as a harmless flirtation."
   340-58 **My . . . mine**] BELLETTE (1978, p. 68): "An heroic attempt to re-establish true judgement and necessary distinction. 'Among the infinite doings of the world' [344] Camillo sees order and pattern, and the speech itself, with its balanced articulation and its periodic and highly subordinated structures, is heard proof not only of Camillo's sanity but of the King's madness."
   341-9 **I . . . end**] WHITE (1913, p. 177): "Simple negligence is a failure to use such care and caution as a reasonably prudent man would exercise under the circumstances, as a result of which another sustains an injury. . . . Wilfullness is a wrongful act, intentionally done, to the injury of another. . . . The Poet makes the speaker attempt to take away the element of wilfulness from his intentional wrongful acts, by the plea that such acts resulted from mere weakness or levity, rather than from a wilfull intent to wrong, while his merely negligent acts were done, 'not weighing well the end', which is a universal characteristic of simple negligence." SMITH (1968, p. 320): "He opposes his royal master, defending himself against unjust charges, and refusing to understand what Leontes is hinting at. . . . He is a plain speaker, whose verse has . . . the ring of a sane man of good sense."
   341 **fearefull**] ROLFE (ed. 1879): "Referring to *coward* [333]."

In euery one of these, no man is free,
But that his negligence, his folly, feare,
Among the infinite doings of the World,
Sometime puts forth in your affaires (my Lord.)   345
If euer I were wilfull-negligent,
It was my folly: if industriously
I play'd the Foole, it was my negligence,
Not weighing well the end: if euer fearefull
To doe a thing, where I the issue doubted,   350
Whereof the execution did cry out
Against the non-performance, 'twas a feare
Which oft infects the wisest: these (my Lord)
Are such allow'd Infirmities, that honestie
Is neuer free of. But beseech your Grace   355
Be plainer with me, let me know my Trespas
By it's owne visage; if I then deny it,
'Tis none of mine.

---

344 Among] Amongst F2-SING1, COL, HUD1, WH1, HAL, DEL
    doings] doing F2-ROWE3
345 Sometime] Sometimes F4-ROWE2, KNT, STAU
    forth∧ . . . Lord.)] ~ . . . . ~ ,∧ mTBY2 *conj.*, THEOBALD (1729) *conj. in*
NICHOLS (1817, 2:359), THEO1+
347 industriously] injuriously HAN
353 infects] affects v1803-SING1, HAL

---

342 **free**] Blameless; see nn. 185, 355, and 933.
343 **But that**] SCHMIDT (1874) does not list this instance, nor is it found in ABBOTT
or FRANZ. Camillo asserts that in general he should be excused for his negligence,
folly, and fear, as these are natural faults, yet he or any man may be blamed for such
shortcomings to the extent they have intruded upon Leontes's affairs. The defects are
elaborated on in 346–53. *But that*, then, seems to mean "except to the extent that."
345 **puts forth**] CALDECOTT (MS 1813–33): "Exhibits itself." SCHMIDT (1875):
"To shoot out, to bud," metaphorically. COLLINS (ed. 1904–24): "The word [*puts*]
is singular, as the substantives in the line [343] are regarded as forming one idea or
alternative single ideas (i.e., *either* his negligence *or*)." The reasons for failures of
concord are myriad, however; see ABBOTT §333.
346 **wilfull-negligent**] MINSHEU (1617, Wilfull): "*Full of his owne will.* [See]
Obstinate, Rash." SCHMIDT (1875): "Done by design" (*OED*, Wilfully 4), but "per-
versely, obstinately" (5) is also possible. ABBOTT (§2): "Two adjectives were freely
combined together, the first being a kind of adverb qualifying the second."
347–9 **if . . . end**] PAFFORD (ed. 1963): "If I deliberately did not treat something
seriously it was due to lack of care and failure to appreciate the importance of the

matter." MAXWELL (ed. 1956, Industriously): "Willfully," corresponding to *wilfull* in 346. ORGEL (ed. 1996, Weighing . . . end): "Sufficiently considering the consequences."

350 **issue doubted**] PAFFORD (ed. 1963): "Doubtful of the outcome."

351-2 **Whereof . . . non-performance**] Paraphrases are as complicated as the expression itself. CAPELL (1783, 2.4:165): "*The execution of which* by another *did cry out against his non-performance* who should have done it; meaning — caused him to be condemn'd, when his '*doubted issue*' [350] prov'd happy." JOHNSON (ed. 1765, Execution), almost impenetrably: "A thing necessary to be done," which WRIGHT & LaMAR (ed. 1966) make "necessity of performance." DODD (1780, 2:103): "Where the . . . doing of the thing, stood in balance against the *not doing it*. Where, considering its *performance*, I hesitated whether it would not be better omitted." MALONE (ed. 1790), comparing 1229-32: Sh. is "entangled . . . ; he *should* have written, either — 'against *the performance*', or — '*for* the non-performance,'" to which MASON (1798, App. p. 32) objects that *execution* and *performance* mean the same. SEYMOUR (1805, 1:159): Camillo means the opposite — "the necessity of the execution reproached or cried out against the non-performance." MOREHEAD (1814, p. 28): "The wisest men are often afraid to do things by doubting the event, which, when they are done, shows that there ought to have been no hesitation in the case." SINGER (ed. 1826) at last arrives at "the execution of which (when done) cried out against the nonperformance of it before," with which MITFORD (1844, p. 127) and most later commentators substantially agree, although COLLINS (ed. 1904-24?), usually accurate, gives the opposite: "And in the course of setting about it, something showed that it ought not to be done." DEIGHTON (ed. 1889): "It was for not doing something that he ought to have done that Camillo apologises." Like SEYMOUR, INGLEBY (1877-81, 2:36), however, believes that Sh. wrote the reverse of what he intended and that "'performance' seems to be meant" by "non-performance." For *doubt* (350), SCHMIDT (1874) gives "to distrust," but "to fear" might also be intended.

353 **infects**] For jealousy as disease, see n. 390-1.

354 **such . . . that**] For *such* with relatival words, see ABBOTT §279. *That* = "as."

allow'd] JOHNSON (1755, To Allow): "To grant license to; to permit" (*OED, v.* 8). RIDLEY (ed. 1935), questionably: "Recognized." BEVINGTON (ed. 1992): "Acknowledged" (*OED, v.* 4).

355 **free of**] *OED* (*a.* 26b, citing this line): "Exempt from." For other adjectival senses, see nn. 185, 812, 871, 933, 2413, 2811.

beseech] For the omission of *I*, see ABBOTT §399.

Grace] SCHMIDT (1874): "Used as an appelation of . . . kings and queens." The other meanings of *grace*, for which see n. 146, make it ironic here.

356-8 **let . . . mine**] DEIGHTON (ed. 1889): "An allusion to a father refusing to acknowledge a child," which is not what Camillo means. See FURNESS in n. 357.

356 **Trespas**] WHITE (1913, p. 175): "Any wrongful act or omission resulting in injury to the person or property of another." *OED* (*sb.* 1, citing this line), less specifically: "A transgression . . . a fault."

357 **By . . . visage**] *OED* (Visage, *sb.* 5, citing this line): A figurative use of Sense 7, "appearance or aspect." DEIGHTON (ed. 1889): "As it really was." FURNESS (ed. 1898): "Give me a particular instance of my trespass, bring me face to face with it."

it's] For *it's* as a possessive pronoun, see n. 1548-1.

357-8 **if . . . mine**] PARRY (ed. 1982): "Because, as an honest man, my word can be relied on."

Leo. Ha' not you seene *Camillo*?
(But that's past doubt: you haue, or your eye-glasse   360
Is thicker then a Cuckolds Horne) or heard?
(For to a Vision so apparant, Rumor
Cannot be mute) or thought? (for Cogitation
Resides not in that man, that do's not thinke)
My Wife is slipperie? If thou wilt confesse,   365 (2A2
Or else be impudently negatiue,
To haue nor Eyes, nor Eares, nor Thought, then say

---

360 doubt: you haue,] ~ , ~ ~ ; THEO1-JOHN2 (−HAN); ~ , ~ ~ , CAM1, GLO,
DYCE2, HUD2-IRV, BUL-ARD1, SIS, PEL1, SIG, PEN2, BEV3
     361 then] that HUD2
     364 Resides] Besides KTLY
          thinke] think it mTBY2 *conj.*, THEO1-v1813 (−MAL), COL2, COL3, STAU, KTLY,
DYCE2, COL4, HUD2
     365 wilt∧] ~ , ROWE1-v1785 (−v1773)
     367 nor Eares] *Om.* DEL; nor ear BUL

359-432 **Ha' . . . blench?**] Coleridge remarks on Leontes's jealousy at n. 181-
92. For the style, see p. 756. CHARLTON (ed. 1916): "Leontes becomes incoherent."
Although his expression is complicated by the tortured parentheses and an ellipsis,
he nevertheless makes sense. See the next n.
     359-65 **Ha' . . . slipperie?**] The basis of the sentence, obscured by the ques-
tion mark after "thought," is "have not you seen or heard or thought my wife is
slippery?" With "(for . . . thinke)," THEOBALD (MS - 1729?) compares "Try what
repentence can, what can it not, Yet what can it, when one cannot repent?" (*Ham.*
3.3.65-6 [2341-2]). MALONE (ed. 1790): "My *Wife is slipperie*," although separated
from "thinke" by a parenthesis, is "evidently to be connected in construction with
it," so that Leontes says, "For cogitation resides not in the man that does not think
my wife is slippery." DEIGHTON (ed. 1889) and others take *thinke* to mean "think
such a thing," so that this parenthesis remains intact; MIRIAM JOSEPH (1947, p. 57)
believes that "the frenzied jealousy of Leontes is emphasized by" the parentheses.
Regarding "for . . . thinke," FURNESS (ed. 1898): "This is not abstract proposition
[sic]. The whole context must be taken together. Have you not thought (says Leontes),
my wife is slippery (for cogitation resides not in the man who does not think *my wife
is slippery*)?" Hence, BETHELL (ed. 1956): "Have you not thought my wife is fickle?—
for the man who does not think so is incapable of thinking." SMITH (1968, p. 321):
The expression is "meaningless, . . . the words of a man losing his faculty for co-
hesive thought," but BETHELL's explanation is clear enough. For more on *slipperie*,
see n. 365. SYMONS (in IRVING & MARSHALL, ed. 1890) would allow THIRLBY's *it* (see
textual n.) after "thinke" to be present though unarticulated; he follows COLLIER (ed.
1842), who asserts that F2 "adds *it* after 'think', but needlessly, the word being clearly
understood." COLLIER later changes his mind, forges the word in the Perkins Folio,
and then asserts (ed. 1858), "Some copies of the second folio add *it*," a piece of
skulduggery that cost WRIGHT (ed. 1891) the pains of examining or having examined
22 copies of F2 located on both sides of the Atlantic. For the record, one more—the
copy at the University of Wisconsin-Milwaukee—also lacks *it*.

RAVENSCROFT (1971, pp. 8-11): "Seen, heard, thought. Surely here we have something very similar to the new rational scientific procedure of empirical observation, verification, and logical deduction. . . . Leontes' exclusive reliance upon the normally accepted human criteria for the real, that is, upon what can be observed and measured by the physical senses, is catastrophically discredited." PAFFORD (ed. 1963): "The situation is tense. Camillo is kept waiting while Leontes works up to this dramatic climax." With the construction, the CLARKES (1879, p. 477) compare the intermingling of "the parenthesis . . . with the context" in 2794-5.

359 **you**] CARRINGTON (1956): "The king . . . speaks to Camillo as a friend. . . . Therefore he addresses him as 'you.'" Since *thou* was used by a superior to an inferior, Carrington's point is that the *you* marks a temporary alteration in the relationship of Leontes and Camillo. See ABBOTT §§231-5 for the general rule and many exceptions. For possible gradations, see nn. 374, 395-7, and 422, but the inconsistencies are so numerous that there may be no rule. Camillo's pronoun, for example, is *your* in 323 but *thee* in 324.

360 **eye-glasse**] JOHNSON (1755, citing this line but giving the wrong sense): "Spectacles." BUCKNILL (1860, p. 125): The cornea, which, diseased, becomes opaque. DEIGHTON (ed. 1889): "The retina." FURNESS (ed. 1898) quotes Thomas Vicary, *The Anatomie of the Bodie of Man* (1546, reissued 1577; ed. F. J. Furnivall, Early English Text Soc. Extra Ser. 53, p. 38) to show that it is neither of these parts of the eye but the "*Humor Vitrus.*" According to *OED* (Humour, *sb.* 3), however, the vitreous humor "fills most of the space between the iris and the retina; formerly including also the denser *crystalline lens.*" *OED* (Eye-glass, *sb.* 1, citing this line only): "The crystalline lens of the eye," a reading that ORGEL (ed. 1996) rejects in favor of FURNESS'S.

361 **thicker**] SCHMIDT (1875, Thick): "Dim, short-sighted," which is, of course, the effect of the thickness. MAXWELL (ed. 1956): "More opaque."

Horne] BOORMAN (ed. 1964): "Probably a reference to the use of thin horn as a transparent covering (as in the old horn books), or possibly to cataract of the eye." Thin "horn . . . offers a natural comparison, but in Leontes' mind *horn* is immediately equated with *cuckold's horn.*"

362-3 **For . . . mute**] DEIGHTON (ed. 1889): "For in cases where the fact is so plain to see there is sure to be plenty of gossip about it." HENLEY (ed. 1902) glosses *Vision* as "spectacle," and *OED* (*sb.* 5, citing this line only), as "a thing actually seen; an object of sight." RIDLEY (ed. 1935, Apparent): "Keen," which causes *Vision* to mean "eyesight." Because of "mute," BOORMAN (ed. 1964) believes "there may be a hunting metaphor here, with 'Rumour' as the name of the hound."

363-4 **for . . . thinke**] PAFFORD (ed. 1963): "For the capacity for thought is not possessed by any man who does not think <this> (i.e., that my wife is slippery)."

365 **slipperie**] JOHNSON (1755): "Changeable; . . . instable." COLMAN (1974): "Sexually unfaithful" (*OED* 5, citing this line). Cf. *slipt* (151), but here the word has physical overtones.

365-7 **If . . . say**] Arguing against ROWE's comma after "wilt," HEATH (1765, p. 205): "The true construction is, 'If thou wilt confess, — then say.'"

confesse . . . Thought] PERRING (1886, p. 174): For clarity, dashes should follow these two words. DEIGHTON (ed. 1889) paraphrases the parenthesis thus created as "you can avoid [confessing] only by impudently declaring that you have neither eyes nor ears nor thought." SCHMIDT (1874, Impudently): "Shamelessly."

366 **negatiue**] *OED* (*a.* 1, citing this line): "Of persons: Making denial of something."

367 **To . . . Thought**] CALDECOTT (MS 1813-33): "To the outrageous extent of saying that you have neither eyes &c."

My Wife's a Holy-Horse, deserues a Name
As ranke as any Flax-Wench, that puts to
Before her troth-plight: say't, and iustify't.   370
   Cam. I would not be a stander-by, to heare
My Soueraigne Mistresse clouded so, without
My present vengeance taken: 'shrew my heart,
You neuer spoke what did become you lesse
Then this; which to reiterate, were sin   375
As deepe as that, though true.
   Leo. Is whispering nothing?

---

368 Holy-Horse] Hobby-Horse ROWE3 +
370 her] a SING1

---

368 **Holy-Horse**] JACKSON (1819, p. 133), ridiculously, prefers this reading to
ROWE's emendation, because the expression is "well known, in allusion to horses, to
mean — a *slippery jade*: and called *holy*, because a *stumbling horse* falls on its knees."
FARMER & HENLEY (1890–1904; 1970, Hobby-horse): "A rantipole [wild] girl; a
wench; a wanton." RIDLEY (ed. 1935): "Prostitute." COLMAN (1974), however: "'A
loose-living person' — female in Sh., though not necessarily a prostitute; male in Jonson, *Epicoene* IV.iii.49." HOWARD-HILL (1972, p. 132): "Crane's spelling 'holly' might
explain" F's reading. But Crane presumably would have written *hobby* or *hoby*, not
holly. For Crane's part in the textual history of *WT*, see pp. 592–8.
   369 **ranke**] The CLARKES (ed. 1865): "Coarse, gross" (*OED, a.* 14, citing this line).
COLMAN (1974): "In heat, lascivious" (*a.* 13). The CLARKES think the word, in addition
to its adjectival function, may work as an adverb modifying *deserues* and meaning
"thoroughly, fully, utterly."
   Flax-Wench] CAPELL (1783 [1774], 1:glos.): "One working in Flax [*OED*, Flax,
sb. 8, citing this line], a spinning Girl." WILSON (ed. 1931): "As a type of coarse
woman." DEIGHTON (ed. 1889): "Possibly with a reference to the nature of flax," by
which he may mean its supposed efficacy as an aphrodisiac. GERARD (1597, p. 445):
"Being taken largely with pepper and honie made vp into a cake, it stirreth vp lust."
   puts to] *OED* (Put, *vb.*[1] 51b, citing this line): "To go to work, 'set to.'" ONIONS
(1986): "Copulate."
   370 **troth-plight**] CAPELL's (1783 [1774], 1:glos.) "The marriage Ceremony; properly, — the Contract preceding" reflects the common idea that betrothal had the force
of marriage. See n. 3363–5.
   say't, and iustify't] DEIGHTON (ed. 1889): "Say that she is unchaste, and prove
your assertion, as you can easily do."
   371–6 **I . . . true**] HUNTER (1965, p. 188): Camillo's "reply to Leontes is completely uncourtierlike in its blunt contradiction." WEINSTOCK (1971, p. 459): His
"spontaneous moral response springs from a natural unreflecting sense of duty."
NELSON (1973, p. 60), by himself: "Camillo does not necessarily worship the perfections of Hermione; he is a loyal servant and considers himself rational, but if he had
any evidence to support Leontes' accusations he might have readily executed the
murder plot against Polixenes." SEXTON (1978, p. 81): "The irony in the speaker's
assumption that someone has misled Leontes emphasizes the king's twisted perception. The power of detraction against goodness is clearly exemplified . . . within
the hero himself, for, as Camillo sees, his base opinion constitutes a 'rebellion' [458]

against his own nobility." LATIMER (1984, p. 127): Camillo's response is "one of anger and desire for revenge, not unlike Leontes' attitude, though in Hermione's defense."

372 **clouded**] JERVIS (1868, To Cloud): "To defame; to stain; to sully" (*OED, v.* 5, citing this line). PIERCE (ed. 1918): Sh. "probably thought of the accusations dimming Hermione's fair reputation as a cloud dims the moon." Cf. *Son.* 33.5-8.

373 **present**] SCHMIDT (1875): "Immediate."

'**shrew**] CALDECOTT (MS 1813-33): "I.e. mischief on! ill betide!" *OED* (*v. Obs.* 1, citing this line): "To curse."

374 **You**] PAFFORD (ed. 1963): "Camillo is so angry that he addresses the king bluntly as 'you' omitting the usual deferential phrase 'my lord', . . . etc."

375-6 **which . . . true**] WARBURTON (ed. 1747): "*I.e.* Your suspicion [actually his speaking of it again] is as great a sin as would be that (if committed) for which you suspect her." RIDLEY (ed. 1935, Though): "Even if." SCHANZER (ed. 1969) prefers *as deep as that* "to refer to the sin committed by Leontes in unjustly accusing her" rather than to Hermione's adultery. TILLEY (1916, p. 77 n.) finds a "depth of masculine nature" revealed by Camillo's refusal "to mention any uncleanness" (cf. n. 2038-9).

377-89 **Is . . . nothing**] HAZLITT (1817, p. 279): "It is only as he [Leontes] is worked up into a clearer conviction of his wrongs by insisting on the grounds of his unjust suspicions to Camillo, who irritates him by his opposition, that he bursts out into [this] vehement strain of bitter indignation: yet even here his passion staggers, and is as it were oppressed with its own intensity." EWBANK (1964, p. 87): "The telescoped syntax and half-finished sentences . . . image the frenzy within. His heated imagination fabricates evidence the very nature of which adds to the sense of rush." ISAACS (1953, pp. 133-4) on echoes in Sh.'s plays: "The mad jealousy of Leontes calls up all the jealous hallucinations of *Othello* . . . and with . . . 'nothing', repeated and reinforced, the echo shifts from *Othello* to *King Lear* in a whirlwind of 'nothings.'" LAWRENCE (1960; 1969, p. 175): "These details . . . may perhaps be regarded as having some foundation in misinterpreted recollections of innocent badinage in the past. Considerable familiarity of manners was customary in Elizabethan times; kissing, for example, was a common form of social salutation." BYLES (1979, p. 88): "Leontes is keen to make Camillo think that his designation of himself as a cuckold is not prompted by his imagination but has been forced on him by his external situation." The king's evidence, however, shifts from events he might have seen, had they occurred, to the thoughts of his supposed betrayers (382 ff.). VICKERS (1971, p. 96) on 379-83: "The symmetry, the very structure of the verse shows the progressive breakdown of Leontes' mind; he is increasingly obsessed with the act, with what they might have done together. . . . The fast growth of the obsession is wonderfully conveyed by the figure *zeugma*, one verb doing duty for several objects, so speeding up the clock and the adulterers' imputed impatience: [quotes 'wishing . . . Midnight'], from the communal time to the time for private assignation." VICKERS continues: "Now to convince himself finally Leontes presents them [in 383-5] deceiving everyone, with an effective use of *anadiplosis* ('but theirs, theirs only'). . . . So far from the first sentence onwards at the end of each question has been suspended the word 'nothing' (the parisonic structure makes it evident that this is understood at the end of each clause): 'Is whispering nothing?/Is leaning cheek to cheek <nothing>?/ Is meeting noses <nothing>?' Having been held in reserve for so long, the word finally comes bursting out [in 385-9], with a quite devastating use of *epistrophe*. . . . In [388] indeed the word forces its way into the language before its time (*ploce*)." VICKERS is echoed by GARBER (1974, p. 166): "The manifest irony here is of course that these things *are* nothing in the sense of Leontes' question—they do not exist and are therefore not evidence of suspicious conduct." See n. 1260-3. COLMAN (1974, p. 17), discussing the inexactitude of much of Sh.'s bawdy language and whether *nothing* sometimes means "pudendum": "A speech like this would seem to be the last word in what Thomas Pyles ['Ophelia's "Nothing,"' *MLN* 64

Is leaning Cheeke to Cheeke? is meating Noses?
Kissing with in-side Lip? stopping the Cariere
Of Laughter, with a sigh? (a Note infallible   380
Of breaking Honestie) horsing foot on foot?
Skulking in corners? wishing Clocks more swift?
Houres, Minutes? Noone, Mid-night? and all Eyes
Blind with the Pin and Web, but theirs; theirs onely,
That would vnseene be wicked? Is this nothing?   385
Why then the World, and all that's in't, is nothing,
The couering Skie is nothing, *Bohemia* nothing,
My Wife is nothing, nor Nothing haue these Nothings,
If this be nothing.

---

380 Laughter] laughing GLO, WH2
380-1 sigh? (a . . . Honestie)] Ff, COL, STAU, DEL2, GLO, KTLY, HUD2, OXF1, CLN2;
~ ; ∧ ~ . . . ~ ? CAP, CAM3, SIS, ARD2, SIG, EVNS, BEV; ~ ? ∧ ~ . . . ~ : ROWE1
etc.
381 on] and BLAIR
383-4 *Verse lines ending* blind . . . only, v1793-KNT1, COL, HUD1, SING2, HAL,
KTLY, KNT3
    383 Noone] the Noone F2-RANN
        Eyes] eyes else WALKER (1860, 3:92) *conj.*, HUD2
    384 Web] the web KTLY

(1949), 322-3] called 'pudendal suggestiveness': *nothing, note, foot, honesty* in a
hymenal form that will break—all these are words which, in one place or another,
Shakespeare uses sexually. But in the pell-mell flow of Leontes's diseased imagination,
'suggestiveness' is the most we can claim. Of the nine *nothings* in those twelve lines,
we cannot point to a single one and say with confidence, 'Just here he means vulva.'"

377-85 **Is . . . nothing?**] HARDINGE (1818, 3:56): "All these are circumstances,
which he must have remarked in a distempered [probably 'deranged'] view upon
other and many other occasions [sic] prior to this parting scene." This supposition
seems highly unlikely.

378 **meating Noses**] DEIGHTON (ed. 1889): "*I.e,* as they kissed."

379 **in-side Lip**] PARTRIDGE (1969) is graphically inconclusive: "Either: with
parted lips alternating thus: male, female, male, female (or vice-versa); or, a kiss that
is either singly or reciprocally lingual."

   Cariere] Either "a short gallop at full speed" (*OED, sb.* 2) or "the short turning
of a nimble horse, now this way, nowe that way" (2b, quoting Baret's *Alvearie*, 1573).
OED puts this line under *sb.* 4 *fig.*, "The height, 'full swing' of a person's activity."
CHARLTON (ed. 1916): "Hence 'the free course.'" MADDEN (1897, p. 298): "The essential characteristic of the career . . . was its abrupt ending, technically known as
'the stop,' by which the horse was suddenly and firmly thrown upon his haunches."
See n. 381 for further horsing.

380 **Note**] Sign. For other instances of noting, see n. 298.

381 **breaking Honestie**] KERSEY (1702, Honesty): "Chastity." *Honesty* or *honest*

occurs in this sense at 670, 769, 832, 986-8, and 3358. WILSON (ed. 1931): "Of transgressing the laws of chastity. 'To break matrimony' was a common sixteenth-century expression for 'to commit adultery', v. [*OED*, Break, *v.* 15d]." VAN DAM (1900, p. 47): For regular meter, the *e* of *Honestie* should be syncopated. For other syncopations of *e*, see nn. 222, 313, 692, 813, 1302, and 2953.

  horsing] SCHMIDT (1874): "To set as on a horse," but PARTRIDGE (1969) finds the word used here "in a transferred sense," meaning that each caresses the other's foot with his or her own, "setting his foot on hers, hers on his" (quoting CHARLTON, ed. 1916), a pedestrious imitation of sexual intercourse. SCHANZER (ed. 1969) thinks "this apparently unique use of the word . . . was . . . sparked off by the equestrian metaphor in" 379. FARMER & HENLEY (1890-1904; 1970) cite Jonson's *Bartholomew Fair* 4.4.231 for *horse* meaning "to possess a woman." ORGEL (ed. 1996): "I.e. mounted, but not on horseback."

  382-3 **wishing . . . Mid-night**] ANSARI (1979, p. 125): "Time is believed [by Leontes] to move with feverish, volcanic haste for them." He actually believes the opposite; he thinks they think time drags. PARRY (ed. 1982): "I.e. wanting the time till bedtime to pass as quickly as possible." ORGEL (ed. 1996): "The fantasy changes: Leontes up to this point has been imagining the lovers together, but they would wish time to move faster only if they were separated." MIRIAM JOSEPH (1947, p. 58) identifies the rhetorical figure as zeugma, one verb serving a number of clauses, "a favorite with Shakespeare." Cf. VICKERS in n. 377-89.

  383 **Houres**] MALONE (ed. 1790, 1.1:xxxvii): Dissyllabic, which would create an 11-syllable line with a trochaic first foot. ABBOTT §484, however: "Monosyllables containing diphthongs and long vowels . . . are often so emphasized as to dispense with an unaccented syllable." In other words, the monosyllable counts as two, one either unaccented or vacant. Considering *noone* such a monosyllable, he gives *houres* one syllable and accents *min*, *no* (*one* unaccented), *mid*, *and*, and *eyes*. See nn. 428, 915, and 1363 for other examples of forced scansion.

  384 **Pin and Web**] COLLIER (ed. 1842) cites FLORIO (1611, *Cataráta*): "A dimnesse of sight occasioned by humores hardned in the eies called a Cataract or a pin and a web." COLLIER's (ed. 1875) subsequent explanation of the term—"a web, as if pinned over the eye"—is doubtful; *OED* (Pin, *sb.*[1] 11): "? characterized by a spot or excrescence like a pin's head, and a film covering the general surface." THEOBALD (MS -1729?) compares *Lr.* 3.4.122 (1896-7), where the disease is a gift of the foul fiend Flibbertigibbet. BEVINGTON (ed. 1992): "The lovers wish to think themselves unobserved."

  385 **That . . . wicked?**] PARRY (ed. 1982): "Who want to copulate in secret."

  385-9 **Is . . . nothing**] GODDARD (1951, p. 650): "Leontes is exactly right, but not in the sense he intends, for it is precisely out the vast realm of Nothing—of pure possibility—that he has summoned these nothings." VYVYAN (1959, p. 100) similarly: "'Something' can spring from 'nothing'. Because, in Shakespeare's view, the soul is a creative power, therefore its contents, seeming nothing, may have tremendous outcomes." JORGENSEN (1962, p. 35): "Leontes' distraction is not only expressed but aggravated by his meditating on the idea of nothingness." Cf. n. 218. STYAN (1967, p. 182): "Shakespeare often guides his speaker with a crescendo . . . by repetitions to simulate a climax of violent thought, as [here]."

  388 **nor . . . Nothings**] PARRY (ed. 1982): "There is no kind of significance in any of the 'nothings'" if this is nothing. BETHELL (ed. 1956): An Elizabethan double negative. "The piling up of negatives in this speech stresses the intensity of Leontes' assertion." For other instances of the double negative, see 463, 900, 1229-32, and 2272, and for the double negative generally, SCHMIDT (1875, pp. 1420-1). The idea that nothing can come of nothing is proverbial (TILLEY N285).

Cam. Good my Lord, be cur'd   390
Of this diseas'd Opinion, and betimes,
For 'tis most dangerous.
    Leo. Say it be, 'tis true.
    Cam. No, no, my Lord.
    Leo. It is: you lye, you lye: 395
I say thou lyest *Camillo*, and I hate thee,
Pronounce thee a grosse Lowt, a mindlesse Slaue,

---

395 you lye, you lye] you lie PEN1
397 a mindlesse] and mindless MAL

---

390 **Good my Lord**] ABBOTT (§13): "The possessive Adjectives, when unemphatic, are sometimes transposed, being really combined with nouns (like the French
monsieur, milord)." Other instances of this transposition occur at 703, 2315, and
3247. The CLARKES (1879, p. 421) find the transposition similar to Italian idiom. For
the opposite, see 194, 293.
    390-1 **be . . . Opinion**] *OED* (Diseased, *ppl.a.* c., citing this line): "In a disor-
dered or depraved condition." MOULTON (1903, p. 66) points out that Camillo's language is similar at 491-4; STAUFFER (1949, p. 353, n. 41) finds "the idea of jealousy
as a disease or infection" also at 221, 289, 353, 390, 401, 403, 491, 507, 532, 537,
639, 1277, and 2930. CLEMEN (1951, p. 197): "The disease-imagery links up with the
notion of taint and stinging things," as in 428. Jealousy as a melancholic disorder is
discussed by BABB (1951, pp. 173-4). BETHELL (ed. 1956): "Sin is a spiritual disease. . . . To Leontes, who is diseased in 'opinion' [SCHMIDT, 1875: 'Judgment'], it
appears that every one else is diseased and he alone well." Yet, as LATIMER (1984,
pp. 127-8) says, he "is considered by those around him as ill rather than evil, and
they treat him accordingly, with concern and tenderness."
    391 **betimes**] JOHNSON (1755): "Soon." SCHMIDT (1874): "Before it becomes too
late."
    392 **For . . . dangerous**] SIEGEL (1950) argues that "Leontes is not merely a
jealous man . . . but a king whose inflamed passions must finally make him dash the
social order to pieces in his frenzy" (p. 304). Archidamus and perhaps Camillo might
agree, but the play concentrates on the destruction of personal relationships and the
family rather than on the social and political consequences of Leontes's madness. The
problem of succession is mentioned, in connection with the death of Mamillius, only
by the oracle, who predicts that the king shall have no heir "if that which is lost, be
not found" (1315-16), a conditional that expresses hope.
    393 **Say it be**] EVANS (ed. 1974): "Suppose it is (dangerous)."
    395-7 **It . . . Slaue**] SANDERS (1987, p. 29): "Peevish vehemence . . . which
confirms its obstinacy by abusive repetition." CARRINGTON (1956): "Observe the contempt in this 'thou' after 'you lie, you lie.'" See n. 359, however.
    397 **Pronounce . . . Slaue**] YOUNG (1928, p. 213): The line is metrical because
of "the successful modulation of quasi-accent in a group of monosyllables; the article
a can fill the stressed place in f[oo]t 2 because the strength of emphasis on stress in
ft. 1 and 3, reducing *thee* and *gross* to insignificance, leaves it capable of supporting
a secondary quasi-accent as part of a group." One suspects nearly the opposite — that
gross, at least, receives full stress.
    grosse] SCHMIDT (1874): "Dull, stupid." Cf. nn. 794, 1031, 1384, and 2031.

Or else a houering Temporizer, that
Canst with thine eyes at once see good and euill,
Inclining to them both: were my Wiues Liuer   400
Infected (as her life) she would not liue
The running of one Glasse.
    Cam. Who do's infect her?
    Leo. Why he that weares her like her Medull, hanging

---

402 The] That KNT3
404 like her] like his THEOBALD (1729) *conj. in* NICHOLS (1817, 2:359), THEO1-
v1773 (−HAN), MAL, SING1, BUL; like a MALONE (1780, 1:143) *conj.*, RANN, COL2, KTLY,
DYCE2, COL4, HUD2, SIG

---

398 houering] SCHMIDT (1874, Hover): "To be irresolute, to waver." CARRING-
TON (1956): "Shifty." *OED* cites this instance as its earliest use of the participial
adjective.
    Temporizer] JOHNSON (1755): "One that complies with times or occasions; a
trimmer [one self-interested and unprincipled]" (*OED* 1, citing this line). The temporizer hovers until certain whether the good or evil side is the better place to light.
HERFORD (ed. 1916-) offers, for *houering Temporizer*, "shifty opportunist." WILSON
(ed. 1931): "Like a hawk hesitating between two objects beneath it." BOORMAN (ed.
1964) thinks "delayer" (*OED* 2) is also meant.
    400-2 were . . . Glasse] HERFORD (ed. 1916-): "If her body were as infected
as her mind [or her conduct] she would die in one turn of the hour-glass." Leontes
mentions the liver as a vital organ, but it may come to his mind because it was
considered the seat of love. DOUCE (1807, 1:61) quotes Bartholomæus, *De proprie-
tatibus rerum* 5.39: "The lyver is the place of voluptuousnesse and lyking of the
flesh." BETHELL (ed. 1956): "Continues the disease metaphor" of 390-1. He finds a
grim play on words in "liuer," "life," and "liue," which, like other puns in Sh.,
"express a point neatly and memorably by suggesting in verbal *form* the relationship
that exists between two *meanings*." WILSON (ed. 1931) approves of DANIEL's idea
that "Liuer" and "Life" have been transposed (see p. 572), but for Leontes there is
nothing conditional in the infection of Hermione's life. With the general idea, cf.
"Better in Health than in good [virtuous] conditions" (TILLEY H285) C. G. SMITH
(1963, no. 150) finds an unconvincing parallel in Leonard Culman, *Sententiae Pueriles*.
    400 Wiues] An old genitive. See FRANZ §64.
    402 The . . . Glasse] Proverbial (TILLEY G132; *Glasse* = "hourglass"), hence
one hour. DELIUS (ed. 1860) compares *1H6* 4.2.35 (1985).
    404 like her Medull] Who wears the medal and what is it exactly? MALONE (1780,
1:143) first suggests that *her* was inadvertently repeated by the compositor from 403.
See textual n. In defense of *her*, STEEVENS (ed. 1793): "Polixenes *wore her, as he
would have worn a medal of her.*" As for the medal, CAPELL (1783, 2.4:165) offers
"the badge of an order," a shot in the dark. CHALMERS (ed. 1823), more reasonably:
"Portrait," expanded by the CLARKES (ed. 1865) to "'her own medal-portrait', or 'a
medal-portrait of herself'" and by SCHMIDT (1875) to "portrait in a locket." Others
seem to think it is simply any metal trinket (*OED, sb.* 1, citing this line and specifying
that the trinket is a disk "bearing a figure"); MACQUOID (1916, 2:114-15) describes

About his neck (*Bohemia*) who, if I   405
Had Seruants true about me, that bare eyes
To see alike mine Honor, as their Profits,
(Their owne particular Thrifts) they would doe that
Which should vndoe more doing: I, and thou
His Cup-bearer, whom I from meaner forme   410

---

406 bare] bear F4-POPE2, HAN, WH2
409 I] Ay CAP+

---

pendants of various shapes worn by both men and women. "A miniature was frequently inserted in the back of these pendants, and sometimes a portrait medallion in cameo set in jewelled ornament formed the obverse." Thus, on the one side is CALDECOTT (MS 1813-33): "As the medal she wears." And on the other, HERFORD (ed. 1916-): "The medallion of her that hangs about his neck," an image that PAFFORD (ed. 1963) renders "as if she were her own miniature portrait pendant about his neck." DEIGHTON (ed. 1889): "The sense is clear, he around whose neck she is so constantly clinging." WILLIAMS (1967, p. 14): "He [Leontes] reduces Hermione to an alluring bauble, symbolizing the lustful arts of the enchantress."

404-5 **hanging . . . neck**] WEBB (1989): "A common motif, often presented to convey intense passion." For the true embrace, see 3322.

405 **who, if**] SEYMOUR (1805, 1:160): A broken construction. "The drift or order of it is changed at . . . 'If.'" Eds. punctuate differently, but all seem to indicate that "who" modifies "*Bohemia*," that "if . . . Thrifts" (405-8) is parenthetical, and that "whom . . . Worship" (410-11) and "who . . . gall'd" (411-13), also parenthetical, modify "thou." Citing ABBOTT §200, KNOWLES (privately): "A *to* is missing: 'who they would do that *to*.'"

406 **bare**] *OED* (Bear, *v*.[1] *str*. 5, citing this line): "To have as a member or part of the body." Or *OED* (Bare, *v*. 1): "Lay bare, uncover." Or the past tense of *bear*, i.e., *bore*; cf. "damned wretch, the curse of her that bare thee" (*2H6* 4.10.77 [2982]). See n. 2066-7.

408 **particular Thrifts**] JOHNSON (1755, Thrift): "State of prospering." HERFORD (ed. 1904): "Private gains."

doe that] I.e., kill him or possibly them (see WEINSTOCK in n. 410).

409 **vndoe more doing**] BETHELL (ed. 1956): "Either 'make further action unnecessary' (on the part of Leontes and his supporters) or 'make further action impossible' (on the part of Polixenes and Hermione)." MALONE (ed. 1790, Doing): "A wanton sense." COLMAN (1974) quotes COTGRAVE (1611, *Besongner*): "To worke, labour . . . ; also, to doe, or leacher with." Thus BOLTZ (ed. 1986): Stop further intercourse (in Ger.). CARRINGTON (1956): "In either case . . . a euphemism for Polixenes' murder." Note the wordplay on "do," "undo," "doing" (see BETHELL in n. 400-2).

I] The change in the entire text from *I*, meaning "yes," to *Ay* begins irregularly in ROWE (ed. 1709), who sometimes modernizes to *ay* (as at 293) and sometimes copies F4's *I* (as at 319; "ay" in ROWE, ed. 1714). As THIRLBY (MS 1725-33?) suggests, eds. from POPE through JOHNSON (ed. 1765), by not adopting *ay*, indicate the personal pronoun, whether or not they intend to.

410 **Cup-bearer**] ORGEL (ed. 1996): "The officer of the royal household in charge of serving the wine. In *Pandosto*, Franion, the Camillo character, is the King's cup-bearer, not his guest's." See p. 623.

Haue Bench'd, and rear'd to Worship, who may'st see
Plainely, as Heauen sees Earth, and Earth sees Heauen,
How I am gall'd, might'st be-spice a Cup,
To giue mine Enemy a lasting Winke:

---

413 gall'd] gall'd thou F2-RANN, COL3, DYCE2, COL4, HUD2, KIT1; gull'd, thou
mLONG *and* GREY (1754, 1:247) *conj.*, RANN; galled,— mTBY2 *conj.*, MAL-COL2,
DYCE1, HAL-KTLY (−CAM1), KNT3, DEL4, CAM3, SIS, PEL1, SIG, PEN2, BEV

---

meaner forme] WEINSTOCK (1971, p. 468): "Leontes commissions the unwilling Camillo to murder [Polixenes] by reminding him of his mean birth," implying
that the lowborn lack moral discrimination. More likely, Leontes reminds Camillo of
a debt of gratitude. MINSHEU (1617, Meane): "Low condition."

forme] The primary meaning is SCHMIDT's (1874) "long seat," alluded to in
411, but "grade or degree of rank . . . or eminence" (*OED*, *sb.* 6) is implied. Hence,
meaner forme is "humbler condition."

411 **Bench'd . . . Worship**] JERVIS (1868, To Bench): "To advance; to dignify."
MOORMAN (ed. 1912): "Given a seat, a sure place, to." *OED* cites *Lr.* and *WT* for the
earliest uses of this word as a verb. *OED* (Rear, *v.*[1] 11, citing this line): "Elevate."
CALDECOTT (MS 1813-33, Worship): "Used as a mark of deference to all persons
holding respectable situations, tho' not having any positive rank." PAFFORD (ed.
1963): "Given a seat above the 'lower messes' [313], an official position, and raised
to a place of honour." For the possible hendiadys, see n. 904-5. BOORMAN (ed. 1964)
detects wordplay on *forme* (= "bench") and "Bench'd." ORGEL (ed. 1996) quotes
OED (Bencher, *sb.* 2): "One who officially sits on a bench; a magistrate, judge, asses-
sor, senator . . . etc."

411-14 **who . . . Winke**] ORGEL (ed. 1996): "Close my enemy's eyes for
good." See n. 414. GROSE & OXLEY (1965, p. 113): A recurring situation in Sh. is that
of "one character urging another to violence: the king and Buckingham in [*R3*], John
and Hubert in [*Jn.*], Cassius and Brutus in [*JC*], Don John and Claudio in [*Ado*], Lady
Macbeth and her husband, Iago and Othello . . . Posthumus and Pisanio in [*Cym.*]."
Cf. n. 657.

412 **Heauen . . . Heauen**] MIRIAM JOSEPH (1947, p. 81) identifies the figure as
antimetabole, "akin to logical conversion in that it turns the sentence around."

413 **gall'd**] MINSHEU (1617, Galle): "Grieue." SCHMIDT (1874): "To injure, to harass, to annoy." PARRY (ed. 1982): This and "made bitter." BEVINGTON (ed. 1992):
"Rubbed, chafed."

gall'd, might'st] YOUNG (1928, p. 214): One word must be expanded to make
regular meter; "I think the tenor requires *mightest* rather than *gall-ed*." But there
may be a vacant syllable at the caesura or a syllable omitted because of emotion, as
in ABBOTT §508 and nn. 1353 and 3245.

be-spice a Cup] AYSCOUGH (ed. 1790): "Poison him." STEEVENS (in REED, ed.
1803) quotes Chapman's trans. of the *Odyssey* (1614?; ed. Allardyce Nicoll, 1956,
10.386-7): "Shee'le . . . spice thy bread With Flowrie poysons."

414 **lasting Winke**] WHITER (1794; 1967, p. 83 n., Wink): "*Sleep* in general, or
with an epithet to be peculiarly applied to a *deep* and a *sound* sleep." THIRLBY (MS
1725-33?) and PORTER & CLARKE (ed. 1908) compare "perpetuall winke" (*Tmp.*
2.1.285 [984]). *OED* (Wink, *sb.*[1]) finds this metonym only in Sh., and the phrase is an
oxymoron, for a wink is a nap. HERFORD (ed. 1916-): "Even Leontes clothes his
incitement to murder in slightly euphemistic phrases." PARRY (ed. 1982): "The line
itself is a verbal 'wink' to Camillo."

Which Draught to me, were cordiall.   415
    Cam. Sir (my Lord)
I could doe this, and that with no rash Potion,
But with a lingring Dram, that should not worke
Maliciously, like Poyson: But I cannot
Beleeue this Crack to be in my dread Mistresse   420
(So soueraignely being Honorable.)
I haue lou'd thee,

---

416 Sir] Sure COL2, COL3
419 Maliciously, like] Maliciously, like a F4-ROWE3; Like a malicious HAN
420 in] *Om.* HARN
421-3 Honorable.) . . . rot:] honourable. | *Leo.* I've lov'd thee.—Make't thy
Question, and go rot: THEOBALD (1729) *conj. in* NICHOLS (1817, 2:359), THEO, WARB,
JOHN, v1773; honourable,ₐ | So lov'd. | *Leo.* Make that . . . rot: HAN; honourable,—
| *Leo.* Make that thy question, and go rot! I have lov'd thee. CAP; honourable!) |
T'have loved the— | *Leontes.* Make . . . rot! CAM3
422-3 *One verse line* v1793+
422 thee,] ~ . F2-POPE2

---

415 **Which Draught**] ABBOTT (§269): "Where definiteness is desired, or where
care must be taken to select the right antecedent," *which* may accompany the repeated antecedent or "a noun of similar meaning supplants the antecedent," here the
latter. For variations, see nn. 736 and 2389.
    cordiall] SCHMIDT (1874): "Reviving the spirits." For the imagery, see n. 303-
4; for more on cordials, see n. 3278. The irony lies in the drink that revives the heart
of Leontes as it stops the heart of Polixenes.
    416 **Sir (my Lord)**] For terms of address similarly repeated, see 1803 and 2997.
    417-19 **I . . . Poyson**] HALE (1678, pp. 43-5): "*Murder* is when a person kill-
eth another of malice" and "an Intention of evil . . . makes a malice." When BAR-
RINGTON (1796, p. 527) holds that *maliciously* "is here used in the sense it bears in
the common forms of indictment for murder," presumably he has something like
HALE's sense in mind, but critics generally do not agree. WARBURTON (ed. 1747): "He
could do it with a dram that should have none of those visible effects that *detect* the
poisoner. These effects he [Sh.] finely calls the malicious workings of poison, as if
[the malicious workings are] done with design to *betray* the user." THIRLBY (MS
1747-53), more accurately: "Yᵗ shall work so as to give no suspicion of the true cause
of his death, of any malice to him." JOHNSON (ed. 1765), disagreeing with WARBUR-
TON: "*Rash* is *hasty* [i.e., taking sudden effect], as in another place [*2H4* 4.4.48
(2422)], *rash gunpowder. Maliciously* is *malignantly*, with effects *openly hurtful.
Shakespeare* had no thought of *betraying the user.*" SCHMIDT (1875, Maliciously)
essentially agrees with JOHNSON ("in an apparently pernicious manner"), as does *OED*
(*adv.* 2, citing this line): "Violently." HUDSON (ed. 1880): "The idea [is] of a poison
that acts so slowly as to be unperceived and unsuspected." DEIGHTON (ed. 1889)
adds: "The emphasis is on *could.*" KNOWLES (privately): "In his talk of poisoning,
Camillo is trying to buy himself some time."
    418 **Dram**] JOHNSON (1755, citing this line): "Such a quantity of distilled spirits
as is usually drank at once." *OED* (*sb.*¹ 3, also citing this line): "1/8 fluid ounce."

. . . hence [a] small draught of . . . spiritous liquor.'' For the word in another sense, see 748 and 2667.

420 Crack] THIRLBY (MS 1733-47?): ''Flaw,'' citing ''honor-flaw'd'' (755). See *OED* (*sb*. 8, citing this line).

dread] The CLARKES (ed. 1865): '''Revered', 'held in awe''' (*OED*, *ppl.a.* 2).

421-4 (So . . . vnsetled] For W. S. WALKER's arrangement of these lines, see pp. 572, nn. 421-2 and 423-4; it requires *vnsetled* to have four syllables. As DYCE (ed. 1857) points out, however, the word has three in 224.

421 So . . . Honorable] MINSHEU (1617, Soueraigne): See ''Chiefe.'' HUDSON (ed. 1880): ''Probably . . . '*she* being so *supremely* honourable' [*OED*, Sovereignly, *adv*. 1, citing this line]; or, it may be, 'she being so perfect in *queenly honour*.''' PARRY (ed. 1982), comparing 372 and 390-2, finds another pun on *sovereign* as a restorative. For the transposition of the adverb, see ABBOTT §421.

421-3 Honorable.) . . . rot] THEOBALD (1729, in NICHOLS 1817, 2:359) paraphrases his emendation: ''Look you, I have lov'd you; but if you make a question of my wife's disloyalty, <I hate you, and> go rot, &c.'' JOHNSON (ed. 1765) explains F: ''*Camillo*, desirous to defend the Queen, and willing to secure credit to his apology, begins, by telling the King that *he has loved him*, is about to give instances of his love, and to infer from them his present zeal, when he is interrupted.'' STEEVENS (ed. 1778) and later PERRING (1885, p. 132) think the antecedent of *that* is ''the love of which you boast,'' but most commentators disagree. MASON (1785, p. 126): ''Leontes . . . takes no notice of that part of Camillo's speech [422], but replies to that which gave him offence—the doubts he had expressed of the Queen's misconduct [419-21].'' SPENCE (1890) paraphrases 423 as ''if you dare to question the truth of my accusation you may go rot.'' Unpersuaded by JOHNSON, CAPELL (1783, 2.4:165) explains that ''I . . . thee,'' which in the MS followed ''rot,'' was turned up by the copyist and that the F printer took the words as Camillo's. MALONE (ed. 1790) disagrees, observing that the comma ending 422 denotes ''an abrupt [interrupted] speech.'' Leontes's reply is ''make that (i.e. Hermione's disloyalty, which is so clear a point,) subject of debate or discussion, and go rot!'' PARRY (ed. 1982), however: ''Camillo seems about to say that he has admired the King (for 'being honourable') just as much as he has admired the Queen.'' PERRING (1886, p. 175), dubiously: Leontes in 423 insinuates ''that Camillo must be false in his professions of loyal attachment [422], because he had not revealed to him the secret of the queen's alleged infidelity.'' FURNESS (ed. 1898): '''That' refers to the Queen's misconduct, and . . . 'Make' is . . . subjunctive: 'If you doubt the queen's unfaithfulness you may go rot.'''

422 thee,] HERFORD (ed. 1916-): ''Camillo uses this pronoun, unusual for a subject to a sovereign, as an appeal to Leontes's memory of their old affection. Leontes is intended to be a considerably younger man.'' See nn. 359 and 395-7. Like some of the 18th-c. eds., though, WILSON (ed. 1931) will have none of this: ''The F. reading is impossible, since a man of Camillo's rank and birth could never address his king as 'thou', still less assure him that he had once loved him.'' Regarding WILSON's emendation, RIDLEY (ed. 1935): ''It is not particularly good in sense, nor does it seem to give much of a point of departure for Leontes' retort.'' PAFFORD (ed. 1963), however: ''There is nothing in the argument that the half-line must mean that Camillo no longer loves Leontes.'' Eds. generally agree with HERFORD, and MARUDANAYAGAM (1983, p. 19) points out that in *Lr*. 1.1. the angry Kent liberally *thou*'s his sovereign. For distinctions between *thou* and *you*, see ABBOTT §§231-5. As PAFFORD notes, Hermione is addressed as ''thou'' in the indictment (1187 ff.), but that is not surprising, for it is a document speaking for the king to a subject. SIMPSON (1911, p. 32) finds that here and elsewhere in Sh., the comma marks an interrupted speech. See n. 674 for a similar use of the semicolon and n. 1387 for a similar use of the colon.

Leo. Make that thy question, and goe rot:
Do'st thinke I am so muddy, so vnsetled,
To appoint my selfe in this vexation?   425
Sully the puritie and whitenesse of my Sheetes
(Which to preserue, is Sleepe; which being spotted,

425–8 *Verse lines ending* Sully . . . sheets, . . . spotted, . . . wasps:) THEO1-
RANN, v1793+ (−CLN2, OXF2); vexation? . . . of . . . being . . . wasps? MAL
426 whitenesse] witness F4

---

423 **question**] SCHMIDT (1875): "Doubt" (*OED, sb.* 1). PIERCE (ed. 1918): "Subject for thought [or discussion]" (*sb.* 3).

    goe rot] COLLINS (ed. 1904–24?): "'You may go and hang yourself', as we say.
Make may be imperative, but is more probably hypothetical subjunctive."

    424–32 **Do'st . . . blench?**] STYAN (1967, p. 181): "This cataract of words,
marked by its rising phrases and run-on lines, periphrases and elliptical sentence-
structure, demonstrates Shakespeare's verse at its most serviceable for rapid pace and
the suggestion of less controlled feeling." GRENE (1967, p. 73): "The causelessness
of the jealousy is exactly what is most important. Leontes himself is aware of this and
tries in his crazy fashion to guard against suspicion."

    424–5 **Do'st . . . vexation?**] RANN (ed. 1787): "As wantonly to involve myself
in such a scene of trouble." MALONE (ed. 1790): "Dost thou think, I am such a fool
as to torment myself, and bring disgrace on me and my children, without sufficient
grounds?" PAFFORD (ed. 1963): "He means that it does not come from within him,
from his imagination, but has been forced on him to designate himself a cuckold."

    424 **so . . . vnsetled**] The CLARKES (1879, p. 521) provide examples of Sh.'s
occasional habit of following a word with another clarifying word, as here.

    muddy] JOHNSON (1755): "Cloudy; dull." *OED* (*a.* 5, citing this line): "Not
clear in mind; confused, muddled."

    vnsetled] JERVIS (1868), wrongly: "Weak; dull." SCHMIDT (1875): "Unhinged,
disturbed" (*OED* 5b). As EVANS (ed. 1974) notes, the word is synonymous with
muddy. BETHELL (ed. 1956) compares *Tro.* 3.3.308–9 (2163–4).

    425 **To**] ABBOTT (§281): I.e., as to.

    appoint] MINSHEU (1617): See "to Ordaine" and "to Assigne"; the CLARKES
(ed. 1865): "'Point out for blame', 'mark out for censure', 'stigmatise', 'asperse'"
(*OED, v.* 18); but SCHMIDT (1874): "to dress myself" (*OED, v.* 15); SCHMIDT compares
"drest in an opinion" (*MV* 1.1.191 [104]), "attired in wonder" (*Ado* 4.1.144 [1807]),
"wrapt . . . in a thousand feares" (*Luc.* 456). LEE (ed. 1907) prefers "'settle' or
'arrange' (a matter of business)" (*OED, v.* 1); WILSON (ed. 1931), "ordain, devote (a
person or thing to some fate)" (*v.* 11). ORGEL (ed. 1996, *Appoint*): "With ironic
legalistic overtones." He quotes *OED, v.* 12: "To ordain or nominate a person . . . *to*
an office, or *to perform* functions" and *v.* 18: "To . . . arraign."

    vexation?] DEIGHTON (ed. 1889): "With a stronger sense than the word has
now." MINSHEU (1617, to Vexe): See "Afflict, Trouble, Molest."

    426 **Sully . . . Sheetes**] PARRY (ed. 1982): "The imagery here unites two ideas.
(i) Leontes has stained his own honour if his suspicions are wrong. (ii) His honour,
like his bed, is stained if his suspicions are right. The sting of the latter (and dominating) idea overwhelms him at [428]."

    427 **Sleepe**] For sleeplessness as a symptom of psychological distress, see KREIDER
(1941, pp. 159–93).

Is Goades, Thornes, Nettles, Tayles of Waspes)
Giue scandall to the blood o'th' Prince, my Sonne,
(Who I doe thinke is mine, and loue as mine) 430
Without ripe mouing to't? Would I doe this? (2A2^{vb})
Could man so blench?
    Cam. I must beleeue you (Sir)
I doe, and will fetch off *Bohemia* for't:
Prouided, that when hee's remou'd, your Highnesse 435

---

428 Goades . . . Tayles] goads, and thorns, nettles, and tails HAN; goads, is thorns, is nettles, tails KTLY
      Waspes)] wasps? Or would I CAP
   430-1 mine) . . . to't?] ∼ ; . . . ∼ ∧ HAN

---

428 **Is . . . Waspes**] See ABBOTT §§484, 509. PORTER & CLARKE (ed. 1908): "A nervous line, alive with dramatic passion." HERFORD (ed. 1916-): "The verse is technically of four feet only, but its slow movement and weight of reiterated stresses disguise the anomaly." BETHELL (ed. 1956): "This list of stinging things shows the sensitive state of Leontes' nerves." For the imagery, see n. 390-1. KNOWLES (privately) compares "O, full of Scorpions is my Minde, deare Wife" (*Mac.* 3.2.36 [1194]).

429 **Giue . . . blood**] *OED* (Scandal, *sb.* 2, citing this line): "Damage to reputation." RIDLEY (ed. 1935): "Question the legitimacy."

431 **ripe mouing to't**] CALDECOTT (MS 1813-33): "Being prompted by *maturely full* proof" (see *OED*, Ripe, *a.* 5). PIERCE (ed. 1918): "Ample cause for it." BEVINGTON (ed. 1992, Ripe): "Urgent" (*OED, a.* 8, approximately). MAXWELL (ed. 1956): "The phrase goes with *appoint, sully, give scandal*."

432 **blench**] GILDON (1710, p. lxviii), somewhat inappropriately: "Sin [*OED, v.*[1] 1: 'To deceive, cheat'], fear." JOHNSON (1755): "To shrink; to start back; to fly off." STEEVENS (ed. 1778): "Fly off from propriety of behaviour" (*OED, v.*[1] 2): "Swerve," to which HERFORD (ed. 1916-) adds "from reason." SCHMIDT (1874): "Be inconstant," which DEIGHTON (ed. 1889) amplifies to "be so fitful, pass so weakly from one course to another." ORGEL (ed. 1996): "'Blench' has implications that contradict Leontes' claim that he is facing an ugly truth: the word means swerve aside, normally to *avoid* something, shy away from something, flinch, avert one's eyes." He refers to *Ham.* 2.2.597-8 (1637-8). MAXWELL (ed. 1956), in the minority: "Deceive himself."

433-9 **I . . . yours**] Camillo introduces provisions that depend on his committing a murder he will not commit, in order to lend conviction to his apparent assent.

433 **I . . . you**] Camillo equivocates. Leontes understands "I am persuaded by your argument." We understand "You are the king and I have no choice." MOULTON (1903, p. 68): "Camillo sees that he must affect to enter into the plot against Polixenes in order to save him." MARSH (1962; 1980, p. 131), differently: "Camillo must either do what he knows to be wrong, or he must break the allegiance to his master, by which he has lived." NEWTON (1986, p. 147), similarly: "Camillo has no option but to agree that Leontes is right." But see the next n.

434 **fetch off**] CALDECOTT (MS 1813-33): "Take, cut off." SCHMIDT (1874): "Make away with." PAFFORD (ed. 1963): "Camillo may be equivocating. . . . 'Fetch off' can also mean 'rescue' [*OED, v.* 16a, first citation 1641; SCHMIDT, 1874, gives no Shn. examples] and that may already be what Camillo intends to do." See n. 448 for another possible equivocation.

435 **remou'd**] EVANS (ed. 1974): "Perhaps ambiguous" in the same way as *fetch off*.

Will take againe your Queene, as yours at first,
Euen for your Sonnes sake, and thereby for sealing
The Iniurie of Tongues, in Courts and Kingdomes
Knowne, and ally'd to yours.   440
  Leo. Thou do'st aduise me,
Euen so as I mine owne course haue set downe:
Ile giue no blemish to her Honor, none.
  Cam. My Lord,
Goe then; and with a countenance as cleare
As Friendship weares at Feasts, keepe with *Bohemia*,   445

---

437 for sealing] for-sealing ANON. *conj. in* CAM1, WH2, NLSN, PEN2; forestalling
KELLNER (1925, p. 13) *conj.*, CAM3
443-4 *One verse line* OXF2

---

436 **at first**] DEIGHTON (ed. 1889): "When first you married her."
437 **thereby**] SCHMIDT (1875): "By that." HERFORD (ed. 1904): "Moreover," but
OED does not find this sense later than 1500 approximately.
437-8 **for sealing . . . Tongues**] WHITE (ed. 1883, For-sealing): "Closing up";
PAFFORD (ed. 1963) also considers *for* as a prefix meaning "fore." SCHANZER (ed.
1969): *For sealing* "can be made to yield adequate sense if taken to mean 'for the
sake of sealing,'" but he finds this construction un-Shn. "It seems highly probable
that *for* here is an intensive prefix, the word meaning 'sealing up close.'" SCHANZER
is supported by *OED* (For-, *pref.*[1] 6 or 7), but *forseal* as a word is not listed. The
CLARKES (ed. 1865) on *sealing*: "'Closing', 'putting a stop to'"; on *Iniurie*: "'Contu-
melious language'" (*OED, sb.* 2), but including "wrong," "harm," "detriment."
SCHMIDT (1875) compares *seel*, "to blind," "with which it [*seal*] is sometimes con-
founded." CAPELL (1783, 2.4:166): "Sealing up tongues that . . . injure by slander,"
which SISSON (1956, 1:197) makes "silencing injurious tongues."
440-2 **Thou . . . none**] PARRY (ed. 1982): "Here and at [453] Leontes declares
an intention which . . . he is incapable of carrying out." See as well nn. 444-5 and
453. SCHANZER (ed. 1969) compares p. 623.
442-3 **Ile . . . Lord**] WALKER (1854, p. 66) attempts to make one verse line by
allowing one syllable to *blemish* and to *to her.*
443-4 **My . . . cleare**] ORGEL (ed. 1996): "One of a number of alexandrines in
the play. F prints 'My lord,' as a separate line, probably because the compositor
needed to fill space on this page." It is true that "My Lord," could have got in what
is now 444, but the phrase was not put on its own line to fill space, because at 467
the running of the SD into the line of text shows that the compositor was saving
space. More likely, the words in 443 were an authorial or scribal addition.
444-5 **with . . . Bohemia**] As ERICKSON (1982, p. 819) points out, Leontes cannot manage this. See 474-5 and nn. 440-2 and 453.
444 **cleare**] MINSHEU (1617): See "pure, transparent, bright." JERVIS (1868): "Serene; cheerful." *OED* (*a.* 14 and 15): "Guileless . . . innocent."
445 **weares**] *OED* (*v.*[1] 7, citing this line): "To exhibit or present (a particular look,
expression, appearance, etc.)."
  keepe with] CALDECOTT (MS 1813-33): "Continue your intercourse with"
(*OED, v.* 45, citing this line). RIDLEY (ed. 1935): "Keep on good terms with."

And with your Queene: I am his Cup-bearer,
If from me he haue wholesome Beueridge,
Account me not your Seruant.
   Leo. This is all:
Do't, and thou hast the one halfe of my heart;   450
Do't not, thou splitt'st thine owne.
   Cam. Ile do't, my Lord.
   Leo. I wil seeme friendly, as thou hast aduis'd me.   *Exit*
   Cam. O miserable Lady. But for me,
What case stand I in? I must be the poysoner   455
Of good *Polixenes*, and my ground to do't,

---

451 thine] thy HARN

---

448 **Account . . . Seruant**] PAFFORD (ed. 1963, at 434): "Camillo's way of saying to himself that he will in fact cease to be Leontes' servant."

449 **This is all**] WRIGHT & LAMAR (ed. 1966): "This is what the matter comes to."

450-1 **Do't . . . owne**] Comparing *Pandosto*, p. 623, PORTER & CLARKE (ed. 1908): "In this terse way, Shakespeare compresses the reward on one side, and the penalty on the other." MIRIAM JOSEPH (1947, pp. 160-1): Antisagoge is a figure, based on antecedent and consequent, which joins to a precept the promise of reward and to its violation, punishment. . . . Leontes later commends Camillo for having disregarded [this] injunction and describes in the very terms of its definition the figure he himself had used [quotes 1347-50 "the . . . done"].

451 **thou . . . owne**] RANN (ed. 1787), wrongly: "Thou art double hearted, a deceiver." ROLFE (ed. 1879): "Thou dost rive thine own; that is, it will be the death of you." DEIGHTON (ed. 1889): "Dost crack thine own by being only half loyal to me." More likely, "you're a suicide," as ROLFE says.

453 **seeme friendly**] BOORMAN (ed. 1964): "From Polixenes' words on entering [468-70], it is clear that Leontes immediately forgets his promise." Or that he is unable to keep it. See nn. 440-2 and 444-5.

454 **for**] ABBOTT (§149): As for.

455-66 **What . . . breake-neck**] BULLOUGH (1975, 8:161) contrasts "Camillo's dignity and brevity" with Franion's agitation (see p. 624). MIRIAM JOSEPH (1947, p. 188): "The most complex form of reasoning is the dilemma, a compound syllogism having for its major premise a compound hypothetical proposition and for its minor premise a disjunctive proposition. . . . Camillo, clearly realizing the dilemma that confronts him, resolves to escape between the horns; he will flee." She also points out Porrus's dilemma in *Pandosto*: "Necessitie . . . want" (p. 634).

455 **What . . . in?**] ABBOTT (§86): "'A' was sometimes omitted after 'what', in the sense of 'what kind of.'" Thus, "In what *a* position am I?"

   poysoner] VAN DAM (1900, p. 53): Pronounced *pois'-ner*; for other syncopations of *o*, see nn. 1917 and 2233 and line 1949.

456 **Polixenes**] Pronounced *Polixin*, according to VAN DAM (1900, p. 114), but this seems improbable. *Polix'nes* is more likely (ABBOTT §468).

   to do't] COLLINS (ed. 1904-24?): "'By doing', 'if I do' — gerundial infinitive." KNOWLES (privately): "My ground for doing it" (ABBOTT §356). MAXWELL (ed. 1956): "To kill Polixenes."

121

Is the obedience to a Master; one,
Who in Rebellion with himselfe, will haue
All that are his, so too. To doe this deed,
Promotion followes: If I could find example   460
Of thousand's that had struck anoynted Kings,
And flourish'd after, Il'd not do't: But since
Nor Brasse, nor Stone, nor Parchment beares not one,
Let Villanie it selfe forswear't. I must
Forsake the Court: to do't, or no, is certaine   465
To me a breake-neck. Happy Starre raigne now,
Here comes *Bohemia*.   *Enter Polixenes.*

---

459 doe] *Om.* ROWE
467 SCENE IV. POPE, HAN, WARB, JOHN

457-64 **one . . . forswear't**] BETHELL (ed. 1956): Here "individual psychology [is compared] with the state, a parallel so familiar . . . that [a] simple reference was in effect a sort of shorthand. If Leontes is in rebellion with himself, it could mean only that the lower elements, the passions, have risen against their natural sovereign, the reason. In this state, says Camillo, he will have his followers be rebels too—but 'rebels' is meant literally this time, for they are to strike an anointed king. . . . 'Anointed' is an important word, reminding us of the almost sacramental power of the unction at coronation." Considering "will . . . so too [458-9]," BROOKS (in PAFFORD, ed. 1963): "Would have all who owe him obedience obey his rebellious self, or, perhaps, would have them also rebel against their true selves." TRAVERSI (1969, 2:302-3): "Camillo's final comment stresses at once the irrationality of his master's behavior . . . and its extension implied in the determination to have 'all that are his so too'. As always, the introduction of passionate division in the mind of the king is followed by a split in the fabric of society, whose unity is only conceivable under royal guidance." ORGEL (ed. 1996) compares *JC* 2.1.63-9 (683-90).

457-9 **one . . . too**] COLERIDGE (1813; ed. Foakes, 1989, p. 175): "Shakespeare in drawing the very worst kings always introduces some corrective of the indignation, lest it should extend too far—as in [this speech]." VELIE (1972, p. 92): "Brutus uses the same image" (*JC* 2.1.67-9 [687-9]).

458 **Rebellion**] WILSON'S (ed. 1931) comment, "'Rebellion' . . . and 're-volt' . . . often used by Shakespeare to mean sudden revulsions of mind and feeling, generally in reference to passion," is truer of the latter word than of the former. See SCHMIDT (1875) for examples.

with himselfe] YOUNG & MOSELEY (ed. 1965): "Against his better self."

459 **so too**] DELIUS (ed. 1860): In rebellion with themselves. DEIGHTON (ed. 1889), in contrast: "Equally disloyal by doing deeds which show no real fidelity to him." WILSON (ed. 1931): Rather, "i.e. in rebellion, but here against 'anointed kings'; cf. [461]." Recent eds. prefer DELIUS.

459-60 **To . . . followes**] ABBOTT (§§356-7): "'To' frequently stands at the beginning of a sentence in [an] indefinite signification." Here the infinitive stands for "if I do." BROOK (1976, p. 110) explains the phrase differently—the infinitive is the object of the verb: "Promotion will follow the doing of this deed."

460-4 **If . . . forswear't**] HUNTER (1845, 1:416): The passage admits "easily of being construed into an intended allusion to that dreadful conspiracy," the Gunpowder Plot, in which the blowing up of Parliament, with King James in attendance, on 1 Nov. 1605 was to signal an uprising of English Catholics. PAFFORD (ed. 1963): "There is biblical authority for the fate of those who strike anointed kings, e.g. *2 Sam*.i.14-15, and a contemporary example in Henri IV and Ravaillac in 1610." THORNDIKE (1901, p. 162) finds here "an echo from Beaumont and Fletcher." He may be thinking of "in that sacred name, The King, there lies a terror, what fraile man Dare lift his hand against it?" (*The Maid's Tragedy*, 2.1.307-9). WEINSTOCK (1971, p. 455): "Camillo takes exception to selfish service. . . . Disloyal as his help in Polixenes' flight may appear to Leontes at first sight, the oracle pronounces Camillo a true subject [1313-14]. Later on, Leontes himself praises him as a man of truth and expresses his thanks for what he now sees to have been loyal service [1343-50]." SUMMERS (1984, p. 29 n.): "Because of the sanctity of *any* anointed king, a courtier ordered to kill one must disobey his own monarch, flee, and undertake a new allegiance: the complex political and moral implications are hardly consoling to simple-minded notions of absolute sovereignty." For an echo of this speech, see 2365-8, and for the supposed allusion to the death of the Queen of Scots, p. 603.

461 **thousand's**] F. W. CLARKE (in FURNIVALL, ed. 1908): "= Thousandes." True or not, in *WT* and in F1 as a whole, only here is the plural of a noun formed with the apostrophe.

struck anoynted Kings] Cf. *Pandosto*, p. 623.

462 **Il'd**] WHITE (ed. 1857) is angry with eds. who render this contraction as *I'd*, because he is convinced the *l* was "pronounced as well as written." That it sometimes was is shown by DOBSON's (1968, 2:451-63) survey of *could*, *should*, and *would*; whether Sh. pronounced the *l* so is unknown, though Holofernes's idea of correct pronunciation (*LLL*, 5.1) is against it. The form is most often found in texts derived from transcripts, including Crane's (*Tmp., MM, Cym.*?). In *WT, Il'd* is preferred by Compositor A, *I'ld* by B. KNOWLES (privately) finds that "in his whole Folio stint, Compositor B divides about evenly on *Ide/Ild*, but strongly prefers *Ild* in Crane plays and in *Lr.*"

463 **Brasse . . . Parchment**] KITTREDGE & RIBNER (ed. 1967): "The various instruments for recording past history."

beares not one] ANON. (MS 1778?-): "Does not . . . contain any example; since there is no instance in history . . . of one man's prospering, who has murder'd a king." *Not* creates a double negative.

464 **Let . . . forswear't**] HERFORD (ed. 1916-): "Since there is no example of such an assassin prospering afterwards, the most utter villain had better in his own interest refrain."

forswear't] KITTREDGE & RIBNER (ed. 1967): "Swear not to do it" (*OED*, Forswear, *v.* 1).

464-5 **I . . . Court**] FOAKES (1971, p. 126): "Why did he [Camillo] not stay behind and attempt, like Paulina and Antigonus, to mitigate the effects of the King's jealous rage?" Cf. n. 2365-6. The obvious answer here is that neither has been trusted by Leontes with all the nearest things to his heart [325] and that neither has been threatened with death if she or he does not murder Polixenes [451].

465-6 **to . . . breake-neck**] COLLINS (ed. 1904-24?): That is, "unless I leave the court." CHARLTON (ed. 1916) finds this "language pulsating with the blood of actual life."

465 **certaine**] SCHMIDT (1874): An adverb.

466 **breake-neck**] JOHNSON (1755): "A fall in which the neck is broken; a steep place endangering the neck." HALLIWELL (ed. 1859): "Complete ruin" (*OED* B., *fig.*).

466-7 **Happy . . . Bohemia**] HUNTER (ed. 1872): "Here comes Bohemia: May a lucky star now be predominant [see n. 283-4]." For other astrological allusions, see n. 1278.

Pol. This is strange: Me thinkes

My fauor here begins to warpe. Not speake?

Good day *Camillo*.   470

    Cam. Hayle most Royall Sir.

    Pol. What is the Newes i'th' Court?

    Cam. None rare (my Lord.)

    Pol. The King hath on him such a countenance,

As he had lost some Prouince, and a Region   475

Lou'd, as he loues himselfe: euen now I met him

With customarie complement, when hee

Wafting his eyes to th' contrary, and falling

A Lippe of much contempt, speedes from me, and

So leaues me, to consider what is breeding,   480

That changes thus his Manners.

    Cam. I dare not know (my Lord.)

    Pol. How, dare not? doe not? doe you know, and dare not?

Be intelligent to me, 'tis thereabouts:

---

471 Hayle] Hoyle F2, F3

475 he had] had he F4-ROWE2

480-1 consider$_\wedge$ . . . Manners.] ~ . . . . ~ ? HUD2

481-2 *One verse line* mCAP2 *conj.*, OXF2

481 changes] changeth GLO, WH2, PEL1

482 (my Lord.)] *Om.* HAN

483 How,] ~ ! CAP-CAM3; ~ ? KIT1; ~ $_\wedge$ mLET *conj.*, PEL1

483-4 dare not? doe not? . . . not? . . . me,] dare not? dare not? you do know, and dare not . . . me: HAN; dare not? do not. . . . not . . . me? CAP, MAL-SING1, HUD1- SING2, COL3, HAL, DEL, COL4; dare not? do not? . . . not? . . . me? v1773; dare not? do not? . . . not . . . me? v1778-RANN, COL1, WH1, KIT1, PEL1, SIG, PEN2; dare not? do not? . . . not . . . me. KNT2; dare not! do not? . . . not . . . me? STAU, HUD2 (me!); dare not! do not. . . . not . . . me? DYCE, KTLY, OXF1, ALEX; dare not! do not. . . . not? . . . me: CAM1, WH2, BUL, NLSN, ARD1; dare not? do not. . . . not? . . . me— CAM3, N&H

    468-81 This . . . Manners] BULLOUGH (1975, 8:161) contrasts the lack of preparation for the disclosure in *Pandosto* (see p. 624).

    469 My . . . warpe] TERRY (1932, p. 32), with those who believe that Polixenes detects hostility in Leontes's attitude at 223: "That is the real reason for his anxiety to cut his visit short." PORTER & CLARKE (ed. 1908): "Polixenes, quick to feel the change in mood before, . . . has now a second and stronger hint of trouble." MIRIAM JOSEPH (1947, p. 146): An example of catachresis, "the wrenching of a word [here *warpe*], most often a verb or adjective, from its proper application to another not proper."

    fauor] KERSEY (1708, Favorite): "One that enjoys the good Will of another," as also in 1273. Cf. 3058.

    warpe] CALDECOTT (MS 1813-33): "Decline, start aside from its even course" (*OED*, *v.* 18 [?]). SCHMIDT (1875): "To change for the worse" (*v.* 19). DEIGHTON (ed. 1889): "To be twisted out of shape" (*v.* 13). *OED* (*v.* 15b, citing this line): "To shrink or shrivel." HARRISON's (ed. 1947) "freeze" seems to be a long shot.

472 **is**] FURNESS (ed. 1898), indicating emphasis: "'What *can be* the news in the Court?'"

473 **rare**] SCHMIDT (1875): "Extraordinary." BOORMAN (ed. 1964): "A certain cynical bitterness here."

474 **countenance**] MINSHEU (1617): "Visage." DEIGHTON (ed. 1889): "Expression."

475 **As**] ABBOTT (§107): "The *if* is implied in the subjunctive [*had lost*]."

475-6 **and . . . himselfe**] BOORMAN (ed. 1964): "Ironic truth."

476 **met**] MAXWELL (ed. 1969): "Greeted."

477 **complement**] SCHMIDT (1874): "Courtesy." BOORMAN (ed. 1964): "Polite greeting."

477-9 **when . . . me**] MASON (1785, p. 126): "Leontes had [at 453] assured Camillo that he would seem friendly to Polixenes . . . but on meeting him, his jealousy gets the better of his resolution, and he finds it impossible to restrain his hatred." SELTZER (1967, p. 139): "Polixenes' account is . . . a literal description of the more or less standard facial 'gesture' for haughty dislike."

478 **Wafting**] JERVIS (1868, To Waft): "To turn; to direct." *OED* (*v.*² 2, citing this line only): "To turn (the eyes) aside with a disdainful movement. *nonce-use.*" HERFORD (ed. 1904): "Turning hastily," a definition unsupported by *OED*.

contrary] SCHMIDT (1874): "The opposite side," i.e., away.

478-9 **falling . . . contempt**] DEIGHTON (ed. 1889): "Drawing down his mouth in a contemptuous manner." *OED* (Lip, *sb.* 2, citing this line) agrees: "To express contempt by the movement of the lip." For *fall* as a transitive verb ("letting fall"), see ABBOTT §291 and *JC* 4.2.26 (1938).

479 **and**] For the unemphatic but accented monosyllable, see n. 891-2.

480-1 **me, to consider**∧ **. . . Manners**] HAPPÉ (1969): "The comma here has the force of a dash," which has the same effect as HUDSON's punctuation, of which WILSON (ed. 1931) approves, because it "would make Camillo's 'I dare not know' a reply to a direct question."

480 **breeding**] COLLINS (ed. 1904-24?): "'Being prepared', 'about to happen.'" RIDLEY (ed. 1935): "Maturing." Cf. n. 63. BOORMAN (ed. 1964) finds "a certain irony . . . remembering Hermione and Leontes' jealous suspicions."

482 **I . . . Lord.)**] COLLINS (1904-24?): Camillo means "'I know, but I dare not tell'; but Polixenes affects not to see this, as it would not suit his purpose." TAYLOR (1972, p. 52), similarly: The words "only make sense, as Polixenes realizes, as some kind of urgent ellipsis indicating that what is known is feared to be spoken."

483-6 **How, . . . not**] FURNESS (ed. 1898): The lines are "all astonishment and bewilderment."

483-4 **How, . . . thereabouts**] For 484, TYRWHITT (in STEEVENS, ed. 1778): "Confess to me that you know." Omitting the comma after *How*, LETTSOM (MS 1840-65) paraphrases the two lines: "How is it you say *dare* not? say *do* not. Do you know, and yet do not know? Speak intelligibly to me." ROLFE (ed. 1879): "What! you dare not? — or is it '*do* not' that you mean? *Do* you know, and yet dare not tell me? You must mean something of the sort." The CLARKES (1879, p. 306), differently: "For, to yourself, what you do know, you must [*be intelligent*]." For *intelligent*, they give (p. 561): "Explicit, communicative, conveyant of intelligence," with which SCHMIDT (1874) and *OED* agree. For *doe not*, EVANS (ed. 1974): "I.e. do you mean you do not?" And PARRY (ed. 1982), for *dare not*: "You cannot 'not dare' to tell yourself something that you know (since you know it whether you like it or not)." PAFFORD (ed. 1963) compares 2299.

483 **How, dare . . . and dare not?**] WRIGHT (1985, 2:379-80): "Polixenes' repetition takes only one line, yet still involves such figures as double alliteration (*d*, *n*) and antimetabole" (repetition in inverse order).

For to your selfe, what you doe know, you must,   485
And cannot say, you dare not. Good *Camillo*,
Your chang'd complexions are to me a Mirror,
Which shewes me mine chang'd too: for I must be
A partie in this alteration, finding
My selfe thus alter'd with't.   490
   Cam. There is a sicknesse
Which puts some of vs in distemper, but
I cannot name the Disease, and it is caught
Of you, that yet are well.
   Pol. How caught of me?   495
Make me not sighted like the Basilisque.
I haue look'd on thousands, who haue sped the better   (2A³

---

485 you doe] do you F3-ROWE2, SIG
489 in] to OXF1
494-5 *One verse line* mCAP2, v1793+ (−COL)
495 How∧] ~ ! mTBY2 *conj.*, CAP, v1778-SING1, HUD, DYCE, HAL, STAU, CAM, GLO,
WH2-ARD1, ALEX; ~ ? KIT1, BEV
497 I haue look'd] I look'd F2 (*sig.* Aa3, *line* 1), F3; I have F2 (*sig.* Aa2ᵛ, *catchword*)

---

484 **Be intelligent**] VAN DAM (1900, p. 135): Run together in pronunciation. Cf.
284.
     'tis thereabouts] SCHMIDT (1875, Thereabouts): "Of that import, or aiming at
that." CHARLTON (ed. 1916): "That must be the case." EVANS (ed. 1974): "I.e. telling
me is probably what you dare not do." PAFFORD (ed. 1963), however: "That's where
the trouble is [i.e., that *I* do not know]."
   485-6 **For . . . not**] The CLARKES (ed. 1865, Must): Elliptical, "be intelligent"
being understood. FURNESS (ed. 1898): "For what you know must be intelligible to
yourself, and you cannot say you dare not tell yourself." EVANS (ed. 1974): "What
you know, you know perforce; daring doesn't enter into it." BETHELL (ed. 1956): "It
must be that you know and dare not admit the fact to *me*." BOORMAN (ed. 1964)
interprets "to your selfe" as "as far as you are concerned." KNOWLES (privately): "All
the commentators seem to miss the point; here is more ellipsis, the stylistic hallmark
of this whole scene. 'What you do know, you must [know], And [what you] cannot
say [to me], you dare not [say],' viz. because you are forbidden, not because you are
ignorant."
   485 **to**] As to (*OED*, To 22, and ABBOTT §188).
   487-90 **Your . . . with't**] PEYRÉ (1984, pp. 146-7): The lucidity of Polixenes
is emphasized to show by contrast the blindness of Leontes: whereas the latter projects his own malady on others, Polixenes . . . always has the capacity to read his
own identity in the other (in Fr.).
   487 **complexions**] SCHMIDT (1874): "External appearance" (*OED, sb.* 5). DEIGH-
TON (ed. 1889): "Colour . . . of the face" (*sb.* 4). Cf. 2443. HERFORD (ed. 1916-),
however, compares 564. FURNESS (ed. 1898): "Refers to Camillo's blanched cheeks,
the sight whereof reacts on Polixenes and causes his to blanch too. . . . Possibly, it

may refer to Camillo's becoming red and white by turns." HAPPÉ (1969): "Perhaps a wider sense . . . of 'disposition'" (*sb*. 3). MOORMAN (ed. 1912), alone but for ORGEL (ed. 1996): "The pale faces [or behavior] of you and Leontes."

488 Which . . . too] HERFORD (ed. 1916-): "As this change affects my own position so closely, I cannot but betray my feeling, also, in my looks." BETHELL (ed. 1956): "The change in Leontes' face and yours shows how my own must appear changed too."

488-90 for . . . with't] The CLARKES (ed. 1865, Alter'd): "Changed," but also "impairs" and "diminishes" or "weakens." Only the first significance is explicitly supported by *OED*. DEIGHTON (ed. 1889): "*I.e.* rather in the way he is treated than in himself." BETHELL (ed. 1956): "For I must be concerned in this alteration, when I find myself altered at the same time," an interpretation that SCHANZER (ed. 1969) renders "for my looks, too, must have changed, reflecting the altered position in which I find myself." BETHELL makes much of the difficulty of the passage, and of its confusion as reflecting Polixenes's disturbed state of mind. He considers and rejects emending "for" to *and*. BOORMAN (ed. 1964): *Alteration* and *alter'd* "probably have the sense of physical change, as in illness; the medical imagery is continued in Camillo's reply." KNOWLES (privately): "If Camillo's and Leontes's faces express unfriendliness, it must be because Polixenes seems no longer a friend to them; he reads his own changed state (from friend to nonfriend) in their looks. Cf. n. 564. *Finding* = 'and find.'"

491-4 There . . . well] For the imagery, see n. 390-1. STEARNS (1865, p. 31): He expresses "himself by a figure, that we can readily conceive of, and yet which, from the nature of things, cannot exist." BETHELL (ed. 1956): "The riddling answer has a long tradition . . . and the Elizabethans and Jacobeans especially loved 'dark meanings.'" One such dark meaning is found by WATSON (1984, p. 320, n. 20): "The guilt [of original sin] transmitted to the child conceived of baptized parents may therefore resemble the illness of Leontes, as Camillo enigmatically describes it." KNOWLES (privately): "Not only riddle but paradox."

492 distemper] COLES (1676): "Sickness." SCHMIDT (1874): "Mental derangement." ONIONS (1986): "Ill humour, bad temper."

493 name] *OED* (*v*.[1] 3, citing this line): "To call . . . by the right name."

494 Of] BEVINGTON (ed. 1992): "From."

yet] BOORMAN (ed. 1964): "Nevertheless or still."

496 Make me not] COLLINS (ed. 1904-24?): "Do not pretend that I [am]."

496-8 sighted . . . so] CAPELL (1783 [1774], 1:glos., Sighted): "Possess'd of Eyes or Sight." WHITE (ed. 1883, Basilisk): "An imaginary monster of the serpent kind." *OED*: He is also called the cockatrice, being half cock, half serpent; he is hatched from the egg of a cock. CHARBONNEAU-LASSAY (1991, pp. 422-3): "Through its eyes, the basilisk discharges waves of its inner poison so destructive that with its look alone it kills whatever human or beast it sees." The idea is proverbial (TILLEY B99 and DENT B99.1). GREY (1754, 1:249) cites Pliny, *Natural History* 8.21 (i.e., 32 for the catoblepas and 33 for the basilisk) and Sir Thomas Browne, *Pseudodoxia Epidemica* 3.7; for more on the basilisk generally, see SEAGER (1896, pp. 24-6). HERFORD (ed. 1916-): "Do not credit me with the basilisk's power to kill with a look." BETHELL (ed. 1956): "The name basilisk (Greek, *basileus* = *king*) has special significance in the context. Polixenes has not been a monarch whose looks killed (i.e. a tyrant) but one who behaved graciously."

497-8 I . . . so] BOORMAN (ed. 1964): "Perhaps a delicate compliment to King James, when the play was acted at Court in 1611 and 1612-13."

497 sped] JOHNSON (1755, Speed): "To have success" (*OED, sb*. 3). COLLINS (ed. 1904-24?), more neutrally: "Fared." For more on *speed*, see n. 1327.

127

By my regard, but kill'd none so: *Camillo*,
As you are certainely a Gentleman, thereto
Clerke-like experienc'd, which no lesse adornes   500
Our Gentry, then our Parents Noble Names,
In whose successe we are gentle: I beseech you,
If you know ought which do's behoue my knowledge,
Thereof to be inform'd, imprison't not
In ignorant concealement.   505
   Cam. I may not answere.
   Pol. A Sicknesse caught of me, and yet I well?
I must be answer'd. Do'st thou heare *Camillo*,
I coniure thee, by all the parts of man,
Which Honor do's acknowledge, whereof the least   510
Is not this Suit of mine, that thou declare
What incidencie thou do'st ghesse of harme
Is creeping toward me; how farre off, how neere,
Which way to be preuented, if to be:
If not, how best to beare it.   515

---

499 are . . . Gentleman] are, certain, gentleman CAP
   thereto_∧] *Om.* POPE1-JOHN2; thereto; v1821
   500 Clerke-like_∧] ~ , mLONG *conj.*, CAP, v1778-HAL (−WH1), KTLY, KNT3, COL4, HUD2
   experienc'd] expedienc'd F2-ROWE3
   514 if to] if it THEO1-JOHN2 (−HAN), v1773

---

498 **By**] PAFFORD (ed. 1963): "For, as a result of" (ABBOTT §146).
   regard] SCHMIDT (1875): "Look."
   498–505 *Camillo* . . . **concealement**] SULLIVAN (1925, 1:lxxxvii): In the second book of GUAZZO's *The civile conversation* (trans. 1581), a speaker says, "Gentry is the daughter of knowledge: and that knowledge doeth gentellise him that possesseth it. . . . For the more good partes bee in a man, the more Gentlemanlike hee is sayde to bee" (ed. 1925, 1:184). "One cannot help assuming that these words were strong in Shakespeare's memory when [he wrote 498–505]." They probably were not; see LIEVSAY (1961, p. 13). See also nn. 2742–3 and 3162–8.
   499 **As . . . thereto**] ABBOTT (§499): "Regular verses of five accents [are sometimes] preceded or followed by a foot, more or less isolated, containing one accent," making "Apparent Alexandrines." He considers *thereto* to be the extra foot. Cf. nn. 77, 185, 190, 1264–5, and 2187.
   thereto] HUNTER (ed. 1872): "And in addition thereto."
   499–502 **thereto . . . gentle**] BROOKS (in PAFFORD, ed. 1963): "There is an echo here of the traditional accounts of Nobility from Juvenal's onwards. Here there is no questioning of the importance of noble ancestors, but the balancing of inheritance and of personal attainment in addition; and this accords with the traditional treatment of the theme." For *gentle*, see n. 502.
   500 **Clerke-like experienc'd**] HUNTER (ed. 1872): Having a clergyman's education. JERVIS (1868): "Learned; scholarly," which accords with SCHMIDT (1874) and

OED (Clerk, *sb.* 4). BEVINGTON (ed. 1992): "Cultivated."

which] ABBOTT (§271): "Which [is used] for 'which thing', often parenthetically."

501 Gentry] SINGER (ed. 1856): "Estate or degree as gentleman" (*OED* 1b). CHARLTON (ed. 1916): "That is, 'rank.'" BOORMAN (ed. 1964): Also "people of high birth." ORGEL (ed. 1996): "With the additional sense of 'good breeding' (*OED* 1c)."

502 In . . . gentle] MINSHEU (1617, Success): Refers to *issue*, "ofspring in blood" (*OED, sb.* 5, citing this line). THIRLBY (MS 1725–33?): "Succession." STEEVENS (ed. 1778): *Gentle* is "opposed to *simple*; alluding to the distinction between the gentry and yeomanry." Thus WHITE (ed. 1857): "By our descent from whom, we have gentility." STEEVENS's speculation that *success* here may mean "success in life" is probably wrong, although BOORMAN (ed. 1964) shares the opinion.

503–4 which . . . inform'd] DEIGHTON (ed. 1889): "The expression is redundant." Probably not, since *knowledge* could mean "understanding" (*OED, sb.* 9). For the expression, KITTREDGE & RIBNER (ed. 1967): "Which it is necessary for me to know." EVANS (ed. 1974): "Would be advantageous for me to learn."

505 ignorant concealement] CAPELL (1783 [1774], 1:glos., Ignorant): "Causing ignorance" (*OED* 3b, citing this line only as a nonce use). DEIGHTON (ed. 1889), similarly: "*Ignorant* [is] used in a proleptic sense, [hence] that concealment which involves ignorance (on my part)." The CLARKES (1879, p. 559): "Uncommunicative, uninforming." HERFORD (ed. 1904): "Under the pretext of ignorance." FURNESS (ed. 1898): "'Imprison not your knowledge in concealment under the plea of ignorance', referring to [483–6], as is shown by the fact that Polixenes reverts at once to Camillo's answer that he could not name the disease which was caught of one who is well." Later eds. usually side with CAPELL. ORGEL (ed. 1996) compares *Tmp.* 5.1.66–8 (2021–3).

507 Sicknesse] For jealousy as disease, see n. 390–1.

509 coniure] PHILLIPS (1706): "To desire earnestly, or to entreat with the most ardent Importunity." For another sense, see n. 3231.

509–10 all . . . acknowledge] DEIGHTON (ed. 1889): "All the duties which honourable men acknowledge to be binding upon them" (*OED*, Parts, *sb.* 8). But PIERCE (ed. 1918): "Traits and qualities" (*sb.* 12).

510–11 whereof . . . mine] RANN (ed. 1787): "A king's request of help" is not the least. HUDSON (ed. 1880): "*Whereof* refers to *parts*." BETHELL (ed. 1956): "The special 'duty' is not strictly Polixenes' petition ('suit'), but the duty of yielding to it, of telling a man of any danger known to be threatening him." PARRY (ed. 1982), however: "And no small part of my honour is involved in this request of mine," which seems off the mark. BEVINGTON (ed. 1992): "Not the least of which is (to answer)" my appeal.

511 declare] ABBOTT (§369): "The Subjunctive after verbs of command [*coniure* (509)] . . . is especially common." See also BROOK (1976, p. 107). Cf. n. 1106.

512–13 incidencie . . . creeping] ANON. (MS 1778?–, Incidencie): "Hap, casualty [accident]." *OED* (*sb.* 1, citing this line as its first instance): "An incidental occurrence or circumstance; an incident"; PAFFORD (ed. 1963) extends this definition to "event *likely to happen*," which is *OED* (*sb.* 2). FURNESS (ed. 1898): "'What impending harm'. An 'incidencie' . . . that 'creeps' is somewhat of a confusion of metaphors." WILSON (ed. 1931): If Sh. "associated 'incidency' with 'insidious', the 'creeping' would naturally follow." Nothing indicates he did, although, as COLLINS (ed. 1904–24?) recognizes, *harm* may mean "evil" in addition to "injury." LEE (ed. 1907) compares *Tim.* 5.1.200 (2444), where *incident* means "contingent."

512 ghesse] HONIGMANN (1965, p. 118) identifies this as a Shn. spelling, also found in F1 *Ado* 1.1.93 (106), F1 *MM* 4.4.6 (2278), and Q1 *Oth.* 3.3.148 (1757). For another, see n. 1904.

514 if to be] DEIGHTON (ed. 1889): "*I.e.* prevented."

    Cam. Sir, I will tell you,
Since I am charg'd in Honor, and by him
That I thinke Honorable: therefore marke my counsaile,
Which must be eu'n as swiftly followed, as
I meane to vtter it; or both your selfe, and me,   520
Cry lost, and so good night.
    Pol. On, good *Camillo.*
    Cam. I am appointed him to murther you.
    Pol. By whom, *Camillo?*
    Cam. By the King.   525

---

520 me] I COL2
523 am] *Om.* F2-F4
    him] *Om.* mF1H *conj.*, ROWE1-POPE2; Sir mTBY2 *conj.*, HAN, CAP; Him [i.e.,
the one] THEO, WARB, JOHN, v1773-SING1, COL1, COL3, STAU, DEL, HUD2, ARD1, N&H,
CLN2; by him mTBY2 *conj.*, KTLY

---

517 **charg'd in Honor**] DEIGHTON (ed. 1889): "Bound by that sense of honour
to which you . . . have appealed [in 509-10]." GURR (1983, p. 423) believes that
Camillo acts out of love, but it rather appears that he is too honest a man to administer
the lingering dram (418).
    518 **marke my counsaile**] KEETON (1930; 1967, p. 149): "Camillo persuades
Polixenes to take entirely the wrong course. Had he stayed and confronted Leontes
with his baseless suspicions one imagines that the lifelong friendship would have
continued uninterruptedly." Camillo, however, probably knows his master too well
to make such a mistake.
    520 **me**] CALDECOTT (MS 1813-33): "The accusative for the nominative" (see
ABBOTT §210). According to COLLINS (ed. 1904-24?), *me* for *I* is emphatic, but neither
ABBOTT nor FRANZ §282 notices this usage.
    521 **Cry . . . night**] WILSON (ed. 1931, Cry): "Imperative mood." Actually fu-
ture indicative. SCHMIDT (1875, Good night, s.v. Night): "Farewell for ever; lost for
ever." FURNESS (ed. 1898): "It is not Polixenes and Camillo who cry 'cry *lost*', but it
is the imaginary cry of spectators who see their doom and bid them an everlasting
farewell. In the phrase 'cry aim' it was not the archer who aimed that so cried; it was
the spectators. That phrase may have been hovering in Camillo's mind, and the
present passage shaped itself on that formula: 'both for yourself and for me there is
the cry of "lost," and so good night to us'. The use of the very phrase 'good night'
implies a group of imaginary friends; no one says it to himself." MAXWELL (ed. 1956),
however: *Good night* means "this is the end (as in modern slang, an expression of
finality)." Its expression requires no group of imaginary friends.
    523 **appointed him**] STEEVENS (ed. 1773, Him): "The person." MALONE (in
STEEVENS, ed. 1793) cites *1H6* 4.7.75 (2309). Commentators generally agree, but the
construction has seemed ambiguous. BOSWELL (ed. 1821): "*By* is understood: I am
appointed *by him*," with which KERMODE (ed. 1963) agrees. ABBOTT (§220), though
he allows that STEEVENS may be right, considers this word the ethical dative—he was
"possibly misled by Boswell," says FURNESS (ed. 1898). For the ethical dative, see n.

Pol. For what?

Cam. He thinkes, nay with all confidence he sweares,
As he had seen't, or beene an Instrument
To vice you to't, that you haue toucht his Queene
Forbiddenly.   530

Pol. Oh then, my best blood turne
To an infected Gelly, and my Name
Be yoak'd with his, that did betray the Best:

---

529 vice] tice HEATH (1765, p. 206) *conj.* ('ntice), DYCE2
532 infected] affected HARN

1598. ROLFE (ed. 1879), who agrees with ABBOTT: "The king has not been mentioned in the conversation thus far, but Camillo is thinking of him. Polixenes, who is *not* thinking of him—or at least only doubtfully—naturally asks" his question.

526 **what?**] WILSON (ed. 1931): "A [question mark] in F. often stands for an exclamation mark," but these words ask a question.

528 **As**] ABBOTT (§107): "Appears to be (though it is not) used . . . for *as if*. . . . The 'if' is implied in the subjunctive [*had seen*]."

Instrument] The CLARKES (ed. 1865): "Motive agent, or operating cause."

529 **vice**] WARBURTON (ed. 1747): "Draw, persuade" (*OED, v.*[1] 2, citing this line). CAPELL (1783 [1774], 1:glos.) has the idea that the word derives from the Vice of the moralities, who "draws," or tempts, and STEEVENS (ed. 1778) adds two other possibilities, to work as if by machinery and "to advise," corrupted. RANN (ed. 1787): "Advise," which he thinks derived from roots meaning "hold together," although neither MINSHEU (1617) nor SKINNER (1671) agrees. Echoing STEEVENS, SINGER (ed. 1826): "Screw or move. . . . A *vice* meant any kind of winding screw," an association made by HANMER (ed. 1743), who thought the function of the tool would be to "hold fast." The CLARKES (ed. 1865): The verb "includes the sense of *viciously* urges or incites," an idea that had also occurred to CALDECOTT (MS 1813-33). BOORMAN (ed. 1964): "Deputy, agent," another secondary meaning. HERFORD (ed. 1916-): "The image hints at Camillo's sense that Leontes's belief was due to his own violent impulse, without any ground in facts." He glosses *vice* simply as "force." On the verb itself, ABBOTT (§290): "Any noun or adjective could be converted into a verb by Elizabethan authors, generally in an active signification."

532 **infected Gelly**] JOHNSON (1755, Gelly, citing this line): "Any viscous body; . . . gluey substance." DEIGHTON (ed. 1889): "A diseased, clotted mass." For jealousy as disease, see n. 390-1.

533 **his . . . Best**] THIRLBY (MS 1725-33?): "Judas." DOUCE (in BOSWELL, ed. 1821): "A clause in the sentence against excommunicated persons was: 'let them *have part with Judas that betrayed Christ.* Amen;' and this is here imitated." This explanation is found as late as LEE (ed. 1907), but any allusion to Christ and Judas is likely to mention betrayal. BAYNE (1916, 1:77): "Polixenes forgets that he is a pagan. . . . Leontes too speaks as a modern" at 326-7. To this biblical allusion, FRYE (1986, p. 163) adds 2289-91. FLEISSNER (1989), in the minority, argues that in keeping with the play's setting, "which evidently is respectably heathen," the reference may, rather, be to Brutus or to an abstraction.

Turne then my freshest Reputation to
A sauour, that may strike the dullest Nosthrill   535
Where I arriue, and my approch be shun'd,
Nay hated too, worse then the great'st Infection
That ere was heard, or read.
    Cam. Sweare his thought ouer
By each particular Starre in Heauen, and   540
By all their Influences; you may as well
Forbid the Sea for to obey the Moone,
As (or by Oath) remoue, or (Counsaile) shake
The Fabrick of his Folly, whose foundation
Is pyl'd vpon his Faith, and will continue   545
The standing of his Body.
    Pol. How should this grow?
    Cam. I know not: but I am sure 'tis safer to
Auoid what's growne, then question how 'tis borne.
If therefore you dare trust my honestie,   550
That lyes enclosed in this Trunke, which you
Shall beare along impawnd, away to Night,

---

538 read] read of mFLV.a.80 *conj.*, KTLY
539 his thought] this though THEOBALD (1729) *conj. in* NICHOLS (1817, 2:359),
THEO1-JOHN2, v1773, COL2, WH1; this thought mTBY2 *conj.*, THEOBALD (1729) *conj.*
in NICHOLS (1817, 2:359), GENT, HUD2, CAM3
547 should] shall JOHN2
549 borne] born F4+

534-7 **freshest . . . Infection**] BUCKNILL (1860, p. 127) notices "the connection between infection and bad smells." Polixenes "imprecates upon himself . . . a
pathological punishment." For jealousy as disease, see n. 390-1.
534 **freshest**] SCHMIDT (1874, Fresh): "Unimpaired." ORGEL (ed. 1996): "Perfectly pure."
    to] FURNESS (ed. 1898) points out that "unemphatic monosyllables in emphatic
places . . . are a characteristic of this play. See lines [540, 548, 551, 566, and 578]
in this very scene." See also n. 891-2.
535 **sauour**] MINSHEU (1617): "Smell."
    strike] CALDECOTT (MS 1813-33): "Instantly and offensively pierce."
    dullest] ORGEL (ed. 1996): "Least sensitive."
536 **arriue**] *OED* (*v.* 5, citing this line): "Make one's appearance."
537 **Infection**] Probably alluding to the plague. Cf. 2929-31.
538 **read**] The CLARKES (ed. 1865): I.e., read of.
539-40 **Sweare . . . Heauen**] JOHNSON (ed. 1773): F may mean "*overswear*
his present persuasion, that is, endeavour to *overcome his opinion* [that you have
touched his queen], by swearing oaths [that you did not] numerous as the stars."
MALONE (in STEEVENS, ed. 1778): "Swear away his jealousy . . . strive, by your oaths,

to change his present thoughts." STAUNTON (ed. 1859): "To swear over = over-swear, is merely to *out*-swear," that is, to be more vehement in denial than he is in accusation, a reading with which DELIUS (ed. 1860) agrees. PAFFORD (ed. 1963): "Endeavour to prevail over his thought [alluded to at 527-30] by the superior power of oaths." The reading has been questioned, however; WILSON (ed. 1931): "There seems no parallel for 'swear over' in this sense." See also FISHER (1985). ORGEL (ed. 1996): "When Shakespeare uses 'overswear' in *Twelfth Night*, it means 'outswear'" (5.1.269 [2435]). KNOWLES (privately), similarly: *Over* is an adverb, "so as to overcome." Cf. *OED* (*a.* 21).

541 **Influences**] JOHNSON (1755, Influence): "Power of the celestial aspects operating upon terrestrial bodies and affairs." COLLINS (ed. 1904-24?): Influence is a "flowing in" of the ethereal fluid emitted by the stars. WHITE (ed. 1857, 3:121) wrongly asserts that "'influence' in Shakespeare's time was a word without a plural"; FURNESS (ed. 1898) gives instances to the contrary. For other astrological allusions, see n. 1278.

541-4 **you . . . Folly**] CREIZENACH (1909; 1916, pp. 333-4) identifies the hyperbole as adynaton "(*e.g.* 'It is more possible for this or that to happen, than for . . . ,' etc.)," a form of paradox (see SONNINO, 1968, p. 191) also found in *MV* 4.1.71 (1977) ff. Regarding the imagery, SPURGEON (1935, p. 307): "The immutability of the laws of nature, working alike in the human and the natural world, is in the poet's mind."

542 **for to**] ABBOTT (§152): "'For to', like 'to', is found used without any notion of purpose, simply as the sign of the infinitive." See also BROOK (1976, p. 95). The CLARKES (ed. 1865): "In the present instance [*for*] aids the metre."

543 **or by**] HUNTER (ed. 1872): Either by.

(Counsaile) shake] PAFFORD (ed. 1963): "Change by reasoning."

544 **Fabrick**] SCHMIDT (1874): "Structure, frame" (*OED, sb.* 3). MAXWELL (ed. 1956): "Creation." KITTREDGE & RIBNER (ed. 1967): "The metaphor is that of a building" (*OED, sb.* 1, "Edifice," citing this line for a figurative use).

544-5 **whose . . . Faith**] JOHNSON (ed. 1765): "This folly which is founded upon settled *belief.*" *Faith* has the same meaning in 3301; for other meanings, see nn. 672, 1193, 1836, and 2307. BETHELL (ed. 1956): "Leontes' 'faith' is belief in Hermione's unfaithfulness." BOORMAN (ed. 1964), differently: In *pyl'd . . . Faith* "there is an ironic undersense of 'faith' in its usual meaning, that is, the foundation of his folly has buried his faith in Hermione."

545-6 **continue . . . Body**] RANN (ed. 1787): "During his life." JERVIS (1868, Standing): "Continuance; duration" (*OED, vbl. sb.* 7a, citing this line). HERFORD (ed. 1904): "As long as his body stands," but *OED* (1d) does not find the word to mean "erect position" until 1709. MOORMAN (ed. 1912): "As long as his body lasts."

547 **How . . . grow?**] The CLARKES (ed. 1865): "How could this [Leontes's suspicion] have originated?" ABBOTT (§325): "*Should* was . . . used in direct questions about the past, where *shall* was used about the *future.*"

551 **enclosed**] PORTER & CLARKE (ed. c. 1903): "Three syllables."

this Trunke] CALDECOTT (MS 1813-33): "My body." DEIGHTON (ed. 1889): "With an allusion to the article of luggage." See nn. 552 and 555.

552 **impawnd**] JOHNSON (1755, To Impawn): "To impignorate [which he defines as 'to pawn'] . . . to pledge." FURNESS (ed. 1898), agreeing with DEIGHTON, thinks this word suggests that by *Trunke* Camillo means "a *chest* or *coffer.*" HERFORD (ed. 1916-), ignoring the doubtful quibble: "Camillo's person . . . will accompany the king as a pledge (*impawn'd*) of his good faith."

to Night] SCHMIDT (1875): "This, or in this, present night," as in line 985. See n. 911, however.

Your Followers I will whisper to the Businesse,
And will by twoes, and threes, at seuerall Posternes,
Cleare them o'th' Citie: For my selfe, Ile put   555
My fortunes to your seruice (which are here
By this discouerie lost.) Be not vncertaine,
For by the honor of my Parents, I
Haue vttred Truth: which if you seeke to proue,
I dare not stand by; nor shall you be safer,   560
Then one condemnd by the Kings owne mouth:
Thereon his Execution sworne.
   Pol. I doe beleeue thee: (2A3
I saw his heart in's face. Giue me thy hand,
Be Pilot to me, and thy places shall   565
Still neighbour mine. My Ships are ready, and
My people did expect my hence departure
Two dayes agoe. This Iealousie

---

560 by] by't HAN
561-3 *Verse lines ending* thereon . . . thee: CAP, V1778-KNT2, DYCE, HAL, DEL, CAM1, GLO, KNT3, HUD2-NLSN, KIT1, ALEX, SIG, EVNS, BEV; *ending* mouth, . . . thee: HAN, COL, SING2, KTLY, ARD1, CAM3, SIS-ARD2 (−MUN), OXF2
562 Thereon . . . sworne] His execution sworn HAN; His execution sworn thereon PEN1
568 Iealousie] jealousy of his WALKER (1860, 2:257 *and* 3:96) *conj.*, HUD2

---

553 **whisper to**] HENLEY (ed. 1902): "Secretly persuade" (*OED, v.* 3, citing this line).
554 **seuerall**] PHILLIPS (1706): "Different" (*OED, a.* 1b). For other meanings, see nn. 312 and 2009.
   Posternes] KERSEY (1702, Postern): "Back-door." ROLFE (ed. 1879): "The smaller gates, the less frequented outlets of the city."
555 **Cleare**] DEIGHTON (ed. 1889), alone: This word "in such a context looks like an allusion to the clearing of goods at a custom-house." *OED* (*v.* 15b, citing this line): "To get (any one) clear of a place." PIERCE (ed. 1918): "Get them away from."
555-6 **put . . . seruice**] CALDECOTT (MS 1813-33): "To service with you, or at your service."
556 **here**] HENLEY (ed. 1902): "*I.e.* in this Court of Sicilia's."
557 **discouerie**] JOHNSON (1755): "Revealing or disclosing any secret." Cf. nn. 647 and 1170.
   Be not vncertaine] MINSHEU (1617, Vn-Certaine): "Doubtfull" (*OED* 3). RANN (ed. 1787): "Do not hesitate." PAFFORD (ed. 1963): "Do not doubt that what I have told you is true."
558 **For . . . Parents**] FURNESS (ed. 1898): "Polixenes had referred to 'our Parents noble names' [at 501]."
559-60 **which . . . by**] DEIGHTON (ed. 1889): "And if you should test my information by speaking to Leontes, I dare not stay to see the result," interpreting *stand by* as does SCHMIDT (1875). The words, however, have other appropriate meanings:

"support . . . protect, defend . . . ; take the side of, be faithful or loyal to" (*OED*, Stand, *v.* 70c) or "abide by (a statement . . . or the like)" (70d). FURNESS (ed. 1898) thinks the last may be meant.

561-3 **Then . . . thee**] Most eds. who adopt CAPELL's lineation expect *condemnd* to be elided, as its spelling suggests, whereas those who follow HANMER presumably expect that the word is to be expanded to *condemned* and the preterit ending to be accented. Exceptions are those eds. who follow F's lineation yet print *condemn'd*—SINGER (ed. 1856) and BETHELL (ed. 1956, CLN2)—or who follow CAPELL yet also print *condemned*—CRAIG (ed. 1891, OXF1), KERMODE (ed. 1963, SIG), and BEVINGTON (ed. 1988, BEV4); some of these editions do not, as a matter of stylistic policy, elide *-ed*. ORGEL (ed. 1996): "Line [561] is a long one, and either the removal of an apparently superfluous *-e* or the removal of a final 'thereon' to the next line [i.e., from 561 to 562] would be a reasonable expedient for a compositor pressed for space."

562 **Thereon . . . sworne**] For *thereon*, SCHMIDT (1875) gives "on it, on that," but *OED* (*adv.* 3), more appropriately: "as soon as that was said." For *his*, CALDECOTT (MS 1813-33): "The condemned party's." Hence HUNTER (ed. 1872): "The execution of that one being thereupon decreed."

564 **I . . . face**] DENT compares "The Face is the index of the heart" (TILLEY F1).

Giue . . . hand] LEIMBERG (1987, p. 130): "Although he has just been betrayed by . . . Leontes, he [Polixenes] dares to accept friendship and offers his own. Thus he acts according to the maxim 'it is required you shall awake your faith' [3300-1], and embraces trust in the middle of treason." For more on hand giving, see n. 172-201.

565 **Pilot**] PORTER & CLARKE (ed. 1908): "Greene gives Franion 'some small skill in Navigation.'" See *Pandosto*, p. 625.

565-6 **thy . . . mine**] JOHNSON (1755, Place): "Office[s]" (i.e., official positions), and STEEVENS (ed. 1793): "*Preferments, or honours.*" The CLARKES (ed. 1865) find both meanings for *place*: "Position as to fortune and spot wherein to dwell." JOHNSON (1755, Neighbour): "To adjoin to; to confine on." For the clause, MALONE (ed. 1790): "Wherever thou art, I will still be near thee." Or HARNESS (ed. 1825): "Thy appointments at court shall be near my person." For *still*, see n. 200.

567 **hence departure**] ABBOTT §429 lists similar adverbial compounds, e.g., *back-return, here-approach*.

568-74 **This . . . bitter**] HERFORD (ed. 1916-): "Polixenes humanely explains and excuses the fierceness of Leontes's anger by the peerless quality of the wife, and his old confidence in the friend, by whom he believed himself injured." ENRIGHT (1970, p. 170): "This goes a long way . . . to preserving Leontes as a figure who can conceivably redeem himself eventually. . . . If Leontes didn't love her [Hermione] enough not to be jealous, at least he loved her too much to be lightly jealous." SOELLNER (1972, pp. 256-7), differently: "Polixenes . . . claims that the passions of great men are part of their greatness. . . . But . . . we must understand the remark in its dramatic context; Polixenes' words are the benevolent excuse of the weakness of a friend. Even if they echo aristocratic prejudice, it was not Shakespeare's." SANDERS (1987, p. 32): "Far from finding something monstrous in the King's suspicion, Polixenes thinks it is all too intelligible. He, too, is a male." TOLIVER (1989, p. 162): "That Polixenes is formally precise points up the command that a genteel style maintains over a nasty business—a Ciceronian style of matched clauses and well-weighed alternatives." RYLANDS (1928, pp. 224-5) finds a similar arrangement of clauses in 1146-8 as well as in passages in *Cym.* and *Tmp.*

568 **Iealousie**] CARRINGTON (1956): "Malice, envy," a sense unsupported by *OED*. SCHMIDT (1874): "Suspicion in love" (*OED, sb.* 4).

Is for a precious Creature: as shee's rare,
Must it be great; and, as his Person's mightie,   570
Must it be violent: and, as he do's conceiue,
He is dishonor'd by a man, which euer
Profess'd to him: why his Reuenges must
In that be made more bitter. Feare ore-shades me:
Good Expedition be my friend, and comfort   575
The gracious Queene, part of his Theame; but nothing
Of his ill-ta'ne suspition. Come *Camillo*,

---

573 to] love to KTLY
575 be] by SIG
        friend, and] friend! Heav'n HAN, CAP, COL2, COL3, COL4; friend! God mTBY4
and SINGER (1853, pp. 72-3) *conj.*, KTLY (Heaven *in* KEIGHTLEY, 1867, p. 200)
        575-6 comfort . . . but nothing] nothing . . . discomfort HUD2
        576 Queene,] Theame;] Ff, ROWE, POPE; ~ ; . . . ~ , THEO1, THEO2, WARB-
CAP, WH2; ~ , . . . ~ , HAN1 *etc.*
        Queene] Queen's WARB, JOHN
        Theame] dream COL2, COL3, COL4

---

569 **as**] CALDECOTT (MS 1813-33): "In that proportion."
570-1 **as . . . violent**] THIRLBY (MS 1733-47?): "As a man's power is, such is
his anger."
571 **conceiue**] SCHMIDT (1874): "Imagine." Cf. n. 914-18.
572 **which**] ABBOTT (§265): "Used interchangeably with Who and That." Cf.
1026, 1991, and 3064.
573 **Profess'd**] OED (*v.* 3): "Make protestation of." THIRLBY (MS 1733-47?): I.e.,
professed friendship (*OED, v.* 3b, *intr.*, citing this line). HUNTER (ed. 1872): Cf. "I
professe my selfe in Banquetting To all the Rout" (*JC* 1.2.77-8 [172-3]).
574 **In**] Probably "on account of" (SCHMIDT, 1874).
        ore-shades] SCHMIDT (1875): "Make dark and gloomy." MAXWELL (ed. 1956):
"Covers."
575-7 **Good . . . suspition**] The passage has been variously paraphrased, and
the explanatory difficulty has been compounded by critics' desire to justify Polixenes's desertion of Hermione in order to save himself. Regarding the flight, SPENCER
(1940, p. 368) expresses the majority opinion: "Polixenes . . . is not to be cen-
sured. . . . His life, in this world of absolute monarchy, is explicitly forfeit.
. . . Polixenes is innocent; it would be natural to suppose that, the irritating object
once removed from sight, Leontes's jealousy would subside. Above all, the plot requires his flight." HEATH (1765, p. 207), explicating: "Bohemia's wish . . . is, That
the expedition he was about to use might be fortunate to himself, and prove a comfort
to the Queen too . . . [as] she could not . . . but be very deeply affected with grief
if any misfortune should befal himself; but . . . he wishes too, that his flight might
not . . . strengthen the King's ill-grounded suspicion." JOHNSON (ed. 1773), on the
wrong track: "Jealousy is . . . the *theme* or subject of the King's thoughts.—Polixenes, perhaps, wishes the queen, for her comfort, so much of that *theme* . . . as is
good, but deprecates that which causes misery. May part of the king's present sentiments comfort the queen, but away with his suspicion." HUDSON (ed. 1852), following STEEVENS (ed. 1778), restates this: "May a speedy departure be my friend, and

bring comfort to the queen, who is part of the theme whereon the king dwells, myself being the other part; but who has really done nothing to justify his ill-taken suspicion." MALONE (in STEEVENS, ed. 1778): "Good expedition befriend me, by removing me from a place of danger, and comfort the innocent queen, by removing the object of her husband's jealousy — the queen, who is the subject of his conversation, but without reason the object of his suspicion." WILSON (ed. 1931) believes that this gloss "remove[s] all difficulties," and RIDLEY (ed. 1935) also accepts it, noting that "*Nothing of* means 'no (legitimate) part of.'"

CAPELL (1783, 2.4:167): Out of Hermione's graciousness "rises her present danger; . . . the jealousy of Leontes is built on it, and had no other foundation." Her graciousness was part of Leontes's theme "but was improperly made so of his suspicion." BECKET (1815, 1:355): "May expedition be my friend and comforter; and may the queen again become his <Leontes'> theme, but without suspicion." HARNESS (ed. 1825) thinks that *his Theame* means "the object of his disquiet" and paraphrases *nothing . . . suspition* as "not suspected by Leontes as I am." HALLIWELL (ed. 1859), improbably: "If ['comfort . . . suspition'] be taken literally, it must be presumed that Polixenes had misapprehended the exact force of Camillo's former speech, and was thinking that he himself was the chief object of the suspicion of Leontes. The meaning then will be — comfort the beautiful queen, who is part of the subject of his thoughts but who has not fallen under his suspicion. . . . Polixenes may be presumed to imagine that he alone had displayed courtesies misinterpreted by Leontes, and that the queen, who had not been seriously suspected, would yet receive comfort from his absence by the then impossibility of a surmise of her bestowing even a faint appreciation on him degenerating into actual suspicion."

Regarding "comfort . . . Theame," CLARK & WRIGHT (ed. 1863), partly repeating MALONE and repeated by SCHANZER (ed. 1969): "We should have expected Polixenes to say that his flight without Hermione would be the best means not only of securing his own safety but of dispelling the suspicions Leontes entertained of his queen." INGLEBY (1877, p. 148): "Let me have good speed for my friend, and the Queen have good speed for her comfort." He interprets *part of* as "a contribution to"; hence, "The king's 'theame' was of the Queen and Polixenes: each contributed to it." Citing *Ant.* 2.2.80 (771), KINNEAR (1883, p. 178) glosses *nothing Of* as "nothing to do with." PERRING (1886, pp. 176-7) interprets *but . . . suspition* as "'She gives no occasion to the king to suspect, however much he may suspect'; she does nothing to *promote* it; and in *that* sense she is 'nothing of it.'" The CLARKES (ed. 1865) would like *expedition* to mean "speed," and *speed* in its turn to mean "success" or "issue." If *expedition* means "voyage" or "journey," as it does in *TGV* 1.3.77 (379), Polixenes is saying, "May my escape befriend me (by saving me), and may comfort befriend the queen." KERMODE (ed. 1963) accepts their interpretation, adding "the vagueness of the expression matches the emptiness of the wish."

McCLENTHEN (1888, p. 169), to whom PAFFORD (ed. 1963) refers, is one of the few critics who believes Polixenes thinks explicitly about the effect his flight will have on Leontes: "May my expedition comfort, that is sustain, encourage, strengthen, or corroborate . . . nothing of the king's ill-taken suspicion; Polixenes not unnaturally fearing that his secret and hasty departure will strengthen or possibly confirm the suspicion entertained by the king." FURNESS (ed. 1898): "May my hasty departure . . . prove my best course, and bring what comfort it may to the gracious Queen whose name cannot but be linked with mine in the King's thoughts, but who is not yet the fatal object of his ill-founded suspicion." Polixenes is "entirely ignorant that Hermione is included in the worst suspicions of the king, and . . . fully impressed with the idea that this flight of his is all that is needed eventually to restore sunshine to the Court." MOORMAN (ed. 1912) approves of FURNESS's interpretation because "though it may at first seem like special pleading . . . it has the inestimable advantage of representing Polixenes' conduct . . . in an altogether favorable light." Ear-

I will respect thee as a Father, if
Thou bear'st my life off, hence: Let vs auoid.
   Cam. It is in mine authoritie to command   580
The Keyes of all the Posternes: Please your Highnesse
To take the vrgent houre. Come Sir, away.   *Exeunt.*

---

579 off, hence:] ~ . ~ : CAM3, KIT1, ARD2, PEN2, EVNS

---

lier, however, COLLINS (ed. 1904-24?) had noted that this interpretation "seems ruled
out by [527-30, 572-4]." SCHÜCKING (1922, p. 198 n.) adds scornfully: "As
if . . . the most indispensable quality of a Shakespearean hero were a highly chivalrous behaviour toward ladies!" BETHELL (ed. 1956) has the unlikely idea that *Expedition* is not the subject of *comfort*; rather, the subject is unexpressed, and Polixenes
means "may speed by my friend and may (God) comfort the gracious queen." KIN-
NEAR (1883, pp. 178-9) had suggested that "'*God*' was probably the original word,
'*and*' being ignorantly substituted to meet the requirement of *the Act* [of Abuses]."
SCHANZER (ed. 1969): "*Nothing . . . suspicion* does not mean that Hermione is not
included in her husband's wrongly conceived suspicions, but that she does not deserve them, though she is part of this *theme* (which here has the meaning of 'matter
for feeling and action')." COLLINS suggests that because *expedition* may mean
"speed" and *speed* may mean "fortune," as in 1327, *expedition* "might also have this
meaning, though there is no other instance." SHERMAN (1902, p. 118), despite the
excuses of other critics: "And so the royal guest sneaks away, . . . never for a moment thinking of the effect his flight may have upon the destiny or welfare of the
Queen." MARSH (1962; 1969, p. 132), more gently: "Polixenes is not uncontaminated
by the concern for self that is destroying Leontes; his later actions prove him to suffer
from the same disease." STOLL (1940, p. 179), who finds that in Sh. and other Elizabethan drama "character does not much reside in the implications of the action,"
compares Polixenes's apparent disregard of Hermione's safety with Macduff's apparent disregard of the safety of his wife and child when he goes to England in *Mac.* 4.3.
    578-9 **I . . . off**] THORNE (1968, p. 35): "Later Camillo is also to bear Florizel's
life off and do him a similar office."
    578 **respect**] MINSHEU (1617): See "Regard, Consideration."
    579 **bear'st . . . hence**] WELLS (in WELLS & TAYLOR, 1987), against emending
the punctuation: "'Bear'st my life off' seems to need some modification." A strong
stop after *off* changes *hence* from "from here" (*OED, adv.* 1) to "go hence, depart"
(*adv.* 2). SCHMIDT (1874) gives "Away, be gone."
    bear'st . . . off] DEIGHTON (ed. 1889): "*I.e.* get me away safe from this country."
    auoid] PHILLIPS (1706): "Quit or leave." PORTER & CLARKE (ed. c. 1903): "De-
part."
    580 **authoritie**] CALDECOTT (MS 1813-33): "Commission, a power with which I
am invested."
    command] *OED* (*v.* 11, citing this line): "To have (a thing) at one's bidding,
or within one's power."
    581 **Posternes**] See n. 554.
    Please] ABBOTT (§361): "Often found in the subjunctive [representing] 'may
it please.'" See 740, 835, 873, 884, and many later instances.
    582 **take . . . houre**] DEIGHTON (ed. 1889): "Seize the opportunity while there
is yet time to do so." COLES (1676, Urgent): "Pressing." As PORTER & CLARKE (ed.
1908) point out, "the hour was less urgent in Greene," where the favorable wind
does not arise for six days. See *Pandosto*, p. 625.

Actus Secundus. Scena Prima.   2.1

Enter Hermione, Mamillius, Ladies: Leontes,
Antigonus, Lords.   585

---

584 *The* SCENE [i.e., Sicilia; the palace] *Continues.* POPE1+ (−PEL1, CLN2, PEN2, OXF2) (*subst.*)
584-5 *Leontes, Antigonus, Lords.*] *Om.* ROWE1+
585 *Lords*] *Lord* F2-F4

---

583 *Actus . . . Prima*] Because of "the proposed departure of Polixenes and Camillo on the *night* of the first day [represented in the play; see 552], and the mission, *since then,* of Cleomenes and Dion to Delphos [800-2]," DANIEL (1879, p. 177) believes that this scene takes place on the second day represented. CLAPP (1885, p. 402): "The next morning apparently." PYLE (1969, p. 31), less exactly: "The opening of the second act, with Hermione expecting to have her baby soon, leads us to suppose that some months have passed, and then, in keeping with the harsh and unnatural mood that is in the ascendant, we are abruptly and disconcertingly abused." He evidently does not believe that the Hermione of Act 1 is obviously pregnant (see n. 49).

COLLINS (ed. 1904-24?): "The whole scene with Mamillius is developed from a passage of Greene ['Comming to the queenes lodging, they found her playing with her yong sonne Gariinter' (see p. 626)]. Further, in Greene (*a*) the Lords believe Pandosto's accusation (contrast lines [740-1]; see p. 626), (*b*) Bellaria herself asks Pandosto to send messengers to Apollo's oracle (see p. 630). Shakespeare's alteration exalts the dignity of Hermione and intensifies the self-will of Leontes." COLERIDGE'S (1813; ed. Foakes, 1989, pp. 104, 175) view that Sh.'s fondness for children inspired this scene exemplifies COLERIDGE's idea that "preparatory to the most horrid scene . . . he [Sh.] gives variety, a pleasing relief, and yet heightens the after pathos" (p. 104). HERFORD (ed. 1916-), similarly: "A scene of serious import is preluded by a passage of charming by-play of no apparent relevance. Mamillius, whispering to his mother the 'sad tale best for winter' [618], is rudely interrupted by the harsh notes of the actual *Winter's Tale* which is about to separate for ever the mother and son thus for a last moment seen in confidential intimacy. The remainder of the scene carries out, with the violence and suddenness habitual in these 'Romance' plots, the consequences, easily to be foreseen, of the flight of Polixenes and Camillo at the end of the previous act. Hermione is hurried off to prison; but the loud and unreserved protests of the courtiers throw the fatuity of Leontes into yet more glaring prominence and increase our assurance that justice will finally triumph."

BETHELL (ed. 1956): "Except for some speeches of Leontes, the verse is simpler and less intense than in Act I. Hermione is the central figure, maintaining her position not by outbursts of passion but by quiet self-control." TRAVERSI (1954, p. 121): In 2.1 Leontes's "jealousy, brought into more direct contact with its object, stands revealed as much more than criminal short-sightedness. It is, indeed, a sensual repulsion of the uncontrolled 'blood' against a right sexual relationship, against natural fertility consecrated, given its proper spiritual context, in the bond of marriage."

584-5 *Enter . . . Lords*] Until recently, eds. did not speculate about why char-

Her. Take the Boy to you: he so troubles me,
'Tis past enduring.
   Lady. Come (my gracious Lord)
Shall I be your play-fellow?
   Mam. No, Ile none of you.   590
   Lady. Why (my sweet Lord?)
   Mam. You'le kisse me hard, and speake to me, as if
I were a Baby still. I loue you better.
   2. Lady. And why so (my Lord?)
   Mam. Not for because   595
Your Browes are blacker (yet black-browes they say
Become some Women best, so that there be not
Too much haire there, but in a Cemicircle,
Or a halfe-Moone, made with a Pen.)
   2. Lady. Who taught'this?   600

589-95 *Four verse lines ending* you. . . . me, . . . love . . . because CAP
589-91 *Verse lines ending* you. . . . lord? mCAP2, v1793-DYCE1, COL3-EVNS; *ending* playfellow? . . . lord? WH1, BEV
592-3 *Prose* HARN
594 2. Lady] *First Lady* COL4
    my Lord] pray, my Lord HAN; my good lord v1793-v1813; my dear lord KTLY
599 Or] *Like* HAN
    a halfe-Moone] half-moon v1793-SING1, HUD1, HAL
600 taught'this] F1, DYCE1, WH1, ARD1, CAM3, PEL1+ *and* K&R; taught this F2-F4, COL1-COL2, COL3, HAL, NLSN; taught ye this DYCE1 *conj.*, DEL, DYCE2, HUD2, WH2, BUL; taught't this ALEX, SIS; taught you this ROWE1 *etc.*

---

acters sometimes appear in entrances, as the men do here, before the action requires them. PIERCE (ed. 1918), however, suggests that actors playing these characters "were probably to be ready when thus mentioned." For what is now accepted as the true explanation, see p. 593.

   584 **Ladies:**] WILSON (ed. 1931, p. 122) finds the colon a "clue suggestive of a playhouse plot." See p. 594 below. Actually, the colon separates those who enter now from those who enter at 628.

   Leontes] All eds. consulted move Leontes's entrance to 628 approximately (see the textual notes), but in some performances he evidently entered here. FOSS (1932, p. 136): His entrance is an awkward snag, because he speaks "twenty-four [or 44] important lines before the group of ladies listening to Mamillius' sad tale become aware of the presence of their King." SPRAGUE (1935, p. 87): "Perhaps, the ladies should notice Leontes a good deal earlier . . . and even if they did the awkwardness might remain." CAVELL (1987, p. 199): "I expect considerable agreement that in Leontes' intrusion we have an Oedipal conflict put before us."

   586-627 **Take . . . eare**] CAZAMIAN (1945, pp. 200-1): The words exchanged between little Mamillius, the ladies-in-waiting, and the queen create an exquisite comedy, so rich in truth to nature that realism could not make it more perfect nor more quietly amusing (in Fr.). CARRINGTON (1956) is reminded of *Mac.* 4.2, in which "Lady Macduff is playing with her son before the murderers sent by Macbeth descend," but nothing here compares with the tension of Lady Macduff's "Sirra, your Fathers dead, And what will you do now?" (30 - 1 [1746 - 7]).

586 **Take . . . you**] MAXWELL (ed. 1956): "Take charge of the boy." MACDONALD (1883, p. 156): "The changefulness of Hermione's mood with regard to her boy [indicates] her condition." PORTER & CLARKE (ed. 1908) add: "She is soon ready for him, neither her disposition nor her love of him being vexed by his importunities, but only her nerves." PAFFORD (ed. 1963) disagrees: "Hermione's opening words are in mock-annoyance."   .

    troubles] *OED* (*v.* 5, citing this line): "Pester[s]."

588 - 612 **Come . . . her**] J. H. S. ARMSTRONG (1969, p. 62): "The court women spoil the boy, encouraging his prattle because he releases in them a mood of gay coquetry and ministers to their vivacity." NEELY (1985, p. 197): "Mamillius's flirtatious banter . . . shows his precosity, not his innocence." See n. 596.

590 **Ile . . . you**] DEIGHTON (ed. 1889): "I will have nothing to do with you."

593 **Baby**] *OED* (*sb.* 1, citing this line): "Formerly synonymous with *child*." But Mamillius clearly means *baby*.

594 **2. Lady**] MAHOOD (1992, p. 45): "Of Hermione's gentlewomen in this scene, the Second Lady sounds a little older and more staid, so it makes sense to identify her with . . . Emilia." See n. 3380, above, for Emilia.

595 **for because**] ABBOTT (§151): *For* means "because," but "the desire of clearness and emphasis led to the addition of *because*." See *OED* (Because B.1) and cf. *Jn.* 2.1.588 (909). For similar repetitions, see 302, 634, 856, 890, 916, 1208, and 1214 - 16.

596 **Your . . . blacker**] *Browes* = *eyebrows* = *forehead* at 192, 222, and 2528. WILSON (ed. 1931): "The boy is being, perhaps deliberately, rude: black brows were not admired." WILSON compares *LLL* 4.3.254 - 6 (1607 - 9) and *Son.* 130, 131, and 132. PAFFORD (ed. 1963), on the other hand, suggests that "feminine make-up" is being ridiculed. He compares the mistress's eyebrow as the object of "the lover's extravagance" in *AYL* 2.7.149 (1128); see KNOWLES (ed. 1977). For the supposed evils of cosmetics, see nn. 599 and 1914 - 16 below. WHITE (1981, p. 104) discovers here "a precocious knowingness that taints the paradise which his [Mamillius's] childhood could represent." See n. 588 - 612.

597 **so**] SCHMIDT (1875): "Provided."

599 **made . . . Pen**] DEIGHTON (ed. 1889): "Delicately shaded as though drawn with a pen." Mamillius probably means, however, that the Lady uses an Elizabethan eyebrow pencil. For the use of blacklead, or graphite, on eyebrows, see Maggie Angeloglou, *A History of Make-up* (1970, p. 45). For allusions to eye paint and other cosmetic abominations, see Thomas Tuke, *A Treatise against Painting* (1616, B2ᵛ, C2ᵛ, et passim).

600 **taught'this**] PAFFORD (ed. 1963), referring to PAFFORD (1961, pp. 175 - 6): "An apostrophe is often used for the omission of a complete word [or words] (e.g., [13, 614, 2094, 2594, 2873, 3263]) as well as for the omission of letters." Apostrophes also stand for words at 719, 724, 1337, 1662, 2063, 3068, and 3160. HOWARD-HILL (1972, p. 129) agrees that here the apostrophe represents a notional word — *ye* or *you* probably, as ROWE thought — and eds. who emend to create an additional syllable no doubt believe, with HERFORD (ed. 1916-), that it "is clearly necessary, and accords with the scansion." BOORMAN (ed. 1964) tries to have it both ways by emending to *y'this*, but *y'* never appears in Shn. texts before pronounced consonants. The apostrophe is probably Crane's, not Sh.'s, and the meter seems against any trace of a syllable's being heard. Yet a pronoun does appear in Sh.'s other uses of *taught this* (*Wiv.* 2.2.206 [965] and *2H6* 4.2.154 [2474]), and here FURNESS (ed. 1898) thinks the pronoun, "if at all pronounced, is to be slurred, like 'This' a good block' in *Lear*" (4.6.183 [2625]). The apostrophe in *Lr.* is editorial, and three other instances of the apostrophe indicating "absorption" found by FURNESS (two in *Tmp.* and one in *MM*)

Mam. I learn'd it out of Womens faces: pray now,
What colour are your eye-browes?
    Lady. Blew (my Lord.)
    Mam. Nay, that's a mock: I haue seene a Ladies Nose
That ha's beene blew, but not her eye-browes.   605
    Lady. Harke ye,
The Queene (your Mother) rounds apace: we shall
Present our seruices to a fine new Prince
One of these dayes, and then youl'd wanton with vs,
If we would haue you.   610
    2. *Lady.* She is spread of late
Into a goodly Bulke (good time encounter her.)
    Her. What wisdome stirs amongst you? Come Sir, now
I am for you againe: 'Pray you sit by vs,
And tell's a Tale.   615
    Mam. Merry, or sad, shal't be?
    Her. As merry as you will.
    Mam. A sad Tale's best for Winter:
I haue one of Sprights, and Goblins.

---

602 are] be F2-JOHN2
606 *Lady*] 2 *Lady* v1773-DEL2 (−RANN, DYCE1), KTLY-COL4 (−DYCE2), OXF1, CLN2
609 youl'd] you'l F4-JOHN2, v1773
611 2. *Lady*] 1. *Lady* MAL-DEL2 (−DYCE1), KTLY, DEL4, COL4, OXF1, CLN2
615-16 *One verse line* mCAP2, v1793+ (−OXF2)
617-20 *Verse lines ending* best . . . Goblins. . . . Sir. mTBY2 *conj.*, HAN; *ending*
winter: . . . sir. v1793-DEL2 (−DYCE1), KTLY-COL4 (−DYCE2), OXF1, CLN2; *ending*
will. . . . one . . . sir. DYCE, CAM, GLO, HUD2-IRV, BUL-PEL1, ARD2, SIG+

---

are in texts printed from Crane transcripts. HALLIWELL (ed. 1859): "The suppression
of the objective case of the personal pronoun after a verb was not of unusual occurrence." He compares "beseech'" (1078). CALDECOTT (MS 1813-33) finds a different
reason for reading with F: The speech "is not necessarily addressed to Mamillius";
the Lady may address the others in mock amazement. KITTREDGE & RIBNER (ed. 1967):
"It has been suggested that baby talk ('taught it') is intended." HAPPÉ (1969): "The
omission suggests he is being teased."
    601 I . . . faces] As well as "by a careful study of women's faces," DEIGHTON
(ed. 1889) finds a "secondary sense of watching the looks with which women examine each other's personal appearance."
    601-2 pray . . . eye-browes?] Turning to the First Lady, Mamillius seems to
ask, "What color are your eyebrows really?"
    603-5 Blew . . . blew] Few explain. The Lady may be speaking literally; she
has applied a cosmetic. But TERRY (1932, p. 28): "Her . . . reply strikes me as one
of those feeble jests some adults wrongly think will 'amuse the children.'" According
to PARRY (ed. 1982), this condition "may result from the cold — or from drinking too
much too often."
    604 mock] MINSHEU (1617): "Scoffe, or iest, a quippe, or a gibe." RANN (ed.

1787): "Fib," which seems related to the adjectival sense given by JOHNSON (1755): "False . . . not real."

607–12 The . . . her] TRAVERSI (1969, 2:305): "The 'rounding' of the queen is here envisaged as part of a natural, beneficent process, 'goodly' and destined, in 'good time', to find its proper fulfillment in maternity. The unsoftened harshness of Leontes' use of 'big' and 'swell' [661–2], with their implication of the grotesque and the deformed, appear[s] in the light of this contrast as a deliberate inversion of nature which will produce its own fruit in the disruption of normal human relationships."

608 Present our seruices] DEIGHTON (ed. 1889): "Respectfully welcome." HAPPÉ (1969, Present): "Offer."

Prince] PAFFORD (ed. 1963): Either masculine or feminine. "The speaker is not assuming that Hermione will have a son." For *prince* as feminine, see *OED* (*sb.* 1b).

609 wanton] JOHNSON (1755): "Play." *OED* (*v.* 1b, citing this line): "To play sportively, heedlessly, or idly." Cf. n. 201 for another use of the word.

612 Into . . . her] Pointing out that trisyllabic terminations are rare in Sh., WALKER (1854, p. 67) tries to make a regular pentameter by allowing *goodly* only one syllable. Cf. n. 1913. ABBOTT (§465), however: "Words frequently drop or soften *-er* . . . especially before a vowel or *h* in the next word." VAN DAM (1900, p. 93) offers *good* (for *goodly*) and *counter*. As it stands, the line is a regular hexameter.

good . . . her] ONIONS (1986, Time): "Happy issue, good fortune." (Encounter): "Light upon, befall." BETHELL (ed. 1956): "May she be safely delivered of her child!"

613 What . . . you?] The CLARKES (1879, p. 417): "Ironically expressed." DEIGHTON (ed. 1889): "Playfully; what are these subjects you are so wisely discussing?" HAPPÉ (1969): "What are you gossiping about?"

614 for you] ABBOTT (§155): "*For* is sometimes *ready for, fit for.*" ABBOTT §405 deals with ellipses after the verb *to be*.

616, 618 sad] Neither SCHMIDT (1875) nor ONIONS (1986) lists this instance. The word may mean "causing sorrow; distressing, calamitous, lamentable" (*OED* 5f), Mamillius's idea of the consequences of supernatural hostility, in contrast to "merry." The two words are again contrasted in 1793–4.

617 as you will] DEIGHTON (ed. 1889): "As you please; it cannot be too merry for my taste."

618 A . . . Winter:] For the connection between this line and the play's title, see n. 0. CHARLTON (ed. 1916): "The suggestion of a sad winter's tale and of church-yards [625], prepares for the entry of Leontes." TINKLER (1937, p. 361), in a debatable assertion: "The fact that the tale is that of the play itself, the tale for Winter, gives a sense of double time, of the action taking place within itself, and this results in a certain distancing of the emotions." KNIGHT (1947; 1966, p. 89): "The 'sad tale' reflects the coming disaster; the boy's words characterize his father, dwelling close . . . to death; the broken story is itself a little tragedy." SITWELL (1948, p. 204): "But it was a child who was speaking, to whom time is long. He could not foresee the spring." HAPPÉ (1969): "The whole play owes much to the mood of mystery and sadness caught in these few lines." FAAS (1984, p. 146): "Mamillius will not speak again, and the winter's tale about the hope of a rebirth in spring, which the opening scene misleadingly invests in his person, will find its fulfillment in others."

619–25 I . . . Church-yard] KNOWLES (privately): "These lines articulate in another form the phantoms in Leontes's mind."

619 I . . . Goblins] SHERMAN (1902, p. 119): "Most children can be scared pretty effectually, as listeners, by tales of ghosts. Here is one who frightens his mother [622] by telling them." Hermione is actually both teasing and encouraging him. KERNAN (1975, 3:447): "Shakespeare's play is also of sprites and goblins, of the strange powers at work in the human mind, and it too begins by a churchyard, the place of death and burial." KERNAN seems to allude to the fate of the prince and to the sup-

Her. Let's haue that (good Sir.)   620
Come-on, sit downe, come-on, and doe your best,
To fright me with your Sprights: you're powrefull at it.   (2A3)
    Mam. There was a man.
    Her. Nay, come sit downe: then on.
    Mam. Dwelt by a Church-yard: I will tell it softly,   625
Yond Crickets shall not heare it.
    Her. Come on then, and giu't me in mine eare.

---

620 good] *Om.* v1793-v1813
626 Yond] Yon' CAP, v1773-SING1, KNT, WH1, HAL
626-7 *Verse lines ending* then, . . . ear. MTBY2 *conj.*, CAP, v1778+ (−CLN2, SIG, BEV, OXF2)

---

posed fate of the queen. SPENDER (1982, 1:238): Mamillius "seems to be saying that the tragedy which will result in his own death is only a tale of 'sprites and goblins'. Whispering to his mother, he and she seem to be at the centre of some mystery compared with which the frenzy of Leontes is only a nightmare."

621-2 **Come-on . . . Sprights**] SCHANZER (ed. 1969): "A poignant touch of dramatic irony: Hermione, still happy and unsuspecting, plays at being frightened by the imaginings of her son, unaware that a few moments later she will be truly frightened by the imaginings of her husband (note also the echo of the words at [1271])."

622 **you're . . . it**] SCHMIDT (1875, Powerful): "You are a master in it." WILSON (ed. 1931): "The usual Shakespearian form is 'y'are'; cf. [n. 294]." In the five comedies examined by HOWARD-HILL (1972, p. 89), *you're* is found only in *WT* (p. 89).

623-5 **There . . . Church-yard**] BETHELL (ed. 1956) finds this man "rather like the penitent Leontes later, who daily visited his wife's tomb," and, on BETHELL's comparison, CROW (1958, p. 303) comments, "The thing seen has become nothing; the eye of the beholder is all." MCPEEK (1969, p. 251 n.), who also beholds: "These lines . . . read like the preparation in a modern motion-picture for a fade out: all that follows somehow seems like the story Mamillius is presumed to tell." GRENE (1967, pp. 72-3): Mamillius's story is "interrupted by the entrance of his crazy father beset by phantoms far more convincing than the goblins of romance."

626 **Crickets**] THIRLBY (MS 1733-47?): "Does he mean the ladies?" He probably does. Sh. generally associates crickets with their chirp, and Beaumont extends this sound to a woman's chatter in *The Coxcomb* 4.3.51: "Lord how shee'le talke some times? tis the maddest cricket——." RANN (ed. 1787): "Pratlers." HERFORD (ed. 1916-): "The phrase emphasizes the boy's masculine contempt for them, conveyed in the preceding dialogue," a judgment that seems too harsh, although Mamillius may take some childish revenge for 607-10. FURNESS (ed. 1898): "This maturity of observation in the little boy throughout this scene has its purpose. The heart of a less precocious child would not have been broken by the ill-treatment of his mother." See 914-18. Crickets may be introduced because, though sometimes associated with cheerfulness and mirth ("As merry as Crickets," *1H4* 2.4.89 [1054]; cf. TILLEY C825), they are, as well, creatures of ill omen; see DYER (1884, pp. 251-2, 516), who also points out (p. 252) that the cricket's "supposed keen sense of hearing is referred to" here.

627 **giu't . . . eare**] PARRY (ed. 1982): "The whispered story probably continues through the next twenty lines or so, while the audience's attention switches to Leon-

   Leon. Was hee met there? his Traine? *Camillo* with
him?
   Lord. Behind the tuft of Pines I met them, neuer   630
Saw I men scowre so on their way: I eyed them
Euen to their Ships.
   Leo. How blest am I
In my iust Censure? in my true Opinion?
Alack, for lesser knowledge, how accurs'd,   635

---

628 SCENE II. POPE, HAN, WARB, JOHN
     Enter L. F2-F4; *Enter* Leontes, Antigonus, *and* Lords. ROWE1 + (*subst.*)
628-9 *One verse line* ROWE1 +
631-3 *Verse lines ending* eyed . . . I MTBY2 *conj.*, NLSN
632 Euen] On even HAN
633-49 How . . . will:] *Marked as aside* COL2

---

tes and his attendants." EDWARDS ("Seeing," 1986, p. 79): "Is [Leontes's] interruption
an allusion to the most famous element of Peele's [*Old Wives Tale*], the electrifying
appearance of Madge's characters as she begins to tell her tale?" *The Old Wives Tale*
"twice mentions 'winter's tale' in its induction" (ed. Binnie, 1980, 85-6, 98-9). For
another possible debt to Peele, see n. 1930-43.
   628-9 **Was . . . him?**] The CLARKES (ed. 1865): "Admirably does the 'he', 'his',
and 'him' . . . , referring to the unnamed Polixenes, serve to indicate the perturbation of the speaker." See nn. 2165 and 2497 for a similar technique. ROLFE (ed. 1879):
The pronouns, however, may indicate only "the continuation of a conversation begun
before the parties come upon the stage."
   628 **Traine**] MINSHEU (1617): "A companie of seruants, attending vpon anie
prince."
   630-2 **Behind . . . Ships**] MCLUSKIE (1988, p. 183): "The stage is divided.
. . . On one part is the static emblem of Hermione as mother . . . , on the other
Leontes is being told the tale of Camillo's escape. As in the case of Sir Smile [273-
89, where he imagines that the world is full of cuckolds], the tale of one treachery
encourages him to see treachery everywhere and he can confidently invite his courtiers to share in his interpretation of the signs [quotes 667 'Looke . . . well']."
   631 **scowre . . . way**] PHILLIPS (1706, Scour away): "Scamper or run away hastily."
     eyed] SCHMIDT (1874): "Observe[d]."
   633-4 **How . . . Opinion?**] BULLOKAR (1616, Censure): "A iudgement: an opinion." DEIGHTON (ed. 1889): "Said ironically: How happy I am in having so rightly
judged my wife and Polixenes: 'just censure' and 'true opinion' are identical in meaning." FURNESS (ed. 1898) disagrees about the tone: "Genuine sincerity." ENRIGHT
(1970, p. 171): "There is some satisfaction in finding yourself even more right than
you had thought." For similar repetitions, see 302, 595, 856, 890, 916, 1208, and
1215.
   635-6 **Alack . . . blest?**] HEATH (1765, p. 208): "Alas would my knowledge had
been less! how accursed am I now in being what I called blest with greater!" BOOR-
MAN (ed. 1964): "I was lucky to realize the truth about Polixenes and my wife, but
that makes it all the worse that I did not know of Polixenes' plan to escape." But this

In being so blest? There may be in the Cup
A Spider steep'd, and one may drinke; depart,
And yet partake no venome: (for his knowledge
Is not infected) but if one present
Th'abhor'd Ingredient to his eye, make knowne   · 640

---

637 drinke; depart] drink a part mTBY4 *conj.*, COL2, COL4

---

interpretation does not lead to the meaning of the unseen spider; instead, PAFFORD (ed. 1963) has, like HEATH, "'Oh that I knew less' (ignorance would be bliss). 'How accursed that I am proved right.'" He cites a parallel in Middleton's *The Witch* (MSR 1694-6) and compares *Oth.* 3.3.342-[3] (1985-6). BEVINGTON (ed. 1992): "Would that there were less for me to know."

636-42 **There . . . Spider**] WRIGHT (1985, 2:384): "In [Sh.'s] later plays, the extended comparison is likely to be drawn from a commoner, or even harsher, frame of reference [than in his earlier], and to be conducted without sentimentality and often in an unconventional form [as here]."

636-8 **There . . . venome**] Leontes does not share the notion that spiders themselves, as well as their bite, are deadly; among the poisons administered to Sir Thomas Overbury, HENDERSON (in STEEVENS, ed. 1785) reports, were "*great Spiders* and *Cantharides.*" As STAUNTON (ed. 1859) remarks, "It would appear, however, that to render the draught fatal, the victim ought to see the spider," although the passage he quotes — from Middleton's *No Wit, No Help Like a Woman's* (ed. Johnson, 1976, 2.1.374-5) — does not support the idea. Nevertheless, as BUCKNILL (1860, p. 127) observes, this "passage would seem to call in question the truth of the old opinion; or at least to express the power of fancy" in the effects of the supposed poison. TOPSELL (1658, p. 787) sensibly decides that swallowing spiders is harmless if they are so: "Our Spiders in *England*, are not so venomous as in other parts of the world, and I have seen a mad man eat many of them, without either death or deaths harm, or any other manifest accident or alteration to ensue. And although I will not deny, but that many of our Spiders being swallowed down, may do much hurt, yet notwithstanding we cannot chuse but confesse, that their biting is poysonlesse, as being without venom, procuring not the least touch of hurt at all to any one whatsoever." PIERCE (ed. 1918): "'In the cup of my family life', says Leontes, 'there has been the spider of adultery; but it did not poison my mind with jealous suffering as long as I did not perceive it.'" SCHANZER (ed. 1969): "The analogy is therefore a precise one, reminiscent of a metaphysical conceit." MARSH (1962; 1980, p. 133): "The spider is in his own mind, and . . . he is the source of the poison." CLEMEN (1951, p. 197): "The collocation of disease, of stinging and poison becomes . . . obvious." See nn. 390-1, 428. STOCKHOLDER (1987, p. 260, n. 4), having surveyed allusions to spiders in other Shn. plays: "When all these associations are taken into account the spider in Leontes' cup can be seen to embody Leontes' fear of woman's sexual charms, which will expose and punish his foul sexuality by reducing him to an insect, and will by devouring him incorporate him into her interior foulness." Additional spider lore may be found in HOTINE (1983).

637 **steep'd**] *OED* (Steep, $v.^1$ 1, citing this line): "Soak."

depart] The CLARKES (ed. 1865): "Be gone unconscious of harm."

639 **infected**] For jealousy as disease, see n. 390-1.

How he hath drunke, he cracks his gorge, his sides
With violent Hefts: I haue drunke, and seene the Spider.
Camillo was his helpe in this, his Pandar:
There is a Plot against my Life, my Crowne;
All's true that is mistrusted: that false Villaine,   645
Whom I employ'd, was pre-employ'd by him:
He ha's discouer'd my Designe, and I
Remaine a pinch'd Thing; yea, a very Trick

641, 642 drunke] drank mFLV.a.80 *conj.*, v1793-v1821, HAL
645 is] I mTBY3 *conj.*, LETTSOM *conj. in* DYCE2, HUD2
647 ha's] hath ROWE1-JOHN2, v1773-MAL

---

641 **gorge**] MINSHEU (1617): "Gullet," not "stomach," as PORTER & CLARKE (ed. c. 1903) and HARRISON (ed. 1947) believe. One cracks it, ROLFE (ed. 1879) says, "by endeavouring to vomit."

642 **Hefts**] HANMER (ed. 1743-4, 6:glos.): "Heavings" (*OED, sb.* 4, citing this line only). STEEVENS (ed. 1778) incorrectly extends this to "what is heaved up." Not used elsewhere by Sh., the word may be adopted here for meter. With a somewhat different meaning, it reappears in 940 as "heauings."

I . . . Spider] VYVYAN (1959, p. 108): "In reality, Leontes had drunk, and dreamed the spider; for it is a creation of his mind. But its venom is no less potent on that account." DENT S749.1 finds the proverbial *digest a spider*, meaning "swallow all injuries," possibly relevant, but WILLIAMS (1994, pp. 339-40) finds in *Tell-Trothes New-Yeares Gift* (1593) "to be a cuckold, and know it not, is no more (sayes some) than to drincke with a flye in his cuppe, and see it not." PILGRIM (1983, p. 26) compares 2807-8 for the "vividness and power and compression" of the image.

643 **this**] Because of "his Pandar," the word refers to the adultery rather than to the escape.

645 **All's . . . mistrusted**] BARTON (1980, p. 144): "The word order . . . is oddly convoluted. [The] inversion draws attention to a rival, and even more important, interpretation" than the overt meaning — that Leontes finds his suspicions borne out. As DAVIDSON (1982, p. 79) puts it: "Indeed he is mistrusting all that is true."

mistrusted] JOHNSON (1755, Mistrust): "Suspect."

645-9 **that false . . . will**] The courtiers would be especially mystified by this; see n. 1341-6.

646 **pre-employ'd**] SCHMIDT (1875): "To employ before another," used by Sh. only here. GARNER (1982, p. 163): A neologism. Since Polixenes, only nine months in Sicilia, could not have pre-employed Camillo, Leontes may have in mind his own specific employment of him to be Polixenes's poisoner (409 ff.).

647 **discouer'd**] HUNTER (ed. 1872): "Disclosed." Cf. nn. 557 and 1170. HERFORD (ed. 1904): "Betrayed."

648 **pinch'd Thing**] HEATH (1765, p. 208): "A mere child's baby, a thing pinch'd out of clouts" (*OED*, Pinch, *v.* 1). Perhaps the right idea; cf. "The good Lady wou'd marry any Thing that resembl'd a Man, tho' 'twere no more than what a Butler cou'd pinch out of a Napkin" (Congreve, *The Way of the World*, ed. Herbert Davis, 1967, 2.1.311-13). AYSCOUGH (ed. 1790) adds, "A puppet for them to move and actuate as they please." Several other interpretations have been offered, however. WARBURTON (ed. 1747), certainly wrong: "Alluding to . . . those who were enchanted, and fastened to the spot, by charms superior to their own." STEEVENS (ed. 1778) provides

For them to play at will: how came the Posternes
So easily open?   650
    Lord. By his great authority,
Which often hath no lesse preuail'd, then so,

---

649 Posternes] postern WH2
650 open] open'd CAP (*text*); open CAP (*errata*)
652-3 often . . . On] hath prevailed oftentimes no less | Than so on HAN
652 hath] have F4-ROWE2

---

quotations to show that *pinch* was used figuratively to mean "distress" or "afflict" (*OED, v.* 7), but also one citation to support HEATH. MASON (1785, p. 127): "Shrunk, or contracted" (*ppl.a.* 2). JACKSON (1819, p. 138): "Leontes means, *that the shoe pinches.*" HARNESS (ed. 1825): "*To pinchin* in Chaucer means *to jeer or banter*" (*MED*, Pinchen, v. 5, "To cavil, object to"?), perhaps intending that a "pinch'd Thing" would be an object of ridicule, the sense given by SCHMIDT (1875, Pinch, vb. 5). KNIGHT (ed. 1841): "Petty and contemptible, shrunk up . . . by poverty or hunger" (*OED, v.* 6).

    STAUNTON (ed. 1859): "*Restrained, nipped, confined* thing." The CLARKES (ed. 1865): "'Galled', 'wounded', 'disabled.'" HUNTER (ed. 1872), evidently interpreting *pinch'd* as "inhibited" or "enfeebled": "One precluded from accomplishing my desire." FURNESS (ed. 1898): "After the shape, the proportions, of his designs have been ruined by 'discovery', as a bladder when it is pricked, he [Leontes] is reduced merely to a pinched and shrivelled thing,—then the association of ideas suggests a trick, a puppet, a toy." LEE (ed. 1907): "A nonentity." *OED* (Pinched, *ppl.a.*, citing this line): "Compressed between the finger and thumb, or two opposing bodies," identified by LOBBAN (ed. 1910) as "his own design and the treachery of Camillo." WILSON (ed. 1931): "I.e. a wretch upon the rack," comparing "If ye pinch me like a Pasty, I can say no more" (*AWW* 4.3.123 [2231]) and citing *OED* (*v.* 5): "To hurt, pain, torture, torment. (In the first two quots. applied to torture on the rack)." Parolles, whose line WILSON refers to, does believe his captors have sent for tortures, yet he probably thinks of pincers rather than the rack. RIDLEY (ed. 1935): "Trapped." CARRINGTON (1956): "Tricked, outwitted." PAFFORD (ed. 1963): "Reduced to futility." BOORMAN (ed. 1964): "Castrated." RUBINSTEIN (1984), in the same territory: "His plan for revenge nipped in the bud and his bud too, his thing (penis . . .) pinched or pruned." HAPPÉ (1969): "Made ridiculous." For Greene's "pinching penurie," see p. 626.

    648-9 **Trick . . . play**] HEATH (1765, p. 208, Trick): "Puppet." *OED* (*sb.* 6b), less specifically: "A trifling ornament or toy." MALONE (ed. 1790) asserts that this word confirms HEATH's explanation of *pinch'd Thing*, but if HEATH is right, the verb should be *play with.* BEVINGTON (ed. 1992) so glosses *play*, but *OED* does not concur; SCHMIDT (1875) gives "To make sport." HAPPÉ (1969, Trick): "Joke." CALDECOTT (MS 1813-33) incorrectly paraphrases "Trick . . . will" as "a card for them to shuffle." PORTER & CLARKE (ed. 1908): "A deft bit of handling, merely, is he for them."

    649-54 **how . . . well**] WILSON (ed. 1931), who believes Leontes to have been a libertine: "Another reference to Leontes' secret vices; cf. note [326]." BETHELL (1947, p. 123): Posterns "may admit spies or secret embassies" rather than a parade of mistresses. PILGRIM (1983, p. 82, n. 2): If Leontes does have "secret vices," "we must suppose [Sh. took over] from his source something (viz. Pandosto's sensuality) that, for whatever reason, he never properly assimilated into his play." SCOTT (1920, p. 149), sensibly: The Lord "is expressing his general mistrust and jealousy of the excessive authority with which Camillo has been invested."

On your command.

   Leo. I know't too well.

Giue me the Boy, I am glad you did not nurse him: 655
Though he do's beare some signes of me, yet you
Haue too much blood in him.

   Her. What is this? Sport?

   Leo. Beare the Boy hence, he shall not come about her,
Away with him, and let her sport her selfe   660
With that shee's big-with, for 'tis *Polixenes*

653-4 *One verse line* v1793+ (−BEV)
654 know't] know JOHN
657 him.] ~ ? HAL
660 *some bear off* MAMILLIUS. CAP, CAM3 (*after* 665), KIT1, SIS (*subst.*); *Exit Mamillius, with some of the Guards.* DYCE, HUD2, BUL; *Exit* MAMILLIUS, *with some of the* Attendants. STAU, OXF1, CLN2; *Exit* MAMILLIUS *and* Ladies. COL4; *Exit Mamillius and a Lady.* PEN1, SIG; *Mamillius is led out.* ALEX, PEN2, BEV, OXF2 (*subst.*)
661 for] *Om.* POPE, HAN

652-3 **Which . . . command**] DEIGHTON (ed. 1889): "Which has often had the same effect . . . as your express order." BOORMAN (ed. 1964, Then so): "Than in this case."

655 **I . . . him**] PEARSON (1957, p. 86): "Many Elizabethan mothers nursed their children because they believed an infant could absorb evil as well as good with the milk it took from the breast." Cf. *Tit.* 2.3.145 (888), *Rom.* 1.3.68 (414), and WILSON (1553; 1982, p. 229). PARRY (ed. 1982): Mamillius was breast-fed by a wet nurse, "as was the habit among the Elizabethan upper classes."

656 **signes of me**] DEIGHTON (ed. 1889): "Marks of personal resemblance."

657 **too . . . him**] DEIGHTON (ed. 1889): "Too large a share in his physical constitution." PARRY (ed. 1982): "Too much of your nature in him." Regarding the situation, GROSE & OXLEY (1965, p. 113): "Repeatedly [in Sh.] we are shown people— usually the heroines—victimized by slander: Hero in [*Ado*], Desdemona, Edgar, Imogen in [*Cym.*]." Cf. n. 411-14.

658 **Sport?**] MINSHEU (1617): See "Pastime, & *to* Play." MACKENZIE (1924, p. 431) finds Hermione's expression "contemptuous anger." BETHELL (ed. 1956), however: "A joke." PAFFORD (ed. 1963): "Hermia . . . asks a similar question [of Lysander; *MND* 3.2.265 (1296)], and so does Lady Percy of Hotspur [*1H4* 2.3.99 (944)]."

659 **hence**] HASLER (1983, p. 204): "From now on, the imperatives *hence, out, away* recur with increasing frequency in his speeches." HASLER points out 949 ff. especially.

   come about] OED (About, *adv.* and *prep.* 3, citing this line): Be "in common intercourse with." Cf. 950.

660 **sport her selfe**] KITTREDGE & RIBNER (ed. 1967): "Amuse herself" (*OED*, Sport, *v.* 1b, citing this line).

661-2 **With . . . thus**] Leontes's view of Hermione's pregnancy contrasts with that of her ladies in n. 607-12. GARBER (1981, p. 149): "He chooses his metaphor [swell] from the language of disease rather than healthful growth."

661 **big-with,**] Referring to MALONE's (ed. 1790) note on a similar shift in pronouns in *Cym.* 3.3.103-5 (1664-6), where the case actually differs, FURNESS (ed. 1898) wants a full stop after this word so that "it will be manifest that the preceding lines are addressed by Leontes to his attendants." Recent eds. find a comma adequate,

Ha's made thee swell thus.

   Her. But Il'd say he had not;
And Ile be sworne you would beleeue my saying,
How e're you leane to th'Nay-ward.   665

   Leo. You (my Lords)
Looke on her, marke her well: be but about
To say she is a goodly Lady, and
The iustice of your hearts will thereto adde
'Tis pitty shee's not honest: Honorable;   670
Prayse her but for this her without-dore-Forme,

662-3 *One verse line* mCAP2, v1803+
663 But Il'd] I'd but HAN
665 Nay-ward] nayword v1803
670 honest: Honorable] honest honourable WH1; honest-honourable WALKER
(1860, 1:22) *conj.*, DYCE2, HUD2

---

however. Because "the line is now a syllable too long," MAXWELL (in PAFFORD, ed.
1963) suggests "that the second *with* may be an interpolation," but the word is
needed for the line to make sense.

   662 **thee**] CARRINGTON (1956): "The very pronoun expresses his contempt. See
[395-6]." But a husband ordinarily uses the informal pronoun when addressing his
wife; see 156, 174-5, and n. 422.

   663-5 **But . . . th'Nay-ward**] PAFFORD (ed. 1963): "'I should merely have to
say he had not and I am absolutely certain you would believe my mere statement
however much you are inclined to the contrary.' . . . Hermione says that it would
only be necessary for her to *say* that she is innocent." ORGEL (ed. 1996): "Hermione's
conditional implies a hypothetical situation, one that she has not yet taken seriously."
CHARLTON (ed. 1916): "Reveals [Hermione's] open nature, and at the same time reflects some credit on Leontes, for Hermione trusts in his love for her."

   663-4 **But . . . sworne**] HUNTER (ed. 1872), wrongly: "If I would but say he
had not, although I am ready to be sworne." For "But Il'd say," FURNESS (ed. 1898):
"'Only I would say', or, perhaps, 'I need but say.'" HERFORD (ed. 1916-): "The
conditional . . . does not, of course, mean that Hermione gives only a qualified or
doubtful denial of the charge; she simply declares how she would meet a charge
which even now she can hardly believe to be seriously made." For further distinctions
between saying and swearing, see 92-3 and 3166.

   665 **to th'Nay-ward**] HANMER (ed. 1743-4, 6:glos.): "To the side of denial, towards the saying of Nay" (*OED*, citing this line only). HANMER distinguishes this word
from *nayword*, which he defines as "By-word: a word of contempt" and as a soldiers'
watchword. Because *nayward* is unique, however, BETHELL (ed. 1956) suggests that
"Nayward" may be an error for *nayword* = "refusal" (*OED*, Nayword², with one
example, dated 1898); ed. 1803 actually printed that word, no doubt by mistake.
PAFFORD (ed. 1963), however, repeating HANMER: "It is not to be confused with
nayword which means a watchword or proverb" (*OED*, Nayword¹).

   666-7 **You . . . well**] HOLBROOK (1964, p. 160): "He assumes a false and stagey
histrionic posture." Perhaps; staginess is not necessarily implied, and Leontes is quite
sincere about the contrast between Hermione's beauty and her dishonesty.

   668 **goodly**] MINSHEU (1617): See "Gallant, & Gorgeous."

   670 **honest: Honorable**] See n. 381. WALKER introduces the hyphen to signify
"honourable with honesty." ORGEL (ed. 1996): "Leontes is decrying the fact that
Hermione's honourable condition is not accompanied by an inner honesty, but it is

(Which on my faith deserues high speech) and straight
The Shrug, the Hum, or Ha, (these Petty-brands
That Calumnie doth vse; Oh, I am out,

---

673 Petty] pretty HAN2

---

to the point that he separates the concepts and assumes that 'honourable' has no moral implications."

671 this her without-dore-Forme] RANN (ed. 1787) compares *Cym.* 1.6.15 (610): "All of her, that is out of doore" — i.e., visible. SCHMIDT's (1875) definition "external" (for which *OED* cites this as its only example) is extended inappropriately by HENLEY (ed. 1902) to "workaday." The CLARKES (1879, p. 421) list other instances of demonstrative and possessive pronouns used together. Cf. 836.

672 faith] SCHMIDT (1874): "Truthfulness." The word means the same in 2348; for different meanings, see nn. 544–5, 1193, 1836, and 2307.

high] Probably "of exalted . . . style; of lofty, elevated, or superior kind" (*OED, a.* 6).

straight] JOHNSON (1755): "Immediately, directly."

673 Shrug . . . Ha] HAPPÉ (1969): "Gestures and expressions which imply Hermione's guilt."

Hum] *OED* (*sb.*[1] 2a, citing this line): "An inarticulate vocal murmur uttered . . . from hesitation, embarrassment."

Ha] *OED* (*sb.*[2] 3): "Expressing hesitation." SCHMIDT (1874): "Expressive of indignation." He points out that *ha* is also joined with *hum* in *Wiv.* 3.5.139 (1807), where Ford learns that, according to Falstaff's plan, he will cuckold himself; and in *Per.* 5.1.84 (2066), where Marina attempts to awaken Pericles.

Petty-brands] WILSON (ed. 1931): I.e., "'the shrugs, the hums, the ha's.'" Following MOORMAN (ed. 1912), HERFORD (ed. 1916–): "Marks of infamy, trifling in appearance, but no less significant than open disgrace." LEE (ed. 1907): "The figure is pursued at [675–6]." CHARLTON (ed. 1916): "Leontes conceives of these things as physical distortions and suffering." BETHELL (ed. 1956): "Their [the court's] praise of her appearance will be followed by a significant gesture or sound instead of praise of her 'honesty.'"

674 vse;] SIMPSON (1911, pp. 60–1): "The semicolon serves to mark a sudden pause or a break in the construction." See n. 422 for a similar use of the comma and n. 1387 for a similar use of the colon.

674–6 Oh . . . selfe] COLLINS (ed. 1904–24?): "Leontes means that calumny [slander] uses these 'petty brands' against innocence, mercy uses them against guilt; he implies that *justice* would go much further, as he proceeds to do himself." HAPPÉ (1969): "Leontes substitutes mercy because the hints about infidelity [673] are really polite, not to say generous, references to the truth rather than slander." With "Calumnie . . . selfe [675–6]," DENT compares "Calumny shoots at the fairest mark" (TILLEY E175) but questions its relevance. HERFORD (ed. 1916–), missing the sarcasm: "Leontes, in spite of his violent language, is confusedly aware that his charge may be false, as is shown by his mission to the oracle. [But see n. 800.] He betrays his confusion also by this unintended assertion that those who 'shrugged', instead of speaking openly of Hermione's character, did so, as calumniators, to suggest unreal guilt, instead of in 'mercy' to veil an actual offense." It is clear, of course, that the shrugs, hums, and ha's are merely figments of Leontes's imagination.

674 out] SCHMIDT (1875): "Aiming or going in a wrong way." MAXWELL (ed. 1956): "Mistaken." With *out*, FURNESS (ed. 1898) compares "Like a dull Actor now, I haue forgot my part, And I am out" (*Cor.* 5.3.40–1 [3390–1]), but as KNOWLES (privately) points out, in *Cor.* the word means "out of things to say," as in *AYL* 4.1.78 (1988).

151

That Mercy do's, for Calumnie will seare   675
Vertue it selfe) these Shrugs, these Hum's, and Ha's,
When you haue said shee's goodly, come betweene,
Ere you can say shee's honest: But be't knowne
(From him that ha's most cause to grieue it should be)
Shee's an Adultresse.   680
    Her. Should a Villaine say so,
(The most replenish'd Villaine in the World)
He were as much more Villaine: you (my Lord)
Doe but mistake.
    Leo. You haue mistooke (my Lady)   685

---

675 do's] doth HAN
     seare] fear ROWE3
678 be't] it be v1793–v1803 (*corrected* m1793 Bod)
682 replenish'd] replenish SING1, HUD1

675-6 **Calumnie . . . selfe**] *OED* (Calumny 1, citing this line): "Slander." The
sentiment is a favorite of Sh.'s: THEOBALD (MS –1729?) finds variations of it at 1006–
7, *MM* 3.2.196–9 (1671–4), *Ham.* 1.2.38 (501), and *Cym.* 3.4.35–9 (1704–8). C. G.
SMITH (1963, no. 269) finds a parallel in Leonard Culman, *Sententiae Pueriles,* and
see DENT E175. For *sear,* MINSHEU (1617) refers to *cautere,* "a searing or hote iron,"
and HENLEY (in STEEVENS, ed. 1785) finds the figurative meaning "*stigmatize* or
brand" in *AWW* 2.1.175–6 (783–4). See n. 673 for *Petty-brands.* REYHER (1947, pp.
594–5) comments on the irony of Leontes's observation. PARRY (ed. 1982), similarly:
Calumniating "is just what Leontes *himself* is doing. . . . Instead of the truth he can
only assert respectable but false motives."

676-8 **these Shrugs . . . honest**] DEIGHTON (ed. 1889): "Before you have time
to add to your commendations of her beauty your admiration of her character, you
are interrupted by these marks of contempt involuntarily exhibited either in gesture
or in words." BETHELL (ed. 1956): "When the person spoken about is infamous, it is
merciful to use a shrug or broken exclamation rather than to speak out her fault."

680 **Shee's an Adultresse**] PAFFORD (ed. 1963): "This plain but vehement exclamation comes with dramatic suddenness after the lengthy and tortuous build-up from
[664]."

681-4 **Should . . . mistake**] JAMESON (1833; 1889, p. 186): "This characteristic composure of temper never forsakes her; and yet it is so delineated that the impression is that of grandure . . . : it is the fortitude of a gentle but a strong mind,
conscious of its own innocence."

682 **replenish'd**] JOHNSON (1755, Replenish): "Consummate. . . . Not proper,
nor in use." CHARLTON (ed. 1916): "Metaphorically (from the root idea of 'full') 'perfect'" (*OED, ppl.a.,* citing this line). LEE (ed. 1907) compares *R3* 4.3.18 (2722); and
PAFFORD (ed. 1963), *LLL* 4.2.26 (1178).

684-5 **mistake . . . mistooke**] KITTREDGE & RIBNER (ed. 1967): "(a) Erred (b)
taken improperly" — (a), as BEVINGTON (ed. 1992) says, "playing bitterly on" (b). *OED*
(Mistake, *v.* 8, citing this line as its first instance) gives (a) only. PAFFORD (ed. 1963)
compares the wordplay at 1013–14. YOUNG & MOSELEY (ed. 1965, Mistake): "To
fornicate"; and COLMAN (1974), on the basis of a quibble in *H5* 3.2.134 (1252): "to
have anal intercourse" — an interpretation that hardly sorts with Hermione's pregnancy.

Polixenes for *Leontes*: O thou Thing,
(Which Ile not call a Creature of thy place,
Least Barbarisme (making me the precedent)
Should a like Language vse to all degrees,   (2A3^{vb})
And mannerly distinguishment leaue out,   690
Betwixt the Prince and Begger:) I haue said
Shee's an Adultresse, I haue said with whom:
More; shee's a Traytor, and *Camillo* is
A Federarie with her, and one that knowes

---

694 Federarie] feodary MAL (10:603) *conj.*, COL2, COL3, COL4; fedary DYCE2,
HUD2, NLSN, CAM3, PEN2, BEV4
     and] *Om.* HAN
694–5 knowes What] knows her To be what KTLY

685–99 **You . . . escape**] SMITH (1972, pp. 175–7), comparing *Cym.* 2.5.13–
35 (1350–72), another passage "in which a husband supposes his wife has been
unfaithful to him": "Both are self-conscious, rhetorical, and tortured in syntax and
strange in vocabulary. . . . There are polysyllabic latinisms, and such words as 'distinguishment' [690] and 'federary' [694] are used by Shakespeare only in this passage." SMITH (1968, p. 322): The speech "is a mixture of affectation and explosive
bombast, of what [PUTTENHAM, 1589] called 'cacozelia' [p. 210] and 'bomphilogia'
[p. 217]." These terms mean "the affectation of new words and phrases" and "pompous speech."
     685–6 **You . . . Leontes**] RUBINSTEIN (1984, Creature): "Leontes may be sug-
gesting a mirror-image of the nature of his own love for Polixenes." For Leontes's
supposed homosexuality, see p. 782.
     686 **Thing**] SEYMOUR (1805, 1:161): The word sometimes expresses "what is pre-
eminently good [as in *Cor.* 4.5.122 (2774)], and sometimes what is extremely the
reverse, as here" (*OED, sb.*¹ 10b, citing this line). CHARLTON (ed. 1916): "Leontes will
not call her, as she is a queen, by the name he thinks she has deserved by the crime
he imputes to her." WATSON (1984, p. 236): "He tries to uphold a verbal distinction . . . even when he believes its real moral basis has collapsed."
     687–91 **(Which . . . Begger)**] BOORMAN (ed. 1964): "But I will not give one of
your rank that name (the equivalent of 'thing'), for fear that ignorant people, following
my example, should use a similar word for all ranks [degrees], and cease to distinguish
decently between the prince and the beggar. (Leontes is thinking of the 'bold'st Titles'
of [698].)" LEECH (1975, p. 87): "There is a strong emphasis on the notion of 'degree',
Leontes . . . holding back from the full reproach he thinks his wife deserves." Cf.
n. 689.
     688 **Barbarisme**] SCHMIDT (1874): "Rude ignorance and want of good manners"
(*OED* 2). SMITH (1968, p. 322): "Rudeness or unpolished language" (*OED* 1). CAR-
RINGTON (1956), not exactly supported by *OED*: "The common people." VAN DAM
(1900, p. 45): Syncopated to *bar-b'rism*.
     689 **degrees**] CARRINGTON (1956): "Ranks."
     690 **mannerly distinguishment**] HAPPÉ (1969): "Distinction appropriate to so-
cial rank."
     692 **Adultresse**] VAN DAM (1900, p. 46) notices the syncopation of the first *e* of
Adulteress. For other syncopations of *e*, see nn. 222, 313, 381, 813, 1302, and 2953.
     693–4 **shee's . . . her**] See *Pandosto*, p. 626.
     694 **Federarie**] JOHNSON (1755, Federary): "A confederate; an accomplice." He

What she should shame to know her selfe,   695
But with her most vild Principall: that shee's
A Bed-swaruer, euen as bad as those
That Vulgars giue bold'st Titles; I, and priuy

---

695 shame] be asham'd HAN
696 But . . . Principall:] *Om.* CAP
696-7 shee's A] she Is a WALKER (1860, 3:98) *conj.*, DYCE2, HUD2
698 That] The HAN
     Vulgars] vulgar F4-POPE2, HAN
     bold'st] bold v1793-v1813

---

lists *fedary* separately, commenting that the word is peculiar to Sh. and defining it as "a confederate; a partner; or a dependant." *OED* (Fedarie) lists *fœdarie* and *federarie* as alternatives, identifying all forms as "var. of *feodary*, FEUDARY . . . used by Shaks. in [this?] sense due to erroneous association with L. *fœdus* [league]." It notes, "The form *federarie*, which would be a correctly formed derivative of *fœdus*, but occurs only [here], is perhaps a misprint or a scholarly correction, as the usual form *fedarie* suits the metre better." The scholarly corrector, if one there was, would probably be Crane. *Fedarie*, however, occurs in *MM* 2.4.122 (1133), *fœdarie* in *Cym.* 3.2.21 (1489); the former is thought to have derived from a Crane transcript, the latter possibly so (see HAAS, 1989, p. 7). KEIGHTLEY (1867, p. 200): "As Polixenes is styled 'her principal' [see n. 694-9], the meaning may be, that she (and Camillo 'with her' [694]) had transferred her allegiance to him." WILSON (ed. 1931): "A feudal tenant, and so, retainer, dependent. Perhaps the error arose through analogy with 'confederate.'" SMITH (1968, p. 322) thinks Sh. drew the word from *fœdus* meaning "base" or "vile" rather than "league" or "alliance."

     694-9 **one . . . escape**] The CLARKES (ed. 1865): *But* means "'only' [cf. n. 711]; and the sentence beginning with 'what' and ending with 'principal' is parenthetical. . . . 'Camillo' [is] the antecedent to 'one that knows', while 'she's' forms the antecedent to 'and privy to this', &c." MALONE (in STEEVENS, ed. 1778), more simply: "One that knows what Hermione should be ashamed of, even if the knowledge of it rested only in her own breast and that of her paramour." SHERMAN (1902, p. 122): "He is trying to scandalize her, and break in any way possible her exasperating repose." CAPELL omits a part (see textual note) because the words are "a disgrace to the passage, to metre hurtful, and no just sentiment." Other critics interpret some of the words slightly differently:

     695 **shame**] JOHNSON (1755): "Be ashamed."

     696 **But**] SINGER (ed. 1856): Used for *be-out* (whatever that may mean).

       Principall] SCHMIDT (1875): "Abettor, accomplice." COLLINS (ed. 1904-24?): "Regarded as directly responsible for the crime." According to *OED, sb.* 2b, the word may have either meaning, but the fact that its 16th-c. illustrations take COLLINS's meaning suggests that Leontes thinks of Polixenes rather than Hermione as the seducer.

     697 **Bed-swaruer**] GILDON (1710, p. lxxii): "One inconstant to his Bed, a Rover, a Debochee" (*OED*, Bed, *sb.* 19, citing this line only; Swerver, "a transgressor").

     698 **That Vulgars**] I.e., to whom the vulgar (ABBOTT §201 and BROOK, 1976, p. 93). Regarding *vulgars*, ABBOTT (§433): "A participle or adjective, when used as a noun, often receives the inflection of the possessive case or the plural." See also BROOK (p. 84). The CLARKES (1879, p. 601): "Common people." HENLEY (ed. 1902): "The herd."

       bold'st] THIRLBY (MS 1747-53): "Bold opposite to modest." SCHMIDT (1874): "Impudent."

To this their late escape.

    Her. No (by my life)   700
Priuy to none of this: how will this grieue you,
When you shall come to clearer knowledge, that
You thus haue publish'd me? Gentle my Lord,
You scarce can right me throughly, then, to say
You did mistake.   705

    Leo. No: if I mistake
In those Foundations which I build vpon,
The Centre is not bigge enough to beare

---

704 throughly, then,] F1-F3, SIS, ARD2, EVNS; throughly, then F4; throughly than ROWE1, ROWE2; throughly then, ROWE3-DEL2, KTLY-HUD2, IRV, BUL, CAM3; throughly then CAM1 *etc.*
706 No: if I] No, if I do HAN, CAP; No, no; if I v1793-SING1, SING2, KTLY, DYCE2, HUD2
707 those] these POPE2-v1773 (−HAN, CAP)

701-3 **how . . . me?**] BETHELL (ed. 1956): How sorry you will be about publicly using such terms of me, when you understand things better; "that . . . me" is in apposition to *this*. BROWN (1962, p. 219): "Even when shocked by his accusation, she thinks of his point of view."

703 **publish'd**] CALDECOTT (MS 1813–33): "Proclaimed." BOORMAN (ed. 1964): "Publicly accused" (*OED, v.* 3, citing this line).

    Gentle my] For the transposition, see n. 390.

704-5 **You . . . mistake**] ERICKSON (1982, p. 826): "Hermione initially suggests that Leontes can never undo the consequences of his deluded accusation." She actually suggests that his admission of error will just barely vindicate her, because the charge is so outrageous.

704 **throughly**] The CLARKES (ed. 1865): "Thoroughly." For the spelling, see n. 1356.

    to say] I.e., "by saying." ABBOTT (§356): A "gerundive use of the infinitive." For other instances, see 886, 1560, 2747, and 2853.

706-9 **if . . . Top**] JOHNSON (ed. 1765): "That is, If the proofs which I can offer will not support the opinion I have formed, no foundation can be trusted."

707 **Foundations**] JOHNSON (1755, Foundation): "The principles or ground on which any notion is raised."

708 **Centre**] RANN (ed. 1787), followed by HARRISON (ed. 1947): "Of the earth." HUNTER (ed. 1872): "The earth [as] the central orb in the Ptolemaic theory." Sh. does use the word in RANN's sense (*OED, sb.* 2a), but most authorities agree that here HUNTER's is intended (2b). See SCHMIDT (1874). BETHELL (ed. 1956): "Continues Leontes' large, cosmic imagery for his assurance, begun in Act I, Scene ii (e.g., [386–9])." Because of 707, however, *OED* prefers a different sense altogether: "A temporary framework supporting any superstructure; now *spec.* the wooden support and 'mould' upon which an arch or dome is supported while building" (*sb.* 13, citing this line). Hence BOORMAN (ed. 1964): "The main area, the core, of the foundations," a reading that may have been anticipated by ANON.'s (MS4, 1790–) "that which bears up the earth."

A Schoole-Boyes Top. Away with her, to Prison:
He who shall speake for her, is a farre-off guiltie,   710
But that he speakes.
  Her. There's some ill Planet raignes:
I must be patient, till the Heauens looke
With an aspect more fauorable. Good my Lords,

---

710 a] *Om.* POPE1-v1773 (−CAP)
     off] of THEO
711 But] In HAN
714 With . . . fauorable] With aspect of more favour HAN

---

709 **A Schoole-Boyes Top**] HOLBROOK (1964, p. 160): "The image . . . suggests the way a kingdom can be poised on a man's infantile whim."
  710 **a farre-off guiltie**] HEATH (1765, p. 208): "Participating in her guilt, at least in a distant degree," or, as PORTER & CLARKE (ed. c. 1903) say, "indirectly." KITTREDGE & RIBNER (ed. 1967): "An accomplice." MALONE (1780, 1:144) compares *H5* 1.2.239 (387). FURNESS (ed. 1898), oddly, finds *H5* no parallel; here, he thinks that *farre-off*, instead of modifying *guiltie*, refers "to any one who intercedes for the Queen . . . *however far removed he may be.*"
  711 **But . . . speakes**] MALONE (1780, 1:144): *But* means "only," as in 696. MALONE (ed. 1790): "In merely speaking" (ABBOTT §128 and BROOK, 1976, p. 102). See n. 1993-4 for this same *but* in a more difficult construction. WILSON (ed. 1931): "By the fact of speaking."
  712-22 **There's . . . perform'd**] JAIN (1948, p. 173): "She neither bewails her lot nor gives way to despair. But she is courageous and collected and submits to the king's will with calm resignation." PYLE (1969, p. 32): "In her composed and timeless contemplation of grief Shakespeare may have thought of her as the human embodiment of Patience on a monument, 'smiling Extremity out of act' (*Per.* [5.1.138-9 (Q2117-18)]). If so, of course, this thought is the origin of the statue scene."
  712-14 **There's . . . fauorable**] GREEN (1890, p. 13): "Hermione . . . in her entire love for him, [seeks] some outward explanation, some force of circumstance." FOAKES (1971, p. 127): She "simply [accepts] what is happening as a kind of misfortune. . . . Some malign influence from the heavens has caused her afflictions."
  712 **ill Planet**] *OED* (Ill, *a.* 3, citing this line): "Pernicious . . . dangerous." DYER (1884, p. 79): "According to vulgar astrology, the planets, like the stars, were supposed to affect, more or less, the affairs of this world." SHUMAKER & HEILBRON (1978, p. 92): "Mars and Saturn, [were thought of] as inveterate evildoers." CUVELIER (1983, p. 36) specifies Saturn, the gloomy planet.
  raignes] Planets reign in that they "have power, sway, or predominance" (*OED, v.* 3 and 3b).
  714 **With . . . Lords**] WALKER (1854, p. 274): "We sometimes find two unaccented syllables inserted between what are ordinarily the fourth and fifth, or sixth and seventh [as here], the whole form being included in one word [*fauorable*]." Cf. 518.
  aspect] CAPELL (1783, 2.4:229): Accented *aspéct.* STEEVENS (ed. 1793): The way "the planets, from their relative positions, look upon each other," to which *OED* (4) adds "transferred to their joint look upon the earth." For other astrological allusions, see n. 1278.
  Good my Lords] For the construction, see n. 390.

I am not prone to weeping (as our Sex   715
Commonly are) the want of which vaine dew
Perchance shall dry your pitties: but I haue
That honorable Griefe lodg'd here, which burnes
Worse then Teares drowne: 'beseech you all (my Lords)
With thoughts so qualified, as your Charities   720
Shall best instruct you, measure me; and so
The Kings will be perform'd.
   Leo. Shall I be heard?

721–2 and . . . perform'd.] *to the Guard.* CAP
723 *seeing them delay.* CAP; *To the guards.* v1778-HUD2 (−CAM1, GLO, DEL4), OXF1-SIS (−NLSN, ARD1, KIT1) (*subst.*)

715–19 I . . . drowne] BETHELL (ed. 1956): "The repeated imagery of wet and dry, water and fire, emphasizes her spiritual power, since she repudiates the element of water, associating herself with its opposite, fire, which was believed to lie highest in the universe and nearest heaven." The fire here, however, is anguish; see n. 719. PAFFORD (ed. 1963) compares *H8* 2.4.70–4 (1426–9). McLUSKIE (1988, p. 176): "Her denial of her sex's frailty grants her dramatic power and distinguishes her from the weaker women who surround her on stage [quotes 726]. However that dramatic power depends upon a set of rhetorical oppositions—'vain dew/honorable grief', burning and drowning—of which woman/not woman is only one. Hermione's denial of her gender is, moreover, given further dramatic twist by succeeding on a stage image in which she is the center of domestic harmony as she listens to her son's whispered story." Hermione denies not her gender but one propensity of it. PORTER & CLARKE (ed. 1908) contrast Pandosto's queen, who "with sighes and teares past away the time" (p. 626).
  716 the . . . dew] DEIGHTON (ed. 1889): "This inability of mine to weep."
    vaine] MINSHEU (1617): "To no purpose."
  717–20 pitties . . . Charities] For similar plurals, see n. 34–6.
  718 Griefe lodg'd] BALDWIN (1943, pp. 199–200) finds the idea "of Grief taking a lodging within a person" in *R2* 2.2.6–9 (958–61) and 5.1.13–15 (2274–6). KNOWLES (privately) adds *Ham.* 1.5.87–8 (771–2). HUNTER (ed. 1872) says that *grief* here means "sense of being aggrieved," but SCHMIDT (1874) gives "sorrow."
    here] BOORMAN (ed. 1964): "An indication of her gesture, to her heart or bosom."
  718–19 burnes . . . drowne] PAFFORD (ed. 1963): "A favorite antithesis." He compares *TGV* 1.3.78–9 (380–1) and *Rom.* 1.2.90–1 (339–40). The *Rom.* passage was previously cited by GILDEMEISTER (ed. 1870).
  719 Worse . . . drowne] DEIGHTON (ed. 1889): "With a fierceness that no flow of tears could quench." More likely, she feels a grief more painful than the kind that tears can assuage.
    'beseech] For the omission of the nominative, see ABBOTT §399.
  720 qualified] SCHMIDT (1875): "Of a kind." PIERCE (ed. 1918), whom most later eds. follow: "Moderated." KITTREDGE & RIBNER (ed. 1967), for example: "Mixed (with kindness)." Cf. 2393. SCHANZER (ed. 1969), however, returns to SCHMIDT: "Of such a nature."
  721 measure] SCHMIDT (1875): "Judge."
  723 Shall . . . heard?] THIRLBY (MS 1725–33?, Heard): "Obey'd" (*OED* 8). DEIGHTON (ed. 1889): "Said with great impatience," for, as FURNESS (ed. 1898) re-

Her. Who is't that goes with me? 'beseech your Highnes
My Women may be with me, for you see   725
My plight requires it. Doe not weepe (good Fooles)
There is no cause: When you shall know your Mistris
Ha's deseru'd Prison, then abound in Teares,
As I come out; this Action I now goe on,

---

marks, the courtiers have stood petrified by astonishment. Their hesitation, according
to HERFORD (ed. 1916-), is "another sign of the general resentment excited by his
calumny." PAFFORD (ed. 1963), slightly differently: "Leontes is impatient at Hermione's collected steadiness." And PYLE (1969, p. 33): "In her easy composure she
unintentionally makes Leontes look absurd." PORTER & CLARKE (ed. 1908) are probably mistaken that "a murmur must have started against the king when he cried 'Away
with her' [709]."

724 'beseech] For the omission of the nominative, see ABBOTT §399.

726 **My . . . it**] CALDER-MARSHALL (1982, p. 246): "Hermione's strong and vulnerable at the same time. Shakespeare . . . seems to have understood that a pregnant
woman has the strength of a lioness because she's not just fighting for herself."

requires] For several senses, see n. 1122.

Fooles] MALONE (ed. 1790), glossing *TN* 5.1.377 (2540): "A term of tenderness
and pity." *OED* gives three examples of the word in this sense, and SCHMIDT (1874)
adds several more. EMPSON (1951, p. 116): "They are only fools from a very elevated
point of view, but to suppose that she merely uses the word as a 'term of endearment'
[*OED*'s gloss] is to underrate the strain and the paradoxical stoicism of the whole
passage." PARRY (ed. 1982), however: "Roughly equivalent to 'poor dears.'" BROOK
(1976, p. 61) points out that in Sh. "terms of abuse are often used as terms of endearment," e.g., Othello's "excellent wretch" (3.3.90 [1691]).

728 **abound in**] *OED* (*v.*[1] 3, citing this line): Be "copious in."

729 **As . . . out**] CALDECOTT (MS 1813-33) asks, "Does it mean 'at the time of
my discharge', or is it 'as I come out of the Ordeal, according to the nature of the
proofs made'?" By identifying it as a "military phrase," however, THIRLBY (MS 1747-
53) indicates that the concealed metaphor is that of a siege. In this context to *come
out* is "'out into the field', *i.e.* to fight" (*OED*, Come, *vb.* 63b) and *action* is "fighting"
generally (*OED* 10) or "a fight" (11). Cf. *Ado* 1.1.299 (288); Claudio says to Don
Pedro, "When you went onward on this ended action," referring to the campaign
just completed. Thus WILSON (ed. 1931): Hermione "is undertaking a campaign for
her honour." BETHELL (ed. 1956), stressing the "strong theological implication in
'grace,'" sees Hermione as a Christian soldier, for "the sufferings of the saints are
traditionally spoken of in military terms."

JOHNSON (ed. 1765, Action), however: "*Indictment, charge*, or *accusation*" (*OED*
8: "A legal process or suit"); he is followed by SCHMIDT (1874). MASON (1785, p. 127)
disagrees, because he thinks the legal sense does not work with "goe on." "Hermione
only means, 'What I am now about to do.'" But HERFORD (ed. 1916-): "The charge
on the grounds of which I am now going to prison (opposed to 'come out' . . .)."
LOBBAN (ed. 1910) finds both the general sense of *action* ("experience") and the
legal ("trial at law") appropriate, whereas SCHANZER (ed. 1969) finds both the legal
and the military senses inappropriate. He suggests that "perhaps the metaphor
. . . is theatrical, *action* meaning 'the acting of plays': 'the part I now have to play.'"
PAFFORD (ed. 1963): "There is an echo of the proverbial belief that afflictions are for
our own good (Tilley, A53)." C. G. SMITH (1963, no. 5) finds parallels in Seneca and
in Leonard Culman, *Sententiae Pueriles*.

Is for my better grace. Adieu (my Lord)   730
I neuer wish'd to see you sorry, now
I trust I shall: my Women come, you haue leaue.
   Leo. Goe, doe our bidding: hence.
   Lord. Beseech your Highnesse call the Queene againe.
   Antig. Be certaine what you do (Sir) least your Iustice   735
Proue violence, in the which three great ones suffer,
Your Selfe, your Queene, your Sonne.

---

733 our] your WARB
   Exit Queen, *guarded; and Ladies.* THEO1+ (*subst.*)

---

730 **for . . . grace**] Because of ambiguity in *grace*, critics differ as to the exact meaning. SCHMIDT (1874): "Divine favour, salvation." WILSON (ed. 1931): "Reputation, credit." DEIGHTON (ed. 1889) rewords the phrase as "for the chastisement and purifying of my nature"; in LEE (ed. 1907) it becomes "for my good." EVANS (ed. 1974): For my "greater honor (when I am vindicated)." BEVINGTON'S (ed. 1992) interpretation— "ennoble me by suffering"— is related to FOAKES'S (1971, p. 128): "Uppermost seems to be the thought that what faces her will strengthen her inwardly, by straining her patience and steadfastness, and so reinforcing her humility in relation to an inscrutable providence." TRAVERSI (1954, p. 123): "The sense of spiritual acceptance is deliberately stressed." MELDRUM (1968, p. 56): "In the final reckoning she will appear to all in greater splendor than before as a direct result of her tribulations." PARKER (1955, pp. 183–4): "The pagan Hermione . . . goes to her undeserved suffering with a devotion strikingly Christian." For other meanings of *grace*, see n. 146.

731-2 **I . . . shall**] MARTIN (1891, p. 33), of her own delivery: "The familiar loving tones were turned to anger and almost imprecation." RICHMOND (1978, p. 341), differently: "Her last words make clear [that] she both loves Leontes and believes that the marriage may survive. The 'passive' feminine role is here a creative one, infinitely superior to male assertiveness." SANDERS (1987, p. 39): "It is her trust in his better nature which reveals to her the necessity of his sorrow."

732 **you haue leaue**] BOORMAN (ed. 1964): "Leontes should nod brusquely when Hermione makes her request at [724–5]." Perhaps not; Hermione may assert an authority even Leontes cannot contravene.

733 **hence**] As the textual notes indicate, Hermione and those accompanying her depart in response to this command. GRANVILLE-BARKER (1912; 1974, p. 20): "After the one outbreak of rage with her, he never looks Hermione in the face, not through her trial, never until she has swooned." This seems doubtful, for Leontes speaks directly to her several times, beginning at 1229. MASEFIELD (1912, p. 229) notices that Hermione has seen her son for the last time; "Mamillius dies before the oracle's message comes to clear her."

734 **Beseech**] For the omission of the nominative, see ABBOTT §399.

735 **your Iustice**] DEIGHTON (ed. 1889): "*I.e.* what you conceive to be justice."

736 **violence**] SCHMIDT (1875): "Power exerted . . . unjustly." MAXWELL (ed. 1956): "Outrage."

   which] ABBOTT (§270): "Sometimes the noun qualified by *which* ['violence' here] is not repeated." See 2428, and for *the whom*, n. 2389.

737 **Your . . . Sonne**] MIRIAM JOSEPH (1947, p. 152): "Catacosmesis . . . the ordering of words from greatest to least in dignity."

Lord. For her (my Lord)
I dare my life lay downe, and will do't (Sir)
Please you t'accept it, that the Queene is spotlesse   740
I'th' eyes of Heauen, and to you (I meane
In this, which you accuse her.)
    Antig. If it proue
Shee's otherwise, Ile keepe my Stables where
I lodge my Wife, Ile goe in couples with her: 745

---

744 my Stables] my Stable F4-ROWE2, JOHN, v1773-RANN, HUD2; my stable-stand
HAN1-WARB, CAP; me stable COLNE (me) *and* COL1 (stable) *conj.*, COL2, COL3, COL4

738-42 **For . . . her**] HIBBARD (1964, pp. 110-11): "Leontes's court
. . . is . . . the healthiest court that Shakespeare depicts in all his works. Paulina,
it is true, accuses one of Leontes's servants of being too obsequious to him [in 938-
41]. But none of this criticism applies to the courtiers themselves. They do not flatter
the King, but speak up for truth and humanity. . . . [The Lord's] powerful plea for
humanity [at 1077-83] saves Perdita's life and, in doing so, assures the land of an
heir. . . . The soundness of the court is in marked contrast to the diseased mind of
the King and prevents his mad excesses from leading to absolute disaster." Paulina
at 930 ff. seems not to share this view of the courtiers, however. SEXTON (1978, p.
85): "The lord . . . has no name; he speaks only a few lines. His heroism is a bright
flash of love." He may be the same lord who later speaks for the others in begging
Leontes to change his purpose. See n. 1077.
    739 **lay downe**] SCHMIDT (1874, Lay 6b): "Give up" (*OED*, Lay, *v.* 51e). "Wager"
also seems possible, however (51d).
    741-2 **I . . . her**] The Lord's reservation is curious. Possibly he makes it because
in Christian belief Hermione, like the rest of us, is spotted by original sin.
    742 **which . . . her**] ABBOTT (§394): "In relative sentences the preposition is
often not repeated." Thus HUNTER (ed. 1872): "Which you accuse her of"; he compares this construction with "this point, which now you censure him" (*MM* 2.1.15
[466]) and *WT* 2302. See FRANZ §542.
    743-62 **If . . . issue**] PARRY (ed. 1982) believes that Antigonus "adopts the
king's own, overheated style of expression." CANFIELD (1989, pp. 58-9): "The grossness of the metaphors reveals latent misogyny. . . . And the threat to spay one's
daughters and even to castrate oneself implies what lies beneath misogyny in general
and Leontes's jealous paranoia in particular: a castrating fear of female sexuality itself."
Antigonus speaks as a defender of the queen, however, an unnatural role for any sort
of misogynist.
    744-5 **Ile . . . her**] A baffling passage, as much so to later as to early commen-
tators. HANMER (ed. 1743-4) emends, glossing his *stable-stand* as "a place where a
Deer-stealer fixes his stand. . . . It came to be applied also to the person." *OED*
confirms the definition, though not the absurd substitution, upon which THIRLBY (MS
1747-53) comments, "Stuff upon stuff." Equally unhelpful is STEEVENS's (ed. 1778)
supposed parallel from Lewis Wager, *Mary Magdalene* (1567, B4): "Where thou dwell-
est, the deuyll may haue a stable."
    MALONE (ed. 1790) makes the first attempt to penetrate the F reading: "Two dis-
tinct propositions may be intended. I'll keep my station [= 'Stables'] in the same
place where my wife is lodged; I'll run every where with her, like dogs that are

160

coupled together." DYCE (1844, pp. 80-1): "If Hermione prove unchaste, I shall have no doubt that my wife is inclined to play the wanton, and therefore I will allow her no more liberty than I allow my horses ['Ile . . . Wife'], or my hounds ['Ile . . . her']." SCHMIDT (ed. 1870, p. 281) suggests a fairly straightforward "Where I lodge my wife, I'll keep my stables, under lock and key" (in Ger.). NICHOLSON (1883-4, p. 124): "If Hermione be not virtuous, no woman can be, and henceforth I'll keep my horses where I keep my wife, *similes cum simili* [like with like]." BOODLE ("*Winter's Tale*," 1885, p. 42) objects that Antigonus actually says *stables*, not *horses*, and *lodge*, not *keep*— "*i.e.*, I'll guard my stables where I lodge my wife," in which gibberish he finds "if Hermione proved false, Antigonus would keep a vigilant eye upon his grooms." HENLEY (ed. 1902), similarly: I will "lock and guard my wife's quarters exactly as I lock and guard the places where I house my brood-mares and kine."

BOORMAN's (ed. 1964) paraphrase is typical of recent ones: "If Hermione is not innocent, I'll be unable to trust my wife except when I can see and feel her; so I'll go about in double harness with her, as if we were horses, and thus we shall make our home the stables." To the same general idea, MAXWELL (ed. 1956) adds, "*stables* intended to suggest a beast to be ridden." KITTREDGE & RIBNER (ed. 1967), however: "I'll treat my wife's lodging as I do my stable, where the mares are kept strictly separate from the stallions." EVANS (ed. 1974): "'I'll guard (*keep*) my wife as I guard my horses' or 'I'll keep my wife away from men as watchfully as I keep my mares from my stallions.'"

Some older interpretations are bizarre. SEYMOUR (1805, 1:161): "He will renounce all belief in his wife's chastity, and have his bedchamber degraded into a stable for *the soiled horse* [as in *Lr.* 4.6.124 (2566)]." BARRY (in COLLIER, ed. 1842): *Stables* (singular) may have "its etymological sense from *stabulum*, a standing-place, abode, or habitation. In that case, Antigonus only says that he will take care never to allow his wife to dwell in any place where he is not." This meaning of *stable* is unknown to *OED*, but for a similar approach, see Crosby below. STAUNTON (ed. 1859) interprets *keep* as "guard" (*OED*, *v.* 14b) or "fasten" (not in *OED* exactly); where he lodges his wife, Antigonus will guard or fasten the stable door, for he will believe her to be as lecherous as Semiramis, who had a yen for horses. LETTSOM (MS 1840-65): "Quite mistaken," but the same idea is suggested by KERMODE (ed. 1963). For *goe in couples* KERMODE adds, "Be coupled by a leash to her, for safety's sake (of course, he means that if the Queen is unchaste, other women must be even more so)." His paraphrase is based on *OED*, Couple, *sb.* 1: "A leash"; *OED*, however, cites this line under *sb.* 1b: "Pairs, twos."

On the basis of a passage in Chapman's *All Fools* (ed. Manley, 1968, 4.1.261-6) and another in Greene's *James the Fourth* (ed. Sanders, 1970, 1.2.58-63), first cited by DYCE (ed. 1864, 9:232), INGLEBY (1875, p. 77): "The phrase to *keep one's stables* was a familiar phrase . . . and meant to keep personal watch over one's wife's or one's mistress' chastity." FURNESS (ed. 1898) was to show INGLEBY's evidence to be largely groundless, although the phrase does mean "to guard." INGLEBY, however, had convinced Joseph Crosby, who in a letter to INGLEBY of 30 Aug. 1876 (Folger Library 131b4) compares "then if your husband haue stables enough youle see he shall lacke no barnes" (*Ado* 3.4.47-9 [1545-7]). INGLEBY observes, "*Stable* is derived from *Stabulum*, from Lat. *sto, stare* to STAND query, is IT not called a *stable* from being a 'STANDING-PLACE?" LETTSOM (MS 1840-65), less biologically: "I'll keep my house like my stables, tying up my wife[;] if she goes abroad, I'll tie myself to her, so that she shall no more be able to get out of my sight than a dog coupled to another can get loose from his companion." FURNESS (ed. 1898): "Stables were used not only for horses but also for horned cattle. Where Paulina lodged, were she unchaste, would be a fitting stable for her husband [he being equipped with the horns of a cuckold]." GOLLANCZ (ed. 1894) reduces earlier labors to "I'll degrade my wife's chamber into a stable or dog-kennel"; RIDLEY (ed. 1935), similarly: "Is it just that he will keep her

Then when I feele, and see her, no farther trust her:
For euery ynch of Woman in the World,
I, euery dram of Womans flesh is false,
If she be.
 Leo. Hold your peaces.   750
 Lord. Good my Lord.
 Antig. It is for you we speake, not for our selues:

---

746 Then] F1-POPE1, MAL, v1821, SING1, OXF1; Than POPE2 *etc.*
  see her,] see, THEO2, WARB-JOHN2
749–51 *One verse line* mCAP2, v1793-ARD2, PEN2+; *two lines ending* be. . . .
lord. SIG

---

as it were in a stall?" WHITE alone (ed. 1883) finds possible an obscure allusion to
Jer. 5:8: "They rose vp in y^c morning *like* fed horses: *for* euery man neyed after his
neighbours wife."
 More generally, CHARLTON (ed. 1916): "The phrase . . . expresses . . . that
trust in one fundamental thing on which the order of the whole universe is
built. . . . It is Antigonus' mode of expressing an utterly annihilating and destructive
supposition by imagery of domestic topsy-turveydom, stables where the ladies' chamber would naturally be." Thus PIERCE (ed. 1918): "I'll consider human beings on a
level with horses in morality." MUNRO (ed. 1957): "The main import of much discussion . . . is that Antigonus states that if Hermione is untrue, all women are, and
he will lodge his wife with his horses and dogs; and never let her go out without
him."
 WILSON (ed. 1931) finds a personal quirk: "Antigonus is a 'horsey' character and
speaks the language of the stable throughout [cf. n. 961–2]."
 746 **Then . . . trust her**] MALONE (1783, p. 21): Although *than* and *then* were
both spelled *then*, the word here is perhaps the adverb of time. On the other hand,
KNIGHT (ed. 1841): "The sentence is comparative: I will trust her no farther *than* I
can see her." CARRINGTON (1956): "The normal order would be, 'No further trust
her than when I feel and see her.'"
 farther] By analogy with *Farre* in 2275, VAN DAM (1900, p. 111) suggests that
-ther be dropped to make a pentameter.
 747–9 **For . . . be**] HORWITZ (1988, p. 7): "It is clear that in rejecting Hermione,
Leontes is . . . erroneously rejecting the very idea of feminine virtue." This might
be clear to us, but Leontes does not believe Antigonus. See n. 750.
 748 **dram**] SCHMIDT (1874): "The smallest quantity." For a more literal meaning,
see n. 418.
 749 **she**] Hermione.
 750 **Hold your peaces**] YOUNG & MOSELEY (ed. 1965): "Leontes's brusque refusal to listen to reason is a trait he has in common with all Shakespeare's obsessed
heroes from Lear to Othello."
 peaces] For use of the plural, see n. 34–6.
 751 **Good my Lord**] For the transposition, see n. 390.
 752–4 **It . . . for't**] WEINSTOCK (1971, p. 450): In Sh. "true servants . . . make
every effort to contradict their masters when necessary, . . . to tell them the truth
to their faces." See n. 970. Antigonus is being diplomatic in ascribing Leontes's insane suspicion to the putter-on.

You are abus'd, and by some putter on,
That will be damn'd for't: would I knew the Villaine,
I would Land-damne him: be she honor-flaw'd,   755   (2A4ª)

---

753 abus'd, and by] abus'd by F2-F4; abused by ROWE1-POPE2, HAN
755 Land-damne] land-damm THEO2, HAN, WARB; land-dam THEO4, JOHN; lamback COL2, COL3; lant-dam HUD2; lam-damn JABEZ (1875) *conj.*, CAM3, PEN2

---

753 **abus'd**] SCHMIDT (1874, Abuse 9): "To deceive."

   putter on] JOHNSON (1755, citing this line): "Inciter, instigator" (*OED*, Putter, *sb.*[1] 8). HENLEY (ed. 1902): "Panderly beast," though it is not clear why a pander would discredit Hermione.

754 **Villaine**] STAUFFER (1949, p. 293): "The villain is man's vile imagination, self-generating, from whose sullen embers jealousy arises like a foul phoenix."

755 **Land-damne him**] A crux that has spawned desperate interpretations and various readings, some, like that of THEOBALD (ed. 1740), unexplained. HANMER (ed. 1743–4, 6:glos.), grotesquely: Take away his life, for "*Land* or *Lant* is an old Word for *Urine* [*OED*, Lant, *sb.*[1]], and to stop the common passages and functions of Nature is to *kill*." STEEVENS (in JOHNSON, ed. 1765, 8:Ii3ᵛ): "Confine him . . . [or] procure sentence to be passed on him here on earth [evidently in contrast to *damn'd* after death in 754]; or . . . interdict him the use of earth . . . [as] in a formal curse." JOHNSON (ed. 1773): "*Rid the country* of him; *condemn* him to quit the *land*." CAPELL (1783 [1774], 1:glos.): Rightly *land-damm*, "to pit, or bury; damm or stop up with . . . Earth." M. H. (1790, p. 306): "Emasculate him"; his or her justification is that "the scene lies in *Sicily*." In *Tit.* (5.3.179–80 [2683–4]) Aaron is set breast deep in earth to starve to death. SCHMIDT (ed. 1870, p. 281) thinks, therefore, that the same punishment is intended here, the F hyphen representing a dash: "I would Land—damn him." He then asserts that the dash should logically be preceded by *would*, and that the MS read "would I knew the villain, I would—Lord, damn him!" (in Ger.). HALLIWELL (ed. 1859): "Either, to condemn [him] to quit the land, to banish, or to curse [him] throughout the land." COLLIER's (1853, p. 187) *lamback* means "beat," and in MS 1858–78? COLLIER wonders fruitlessly whether that word bears "some relation to *lamb-skin* in . . . [Thomas] Shelton's [trans. of] *Don Quixote* [1612, p. 4]: 'for a good opportunity . . . that he might lamb-skin and trample him into powder.'"

   PERRING (1885, pp. 137–8) thinks either that *damne* sums up the ferocious treatment Antigonus would have accorded the villain (the challenge, the duel, the triumph that leaves the adversary "no ground to stand upon," etc.) or that *Land-damne*, being "the title of a high magistrate of a Swiss canton," might indicate the "sort of authority" Antigonus desires. The Swiss connection was made by KILGOUR (1875), whose etymology is scorned by SKEAT (1875) and by MARX (1875), who favored JOHNSON's explanation. This explanation MARX could have found in SMITH (1874, p. 14 n.), who attributes it to HUNTLEY (1868), who probably got it from HALLIWELL (ed. 1859), from whom he also may have derived his alternate gloss, "To abuse with rancour." *OED* (*v.*, citing this line only): "? To make a hell on earth for (a person). . . . The alleged survival of the word in dialects, with the sense 'to abuse with rancour' [*EDD*], appears to be imperfectly authenticated." *EDD* had taken *landam* and *landan* as alternative forms and had cited *land-damn* only in ANON. (1891, *Works*), who reports it "near half a century ago . . . not unknown in folk-speech in the West Riding of Yorkshire." HALLIWELL (1852, Land-damn) had mentioned *landan, lantan,* and *rantan* as Gloucestershire words, and THORNCLIFFE (1875) reports *lan-dan* and *land-damn* in use in

I haue three daughters: the eldest is eleuen;
The second, and the third, nine: and some fiue:
If this proue true, they'l pay for't. By mine Honor
Ile gell'd em all: fourteene they shall not see
To bring false generations: they are co-heyres,   760

---

757 some] sonnes F2-POPE2

---

the Midlands "forty years ago" in connection with a noisy method of denouncing wrongdoers. WEDGWOOD (1875) thinks the word "is a mere representation of continued noise." MACKAY (1884, pp. 44-5), on the basis of a strange Celtic derivation, arrives at "I will damn him, aye, and scourge him also with a bull's pizzle." FARMER & HENLEY (1890-1904; 1970) flatly guess at "proclaim him infamous." MAXWELL (ed. 1956): "The *damn* reveals the meaning of this 'mysterious compound,'" but he does not say what that may be; perhaps he would agree with BOORMAN (ed. 1964) that the term is "an emphatic form of 'damn.'"

PAFFORD (ed. 1963) tentatively suggests "an unrecorded dialect form of . . . *lambaste*," a gloss that may have given rise to KERMODE's (ed. 1963) "severely beat (?)." Among others, MALONE (1783, p. 21) believes that the true reading has been lost: *Damne* has been incorrectly brought down from 754, or (ed. 1790) "the transcriber was deceived by the similitude of sounds." SCHANZER (ed. 1969): "A nonceword, made up . . . from the *damn* of the preceding line and the verb 'to lam' ('to thrash') [this being misread], and . . . [the meaning is] 'I would thrash him unmercifully.'" EDWARDS (1975, p. 39): "One of the worst consequences of being found guilty [of treason] was that a nobleman was attaindered or attainted in blood. . . . He and his posterity lost all title of nobility . . . and . . . his lands and demesnes were confiscated. . . . [Hence] land-damn." BETHELL (ed. 1956) sums up: "Its meaning is unknown but it must be an energetic expression." For proposed emendations, see p. 574.

756-7 **I . . . fiue**] BOORMAN (ed. 1964): "We hear no more of these convenient . . . children." Girls of nine, however, are also mentioned by Paulina at 1369.

757 **some**] THEOBALD (ed. 1733) prints *some* because he recognizes it means "about" (RITSON, 1783, p. 69, and *OED, a.* 9), as in *Lr.* 1.1.19 (22) and 1.2.5 (339). If F2's "sonnes" were the reading, MALONE (ed. 1790) points out, "the second and third daughter would both be of the same age. . . . Besides; daughters are by the law of England co-heirs [760 and n.], but sons never."

758 **they'l pay for't**] CARRINGTON (1956), oddly: "Presumably meaning that they will be 'honour-flaw'd' too." Antigonus means they will be spayed; see n. 759.

758-62 **By . . . issue**] DRAPER (1985, pp. 21-2): "The deprivation of family relationship which he [Leontes] is in the process of inflicting on himself . . . is curiously mirrored [here]. Such violence of language . . . betrays the corruption that has infected him [Antigonus] and the other courtiers, even though it has not completely blinded his judgement."

759 **Ile . . . all**] MALONE (in BOSWELL, ed. 1821) demonstrates that the operation was performed on women; he refers to John Bulwer, *Anthropometamorphosis* (1650, pp. 208 ff.), which describes female castration as practiced by some ancient and exotic peoples. Nothing indicates that Sh. knew Bulwer's sources, and he cannot have known his book. WRIGHT & LAMAR (ed. 1966, Geld): "Spay; deprive of ovaries [*OED, v.*[1] 1b], possibly with the secondary sense of 'cut off', as is done to superfluous shoots of a plant [3]."

759-60 **fourteene . . . generations**] Probably "they shall not at fourteen bring

And I had rather glib my selfe, then they
Should not produce faire issue.
  Leo. Cease, no more:
You smell this businesse with a sence as cold

---

forth false generations because I will have gelded them, Hermione's infidelity having proved that no woman can be true."

759 **fourteene**] YOUNG & MOSELEY (ed. 1965): "The usual age for marriage in Elizabethan times." This opinion is supported by CAMDEN (1952, p. 93), but MC-MURTRY (1989, p. 116) has data indicating "a mean of just over nineteen years for [aristocratic] brides." See also STONE (1977, p. 49). HANKINS (1978, p. 65): "The beginning of puberty." Both Juliet and Miranda are 14 or close to it.

760 **bring**] SCHMIDT (1874): "Beget."

    false generations] DEIGHTON (ed. 1889): "Adulterous progeny," or, as HERFORD (ed. 1904) says, "bastard offspring." COLLINS (ed. 1904-24?): Contrast "faire issue" (762).

    co-heyres] PIERCE (ed. 1918): "Equal heirs in default of sons" (*OED* b., citing this line). That the four daughters of Sir Thomas Spencer (d. 1684/5) were his co-heirs was significant enough to be mentioned in the father's epitaph (see STONE, 1977, plate 8). PARRY (ed. 1982): "They inherit the shameful propensity of Hermione [because of 747-9]." Antigonus, however, is positive that Hermione's flesh is not false.

761-2 **I . . . issue**] PAFFORD (ed. 1963): "Apparently the point of this is simply to show the extent of Antigonus' feelings; for to geld (glib) himself can have nothing to do with the children which his daughters and joint heiresses may produce. But perhaps 'them' has been lost after 'glib.'" WRIGHT & LAMAR (ed. 1966): "Antigonus means that he would deprive himself of a posterity to inherit his land, which would be the effect of preventing his daughters from having children." ENRIGHT (1970, p. 173): "Perhaps what Antigonus means is that he would rather have gelded himself at the start than father daughters who 'should not produce fair issue.'"

761 **glib**] Castrate, geld, related by JOHNSON (1755) to the adj. *glib*, "smooth" (see *OED, a.* and *adv.* and *v.*¹ 1). OED (*v.*²), labeling the verb "app. a corruption of LIB *v.*," cites only two examples, this line and James Shirley's *St. Patrick for Ireland* (c. 1637-40; 5.1, 4:430). For *glib'd, EDD* also gives "castrated," citing only this line and an annotation by Sir Frederic Madden in Pierce Egan's copy of Grose's *Classical Dictionary of the Vulgar Tongue* (1823). Yet ANON. (MS c. 1750) asserts, "Yᵉ word is yet in use in Yorkshire for geld," and STEEVENS (ed. 1773) claims that "*glib* is at this time current in many counties." GREY (1754, 1:250), nevertheless, suspects the word should be the more common *lib* (*OED, v.*¹), found by him in Richard Brome's *The Court Beggar* (Pearson's *Dramatic Works*, 1873, 1:243) and by STEEVENS in John Ford, *The Fancies, Chaste and Noble* (ed. Dominick J. Hart, 1985, 1.2.115-16) and elsewhere.

762 **faire issue**] RANN (ed. 1787): "A legitimate offspring."

764-7 **You . . . feele**] FRYE (1986, p. 162): Leontes "says he smells and feels and tastes [at 783 presumably] his situation, but seeing and hearing, the primary senses of the objective, he takes less account of." But for the possible importance of Leontes's seeing and hearing, see n. 121-3, and here he clearly says he sees the business.

764 **smell this businesse**] *OED* (Smell, *v.* 6b): "To take or get a slight touch or taste *of.*" PAFFORD (ed. 1963): A common idiom in Sh. PAFFORD compares 2555-6, as well as *1H4* 1.3.277 (605) and *Oth.* 5.2.191 (3476).

    cold] JOHNSON (1755, citing this line): "Not having the scent strongly affected." *OED* (citing this line), SCHMIDT (1874), and probably JOHNSON, too, considers the word as used here a hunting term.

As is a dead-mans nose: but I do see't, and feel't,   765
As you feele doing thus: and see withall
The Instruments that feele.

---

765 but I do] I POPE1-v1773 (−CAP), v1793-v1821
766 feele] feeling HARN
       thus] this LETTSOM *conj. in* DYCE2, HUD2
       Laying hold of his arm. HAN, DYCE2, HUD2, KIT1, EVNS, BEV3 (*subst.*); *sinking
his brows.* JOHN (*text*); *striking his brows.* JOHN (*errata*), v1773-v1785; indicates a
thing shown or pointed to CAP; *Striking him.* RANN; *touching* ANTIGONUS. WH1;
Pinching his arm. COL4, PEL1 (*subst.*); *he tweaks his nose* CAPN *conj.*, CAM3
767 that] I HAN; that you HEATH (1765, p. 210) *conj.*, HUD2

---

765 **As . . . feel't**] According to FLEAY (1881, p. 58), "a true Alexandrine," the
second syllable of the final foot being accented. "As is a" may be elided without
accent, however.
   is a] The CLARKES (ed. 1865): I.e., is that of a.
   766-7 **As . . . feele**] What are the instruments and do they receive the feeling
or transmit it? HEATH (1765, p. 209): "The instruments we employ in doing any thing
do not feel, but are felt"; for his proposed emendation, see p. 575. Regarding JOHN-
SON's SD, TOLLET (in STEEVENS, ed. 1778), similarly: "Leontes might feel a stroke upon
his brows, but could not see the instruments that feel, i.e. his brows." RANN (ed.
1787) glosses *feele* in 767 as "touch you." MALONE (ed. 1790), regarding *instruments*:
"My fingers"; for Sh.'s use of the word to mean "bodily organs" (*OED, sb.* 4), he
refers to *Cor.* 1.1.101 (103). SINGER (ed. 1856): "As you . . . *now* feel my doing this
to *you*, and *as you now see . . . my fingers.*" HUNTER (ed. 1872): "As sensibly as
you feel your hands move, and see the hands that feel." WILSON (ed. 1931) glosses
instruments as "(i) Leontes' fingers; (ii) Hermione and Polixenes." Later eds. generally
agree with RANN and MALONE, although EVANS (ed. 1974) follows WILSON.
   766 **doing thus**] THIRLBY (MS 1733–47?): "Does he mean the act of kind?" —
one of his stranger speculations. STEEVENS (ed. 1778): "Some stage direction seems
necessary." As the textual note indicates, however, many eds. supply no SD, Sh.'s
intention being uncertain. See also conj. emendations, p. 574. MALONE (ed. 1790),
who reiterates THEOBALD's idea that the beard at 1092 is Antigonus's, asserts that
"Leontes must here be supposed to lay hold of either the beard or arm, or some other
part, of Antigonus," an interpretation HARDINGE (1800, p. 70) regards as ridiculously
literal minded, although it satisfies BENDA (ed. 1825). In addition, BETHELL (ed. 1956):
"Presumably Leontes tweaks Antigonus' nose . . . as he refers in the previous line
to 'a dead man's nose.'" LEE (ed. 1907): "Apparently Leontes here grasps Antigonus's
hand in his own. The 'instruments' are doubtless Antigonus's fingers, which 'feel'
Leontes' movement." PAFFORD (ed. 1963): "Perhaps Leontes merely performs an action of 'feeling' something — as of grasping one hand with the other." KERMODE (ed.
1963): "Leontes here strikes either Antigonus or himself. 'But I see it and feel it with
immediate, vital force, as you do when you strike yourself thus <or, when I strike
you thus> — you feel it and see the hands that inflicted the pain.'" SELTZER (1967, p.
138) believes that Leontes gives Antigonus a hard pinch; SCHANZER (ed. 1969) says
that "Leontes is striking against a wall or chair with his fingers, which can then fitly
be called *The instruments that feel*, without giving to *feel* the rather forced meaning
of 'touch.'" PROUDFOOT (1976, p. 74): "The implied action, Leontes' striking his
hand, presumably against his throne, suggests not so much conviction as the desperate

Antig. If it be so,
We neede no graue to burie honesty,
There's not a graine of it, the face to sweeten 770
Of the whole dungy-earth.
    Leo. What? lacke I credit?
    Lord. I had rather you did lacke then I (my Lord)
Vpon this ground: and more it would content me
To haue her Honor true, then your suspition 775
Be blam'd for't how you might.
    Leo. Why what neede we
Commune with you of this? but rather follow
Our forcefull instigation? Our prerogatiue

---

775 her] your ROWE2-POPE2, HAN

    suspition∧] Ff; ∼ ; ROWE1-KNT2, HUD1, SING2, WH1, HAL, DEL2, KTLY, KNT3;
∼ , COL1 *etc.*

    778 of . . . but] for . . . but F2-POPE2; for . . . not HAN

---

search for evidence palpable enough to be unambiguous." Or he may passionately
drive a fist into the palm of the other hand.

    withall] SCHMIDT (1875): "Together with this, at the same time." Cf. n. 2563
for the word in another sense.

    769 **honesty**] See n. 381.

    770 **face**] SCHMIDT (1874): "Surface."

    sweeten] *OED* (*v.* 2, citing this line): "To free from offensive taste or smell; to
render fresh."

    771 **dungy-earth**] Used also in *Ant.* 1.1.35 (46) and 5.2.7-8 (3207-8). The
CLARKES (1879, p. 318, Dungy): "Foul, rank-smelling." By p. 548 they have changed
to "material." PAFFORD (ed. 1963): As in *Ant.*, "'the base earth' which cannot be
sweetened because no honesty exists to do so." NOBLE (1935, p. 239): "Suggests the
contemptuous 'dung [for] the earth' of Ps. [83:10]."

    772 **credit**] JERVIS (1868): "Credibility."

    773 **lacke**] CALDECOTT (MS 1813-33): "Came short, were in this delicate point
found deficient."

    774 **Vpon this ground**] Anticipated by CALDECOTT (MS 1813-33), DEIGHTON
(ed. 1889): "In this matter." BOORMAN (ed. 1964): "On such evidence."

    776 **Be . . . might**] DEIGHTON (ed. 1889): "However men might blame you for
so hastily suspecting her."

    777-86 **Why . . . ours**] NEWTON (1986, p. 147): "Force is only a last resort, for
Leontes is no tyrant. He is first of all intent on persuasion." However, HARRISON (ed.
1947): "Leontes, being unable to persuade his Lords by argument, falls back on his
dignity and speaks with the royal 'We.'"

    777-9 **Why . . . instigation?**] ABBOTT (§385): "The negative is *implied* in the
first verb through *the question*, 'Why need we?' *i.e.* 'We need not'. [For *what* as *why*,
see ABBOTT §253.] The second verb *must not be taken interrogatively*, and thus it
omits the negative . . . *i.e.* 'Why need we commune with you? we need rather follow our own impulse'. Else, if both verbs be taken interrogatively, 'but' must be taken
as 'and *not*': 'Why need we commune with you, and *not* follow our own impulse?'"

    778 **Commune**] SCHMIDT (1874): "Take counsel."

Cals not your Counsailes, but our naturall goodnesse   780
Imparts this: which, if you, or stupified,
Or seeming so, in skill, cannot, or will not

778-81 **this . . . this**] The unexpressed referents are Hermione's infidelity, the
"truth" alluded to in 783. Or the second *this* may refer to what Leontes is saying,
"this explanation," since he is not obliged to account for his actions.

778 **but rather**] The CLARKES (1879, p. 312): Sh. "occasionally has a form of
question where the word 'not' is elliptically understood." Here one understands "but
[why should we *not*] rather." HENLEY (ed. 1902): "And not."

779 **forcefull**] SCHMIDT (1874): "Powerful" (*OED, a.* 1). WILSON (ed. 1931): "Impetuous" (*a.* 2). HAPPÉ (1969): Having "full authority." Used by Sh. here only.

instigation] MINSHEU (1617, To Instigate): See "*to* Incite, Prouoke, *and to*
Incense." The word often indicates a prompting to evil. HUDSON (ed. 1880), however:
"To be taken [here] in a good sense: 'the strong prompting of our own judgment or
understanding.'" MAXWELL (ed. 1956): "Incentive." EVANS (ed. 1974): "Motive for
action."

779-80 **Our prerogatiue . . . Counsailes**] CALDECOTT (MS 1813-33): "Enabling us to dispense with . . . your advice." WHITE (1913, pp. 180-1), more fully:
"The arbitrary power vested in the King, to do good and not evil. . . . In such matters as that here considered, [he] did not have to take the counsel of his courtiers,
but was permitted to follow such promptings as his own conscience suggested."
HARRISON (ed. 1947), differently: "As your King I am under no obligation to ask your
advice." DAVIS (1884, p. 127): "The Tudor and Stuart conception of the extent of the
prerogative is asserted here."

779 **prerogatiue**] VAN DAM (1900, p. 67): Pronounced *prerog'tive*.

780 **Cals not**] CARRINGTON (1956): "Has no need of." HAPPÉ (1969): "Does not
have to consult."

781 **Imparts**] SCHMIDT (1874): "Communicates." MAXWELL (ed. 1956): "Be-
stows."

which] LETTSOM (MS 1840-65): "I.e. with regard to *which. Which* refers not
to supposed crime, but to the act of imparting it to [them], & . . . taking counsel
with them." See ABBOTT §249. COLLINS (ed. 1904-24?): "*Which* is superfluous, as
there is a change in construction after it, owing to the parenthesis, and an additional
object (*truth*) is given to *relish*." WILSON (ed. 1931): "Both 'which' [= 'in respect of
which'] and 'a truth' are the objects of 'relish.'" He compares the construction with
2891-2. WILSON is followed by SCHANZER (ed. 1969), though it is hard to see how
which could ever be construed as the object of *rellish*. BETHELL (ed. 1956): "It has
no grammatical place in the sentence but merely indicates a general connexion with
what has gone before."

or] FRANZ §586: Either.

stupified] SCHMIDT (1875): "Stupid." ORGEL (ed. 1996): "Stunned" (*OED, v.*
2).

782 **seeming so**] PAFFORD (ed. 1963): "Cunningly pretending."

in skill] RANN (ed. 1787): "Through design." LETTSOM (MS 1840-65): "Artfully." JERVIS (1868, Skill): "Cunning," a definition with which SCHMIDT (1875) and
ONIONS (1986) concur. Thus LEE (ed. 1907): "Of cunning purpose." Although *OED*
defines *cunning* as "skill" (*sb.* 3), it does not give "cunning" for *skill*. Hence MAXWELL
(ed. 1956): "Discernment" and KERMODE (ed. 1963): "Reason" (both *OED, sb.*[1] 1).
Cf. n. 1969-71.

Rellish a truth, like vs: informe your selues,
We neede no more of your aduice: the matter,
The losse, the gaine, the ord'ring on't,   785
Is all properly ours.
   Antig. And I wish (my Liege)
You had onely in your silent iudgement tride it,
Without more ouerture.
   Leo. How could that be?   790
Either thou art most ignorant by age,
Or thou wer't borne a foole: *Camillo's* flight
Added to their Familiarity
(Which was as grosse, as euer touch'd coniecture,

---

783 a] as mTBY2 *conj.*, CAP-v1813 (−MAL), SING, KTLY, HUD2, OXF1
785-7 *Verse lines ending* all . . . liege, mTBY2 *conj.*, THEO1-ARD2, PEN2+; *ending* on 't, . . . liege, SIG
   786 Is] are HAN
       all properly] properly all POPE
   787 I] I do HUD2

---

   783 **Rellish**] SCHMIDT (1875): "To taste, and hence to feel, to perceive." PIERCE (ed. 1918): "Appreciate" (*OED, v.*[1] 3d, citing this line). For the literal sense, see 3130.
   a] Regarding eds.' change to *as,* MALONE (ed. 1790): "A wish to reduce our author's phraseology to the modern standard."
   like vs] DEIGHTON (ed. 1889): "As clearly as we can."
   informe your selues] *OED* (*v.* 6, citing this line): "Learn." KITTREDGE & RIBNER (ed. 1967): "Be well assured."
   785-6 **the ord'ring . . . ours**] DEIGHTON (ed. 1889): "The management . . . of it [is] specially ours." *On't* as "of it" occurs frequently, in *WT* at 857, 916, 1162, 1802, 2035, 2115, 2153, and 2520; see ABBOTT §182. WILSON (ed. 1931, Properly): "By right" (*OED* 1a), but RIDLEY (ed. 1935): "Peculiarly" (*OED* 1b). Hence BETHELL (ed. 1956): "Exclusively mine"; but PAFFORD (ed. 1963): "By natural right our own."
   786 **ours**] CAPELL (1783, 2.4:228): A dissyllable (thus validating THIRLBY's relineation of 785-7). VAN DAM (1900, p. 11) gives many other instances of words in which "the letter *r* may constitute a syllable by itself."
   788 **tride**] SCHMIDT (1875): "To examine, to inquire into in any manner." See n. 1580 for another sense.
   789 **ouerture**] JOHNSON (1755): "Disclosure; discovery." CALDECOTT (MS 1813-33): "'Publishing her' . . . without any *open* act or declaration."
   791 **ignorant**] CALDECOTT (MS 1813-33): "Lost everything you ever learnt, are become superannuate & unapprehensive." JERVIS (1868, Ignorant): "Dull; stupid; wanting discernment." SCHMIDT (1874) agrees, although *OED* mentions none of JERVIS's synonyms.
   by] ABBOTT (§146): "In consequence of."
   793 **Familiarity**] PAFFORD (ed. 1963): "Public intimacy." PARRY (ed. 1982): "Sexual intimacy." To make the line scan, SCHANZER (ed. 1969), following VAN DAM (1900, p. 14), wants this word to have six syllables; according to *OED*, it does.
   794-7 **Which . . . deed**] PIERCE (ed. 1918): "Which was as gross as was ever found by a suspicion (conjecture) that lacked sight <of their crime> only, lacked

That lack'd sight onely, nought for approbation   795
But onely seeing, all other circumstances
Made vp to'th deed) doth push-on this proceeding.
Yet, for a greater confirmation

---

797 doth] do JOHN1-v1778 (−CAP)

---

nought for proof (approbation), except actually seeing them in sin—with all the circumstances pointing (made up) to the deed—all these, etc." BETHELL (ed. 1956): The parenthesis should begin with "That." SMITH (1968, p. 324): "Empty ratiocination . . . a palsied attempt at convincing definition."

 794 **grosse**] SCHMIDT (1874): "Palpable." Cf. nn. 397, 1031, 1384, and 2031.

 touch'd coniecture] HUDSON (ed. 1880, Touch): "To *stir*, to *move*, to *rouse*" (SCHMIDT, 1875, 11c). HERFORD (ed. 1904): "Roused suspicion." MOORMAN (ed. 1912), comparing *touch'd* with *Oth.* 3.3.81 (1681): "As conjecture ever put to the test." HERFORD (ed. 1916-), oppositely: "Put conjecture, or suspicion, to the test; implying that it proves the suspicion just by putting the fact suspected beyond doubt." COLLINS (ed. 1904-24?): "Such an inversion is very ugly, especially in view of the next line, where *sight* is, of course, object." EVANS (ed. 1974): "Conjecture reached to."

 795 **approbation**] *OED* (1): "Confirmation, . . . proof."

 796 **seeing**] KNIGHT (ed. 1841): "Used as a noun." Following F1 in putting a comma after the word, SINGER (ed. 1856), however, arrives at "that wanted nothing but proof to be seen" rather than "that wanted nothing for proof but to be observed." HERFORD (ed. 1916-): "The proof was convincing even without ocular evidence."

 circumstances] SCHMIDT (1874): "Something attending and affecting a fact or case." He finds three variations of this basic meaning present in *WT*; see nn. 1192, 2837, and 3041.

 797 **Made . . . deed**] CALDECOTT (MS 1813-33): "Equivalent to proof of fact."

 Made vp] SCHMIDT (1875, To make up): "To complete, to make full, to accomplish." Hence COLLINS (ed. 1904-24?): "Being complete," but BOORMAN (ed. 1964): "Approached very near to"; EVANS (ed. 1974): "Added up."

 push-on] WILSON (ed. 1931): "Press forward, urge on" (*OED*, Push, *v.* 11, citing this line). These words are again hyphenated at 2619.

 798-805 **Yet . . . well?**] Various reasons are found for Leontes's consulting the oracle, including none. CRAIG (1948, p. 334): "Just why he [Leontes] does so is not very clear, since to all intents and purposes he is still a lunatic." LLOYD (in SINGER, ed. 1856, 4:139): Unlike Greene (see p. 630), "Shakespeare made the reference to the oracle originate with the accuser, and this proof of respect for it, on his part, renders his sense of impiety in insulting it, and consequent confession of guilt and subjection to its predictions, consistent and natural." HERFORD (ed. 1916-, pp. xv-xvi): "This is ascribed, in the play, solely to the tardy qualms of Leontes' conscience, hitherto completely impervious to doubt," a minority opinion. It is one shared, however, by LEECH (1958, p. 24), who takes the consultation, along with the modification of his order "that the new-born child must at once be killed" (1085-7), as a sign that Leontes is "not without mercy." KNIGHT (1947; 1965, p. 85), similarly: "Tyrant though he be, he can still think constitutionally. Though absolutely certain, he is not yet quite certain that his certainty can maintain itself: paradoxes abound." SCHANZER (ed. 1969): "By making the idea . . . originate with Leontes . . . , Shakespeare con-

(For in an Acte of this importance, 'twere
Most pitteous to be wilde) I haue dispatch'd in post,   800
To sacred *Delphos*, to *Appollo's* Temple,
Cleomines and *Dion*, whom you know
Of stuff'd-sufficiency: Now, from the Oracle

---

800 I haue] I've HAN

---

trived to make him much more sympathetic than Pandosto," another minority opinion but one endorsed by PILGRIM (1983, p. 25). BELLETTE (1978, p. 69): "Leontes, beyond words, craves the Word. He turns instinctively to the divine pronouncements of Apollo as a guarantee against the terrifying possibility that . . . 'the world, and all that's in't, is nothing' [386]. It is not so much justification that Leontes seeks, or the semblance of legality, but the Word which endorses a felt truth and extends beyond itself the validity of a private vision." KNOWLES (privately): Leontes has already had from Camillo a defense of Hermione's spotless reputation (371–6, 419–21), and can anticipate (and gets) more of the same from the other courtiers; therefore, before making a public accusation he assures acceptance of his opinion, to him a certainty, by sending for 'confirmation' from Apollo's oracle, as he says, to "Giue rest to th'mindes of others" (809).

800 **Most . . . wilde**] CALDECOTT (MS 1813–33): "A sad thing to be precipitate." ROLFE (ed. 1879, Wild): "Rash." Cf. 2403 and 2435. The CLARKES (ed. 1865): "An exquisite satire upon human auto-blindness; especially when we find how he behaves when this very oracle is delivered."

I haue dispatch'd] PORTER & CLARKE (ed. 1908): "Shakespeare thus makes Leontes do of his own motion what Greene makes him do only after Hermione had proposed it [*Pandosto*, p. 630]. Perhaps his motive for the change was three-fold: to hurry the action so as to make the arrival of the ambassadors with the sealed oracle the climax of the trial-scene procedure; to show that Leontes was sincere and not incapable of fairness; and to make the queen's appeal absolutely independent of any prejudice of the oracle in her favor, since it had cleared her in advance of her appeal." PYLE (1969, p. 38): "He has already dispatched his deputation . . . : that is to say, he has forejudged the issue, for he can have done so only before he knew his plan to poison Polixenes had miscarried." But the plot of *WT* is not so meticulously devised. VAN DAM (1900, p. 30) thinks Sh. intended the aphetised forms *I've* and *spatch'd*.

in post] SCHMIDT (1875): "In haste" (*OED*, Post, *sb.*[2] 8d). SYMONS (in IRVING & MARSHALL, ed. 1890): "As we say now *post-haste*."

801 **Delphos**] See n. 1147 for the isle of Delphos and its oracle.

Appollo's] *OCD*: The equivalent spelling is found in Greek. Apollo's functions include prophecy, and "he is often associated with the higher developments of civilization, approving codes of law" and with the care of flocks and herds. Delphi is his chief oracular shrine. As Phoebus, he was invested with many attributes of Helios, the sun. See n. 1938.

803 **Of stuff'd-sufficiency**] JOHNSON (ed. 1765): "Of abilities more than enough" (*OED*, Sufficiency 4 and Stuff, *v.*[1] 8). *Sufficiency* does not mean "credibility," as suggested by AS YOU LIKE IT (1789, p. 711). BOSWELL (ed. 1821) refers to F1's "stuffe o' th'conscience" (*Oth.* 1.1.2 [205]), and JOHNSON (ed. 1765) defines *stuff* there as "essence" (*OED* 3). The word here, however, means "crammed full of"; cf. *Ado* 1.1.56 (54). CALDECOTT (MS 1813–33): "Completely accomplished."

They will bring all, whose spirituall counsaile had
Shall stop, or spurre me. Haue I done well?   805
   Lord. Well done (my Lord.)
   Leo. Though I am satisfide, and neede no more
Then what I know, yet shall the Oracle
Giue rest to th'mindes of others; such as he
Whose ignorant credulitie, will not   810
Come vp to th'truth. So haue we thought it good
From our free person, she should be confinde,
Least that the treachery of the two, fled hence,
Be left her to performe. Come follow vs,
We are to speake in publique: for this businesse   815
Will raise vs all.
   Antig. To laughter, as I take it,
If the good truth, were knowne.   *Exeunt*

---

805 Shall] I shall WH2, NLSN
    me] me on HAN, HUD2
805-6 *One verse line* MCAP2, KTLY
809 *Points at Antigonus.* FURNESS (ed. 1898) *conj.*, EVNS
811 haue we] we have F3-POPE2, HAN
817-18 *Marked as aside* HAN, JOHN1+

---

804 **all . . . had**] DEIGHTON (ed. 1889): "Everything that is necessary
. . . being received." BETHELL (ed. 1956, All): "All we need to know." PAFFORD (ed.
1963): "The whole truth . . . when received."
  805 **stop . . . me**] LEE (ed. 1907): "Withhold me or press me forward."
  807-9 **Though . . . others**] CLARKE (in FURNIVALL & CLARKE, ed. 1908): "It is
entirely in harmony with the tyranny and self-confidence of Leontes that he should
anticipate the decision, which he regards as a merely formal ceremony which can
have no possible result other than to confirm his own opinion."
  807 **satisfide**] SCHMIDT (1875, Satisfy): "To convince."
  809 **such as he**] FURNESS (ed. 1898) wonders why eds., "in their fondness for
superfluous stage-directions, have not here inserted: 'Pointing to Antigonus.'" MOOR-
MAN (ed. 1912), however: The pronoun's antecedent may be indefinite — *anyone*.
  810-11 **credulitie . . . th'truth**] SEYMOUR (1805, 1:162): "Confidence in the
Queen's purity will not suffer him to perceive her true character." CALDECOTT (MS
1813-33): "Follow up & reach it [the truth] by necessary investigation." *OED* (Come,
v. 69h, citing this line): "Rise to the level of." PARRY (ed. 1982): "Be brought to
understand [it]."
  811 **So**] BETHELL (ed. 1956): "*Because* she is guilty, and *until* the oracle pronounces on the matter."
  812 **From . . . confinde**] RANN (ed. 1787): "She should be debarred all access
to our person; from conversing freely with." For *free*, however, SCHMIDT (1874):
"Accessible to all" and, as HERFORD (ed. 1916-) says, "therefore to be guarded from
the supposed 'treachery' of Hermione." For other adjectival senses, see nn. 185, 355,

871, 933, 2413, and 2811; here HAPPÉ (1969) prefers "honourable, noble," as in 2413, as well as "innocent." HERFORD finds a similar use of *from* ("remote from") in *Tim.* 4.3.526 (2180). BOORMAN (ed. 1964) notes "a rhetorical effect in the contrast of 'free' and 'confined.'"

813-14 **Least . . . performe**] PAFFORD (ed. 1963, Treachery): "The plan to murder me." JOHNSON (ed. 1765): "He has before declared, that there is a *plot against his life and crown* [644], and that *Hermione* is *federary* with *Polyxenes* and *Camillo* [692-4]." DEIGHTON (ed. 1889): "For fear that she may have been left behind to carry into execution the treachery planned by Polixenes and Camillo; or, lest it be left to her to carry, etc." CARRINGTON (1956): "He imagines that Polixenes planned to do to him what he planned to do to Polixenes."

813 **treachery**] VAN DAM (1900, p. 48): For regular meter, read *treach'-ry*. For other syncopations of *e*, see nn. 222, 313, 381, 692, 1302, and 2953.

814 **follow vs**] For the exit cue, see n. 3182.

815 **We . . . publique**] BOORMAN (ed. 1964): "Leontes's accusation of Hermione is given wider publicity than even at the trial later (cf. [1280-1])."

816 **raise vs all**] RANN (ed. 1787): "Call forth the exertion of all our faculties." For *raise*, however, JOHNSON (1755) gives "To excite"; for the phrase, DEIGHTON (ed. 1889): "Cause a commotion among us." SCHMIDT (1875, Raise): "Rouse." So WILSON (ed. 1931): "Rouse us all to action." BETHELL (ed. 1956): "But Leontes is complacent about his 'smartness' in detecting the supposed adultery and plot, and seems pleased at the prospect of a public speech, so that there may be the added sense of *raise* = *elevate, dignify*. . . . King James I was proud of his own detective work and professed to have discovered the Gunpowder Treason just in the nick of time. . . . The example of a king who took pride in secret service activities might well have suggested a Leontes who hoped to be raised in his people's esteem by a similar display of cleverness." Among eds., BETHELL alone holds this opinion.

817-18 **To . . . knowne**] BETHELL (ed. 1956): "Perhaps addressed more to the audience than to his fellow lords." KNIGHT (1947; 1965, p. 86): "Of all Shakespeare's jealous husbands, Leontes is most like Ford [in *Wiv.*], existing in almost comic objectivity, though without one atom's loss of tragic intensity." PYLE (1969, p. 39), however, believes that the purpose of the comment is to avoid a tragic emphasis. McDONALD (1985, p. 321): "Antigonus not only reverses the meaning of Leontes' words, but also radically alters the tone at the end of the scene." Michael TAYLOR (1982, p. 227), similarly: "The play's true status as a tragicomedy is startlingly and ingenuously revealed." FIEDLER (1972, p. 150): "There is something essentially comic about a jealous husband—the sense that his anguish, whether justified or not, is a fitter occasion for laughter than for tears." MARSH (1962; 1980, p. 134): The business "seems a mistake that will soon be discovered, and laughed at when the truth is known. In fact, it is a mistake that costs him [Antigonus] his life."

Scena Secunda.   2.2 (2A

Enter Paulina, a Gentleman, Gaoler, Emilia.   820

Paul. The Keeper of the prison, call to him:
Let him haue knowledge who I am. Good Lady,
No Court in Europe is too good for thee,
What dost thou then in prison? Now good Sir,
You know me, do you not?   825

Gao. For a worthy Lady,

---

819 SCENE III. POPE, HAN, WARB, JOHN

820 *A* PRISON. POPE1-JOHN2, v1773-RANN, CAM1, GLO, IRV, BUL, ARD1, KIT1-SIS, ARD2, SIG, EVNS, BEV (*subst.*); *Outer-Room of a Prison.* CAP, MAL-DEL2, KTLY-WH2, OXF1, NLSN, CAM3 (*subst.*)

    a . . . Emilia] *and a Gentleman* ROWE1-JOHN2, v1778 (*subst.*); *and a Gentleman, with other Attendants* HAN, CAM1, GLO, WH2, IRV, NLSN-ALEX, PEN2+ (*subst.*); *attended* CAP, MAL-DEL2, KTLY-HUD2, OXF1, BUL, SIS (*subst.*); *and Gentlemen* v1773

    821 *Exit Gent.* [or *Attendant*] ROWE1-JOHN2, v1773-EVNS (−ARD2), OXF2 (*subst.*); *to an Att.* CAP; *Gentleman goes to the door.* BEV

    822 knowledge] the Knowledge ROWE

    who] whom F2-POPE2

    825 *Re-enter Gentleman* [or *Attendant*] *with the Goaler.* ROWE1-JOHN2, v1773-CLN2, SIG-EVNS, OXF2 (*subst.*); *Enter Gaoler.* CAP, ARD2, BEV

---

    819 *Scena Secunda*] DANIEL (1879, p. 177): "*An interval* of twenty-three days is now to be supposed" (see 1134-5). PORTER & CLARKE (ed. 1908): "Paulina has no prototype in Greene's tale [*Pandosto*] and is invented . . . to take the plot on far beyond Greene's. She is shown at once to be of importance, both in rank and character. . . . She is a woman of independent means to back her independent character." HERFORD (ed. 1916-): "It is characteristic of the 'Romance' technique that Paulina, the most forceful person in the play, and, when the frenzy of Leontes has spent itself, the chief controller of its issues, here emerges suddenly and without the least preparation, for the first time. But her first words bring her vividly before us as a woman of natural power and authority, indignant at the fate of her slandered mistress, and bent on plain speech to its author, but biding her time with entire self-control." CHARLTON (ed. 1916), however: "Her impetuosity [in introducing Perdita to Leontes] prepares us for condoning in some slight degree the utter villainy of the king, since he is exasperated by Paulina's trumpet tongue." Cf. 859-61. MACKENZIE (1924, p. 433): She is "Beatrice [in *Ado*] grown elderly," though the ages of her daughters (756-7), if Sh. remembers she has any, suggest that she is not much advanced in years. BETHELL (ed. 1956): "Her forthrightness is akin to that of Antigonus but without his crudity of metaphor."

    821-4 **The . . . prison?**] PAFFORD (ed. 1963): "['The . . . am'] is addressed to the Gentleman who then summons the Gaoler. From 'Good lady' to 'prison' is soliloquy on Hermione."

And one, who much I honour.
  Pau. Pray you then,
Conduct me to the Queene.
  Gao. I may not (Madam)   830
To the contrary I haue expresse commandment.

827–8 *One verse line* mCAP2, v1793+ (−OXF2)
827 who] whom F2-SING2, COL3, HAL, DEL, KTLY, KNT3, WH2, OXF1, CAM3, PEL1, SIG
829–45 *Fifteen verse lines ending* Madam; . . . commandment. . . . a-do . . . from . . . lawful, . . . them? . . . madam, . . . I . . . her: . . . be . . . Well, well; . . . pr'ythee. . . . stain a stain, . . . gentlewoman, . . . Lady? HAN; *thirteen, ending* madam; . . . commandment. . . . honour . . . visitors! . . . women? . . . madam, . . . I . . . her: . . . be . . . pr'ythee. . . . stain a stain, . . . gentlewoman, . . . lady? JOHN; *fourteen, ending* queen. . . . contrary . . . ado, . . . from . . . lawful, . . . them? . . . madam, . . . I . . . now, . . . must . . . conference. . . . ado, . . . colouring.— . . . lady? CAP-RANN; *fourteen, ending* queen. . . . contrary . . . ado, . . . from . . . lawful, . . . them? . . . put . . . bring . . . her. . . . present . . . pr'ythee. . . . stain a stain, . . . colouring. . . . lady? MAL; *fifteen, ending* queen. . . . contrary . . . ado, . . . from . . . lawful, . . . them? . . . put . . . bring . . . her. . . . madam, . . . conference. . . . pr'ythee. . . . stain a stain, . . . colouring. . . . lady? v1793-SING1, SING2, HAL, KTLY; *fifteen, ending* queen. . . . contrary . . . ado, . . . from *then as* F1 [837–8, 839–40 *linked*] mTBY3 *conj.*, KNT, COL, WH1, STAU, OXF1, BUL, KIT1, SIS; *fifteen, ending* queen. . . . contrary . . . ado, . . . from . . . lawful, . . . them? . . . put . . . bring . . . her. . . . madam, *then as* F1 HUD1; *fifteen, ending as* CAP *through* 836 I *then as* F1 [837–8, 839–40 *linked*] DYCE, DEL, HUD2; *fifteen, ending* madam: . . . commandment. . . . ado, . . . from *then as* F1 [837–8, 839–40 *linked*] CAM, GLO, WH2, IRV, NLSN, ARD1, PEL1-PEN2; *fourteen, ending* madam; . . . commandment, *then as* F1 [837–8, 839–40 *linked*] ALEX; *thirteen, ending* madam: . . . commandment. . . . honesty . . . visitors. . . . women? . . . madam, . . . I . . . her.— . . . must . . . prithee. *then as* F1 EVNS; *fifteen, ending* madam. . . . commandment, *then as* F1 [837–8 *linked*] BEV; *seventeen, ending* queen. . . . contrary . . . ado . . . from *then as* F1 OXF2

---

821 **call to him**] DEIGHTON (ed. 1889): "Call out to him, not exactly the same as call, summon, him."
822 **haue knowledge**] PAFFORD (ed. 1963): "Be informed."
827 **who**] ABBOTT (§274): "The inflection of *who* is frequently neglected." Cf. 1207, 2353, 2502, and 2860.
829–45 **Conduct . . . Lady?**] For an arrangement of these lines depending heavily on aphæresis and syncopation (e.g., *contrar, vis'tors, wim* [for *women*]), see VAN DAM (1900, p. 51).
831 **To . . . commandment**] MARTIN (1893, p. 354): "He [Leontes] has given express orders that Paulina is not to be admitted." COLLINS (ed. 1904–24?): "He is forbidden to admit anyone."

Pau. Here's a-do, to locke vp honesty & honour from
Th'accesse of gentle visitors. Is't lawfull pray you
To see her Women? Any of them? *Emilia?*

Gao. So please you (Madam)   835
To put a-part these your attendants, I
Shall bring *Emilia* forth.

Pau. I pray now call her:
With-draw your selues.

Gao. And Madam,   840
I must be present at your Conference.

Pau. Well: be't so: prethee.
Heere's such a-doe, to make no staine, a staine,
As passes colouring. Deare Gentlewoman,

---

834 her] the ROWE1, ROWE2
835 So] If it so HAN
838 pray now] pray you now F2-v1803 (−HAN); pray you RLTR
839 *Exeunt Gent.* &c. THEO1-EVNS, OXF2 (*subst.*); *Gentleman and attendants withdraw.* BEV
841 your] all your HAN
842 Well] Well, well; HAN
       Enter Emilia. F2-THEO4; *Exit* Gaoler. JOHN1+ (*subst.*)
844 [*After* colouring.] *Enter* Emilia. JOHN, v1773; *Re-enter* Keeper, *with* EMILIA. CAP, v1778+ (*subst.*)

---

832 **a-do**] MINSHEU (1617, Much Adoe): See "Trouble, Disturbance." CALDECOTT (MS 1813-33): "Work afoot."
       honesty] See n. 381.
833 **Th'accesse**] PORTER & CLARKE (ed. c. 1903): "Stress on second syllable."
       gentle] BOORMAN (ed. 1964): "Respectable." Since the visitors would share honesty and honor with Hermione, they would presumably be "not violent, harmless" as well as "well born" (both SCHMIDT, 1874, although he does not cite this instance of *gentle*).
       lawfull] MAXWELL (ed. 1969): Her tone is satirical.
836 **put a-part**] CARRINGTON (1956): "Send away."
       these your] For the demonstrative and possessive pronouns used together, see n. 671.
841 **Conference**] SCHMIDT (1874): "Discourse, conversation."
844 **As passes colouring**] CALDECOTT (MS 1813-33, Colouring): "The dying in all the colours of the rainbow." JERVIS (1868): "Exaggeration; heightening." HUDSON (ed. 1880): "To *pass* is . . . to *outstrip*, to *go beyond*, to *surpass*: [*OED* 19]. To *colour* often means to *palliate*, to *disguise*, to *make specious* [*OED* 3]." Most critics assume that the allusion is to the dyer's art and falsity, although SCHMIDT (1874) recognizes two senses of *colour* as a verb, "to dye" and "to give a specious appearance"; he glosses the word here as "to dye." Thus CARRINGTON (1956): "As black as possible." PIERCE (ed. 1918), however, chooses the second sense, which yields, as YOUNG & MOSELEY (ed. 1965) put it, "the futility of Leontes's attempt to prove Hermione's guilt is obvious." HERFORD (ed. 1916-) finds another type of creativity: "As

How fares our gracious Lady?   845
   Emil. As well as one so great, and so forlorne
May hold together: On her frights, and greefes
(Which neuer tender Lady hath borne greater)
She is, something before her time, deliuer'd.
   Pau. A boy?   850
   Emil. A daughter, and a goodly babe,
Lusty, and like to liue: the Queene receiues

---

845 our] one F2

---

outdoes the arts of the painter. They are more bent upon making Hermione's stainless character look black than a painter is to cover his white canvas with colour. The barely hinted figure is not quite coherent, since the process of painting does not involve the 'ado' required to make the slander upon Hermione plausible." WILSON (ed. 1931): "It is the 'ado to make no stain a stain' which 'passes colouring' (= the dyer's art)." NEILSON & HILL (ed. 1942) add "excusing." So BETHELL (ed. 1956): "'There is more leuen here to make what is no stain into a stain (i.e. to make the innocent appear guilty) than the dyer makes' — in dyeing ('colouring') a garment. *To colour* also means *to make plausible* and *to palliate, excuse*: thus 'as passes colouring' means, in addition to the literal sense given above, 'as passes all plausibility' (Leontes' 'ado' lacks the colour of truth) and 'as passes all excuse' (it is beyond excusing)." BEVINGTON (ed. 1992): "With a pun on *stain*, 'coloring', in [843]." COLLINS (ed. 1904-24?): "In either interpretation [*stain* as 'disguise' or as 'palliate'] the word *colouring* is suggested by the literal sense of *stain*, while in the second view *colouring* is an actual part of the metaphor." For "o're-dy'd Blacks," see n. 208.

847 **May hold together**] The meaning is evidently so obvious that few eds. provide a gloss, but the glosses provided are odd. CALDECOTT (MS 1813-33): "May be expected to profess herself. The phrase seems to have been chosen in reference to her present situation; that of having just 'fallen to pieces.'" SCHMIDT (1874, Hold 2c): "Not to fall in pieces." HUDSON (ed. 1880): "To *hold together*, to *stand together*, is to *be consistent*, and so to *be possible*," which seems entirely off the mark. *OED* (*v.* 43): "To continue in union or connexion; to remain entire; to cohere. *lit.* and *fig.*" This is obviously a figurative use, perhaps "remain in control of herself." KNOWLES (privately) prefers "as one may reconcile such greatness with such forlornness" or "as one so great and [one] so forlorn may consist in the same person."

On] SCHMIDT (1875): "Denoting the ground or occasion of anything done." ROLFE (ed. 1879): "In consequence of." See ABBOTT §180.

848 **Which**] DEIGHTON (ed. 1889): "Than which."

849 **She . . . deliuer'd**] PORTER & CLARKE (ed. 1908): "Shakespeare's special touch of nature to show how her woes grieved her."

something] Somewhat. See n. 224. WALKER (1860, 1:222): Accented on the second syllable. Cf. "nothing" (2210).

852 **Lusty**] JOHNSON (1755): "Vigorous; healthy."

like to liue] SCHMIDT (1874, Like, adj. 3): "Having a certain air, a look indicative of something." PIERCE (ed. 1918), however: "Likely" (adj. 4). STONE (1977, pp. 68-70) shows that infant mortality in Sh.'s time was very high by modern standards. From 1590 to 1610, more than 25% of the nobility died before reaching age 15, and the children "most at risk were new-born infants" (p. 68).

Much comfort in't: Sayes, my poore prisoner,
I am innocent as you.
   Pau. I dare be sworne: 855
These dangerous, vnsafe Lunes i'th'King, beshrew them:
He must be told on't, and he shall: the office

---

856 vnsafe] unsane COL2, COL3
    i'th'] o'the MTBY2 *conj.*, CAPN (V.R.), v1773-KNT1, KNT3
857 on't] of it POPE, HAN
    he] *Om.* ROWE1-POPE2, HAN

853-4 **my . . . you**] WATSON (1984, p. 246): Sh.'s audience, "highly conscious" of original sin, would have found "her phrasing . . . dangerously general." She commits "the sin of moral complacency." No one else thinks so.

854 **I . . . you**] DENT compares "As innocent as a newborn Babe" (TILLEY B4).

you] BOORMAN (ed. 1964) interprets the comma following this word in F1 as "perhaps suggesting that Emilia is interrupted by Paulina." Since the grammar is complete and an interruption pointless, other eds. change to a period. See p. 567.

855-61 **I . . . more**] MARTIN (1891, p. 12): "In hot anger she [Paulina] exclaims, 'I dare be sworn!'—and in the words that follow shows the clear commonsense and fearless courage of which she gives remarkable proofs at a later stage. From first to last she regards the conduct of Leontes as simple madness."

855 **I . . . sworne**] PARRY (ed. 1982): "I'll take my oath on (the truth) of that."

856 **dangerous**] STAUNTON (ed. 1859): "Biting, caustic, mischievous." The CLARKES (ed. 1865): "'Severe', 'sharp', 'keen.'" The CLARKES (1879, p. 610): Thus not a pleonasm, for the word is used in these senses "more than its directer sense of 'perilous.'" *OED* does not concur.

dangerous, vnsafe] For similar repetitions, see 302, 595, 634, 890, 916, 1208, and 1215.

Lunes] HANMER (ed. 1743-4, 6:glos.): "Fits of Lunacy or frenzy, mad freaks" (*OED*, Lune[2] *pl.*, citing this line as its first example). HUDSON (ed. 1880) is mistaken in saying that the term "is not met with in any other English writer," but its later uses may derive from this one. *OED* makes a connection with *Line* (*sb.*[2] 29), "used by Shaks. in *pl.* for: 'Goings on', caprices or fits of temper. <Cf. the Warwickshire dial. phrase *on a line* = in a rage.>" Since *lines* is found in F *Wiv.* 4.2.22 (1918) and F *Tro.* 2.3.130 (1335), *lunes* here may be an error for that word; on the other hand, some eds. substitute *lunes* for *lines* in *Wiv.* STEEVENS (ed. 1778), who thinks the word means "a leash for a hawk," has the wrong meaning here (Lune[1]), though in this sense it twice appears in Greene's *Mamillia*, pt. 2 ([1583?]). HARNESS (ed. 1825), straight-facedly perhaps: "It was suggested by Mr. Kemble that *lunes* was a Spanish term, expressing the cry of a restive mule."

beshrew] HANMER (ed. 1743-4, 6:glos.): "An Imprecation . . . *ill betide.*" PHILLIPS (1706): "Curse" (*OED*, *v. arch.* 3b and 3).

857 **must . . . on't**] See n. 785-6 and, for the passive construction, *OED* (Tell, *v.* 8b, citing this line).

857-8 **the . . . best**] STOPES (1916, p. 34): "She sets out single-handed, as a Lady-Knight, to beard the King in his den, and try to do alone what a whole Court of men had feared to attempt in combination."

857 **office**] JOHNSON (1755): "Business." A verb at 253, this word as a noun appears in other senses at 1121, 2440, and 2820.

Becomes a woman best. Ile take't vpon me,
If I proue hony-mouth'd, let my tongue blister.
And neuer to my red-look'd Anger bee   860
The Trumpet any more: pray you (*Emilia*)
Commend my best obedience to the Queene,
If she dares trust me with her little babe,
I'le shew't the King, and vndertake to bee
Her Aduocate to th'lowd'st. We do not know   865

858–9 me, . . . blister.] ~ . . . . ~ ; THEO1+
859 mouth'd] mouth WARB
864 shew't] show it to PEN1

---

858 **Becomes**] SCHMIDT (1874, Become): "Suit[s]."
859–61 **If . . . more**] PYLE (1969, pp. 41–2): She indicates "her intended method of approach, which . . . is speaking. . . . In this she is in evident contrast with conventional ideals of womanly excellence . . . and, so considered, the part contains an inherent element of comedy."
859 **hony-mouth'd**] SCHMIDT (1874): "Sweet and smooth in speech." DENT compares "Honey in his mouth" (TILLEY H547).
    let . . . blister] DYER (1884, p. 266): "A lie produces a blister on the tongue." See TILLEY R84.
860–1 **to . . . Trumpet**] WILSON (ed. 1931), followed by KERMODE (ed. 1963) and some later eds., asserts that "heralds were loud-voiced persons dressed in red and often bore candid, or insulting, messages; their 'trumpet' was a man who preceded them" (SCHMIDT, 1875). BOORMAN (ed. 1964) quotes Dekker's *The Gull's Hornbook* (1609): "Present not yourself on the stage . . . until the quaking Prologue hath by rubbing got colour into his cheeks, and is ready to give the trumpets their cue that he's upon point to enter" (ed. McKerrow, p. 52), but this advice has nothing to do with anger. The tongue itself is a herald in *AWW* 5.3.46 (2752); here it is WILSON's trumpeter or a musical instrument capable of a blast. Cf. 865 and the trumpet-tongu'd angels of *Mac.* 1.7.19 (493).
860 **red-look'd**] MAXWELL (ed. 1956): "Red-faced." ABBOTT (§294): A passive verb, "found mostly in the participle." He compares "leane-lookt prophets" (*R2* 2.4.11 [1295]). CARRINGTON (1956), incorrectly: "Making me red in the face."
862 **Commend**] SCHMIDT (1874): "Recommend" (*OED*, *v.* 2a). PORTER & CLARKE (ed. c. 1903): "Consign." EVANS (ed. 1974): "Deliver."
865 **Aduocate**] Because Rabelais, according to FARMER & HENLEY (1890–1904; 1970), uses *advocatière* to mean "ponce" or "pimp" ("Pantagrueline Prognostication 5," *Œuvres complètes*, ed. Boulenger & Scheler, Bruges, 1955, p. 902), RUBINSTEIN (1984) holds that *Aduocate* would be understood as "procurer, bawd," although that sense here makes no sense. SCHMIDT (1874): "One who pleads the cause of another." See further at nn. 970, 2622, and 2993.
    to th'lowd'st] CALDECOTT (MS 1813–33): "Open-mouthed, and in the highest tone." SCHMIDT (1874, Loud): "Speaking at the top of the voice" (*OED*, *a.* 5, citing this line). Paulina evidently means this rather than "emphatic or vehement in expression" (*OED*, *a.* 2), because of the contrast, in 867, with the child's silence.

How he may soften at the sight o'th'Childe:
The silence often of pure innocence
Perswades, when speaking failes.
    Emil. Most worthy Madam,
Your honor, and your goodnesse is so euident,   870
That your free vndertaking cannot misse
A thriuing yssue: there is no Lady liuing
So meete for this great errand; please your Ladiship
To visit the next roome, Ile presently
Acquaint the Queene of your most noble offer,   875
Who, but to day hammered of this designe,

---

870 is] are COL2
876 of] on HAN

---

866 **soften**] *OED* (*v.* 7, citing this line): "To become more gentle, tender, or emotional."

867-8 **The . . . failes**] PAFFORD (ed. 1963) compares the "prone and speechlesse dialect" of *MM* 1.2.183 (276). LIVINGSTON (1969, p. 344): "But neither truthful words nor the silent forms of innocence can move a mad king." BLAKE (1983, p. 107): "*Often* is usually regarded as an adverb qualifying *perswades.* Yet . . . the middle of a nominal group . . . is an unusual place to locate an adverb. [It may instead] be taken as an adjective. This would then make the sentence mean 'The continual silence of pure innocence persuades. . . .'" *Often* is occasionally an adjective (see *AYL* 4.1.18 [1934]); here, however, it is probably an adverb, not put at the end of the line because there it would create a bad pentameter.

870 **is**] The verb is singular because "two . . . singular nouns precede" it (ABBOTT §336). For other subject-verb disagreements, see nn. 237, 920-1, 1636-7, 1643, and 1724. COLLINS (ed. 1904-24?) believes instead that "*honour and goodness* [are] regarded as a single notion." For F2's treatment of this construction, see n. 30.

871 **free**] SCHMIDT (1874, Free 10): "Guiltless, innocent, harmless"—a reading that, because of the restrictions placed upon Hermione (830-1) and possibly upon the baby (885-7), is not impossible, despite FURNESS's (ed. 1898) patronizing objection ("not based on English authority"). FURNESS prefers "freely offered." Hence, MAXWELL (ed. 1956): "Voluntary." SCHMIDT (1874, Free 11): "Of a pure and generous mind, . . . gentle, gracious," the choice of EVANS (ed. 1974). For other adjectival senses, see nn. 185, 355, 812, 2413, and 2811.

    misse] *OED* (*v.*[1] 6): "Fail to get."

872 **thriuing yssue**] PIERCE (ed. 1918): "Successful result." UPHAUS (1981, p. 75): Refers "both to the birth of Perdita and to the, presumably, successful reversal of Leontes's jealousy as a result of that birth." The reference to Perdita's birth seems quite unlikely.

873 **meete**] SCHMIDT (1875): "Proper, fit."

873-4 **please . . . roome**] THIRLBY (MS 1725-33?): "Foolishly order'd [if thus] Shakespear." He refers to 884, where Emilia asks Paulina to "come something neerer." There is no inconsistency, however; see n. 884.

873 **please**] ORGEL (ed. 1996): "If it please."

    Ladiship] VAN DAM (1900, p. 57): Pronounced *lad'-ship.*

874 **presently**] MINSHEU (1617): See "Immediatelie." Cf. 3290.

876 **hammered of**] ANON. (MSFL 1733-): "Contrived it in her mind" (*OED, v.*

But durst not tempt a minister of honour
Least she should be deny'd.
   Paul. Tell her (*Emilia*)
Ile vse that tongue I haue: If wit flow from't   880
As boldnesse from my bosome, le't not be doubted
I shall do good.
   Emil. Now be you blest for it.
Ile to the Queene: please you come something neerer.

---

884 *Exit marked by* CAM3

2a). JERVIS (1868): "To make mention; to dwell upon" (4b). HERFORD (ed. 1916-): "Her mind was urgently possessed by it. . . . Used in Shakespeare of strong and persistent desires or intentions entertained but not yet urged." He compares *TGV* 1.3.18 (320). CHARLTON (ed. 1916): "Was shaping (with the metaphor of forging) or kept on urging (with the more obvious metaphor of the repeated strokes of the hammer)." RICO (1985, p. 291): "Throughout . . . the second act, the imagery of hardness and coldness refers as much to Leontes' jealousy as to Hermione's constancy. . . . This community's recovery depends on a 'design' that Paulina and Hermione have 'hammered of.'" But in this—RICO's only example of the imagery—Hermione alone was hammering. The idea of appealing to Leontes's pity by showing him his newborn daughter occurred to each independently, an indication of its fundamental power. ABBOTT (§175) considers that *of* is used metaphorically for *on*; the design is regarded as the object from which or toward which the action proceeds.

   877 **tempt**] CALDECOTT (MS 1813-33): "Solicit" (*OED*, *v.* 5). CHARLTON (ed. 1916): Perhaps the word "has a suggestion of its derivative 'attempt'. Hence 'venture to solicit'" (*v.* 3c). WILSON (ed. 1931): "Make approaches to." RIDLEY (ed. 1935): "Try" (*v.* 1 or 3).

   minister of honour] COLLINS (ed. 1904-24?): "Honourable messenger." HARRISON (ed. 1947): "A high official of the court."

   880 **wit**] JOHNSON (1755): "The powers of the mind; the mental faculties; the intellects. This is the original signification." FURNESS (ed. 1898): "Here modified into *keenness, tact, address.*" WILSON (ed. 1931): "Words of wisdom, for the king's good."

   881 **As . . . bosome**] PARRY (ed. 1982): "As there is forthrightness in the way I feel." For *bosome*, see n. 327.

   boldnesse] SCHMIDT (1874): "Courage."

   le't] The unusual form may be Crane's representation of one-syllable pronunciation. The line is hypermetrical, nevertheless.

   884 **please . . . neerer**] FURNESS (ed. 1898), puzzled, speculates "that Paulina is not actually inside the Prison, but stands without at the Gate or Entrance, and Emilia asks her to come further within it." Instead of "A Prison" or an "Outer-room of a Prison," where many eds. set it, the scene, according to FURNESS, should be "At the Gate of a Prison," for "Paulina's very first words [quotes 821] betoken that she is outside the prison and is summoning him [the Jailer] to the entrance." The scene is not precisely located, although Emilia's mention of a "next roome" (874) suggests an interior. The present words, rather than indicating a location, could mean only that the women whisper briefly before Emilia exits. WILSON (ed. 1931), however: "The two are on the outer stage; and as Emilia speaks she motions with her hand towards the inner stage or one of the side doors, and then exits"—to "visit the next roome," as BETHELL (ed. 1956) notes.

   something] Somewhat. See n. 224.

Gao. Madam, if't please the Queene to send the babe,   885
I know not what I shall incurre, to passe it,
Hauing no warrant.
    Pau. You neede not feare it (sir)
This Childe was prisoner to the wombe, and is
By Law and processe of great Nature, thence   890
Free'd, and enfranchis'd, not a partie to
The anger of the King, nor guilty of

887-8 *One verse line* mCAP2, v1793+ (−HARN, KNT, HAL, STAU)
889 This] The ROWE1-SING1 (−CAP), COL, HUD, DYCE, HAL, DEL, IRV, OXF1, SIS, CLN2

---

886 **to passe it**] ABBOTT (§356): "As the consequence of, or *for*, letting it pass."
For the indefinite use of the infinitive, see n. 704 and cf. 1560, 2747, and 2853. *OED*
(Pass, *v.* 43, citing this line as its first instance): "To . . . allow . . . to go
. . . through." KITTREDGE & RIBNER (ed. 1967): "Allowing it to leave the prison."
    889-93 **This . . . Queene**] BUCKNILL (1860, p. 128): Paulina alludes to "the
merciful theory of the English law, that an unborn child is innocent of the guilt of its
mother; a theory carried out to the reprieve of a person condemned to death if she
be found pregnant, until parturition . . . has separated the guilty from the innocent
life." PHILLIPS (1972, p. 47) believes "the question [is] whether a child . . . born to
a mother . . . in prison is also a prisoner or is by nature born free." WILLIAMS (1967,
p. 13): She places "mocking stress on the legal terminology Leontes has distorted."
TRAVERSI (1954, pp. 125-6): "The first direct enunciation of one of the main
themes . . . : the function of new-born innocence as a healing power in redressing
the excesses that spring from the distortion of sexual feeling." HORWITZ (1988, p.
10): "Although she mentions freedom and enfranchisement, her reference to 'law
and process' frames and controls the natural process of birth, denying the randomness
that so threatens Leontes."
    890 **Law and processe**] For the possible hendiadys, see n. 904-5. SCHMIDT
(1875, Process): "The way and order in which something goes forward or happens,"
here childbirth. CARRINGTON (1956): The word here also means "(legal) proceeding"
(*OED*, *sb.* 7). The obvious contrast is with the perverted law and process of Leontes's
sessions (3.2). For similar repetitions see 302, 595, 634, 856, 916, 1208, and 1215.
    891 **enfranchis'd**] BETHELL (ed. 1956): "Given the rights of a free man (after
slavery or serfdom) [*OED* 1]; also, freed from prison [2]. . . . The child (i) attains
personality, and (ii) is no longer 'prisoner to the womb.'" The child is "free'd" by
the law of Nature, being innocent of any wrongdoing, and "enfranchis'd" by the
process of Nature, being released from the womb's confinement.
    891-3 **not . . . Queene**] MARSH (1962; 1980, p. 134): "The overriding law of
nature . . . does not carry guilt over from generation to generation. Leontes, in denying the parentage of his own child, and in making her the object for his revenge,
is denying this law of nature."
    891-2 **to . . . of**] ABBOTT (§457): "Sometimes an unemphatic monosyllable is
allowed to stand in an emphatic place, and to receive an accent. This is particularly
the case with conjunctions and prepositions at the end of the line." *WT* has many
instances, including 479, 534, 548, 566, 578, etc.

(If any be) the trespasse of the Queene.
    Gao. I do beleeue it.
    Paul. Do not you feare: vpon mine honor, I   895
Will stand betwixt you, and danger.   *Exeunt*

Scæna Tertia.   2.3

894–6 *Two verse lines ending* upon . . . danger. CAP, MAL-SING1, SING2, HAL, KTLY; *ending* I . . . danger. DEL; *three, ending* it. . . . honour, . . . danger. OXF2
896 betwixt] 'twixt POPE1-SING1, SING2, HAL, KTLY, DYCE2, HUD2, OXF2
897 SCENE IV. POPE, HAN, WARB, JOHN

---

893 **If any be**] Regarding *If any be*, PAFFORD (ed. 1963): "If there be any guilt." HERFORD (ed. 1916–): "Paulina . . . guards against the inference . . . that she admits the queen's guilt."

894–6 **I . . . danger**] WALKER (1860, 3:100), commenting on eds.' attempts to regularize these lines: "Shakespeare very frequently concludes his scenes with a seven-syllable line; so that any objection to such an arrangement of the lines in such a situation, as being out of place, is unfounded." As well as in *WT* and in *TNK* 5.4.136–7, instances may be found in *Lr.*, *Mac.*, and *Oth.*, WALKER says, but he gives no references.

897 *Scæna Tertia*] HERFORD (ed. 1916–): "The tragic plot moves toward its climax with the swiftness usual in the Romances; Paulina is repelled, and the newborn child condemned to the fire. But in keeping with the same 'Romantic' technique, the edge of the tragic menace is turned in this very scene; Leontes consents to sentence the child, instead of being destroyed, to be cast away in a 'desert place' where 'chance', as every reader of Romance knows[,] will cause it to be found and reared; and at the close the messengers from 'Delphos' return with Apollo's decree, their unexampled speed [1132–3] reflecting their eager hope that the divine voice would destroy the groundless calumny. Paulina's demeanour to Leontes is admirably free from mere rudeness, on the one side, and from any regard for the 'divinity (which) doth hedge a king', but which the king himself has so grossly violated, on the other." HERFORD compares Kent's "vainly stemming the passion of Lear." CHARLTON (ed. 1916): "The problem immediately before Shakespeare [in this scene] is to bring the monstrous inhumanity of this [Perdita's fate] within the range of human possibility: and this he does by a succession of suggestions and devices the general tone of which is exemplified by the indirect and semi-pathetic appeal of the first line: the inhuman madman is beyond our sympathy, but the sleepless sufferer may extort it." BETHELL's (ed. 1956) description is rather odd: "The opening . . . is highly serious but the tone changes to what is almost music-hall farce, with the slanging match between Leontes and Paulina and jokes about henpecked husbands, then modulates into a quiet but tense conclusion."

Enter Leontes, Seruants, Paulina, Antigonus,
and Lords.

Leo. Nor night, nor day, no rest: It is but weaknesse   900

---

898 *The* PALACE. POPE1+ (−PEL1, CLN2, PEN2, OXF2) (*subst.*)

898–9 *Enter . . . Lords.*] *Enter* Leontes, Antigonus, *Lords, and other Attendants.*
ROWE1-JOHN2, v1773-HAL, DEL2-ARD1, KIT1-CLN2, SIG (*subst.*); ANTIGONUS, *and Lords,*
waiting, and other Attendants. Enter LEONTES. CAP, STAU, OXF2, BEV4 (*subst.*); LEON-
TES *alone, discovered.* KEM1, CAM3, ARD2, PEN2 (*subst.*); *Enter* LEONTES; SERVANTS
keeping the door. EVNS, BEV3

898–9 *Enter . . . Lords*] WILSON (ed. 1931): "The order of these names, as
elsewhere in the text, denotes the order of entry." Although they differ somewhat in
form, the SDs of eds. call for similar action. Leontes is alone or, if the Lords and others
are present, they are at some distance. After the Servant enters at 909 and reports on
Mamillius, Leontes orders, "Leaue me solely." At 928–9 the Lords intercept Paulina,
but Leontes is unaware of her presence until 945. PAFFORD (ed. 1963): There "Paulina
and the others do not enter far on the stage or else the stage is in some way divided.
They can be seen and heard by the audience but not by Leontes." HOWARD-HILL
(1972, p. 130) notices that "the Babe is omitted from" this SD (see the textual notes).
The babe would have been a doll, however, and the F SDs do not specify props.

898 *Antigonus*] BROWN (1962, p. 219): "The most fluently politic of Leontes'
courtiers," in contrast to his wife, Paulina.

900–8, 919–27 **Nor . . . againe, See . . . powre**] GREEN (1890, p. 14): "His
diseased mind is now his prison house, his accusing conscience his sleepless jailer."
PAFFORD (ed. 1963), more accurately: "Leontes' soliloquy, his tormented mind seeking relief in plans for savage vengeance, makes clear that Paulina's mission could
hardly be worse timed, and prepares for the brutal sentence on the child and on
Antigonus." BEVAN (1967, p. 61): "His desire for 'present revenge' must be glutted
by one death at least, if not Polixenes' then Hermione's. Paulina calls him 'mad' [987];
for his actions, which might [possibly] have been undertaken for honour, make him
dishonourable, thus defeating any justifiable end [quotes 1004–6]." BEVAN's point is
that dispassionate revenge should be undertaken for the reparation of a man's honor,
although when the offense is adultery, the revenge must be kept secret to avoid public
dishonor.

900 **Nor . . . rest**] GREEN (1890, p. 14): "Hermione is a free spirit no bars can
fetter. The immured, the prison-bound is he whose soul is hampered, the cruel, jealous king." DEIGHTON (ed. 1889): "A double negative." HUSSEY (1992, p. 233): The
"apparently casual syntax [gives] the impression of thought being turned immediately
into speech." Linking these words with 1141–2, P.A.C. (1892, p. 516): "In Greene
and in Shakespeare the King wishes the Queen's death because he is uncomfortable
so long as she lives, and he prefers his comfort to aught else, taking it as his conjugal
right and royal prerogative."

900–2 **but . . . being**] PAFFORD (ed. 1963): "With the *F* punctuation the meaning would be 'It is weakness to take the matter in this way: it were absolute weakness
if the cause of the trouble were no longer alive.'" HAPPÉ (1969), similarly: "It is simply
weakness to be so overcome by my weakness and anxiety: it would be the essence
of weakness still to be overcome if Hermione, the cause, were dead." With COLLIER's
punctuation, HAPPÉ continues, "*meere weaknesse* repeats the idea without suggesting that the continued survival intensifies the state of weakness."

To beare the matter thus: meere weaknesse, if
The cause were not in being: part o'th'cause,
She, th'Adultresse: for the harlot-King
Is quite beyond mine Arme, out of the blanke
And leuell of my braine: plot-proofe: but shee,   905
I can hooke to me: say that she were gone,

---

901 weaknesse,] ~ . COL, HUD1, DYCE, STAU-GLO (−CAM1), DEL4+

---

901 **thus**] DEIGHTON (ed. 1889): I.e., "without making any effort to avenge my-self."

    meere] JOHNSON (1755): "Such and nothing else; this only." So spelled else-where in *WT*, 1322 and 1326.

    902 **cause . . . cause**] SCHMIDT (1874): "Referring to persons, = author." WILSON (ed. 1931): "In its ordinary sense, but with reference also to its common meaning of 'disease'" (*OED, sb.* 12). Cf. 941.

    in being] SCHMIDT (1874, Being): "Life, existence." KITTREDGE & RIBNER (ed. 1967): "Alive."

    part o'th'cause] ROLFE (ed. 1879) compares 576. KERMODE (ed. 1963), differ-ently: "Leontes interrupts himself, remembering that Polixenes is inaccessible, so that only part of the cause of his agony is within his power to destroy."

    902–6 **part . . . me**] HAPPÉ (1969): "A tormented aside."

    903 **harlot-King**] GREY (1754, 1:250), incorrectly: A king who makes harlots. For *harlot*, CALDECOTT (MS 1813–33): "False." HALLIWELL (1852): "A low depraved class of society, the ribalds, and having no relation to sex." *OED* (*sb.* 1), agreeing, adds, "In later use (16–17th c.), sometimes a man of loose life, a fornicator; also, often, a mere term of opprobium or insult." Like CALDECOTT, however, WILSON (ed. 1931) regards the word here as an adjective— "lewd."

    904–6 **beyond . . . me**] MOORMAN (ed. 1912): "It is the custom of Shakespeare to pass lightly from one metaphorical expression to another; [here] passing from the levelling of a gun [see n. 904–5] to the grappling of ships in a naval encounter by means of grappling-hooks." HERFORD (ed. 1916–) adds that "beyond mine Arme" suggests capture. All are images of physical conflict, of course.

    904–5 **out . . . braine**] JOHNSON (ed. 1765): "Beyond the *aim* of any attempt that I can make against him. *Blank* and *level*, are terms of archery" or, according to DOUCE (in STEEVENS, ed. 1793), gunnery. *Blank* refers to the target's white center (*OED, sb.* 2); *leuell*, either to the act of aiming (*OED, sb.* 9a, citing this line) or to the mark aimed at (9b). See n. 1258–9 and cf. "As leuell as the Cannon to his blanck" (*Ham.* 4.1.42 (2628 + 2), glossed by EVANS (ed. 1974) as "with aim as good" as the cannon to its "target." ENRIGHT (1970, p. 175): "In [1258] Hermione is to point out that it is not the level of his brain that her life stands in, but in the level of his dreams." WRIGHT (1981, p. 190) lists two instances of hendiadys in *WT*. He says privately that taking sense 9a for *leuell*, he counts this expression as one; for the other, see n. 2951–2. There is no hendiadys in 890, since "Law and processe" are not the same thing.

    905–6 **shee . . . me**] HUDSON (ed. 1880): "She *whom* I have within my grasp." *She*, however, is probably substituted for *her*; see ABBOTT §211 and FRANZ §287g. For *hooke to me*, SCHANZER (ed. 1969): "Get hold of (the metaphor derives from the use of the grappling-hook in sea-fights)," an idea that accords with that of "blanke And leuell."

    906 **say that**] BROOK (1976, p. 99): One of several phrases "used to express conditions." Others include *upon condition* and *provided (that)*.

Giuen to the fire, a moity of my rest
Might come to me againe. Whose there?
    Ser. My Lord.
    Leo. How do's the boy?   910
    Ser. He tooke good rest to night: 'tis hop'd
His sicknesse is discharg'd.
    Leo. To see his Noblenesse,

908-13 *Four verse lines ending* there? . . . rest . . . discharg'd. . . . nobleness!
HAN, RID; *ending* lord? . . . to-night; . . . see, . . . nobleness! v1793-SING1, HAL;
ending lord? . . . to-night; . . . discharg'd. . . . nobleness! KNT, HUD, DYCE, WH,
CAM, GLO, IRV, BUL-ARD1, KIT1-PEL1, ARD2, PEN2, EVNS, OXF2; *three, ending* lord. . . .
to-night: . . . nobleness! COL, SING2, STAU, DEL, KTLY, CLN2; *four, ending* lord? . . .
boy? . . . to-night; . . . nobleness! OXF1; *ending* lord! . . . boy? . . . hoped . . .
nobleness! mCAP2, SIG, BEV
    909 *Enrer.* F2; *Enter.* F3, F4; *Enter an Attendant.* ROWE1-RANN (−CAP), CAM3,
ARD2, PEN2, OXF2, BEV4 (*subst.*); *advancing.* CAP, MAL-HUD2 (−COL, DEL, CAM1, GLO),
OXF1, BUL, SIS, CLN2, EVNS, BEV3 (*subst.*)
    911 to night: 'tis] to-night and it is CAP
    913-14 Noblenesse, . . . Mother.] ∼ , . . . ∼ , F2, F3; ∼ . . . . ∼ , F4-CLN2,
SIG, PEN2, BEV3+

---

    907 **Giuen . . . fire**] GREY (1754, 1:251): "Alluding to the punishment
. . . for . . . treason in women." Men guilty of high treason were hanged, drawn,
and quartered; see UNDERHILL (1916, 2:398-9). WILSON (ed. 1931): Leontes "considers Hermione guilty both of high and petty treason," the former being a violation of
allegiance to the sovereign or state, the latter being the murder of a husband by his
wife or the contrivance of it (*OED*). Cf. the indictment (1187-91).
    moity] *OED* (Moiety 2b, citing this line): "Small part," with which ONIONS
(1986) agrees. KERMODE (ed. 1963), however: "Half" (*OED* 1). Probably the former,
as explained in n. 1213.
    908 **Whose there?**] ORGEL (ed. 1996): "A command for attendance, not a ques-
tion."
    910 **How . . . boy?**] YOUNG & MOSELEY (ed. 1965) find that Mamillius's "sick-
ness and death is symbolic of the destruction of trust between Leontes and Hermione." WELLS (1994, p. 343): "The illness that afflicts Mamillius bears a symbolical
relationship to his father's growing mental sickness, even though Leontes ascribes it
(accurately in one sense) to 'the dishonour of his mother' [914]."
    911 **Ser.**] This may be the same servant who announces the return of Cleomines
and Dion at 1127. For his possible reappearance late in the play, see n. 2855.
    to night] SCHMIDT (1875): "Last night." See nn. 552 and 935 for another mean-
ing.
    912 **discharg'd**] SCHMIDT (1874): "Dismiss," figuratively. DEIGHTON (ed. 1889):
"Got rid of."
    913 **To see**] DEIGHTON (ed. 1889): "How wonderful to witness." BETHELL (ed.
1956): "Imagine."
    913-14 **Noblenesse, . . . Mother.**] ORGEL (ed. 1996), regarding F4's punctu-
ation: "There is no textual justification for this; and since it provides Leontes with a
neater and more rational train of thought, it is dramatically undesirable."

Conceyuing the dishonour of his Mother.
He straight declin'd, droop'd, tooke it deeply,   915
Fasten'd, and fix'd the shame on't in himselfe:
Threw-off his Spirit, his Appetite, his Sleepe,
And down-right languish'd. Leaue me solely: goe,

---

915 declin'd . . . deeply] declin'd, and droop'd, took it most deeply HAN; declin'd
upon't, droop'd, took it deeply CAP; declin'd, droop'd, took it deeply, and KTLY;
declin'd, took it deeply PEN1
918 *Exit Attendant.* THEO1+ (*subst.*)

914-18 **Conceyuing . . . languish'd**] BUCKNILL (1860, p. 128): Leontes "gives
exactly the symptoms to be expected in such a case of nervous disturbance in a child,
arising from grief and shame." FURNESS (ed. 1898): "Leontes is trying to justify to
himself his own brutality by attributing to Mamillius emotions far beyond his tender
years. It is not to be supposed that so young a child, however precocious intellectually,
would know anything of the real disgrace imputed to his mother; all that he saw and
appreciated were the terrifying looks and brutal violence of his father and his mother's
grief; added to this, came the separation from his mother, and his little heart broke."
However, for *conceiving*, CALDECOTT (MS 1813-33): "Having a quick feeling & sense
of." SCHMIDT (1874): "To form an idea of, to imagine." Hence, BEVINGTON (ed. 1992):
"Grasping the enormity of [his mother's disgrace]." CHARLTON (ed. 1916): "Leontes'
attribution of the cause of the illness of Mamillius to a nobleness of nature languishing
for his mother's crime serves in some small measure to redeem Leontes in our esteem:
he has some conception of nobleness. And . . . the real cause of the illness adds to
the pathos of Hermione's innocence." TRAVERSI (1954, p. 126), oppositely: "This
sickness . . . Leontes characteristically misinterprets to fit in with his own obsession." PARRY (ed. 1982) finds Leontes's interpretation "wishful thinking rather than
sensible diagnosis." ERICKSON (1982, p. 821), similarly: "Preoccupied with himself,
he cannot see that his son's 'languish' and loss of 'appetite' stem from maternal deprivation, which causes the boy's death." SANDERS (1987, p. 34): "A mute anguish of
bewilderment, which will fasten and fix all the shame in itself rather than accuse
those it loves." Because he thinks "conceyuing" carries on "the play's ideas of pregnancy," CAVELL (1987, p. 194): "The lines . . . project [Leontes's] identification
with his wife."
    915 **straight**] BAILEY (1721): "Presently."
    droop'd] PORTER & CLARKE (ed. 1908): "The time of a foot is filled with one
long syllable. The line is regular as to the number of stresses, five."
    tooke it deeply] DEIGHTON (ed. 1889): "Felt it most keenly; but perhaps with
an allusion to taking, catching a disease."
    916 **Fasten'd**] The sense is repeated in "fix'd" (*OED, v.* 10b, citing this line). For
similar repetitions, see 302, 595, 634, 856, 890, 1208, and 1214-16.
    shame] PORTER & CLARKE (ed. 1908): "The king interprets the child from his
prejudiced point of view. It is likelier that he grieved over the discord."
    on't] Of it. See n. 785-6 for the expression.
    917 **Threw-off**] DEIGHTON (ed. 1889): "Lost . . . though with the idea of his
doing so voluntarily, actively."
    Spirit] SCHMIDT (1875): "Vivacity, mettle, fire" (*OED, sb.* 13).
    918 **down-right**] JOHNSON (1755): "Completely." SCHMIDT (1874): "Directly."
    solely] MASON (1785, p. 127): "Alone" (*OED, adv.* 1b, citing this line). *OED*:
The word is "passing into adj."

See how he fares: Fie, fie, no thought of him,
The very thought of my Reuenges that way   920
Recoyle vpon me: in himselfe too mightie,
And in his parties, his Alliance; Let him be,
Vntill a time may serue. For present vengeance
Take it on her: *Camillo*, and *Polixenes*
Laugh at me: make their pastime at my sorrow: 925

---

921 Recoyle] Recoils mTBY3 *conj.*, HAN, KTLY
922 *Om.* F2-ROWE3
     And] *Om.* CAP, RANN
     Alliance] alliances mTBY4 *conj.*, mCAP2, CAPN *conj.*, RANN
922-3 him be, Vntill] him | Be 'till HAN

---

919 **he . . . him**] The CLARKES (1879, pp. 657 and 709): Mamillius
. . . Polixenes. COLLIER (ed. 1842): "Coleridge called this, in his lectures in 1815, an
admirable instance of propriety in soliloquy, where the mind leaps from one object
to another . . . the operation here being perfectly intelligible without mentioning
Polixenes." CHARLTON (ed. 1916): "He cannot drive Polixenes' image from his mind,
but is haunted by it and goaded to fury." See 924-7.
     Fie] MINSHEU (1617, Phy): "A voice of misliking, as a stincke." HARDINGE (1818,
3:63): "Shame."
     920-1 **The . . . me**] HOLBROOK (1964, p. 162) mistakenly believes that Leontes
thinks of Mamillius rather than of Polixenes: "Leontes himself has an inkling (in this
lies his deepest suffering—and Shakespeare's profoundest perception) that he is but
projecting on his wife and son 'bad' elements from within himself."
     thought . . . Recoyle] The lack of agreement between singular subject and
plural verb stems from the intervention of the plural *reuenges* (ABBOTT §412). BROOK
(1976, p. 66) gives other examples of false concord. For other instances in *WT*, see
nn. 237, 870, 1636-7, 1643, and 1724.
     921 **Recoyle**] SCHMIDT (1875): "Rebound"; as PARRY (ed. 1982) says, causing
"more pain than comfort." HERFORD (ed. 1904): The thought "is instinctively rejected
as infeasible."
     922 **parties**] SCHMIDT (1875, Party 7): "Ally, confederate."
     Alliance] JOHNSON (1755): "Relation by any form of kindred." FURNESS (ed.
1898), commenting on CAPELL's addition of *s*: "The sibilant termination of the singular
does duty for the plural." See BROOK (1976, §260).
     922-3 **Let . . . serue**] ENRIGHT (1970, p. 175): "It will be a long time indeed,
but it will serve: Leontes is to espouse the cause of the runaway Florizel against his
father."
     923 **Vntill . . . serue**] FURNESS (ed. 1898): "Until the chance come."
     923-4 **For . . . her**] PORTER & CLARKE (ed. 1908): "Shakespeare did not find
in Greene the [subtle] instigation of the king to wreak his rage on Hermione which
he expresses in the rankling love of her which gave him 'Nor night, nor day, no rest'
[900] . . . and . . . 'say that she were gone, . . . a moity of my rest might come
to me again' [906-8]."
     924 **Take it**] MOORMAN (ed. 1912): "Let me exercise it."
     924-5 ***Camillo* . . . sorrow**] TRAVERSI (1954, p. 127): "The tendency to feel
himself ridiculed, to regard his self-esteem as subject to affront, has from the first been
a factor in Leontes' passion-driven behaviour."
     925 **pastime**] HAPPÉ (1969): "Joke, entertainment."

They should not laugh, if I could reach them, nor
Shall she, within my powre.

Enter Paulina.

Lord. You must not enter.
Paul. Nay rather (good my Lords) be second to me: 930
Feare you his tyrannous passion more (alas)
Then the Queenes life? A gracious innocent soule,
More free, then he is iealous.

---

928 SCENE V. POPE1, HAN, WARB, JOHN; SCENE VI. POPE2
    Ad. *with a Child* ROWE1 + (*subst.*); and ad. ANTIGONUS, *lords, and the servant*
. . . CAM3, PEN2, OXF2, BEV4 (*subst.*); as CAM3 except *servants* ARD2; as CAM3 except
om. *and the servant* EVNS, BEV3

---

928 **Enter Paulina**] See n. 898–9 for the blocking. GREG (1955, p. 416), comparing 1437: "It should have been specified that Paulina is carrying the baby." SPEN-
CER (1966, p. 51): Because boys took women's parts, mothers with babies do not
appear in Sh. "Shakespeare knows how to avoid embarrassment." When babies do
appear—in *H8* 5.5.0.5–7 (3357–60) and here—they are carried on by other women.
Why this is not just as embarrassing, SPENCER does not say.
    929–45 **You . . . hoe?**] PARRY (ed. 1982): "Until [945] Leontes 'freezes' (plot-
ting his action against Hermione?) while the audience's attention switches across the
stage to the new arrivals."
    930 **good my Lords**] For the transposition, see n. 390.
        second] JOHNSON (1755): "A supporter." *OED*, however, citing this line only,
considers the word an adjective; it quotes SCHMIDT (1875): "Helpful, lending assistance."
    931–2 **Feare . . . life?**] BETHELL (ed. 1956): "Are you more afraid *of* his unjust
anger than you are afraid *for* the life of the queen?"
    931 **tyrannous**] WILSON (ed. 1931): "Cruel, as always in Shakespeare." Accord-
ing to SCHMIDT (1875), however, the word in this context and in two other instances
means "despotic, unjustly severe." Cf. 1180. VAN DAM (1900, p. 115) wants to pronounce the word as *tyran.*
    932 **Then**] The CLARKES (1879, p. 298): I.e., than for.
        gracious] See n. 1639.
        innocent] VAN DAM (1900, p. 66): Pronounced *in'cent.*
    933 **free**] SEYMOUR (1805, 1:163), citing *MM* 3.2.41 (1528): "Blameless" (*OED,
a.* 7); SINGER's (ed. 1856) extension to "chaste" (i.e., free from unchastity) is accepted
by FURNESS (ed. 1898). WHITE (ed. 1857, 2:254): "Of an open, kindly, generous nature. . . . *Hermione* in her innocence, was more frank and generous in her construction of others than *Leontes* was jealous in his." LETTSOM (MS 1840–65): "Free-spirited,
honourable [*OED, a.* 3], pure." ROLFE (ed. 1879) compares "make mad the guilty and
appall the free" (*Ham.* 2.2.564 [1604]), in which the juxtaposition of the two adjectives supports Seymour's gloss on *free*. For the line, CALDECOTT (MS 1813–33): "More
free from faults than he is willing to impute them." BETHELL (ed. 1956), slightly differently: "Whose freedom from the sin which is the ground of his jealousy is greater
than that jealousy itself." Allowing the general sense of "innocent," COLLINS (ed.
1904–24?) thinks the primary sense is "[free] from the guilt of this particular crime,
whereas *innocent* has a general reference." Cf. n. 871 for other senses.

Antig. That's enough.

Ser. Madam; he hath not slept to night, commanded   935
None should come at him.

Pau. Not so hot (good Sir)
I come to bring him sleepe. 'Tis such as you
That creepe like shadowes by him, and do sighe   (2A
At each his needlesse heauings: such as you   940
Nourish the cause of his awaking. I

---

934 *Marked as aside* CAP
935 *Ser.*] F1-POPE2, HAN1-JOHN2, v1773-RANN, ARD2, SIG, PEN2, OXF2, BEV4; *Atten.*
[*within.*] THEO; 2. *A.* CAP, DYCE, STAU, CAM1, GLO, HUD2-CAM3, ALEX, SIS, CLN2, EVNS,
BEV3 (*subst.*); 1. *Attend.* MAL *etc.* (*subst.*)
        night, commanded$_\wedge$] $\sim$ $_\wedge$ $\sim$, WARB
936 at] near ROWE

---

934 **That's enough**] CALDECOTT (MS 1813-33), obscurely: "That, to be such
[gracious and innocent], cannot be less than a clear character." DEIGHTON (ed. 1889):
"More than enough, for he is absurdly . . . jealous," with which SCHMIDT (1874,
Enough) agrees. Thus the remark confirms what Paulina says. Sh. does not use this
expression to mean "That's sufficient; be quiet!"

935 **to night**] SCHMIDT (1875): "This, or in this, present night." See n. 911 for
another meaning.

936 **come at**] CALDECOTT (MS 1813-33): "Approach, come to" (*OED, prep.* 12b,
citing this line).

937-44 **Not . . . sleepe**] DONAWERTH (1984, p. 67): "Purgative words are a
metaphor for the wise counsel that Leontes needs to conquer his jealousy. . . . The
humane speaker here is not one who represses passion, but one who unites the forces
of her personality and . . . pours forth her inward passions and her secret thoughts
in an honest cause."

937 **Not so hot**] BETHELL (ed. 1956): "Don't be so impatient." KITTREDGE & RIB-
NER (ed. 1967): "Angry." BOORMAN (ed. 1964): "The [Servant] tries to bar Paulina's
way."

938-41 **'Tis . . . awaking**] BUCKNILL (1860, p. 129), quoting Florence Nightingale, *Notes on Nursing* (1860, p. 26): "Slight noises which excite attention are far
more destructive to the repose of the patient than much louder noises which are
decided and undisguised." STEARNS (1865, p. 31) agrees: "An officious attendance
upon the sick does more harm than good." PRESTON (1978, p. 425): "Paulina accuses
the fawning courtiers who do not press the point of Hermione's innocence." MUIR
(1957, p. 247): Sh. borrows from "a description of the effect of the Queen's death
on the common people" in *Pandosto*: "they went like shadowes, not men" (see p.
632).

940 **each**] ABBOTT (§12): "'All' or 'each one of.'"

        heauings] SCHMIDT (1874): "Deep sigh[s]." Citing *OED* (Heave, *v.* 8), ORGEL
(ed. 1996): "Groans."

941 **cause**] See n. 902 for the association with disease, here of the imagination.

        awaking] *OED* (*vbl. sb.*), citing this line: "The rising, or arousing, from sleep."
BOORMAN (ed. 1964): "Sleeplessness."

941-4 **I . . . sleepe**] BETHELL (ed. 1956): "Her plain speech and her medicinal
purpose support her function as a symbol of Leontes' conscience." DONAWERTH

Do come with words, as medicinall, as true;
(Honest, as either;) to purge him of that humor,
That presses him from sleepe.
    Leo. Who noyse there, hoe?   945
    Pau. No noyse (my Lord) but needfull conference,
About some Gossips for your Highnesse.
    Leo. How?

---

945 Who] What F2+

(1984, p. 67): "Paulina's speech is medicinal in a higher sense, one recognized by Sir Thomas Elyot when he recommends that cure of the affections [emotions] requires the help of a person 'wyse and well learned in morall philosophye.'" THORNE (1968, p. 36): "The irony . . . lies in the fact that she is actually carrying in her arms the instrument that, years later, will purge Leontes of the evil in him."

    942 **as . . . true**] HAPPÉ (1969): "Her words will cure the mental sickness of Leontes, and they are also true."

    medicinall] KITTREDGE & RIBNER (ed. 1967): "Healing." ROLFE (ed. 1879) and VAN DAM (1900, p. 50): Pronounced *méd'cinal*. CERCIGNANI (1981, p. 281) agrees, but see DOBSON (1968, 1:360). For other syncopations of *i*, see nn. 162, 313, and 3369. FURNESS (ed. 1898), however: Neither "*mèd'cinàl* or *medicìnal*. It is quite possible to read this line without a jar, and yet throw the accent on the second syllable of 'medicinal', care being taken to show that 'as medicinal' is a parenthesis by a slight pause before and after it."

    943 **Honest, as either**] WARBURTON (ed. 1747): "*I.e.* whose subject is the Queen's innocence: otherwise there would be a tautology." FURNESS (ed. 1898): "Paulina here refers to herself. She is as honest in intention as either healing or truth." PAFFORD (ed. 1963): "I.e. 'my words are indeed both medicinal and true.'" KNOWLES (privately): "She repeats this defense in 965–6: I am your 'Physitian' (medicinal), your 'Counsailor' (true), and 'loyall [honest] Seruant.'"

    humor] SCHMIDT (1874): "Fancy, conceit, caprice." HERFORD (ed. 1904): "Capricious mood." ORGEL (ed. 1996): "Mental illness." Paulina's "medicinall" words are intended to effect a cure by purging Leontes of the detrimental humor afflicting him. MAXWELL (ed. 1956), uncertain of the humor's identity: "That of the four humours which, by having become predominant, prevented sleep." DRAPER (1945, pp. 53–4) identifies choler as the source of jealousy.

    944 **presses**] SCHMIDT (1875, Press): "To drive from, to keep from." HAPPÉ (1969): "Weighs upon him and prevents sleep." ORGEL (ed. 1996): "The metaphor changes its reference from medicine to judicial torture."

    945 **[What] . . . hoe?**] BOORMAN (ed. 1964, Noise): "Quarrelling," although *OED*'s last citation of the word in this sense is dated 1530. SCHANZER (ed. 1969): "These words suggest that the altercation of [929–44] is meant to take place out of the hearing of Leontes."

    hoe?] The CLARKES (1879, p. 463): Expressing "angry inquiry."

    946–7 **No . . . Highnesse**] PARRY (ed. 1982): "She has not come with mere chit-chat but for a necessary discussion . . . about the choice of godparents [*OED*, Gossip, *sb.* 1a] for his new baby." The gossips are for Leontes only, in that they would oblige him (*sb.* 1c), but, as PORTER & CLARKE (ed. 1908) point out, the word startles him. Paulina has assumed a jolly tone, as though nothing untoward has happened.

    948 **How?**] The CLARKES (1879, p. 464): Expressing an "angry inquiry."

Away with that audacious Lady. *Antigonus*,
I charg'd thee that she should not come about me,   950
I knew she would.
    Ant. I told her so (my Lord)
On your displeasures perill, and on mine,
She should not visit you.
    Leo. What? canst not rule her?   955
    Paul. From all dishonestie he can: in this

949-51 **Away . . . would**] FRYE (1962, p. 239): "Leontes (as he himself points out [at 1050-2]) falls far short of being a somber demonic tyrant . . . and can only alternate between bluster and an uneasy sense of having done wrong [as here]." BETHELL (ed. 1956): "The first note of comedy. Leontes has clearly been scared of Paulina all along and, while forbidding her the court, has been gloomily conscious that she would disobey him. Allegorically this applies to the way in which conscience breaks through the mental barriers we erect to keep out the thought of our sin. Shakespeare makes a *serious* point comically, as elsewhere in this play, especially [3.3]." MOWAT (1976, p. 25): The "comic outburst . . . reveals his dread of the scolding but powerless female [, after which] we cannot continue to suffer with him as with a tragic hero."

949 **audacious**] JOHNSON (1755): "Bold; impudent; daring; always in a bad sense."

950 **I . . . me**] Cf. n. 831. Leontes has ordered that Paulina be kept from him as well as from Hermione. For *come about*, see n. 659.

953 **On . . . perill**] BOORMAN (ed. 1964): "At the risk of your displeasure."

    and on mine] BOORMAN (ed. 1964): "There should be a marked pause after 'peril', so that this sounds like a wry (and amusing) after-thought, prompting Leontes' scornful comment in the next line." Or Antigonus may plead that his command has been reinforced by reference to the highest public and private authority. Leontes's question (955), emphasizing that Paulina is there despite the authorities, comes from one who thinks he could not rule his own wife. BROWN (1962, p. 219): "In a bizarre way there is a parallel between the two husbands." See n. 956-9.

955 **canst not**] For the omission of *thou*, see ABBOTT §241.

956-9 **From . . . me**] SIMPSON (1950, p. 123): "Without waiting for her husband's reply, Paulina takes up the challenge and turns the sneer to the king's disadvantage. . . . The urgency of the occasion . . . condones any semblance of bad manners. Conventions and etiquette are for the shallows of experience, not the great tides of emotion." STYAN (1975, p. 29) on parallelism in the play: "The lady Paulina presents [here] a far less submissive Hermione and her husband Antigonus a far more hapless Leontes. 'What . . . her?' cries the tyrant . . . , and by comic perspective . . . we see in a moment the natural inversion of jealousy and servility. Leontes faced with a Paulina is quite at a loss, and the shaping of the action at this critical point is not to present us with a second foundering marriage, but to float us from one mood to another, preparatory to the reversal." DUSINBERRE (1975, pp. 90-1): "A husband's villainy annuls his wife's duty to him. . . . The retort [to Leontes] comes not from a wife, but from an individual capable of distinguishing good from evil without the intervention of a third party. . . . Women can be for God only as well as men." WAYNE (1985, p. 180) believes, however, that "Antigonus dies through a chain of circumstances that originated with Paulina's outburst. . . . Slander and shrewish speech are accorded a symbolic power that can lead, however indirectly

(Vnlesse he take the course that you haue done)
Commit me, for committing honor, trust it,
He shall not rule me.

   Ant. La-you now, you heare,   960
When she will take the raine, I let her run,
But shee'l not stumble.

   Paul. Good my Liege, I come:

---

958 it] me HAN
960 La] Lo POPE1-JOHN2, v1773, v1778, RANN, v1793-KNT1, COL, HUD, DEL
962 *Marked as aside* CAM3, SIS, EVNS

---

and inadvertently, to death." Regarding Paulina's words, the parenthesis rightly concludes with "honor" in 958.

956 **dishonestie**] MINSHEU (1617, to Dishonest): See "Pollute, . . . Disgrace."

958 **Commit . . . committing**] DEIGHTON (ed. 1889): "'Commit' and 'committing' are used in two different senses ['send to prison' (*OED* 3) and 'perpetrating' (6)], and in the latter case the sarcasm consists in applying to the word 'honour' a term which is properly applied to what is dishonourable, sinful, criminal." WHITE (1913, p. 183): She "plainly gives the King to understand that she will not be lawfully committed, unless . . . as he had done with Hermione, [he] commit her to jail for acting honorably. . . . For until lawful trial and conviction, she could not be committed." BETHELL (ed. 1956): "By this witty use of the unexpected it is implied that, to Leontes, 'honour' is a crime." ORGEL (ed. 1996): "'Sin' is the word one would expect after 'committing.'"

   trust it] BETHELL (ed. 1956): "Be quite sure."

960 **La-you**] KNIGHT (ed. 1842), inaccurately: Both *la* and *lo* "mean *look you*; but *la* is used affectedly, or ironically as in this case." *OED* distinguishes more firmly, however: *La* or *la you* is "an exclamation . . . to introduce or accompany a conventional phrase . . . or to call attention to an emphatic statement," whereas *lo* is equivalent to modern "Oh!" or to "Look! See! Behold!" For *la you*, SCHMIDT (1874) has it both ways, however: "Look, behold, there you have it." SCHANZER (ed. 1969): "'There now' . . . accompanied by some gesture of resignation." COLLINS (ed. 1904-24?) finds *you* to be the ethical dative, for which see n. 1598. For a nearly identical expression, see 178.

   you heare] BEVINGTON (ed. 1992): "You hear how she will go on talking."

961-2 **When . . . stumble**] STEARNS (1882, p. 146): "Even a stumbling horse will not stumble when going at full speed." According to DEIGHTON (ed. 1889), however, what Antigonus means is that "nothing will stop her gallop until she pulls up of her own accord from mere weariness." ORNSTEIN (1986, p. 222): "Paulina may be headstrong but she is not confused or blind." KERMODE (ed. 1963): "Antigonus, as usual, speaks of his wife as if she were a horse" (see n. 744-5). HENDERSON & MCMANUS (1985, p. 119) find the same imagery in SWETNAM's misogynistic *Arraignment of . . . Women* (1615; 1985, p. 209).

961 **take the raine**] YOUNG & MOSELEY (ed. 1965): "Take the bit between her teeth."

963-9 **Good . . . Queene**] MIRIAM JOSEPH (1947, p. 273): "By parrhesia one is humbly respectful or, if necessity demands, courageously outspoken in addressing those whom he ought to reverence or fear," as here.

963 **Good my Liege**] For the transposition, see n. 390.

And I beseech you heare me, who professes
My selfe your loyall Seruant, your Physitian,   965
Your most obedient Counsailor: yet that dares
Lesse appeare so, in comforting your Euilles,
Then such as most seeme yours. I say, I come
From your good Queene.
   Leo. Good Queene?   970
   Paul. Good Queene (my Lord) good Queene,
I say good Queene,

---

964 professes] profess ROWE3 -v1813 (−MAL), SING1, HAL, GLO, DYCE2, COL4-WH2,
BUL, CAM3, SIS, PEL1, SIG
   966 dares] dare mTHEO1 *conj.*, v1793-SING1, HAL, GLO, DYCE2, COL4-WH2, CAM3,
PEL1
   968 seeme] seems POPE2-JOHN2 (−HAN), v1773
   969−72 *Verse lines ending* lord, . . . good Queen; POPE1-JOHN2, CAM1, GLO,
WH2, IRV, NLSN, ARD1, PEL1; *ending* queen! [970] . . . good queen; [972] mTBY2
conj., CAP, v1773-DEL2, KTLY-HUD2, OXF1, BUL, KIT1, ALEX, SIS, CLN2-SIG, PEN2, EVNS;
ending queen. . . . queen! [970] . . . good queen, CAM3, BEV, OXF2
   970 Queene?] ∼ ! CAP, HAN3-SIG (−RLTR, RID, KIT1, PEL1)

964−6 **professes . . . dares**] The CLARKEs (ed. 1865): "The verb[s] being put
thus into the third person, [give] the excellent effect of Paulina's speaking of another,
while she thus confidently speaks of herself and her own fidelity." KINNEAR (1883,
pp. 180−1): "In this and similar constructions, *who* is followed by the *verb* in the
third person, but takes the *personal pronoun* and *personal possessive* in the first."
He compares *Cor.* 4.5.65−8 (2722−5) and *H8* 1.1.224−6 (313−15). See WALKER
(1860, 1:233 ff.) and nn. 966 and 1055. PAFFORD (ed. 1963), however, believes that
Paulina becomes ungrammatical through excitement.
   965 **your Physitian**] PARRY (ed. 1982): "She means what she said at [941−4]."
   966 **Counsailor**] VAN DAM (1900, p. 60): Pronounced *couns(el)-lor.*
   966−8 **yet . . . yours**] CAPELL (1783, 2.4:168): "I have less power to shew my
obedience" in "encouraging you by a vicious compliance to persist in those evils
. . . than have some about you whom you take for your greatest friends [or most loyal
subjects]." PORTER & CLARKE (ed. 1908): *Dares* is "an example like *professes*
[964] . . . of an ungrammatical plural in place of the singular; for *I* is still the subject."
   967 **comforting your Euilles**] MASON (1785, p. 128): *Comforting* has its legal
sense (*OED*, Comfort, *v.* 2: "Abet, countenance"). RANN (ed. 1787): "Confirming you
in the practice of evil, through a vicious complaisance." *OED* (*v.* 6, citing this line),
however: "To relieve, assist (in sickness, affliction, etc.)." DEIGHTON (ed. 1889):
"*Evils* is here used ambiguously of his folly as well as his troubles." Thus BOORMAN
(ed. 1964): "Also . . . in helping you in your troubles."
   968 **seeme yours**] MOORMAN (ed. 1912): "Seem to be your most loyal servants."
BETHELL (ed. 1956): "Hers is a deeper loyalty than theirs, for she shows him his faults
while they pander to them."
   970 **Good Queene?**] RUBINSTEIN (1984): A sarcastic pun on *good* (lubricious, as
a whore is good) *quean* (VERSTEGAN [1605]: "A dishonest woman of her body").
Much more obvious, however, is Leontes's sarcastic emphasis on *good* and Paulina's
refutation of his sarcasm by her reiteration of the word in 971−2 and again in 978−
9. For Paulina's contradiction as a mark of a good servant, see n. 752−4.

And would by combate, make her good so, were I
A man, the worst about you.
   Leo. Force her hence.   975
   Pau. Let him that makes but trifles of his eyes
First hand me: on mine owne accord, Ile off,
But first, Ile do my errand. The good Queene
(For she is good) hath brought you forth a daughter,
Heere 'tis. Commends it to your blessing.   980
   Leo. Out:

---

973 so] *Om.* ROWE
   good$_\wedge$ so,] $\sim$, $\sim$ $_\wedge$ mTBY2 *conj.*, THEO1+
974 the] on th' WARB (*attrib. to Hanmer by* CAM1)
977 mine] my SING1, HUD1
980 *Laying down the Child.* ROWE1+ ($-$RLTR) (*subst.*)

---

973 **combate**] MINSHEU (1617): "A formall triall of a doubtfull cause or quarrell
by . . . two Champions" (*OED, sb.* 1). WILSON (ed. 1931): "According to the laws
of chivalry a lady's honour might be vindicated if her champion won."
   make her good] The CLARKES (ed. 1865): "Prove her good." HARRISON (ed.
1947): "Restore her good name."
   974 **worst**] EDWARDS (1753, p. 18): "*Weakest,* or *least war-like.*" CALDECOTT
(MS 1813–33), similarly: "Of the least skill & courage." JOHNSON (ed. 1765), however:
"Lowest [in rank]." PORTER & CLARKE (ed. 1908): "If she were, she says, the basest
of your subservient idle men here, she would champion the queen in combat against
him." KITTREDGE & RIBNER (ed. 1967): "The vindication of a slandered queen by
combat in her behalf, often by a lowly person, is a common motif of folk romance."
   976–88 **Let . . . honest**] GOURLAY (1975, p. 382): "Shakespeare presents Paulina first as a negative female stereotype, a comic scold. Leontes tries to dismiss her
as a shrew, a mere 'Dame Partlet' [see n. 992]. . . . From the start, the lines of battle
are clearly drawn between two kinds of power: Paulina's female tongue versus Leontes' masculine rule."
   977 **hand**] JOHNSON (1755): "To seize; to lay hands on" (*OED, v.* 1, citing this
line). See n. 2170 for a figurative use.
   on . . . accord] *OED* (5b, citing this line): "Of one's own spontaneous
motion."
   off] *OED* (*adv.* 9, citing this line): "Used with ellipsis of . . . *go* . . . so as
itself to function as a vb."
   979 **is**] DEIGHTON (ed. 1889): "Emphatic."
   980–1 **Heere . . . Out**] SIMPSON (1955, p. 85): A "pause before the final strong
syllable is found only in the later plays. . . . Sometimes the dialogue changes over
at this point."
   980 **Heere 'tis**] ENGLAND (1982, p. 75): This "dramatic unveiling [prefigures] the
later unveiling of Hermione."
   blessing.] Eds. agree that here Paulina lays the baby down, although those
words do not appear in F1. Nevertheless, BLUESTONE (1974, p. 75) observes that Sh.
here "makes literal a metaphorical expression in *Pandosto*: the courtiers, hearing that
the king plans to burn his wife and daughter, 'sought by perswasions to diuert him
from this bloody determination: laying before his face the innocencie of the child'"
(see p. 628 below).

A mankinde Witch? Hence with her, out o'dore:
A most intelligencing bawd.
   Paul. Not so:
I am as ignorant in that, as you,   985
In so entit'ling me: and no lesse honest
Then you are mad: which is enough, Ile warrant
(As this world goes) to passe for honest.
   Leo. Traitors;
Will you not push her out? Giue her the Bastard,   990

---

982 **mankinde Witch**] In Adrianus Junius, *The Nomenclator*, trans. John Higgins
(1585, 19b), SINGER (ed. 1826) finds *virago* defined as "a manly woman, or a mankind
woman." THEOBALD (ed. 1733): "*Bold* and *masculine*" (*OED, a.*[1] 3, citing *Cor.* 4.2.16
[2524]). JOHNSON (ed. 1765): "Violent, ferocious, and mischievous" (*a.*[2]). Supporting
"masculine," MASON (1785, p. 128) cites *mankind* as an adjective in Massinger, *The
Guardian* 1.2.40; Jonson, *The Forest* 10:13; Beaumont & Fletcher, *The Woman Hater*
3.1.209; and Fletcher, *Monsieur Thomas* 5.1.52. Massinger, however, also uses the
word to mean "ferocious" in describing a woman who has just been called "brach"
(i.e., bitch; *The City Madam* 3.1.51). *OED* points out that *a.*[1] 3 and *a.*[2] are "sometimes
indistinguishable." For *Witch*, SCHMIDT (1875): "Term of reproach for an old and ugly
woman." For the phrase, the CLARKES (ed. 1865): "A witch of the masculine sex."
HERFORD (ed. 1916-) believes that Leontes uses the word "to explain his helpless
cowering before Paulina's resolute will and scarcely concealed indignation." ERICK-
SON (1982, p. 822): "Since patriarchy distributes power according to sexual roles,
Paulina's illegitimate assertion of power upsets the system. She is automatically labeled
'masculine' for usurping male prerogatives." Disobeying her husband and speaking
too frankly and vehemently to her king would not seem to be such prerogatives,
however. For *mankinde*, RIDLEY (ed. 1935), oddly: "Mad."

   o'dore] Seems to be added for emphasis rather than as a specific direction. Cf.
Wiv. 4.2.184 (2067), *2H4* 2.4.212 (1232), *JC* 3.2.179 (1716), and *Tmp.* 3.2.70 (1422).

   983 **intelligencing**] CAPELL (1783 [1774], 1:glos.): "Intelligence-giving" (i.e., spying). SCHMIDT (1874): "Going between parties" (i.e., pimping, as HENLEY, ed. 1902,
says). Either meaning or both may apply, although *OED* (citing this line) prefers CA-
PELL. PORTER & CLARKE (ed. 1908): "Leontes insinuates that she is making it her
interest to take part with the escaped traitors as well as with the imprisoned one,
which is why Paulina replies [as she does in 985], i.e., in why they went or in such
a rôle as he is to accuse her."

   985-6 **I . . . me**] BETHELL (ed. 1956): "I am as ignorant of the profession of
bawd . . . as you are of me in giving me that name."

   985 **ignorant**] PAFFORD (ed. 1963): "Uninformed, unskilled," as in *Cym.* 3.2.23
(1492). Her "ignorant" plays off his "intelligencing" (983).

   986 **entit'ling**] SCHMIDT (1874, Entitle): "To call." EVANS (ed. 1974): "A contraction of the old spelling *entituling*."

   986-8 **honest . . . honest**] See n. 381. She is responding to "bawd" (983).

   987-8 **which . . . honest**] DEIGHTON (ed. 1889): "If I am as honest as you are
mad, I shall easily pass muster for honesty." BETHELL (ed. 1956): "To tell a king to
his face that he is mad would be . . . a remarkable feat of plain speaking."

   988 **As . . . goes**] DENT W884.1: "Thus (How) goes (fares) the World."

   990 **Bastard**] PAFFORD (ed. 1963): "Leontes' horror of bastardy foreshadows Perdita's (cf. [1910-11])."

Thou dotard, thou art woman-tyr'd: vnroosted
By thy dame *Partlet* heere. Take vp the Bastard,
Take't vp, I say: giue't to thy Croane.
    Paul. For euer
Vnvenerable be thy hands, if thou   995

---

991 thou] that CAP
992 thy] the ROWE3
993 thy] the F2-ROWE3
995 be thy] by the F4

991–2 **Thou . . . heere**] BROWN (1962, p. 219): "He [Leontes] tries to reduce her claims to the exaggerations of marital comedy."

991 **dotard**] MINSHEU (1617, Doater): "A sottish, foolish . . . fellow, a foppe." SCHMIDT (1874): "A man whose intellect is impaired by age." Most recent eds. agree with MINSHEU, because Antigonus does not seem antiquated.

    woman-tyr'd] STEEVENS (ed. 1773): "*Peck'd* by a woman [*OED*, Woman, *sb.* 7]. The phrase is taken from falconry" (*OED*, Tire, *v.*² 2: "To pull or tear with the beak"). MASON (1785, p. 128): "Henpeck'd." CAPELL (1783 [1774], 1:glos.), confusing *tyr'd* with *tire*, headdress: "Whose head is . . . comb'd, by his Wife."

    vnroosted] JOHNSON (1755): "Driven from the roost ['on which a bird sits to sleep']." *OED* (*v.*1 *fig.*, citing this line). "Dislodge or force out of a place."

992 **dame *Partlet***] HANMER (ed. 1743–4, 6:glos.): "A name given to a hen" (*OED*, Partlet¹, citing this line). According to *OED* (Partlet²), the word was "orig. a neckerchief of linen or the like; a collar or ruff," and so perhaps also an adornment on Paulina's dress. GREY (1754, 1:252): "An allusion to the . . . *Tale of the Nunn's Priest*, in Chaucer." GREY refers as well to Pertelok in Gavin Douglas's trans. of Vergil's *Aeneid (Poetical Works*, ed. John Small, 1874, 4:85:7). Following BENDA (ed. 1825) and DELIUS (ed. 1860), WILSON (ed. 1931): "The hen in *Reynard the Fox.*" *OED*: "Used as the proper name of any hen . . . ; also applied, like 'hen', to a woman." In *1H4* 3.3.52 (2054), Falstaff addresses the ruffled Hostess as "dame Partlet the hen." Paulina has unroosted (perhaps punning on *unroostered*) Antigonus by henpecking him. PORTER & CLARKE (ed. 1908): "There is much human nature in chickens."

993 **Croane**] VERSTEGAN (1605, p. 334): "An old yeow [ewe], and applyed in anger vpon an old or elderly woman" (*OED*, *sb.* 1 and 2). SCHANZER (ed. 1969) thinks the second sense "would have little pertinence. . . . Paulina's loud reproaches, after being compared to the angry clucking of a hen, are now likened to the bleating of an old ewe." The furious Leontes, however, wants to strike back, and name-calling need not be accurate. KNIGHT (1947; 1965, p. 87) finds in *Partlet* and *Croane* "unchivalrous, ugly, scorn, the horror almost of woman as woman . . . the latter suggesting witchcraft."

995–6 **Vnvenerable . . . basenesse**] JOHNSON (ed. 1765): "*Paulina* forbids him [Antigonus] to touch the Princess under that appellation [bastard]. *Forced* is *false*, uttered with violence to truth" (*OED*, *ppl.a.* 1). Cf. nn. 1165, 1844. WARBURTON (ed. 1747) had understood *forced* as "unnatural" (*OED*, *ppl.a.* 3c), and WHITE (ed. 1883) glosses it as "violent," which is not exactly supported by *OED*. For *baseness*, JOHNSON (1755) gives both "Meanness" and "Bastardy."

995 **Vnvenerable . . . hands**] CALDECOTT (MS 1813–33): "May respect no longer attend the deeds of thy hands." SCHMIDT (1875, Unvenerable): "Contemptible"; *OED* cites this instance in *WT* as the first use of the word.

Tak'st vp the Princesse, by that forced basenesse
Which he ha's put vpon't.

    Leo. He dreads his Wife.

    Paul. So I would you did: then 'twere past all doubt
Youl'd call your children, yours.   1000

    Leo. A nest of Traitors.

    Ant. I am none, by this good light.

    Pau. Nor I: nor any
But one that's heere: and that's himselfe: for he,
The sacred Honor of himselfe, his Queenes,   1005 (2A5
His hopefull Sonnes, his Babes, betrayes to Slander,

1002-3 *One verse line* mCAP2, v1793+ (−WH1)
1006 his] this mTBY2 *conj.* (*withdrawn* mTBY3), CAP

996-7 **forced . . . vpon't**] PAFFORD (ed. 1963): "'Under that false title of bastard which he has unnaturally thrust on it' or 'accepting that description of it as bastard which he has falsely thrust upon it'. Antigonus is to act like someone who refuses to answer to a name or title he repudiates—but the repudiation is to be on behalf of the child."

996 **forced**] The CLARKES (1879, p. 629): "In the peculiar sense of 'perverted from truth', 'wryed from fact', 'false.'" Cf. "forc'd thoughts" (1844) as well as "forcing" (1165). MOORMAN (ed. 1912): "Used in the sense of strained, distorted, and the meaning . . . is accordingly that distorted application of the word bastardy."

998-9 **He . . . did**] KNOWLES (privately): "Paulina puns on *dread*: Leontes means 'fear'; she means 'venerate.'" *OED* (*v.* 1) includes both meanings.

998 **He . . . Wife**] PARRY (ed. 1982): "Antigonus makes no move to pick up the baby."

999 **So . . . did**] BROWN (1962, p. 220): "Leontes has put himself into a position that is potentially ridiculous as well as painful."

1000 **yours**] ORGEL (ed. 1996): "Under English law, the children of a legally married woman were legitimate, and therefore entitled to inherit, even if the husband denied paternity." THIRLBY (MS 1725-33?) marks this word "*subintell*[*igitur*]," an inaudible addition. Leontes thus would understand "I wish you did dread your wife; then doubtless you'd call your children [to you]." But to "children" Paulina adds "yours" under her breath. No one else thinks this.

1002 **by . . . light**] BEVINGTON (ed. 1992): "By the light of day, or, by my eyesight. (A common oath.)" FURNESS (ed. 1898) believes "this unusual oath" was suggested by 1001. "Is there not somewhat of *concealment* in the idea of a *nest* which prompts Antigonus to swear by the light of day which shines everywhere and reveals all things? or is it that Shakespeare merely wishes us to be made conscious of the bright light of heaven shining down on this dark and tragic scene?" Probably neither; the oath is Trinculo's in *Tmp.* 2.2.144 (1188), and it is also found in *TNK* 2.2.264 (Fletcher). The asseveration (*OED*, Light, *sb.* 2b and SCHMIDT, 1874, 1) occurs some half dozen times. EVANS (ed. 1974), however: "By my eyesight," a gloss that may derive from SCHMIDT (1874, Light 3): "the power of seeing." LEE (ed. 1907), not taking the words as an oath: "In this full light of day."

1006 **hopefull**] PARRY (ed. 1982): "'Hoping to succeed to the throne' and 'in whom we have high hopes.'"

Whose sting is sharper then the Swords; and will not
(For as the case now stands, it is a Curse
He cannot be compell'd too't) once remoue
The Root of his Opinion, which is rotten,   1010
As euer Oake, or Stone was sound.
   Leo. A Callat
Of boundlesse tongue, who late hath beat her Husband,
And now bayts me: This Brat is none of mine,

1011 sound] found F2-ROWE2
1014 This] That v1785, v1793

---

his Babes] MALONE (ed. 1790), recognizing that these words might be taken to be an appositive, identifies the babe as the "female infant."

betrayes] HAPPÉ (ed. 1969): "Leaves open to."

1006-7 **Slander . . . Swords**] SINGER (ed. 1856) compares "Slander, whose edge is sharper than the Sword" (*Cym.* 3.4.33-4 [1704-5]). Cf. also "Slander leaves a score (scar) behind it" (TILLEY S522), and DENT S521.1, who nevertheless questions whether the expression is proverbial. DENT adds, "Wounds hurt (cut) more than swords" (TILLEY W839). C. G. SMITH (1963, no. 270) finds a parallel in Publilius Syrus, *Sententiae.*

1007-11 **and . . . sound**] PAFFORD (ed. 1963): "And he will never change <once remove> the source of his opinion, which is as rotten as ever oak or stone were sound because, things being as they are <i.e., he being a king>, it is a tragedy that no one can make him change."

1009 **He . . . too't**] YOUNG & MOSELEY (ed. 1965, Too't): "To change his opinion." FURNESS (ed. 1898): "On account of his supreme, autocratic position."

1009-10 **remoue The Root**] DEIGHTON (ed. 1889): "Root out."

1010-11 **is rotten, As**] For the omission of the first *as* [*as rotten*], see ABBOTT §276. FURNESS (ed. 1898): "It is not impossible to suppose that the first *as* is absorbed in 'is.'"

1012-36 **A . . . Subiect**] HARTWIG (1972, p. 112): "The comic distance achieved through establishing the characters in their stock positions—Paulina as a shrew, Antigonus as her hen-pecked and ineffectual husband, and Leontes as the long-suffering victim of her tongue—works both to remove Paulina from a wholly commendable position and also to dispel the pathos of Leontes' grappling with his sorrow." According to HENDERSON & McMANUS (1985, p. 119), Leontes's invocation of the stock roles allows him "to avoid a direct response to her [Paulina's] rational assertions of Hermione's innocence." DUSINBERRE (1975, p. 220): "Fearless speech spells shamelessness, a masculine disregard for feminine propriety." The situation recurs at 1229-32.

1012 **Callat**] COCKERAM (1623): "A lewd woman" (*OED*, Callet, *sb.* 1). POPE (MS -1723): "A scold, a lozel [see n. 1032], a lazy lubber [drudge, scullion]" (*OED*, *sb.* 2, citing this line: "Sometimes perhaps = 'scold' as in the vb."). Both PARTRIDGE (1969) and COLMAN (1974) give sense 1, but "boundlesse tongue" suggests that sense 2 is correct. MACKAY (1884, p. 58) finds the word connected with the Celtic for "old woman." For other possible derivations, see *OED*.

1013 **boundlesse**] SCHMIDT (1874): "Unconfined, unbridled."

1013-14 **beat . . . bayts**] ELLIS (1871, 3:924): "It is absolutely essential to the cutting sarcasm that *beat, bait* should have been differently pronounced," that is, *beat* should not be pronounced with a long *a*. WHITE (ed. 1883), on the other hand,

It is the Issue of *Polixenes*.   1015
Hence with it, and together with the Dam,
Commit them to the fire.
    Paul. It is yours:
And might we lay th'old Prouerb to your charge,
So like you,'tis the worse. Behold (my Lords)   1020
Although the Print be little, the whole Matter
And Coppy of the Father: (Eye, Nose, Lippe,

---

believes that the play on these words depends on their being pronounced identically. CERCIGNANI (1981, p. 235) agrees with ELLIS: "The word-play is based on antithesis, not identity." For *bayts*, HUDSON (ed. 1880): "Bark at [SCHMIDT, 1874, vb. 1: 'To attack with dogs'], . . . harass [SCHMIDT 2]," but in *Shr.* 4.1.95-6 (1829-30) the same words, used with respect to kites (the bird), mean to beat the wings and to flutter (*OED*, Bate, *v.*[1] 2). PORTER & CLARKE (ed. c. 1903): "Harass, seek, annoy" (*OED*, Bait, *v.*[1] 2 and 4 *fig.*). Here too CERCIGNANI (p. 14) thinks "the use of a single vowel would certainly destroy the forcefulness." For similar wordplay, see 684-5. PAFFORD (ed. 1963): "That Leontes can pun even in his fury is typically Shakespearian."

1016-17 **Hence . . . fire**] SCHANZER (ed. 1969) compares *Pandosto*; see p. 628.

1016 **Dam**] For the use of *dam*, see n. 1385.

1017 **Commit . . . fire**] See n. 907. *OED* (Commit, *v.* 2, citing this line): "Consign." For a possible inspiration of this idea, see n. 1062. GRENE (1967, p. 79): "Leontes orders . . . Perdita to be exposed *before* the guilt of the mother has been proved by the court and by the verdict of Delphi." Leontes is sure, of course, that the crime so apparent to him will be equally apparent to the court and the oracle.

1018-30 **It . . . Husbands**] DRAPER (1985, p. 23): "Her reiteration of the close resemblance between the father and the child exacerbates Leontes' anger to the point where he orders not only that she be pushed out of doors [949 ff.], but also that the child be burnt to death [1017, 1062]."

1020 **So . . . worse**] THIRLBY (MS 1733-47?) quotes RAY (1678, p. 354): "They are so Like that they are the worse for it" (TILLEY L290). HENLEY (ed. 1902) gives another version: "The Devil calls him his white son: he is so like him that he looks the worse for it." LEE (ed. 1907) quotes another, inapposite, proverb: "'The better, the worse' (of a good deed productive of evil consequences)" (B333).

1021-5 **Although . . . Finger**] BLADES (1872, p. 42), in *Print, Matter, Coppy, Mold*, and *frame*, "five distinct typographical words, three of which are especially technical," finds evidence to prove Sh. a printer, evidence just as strong as that used to prove Sh. a schoolmaster, a lawyer, a soldier, or a Roman Catholic. BLADES is amusing himself, but the conceit is real. Like Hermione here, Florizel's mother, at 2880-1, "did print" a copy of Polixenes. MUIR (1960, p. 24) finds the same comparison in *Edward III* (ed. Brooke, 1908, 4.4.128-9 and 5.1.3) as well as "the juxtaposition of *face, matter*, and *printed*" (4.5.26-8). EGAN (1975, p. 64) alone takes *print* to mean "painting" and nature to be the artist.

1021 **Matter**] SCHMIDT (1875): "Contents."

1022 **Coppy**] The CLARKES (ed. 1865), comparing *Err.* 5.1.62 (1531): "Abundance, store," evidently with reference to "the whole Matter" (1021). Their "transcript or duplicated imitation" is more appropriate. The CLARKES (1879, p. 543): "Copious transcript." Although many eds. reflect it, the idea of "abundance" (*OED, sb.* 1) may be a false lead. "Reproduction, image" (*sb.* 4) seems to be the principal idea; to illustrate it, *OED* quotes "my brother hath a daughter, Almost the copie of my child thats dead" (*Ado* 5.1.298-9 [2373-4]). For *coppy out of*, see n. 197.

The trick of's Frowne, his Fore-head, nay, the Valley,
The pretty dimples of his Chin, and Cheeke; his Smiles:
The very Mold, and frame of Hand, Nayle, Finger.)   1025
And thou good Goddesse *Nature*, which hast made it
So like to him that got it, if thou hast
The ordering of the Mind too,'mongst all Colours

1023 Valley] valleys HAN, CAP, RANN, KTLY, DYCE2, HUD2
1024 *Verse lines ending* cheek, . . . smiles, GLO, WH2, NLSN
    pretty] *Om.* HAN
    his Smiles:] *Om.* v1778 *conj.,* CAP, RANN
1025 of Hand] of his Hand ROWE1, ROWE2
1027 hast$_\wedge$] ~ — HAL

1023 **trick . . . Fore-head**] KNIGHT (1947; 1965, p. 90): A "pretty irony . . . :
Leontes' ugly wrath at this instant is reflected in the baby's puckered brow."
    trick] HANMER (ed. 1743–4, 6:glos.): "The Air, or that peculiarity in a face,
voice, or gesture, which distinguishes it from others" (*OED, sb.* 8b). RANN (ed. 1787),
citing *Jn.* 1.1.85 (93): "Striking resemblance." FURNESS (ed. 1898), followed by HEN-
LEY (ed. 1902) and others, thinks the word here is a heraldic term (*OED* 10: "A sketch
in pen and ink of a coat of arms"), an idea that seems learnedly irrelevant.
    Valley] *OED* (*sb.* 3, citing this line): "A depression . . . suggestive of a valley."
Cf. *EDD*: "Also in form *velley.* . . . Any small channel or hollow, as a drain or gutter
in a roof." Critics disagree on the location of Perdita's. SCHMIDT (1875): "Apparently
explained by *the pretty dimples* as its apposition." FURNESS (ed. 1898): "Some characteristic of a frowning forehead (which let us hope Perdita outgrew)." TANNENBAUM
(1928, p. 362; reiterated in TANNENBAUM, 1932): "The dimple in the middle of the
upper lip, . . . the 'philtrum.'" WILSON (ed. 1931): "Perhaps the cleft of the chin."
PAFFORD (ed. 1963): "The hollow under the lower lip?"
    1024 **The . . . Smiles:**] Some eds. try to rectify this hexameter by relining or by
omitting words. MALONE (ed. 1790) thinks instead that *dimples* may be elided to one
syllable, an idea HARDINGE (1801, pp. 43–4) understandably finds silly. Although he
does not use the plural elsewhere, Sh. never elides *dimple* (*Ven.* 242) or *dimpled*
(four instances) or, for that matter, *simple.* Regarding STEEVENS's omission, LETTSOM
(MS 1840–65): "In fact *his smiles* merely explains the rest of the verse." For other
emendations, see p. 576.
    1026 **Goddesse *Nature***] MOORMAN (ed. 1912, p. xxiii): "Shakespeare has gath-
ered about the action . . . something of the atmosphere of classical Greece. No
Christian sentiment is permitted to fall from the lips of any of the characters." Classical
deities are alluded to—Jove (thrice), Apollo (a dozen times), the numerous gods and
petty gods of 4.4. BETHELL (1947, pp. 37–8) regards "the religious atmosphere as
emphatically Christian, while the pagan suggestions give authenticity to the story and
serve to 'distance' the Christian attitudes, presenting them in a new setting so as to
counteract the deadening influence of familiarity and escape . . . controversy over
minor theological questions." BETHELL's evidence includes "Whitson-Pastorals"
(1949), the hereditary imposition (137–8), the many allusions to grace (see n. 730,
for example), Judas Iscariot (see n. 533), and other Christian allusions.
    which] For this use of the relative, see n. 572.
    1027 **got**] JOHNSON (1755, Get): "Beget upon a female."
    1028 **ordering . . . Mind**] DEIGHTON (ed. 1889): "Regulating of its complex-
ion, character." HAPPÉ (1969): "Power of arranging."

No Yellow in't, least she suspect, as he do's,
Her Children, not her Husbands.   1030
   Leo. A grosse Hagge:
And Lozell, thou art worthy to be hang'd,
That wilt not stay her Tongue.
   Antig. Hang all the Husbands

1033 That] Thou ROWE2-POPE2

Colours] Eds. probably take this word to mean "hues," although none glosses it except ORGEL (ed. 1996), who interprets it as "characters, natures" by analogy with *Lr.* 2.2.138 (1218).

1029-30 **No . . . Husbands**] *OED* (Suspect, *v.* 2 and 2b, citing this line): "To imagine or fancy something, esp. something wrong . . . with slight or no proof . . . with obj[ect] and compl[ement]." ANON. (MS c. 1750): Let there be "no jealous part [see n. 1029] in ye Child's mind least she wh[en] married & a mother of Children sh[ould] suspect her Children not her Husbands, as ye now King, her Father, suspects his Children not his own." Later commentators find the supposition absurd. MALONE (ed. 1790): "No suspicion that the babe . . . might entertain of her future husband's *fidelity*, could affect the legitimacy of her offspring. Unless she were *herself* a 'bed-swerver', (which is not to be supposed,) she could have no doubt of his being the father of her children." LETTSOM (MS 1840-65): "Paulina hints that Leontes's suspicions of the legitimacy of the babe were as ridiculous as those of a jealous wife would have been." KIESSLING (1977, pp. 94-5), alone: "Perdita, were she to inherit her father's 'yellow', might either (1) come to suspect that her children were fathered not by her husband but by a spirit assuming the shape and form of her husband, or (2) come to suspect that her children were changelings." Critics disagree as to whether the illogic is intentional. MALONE (ibid.) thinks Sh. forgot "the difference of sexes." STEEVENS (ed. 1793) believes that the "seeming absurdity . . . [is] preferable to languid correctness"; HARDINGE (1800, p. 69), that Paulina is being sarcastic; ROLFE (ed. 1879), that she is excited. BENDA (ed. 1825): Sh. made Paulina's illogic overt in order to draw attention to the illogicality of the king's jealousy. Sh. accurately describes someone so angry as to have lost his senses (in Ger.). MCIVER (1979, p. 345) has the same idea: "The absurdity of this comparison underlines and insists upon the absurdity of Leontes' deluded perceptions." MAXWELL (ed. 1956) agrees, and BETHELL (ed. 1956) finds this another comic strand closely interwoven, in this scene, with the serious. ORGEL (ed. 1996): "There is no reason to assume that Paulina does not mean exactly what she says, . . . that it would be as fantastic for Perdita to suspect the legitimacy of her children as it is for Leontes to do so."

1029 **Yellow**] CALDECOTT (MS 1813-33): "The colour of jealousy" (*OED, sb.* 1c, citing this line). HUNTER (1845, 1:418-19) refers to the "greene and yellow melancholly" of *TN* 2.4.113 (1003). *OED* finds *yellow* in this sense no earlier than 1602.

1031 **grosse**] SCHMIDT (1874): "Blunt, rude." Cf. nn. 397, 794, 1384, and 2031.

1032 **Lozell**] REED (ed. 1785) refers to VERSTEGAN (1605, p. 335): "A *Losel* is one that hath lost neglected or cast of his own good and welfare, and so is become lewd & carelesse of credit and honesty." BULLOKAR (1616): "A lout, sometime a craftie fellow." PHILLIPS (1706): "A lazy Lubber, a slothful Booby." SCHMIDT (1874): "A faint-hearted, cowardly fellow," a sense not supported by *OED* (Losel, *sb.*).

1033 **stay**] See n. 59.

1034-6 **Hang . . . Subiect**] MOORMAN (ed. 1912, Hang): "If you hang." FURNESS (ed. 1898) agrees with ANON. (p. 576) that this speech is an aside, for "Leontes

That cannot doe that Feat, you'le leaue your selfe   1035
Hardly one Subiect.
    Leo. Once more take her hence.
    Paul. A most vnworthy, and vnnaturall Lord
Can doe no more.
    Leo. Ile ha' thee burnt.   1040
    Paul. I care not:
It is an Heretique that makes the fire,
Not she which burnes in't. Ile not call you Tyrant:
But this most cruell vsage of your Queene

---

by reiterating his previous command [1037] conveys the impression that he has not
heard Antigonus speak." BETHELL (ed. 1956) to the contrary: "The perennial joke.
The tone is now so completely of the music-hall that normal courtly politeness is
forgotten."

1037 **Once more**] CARRINGTON (1956): "The servants are slow to obey him."

1038-9 **A . . . more**] KNOWLES (privately): "If she addresses Antigonus, she
means 'a most unworthy husband can do no more than remove me'; if Leontes, there
is no worse thing a magistrate can do than to order the deaths of innocent members
of his family." See n. 1038.

1038 **vnnaturall**] *OED* (*a.* 2b): "Devoid of natural feeling."

Lord] DEIGHTON (ed. 1889): "Husband." Leontes's response, however, suggests that she may address him. See PARRY, n. 1043.

1042-3 **Heretique . . . in't**] THIRLBY (MS 1733-47?, Heretique): "Alluding . . . to the kings wrong belief of his wife." PORTER & CLARKE (ed. 1908):
"There's many a true believer burned for a heretic, which the burning has no power,
therefore, to make her. Rather in her resides the power to be heretical and not in the
external thing, the fire." PAFFORD (ed. 1963): "Dr [BROOKS] points out that the further
sense conveyed is 'If she is innocent the fire becomes something other than the
instrument of justice: it is an instrument of tyranny.' Paulina is saying that not every
execution of a woman at the stake is what it purports to be: that depends entirely on
whether she is a heretic or not: and, as for herself, Paulina is asserting that like the
martyrs so burned, she would also be a witness to the truth and, furthermore, she is
ready for her fate, she will not be silenced in her witness." ORGEL (ed. 1996), more
simply: "I.e. you are the heretic, not I." HOPPIN (1906, pp. 126-7): Perhaps an allusion to John Huss, the Bohemian reformer, who was burned as a heretic in 1415.
WILSON (ed. 1931): "Perhaps a reference to the fires of Smithfield in Mary's reign."
SCHANZER (ed. 1969): This was the most extreme punishment for that crime. "Paulina
wittily applies it to the heresy of lacking faith in Hermione." Regarding "the assignment of theological and ethical comments to pagan characters" in Sh.'s works, R.M.
FRYE (1963, p. 114, citing this instance): "There are a few anachronisms, and
. . . these are minor." ABBOTT (§§259-60) deduces Sh.'s rules for the use of *that*,
who, and *which*. Here (§260) *that* = "by nature, of necessity"; *which* distinguishes
an accidental fact.

1043 **which**] For *which* as *who*, see ABBOTT §265.

Tyrant] COCKERAM (1623): "A cruel bloudy prince." WILSON (ed. 1931):
"Cruel monster." BETHELL (ed. 1956): "The worst name that could be applied to a
king." See n. 1362. PARRY (ed. 1982) points out that "she has already called him a
madman [986-7], a traitor [1004], a jealous fool [1027 ff.], and 'a most unworthy and
unnaturall lord' [1038]."

(Not able to produce more accusation   1045
Then your owne weake-hindg'd Fancy) somthing sauors
Of Tyrannie, and will ignoble make you,
Yea, scandalous to the World.
    Leo. On your Allegeance,
Out of the Chamber with her. Were I a Tyrant,   1050
Where were her life? she durst not call me so,
If she did know me one. Away with her.
    Paul. I pray you doe not push me, Ile be gone.
Looke to your Babe (my Lord) 'tis yours: *Ioue* send her
A better guiding Spirit. What needs these hands?   1055
You that are thus so tender o're his Follyes,
Will neuer doe him good, not one of you.
So, so: Farewell, we are gone.   *Exit.*
    Leo. Thou (Traytor) hast set on thy Wife to this.
My Child? away with't? euen thou, that hast   1060

1046 somthing] sometimes ROWE
1048 the] all the POPE, HAN
1051 durst] dost F4
1055 better guiding] better-guiding WALKER (1860, 1:37) *conj.*, DYCE2, KNT3,
HUD2, BUL
        needs] neede F2-HAL (−DYCE1), KTLY-HUD2 (−DEL4), OXF1
1059 SCENE VI. POPE, HAN, WARB, JOHN
    1060 Child? . . . with't?] Ff; ∼ ! . . . ∼ ! KNT, WH1, HAL, KTLY, OXF1, CAM3,
ALEX, CLN2; ∼ ? . . . ∼ . ROWE1 *etc.*
        thou,] thou, thou THEO1-JOHN2 (−HAN)

    1045 **Not able**] BEVINGTON (ed. 1992): "You not being able." For the omission
of the participle, see ABBOTT §381.
    1046 **weake-hindg'd**] SCHMIDT (1874, Hinge): "That on which a thing turns or
depends." For *weak-hinged*, SCHMIDT (1875) gives "ill-founded." WILSON (ed. 1931):
"Crazy, rickety." HAPPÉ (1969): "Unbalanced." FURNESS (ed. 1898): "This cannot
refer to the metal double joints . . . on modern doors, but rather to the *hooks* or
staples on which doors were anciently hung, [like] the 'hook-and-eye' hinges on
which gates swing." He cites COTGRAVE (1611): "Gonds d' vne porte. *The hookes,
or hindges of a doore.*" OED (*a.* 23a) cites this instance only.
    Fancy] SCHMIDT (1874): "A thought not founded on reason, but on imagina-
tion," as also at 1368. See nn. 2335 and 3256 for related meanings. HAPPÉ (1969):
"The word is also used by Shakespeare to mean *love*, and the implication here may
be that the accusation is a result of distorted love," which seems improbable.
    somthing] somewhat. See n. 224. PARRY's (ed. 1982) "strongly" is what Pau-
lina means, however.
    1048 **scandalous**] OED (*a.* 2, citing this line): "Guilty of grossly disgraceful con-
duct, infamous."
    1049 **On your Allegeance**] HARRISON (ed. 1947): "The most solemn of all com-
mands; to disobey is high treason." ORGEL (ed. 1996) compares *Lr.* 1.1.166 (181).

1050 **Tyrant**] KERMODE (ed. 1963): "Paulina avoided calling him tyrant, but in coming close to so doing reminded him that this interpretation might all too easily be put upon his actions." Perhaps, instead, Leontes confesses what he knows he is even as he denies it. HUNTER (1965, p. 189): "Clearly, his subjects do not fear Leontes because he is usually not frightening. Their mode of addressing him makes it plain that they can ordinarily expect common sense and justice at his hands."

1053 **I . . . gone**] FREY ("Tragic Structure," 1978, p. 116): "Paulina's final speech points graphically to what must be happening onstage." See also n. 1055. JONES (1977, p. 271): "The way Paulina is got off the stage . . . makes a curiously sharp effect. . . . The violence offered the plain-speaking Paulina is not true tyrannical violence—hardly more than the apologetic nudging of essentially polite courtiers." JONES compares Seneca's *Agamemnon* (1003-4), in which Clytemnestra orders that Cassandra be dragged away and Cassandra replies, "Ne trahite, vestros ipsa praecedam gradus" [Drag me not, I will precede your going]. PITT (1981, p. 130): Paulina's "frostily courteous response reflects her sublime sang-froid." Lines 1053-8 are hardly imperturbable, however. See n. 1055.

1054 **Looke . . . Babe**] PORTER & CLARKE (ed. 1908): "This shows that she left the child where she had laid it, at his feet, presumably, for he says, at the time, ['Take vp the Bastard' (992), etc.]."

Looke to] *OED* (Look, *v*. 21c): "To attend to, take care of."

1055 **A . . . Spirit**] HUDSON (ed. 1880): "A spirit who will guide her better, or take better care of her . . . ; for *her* [1054] . . . must refer to *babe*." *OED* (Spirit, *sb*. 8, citing this line): "A particular character, disposition, or temper existing in . . . a person." ABRAMS (1986, p. 159), however, associates these words with the "powerfull Spirit" of 1118: "The angelic advocate or tutelary genius whom these words conjure is Hermione, who, appearing to Antigonus in a dream, names her daughter in Leontes's default and safely guides it to Bohemian shores."

What . . . hands?] ROLFE (ed. 1879): "Referring to the persons who are putting her out of the room." Antigonus, according to MOORMAN (ed. 1912), but the king's order (1049-50) may be general. PARRY (ed. 1982) suggests Leontes himself may manhandle her. NEILSON & HILL (ed. 1942): "You don't have to push me out." ORGEL (ed. 1996): "'Keep your hands off me.'"

needs] LETTSOM (MS 1840-65): "Note the superfluous *s* for *professes* [964]." This *s* is not superfluous, however; the verb is impersonal (ABBOTT §297), and, despite the critics' search for one, no agent is specified. Cf. n. 964-6 for a similar construction. For F2's change, see n. 30.

1056, 1061 **tender o're**] KITTREDGE & RIBNER (ed. 1967): "Gentle with." HAPPÉ (1969, Tender): "Compassionate." FURNESS (ed. 1898) is only technically right that Sh. uses this phrase only here. *Tender ouer* in the same sense is found in *Cym*. 5.5.87 (3357).

1056 **Follyes**] SCHMIDT (1874): "Absurd acts."

1058 **we**] Since Paulina enters unaccompanied at 928, the plural pronoun suggests that, despite the *Exit*, one or more of the courtiers leave with her. As COLLINS (ed. 1904-24?) says, she acts "somewhat ill-advisedly" in leaving Perdita, but she no doubt cannot imagine that Leontes would do the baby harm. SANDERS (1987, p. 42): "Her action [dramatizes] the unthinkableness of the thing Leontes now does."

1059 **set on**] SCHMIDT (1875): "Incite . . . instigate." HAPPÉ (1969): "Put her up to it."

1060 **My Child?**] The CLARKES (1879, p. 326): *My*, "where the rhythmical accent does not . . . lie," is emphasized, "thus producing doubly impressive effect." Cf. 2574.

with't?] I.e., with't!

1060-1 **euen . . . hence**] PORTER & CLARKE (ed. 1908): "Antigonus . . . is hovering with benignant interest over the baby."

A heart so tender o're it, take it hence,
And see it instantly consum'd with fire.
Euen thou, and none but thou. Take it vp straight:
Within this houre bring me word 'tis done,
(And by good testimonie) or Ile seize thy life,   1065
With what thou else call'st thine: if thou refuse,
And wilt encounter with my Wrath, say so;
The Bastard-braynes with these my proper hands
Shall I dash out. Goe, take it to the fire,
For thou sett'st on thy Wife.   1070

    Antig. I did not, Sir: (2A
These Lords, my Noble Fellowes, if they please,
Can cleare me in't.

    Lords. We can: my Royall Liege,
He is not guiltie of her comming hither.   1075

    Leo. You're lyers all.

    Lord. Beseech your Highnesse, giue vs better credit:
We haue always truly seru'd you, and beseech'
So to esteeme of vs: and on our knees we begge,
(As recompence of our deare seruices   1080
Past, and to come) that you doe change this purpose,
Which being so horrible, so bloody, must
Lead on to some foule Issue. We all kneele.

    1061 so] to DEL2
    1065-6 (And . . . call'st] And . . . seize | Thy life, with all that's HAN
    1068 Bastard-braynes] bastard's brains mTBY *and* HEATH (1765, p. 210) *conj.*,
HUD2, WH2
    1070 sett'st] sett'd'st HAN
    1072 These] The POPE, HAN
    1074 *Lords.*] Ff, THEO3, CAM1, GLO, WH2, BUL-PEL1, ARD2+; 1 & 2 *Lord.* WH1;
Lord. ROWE1 *etc. (subst.)*
    1077 *Lord.*] *Lords.* ROWE1-THEO4 (−HAN)
    1078 always] alway HAN3
        beseech'] beseech you ROWE1-THEO3, THEO4-JOHN2, v1773, COL2, COL3,
CAM1-DYCE2, HUD2, IRV, OXF1, ARD1, PEL1; beseech ye RLTR
    1079-80 *Verse lines ending* knees . . . service HAN
    1080 seruices] service HAN

1062 **And . . . fire**] ROWSE (1963, p. 429) wonders "whether the theme of the baby consigned to the fire may not echo the contemporary story of the Darrells, by which the Pophams were supposed to have succeeded to their house, Littlecote." According to John Aubrey, Sir John Darrell murdered his bastard child and burned its body in the fireplace. Discovered, Darrell saved his life by bribing Sir John Popham, Lord Chief Justice, with the gift of his "noble Howse, parke, and mannor" (*Brief Lives*, ed. Dick, 1949, pp. 245-6). Whether or not this story is echoed, the baby and the fire come from *Pandosto*. See p. 628.

1063 **straight**] See n. 915.

1065 **by good testimonie**] BOORMAN (ed. 1964): "With satisfactory proof."

seize] MINSHEU (1617, Seise): "Lay hold or hands on." According to FURNESS (ed. 1898), the word is the legal term, but he does not specify which of the legal term's several meanings he is referring to. Perhaps "to take possession of by force" (*OED*, *v*. 6). WILSON (ed. 1931): "Confiscate" (5b?).

1067 **wilt encounter with**] *OED* (*v*. 1b): "To meet as an adversary; to confront in battle." ABBOTT (§348): "The future is often used where we should use the . . . subjunctive."

1068 **Bastard-braynes**] WALKER (1860, 1:261-2) lists a few other "instances in which a hyphen has usurped the place of the final *s*."

proper] JOHNSON (1755): "One's own."

1072 **Fellowes**] The CLARKES (ed. 1865): "'Equals', 'peers', 'colleagues.'" PORTER & CLARKE (ed. c. 1903): "Comrades."

if they please] For *please* as a personal verb in this expression, see ABBOTT §297.

1073 **in't**] YOUNG & MOSELEY (ed. 1965): "*I.e.* of the accusation."

1074 **Lords**] FURNESS (ed. 1898): "There is something slightly unnatural in this harmonious chorus of Lords," which is probably not intended to be a chorus. For an arrangement other than those offered in the textual notes, see pp. 576.

1077 **Lord**] Believing that this Lord and the one in 2.1 are identical (see n. 738-42), the CLARKES (ed. 1865): "The character of this speaker is delineated with so much moral beauty throughout (from that speech of chivalrous loyalty to his queen, and courageous loyalty to his king [738 ff.] down to the present earnest remonstrance), that in the play of any other dramatist it would have assumed name and shape as a personage of importance; whereas, in Shakespeare's wealth of resource, and care in finishing even the most subordinate parts among his *dramatis personæ*, it merely figures as 'First Lord.'" Regarding the remonstrance (1077-83), TOLIVER (1989, pp. 154-5): "Even while Bohemia is still a long way off, we know that something is decidedly not right in the Sicilian combinations of high protocol and stress, as in this still appeal. . . . The trial issues other such fossilized statements."

Beseech] For the omission of the nominative, see ABBOTT §399.

giue . . . credit] MINSHEU (1617, Credit): "Trust." COLLINS (ed. 1904-24?): "Believe better of us."

1078 **beseech'**] WHITE (ed. 1857): The apostrophe "marks the arbitrary elision of 'you.'" He compares "taught 'this" (600), but see that n., and for the omission of the nominative, see ABBOTT §399.

1079 **So . . . vs**] *OED* (Esteem, *v*. 5b, citing this line): "Have (such and such) an opinion *of*." BETHELL (ed. 1956): "To understand that we have done so."

1080 **deare**] The CLARKES (ed. 1865): "'Sincerely devoted', 'faithfully dedicated', 'earnestly given.'" BOORMAN (ed. 1964): "Valuable." ORGEL (ed. 1996): "Both loving and valuable."

1083 **Issue**] MINSHEU (1617): "The end of a matter."

Leo. I am a Feather for each Wind that blows:
Shall I liue on, to see this Bastard kneele,   1085
And call me Father? better burne it now,
Then curse it then. But be it: let it liue.
It shall not neyther. You Sir, come you hither:
You that haue beene so tenderly officious
With Lady *Margerie*, your Mid-wife there,   1090
To saue this Bastards life; for 'tis a Bastard,
So sure as this Beard's gray. What will you aduenture,
To saue this Brats life?
    Antig. Any thing (my Lord)
That my abilitie may vndergoe,   1095
And Noblenesse impose: at least thus much;
Ile pawne the little blood which I haue left,
To saue the Innocent: any thing possible.
    Leo. It shall be possible: Sweare by this Sword
Thou wilt performe my bidding.   1100

1084 I am . . . blows:] Am I . . . blows? COL2
       Feather] Father F4, ROWE
1086 Father] Feather F4
1090 Mid-wife] mild wife CAPN *conj.*, RANN
1092 this] thy MTBY3 *and* MCOL1 *conj.*, COL, HUD, DYCE, OXF1
1096 least] last F2-F4
1097 which] that HUD2
1098 any thing] what's HAN

1084–8 **I . . . hither**] PILGRIM (1983, p. 32): "It is here that schizophrenia is most apparent."
    1084 **I . . . blows**] DENT compares "As wavering as Feathers in the wind" (TILLEY F162). DEIGHTON (ed. 1889): "Said with the ironical contempt of one who believes strongly in his own firmness, though he immediately afterwards [1087] justifies by his vacillation the very opinion at which he is sneering." HERFORD (ed. 1916–), differently: "Leontes naïvely betrays the weakness of conviction and will which underlies his violence"; HERFORD also notes (p. xvi), "we . . . witness the kaleidoscopic incoherence of a character which is at bottom only a string of moods." YOUNG & MOSELEY (ed. 1965): "Leontes's speeches from now on seem to indicate an indecision (perhaps due to the partial working of Paulina's stratagem) about the fate of Perdita. Doubt is beginning to creep in; Perdita's influence as a reconciling factor is beginning to be felt."
    1087 **be it**] The CLARKES (1879, p. 406): "Be it <so>," or as MAXWELL (ed. 1956) has it, "so be it." BETHELL (ed. 1956): "Leontes relents momentarily" and thereby "shows himself not without mercy" (see n. 798–805).
    1089 **officious**] SCHMIDT (1875): "Meddling." SCHANZER (ed. 1969): "The conjunction with *tenderly* suggests . . . the obsolete . . . 'ready to do kind offices' [*OED* 1]." If so, Leontes is sarcastic. Cf. "tender" at 1056 and 1061.
    1090 ***Margerie***] SCHMIDT (1875): "Vulgar form of Margaret. . . . [Here] a term of contempt." Sh.'s Margeries (always spelled *-ie*) are a sailor's girlfriend in *Tmp.*

2.2.48 (1087), Mrs. Gobbo in *MV* 2.2.89-91 (651-3), and a witch in *2H6* 1.2.75 (350). WILSON (ed. 1931) believes the name alludes to *margery-prater*, a cant word for a hen (see FARMER & HENLEY, 1890-1904; 1970), and "is therefore a variant on 'dame Partlet' [992]."

Mid-wife] THEOBALD (1729, in NICHOLS, 1817, 2:360): "Does the King mean to reflect on Antigonus's wife, as if she would be a party-bawd, to conceal the adultery, and save the child?" CAPELL (1783, 2.4:169), though he dislikes it, explains the F reading: "Paulina's bringing the child *in* [is] held a bringing it *forth* by" Leontes. HALLIWELL (ed. 1859), more simply: "He calls her midwife in contempt, because she brought the child into his presence." HOENIGER (1992, p. 42) believes that Paulina actually assisted Hermione at Perdita's birth, but that seems an unlikely office for a great lady. Nevertheless, ORGEL (ed. 1996): "The term implicates Paulina in both the birth of the child and the concealment of its true paternity. The midwife's oath . . . included a promise not to 'permit or suffer that woman being in labour or travail shall name any other to be the father of her child, than only he who is the right true father thereof.'"

1092 **this**] THEOBALD (1729, in NICHOLS, 1817, 2:360) asserts, regarding his conjectural *his* (see p. 576), "*I.e.* Antigonus's. . . . It is very plain, from [2.1], the Prince was a very young boy: and, [at 233-4] the King says that looking upon the child, he was moved to throw off 23 years in thought, . . . so that, allowing the child to be eight years old, the father could be but 31." Adducing the same evidence, MALONE (ed. 1790) agrees. For Antigonus's age, see nn. 1097 and 1548-9. CALDECOTT (MS 1813-33), however: "But anxiety & care will shed untimely snows" (cf. *Rom.* 4.5.28 [2606]), and Sh. was an inexact measurer of time: Leontes "means his own beard." Editorial indecision is perfectly illustrated by HERFORD (ed. 1904), who glosses "Antigonus'," and HERFORD (ed. 1916-), who glosses "his own." Favoring *thy*, DYCE (ed. 1857) points out that *this* may have been induced by the same word in 1091 and 1093 and, citing 2260-1, that its juxtaposition with *you* does not make *thy* impossible. Comparing 766-7, BETHELL (ed. 1956) decides that "the king probably pulls Antigonus' beard." SCHANZER (ed. 1969): "Perhaps Leontes is meant to pull Antigonus's beard, though it would suffice if he pointed at it." Cf. n. 766.

aduenture] Dare, risk. See n. 95.

1095-6 **my . . . impose**] SCHMIDT (1875, Undergo 3): "Perform." KITTREDGE & RIBNER (ed. 1967): "I am capable of doing [anything] that a noble person would ask me to do."

1097-8 **Ile . . . possible**] STOPES (1916, p. 35): "This pledge he is called on to redeem, and thereby really becomes the means of saving the innocent." PORTER & CLARKE (ed. 1908): "Antigonus thus foretold his own death."

1097 **pawne**] MINSHEU (1617, a Paune): "Pledge," with which JOHNSON (1755, citing this line) agrees. SCHMIDT (1875) distinguishes a slightly different meaning, "to stake," which *OED* considers a figurative use.

little blood] PAFFORD (ed. 1963): "Antigonus is elderly." Cf. 1092. PARRY (ed. 1982): "As one grew elderly one's life-blood diminished in quantity."

1099 **Sweare . . . Sword**] STEEVENS (ed. 1778): "By the cross on the handle of a sword." NARES (1876; 1905, Sword, swearing upon): The cross is not on the sword but formed by the "straight transverse bar" that separates blade and hilt. BETHELL (ed. 1956): "This Christian custom is introduced at an important point in the play: the Cross figures in the disposal of Perdita as it does in her finding." The cross at Perdita's finding, however, is an egregious anagogical invention; see n. 1553-4. As for the custom, it is mentioned again at 1304, where the sword of Justice seems devoid of Christian associations. KNOWLES (privately): "The sword was the emblem of authority (*OED* 2), military courage and honesty (*H5* 2.1.100 [600], *Lr.* 2.2.72-3 [1145-6]), knighthood (*R2* 1.1.78 [83]), justice (*OED* 5, *2H4* 5.2.114 [2998]). When he swears by his sword (1.3.82 [399]), Antony is not anticipating the cross."

Antig. I will (my Lord.)
Leo. Marke, and performe it: seest thou? for the faile
Of any point in't, shall not onely be
Death to thy selfe, but to thy lewd-tongu'd Wife,
(Whom for this time we pardon) We enioyne thee,   1105
As thou art Liege-man to vs, that thou carry
This female Bastard hence, and that thou beare it
To some remote and desart place, quite out
Of our Dominions; and that there thou leaue it
(Without more mercy) to it owne protection,   1110
And fauour of the Climate: as by strange fortune
It came to vs, I doe in Iustice charge thee,
On thy Soules perill, and thy Bodyes torture,
That thou commend it strangely to some place,
Where Chance may nurse, or end it: take it vp.   1115
Antig. I sweare to doe this: though a present death
Had beene more mercifull. Come on (poore Babe)
Some powerfull Spirit instruct the Kytes and Rauens
To be thy Nurses. Wolues and Beares, they say,
(Casting their sauagenesse aside) haue done   1120

1102 thou?] ~ ; COL, SING2, WH, STAU, DEL, KTLY, PEL1, BEV; ~ ! OXF1, CLN2
1110 more] much F2-POPE2
     it] its F3-OXF1 (−WH, STAU), SIG, PEN2, BEV4
1114 strangely to some] to some stranger HAN
1115 Chance] Change F3, F4

1101 **I . . . Lord**] PAFFORD (ed. 1963): "He touches the sword."
1102 **seest thou?**] DEIGHTON (ed. 1889): "Take care to [perform it]." Eds. who transform F's question mark to an exclamation point (as DEIGHTON does) mean "See to it!" Those who keep the question mark mean, as WRIGHT & LAMAR (ed. 1966) say, "Do you understand?"
     faile] JOHNSON (1755): "Omission; non-performance." Also at 2759. EVANS (ed. 1974): "The regular Elizabethan form." For the part of speech, see n. 2931.
1104 **lewd-tongu'd**] HUDSON (ed. 1880): "*Lewd* meant vulgar or ignorant" (*OED* 3, 4). The CLARKES (ed. 1865): "Wicked-tongued" (*OED*, Lewd 5). PARRY (ed. 1982): "Foul-mouthed."
1105 **Whom**] KNOWLES (privately): "Substituted for the accusative *her*, object of 'we pardon.'"
1105-11 **We . . . Climate**] HOLBROOK (1945, pp. 173-4), perhaps seriously: "It is possible that the errand . . . presents a welcome alternative to more of his [Antigonus's] wife's dictatorship." HOLBROOK (1964, p. 165): "'Liegeman' he calls Antigonus, to command his obedience. . . . Antigonus is made the instrument of Perdita's exposure, on his '*honour*,'" because as the vassal of the king he is bound by oath to serve him.

1105 **enioyne**] SCHMIDT (1874): "Bind" (*OED, v.* 2e, citing this line).

1106 **As . . . vs**] JOHNSON (1755, Liege-man): "Subject." *Liege* is "Sovereign; superior lord." RANN (ed. 1787): "On thy allegiance."

carry] For the subjunctive, see n. 511.

1110 **it**] ABBOTT (§228): "An early provincial form of the old genitive," which recurs at 1279. Despite CRAIK's (1859, pp. 98–100) discussion of possessive *it* and their own and STAUNTON's observation of the form in nearly a dozen Shn. texts, CLARK & WRIGHT (ed. 1863): "We think it most probable that Shakespeare would not deliberately have written *it* for *its*, or *his*, except when imitating the language of rustics or children." ROLFE (ed. 1879), however: SCHMIDT (1874) lists 14 certain instances of *it* meaning "its"; "in seven of these it is in the combination *it own*." For *it's* as a possessive pronoun, see n. 230–1.

1111 **fauour**] CARRINGTON (1956), unsupported by *OED*: "Treatment, without our sense of *kindly* treatment." SCHMIDT (1874): "Friendly disposition," evidently ironically.

1111–15 **as . . . end it**] SCHANZER (ed. 1969) refers to *Pandosto*; see p. 628.

1111 **strange**] CALDECOTT (MS 1813–33): "Unaccountable" (*OED, a.* 10, adding "abnormal, . . . difficult to take in"). WALKER (1860, 2:288): "Alien, foreign; it being, as he maintains, the child of a foreigner," an interpretation that seems unlikely, although SCHMIDT (1875) agrees. See n. 1114.

1112 **in Iustice**] WILSON (ed. 1931): "The foreign bastard is an intruder and deserves banishment."

1114 **commend**] MINSHEU (1617): "Commit" (*OED, v.* 1). SCHMIDT (1874): "Deliver."

strangely] JOHNSON (ed. 1765): "As a stranger," or, as MOORMAN (ed. 1912) has it, "as though it were of alien birth." Eds. generally agree, but not SCHMIDT (1875, p. 1418b): "In the situation of a stranger; so as not to be known there," "the adverb not expressing a manner or degree, but a state and condition." Thus COLLINS (ed. 1904–24?): "*I.e.* take it to a foreign country." BETHELL (ed. 1956): "With a reference back to [1111]."

1115 **nurse, or end**] DENT compares "Either Mend or end" (TILLEY M874). MOORMAN (ed. 1912) compares 1168. SCHMIDT (1875, Nurse): "To bring up."

1116 **I . . . this**] SHERMAN (1902, p. 128), oddly: "Except that this man had been henpecked so thoroughly, he would have withheld consent."

present] SCHMIDT (1875): "Immediate."

1117 **Come . . . Babe**] GRANVILLE-BARKER (1912; 1974, p. 20): "Little dignity is left to Leontes; and when any is restored to the scene, it is to Antigonus it falls as he takes the child in his arms to depart." In doing so, PYLE (1969, p. 46) remembers, he places himself under his wife's curse (994–7).

1118–19 **Some . . . Nurses**] GREY (1754, 1:253): An allusion to God's commanding the ravens to feed Elijah (1 Kings 17:4). NOBLE (1935, p. 247): A "possible reminiscence."

1118 **Spirit**] ABBOTT (§463): Monosyllabic. For its possible identity, see n. 1055.

1119–21 **Wolues . . . Pitty**] GREY (1754, 1:253): Alluding to "*Romulus* and *Remus*, who were said to have been nursed by a *wolf.*" SMITH (1972, pp. 4–5): That legend "may have been coupled in his [Sh.'s] mind with a recollection of the bear as nurse in" *Valentine and Orson*, a romance "there is reason to believe Shakespeare knew." The reason, however, is merely that the romance is known to have been read by a contemporary of Sh.'s. PAFFORD (ed. 1963): "The hope about wild beasts here is ironically falsified in the fate of Antigonus." For more on Elizabethan bears and wolves, see SEAGER (1896, pp. 29–31 and 346–51), and for these lines as ironical anticipation, see n. 1500.

Like offices of Pitty. Sir, be prosperous
In more then this deed do's require; and Blessing
Against this Crueltie, fight on thy side
(Poore Thing, condemn'd to losse.)   *Exit.*

    Leo. No: Ile not reare   1125
Anothers Issue.   *Enter a Seruant.*

    Seru. Please' your Highnesse, Posts
From those you sent to th'Oracle, are come
An houre since: *Cleomines* and *Dion*,
Being well arriu'd from Delphos, are both landed,   1130
Hasting to th'Court.

    Lord. So please you (Sir) their speed
Hath beene beyond accompt.

    Leo. Twentie three dayes
They haue beene absent: 'tis good speed: fore-tells   1135
The great *Apollo* suddenly will haue
The truth of this appeare: Prepare you Lords,   (2.
Summon a Session, that we may arraigne
Our most disloyall Lady: for as she hath
Been publikely accus'd, so shall she haue   1140
A iust and open Triall. While she liues,
My heart will be a burthen to me. Leaue me,
And thinke vpon my bidding.   *Exeunt.*

    1122 do's] doth v1803-COL2 (−KNT2), WH1-DEL2, DEL4, COL4, OXF1

    1124 *Exit*] Ad. *with the Child* ROWE1 + (*subst.*)

    1126-7 *One verse line* mCAP2, v1793+ (−WH1)

    1126 *Enter a Seruant.*] *Om.* CAP, MAL-HUD2 (−CAM1, GLO)

    1127 *Seru.*] 2. *A.* CAP, DYCE, STAU, HUD2; 1. *Attend.* MAL-SING2, WH1-HAL, DEL2, KTLY, KNT3-COL4

    1135 'tis good speed:] this good speed∧ POPE1-JOHN2, RANN; 'Tis good speed and KTLY

    1136 The] That mTBY2 *conj.*, RANN

    1121 **Like**] SCHMIDT (1874, adj. 1): "Equal." MOORMAN (ed. 1912): "Similar" (SCHMIDT 2).

    offices of Pitty] JOHNSON (1755, Offices, citing this line): "Act of good or ill voluntarily tendered." For other senses, see nn. 857, 2440, and 2820. According to LENZ (1986, p. 98), the bear's "peculiar office of pity" is to dine on Antigonus rather than on Perdita. See n. 1500.

    1121-2 **Sir . . . require**] DEIGHTON (ed. 1889): "A sort of farewell, as though Antigonus knew that he was never to see the king again."

    1122 **In more**] EVANS (ed. 1974): "In more ways (?) or to a greater degree (?)."

    do's require] RODERICK (1758, p. 212): "Could with any right *demand*, or in reason *expect*." CALDECOTT (MS 1813-33): "Intitle you to." SCHMIDT (1875, Require 2) agrees: "To render necessary, to need, to want. . . . Passing into the sense of to deserve" (*OED, v.* 6b). See n. 1240.

1122–4 **Blessing . . . losse**] RODERICK (1758, pp. 212–13): "The *Blessing* of heaven . . . protect the poor child, *condemned to be exposed*, against the intended effects of its father's *Cruelty*." To reinforce this meaning, RODERICK wishes, unnecessarily, to change "this Crueltie" to "*his* Cruelty." CAPELL (1783, 2.4:169, Loss): "Perdition" (i.e., *OED, sb.*[1] 1: "Ruin, destruction"). However, MALONE (1790) points out that *losse* cannot mean "destruction" because, at 1492–3, Antigonus speaks of Perdita's being "expos'd To losse, and what may follow." Thus the meaning can be "diminution of one's possessions or advantages; detriment or disadvantage involved in being deprived of something, or resulting from a change in conditions" (*OED, sb.*[1] 5), or, as SCHMIDT (1874) has it, "the state of being cast off and discarded." Exposure is the consequence rather than the loss itself, and, at 1492–3, Antigonus means "abandonment and death." LEE (ed. 1907), comparing 1493, points out that BARET (1580) gives as one meaning of *loss* "hurt: properly things cast out of a shippe in time of tempest." MOORMAN (ed. 1912) makes it "perdition" (total destruction presumably).

1123 **Against**] MOORMAN (ed. 1912): "To counteract."

1124 **Poore Thing**] The Shepherd uses these words when he discovers Perdita at 1517.

1125–6 **No . . . Issue**] PORTER & CLARKE (ed. 1908): "A hardening of the king's heart, which shows that it was a little inclined to soften."

1127 **Please' your Highnesse**] The construction is discussed by ABBOTT §297. PAFFORD (ed. 1963) thinks that "*Please*' is perhaps a misprint for '*Please*."

Posts] MINSHEU (1617): "Messenger[s] in hast."

1128 **th'Oracle**] *OED* (*sb.* 1, citing this line): "The mouthpiece of the deity; the place or seat of such instrumentality." See n. 1298 for another meaning.

1129 **An houre since**] PYLE (1969, p. 46): "By delaying the news for an hour, [was] chance giving Leontes time to seal his own fate and that of the child, which hung so precariously in the balance [1086–8]?"

1130 **well**] SCHMIDT (1875): "In such a state . . . as one would wish." COLLINS (ed. 1904–24?): "Happily, without misfortune."

Delphos] See n. 1147.

1133 **beyond accompt**] SCHMIDT (1874, Account): "Computation" (*OED* 1). FURNESS (ed. 1898), however: "Beyond any of which we have account, unprecedented" (*OED* 16). SCHANZER (ed. 1969): "Probably 'beyond explanation'" (*OED* 8).

1134 **Twentie three dayes**] COLLINS (ed. 1904–24?) points out that Greene makes the travel time to Delphos "within three weeks"; see p. 630. "Shakespeare makes the speed more miraculous by making them travel the double journey in this time. Shakespeare is not of course troubling about the fact that Greene's messengers are starting from Bohemia, his own from Sicily." CARRINGTON (1956): "Such a realistic touch of circumstantial detail gives the truth of fact to fiction."

1135–6 **fore-tells The**] The CLARKES (ed. 1865): A nominative is understood before *fore-tells*, and *that* "is elliptically understood before 'the.'" See ABBOTT §§399–402 and FRANZ §306.

1136 **suddenly**] SCHMIDT (1875): "Immediately."

1138 **Session**] SCHMIDT (1875): "The sitting . . . of a court of justice" (*OED, sb.* 4, citing this line). For *sessions*, see n. 1176.

1140–1 **so . . . Triall**] GARDNER (1980, p. 62): This statement registers in Leontes's favor. "Nor is he without the desire to deal fairly." But the next words show that the presiding magistrate has already reached a verdict and pronounced the sentence.

1141–2 **While . . . me**] See n. 900.

1143 **thinke . . . bidding**] DEIGHTON (ed. 1889): "Take care that it [my will] is performed."

Actus Tertius. Scena Prima. 3.1

Enter Cleomines and Dion. 1145

Cleo. The Clymat's delicate, the Ayre most sweet,
Fertile the Isle, the Temple much surpassing

1144 *Actus Tertius. Scena Prima.*] Act 2, last scene THEOBALD (1729) *in* NICHOLS (1817, 2:369), KEM

1145 SCENE, *a Part of Sicily near the Sea-side.* THEO1-JOHN2, v1773-RANN, CAM1, GLO, WH2, OXF1, ARD1 (*subst.*); *The same* [i.e., Sicilia]. *A Street in some Town.* CAP, MAL-COL3, STAU-DEL2, KTLY-HUD2, IRV, BUL, NLSN (*subst.*); DELPHI, *near the Temple of* APOLLO. HAL; *Before an inn upon a high road in Sicilia* CAM3, ARD2 (*subst.*); *Sicilia. On the road.* KIT1-SIS, SIG, EVNS, BEV (*subst.*)

Dion] Ad. *with Attendants* JOHN, v1773; *and an* Attendant WALKER (1860, 3:101) *conj.*, DYCE2, HUD2; *attended* IRV

1147 Isle] Soil WARBURTON *conj. in* THEO1, HAN, CAP

1144 ***Actus Tertius.***] NEVO (1987, p. 116): "Act III consists of three scenes symmetrically divided to form a triptych. The two flanking scenes suggest the two antagonistic drives which tragicomedy commingles." THEOBALD (1729, in NICHOLS, 1817, 2:361) argues that this scene should conclude Act 2. At 1127 ff., Cleomines and Dion have arrived from Delphos, but at 1172 they have not reached the court, "and yet the very next scene [3.2] opens with . . . the Queen's trial, the determination of which was to await the answer of the oracle. This hurries the action on with somewhat too much precipitation." THEOBALD does not alter the scene's number in his ed. 1733, however. Although the act division is probably scribal (see p. 594), the question could be relevant: according to JEWKES (1958, pp. 100-1), act division in public-theater plays became more frequent from about 1607 on; hence Sh., rather than Crane or someone else, may have decided where acts were to begin. For another disputed act division, see n. 1578.

Scena Prima.] WELSFORD (1927; 1962, p. 288): "Dramatically [this] conversation is unnecessary." She probably means that it does not advance the plot, but several eds. find the scene useful in other ways. HERFORD (ed. 1916-): "The messengers sent to consult the oracle are now on their way home, bearing Apollo's response in a sealed packet. They are still full of the wonderful and 'unearthly' [1153] impression made by the temple and its ceremonies; and while hoping fervently for Hermione's acquittal, are confident that the oracular reply will be 'something rare' [1170] in any case; for Hermione's guilt divinely attested, would be an even greater prodigy than the king's infatuation." BROOKE (1905; 1913, p. 264): "This happy, gentle picture relieves the mind, oppressed with the furies of the last act." GRANVILLE-BARKER (1912; 1974, p. 24) finds the scene "a model 'bridge' from the raucous revilings of Leontes over the helpless child to the dignity of the scene of the trial." SPRAGUE (1935, p. 188): It "lends dignity to the oracle, and we become more eager to know what it contains." MINCOFF (1941, p. 40): The scene "serves to underline the importance of the oracle and to increase the tension, separates the two scenes in which Leontes appears surrounded by his court." PRICE (1948, pp. 102, 108): The "scene has little or nothing to do with the plot. . . . [Rather] it may be said to mirror the play . . . [in order] to shed light upon his [Sh.'s] central thought. . . . He wishes to invest with the utmost authority the twofold function of the gods. They save Hermione and they decree the punishment Leontes is to suffer." BETHELL (ed. 1956): "The turning-point of the play. We have so far followed the uninterrupted course of an evil passion. We now note the beginning of a divine action which will encounter and conquer it. A pagan religious service is described in the language of Christian devotion, so as to express the power and mystery and beneficence of God, who providentially orders the lives of men and brings good out of evil." The language does express devotion, but the oracle's voice is like Jove's thunder (see n. 1156) and the presiding spirit is specifically Apollo's. Nevertheless, as YOUNG & MOSELEY (ed. 1965) say, "Shakespeare is here allowing the supernatural in the plot to begin to direct the course of the play." GILBERT (1979, p. 237): "The dramatic value of the scene lies in its quiet, its non-violence, even in its lack of action; we are reminded of a different world and of the possibilities of order." PARRY (ed. 1982): The messengers' "comments on [the oracle] throw into relief—and make a brief respite from—the sense of oppression that the play has steadily built up since [1.2]. At the court of Sicilia reverence and ceremony have been notably *absent* from the conduct of affairs." R. P. KNOWLES (1982, p. 275): "Coming before the trial scene in which Hermione pleads 'Apollo be my judge' [1295], it prepares our expectations that ultimately 'something rare . . . will rush to knowledge' [1170-1]."

As to locale, HALLIWELL (ed. 1859): "Apparently . . . in Delphi, soon after Cleomenes and Dion had visited the oracle, the allusion to the happy issue of the journey [1159-61 presumably] referring to the accomplishment of the object of their mission, not necessarily including their return to Sicily. . . . The temple was some distance from the sea, and they required fresh horses [at 1171], not for their last stage in Sicily, but to take them with the utmost rapidity down to their ship." FURNESS (ed. 1898): "It adds greatly to Halliwell's argument that Cleomenes says 'The Climate is delicate' [1146], not '*was* delicate.'" If HALLIWELL is right, 3.1 takes place before 2.3, but, as the textual notes show, recent eds. avoid that confusing sequence by locating the scene in Sicilia. Following KOPPEL (1874, p. 289), FURNIVALL (ed. 1908) puts it at "An Inn, one post from the Capital," and F. W. CLARKE (in FURNIVALL, ed. 1908) notes, "Line [1171] implies that the Riders had brought in tired horses, and had not just landed, as some Eds. make them." They probably allude to those eds., like CLARK & WRIGHT (ed. 1864), who place the scene at "*A sea-port in Sicilia.*" TANNENBAUM alone (1928, pp. 363-4) thinks the lords "are now at an inn in the capital of Sicilia . . . and are preparing their respective reports."

1145 *Enter . . . Dion*] WALKER (1860, 3:101): An attendant is needed to receive the order given in 1171, as DYCE (ed. 1864) and HUDSON (ed. 1880) indicate. Eds. who add more attendants may consider a large retinue appropriate to the rank of the king's emissaries.

1146-8 **The . . . beares**] Regarding the arrangement of the clauses, see n. 568-74. BETHELL (ed. 1956): "Images of natural goodness and fertility to express the supernatural goodness of the Creator." HOLBROOK (1964, p. 166) compares *Mac.* 1.6.1-8 (434-42), where the Creator is quite ironical.

1146 **delicate**] SCHMIDT (1874): "Delicious" (i.e., delightful). JOHNSON (1755), like SCHMIDT, quotes "The ayre is delicate" (*Mac.* 1.6.10 [444]): "Pure, clear."

1147 **Isle**] A famous discrepancy. WARBURTON (in THEOBALD, ed. 1733) objects, "But the Temple of *Apollo* at *Delphi* was not in an *Island*, but in *Phocis* on the Continent." Later WARBURTON (ed. 1747) adds, "Either *Shakespear*, or his Editors, had their heads running on *Delos*, an island of the *Cyclades*." The mistake is sometimes attributed—by UPTON (1746, pp. 40-1), for example—to Sh.'s ignorance, and

The common prayse it beares.
  Dion. I shall report,
For most it caught me, the Celestiall Habits,   1150
(Me thinkes I so should terme them) and the reuerence
Of the graue Wearers. O, the Sacrifice,
How ceremonious, solemne, and vn-earthly
It was i'th'Offring?
  Cleo. But of all, the burst   1155
And the eare-deaff'ning Voyce o'th'Oracle,
Kin to *Ioues* Thunder, so surpriz'd my Sence,
That I was nothing.

1149 I shall] It shames WARBURTON *conj. in* THEO1, WARB
1150 For most] Foremost WARB
     it] they HAN

---

the information to which WARBURTON alludes was available in the 16th c. COOPER (1565) glosses *Delphicum oraculum* as "the aunswere made at the temple of Apollo in Delphos" and *Delphos* as "a citie in the countrey called *Phocis*, on a mountayne in Greece called *Parnassus*: there was the great & famous temple of Apollo called *Delphicus*, where the diuell gaue aunsweres by women, which there serued for the purpose." (COOPER's diabolical spokeswomen contrast sharply with the divine, yet powerful, oracle described by Cleomines and Dion in 3.1.) Yet SPENCER (1952, p. 200) shows that "in the early seventeenth century, the island famous in antiquity as Delos, the sacred birthplace of Apollo, *was* commonly known as Delphos," in part because of the colossal statue of Apollo found there. The island even had an oracle, referred to in *Aeneid* 3.73-101. Sh. was, in fact, "writing in accordance with the state of knowledge in his own time" (p. 202), as was Greene; Delphos is an isle in *Pandosto* just as Bohemia is there a maritime nation. See n. 1440 and pp. 630 and 675. PAFFORD (ed. 1963): Other Delphic isles are found in Greene, *Menaphon* (1598); in Moraes, *Palmendos*, trans. Mundy (1589); in Sabie, *Fissher-mans Tale* (1595); in Forde, *Parismus* (1598); and in *The Thracian Wonder* (1590-c. 1601). As MUIR (1957, p. 244) points out, *Parismus* had already provided Bohemia with a seacoast. For GERVINUS's opinion that these geographical "mistakes" are intentional, see n. 0.

As to the oracle, BOORMAN (ed. 1964) finds it "remarkable for its plain replies to questions, whereas the Oracle at Delphi gave cryptic and ambiguous replies. The oracle read aloud [at 1313-16] . . . is largely straightforward, even blunt, of a type more likely to have come from Delos than from Delphi." It is dramatically necessary, however, that the oracle be powerfully clear and unambiguous, as Sh. understood when he read it in *Pandosto*; when a mysteriously allusive supernatural communication was needed, as in *Cym.* 5.4.138-44 (3176-82), that too was forthcoming. R. P. KNOWLES (1982, p. 274), discussing Shn. theophanies: *WT* "carries farther the movement in the last plays away from the intimation of providential control toward full identification with artistic control by employing Apollo . . . as the presiding deity . . . and by relegating the deity as deity to a more minor place in the story. The oracle, nevertheless, plays an important role in effecting the shift from the Dionysian first half of the play, with its confusion, noise, and pain, to the Apollonian second half of harmony and healing."

1148 **common**] SCHMIDT (1874): "General."

1149–54 **I . . . i'th'Offring?**] CHARLTON (ed. 1916): "Reference to the gravity and reverence of the priests lends a dignity and conviction to the oracle. . . . It gives just the proper atmosphere for what is to follow—the justification of Hermione." BETHELL (ed. 1956): "Cleomenes has described the effects of divine goodness in the *natural order* [1146–8]; now Dion gives a condensed description of the *supernatural* quality of religious worship." RICHMAN (1990, p. 124): Sh. "conveys Dion's honest reaction to the oracle and his genuine difficulty in finding adequate language for extraordinary experience and emotion. At the same time, he mildly satirizes the courtier's desire to find the *mot juste*." BOWDEN (1899, p. 288) finds the religious doctrines represented in *WT* "Tridentine rather than Olympian." He adds, "The idea of the sacrifice of the mass [may] be here indirectly suggested" (p. 290).

1150 **For . . . me**] RANN (ed. 1787): "What struck me most."

it] JOHNSON (ed. 1765): "*It* may relate to the whole spectacle." The CLARKES (ed. 1865): "In reference to the effect collectively produced by several objects . . . 'the celestial habits', &c."

caught] JOHNSON (1755, Catch): "To charm." *OED* (*v.* 37): "To captivate."

Celestiall Habits] JOHNSON (1755, Habit): "Dress; accoutrement." PARRY (ed. 1982): "Heavenly costumes."

1153 **ceremonious**] *OED* (*a.* 2, citing this line): "Accompanied with rites, religious or showy."

vn-earthly] JOHNSON (1755): "Not terrestrial."

1155–8 **But . . . nothing**] BELLETTE (1978, p. 69): "The speech prefigures Leontes' collapse in the trial scene and the reduction of that self to nothing which would have destroyed the world." Leontes does not collapse all at once, however; the news of Mamillius's death (1326–7) is followed by Hermione's collapse (1331 ff.) and that by the report of her death (1388).

1155 **burst**] MOORMAN (ed. 1912): "The breaking out into speech." Cf. *Cym.* 4.2.106 (2385).

1156–7 **eare-deaff'ning . . . Thunder**] HARDINGE (1818, 3:66): Since the Sicilians do not know what the oracle has pronounced, the voice is "inarticulate of course, or intelligible only to the initiated." To put a fine point upon it, the latter is evidently the case, for the words are written down and sealed. To BETHELL (ed. 1956), the thunderous oracle "recalls the giving of the Law on Mt. Sinai," and PAFFORD (ed. 1963) notes that "thunder or thunderous noise is usual with any theophany." He cites *Cym.* 5.4.92.1–2 (3126–7) and Ariel like a harpy in *Tmp.* 3.3.52.1 and 3.3.82.1 (1583, 1616). See nn. 1330–1 and 1444–5 for reiterations of Cleomines's experience.

1157 **surpriz'd**] The CLARKES (ed. 1865): "'Overcame', 'overpowered'" (*OED*, *v.* 1b, citing this line).

Sence] LETTSOM (MS 1840–65), referring to WALKER (1854, p. 248), suggests that this word may be a collective singular (*OED*, *sb.* 4b).

1158 **I was nothing**] DEIGHTON (ed. 1889): "Utterly bewildered, and conscious only of my insignificance." MAHOOD (1992, p. 80): "The self-surrender that [is] the right prelude to the operation of divine grace."

Dio. If th'euent o'th'Iourney
Proue as successefull to the Queene (O be't so)   1160
As it hath beene to vs, rare, pleasant, speedie,
The time is worth the vse on't.
    Cleo. Great *Apollo*
Turne all to th'best: these Proclamations,
So forcing faults vpon *Hermione,*   1165
I little like.
    Dio. The violent carriage of it
Will cleare, or end the Businesse, when the Oracle
(Thus by *Apollo's* great Diuine seal'd vp)
Shall the Contents discouer: something rare   1170
Euen then will rush to knowledge. Goe: fresh Horses,
And gracious be the issue.   *Exeunt.*

1162 time . . . vse] use . . . time HAN, WARB, CAP
    the] to WH2
1164 these] the ROWE2
1168-70 cleare, . . . Businesse, . . . discouer:] ~ , . . . ~ ; . . . ~ , JOHN1-
ALEX (−RLTR), PEL1+; ~ ; . . . ~ , . . . ~ , SIS
    1171 Goe . . . Horses,] *To Attendant* DYCE2, HUD2

1159-62 **If . . . on't**] MALONE (ed. 1790): "If the event prove fortunate to the
queen . . . the happy issue of our journey will compensate for the time expended
in it, and the fatigue we have undergone."
    1159 **th'euent**] COCKERAM (1623): "The ende of a thing."
    1161 **rare**] MINSHEU (1617): See "Excellent, & Singular."
    1162 **The . . . on't**] JOHNSON (ed. 1765): "The time which we have spent in
visiting *Delos* has recompensed us for the trouble of so spending it." Most commentators seem to understand *use* generally, as "employment"; SCHMIDT (1875), for example: "The time is worth having been used, i.e. spent most usefully." HENLEY (ed.
1902), however: "Interest charged and paid," a reading that may derive from SINGER's
(ed. 1826) quotation of Florio's trans. of Montaigne: "The common saying is, the time
we live, is worth the mony we pay for it" (*Essays*, 1603; introd. Saintsbury, 1892, 1:
75). WILSON (ed. 1931), similarly: "Profit, advantage" (that it brought, presumably).
For *on't* as "of it," see n. 785-6.
    1163-4 **Great . . . th'best**] DENT compares the proverbial "God turn all to
good" (G227.1).
    1164-6 **these . . . like**] BLAKE (1983, p. 120): "The placing of the object first
in the clause is but common . . ., but Shakespeare frequently extends the nominal
group acting as object by including one or more qualifiers. . . . The longer the
qualifier, the more unexpected it is to find that the first nominal group is not the
subject."
    1165 **forcing**] The CLARKES (ed. 1865): "'Falsely imputing', 'wrongfully charg-
ing.'" Cf. nn. 995-6 and 996-7.

Scœna Secunda.   **3.2**

1167 **violent . . . it**] SCHMIDT (1874, Carriage): "Management." DEIGHTON (ed. 1889): "The headstrong manner in which Leontes has proceeded." BETHELL (ed. 1956): "Rapid pushing-on" of it.

1168 **cleare, or end**] BETHELL (ed. 1956): "I.e. clear it up (favourably for Hermione) or end it (in her condemnation)." Cf. n. 1115.

1168–72 **when . . . issue**] FREY ("Tragic Structure," 1978, p. 121), alone: "The whole image is one of birth as the seal gives way, the contents are discovered, and what is rare bursts forth."

1169 **Diuine**] SCHMIDT (1874): "Priest." WILSON (ed. 1931), for *great Diuine*: "Chief Priest," but *great* may mean, rather, "eminent" or "lofty."

1170 **Contents**] PORTER & CLARKE (ed. c. 1903): "Stress on second syllable."

discouer] KERSEY (1708): "Reveal, to make manifest." See 2602. YOUNG & MOSELEY (ed. 1965): "The oracle reveals its own contents by being opened."

rare] Unusual. See n. 1161.

1171 **rush to knowledge**] KITTREDGE & RIBNER (ed. 1967): "Quickly make itself known."

fresh Horses] TANNENBAUM (1933, p. 27): "Can there be any question . . . that Shakspere not only never brought a horse on the stage . . . but that he avoided doing so?" Not to mention bears; see n. 1500. PAFFORD (ed. 1963): "This shows that the messengers have travelled some distance since they landed and the scene is therefore inland."

1172 **gracious**] JERVIS (1868): "Prosperous." *OED* (*a.* 7, citing this line) adds, "Happy, fortunate." See n. 1639.

issue] MINSHEU (1617): "The end of a matter."

1173 *Scœna Secunda*] SCHANZER (ed. 1969): "Shakespeare has here fused two court scenes in *Pandosto* which are separated by several weeks [pp. 629–31]. In each the Queen is accused in open court and defends herself eloquently; some of her words are echoed in Hermione's speeches [1202–6, 1219–21, 1293]. In *Pandosto* the King immediately accepts the truth of the oracle and repents his actions. By making Leontes blasphemously deny its truth, Shakespeare is able to punctuate his trial-scene with a crescendo of climaxes, culminating in Paulina's report of the Queen's death." STUDING (1970, p. 63): The scene "is governed as much by *mise en scène* [the physical events] as by the language itself. . . . Its entire structure is based on a series of interrupting spectacular occurrences which eventually shatter the false display of sophisticated stately order and justice." PYLE (1969, pp. 49–50): "The scene falls into three sections. The first consists chiefly of Hermione's speech in her own defence and ends with the reading of the oracle and the momentary rejoicing [1317–18]. The second covers the death of Mamillius, the apparent death of Hermione, Leontes' intended reconciliation and his public confession [1319–57]. In the third Hermione's death is confirmed, and Leontes resolves upon a life of unbroken remorse."

SPENCER (1940, p. 369): It "is dominated by the women—first by Hermione and then by Paulina; it is one of the best-acting trial scenes in drama." BROWN (1962, p. 221): The order with which the scene begins "is soon broken: Hermione protests her

Enter Leontes, Lords, Officers: Hermione (as to her
Triall) Ladies: Cleomines, Dion.   1175

Leo. This Sessions (to our great griefe we pronounce)
Euen pushes 'gainst our heart. The partie try'd,
The Daughter of a King, our Wife, and one
Of vs too much belou'd. Let vs be clear'd
Of being tyrannous, since we so openly   1180
Proceed in Iustice, which shall haue due course,
Euen to the Guilt, or the Purgation:

1174 SICILY. POPE; *ad.* SCENE *represents a Court of Justice.* THEO1 + (−PEL, CLN2,
PEN2, OXF2) (*subst.*)
1174–5 *Enter . . . Dion*] *Enter* Leontes, *Lords, Officers,* Hermione, *as to her
Trial, with* Paulina *and Ladies* ROWE1-POPE2; Leontes, *Lords, and Officers, appear
properly seated* THEO1+ (*subst.*)
1176 Sessions] Session THEO1-RANN, DYCE2, HUD2, PEN1, SIG
      pronounce] pronounce it KTLY

---

innocence before she is called to make a statement and Leontes is stung to sudden
personal controversy, denial and expression of pain. Proper procedure is abandoned:
the king is accuser as well as sole judge; there is no counsel, no evidence is brought
forward; the 'normal' course of criminal justice is reversed, and Hermione is guilty
until she can prove herself innocent. Only when she refers to the oracle is public
ceremony restored." HERFORD (ed. 1916–): "The god's emphatic declaration of her
innocence is the turning-point of the plot. The king resists for a moment; but, immediately after, the death of Mamillius is announced; Hermione faints and is carried
out, Leontes surrenders without reserve, and abjectly implores pardon from the god.
Then Paulina rushes in, and pours upon the king a torrent of grief and anger. But the
first sign of his repentance abruptly checks its flow . . . and she humbly asks pardon
for her feminine rashness and folly." But see n. 1417–23. Some eds. carefully set this
scene out of doors because of 1284.
    DANIEL (1879, p. 178): The fourth day represented in the play. CLAPP (1885, p.
402), however, places it "a very few days" after 3.1.
    1174–5 *Enter . . . Dion*] GREG (1955, p. 416): "Paulina is present, she speaks
at [1332] and later; . . . a Servant enters at [1323]." PAFFORD (ed. 1963): "The
massed entry . . . is unusual only in that it is incomplete."
    Hermione . . . Triall] MARTIN (1891, p. 15): "This is a scene which makes
a large demand upon the resources of the actress, both personal and mental. With
enfeebled health, and placed in a most ignominious position, Hermione must be
shown to maintain her queenly dignity, and to control her passionate emotion under
an outward bearing of resigned fortitude and almost inconceivable forbearance." Critics compare the trial of Queen Katherine in *H8* 2.4. For example, KNIGHT (1947;
1965, p. 93): "The calm yet condemnatory scorn of Hermione's manner shows a close
equivalence to that of Queen Katherine."

1176-82 **This . . . Purgation**] HARDINGE (1818, 3:60): "The King is the only accuser, the only advocate, the only witness, the only judge, and the only executive government!" His tone is that of "*counterfeit solemnity*, and restraint upon his fury (boiling in him all the time, prepossessed, and predetermined)." KEETON (1930; 1967, p. 151): "In Shakespeare's day . . . persons accused of treason had no right to representation, nor to see a copy of the indictment before the trial."

1176-7 **This . . . heart**] PYLE (1969, p. 50): "Plain hypocrisy."

1176 **Sessions**] According to *OED* (Session, 2c), which labels the usage *rare*, the plural may have singular sense and construction. The form is found again at 1322. Yet, as LETTSOM (in DYCE, ed. 1864) points out, Leontes's word is "Session" at 1138 [and 2568], and DEIGHTON (ed. 1889) remarks that Sh. "does not appear to have elsewhere used the plural form of this word with an adjective in the singular."

1177 **Euen . . . heart**] DEIGHTON (ed. 1889): "*Even* goes with *heart*," that is, the grief pushes against his very heart. Cf. n. 1182. STEEVENS (ed. 1793) compares "euery minute of his being, thrusts Against my neer'st of Life" (*Mac.* 3.1.116-17 [1120-1]), where eds. gloss *neer'st of Life* as "vitals." PARRY (ed. 1982): Leontes's "words will soon prove only too true."

The partie try'd] BLAKE (1983, p. 101): "The defendant to be judged."

1178 **Daughter . . . King**] Cf. 1213 and 1299.

1179 **Of**] The CLARKES (ed. 1865): "By."

1179-82 **Let . . . Purgation**] CHARLTON (ed. 1916): "Leontes is haunted by the fear of being considered tyrannous: and this surely is one touch of nature which secures for him some little of our regard." WILSON (ed. 1931): "Paulina's accusation [1042-8] rankles." KEETON (1930; 1967, p. 150): "His jealousy has convinced him of her guilt, and yet . . . he can scarcely believe her guilty. Accordingly, he decides upon a public trial, in order that others may become as convinced as he is, and so, eventually, his own last doubts may be removed. He deliberately tortures himself by re-examining the whole matter in the public eye." One doubts Leontes's last doubts, however; he fully expects his judgment to be confirmed by the oracle.

1180 **tyrannous**] For the meaning, see n. 931.

1182 **Euen . . . Purgation**] FURNESS (ed. 1898): The sentence may be unfinished, an indication of "the excessive perturbation of mind in Leontes." Later eds. do not consider the sentence unfinished.

Euen] Anticipated by THIRLBY (MS 1725-33?), RODERICK (1758, p. 213): *Even* is not an adverb — *etiam* (quite) — but an adjective — *æqualis* (just, impartial). RANN (ed. 1787): "Unbiass'd." By *equal,* AYSCOUGH (ed. 1790) and VALPY (ed. 1833) also mean "impartial" (*OED, a.* 12). DEIGHTON (ed. 1889), on the other hand, thinks *even* has "the more ordinary sense of extent; the regular course of justice is to proceed until the guilt or innocence of Hermione is fully established."

Purgation] ROLFE (ed. 1879): "Exculpation" (*OED*, 4, quoting this line). WILSON (ed. 1931, citing the word in *AYL* 1.3.53 [514] and 5.4.44 [2621] and *Ham.* 3.2.306 [2176]): "A theol[ogical] not a legal term," but *OED* may not bear him out. See *LLL* 3.1.126 (892) and KNOWLES (*AYL*, ed. 1977, n. 514). BERGERON (1984, p. 5) prefers "catharsis."

Produce the Prisoner.
Officer. It is his Highnesse pleasure, that the Queene
Appeare in person, here in Court.   *Silence.* 1185
Leo. Reade the Indictment.

1183-5 Produce . . . Court.] *Verse lines ending* pleasure . . . court. OXF2

1185 *Silence.*] F1, COL, HUD1, CLN2; *Silence. Enter* [flush right] F2-F4; *as dialogue given in a new line to* Crier *after* 1186 CAP, *after* 1185 DYCE, HUD2; *as dialogue cont. in a new line to* Officer CAM3, OXF2; *in one verse line to* Officer ROWE1 *etc.*

Hermione *is brought in, guarded;* Paulina, *and Ladies, attending.* after *Silence.* THEO1-JOHN2, v1773-ARD1, KIT1, SIS-ARD2, BEV; *after* Court. CAP, CAM3, ALEX, SIG-EVNS, OXF2

1185 *Silence.*] COLLIER (ed. 1842), encouraged to think this word a SD by "*silent all*" in *3H6* 4.3.22 (2247): "The word . . . was probably meant to mark the suspense, that ought to be displayed by all upon the stage, on the entrance of Hermione." DYCE (1844, p. 823), rejecting the analogy, would assign the word as dialogue to a Crier or Officer because of Wolsey's "Let silence be commanded" in *H8* 2.4.2 (1351), essentially the solution of CAPELL (ed. 1768). The CLARKES (1879, p. 467), comparing Austria's "Peace" and Faulconbridge's mocking "Heare the Cryer" (*Jn.* 2.1.134 [431-2]): "Faulconbridge likens Austria's exclamation . . . to the proclamation, 'Silence!' made by criers in courts of justice." HALLIWELL (ed. 1859) thinks the distinction is without significance, since "the practical effect in representation is the same," but the representation itself is not. WILSON (ed. 1931), who also gives the word to the Officer: "The exclamation is . . . occasioned by the murmurs of the crowd as Hermione enters, and seems to have been written separately from the rest of the speech in the copy because it *was* separated from it by the Queen's entry, which is there of course not given." HOWARD-HILL (1972, p. 132): The italics result from Ralph Crane's "use of italic handwriting for emphasis."

Regarding the trial itself, VENEZKY (*Pageantry*, 1951, p. 125): "The audience is immediately sympathetic with the accused Queen who must defend herself in the cold and formal setting of a court." Because of the elaborate SD in *H8* 2.4.0.1-19 (1332-49), VENEZKY believes that here too "a careful attention to the arrangement of the principals" should be paid. This may be so, even though the *H8* SD could be Fletcher's (see Fredson Bowers, ed., in *The Dramatic Works in the Beaumont & Fletcher Canon*, 7:4 and n. 7). Another direction in *H8*, at 2.4.12.1-3 (1363-5), follows a Crier's formal summons of Queen Katherine to her trial: "*The Queene makes no answer, rises out of her Chaire, goes about the Court, comes to the King, and kneeles at his Feete. Then speakes*" (ed. 1623, sig. v2ᵛ). HONIGMANN (1989, pp. 185-6): "The *Henry VIII* stage-direction spells out what must have happened in *The Winter's Tale*. Hermione, like Katherine, is asked to appear at court, and evidently walks to her appointed place. '*Silence*' . . . looks like a stage-direction, and should not be altered since it makes good sense as one. It tells us that a very special silence is required. Not the short 'pause' of modern play-texts, but a protracted silence at the end of which Hermione stands face to face with Leontes . . . like a statue. The unusual stage-direction . . . may point forward to the statue-scene, where Leontes and Hermione once more face one another [quotes 'I . . . wonder' (3209-10)]."

1186 **Reade the Indictment**] CAMPBELL (1859, p. 60): "Although the indictment is not altogether according to English legal form, . . . we lawyers cannot but wonder at seeing it so near perfection in charging the treason, and alleging the overt act

Officer. Hermione, *Queene to the worthy* Leontes, *King of*
Sicilia, thou art here accused and arraigned of High Trea-
son, in committing Adultery with Polixenes *King of Bohemia,*
and conspiring with Camillo *to take away the Life of our Soue-*   1190 (2A5ᵛᵇ)
raigne Lord the King, thy Royall Husband: the pretence whereof
*being by circumstances partly layd open, thou (*Hermione*) con-*
trary to the Faith and Allegeance of a true Subiect didst coun-
saile and ayde them, for their better safetie, to flye away by
Night.   1195

1191 *whereof*] thereof KNT
1192 *circumstances*] *circumstance* F2-ROWE2, HAL
1194 *flye*] *flee* F3, F4

---

committed by her." Although "the trial . . . belonged to no time or place," KEETON
(1930; 1967, p. 154) finds that "Hermione is regularly indicted, in proper English
form, for adultery and conspiracy to murder the King, both of which are treason
under the Statute of 1351." MONTMORENCY (1930, p. 800), struck by KEETON's observation (pp. 155-6) that, instead of counsel for the crown, the king himself conducts the prosecution, suggests that *WT* was "written . . . in Stratford out of reach
of the Gentlemen of the Temple [i.e., lawyers]," whom Sh. usually consulted on legal
points. PHILLIPS (1964, p. 187), however: "Shakespeare's imagination was working
on an old legend," which is true in spirit at least.

   Indictment] WHITE (1913, p. 185): "A written accusation . . . of a crime or
misdemeanor, presented to and preferred upon the oath or affirmation of a grand
jury. . . . Used here as a synonym for information, which is a charge of crime, preferred by a public prosecutor."

   1187-95 **Hermione . . . *Night*]** For the indictment's use of "thou" rather than
"you," see n. 1358. HOWARD-HILL (1972, p. 77): "In *WT* there are two longer passages
in which roman names are conspicuous [this and 1313-16], both set by compositor
A [see p. 589]. The typography is just what might be expected if the compositor had
had Crane's calligraphic transcript before him." See p. 592.

   1188 *arraigned*] *OED* (*v.*¹ 2, citing this line): "To indict before a tribunal."

   1190-1 *conspiring . . . Husband*] MACKENZIE (1924, p. 435): "To the prior
charge of adultery has been added a fresh one." The charge is fresh, but Leontes has
suspected a plot against his life since Polixenes and Camillo made their escape. See
644.

   1191-5 *pretence . . . Night*] SCHANZER (ed. 1969) compares "their pretence
being partly spyed, shee counselled them to flie away by night" (*Pandosto*, p. 629).

   1191 *pretence*] JOHNSON (ed. 1765, citing *TGV* 3.1.47 [1116]): " A *scheme laid,*
a *design formed*" (*OED, sb.* 3). KNIGHT (ed. 1854, glos.): "Intention." See also *Mac.*
2.3.137 (900), *Cor.* 1.2.20 (336).

   1192 *circumstances*] SCHMIDT (1874): "Occurrence, accident." For related
meanings, see nn. 796, 2837, and 3041; SCHMIDT's gloss for 3041 — "Facts from which
a certain presumption arises, which give evidence of some truth" — perhaps is preferable here.

   layd open] CARRINGTON (1956): "Revealed."

   1193 *Faith*] SCHMIDT (1874): "Fidelity." For other meanings, see nn. 544-5, 672,
1836, and 2307.

Her. Since what I am to say, must be but that
Which contradicts my Accusation, and
The testimonie on my part, no other
But what comes from my selfe, it shall scarce boot me
To say, Not guiltie: mine Integritie   1200
Being counted Falsehood, shall (as I expresse it)
Be so receiu'd. But thus, if Powres Diuine

1198 The] *Om.* POPE2

1196-1228 **Since . . . Graue**] FURNIVALL (ed. 1877?, p. xcii): "If we contrast her [Hermione's] noble defence of herself against the shameless imputation on her honour, with the conduct of earlier women in like case, the faltering words and swoon of Hero [*Ado*], the few ill-starred sentences of Desdemona [*Oth.*], saying just what would worst inflame her husband's wrath, the pathetic appeal yet submission of Imogen [*Cym.*], we see how splendidly Shakspere has developed in his last great creation." KITTREDGE (ed. 1936, p. 432): Hermione's "whole defensive argument . . . is Greene's prose turned into poetry." See p. 629. GREENE (1982, p. 10): Woman in *WT* "is powerful only insofar as she fulfills biological and social roles that nurture and redeem an erring Leontes. Even [here] Hermione offers a self-defense and self-justification in terms of her relation to husband, son, and her father the king." That is true, but adultery would be regarded as a criminal betrayal of her husband, a contamination of her hopeful son's legitimacy, and a disgrace to her own royal line.

1196-1202 **Since . . . receiu'd**] KENNEDY (1942, p. 162): "Hermione's oration represents at once . . . the best of Shakespeare's work in the structure of the oration in itself and the best of his work in the dramatic integration of the oration as a vital part of plot development." KENNEDY outlines her entire defense (pp. 113-14). DUSINBERRE (1975, p. 53): Since "a woman's chastity included all other virtues . . . Hermione can offer no defense of her innocence because she has no identity apart from the chastity which has been discredited." KNOWLES (privately) responds: "But even in this speech Hermione appeals to other aspects of her 'identity' — patience, truth, royal birth and dignity, royal status, and honor." HORWITZ (1988, p. 9) seems to agree with DUSINBERRE: "Once Leontes brands her as the image of deceit, her language is totally disabled." Earlier critics, however, stress Hermione's dignity and power. BETHELL (ed. 1956), for example: "In this and the following speeches of Hermione, she is making a public defence of her conduct. . . . The actress . . . should deliver these speeches with a more formal manner of diction and gesture than in her usual dialogue." His paraphrase of these lines is "since all I can say in my defence will be a denial of the charge, and since there is no one to give evidence for me except myself, it will not be any use ['scarce boot me'] to say 'Not guilty': my innocence is already taken as guilt, and when I plead my innocence it will be taken in the same way." Cf. n. 1200-2.

WILLIAMSON (1962, p. 14), who believes Sh. lived and died a Roman Catholic: "Hermione's defence . . . opens with the very words with which Blessed Edmund Campion opened his defence . . . : 'Since what I am to say must be but that which contradicts my accusation, and the testimony on my part no other but what comes from myself, it shall scarce boot me to say "Not Guilty."'" KEETON (1930; 1967, p. 155): "Campion's trial was long remembered and discussed, for the courage and high character of the accused, and pamphlets recounting it were common. Shakespeare

Behold our humane Actions (as they doe)
I doubt not then, but Innocence shall make
False Accusation blush, and Tyrannie   1205

1203 Actions∧ (as they doe)∧] ~ , (~ ~ ~)∧ CAP, v1778-RANN, COL2, COL3, DEL2; ~ ∧ (~ ~ ~), SING, DYCE1, STAU, DEL4, COL4, CAM3, KIT1, ARD2, EVNS
1205 Accusation] Accusations F2-POPE2, HAN

---

may well have seen one of them, from which the words may be derived, but . . . they do not appear at any point in the account given in the State Trials." As for Sh. and the Roman Catholic clergy elsewhere, KEETON recalls the allusion to Father Garnet the equivocator in *Mac.* 2.3.8-11 (751-4). BERGERON (1984, p. 4): "Hermione stands alone: defendant and sole legal counsel. . . . Solitary and vulnerable, she must make the best case for herself." Hermione specifically means, BERGERON says, that she can call no witness to testify that she never committed adultery. "She cannot counter with tangible proof" (p. 5). Her defense is her integrity; that being counted falsehood, she must refer herself to the just and omniscient Apollo. The same is true of the conspiracy charge (1190-1).

1199-1206 it . . . Patience] MIRIAM JOSEPH (1947, p. 249): "Apocarteresis is the casting away of all hope in one direction and turning to another for aid, as [here]."

1199 boot] MINSHEU (1617): "Helpe, succour, aid and advantage."

1200 Not guiltie] HOLBROOK (1964, p. 166): "Her plea . . . recalls Polixenes' earlier recollection of innocence in childhood [137-8]."

1200-2 mine . . . receiu'd] JOHNSON (ed. 1765): "That is, my *virtue* being accounted *wickedness*, my assertion of it will pass but for a *lie*. *Falsehood* means both *treachery* and *lie*." TOLIVER (1989, p. 173): *Integritie* "in this case means marital fidelity and love as professed."

1202 But thus] DEIGHTON (ed. 1889): "But as I have to speak, this is what I say." Unlike Bellaria in *Pandosto*, Hermione is not eager to defend herself in public examination.

1202-6 if . . . Patience] MALONE (ed. 1790) compares *Pandosto*; see p. 631. SHERMAN (1902, p. 130): "Her absolute, unshrinking faith in moral order has allied the powers of the universe in her defence, and made the august tribunal seem but a cheap and sorry spectacle." SANDERS (1987, pp. 46-7): "Not to doubt at such a moment shows a brave magnanimity, especially since she holds out to herself no hope of their intervention, only of their beholding."

1203 humane] *OED*: "A common earlier spelling of HUMAN which became restricted after 1700 to a particular group of senses." The word, in this spelling, is also found in 2774. See n. 1350 for the modern sense.

as they doe] The CLARKES (1879, p. 476): "Shakespeare's parentheses are frequently of very condensed significance, containing much earnestness and wisdom put into extremely small space." WILSON (ed. 1931): "The brackets add great emphasis to the words." They do the same for "as . . . it" in 1201 and "my Lord" in 1206, even though the brackets are probably Crane's. As BETHELL (ed. 1956) notes, "The three monosyllabic words occurring together call for emphasis."

1204-6 Innocence . . . Patience] BETHELL (ed. 1956): "Personifications somewhat soften what is in effect a counter-accusation directed at Leontes." PAFFORD (ed. 1963): "That a clear conscience does not fear false accusation is proverbial" (TILLEY C597).

1205-6 Tyrannie . . . Patience] COLLINS (ed. 1904-24?): "*I.e.* you, as a tyrant,

Tremble at Patience. You (my Lord) best know
(Whom least will seeme to doe so) my past life
Hath beene as continent, as chaste, as true,
As I am now vnhappy; which is more
Then Historie can patterne, though deuis'd,   1210
And play'd, to take Spectators. For behold me,
A Fellow of the Royall Bed, which owe

1207 Whom] Who ROWE1+ (−NLSN); Who N&H
1208 as true] and true ROWE1, ROWE2
1212 owe] owes v1785

---

tremble before me, as suffering your tyranny." KITTREDGE & RIBNER (ed. 1967): "The cruel accuser will be overcome by the fortitude of the accused."

1206 **Patience**] ORGEL (ed. 1996): "With an overtone of its original sense, 'suffering'" (Latin *patientia*).

1206-28 **You . . . Graue**] BERGERON (1984, p. 5): "Hermione's first argument rests on establishing the 'ethos' of the speaker, that is, her moral, credible, and upright nature."

1207 **Whom**] For confusion of *who* and *whom*, see ABBOTT §274 and for other instances, *WT* 2184 and 2266. ORGEL (ed. 1996), having cited examples in *Tmp.*: "These may be simply errors (and it may be relevant that both texts [*WT* and *Tmp.*] derive from Ralph Crane copies); but they may also be expressive: all occur at moments of high anxiety, and seem to show the character—or Shakespeare on the character's behalf—changing direction abruptly in mid-sentence."

will] BOORMAN (ed. 1964): "Wish to."

1208 **continent**] PHILLIPS (1706): "Temperate, Chaste, Sober."

true] KERSEY (1702): "Genuine, faithful, unfeigned." The three adjectives Hermione employs all mean, among other things, "sexually pure." For similar repetitions, see 302, 595, 634, 856, 890, 916, and 1215.

1209 **vnhappy**] HUNTER (ed. 1872): "Unfortunate."

1209-11 **which . . . Spectators**] MALONE (ed. 1790, Which): "Which unhappiness." BETHELL (1956): "Hermione's words (*a*) emphasize her grief (in the play world) and (*b*) apologize to the audience for the inadequacy of the dramatic medium. The actress should treat the real audience as part of the stage audience and include them in a sweeping gesture at the word 'spectators'. The audience itself is thus given a double status: (*a*) as real-world audience, receiving the playwright's apology; (*b*) as stage audience, caught up into the story."

1210 **Historie**] WILSON (ed. 1931): "Story of any kind, often (as here) = dramatic story, tragedy." *OED* (*sb.* 6a): "A historical play." With only a few exceptions, however, Elizabethan tragedies purported to be histories.

patterne] JOHNSON (1755, citing this line): "Serve as an example." SCHMIDT (1875) adds "precedent."

1211 **take**] RANN (ed. 1787): "Gain the applause of." JERVIS (1868): "Captivate" (*OED, v.* 10). HUNTER (ed. 1872): "Excite the passions." CARRINGTON (1956): "Bewitch, charm." See nn. 97 and 1933.

1212 **owe**] HANMER (ed. 1743-4, 6:glos.): "Possess; [implying] an absolute right . . . in the thing possessed"— i.e., own.

A Moitie of the Throne: a great Kings Daughter,
The Mother to a hopefull Prince, here standing
To prate and talke for Life, and Honor, fore   1215
Who please to come, and heare. For Life, I prize it
As I weigh Griefe (which I would spare:) For Honor,

1215 for] of OXF1

1213 **Moitie**] CAWDREY (1604): "Halfe." Dictionaries continue so to define the word through JOHNSON (1773), but according to *OED*, as early as *Luc.* (1594, Dedication) the meaning had become the less precise "share," "portion," or "lesser portion." See n. 907.

1214 **hopefull**] JOHNSON (1755): "Promising." KITTREDGE & RIBNER (ed. 1967): "With expectations of succeeding to the throne."

1214-16 **here . . . heare**] BETHELL (ed. 1956): "Hermione's distaste for the vulgar publicity . . . comes out in these lines, especially in 'prate and talk'. ('Prate' = *chatter idly* contemptuously reduces the court proceedings to a sort of idle gossip.)" For *prate* MINSHEU (1617) refers to the verbs "to Cackle, & to Babble." HAPPÉ (1969): "Hermione implies that her cause is already lost." KNOWLES (privately), however: "She complains of the indignity of her position, not the hopelessness of her plea." The CLARKES (1879, p. 610): The "second verb [*talke*]," which bears "almost similar meaning with the first, [gives] emphasis and additional force to the phrase."

1215 **prate and talke**] For similar repetitions, see 302, 595, 634, 856, 890, 916, and 1208.

1216-17 **For . . . spare**] JOHNSON (ed. 1765): "*Life* is to me now only *grief*, and as such only is considered by me, I would therefore willingly dismiss it," or, as CLARK & WRIGHT (ed. 1863) put it, "Hermione now holds life and grief to be inseparable and would willingly be rid of both." JOHNSON (ed. 1773) adds, "*To spare* any thing is to *let it go, to quit the possession of it.*" STAUNTON (ed. 1859) thinks, oddly, that *griefe* is wrong, because "Hermione means that life to her is of as little estimation as the most trivial thing which she would part with [e.g., 'a straw' (1289)]. . . . Could she speak of 'grief' as a trifle?" The CLARKES (ed. 1865) find *spare* ambiguous, "used partly in its sense of 'part with' . . . ; partly in that of 'forbear from destroying', or 'shield from destruction'; partly in that of 'avoid encountering.'" They paraphrase: "I estimate life as I estimate grief,—things that I could willingly part with, while the one I would avoid destroying, and the other I would avoid encountering." WILSON (ed. 1931): "The more grief I have—and every moment I live now throws new grief into the scales—the less I prize life; I would willingly spare (i.e. keep back . . .) grief, but I have no wish to spare (i.e. save) life." REESE (1953; 1980, pp. 366-7): "Sometimes the concentration of meaning is so intense that various interpretations are possible . . . : *spare* can have the meanings of *part with, pardon,* and *avoid.* . . . Shakespeare has brought word-play to a pitch where a single statement will dissolve into infinite shades of meaning." REESE's paraphrase is close to that of the CLARKES', however. SANDERS (1987, p. 43): "The numbing cadence gives us the flatness of her misery."

1216 **For**] As for. Cf. the same marker at 1217, 1238, and 1248, as Hermione addresses, in turn, the charges stated or implied by the indictment.

1217 **weigh**] HAPPÉ (1969): "Value" (*OED*, *v.*[1] 13).

'Tis a deriuatiue from me to mine,
And onely that I stand for. I appeale
To your owne Conscience (Sir) before *Polixenes*   1220
Came to your Court, how I was in your grace,
How merited to be so: Since he came,

1222 How] Now AYS2

1218 **'Tis . . . mine**] STEEVENS (ed. 1778): Probably borrowed from Eccles. 3:
11. He then quotes the verse from the Authorized Version — with which Sh. may have
been unfamiliar, as FURNESS (ed. 1898) notes. Verse 14 in the Geneva Bible, however,
is very similar: "Mans glorie cometh by his father's honour, & the reproche of yᵉ
mother is dishonour to the children." According to SINGER (ed. 1856), this "sentiment . . . cannot be too often impressed on the female mind."
    deriuatiue] *OED (sb.* 1, citing this line): "A thing flowing, proceeding, or orig-
inating from another." JERVIS (1868): "An inheritance."
    1219 **stand for**] SCHMIDT (1875): "Fight for." The expression may also be taken
literally — "stand here for."
    1219-28 **I appeale . . . Graue**] The "theologically loaded terms in this speech"
suggest to WATSON (1984, p. 245) that "Hermione shares to some extent her husband's moral presumption," because she thinks she could gain grace by merit, because she seems unaware that she is tainted by original sin, and because, in 1225-6,
she seems to deny her own concupiscence, "the fallen susceptibility of the human
will."
    1219-21 **I appeale . . . grace**] SCHANZER (ed. 1969): An echo of *Pandosto*. See
p. 632.
    1220 **To . . . *Polixenes***] ABBOTT (§469): "Polysyllabic names often receive but
one accent at the end of the line in pronunciation. Proper names, not conveying, as
other nouns do, the origin and reason of their formation, are of course peculiarly
liable to be modified; and this modification will generally shorten rather than lengthen
the name. . . . Less frequently [modification occurs] in the middle of the line." For
other instances of name shrinking, see 2844-5, 2864-5, and 3214.
    Conscience] SCHMIDT (1874): "Private judgment, inmost thoughts."
    1221 **grace**] JOHNSON (1755) "Favour." For other meanings of *grace*, see n. 146.
    1222-4 **Since . . . thus**] JOHNSON (ed. 1765) makes the sentence interrogative.
STEEVENS (ed. 1778): "An *uncurrent encounter* seems to mean an irregular, unjusti-
fiable congress"; hence, "in what base reciprocation of love have I caught this strain."
SEYMOUR (1805, 1:163-4) objects that *encounter* in a "gross sense" is inappropriate
for Hermione; he paraphrases (1:164): "I offer it to your conscience to determine
with what unwarrantable action I have exceeded the rules of propriety and decorum,
so as to deserve this dishonour." AMYOT (in COLLIER, ed. 1842): "Beloved as I was
by you before Polixenes arrived . . . how has it happened that I have had to struggle
against so untoward a current, as to appear thus before you in the character of a
criminal." VERPLANCK (ed. 1845): "In what unusual interview have I so erred as to
expose myself to the appearance of guilt?" HUDSON (ed. 1852): "*Encounter so uncurrent* is *unallowed* or *unlawful meeting. — Strain'd* means *swerv'd* or gone astray
from the line of duty. . . . *To appear thus* is *to seem guilty*." MUNRO (ed. 1957)
alone interprets "strayn'd t'appeare thus" as "exerted myself to appear thus <worthy
of your favour [1222]>."
    Most recent commentators paraphrase much as does LEE (ed. 1907): "With what

With what encounter so vncurrant, I
Haue strayn'd t'appeare thus; if one iot beyond
The bound of Honor, or in act, or will   1225
That way enclining, hardned be the hearts
Of all that heare me, and my neer'st of Kin

1223-4 I Haue . . . thus;] have | I . . . thus? HAN, CAP; I | Have . . . thus?
v1773-v1785; have I | . . . thus? KTLY
  1224 strayn'd] stray'd MASON (1785) *conj.* (*withdrawn*), COL2, COL3, COL4
    thus;] ~ ? HAN, CAP-v1785
  1225 bound] bounds ROWE1-JOHN2, v1773
    or∧ in] ~ , in CAP-SING2 (−VALPY, HUD1), WH1, HAL, DEL, KTLY, KNT3

---

unwarrantable familiarity of intercourse have I so exceeded bounds as to be condemned to figure as defendant in this kind of suit?" MOORMAN (ed. 1912): "In what
way have I exceeded the bounds of propriety in my behaviour towards Polixenes that
I should appear thus in a court of justice?" WILSON (ed. 1931): "The whole point of
the appeal is its delicacy: 'strain' = to depart *in spirit* from the path of duty; 'encounter' = external behaviour; 'uncurrent' = a little out of the ordinary." BETHELL
(ed. 1956): "The argument is *a fortiori*: 'I have not even broken the conventions, let
alone committed adultery.'" SCHANZER (ed. 1969): "The difficulty . . . is caused
chiefly by a shift in the nature of the appeal: Hermione first begs Leontes to *remember*
how, before the arrival of Polixenes, her behaviour merited his love, and next begs
him to *make known* how, after the arrival of Polixenes, her behaviour merited his
arraignment of her." FURNESS (ed. 1898) thinks the passage may be unfinished.
    1223 **encounter so vncurrant**] DOUCE (1807, 1:351), strangely, but followed by
KNIGHT (ed. 1841), thinks the "metaphor taken from tilting," an *uncurrent encounter*
being an irregular passage of arms; "or in plainer terms, *whether I have deviated
from the paths of honour and* forcibly *obtruded myself on this tribunal.*" COLLIER
(ed. 1858): "So unusual a course," which accords with *OED*, Encounter (*sb.* 3), "behaviour," and Uncurrent (*a.* 2), "not commonly accepted or recognized." WHITE (ed.
1883), however, suggests "intercourse so unallowable, (in Fr.) *inconvenable* [im-
proper]." HAPPÉ (1969) for *encounter* proposes "way of welcoming" and for *vncur-
rent*, "objectionable, extraordinary." ORGEL (1991, pp. 431-3) thinks that here and
at 1285 the obscurity is part of the meaning.
    1224 **strayn'd**] *OED* (Strain, *v.*¹ 11b): "To transgress the strict requirements of
[one's conscience]." STEEVENS (in JOHNSON, ed. 1765, 8:Ii3ᵛ, citing *Tim.* 2.2.217-18
[888-9]): "Caught a wrench in my character." MALONE (1780, 1:144): "Swerve" (as
in *Bed-swaruer* [697]). About this gloss, MALONE had changed his mind; in his Notebook (1777-80) he conjectures that *strayn* here means "draw tight," yielding "by
what irregular commerce have I *stretched* my reputation." STEEVENS (ed. 1773) cites
Wiv. 2.1.91 (630). KEIGHTLEY (1867, p. 201, citing *straining* in 2313): "'Strain'd'
signifies pulled against the line of my duty as a wife — a metaphor taken from dogs in
a leash." This seems quite unlikely, yet it is at least as helpful as MADDEN's (1897, p.
54 n.) quoting *The Noble Arte of Venerie or Hunting* (1575) to the effect that a fast-
running hart is said to strain. SCHMIDT (1875, Strain): "Perhaps = brought about,
contrived."
    thus] CAPELL (1783, 2.4:170): "Where I do" (i.e., in this place). EVANS (ed.
1974): "I.e. on trial for adultery."
    iot] ORGEL (ed. 1996) "Iota, the smallest letter, hence the least bit."
    1225-6 **or in . . . enclining**] DEIGHTON (ed. 1889): "Or if I have inclined that

229

Cry fie vpon my Graue.

   Leo. I ne're heard yet,

That any of these bolder Vices wanted   1230

Lesse Impudence to gaine-say what they did,

Then to performe it first.

   Her. That's true enough,

Though 'tis a saying (Sir) not due to me.

   Leo. You will not owne it.   1235

   Her. More then Mistresse of,

1230 these] those F4-JOHN2, v1773
1236 Mistresse] I'm Mistress HAN, KTLY

---

way in will or act." *Or . . . or*, however, means "either . . . or." Hence, "either in act or in desire."

   1228 **fie**] HARDINGE (1818, 3:63): "Shame."

   1229-32 **I . . . first**] JOHNSON (ed. 1765): "According to the proper . . . use of words, *less* should be *more*, or *wanted* should be *had*. . . . Two negatives did not originally affirm, but strengthen the negation." So EVANS (ed. 1974): "I.e. were more wanting in. *Less* . . . intensifies the idea of deficiency in *wanted*" (*OED, a.* 4, citing this line). RITSON (1783, p. 70): "You . . . who have had sufficient impudence to do what I charge you with, can be at no loss for impudence to deny [gainsay; *OED*, *v.* 1] it," with which SEYMOUR (1805, 1:164) and most others agree. The CLARKES (ed. 1865), however, like INGLEBY (1875, pp. 156-7), take *lesse* to be an adverb: "'I ne'er heard that these vices less wanted impudence to gainsay what they did, than to perform it at first.'" For *wanted less*, COLLINS (ed. 1904-24?): "*I.e* required *more.*"

   As for significance, CHARLTON (ed. 1916), questionably: "Leontes appeals to proverbial generalities and common beliefs. This is not only an indication of his character: it has a peculiar dramatic value in that the truisms add a semblance of truth to his side of the case." Rather, he makes it impossible for Hermione to appear as her own character witness, and, as DUSINBERRE (1975, p. 220) says, "He interprets her eloquence as effrontery, urging condemnation of her not for what she says, but for saying it at all." Cf. n. 1012-36. KENNEDY (1942, p. 44): "The denunciatory outbursts of Leontes contrast with the calm, ordered rhetoric of Hermione's defense." PARRY (ed. 1982): "His tone is derisive, sneering." See n. 733 for the opinion that Leontes does not look at Hermione as he speaks these and subsequent lines.

   1230-2 **any . . . first**] DESSEN (1986, p. 173, n. 18): A possible allusion to the Vice of the morality play. KNOWLES (privately): "Unlikely, since the Vice was always a male clown."

   1231 **Impudence**] *OED* (2, citing this line): "Shameless effrontery."

   1234 **due**] SCHMIDT (1874): "Appropriate." ROLFE (ed. 1879): "Applicable" (*OED, a.* 9).

   1235 **owne**] SCHMIDT (1875): "Confess." PARRY (ed. 1982): "Accept" (as yours). BLAKE (1983, p. 128): 1236-8 "seems to be a reply to a question and so a question mark after [1235] would seem both possible and appropriate." Eds. have not thought so.

   1236-8 **More . . . acknowledge**] The elliptical expression causes minor disagreement. CALDECOTT (MS 1813-33), for "More . . . Fault": "More than belongs to me of that quality [imputed to me as] vice." HUNTER (ed. 1872): "Any more than

Which comes to me in name of Fault, I must not
At all acknowledge. For *Polixenes*
(With whom I am accus'd) I doe confesse
I lou'd him, as in Honor he requir'd: 1240
With such a kind of Loue, as might become
A Lady like me; with a Loue, euen such,
So, and no other, as your selfe commanded:
Which, not to haue done, I thinke had been in me

1237 Which] What ROWE1-v1773 (−HAN, CAP)

I am mistress, or cognisant, of which comes to me in the name of fault, I must not,
&c." ROLFE (ed. 1879): "I must not acknowledge more faults than belong to me [than
I have]," with which many later eds. generally concur. CARRINGTON (1956), for example: "Myself to be guilty of more than ordinary faults." However, WHITE'S (ed.
1883) "I must not confess to more than I am accused of" also has proponents; LEE
(ed. 1907) alters it to "it is not for me in any way to admit more knowledge of the
grounds of the imputation made against me than I learn from the terms of the charge."
Both invoke the meaning of *acknowledge* favored by the *OED*, which cites this instance. HERFORD (ed. 1904) thinks a line was omitted; after another look, HERFORD
(ed. 1916–) explains: "'More than mistress of' stands for 'conduct exceeding what I
have myself committed', and is virtually subject to 'which . . . fault', i.e. which is
charged against me." Hence MOORMAN (ed. 1912): "*Fault* here is to be regarded as
standing in opposition to . . . *bolder vices* [1230]. Hermione acknowledges that
she is answerable for (*mistress of*) shortcomings to which the name 'faults' may be
given, but not for the crime of adultery." PIERCE (ed. 1918), differently: "I must not
at all acknowledge that I am guilty (mistress) of anything more than <that> which
is counted against me as fault <namely, my innocent hospitality toward Polixenes>."
PAFFORD (ed. 1963) agrees: "'I must not admit being answerable for anything more
than that which is now being called a fault'. She refers to her friendship with Polixenes
of which she goes on to speak." ADAMS (1989, p. 97): "The sentence is given to us
in elegant disarray." KNOWLES (privately) expands the ellipses: "[To be] more than
mistress of [that] which . . . fault," a reading that yields "I am in control of [mistress
of; *OED*, *sb.* 4], not owner of, the faults imputed to me."

    1238-48 **For . . . yours**] NATHAN (1968, p. 24): "Two things distinguished her
attitude; Polixenes was a king and her husband's dearest friend. She could, and did,
jest with Polixenes as with an equal. . . . Too, she treated Polixenes as her own
friend, as she felt bound to do." BERGERON (1984, p. 6) considers that Hermione now
offers "logical proof" of her innocence, but she cannot do that; see n. 1196-1202.

    1240-3 **I . . . commanded**] WATSON (1984, p. 241) compares Desdemona's
"I neuer did Offend you in my life: neuer lov'd *Cassio*, But with such generall war-
rantie of Heauen As I might loue" (*Oth.* 5.2.58-61 [3310-13]).

    1240 **as . . . requir'd**] RODERICK (1758, p. 213): "With such a pure love, as the
honour and dignity of his royal character demanded on my part." PAFFORD (ed. 1963),
similarly: "As, in view of his position and mine, he had a natural right to expect." For
require, see n. 1122. MALONE (ed. 1790) compares *Pandosto*; see p. 632.

    1241 **become**] KITTREDGE & RIBNER (ed. 1967): "Be proper to."

    1242-3 **a Loue . . . commanded**] PAFFORD (ed. 1963) compares "which of
your Friends Haue I not stroue to loue" (*H8* 2.4.29-30 [1383-4]).

231

Both Disobedience, and Ingratitude   1245
To you, and toward your Friend, whose Loue had spoke,
Euen since it could speake, from an Infant, freely,
That it was yours. Now for Conspiracie,
I know not how it tastes, though it be dish'd
For me to try how: All I know of it,   1250
Is, that *Camillo* was an honest man;
And why he left your Court, the Gods themselues
(Wotting no more then I) are ignorant.
    Leo. You knew of his departure, as you know
What you haue vnderta'ne to doe in's absence.   1255
    Her. Sir,   (2A6
You speake a Language that I vnderstand not:

1245 Ingratitude] in gratitude F4
1246 Friend] friends F2-POPE2
1254-5 know . . . haue] Know what You've WALKER (1860, 3:101) *conj.*, DYCE2,
HUD2, IRV
1255-6 *One verse line* WALKER (1860, 3:101) *conj.*, KTLY, DYCE2, HUD2, IRV, SIG
1256-7 *One verse line* CAP

1245-6 Disobedience . . . Friend] HUNTER (ed. 1872): "Disobedience to you
and ingratitude toward your friend." With this construction he compares 1348-50.
For *ingratitude*, SCHMIDT (1874) gives "unthankfulness," a reading that may fit, since
Polixenes's gift of friendship deserved Hermione's thanks. "Disagreeableness; unfriendliness, unkindness" (*OED* 2) is also possible.
    1246-8 whose . . . yours] BLAKE (1983, p. 108): "The two adverbs *from an
Infant* and *freely* are found after the second clause. They may both refer to the second
clause 'since it could readily speak from infancy' or to the first clause 'whose love
had readily proclaimed from childhood', or they may be divided in reference to both
the preceding clauses 'whose love had readily proclaimed from the very moment it
could speak in childhood.'" STAUNTON (1874, p. 864): "Note . . . that the professed
love of Polixenes to her husband is particularly dwelt on." PAFFORD (ed. 1963) compares 130-8.
    1249-50 I . . . how] RANN (ed. 1787): "Forms a part of my charge, and I am
put to answer about it." *Dish*, however, means "serve up" (*OED*, *v.*[1] 2, citing this
line). BETHELL (ed. 1956), more clearly: "'I do not know what it feels like to be a
conspirator, though you are doing your best to make me feel like one.' (Conspiracy
is being 'dished up' in the indictment for her to taste.)" PAFFORD (ed. 1963), clearer
yet: "I do not know what it tastes like and should not know even if it were put before
me to taste." PILGRIM (1983, p. 57) compares the similarly homely imagery of 100
and 161-2.
    1251 was] FURNESS (ed. 1898): Emphatic.
    1253 Wotting . . . I] RODERICK (1758, p. 213): "If they know no more of it than
I do." For the participle to express a condition, see ABBOTT §377.
    1255 What . . . absence] BETHELL (ed. 1956): "I.e. to murder Leontes."
    1257 You . . . not] PAFFORD (ed. 1963) compares "I vnderstand a fury in your
words, But not the words" (*Oth.* 4.2.32-3 [2724-2724+1]).

My Life stands in the leuell of your Dreames,
Which Ile lay downe.

    Leo. Your Actions are my Dreames.   1260
You had a Bastard by *Polixenes*,
And I but dream'd it: As you were past all shame,
(Those of your Fact are so) so past all truth;
Which to deny, concernes more then auailes: for as

1262 were] are HAN
1263 are so) so] are) so you're HAN
1264 Which] *Om*. CAP
1264-5 auailes . . . cast] avails: | For as thy brat's cast HAN; avails: | For as | Thy
. . . cast v1793-v1813, KNT1, DYCE2

    1258-9 **stands . . . downe**] For *leuell*, see n. 904-5. JOHNSON's (ed. 1765) "be
within the reach" STAUNTON (ed. 1859) makes "within the range or compass" (*OED*
9a). HUDSON's (ed. 1852) "to stand within the *level* of a gun is to stand in a direct
line with its mouth" is *OED*'s "line of fire." HALLIWELL (ed. 1859), anticipated by
CALDECOTT (MS 1813-33): "My life, which I place at your disposal, is the aim or
object of your imagination" or, as BOORMAN (ed. 1964) puts it, "as a target for your
fancies." The CLARKES (ed. 1865): I.e., "her life lies at the mercy of his false fancies."
For the reference of "Which" to "Life" rather than to "Dreames," see ABBOTT §§261-
2; BOORMAN, however, thinks the reference ambiguous: "(*a*) Which (life) I'll sacrifice
or (*b*) Which (fact) I'll insist upon." For *lay downe*, see n. 739.
    1260-3 **Your . . . truth**] For "And . . . it," MOORMAN (ed. 1912): "And this,
you say, was but a dream of mine." VYVYAN (1959, p. 114): "Every word of this—as
he comes to realize later—is false of her and true of him." See n. 377-89.
    1260 **Your . . . Dreames**] DEIGHTON (ed. 1889): "What you call my dreams
[delusions] are your actions." Or, more likely, "I have nightmares about what you
did." YOUNG & MOSELEY (ed. 1965): "Leontes is being ironical."
    1263 **Those . . . Fact**] PHILLIPS (1706, Fact): "Act, Action, or Deed." Although
his dictionary accepts this definition, JOHNSON (ed. 1765) is convinced the word here
must mean "guilt" (*OED* 1c); he thus prefers to read *pack*. MALONE (ed. 1790), however, establishes *fact* as correct by reference to *Pandosto*; see p. 629. Even so, BECKET
(1815, 1:358), wrongly: "*Faction* or *party*." SCHMIDT (1874): "Evil deed, crime"
(*OED* 1c: "In the 16th and 17th c. the commonest sense"). For the phrase STEEVENS
(ed. 1778) gives "those who have done as you do," and HERFORD (ed.
1916-), "adultresses like you."
    1264-5 **Which . . . selfe**] ABBOTT (§499) scans these lines by moving *for as* to
1265 and considering it as an isolated foot there. See nn. 77, 185, 190, 499, and 2187.
    1264 **Which . . . auailes**] CAPELL (1783, 2.4:170) takes *to deny* substantively
(i.e., your denial) and glosses *concernes* as "gives concern, *i.e.* sorrow." For *concernes . . . auailes*, RANN (ed. 1787), incorrectly: "Tends but to add to my concern,
without advancing your cause." MALONE (ed. 1790): "It is your *business* to deny this
charge, but the mere denial will be useless; will prove nothing." BOSWELL (ed. 1821,
1:584) considers *more* to be confused with *less*. Later critics differ as to who is concerned and who availed. DEIGHTON (ed. 1889): "To deny which may be a matter of
importance to you, but will have no effect upon me." HALLIWELL (ed. 1859), alternatively: "The denial is your business, but it avails thee nothing." LEE (ed. 1907),
somewhat differently: "The denial [is] a point of interest but of no practical utility."

Thy Brat hath been cast out, like to it selfe,   1265
No Father owning it (which is indeed
More criminall in thee, then it) so thou
Shalt feele our Iustice; in whose easiest passage,
Looke for no lesse then death.
    Her. Sir, spare your Threats: 1270
The Bugge which you would fright me with, I seeke:
To me can Life be no commoditie;
The crowne and comfort of my Life (your Fauor)
I doe giue lost, for I doe feele it gone,
But know not how it went. My second Ioy,   1275
And first Fruits of my body, from his presence
I am bar'd, like one infectious. My third comfort
(Star'd most vnluckily) is from my breast
(The innocent milke in it most innocent mouth)
Hal'd out to murther. My selfe on euery Post   1280
Proclaym'd a Strumpet: With immodest hatred
The Child-bed priuiledge deny'd, which longs
To Women of all fashion. Lastly, hurried

1265 like] left KEIGHTLEY *conj. in* CAM1, HUD2
1268 Shalt] Shall COL3, HUD2
1271 would] will v1778-RANN
      me] we CAP (*text*), HAN3; me CAP (*errata*)
1276 And] The ROWE2-JOHN2, v1773
1279 it] its mFLV.a.80 *conj.*, ROWE1-DEL2 (−WH1, STAU), DYCE2-IRV (−WH2), PEN2, BEV4
1281 Strumpet: . . . hatred∧] ~ ∧ . . . ~ ; mTBY3 *conj.*, HAN, WARB, CAP, RANN

MAXWELL's (ed. 1956) "implicates" for *concernes* is an interesting departure, but recent eds. essentially agree with KERMODE (ed. 1963): "Is more trouble to you than it's worth."

1265 **like . . . selfe**] DEIGHTON (ed. 1889): "With the disgrace that properly belongs to it." NEILSON & HILL (ed. 1942): "As a bastard should be." LUDWIG (1974, p. 376): "The phrase seems to make sense; we can infer meaning [NEILSON & HILL's]. But such sense must be inferred from the context, not read out of the words." HAPPÉ (1969): "As is appropriate to it."

1266 **owning**] *OED* (Own, *v.* 3a, citing this line): "Acknowledge as one's own."

1266-7 **which . . . it**] DEIGHTON (ed. 1889): "In which matter it is you who are to blame, not the child."

1268-9 **in . . . death**] SCHMIDT (1875, Passage): "Course, process." HUDSON (ed. 1880): "'Whose easiest passage' is whose *lightest sentence*; *whose* referring to *justice*. 'Death is the mildest sentence that justice can pass upon you.'" WILSON (ed. 1931): "He hints at torture."

1270-95 **Sir . . . Iudge**] SANDERS (1987, p. 44): Sh. "never so wonderfully caught the *power* of a woman's voice as here—its capacity to be all feeling and flexibility, yet at the same time as implacable as steel."

1270-85 **Sir . . . limit**] BERGERON (1984, p. 7) identifies this stage of Hermione's defense as "pathetic persuasion." See nn. 1206-28 and 1238-48 for earlier stages. "The pathetic proof also proceeds logically, step by step."

1271 **Bugge**] MINSHEU (1617): "Bugbeare, or Scar-crow. . . . [See] Hobgoblins." JOHNSON (1755): "A walking spectre . . . a false terrour to frighten babes." DENT compares "Bugs (Bugbears) to scare babes" (TILLEY B703). BETHELL (1947, p. 20): "Her attitude is one not of Stoic or Epicurean contempt but of Christian resignation." In what follows, however, Hermione counts her losses, to which death would bring an end.

1272 **commoditie**] WHITE (ed. 1857): "Profit." Sh. does use the word in this sense (*OED* 2c; frequently in *Jn.*, for example), but SCHMIDT (1874) considers the significance here to be "convenience" (1 or 2). HUNTER (ed. 1872) and most later critics, however: "Advantage"; HERFORD (ed. 1904): "Object of desire"; CHARLTON (ed. 1916): "Of pleasure (because convenient or fitting)." WILSON (ed. 1931) objects to this expansion of meaning: "'Commodity' is a commercial term." PORTER & CLARKE (ed. 1908) would agree: "No article of value to trade for or desire."

1273 **crowne and comfort**] MALONE (ed. 1790): "Supreme blessing." WRIGHT & LAMAR (ed. 1966): "Crowning happiness."

Fauor] JOHNSON (1755): "Propitious aspect." See n. 469.

1274 **giue**] CALDECOTT (MS 1813-33): "Yield; give up, as." With the idiom, WILSON (ed. 1931) compares "mens reports Giue him much wrong'd" (*Ant.* 1.4.39-40 [471-2]) and glosses "consider, set down as."

1275-85 **My . . . limit**] DAVIES (1986, p. 155): "Visual details such as the breastmilk on the mouth of the suckling girl-baby forcibly weaned . . . ; the mother's need to be with her boy-child; the exposure of her name to slander and her body in its post-natal weakness to the outdoor trial[;] each image connotes rape." KNOWLES (privately): "None connotes rape."

1276 **first . . . body**] HARDINGE (1818, 3:64): "I wish the description of her child had been more delicate."

1278 **Star'd most vnluckily**] STEEVENS (ed. 1773): "Born under an inauspicious planet." MOORMAN (ed. 1912, Star'd): "Fated" (*OED, ppl.a.* 4, citing this line). For its part of speech, see n. 2931. SYMONS (in IRVING & MARSHALL, ed. 1890, 7:378) finds other astrological allusions in 283-4 and 466 as well as in the mention of influences in 541. See also nn. 712-14, 712, and 714.

1279 **The . . . mouth**] ABBOTT (§468): In scanning, "any unaccented syllable of a polysyllable . . . may sometimes be softened and almost ignored," so *innocent* here becomes "*í*nn*o*cent" both times, the *o* being elided.

it] See n. 1110. For *it's* as the possessive, see n. 230-1.

1280 **Hal'd . . . murther**] FLEAY (1881, p. 59) scans Hal'd out | to mur | *ther* | |, *ther* being a "Mid-line (female or double or) Extra syllable."

Hal'd] MINSHEU (1617, Hale): See "Pull, Draw."

Post] DYCE (ed. 1864-7, 9:393-4): "At the doors of sheriffs were usually set up ornamental posts, on which royal and civic proclamations were fixed." See *Pandosto*, p. 626.

1281 **immodest**] JOHNSON (1755): "Unreasonable." The CLARKES (ed. 1865): "'Immoderate', 'excessive', as well as 'indecent', 'unseemly.'"

1282-3 **The . . . fashion**] KAIL (1986, p. 96): "It was not uncommon for another pregnancy to occur before a woman had recovered from the effects of the previous one." KAIL thus thinks the privilege refers specifically to a cessation of sexual intercourse. Hermione actually refers to the necessary period of recuperation, the length of which varied. ECCLES (1982, p. 96): "Although ordinary women got up about the third day the unanimous advice of authors [of works on obstetrics] was that the longer the woman stayed in bed the better, even up to a fortnight, a recommendation only feasible for leisured women." GREENBLATT (1988, p. 132): "Leontes has denied

235

Here, to this place, i'th' open ayre, before
I haue got strength of limit. Now (my Liege)   1285
Tell me what blessings I haue here aliue,
That I should feare to die? Therefore proceed:
But yet heare this: mistake me not: no Life,
(I prize it not a straw) but for mine Honor,
Which I would free: if I shall be condemn'd   1290
Vpon surmizes (all proofes sleeping else,
But what your Iealousies awake) I tell you
'Tis Rigor, and not Law. Your Honors all,
I doe referre me to the Oracle:
Apollo be my Iudge.   1295

1285 limit] limbs F3-POPE2, HAN
    Now] And now POPE, HAN
    1288 no] my WH1, HUD2; for KEIGHTLEY *conj. in* CAM1, DYCE2, BUL, KIT1, SIG; no K&R
    no₍ₐ₎] ~ ! mTBY3 *conj.*, HAN, v1778-SING1 (−RANN), COL1-SING2, COL3, HAL, KTLY, KNT3

---

his wife the 'child-bed priviledge' because he believes that her adulterous body is defiled beyond redemption. . . . This nausea [at the thought of the female body] appears to be awakened in some obscure way by Hermione's pregnancy, as if what it revealed was beyond the power of any ritual to cleanse." GREENBLATT may think the "priviledge" is the service called "The Churching of Women." Jews held that after childbirth, a woman is unclean and requires purification (Lev. 12). The Anglican service that descends from the Jewish rite was identified as "The Order of the Purification of Weomen" by the 1549 Prayer Book, but the name was changed in 1552 and subsequently to "Thankes giuing of Women." Despite its 1549 name, the service had not regarded the woman as contaminated since the time of Gregory the Great (590-604). See SHEPHERD (1950, p. 305). Defilement from adultery is another matter, of course.

1282 **priuiledge**] SCHMIDT (1875): "A particular right."

longs] ABBOTT (§460): This truncated form of *belongs* also occurs in *H5* 2.4.80 (974) and *H8* 1.2.32 (360). Cf. n. 2666.

1283 **fashion**] WALKER (1860, 2:348): "Rank." FURNESS (ed. 1898): "Generally understood [as] 'degrees, high and low, alike.'" SCHMIDT (1874), more generally: "Kind, sort."

1284 **i'th' open ayre**] WILSON (ed. 1931): "The fresh air was considered most dangerous to invalids by doctors." He compares *TN* 3.4.132 (1653-4) and *JC* 2.1.264-7 (902-5). TILLEY A93: "Fresh Air is ill for the diseased or wounded man." PAFFORD (ed. 1963): "Hermione may mean that she had to make a journey in the open air, but the phrase seems to qualify 'this place.'" BOORMAN (ed. 1964): "Also . . . the strain on Hermione of this open, public trial (cf. [1280-1])."

1285 **strength of limit**] THEOBALD (ed. 1733): "I.e. Strength enough for coming abroad, going never so little a way." HEATH (1765, p. 212): "Before I have recovered that degree of strength, which women in my circumstances usually acquire by a longer confinement." RANN (ed. 1787): "Strength to pass my chamber's *limit*." SCHMIDT (1874), like *OED* (*sb*. 2f, citing this line as the only example), gives both "the time of lying-in before leaving childbed? [and] limited, prescribed strength?" — the latter being MASON's (1785, p. 130) interpretation. Modern eds. generally prefer the former. Yet WHITE's (ed. 1883) "bounds" (*OED, sb*.1) is possible if *of limit* can signify "to pass bounds," and MAXWELL (ed. 1956) interprets *of limit* as an adjectival phrase— "limited." STEEVENS's (ed. 1773, 10:Mm2) idea, repeated by NARES (1876; 1905)—that *limit* as used in W. Bettie's *Historie of Titana* [sic], *and Theseus* (1636; 1st ed. 1608) means "limb"—is wrong. As MASON recognizes, there it means "contour (of the human form)" (*OED, sb*. 1b). HUDSON (ed. 1880): If *of* is equivalent to *by*, the sense would be "before I have got strength *by seclusion*." *Of* is not *by*, however, except in a few special uses (see *OED* 12b and 59 and ABBOTT §168). CARRINGTON (1956), without authority: "Sufficient." BECKET (1815, 1:359) absurdly suggests that *lineaments*, contracted to *line'mets*, appeared to be *limits*. For the possibility that the obscurity is intentional, see n. 1223.

1285-95 **Now . . . Iudge**] BERGERON (1984, p. 7): The peroration of her defense. See nn. 1206–28 and 1238–48 for earlier rhetorical stages.

1285-7 **Now . . . die?**] MIRIAM JOSEPH (1947, p. 215): "By the figure anacoenosis the speaker asks counsel of his hearers," as here.

1288 **no Life**] CAPELL (1783, 2.4:170–1): "Life is not ask'd of you, that is not my concern." In support of changing *no* to *for*, DYCE (ed. 1864) compares 1216. FURNESS (ed. 1898): "With [1287], Hermione ends her defence, by commanding the trial to proceed. Then the thought of a sullied name flashes upon her, and that she has not with sufficient emphasis contended for the preservation of her honour; she hastily resumes, but fearing lest the king should . . . suppose that it is to plead for life . . . she exclaims: 'Mistake me not! No life! Give me not that! I prize it not a straw'. . . . The lines from 'mistake me not' to 'I would free' [1290], inclusive, are parenthetical." HERFORD (ed. 1916-): "Hermione is too eager to repel the idea that she is asking for life to heed exact syntax."

1289 **prize . . . straw**] DENT compares "Not care (give) a straw" (TILLEY S917).

1290 **free**] SCHMIDT (1874): "Acquit . . . absolve" (*OED, v*. 2e, citing this line). Cf. 2277. For adjectival senses, see n. 185.

1290-3 **if . . . Law**] WHITE (1913, pp. 184–5): "Legal evidence consists of those facts within the knowledge of the witnesses called . . . as distinguished from all comments, arguments or 'surmises' as to facts not within the knowledge of the witnesses. . . . Hearsay, or 'surmises', . . . is never admitted in controversies in a legally constituted court." MIRIAM JOSEPH (1947, p. 220): "Aphorismus is a figure which reprehends by raising a question about the proper application of a word," here *surmizes*.

1291 **proofes**] Citing *Oth*. 3.3.324 (1964) and *H8* 2.1.16 (843), PAFFORD (ed. 1963): "Written evidence." The word may have this meaning (*OED, sb*. 1b [*b*]), but there is no indication here that a special sense is required. SCHMIDT (1875): "A convincing token or argument," as at 2943 and 3042.

  sleeping] SCHMIDT (1875): "Denoting . . . entire repose or quiet."

  else] Probably SCHMIDT (1874): "Except this"; hence, "no arguments being raised against me but surmises."

1293 **Rigor . . . Law**] PHILLIPS (1706, Rigour): "Harshness, Sternness, Cruelty, utmost Extremity." WILSON (ed. 1931): "I.e. the rigour of the law without its legality." KERMODE (ed. 1963): "Tyranny, not justice." The expression comes from *Pandosto*; see p. 630.

1294 **referre**] MINSHEU (1617): "Commit, or put vnto [for decision]" (*OED, v*. 5, citing this line).

Lord. This your request
Is altogether iust: therefore bring forth
(And in *Apollo's* Name) his Oracle.
Her. The Emperor of Russia was my Father.

1296 SCENE III. POPE, HAN, WARB, JOHN
        Enter Dion and Cleomines. F2-JOHN2, v1773-RANN
1298 *Exeunt certain Officers.* CAP, MAL+ (*subst.*)

1298 **Oracle**] *OED* (*sb.* 2, citing this line): "A response . . . given usually by a priest or priestess of a god . . . by his inspiration. . . . For the most part obscure or ambiguous." See n. 1128 for another meaning. FRYE (*Perspective*, 1965, p. 125): "In three of the romances a deity, Diana in *Pericles*, Jupiter in *Cymbeline*, and a hidden and off-stage Apollo [here], brings about or is involved in the conclusion." Cf. 3332-5. Regarding the *exeunt* supplied by eds. here and the reentry at 1303, PAFFORD (ed. 1963): "Cleomenes and Dion . . . could quite well have been in the Court from the outset and be simply brought forward at [1303]. However, there is perhaps greater dramatic and stage effect in sending officers for them and bringing them in with some ceremonial." TREWIN (1978, p. 263): "I once saw the scroll brought in among what seemed to be the flames of a chafing-dish."

1299-1303 **The . . . Reuenge**] GREEN (1890, p. 21): "No wish for a father to justify or revenge the bitter wrong; only the cry of the daughter for the dear love and sympathy forever gone." BETHELL (ed. 1956), dubiously: "A conventional aside, intended to convey to the *real* audience what she is feeling but would not in fact speak aloud." Eds. do not treat the speech as an aside, however.

1299 **Emperor of Russia**] KNIGHT (ed. 1841, Comedies 2:340): He "represents some dim conception of a mighty monarch of far-off lands." In *Pandosto* he is the father of Egistus's (= Polixenes's) wife rather than of Bellaria (= Hermione); see p. 626. CHARLTON (ed. 1916): "The mention of her father [gives] a sense of majesty and pathos." PAFFORD (ed. 1963) adds, "And the old feeling of tragedy as being 'de casibus virorum illustrium' [about the fall of illustrious people]." HERFORD (ed. 1916-): "It is likely that both Greene and Shakespeare were thinking of the contemporary Tsar of Muscovy, Ivan the Terrible . . . since he had excited notoriety at the English court by his mission to England to obtain the hand of one of Elizabeth's maids of honour as his consort. His envoys are chafingly glanced at in *Love's Labour's Lost* [5.2.120 ff. (2011 ff.)]." Sh. does not allude specifically to Ivan, however, for his "known disposition towards offenders was notoriously at variance with that ascribed by Hermione to her father." ANDERS (1904, p. 231): 16th-c. English searches for a northeast passage "led to an important trade with Russia in the White Sea." Thus references to that country and to searches for the passage might be expected. They occur in *MM* 2.1.134 (586) and 3.2.88 (1577), *H5* 3.7.144 (1772), *Mac.* 3.4.99 (1377), and *TN* 3.2.27 (1407), as well as in *LLL* and *WT*.

As for this allusion, FELPERIN (1972, p. 218): "Shakespeare often endows his major characters with a life that extends beyond the confines of the immediate action, and of which we catch fleeting glimpses as they speak or are spoken of by others." Thus ROCKAS (1975, p. 8) is mistaken that the mention of this Russian emperor and of Smalus, the king of Libya (2916), indicates only "the concern with father kings in the play," and Mark TAYLOR (1982, p. 130) is probably mistaken as well: "For Hermione he is emperor first and father second. Does this not show his authoritarian posture?" ERICKSON (1982, p. 825), similarly: "She submits her case to an earlier patriarchal

Oh that he were aliue, and here beholding   1300
His Daughters Tryall: that he did but see
The flatnesse of my miserie; yet with eyes
Of Pitty, not Reuenge.
   Officer. You here shal sweare vpon this Sword of Iustice,
That you (*Cleomines* and *Dion*) haue   1305
Been both at Delphos, and from thence haue brought
This seal'd-vp Oracle, by the Hand deliuer'd
Of great *Apollo's* Priest; and that since then,
You haue not dar'd to breake the holy Seale,
Nor read the Secrets in't.   1310
   Cleo. Dio. All this we sweare.

1303 *Re-enter Officers, with* CLEOMINES, *and* DION, *bringing in the Oracle.* CAP,
MAL + (*subst.*)
   1304 this] the F2-RANN (−CAP, v1785)
   1310-11 *One verse line* mCAP2, v1773+ (−OXF2)

---

authority." But Hermione invokes him not for his authority, which would take the
form of revenge upon Leontes, but for a father's love and pity and, by the way, to
contrast the greatness of her line with the sordidness of her situation. HERFORD (ed.
1916-): "Hermione expresses the merciful attitude towards evildoers characteristic
of 'Romances' in its extremest form, for the evildoer has not yet either repented (like
Iachimo) or been convicted (like Caliban and his associates)."

   1301 **Tryall**] ESTRIN (1985, p. 179): "Both a literal judgment . . . and an endurance test."

   1301-3 **that . . . Reuenge**] SUNDELSON (1983, p. 4): "Hermione immediately
gets the attentions she asks for, not from her true father but from Apollo [,who] seems
to take the revenge she herself renounces."

   1302 **The . . . miserie**] JOHNSON (1755, Flatness): "Dejection of state"; in ed.
1765, he glosses: "How low . . . I am laid by my calamity." BECKET (1815, 1:359),
more appropriately: *Flatness* means "absoluteness, completeness" (*OED* 5b, citing
this line only). MOORMAN (ed. 1912): "Abjectness." PAFFORD (ed. 1963) thinks "the
word also gives the sense of 'unrelieved expanse'" (like the Russian steppes of her
father's country, presumably), an idea reiterated in MAXWELL's (ed. 1969) "uniform-
ity" (*OED* 3, possibly, though the first citation is from 1702). VAN DAM (1900, p. 47):
For regular meter, the medial *e* of *miserie* should be syncopated. For other syncopations of *e*, see nn. 222, 313, 381, 692, 813, and 2953.

   1304-10 **You . . . in't**] CAMPBELL (1859, p. 60): "The messengers . . . are
sworn to the genuineness of the document they produce almost in the very words
now used by the Lord Chancellor when an officer presents at the bar of the House
of Lords the copy of a record of a court of justice." For other legalisms, see nn. 112
and 2402.

   1304 **You . . . Iustice**] See n. 1099 for swearing upon a sword.

   1311 *Cleo. Dio.*] HONIGMANN (1976, p. 123): "When the text names two speakers, instead of using the speech prefix '*Both*', it is . . . likely that simultaneous 'choric' speech is required."

   sweare] PAFFORD (ed. 1963): "Here they touch the sword of justice."

Leo. Breake vp the Seales, and read.

Officer. Hermione *is chast,* Polixenes *blamelesse,* Camillo
a true Subiect, Leontes *a iealous Tyrant, his innocent Babe*
truly begotten, and the King shall liue without an Heire, if that   1315
which is lost, be not found.

1313 *chast*] *cast* F2

1312 **Breake . . . read**] At this point HARDINGE (1818, 3:67) would have Paulina
"in a fit of religious passion, fall down and invoke the Gods." BERGERON (1985, p.
162), alone: "That breaking is emblematic of the splitting of the family bond." To the
reading and interpretation of the oracular text, he compares (p. 239, n. 37) Christ's
reading from Isaiah in the synagogue (Luke 4:17–21).

    Breake vp] SCHMIDT (1874): "To rend apart" (*OED*, Break, *v.* 2a and 56b).

    1313–16 **Hermione . . . *found***] CRANE (1951, p. 121): "The confusion of the
trial-scene is pierced through by the short, bald phrases of the oracle." PAFFORD
(1959, p. 161): "Music . . . is sensed as having been in the background. . . ." The
staccato phrases do not suggest it. BERGERON (1984, p. 8): "The oracle parallels in
some respects the indictment [1187–95] . . . even to the point of naming the characters . . . in the same order." MALONE (ed. 1790): "This is almost literally from
[Greene's] novel"; see p. 631.

    COLERIDGE (1813; ed. Raysor, 1960, 1:107), supported by QUILLER-COUCH (ed.
1931, p. xx), complains that the oracle should have provided "some ground for Hermione's seeming death and . . . concealment"—for example, "'Nor shall he ever
recover an heir if he have a wife before that recovery.'" SCHANZER (ed. 1969, on
3337–40): He "needed only to change one word in the oracle . . . 'and the king
shall live without a *wife.*" FURNESS (ed. 1898) objects: "With such a clause
. . . Paulina's   occupation   would   thereafter   have   been   gone. . . . Above
all, . . . the meaning and effect of the play would have been distorted. . . . Had
Leontes been restrained from remarrying by the words of an Oracle and not by heart-
broken contrition and devotion to Hermione's memory, he would never have won
from us that pity which goes far to help us forgive him." PAFFORD (ed. 1963): "Shakespeare does not wish to hint that Hermione may be living. On the contrary he repeatedly emphasizes that she is dead (e.g. [1388, 1484, 2823, 3354])."

    MOULTON (1903, pp. 70–1) places the oracle in a scheme of loss and restoration.
Leontes has lost his wife, his son, his daughter, his friend, his minister (Camillo), and
his loyal servant (Antigonus). "But in its latter clauses the oracle is the dim revelation . . . [of] sixfold restoration: the wife is to be received as from the tomb, the
friend to be again embraced in Sicilia; the lost babe will reappear a lovely daughter;
the lost son will be replaced by a son-in-law. . . . Camillo will return, unable to live
without his king; and if Antigonus himself has been caught in the doom of which he
is the minister, it is his widow, the faithful Paulina, to whom has been committed the
chief ministry of restoration." KERNAN (1975, 3:455): "The oracle . . . declares her
innocence in clear, direct terms, and by doing so guarantees that at some great distance from the fevers and hatreds of life there is a presence, a serenity, which knows
the truth of things in this world and will speak, when questioned, to make the truth
known."

    FELPERIN ("Deconstruction," 1985, p. 8), deconstructing Apollo, finds the words
of the god not clear and direct but "disturbingly difficult to verify or validate. . . .
The god's language without the god to back it up is a bit like paper currency without

Lords. Now blessed be the great *Apollo*.
Her. Praysed.
Leo. Hast thou read truth?
Offic. I (my Lord) euen so as it is here set downe.   1320
Leo. There is no truth at all i'th'Oracle:
The Sessions shall proceed: this is meere falsehood.   (2A6^b)

1319-20 *Verse lines ending* so . . . down. CAP, v1793+ (−OXF2)
1319 truth] the truth F3-POPE2, HAN
1320 it is] *Om.* HAN
1322 Sessions] Session THEO1-RANN (−CAP), DYCE2, HUD2
    Enter Servant. ROWE1+ (*subst.*)

---

any gold behind it. It becomes unstable, subject to the vagaries of special interests and private speculation, with all their devaluing effect. Once cut off from the presence of their divine speaker, with his univocality of meaning and intent, Apollo's words enter the realm of . . . the interpretable." The Lords who exclaim at 1317 seem to have found nothing disturbing, however, and we see immediately what happens to the one who devalues those words. LASCELLES (1959, p. 84): "What would have happened if Leontes had accepted the truth thus delivered? The prediction that 'the king shall live without an heir' would have been inexplicable; indeed, at the time when it was entrusted to the messengers, Leontes would still have a wife and two children with him. But, possessed by the insane conviction that he and oracular truth are ranged together against false seeming, he does not wait for the revelation: he condemns the child he supposes Polixenes' to death. It is Shakespeare's way to accept character as the ultimate source of event." ARTHOS (1964, p. 185): "It is the oracle and not the death of the child that is the climax of the first movement of the play, the high point that looks towards the resolution." For more on the oracle, see n. 3338-40, and for the names set in roman, n. 1187-95.

1313-14 **Hermione . . . *Tyrant*]** HUNTER (*The Malcontent*, ed. 1975, p. 28 n.) compares "Maquerelle is a cunning bawd; I am an honest villain; thy wife is a close drab; and thou art a notorious cuckold" (1.3.89-91). BROOK (1976, p. 170): "*Parison* is the figure in which several successive phrases or clauses are of corresponding structure."

1315 *truly*] OED (*adv.* 4c): "Rightfully, legitimately." *OED* finds the word in this sense only here and in *Mac.* 5.2.26 (2206).

liue . . . Heire] HERFORD (ed. 1916-): "Perdita . . . is formally described as his heir (with Florizel) in [3192]." He is mistaken; Florizel and Perdita are there called "Heires of your [Leontes's and Polixenes's] Kingdomes," she of Sicilia, he of Bohemia.

1317 **Now . . . *Apollo*]** LLOYD (in SINGER, ed. 1856, 4:136): "The retributive edict of the Delphic oracle harmonizes admirably with the staid and solid glory of the nature of Hermione. . . . The god of the oracle directs the path of Antigonus to Bohemia to expose the infant, and . . . the same power directed the hawk of Florizel . . . across the walk of the gentle shepherdess, and aided and governed the track of fortune to the end."

blessed] PORTER & CLARKE (ed. c. 1903): "Two syllables."

1321-2 **There . . . falsehood]** HARDINGE (1818, 3:66-7): "He means that it [1313-16] is not a *faithful* copy or *picture* of the Oracle, not that of the words of the God, that *he* is to be accused. A part of the Oracle being that he die without *an heir* ['liue', actually; see 1315], and the last account of Mamillius being that he was

241

Ser. My Lord the King: the King?
Leo. What is the businesse?
Ser. O Sir, I shall be hated to report it.   1325
The Prince your Sonne, with meere conceit, and feare
Of the Queenes speed, is gone.
Leo. How? gone?

1328 How?] ~ ∧ POPE1-JOHN2

---

better [911-12], nor any peril of his life being suspected, he naturally doubts the *integrity of this menace.*" HUDSON (ed. 1852): Leontes "will not suffer the truth of the charge to stand in issue. Accordingly he rejects the answer as soon as he finds it clashing with his opinion: if the god confirms what he already thinks, then his [Apollo's] authority is unquestionable; if not, then he is no god." SNIDER (c. 1890, p. 478): "The oracle . . . tells only what everybody knew already. . . . It simply gives in a religious form the universal conviction of the time. Why, then, does the Poet employ the oracle? Because he wishes to portray the negative conduct [of] Leontes in its completeness and final culmination. He is made to deny religion—or, the profoundest principle of his nation and his age." DRAPER (1985, pp. 24-5): "A piece of outrageous blasphemy." PARTRIDGE (1982, p. 3): "The Aristotelian *peripeteia.*"

1322 **Sessions**] see n. 1176.

meere] JOHNSON (1755): "Such and nothing else." For the spelling, see n. 901.

1323 **the . . . King**] The CLARKES (1879, p. 425): Iteration used "to express anguish," as also in 1545. For other uses, see 75, 1387, 1958, and 2807.

1324 **businesse**] THIRLBY (MS 1725-33?): "Matter."

1325 **to report**] ROLFE (ed. 1879): "For reporting." For the "Infinitive, indefinitely used," see ABBOTT §356.

1326-7 **The . . . gone**] ARTHOS (1964, pp. 172-6): "It was not only the idea of his mother's wrong that killed Mamillius, it was also his trust in the world she represented. . . . The evil Leontes invented terrified the boy. The child has been able to play with the thought of being frightened by evil spirits, but notions like this [Hermione's dishonor] would kill him." MORO & WILLEMS (1982, p. 36), more simply: "Young Mamillius cannot bear the separation from his mother and dies." FRYE (1986, p. 163): He dies "from shame at the accusation of his mother." Mark TAYLOR (1982, pp. 5-6): "Since Mamillius is a small child, since his role, too, is small, since his death is occasioned by sentiment not action . . . we regard it as mainly pathetic, an event stimulating pity and sadness . . . but no grander emotion. It is also the price Leontes must pay."

1326 **meere conceit**] KERSEY (1702, To conceit): "Imagine." SCHMIDT (1874, Conceit): "Conception, idea, image in the mind." Hence CARRINGTON (1956): "Out of sheer imagination." For the spelling of *meere*, see n. 901.

conceit, and feare] DEIGHTON (ed. 1889): "A hendiadys for 'fearful apprehension,'" but not considered so by WRIGHT (1981). SCHANZER (ed. 1969): "Thinking about and worrying over."

1327 **speed**] JOHNSON (ed. 1765): "The *event* [outcome] of the Queen's trial." SCHMIDT (1875) glosses "with . . . speed" as "fear, that the queen might not succeed," *speed* being "good fortune" (*OED, sb.* 3). See n. 497 and line 1488. HALLIWELL's (ed. 1859) "*Fortune*, not necessarily in the sense of success" is not supported by *OED*. ANSARI (1979, p. 128) believes that Mamillius dies "in desperation when the . . . notion of Hermione committing adultery . . . reaches him."

Ser. Is dead.

Leo. Apollo's angry, and the Heauens themselues   1330
Doe strike at my Iniustice. How now there?

Paul. This newes is mortall to the Queene: Look downe

1331   now∧ there?] ~ ? ~ ! JOHN
       Her. *faints.* ROWE1 + (*subst.*)

1329 **Is dead**] Describing Mary Anderson as Hermione (see p. 806), FOSS (1932, p. 136): "When she heard of the death of Mamillius [she] drew a cloak over her face and stood for full [sic] thirty seconds before falling headlong." ELLIS (1947, p. 133): in *WT*, "where Leontes loses Mamilius [sic] as Shakespeare lost his Hamnet, Leontes represents both Plutarch and Shakespeare in his disinclination for superficial chatter about a dreadful depth of loss. Plutarch and Shakespeare had exchanged a handshake in the dark. With Plutarch, the dead child was only a daughter." THORNE (1982, p. 89): "Leontes' son . . . dies in his stead so that the suffering king may go on to the spiritual regeneration effected through the mock death of his wife and the fertility mission of his daughter." "Fertility mission" may allude to Perdita's exile from barren Sicilia and her return as Florizel's intended wife after her identification with Bohemian natural abundance.

1330-1 *Apollo's* . . . **Iniustice**] HOY (1964, p. 270): "The scales fall from Leontes's eyes, and he regains his senses as suddenly as he had previously taken leave of them." HERFORD (ed. 1916-): "Leontes's sudden surrender . . . again exemplifies the abrupt changes characteristic of the technique of the 'Romances.'" ORNSTEIN (1986, p. 224): It rather "suggests that his defiance required a tremendous effort of will and there is immense relief . . . in his submission." MOWAT (1969, p. 41), however: "His reaction is that of a child . . . who has been discovered by angry parents in the midst of mischief: 'Apollo's angry.'" CHAMBERS (1925, p. 296): "The justification of Providence . . . is the conscious intention which informs the romantic theme; and the supernatural intervention of Apollo represents, in accordance with the ordinary use of the supernatural by Shakespeare, an acknowledgment of the ultimate mystery which, in the last resort, the conception of Providence involves." FRIPP (1938, 2:736): "A clap of thunder shakes the palace." For this sound effect in productions of the play, see p. 803. SPRAGUE (in SPRAGUE & TREWIN, 1970, p. 130, n. 14) describes "a terrifying picture in the *Illustrated Sporting and Dramatic News*, 23 September 1876, of the lightning flash as it was simulated in a contemporary production at Liverpool." WHEELER (1980, p. 164): "Even the oracle of Apollo is powerless to free Leontes from his delusion until news comes of Mamillius' death. . . . Mamillius dies when he is deprived of the essential maternal presence Leontes destroys in fantasy." BATE (1993, p. 223): "Cleomenes' association of Apollo's oracle and Jove's thunder [1155-8] has been borne out." HANKINS (1978, p. 237) is reminded "of the death of the first-born as one of the plagues of Egypt (Exod. 12: 29)." For a further exhibition of Heaven's anger, see 1442-5.

1331 **strike**] For other instances of striking, see n. 283.

   How now] See n. 201.

1332 **This** . . . **Queene**] PYLE (1969, p. 61 n.): "Making her [Paulina] say . . . that the queen is dying helps to authenticate . . . her later report of her death [1387 ff.]." DRAPER (1985, p. 25): "This is the absolute climax of the play's wintry movement. The King has virtually destroyed his own family and left himself, and the state also, with no possibility of continuity."

   Look downe] BOORMAN (ed. 1964): "Leontes should be sitting in a high throne." Maybe, but as Hermione is prostrate, Leontes sitting in anything would be above her.

And see what Death is doing.

   Leo. Take her hence:
Her heart is but o're-charg'd: she will recouer.   1335
I haue too much beleeu'd mine owne suspition:
'Beseech you tenderly apply to her
Some remedies for life. *Apollo* pardon
My great prophanenesse 'gainst thine Oracle.
Ile reconcile me to *Polixenes*,   1340
New woe my Queene, recall the good *Camillo*
(Whom I proclaime a man of Truth, of Mercy:)

1335 *Exeunt* Paulina *and Ladies with* Hermione. ROWE1-RANN; *at* 1338 MAL+ (*subst.*)
   1336 SCENE IV. POPE, HAN, WARB, JOHN
   1342 of Mercy] and mercy HARN

   1333 **see . . . doing**] GRINDON (1930, pp. 27-8), a spiritualist: "Not so, her etheric body slipped out of the physical and immediately went in search of her baby." See n. 1478. More or less similarly, ORTEGO (1970, p. 33): "Hermione succumbs to a spell."
   1335 **Her . . . recouer**] Michael TAYLOR (1982, p. 234): "Leontes remains astonishingly, ingenuously optimistic." RIEMER (1987-8, p. 23): "His assertion . . . is not the product of some superior diagnostic skill, but the result of [his] inability to contemplate the consequences of his own wrongdoing." He is, however, right.
   o're-charg'd] MAXWELL (ed. 1956): "Too full (of grief)."
   1336-57 **I . . . blacker?**] JOHNSON (ed. 1765): "This vehement retractation of *Leontes*, accompanied with the confession of more crimes than he was suspected of, is agreeable to our daily experience of the vicissitudes of violent tempers, and the eruptions of minds oppressed with guilt." The threat of death and the encouragement of reward are implied in 423-32 rather than stated. See n. 1409 for JOHNSON's similar description of Paulina. HARRISON (1927, p. 40): "It is the familiar tragedy of the weak man who mistakes obstinacy for strength and breaks himself rather than acknowledge his own mistakes. But his repentance is as extravagant as his grief." SCOTT (1920, p. 151): "In the speech of newly dawned repentance Hermione is mentioned only once [1341]; all the contrition is directed to Polixenes and Camillo." HUNTER (1965, p. 62): The "revelation of guilt is often a revelation to the sinner as well as to the society that discovers him to be guilty—as when . . . the death of Mamillius suddenly and irrationally convinces Leontes that he has wronged his wife."
   1336 **I . . . suspition**] CAVELL (1987, p. 196): "The statement merely expresses his regret that he *believed* his suspicion too much. How much would have been just enough?" It probably expresses "I have believed my suspicion, any of which would have been too much." The king has just heard the oracle proclaim that "Hermione is *chast*."
   1337 **'Beseech**] For the omission of the nominative, see ABBOTT §399.
   1341 **woe**] I.e., woo.
   1341-6 **recall . . . *Polixenes***] GRENE (1967, p. 76): "That the courtiers do not understand [645-9] seems very likely, since it is only when his delusion is at an end that Leontes announces the truth as something quite new to them."

For being transported by my Iealousies
To bloody thoughts, and to reuenge, I chose
Camillo for the minister, to poyson   1345
My friend *Polixenes*: which had been done,
But that the good mind of *Camillo* tardied
My swift command: though I with Death, and with
Reward, did threaten and encourage him,
Not doing it, and being done: he (most humane,   1350
And fill'd with Honor) to my Kingly Guest
Vnclasp'd my practise, quit his fortunes here

1343 **transported**] SCHMIDT (1875, Transport): "To hurry away by violence of passion." For a related meaning, see n. 3268.

1345 **minister**] CARRINGTON (1956): "Agent."

1346–51 **which . . . Honor**] HOLBROOK (1964, p. 168): "Leontes' . . . verse at last resumes the balanced movement of sanity, of wise consideration, recognizing painfully the good values and norms."

1347–50 **the . . . done**] See n. 450–1 for the rhetorical figure.

1347–8 **tardied . . . command**] THEOBALD (1726, p. 11): "It is . . . familiar with him [Sh.] to make *Verbs* out of *Adjectives*." Theobald offers *tardied* as an example, glossing it "stopp'd, made slow, or tardy" (*OED*, *v.*, citing this line as the first of two instances). For other adjectives created from verbs, see ABBOTT §290 and MIRIAM JOSEPH (1947, p. 63). For the phrase, COLLINS (1904–24?): "Delayed to execute my command, which enjoined swiftness." MALONE (ed. 1790): "Our author has closely followed Greene"; see p. 632.

1348–50 **though . . . done**] HUNTER (ed. 1872): "Though I did threaten him not doing it with death, and encourage him, it being done, with reward." With the construction, he compares 1245–6; see also 2203–4 and ABBOTT §378. BLAKE (1983, p. 102): "The final line means 'If he did not do it, and if it was done', and each clause refers respectively to the *threaten* and *encourage* of the previous line." CORSON (1889, p. 375) calls this figure a "respective [or restrospective] construction." BETHELL (ed. 1956): "In rhetoric it is treated as a species of *isocolon*, a figure concerned with rhythm, since it produces equality among the different parts of the sentence." COLLINS (ed. 1904–24?): "A triple instance . . . where *abc, def* is put into the form *ad, be, cf*; cp. a double instance in [1393]." Another triple is found in *Ant.* 4.15.25–6 (3030–1), a double in *Mac.* 1.3.60 (160–1).

1350 **Not . . . humane**] SCHMIDT (1875, p. 1413a) scans by counting *doing* and *being* as monosyllables and stressing the second syllable of *humane* rather than the first, as usual in Sh.; but, as HAPPÉ (1969) notes, the word here means "humane" rather than "human," as it does at 1203 and 2774, and the stress is thus normal. For the spelling, see n. 1203.

Not . . . done] For "being done," LETTSOM (MS 1840–65): "And *it* being done" (ABBOTT §378). MOORMAN (ed. 1912): "The [entire] phrase refers to 'death' and 'reward' respectively; death will be Camillo's lot for not slaying Polixenes, reward if he slays him."

1352 **Vnclasp'd my practise**] HUNTER (ed. 1872): "Revealed my design." HERFORD (ed. 1904, Practise): "Knavery."

(Which you knew great) and to the hazard
Of all Incertainties, himselfe commended,
No richer then his Honor: How he glisters   1355
Through my Rust? and how his Pietie

1353 hazard] certaine hazard F2-SING1 (−MAL), COL3, DEL, DYCE2, KNT3, COL4,
HUD2, OXF1, BUL, CAM3, KIT1, N&H, ALEX, SIS, ARD2, OXF2; hazard boldly KTLY
    1354-5 commended, . . . Honor:] ∼ . . . . ∼ , STAU
    1356 Through] F1-RANN, IRV, NLSN, PEL1, CLN2, SIG+ ; Thorough mTBY3 *conj.*,
MAL *etc.*
        my Rust] my darke Rust F2-RANN, NLSN

1353 **hazard**] As the more natural expression, MALONE (in STEEVENS, ed. 1785)
prefers *fearful hazard* to F2's *certain*. Subsequently, in MALONE (ed. 1790) he adds
doubtful as another possibility. STEEVENS (ed. 1793) prefers *certain* because of "sure
vncertaintie" in *Err.* 2.2.185 (580), which BEVINGTON (ed. 1980), e.g., glosses "undoubted illusion." The connection between *WT*'s passage and the one in *Err.* is remote, yet the decision of many eds. to follow F2 repudiates MALONE's adverse opinion
of *certain*. LETTSOM (in WALKER, 1860, 3:102 n.) attempts to refute MALONE by citing
other certain uncertainties, including "Her certaine sorrow writ vncertainely" (*Luc.*
1311). MIRIAM JOSEPH (1947, pp. 83–4), however, considers that *certain* with "Incertainties" creates a polyptoton, the repetition of words derived from the same root,
a figure used by Sh. a dozen times elsewhere. For other suggestions, see p. 577.
BOSWELL (ed. 1821) points out that no emendation may be required, since many other
lines in Sh. are as defective as F1's. ABBOTT (§508) finds that some lines he considers
to be regular omit a syllable or even a foot when "a marked pause" occurs, here
between *great* and *and*. Cf. 3245.
    1354 **Incertainties**] SCHMIDT (1874): "Doubtfulness, precariousness." For the
form, see n. 2761.
        commended] Committed. See n. 1114.
    1355 **No . . . Honor**] RANN (ed. 1787): "Rich only in; no better equipped than
with his integrity; furnished with no other safeguard." HUNTER (ed. 1872): "With no
other riches than his honour." BOORMAN (ed. 1964): "[2466–7] repeats that Camillo
left all his fortune in Sicilia."
    1355-7 **How . . . blacker?**] BROWN (1962, p. 222): "In fastening on Camillo's
truth, Leontes is making a personal valuation and showing that he had been concerned
for himself not for Hermione." Cf. n. 1428–34.
    1355-6 **How . . . Rust?**] HUNTER (ed. 1872): "How brightly he shines by con-
trast with my rusty stains." SCHMIDT (1874, Glister): "To shine, to sparkle." KIT-
TREDGE & RIBNER (ed. 1967): "The metaphor is that of polished and rusty armour."
Rust, however, was used generally to mean "moral corrosion" (*OED, sb.*[1] 2, citing
this line).
    1356 **Through**] SINGER (ed. 1856): Disyllabic, as THIRLBY's reading indicates. The
word occurs six times in *WT*, never as *thorough*. Even *thoroughly* is "throughly" at
704. In 704, 1926 (twice), 1965, and 3198 it is monosyllabic; at 2383, however, it is
disyllabic, and DELIUS (ed. 1860) finds it disyllabic in *MV* 3.2.302 (1660). ABBOTT
(§§477 ff.) discusses various ways in which words may be lengthened. As for this line,
BOORMAN (ed. 1964): "A strong pause after [Rust?] has a similar effect [to that of
disyllabic *through*]." ORGEL (ed. 1996): "In speaking, the initial foot is heard as an
iamb because of the feminine ending of [1355]."
        Pietie] SCHMIDT (1875): "Used with some latitude, = virtue in general." PARRY

Do's my deeds make the blacker?
   Paul. Woe the while:
O cut my Lace, least my heart (cracking it)
Breake too.   1360
   Lord. What fit is this? good Lady?
   Paul. What studied torments (Tyrant) hast for me?

1357 SCENE V. POPE, HAN, WARB, JOHN
    Enter Paulina. ROWE1+ (*subst.*)
1360-1 *One verse line* MCAP2, ARD, KIT1, SIS, PEL1, PEN2+
1361 What] Alas! What HAN
1362 hast] hast thou KTLY

(ed. 1982): "The word sums up all the qualities—of goodness, truth, mercy, humanity and honour—that Leontes here confesses he has profaned."

1358 **Paul.**] PYLE (1969, pp. 56-7): She is "not simply the lady who has been absent . . . seeking to revive her [Hermione]. She is also retributive justice, knowing . . . the detail that Paulina could not know [1375-6; see n.]. . . .Thus the trial of Hermione resolves itself into the trial of Leontes." As Justice, she addresses the king as *thou* (as Hermione was addressed in her indictment [1187-95]) rather than the more formal and respectful *you*.

Woe the while] The CLARKES (ed. 1865): "Ah, woful time." The expression also occurs in *H5* 4.7.75 (2603) and *JC* 1.3.82 (522); on the latter instance, CRAIK (1857; 1867, p. 195) comments, "Commonly understood to mean, alas for the present time."

1359-60 **O . . . too**] FURNESS (ed. 1898): "It may be that Shakespeare wished us to perceive by this chilling dash of rant that Paulina lacked the earnestness which should be hers if she were really convinced that the queen was truly dead. And yet we must not here doubt her sincerity . . . nor must we examine even the rest of Paulina's speech too curiously. She was not present when Leontes made his confession, and yet she knows every detail of it. . . . See note on [1375-6]." PILGRIM (1983, p. 60): "At this stage even she must have believed that Hermione was really dead." At 1332-3, Paulina thinks Hermione is in danger of dying. Here whether she believes her dead or has begun her deception is immaterial, as she would say the same thing in either case. MUIR (1977, p. 267): "Paulina swears that Hermione is dead; Leontes says later that he viewed the bodies of his wife and son [he actually asks at 1426-7 that he be taken to view them; that he did see them seems a legitimate assumption]; and Antigonus' dream [1458 ff.] . . . , all these things reinforce the conviction that Hermione has died. For the audience to share in Leontes' feelings in the last scene . . . , it was necessary for Shakespeare to indulge in unprecedented obfuscation." DRAPER (1985, p. 25): "Death is what it seems to be. Paulina is emphatic that it is so, and the audience are given no hints that it might be otherwise."

1359 **Lace**] Laces fastened the bodice; see CUNNINGTON & CUNNINGTON (1972, p. 82) and *OED* (Lace, *sb.* 3). Distressed ladies need relief from this confinement in *R3* 4.1.33 (2512, Queen Elizabeth) and in *Ant.* 1.3.71 (385, Cleopatra).

cracking it] SCHMIDT (1874, Crack): "To break with a noise, to split." These actions may seem inappropriate for a lace, "a string or cord" (*OED*, *sb.* 3), but under great stress a ship's rigging and a person's heartstrings also crack (*OED*, *v.* 13).

1362-89 **What . . . yet**] STRACHEY (1906; 1922, p. 58): "Nowhere are the poet's metaphors more nakedly material; nowhere does he verge more often upon a sort of brutality of phrase, a cruel coarseness." STRACHEY compares the imagery of

What Wheeles? Racks? Fires? What flaying? boyling?
In Leads, or Oyles? What old, or newer Torture
Must I receiue? whose euery word deserues   1365
To taste of thy most worst. Thy Tyranny
(Together working with thy Iealousies,
Fancies too weake for Boyes, too greene and idle
For Girles of Nine) O thinke what they haue done,
And then run mad indeed: starke-mad: for all   1370
Thy by-gone fooleries were but spices of it.
That thou betrayed'st *Polixenes*, 'twas nothing,
(That did but shew thee, of a Foole, inconstant,

1363 Racks? Fires] what racks? what fires KEIGHTLEY *conj. in* CAM1, KTLY
        flaying? boyling?] F1, v1778-v1821, CAM1, GLO, WH2, BUL, ARD, SIS; flaying?
boyling? Burning, F2-ROWE2, POPE1-JOHN2, v1773; Flaying? Boiling? Burning. ROWE3;
flaying, rather? boiling∧ CAP; flaying? burning, boiling∧ mTBY2 *conj.*, COL2; flaying?
or what boiling∧ DYCE2, HUD2; flaying? boiling, v1793 *etc.*
    1364 Leads . . . Oyles] lead . . . oil mTBY3 *conj.*, COL2, DYCE2, COL4, HUD2
        newer] new F2-ROWE3
    1365 euery] very F2-ROWE3
    1371 but] *Om.* THEO1
        of] for F2-ROWE1
    1373 thee, of] thee off, WARB
        Foole] Soul THEOBALD (1729) *conj. in* NICHOLS (1817, 2:361-2), THEO, HAN,
WH2

272-89. LEGOUIS (ed. 1936, pp. xiii-xiv): When she returns, does Paulina believe
Hermione dead . . . or does she play a convincing rôle in order to confirm the death
of the queen? The poet has cast a shadow on everything that concerns the supposed
death of Hermione; he has thus allowed certain critics to suspect Paulina of trickery. . . . One must reject that interpretation. . . . She is sincere in her vehemence.
She invites the courtiers to view the queen deprived of life. When one shows her the
king's prostration from remorse and sorrow, her fury is calmed (in Fr.). SIEMON (1974,
p. 14): "The dramatic effect of this outburst is to suggest that, under the pressure of
grief too great to be borne, Paulina has momentarily broken down. . . . There is
nothing to suggest that she has been dissembling. . . . The emotional
force . . . can only be taken to mean that Hermione is dead and that Paulina knows
it." ESTRIN (1977, p. 38 n.) accuses SIEMON of ignoring "the deliberate hyperbole of
Paulina's language," but the anguish is real despite the discrepancy of fact. MCDONALD
(1985, p. 322): "As the tirade unfolds, we perceive that Paulina's joint purposes are
intertwined: she will simultaneously condemn Leontes and reveal his most appalling
crime. The first objective waits upon the second, which remains unknown until the
conclusion. . . . Every folly and act of cruelty must be compared with Leontes' last
incomparable outrage." PARRY (ed. 1982): "Paulina in effect torments *him*, while
holding back her heart-breaking news."
    1362-6 **What . . . worst**] The CLARKES (1879, p. 77): "Paulina, hissing out her
detestation . . . , utters a sentence sibilant with ss" (e.g., *s*tudied torment*s*, ha*s*t,
wheel*s*).
    1362 **studied**] SCHMIDT (1875, Study): "To devise; . . . to be intent on." DEIGH-
TON (ed. 1889): "Prepared with studious malignity" (*OED, ppl. a.* 1, citing this line).

Tyrant] BETHELL (ed. 1956): "Paulina has now overcome any previous reluctance she may have had [so to call Leontes; see 1043 and n.]. . . . No doubt she is meant . . . to believe at this point that the queen is really dead, so that her grief is the psychological occasion of her outburst." See n. 1359-60 for the question of her belief.

1363 **Wheeles]** *OED* (*sb.* 2): "A large wheel, or contrivance resembling one, used in various ways as an instrument of torture or punishment."

Racks] *OED* (*sb.*³ 1): "An instrument of torture . . . consisting (usually) of a frame having a roller at each end; the victim was fastened to these by the wrists and ankles, and had the joints of his limbs stretched by their rotation."

Fires] MALONE (ed. 1790, 1.1.xxxv): "A dissyllable." HARDINGE (1801, pp. 20-2) heartily disagrees. So does ABBOTT (§484), who gives *boyling* three syllables (see n. 383). An example of two-syllable *fire*, however, is given by CERCIGNANI (1981, p. 356).

flaying? boyling?] MOORMAN (ed. 1912): "The addition of *burning* [by F2] . . . seems superfluous. It may have been added for the sake of the metre [it clearly was], but the pauses after almost every word in this line make it long enough."

1364 **In . . . Oyles?]** COLLINS (ed. 1904-24?): "In molten lead or boiling oil." WHITE (1913, p. 186): During the reign of Henry VIII, 17 persons in the family of the Bishop of Rochester and several others were poisoned by one Richard Roose. This offense "raised a kind of indignation in the legislature; and it was declared . . . that the said poisoning should be adjudged high treason, and that Richard Roose [and others who committed his crime] should . . . be boiled to death."

old] The CLARKES (1879, p. 287): "Long-used."

1365 **deserues]** SCHMIDT (1874, Deserve): "Merit; applied to good and evil."

1366-85 **Thy . . . Dam]** Compare *Pandosto*, p. 632.

1366 **To . . . worst]** The CLARKES (ed. 1865): *Most worst* is a double superlative (see n. 213). PAFFORD (ed. 1963): "With accent on *most*."

1368 **Fancies]** See n. 1046.

greene . . . idle] SCHMIDT (1874): "Inexperienced, raw . . . silly."

1369 **Girles of Nine]** Such as her daughter. See 757.

1370 **starke]** SCHMIDT (1875): "Absolutely, quite."

1371 **spices of it]** HUNTER (ed. 1872): "Samples of madness." SCHMIDT (1875): "Served only to season it, to give it a zest," to which FURNESS (ed. 1898) objects. To FURNESS, the word "may be equivalent to its doublet, *species* [*OED*, *sb.* 3 and 4] . . . ; if so, a paraphrase of the passage may be: — 'all thy by-gone fooleries were but in the same kind with thy tyranny'. Or it may mean (and this seems to be the more probable), *a small quantity* [*sb.* 5b] . . . 'all thy by-gone fooleries were but a modicum of thy tyranny', or 'in comparison with it'. Herein the phrase finds a correspondence with [1376-7: 'poore . . . by']." Eds. generally follow HUNTER. PIERCE (ed. 1918): "Foretastes."

1373-4 **of . . . ingratefull]** THEOBALD (ed. 1733) reads *Soul* because "Foole" is "too gross and blunt in Paulina"; however, as COLERIDGE (1813; ed. Raysor, 1960, 1:108) observes, Paulina uses the very word THEOBALD objects to, describing the king as "grosse and foolish" at 1384. JOHNSON (ed. 1765): "*It show'd thee* first *a fool*, then *inconstant and ungrateful*." CAPELL (1783, 2.4:171): You were inconstant and ungrateful because you always were a fool. COLERIDGE, who believes F1 authentic because "the involved grammar is Shakespearian," paraphrases as "shew thee, being a fool naturally, to have improved your folly by inconstancy."

Citing *AWW* 4.3.31 (2132), where he supplies other instances, MALONE (ed. 1790) points out that *damnable* is an adverb; see n. 2364, FRANZ §241(c), and ABBOTT §1 for similar usages. Discovering another parallel in *AWW*— "You shall find of the King a husband" (1.1.6 [11])—WHITE (ed. 1857): "A French construction . . . meaning 'That did but show thee a fool', &c." SCHANZER (ed. 1969) more appropriately cites "Henry . . . Is, of a King, become a banisht man" (*3H6* 3.3.24-5 [1751-2]). HAL-

And damnable ingratefull:) Nor was't much,
Thou would'st haue poyson'd good *Camillo's* Honor,   1375
To haue him kill a King: poore Trespasses,
More monstrous standing by: whereof I reckon
The casting forth to Crowes, thy Baby-daughter,
To be or none, or little; though a Deuill
Would haue shed water out of fire, ere don't: 1380
Nor is't directly layd to thee, the death

1377 whereof] wherefore F4-ROWE3
1378 to] of F4
      thy] the F2-F4

LIWELL (ed. 1859), by contrast, thinks "the genitive [possessive] case of a noun was sometimes used instead of the adjective, so that *of a fool* simply means, foolish." STAUNTON (ed. 1859): "'*Of* a fool,' is the same as '*for* a fool.'" ABBOTT (§173), however: *Of* is applied "to any influencing circumstance, in the sense of 'as regards', 'what comes from.'" Here, therefore, "'as regards a fool', 'in the matter of folly.'" CHARLTON (ed. 1916),: "*I.e.* in thy capacity of fool."

   1375-6 **Thou . . . King**] MALONE (1780, 1:144): "No one had charged the king with this crime except himself [at 1343-6], while Paulina was absent," having exited with Hermione at 1335 approximately. A few critics seek a logical basis for the accusation. PYE (1807, p. 113): Camillo, who was on good terms with Paulina (see 3356-7), may have told her before he fled. HARNESS (ed. 1825): The words "may allude to the reproach of treason against himself, which Leontes cast on Camillo." Leontes does not specifically accuse Camillo of treason, though he comes close at 328-37; Antigonus, however, is said to be one of a nest of traitors (1001). The CLARKES (ed. 1865) are impatient with critics who are bothered by such small discrepancies, and CALDECOTT (MS 1813-33) finds in 1548-9 another instance of a fact known to Sh.'s "auditory" but not "in the knowledge of the speaker," a point elaborated by the CLARKES (1879, pp. 18 and 501). HAPPÉ (1969): "The effect of her statement is to suggest her reliability and truthfulness."

   1376 **To haue him**] BETHELL (ed. 1956): "By making him."

   1376-7 **poore . . . by**] HUNTER (ed. 1872): "Slight . . . when viewed alongside of more monstrous ones."

   1377 **More . . . by**] WILSON (ed. 1931; 1950): "I.e. in comparison with others more monstrous." Regarding this interpretation as possible, EVANS (ed. 1974) adds, for *standing by*, "To follow (?)" CARRINGTON (1956), however: "To be revealed, ready to come forward," an extension of *OED*, Stand, *v.* 91a.

   1378 **Crowes**] SCHMIDT (1874) identifies this bird as *Corvus cornix*, the hooded crow; HARTING (1871, p. 110) says it is *Corvus corone*, the carrion crow.

   1380 **water . . . fire**] STEEVENS (ed. 1773): "Tears of pity o'er the damn'd." HALLIWELL (ed. 1859): "Tears of pity even from his fiery abode." The CLARKES (ed. 1865): "Tears from burning eyes." BETHELL (ed. 1956): "Implying pity in the least likely place, (*a*) because devils have no pity and (*b*) because water is the element opposed to fire." DENT questionably compares "To fetch (wring) Water (blood) out of a stone (flint)" (TILLEY W107).

   1381 **Nor is't**] DEIGHTON (ed. 1889): "*It* is redundant; or rather, perhaps, there is a confusion of constructions between 'Nor is it laid to thee that thou didst kill', etc. and 'Nor is the death of the prince laid to you.'"

Of the young Prince, whose honorable thoughts
(Thoughts high for one so tender) cleft the heart
That could conceiue a grosse and foolish Sire
Blemish'd his gracious Dam: this is not, no,　　　　　　1385
Layd to thy answere: but the last: O Lords,
When I haue said, cry woe: the Queene, the Queene,

1383 **high**] SCHMIDT (1874): "Deserving . . . respect." BOORMAN (ed. 1964): "Noble."

tender] VERPLANCK (ed. 1845): "I.e. Tender in years."

1384 **conceiue**] SCHMIDT (1874): "To form an idea; to imagine; to think." HAPPÉ (1969): "Even contemplate."

grosse and foolish] SCHMIDT (1874, Gross): "Rude, base." Cf. nn. 397, 794, 1031, and 2031. WRIGHT & LAMAR (ed. 1966) consider this a hendiadys, "greatly foolish." For more on the hendiadys, see n. 904-5.

Sire] *OED* (sb. 7): "A male parent of a quadruped. . . . Correlative to *dam*."

1385 **Blemish'd**] SCHMIDT (1874): Dishonored.

Dam] ROLFE (ed. 1879): "Elsewhere [213 and 1016] applied only in contempt to a human mother." *OED* (*sb.*² 3, citing this line) agrees. SYMONS (in IRVING & MARSHALL, ed. 1890): Paulina "was not a squeamish person; and it is quite characteristic of her to use a word of this sort affectionately." In *3H6* 2.2.135 (1012), Queen Margaret uses the terms for the handsome mother and father of the foul stigmatic Richard; here *dam*, modified by *gracious*, follows from the insulting *sire* of 1384.

1386 **Layd . . . answere**] DEIGHTON (ed. 1889): "Brought against you as a crime for which you will have to answer." SCHMIDT (1874, Answer): "Account." WILSON (ed. 1931): "Lit. reply to a charge, hence—charge." PARRY (ed. 1982): "Her point is that though Leontes may not be *directly* responsible for Mamillius' death, he *is* so for Hermione's."

1386-95 **O . . . Gods**] SPENCER ("Artistry," 1970, p. 74): "There is a special bond of confidence between the audience and Paulina. . . . And yet into her mouth is put the announcement . . . that Hermione is dead. . . . It is a unique deception . . . unique, at any rate, in Shakespeare's maturity. The only parallel is that in *The Comedy of Errors* Shakespeare does conceal from the audience that Aemilia . . . is living in Ephesus as abbess of the local convent." For more Shn. misleading, see n. 1458-83.

1387 **said**] STAUNTON (ed. 1859): "Done." PAFFORD (ed. 1963): "Said my say."

woe:] SIMPSON (1911, pp. 71-2): The colon marks an interrupted speech. "The broken utterance may be resumed with a new turn of expression when the speaker has been completely overpowered by the emotion of the moment. . . . The colon marks the interval of silence." See n. 422 for a similar use of the comma and n. 674 for a similar use of the semicolon.

1387-8 **the Queene, the . . . dead**] LUDWIG (1974, p. 369): "Hermione's death is what the trial scene is aiming toward; Leontes describes the justice he will execute on his wife as one 'in whose easiest passage / Look for no less than death' [1268-9]. Leontes' wish comes true at exactly the moment he ceases to wish it." So it would appear, but it is not entirely certain that Paulina believes what she so vehemently says. Some think she does. STEARNS (1865, p. 32): "We are to understand . . . that the queen had fallen into a cataleptic state, brought on by combined physical and mental suffering." HARRISON (ed. 1947): "Paulina at this moment . . . believe[s] Hermione to be dead indeed. It is not disclosed how Hermione was later found to be

The sweet'st, deer'st creature's dead: & vengeance for't   (2A6

Not drop'd downe yet.

    Lord. The higher powres forbid.   1390

    Pau. I say she's dead: Ile swear't. If word, nor oath

Preuaile not, go and see: if you can bring

1388 deer'st] *Om.* HAN

1389 drop'd] drop JOHN, v1778 (*text;* dropp'd *in errata*)

---

alive. Nor is the audience allowed to believe otherwise until the very end." See n.
1483-6. B. EVANS (1960, p. 290): "He [Sh.] tells us flatly that we can have no true
comfort, because what has happened is beyond remedy." HOROWITZ (1965, p. 75):
"Indeed, Hermione's reported death is but the symbolic realization of her actual condition, because Leontes has bereft her of all reasons for living." BARKAN (1986, p.
284): "Leontes and Hermione are not independent organisms but a pair of Shakespearean twins, two halves of a single system. The husband treats the wife lovelessly,
and she becomes a stony lady." BARTON (1980, p. 140), arguing that in his last plays
Sh. subordinates consistency of character to action or immediacy of dramatic effect:
"Paulina, of course, is lying—or, at least, she seems to be from the vantage point of
the fifth act. In [this] scene . . . , one must assume that she . . . is half crazed with
shock and grief, expressing the truth of the situation. For the theatre audience at this
point in the play, Hermione . . . is indeed dead. Paulina's voice is faithful to the
action." KNOWLES (privately) remembers that at 1426-7, Leontes asks to be brought
to "the dead bodies of my Queene, and Sonne." Presumably he is, and is convinced
that both are dead, as we learn later in the play. Taking "Ile" [1391] to express
futurity, FOWLER (1978, p. 47): "Few notice that she does not actually swear," but
that is mere tense splitting. On the other hand, QUILLER-COUCH (1917, p. 258):
"If . . . we know our Shakespeare of old, we ought to have guessed in Paulina's
protestations a something held up her sleeve." SPRAGUE (1935, p. 159 n.), however:
"Familiarity with Shakespeare's methods would, as I see it, work exactly the other
way." ORNSTEIN (1986, p. 224): "In any event, she is determined, like Leontes, to
impose her 'truth' by sheer insistence."

    1387 the . . . Queene] The CLARKES (1879, p. 426): Iteration to express sob-
bing. For other uses, see 75, 1323, 1545, 1958, and 2807.

    1388 The . . . for't] WALKER (1854, pp. 168, 272) considers this line to have a
trisyllabic termination—*vénge ance for't* presumably.

    sweet'st, deer'st] ABBOTT (§473): "Est in superlatives is often pronounced st
after dentals and liquids."

    1389 Not . . . yet] KITTREDGE & RIBNER (ed. 1967): "Sent from heaven." DEIGH-
TON (ed. 1889) adds, "*I.e.* as we might have expected."

    1392-5 if . . . Gods] HUNTER (ed. 1872): "I will worship you as [a] divine be-
ing, thus quickening the dead." LLOYD (in SINGER, ed. 1856, 4:128) finds these words
"perhaps . . . a slight hint" that Hermione is alive after all. See n. 2819-29. FOWLER
(1978, p. 50): "It may be wrong to think of Paulina as keeping Hermione from Leontes.
She encouraged him from the beginning to visit, even to kiss, the 'dead' Hermione."
But this is a taunt, not an invitation, and hostesses do not call prospective guests
"Tyrant." GARBER (1974, pp. 169-70): Paulina's avowal suggests "the very possibility
she denies. The scene thus becomes a dramatic anticipation of the denouement, an
emphatic statement of the impossibility and irrationality of something which will turn
out to be true."

    1392 Preuaile not] BOORMAN (ed. 1964): "Are useless."

Tincture, or lustre in her lip, her eye
Heate outwardly, or breath within, Ile serue you
As I would do the Gods. But, O thou Tyrant,   1395
Do not repent these things, for they are heauier
Then all thy woes can stirre: therefore betake thee
To nothing but dispaire. A thousand knees,

1393 eye∧] F1-F3, POPE; ~ , ROWE, THEO1-DEL2, KTLY, KNT3-COL4, OXF1, CAM3,
CLN2, K&R, PEN2+; ~ ; F4 *etc.*
1396-7 Do . . . stirre:] Dot . . . stirre: F2; Dost . . . stir: F3-ROWE3; Dost . . .
stir? POPE
1397 Then] That ROWE2, ROWE3
      woes] vows WARBURTON *conj. in* HAN2, HAN

1393-4 **Tincture . . . within**] BLOUNT (1656, Tincture): "Colour." MAXWELL
(ed. 1956): "Color to the lip or brightness to the eye." BUCKNILL (1860, p. 131):
"Although it is confessedly a difficult medical problem to fix upon certain signs of
the recent cessation of life," the signs Paulina gives— "the pallor, the lustreless eye,
the cessation of breath, and the loss of animal heat"—in a real case would be strong
evidence of death.
      1394 **Heate outwardly**] KITTREDGE & RIBNER (ed. 1967): "External heat (adverb
used as adjective)."
      1395-1402 **But . . . wer't**] BETHELL (ed. 1956): "For a brief time Paulina coun-
sels despair. Her attitude is that of the Old Testament: Leontes has sinned too deeply
for recovery." At 1409 ff. she seems to reverse herself, however; see nn. 1409 and
1417-23.
      1396 **repent**] COLLINS (ed. 1904-24?): "Do penance for," but neither *OED* nor
SCHMIDT (1875) recognizes this meaning.
      1396-7 **heauier . . . stirre**] HUNTER (ed. 1872): "Too heavy a load of guilt for
all thy acts of penance to stir," glossing *heauier* in effect as "weightier." KITTREDGE
& RIBNER (ed. 1967) make it "sadder." SCHMIDT (1874): "The different significations
often scarce distinguishable, as they afford much scope to quibbling." For *stirre*,
SCHMIDT (1875): "Move"; MOORMAN (ed. 1912): "Remove"; WILSON (ed. 1931):
"Shift"; MAXWELL (ed. 1956): "Alter"; BETHELL (ed. 1956): "I.e. atone for"; HAPPÉ
(1969): "Ease." For *woes*, WILSON (ed. 1931): "Cr[ies] of woe, lamentation[s]." Thus,
"lamentations can move."
      1397-1401 **therefore . . . perpetuall**] For these lines as evidence of Sh.'s re-
ligious views, see n. 324-8.
      1398-1402 **A . . . wer't**] BROOK (1976, p. 169): "*Hyperbole*, or exaggeration,
is especially used by women characters" in Sh. This passage illustrates "hyperbole
for vituperation." CLEMEN (1951, p. 199) finds it especially significant: "This magnificent and terrible image marks another decisive stage of the tragic development in
the first three acts. It expresses the sense of Leontes' irretrievable guilt and its effect
upon us is the more forcible as it is the only fully executed image in this scene. . . . It
forebodes the storm of the next scene." KRIER (1982, pp. 350-1): The "imagery is
all of sterility, desolation, manacling isolation, and suffering. In fact Leontes' next
sixteen years will be much like this; but even such a horrible time will work to his
renewal." LAROQUE (1974, p. 11): "Leontes' madness has transformed Sicilia into a
waste land, steeped in perpetual fast and mourning." HANKINS (1978, p. 56): "The
final sentence envisions some form of purgatorial expiation," but Paulina is saying

Ten thousand yeares together, naked, fasting,
Vpon a barren Mountaine, and still Winter   1400
In storme perpetuall, could not moue the Gods
To looke that way thou wer't.
    Leo. Go on, go on:
Thou canst not speake too much, I haue deseru'd
All tongues to talke their bittrest.   1405

---

just the opposite. HANKINS (1956, p. 492) had previously found "the barren mountain, winter, and perpetual storm . . . reminiscent" of the 12th-c. *Vision of Tundale*, in which the nobleman's wandering soul observes, among other hellish wonders, "a vast mountain over which was a narrow road, on the one side of which was fire and on the other ice and snow" (see Howard Rollin Patch, *The Other World* [Cambridge, Mass., 1950, p. 112]). As FREY ("Tragic Structure," 1978, p. 119) points out, "Paulina, at least momentarily, denies Leontes the power of effective repentance. . . . Shakespeare's materializing imagination will immediately produce a wintry storm and present onstage the violent death of Antigonus." ERICKSON (1982, p. 822): "Leontes plays the role of obedient son to mother Paulina, who dictates a period of 'fasting' to compensate for the oral deprivation Leontes imposed on Mamillius." ERICKSON apparently means Mamillius's loss of appetite (917).

    1398-9 **A . . . together**] COLLINS (ed. 1904-24?): "'A thousand prayers lasting for ten thousand years'; *i.e.* if you were to pray for ten thousand years. *Naked, fasting* agrees with the implied subject." But see the next n.

    1399 **together**] SCHMIDT (1875): "Without intermission."

    naked, fasting] The CLARKES (1879, p. 750): A spirited personification. FURNESS (ed. 1898): "But can 'fasting' be predicated of 'knees'? The subject must be *all this*, or a similar phrase. 'Knees' are merely equivalent to *prayers*; and 'naked' and 'fasting' refer to him who offers the prayers." DEIGHTON (ed. 1889): The knees are naked; the suppliants to whom they belong are fasting.

    1400 **still**] Always, continuously. See n. 200.

    1401 **could not moue**] DEIGHTON (ed. 1889): "The subject is 'A thousand loves [i.e., knees].'"

    1402 **To . . . wer't**] DEIGHTON (ed. 1889): "To turn their eyes in your direction." More literally, to look in the direction where you were. BOORMAN (ed. 1964): "I.e. to look upon you with favour."

    1403-5 **Go . . . bittrest**] GRIFFITH (1775, p. 109): "Our suffering, upon true penitence and contrition, not only [accepts?] all reproach thrown out against us with meekness and submission, but even encourag[es] and augment[s] the abuse, by joining in our own condemnation. This may possibly arise from a strong wish, or sanguine hope, that such a voluntary penance may in part be accepted, both by heaven and the world, as some sort of atonement for our crimes." GRIFFITH cites a further instance in 1424-35. HARTWIG (1972, p. 114): "In submitting to the shrew, Leontes makes partial amends for his previous tyranny. Paulina's fury does not abate easily, however, and she extends the verbal punishment of Leontes beyond humane limits [1409-23]. Her intense and bitter accusations produce another important effect aside from absorbing part of the hostility that Leontes' actions have generated: they convince the audience that Hermione is, in fact, dead." The audience, having no reason to disbelieve the vehement Paulina, has believed it from 1388.

    1405 **tongues to talke**] ABBOTT (§354): In impersonal sentences the infinitive with a noun may serve as subject or object (as here). Cf. 2775 and 1365-6. *Impersonal* means "not pertaining to . . . any particular person" (*OED* A.2).

Lord. Say no more;
How ere the businesse goes, you haue made fault
I'th boldnesse of your speech.
    Pau. I am sorry for't;
All faults I make, when I shall come to know them,   1410
I do repent: Alas, I haue shew'd too much
The rashnesse of a woman: he is toucht
To th'Noble heart. What's gone, and what's past helpe
Should be past greefe: Do not receiue affliction
At my petition; I beseech you, rather   1415

1414 receiue] revive LETTSOM *conj. in* DYCE1 (*errata*), HUD2
1415 my petition; . . . you,] my petition, . . . you, F2-F4, HUD2; my petition,
. . . you; ROWE1-HUD1, SING2, WH1, HAL, KTLY, PEN2; repetition, . . . you; COL2,
COL3, COL4

1407 **made fault**] KITTREDGE & RIBNER (ed. 1967): "Done wrong." For a similar
construction, see 151. The same idiom is found in *Luc.* 804 and *Son.* 54.6. See also
2728.

1409 **I . . . for't**] JOHNSON (ed. 1765): "Another instance of the sudden changes
incident to vehement and ungovernable minds." See n. 1336-57. HARDINGE (1818,
3:68), on the other hand: "How sweet is her answer! how noble! how ingenuous!"
Similarly, HERFORD (ed. 1916-): "Paulina's sudden relenting, at the first sign of Leontes's recognition of the wrong, again exemplifies the 'surprise' technique of the later
plays." WAYNE (1985, p. 181): "It is a fine joke on the tradition that after the shrew
had so often been forced to submit, here she does so too readily, and mistakenly, to
the wrong person." None seems to recognize that Paulina's assault on Leontes continues. See n. 1417-23.

1411-12 **Alas . . . woman**] HENDERSON & MCMANUS (1985, p. 54): Paulina
"expresses anxiety of being thought a shrew." At p. 119 they say, "Part of her [Pau-
lina's] complexity is ambivalence at her own assertiveness: . . . she apologizes to
him [Leontes] by casting herself into a stereotype. . . . As he once ignored her
words, so he commits himself to respecting all the words she shall utter in the future
[at 2812]." See the next n., however.

1412-13 **he . . . heart**] BOORMAN (ed. 1964): "Note the stage-direction in the
text." PARRY (ed. 1982): "Leontes is no doubt slumped, or bowed down, with grief."
Cf. nn. 2134-5, 2190, and 2634-5. GARDNER (1980, p. 63): "The sudden tenderness
that she feels for him is surely a guide for the audience." Paulina's forte is indirection,
however; see n. 1417-23.

1413-14 **What's . . . greefe**] "Never Grieve for that you cannot help" (TILLEY
G453). DENT also compares "Past Cure past care" (TILLEY C921). LEE (ed. 1907) finds
similar proverbial sayings in *R2* 2.3.171 (1282), *LLL* 5.2.28 (1915), and *Mac.* 3.2.11-
12 (1165-6). CALDECOTT (MS 1813-33) finds "in this sudden change of Paulina's
manner . . . much art & address, as well as Nature and Feeling."

1414-15 **Do . . . petition**] MINSHEU (1617, Petition): (1) "*Request . . .
supplication.*" (2) Generally signifies "*all* intreaties *made by an* inferior *to a* superior."
HUNTER (ed. 1872): "Do not give yourself up to affliction; at my petition, do not."
HUDSON (ed. 1880), confusedly: "'I beseech you, rather let me be punished as *at my
own request*'; that is, at her request, and not as by the sentence of the King." DELIUS
(ed. 1860) is echoed in part by FURNESS (ed. 1898): "Because I have entreated you to

Let me be punish'd, that haue minded you ·
Of what you should forget. Now (good my Liege)
Sir, Royall Sir, forgiue a foolish woman:
The loue I bore your Queene (Lo, foole againe)
Ile speake of her no more, nor of your Children: 1420
Ile not remember you of my owne Lord,
(Who is lost too:) take your patience to you,
And Ile say nothing.
    Leo. Thou didst speake but well,

1418 woman:] ~ ∧ POPE, HAN2
1422 take your . . . you] take you your . . . you ROWE3-CAP, DYCE2, HUD2,
KIT1; take your own . . . you AYS; take your . . . you, sir KTLY
1424 speake] say JOHN

---

be afflicted, do not give way to it." Paulina "now withdraws her words ['Thy . . . it'
(1366-71), 'But . . . dispaire' (1395-8)], and begs him not to be afflicted by them."
    1416 **minded**] JERVIS (1868): Reminded.
    1417-23 **Now . . . nothing**] GENTLEMAN (ed. 1774): "There is great art in pre-
tending she means not to wound him, yet strikes him three times." GRIFFITH (1775,
p. 109): "Her vindictive spirit appears plainly not to have yet subsided, but only taken
a different course, . . . for she continues still to accumulate her charges against him,
as if only by way of enumerating the articles of her forgiveness."
    1417-18 **Now . . . Royall Sir**] FURNESS (ed. 1898) seems to contradict the opin-
ions expressed in n. 1417-23: "The repetition betokens . . . deep emotion and entreaty. Paulina imagines that the King does not listen to her, so deeply bowed is his
head and closely veiled are his eyes."
    1417 **good my Liege**] For the transposition, see n. 390.
    1418 **a foolish woman**] Regarding the sincerity of this, see n. 956-9.
    1419 **Lo, foole againe**] According to the CLARKES (1879, p. 465), *lo* is said "self-
rebukingly." PAFFORD (ed. 1963), however: "All the same, Paulina constantly *does*
remind him of those he has injured."
    1420 **Ile . . . Children**] TREWIN (1978, p. 264): "The fifth act suggests that she
goes on doing so for sixteen years."
    1421 **remember**] JOHNSON (1755): "Remind."
    1422-3 **Who . . . nothing**] In scanning, COLLIER (ed. 1875) gives *patience*
three syllables. ABBOTT (§480) gives *your* two, because monosyllabic words preceded
by a long vowel or diphthong (e.g., *fear*, *fire*) "are frequently so pronounced." He
finds an emphatic antithesis in *your*. KNOWLES (privately) thinks "the pause at the
colon serves as an unaccented syllable."
    1422 **Who . . . too**] LETTSOM (MS 1840-65): "Antigonus was not yet lost; much
less known to be so." PARRY (ed. 1982) believes that her intuition is at work; LENZ
(1986, p. 97), that Sh., disregarding the logic of the plot, prepares us for the bear;
and HATTORI (1982, p. 96), that "we are allowed no time to ponder the question"
and that this scene occurs later than 3.3. See n. 1436 and, for *lost*, n. 1122-4.
    take . . . you] ROLFE (ed. 1879): "Have patience; as in [*H8* 5.1.105 (2901-
2)]," Sh.'s scene. DENT compares "Take a man's (good) Heart to thee" (H328.1).
    1424-35 **Thou . . . sorrowes**] See n. 1403-5 for the acceptance of reproach
as a kind of penance.
    1424 **but**] The CLARKES (ed. 1865): "'No other than', 'only.'"

When most the truth: which I receyue much better,   1425
Then to be pittied of thee. Prethee bring me
To the dead bodies of my Queene, and Sonne,
One graue shall be for both: Vpon them shall
The causes of their death appeare (vnto
Our shame perpetuall) once a day, Ile visit   1430
The Chappell where they lye, and teares shed there

1429-30 (vnto . . . perpetuall)] ∧ ~ . . . ~ ; ROWE1+

1426-35 **Prethee . . . sorrowes**] WAIN (1964, p. 221): "Mamillius is dead, Perdita presumed so, and Hermione [evidently] has died. Under this threefold blow, Leontes, his life given over to repentance, becomes 'the man [who] dwelt by a churchyard' [623-5] and acts out the sad winter's tale." Considering the passage as typical of the style of the last plays, FRYE (1970, p. 195): "The rhythm here is pronounced, and . . . the irregularities . . . are sufficient to provide an underlying tension with the blank verse pattern: four lines end on unstressed syllables [1425, 1426, 1430, 1432], four sentences begin after full stops in the middle of the line, and all the lines except one [1427] are fully enjambed. Even more characteristic . . . is the remoteness of its emotions . . . : Leontes must ask to be 'led' to 'these sorrows', as though they existed objectively at some remove from his own immediate experience. . . . We must never abandon hope that grief will be overcome with gladness, so . . . Leontes declares that tears 'shall be my recreation.' "

1426-32 **Prethee . . . recreation**] As lines 3353-5 indicate, Leontes does see Hermione's body and he does pray at her grave daily. At 3353-5, Leontes understandably does not mention Mamillius.

1428-34 **Vpon . . . it**] BROWN (1962, pp. 222-3): "No love is reawakened when Leontes is forced to recognize Hermione's truth. Paulina speaks of the 'sweet'st, dear'st creature' [1388], but Leontes does not. In his isolation . . . he has turned from accusation to grief and guilt: fearing dispossession he has neither given in love nor received its bounty; now his physical isolation mirrors that of his heart." Cf. n. 1355-7. PYLE (1969, p. 62): "He who scorned Antigonus for being 'woman-tired' [991] now humbly bows to Paulina's rule."

1428 **One . . . both**] CARRINGTON (1956): "The funeral of Hermione was either forgotten or it was a sham." NATHAN (1957), however, thinks there may have been a funeral which Leontes, according to custom, did not attend, for in none of his plays does Sh. "portray a burial scene with the husband following the corpse of his wife."

them] DEIGHTON (ed. 1889): "The one grave which contains the two bodies." HAPPÉ (1969): "I.e. the gravestones."

1430-4 **once . . . it**] YOUNG (1972, p. 135): "For sixteen years both he and Hermione will be, in effect, outside time, suspended beyond the tragic, linear movement which brought them to this fate, and not yet part of the comic, cyclic phase which will restore them to Perdita and to each other." KERNAN (1975, 3:413): He accepts "his guilt in Christian humility." SANDERS (1987, p. 56): "Leontes' proposals for his future 'recreation' sound perilously close to a cult of guilt. . . . Yet he isn't proposing to fade wispily into a necrophiliac revenant: there is some strenuousness in his resolutions, and some manfulness."

1430 **Our**] DEIGHTON (ed. 1889): "Speaking as a king."

Shall be my recreation. So long as Nature
Will beare vp with this exercise, so long
I dayly vow to vse it. Come, and leade me
To these sorrowes.   *Exeunt*   1435

1432-5 *Four verse lines ending* nature . . . exercise, . . . Come . . . sorrowes.
JOHN1-v1773; *ending* nature . . . long . . . Come, . . . sorrowes. v1778-RANN, PEN2;
ending as . . . exercise, . . . Come, . . . sorrowes. v1793- SING1, HAL; *ending* long
then as v1793 KTLY
    1432 So] *Om.* HAN
    1435 To] Unto WALKER (1860, 1:271) *conj.*, GLO, DYCE2, HUD2, WH2, PEL1
        sorrowes] my sorrows HAN, CAP

1432-5 **Shall . . . sorrowes**] SCHANZER (ed. 1969) likes the lineation of ed.
1778 because "the long pause after *Come*, which fills out the line, is an expression
of the king's anguish."
    1432 **recreation**] JOHNSON (1755): "Relief after toil or pain." SCHMIDT (1875)
believes that the word is used (ironically) in its usual sense of "diversion, amusement,"
but FURNESS (ed. 1898) prefers the Latin sense "restoration to health, re-creation."
HERFORD (ed. 1916-): "Amusement." He rejects "restoration" because of Leontes's
dedication of himself to a lifetime of grief (1432-4), but CHARLTON (ed. 1916) does
not: "The means of bringing me back to life and sanity." WILSON (ed. 1931) sides
with HERFORD; BETHELL (ed. 1956) prefers both *pastime* and *recreation*, "used of
Leontes' spiritual health." MARSH (1962; 1969, p. 139): "His tears, and his full realization of what he has lost, are in the truest sense his recreation, his rebirth back into
life."
    1433 **beare vp**] JOHNSON (1755, citing this line): "Stand firm without falling."
JOHNSON (1773): "Not to sink; not to faint or fail." ORGEL (ed. 1996): "Endure."
    exercise] SCHMIDT (1874): "Act of devotion." Though not for this passage, he
also gives "any kind of habitual practice," a meaning that SCHANZER (ed. 1969) believes is also intended here. BETHELL (ed. 1956): "The obvious meaning of both words
[this and *recreation*] in their context is metaphorical, taken from sport, and their
deeper meaning literal."
    1434 **I . . . it**] HUNTER (ed. 1872): "I vow to use it daily." As to the position of
the adverb, he compares "That you to day promised to tell me of" (*MV* 1.1.121 [130])
and "Of some thing nerely that concernes your selues" (*MND* 1.1.126 [135]). KIT-
TREDGE & RIBNER (ed. 1967, Use it): "Carry it on."
    1434-5 **Come . . . sorrowes**] FREY (*Vast Romance*, 1980, pp. 137-8): "To
witness Leontes reaching for Paulina's hand . . . is to measure the distance he has
traveled. The first image we had of him was [at 32], but then we saw Hermione take
her hand from Leontes and give it to Polixenes, and we heard Leontes' ranting disgust
[188]. . . . Now . . . he demonstrates graphically the degree to which his misogyny and his mistrust of human contact have been replaced by a search for sympathy
and trust." No ed. collated directs that Leontes reach for Paulina's hand. DRAPER
(1985, p. 26): "The scene—and the play's first movement—ends with Leontes in a
posture of penitence that is unqualified, and which he envisages as lasting for the rest
of his life. It is a penitence, however, performed for its own sake, without belief that

Scæna Tertia.   3.3

it will win him any kind of compensation. The one word that may ambiguously carry a more positive suggestion is 'recreation,'" for which see n. 1432. RIEMER (1980, p. 134): "The play's narrative comes to a catastrophic and unsatisfactory conclusion before the end of Act III is reached—unsatisfactory because few of the demands of drama and of the theatre have been fulfilled. It is no more than a sordid tale of sexual mistrust which has its unfortunate and not at all edifying conclusion. Because of these foreshortenings, the audience comes to expect a reversal of fortunes: the play is clearly too short to end at the conclusion of III. ii. . . . . There is no direction for the play to take but towards happiness and reconciliation."

1435 **sorrowes**] DEIGHTON (ed. 1889): "These sorrowful sights, the dead bodies of his wife and child," but Leontes may mean only the life of repentance he has just described. GRENE (1967, p. 80): "This is the guise in which we are to find him again when we revisit Sicilia." UPHAUS (1981, p. 76): "All possible avenues of individual initiative have [now] been exhausted, save for the cryptic verdict from Apollo which, in the eyes of the characters, may appear superfluous. . . . The play's tragic action has spent itself, but the play also seems to be at a standstill."

Exeunt] Leontes now disappears until 5.1 (2725), approximately one-third of the play later. DAY & TREWIN (1932, p. 94) tell how F. R. Benson, performing in Stratford in 1903, went rowing on the Avon during the hiatus, overstayed the time, and reentered wearing his gray flannels.

1436 *Scæna Tertia*] DANIEL (1879, p. 178): "*An interval* of a few days must be allowed for Antigonus's journey." This is the fifth day represented. HUDSON (1855; 1872, 1:455): "While the play . . . divides itself into two parts, these are skilfully woven together by a happy stroke of art. [This] scene . . . not only finishes the action of the first three [acts], but by an apt and unforced transition begins that of the other two; the two parts of the drama being smoothly drawn into the unity of a continuous whole by the introduction of the old Shepherd and his son at the close of the one and the opening of the other. This natural arrangement saves the imagination from being disturbed by any yawning and obtrusive gap of time, notwithstanding the lapse of so many years in the interval." KNIGHT (1947; 1965, p. 97): "Our action enters, as it were, the elemental background of all tragedy; the wild and rugged Bohemian coast, with threatening storm. We are behind the scenes, where the organizing powers fabricate our human plot." HERFORD (ed. 1916-) is less favorably impressed: "This scene distinctly resembles in topic various scenes of the other Romances—the storm-scene in *The Tempest*, the hunting-scene in *Cymbeline*—but has no pretensions to dramatic quality. The fate of Antigonus is too unrelated to his character or actions to be tragic, too sudden or casual to be even moving; and for modern audiences it comes dangerously near to undesigned comedy—a lapse even in the confessedly loose Romance technique. The harrowing details later provided [at 1525 ff.] do not alter the case." According to CHARLTON (ed. 1916), these harrowing details "are presented to us from a fresh and a jovial standpoint: we hear of them

*Enter Antigonus, a Marriner, Babe, Sheepe-
heard, and Clowne.*

Ant. Thou art perfect then, our ship hath toucht vpon
The Desarts of *Bohemia.*   1440

1437 *A desart Country; the Sea at a little distance.* ROWE; ad. *Changes to Bohemia.* POPE1+ (−PEL1, CLN2, PEN2, OXF2) (*subst.*)
    a Marriner] Mariners HAL
1437-8 *Sheepeheard, and Clowne*] Om. ROWE1+
1440-1 *One verse line* mCAP2, v1793+

---

out of the mouth of a simple shepherd and his more simple son, the Clown. We know
it is a lucky day and that good deeds and joy are to come from it." COGHILL (1958,
p. 35): "We are passing from tears to laughter, from death to life." UPHAUS (1981, p.
77) elaborates: Shakespeare uses "this short scene as the exhaustion of tragedy (in
death) and the provisional entrance of pastoral comedy (in the natural reemergence
of life associated with spring)." PARRY (ed. 1982): "This scene's pivotal function . . . is marked in the shift from Antigonus' courtly verse to the old Shepherd's
rustic prose. . . ." BROWN (1962, p. 223): "The course of the narrative, which had
been largely controlled by his [Leontes's] actions, now seems more the result of
chance or fate." HATTORI (1982, p. 97): "Despite its finality [3.2] or indeed the entire
tragic first half of the play does not seem to depart altogether. We *do* care about
Paulina's [lost lord]. . . . How did he die? How does she know? . . . What has
happened to the baby? The business of this scene is to answer these questions immediately. . . . It is a kind of flashback."
    1437 *Antigonus*] CHARLTON (ed. 1916): He makes "Perdita's coming to Bohemia
a thing designed and not merely fortuitous as it is in Greene"; see p. 633. BETHELL
(ed. 1956): "The name Antigonus occurs in Plutarch [see n. 3374 above] but also in
Josephus' *Antiquities of the Jews* (which would be familiar in Shakespeare's day),
where it is borne by . . . the last truly Jewish king of Judaea, who was
. . . succeeded by the non-Jewish Herod, in whose reign Our Lord was
born. . . . This transition scene [3.3] is thus surely intended to represent the movement from Old Testament to New, . . . from the spiritual death of sin to the new
life of grace, as we move from tragedy to comedy." Whatever one may think of the
movement from the Old to the New Testament, Sh. may have known of Josephus,
though indirectly. Because of an allusion to "the Mutines of Ierusalem" in *Jn.* 2.1.378
(692), THEOBALD (1909, p. 394) thinks Sh. must have read "the original text of Josephus"; it has subsequently been shown that "the story was well known c. 1590,"
there having been at least one play on the civil war in Jerusalem (see E. A. J. Honigmann, ed. *Jn.*, 1965, 2.1.378 n.). Nevertheless, the chance of the Jewish Antigonus
being recognized in Sh.'s character is nil.
    1438 *Clowne*] He enters at 1520. Antigonus departs for good at 1500. WEBSTER
(1942, p. 45) suggests that one actor took both parts.
    1439-40 **Thou . . . Bohemia**] SPRAGUE (1935, pp. 34-5) quotes Sidney—"the
player, when he cometh in, must ever begin by telling where he is"—and adds "sometimes the information is contained in [a] question and merely corroborated in the
reply."
    1439 **perfect**] JOHNSON (1755, citing this line): "Safe; Out of danger." This is
wrong. JOHNSON (ed. 1765): "*Certain, well assured,* or *well informed*" (JOHNSON,

1773, and *OED, a.* 6, citing this line). REA (1932, p. 84), pointing out that Sh. some-times falls naturally into the language of the theater (e.g., "that question's out of my part" [*TN* 1.5.179 (474)]), cites this as an instance.

1440 Desarts] MINSHEU (1617, Desart): "Solitarie place." See "Wildernesse."

Bohemia] SNIDER (1877, 2:71): "Bohemia . . . is wholly different [from Si-cilia]; it is a poor, mountainous, uncivilized region, inhabited by shepherds. But it is free from the strife and calamity of Sicilia; its people are simple and humble, yet at the same time they are joyous and humane. . . . Pastoral life . . . a primitive con-dition of man, almost before evil enters and introduces strife, will be de-picted. . . . Bohemia is . . . the means whereby those whom Leontes has driven away are restored to him."

JONSON ("Conversations," 1:138): "Sheakspear jn a play brought jn a number of men saying they had suffered Shipwrack jn Bohemia, where y^r is no Sea neer by some 100 Miles." (Because of "a number," HALLIWELL, ed. 1859, alters *a Marriner* in 1437.) GILDON (1710, p. 336): "The making *Bohemia* of an Inland, a maritime Country" is copied from *Pandosto*, in which Sicilia also has a coast (see p. 633), yet HANMER (ed. 1743–4), to prove Sh. above such an error, devises a crazy explanation: Although Sh. found *Bohemia* in "the paltry old book of *Dorastus* and *Faunia*, . . . he removed this impropriety and placed the scene in *Bithynia*, which . . . the first Transcribers or Printers" might have corrupted back to *Bohemia*. LENNOX (1753, 2:87), sensibly, will have none of this: Sh. in *TGV* "makes *Protheus* [sic] travel from *Verona* to *Milan* by Sea. Yet both those Cities are inland. . . . Unless this Blunder can be also charged upon the Transcribers, or Printers, 'tis reasonable to suppose that *Shakespear*, who was guilty of the one, might be so of the other." Moreover, MALONE (ed. 1790) observes that JONSON's remark was made in 1619, before *WT* was printed. KNIGHT (ed. 1842, p. 13): "It is quite impossible to imagine that he who, when it was necessary to be precise, as in the Roman plays, has . . . perplexed this play with such anom-alies through ignorance or even carelessness."

Where Greene, from whom the location of the Delphic oracle on an isle also derives (see n. 1147), found a coastal Bohemia is unknown, though BULLOUGH (1975, 8:119) notes that he was generally indebted to "romances such as the Spanish *Mirror of Knighthood* . . . and the *Amadis de Gaule*," from which the name *Garinter* was drawn. Possibly one of these works was *Florambel de Lucea*, which, as O. T. (1904) remarks, gives Bohemia *un puerto llamado Esterlin*, according to Clémencin's note on *Don Quijote* (ed. 1833, 1.3:381). The five books of *Florambel* were published in Spain in 1532, rpt. 1548. The reference to Bohemia occurs in book 2. CAPELL (1783, 2.4:169), wildly: Although he rejected the names of Greene's characters "partly from judgment and partly from his ear's goodness," Sh. could not alter the name of Polix-enes's maritime kingdom because its connection with Sicilia had been too firmly fixed in the public's mind by *Pandosto*. This is probably nonsense. LANG (1894, p. 716): "This process [of national inversion] makes it inevitable that Bohemia [as well as Sicilia] must have a seaboard." FARMER (in STEEVENS, ed. 1778) found in *The Life of Edward Lord Herbert of Cherbury* (1770, p. 134) that De Luynes, the favorite of Louis XIII but no favorite of Lord Herbert's, "when there was a question made about some business in Bohemia, . . . demanded whether it was an inland Country, or lay upon the Sea?" The idea in another form seems to be repeated by COLLIER (1836, p. 21), who finds in *Taylor his Trauels . . . to . . . Prague* (1620, sig. A2^v): "*Gregory Gandergoose*, an Alderman of *Gotham* catches me by the goll, demaunding if *Bo-hemia* bee a great Towne . . . and whether the last fleet of shipps be ariued there." Even LIPPMANN (1891), having noticed a similar confusion in Tschamser's *Annals of the Barefooted Friars of Thann*, argues that *Bohemia* actually signifies *Apulia*, the region in southern Italy. JUSSERAND ("*Winter's Tale*," 1925; 1968, p. 229) reports a proposal "to understand Styria [in Austria], which was under Bohemian rule in 1270."

ULRICI (1839; trans. 1876, 1:256–7): "It is still very doubtful whether Shakspeare

did not intentionally insert these supposed proofs of schoolboy ignorance, in order . . . to intimate that his poems had their roots in the free, shifting soil of
fancy, . . . to raise the spectator . . . into the sunny regions of poetry." BETHELL
(ed. 1956): "It would appear . . . that there was a joke of the 'Swiss navy' type
current about 1620 both in England and abroad, of which the subject was Bohemia's
well-known non-existent coastline. Perhaps it originated from *Pandosto*, which was
widely known and had been translated into French in 1615. It could scarcely have
arisen from the unpublished *Winter's Tale*. It is, however, unlikely that a joke so
widespread would arise from a piece of bad geography in a novel at a time when
such mistakes were not uncommon. If it were an old joke of unknown origin, then
Shakespeare, and even Greene, might have been aware of it and used the sea-coast
of Bohemia to imply that the Bohemia of this 'old tale' is to be found not on the
contemporary map of Europe but in the realms of the imagination." If everyone knew
the joke, why was JONSON not amused? Because, according to GURR (1983, p. 422),
"it was Jonson whom Shakespeare was teasing for his insistence on realism. . . .
Jonson fell precisely into Shakespeare's trap. . . . Shakespeare knew what he was
doing, because in order to give Bohemia its coast he deliberately switched the two
kingdoms of *Pandosto* . . . to flout geographical realism, and to underline the unreality of place in the play." If this is so, then Greene teased JONSON first; for the
deliberate invocation of unreality, cf. KNIGHT and SIMROCK, below. Following
BETHELL, MUIR (*Last Periods*, 1961, p. 46): The change "was presumably a hint to
the audience that his action was not to take place in the real Bohemia—to whose
ruler Princess Elizabeth was to be married—but somewhere beyond space or time."
MUIR is probably mistaken: in 1611, when *WT* was performed (see p. 602), Queen
Anne was busily trying to arrange a marriage between Princess Elizabeth and King
Philip of Spain. The marriage contract with Frederick V, the Elector Palatine, was
signed on 16 May 1612 and the marriage took place in 1613 (*DNB*, 6:652-3).

After and because of Sh., the seacoast persisted. FARMER (in STEEVENS, ed. 1773,
10:Pp4ᵛ) remembers that in *Tristram Shandy* the king of Bohemia takes "great pleasure and delight in navigation and all sorts of sea-affairs" (ed. Melvyn New & Joan
New, 1978-84 , 2:692; they observe in 3:513-14 that Sterne may have derived the
Shn. idea from Burke). ANON. (1811) perhaps facetiously, although HALLIWELL (8:36-
7) takes the point seriously: During the reign of Ottocar II, Bohemia extended to the
Adriatic, so that—in the mid-13th c.—the country did have a seacoast. KNIGHT (ed.
1841, Comedies 2:340-1) should have put the whole matter to rest: "Bohemia is but
the name for a wild country upon the sea. . . . Jonson . . . committed the unfair-
ness of imputing to Shakspere the fault, if fault it be, which he knew to be the common
property of the romantic drama." SIMROCK (1831; 1850, p. 103), similarly: "We think
that this error rather suited the fabulous nature of the story, which runs into the
region of fable and the age of poesy, better than the most accurate geographical
definition." HUNTER (1964, pp. 40-1) notes that Sh. "was not exceptional in this
[geographical inexactitude]," for writers of romances used place-names "for their
associations, not for their reality." VERPLANCK (ed. 1845) nevertheless learnedly observes that Bohemia takes its name from the ancient Boii, two branches of which
lived on the coast, as a scholar like Greene would have known. Similar geographical
and historical speculations may be found in KOZMIAN (1875), LATHAM (1877), and X
(1904); other attempts to show that in remote times Bohemia had a coast or that
certain coastal places were known as Bohemia are summarized by FURNESS (ed. 1898).

By the early 20th c., the matter had been drawn into perspective; JUSSERAND (in
LEE, ed. 1907, p. xiii): Sh.'s "one general rule was that all distant towns are by the
seaside; and if they are not, they should be and shall. The Rome, the Mantua, the
Padua, the Verona, the Milan, the Florence of his stage are all washed by the sea."
KITTREDGE (ed. 1936) restates KNIGHT: "Had Bohemia a seacoast? Yes. When? At some
indeterminate date B.C., when Leontes was king of Sicilia—that Leontes who married

Mar. I (my Lord) and feare   1441
We haue Landed in ill time: the skies looke grimly,
And threaten present blusters. In my conscience

1441 my Lord] *Om.* HAN

---

a daughter of the Emperor of Russia and was a boyhood friend of Polixenes, King of
Bohemia." For GERVINUS's opinion that the "mistakes" in the plot were deliberate,
seen nn. 0, 1147, 1440, and 1548–9. HARTWIG (1972, p. 125 n.), too, finds the error
no error: "In a play where other anomalies and anachronisms figure so clearly in the
methods of self-conscious artistry, surely this error has a similar effect of drawing the
audience's attention to a 'fact' which is 'fiction.'" Rather oddly at this late date, BUL-
LOUGH (1975, 8:125): "The most probable explanation is that Sicily was well known
for crimes of jealousy and revenge, while Bohemia with its fabled sea-coast was currently a frequent centre for romantic adventure." FREY (*Vast Romance*, 1980, p. 15)
also: "Suppose the error was intended. Suppose that Shakespeare knew as well as the
next man that he was telling a 'fabulous' tale and that the association in space of a
seacoast with Bohemia was no odder than, say, his association, in time, of Julio Romano with the Delphic oracle, and that both associations could help support an
atmosphere of dreamed reality." Despite CAPELL and the rest, one wonders how many
in the audience would have recognized the mistake; neither *Sicilia* nor *Bohemia*
could have been an Elizabethan commonplace.

Discussing Sh.'s "anachronisms and anatopisms" generally, SQUIRE (1935, p. 32):
"This sort of 'error' resembles a good many other things in the theatre: everything
depends on whether the audience 'minds', whether its illusion is, however slightly,
impaired." One guesses that in this instance the audience is perfectly indifferent. As
for Bohemia's place in the plot, LETTSOM (MS 1840–65): "A[ntigonus] seems to have
intended to go to Bohemia, perhaps in consequence of the dream or vision. It would
perhaps have been better and more natural if Leontes had enjoined him to expose
the child in the territory of its supposed father." In the dream, Hermione does not
order the child taken to that country; when she appears, the ship evidently lies off
its coast. For more on the question and Sh.'s use of *Pandosto* generally, see p. 656.

1442–3 **We . . . blusters**] THIRLBY (MS 1747–53) asks a practical question:
"Then are you not safer on shore than aboard?" The Mariner, however, may hope to
prevent his ship's being driven onto the lee shore, which, unhappily for him, is what
happens.

1443 **present blusters**] TAYLER (1964, p. 129): "A storm at sea [is] the archetypal
image of birth and death." Because Antigonus and the ship are lost but Perdita is
found, "the scene . . . recalls the disruption and chaos of the earlier action
and . . . anticipates the restoration of harmony in the last act." Cf. 1553–4. Of the
many storms in Sh.'s plays, KNIGHT (1932, p. 26): "Plots vary, tempests persist. It is
always the same tempest. . . . Ultimately we must call the Shakespearian tempest
something like this: 'Shakespeare's intuition of discord and conflict'. But even that is
to translate the symbol: therefore we should improve it to 'Shakespeare's intuition of
tempestuousness at the heart of existence.'" BLUESTONE (1974, p. 168): "The storm
indicates moral disorder. Without doctrinaire or moralistic insistence, the storm descends in retribution for the abandonment of Perdita."

present] SCHMIDT (1875): "Immediate." SCHANZER (ed. 1969): "Imminent."

blusters] JOHNSON (1755): "Roar; noise; tumult." SCHMIDT (1874): "Boisterous
tempest."

In my conscience] SCHMIDT (1874): "In truth, indeed" (*OED* 9). MAXWELL
(ed. 1956): In my opinion. KERMODE (ed. 1963) thinks "something of the modern
meaning" is also present.

The heauens with that we haue in hand, are angry,
And frowne vpon's.   1445
   Ant. Their sacred wil's be done: go get a-boord,
Looke to thy barke, Ile not be long before
I call vpon thee.   (2A6^{vb}
   Mar. Make your best haste, and go not
Too-farre i'th Land:'tis like to be lowd weather,   1450
Besides this place is famous for the Creatures
Of prey, that keepe vpon't.
   Antig. Go thou away,
Ile follow instantly.
   Mar. I am glad at heart   1455
To be so ridde o'th businesse.   *Exit*
   Ant. Come, poore babe;
I haue heard (but not beleeu'd) the Spirits o'th'dead

1445 *Om.* HARN
1446 go get] get F2-F4; get thee ROWE1-JOHN2
1448-9 *One verse line* mCAP2, VALPY, OXF1, CLN2, SIG, BEV, OXF2
1448 vpon] on HAN
1450 Too-farre] Too fair AYS2
1454-8 *Four verse lines ending* instantly. . . . business. . . . heard, . . . dead
JOHN, v1773; *three, ending* heart . . . babe:— . . . dead mCAP2, v1793+

1444-5 **The . . . vpon's**] For similar exhibitions of Heaven's anger, see nn.
1156-7 and 1330-1.
   1444 **that . . . hand**] KITTREDGE & RIBNER (ed. 1967): "What we are doing."
   1447 **barke**] MINSHEU (1617): "Little shippe, or great boat, or hoy [small coastal
vessel]." Bohemia must have lain at no great distance from Sicilia.
   1450 **i'th Land**] RIDLEY (ed. 1935): "Inland."
     lowd weather] TREWIN (1978, p. 264) refers to the storm as a blizzard, but
lowd means simply "loud" (*OED, a.* 1b). SCHMIDT (1874, Loud): "Boisterous, turbulent."
   1451-2 **this . . . vpon't**] HERFORD (ed. 1916-): "This is Antigonus's (and our)
only warning of his coming fate," for which see n. 1500. For another, remote, warning, see 1119.
   1452 **keepe**] HUNTER (ed. 1872): "Have their haunts." The CLARKES (1879, p.
563): "Dwell."
   1455-6 **I . . . businesse**] WEINSTOCK (1971, p. 458): "Shakespeare . . . has
the sailor pay with his life for committing a sin of omission," that is, for not intervening
to save Perdita. He contrasts (p. 459) Camillo's effort to stem Leontes's slander of
Hermione (371-6).
   1458-95 **I . . . this**] TILLYARD (1938, p. 77): "There is nothing in the play so
melodramatic, so remote from ordinary life as this speech." BETHELL (ed. 1956): "The
verse . . . at times seems to burlesque an outmoded type of melodramatic 'vision'
poetry—such as *The Mirror for Magistrates*, with its series of informative ghosts—
and this prevents the audience from taking it too seriously and leaves them emotionally free to speculate about the nature of the vision." BETHELL goes on to describe the

"surprising mixture of stylized burlesque and serious significance" (e.g., the positions of the head, the three bows, the gasp), which he considers parodic of "an earlier style." Others discover no parody. HOLBROOK (1964, p. 173): The speech is "formal, distanced, masque-like." NEVO (1987, p. 117): "It is a premonition of his own death."

1458–83 **I . . . this**] Several explanations of Antigonus's remarkable experience have been offered. One is that he may have seen a ghost or something so like a ghost as hardly to be distinguished. CLARK (1936, p. 167): "The one instance in Shakespeare where the supernatural presence of a living being is recorded." (But see SCHANZER below.) WILSON (ed. 1931): "Antigonus touches upon one of the standing controversies of the age, and declares himself on the side of the Protestant doctors," though which side that was is unclear. WILSON refers to his own introduction to LAVATER (1572; ed. 1929), in which two Protestant attitudes toward ghosts are described: "The orthodox Protestant conclusion was that ghosts, while occasionally they might be angels, were generally nothing but devils, who assumed the form of departed friends or relatives in order to work bodily or spiritual harm" (p. xvi). Yet a few people were "frankly and entirely skeptical. . . . Apparitions are either the illusion of melancholic minds or flat knavery on the part of some rogue. . . . The doctors thus furiously raged together over the meaning of spectral appearances" (p. xvii). CRAIG (1948, p. 335): Hermione's appearance "in a vision . . . seems to indicate that Shakespeare [at this point in the play's composition] thought of Hermione as dead" (see n. 2724). BETHELL (ed. 1956) adds: "The traditional Catholic attitude (to which a High Anglican would incline) was that for some purposes, good and ill, the dead were themselves permitted to return. Antigonus, it seems, had previously taken the Protestant line [that a spirit had assumed human form or that the figure was illusory] but was converted by the vision he goes on to describe. The matter is complicated for the audience by the fact that *in this instance* he was wrong: Hermione was not dead. Was the vision angelic (to assure the proper disposal of Perdita) or diabolic (attempting to induce despair in Antigonus and the destruction of Perdita), or was it meant to be an appearance of Hermione's separated soul during the period of her unconsciousness after the trial? The audience does not yet know that Hermione is alive: they would be divided into the well-known Protestant and Catholic camps, since the evidence appeared compatible with either theory. Later, at the end of the play, if their minds recurred to the vision, both parties would be forced to a reconsideration and possible revision." One wonders whether these doctrinal distinctions would occur to anyone at a compelling moment in a theatrical fiction (or later).

Restating a point made by HUNTER (1954, p. 25), MUIR (1969, pp. 93–4): "The vision behaves as a ghost, chooses a name for her daughter, and prophesies Antigonus' death. I think there can be no doubt that even if Shakespeare did not intend Hermione to be dead at this point in the play, he intended us to think so." This seems obvious; if Hermione is not believed dead, the statue scene (5.3) could create wonder only in the characters, not in us. Hence PARRY (ed. 1982), among others: "The account of his vision . . . confirms our impression that Hermione is dead." SCHANZER (ed. 1969, p. 15), moreover: "There is no precedent in Elizabethan drama for the spirit of a living person appearing to others either in dream or waking." KNOWLES (privately), however: "Certainly one can have a guilty or premonitory dream of living persons, as Clarence does of Richard [*R3* 1.4.9–63 (845–99)], and that may be all that happens here." SPENCER ("Artistry," 1970, p. 74), nevertheless: "We do not expect to be misled by his [Antigonus's] conviction that Hermione is dead, any more than we expect to be told a direct lie by Paulina [in 1386–95]. Shakespeare seems to have been taking great care to deceive us." PROUDFOOT (1976, p. 72): The "simplest effect [of the apparition] is to reinforce our sense that she is dead (though our scepticism may be aroused by the ghost's lies)." Proudfoot's parenthesis is puzzling; the ghost is entirely truthful.

A minority holds that the figure is not exactly a ghost but some other spiritual

May walke againe: if such thing be, thy Mother
Appear'd to me last night: for ne're was dreame   1460
So like a waking. To me comes a creature,
Sometimes her head on one side, some another,
I neuer saw a vessell of like sorrow
So fill'd, and so becomming: in pure white Robes

1461 a waking] awaking mTBY4 *conj.*, PEN1, SIG
1462 on] is on F2-F4
1463 sorrow$_\wedge$] $\sim$, CAP+
1464 becomming] o'er-running COL2, COL3, COL4, HUD2

---

manifestation. MACDONALD (1883, p. 156): "Convinced of the reality of the vision, Antigonus obeys; and the whole marvellous result depends on this obedience. Therefore the vision must be intended for a genuine one. But how could it be, if Hermione is not dead . . . ?" The answer is that "at the time she appeared to him, she was still lying in that deathlike swoon, into which she fell when the news of the loss of her son reached her." RANNEY (1893, p. 500), similarly: "In times of great personal distress . . . there is something that may leave the body, having sufficient resemblance to the living form as to be recognized by others. . . . It is a phantasm of the living. . . . Believing himself to have been awake and in his normal mind, his [Antigonus's] inference is that Hermione is dead—a very reasonable one." The reasonable view of this matter, if one is possible, is SCHANZER's (ed. 1969): "Shakespeare leaves us purposely uncertain whether what Antigonus experienced was a dream or an apparition." For "the shadows of a dream" that become "visible hallucinations," see LITTLEDALE (1916, 1:534-6).

1461 **waking**] *OED* (*vbl. sb.* 1, citing this line): "The action of remaining awake or sitting up at night." KNOWLES (privately): "A participle used elliptically for a substantive: 'a dream so like a waking perception.'"

1462 **some**] CAPELL (1783 [1774], 1:glos.): "Some times."

another] For *another* as *the other*, see ABBOTT §88.

1463-4 **I . . . becomming**] CAPELL (1783, 2.4:172): A "scripture-metaphor . . . : the image . . . of extream sorrow, managed with great decorum." Possibly CAPELL is thinking of Mary Magdalene, who washed Christ's feet with her tears (Luke 7:37-8) and who wept again at the sepulchre (John 20:11), or, like HERFORD (ed. 1916-), simply of "the weaker vessel" (1 Pet. 3:7). For *vessell*, SCHMIDT (1875): "A person," and WILSON (ed. 1931): "Commonly used of the body, as the receptacle of the soul." Both WILSON and SCHMIDT cite "Now is that Noble Vessell full of griefe" (*JC* 5.5.13 [2655]). PAFFORD (ed. 1963): "The association of a woman in flowing white robes with a ship under full sail was probably traditional by 1611." His only evidence, however, is Romeo's "A sayle, a sayle," followed by Mercutio's "Two two, a shert and a smocke," with reference to the approach of the Nurse and Peter (*Rom.* 2.4.102-3 [1202-3]). Moreover, it is hard to see how the analogy is useful here, despite the fact that Antigonus was seaborne.

For *becoming*, MINSHEU (1617) gives "decent"; JOHNSON (1755), very suitably for this instance, "that which pleases by an elegant propriety; graceful" (*OED, ppl.a.* 1). STAUNTON (ed. 1859), citing "becomed" in *Rom.* 4.2.26 (2452): "Self-restrained," but the word there is usually glossed as "befitting." LETTSOM (in DYCE, ed. 1864) objects that "becomming" can be applied neither to *vessel* nor to *Hermione.* "A *becoming bonnet, colour,* or *attitude,* I can understand; but what can be said to *a becoming young lady,* or *a becoming queen?*" DEIGHTON (ed. 1889) answers that "it was the sorrow that was so 'becoming' to her," and SYMONS (in IRVING & MARSHALL, ed.

Like very sanctity she did approach   1465
My Cabine where I lay: thrice bow'd before me,
And (gasping to begin some speech) her eyes
Became two spouts; the furie spent, anon
Did this breake from her. Good *Antigonus*,
Since Fate (against thy better disposition)   1470
Hath made thy person for the Thrower-out

1469 from her] her from PEL1

1890) notes that Antigonus describes "grief . . . rather enhancing the beauty of a
countenance than deforming it." WILSON (ed. 1931): "So . . . becoming" refers
"both to the person and the vessell," meaning "(*a*) so complete and so beautiful, (*b*)
so full and yet still becoming full." BETHELL (ed. 1956) considers "vessell
. . . sorrow" to be "at the same time *sorrowful creature* and *jar of tears*. 'So fill'd'
goes with the second meaning. 'So becoming' does not fit with either meaning in
strict grammar; expand: '. . . so filled and to which the being filled was so becoming.'" WRIGHT & LAMAR (ed. 1966), more simply: "So full of becoming sorrow."

FURNESS (ed. 1898), strangely, prefers COLLIER's *o'er-running*, because Hermione's
eyes become "two spouts" (1468), and MOORMAN (ed. 1912), too, wants "some word
conveying the idea of overflowing." See p. 577. For SCHANZER (ed. 1969) the crucial
point is the position of the comma in 1463-4: "Though both readings [F's 'sorrow
So fill'd' and emended 'sorrow, So fill'd'] make good sense, the [emended]
one . . . seems the more satisfactory." SCHANZER does not gloss the F reading. If it
means "I never saw such a sorrowful container (= person) filled in such a beautiful
way," the sense does not seem excellent.

1465 **very sanctity**] BOORMAN (ed. 1964): "Holiness [*OED*, Sanctity 1, citing this
line] itself." In the account of the dream and particularly here, BROWN (1962, p. 224)
finds "a reminiscence of the ceremonial order of the oracle." MUELLER (1971, p. 227):
She "is a *donna angelata*, like Milton's 'late-espoused saint.'"

1466 **Cabine**] SCHMIDT (1874): "Apartment in a ship" (*OED*, *sb.* 5). The word
was probably understood in this sense until WILSON (ed. 1931) observed that *OED*
offers a more appropriate meaning: "A berth (in a ship)" (5b).

1466-9 **thrice . . . her**] PYLE (1969, p. 63): "The forced, theatrical air of a
Senecan ghost."

1467-8 **her . . . spouts**] GARBER (1974, p. 172): Alludes to "Niobe . . . , who
turns into a fountain and weeps for the loss of her children" (Ovid, *Met.* 6.148 ff.,
trans. Miller). Other weepers who may be alluded to appear in n. 1463-4.

1468 **furie**] CALDECOTT (MS 1813-33): "I.e., storm, flood." ROLFE (ed. 1879):
"Passionate burst of grief." TANNENBAUM (1928, p. 365): "Antigonus [applies] the
opprobrious term 'fury' to Hermione."

anon] MINSHEU (1617): See "Immediately."

1469-76 **Good . . . call't**] MCDONALD (1985, p. 325): "Hermione['s] . . .
innocence is usually expressed in uncommonly plain language. When Antigonus
. . . quotes the ghost's instructions to him, 'Hermione's' style becomes complex and
periodic."

1471-2 **made . . . Thrower-out Of**] CALDECOTT (MS 1813-33): "Destined
thee . . . to be the person who was to make a castaway." SPEVACK (1989, p. 4):
"A . . . Shakespearean device for establishing or enforcing derogatory or ironic assertions is the noun phrase . . . consisting of a verb plus the agential suffix *-er* and
a place adverb or preposition."

Of my poore babe, according to thine oath,
Places remote enough are in *Bohemia*,
There weepe, and leaue it crying: and for the babe
Is counted lost for euer, *Perdita*   1475
I prethee call't: For this vngentle businesse
Put on thee, by my Lord, thou ne're shalt see
Thy Wife *Paulina* more: and so, with shriekes
She melted into Ayre. Affrighted much,
I did in time collect my selfe, and thought   1480
This was so, and no slumber: Dreames, are toyes,
Yet for this once, yea superstitiously,
I will be squar'd by this. I do beleeue

1472 thine] thy PEN2
1474 weepe] wend COL2, COL3, DYCE2, COL4, HUD2
1475 euer,] ever, ever ROWE1; ever and ever, ROWE2-JOHN2 (−HAN)
1477 shalt] shall HARN, PEN1

1473-4 **Places . . . crying**] PYLE (1969, p. 63): "Antigonus's commission is vague ['commend it strangely to some place' (1114)]. . . . [Bohemia] is not the result of whim or chance, but of Hermione's guiding hand." KNOWLES (privately): "Only if Hermione is a real spirit. More likely, providence is guiding events."

1474 **weepe . . . crying**] Despite his emendation, COLLIER (1852, p. 212) adequately explains F: "Leave the infant crying, while you cannot refrain from tears yourself." See n. 1493.

    for] DODD (1752, 1:141): "Because" (*OED, prep.* 21a, and ABBOTT §151).

1475 **counted**] SCHMIDT (1874, Count): "Account."

    Perdita] See n. 3378 above. PAFFORD (ed. 1963) compares "the similar naming of Marina 'for she was born at sea' (*Per.* [3.3.13 (1325)])." PYLE (1969, p. 126 n.) observes that the child is named in Antigonus's dream, yet is spoken of by Hermione and Paulina as "our Perdita" (3332). "Accordingly, he [Antigonus] left a note with the name of the child [1489], so that she came to be known as Perdita in Bohemia. . . . It appears that Hermione gave the child its name in her own mind, communicating it (by thought transference!) to Antigonus in his dream, and telling it personally to Paulina." Mark TAYLOR (1982, p. 22), similarly: "In some mysterious way, evidently, she really did go to Antigonus, give him her daughter's name, judge him, and warn him of his fate. He is right to think the appearance more real than a dream." THATCHER (1992, p. 8): "Either we accept that Antigonus's dream accurately reflected an actual choice of name on the part of the real Hermione before or after his dream or . . . that Shakespeare has neglected to show, by providing a clear and material mode of transmission (e.g., a letter from Hermione or Paulina, transmitted through Antigonus to the shepherd), how the name actually adopted by the real Hermione (and by Paulina) coincided with the name Perdita bore."

1476 **vngentle**] SCHMIDT (1875): "Unkind, harsh." BETHELL (ed. 1956): "Ignoble."

1478 **shriekes**] SCHANZER (ed. 1969): "The typical cry of a ghost." Ghosts in Sh. shriek in *JC* 2.2.24 (1011); they also squeal, squeak, gibber, cry out, and, like Hamlet's father, talk. None of these utterances seems very typical. GRINDON (1930, p. 28), a spiritualist: "What caused those shrieks? The answer to-day is simple and sure. The etheric vision is more extended than the physical, and the future is clearer. Hermione would actually see the bear tearing Antigonus to pieces."

1479 **melted**] *OED* (Melt, *v*.¹ 2d, citing this line): "Vanish, disappear."

1481 **so**] THIRLBY (MS 1733–47?): "Real, wʰ it seem'd."

1481-3 **Dreames . . . this**] MINSHEU (1617, Toies): See "Trifles." SEYMOUR (1805, 1:66): "A superstitious man, who would yet persuade himself that he is a reasonable man, will affect to despise a propensity which, at the same time, he is unable to resist." ROFFE (1851, p. 25) holds that Antigonus has experienced a prophetic dream and, not very logically, that because its prophecy is fulfilled, "the just inference is, that the Skepticism belongs to Antigonus alone, the Belief [in such dreams] to the writer of the work."

1482 **superstitiously**] FURNESS (ed. 1898) quotes COTGRAVE (1611, *Superstitieusement*): "Ouerscrupulously, ceremoniously, curiously [very carefully]." JERVIS (1868), incorrectly: "Reverently." SCHMIDT (1875): "With erroneous religion," the current meaning (*OED*, *adv.* 1, citing this line). WILSON (ed. 1931): "I.e. contrary to Protestant doctrine which held that 'the spirits o'th' dead' may not 'walk again.' Cf. [n. 1458-83]." LAROQUE (1982, p. 26): "By choosing to follow superstition against the voice of his reason, Antigonus will save the life of Perdita and lose his own, as he is briefly to find out. The tempest-beaten coast of Bohemia is full of ambiguities and contradictions which are not wholly justified by the devious ways of Apollo to men nor by the entangled ironies of the dramatic construction."

1483 **squar'd by this**] PECK (1740, pp. 223–4): Sh. uses this word in opposed senses, "to express an *agreement* [and] to express a *quarrel*." Appropriate here is JOHNSON (1755, to Square): "To regulate; to mould; to shape." CALDECOTT (MS 1813–33): "Suffer myself to be governed by this suggestion." Cf. 2786. PECK's second sense may be found in, e.g., *MND* 2.1.30 (400).

1483-6 **I do . . . Polixenes**] LETTSOM (MS 1840–65): "This inference is scarcely warranted by the vision, and not at all in accordance with the confidence before expressed by Antigonus in the innocence of Hermione nor with the appearance of the visionary figure in pure white robes like very sanctity [1464-5]." HARRISON (ed. 1947): "This is a further [see n. 1387-8] and deliberate misleading of the audience at the same time as it is shown that the babe is saved. It is curious that Antigonus should at this point believe in Hermione's guilt." PAFFORD (ed. 1963) does not find it so: "It is clear that Hermione's appearance to Antigonus convinces him of her guilt." She also convinces him, PYLE (1969, p. 64) adds, "that the oracle had condemned her and that she had been executed." EGGERS (1977, p. 39): "That Antigonus interprets his dream as proof of Hermione's guilt should make the audience distrust the dream, even if not all the truth about her is yet known." BETHELL (ed. 1956): "Visions can mislead or they can be wrongly interpreted." Distinguishing between Puritan and High Church positions on the veracity of spirits, BETHELL concludes that Antigonus "hastily attached to his vision an interpretation which his moral sense should have repudiated; the doubtful—for it may be diabolic—vision weighs more with him than what he knows of Hermione's purity. It is significant that he is converted to the unbelief . . . immediately before being eaten by the bear." But as LETTSOM notices, the vision says nothing pertaining to Hermione's guilt or innocence. SCHANZER (ed. 1969, pp. 24–5): "Leontes [has become] utterly isolated, no arguments or abuse succeeding in making others share his delusions. Why he [Sh.] should have chosen to impair this image by making Antigonus confess to a belief in Hermione's guilt just before his death . . . is one of the puzzles for which no ready answer is available." The answer is available to those who think that Hermione's survival was Sh.'s second thought. See n. 1458-83.

Hermione hath suffer'd death, and that
Apollo would (this being indeede the issue   1485
Of King *Polixenes*) it should heere be laide
(Either for life, or death) vpon the earth
Of it's right Father. Blossome, speed thee well,
There lye, and there thy charracter: there these,
Which may if Fortune please, both breed thee (pretty)   1490

1488 well,] ~ ? SING1
1490 thee (pretty)] thee (Pretty) [*with* (Pretty) *hung near right margin as if part of* 1491 *turned up*] F4; thee, Pretty one, ROWE1-v1773 (−CAP), KTLY; thee pretty, HARN, KNT, WH1, HAL

1486 **it . . . laide**] HERFORD (ed. 1916-): "Antigonus is thus made deliberately to leave the child in the land of its reputed father. Shakespeare has thus diminished the play of chance in the connexion of the two parts of his plot. In Greene the exposed child's fate is committed to, and determined by, 'Fortune' alone." (See p. 633.)

1487 **earth**] SCHMIDT (1874): "The country, the land."

1488 **it's**] For *it's* as a possessive pronoun, see n. 230-1.

   right] KERSEY (1702): "True."

   Blossome] SCHMIDT (1874): "Figuratively, a hopeful child." BETHELL (ed. 1956): "Alluding to the child's beauty and fragility." The epithet anticipates Perdita as the goddess Flora in 4.4, and COTTRELL (1964, p. 75) finds it "the link between the winter of jealousy and the spring of forgiveness." KNIGHT (1947; 1965, p. 98): Antigonus "buries it [the baby], as a seed, to live or die . . . ; entrusting it to forces beyond man's control." MARSH (1962; 1969, p. 140) quotes, "How with this rage shall beauty hold a plea, Whose action is no stronger than a flower" (*Son.* 65).

   speed thee] For *speed*, see n. 1327. ABBOTT (§212): Rather than as a reflexive, *thee* seems to have been added to imperatives not commanding motion only for euphony. Cf. 1555, 1555-6.

1489 **charracter**] WARBURTON (in THEOBALD, ed. 1733) finds an allusion to the doctrine of signatures: "The *Naturalists* and *Botanists* pretending, that the *Qualities* of every *Plant* may be known by its *Mark* or *Character*, which, they say, Nature has impress'd on it; after he [Antigonus] had called the Child *Blossom*, he straight makes an Allusion to that Opinion." STEEVENS (ed. 1778), more sensibly: "The writing afterwards discovered with Perdita" (see nn. 3044 and 3045). COLLIER (ed. 1842): "Description, with the name 'Perdita', as prescribed in the dream of Antigonus." STAUNTON (ed. 1859), strangely, thinks the writing is "ciphers."

   there these] The CLARKES (ed. 1865): "Queen Hermione's mantle and jewel, the gold and other contents of the 'fardel' mentioned [at 2591, 2600, 2636, etc.]. They are what he hopes will cause this pretty one to be bred up well, and yet remain hers; the gold spent in rearing her, the mantle and jewel kept as proofs of her royal birth." WILSON (ed. 1931): "That the gold was in a box is clear from [2637]." WATSON (1984, p. 253): "Her breeding will depend more on the kindly nature of the shepherds than on these civilized Sicilian artifacts."

1490-1 **Which . . . thine**] JOHNSON (1755, Breed): "Educate" (*OED, v.* 10b), in which most eds. concur, often giving the equivalent "bring up" or "rear." SYMONS (in IRVING & MARSHALL, ed. 1890): "Keep" (not exactly supported). Regarding "still rest thine," HERFORD (ed. 1916-): Antigonus means "either that the ornaments would

And still rest thine. The storme beginnes, poore wretch,
That for thy mothers fault, art thus expos'd
To losse, and what may follow. Weepe I cannot,
But my heart bleedes: and most accurst am I
To be by oath enioyn'd to this. Farewell,   1495
The day frownes more and more: thou'rt like to haue
A lullabie too rough: I neuer saw

1492 art] are KNT1

---

be more than enough to pay for Perdita's rearing, or that, as a token of her high birth, they would induce her lowly discoverers to bring her up in the hope of reward, while remaining her possession." HERFORD does not say how Antigonus knows of the lowly discoverers. STAUNTON (ed. 1859): "Which [good speed] may happen, despite thy present desolate condition, if Fortune please to adopt thee (thou pretty one!) and remain thy constant friend; [1489] being . . . parenthetical." HUNTER (ed. 1872), similarly: "Which treasures, if Fortune please, may both serve to breed thee, thou pretty one, and continue to be honestly appropriated to thee," or, as MOORMAN (ed. 1912) puts it, "remain unspent for your subsequent use."

1490 **pretty**] MOORMAN (ed. 1912): "Pretty one." BLAKE (1983, pp. 107–8), however: "*Pretty* could be interpreted as an adverb (or even an adjective, for that matter) referring back to *breed*. To *breed pretty* would mean 'to bring up elegantly or in a courtly manner' . . . because the riches will suggest to the finder that the foundling is someone of substance."

1491 **wretch**] KERSEY (1702): "*An unfortunate*, or *forlorn creature.*" JOHNSON (1755): "It is sometimes a word of tenderness."

1492 **thy mothers fault**] PORTER & CLARKE (ed. 1908): Antigonus "is sorry for her [Hermione], but does not quite dare to continue to oppose the king's word, or at least he is ready, formally, to suppose 'there is something in it'. . . . He set out on his voyage before the Oracle had spoken."

1492-3 **expos'd . . . follow**] Misunderstanding MALONE's remarks on 1122–4, MOORMAN (ed. 1912) suggests that *losse* here means "loss of parents and home." ORGEL (ed. 1996), comparing 1124, rightly prefers "both ruin and estrangement" (*OED, sb.*[1] 1 and 2c). WILSON (ed. 1931): "I.e. perdition and perhaps being torn in pieces by the 'creatures of prey' [1451–2]."

1493 **Weepe I cannot**] WHITE (1854, p. 294): "The vision enjoined tears upon him as a becoming accompaniment to his sad duty [1474]." Antigonus does not disobey, however, for his bleeding heart expresses more sorrow than weeping. BOORMAN (ed. 1964): "Perhaps because one cannot properly repent a sin while continuing to commit it?" — an idea, as he recognizes, that is doubtfully applicable.

1495 **enioyn'd to this**] KITTREDGE & RIBNER (ed. 1967): "Obliged to do this."

1496-8 **thou'rt . . . clamor?**] BRANDES (ed. 1905, p. xix) compares "Thou art the rudelyest welcome to this world, That euer was Princes Child" (*Per.* 3.1.30–1 [1144–5]).

1496 **thou'rt**] See n. 294.

1497 **lullabie**] MALONE (ed. 1790) refers to "Shalt thou haue the whistling winds for thy Lullabie" (see p. 628).

A . . . rough] PAFFORD (ed. 1963): "This, and the 'blusters' in [1443], echo the 'more blusterous birth had neuer Babe' of *Per.* [3.1.28 (1143)]."

The heauens so dim, by day. A sauage clamor?
Well may I get a-boord: This is the Chace,
I am gone for euer.   *Exit pursued by a Beare.*   1500

1498-1500 **A . . . euer**] ADELMAN (1973, pp. 166-7): "The metaphors of the earlier plays become the literal actions of the romances. Lear says to Kent in the storm, '. . . where the greater malady is fixt, The lesser is scarce felt. Thou'dst shun a Beare, But if thy flight lay toward the roaring sea, Thou'dst meete the Beare i'th' mouth' [3.4.8-11 (1788-91)]. . . . In *The Winter's Tale* precisely this metaphor will become the literal action." RANDALL (1985, p. 90): "The shock of the bear-scene is positioned between two other major and more or less equidistant shocks . . . the explosion of Leontes' jealousy, and . . . the coming to life of Hermione's statue. . . . At the middle of the play, with seven scenes having been played and seven scenes to go, Shakespeare placed his bear." JOHNSON (ed. 1765): "This clamour was the cry of the dogs and hunters; then seeing the bear, he cries, *this is the chace*, or, the *animal pursued*." CALDECOTT (MS 1813-33) partly agrees: "Hearing the confused cry of dogs & hunters, he first merely says, 'tis . . . time for him to get aboard: but perceiving a Bear in pursuit of him he exclaims, Tis *myself* I now find that am the Chase, & I am lost for ever." For *chase*, MINSHEU (1617) gives "hunt." Nevertheless, later eds. generally follow JOHNSON, though SCHANZER (ed. 1969) objects: "(1) If the hunters are in such close pursuit of the bear that their voices can be heard off stage, it does not make sense that they let him devour Antigonus at their leisure, and are never heard of again; (2) the epithet *savage* is far more suited to the growling of the bear than to the cry of the dogs and hunters. The word *clamour* was used of any 'loud vocal noise of beasts and birds' [*OED*]; (3) *Well may I get aboard!* suggests a threat to Antigonus's life, which fits the bear but not the hunt. *The chase* then means not 'the hunted animal' . . . but rather 'the hunt.'" Points (2) and (3) may be valid, but as for (1), who knows what sense boiled-brains will make? BETHELL (ed. 1956) believes that "This is the Chace" may mean "I'll have to run for it," and to FREY (*Vast Romance*, 1980, p. 150), "at least some modicum of onstage pursuit" is suggested. FREY imagines "a circuit or two around the stage circumference — Antigonus rushing, arms outstretched in horror, the bear lumbering after, Perdita in the center oblivious." BATE (1993, p. 224), an animal advocate: The bear "chases Antigonus because it is being chased itself. . . . It is only because the bear is frightened that it kills Antigonus." CARRINGTON (1956): His death fulfills "the prophecy in his dream [1477-8]." RALEIGH (1907, pp. 137-8): "His part in the play is over. Sixteen years are to pass, and new matters are to engage our attention; surely the aged nobleman might have been allowed to retire in peace. Shakespeare thought otherwise; perhaps he felt it important that no news whatever concerning the child should reach Leontes."

Critics differ on the artistic success of both the event and the agent. HERFORD (ed. 1916-): "This is the only death in Shakespeare which justly provokes us. Its evident object, to relieve the play of a person who has no further function in it, is effected in a way epic rather than dramatic. The suddenness of the catastrophe, and the introduction of an animal, almost as a *dramatis persona*, strain even the 'surprise technique' of the Romances to the utmost. . . . The introduction of the *hunt* (not in Greene) at least provides a motive to explain both the bear and the presence of the shepherds on the shore." PARROTT (1949, p. 111) puts the bear in the same category as the pirate ship in *Ham.* and Valentine's leading the outlaw band in *TGV*, "a curious example of Shakespeare's occasional carelessness, or, perhaps, poverty of invention, when confronted with some pressing problem of dramatic construction." CARRINGTON (1956) finds "the tearing of Antigonus by the bear the most ludicrous incident in Shakespeare. It is harrowing, not tragic, because it is accidental and not related to his character or actions." If Antigonus is torn, however, we do not see it; as VELIE (1972, p. 101) notes, quoting the SD: "The bear catches and kills Antigonus offstage." STOPES (1916, p. 35): "Why the dramatist should destroy the best Lord of the batch, is not clear, unless it be to teach that he should not have kept his oath, when it led him to a greater sin than oath-breaking." CHARLTON (ed. 1916): "Antigonus's death has some symbolical propriety, since he believed Hermione to be guilty [1485-6], and we are reminded [1476-8] that he suffers for his share in this 'ungentle business'. By it, we know on whose side the gods are." FOAKES (1971, p. 95) is unmoved: "No one is much troubled . . . for [the death is] presented within the detached perspective of a dramatic structure which treats death as a detail in the pattern of existence." KNIGHT (1947; 1965, p. 98) also finds symbolism: "Shakespeare is moulding even from his own past imagery. His recurrent association of tempests with rough beasts, especially bears (as at [*Lr.* 3.4.9-11 (1789-91)]), is here actualized." WAIN (1964, p. 218): "Both bear and storm seem to typify the intervention of that 'nature' which humbled Lear and Gloucester, the pitiless power which beats men to their knees. But . . . the storm proves to be a fruitful turmoil [quotes 1553-4]." Similarly, NEWMAN (1988) alludes to the Candlemas Bear; this creature returned groundhoglike to hibernation, and the world returned to cold weather, if he saw the sun when he awoke on 2 Feb. Since he sees present blusters, this "bear, though mortal to Antigonus, signals the end of winter, and an upturn in the dramatic weather."

BOAS (1963) finds the episode not only as intolerable as the blinding of Gloucester (*Lr.* 3.7) but virtually unproducible, a comic event inconsistently following the tragic soliloquy of Antigonus. MIKO (1989, p. 261): "We and the shepherds enjoy a ghastly joke." SPENCER ("Artistry," 1970, p. 75): Sh. wants to insulate us from any strong feeling about his [Antigonus's] death. He intends us to be, in the Brechtian sense, 'estranged' or 'alienated' from what is going on; to limit our feelings to considering what a remarkable thing it is to bring that ferocious bear onto the stage." COLIE (1974, pp. 268-9), similarly: "The absolute rejection of verisimilitude in this episode moves us away from tragic expectation to another mode, one which assumes as its own ground unreality, impossibility, and exaggeration. The horrible death, furthermore, is *told* in the shepherdly clown's rustic malapropisms—turned into a topic for laughter. Indeed, as we stand off from *The Winter's Tale*, the Antigonus episode comes to stand for a great deal in the play's technique, as the dramatist strips his presentation of the usual modes of dramatic persuasion to belief: in this schematic *sinopia* of a play devices are forced beyond their own limits to point unequivocally at their thematic and technical significances." COLIE does not identify the significances to which this device points so unequivocally. PARRY (ed. 1982), though, agrees: "A certain 'pantomime' spirit reigns over the removal of Antigonus: in the 'new world' of Bohemia it is not a tragic event. In so far as his death can be seen as a sudden retribution for a contradiction of the truth [1483-8], it may be regarded as a kind of echo—almost a pastiche—of the climax of the trial scene." ABARTIS (1977, p. 100), more convincingly: "Antigonus' death breaks the link with the tragic world of Sicilia." Or, as DAVIES (1986, p. 164) puts it, "His [Antigonus's] blood atones for his generation, his tribe and his gender." CARRINGTON (1956, p. 11), a gastronome, finds "it strange that the bear is bothered to chase a tough old man when a tender babe lay ready on the grass." BATE (1993, pp. 226-7) attempts a connection with Callisto, a nymph transformed into a bear, who was depicted in Thomas Heywood's *The Golden Age* (1609-11). See p. 692. BRYANT (1963, p. 393): "It seems likely that Shakespeare was spoofing the clichés of storms and wild animals" found in pastoral romances. BULLOUGH (1975, 8:125-7) reviews sources from which the bear may have been drawn, including Sidney's *Arcadia* (1590 version), Spenser's *The Faerie Queene* (6.4), Emanuel Ford's *Parismenos* (1599), and *Mucedorus*.

1499 **Well . . . a-boord**] DEIGHTON (ed. 1889): "It is high time that I got aboard, or, May I get safely aboard!"

This . . . Chace] Draper (1985, p. 28): "Suggests a comic reversal of human-hunter and animal-quarry. . . . The episode is tragic, comic, melodramatic, farcical—all at once."

1500 **Exit . . . Beare**] The ridiculous idea that the bear was real—which, according to Lawrence (1935, p. 25), originated with Paul Mönkemeyer—was also advocated by Thorndike (1916, p. 195). Thorndike had previously suggested that the satyr dance in 4.4 was borrowed from Ben Jonson's *Oberon*, performed on 1 Jan. 1611 (see n. 2164). "Even the bear that devours Antigonus may have been one of the white bears that drew the chariot [for the grand entrance] of Oberon," impersonated by Prince Henry. Two polar bears were employed on that occasion, the animals being "on either side guarded by three *Syluanes*, with one going in front" (*Oberon* 10: 297-8). The sylvans may have been bearwards, and the situation is obviously very different from that in *WT*, where the unaccompanied animal ought to rear ferociously, not amble amiably. According to the correspondence quoted by Briley (1955, pp. 107-8), these bears were real, although Hosley (1967, pp. 49-50) and Bradbrook ("Dramatic Romance," 1976, p. 88) think not. To Quiller-Couch (1917, pp. 264-5), however, it is unnecessary to imagine a borrowed polar bear: The plot has reached a point at which "all we now have to do as a matter of stage-workmanship is to efface Antigonus. But why introduce that bear? . . . Why . . . not engulf Antigonus with the rest [the mariners who drown in the shipwreck]? I can discover no answer to that. . . . My private opinion . . . is that the Bear-Pit [Bear Garden] in Southwark . . . had a tame animal to let out, and the Globe management took the opportunity to make a popular hit."

Spens (1922, pp. 86-7) takes Thorndike's idea in another direction: In the popular old play *Mucedorus* (possibly acted as early as 1588), the heroine is saved from a bear by the disguised hero-prince. "That bear is clearly the same as that which pursues and kills Antigonus so unnecessarily. . . . It is unlikely that there was more than one bear provided originally for baiting and yet tame enough to be allowed to run free across the stage." Therefore, Antigonus's consumption "is an alternative and very early version of his disappearance, retained in the Folio text because it had shared with the scene in 'Mucedorus' an enormous popularity." Chambers (1923, 4:35) conjectures "that both episodes were inspired by the successful bear in Jonson's *Mask of Oberon* . . . to which there is also an allusion in his *Love Restored* of 6 Jan. 1612." In *Love Restored*, however, Robin Goodfellow mentions "the fighting beare of last year" (91), which Herford & Simpson identify with "the fellow i' the beare's skin" of *Bartholomew Fair* 3.4.131-2, "an actor who belonged to the Fortune Theatre" and who was the subject of a ballad entitled *The men* [sic] *bayted in a beares skynn &c.* (H&S 10:198)—clearly not a member of Prince Henry's team. Chambers (1930, 1:489) withdraws his incorrect statement that the *Mucedorus* bear was inspired by the bear in *Oberon*.

To return to *WT* and *Mucedorus*, Rhodes (1923, pp. 99-100), who erroneously believes that *WT* was an assembled text (see n. 2164 and p. 591), finds the SD to be the work of the assembler: "From reading the scene . . . [one sees] nothing [that] would have shown the actual appearance of a bear in pursuit of Antigonus, unlike . . . *Mucedorus* where the clown falls over a bear. . . . But in *The Winter's Tale* the Clown's account of the bear eating Antigonus [1546-7] is enough, . . . and only the recollection of a performance could account for the insertion" of the SD. *Mucedorus* was first published in 1598 (rpt. 1606); ed. 1610 is "amplified with new additions, as it was acted before the Kings Maiestie" in that year. The text of the early eds. requires only a bear's head as a prop. In ed. 1610, however, the clown announces that he has been frightened by a bear, which is now following him. So that he will not again be surprised, he begins to walk backward. Then, "*As he goes backwards the Beare comes in, and he tumbles ouer her and runnes away*" (sig. B1). In the earlier eds., as well as in ed. 1610, the bear is referred to by both the masculine pronoun and the feminine (e.g., "behould his head" [ed. 1598, sig. A3ᵛ] and "I see her wite [sic] head and her white belly" [B1]). Having missed a gender, RHODES continues: SPENS's idea that there could have been only one performing bear appearing both in *Mucedorus* and in *WT* "is shattered by finding that it was a she-bear in *Mucedorus* and a he-bear in *The Winter's Tale*." How the difference would be revealed is not discussed. Nevertheless, WRIGHT ("Animal Actors," 1927, p. 663) is almost persuaded: "Perhaps the [*Mucedorus* bear] was artificial, but since real trained bears were plentiful, it is not impossible that an actual bear sometimes graced the stage." REYNOLDS (1959, p. 263) reports the opinion of L. Harrison Matthews, a director of the Zoological Society of London, that "there is no reason at all why a living bear should not have been used in the production of . . . *Mucedorus*." As for *WT*, WILSON (ed. 1931) had already been convinced: "It can hardly be doubted that Antigonus was pursued by a polar bear on the shores of Bohemia in full view of the audience at the Globe." RIDLEY (ed. 1935) agrees: "It looks as though about this time there was a favorite (and well-trained) bear available, as much of a draw, one may imagine, as a star film-dog."

WEBSTER (1942, p. 45) believes him ("It used to be a real bear"), as does GURR (1992, p. 200), although GURR (1983, p. 424) had favored "a man in a bearskin." PAFFORD (ed. 1963), after reviewing opinions to the contrary: "The likelihood is that the bear was real since the remark at [1569–70] could only be made by someone with a knowledge of tame bears." This is absurd; one does not require an introduction to any carnivore to know that it is curst when it is hungry. As for bruin's treacherous nature, Sh. "may have known better about a particular bear," the one that inspired 1569–70. PAFFORD also reports the opinion of James G. McManaway "that the idea may come from the current knowledge of Barents' voyages on which at least two men were 'torn to pieces' by polar bears (cf. G. de Veer, *The true . . . Description of three Voyages*, trans. William Phillip, 1609 [Repr. Hakluyt Soc. 1876. See p. 63 (of that ed.)]). Dutch and German editions [1598, 1599] had pictures [Hakluyt Soc., p. 62] showing a bear tearing at a man's shoulder (cf. [1537])." PAFFORD adds, "The episode in *2 Kings* ii.24 would also be well known"; in it, Elisha, angry with the little children of Bethel who had called him baldheaded, "cursed them in the Name of the Lord. And two bears came out the forest, and tare in pieces two and fourtie children of them."

QUENNELL (1963, p. 323 n.) leaves the case open, and LENZ (1986, p. 97), pointing out the ursine preparation at 1119 and 1451–2, admits the possibility, though (pp. 99–100) he thinks the bear is as laughable as the Clown's report of him (1546–7). STYAN (1975, p. 34) discovers dramatic architecture: "Only the actuality of this bear could touch both horror and farce at the same time, and thus swiftly and without a word build a bridge between the tragedy of Hermione and the comedy of the Shepherds." If this were true, the stage history of *WT* would be thick with bears, but not a single production on record employs one. HARDMAN (1985, p. 232), bearing in mind that horror should be the effect of the slaughter: "Any real bear trusted to pursue Antigonus without taking a small bite from time to time would have been too tame: paradoxically, an actor imitating a bear would be far more frightening. . . . The real would be less convincing than the artificial." WILES (1987, p. 170) discovers symbol: "If this hypothesis [that the bear was live and polar] is correct, then we can see how Shakespeare used the bear-as-actor to convey subtleties of meaning. The whiteness in its theatrical context signifies the cruel winter of *The Winter's Tale*: the bear's exit heralds scenes of spring and pastoral regeneration. The white bear connotes purity, also exoticism, also—as a royal possession [e.g., King James's]—the royalty of the foundling. The Bear . . . is a complex sign."

The sensible remarks of LAWRENCE (1935, p. 26) should have ended the controversy over the live bear before it began: "There were no tame bears in the old Bear Garden. Constant baiting had rendered them all ferocious. Few full-grown bears are to be trusted in an unmuzzled state, bruin being by nature treacherous, yet the bear that chased Antigonus came in free and undirected, and went off in a particular way as quickly as it came. . . . What need was there to seek for it [a live bear] when playgoers were accustomed to see property bears in situations both of a serious and a comic nature?" A serious bear may appear in the allegorical dumb show beginning *Locrine* (ed. Gooch, 1981, 1.1.1.3–4): "*Let there come forth a* Lion *running after a* Bear *or any other beast*"; a comic one does appear in *Mucedorus*. For animals on the Elizabethan stage generally, see LAWRENCE (pp. 9–27), and for Sh.'s handling of an animal that could not be represented by a costumed actor, see n. 1171.

Production is again discussed by COGHILL (1958, p. 34), who concludes: "The practical aspects . . . make it certain that no Harry Hunks or Sackerson [fighting bears] was borrowed for *The Winter's Tale* from the bear-pit next door." Regarding the one in *Mucedorus*, BULLOUGH (1975, 8:127–8): "It would be a brave Mouse indeed who would undertake daily to walk backwards on to a real bear and fall over it. Proponents of the 'live bear theory' could speedily end the controversy by trying the feat once or twice." HARRISON (ed. 1947): "A bear rampant is of all beasts the most easily personated by a man," and, as several critics note, the inventory taken on 10 Mar. 1598 of the properties of the Lord Admiral's Men includes "j beares skyne" (*Henslowe's Diary*, ed. Foakes & Rickert, p. 319). The Lord Admiral's Men did not perform *WT*, but if one company could have a bear's skin, so could another. BRAD-BROOK ("Open Form," 1976, p. 209): "There is no doubt that the bear . . . is a human bear. How, otherwise, could the play be repeated anywhere but on Bankside?" It was performed on Bankside when Forman saw it, but it was also given a half-dozen times at court (see p. 798). The question is not unanswerable, however, for the bear proponent might insist that only the Globe got the real ursine thing. ROBERTS (1980, p. 81) nevertheless speaks of "the visibly artificial bear."

His artificiality is sometimes emphasized on the stage. FOSS (1932, p. 139): In Granville-Barker's 1912 production, "a first experiment of fanciful unreason, . . . a man dressed in furs walked on and solemnly waltzed off with Antigonus." SPEIRS (1957, p. 334 n.) also finds a "strange mixture of buffoonery and horror of death. Cf. also the Porter of Hell-gate scene in *Macbeth* and the element of grotesque in *Lear*, and the 'rural fellow' with the basket of figs in *Antony and Cleopatra*." COGHILL (1958, pp. 34–5) agrees: "The terrible and the grotesque come near to each other in a *frisson* of horror instantly succeeded by a shout of laughter." Shouts of laughter have so far gone unreported by reviewers, but for the mixture of tones, see further in n. 1525–51. BERRY (1981, p. 133), similarly: "The death of poor Antigonus is no laughing matter. But it becomes so. Laughter is the principle of indecorum, an audible and visual paradox here. It is the first sign of the coming reassurance that life renews itself." Finding *authority* and *bear* associated in 2682–3, BERRY continues, "The bear is the result if not the agent of Leontes' orders. May we not see the bear as figuring the impulse of ridicule directed against the tyrant?" COLIE (1974, p. 268): "The throw-away death of Antigonus, with the astonishing (marvelous—and thus properly pas-toral) stage-direction . . . , suggests that in spite of its horror, the play is about to turn around to match in unpredictability Antigonus' unpredictable death." GURR (1983, p. 424), similarly: "Tragic realism is transformed into comedy through the exploitation of theatrical illusion, and the tragic half of the play gives over to the comic half." ADAMS (1989, p. 109): "The straightfaced levity of this central instant [the throwaway death] says something about the quirky nature of the action as a whole. 'I love a ballad but even too well', the Clown has declared, 'if it be doleful matter merrily set down; or a very pleasant thing indeed and sung lamentably' [2013–15]. An audience could hardly expect fairer warning."

The merry bear invented by this cluster of critics has seldom been seen in recent productions. According to MALE (1984, pp. 14–17), in 1969 (Trevor Nunn, director) the bear was a fiercely costumed actor, wearing 8-inch platform boots, at whom nobody laughed; in 1976 (John Barton and Trevor Nunn, directors) "an actor wearing a bear mask, carrying a staff decorated with human skulls, confronted Antigonus and reappeared moments later as Time"; in 1981 (Ronald Eyre, director) a "gigantic bear-like shadow" created an "uncanny and frightening" effect.

KNIGHT (1947, p. 98): "We must take the bear seriously, as suggesting man's insecurity in the face of untamed nature; indeed, mortality in general." BIGGENS (1962, p. 8), who capably reviews the bear's critical history: "From the end of [3.2] until the last Act Hermione is believed to be dead, and Leontes is, figuratively, dead too, until restored to the living world by reunion with his reincarnated queen. . . . The dramatic irony of the bear-scene focusses Leontes' now dead brutality and false suspicion on Antigonus, in order to destroy them *dramatically*. . . . Through Antigonus the tragic world of Leontes' jealousy is finally manifested and symbolically destroyed." HOLBROOK (1964, p. 171) cautions against trying to explain this "most bizarre of stage directions . . . by supposing the availability of some convenient animal at the Globe. The bear is no comedy item, nor is the use of it mere expediency—to the Elizabethans bears would be familiar as dangerous beasts . . . savage and predatory, and would be unconsciously associated with brutal sadistic feelings." HOLLAND (1964, p. 287): "The bear, like [Sh.'s] other references to animals, images the human situation, here the unnaturalness, the savagery, of exposing . . . Perdita." ROCKAS (1975, p. 7) discovers a different irony in Antigonus's earlier "Wolues and Beares, they say, (Casting their sauagenesse aside) haue done Like offices of Pitty" (1119–21). RANDALL (1985, pp. 94–5) finds the bear doubly important: "The sacrifice of Antigonus is a major gesture to counterbalance Leontes' wrongdoing. The effect of Antigonus' death is to help set the moral ledger straight without killing the father-king. . . . [The] bear is . . . a means of evening up dramatic accounts. . . . [Moreover,] the highly theatrical climax that comes just before the close of the play [the statue's vivification] may be seen to gain some of its impact from its multiple contrasts to [this] highly theatrical action." BURTON (1988, p. 193): "Antigonus may perhaps be regarded as that aspect of man which 'sacrifices' itself in fatherhood in order that his child may thrive."

Regarding Sh.'s possible source of inspiration, NICHOLS (1828, 2:259) notes that on 23 June 1609 the king, with other members of the royal family and "divers great Lords," witnessed a bear that had killed a child defend itself successfully against lions and dogs; the animal survived until 5 July, when it was "bayted to death upon a stage." BLISSETT (1971, p. 57 n.) thinks "this striking and recent incident" involving a king, a bear, and a child "quite possibly stirred his [Sh.'s] imagination and suggested a new combination of its elements on a more exalted stage." BLISSETT (p. 57 n.) is mistaken that a bear also appears in Ulpian Fulwell's *Like Will to Like* (1568); a dancing bear is merely mentioned there (MSR 104). For a comparison of the dramatic effect of the bear with that of the tempest in *Tmp.*, see WILLIAMS (1995, pp. 1–4). As an example of dramatic convenience, KITTO (1954, p. 66) compares this stage direction with the gadfly in Aeschylus's *Prometheus*.

1501 **Shep.**] MOULTON (1893, pp. 352–3 n.) finds the complication of the plot marked by verse and its resolution by prose, the transition occurring exactly here. MOULTON (1903, p. 71): "A change from verse to prose appropriately ushers in the passage from high life, with grand passions and court intrigues, to the remote recesses of the country, and the rude pastoral manners in which poetry has always sought its golden age." STEINER (1961, p. 249): "The comedy and the prose belong to low life, the grief and the poetry to high. . . . In *The Winter's Tale* the use of prose precisely marks the limits of the pastoral. The clown, the servant, and the shepherds speak in prose though poetry knocks at every door." As STEINER notes (p. 250), there are exceptions: Gentlemen speak prose in 1.1 and 5.2, as do Polixenes and Camillo in 4.2 and Polixenes amid the shepherds (as at 2026); so do the Oracle (1187–95) and Camillo addressing Autolycus (2510–19). HUNTER (1965, p. 196): "The bear's exit is

Shep. I would there were no age betweene ten and three and twenty, or that youth would sleep out the rest: for there is nothing (in the betweene) but getting wenches with childe, wronging the Auncientry, stealing, fighting, hearke you now: would any but these boylde- braines of nineteene, and two and twenty hunt this wea-

1505

1501 SCENE VII. POPE, HAN, WARB, JOHN
    Enter a Shepheard. F2+ (*subst.*)
    were] was KNT
1501-2 ten . . . twenty] thirteen and three and twenty HAN, CAP; ten and three [13] and twenty RANN; sixteen and three-and-twenty CAM1 *conj.*, GLO, HUD2, WH2, OXF1; ten and twenty KTLY; ten and three-and-twenty HARN-CAM1, DYCE2-COL4, IRV, BUL+ (−ALEX, SIS)
1505 fighting,] fighting— [*Horns.*] WH2, NLSN, ALEX, EVNS

---

followed immediately by the entrance of a more obviously symbolic figure — the good shepherd." EVANS (1965, p. 64): "With the Shepherd's entry romance and comedy and reconciliation return, and remain to the end." KNIGHT (1947; 1965, pp. 98-9): "Both the Shepherd and his son are thoroughly at home in this weird place; its awe-inspiring quality fades. . . . Bears are no terror to them, they know their ways: [quotes 'they . . . hungry' (1569-70)]. The scene wakes into semi-humorous prose, sturdy commonsense, and simple kindliness."

MOULTON (1903, p. 76) locates another dimension: "In the physiological world healing is in the main a process of Nature. . . . So here, we [seem] to move a step nearer to Nature as we [pass] from the specialised life of the court to pastoral simplicity." FARRELL (1975, pp. 217-18) finds a joke implied in "I am gone foreuer": "for instantly the old Shepherd enters . . . [who] actually continues Antigonus' role, but as a wish-fulfillment version of it." LINDENBAUM (1972, p. 19) thinks the Shepherd is "used to provide a parody of Polixenes' response to the onset of sexual passion in youth [at 141-5]." STUDING (1982, p. 219), determined to show that pastoral Bohemia is just as vile as courtly Sicilia: "Suggestively, the references to 'youth', 'getting wenches with child', 'stealing', and 'fighting' point to the complexities of the Leontes-Polixenes conflict. In this context, 'wronging the ancientry' recalls Leontes' violation of kingship by his tyrannic impositions on his aged counselor, Camillo, and, for that matter, the entire court. Even the plight of the Shepherd's two best sheep, who have been scared away and are now lost and liable prey for the wolf, brings to mind Leontes' treatment of Mamillius and Perdita; at the same time, it forecasts the oncoming danger of Florizel and Perdita at the hands of Polixenes." STUDING continues in this vein. For an unlikely connection between the bear and Perdita, see n. 1511, *Barne?*

1501-19 **I . . . Whoa-ho-hoa**] "Might not this speech be made verse?" asks THIRLBY (MS 1725-33?). The answer, of course, is no. See n. 1612.

1501-7 **I . . . weather?**] STONE (1977, pp. 376-7): "The problem of adolescence, and the nuisance it causes to society, were familiar enough . . . especially as the time-lag between sexual maturity and marriage got longer and longer. The shepherd . . . must have struck a familiar chord."

1501 **ten**] ANON. (MS c. 1750): "Surely . . . too young for either sex, in England however, to begin getting Wenches &c." PAFFORD (ed. 1963), nevertheless: Ten is considered "too young for the offences mentioned. But it is not too young for some of them . . . : the passage makes no claim that all the offences are committed at every stage of the age group." As evidence of Bohemian juvenile delinquency, he cites 1559-60. In support of their textual change, CLARK & WRIGHT (ed. 1863): "If written in Arabic numerals 16 would be more likely to be mistaken for 10 than 13, which Capell [HANMER] suggested. . . . Another mistake of one number for another occurs [1617], but this may have been a mistake on the author's part." LETTSOM (MS 1840-65), however, holds to HANMER's emendation, "for 13 & 3 & 20 suit each other better in speaking than 16 & 3 & 20." DEIGHTON (ed. 1889) objects: "*Ten* marks extreme boyishness, *sixteen* does not." He prefers *ten* as indicating "mere boyishness" and *three and twenty* "years of discretion." PIERCE (ed. 1918) favors *ten*, because Sh. "was representing an ignorant and excited man," to which WILSON (ed. 1931) adds that "his 'ten' raises a laugh." GILDEMEISTER (ed. 1870), however: "'Nineteen' is to be preferred, which the Shepherd himself mentions a few lines further on." He is not alone in this opinion; see p. 578.

1502 **the rest**] CAPELL (1783, 2.4:172): "The years between."

1503-5 **for . . . fighting**] NEELY (1978, p. 189), citing 1559-60: "He speaks from experience, it seems." See n. 1559-60.

1503 **betweene**] OED (quasi-*sb*., citing this line and one other instance): "An interval of time."

1503-4 **getting . . . childe**] BATE (1993, p. 224): "The discovery of the baby . . . seems to him to be further evidence of this."

1504 **wronging the Auncientry**] HUNTER (ed. 1872): "Sullying the honour of ancient rank," a gloss subsequently modified. LOBBAN (ed. 1910, Wronging): "Deceiving," which is probably too specific. SCHMIDT (1875, Wrong): "Harm, . . . injure." JERVIS (1868, Ancientry): "Gentry." OED, however, gives "elder people, elders" (Ancientry 3, citing this line). SCHMIDT (1875, p. 1422a): "Old people," the abstract for the concrete, a kind of metonymy. Cf. nn. 2278 and 2642. SCHANZER (ed. 1969): "He is thinking of himself. In contrast to the shepherd in *Pandosto*, he is depicted as an old man, already sixty-seven when he finds the child [16 years later he gives his age as 'fourescore three' (line 2300)]. . . . He has to be an old man for Shakespeare's purposes. But the change of age makes his supposed paternity of Perdita much less credible."

1505 **hearke you now**] BETHELL (ed. 1956): "Spoken directly to the audience, as all this speech is." KNOWLES (privately): "An introduction to the following concrete examples of the foolishness of youth." PARRY (ed. 1982): "He assumes that the offstage noise of the bear killing Antigonus is coming from a hunting party." Eds. who call for *horns* obviously think otherwise. For pronouns with imperative verbs, see FRANZ §649.

1505-6 **boylde-braines**] CALDECOTT (MS 1813-33): "Restless, as if by such a process bubbling up." The CLARKES (ed. 1865), more aptly: "Brains inapt to judge wisely, but active to work rashly"; SCHMIDT (1874), similarly: "Hot-headed fellows." Citing "seething braines" (*MND* 5.1.4 [1796]) and "thy braines . . . boile within thy skull" (*Tmp*. 5.1.59-60 [2015-16]), HUDSON (ed. 1880, 7:95) speculates that "the expression grew from the heat or fever that was understood or supposed to agitate the brain" under the stress of love, madness, or melancholy. "Here the phrase means the same as our 'mad-brained youth.'" SCHANZER (ed. 1969): "Probably 'addle-brained youths', rather than 'hotheads' or 'lunatics.'" OED gives no example of the term but this, but ORGEL (ed. 1996) finds SCHANZER's variety of boiled brains in the *Tmp*. and *MND* lines cited above.

ther? They haue scarr'd away two of my best Sheepe,
which I feare the Wolfe will sooner finde then the Maister; if any where I haue them, 'tis by the sea-side, brou-
zing of Iuy. Good-lucke (and't be thy will) what haue   1510
we heere? Mercy on's, a Barne? A very pretty barne; A
boy, or a Childe I wonder? (A pretty one, a verie prettie
one) sure some Scape; Though I am not bookish, yet I
can read Waiting-Gentlewoman in the scape: this has   (2l

1510 of] on v1793-v1813; the OXF1
     thy] the F2-ROWE2
1510-11 haue we] we have ROWE2
1511 heere?] Ad. *Taking up the Child.* ROWE1-DEL2 (−CAP, WH1), KTLY, DEL4,
OXF1, ALEX; *Seeing the Child.* DYCE2, COL4, HUD2, BUL, KIT1, SIS, ARD2, OXF2, BEV4
     A very] very RID
1512 boy, . . . Childe] god, or a child WH1, HUD2; boy- or a maid-child KEIGHTLEY
conj. in CAM1, KTLY

1507 **scarr'd**] MANNING (1929, pp. 42-3): The spelling testifies to the *a* of *hard*
and *guard*. This is not borne out by DOBSON (1968). Both KÖKERITZ (1953, p. 179)
and CERCIGNANI (1981, also p. 179) indicate the *a* of *dare*.
     two . . . Sheepe] HEIMS (1988, 4:6): In *Pandosto* only one sheep is missing;
see p. 634. Sh. doubled the number in order to "recall the 'twinned lambs'
[130], . . . sundered by a kind of wolf, . . . sexual jealousy." Which seems quite
unlikely.
     1509-10 **if . . . Iuy**] MALONE (ed. 1790): See *Pandosto*, p. 634. PORTER &
CLARKE (ed. 1908, Iuy): "Sea-weed, perhaps." SAVAGE (1923, p. 43) alludes to "the
little known fact, that sheep often browse upon the ivy [*Hedera helix*]." DENT (1971,
p. 66) finds ivy a surprising fodder. Yet, as COLLIER (MS 1858-78?) notices, in *Menaphon* (6:36) Greene once again mentions that "ewes and lambes were straggled
downe to the strond to brouse on the sea iuie." *OED*, referring only to Greene's use
of the word, suggests that the ivy may be sea holly (eryngo). Professor David Thomas
of the Department of Meat and Animal Science of the University of Wisconsin, a
specialist in the diet of sheep, reports that they will eat anything, including *Hedera
helix*. ORGEL (ed. 1996): "Wild sheep . . . will graze on seaweed, and this may be
the plant intended."
     1509 **haue**] PAFFORD (ed. 1963): "Find."
     1509-10 **brouzing of**] ABBOTT (§178): I.e., in the browsing of ivy; *brouzing* is
a verbal noun rather than a participle.
     1510 **Good-lucke . . . will**] BETHELL (ed. 1956, Thy): "God's." SCHANZER (ed.
1969): "The reference is to the search for the sheep, not to the finding of the child."
     1510-11 **what . . . heere?**] A proverb (DENT W280.2). PROUDFOOT (1976, p.
77): "No line in the play so invariably provokes happy laughter as [this]."
     1511 **heere?**] FURNESS (ed. 1898): Eds. who have the Shepherd take up the child
at this point overlook "Ile tarry till my sonne come" at 1518. "Possibly, the child is
not lifted from the ground until [1556]. It is hardly likely that the old man, while
listening to his son's account of the ship-wreck, stands holding the child in his arms."

Eds. who do not supply a SD here do not supply one at all, as the exact place of the child's being taken up is uncertain. See n. 1517-18.

1511-14 **Mercy . . . scape**] VICKERS (1968, p. 416): "His wheezy syntax [shows] his age." BROOK (1976, p. 183): "The most noticeable characteristic of the speech of Shakespeare's old men is that they speak in short, jerky sentences, as though out of breath."

1511 **Barne?**] BLOUNT (1656): "Child." *OED* (Bairn, citing this line): "A son or daughter. (Expressing relationship, rather than age.)" But that cannot be the case here. WELLS (in WELLS & TAYLOR, 1987): Sh.'s "only other direct use [of the word] is by Lavatch [*AWW* 1.3.25 (354)]; he probably regarded it as dialectal. (It also occurs as a pun on [*barns, Ado* 3.4.49 (1546)])." HOLLAND (1964, p. 295), dubiously: Because "the word is the old past participle of the verb 'to bear,'" Sh. may connect it with Antigonus's bear (1500), "a deadly savage form of the idea,'" whereas this is "a life-giving version." Moreover, when the kings were "barnes," they were "twyn'd Lambs" (130); "at the point when the shepherd or *pastor* is looking for his lost sheep, [they] are themselves lost, estranged, separated by a bearlike savagery." *OED* does not give *barne* as a past participle of *bear*.

1512 **boy**] WHITE (ed. 1857), believing that *child* could mean only "boy" (as does NARES; see the next n.), emends to *god* because of "thought assuredly, that it was some little God" (*Pandosto*; see p. 634).

Childe] RANN (ed. 1787): "Girl." *OED* (*sb.* 1b, citing this as its earliest instance): "Girl-baby." *OED*'s other citations indicate that the word in this sense remained a provincialism, and perhaps it was adopted here on that account, although PAFFORD (ed. 1963) finds the word used by a lawyer in Greene's *James the Fourth* (ed. Sanders, 1970, 5.4.103). ONIONS's (1986) assertion that "*my child* is always used by S[h]. of a daughter e.g. [*Tmp.* 5.1.198 (2177), *Ado* 4.1.76 (1735), *Lr.* 4.7.69 (2825)]" is irrelevant here, since the pronoun is lacking, and boys elsewhere are called *child* (e.g., *Wiv.* 4.1.47 [1863] and 63 [1877] and *Jn.* 2.1.159 ff. [460 ff.]). WILSON (ed. 1931): A west-country word "and west country dialect was the conventional speech of yokels on the Elizabethan stage." KNIGHT (ed. 1854, glos.): "There is a vulgar joke yet of asking, on a birth being announced, is it a boy or a child?" NARES (1876; 1905), however, thinking *child* refers only to boys or young men, believes that in his simplicity the Shepherd reverses common usage. THIRIOLD (1876) cites a possible instance in sophisticated speech in *Philaster* 2.4.59-61: "If he [any usurper] have any child, It shall be crossely match'd: the gods themselves Shall sow wilde strife betwixt her Lord and her." But here the intervening *it* suggests that by the time he reached the *hers*, Fletcher had lost control of the antecedent.

1513 **Scape**] JOHNSON (1755): "Loose act of vice or lewdness" (*OED*, *sb.*[1] 2). RANN (ed. 1787), wrongly: "Chance bargain." FARMER & HENLEY (1890-1904; 1970): "An act, or effect, of fornication." The CLARKES (1879, p. 588), more delicately: "Prank, irregularity, wild freak."

1513-14 **yet I . . . scape**] VICKERS (1968, p. 417): "The kind of conclusion that Leontes has drawn, and both are wrong." DUSINBERRE (1975, p. 52), however: "Chastity in women has never been the shibboleth to the working classes that it is to the upper classes. . . . The Shepherd . . . assumes her [Perdita] to be the bastard not of a great lady but of a working woman." Although she worked by attending another, a waiting gentlewoman was not working class in the modern sense; she was an "upper servant" (SCHMIDT, 1875), originally a woman of good birth (*OED*, Gentlewoman 2). She might be sexually adventurous nevertheless; Margaret, Hero's waiting-gentlewoman in *Ado*, entertains Borachio in a way that causes Hero to be thought unchaste. Gentleman servants appear in 5.2; see n. 3009.

1514 **reade**] A modest pun on *read* as "peruse" (*OED*, *v.* 5b) and "make out the . . . nature of" (5d, citing this line). For a similar use, see n. 1997, *reade*.

beene some staire-worke, some Trunke-worke, some be-   1515
hinde-doore worke: they were warmer that got this,
then the poore Thing is heere. Ile take it vp for pity, yet
Ile tarry till my sonne come: he hallow'd but euen now.
Whoa-ho-hoa.

Enter Clowne.   1520

Clo. Hilloa, loa.

Shep. What? art so neere? If thou'lt see a thing to
talke on, when thou art dead and rotten, come hither:
what ayl'st thou, man?

Clo. I haue seene two such sights, by Sea & by Land: 1525

1520 *After* 1523 DYCE, STAU, DEL, HUD2, BUL
1521 *Clo.*] *Clo.* [*Within.*] DYCE, STAU, DEL, HUD2, BUL (*subst.*)

1515-16 **some staire-worke . . . worke**] SPEVACK (1989, p. 5) compares this instance of Sh.'s compounding of words and phrases for satirical purposes with such others as Hotspur's "Sword and Buckler Prince of Wales" (*1H4* 1.3.230 [558]). For the several types of work, SCHMIDT (1874) gives, e.g., "what is made behind the door" and (1875) "work made on a chest" or "on a staircase." PAFFORD (ed. 1963, Staire-worke): "A clandestine love affair in which the lover got access to his mistress by back or secret stairs." SCHANZER (ed. 1969): "Not . . . the way in which the lover got access to his mistress . . . but rather to the places where the furtive copulation took place." *OED* (Trunk, *sb.* 18, citing this line only): "Secret or clandestine action, as by means of a trunk." Like WILSON (ed. 1931), *OED* may be thinking of Iachimo's trunk work in *Cym.*, where Iachimo is in rather than upon it, but for a work upon a trunk, see n. 2023-4. MAXWELL (ed. 1956): "A pun on *trunk* meaning (1) a secret place [like a chest or coffer, presumably (*OED*, *sb.* 6)] (2) the body apart from the head and limbs."

worke . . . worke . . . worke] SCHANZER (ed. 1969): "Used repeatedly by Shakespeare in the sense of 'sexual intercourse.'" COLMAN (1974) lists three other instances in Sh.

1516 **got**] SCHMIDT (1874, Get): "Beget." For *get* in this sense, see *OED* (*v.* 26).

1517 **poore Thing**] Also Antigonus's words at 1124. PYLE (1969, pp. 66-7): "The Antigonus spirit . . . lives on, in the old Shepherd, in a world where there is no curse on one who does so [pities the child], but rather rich reward."

1517-18 **Ile . . . come**] FURNESS (ed. 1898): "This may mean, of course, 'I'll take up the babe and then tarry till my son come' but it may, also, mean 'I'll take it up,—yet, no—I'll wait till my son come.'" CREIZENACH (1909; 1916, pp. 301-2), choosing the former, observes that a "popular device was to send the clown [e.g., Shepherd] on to the stage carrying a baby in swaddling clothes, with which he plays all kinds of tricks." CREIZENACH cites this instance.

1518 **he . . . now**] SHIRLEY (1963, p. 190): "Only seldom is there a shout off stage" to provoke this remark. None of the eds. collated calls for it.

hallow'd] SCHMIDT (1874): "To call or shout to with a loud voice."

1519-21 **Whoa-ho-hoa . . . loa**] WHITE (ed. 1857) thinks the final *a*'s are meant to be pronounced. *OED*, however, indicates one syllable for *whoa* and gives *hoa* as a variant spelling of *ho*, *hilloa* of *hillo*, and *loa* of *lo*.

1521-77 **Hilloa . . . on't**] BOOTH (1981, p. 57): "Antigonus . . . is succeeded

282

on the stage by a shepherd . . . who is shortly joined by the clown, who describes what *he* has found while his father was seeking lost *sheep*. The description yaws frantically and comically between the lost *ship*, 'boring the moon' [1533-4], and the bear dining upon the gentleman." HARDMAN (1985, p. 233): "The dialogue . . . may be seen to parallel the one between the courtiers [1.1]; it is the first time there has been any prose since then: it is like a new beginning. . . . The shepherds introduce romantic comedy as the courtiers introduced tragedy."

DELIUS (1870, p. 250) finds the shepherds' prose to be more finely worked than that spoken by clowns in earlier plays. For example, the Clown's simultaneous description of the shipwreck and the fateful end of Antigonus (1530-47) can be counted among the most outstanding examples of virtuosity in prose style. WILLIAMS (1967, p. 8), however: The Clown's "report is a series of independent clauses, indicating the humorous inability of a mind to structure or subordinate what it sees."

1521 **Hilloa, loa**] The CLARKES (1879, p. 463): Expressing "rustic shouting."

1522 **What? . . . neere?**] PARRY (ed. 1982): "His son's greeting-cry is probably unexpectedly loud and close, making the old man jump."

1522-3 **If . . . hither**] BETHELL (ed. 1956): "Shakespeare's 'clowns' . . . are frequently comic through their unintentional breaches of logical and rhetorical propriety." This Clown garbles a proverb: "Men will talk on it when we be dead, do what we can" (TILLEY M562).

1523 **talke on**] KITTREDGE & RIBNER (ed. 1967): "Be spoken about."
  dead and rotten] Proverbial (DENT D126.1).

1525-51 **I . . . footing**] QUILLER-COUCH (1917, pp. 62-3), observing that Sh. employs shipwreck as a plot device in *Err.*, *Per.*, *TN*, and *Tmp.*: "By shipwreck Perdita is abandoned on the magical seacoast of Bohemia." But Perdita would have been abandoned whether or not the ship was lost; the shipwreck and the bear appear, rather, to sever all links with Sicilia. See n. 1498-1500. COLLINS (1880, p. 742), strangely: "It is . . . very difficult to see why the poet has [here] selected prose in preference to verse. The subject is impressive, the treatment is serious, the [play as a whole is] for the most part in verse." BETHELL (ed. 1956) provides an answer; the subject is serious but the treatment clearly is not: "A storm at sea usually symbolizes human passions, since in the analogy of microcosm (man) and macrocosm (the physical universe) *blood* corresponds to *sea*, and blood is the physical basis of the passions. The ship and its crew thus perish in the storm as we move from the tragic episodes in Sicilia to new life in Bohemia: tragedy takes its victims and itself dies before our eyes. Antigonus, the last to disbelieve in Hermione's innocence, perishes at the same time, to the audience's laughter [see n. 1500 for the death as horrible; BETHELL's idea, however, is shared by such other critics as QUENNELL (1963, p. 323)]. These deaths are made comic because good is to come out of ill and, this being the law of the universe, death is not a final or irremediable evil. . . . The Clown labours to be expressive but . . . he persistently uses figures of diminution: (*a*) the bodkin [1527]; (*b*) 'boring the moon', as with an auger [1533-4]; (*c*) the cork in the hogshead [1535-6]; (*d*) the flapdragon [1539-40] — all refer to small and familiar objects. . . . The Clown uneasily moves between one part of his tale and another, from the ship to Antigonus and back again, with his comments on the process: 'but that's not to the point' [1531]; 'And then for the land-service' [1536]; 'But to make an end of the ship' [1539]. Observe also (*a*) 'land-service', which could only be jocular and so is out of place; (*b*) balance of phraseology with comic effect (not intended by the Clown) owing to the forcing of the later phrase into conformity with the earlier; so that the 'poor gentleman' is said to 'roar' . . . and the bear to 'mock' him [1541-2]."

CRANE (1951, p. 121): "The distortion . . . in the Clown's description provides us . . . with the transition from the melodrama of the first three acts to the pastoral beauty of the fourth and the recognition and reconciliation of the fifth." VICKERS (1968, pp. 417-18): "This muting of potential seriousness is done partly through the

but I am not to say it is a Sea, for it is now the skie, betwixt the Firmament and it, you cannot thrust a bodkins
point.

    Shep. Why boy, how is it?

    Clo. I would you did but see how it chafes, how it ra-   1530
ges, how it takes vp the shore, but that's not to the point:
Oh, the most pitteous cry of the poore soules, sometimes
to see 'em, and not to see 'em: Now the Shippe boaring
the Moone with her maine Mast, and anon swallowed
with yest and froth, as you'ld thrust a Corke into a hogs-   1535
head. And then for the Land-seruice, to see how the
Beare tore out his shoulder-bone, how he cride to mee
for helpe, and said his name was *Antigonus*, a Nobleman:

1530 chafes] chases WARB
1531 takes] rakes HAN
1533 not] then, not CAP, HUD2
1536 for] *Om.* ROWE2-POPE2, HAN
        Land-seruice] land-sight HAN

---

imagery, which is not merely 'homely' but innocuous, as in [1526-8], which suggests nothing more dangerous than thrusting a needle . . . in a piece of cloth. . . . He is made to . . . report both disasters simultaneously, gets . . . completely mixed up . . . and reduces the tragic loss to a comic turn." COGHILL (1958, p. 35): Sh. "deliberately underlined the juxtaposition of mood, achieved by the invention of the bear, in the speeches . . . of the Clown, grisly and ludicrous, mocking and condoling. . . . This is a dazzling piece of *avant-garde* work . . . the transformation of tragedy into comedy . . . the revenge of Nature on the servant of a corrupted court." HOLBROOK (1964, p. 174), similarly: "It is painful but it is comic: it is clowning such as accompanies death in the folk-ritual: it is one way for us to accept death, by a resigned wry grimace." EDWARDS (*Progress*, 1986, p. 170): "All the narrative links in *The Winter's Tale* emphasize the insubstantiality and indeed the absurdity of the story. The Clown makes a comic business of his gruesome tale of the preposterous coincidence of the bear and the shipwreck, by which all witnesses to the abandonment of Perdita are destroyed at a stroke. This whole contrivance is Shakespeare's addition to Greene's story." HONIGMANN (1981, p. 114) also finds that the bear comes "at the point where the play modulates from one mood to another" and is in this respect like the bed-trick in *MM*, the 'Cinna the poet' scene in *JC*, and the porter scene in *Mac.* HALE (1985, p. 152): "He mangles the story as the bear does the gentleman!" SCHANZER (ed. 1969): "The Clown's account . . . is purposely made to sound ridiculous in order to 'distance' them [the deaths] . . . and so to reduce their horror and pathos. . . . It is done chiefly (1) by making the Clown, anxious to narrate both calamities at the same time, scuttle to and fro between them; (2) by means of the figurative language he employs. The comic effect . . . results from the discrepancy between extraordinary and fearful events and the homely and trivial manner in which these are described." PAFFORD (ed. 1963) compares Miranda's description of the storm and shipwreck in *Tmp.* 1.2.2-13 (83-94), similar in detail but very different in style.

    MARSH (1962; 1980, p. 141) emphasizes the negative: "All is confusion, all order gone, mirroring . . . some great moral confusion. The sailors and Antigonus die, Perdita is cast away to face the violence of the natural world, because of Leontes's sin."

1526-8 **but . . . point**] FALCONER (1964, p. 42): "In violent gales and tempests all distinction between air and sea is lost. Spray rises in curtains . . . and everything becomes enveloped in thick haze." He quotes further instances of the invasion of sky by sea from Sh. and others. MIRIAM JOSEPH (1947, pp. 179-80) cites these lines as an example of the figure syllogismus, in which the mind leaps from "a single vivid suggestion . . . to the desired inference without adverting to the process of reasoning which underlies it."

1527 **bodkins**] A pointed instrument or weapon (*OED*).

1530-1 **how it chafes . . . rages**] BLISSETT (1971, pp. 64-5): "The beast and the storm play their parallel roles concurrently. . . . The Clown [speaks here] not of the bear but of the sea; and by similar transference, he exclaims at 'how the poor souls roared' [1540]."

1530 **chafes**] *OED* (*v.* 10c, citing this line): "To fret, fume, or rage."

1531 **takes vp**] HUDSON (ed. 1880) guesses at "something in the sense of *devour*," which MOORMAN (ed. 1912) makes "swallows up." SCHMIDT (1875) has two meanings: "To rebuke, to rate, to scold" (a sense consonant with *chafes* as "frets against") and "to oppose, to encounter." DEIGHTON (ed. 1889), finding SCHMIDT too elaborate: "Encroaches upon, engulfs." Eds. usually adopt SCHMIDT's first gloss, though WILSON (ed. 1931) adds "cope[s] with" and PAFFORD (ed. 1963), "contends with, rebukes."

1533-40 **Now . . . it**] TURNER (1971, p. 152): "The storm is like the fermentation in a barrel of beer: the decay of one thing but the brewing up of something better. . . . Perhaps there is even a suggestion of the effects of strong drink: forgetfulness, loss of care, sleep, . . . an almost dreamlike detachment, so that we may see the two halves of the play in proper perspective." KNOWLES (privately): "The image is mainly pictorial, not thematic."

1533-6, 1539-40 **Now . . . head, But . . . it**] CLEMEN (1951, p. 199), oddly: "The Clown's prose-observations on the storm express a far more realistic point of view" than the Mariner's (1442-5) or Antigonus's (1496-8). DRAPER (1985, p. 28): "A brilliant exercise in the tragic-comic grotesque."

1533 **boaring**] PORTER & CLARKE (ed. c. 1903): "Perforating" (*OED*, Bore, *v.*¹ 1).

1534 **anon**] Immediately. See n. 1468.

1535 **yest**] JOHNSON (1755): "The foam, spume, or flower of beer in fermentation; barm." SCHMIDT (1875): "Spume or foam of water." *OED*'s first citation of the word in this sense (Yeast, *sb.* 3) is of this line, although "yesty waves" are found in *Mac.* 4.1.53 (1583). PARRY (ed. 1982): "At other moments the ship is submerged and covered with spray and froth, like a cork bung when it is driven into the barrel it has been sealing."

as you'ld] CALDECOTT (MS 1813-33): "Just as if you were to."

1536 **Land-seruice**] JOHNSON (1755): Service on land as opposed to service at sea. *OED*: "Military, as opposed to naval, service." SCHMIDT (1875): Used improperly to mean "the mischief happening on land." FURNESS (ed. 1898), however, thinks that *seruice* here means a "course of dishes at table" (SCHMIDT's gloss for *service* in *Ham*. 4.3.24 [2689]; *OED*, Service¹ 25c) and "that the clown says, in effect: — 'And then to see what was dished up on land.'" Later eds. find both meanings present. ORGEL (ed. 1996): "The foot-soldier Antigonus, as opposed to the sailors just described."

1537-8 **how . . . helpe**] VICKERS (1968, p. 419): The "grotesque point is that our observer has been so caught between the two spectacles that he did not stir, and in vain did the man cry for help." But how was the observer to part the roaring bear and the shoulder bone? For more on shoulder bones, see n. 1740-1.

1538 **said . . . Nobleman**] BRANDES (ed. 1905, p. xx), commenting on *WT*'s

But to make an end of the Ship, to see how the Sea flap-
dragon'd it: but first, how the poore soules roared, and   1540
the sea mock'd them: and how the poore Gentleman roa-
red, and the Beare mock'd him, both roaring lowder
then the sea, or weather.

    Shep. Name of mercy, when was this boy?

    Clo. Now, now: I haue not wink'd since I saw these   1545
sights: the men are not yet cold vnder water, nor the
Beare halfe din'd on the Gentleman: he's at it now.

    Shep. Would I had bin by, to haue help'd the olde
man.

    Clo. I would you had beene by the ship side, to haue   1550
help'd her; there your charity would haue lack'd footing.

    Shep. Heauy matters, heauy matters: but looke thee
heere boy. Now blesse thy selfe: thou met'st with things
dying, I with things new borne. Here's a sight for thee:

    1543 or] or the CAP
    1546 yet] *Om.* ROWE1, ROWE2
    1548-9 olde man] Nobleman THEOBALD (1729) *conj. in* NICHOLS (1817, 2:362),
THEO, HAN, HUD2, BUL
    1550-1 *Marked as aside* THEO1-SING1 (−HAN, CAP), HUD1, SING2, HAL, KTLY,
CAM3
    1550 ship] ship's COL, HUD1, DEL, OXF1, PEN1, SIG
    1551 there] but there HAN
        there . . . footing] *Marked as aside* HUD2
    1553 met'st] meet'st F4-JOHN2, v1773

"playfulness of expression which gives a certain raillery to incidents which would otherwise be horrible": "It does not seem very likely that the unfortunate man's chief anxiety
while the bear was tearing him to pieces would be to inform the shepherd of his name
and rank." FARJEON (1949, p. 77), from his own review of the 1925 Old Vic production:
"Antigonus . . . seems to have been a man of great presence of mind. . . . In the
teeth of a savage beast I, too, would cry for help, but I should be too much put about
to think of adding, 'My name is Herbert Farjeon, a dramatic critic.'"

    1539 **to . . . Ship**] DEIGHTON (ed. 1889): "To finish my story about the ship;
with an allusion to the sea having made an end of it, *i.e.* sunk it."

    1539-40 **flap-dragon'd it**] JOHNSON (1755, Flapdragon): "A play [amusement],
in which they catch raisins out of burning brandy, and, extinguishing them by closing
the mouth, eat them." Hence, to *flapdragon*: "To swallow" (*OED*, *v.* [*nonce-wd.*]),
citing this line only). For more on the part of speech, see n. 2931. Because the raisin
"would be agitated in the liquid," HALLIWELL (ed. 1859) finds "this somewhat strange
metaphorical verb" justified. STAUNTON (ed. 1859): "Swallowed it as our old revellers
did a flapdragon" or raisin. CHAMBERS (ed. 1907), wrongly: "Flattened." Flapdragons
also appear in *LLL* 5.1.42 (1781) and *2H4* 2.4.246 (1268); *snapdragon* was later used
in the same sense (*OED*, Snapdragon 4), but that word does not appear in Sh.

    1541 **mock'd**] THIRLBY (MS 1725-33?): I.e., "by imitating." Sh.'s use of the var-
ious senses of *mock* is explored by BEREK (1978); see further in n. 3207-8.

1541-2 **how . . . him**] ORGEL (ed. 1996): "I.e. a bear-baiting in reverse, with the bear doing the baiting."

1544 **Name**] *OED* (*sb.* 11b, citing this line): "In adjurations, orig. by solemn reference to God, Christ, or the saints, but latterly with various substitutions for the names of these, the phrase freq. becoming a mere adjuration." KNOWLES (privately): "Elliptical for 'in the name of.'"

1545 **Now, now**] The CLARKES (1879, p. 425): Iteration used "to express agitation," as also in 1323. For other uses, see 75, 1387, 1958, and 2807.

1546-54 **the men . . . borne**] STAUFFER (1949, p. 298): The Clown "is ridiculously inept at expressing pity for the shipwrecked sailors and the slaughtered Antigonus. . . . The old shepherd takes the news with the calm philosophy of Justice Shallow meditating on death and the price of bullocks at Stamford fair" (in *2H4* 3.2.40-3 [1568-9]).

1546 **cold**] MAXWELL (ed. 1969): "Dead."

1546-7 **nor . . . now**] MAHOOD (1957, p. 156): "He sees Antigonus's fate from the bear's point of view." But 1536-8 are surely from the Clown's.

1548-9 **Would . . . man**] BERKELEY & KARIMIPOUR (1985, pp. 94-5), who believe the Clown should have "battled the bear," take this as "an implied reproof." THEOBALD (1729, in NICHOLS, 1817, 2:362), asks, "How came the *Shepherd*, who did not see Antigonus, know him to be an *old* man?" He adds, "His son . . . [at 1538], acquaints us he was a NOBLEMAN," which THEOBALD thinks is the true reading here. STEEVENS (ed. 1773): "The Shepherd infers the age of Antigonus from his inability to defend himself," later adding (ed. 1778) "or perhaps Shakespeare, who was conscious that he himself designed Antigonus for an *old* man, has inadvertently given this knowledge to the Shepherd." CAPELL (1783, 2.4:172), similarly: The Shepherd "presumes he [Antigonus] was old because he himself was." MALONE (ed. 1790): *Old* may have been inadvertently omitted before "Gentleman," 1547. For GERVINUS's opinion that such discrepancies are intentional, see n. 0.

1550-1 **I . . . footing**] THEOBALD (1729, in NICHOLS, 1817, 2:362): "Does this ungracious Clown wish his father to have been by the ship-side to have been drowned?" He considered emending (see p. 578), but later, having decided the answer is yes, he makes the speech an aside. FURNESS (ed. 1898) objects "that the speech is that of a Clown . . . from whom any absurd sentiment or perverted expression is to be expected." For "there . . . footing," DEIGHTON (ed. 1889): "There would have been no opportunity for your charitable help; with a reference to the literal meaning of his not being able to set foot on the vessel." BOORMAN (ed. 1964): "Would not have had a leg to stand on." WILSON (ed. 1931), wrongly: "While the Clown pretends to his father to be much affected by the double disaster he has a secret understanding with the spectators that he is only fooling the old man. The words 'your . . . footing' seem to refer to the fashion of the day for establishing charitable foundations . . . , such establishments, of course, not being encouraged by heirs, of whom the Clown was one." WILSON refers to *OED*, Footing, *vbl. sb.* 7 and 8, but neither definition connects *footing* specifically with charitable institutions, although they are mentioned in the glosses of some later eds. ORGEL (ed. 1996), however, finds wordplay between *foundation* and *footing*, which seems likely. PAFFORD (ed. 1963): "In [1548-9] the Shepherd has cast a slight on the Clown's courage: here the Clown implies that the Shepherd is such a braggart that he could no doubt have saved the ship. It is typical yokel back-chat."

1552 **Heauy**] MINSHEU (1617): "Sad." The CLARKES (ed. 1865): "Grievous."

1553-4 **Now . . . borne**] HARDMAN (1985, p. 229): "Reflecting a well-known passage from the essay (or rather essays) *De Tragoedia et Comoedia* by the fourth-century grammarians Evanthius and Donatus, frequently printed in Renaissance school editions of Terence: ' . . . in tragoedia fugienda vita, in comoedia capessenda exprimitur.'" BETHELL (ed. 1956): "The tone changes suddenly to extreme seriousness. The actors can convey this by a solemn pause while the Clown looks at the

Looke thee, a bearing-cloath for a Squires childe: looke   1555
thee heere, take vp, take vp (Boy:) open't: so, let's see, it
was told me I should be rich by the Fairies. This is some
Changeling: open't: what's within, boy?

    Clo. You're a mad olde man: If the sinnes of your
youth are forgiuen you, you're well to liue. Golde, all   1560
Gold.

    Shep. This is Faiery Gold boy, and 'twill proue so: vp
with't, keepe it close: home, home, the next way. We

    1558 open't . . . boy?] *Om.* v1785
    1559 mad] made mTBY2 *conj.,* THEOBALD (1729) *conj. in* NICHOLS (1817, 2:362-
3), THEO, HAN, JOHN1, CAP, v1773+
    1562 'twill] will THEO1-v1773 (−HAN, CAP)

---

infant as if awe-stricken and then makes the sign of the Cross. [I.e., 'blesse thy selfe'
(*OED*, Bless, *v.*[1] 2). For a cross that actually exists in the play, see. n. 1099.] For a
moment there is almost a tableau, . . . a Nativity scene . . . interpreted by the dialogue: 'things dying ["the old man"] . . . things new born'. Baptism is new birth,
according to the Scriptures, and baptism is indirectly referred to below: 'a bearing
cloth for a squire's child!' Now, in this scene, Leontes' 'old man' and the world of sin
are drowned and consumed, that his new life, symbolized by Perdita, may grow. There
is a triple reference (*a*) on the story level, to the renewed fortunes of Leontes; (*b*) to
spiritual regeneration by baptism into the Church; (*c*) to the historical events of the
Incarnation and Crucifixion, by which new life has been won for the world." PAFFORD
(ed. 1963) declines to be exalted: "Surely few will see these things in the passage.
There is no change of tone; the picture continues the counter-boasting, showing the
Shepherd triumphantly displaying, with some natural cupidity, what *he* has found."
Referring to BETHELL and to TRAVERSI (1938, p. 137), PAFFORD continues: "Whatever
importance is attached to the remark it must be agreed that it is a simple statement
of fact in language completely fitting to the occasion and to the speaker. . . . The
old man, tired of his son's boasting, now wants to show his own find. At the same
time . . . Shakespeare often allows his comic dialogue to carry a serious theme."
"Boasting" seems hardly the word for it, though HARTWIG (1972, p. 127) finds that
the Clown takes "pride in his narrative skill." SMITH (1966, p. 49): "The constructive-
destructive dialectic of Nature is emphasized by the juxtaposition of birth and death,
as well as by the change of setting from courtly to pastoral and of tone from tragic
to comic." SMITH's opinion of the tone is reiterated by FRYE (1970, p. 151) in terms
of structure: "This shift of attention from the death of the old to the birth of the new
marks the [play's] major turning point." HAPPÉ (1969): The line is "a pivot upon
which the worlds of Bohemia and Sicilia are balanced."

    1555, 1555-6 **Looke thee**] For the construction, see n. 1488, *speed thee.*
    1555 **bearing-cloath**] PERCY (in STEEVENS, ed. 1773): "The fine man-
tle . . . with which a child is usually covered, when it is carried to church to be
baptized" (*OED*, Bearing, *vbl. sb.* 17, citing this line). Gloucester insults Winchester
with "Thy Scarlet Robes, as a Childs bearing Cloth, Ile vse, to carry thee out of this
place" (*1H6* 1.3.42-3 [408-9]). PAFFORD (ed. 1963): "Presumably the ['Mantle of
Queene *Hermiones*' (3042-3)]."

    Squires childe] SCHMIDT (1875, Squire): "A gentleman next in rank to a knight." DEIGHTON (ed. 1889): "*I.e.* one [a child] of high degree." Evidently *squire* is something more exact than *country gentleman*, for *OED* does not find the word in this sense until later than *WT* (*sb.* 5). BETHELL's (ed. 1956) interpretation seems right: "The highest rank he is accustomed to."

1556-7 **it . . . Fairies**] PAFFORD (ed. 1963): "Foretold to me that by means of the fairies I should be made rich." Fairies had favorites, like Dapper in Jonson's *The Alchemist*. See DYER (1884, p. 21). NICHOLS (1981, pp. 176-7): "We are moving from a world in which sprites and goblins frighten men [618-19] to one in which fairies are thought to bring joy."

1558 **Changeling**] GREY (1754, 1:257): "An allusion to the vulgar notion of *fairies* changing children in the cradle." He compares *1H4* 1.1.86-9 (89-92) and *FQ* 1.10.65. COLLIER (ed. 1858, 6:glos.) adds Gypsies to the perpetrators, an idea with which *OED* does not concur. According to *OED*, the changeling is the stupid, ugly child left for the beautiful stolen one; but Sh. (*MND* 2.1.23 [393], etc.) uses the word to mean a beautiful mortal child—in *MND*, not stolen but adopted.

1559 **mad**] The Clown is not sophisticated enough to think his father insane for believing in the prophecy. To support his change to *made*, meaning "whose fortune is made" (DYCE, 1859, p. 81; cf. *OED, ppl.a.* 7), THEOBALD (1729, in NICHOLS, 1817, 2:362-3) cites the word in the same sense in *MND* 4.2.19 (1764) and *TN* 2.5.146 (1160). (It is repeated in *TN* 3.4.55 [1574].) THEOBALD (ed. 1733) adds non-Shn. instances. FARMER (in STEEVENS, ed. 1773, 10:Pp5): "The word [*made*] is borrowed from the *novel*"; see p. 635. *Mad* and *made* also seem confused in *Tro.* 2.2.56 (1041) (Q *madde*, F *made*) and *2H4* 2.1.113 (705) (Q *made*, F *mad*). As BECKET (1815, 1: 130) notes, though, *mad* was an acceptable spelling of *made* (*OED*, Make, *v.*[1] Forms). WILSON (ed. 1931) considers that "the Clown may be quibbling upon 'mad.'" He compares *1H4* 2.4.492 (1453), where Q and F *made* is changed by F3 and some later eds. to *mad*, but he does not explain how that disputed reading indicates a quibble here. PAFFORD (ed. 1963), who emends because of the *Pandosto* correspondence, thinks that "'mad' could be defended in the sense of *happy, joyous*," but *OED* does not very strongly bear him out ("extravagant in gaiety; wild," *a.* 7).

1559-60 **If . . . you**] EATON (1860, p. 172): From Ps. 25:7—"Remember not the sinnes of my youth." NOBLE (1935, p. 247) adds, "the sinne of his youth" (Job 20:11). PAFFORD (ed. 1963) thinks "the phrase recalls [1501-6]—with a little irony." Critics who take the Clown seriously (see n. 1503-5, for example) disregard his genius for the inapposite.

1560 **you're . . . liue**] ABBOTT (§356): "'You are well off *as regards living*,' resembles our modern 'you are well to do'" or, as DEIGHTON (ed. 1889) puts it, "You have a happy life before you." BOORMAN (ed. 1964) more nearly catches the remark's comic inconsequence: "You'd do well to live." MOORMAN (ed. 1912), citing *MV* 2.2.53 (615), makes it "well to do," but the expression in *MV* seems to be a malapropism (EVANS, ed. 1974, notes, "Perhaps Gobbo supposes that the phrase means 'in good health'"). Here EVANS agrees with MOORMAN, however, adding "with pun on the sense 'living in virtue.'" For the indefinite use of the infinitive, see n. 704 and cf. lines 886, 2747, and 2853.

1562-3 **Faiery . . . close**] CALDECOTT (MS 1813-33): *Faiery Gold* alludes to "gifts of good omen left behind them, the rewards . . . of well doing." HALLIWELL (ed. 1859): "The revelation of any fairy gifts . . . entail[s] disaster." Cf. Field, Fletcher, and Massinger, *The Honest Man's Fortune*: When ladies who have been kissed "talke once, tis like fairy-money, They get no more close kisses" (5.1.57-8). SCHMIDT (1874, Close): "Secret."

1562 **proue so**] JOHNSON (1755, Prove): "To be found in the event." PARRY (ed. 1982): "I.e. it must be treated accordingly."

1563 **next**] MINSHEU (1617): See "Neare & hard By." Citing *1H4* 3.1.264 (1805), MALONE (ed. 1790): "Nearest." Cf. n. 277. HUNTER (ed. 1872): "Most direct," a read-

are luckie (boy) and to bee so still requires nothing but
secrecie. Let my sheepe go: Come (good boy) the next   1565
way home.

Clo. Go you the next way with your Findings, Ile go
see if the Beare bee gone from the Gentleman, and how
much he hath eaten: they are neuer curst but when they
are hungry: if there be any of him left, Ile bury it.   1570

Shep. That's a good deed: if thou mayest discerne by
that which is left of him, what he is, fetch me to th'sight
of him.

Clowne. 'Marry will I: and you shall helpe to put him
i'th'ground.   1575

Shep. 'Tis a lucky day, boy, and wee'l do good deeds
on't.   *Exeunt*

1569 when] *Om.* OXF1
1570 it] him OXF1

---

ing that *OED* (*a.* 1b) confirms. In 1567 the Shepherd goes home the next way,
whereas the Clown detours to dispose of Antigonus's remains (1567-70).

1564 **still**] Always. See n. 200.

1569 **curst**] HENLEY (in MALONE, 1780, 2:703): "Mischievous." STAUNTON (ed.
1859): "Malicious, dangerous" (*OED, ppl.a.* 4b: "Savage, vicious"). MAXWELL (ed.
1956): "Mean." PAFFORD (ed. 1963): "This sort of knowledge could only be held by
someone familiar with bears in captivity," but the familiarity need not have been
firsthand. See p. 816.

1570 **it**] VICKERS (1968, p. 420): "Antigonus finally becomes left-overs . . .
reduced to a pronoun."

1571 **a good deed**] BETHELL (ed. 1956) suggests a most unlikely allusion to Tobit
12:13: "Thy good dede was not hid from me." PAFFORD (ed. 1963): "To bury the
dead is by ancient and widespread tradition a good deed."

1572 **what he is**] KITTREDGE & RIBNER (ed. 1967): "(a) His identity (b) his social
position."

1572-3 **th'sight of him**] (1) To see him. (2) To his sight (that he may see me,
now sadly impossible). CLARK & WRIGHT (ed. 1863): "Capell's copy of the first Folio
has distinctly 'fight'. A copy in the possession of the Rev. N. M. Ferrers, Fellow of
Gonville and Caius College, has as distinctly 'sight.'" HINMAN (1963) records no such
press variant, however, and the *si* and *fi* ligatures are very similar.

1574 **'Marry**] SCHMIDT (1875): "An exclamation supposed to have been derived
from the name of the Holy Virgin, used [here] as an expletive particle, = why. . . .
Followed by an inversion of the subject in answers." SCHMIDT gives another meaning,
however, which is more appropriate here — "indeed, to be sure."

1576-7 **'Tis . . . on't**] LAWLOR (1962, p. 98): "The first note of hope in the
play." WALKER (1860, 2:170) suggests that "Thrive and do good," to which he finds
this expression related, may be proverbial, but DENT does not list it. LEE (ed. 1907):
The words are found in *2H6* 4.3.15 (2526). PAFFORD (ed. 1963): "Perhaps an echo
of the proverb 'The better the day the better the deed' (Tilley D60)." DEIGHTON (ed.

Actus Quartus. Scena Prima.   **4.1** (2B1ᵇ)

1578 *After* 1611 THEO, WARB, JOHN
  Scena Prima.] *Om.* CAP-BUL (−v1773, CAM1, GLO, WH2)

1889): "The reference to lucky and unlucky days is frequent in Elizabethan literature, and in the old almanacs they were marked; but it has not been shown that to do good on . . . lucky [days] was regarded as especially incumbent."

1577 **Exeunt**] SEWELL (1945, p. 222): "There is a close connection between the distribution of stage time and the credit granted by the audience to the movement of passion, the sequence of moods, the procession of events. In the first three acts . . . Shakespeare seems not to have given himself sufficient stage time to give proper authority to the quickening and development of Leontes' jealousy. In consequence, ideal time is unconvincing." Ideal time seems to be the imaginary time required for the fictional action and "movement of passion" (p. 212). SEWELL'S is a minority opinion.

1578 **Actus . . . Prima.**] THEOBALD (ed. 1733) makes Time's speech a separate postscript to Act 3, and WARBURTON (ed. 1747) makes it the conclusion of that act rather than the beginning of 4. HEATH (1765, p. 213), though convinced by "the insipid flatness of the sentiment, that this Chorus is an interpolation of the players," nonetheless would retain it at the beginning of Act 4 because "its purpose is to prepare . . . for a new scene of action, at a greatly distant time, in a different court, and in which new personages are introduced." (See n. 1144 for another disputed act division.) CAPELL (1783, 2.4:172): "This '*Chorus*' is like all Shakespeare's others—a prologizer, introductive of an action that succeeds his entry immediately: The address is of the utmost use here." GILBERT (1979, p. 238): "He appears *after* the important choices have already been made. . . . Leontes has already vowed repentance. The Old Shepherd . . . has already decided to care for the foundling. So Time may be seen both as a force directing the play's characters and as a force created by their own moral choices." JONES (1971, p. 68) hypothesizes that *WT*, like the tragedies and histories, "divide[s] into two unequal movements (corresponding roughly to the first three acts and the last two acts) and . . . the division between them is such as to make it likely that in performance a major interval [i.e., a suspension of performance] took place." No direct evidence has been found, however, of an interval in the performance of any English Renaissance play. Regarding the unequal parts, GRENE (1967, p. 68) praises *WT*'s "compression and neatness of structure."

The chorus is either unworthy of Sh. or another manifestation of his genius. PANOFSKY (1939, p. 81): "A mere device." CARRINGTON (1956): "He [Sh.] is getting careless, and he takes the line of least resistance." COGHILL (1958, p. 36), however: "He [Time] shows us we are being taken beyond 'realism' into the region of parable and fable, adumbrated in the title of the play. Time stands at the turn of the tide of mood, from tragedy to comedy. . . . Time is at the heart of the play's mystery." DOBREÉ (1960, p. 143): "Time . . . , plugging a gap of sixteen years, shows how shaky the idea of time is. . . . Before long the brilliant 'now' will be just like an old and faded story." HOY (1964, p. 270): "The last two acts [of *WT*] function as a kind of satyr play to the tragedy enacted in the first three. The presenter is, appropriately, Time, which throws a choral bridge over the sixteen-year interval that separates the tragic circumstance from its comic resolution. The sin which time brings to birth is atoned for in the fulness of time, and with atonement comes the restoration of certain at least of those who have been lost." QUINONES (1965, p. 347): "In the sonnets, Time cheers and checks; in the romances, it checks and then cheers. But in [this speech] there is no indication of either a benevolent or an inimical order of things. Time tries all, both good and bad. But in its expression of Time's power, the speech is in accord with the impression of the last plays. These plays deal with elemental things, and Time is one of the great elements." WALLER (1970, p. 136): "Time has taken over the function of the traditional conception of Providence. . . . Providence becomes identified with the chances Time brings to man and the reactions it provokes in him."

Regarding Time's function, GILDON (1710, p. 335): "*Shakespear* himself was sensible of this Grossness of making the Play above sixteen Years, and therefore brings in Time . . . to excuse the Absurdity." KOLBE (1930, p. 100): "Shakespeare's theory was . . . that the imagination can jump a lifetime as easily as a week, and his defence of this theory is elaborated in the choruses of *Henry V*. The lapse of time in *Macbeth* is greater than sixteen years, but there the development is so skilfully managed that there is no need to apologise for it." LÜDERS (1870, p. 282) believes that Time's function in *WT* as a deus ex machina derives from *Pandosto*, which is subtitled *The Triumph of Time*. SKOTTOWE (1824, 2:296): "The interval . . . is easily passed over in narration; but it was a serious difficulty in the play. The dramas of his predecessors and contemporaries furnished Shakespeare with abundance of precedent for the expedient he adopted." Time and his hourglass appear in an earlier pastoral romance, *The Thracian Wonder* (1590–c. 1601), but there he reminds the Chorus to keep the narrative moving. Soon after *WT*'s composition, Time's chorus was imitated in the anonymous *Tom a Lincoln* (c. 1611; MSR, ed. Richard Proudfoot, lines 122 ff.); see n. 94 for another imitation. SPIVACK (1958, pp. 310–11) finds Time to be the kind of abstract figure derived by Sh. from the morality plays; outside the play, he is "as clearly distinguished from the essential plot and its normal inhabitants as a frame is from its picture." CALDER–MARSHALL (1982, p. 248): "We have moved from a winter's tale to a summer's tale."

PAFFORD (ed. 1963, pp. 167–8) lists several modern discussions of "emblematic representations of Time" and quotes from Henry Peacham, *The Gentlemans Exercise . . . in Lymning, Painting*, [etc.] (1612, pp. 111–[12]): "An old man in a garment of starres, vpon his head a Garland of Roses, eares of Corne and dry stickes, standing vpon the Zodiack (for he hath his strength from heauen) holding a looking glasse in his hand, as beholding onely the present time[,] two children at his feete, one fat, and well liking, the other leane, writing both in one booke[;] vpon the heade of one, the sunne[;] vpon the other, the Moone. Hee is commonly drawne vpon tombes in Gardens, and other places an olde man bald, winged [*WT* 1583] with a Sith and an hower glasse [1595]." ORGEL (ed. 1996): "Cesare Ripa makes Time winged on the authority of Virgil, '*volat Tempus irreparabile*' (Time flies inexorably), *Iconologia* (Padua, 1611), p. 511; the Virgilian phrase is *fugit irreparabile Tempus* (*Georgics* 3.284, and compare *Aeneid* 10.467)." See also PANOFSKY (1939, pp. 71 ff.). SCHANZER (ed. 1969): "The scythe . . . may have been omitted on the stage in order to emphasize his role in the play as revealer rather than destroyer." CHEW (1939, pp. 85, 106–7): Time is described in Marston's *Insatiate Countess* as "as old bald thing" (ed. Melchiori, 1984, 2.1.32–3); he is also bald in *Err.* 2.2.70 (464). Proverbially Time is female, bald behind but with a forelock (TILLEY T311), but CHEW (p. 108) gives an example of a masculine Time so unadorned and adorned.

Songs aside, Time is given the only rhyme in the play.

Actus Quartus.] CLAPP (1885, p. 402): "The time of the [first] three scenes of Act IV . . . evidently does not exceed two or three days." See nn. 1612 and 1795.

Enter Time, the Chorus.

Time. I that please some, try all: both ioy and terror   1580
Of good, and bad: that makes, and vnfolds error,

1579 the] as THEO1-v1821, SING, KNT, DYCE, WH1, HAL, STAU, DEL, KTLY, HUD2
1581 makes, and vnfolds] Ff, WH, CAM1, GLO, NLSN+; mask and unfold THEOBALD
(1730) *conj. in* NICHOLS (1817, 2:609), THEO; masks and unfolds BUL; make and unfold
ROWE1 *etc.*

THORNDIKE (1901, pp. 162-3): In Act 4, "Shakspere is only giving an original development to the inevitable idyl. . . . The business of a girl gathering flowers [which
is not found here] in March [which is not the month represented; see n. 1887] had
been seen on the stage before Shakspere was born [he provides one instance]. The
business of the shepherds and shepherdesses was also an old and popular theatrical
convention, and the dance of satyrs was an entertainment probably directly borrowed
from a court masque [i.e., *Oberon*; see p. 855]. The reality given to these conventions
and to the equally conventional love story is Shakspere's own, and is secured largely
by the introduction of comic characters from real life [which the Shepherds are not]."
    1580-1 **I . . . vnfolds**] ABBOTT (§247): "The Relative . . . frequently (1) takes
a *singular* verb, though the antecedent be *plural*, and (2) the verb is often in the
third person, though the antecedent be in the *second* or *first*." Here "the distance of
the relative [*that* (1581)] from the antecedent [*I*] . . . makes a difference." HERFORD
(ed. 1904), on the other hand, believes that the conception changes: "The antecedent,
Time, is irregularly thought of as the person described only, not as the person speaking." PAFFORD (ed. 1963) thinks that *I am he* may be understood before *that*.
    1580 **I . . . all**] Proverbial (TILLEY T336).
        try] MINSHEU (1617, Trie): "[1] Proue, or assay [2] examine." SCHMIDT (1875):
"To examine by a test." TURNER (1971, p. 153): "To 'try' something is to refine away
and reject that which cannot endure in it. If Man is wholly a temporal being, then he
is wholly subject to the laws of time — of decay and fate: when time tries him, he will
be found wanting in that which endures, that which is independent of time." HAPPÉ
(1969): "The 'test of time' is still a proverbial phrase." For *try* in a slightly different
sense, see n. 788.
    1580-1 **both . . . error**] The CLARKES (ed. 1865): I.e., "that am both joy and
terror." DEIGHTON (ed. 1889): "The joy of the good and the terror of the bad."
PAFFORD (ed. 1963), however, compares "O time thou tutor both to good and bad"
(*Luc.* 995); and, following HUNTER (1965, p. 197), SCHANZER (ed. 1969) paraphrases
Time's words as "'the joy as well as the terror of good and bad alike'. This [SCHANZER
says] accords much better not only with the facts of life but also with the words that
follow: by making error, Time is the joy of the bad and terror of the good; by unfolding
it, the terror of the bad and joy of the good." ALMASY (1981, p. 120) cites instances
of the simultaneous experience of the opposites at 3025-9, 3053-6, 3059-61, 3081-
2, and 3277-8.
    1581 **makes . . . error**] That wrong may be covered by a folded or tightly wo-
ven cloth is reiterated in *Lr.* 1.1.283-4 (307-8), and THEOBALD (1730, in NICHOLS,
1817, 2:609) changes "makes" to *maske* because "a contrast in the terms seems
plainly designed." Defending F, STEEVENS (ed. 1773): "*Departed time* renders many
facts obscure, and in that sense is the cause of error. *Time to come* brings discoveries
with it." RANN (ed. 1787): "Occasion absurdities by the portion of me that is past,
and develope [sic] them in my progress." SCHMIDT (1875), who does not list this

Now take vpon me (in the name of Time)
To vse my wings: Impute it not a crime
To me, or my swift passage, that I slide
Ore sixteene yeeres, and leaue the growth vntride   1585
Of that wide gap, since it is in my powre

1585 growth] gulf WARB, (*withdrawn* mWARB)
1586-8 gap, . . . Custome.] ~ . . . . ~ , SING2 (*attrib. to* J. LLOYD *by* CAM1)

---

instance specifically, evidently assigns to *make* its usual significance, "to produce, to cause"; for *unfold*, he gives "to reveal." FURNESS (ed. 1898) suggests that "'makes' and 'unfolds' do not refer to Time, but to the 'good' and the 'bad.'" He paraphrases, "I, who please some, try all, and am both the joy and terror of the good man, as well as the bad man who makes and unfolds error." "This interpretation," he continues, "does away with the irregularity of construction in having two verbs in the 3rd pers., 'makes and unfolds', placed between two verbs in the 1st pers.: 'please' and 'take', and all four with the same nominative." MOORMAN (ed. 1912), who is followed by later eds., disagrees: "Who am both the cause of misunderstandings and the remover of these misunderstandings." LETTSOM (MS 1840-65), oddly: "It seems odd that S. did not write *unmake*."

1582 **in . . . Time**] DEIGHTON (ed. 1889): "Under the name; *not* in behalf of." PAFFORD (ed. 1963): "With the authority" of Time. BETHELL (ed. 1956): "The audience must be told who he is"—a doubtful reading, though Sh. may have been playing safe. For the ubiquity of the figure, see n. 1578.

1583-5 **Impute . . . yeeres**] "Like an old Tale still," *WT* systematically violates the unities, here the unity of time. Sir Philip SIDNEY (1595; 1912, 3:38) had complained in his *Defense of Poesie*: "Now of time, they [playwrights] are much more liberall [than of place]. For ordinarie it is, that two yoong Princes fall in love, after many traverses she is got with childe, and delivered of a faire boy: he is lost, groweth a man, falleth in love, and is readie to get an other childe, and all this in two houres space: which howe absurd it is in sence, even sence may imagine." This idea persists in various ways (see, e.g., BOORMAN, ed. 1964)—perhaps not altogether irrelevantly, for in *Tmp*. Sh. does observe the unities, including that of time. PROUDFOOT (1966, p. 240) speculates that "the unwonted concern about the unity of time [here] might possibly have had its origin in critical argument between Shakespeare and Jonson, perhaps about *Pericles*." SCHANZER (1975, p. 59): Jonson himself, using Cordatus as his spokesman (*Every Man Out*, Ind. 266-70), argued for needful innovation in drama, as SCHANZER believes Time does here, but elsewhere also ridiculed "the extravagant excesses of romantic drama" (*Every Man In*, Prol. 7-9).

1583 **Impute . . . crime**] PYLE (1969, p. 71): "No serious objection should be raised." SPENCER ("Artistry," 1970, p. 73): "He means: 'I realise I am playing a trick upon you, and I know all the critics condemn this kind of device.'"

1584-8 **I . . . Custome**] PYLE (1969, p. 72): "With solemn levity he [Sh.] refers the question of the unity of time to the arbitration of Time himself. Time civilly admits that sixteen years is a 'wide gap', but exercising his power to 'plant and o'erwhelm' convention announces a *fait accompli*."

1585 **sixteene**] At 1617, Camillo has been away from his country for fifteen years, but Forman, as PAFFORD (ed. 1963) observes, heard *sixteen*. See p. 606. HONIGMANN

(1965, p. 138, n. 3): "Probably the same number should have been given both times: the gap between Camillo's departure (Act I) and the end of Act III (to which the chorus refers) could only be a matter of weeks." HONIGMANN (1989, p. 204) later suggests that this Shn. inconsistency and others resulted from Sh.'s writing while his company was on the road; he had left his books and papers in London. As for the number itself, it had to be great enough for Leontes's period of mourning to be impressive yet not so great that he and Hermione would have become antiquities by the time of their reunion. Perdita's age is also a factor. HARBAGE (1952, p. 238): "Juliet is . . . not quite fourteen in Shakespeare [*Rom*.]. . . . Miranda [*Tmp*.] fifteen, and Mariana [*Per*.] fourteen. Whenever the age of the heroine is optional in his sources, Shakespeare makes it extremely young. To Frank Harris this seemed evidence of his 'fierce sensuality'. Rather it is evidence of his impulse . . . to portray in woman complete absorption in the lover, complete isolation from all other men." HARRIS (1909) describes Sh.'s sensuality as "overwhelming" (p. 381), "tortured," and "excessive" (p. 385). Another factor affecting Perdita only, according to HOLMES (1960, p. 214), is that her part would be taken by the same boy who played Mamillius. FOWLER (1978, pp. 56-7) notices that "the subtle *simplesse* of [the] speech finds matching form in sixteen couplets. . . . As a square number, and especially as the square on the tetrad, it [16] symbolized virtue and justice. Particularly, it meant the ordering of the psyche. . . . Leontes himself speaks of his repentance in a similar mathematical metaphor [in 2785-6]."

1585-6 **and . . . gap**] HEATH (1765, p. 214): "And leave unexamined what had been the product of that wide gap of time he was sliding over, that is, of sixteen years." MALONE (1780, 1:145): *Growth* in the sense of "product" (*OED*, Growth[1] 4) is reiterated in 1595. PORTER & CLARKE (ed. c. 1903): "Progress"; PORTER & CLARKE (ed. 1908): "Life in process of development." KAMACHI (1979, p. 28): "Something new, fresh and positive is anticipated in the repeated use of the word 'grow' [also found in 1603]." JOHNSON (ed. 1765): "*Untried* is not, perhaps, the word which he [Sh.] would have chosen, but which his rhyme required." He does not again use *untried*, but *try* meaning "examine" or "test" occurs frequently—e.g., at 788. HENLEY (ed. 1902) and MAXWELL (ed. 1956), somewhat inaccurately: "Untold." BETHELL (ed. 1956): "'Untried' means either that the sixteen years growth is *unattempted* by the dramatist or *not tested, not sampled*, by the audience—or it may mean both." KERMODE (ed. 1963): "Time asks to be excused from detailed accounts of the interim period and its developments, for instance Perdita's childhood." SPENDER (1982, 1: 234): "He has no intention of telling us what the characters have been up to in the meantime."

1586 **wide gap**] BETHELL (ed. 1956): Cf. "this great gap of time" (*Ant*. 1.5.5 [527]). Time passes the words on to Leontes; see 3368.

1586-8 **since . . . Custome**] JOHNSON (ed. 1765): "He who has broke so many laws may now break another; . . . he who introduced every thing may introduce *Perdita* on her sixteenth year; and he intreats that he may pass as of old, before any *order* or succession of objects, ancient or modern, distinguished his periods." CAPELL (1783, 2.4:173): "The '*law* and *custom*' . . . mean those of the drama"; Time excuses "those breaches in the drama's establish'd unities which the poet is led into by his '*tale*.'" HUDSON (ed. 1880): "He seems to mean, that he who overthrows every thing, and makes as well as overwhelms custom, may surely infringe the laws of his own making." DEIGHTON (ed. 1889): "The two most durable of institutions, are still powerless against the innovations of time." BETHELL (ed. 1956): "The dramatist in ignoring the critics' laws about time is only doing what Time himself does with laws and customs in general." KERMODE (ed. 1963): "Time 'plants' Custom but not Law. Custom lacks the authority of Law, and relates to erroneous Opinion; hence the contemporary use of the word in attacks on such ceremonies of the Roman Church as

To orethrow Law, and in one selfe-borne howre
To plant, and ore-whelme Custome. Let me passe
The same I am, ere ancient'st Order was,
Or what is now receiu'd. I witnesse to   1590
The times that brought them in, so shall I do
To th'freshest things now reigning, and make stale

1588-90 Custome. . . . am, . . . receiu'd.] ~ , . . . ~ . . . . ~ , SING2
1588 passe‸] ~ — CAM3, SIG
1590 witnesse] witness'd mTBY3 *conj.*, CAP, SING2, KTLY, HUD2

---

seemed to Protestants without Scriptural authority.'' This distinction is in general borne out by SCHMIDT (1874), who for *law* gives ''a rule prescribed by the supreme power of a state'' or ''any rule of direction''; for *custom* he gives ''common use, received order.''

SCHANZER (ed. 1969) offers another interpretation: ''The *law* referred to is evidently that [which] limited the action of a play to one day. . . . Shakespeare wittily makes Time defend his own most blatant violation of the unity of time in this play by having him point out that all such laws and customs are of no permanent validity. The crime referred to in [1583] is therefore that of violating the rule of the unity of time, rather than . . . that of failing to stage the events of the intervening sixteen years.'' MACKINNON (1988, p. 140): ''He shows himself as a ravening destroyer, who breaks down both the subtle creation of 'law' and the humbler ordering of 'custom.''' Time says he can do these things, not that he has done them. PAFFORD (ed. 1963) finds the ideas reiterated from *Luc.* 876, 880, 930-2 and *Son.* 115.

1587 **one . . . howre**] For *selfe-borne*, CAPELL (1783 [1774], 1:glos.): ''Springing or born from myself,'' but the CLARKES (ed. 1865): ''One and the same.'' For various uses of *self*, including this compound, see ABBOTT §20. For the phrase, HERFORD (ed. 1916-), following CAPELL: ''A single hour of my own begetting. All hours are thought of as Time's offspring; all are thence, for Time, 'self-born'; the point here, however, is not this, but that in a *single* hour Time can 'plant' and destroy a custom. . . . 'Self' [has] its original sense of 'same' [*OED, a.* 1].'' TURNER (1971, p. 150), somewhat differently: ''Perhaps implies that since the past is dead, every hour is self-generating; the present has a superficial resemblance to the immediate past, but that is all.'' CHARLTON (ed. 1916): ''He has the power to overthrow his own law by sudden revolution.'' COOPER (1923, p. 133) believes that the reference is to the Aristotelian unities rather than law in general; ''The 'laws' of place and time in this 'poem unlimited' are manfully overthrown by an artist who regards action as the important thing.''

1588 **plant . . . Custome**] THIRLBY (MS 1733-47?): ''P[lant] one & o['erwhelm] another.'' LOBBAN (ed. 1910): ''In one and the same hour to make and unmake precedent.''

1588-90 **Let . . . receiu'd**] RANN (ed. 1787): ''Conceive of me now, as of old, before any regular succession of events was established, or the terms *ancient* and *modern* known." HUNTER (ed. 1872), similarly: "Let me pass for the same that I am before the most ancient social order existed, or that which is now recognized." HER-FORD (ed. 1904): "Time pleads that as he can bring about sudden revolutions, he is not deserving his character in passing suddenly over the slow changes of sixteen years. . . . But the following ['ere . . . was'] does not very well connect with ['I witnesse . . . in']." For *passe*, the CLARKES (ed. 1865): "'Pass by, or on', and 'pass for'"; BOORMAN (ed. 1964): "Be accepted." CHARLTON (ed. 1916): "Time's words, with their use of *am* for *was* [1589], are an outward sign that the distinction of past and present is broken down by him. In the same way *witness* [1590] is used in the present tense instead of the past." KERMODE (ed. 1963), who follows WILSON (ed. 1931) in punctuating after "passe": "Let me pass over that gap; I alone remain un-changed from the beginning—and have passed over that far greater gap." Summing up, KITTREDGE & RIBNER (ed. 1967): "Let me (time) move unchanged from the era before all forms of civilization began to the present, which inherits these forms from earlier times. This seems to be the general meaning, time being conceived of as eternal and universal." SCHANZER (ed. 1969) interprets *ancient'st Order* as "oldest injunc-tions." Time's relationship to eternity naturally prompts religious considerations. With this passage THIRLBY (MS 1725-33?) compares Christ's words: "Before Abraham was I am" (John 8:58), and WILSON punctuates after *passe* to convey the idea of "the attribute of Jehovah ('I am' [Exod. 3:14]), which [Sh.] applies to Time." In a long note, BETHELL (ed. 1956) observes that "time considered apart from our day-to-day experience is an eternal present" and that "past, present and future are all on the same level in the judgement of eternity." KNOWLES (privately): Time "is being face-tious: 'Let me, before your eyes, pass through sixteen years without any signs of aging [such as are evident in Hermione (3217-18)], since my appearance hasn't changed from the earliest age until the present.'"

1588 **Let me passe**] PARRY (ed. 1982): "Both 'accept me' and 'allow me to go by.'"

1589-91 **ancient'st . . . in**] PAFFORD (ed. 1963): Cf. *Luc.* 939-41.

1589 **was**] ELLIS (1871, 3:956): *Was* also rhymes with *pass* in *Ham.* 2.2.418 (1463) and *Son.* 49.5-7. Elsewhere Sh. rhymes it with *ass*, *grass*, *glass*, and *lass*.

1590 **receiu'd**] SCHMIDT (1875, Receive): "Acknowledge." SCHANZER (ed. 1969): "Accepted as a rule."

witnesse] *OED* (*v.* 2a, citing this line): "Testify."

1591 **them**] DEIGHTON (ed. 1889): "The ancient order of things." HENLEY (ed. 1902): "And 'what is now received.'"

1591-2 **do To**] PARRY (ed. 1982): "Observe the passing of."

1592 **th'freshest . . . reigning**] SCHMIDT (1874, Fresh): "Holding good, un-changing, constant." KITTREDGE & RIBNER (ed. 1967): "Newest things of the present time." EDWARDS (*Progress*, 1986, p. 149): "He is inexorable time, whose hand is upon Florizel and Perdita."

1592-4 **make . . . it**] HAPPÉ (1969): "I shall make this shining present seem as dull to the future, as I have already made the past (when the story took place) dull by comparison with the present." WILSON (ed. 1931) compares *Tro.* 3.3.171-4 (2023-6); PAFFORD (ed. 1963), *Luc.* 939, 944-7.

The glistering of this present, as my Tale
Now seemes to it: your patience this allowing,
I turne my glasse, and giue my Scene such growing   1595
As you had slept betweene: *Leontes* leauing
Th'effects of his fond iealousies, so greeuing
That he shuts vp himselfe. Imagine me
(Gentle Spectators) that I now may be
In faire Bohemia, and remember well,   1600

1596-8 leauing∧∧ . . . iealousies, . . . himselfe.∧] F1, ROWE; ~ ∧∧ . . . ~ ,
. . . ~ ,∧ F2-F4, COL, WH1, KTLY, OXF2; ~ ∧∧ . . . ~ ∧ . . . ~ ;∧ POPE, KIT1, SIS;
~ ∧∧ . . . ~ , . . . ~ ;∧ THEO1-JOHN2, DYCE1, IRV; ~ ∧∧ . . . ~ ; . . . ~ ;∧ CAP-
KNT2, HUD1, SING2, HAL, KNT3; ~ ,— . . . ~ ∧ . . . ~ ;— STAU, K&R *etc*.
1597 Th'effects] To th' effects KEIGHTLEY *conj. in* CAM1, KTLY

1593 **glistering . . . present**] RANN (ed. 1787): "The glare of novelty, which
marks the manners of to-day." With *glistering*, "brightness," cf. n. 1355-6; and for
this present used to identify the play's world with the real world, see n. 274-8.

my Tale] LINDENBAUM (1972, p. 3): Time is "the author of the play in which
he appears." Time's tale would naturally be an old one. KERMODE (ed. 1963) alone
takes "my Tale" to refer to this speech, which interrupts the play.

1594 **seemes**] CHARLTON (ed. 1916): "Seems stale."

it] LETTSOM (MS 1840-65): "I.e. *this present*," rather than *glistering*, which
FURNESS (ed. 1898) takes to be the antecedent. ROLFE (ed. 1879) agrees with LETTSOM:
"Seems stale to *this present*." BOORMAN (ed. 1964): "The reality of which it [my tale]
tells." KNOWLES (privately): "Compared to it."

1594-6 **your . . . betweene**] TURNER (1971, p. 150): "As teller of the tale, Time
in a sense represents the dramatist himself; . . . the 'growing' is the growth of the
tiny heap of sand [in the hourglass], as well as an indication of the fruitful and creative
effects of time. The image of sleep . . . convey[s] the idea of healing; and it has the
more mysterious connotations of dream, of the fantasy that is truth. . . . Time's
speech not only conducts us across the widest gap of mood and of imagined time in
Shakespeare, it also plumbs the very nature of time; the change is not a mere scene-
change, but Change itself."

1594 **your . . . allowing**] PORTER & CLARKE (ed. 1908): "Letting all this be supposed, as to Time's effects on conditions real and artistic." SPENCER ("Artistry," 1970,
p. 73): I.e., "If you will forgive me for what I'm doing."

1594-5 **allowing . . . growing**] ELLIS (1871, 3:961) finds similar rhymes elsewhere in Sh. — e.g., *low / cow* in *Ado* 5.4.48-9 (2603-4); *brow / grow* in *Ven*. 139-
41; and *glow / brow* in *Ven*. 337-9.

1595 **I . . . glasse**] SCHANZER (1964, p. 79): "Time marks the great break between the two halves of the play, but also creates in us a feeling of repetition. Both
parts of the hour-glass look alike, and it may not be too fanciful to think that this fact
enhances our sense of the similarity of the shape and structure of the two halves."
ORGEL (ed. 1996): "The time occupied by the play is thus half over, and that half has
lasted an hour. If this is to be taken literally, it implies that the text must have been
cut for performance by at least a third. The claim that theatrical performances lasted

only two hours is all but universal in the period." RUNDUS (1974, pp. 124–5): Instead of an hourglass, Time may be equipped with a mirror, though a "much less likely possibility," especially as the glass is turned. As for the hourglass, he finds (p. 125) a Renaissance instance of its representing Youth or Age, "depending upon whether the superior part of the glass was empty or full. Thus . . . one reason for Time's turning his hourglass is to show the upper part full and hence a potential for growth-life renewed; but also this action indicates that his concern will now be with Youth . . . and spring." MACKINNON (1988, p. 141), who thinks the glass a mirror: "He directs his mirror to a new point, and he is seen as a reflecting rather than a controlling agent." If he can "try all" (1580), however, he is clearly in control.

Scene such growing] HUNTER (ed. 1872): "Enacted story [i.e., play] such advancement." LAWRENCE (1937, pp. 10–11) finds that *growing* makes clear the significance of "the swelling act" in *Mac.* 1.3.128 (238) and the "swelling scene" in *H5* Prol. 4 (5). PARRY (ed. 1982): Cf. 1585. "'Growth' is the keynote of the Bohemia sequence of the play."

1596 **As**] The CLARKES (ed. 1865): "As if." See ABBOTT §107.

betweene] DEIGHTON (ed. 1889): "Through the interval which must have elapsed." KITTREDGE & RIBNER (ed. 1967): "While all of this intervening action took place."

1596–8 *Leontes . . . me*] THIRLBY (MS 1733–47?): *Leontes* is in the accusative (objective) case. According to HAPPÉ (1969), the sentence then becomes "I turn my glass . . . leaving Leontes so grieving over the results of his mad jealousy that he shuts himself up." STAUNTON (ed. 1859), who construes similarly, points out that if "Th'effects . . . himselfe" is not a parenthesis, the meaning is that Leontes leaves "the consequences of his foolish jealousies, . . . at the same time . . . so 'grieving' over them that he shuts himself up." That *leaving* means "allowing Leontes to remain in this state," he notes, is borne out by *Pandosto* (see p. 633). HUNTER (ed. 1872), however, detects two inversions: "Leaving Leontes, so grieving the effects, &c." HUDSON (ed. 1880), similarly: "Imagine me leaving Leontes, *who* so *grieves* th'effects of his fond jealousies that he shuts up himself." For the dramatic purpose of the reference to Leontes, see n. 1635.

1597 **fond**] MINSHEU (1617): "Foolish." For other meanings, see n. 2270.

1598 **himselfe.**] MUNRO (ed. 1957): "The punctuation . . . is a case of strong internal stopping." MCKERROW (1939, p. 42) had alluded to "rather numerous cases in which a clause is separated by a major stop, such as a semicolon, colon, or full point, from another to which it logically belongs, while at the same time it is only separated by a comma from one with which it has much less close logical connection." Cf. 2281. WELLS (in WELLS & TAYLOR, 1987) does not agree about the logical affinity; he considers "the passage . . . ambiguous." ALEXANDER (1945, p. 77): "Where do we find the most remarkable instances of this . . . punctuation? . . . In those very texts that are judged by the best authorities to have been printed from Shakespeare's own manuscript." That is not the case with *WT*, however. ORGEL (ed. 1996): "F's punctuation, which makes 'my scene' leave Leontes, is unexceptionable, especially in a speech that is otherwise so contorted and elliptical."

me] MASON (1785, p. 131): "*With me* or . . . *for me*," the ethical dative, for which see ABBOTT §220 and VISSER (1984, §320). SINGER (ed. 1826) calls the construction a Fr. idiom, which it is, but it is also found in Old English. Cf. n. 1626–9.

1600 **In faire Bohemia**] PYLE (1969, pp. 73–4): "With Leontes, shut up with his grief, time presumably stands still; and therefore, it seems, Time goes to Bohemia." In so doing, he carries us into the green world of FRYE (1949, p. 68): the forest of *TGV*, the fairy world of *MND*, the Forest of Arden of *AYL*, the Windsor Forest of *Wiv.*

I mentioned a sonne o'th'Kings, which *Florizell*
I now name to you: and with speed so pace
To speake of *Perdita*, now growne in grace
Equall with wond'ring. What of her insues
I list not prophesie: but let Times newes   1605
Be knowne when 'tis brought forth. A shepherds daughter
And what to her adheres, which followes after,
Is th'argument of Time: of this allow,
If euer you haue spent time worse, ere now:
If neuer, yet that Time himselfe doth say,   1610
He wishes earnestly, you neuer may.   *Exit.*

1601 I mentioned a] I mention here a F2-THEO2, WARB-JOHN2, v1773; There is a HAN; A mention'd HUD2
     which] whom POPE1-JOHN2
     1610 neuer, yet$_\wedge$] ~ $_\wedge$ ~ , mTBY4 *conj.*, CAP, v1778-KNT2, SING2, WH1, HAL, KTLY, KNT3

1601 **I mentioned**] LEE (ed. 1907), taking the past tense to indicate a mention of Florizel prior to this one, thinks 242 ff. is being referred to, Time "vaguely assuming responsibility for their [the kings' lines] utterance." PAFFORD (ed. 1963), similarly: "Time is simply referring to the mention earlier in the play—in time just past." TURNER (1971, p. 149) and EVANS (ed. 1974) take these earlier lines to be part of "Times newes" (1605). As BETHELL (ed. 1956) says, "Time is imagined as the narrator of the whole story." PYLE (1969, p. 74) elaborates: The idea that the play is Time's story "is a neat and pleasant fancy worked out in harmony with the mood of easy good humour in which the whole passage is written. . . . It playfully justifies Time's intrusion as Chorus [and] it stimulates a state of expectancy . . . regarding Perdita and her affairs." ROBERTSON (1930, p. 133) thinks that the words imply "a previous prologue, which has been dropped" (see p. 586). What Time means is "don't forget I spoke earlier of the king's son; I now tell you he is named Florizel." NUTTALL (1966, p. 39), however, suggests that Sh. himself took the part of Time and that the personal pronouns are jests.
     1602 **speed so pace**] LEE (ed. 1907): "With equal haste go forward." BETHELL (ed. 1956): "Move forward in an orderly fashion." *OED* considers this usage a transferred sense of the verb, which is used in its conventional sense in line 1780.
     1603 **growne in grace**] BETHELL (1947, p. 90): "At once reminiscent of Hermione."
     grace] JOHNSON (1755): "Natural excellence." For other meanings of *grace*, see n. 146.
     1604 **Equall with wond'ring**] KERSEY (1702, To wonder at): "*Admire*, or *be surpriz'd*." HUNTER (ed. 1872): "To a degree commensurate with the utmost stretch of wonder." Or LEE (ed. 1907): "To an extent that justifies no less wonder or admiration." LOBBAN (ed. 1910): "Her beauty as great as the general admiration of it."

1605 **list**] JOHNSON (1755): "Choose."

prophesie] ABBOTT (§349): A present infinitive with *to* omitted.

1605-6 **let . . . forth**] TURNER (1971, p. 149): "Time says fairly explicitly that the story which follows is to be told by himself." Regarding *newes . . . 'tis*: in Sh., *news* may be construed as either singular or plural. See FRANZ §194 and *OED* (*sb.* [*pl.*] 2 and 2b). PAFFORD (ed. 1963) compares *Per.* 2. Cho. 39-40 and 3. Cho. 55-6.

1606-7 **daughter . . . after**] THIRLBY (MS 1733-47?): *After* is "pronounc'd a'ter," so that it rhymes with 1606. But see the following. *After* and *daughter* also seem to rhyme in *Shr.* 1.1.239-40 (547-8), which, ELLIS (1871, 3:963) observes, "may be meant as ludicrous"—and here, too, perhaps. PAFFORD (ed. 1963), finding in Joshua Sylvester's trans. of Du Bartas's *Divine Weeks and Works* (1605) rhymes on *water / matter* (p. 10) and *matter / after* (p. 11) and in *Posthumus Bartas* (1607) on *water / heerafter* (p. 29), concludes that Sh. pronounced it *atter*. Yet DOBSON (1968, 2:519): "All rhymes involving *after* are to be regarded as special cases, in view of the surviving dialectal pronunciations." Since *OED* records *dafter* as a 16th-17th-c. variant of *daughter*, CERCIGNANI (1981, p. 325): The rhyme here and in *Shr.* does not show that in pronunciation Sh.'s *after* had lost its *f*. That loss is shown, however, in *Lr.* 1.4.317-21 (837-41)—*caught her / daughter / slaughter / halter / after*.

1607 **to her adheres**] The CLARKES (ed. 1865): "Concerns her, or pertains to her story." *Adheres* appears to be *OED* (*v.* 1b *fig.*).

which followes after] DEIGHTON (ed. 1889): "An account of which will be given later on." PARRY (ed. 1982), however: "Which is about to take place."

1608 **th'argument of Time**] For *Time* RANN (ed. 1787) gives "the present time" but LOBBAN (ed. 1910) the "Chorus, Time," as also in 1610. KIRSCH (1981, pp. 166-7): "A similar conception of time is stated in . . . Spenser's 'Mutability Cantos' [*FQ* 7.7.58-63]. . . . Spenser's passage has often been used by critics as a gloss to explain 'th'argument of Time' . . . and [the sense?] of providential immanence we experience in the last plays." However pertinent such a gloss might be, no critic consulted for this ed. provided it.

argument] JOHNSON (1755): "Subject" (*OED* 6).

1608-11 **of this . . . may**] CHALMERS (ed. 1823, Allow), perhaps influenced by MALONE's gloss at 267: "Approve." SCHMIDT (1874), however: *Allow* with *of* means "permit." PAFFORD (ed. 1963): "'Allow' governs both 'this' and 'that Time himself doth say'. 'If you have ever spent time less agreeably than now [or] if you have never spent time less agreeably please admit all the same that Time assures you he [only] wishes with all his heart that you never may.'" CARRINGTON (1956): The allusion is to time spent in the theater. MACKINNON (1988, p. 142): The lines "remind us that Time is an actor . . . and thus tend to diminish his potential symbolic status." FREY (*Vast Romance*, 1980, p. 142): *This* refers back to "th'argument of Time" and forward to "Time's wishes for time well spent." NICHOLS (1981, p. 177): "By concluding with an expression of goodwill for all its audience, Time surprises us, inasmuch as Time began by proclaiming an indifference to man."

1609-11 **If . . . may**] *OED* (Worse, *adv.* 1c, citing line 1609): "Carelessly . . . imperfectly." PORTER & CLARKE (ed. 1908) take *that* in 1610 to be demonstrative—"that aforesaid *Time*." BETHELL (ed. 1956) similarly: "Yet that time (which you are spending so badly) does himself say that he wishes you never may (spend time worse in the future)." MOORMAN (ed. 1912) takes *that* to be relative: "If you have never spent time so unprofitably, then at least approve of this, that Time himself, etc." ORGEL (ed. 1996): "Yet allow that." PARRY (ed. 1982): "His implication is that he does not think that 'his' play is as bad as all that!"

Scena Secunda.   4.2

Enter Polixenes, and Camillo.

Pol. I pray thee (good *Camillo*) be no more importunate: 'tis a sicknesse denying thee any thing: a death to   1615
grant this.

1612 *Scena Secunda*] SCENE I CAP, v1773-STAU, KTLY-HUD2, OXF1, BUL
1613 *Court of* Bohemia. POPE1-NLSN, ARD1+ (−PEL1, CLN2, PEN2, OXF2) (*subst.*);
Before the palace of Polixenes. RLTR

1612 ***Scena Secunda.***] DANIEL (1879, p. 178): The sixth day represented, 16 years
after Day 5, with which 4.1 is occupied. DELIUS (1870, p. 250) finds in this expository
scene the same affected euphuistic prose as that of 1.1. BETHELL (ed. 1956), rather
differently: "The conversation is in prose, being chiefly concerned with matters of
fact." HEIMS (1988, p. 6): "The very first business of the play is recapitulated when
the struggle between a person who wishes to depart and another who is adamant
that he remain becomes a conflict between Polixenes and Camillo," an idea rediscovered by HUSSEY (1992, p. 234). THIRLBY (MS 1725–33?) wonders if "a good deal
of this scene [might] be made verse." No ed. has tried. See n. 1501–19.
    1613 ***Enter . . . Camillo.***] For KNIGHT's praise of this scene's opening, see p.
659. COLLINS (ed. 1904–24?): "This scene, in its effect on the spectator's mind, is an
integral part of the action, though nothing actually happens in it. Further, the introduction of figures already familiar makes the gap of sixteen years seem less abrupt
than if we had been suddenly introduced to a new set of characters." FOWLER (1978,
p. 62): "The analogy between Polixenes and Leontes [extends] to such details as
importunate jealous hospitality." Mark TAYLOR (1982, pp. 26–7): "Setting aside their
first scenes . . . acts 1 and 4 have remarkably similar beginnings. In 1.2 Leontes . . . protests against Polixenes' decision to leave. . . . In 4.2 Polixenes, grateful
for the fifteen years Camillo has served him in Bohemia, protests against Camillo's
desire to return to, and die in, his native land. . . . The duplication suggests that the
two kings are [largely] interchangeable . . . the motives and purposes of one identical with those of the other. . . . The Kings are the same age; they grew up together . . . ; the grown son of one reminds Paulina of the dead son of the other
[2869–72], born at nearly the same time; both Kings are capable of towering rages
directed toward their children; and their reunion at the end of the play is one measure
of restored harmony." See n. 1614–16. CHARLTON (ed. 1916): "We are made to know
at once that the mellowing of years has brought the desire for home ties, and has
produced a penitence which bodes well for the ultimate reunion of broken bonds."
    1614–22 **I . . . departure**] PAFFORD (ed. 1963): "These lines prepare us for
Camillo's motive at [2365–70] and his part in Florizel's and Perdita's flight to Leontes'
court and in the pursuit by Polixenes. Cf. [2544–9]."
    1614–16 **I . . . this**] HILLMAN (1979, p. 18): "Concern over his son . . .
informs his general air of sombre anxiety."

Cam. It is fifteene yeeres since I saw my Countrey:
though I haue (for the most part) bin ayred abroad, I desire to lay my bones there. Besides, the penitent King
(my Master) hath sent for me, to whose feeling sorrowes   1620
I might be some allay (or I oreweene to thinke so) which
is another spurre to my departure.

Pol. As thou lou'st me (*Camillo*) wipe not out the rest
of thy seruices, by leauing me now: the neede I haue of
thee, thine owne goodnesse hath made: better not to   1625
haue had thee, then thus to want thee, thou hauing made

1617 fifteene] sixteen HAN, CAP, RANN, HAL, DYCE2, HUD2, OXF2
1618 bin] being F4-ROWE3

1617 **fifteene**] In favor of HANMER's *sixteen*, STEEVENS (ed. 1773) refers to 1585;
in ed. 1785 he adds 3221 and 3243. Most critics prefer to let the discrepancy stand,
believing that it is of no consequence or that Camillo is not speaking precisely. The
CLARKES (1879, p. 777): "One of those variations in statement which come naturally
from a person supposed to talk without strict precision of a past period." BETHELL
(ed. 1956) thinks "this . . . sort of inaccuracy . . . makes him [Sh.] seem so 'natural.'" WELLS (in WELLS & TAYLOR, 1987), however: "It could be a compositor's or
scribe's misreading of a roman numeral [xvi read as xv] (cf. [*MM* 1.2.167 (261)]
where, in another Crane play, xiv seems to have been misread as xix)." For still
another possible numerical error, see n. 1501, *ten.*

1618 **for . . . part**] FURNESS (ed. 1898), noticing that the transpired time is on
several occasions given as sixteen years (1585, 3221, 3243): Has Camillo not been
continuously at the court of Polixenes during the years just past? PORTER & CLARKE
(ed. 1908): The expression "may be meant to suggest one return [to Sicilia], to close
his affairs there." It is much more likely to be a simple discrepancy.

ayred abroad] JERVIS (1868, Ayred): "To live; to breathe; to enjoy the air," with
which *OED* (*pple.* 2) substantially agrees, considering this a figurative application of
"exposed to the open air" (1). SCHMIDT (1874): "To lead forth, to lead about," as though
Camillo were a poodle. BETHELL (ed. 1956): "Breathed foreign air, lived abroad."

1620 **feeling**] HERFORD (ed. 1904): "Keenly felt." BLAKE (1983, p. 75): "Participles . . . have a passive sense when used in a nominal group."

1621 **allay**] JERVIS (1868): "Mitigation; alleviation." BETHELL (ed. 1956): "Solace."

oreweene] JOHNSON (1755): "Think too highly" (*OED, v.* 2). SCHMIDT (1875):
"Presume" (*OED, v.* 1).

1622 **spurre**] *OED* (*sb.*[1] 4b, citing this line): "Incentive."

1624–5 **the . . . made**] HAPPÉ (1969): "Your own good services have made me
dependent upon you."

1625–6 **better . . . want thee**] Michael TAYLOR (1982, p. 234), alone: "Curiously petulant."

1626 **want**] The CLARKES (ed. 1865): "'Stand in need of', 'be without.'" EVANS
(ed. 1974): "Lack, i.e. lose."

1626–9 **thou . . . done**] BETHELL (ed. 1956): "Camillo, an expert administrator,
has started enterprises of State, that only he can carry through. If he leaves Polixenes
without completing these tasks, he does in effect take away with him the good that
he has done." CALDECOTT (MS 1813–33, Made me): "Originated, or induced me to
embark on," but more likely the ethical dative again—"made for me"; see n. 1598.

303

me Businesses, (which none (without thee) can sufficiently manage) must either stay to execute them thy selfe,
or take away with thee the very seruices thou hast done:
which if I haue not enough considered (as too much I   1630
cannot) to bee more thankefull to thee, shall bee my stu-
die, and my profite therein, the heaping friendshippes.
Of that fatall Countrey Sicillia, prethee speake no more,
whose very naming, punnishes me with the remembrance

1627 Businesses] Business F4-ROWE3
1632 heaping] reaping MTBY3 *conj.*, WARB
      friendshippes] friendship HAN
1634 naming] name WH2

1627-8 **(which none (without thee) . . . manage)**] Regarding brackets
within brackets, SIMPSON (1911, p. 98): "This clumsy device is used occasionally, not
only in a long parenthesis, where there might be some excuse for it, but even within
the compass of a single line." This is his only Shn. example.
   1627 **without**] SCHMIDT (1875, citing this line only): "Except . . . or = wanting
thee and thy help?"
   1627-8 **sufficiently**] *OED* (*adv.* 2, citing this line): "Satisfactorily; hence,
fully . . . quite."
   1630 **considered**] DEIGHTON (ed. 1889): "In the way of reward." Cf. n. 2676.
   1631-2 **to bee . . . friendshippes**] HEATH (1765, p. 214): "And all the profit
I propose to myself in this study of mine to be more friendly to you in the future is,
the heaping still more friendships on thee, and by that means laying still stronger
obligations on thee to continue with me." JOHNSON (ed. 1765): "I will for the future
be more liberal of recompence, [so] that as I heap benefits I shall heap friendships,
as I confer favours on thee I shall increase the friendship between us." CAPELL (1783,
2.4:173): "This natural increase . . . he calls — his 'profit'" (see n. 1632). MALONE
(ed. 1790): *Friendshippes* is used "merely for friendly offices." The CLARKES (ed.
1865): "Friendly benefits, tokens of friendship." SCHMIDT (1874), questionably: "Receiving plenty of good services." MOORMAN (ed. 1912): "Friendly feelings." DEIGH-
TON's (ed. 1889) objection that "Polixenes could hardly mean that the heaping of
friendly offices on Camillo was his *profit*" seems answered by PIERCE's (ed. 1918)
"increase in friendly acts" as just that, although the acts could be performed by either
or both. ABBOTT (§178) considers the replacement of gerunds by participles in such
constructions.
   1632 **profite**] HUNTER (ed. 1872): "My progress or advancement."
      therein] THIRLBY (MS 1733-47?): "In my study."
   1633-8 **Of . . . son?**] DRAPER (1985, p. 351): Like Leontes and Camillo, "Polixenes . . . lives in memory, burdened with a past that refuses to fade [although he]
has more recent concerns to temper his bitterness." TOLIVER (1989, p. 163): "Camillo
should not require so elaborate a reminder of Sicilia or need to be told who Florizel
is. But the audience requires information and must be made to realize Polixenes'
attitude toward his earlier misfortune. . . . The word 'brother' suggests that, whatever the new relation between the two countries becomes, it will remember the old
one." Polixenes has set aside the animosity he might justly have felt because of Leontes's attempt on his life.

of that penitent (as thou calst him) and reconciled King   1635   (2B1^{va})
my brother, whose losse of his most precious Queene &
Children, are euen now to be a-fresh lamented. Say to
me, when saw'st thou the Prince *Florizell* my son? Kings

1637, 1643 are] is mCOL2 *conj.* (1637), KTLY

1635 penitent . . . reconciled] PYLE (1969, p. 76): "Leontes, whom Time the
Chorus spoke of as shut up with his grief [1598], has now stirred himself, has sent
for Camillo and reconciled himself with Polixenes. . . . These things he resolved to
do sixteen years before in the first flush of his repentance [1340-2]. The fact that he
has done so now combines the effect of foreshortening of time with the suggestion
of spiritual growth in Leontes." PAFFORD (ed. 1963): "Here and at [1596-8] Shakespeare is at pains to keep the absent not wholly absent from our minds."
      as . . . him] PAFFORD (ed. 1963): "As thou <rightly> callest him." EVANS
(ed. 1974): "To use your own word." Polixenes does not express disagreement.
      1636-7 losse . . . are] Subject and verb do not agree, because of the interven-
tion of the plural *Queene & Children*, a "confusion of proximity" (ABBOTT §412).
For other failures of concord, see nn. 237, 870, 920-1, 1643, and 1724.
      1637 euen now] BOORMAN (ed. 1964): "Perhaps a suggestion that this is the
anniversary of Hermione's 'death', and of the loss of Mamillius and Perdita." This is
unlikely; *euen* serves "to introduce what is less expected" (SCHMIDT, 1874), and
Polixenes means "now, even after such a long time."
      1638-41 Kings . . . Vertues] The glosses of earlier eds. are summed up in KER-
MODE's (ed. 1963) paraphrase: "It is as hard for kings to bear the disobedience and
ill conduct of their children as to lose them when convinced of their virtues." For
another possibility, see n. 1640. PAFFORD (ed. 1963): "Polixenes seems to compare
Florizel to his disadvantage with the promise of Leontes' son, the dead Mamillius.
Comparison of the two is suggested in [Act 1 (esp. 245-58) and Act 5 (esp. 2869-
72, 2886-9)] and these comparisons are significant since Florizel is to be heir both
to Bohemia and Sicilia, and to replace, as far as is humanly possible, the loss of Mamillius." BROOKS (in PAFFORD, ed. 1963): "In *1H4* . . . the king compares Hal to his
disadvantage with Hotspur and laments the fact that he keeps company with those
socially beneath him. Hal, when enacting his father's probable reception of him, uses
the phrase 'ungracious boy' [2.4.445 (1403)]." NEELY (1978, p. 184): "Polixenes—
extraordinarily—views his son's rebelliousness as comparable to Leontes'
loss. . . . His tirade . . . suggests that he views his son's achievement of sexual
maturity as confirmation of his own impotence, as deterioration into second, unwelcome childhood [cf. 2232-7]." Other critics seem unaware of this possibility. SAN-
DERS (1987, p. 67): "There is really no comparison at all between his loss and Leontes'.
Yet to this gloomy and . . . possessive father, the loss is just as total." HILLMAN
(1979, pp. 17-18): "A king's immortality, bound up with the perpetuation of the
royal dignity, would be particularly vulnerable to the deviance of an only son and
heir. Such vulnerability may be detected behind Polixenes' veiled complaint to Camillo that Florizel's behaviour threatens to subject him to the effects of childlessness."
PARRY (ed. 1982) finds the "assertion . . . of very doubtful validity! Polixenes, as a
father, has grown severe with the passing of time." Sh. is adapting him to a new role,
that of adversary. ANDREWS (1972) believes Sh. bases Florizel's dereliction on Sidney's
story of Prince Plangus of Iberia in *Arcadia* 2.15 (ed. Evans, pp. 312 ff.). Plangus had
an affair with a married woman, as in Beaumont & Fletcher's *Cupid's Revenge*. The
resemblance is slight.

are no lesse vnhappy, their issue, not being gracious, then
they are in loosing them, when they haue approued their   1640
Vertues.

    Cam. Sir, it is three dayes since I saw the Prince: what
his happier affayres may be, are to me vnknowne: but I
haue (missingly) noted, he is of late much retyred from
Court, and is lesse frequent to his Princely exercises then   1645
formerly he hath appeared.

    Pol. I haue considered so much (*Camillo*) and with
some care, so farre, that I haue eyes vnder my seruice,
which looke vpon his remouednesse: from whom I haue
this Intelligence, that he is seldome from the house of a   1650
most homely shepheard: a man (they say) that from very
nothing, and beyond the imagination of his neighbors,
is growne into an vnspeakable estate.

    Cam. I haue heard (sir) of such a man, who hath a
daughter of most rare note: the report of her is extended   1655
more, then can be thought to begin from such a cottage.

    Pol. That's likewise part of my Intelligence: but (I

1644 missingly] musingly HAN, COL2, COL3, COL4, HUD2; missing him WARB

1648 care, so farre,] F1-F3, RLTR, RID; ~ ∧ ~ ~ , F4-JOHN2; ~ ; ~ ~ , CAP, HAN3 *etc.*

1657 part] a part THEO1-v1773 (−HAN, CAP)

    but] and THEO, HAN, CAP, RANN, KTLY, HUD2

1657-8 but (I feare)] ~ , ~ ~ ∧ v1778-HUD2 (−RANN, COL, DEL, CAM1, GLO), OXF1, BUL

1639 **vnhappy**] Unfortunate. See n. 1209.

    gracious] SCHMIDT (1874): "In a state of heavenly grace." MINSHEU's (1617) *Gratious* synonyms, however, are more secular: "Acceptable, Courteous, Benigne, Gentle." JOHNSON (1755, citing this line): "Virtuous; good." LEE (ed. 1907): "Well conducted," meaning "well behaved." EVANS (ed. 1974): "Having princely qualities." The word occurs 14 times in *WT*, often as "a courteous epithet in referring to kings, queens" (*OED* 4b) but often, more exactly, as "fortunate, prosperous" (see n. 1172) and "endowed with divine grace" (932 probably; *OED* 6). For *grace*, see n. 146.

    1640 **they haue**] HERFORD (ed. 1904): "I.e. the children," contrary to KERMODE in n. 1638-41.

    approued] JOHNSON (1755, Approve): "Prove." WRIGHT & LaMAR (ed. 1966): "Demonstrated."

    1643 **happier**] BETHELL (ed. 1956): "I.e. than the 'princely exercises' referred to [at 1645]."

    are] ORGEL (ed. 1996): "For 'is,' as at line [1637]." For other subject-verb disagreements, see nn. 237, 870, 920-1, and 1724.

    1644 **(missingly) noted**] Variously interpreted. THIRLBY (MS 1733-47?): An oxymoron. HEATH (1765, p. 215): "Like a person that hath missed him, or, as I found him missing." STEEVENS (ed. 1773): "At *intervals*, . . . occasionally." SEYMOUR

(1805, 1:167): "Refers to the blank . . . in the court assemblies occasioned by the prince's absence." CAPELL (1783 [1774], 1:glos.): "With Regret, such as follows the Absence of what one misses," a reading with which SCHMIDT (1875) and ONIONS (1986) agree. *OED* (Missing, *ppl.a.*, citing this line as its only instance): "With a sense of loss." HUNTER (ed. 1872) sums up several possibilities: "Noted while missing him; noted, and missed him, or regretted his absence while I noted." KERMODE (ed. 1963) wittily finds another: "He noted not the Prince but his absence." For other instances of noting, see n. 298.

1645 **frequent to**] The CLARKES (ed. 1865): Frequent "in attention to." SCHMIDT (1874): "Addicted" to (*OED*, *a.* 5, citing this line). ORGEL (ed. 1996): "Frequently at."

exercises] WILSON (ed. 1931): "Athletics, field sports, military exercises."

1647 **considered so**] WRIGHT & LAMAR (ed. 1966): "Believed as."

1648 **so farre**] BOORMAN (ed. 1964): "To the extent."

eyes . . . seruice] LEE (ed. 1907): "Spies."

1649 **looke . . . remouednesse**] *OED* (Removed, *ppl.a.* 3, citing this line): Remote[ness]. The CLARKES (ed. 1865): "Watch him in his retirement [from court]." WILSON (ed. 1931): "There would be nothing distasteful to Elizabethans in the notion of a royal father thus setting spies upon his son." He does not corroborate.

1650 **Intelligence**] COLES (1676): "Notice or information."

from] SCHMIDT (1874): "Away from, far from," as in 812.

1651 **homely**] MINSHEU (1617): See "Plaine, Common, Ordinarie, Countrey."

1651–2 **very nothing**] HAPPÉ (1969): "Nothing itself." ORGEL (ed. 1996, Very): "Absolutely."

1652 **imagination**] LOBBAN (ed. 1910): "Understanding." SCHMIDT (1874): "Conception, idea, thought," with which eds. generally agree.

1653 **is . . . estate**] JOHNSON (1755, Unspeakable): "Not to be expressed." BETHELL (ed. 1956): "Huge." ROLFE (ed. 1879): "Has become surprisingly rich." For the Shepherd's wealth, see n. 1701–3. STUDING (1982, p. 220): In addition to acquiring money, the Shepherd "has assumed courtly values," but he is not only "most homely" here but later uncorrupted by his elevation to the gentry (see 3160–1).

1655–6 **note . . . cottage**] SCHMIDT (1875, Note): "Distinction or eminence" (*OED*, *sb.*² 19). ROLFE (ed. 1879): "Notoriety, fame" (19b). CARRINGTON (1956, Is extended): "Reaches proportions." SCHMIDT (1874, Begin): "Take rise." Thus BETHELL (ed. 1956): "She is much more widely known than you would expect for one in such a lowly position." PAFFORD (ed. 1963), however: The report of her "must originate from someone of importance." BOORMAN (ed. 1964): "Camillo is perhaps hinting that Florizel has spread her fame." The later opinions seem doubtful. What person of importance? Not Florizel, surely, who would risk discovery of his entirely unsuitable romance. For other instances of noting, see n. 298.

1657 **That's**] LETTSOM (MS 1840–65): "Refers to the beauty of Perdita." BETHELL (ed. 1956): *That* = "what you have heard about the shepherd's daughter."

but] STAUNTON (ed. 1859): "To boot," by which he probably means that the word emphasizes "the introduction of a distinct or independent fact" (*OED* 25). ROLFE (ed. 1879): Perhaps the conjunction "refers to something implied rather than expressed. Camillo refers to the reports of the daughter's beauty merely as an additional bit of intelligence, apparently not connecting it with Florizel's visits to the cottage; Polixenes, perceiving this by his tone and manner, says, . . . 'I, too, have heard of the pretty daughter, *but* [to *me* it isn't a fact without significance, for] I fear she is the attraction that draws my son thither.'" KINNEAR (1883, p. 185): "I fear *but* the angle"; he compares 1993, which he understands as "I have it but." COLLINS (ed. 1904–24?): "The connection is, 'that may be good in itself, but is bad for me, for. . . .'" PORTER & CLARKE (ed. 1908): "Nothing but that (*I feare*), *i.e.*, that *part of my* information being the bait, etc." BETHELL (ed. 1956): "*But* [introduces] the point against her." An omission seems more likely, however.

feare) the Angle that pluckes our sonne thither. Thou
shalt accompany vs to the place, where we will (not appearing what we are) haue some question with the shep-   1660
heard; from whose simplicity, I thinke it not vneasie to
get the cause of my sonnes resort thether. 'Prethe be my
present partner in this busines, and lay aside the thoughts
of Sicillia.

   Cam. I willingly obey your command.   1665
   Pol. My best *Camillo*, we must disguise our selues.   *Exit*

Scena Tertia.   4.3

Enter Autolicus singing.

1658 Angle] Engle THEO
1659 not] nor ROWE2, ROWE3
1666 *Camillo,*] ~ — THEO1+ (−HAN)
   Exit] *Exeunt* ROWE1+
1667 *Scena Tertia*] SCENE II WARB, JOHN1-DEL2, KTLY-HUD2, OXF1, BUL
1668 *The Country.* POPE1-JOHN2, v1773-RANN (*subst.*); *Fields near the Shep-*
herd's. CAP; *A Road near the Shepherd's Cottage.* MAL+ (−PEL1, CLN2, PEN2, OXF2)
(*subst.*)

1657-8 **I . . . Angle**] STAUNTON (ed. 1859): "The attractions of that girl form
part of my intelligence, and they are, I apprehend, the angle which draws the prince
there." HUNTER (ed. 1872): "But I fear that is the angle." DEIGHTON (ed. 1889),
however, wishes *I feare* to be parenthetical, as in F. "The meaning will then be, 'That
also is a *part* of what I have heard; but, I fear, the *sole* attraction to him.'" PAFFORD
(ed. 1963): "But I fear [this girl to be] the baited hook."
   1658 **Angle**] MINSHEU (1617): "To fish with." PHILLIPS (1706): "A Fishing-rod"
(*OED, sb.* 1: "A fishing-hook; often in later use extended to the . . . tackle . . . and
the rod"). HEATH (1765, p. 215): "A bait," a metaphorical extension, essentially the
meaning given by THEOBALD (ed. 1733), who emends to *Engle*—"*the* Siren, *the* De-
coy, *the* Invitation." ABARTIS (1977, p. 103): Polixenes uses "one of those striking
fishing metaphors that recalls Leontes [at 262]." BECKET's (1815, 1:360-1) idea that
angle here means "horoscope" or "degree of the ascendant" is unlikely, as is the
CLARKES' (ed. 1865) notion that there is a "remote reference to the pun between the
Latin words *Angli*, English, and *angeli*, angles."
   1659-60 **not . . . are**] KITTREDGE & RIBNER (ed. 1967): "In disguise." FREEBURG
(1915, pp. 157-8), pointing out that Sh. "borrowed almost all of his disguise situa-

tions," assumes he borrowed this one as well. "The royal father's spying on his son and the theatrical unmasking . . . are not in Greene's novel, but such a situation was . . . a well established tradition in the plays immediately preceding" *WT.* The disguises Camillo and Polixenes adopt are never specified, but the two are so altered that Florizel does not recognize them, and they do not specifically identify themselves until they break the disguise in 4.4 (Polixenes at 2260).

1660 **question**] MALONE (ed. 1790, citing *MM* 2.4.90 [1098]): "Talk" (SCHMIDT, 1875, 7). See n. 2965.

1661 **not vneasie**] CALDECOTT (MS 1813–33) interprets the *not* as an intensifier: "I.e. attended with much difficulty." COLLINS (ed. 1904–24?) agrees. Unlike the double negative at 1229–32, however, the *not* here cancels the negative prefix *un-*; because of the Shepherd's simplicity, the task will be easy. According to SCHMIDT (1875), Sh. uses *uneasy* to mean "difficult" only here and in *Tmp.* 1.2.452 (605).

1663 **present**] SCHMIDT (1875): "Instant, immediate," as at 373. Or possibly JOHNSON (1755): "Being at hand," as at 2092.

1665 **willingly**] PORTER & CLARKE (ed. 1908): "Camillo endears himself to us by his disinterested love of doing things worth doing. He is apparently not appeased especially by the king's offer to reward him . . . but he *willingly* stays in Bohemia when it is proposed to do the young prince a useful service."

1666 **best *Camillo***] The CLARKES (ed. 1865): Cf. "best Brother" (226).

1667 ***Scena Tertia***] Regarding 4.3 and 4.4, BOODLE ("Theory," 1885, p. 318): "That most of Shakespeare's plays have unity of a certain nature is sufficiently clear; but it is quite evident that unity in Aristotle's sense they have not. Incidents are multiplied such as . . . the rustic scenes in [*WT*], which have little bearing upon the main action of the play, but yet are necessary to Shakespeare's art to throw a clear light upon the characters of his protagonists — [here] the shepherd princess Perdita." For the place of this scene in the play's time scheme, see n. 1795. HERFORD (ed. 1916–): "This scene gives us a pleasant first taste of Autolycus's quality." He "establishes his superiority" to the Clown "by sheer native aptitude and want of scruple." LAROQUE (1974, p. 8): Autolycus's "merry song of summer . . . contrasts with the wintry barrenness of Sicilia."

1668 ***Autolicus***] MACNEICE (1967, p. 233): "Gabbing earth Hot from Eastcheap — Watch your pockets when That rogue comes round the corner, he can slit Purse-strings as quickly as his maker's pen Will try your heartstrings in the name of mirth." PYLE (1969, p. 78): "He bursts upon the play unannounced, altering its tone, its point of view, enlarging its scope, at least for a time." MCFARLAND (1972, p. 131): "Autolycus appears, singing the carefree words that we recognize as the symbol of transformation to the ideal realm of pastoral." HAPPÉ (1969): "This lyric is associated with spring and with the regeneration that begins at this point in the play." TAYLOR (1973, p. 353): "When he first appears he brings with him a great sense of relief, because we have been subjected for three acts to the heavy passion of Leontes and its destructive consequences. He is unfeeling [quotes 1683] and we are pleased by the thinness of his good cheer." NOBLE (1923, p. 94): "His entrance is one of the most effective in the comedies — the gay, careless, and unscrupulous character of the man is at once conveyed. . . . The song [is] used as a soliloquy." IDEM (1926; 1927, p. 131): "The song . . . mitigates the meanness of the theft Autolycus is about to commit. . . . It is song which makes Autolycus a tolerable and lovable stage character." WRIGHT ("Extraneous Song," 1927, p. 264) disagrees: "Autolycus is a clown and only a clown. . . . His songs are mere extraneous clown songs with no dramatic value outside the clown scenes which are themselves extraneous."

When Daffadils begin to peere,
With heigh the Doxy ouer the dale,   1670
Why then comes in the sweet o'the yeere,
For the red blood raigns in y *winters pale.*

1670 *heigh*] *hey* HAN, DYCE, STAU, HUD2, BUL, SIS
1671 *comes*] *come* WARB
1672 *For . . . winters*] Ff; *For . . . o'er the winter's* HAN; *'Fore . . . reins-in the winter* WARB; *For . . . winter* v1773; *For . . . Winter's* ROWE1 *etc.*

1669–90 *When . . . auouch-it*] *WT* has seven songs, these two; "Iog-on, Iog-on" (1791–4); "Lawne as white as driuen Snow" (2044–55); "Get you hence," a three-part catch (2118–33); and "Will you buy any Tape" (2139–44). Autolycus, joined in the catch by Mopsa and Dorcas, sings them all, and all occur in this act. This song and "Iog-on" are labeled "nonsensical" by BURNEY (1776–89; 1935, 2:272). GOSSE (1916, p. 53), exaggerating in the other direction: "The rogue-songs are intensely human and pointedly Shakespearean. . . . They are an integral part of the drama. They complete the revelation of the complex temperament of Autolycus, with his passion for flowers and millinery, his hysterical balancing between laughter and tears, his impish mendacity, his sudden sentimentality." LONG (1961, p. 71): "The scene shifts . . . to the countryside, and the new setting is established by Autolycus, . . . a sympathetic rascal. That such a character can immediately enlist . . . sympathy . . . is due, in large measure, to the fact that he is singing a lilting song." NEILSON (ed. 1906, p. 419): For Autolycus and for this song, "hints may have been derived from Tom Beggar in Robert Wilson's *Three Ladies of London* ([published in] 1584)." The slight resemblance, however, lies in the appearance in both works of commonplaces of the literature of knavery; e.g., Tom Beggar and his comrades sing "*Our fingers are lime-twigges, and Barbers we be, To catch sheetes from hedges most pleasant to see*" (ed. Mithal, 1988, lines 1578–9)—verses signifying only that sheets drying on hedges were sometimes snitched by petty thieves. CHANDLER (1907, 1:53) speaks of the song as being "in the vein of Autolycus." BETHELL (ed. 1956): "This song is *not* an Elizabethan 'nature' lyric but a product of Jacobean wit which incidentally parodies Elizabethan simplicities. . . . Shakespeare takes the usual poetic ingredients—spring, flowers, birds—and sets them in contrast with the petty thief and his immoral companions [BETHELL, 1947, p. 46: 'the nasty sneak-thief and his unlovely companions']. The humour lies in the unexpectedness of some of the words, e.g. 'doxy' after, and in alliteration with, 'daffodils.'" But hearts and flowers would not be expected from someone who looks like Autolycus. For *doxy*, see n. 1670. As for the occasion, AUDEN (1957, p. 42): "Singing is one of Autolycus' occupations, so he may be allowed a good voice, but [this] is an impromptu song. He sings as he walks, because it makes walking more rhythmical and less tiring, and he sings to keep up his spirits. His is a tough life, with hunger and the gallows never very far away, and he needs all the courage he can muster." BROWN (*Shakespeare's Plays,* 1966, p. 99): "The words . . . invite mimicry and business on the four-times repeated 'With heigh!', and on the 'tirra-lirra' for lark-song and the contrasting references to thrush and jay." LONG (1961, p. 71): "The obvious use [of the music] is to change the character of the plays from tragic to comic," but Father Time did that job in 4.1 (see n. 1578).
    1669 *When . . . peere*] PYLE (1969, p. 80) finds this "an anticipatory link with Perdita."

Daffadils] SCHMIDT (1874): "Probably the snowdrop." ELLACOMBE (1896, p. 74), however: "The Wild Daffodil (*Narcissus Pseudo-narcissus*)," with which DE BRAY (1982, p. 14) agrees.

1669-71 **peere . . . yeere**] This rhyme seems unexceptional, yet ELLIS (1871, 3: 965) finds that *year* also rhymes with *dear*, which rhymes with *there* (at 1683-5 and *2H4* 5.3.19-20 [3049-50]) and with *wear* (*Lr.* 1.4.166-8 [680-2]). Cf. 2140-4.

1669 **peere**] MINSHEU (1617): "Peepe." JOHNSON (1755): "By contraction from *appear*"; cf. n. 1800. CROSBY (1878; 1986, p. 307) is ecstatic over the word: "You can fancy the sweet little buds & flowers just *peering out*, making their first shy, retiring début on the earth." Flora herself peers, at 1799-1800.

1670-8 **heigh . . . hey . . . heigh**] PAFFORD (ed. 1963): "The spellings . . . may represent some difference in pronunciation and meaning. In [1670 and 1674] the use may be only exclamatory. The country dance, or its tune, may be referred to in [1678]." PAFFORD evidently intended to print *hey* rather than *heigh* in 1678. According to *OED* (*sb.*⁴), the dance is one with "a winding or serpentine movement, or being of the nature of a reel." *OED* gives identical pronunciations for the two spellings, the vowels having the sound of the vowels in *rain*. See also n. 1677-9.

1670 **Doxy**] COTGRAVE (1611, *Gueuse*): "A woman begger, . . . a great, lazie, and louzie queane; a Doxie." GROSE (1785, Doxies): "She beggars, wenches, whores." BROOK (1976, p. 57) calls the word a euphemism, as he does *aunt* in 1679. SALGADO (1977, p. 122): Because virgin beggarwomen were called *dells* and not *doxies*, "Autolycus . . . is perhaps expressing his taste for the mature woman rather than the inexperienced girl."

1671 **sweet o'the yeere**] *OED* (Sweet, *sb.* 3, citing this line): "The pleasant part *of* something." Cf. "the sweete a'th night" (*2H4* 5.3.51 [3076-7]). MALONE (ed. 1790, 10:603): "Because in that season maidens put out their sheets to bleach on the hedges." LEE (ed. 1907) points out, however: In *A Wife for a Month*, Fletcher has a courtier choose April as "the sweet o'th year": then I would, he says, "kisse my wench upon the tender flowrets, Tumble on every Greene, and as the birds sung, Embrace and melt away my soule in pleasure" (2.1.35-8).

1672 **For . . . pale**] On *raigns in*, NEVO (1987, p. 123): "Reins in? rains in?" in addition to "is king in." MOORMAN (ed. 1912): "It is uncertain whether *pale* means (1) paleness [*OED, sb.*²], or (2) fenced area, enclosure [*sb.*¹ 3]." FARMER (in STEEVENS, ed. 1773, 10:Pp5) finds another possibility: (3) "Dominion" (*sb.*¹ 4), which KNIGHT (ed. 1838, 2:368) interprets as "boundary" (*sb.*¹ 2c) but which HAPPÉ (1969) connects with "an area ruled by winter"; the Pale, he says, was an "area of Ireland ruled by the English from 1547." There were also English Pales in France and in Scotland, though it is doubtful that any of them is relevant here. *OED* itself (*sb.*¹ 5) considers that, in this figurative use, "the senses 'limits', 'bounds' [2c] and 'area' or region [4] become indistinguishable." HEATH (1765, p. 216), choosing (1), "paleness": "For though the winter is not quite over, the red blood resumes its usual vigor." STEEVENS (ed. 1773) supplies examples of (2), "enclosure," from *H5* 5. Prol. 9-10 (2859-60), *Ant.* 2.7.74 (1412), and *1H6* 4.2.45 (1996). Hence, RANN (ed. 1787): "Now flows briskly, though within the confines [pale] of winter, but just on the edge of spring." PYE (1807, p. 114) disagrees: "Nine out of ten readers would understand . . . the red blood of spring now has dominion [definition 3] over the pale [definition 1] occasioned by the coldness of winter." Most critics follow him, although some, such as SINGER (eds. 1826 and 1856) and CHARLTON (ed. 1916), find both definitions 1 and 2 present. ARMSTRONG (1946, pp. 14-16): *Pale* suggests a pale object, the white sheet of 1673, which is immediately followed by *birds* (in 1674) and that image by the sheets and the kite of 1691, an image cluster associated with death, which becomes explicit in 1698. See n. 1691-8. TRAVERSI (1955, p. 139): *Winter's pale* "connects [this] episode . . . with the play's title, and establishes a relationship between the

The white sheete bleaching on the hedge,
With hey the sweet birds, O how they sing:
Doth, set my pugging tooth an edge,   1675
For a quart of Ale is a dish for a King.

The Larke, that tirra-Lyra chaunts,
With heigh, the Thrush and the Iay:
Are Summer songs for me and my Aunts
While we lye tumbling in the hay.   1680

1675 *pugging*] *progging* HAN, WARB, CAP; *prigging* mTBY2 *conj.*, COL2
       an] *on* THEO1-CLN2, BEV, OXF2
1677 *that*] *with* ROWE1-POPE2
       Lyra chaunts] *Lyrachaunts* F3; *Lycrachaunts* F4
1678 *With heigh,*] F1; *With hey, with hey* ROWE1-JOHN2, v1773-v1813, SING2,
DYCE, HAL, STAU, KTLY, HUD2, BUL, SIS; *With heigh! with, hey!* v1821, KNT, CAM3; *With
heigh, with hey etc.* F2 *etc.*
       Iay] *lay* F3-ROWE2
1679 *Summer*] *Summers* F4

---

birth of spring in the heart of winter and the affirmation of the warm, living 'blood'
of youth against the jealousy and care-laden envy of age, an affirmation shortly to be
confirmed in the contrast between the young lovers and their elders." CAPELL alone
(1783, 2.4:173) applies the expression to Autolycus himself: "The *blood* . . . is—
his own blood; which then begins to excite him to cross the dale to his doxy."

       red blood] CROFT (1810, p. 11): "In the spring the blood turns redder from
the nitrous particles which the arterial veins inhale from the vegete, elastic, or livelier
air than what remains in a more torpid state in winter." MAHOOD (1957, p. 156):
"*Blood*, . . . when used in the first part of the play, often carries a connotation of
'lust' [see 135-6, possibly 657]. . . . Now . . . it represents a passion as natural and
inevitable as the sap that rises in the spring."

       1673 *bleaching*] MINSHEU (1617): "Making white, or drying in the sunne." From
LLL 5.2.906 (2872), MALONE (in STEEVENS, ed. 1793) quotes Spring's description of
himself as the time when "Maidens bleach their summer smockes [undergarments]."

       hedge] Where laundry was spread to dry and, as HAPPÉ (1969) remarks, the
"source of shirts for Falstaff's men" (*1H4* 4.2.47-8 [2421-2]).

       1674 *hey*] WILSON (ed. 1931) objects to the substitution of *heigh* (as in 1670) for
this word, since the two are distinguished by *OED*. *Heigh* is "an exclamation used as
a call of encouragement" (*OED* quotes this line). *Hey* "is sometimes used in the
burden of a song with no definite meaning."

       1675 *Doth . . . edge*] COLLINS (ed. 1904-24?): "The sight of the sheet gives
him a desire to steal it and sell it for ale."

       set . . . an edge] *OED* (Edge, *sb.* 2c, "To . . . set an edge upon"): "To stim-
ulate, incite." Although he reads *on*, KNIGHT (ed. 1841) allows that the article and
not the preposition may be the proper form of the idiom; the phrase means, according
to PAFFORD (ed. 1963), "'to set an edge on', 'to sharpen', hence 'to whet the appetite.'" SCHANZER (ed. 1969) finds *on edge*, expressing revulsion (*OED*, Edge, *sb.* 4) to
be "the opposite sense from the one required."

pugging] Many meanings have been offered, including none at all—CAPELL (1783, 2.4:174): "There is . . . no such word as *Pugging*." THIRLBY (MS 1747-53): "In Gypsies language signifies stealing." BECKET (1815, 1:361): "*Pugging tooth*" is a "sweet tooth, a colt's tooth. *Puggy* is a word of endearment . . . in speaking of a girl, a little maid" (see PARTRIDGE, 1967). B. E. (1699, Pug), however: "A nasty Slut, a sorry Jade"; hence, "lecherous" is a possibility. Though COLLIER (ed. 1842) mentions *puggard*, "a well known kind of cheat" (*OED* lists one instance), he thinks that the word should probably be *prigging* (see n. 1769). His first inclination is supported by PAFFORD (ed. 1963), who finds *puggard* = "thief" in Middleton & Dekker, *The Roaring Girl* (ed. Gomme, 1976, 5.1.301). COLLIER (ed. 1858, 6:glos.); however, gives for *pugging tooth* "a thieving habit, or propensity," the meaning doubtfully assigned by *OED* (citing this line as its only example). *OED*'s suggestion that the word may be the present participle of the verb *pug*, meaning "pull, tug," leads KERMODE (ed. 1963) to note that "perhaps Autolycus is thinking of his sheet-stealing; he is all set to begin snatching them off the hedges." WILSON (ed. 1931) agrees, adding that "the tooth is proverbial" and citing *AWW* 2.3.42 (934) and TILLEY T431. H. B. J. (1853), connecting *pugging* with "grinding" (perhaps *OED*, *v*.² 2, remotely), thinks "Autolycus means his molar—his grinding tooth," but, as FURNESS (ed. 1898) observes, that sense is irrelevant. FURNESS records several similar wild shots, like WALTER's (1890; 1896, p. 47) connection of the word with *peg tooth* and MOORMAN's (ed. 1912) with *pug-tooth*; both terms mean canine or eyetooth. BETHELL (ed. 1956) believes that Sh. intends a pun involving *pugging* as stealing and as the eyetooth.

1676 **For . . . King**] DEIGHTON (ed. 1889): "If this has any real connection with the former line, it means 'for by the sale of the stolen sheets I could buy a quart of ale, which is a beverage fit for a king.'" Following the CLARKES (1879, p. 808), DEIGHTON interprets *dish* as "cup" (*OED*, *sb*. 1b), but *OED* defines the word as "a distinct article or variety of food" (2, citing this line).

dish . . . King] Proverbial (DENT D363.1).

1677 **tirra-Lyra**] COTGRAVE (1611) glosses Fr. *tirelire* as "the warble, or song of a Larke." *OED* follows suit, citing this line as its first instance. WHITE (1783, p. 934) finds larks singing *tire-lire* or *tirile tirile* in du Bartas and in Linnæus, and MALONE (ed. 1790) finds that Thomas Moffet in *The Silkewormes and their Flies* (1599) fancifully calls larks *Tyry-tiry-leerers*. DOUCE (1807, 1:353): Crows and even the Christmas shepherds sing similar words.

1677-9 **chaunts . . . Aunts**] To MANNING (1929, p. 63), the spelling indicates that *aunts* would be pronounced *ants*. CERCIGNANI (1981, p. 214), however, finds the vowel to be that of *awe* and *law*.

1678 **With heigh**] Against the usual emendation required by the meter—another *with heigh* or *hey*—is the single occurrence of the words at 1670 and 1674. NOBLE (1923, p. 97) thinks "the one 'With heigh' will do perfectly well by lengthening the value of the note on 'heigh'—it can be represented in print by 'he . . . . igh', and so printed will suitably convey the ecstasy precedent to the closing lines (Autolycus is not standing still while he sings)." DYCE (ed. 1857), nevertheless: "Perhaps the name of some bird has dropped out." Only KINNEAR (1883) has answered the challenge implied; see p. 579.

Iay] WILSON (ed. 1931): "Perhaps in reference to the 'aunts.'" He compares *Wiv.* 3.3.42 (1385), where *jay* means "loose woman."

1679 **Aunts**] B. E. (1699, Aunt): "Bawd." GROSE (1785): "A title of eminence for the senior dells [strumpets]." PARTRIDGE (1969): "A whore, a wanton." THIRLBY (MS 1733-47?) refers to RAY (1678, p. 227): "She is one of mine Aunts that make mine uncle go a begging"; SYMONS (in IRVING & MARSHALL, ed. 1890) cites Dekker, *1 The Honest Whore*: "to call you one of my naunts, sister, were as good as to call you arrant whoore" (1.2.121-2). See n. 1670.

I haue seru'd Prince *Florizell*, and in my time wore three
pile, but now I am out of seruice.

> *But shall I go mourne for that (my deere)*
> *the pale Moone shines by night:*
> *And when I wander here, and there*   1685
> *I then do most go right.*
> *If Tinkers may haue leaue to liue,*
> *and beare the Sow-skin Bowget,*
> *Then my account I well may giue,*
> *and in the Stockes auouch-it.*   1690

My Trafficke is sheetes: when the Kite builds, looke to

1683 *But*] *Om.* v1785
1685 *here,*] ~ ∧ F3+
1686 *most go*] *go most* POPE1-MAL (−CAP)

1681 **I . . . Florizell**] See n. 2593.
1681-2 **three pile**] STEEVENS (ed. 1778): "Rich velvet." *OED (sb.*, citing this line): "Applied to velvet in which the loops of the pile-warp (which constitute the nap) are formed by three threads, producing a pile of treble thickness." LINTHICUM (1936, p. 126), however: "Velvet was . . . made in two piles upon a ground of satin. Since this makes three heights, if the satin ground is counted as one, it is probably [*WT's* three pile]." In *MM* 1.2.32 ff. (128 ff.) the words create an off-color pun, but they seem innocent here. FRIPP (1938, 2:739) thinks, improbably, that the pox is indicated, because velvet patches were used as covering for lanced syphilitic sores (see *AWW* 4.5.94-8 [2576-80] and possibly *MM* 1.2.31-4 [127-30]). PORTER & CLARKE (ed. 1908), also improbably: "Referring not to richness of attire merely, but to the fine livery of a smug servant, plush breeches being the badge of a flunkey."
1682 **out of seruice**] RUBINSTEIN (1984, Eleven) believes that the service is not only princely but copular. Lines 1679-80 are present tense, however.
1683-90 **But . . . auouch-it**] BROWN (*Shakespeare's Plays*, 1966, p. 99): This song contrasts "in mood with the first. . . . The imitation of the forlorn lover is quickly revalued as a prelude to mischief when [1687-90] presents Autolycus again as an adventurer. . . . Even here there is a usual twist, for he will 'avouch' his account in the stocks as if formally claiming right while being punished for wrong." The meaning of *auouch* is somewhat uncertain, however; see n. 1690.
1684 **the . . . night**] BETHELL (ed. 1956): I.e., "No, I have the moonlight to steal by." On auspicious evenings, Sh.'s moons are bright or silvery. When the moon is pale, however, as at *TGV* 4.2.100 (1724), *R2* 2.4.10 (1294), *1H4* 1.3.202 (526), and *Tit.* 2.3.231 (985), danger or distress is implied. Here the implication seems to be the danger that accompanies dishonesty. NOBLE (1923, p. 95): "He will be able to see sufficiently to carry on his petty larcenies and enjoy fair security."
1686 **go right**] DEIGHTON (ed. 1889): "The right path *for me, i.e.* I am most successful in my thieving." LOBBAN (ed. 1910): "Most to the purpose." KNOWLES (privately): "A pun on *right* as 'correctly, straight ahead' [*OED, adv.* 1]. By wandering back and forth, I get straight at what I want, do the thing that is right for me." PAFFORD

(ed. 1963): "For a vagabond, since he has no specific destination, all directions are the right direction."

1687–8 Tinkers . . . Bowget] *OED* (Tinker, *sb.* 1): "A craftsman (usually itinerant) who mends pots, kettles, and other metal household utensils." HARMAN (1567, sigs. E1-1ᵛ): "These dronken Tynkers called also Prygges, be beastly people. . . . With picking and stealing mingled wᵗ a litle worke for a coullor, they pass their time." Christophero Sly in *Shr.* is Sh.'s good-natured example of the type. Autolycus's point may be that if people such as tinkers are tolerated, then he, too, has some chance, though the stocks are probably inevitable (1690); or, as PAFFORD (ed. 1963) puts it, "if tinkers are allowed to trade . . . if they put me in the stocks [I] can show my calling <i.e. that I am a tinker and not a vagabond and therefore should be released>." *Beare . . . Bowget* may mean simply "ply their trade," but the budget may have additional significance. Because receivers of stolen goods had to transport them somehow, containers carried by wanderers were suspect (see Edward Hext's letter [BL MS Lansdowne, 81, no. 62] quoted by AYDELOTTE (1913, 1:170). Autolycus thus could be asserting the right to bear his pack as long as tinkers are permitted to bear their budgets. Or, as BETHELL (ed. 1956) says, he may think of passing himself off as a tinker. He would answer for (SCHMIDT, 1874, Avouch) this impersonation in the stocks, where tinkers inevitably wind up because they are all dishonest. So the point becomes ironical; Autolycus vindicates himself by comparison with notorious thieves. NOBLE (1923, p. 95), therefore, seems to be wrong: "To be a tinker is a lawful calling, and accordingly he can carry a tinker's knapsack on his back and, if apprehended by the law, can plead such an occupation as a plausible explanation of the bag's contents."

1688 Bowget] MINSHEU (1617): "Bag." *OED* (Budget 1): "Usually of leather"; Autolycus does not say why he prefers pigskin. SYMONS (in IRVING & MARSHALL, ed. 1890) thinks Sh. "deliberately misspelt the word for the sake of the rhyme," but *OED* indicates that *bow-* was a legitimate form.

1689 account] SCHMIDT (1874): "Explanation given to a superior, answering for conduct." BOORMAN (ed. 1964): "Or financial reckoning."

1690 Stockes] JOHNSON (1755): "Prison for the legs." HUDSON (ed. 1880): "A common engine in which certain offenders were punished; being fastened by the ankles, and sitting with their legs in a horizontal position."

auouch-it] SCHMIDT (1874 Avouch): "Answer for." HARRISON (ed. 1947): "Corroborate." BOORMAN (ed. 1964): "Or certify (the financial reckoning)"; see n. 1689. See nn. 3072–3 and 3359 for another meaning. The hyphen may be Crane's; see p. 594.

1691–8 My . . . it] FENTON (1930, p. 11): "Because of its personal appeal, the direct address is one of the surest ways of rousing them [the audience] from boredom or indifference. . . . In some instances too, the effect is less of the actor's stepping out of his world, than of drawing the auditors into it." BETHELL (1944, pp. 50–2): "At his first appearance he gives a summary history of himself. . . . Not only is it addressed directly to the audience but a person such as Autolycus would never in reality achieve such neat and objective self-description. . . . The speech, in effect, constitutes a 'character of a rogue' in the Theophrastan manner . . . [, an] old-fashioned stage technique [that] draws attention to the play as play." BROOKS (in PAFFORD, ed. 1963): "The style . . . is similar to that of the 17th-cent. 'Character' as written by Overbury and Earle." RUSSELL (1967, pp. 113–14 n.), however, identifies the "formal self-identifical" as a characteristic of the Vice. ARMSTRONG (1963, p. 16) discovers an image cluster: "Pick out the significant words and we find—sheets—kites—linen—die—hanging—life to come. See what has happened! Once the kite came on the scene—evoked by blood, pale, sheet, and bleaching—thought veered round to death and the hereafter—and, incidentally, bed-linen suggested sleep. Shakespeare was unwittingly being trailed at the tail of a chariot of his own fashioning."

lesser Linnen. My Father nam'd me *Autolicus*, who be-
ing (as I am) lytter'd vnder Mercurie, was likewise a   (2B
snapper-vp of vnconsidered trifles: With Dye and drab,
I purchas'd this Caparison, and my Reuennew is the silly   1695
Cheate. Gallowes, and Knocke, are too powerfull on
the Highway. Beating and hanging are terrors to mee:

1692-3 *Autolicus* . . . Mercurie,] *Autolicus*, being litter'd under *Mercury*; who,
as I am, WARBURTON *conj. in* THEO1, THEO, WARB, JOHN
   1695 this] *Om.* F2-ROWE3
      silly] sly HAN
   1696 Knocke] knocks mTBY2 *conj.*, HAN
   1697 Highway] highways HUD2

1691 **My . . . sheetes**] STEEVENS (ed. 1773): "I am a vender [sic] of sheet ballads, and other [unbound] publications," quibbling on *sheets* as bedclothes, as in line
1673. MASON (1785, p. 133) objects to the supposed allusion to printed matter, because "Autolycus does not yet appear in the character of a ballad-singer." KITTREDGE
& RIBNER (ed. 1967), more probably: "My business is selling sheets (presumably stolen
from hedges)."
   1691-2 **when . . . Linnen**] PECK (1740, p. 241) alludes to the kite's removal
to her nest of "caps, cravats, ruffles," and the like. Autolycus means, PECK says, "I fly
at higher game, or larger linnen." JOHNSON (ed. 1765, 8:Ii3ᵛ): "I leave small linen for
the kite to line her nest with." PHELPS (in HALLIWELL, ed. 1859): He "may mean that
though the purloining of sheets is his ordinary traffic, yet that when necessity com-
pells (i.e., 'when the kite builds',) he does not disdain lesser linen." HERFORD (ed.
1904), however: "Autolycus is drawing an illustration, not a contrast, from the kite's
procedure; 'You look after your small linen when the kite builds; for the same reason
look after your sheets now.'" But now — when daffodils begin to peer — is when the
kite builds. BETHELL (ed. 1956): "He *compares* himself to the kite and so wittily
diminishes the size of the sheets and, by implication, the heinousness of his crime!"
BOORMAN (ed. 1964): *Kite* is "used also for 'rogue, sharper' [*OED, sb.* 2]." CALDECOTT
(MS 1813-33) is mistaken that *lesser linen* means "underclothes," although *linen* has
this significance elsewhere; see *MND* 4.2.40 (1784). RIDLEY (ed. 1935) thinks "there
is doubtless an allusion to the practice of the thieves who with a hook on the end of
a long stick pulled down from windows articles there hung out," but it is equally
doubtless that sheets would not be hooked in that fashion. For *Kite*, see p. 654.
   1692-3 *Autolicus* . . . **Mercurie**] KREIDER (1935, pp. 9-10): Clowns "are
proud of their names [and] their type characteristics." Similar gratuitous introductions
occur in Chapman, *The Blind Beggar of Alexandria* (ed. Holaday, 1970, 2.23-5) and
in Jonson, *Every Man out of his Humour* 1.2.5-8 and *Volpone* 2.1.25 ff. SCHANZER
(ed. 1969): The *who* refers to "My Father." For Autolycus's lineage, see n. 3385,
above.
   1693 **lytter'd vnder Mercurie**] EVANS (ed. 1974): "(1) Begotten by Mercury; (2)
born when the planet Mercury was in the ascendant." That "Mercurie" is in roman
rather than italic type suggests that it, like "Moone" (e.g., 542, 1534) and "Sun" (e.g.,
130, 1717), was considered a common noun. MAVEETY (1966, p. 274): "The comic
astrological reference explains his natural tendency to sin [and] . . . his thievish
proclivities." RUBINSTEIN (1984, Mercury): Autolycus's mother may have suffered
from a venereal disease, for which mercury was the treatment.

1694 **snapper-vp . . . trifles**] *OED* (Snapper, *sb.*[1] 3, citing this line): "One who . . . seizes upon a thing quickly." PARRY (ed. 1982): "A way of avoiding saying 'a petty thief.'" SPENCER (1940, p. 368): He "is not out to make a name for himself in the annals of crime. He modestly sees himself as no big shot."

vnconsidered] RANN (ed. 1787): "Insignificant." *OED (ppl.a.*, citing this line): "Not considered or thought of." CARRINGTON (1956): "Not properly looked after."

1694–5 **Dye . . . purchas'd**] HAPPÉ (1969, Dye): "Singular form of *dice.*" VERSTEGAN (1605, Drabbe): "Foule or filthy woman." PERCY (in STEEVENS, ed. 1773): "With gaming and whoring, I brought myself to."

1695 **purchas'd**] MINSHEU (1617, Purchase): "Procure" (*OED, v.* 4). This meaning does occur in Sh. (see SCHMIDT, 1875), but CLARKSON & WARREN (1942; 1968, p. 105) gloss the word here as "to acquire by irregular means, as by force, stealing, cheating, etc." They compare Marlowe, *Edward II* 2.2.197 and Fletcher & Massinger, *The Little French Lawyer* 1.1.213.

Caparison] MINSHEU (1617): See "Trappings for Horses" (*OED* 1). HANMER (ed. 1745): I.e., his "poor ragged cloaths." *OED* 2: "Outfit."

Reuennew] WILSON (ed. 1931): "A grand word, like 'caparison,' for his small takings."

1695–6 **silly Cheate**] WARBURTON (ed. 1747) glosses *silly* as "simple, low, mean" (*OED, a.* 3 and 3b); SCHMIDT (1875) adds "petty." *Cheate* in this context may mean (a) stolen goods, (b) an "article or thing" (*OED, sb.*[1] 3, citing this line), (c) a swindle or fraud, or (d) a dupe. For (a), *OED* cites HOLME (1688, 3.168): "A stolen thing." See Greene, *The Thirde and Last Part of Conny-catching* (1592; ed. Harrison, 1923, pp. 46–7): "A Cunning villaine, that had long time haunted this Cittizens house, and gotten many a cheat which he carried awaye safely." *The silly Cheate* thus could be any petty theft, the sense understood by CAPELL (1783, 2.4:174) and RANN (ed. 1787). For definition b, *OED*'s authority is HARMAN (1567, sigs. G3ᵛ-4), who in his glossary of "Peddelars Frenche" lists such terms as *a smelling chete* (a nose), *a belly chete* (an apron), and *a grunting chete* (a pig). *The silly Cheate*, therefore, might be anything mean or low. Definition c is derived by ONIONS (1953) as follows: "(1) Escheat, i.e. property which falls to the lord by forfeit or fine, (2) booty, (3) a stolen thing . . . , (4) a fraud." The etymology is omitted from ONIONS (1986), though the definition is retained. It fits the context, of course, and accords with Sh.'s use of the verb — e.g., at *Err.* 4.3.79 (1260) and *LLL* 4.3.288 (1637). For definition d, see THIRLBY (MS 1725–33?). Referring to line 1788, where the word is again used, he notes, "The Gipsies language . . . meaning . . . the silly man; or, I live by the simple"; *cheat* becomes "the one cheated" by metonomy. As PAFFORD (ed. 1963) puts it: "The foolish simpleton is my source of income." One may choose any or all of these meanings or a combination; HENLEY (ed. 1902), for example, glossing *silly* as "feeble, ill" and *cheat* as "dodge": "Probably a combination of 'chucking a dummy' and 'kidding a mug'; *i.e.* feigning helplessness or illness, and gulling a simpleton." PORTER & CLARKE (ed. 1908): "Petty thievery, not bold highway robbery, [is] his forte."

1696–7 **Gallowes . . . Highway**] JOHNSON (ed. 1773): "The resistance [knock] which a highwayman encounters in the fact [crime], and the punishment which he suffers on detection [gallows], withold [sic] me from daring robbery." For *Gallowes, and Knocke*, PIERCE (ed. 1918): "Fear of hanging and of the officer's blow." For *powerfull*, SCHMIDT (1875): "Forcible." BETHELL (ed. 1956): "That Autolycus does fear hanging, though limiting himself to petty theft, is made clear by [2505]."

1697 **Beating and hanging**] COLLIER (ed. 1858): "He should rather have said, 'hanging and beating', in order to correspond with 'gallows and knock.'" FURNESS (ed. 1898): Sh. "sometimes uses a chiasm, or criss-cross construction, as here" and as in *MV* 1.3.23–4 (347–8) and 3.1.63 (1273–4).

For the life to come, I sleepe out the thought of it. A
prize, a prize.

Enter Clowne.   1700

Clo. Let me see, euery Leauen-weather toddes, euery
tod yeeldes pound and odde shilling: fifteene hundred
shorne, what comes the wooll too?
Aut. If the sprindge hold, the Cocke's mine.
Clo. I cannot do't without Compters. Let mee see,   1705
what am I to buy for our Sheepe-shearing-Feast? Three

1700 SCENE III. WARB, JOHN
1701 Leauen-weather] eleven Weather ROWE1-THEO2, WARB-JOHN2, v1773; eleventh weather HAN
1701-2 weather$_\wedge$ . . . yeeldes$_\wedge$]~ — . . . ~ — MALONE (1783, pp. 21–2)
conj., MAL-v1813, SING, KNT, KTLY (~ $_\wedge$ . . . ~ $_\wedge$ MAL 10:604); ~ $_\wedge$ . . . ~ —
v1821, COL, HUD1, WH1, HAL-DEL2
1702 tod] told F2-F4
        pound and odde] a pound and one odd HAN
        shilling] shillings F4-ROWE2
1703 too] to F3-THEO1, HAN, CAP+
1704 *Marked as aside* ROWE1+
1706 am I] I am COL1, WH1, DEL2, COL4
1706-17 *Words indicated as read*: 1706-7 Three . . . rice, 1714 saffron, 1714–
15 mace: dates, 1715-16 nutmegs . . . ginger, 1716-17 four . . . sun CAP, v1778-
SING1, SING2, COL4; 1706-7 Three . . . rice KNT1, KNT2, KTLY, OXF1; 1706-7 Three
. . . rice, 1715-16 nutmegs . . . ginger, 1716-17 four . . . sun COL1-COL3, STAU,
DEL

1698 **For . . . it**] PAFFORD (ed. 1963), following BETHELL (1947, p. 128): "'As
for the future, I don't worry about it' or 'As for the life hereafter I don't worry about
it.'" Most critics understand the latter sense, although the former is preferable. COLE-
RIDGE (1813; ed. Raysor, 1960, 1:108), who believes Autolycus to be a decayed courtier: "Fine as this is, and delicately characteristic of one who had lived and been reared
in the best society, and had been precipitated from it by 'die and drab'; yet [it is] a
note out of time and not coalescing with that *pastoral* tint of the 4th Act." The idea
is "too Macbeth-like" for Autolycus, COLERIDGE says, Macbeth having spoken of eternity as "the life to come" (1.7.7 [481]). LLOYD (in SINGER, ed. 1856, 4:135): "It is
quite consistent with his [Autolycus's] nature; it expresses a latent superstition or
conscientiousness that is still more decidedly marked in his last scene, and that gives
contrast and countercharge to his roguery, even as in the case of Camillo we trace a
line of prudence darkening almost into duplicity." FURNESS (ed. 1898), however: *The
life to come* [which is reminiscent of "the life of the world to come" in the Nicene
Creed] does not mean eternity to Autolycus; it simply means "tomorrow." "The
thought of what the next day may bring shall never break his slumber; all thoughts
of his future living shall be forgotten in sleep." In a long note, PAFFORD concludes
that because Autolycus is an atheist, he is referring to the here and now rather than
to the hereafter. WILSON (ed. 1931) compares *time to come*, for which see n. 2351,

318

and PAFFORD compares *sleepe out* meaning "be oblivious to," in 1502 (cf. *OED*, Sleep, *v.* 9a, citing this line). See also p. 762.

1699 prize] COLES (1676): "Booty." MAXWELL (ed. 1956): "Or one from whom it may be taken."

1701-3 Let . . . too?] WILSON (ed. 1931): "The Clown is reckoning up his father's income." MINSHEU (1617): "Todde of wooll [weighes] 28 pound, *or* two stone [here, as MALONE, ed. 1790, recognizes, *toddes* is a verb; *OED* finds no other such use of the word until the late 18th c.]. . . . WEATHER [i.e., wether] . . . gelded sheepe." *Leauen* is a clipped form of "eleven" (*OED*, citing this line). PETER (1788, p. 767): "The fleeces of every eleven weathers would, upon the average, *tod*, (i.e. weigh a tod). . . . Where fleeces are the largest, three to the tod is . . . the average." AS YOU LIKE IT (1789, p. 712) continues: Small sheep "seldom cut more wool than from two to three pounds each; therefore, eleven fleeces to make a tod . . . is a very proper number. That a tod should sell for 21s. is . . . a probable price." His calculations are similar to those of UNWIN (1916, 1:329 n.). In *A Compendious or Briefe Examination of . . . Complaints*, attributed to William Stafford (1581; ed. 1876, pp. 28, 35-6), WHITE (ed. 1857) finds that during the 30 preceding years, prices had risen 50% and that 30 years before, wool had brought "a marke the Todde." As the value of the mark was 13s. 6d., in 1581 the price of a tod would have been almost exactly a "pound and odde shilling," or 21s. In addition, HOTSON (1930) discovered that in Trinity term, 1599, Sh.'s father sued to collect £21 (plus damages), the cost of 21 tods of wool bought from him in 1568 but not paid for; HOTSON thinks inflation would have added the odd shilling by the time of *WT*. Stratford prices given by HULME (1962, p. 334) are comparable. Though Sh.'s father canceled the inquiry, THIRLBY (MS 1725-33?) pertinently asks, "Is this a sign of unspeakable estate [line 1653]?" It is a substantial sum. According to RITSON's calculations (in STEEVENS, ed. 1793), the Shepherd's wool will bring a total of £143 3s., about half the amount generated annually by an estate that provided a gentleman a handsome living; in Middleton's *A Trick to Catch the Old One* (1605?), an income of £300 a year is said to be "no toye sir" (ed. Barber, 1968, 4.2.45). The CLARKES (ed. 1865) note, however, that the "vnspeakable estate" was probably created as much by the fairy gold found with Perdita (1560-2) as by sheep farming.

1702 odde] SCHMIDT (1875): "Indefinitely exceeding any number specified" (*OED, a.* 4b). HERFORD (ed. 1904), however: "One" (*a.* 1). CARRINGTON (1956): "A guinea in all."

1704 If . . . mine] THIRLBY (MS 1725-33?): "A springe [snare for small birds, often a noose made of hair] to catch a woodcock [simpleton]" was proverbial (TILLEY S788 and *OED*, Springe, *sb.* 2). THEOBALD (MS -1729?): See *Ham.* 1.3.115 (581). HUNTER (ed. 1872): "The woodcock was supposed to have no brains," a supposition, says NARES (1876; 1905), "founded on [its] character, certainly not on any examination of the fact." BROWN (*Shakespeare's Plays*, 1966, p. 99): Autolycus "lets the audience share his hope of successful trickery and at once goes into a new imitative routine."

1705 Compters] STEEVENS (ed. 1793): "Small circular pieces of base metal," used for calculating (*OED*, Counter, *sb.*³ 1a, citing this line).

1706 buy] RAYNER (in PAFFORD, ed. 1963) supplies the following "approximate prices in money values of the time" per lb.: sugar, 1s. 4d.; currants, 5d.; rice, 6d.; saffron, 2s. 6d. (an oz.); mace, 16s.; nutmegs, 6s.; ginger, 2s. 8d.; prunes, 3d.; raisins, 10d. Wool fetched 23s. a tod.

Sheepe-shearing-Feast] HAZLITT (1905, 2:541): "On the day they begin to shear their sheep, they provide a plentiful dinner for the shearers and their friends who visit them on the occasion: a table, also, if the weather permit, is spread in the open village for the young people and children. The washing and shearing of sheep is attended with great mirth and festivity." He gives 16th-c., 17th-c., and later refer-

pound of Sugar, fiue pound of Currence, Rice: What
will this sister of mine do with Rice? But my father hath
made her Mistris of the Feast, and she layes it on. Shee
hath made-me four and twenty Nose-gayes for the shea-   1710
rers (three-man song-men, all, and very good ones) but
they are most of them Meanes and Bases; but one Puritan amongst them, and he sings Psalmes to horne-pipes.

1712 Meanes] Mean ROWE1, ROWE2

---

ences. PAFFORD (ed. 1963): According to Michael Drayton's "Ninth Eglogue" (in
Works, ed. Hebel, 2:564-70), "sheep-shearing takes place late in June, but from
[1887] this feast is clearly later." See n. 1887 for more on the time of the festival.
PAFFORD thinks the eclogue, printed in 1606, may have influenced Sh.; there are some
general similarities between it and the play, noted by Kathleen Tillotson in Hebel's
ed. (5:186-7). For more on the festival, see n. 1800.

1706-7 **Three pound . . . fiue pound**] For the singular in this usage, see
FRANZ §190.

1707 **Currence**] GERARD (1597, p. 727): "Currans, or small Raisins."

1707-8 **What . . . Rice?**] According to *OED*, rice was imported into England as
early as 1234. SAVAGE (1923, p. 347) thinks his question arises because the Clown
does not know "it was used in cookery . . . made into pottage with boiled milk, to
which was added currants, raisins, and spices," other items on the shopping list.
CHARLTON (ed. 1916): "This sly question . . . may have been suggested by the
Clown's recalling the practice of throwing rice at married couples . . . for, of course,
he had seen much of Florizel lately." In the 17th c., however, rice was not used for
this purpose; see Edward Westermarck, *The History of Human Marriage* (1921, 2:
476). RUBINSTEIN (1984, Eleven), impossibly, finds a possible pun on *rise* in a bawdy
sense.

1709 **layes it on**] SCHMIDT (1874, Lay 12), incorrectly here: "To fall to work with
might and main, to do one's best, especially in fighting" (*OED*, Lay, $v.^1$ 55c). PAFFORD
(ed. 1963, citing *AYL* 1.2.106 [271] and *Tmp*. 3.2.151 [1510]): "Does it well, thoroughly," but this sense is not exactly borne out in those plays or in *OED*. *OED* (55e):
"To be lavish in expenses." ONIONS (1986): "Do[es] it in good style." WILSON (ed.
1931), trying to bolster his interpretation of 1550-1: "As heir, he [the Clown] resents
this squandering of his inheritance." See n. 2059.

1710 **made-me**] *Me* is an ethical dative. See n. 1598.

four and twenty] THEOBALD (1729, in NICHOLS, 1817, 2:208 n.): Possibly the
number alludes to "the King's Band of music," called "the Twenty-four," the Puritan
(lines 1712-13) being one among them. The idea is not reiterated in THEOBALD's
1733 ed. or elsewhere.

1711 **three-man song-men**] WARBURTON (1729, in NICHOLS, 1817, 2:208 n.): A
three-man songman is "a singer of catches, which was then, and is now, in three
parts." The three parts are treble, tenor, and bass. THEOBALD (ibid., 2:242) had
thought such a songman "could sing all the three parts in any musical composition"
having them, but in his ed. 1733 he gives WARBURTON's gloss. UPTON (1748, p. xl):
"A Three-m[a]n song [is] *a song to be sung by three men*" (*OED*, *a.*, citing this line),

or, as SQUIRE (1916, 2:47) says, "a trio for male voices." NAYLOR (1931, p. 83): "Shakespeare [at 2113 ff.] is strictly historical in making a pedlar, and two country lasses, capable of 'bearing a part' in a composition of this sort." MALONE (ed. 1790, 10:604): FLORIO (1611) glosses *berlingózzo* as "A drunken or three mens song," such as the one sung by Sir Toby, Sir Andrew, and the Fool in *TN* 2.3.75.1 (770). COOPER (1977, p. 55): "The shepherds of the Wakefield *Secunda Pastorum* sing a three-part song." ORGEL (ed. 1996): "The term 'three-man song' signified at various periods a round or madrigal, a harmonized song for three voices, and a piece with improvised parts in the alto and bass while the tenor carried the tune."

1712 **Meanes**] Authorities disagree. STEEVENS (ed. 1778): "Trebles," changed to "tenors" in ed. 1785. PORTER & CLARKE (ed. 1908): "Between tenor and treble." ONIONS (1986): Tenor or alto (intermediate between treble and bass). HERFORD (ed. 1904): "It is probably meant that there were few *counter-tenors*, the highest male voice." COLLINS (ed. 1904-24?): "Altos." ORGEL (ed. 1996): "Means are boy altos or adult counter-tenors, voices in the range between tenor and treble."

Meanes and Bases] CAPELL (1783, 2.4:174) thinks this witticism too good for the Clown and too obvious for explanation. It turns on *mean* = (1) the singer of a middle part and (2) low, contemptible and on *bass* = (1) the singer of the lowest voice part and (2) base, worthless. Cf. "The meane is dround with you[r] vnruly base" (*TGV* 1.2.93 [256]).

Bases;] SCHANZER (ed. 1969) argues that the semicolon makes "the Clown remark that there is only one Puritan among them, as if Puritan and treble voice were synonymous, which they were not." He substitutes a dash, "which makes the Clown add: 'except for one Puritan amongst them (who takes the treble part) and he sings psalms even to lively dance-tunes.'" Although no earlier ed. comments, it seems unlikely that the semicolon (or colon in some early eds.) conveys the meaning SCHANZER says it does. Some recent eds. prefer a comma; some adopt his gloss.

1712-13 **Puritan . . . horne-pipes**] *OED* (Puritan, *sb.* 1, citing this line): "A member of that party of English Protestants who regarded the reformation of the church under Elizabeth as incomplete, and called for its further 'purification'." DOUCE (1807, 1:355), without substantiation: Puritans commonly burlesqued Catholic plainsong "by adapting vulgar and ludicrous music to psalms and pious compositions." Referring to Thomas Warton's *History of English Poetry*, sec. 45 (probably 4:125-6 in W. Carew Hazlitt, ed., 1871), KNIGHT (ed. 1841): "In the early days of psalmody it was not unusual to adapt the popular secular tunes to versions of the psalms." DEIGHTON (ed. 1889) glosses *to horne-pipes* as "to the accompaniment of hornpipes," wind instruments that, according to *OED* (1), are "said to have been so called from having the bell and mouthpiece made of horn." Following WORDSWORTH (1880, p. 271), FURNESS (ed. 1898), asking, "Who was there to accompany him?" believes that "he sings Psalms to the lively tunes to which Horn-pipes were danced." Hornpipes as dances were "of a lively and vigorous character, usually performed by a single person, orig. to the accompaniment of the wind instrument" (*OED* 2). Possibly FURNESS is right; H. COLERIDGE (1851, 1:143) remarks that "some of the modern evangelicals have adapted hymns to Moore's Melodies, and to most of the fashionable songs, quadrilles, waltzes, &c. — thinking it hard, as they say, that Satan should have all the good music to himself." Yet since the Clown is speaking generally, the question of who accompanies the Puritan does not arise, and *OED* does not find *hornpipe* used to mean a piece of music until 1789.

BALDWIN (1943, p. 198) recognizes the amusing incongruity — he quotes Mistress Ford on Falstaff's disposition and the truth of his words: "they do no more adhere and keep place together than the hundred Psalms [Hundredth Psalm] to the tune of 'Green-sleeves'" (*Wiv.* 2.1.61-3 [606-8]) — but comments on "the ill-taste of those who sang the metrical psalms to such secular tunes as by nature or associations did

I must haue Saffron to colour the Warden Pies, Mace:
Dates, none: that's out of my note: Nutmegges, seuen;   1715
a Race or two of Ginger, but that I may begge: Foure
pound of Prewyns, and as many of Reysons o'th Sun.

    Aut. Oh, that euer I was borne.

    Clo. I'th'name of me.

1714 Warden Pies] Wardens Pies ROWE1, ROWE2; warden-pipes HAN3
1717 pound] pounds KNT3, WH2, NLSN
    many of Reysons] many raisins POPE1-MAL (−CAP)
1718 *Groveling on the Ground.* ROWE1+ (−SIG) (*subst.*)
1719 me.] ~ − ROWE1-ARD1 (−RLTR), SIS, PEL1, EVNS, BEV3

---

not befit the sacred character of the psalms, and he [Sh.] has given some hints as to what kind of people were guilty of this type of confusion." Ill taste, however, may have had little to do with it; despite Ford, "Greensleeves" "was converted to a pious use" shortly after it was registered for publication in 1580 (*The Hymnal 1940 Companion*, 3rd ed., p. 30; see also FIRTH, 1916, 2:518-19) and today is happily sung as "What Child Is This" (*Hymnal 1940*, no. 36). PAFFORD (ed. 1963) thinks the allusion is rather to the Puritans' vocal style; he quotes HOLDEN (1954, pp. 102-3): "According to the stage writers . . . psalms were delivered in a high nasal tone"; HOLDEN does not say the psalms were sung, though. The point may be merely the amusing incongruity, or, as NAYLOR (1931, p. 84) says, "The tune of the hornpipe would tend to show that the Old Adam was not all put away yet." ORGEL (ed. 1996), quite differently: "The puritan sings psalms *even* to hornpipes—i.e. he is not averse to music, but no music is secular for him." LOBBAN (ed. 1910): The Puritan is "another anachronism." Evidently the reference to the figure is also a merely casual one; according to THOMPSON (1903, p. 250), "study of Shakspere's plays . . . for the purpose of finding definite allusion to the religious controversy of the 17th century, will not be fruitful." SYMMES (1903, p. 174): A truly significant feature of the magnificent greatness of Sh. is the absence of any mean and satirical allusion to his contemporaries and their work. Perhaps we have here and there a word against the Puritans [as here and in *TN* 2.3.151 ff. (834 ff.)] (in Fr.). For lines 1712-13 as evidence of Sh.'s own religious views, see n. 324-8. PORTER & CLARKE (ed. 1908): "In other words he was a merry unobjectionable Puritan."

    1714 **Saffron**] *OED* (*sb.* 1, citing this line): "The dried stigmas of *Crocus sativus*." Recipes for "chare de wardoun leche" (sliced wardens) and "wardonys in syryp," given by ANDERSON (1962, pp. 56-7), call for saffron. Regarding saffron, GERARD (1597, pp. 124-5) says, "The Chiues [stigmas] steeped in water, serueth . . . to colour sundry meates and confections. It is with good successe giuen to procure bodilie lust," but it is unlikely that lust lurks in this market list. See also HARRISON (1587; 1968, p. 354), BEISLY (1864, pp. 71-3), and SEAGER (1896, p. 269).

    Warden] MINSHEU (1617): A "great Peare." ELLACOMBE (1896, p. 211) accepts the idea that the name derives from Wardon Abbey in Bedfordshire, the armorial bearings of which include three pears, but *OED* (*sb.*[2] b, citing this line) runs the indebtedness the other way. AS YOU LIKE IT (1789, p. 712): Because wardens are a Christmas treat, Sh. would not have introduced "them at a sheepshearing at Midsummer; a church-warden pye he might mean." One should not take him seriously; there seems to have been no such dish as a church-warden pie. As STEEVENS (ed. 1793) notes, Jonson merely punned on the name of the pear in *The Gypsies Metamorphosed*, where Cocklorell serves the Devil "A deputie Tart, a Churchwarden Pye." For the season of sheepshearing, see n. 1887. WISE (1861, p. 96): "A [true] warden-pie is, to this day, in Warwickshire, called a warden-cob, and consists merely of a warden-pear wrapped in a coat of paste, and then baked, forming a most primitive dish." PROTHERO (1916, 1:372): "There were also Warden apples." For more about wardens, see BEISLY (1864, pp. 73–4) and SEAGER (1896, p. 336); PORTER & CLARKE (ed. 1908) give an early recipe for the pie.

   Mace] JOHNSON (1755): "A kind of spice. 'The nutmeg is inclosed in a threefold covering, of which the second is *mace*.'" Both are products of the *Myristica fragrans*, an evergreen tree native to the Moluccas.

   1715 **my note**] WHITE (ed. 1857): "'Matters of which I am to take note' [*OED*, *sb.*² 14b]; not ' . . . my list,'" because the Clown would have been illiterate. SCHMIDT (1875), a believer in rustic literacy: "Letter, billet." Some eds. concur, but WILSON (ed. 1931), following COLLINS (ed. 1904–24?): "Had it [the list] been written, the Clown would not have mentioned 'dates' at all, since that item could not have appeared." PAFFORD (ed. 1963): "He thinks of dates but, referring to his list, sees that they are not there; or, less probably, that they have been struck out. The Clown, like Mopsa and Dorcas, can read." PAFFORD believes that *note* in 51 means "written record." BOORMAN (ed. 1964): The Clown takes the list out of his pocket as he says "Let me see" (1705). For other instances of noting, see n. 298.

   seuen] DENT (1971, p. 81) complains that this word has never been "explained or even questioned." The word means one more than six, nutmegs enough to flavor the warden pies and such other festive dishes as fritters and tansy and bread puddings, as well as legs of mutton and carbonadoed tongues. Nutmegs remaining could be added to one's pomander (see n. 2475). See Gervase Markham, *The English Housewife* (1631, pp. 70–151).

   1716 **Race**] BAILEY (1721): "A Root, as of Ginger" (*OED*, *sb.*⁶); the plant is an East Indian perennial herb. LANGLIN's (1884; 1883–4, p. 187) suggestion that the word is a provincialism meaning "rasped . . . grated" does not accord with the context. The ginger would probably be used for gingersnaps, like those knapped by the gossip in *MV* 3.1.8–9 (1226–7).

   1717 **Prewyns**] SEAGER (1896, p. 251): "Prunes . . . were usual refreshments in houses of evil repute . . . ; but prunes were also used by respectable people. . . . Prunes were made into tarts." SEAGER may not have intended to pun.

   Reysons o'th Sun] WHITE (ed. 1857) quotes from Thomas Cogan, *The Hauen of Health* (1584, pp. 96–7): "They be of two sortes, . . . great Raysons and smal Raysons, otherwise called Corans [currants]. The greatest sort are called raysons of the sunne," having been sun dried.

   1718 **Oh . . . borne**] Proverbial (DENT B140.1). As CHANDLER (1907, 1:237) notes, this very trick is found in GREENE (*Second Pt.*, 1592; 1922, p. 41). See p. 673. KNIGHT (1947; 1966, p. 101): "A clear parody of the parable of the Good Samaritan." HARTWIG (1978, p. 100), in addition, finds "suggestive parody" of Leontes's "I haue drunke, and seene the Spider" (642) and "Nor night, nor day, no rest" (900).

   1719 **I'th'name of me**] PITMAN (ed. 1834): "A vulgar exclamation," here expressing surprise. KENRICK (1765, p. 87): "The Clown, instead of crying out the name of heav'n, exclaimed in the name of himself [as in such expressions as] *for the* SOUL *of me*, *for the* LIFE *of me*, *for the* HEART *of me*, &c." STEEVENS (ed. 1773) compares "Before me she's a good wench" (*TN* 2.3.178 [869]); see also *Cor.* 1.1.120 (123). KNOWLES (privately): "Bobadill, a specialist in absurd oaths, says, 'Bodie o'me' (Jonson, *Every Man in his Humour* 1.4.84, 1.5.16, 4.9.69)." BARCLAY (1766): "The ME is

Aut. Oh helpe me, helpe mee: plucke but off these   1720
ragges: and then, death, death.
Clo. Alacke poore soule, thou hast need of more rags
to lay on thee, rather then haue these off.
Aut. Oh sir, the loathsomnesse of them offend mee,
more then the stripes I haue receiued, which are mightie   1725
ones and millions.
Clo. Alas poore man, a million of beating may come
to a great matter.
Aut. I am rob'd sir, and beaten: my money, and apparrell tane from me, and these detestable things put vp-   1730
on me.

1724 offend] offends F2+ (−DYCE, STAU, DEL, IRV, BUL, NLSN, ALEX, CLN2, PEN2,
EVNS, OXF2, BEV4)

---

emphatically pronounced," though he does not say why. PORTER & CLARKE (ed.
1908): "The Clown swears by his Christian name, the name given him in baptism."
M. H. (1790, p. 306), unconvincingly except to GOLLANCZ (ed. 1894) and CHARLTON
(ed. 1916): As he was about to exclaim *mercy* [cf. 1544], "his voice failed." HERFORD
(ed. 1904): "*Me* would have suggested a wrong sound" if *mercy* had been intended.
Most recent eds. follow KENRICK. WILSON (ed. 1931), improbably, though not to
RIDLEY (ed. 1935) and others: "In view of the absurd statute against blasphemy upon
the stage, such an expression would raise a laugh." He alludes to An Act to Restrain
the Abuses of Players, 1606, which forbade, in performances, the jesting with or
profanation of the name of God. ORGEL (ed. 1996) compares "for the life of me," an
expression Sh. does not use, and "Before me, she's a good wench" (*TN* 2.3.178 [869]).

1720-1 **these ragges**] HARTWIG (1972, p. 118): "Autolycus is disguised as his
own victim."

1721 **death, death**] STYAN (1975, p. 151): "The thief must perform outrageously
like one in the throes of death in order to pick the Shepherd's pocket, then make a
lightning recovery [1747 ff.] in order to shake off the benefactor who will not desist
from helping him."

1724 **loathsomnesse**] HAPPÉ (1969): "In smell and appearance."

offend] DYCE (ed. 1857, 2:168): A plural verb may follow "a nominative singular when a genitive [possessive] plural intervenes." For similar lack of agreement,
see nn. 237, 870, 920-1, 1636-7, and 1643.

1725 **stripes**] MINSHEU (1617, Stripe): "Blowe." SCHMIDT (1875): "A stroke made
with a lash," usually as punishment (cf. *Ant.* 3.13.152 [2332]). If so, Autolycus nearly
gives himself away; an innocent victim should have received none of these. Cf. his
confusion of virtues and vices at 1756-9. RUBINSTEIN (1984) finds that this word and
others associated with Autolycus have sexual significance.

1727-8 **a . . . matter**] DEIGHTON (ed. 1889): "When you come to reckon it, a
million of beating amounts to a good deal; an adage worthy of Dogberry." CARRING-
TON (1956), dubiously: "Emphasis on the *a, i.e.* only *one* million strokes." BOORMAN
(ed. 1964), even more so: "There may be a pun linking 'a million of beating' to 'matter'
('a maker of mats')."

Clo. What, by a horse-man, or a foot-man?

Aut. A footman (sweet sir) a footman.

Clo. Indeed, he should be a footman, by the garments
he has left with thee: If this bee a horsemans Coate, it   1735
hath seene very hot seruice. Lend me thy hand, Ile helpe
thee. Come, lend me thy hand.

Aut. Oh good sir, tenderly, oh.

Clo. Alas poore soule.

Aut. Oh good sir, softly, good sir: I feare (sir) my   1740
shoulder-blade is out.

Clo. How now? Canst stand?

1732 What, by∧] ~ ∧ ~ , STAU

1733 footman.] ~ ? KNT2

1735 has] hath THEO2-COL2 (−HAN, CAP), WH1-HAL, DEL, KNT3, COL4, OXF1, PEN1,
CLN2

1737 *Helping him up.* ROWE1-DEL2 (−CAP, MAL), KTLY+ (−WH2, IRV, NLSN, ARD2,
EVNS) (*subst.*)

1732-5 **a horse-man . . . thee**] FURNESS (ed. 1898): "There may be significance in the hyphens and the lack of them: 'Was it a man on horseback or a man on
foot?' asks the Clown. 'It was a footman, a servant', answers Autolycus. 'It must indeed
have been a fellow who footed it, a downright tramp, to judge by his clothes', responds the Clown."

1735-6 **If . . . seruice**] HUDSON (ed. 1880): "The Clown quibbles on *footman*
and *horseman*, using them here as military terms. A mounted soldier must have been
in a hard fight, to have had his coat so spoiled." WILSON (ed. 1931): In addition to
"foot soldier," "'Footman' meant also a 'footpad,' and the Clown is perhaps intended
to confuse the two." *OED*'s first record of the word in this sense is dated 1615.
PAFFORD (ed. 1963): "The highwayman . . . has always been more aristocratic than
the footpad," who, as BOORMAN (ed. 1964) notes, is "likely to be ill-clad." For *to see
service*, *OED* (Service[1] 12d, citing this line): "To have experience of warfare. Hence
(in perfect tense) of a thing, to have been much used or worn." For *hot*, SCHMIDT
(1874, Hot 4): "Furious."

1740-1 **I . . . out**] BUCKNILL (1860, p. 131): The bear may have extracted the
shoulder bone of Antigonus, but Autolycus errs in saying his is out, for "the shoulder-
blade . . . cannot be dislocated ['out']." As FURNESS (ed. 1898) suggests, Autolycus
is less anatomical than BUCKNILL. FRYE (*Natural Perspective*, 1965, p. 115) finds here
a "very curious" echo of 1537, and PROUDFOOT (1976, p. 73) considers the doubling
of Antigonus and Autolycus in performance; he is unenthusiastic about the idea,
"though there is shoulder-bones in both." But as HOENIGER (1976, p. 7) inquires,
"Did the echo result from conscious design or quirks of Shakespeare's imagination?"
BLISSETT (1971, p. 55): One of the "various symmetries of stasis" in the play. Cf. n.
3313 for another.

1742 **How now?**] See n. 201.

Aut. Softly, deere sir: good sir, softly: you ha done
me a charitable office.

Clo. Doest lacke any mony? I haue a little mony for   1745
thee.

Aut. No, good sweet sir: no, I beseech you sir: I haue
a Kinsman not past three quarters of a mile hence, vnto
whome I was going: I shall there haue money, or anie
thing I want: Offer me no money I pray you, that killes   1750
my heart.

Clow. What manner of Fellow was hee that robb'd
you?

Aut. A fellow (sir) that I haue knowne to goe about
with Troll-my-dames: I knew him once a seruant of the   1755

1743 *picks his Pocket.* CAP, v1778+ *(subst.)*
1755 Troll-my-dames] troll-| madams WARBURTON *conj. in* HAN2, HAN, CAP, OXF2

1743–4 **Softly . . . office**] McFARLAND (1972, p. 132): "The picking of the
Clown's pocket mockingly prefigures the 'sheep-shearing' scene that follows." HART-
WIG (1978, p. 99): "The manipulation of the audience's sympathies . . . is similar
to that employed in the Sicilian scenes earlier. There we wanted Hermione's honor
to be defended against Leontes' accusations; here, we want Perdita's plans to be
protected. The Clown, as the displaced victim for Perdita, becomes a comic parallel
to Hermione," which seems impossible.

1743 **Softly**] *OED* (*adv.* 10, citing this line): The equivalent of Soft (*adv.* 8), for
which see n. 2224.

1743–4 **you . . . office**] DRAPER (1985, p. 30): The execution of CAPELL's SD
makes these words comically ambiguous.

1744 **office**] SCHMIDT (1875): "An act of good will." For another sense, see n.
1121. "With this false piety," PAFFORD (ed. 1963) compares GREENE (*Second Pt.*,
1592; 1922, p. 31): "In Paules . . . the foist [pickpocket] as deuoutly as if he were
som zealous person, standeth soberly, with his eies eleuated to heauen, when his
hand is either on the purse or in the pocket."

1747 **No . . . no**] THIRLBY (MS 1725–33?): "Perhaps he had pick'd his pocket
before." Which he had, of course.

1748 **past**] SCHMIDT (1875): "More than."

1750–1 **that . . . heart**] *OED* (Kill, *v.* 7c): "To depress or discourage one completely." STEEVENS (ed. 1793) compares *H5* 2.1.88 (587) and CALDECOTT (MS 1813–
33), *AYL* 3.2.246 (1440). BOORMAN (ed. 1964): "Ironically true, if the Clown finds
his money gone." PARRY (ed. 1982), too literally: "My heart can't stand it."

1752 **manner**] *OED* (*sb.*[1] 9, citing this line): "Kind, sort."

1755 **Troll-my-dames**] COLES (1676, Trou-madam): "Troll-madam, or Pidgeon-
holes." NARES (1876; 1905): "Played with a board, at one end of which are a number
of arches, like pigeon-holes, into which small balls are to be bowled." Most eds. gloss
after this fashion, but it is obvious that the supposed fellow is not strolling with a
game board. COTGRAVE (1611, Trou Madame): "Called Trunkes, or the Hole." GEN-
TLEMAN (ed. 1774): "Nine holes," probably a different game, for troll-madam has 11,
according to FARMER (in STEEVENS, ed. 1773, 10:Pp5). FARMER quotes John Jones, *The*

Prince: I cannot tell good sir, for which of his Vertues it was, but hee was certainely Whipt out of the
Court.

   Clo. His vices you would say: there's no vertue whipt   (2B2ᵃ)
out of the Court: they cherish it to make it stay there;   1760
and yet it will no more but abide.

   Aut. Vices I would say (Sir.) I know this man well,
he hath bene since an Ape-bearer, then a Processe-seruer

1761 but] not COL3
1762-3 well, he] well; then he HAN3

Benefit of the Auncient Bathes of Buckstones (18 Jan. 1572, sig. C4), who adds that
troll-madam was much played by women. RIDLEY (ed. 1935), without evidence, asserts that because the game was played by women, "the players themselves" were
called by its name. MADDEN (1897, p. 131) suggests that *troll* means "doxy," an idea
developed by BOORMAN (ed. 1964) and more fully by SCHANZER (ed. 1969): "Since
'to troll' also meant 'to stroll' [*OED, vb.* 1], as well as 'to circulate, be passed round'
[*vb.* 6], it seems likely that Autolycus . . . [alludes] to loose women, his *aunts*." The
resemblance of *troll* to *trull* ("prostitute"), which could be spelled *troul*, may also
be significant.
   1756-7 **Vertues**] SCHMIDT (1875, Virtue): "Any good quality, merit, or accomplishment," probably applies, although he does not cite this instance. HARTWIG (1972,
p. 119): "The Clown ignores the other meanings of 'virtue' (power, and the skill of
manipulation)." So, evidently, does *OED; virtue* as "power" usually refers to the
efficacy or worth of stones or plants (*sb.* 9a and b). RUBINSTEIN (1984), wildly: "Sexual
exploits, which included being a servant (lover or pimp) of the Prince."
   1759 **vices**] KERMODE (ed. 1963): "The Clown fails to see Autolycus' little joke."
   1761 **but**] ABBOTT (§127): "*But* in the sense of *except* frequently follows negative
comparatives, where we should use *than*."
   abide] MINSHEU (1617): "Tarrie." JOHNSON (ed. 1765): "*Sojourn*, to live for a
time without a settled habitation" (*OED, v. str.* 8). RANN (ed. 1787) finds a secondary
meaning— "tolerate" (*OED* 16 or 17), which for *no . . . abide* yields "barely endure
the air of it." BECKET (1815, 1:362) thinks the alternative meaning is "*forbear
. . . refrain* from exercising its powers" (*OED* 15). The CLARKES (ed. 1865): "The
Clown probably uses the word 'abide', as thinking it means something less than
'stay'; or he uses 'but' with the effect of 'but just', 'but barely.'" HERFORD (ed. 1916-):
"His phrase is more pretentious than exact," and intended to be comic, WILSON (ed.
1931) thinks. TILLEY (1930, p. 117 n.): He mistakenly substitutes *abide* for *away*.
BETHELL (ed. 1956), however: "This satire on the court . . . recalls the unhealthy
atmosphere of the court of Sicilia during Leontes' jealousy." Not to many, one suspects. HULME (1958, p. 385): "Intended, I suggest, to echo the proverb 'Things well
fitted abide' ([TILLEY T207,] first record 1640); 'if Virtue felt herself at home she would
remain at court' [*OED* 1]. But by adding the 'no more but' qualification the clown
has given *abide* a second sense, quite opposed to that in the proverb, namely, 'to
stay only for a moment, to pause before going on [*OED* 2].'"
   1763 **an Ape-bearer**] *OED* (Ape, *sb.* 8, citing this line): "A strolling buffoon."
STAUNTON (ed. 1859): His occupation "was to instruct apes in their tumbling, and to
exhibit the learned animals for a consideration to the public." KNIGHT (ed. 1841)
refers to Jonson's assurance in *Bartholomew Fair* that the play will not represent "a

(a Bayliffe) then hee compast a Motion of the Prodigall
sonne, and married a Tinkers wife, within a Mile where   1765
my Land and Liuing lyes; and (hauing flowne ouer ma-
ny knauish professions) he setled onely in Rogue: some
call him *Autolicus*.

1765 Mile] mile of MTBY4 *conj.* (of *or* o'), KEIGHTLEY *conj. in* CAM1, KTLY
1767 in] in a THEO2-RANN (−HAN, CAP)

Iugler with a wel-educated Ape to come ouer the chaine, for the *King* of *England*,
and backe againe for the *Prince*, and sit still on his arse for the *Pope*, and the *King*
of *Spaine!*" (Ind. 17-20). To demonstrate the copiousness of Sh.'s vocabulary, CHAL-
MERS (1797, p. 210) points out that this word and "more than a thousand" others
used by Sh. do not appear in JOHNSON (1755).

   Processe-seruer] *OED* (Process 31b, citing this line): "A sheriff's officer who
serves processes or summonses."

   1764 **(a Bayliffe)**] In response to CLARK & WRIGHT's (ed. 1863) conjecture "to
a bailiff," LETTSOM (MS 1840-65) asks if bailiffs and process servers are not the same.
They are; *OED* (Bailiff 2, citing this line): "An officer of justice under a sheriff, who
executes writs and processes, distrains, and arrests."

   compast] SCHMIDT (1874, Compass): "Obtain" (*OED, v.*[1] 11b). MAXWELL (ed.
1956): "Devised" (1). HULME (1962, pp. 308-9) adds "to make a circuit" (5). She
comments, "'Compast' meaning 'obtained' would be, as it were, parallel to 'married'
[1765]; in the sense 'took on tour' it would go with the travelling of the tinker's wife,
the ape-bearer and the process-server; the puppet-show which Autolycus got hold of
he would take from fair to fair."

   Motion] HANMER (ed. 1743-4): "Puppet-shew" (*OED, sb.* 13, citing this line).
To prove that a puppet show about the Prodigal Son would not be extraordinary,
KNIGHT (ed. 1841) quotes *Bartholomew Fair*, in which Lanthorne Leatherhead remembers motions he has produced: "*Ierusalem* was a stately thing; and so was *Nin-
iue*, and the citty of *Norwich*, and *Sodom* and *Gomorrah*" (5.1.8-10). See also Herford & Simpson's notes in *Ben Jonson* 10:208. For "compast . . . sonne," BOORMAN
(ed. 1964) unconvincingly suggests, in addition, "had a desire to be the Prodigal Son
(i.e. decided to settle down)." JONAS (1918, pp. 402-3) finds other theatrical allusions
at 269-71, 1210-11, 1948-9, 2467-9, 2533-4, 3088-9, and 3365-9.

   1764-5 **Prodigall sonne**] See Luke 15:11-32.

   1765 **Tinkers wife**] For tinkers, see n. 1687-8; their wives presumably are no
less undesirable than the tinkers themselves. BRANDES (ed. 1905, 4:xvi), taking him
seriously, thinks Autolycus actually marries such a woman "and settles down as a
confirmed rogue."

   1766 **Land and Liuing**] DEIGHTON (ed. 1889): "Land and property, almost equivalent to landed property, an ambitious term used to impress the clown with an idea
of the speaker's social position." A singular verb follows, "because the notion is a
single one" and the three words could be telescoped into *living* alone (see *OED*,
Living, *vbl. sb.* 4).

   flowne ouer] BETHELL (ed. 1956): "Passed quickly through."

   1767 **setled**] *OED* (*v.* 8, citing this line): A figurative use of the word, meaning
"to alight *on* something," which accords with "flowne ouer" (1766).

   in] RIDLEY (ed. 1935): "Into the part of." CARRINGTON (1956): "As a." ORGEL
(ed. 1996): "Upon that of."

Clo. Out vpon him: Prig, for my life Prig: he haunts
Wakes, Faires, and Beare-baitings.   1770

Aut. Very true sir: he sir hee: that's the Rogue that
put me into this apparrell.

Clo. Not a more cowardly Rogue in all *Bohemia*; If
you had but look'd bigge, and spit at him, hee'ld haue
runne.   1775

Aut. I must confesse to you (sir) I am no fighter: I am
false of heart that way, & that he knew I warrant him.

1769 Prig . . . Prig] prig . . . prig [Prig *not as an alias*] POPE1 +
1770 Beare-baitings] Bear-baiting ROWE1, ROWE2
1772 this] his ROWE3-POPE2
1777 of] at JOHN, v1773-MAL

Rogue] WILSON (ed. 1931): "Something of a quibble . . . as 'rogue' . . . was practically equivalent to 'vagrant, vagabond,'" a notion that MINSHEU (1617) bears out. BOORMAN (ed. 1964): "The metaphor 'flown over' (with its sense of 'dabbled in') is concluded in 'settled'—the knave comes home to roost."

1768 **Autolicus**] Because the biographical details are specific, GRANVILLE-BARKER (1912; 1974, pp. 21–2) thinks that Autolycus may be "something of a portrait" of a real person.

1769 **Prig . . . Prig**] *OED* (*sb.*³ 2, citing this line): "A thief," not a "pert, conceited, saucy" fellow, as JOHNSON (1755) says—that sense was not current until the late 17th c. (*OED, sb.*³ 3 and 4). WHALLEY (in STEEVENS, ed. 1785), referring to the character Prig in Beaumont, Fletcher, and Massinger's *Beggars' Bush*, recognizes that the Clown is using a canting term (see n. 1687–8). Possibly, too, the word here, as in *Beggars' Bush*, is a proper rather than a common noun, Autolycus's victims having given him the name "Prig." AWDELEY (1575, sig. A2) notes that "a Prygman goeth with a stycke in hys hand like an idle person. His propertye is to steale cloathes of the hedge."

for my life] SCHMIDT (1874): "As sure as I live."

1770 **Wakes**] MINSHEU (1617): "Countrie feasts." *OED* (*sb.*¹ 4b, citing this line): "The local annual festival of an English (now chiefly rural) parish, observed (originally on the feast of the patron saint of the church . . .) as an occasion for making holiday." See DYER (1884, p. 331).

Beare-baitings] *OED* (*vbl. sb.*): "The sport of setting dogs to attack a bear chained to a stake." LEE (1916, 2:431): "Men of fashion, tradesmen, mechanics, apprentices, were all united in an enthusiastic patronage" of bearbaiting, and the events often attracted huge crowds. The huge crowds in turn attracted pickpockets; as PAFFORD (ed. 1963) says, at 2568–9 Autolycus mentions similar events that yield "a carefull man worke."

1774 **look'd bigge**] KITTREDGE & RIBNER (ed. 1967): "With a stern expression." EVANS (ed. 1974): "Put on a bold front." *Big* in this expression, however, means "haughty, pompous, pretentious" (*OED, a.* 8b).

1777 **false . . . way**] DEIGHTON (ed. 1889): "My heart [courage] fails me in any matter of that kind." PARRY (ed. 1982): "Perhaps he speaks in his 'own' voice, inadvertently—and 'covers up' with the next remark."

 Clo. How do you now?

 Aut. Sweet sir, much better then I was: I can stand,
and walke: I will euen take my leaue of you, & pace soft-   1780
ly towards my Kinsmans.

 Clo. Shall I bring thee on the way?

 Aut. No, good fac'd sir, no sweet sir.

 Clo. Then fartheewell, I must go buy Spices for our
sheepe-shearing.   *Exit.* 1785

 Aut. Prosper you sweet sir. Your purse is not hot e-
nough to purchase your Spice: Ile be with you at your
sheepe-shearing too: If I make not this Cheat bring out
another, and the sheerers proue sheepe, let me be vnrold,
and my name put in the booke of Vertue.   1790

1778 you] you do F4-POPE2, HAN
1781 Kinsmans] kinsman ARD1
1782 the] thy F4-RANN (−CAP)
1784 fartheewell] farewell F2-v1773 (−CAP)
   go] goe to F2-F4, ROWE3-RANN (−CAP); go and ROWE1, ROWE2
1789 vnrold] enrolled mTBY2 *conj.*, COL2, COL3, COL4
1790 in] into ROWE2-RANN (−CAP)

 1780-1 **pace softly**] ROLFE (ed. 1879): "Walk along slowly." See n. 1602 for
another sense of *pace*.

 1781 **towards**] See n. 3006.

 1782 **bring**] SCHMIDT (1874): "Accompany."

 1784-5 **Then . . . sheepe-shearing**] KNIGHT (1947; 1965, p. 101): "The
Clown says [this] with a broad grin on his vacant face."

 1786-7 **Your . . . Spice**] The purse is cold because empty. DEIGHTON (ed.
1889): "A reference to the hot nature of spices [SCHMIDT, 1874, Hot 7, jocularly], and
perhaps also to 'warm' in the sense of comfortable, well provided." See n. 1938 for
another association.

 1788 **Cheat**] KERSEY (1702): "Cheating trick." See n. 1695-6.

   bring out] THIRLBY (MS 1747-53): "Produce." BETHELL (ed. 1956): "He now
knows about the sheep-shearing." WILSON (ed. 1931): "I.e. he will procure his pedlar's outfit with the proceeds of his pickpocketing."

 1789 **sheerers proue sheepe**] RABKIN (1981, p. 131): "He will add a new meaning to sheep-shearing." *OED* (Sheep, *sb.* 2e, citing this line): "With suggestion of
'fleecing' or robbing."

   vnrold] WARBURTON (in THEOBALD, ed. 1733): Dismissed from the gang of
beggars of which he is a member. DEIGHTON (ed. 1889): "As though it were an
honourable fraternity such as the Inns of Court, or the various trade guilds." Yet
GREENE (*Second Pt.*, 1592; 1922, p. 35): says that "our nips and foists . . . haue a
kind of fraternity or brother-hood amongst them, hauing a hall or place of meeting,
where they confer of waightie matters, touching their workmanship."

 1790 **booke**] *OED* (*sb.* 4 *fig.* c, citing this line): "With allusive reference to various
real or reputed books." Its first three references to the word in this sense are Shn.

Song.   *Iog-on, Iog-on, the foot-path way,*
         And merrily hent the Stile-a:
         A merry heart goes all the day,
         Your sad tyres in a Mile-a.   *Exit.*

Scena Quarta.   4.4

1792 *hent*] *hend* HAN, CAP, v1773
1795 *Scena Quarta*] SCENE III CAP-RANN, v1793-DEL2, KTLY-HUD2, OXF1, BUL;
SCENE II MAL

1791–4 *Iog-on . . . Mile-a*] See n. 1669–80 and p. 851. REED (ed. 1785):
"These lines are part of a catch printed in '[N. D.'s] *an Antidote against Melancholy,
made up in Pills compounded of witty ballads, Jovial Songs, and merry catches,*
1661'" (ed. J. P. COLLIER, 1870, p. 9). Catch 28 begins with these four lines and adds
eight more.
    1791 *Iog-on*] *OED* (*v.* 4, citing this line): "Trudge."
    foot-path] *OED* (citing this line): "A path for foot-passengers only."
    1792 *hent*] COCKERAM (1623): "To catch or lay hold of" (*OED*, *v.* 1). Sh. uses the
word as a verb, "occupy," in *MM* 4.6.14 (2342) and as a noun, "grasp," in *Ham.*
3.3.88 (2363). SCHMIDT's (1874) "to take, to clear, to pass beyond" extends the action
to its effect. PORTER & CLARKE (ed. 1908): "Possibly, as a horse 'takes' a fence, or at
least 'to take', or seize hold of in order to jump."
    1792–4 *Stile-a . . . Mile-a*] Regarding the *-a,* JOHNSON (1755): "Used in bur-
lesque poetry to lengthen out a syllable, without adding to the sense." *OED* (A, *inter.*
4, citing this line): "Probably originating in the necessary retention of M[iddle]
E[nglish] final *-e* where wanted for measure."
    1793–4 *A . . . Mile-a*] Proverbially, the two hearts may endure equally, though
sometimes merriment is given a slight edge. "As long lives a merry Man as a sad" is
TILLEY's main form (M71), but variants add, e.g., "and longer by a day." On the other
hand, COLLIER (ed. 1842) finds "*A merry heart lives long-a*" (TILLEY H320a) in Beaumont's *The Knight of the Burning Pestle* 1.302 (1:24). BROWN (*Shakespeare's Plays,*
1966, p. 100): The lines give "a further opportunity for mimed action." STAUFFER
(1949, p. 299): "He acts out Florizel's counsel: ['Apprehend Nothing but iollity. . . .
Be merry (Gentle)' (1825–6, 1849)]."
    1794 *sad*] Melancholy. See n. 616, 618.
    tyres] MALONE (ed. 1790): "A dissyllable," which may be so in Ireland and
Virginia but probably not here.
    1795 *Scena Quarta*] SCHANZER (ed. 1969): "In *Pandosto* there is no sheep-shear-
ing feast, only 'a meeting of all the farmers' daughters in Sicilia, whither Fawnia was
also bidden as mistress of the feast' [see p. 637]. It is on her return from this feast
that she and the Prince first set eyes on each other."
    HERFORD (ed. 1916–): "This 'scene', one of the longest in Shakespeare, is dra-
matically a succession of scenes, in which different persons take part; the same place,

the green-sward before the shepherd's cottage, being . . . the 'scene' of all of them. . . . After a prelude (Florizel and Perdita) we have (1) the festival, with the dialogue of Polixenes and Perdita [1860–2005]. (2) Autolycus and the Clown and the shepherd girls' homely comedy in contrast to the high poetry of (1) [to 2165]. (3) Polixenes's intervention; tragedy, or at least tragic 'pity and terror', contrasted with the previous idyll [to 2309]. (4) Camillo's plot with Florizel [to 2553]. (5) Autolycus makes game of the Shepherd [to 2723]." For a different interpretation of the location, see ORGEL at the end of this note.

FERGUSSON (1959; 1970, p. 298): "The scene is a set-piece, like a masque; the story pauses, and we are invited to enjoy the music, the dances, and the poetry. Its interwoven themes of winter and spring, age and youth, guilt and innocence, pull together the imagery of the whole play." PYLE (1969, pp. 81–2): "A scene outstanding even in Shakespeare for its poetical and visual beauty." DEIGHTON (ed. 1889, p. xxxiv), writing for Indian students: "However deeply the noble character and undeserved sufferings of Hermione may be felt, the first thought that comes into an Englishman's mind when *The Winter's Tale* is mentioned, is the thought of Perdita among her flowers and friends." BETHELL (ed. 1956): "With its mixture of lovely poetry and earthy humour, it [this scene] reveals the best side of country life, while not ignoring its less attractive qualities—the crudity of the Clown and the general credulity which allows Autolycus an easy success. . . . The love of Florizel and Perdita, frankly sexual yet completely chaste, contrasts strongly with the morbid sophistication of Leontes in his jealousy." HARTWIG (1972, p. 119) : "In the same way that Carnival acts as an exorciser of evil spirits, the sheep-shearing celebration purges the play of its melancholy." SALINGAR (1974, p. 13): "Through this scene as a whole, with its blend of folklore and mythology, there runs a strong suggestion that this festive moment is to coincide with a change in the direction of the story." FRYE (1978, p. 38): "The sense of 'great creating nature' as an integral part of what man's life ought to be comes to a focus in the sheep-shearing festival, a masque scene in which the dance of the twelve satyrs forms the antimasque." RABKIN (1981, p. 118) finds another direction: "When . . . we see the tragedy of middle age dissolve into the comedy of youth . . . we remember that before the tragic events . . . Leontes and Polixenes had spent a childhood like the childhood of Florizel and Perdita . . . and we become aware of a world in which time moves cyclically in a process of eternal renewal." PARRY (ed. 1982): "The scene explores the nature of Nature and its relation to the nature of Art (in particular the art of disguise). . . . This . . . [is] the subject of discussion between the lovers at their first (and disguised) appearance."

LLOYD (in SINGER, ed. 1856, 4:135): "The pastoral scenes and incidents come upon us by as quick and startling a turn as the jealousy of Leontes upon his exaggerated hospitality." GREG (1906, p. 411), much in the minority: "It is characteristic of the shepherd scenes of that play [*WT*], written in the full maturity of Shakespeare's genius, that, in spite of their origin in Greene's romance of *Pandosto*, they owe nothing of their treatment to pastoral tradition, nothing to convention, nothing to aught save life as it mirrored itself in the magic glass of the poet's imagination." CHAMBERS (1925, p. 300), however: "Essentially this is Shakespeare's picture of a rustic merry-making. . . . It is an exercise in pastoral . . . the poetry of the reaction from civilization, [having a] tendency, intelligible enough even if illusory, to exalt the simplicity and content of the meadows above the pomps of mortal state." STYAN (1965, p. 87): "Pastoral comedy slips into homely farce, and the romantic into the tragic." For ingenuity, he compares *TN* 3.4. JACQUOT (1972, pp. 167–8) notes "some analogies with the masque. Florizel sees Perdita in her 'unusual weeds' [1798] as Flora, and compares himself to the gods 'humbling their deities to love' [1827]. Ovidian mythology also abounds in Perdita's memorable evocation of spring flowers [1926 ff.]. The Prince in his vows and Perdita in her floral games praise with equal felicity the state of virginity, the temperate fires of chaste love, and nuptial joys. Such themes are also expressed with sustained poetry in Campion's masque of Lord Hayes." YUNE (1973, p. 57): "This scene with Perdita who creates the world of spring, love and life is contrasted to the preceding dark world of aged Leontes. In this setting of idyl, the man Polixenes and young Perdita are again contrasted as the two forces of destruction and creation." MARSH (1962;1969, p. 143): "Though it takes the form of a pastoral, this scene is not set in Arcadia. Death and evil intrude . . . and have to be met by love and faith and a belief in the value of life." STUDING (1982, p. 221) seems to agree: "Very clearly, Bohemia and its rural regions have become a haven for exiles and outcasts." GREER (1986, pp. 105–6): "The symbolism of the celebration may be far more important to the play's structure than we can now realize. The Shepherd, like Leontes, has lost a wife. . . . Leontes lost a wife because he misinterpreted the welcome she gave to his guest. . . . The sheep-shearing is the heart of the play and Autolycus's assault on the gullibility of the shepherds one of its main sources of tension."

A few critics find the scene's principal inspiration in sources other than pastoral. HARRISON (1940, p. 41): This "scene . . . seems to have been written with Spenser's earthly paradise on the Isle of Idleness in view" (*FQ* 2.6.12 ff.). This seems doubtful, although there are a few resemblances—e.g., "The lilly, Ladie of the flowring field, The Flowre-deluce, her louely Paramoure, Bid thee to them thy fruitlesse labours yield, And soone leaue off this toylesome wearie stoure . . ." (st. 16). SPEIRS (1957, p. 333 and n.), in connection with the Yule feast in the Towneley *Second Shepherds' Play*: "What has . . . taken possession of the Christian cycle here, and re-created it, is the tradition of pre-Christian dramatic rituals. . . . Shakespeare later is still drawing on the same source, as in the sheep-shearing festival. . . . Even if Shakespeare as a child did not see the Mystery Cycle himself he would have been told about the old performances by those who had seen them."

Because of the intervention of 4.3, DANIEL (1879, p. 178) places this scene one day later than 4.2, thus in the seventh day represented. Regarding the scene's own time scheme, BERRY (1981, pp. 121–4): "The living present—so Shakespeare postulates—can only exist in relation to past and future. . . . The richly varied flowers express Shakespeare's concept here, as they move forth and back in the natural cycle of time. . . . Daffodils [mentioned by Autolycus at 1669 ff.], in the south of England, appear in March. . . . There is an easy assumption that Autolycus is singing *in*, as well as *of*, March. . . . After the transition of the undatable second verse, Autolycus looks forward to high summer—or sings from within it. So there is a time-movement within his song, spring/summer. . . . Autolycus encounters the Clown on his way to make purchases for the sheep-shearing feast. Now this feast was always a midsummer affair. . . . The suggestion . . . is of the passage of time, since the entire movement takes Autolycus' opening line as its point of departure. . . . The feast is presumed to follow the Clown's errand. Yet Florizel's initial address . . . mentions [1800], and apparently fixes the time at, April. . . . Perdita/Flora is an emblem of spring—even in midsummer. She becomes a fusion of spring and summer. . . . The symbolism [of the flowers offered by Perdita at 1880] points to winter, while the actuality stands at midsummer. . . . The syntax [of 1887–90] is most artful. The present participle [*growing*] implies that the season of the statement was late summer [but] Perdita means '*when* the year grows ancient. . . . ' So [she] reifies the literal, natural present of the scene with [1916–21]. It is a courtly adjustment of decorum, and symbol and literal now fuse. . . . Finally, Perdita calls [at 1926–8] for the flowers of spring—already past—for Florizel. . . . Just as the movement opened with spring looking forward to summer, it closes with summer looking back—or forward—to spring." NELSON (1973, p. 59) is mistaken that "the pastoral scene . . . evidently takes place in late autumn." According to TOPSELL (1658, p. 484), "the common time whereat we [English] shear Sheep is in *June*, and Lambs in *July*." PROTHERO (1916, 1:355): "Ryelands and Cotswold sheep [were] shorn in June."

Enter *Florizell, Perdita, Shepherd, Clowne, Polixenes, Ca-*   1796
millo, Mopsa, Dorcas, Seruants, Autolicus.

Flo. These your vnvsuall weeds, to each part of you
Do's giue a life: no Shepherdesse, but *Flora*

1796 SCENE, *the Prospect of a Shepherd's Cotte.* THEO, WARB, JOHN, DYCE, STAU,
DEL, COL4, HUD2, OXF1, BUL, KIT1, ARD2, SIG, EVNS (*subst.*); *A Room in the Shepherd's
House.* CAP, CAM3 (*subst.*); *The old Shepherd's House.* HAN1 *etc.* (−PEL1, CLN2, PEN2,
OXF2)
    1796-7 *Shepherd . . . Autolicus*] Om. ROWE1-CLN2, SIG+; *followed, at a little
distance, by* SHEPHERD . . . *Servants* [*omitting* Autolicus] ARD2
    1799 Do's] Do THEO1-SIG (−KTLY, NLSN, CLN2)

As for location, ORGEL (ed. 1996): "The scene begins indoors (see lines [2006-7]
and [2163]), but by the time the Clown and Shepherd enter at [2566] it seems to be
outside — see especially lines [2705-7]."
    STUDING (1970, p. 70) alone finds "the conversation between Florizel and Perdita
. . . much more artificial than we would expect from a betrothed couple; . . . the
lovers are much more caught up in artifice and show than in true love."
    1796 *Florizell, Perdita*] KERMODE (1963, p. 35): "Unlike the lost Marina [in
Per.], and Imogen in Wales [in *Cym.*], Perdita does not know she is noble; but as she
plays at being a queen her royalty speaks in her actions. She is endowed with strong
suggestions of divinity; 'no Shepherdesse, but *Flora*' [1799]. . . . Here, with great
deliberation, Shakespeare repeats the device by which Marina first appeared with
flowers by the sea [*Per.* 4.1.12.1 (1436)]." MCIVER (1979, p. 344): Perdita "is an
actress playing the part of a princess who thinks she is a shepherdess playing the part
of Flora." BOOTH (1979, pp. 118-19): "If the actor who played Mamillius were now
playing Perdita, the jumble would be sufficient nearly to unfurnish an audience of
reason." He is speaking primarily of 2879 ff., where Leontes meets "the boy dressed
as Perdita [who] would — in theatrical fact — be Leontes' lost son Mamillius," but the
resemblance might also be perceived here.
    1798-1812 **These . . . glasse**] PAFFORD (ed. 1963): "That the flimsiest disguise
is always a complete success is the most common stage convention." SMITH (1972,
p. 98), however: "Perdita and Florizel are in costume, but they are not disguised;
everybody recognizes them. The purpose is not deception; it is to contrast the festive
merriment of the feast, with its traditional aura of sexual laxity, with the innocence
of the lovers." The beauty of the opening speeches obviates the vulgar possibilities,
mentioned by PETERSON (*Time*, 1973, p. 171), that Perdita "may be angling for a
prince, Florizel may be seeking only a tumble in the hay. The quality of love remains
unknown even to lovers until it is revealed by the trials of time and adversity."
    1798-1802 **These . . . on't**] WEINSTEIN (1971, p. 102), alone: "His lyric and
extravagant devotion to Perdita atones, as it were, for the harsh brutality of Leontes'
earlier insults to Hermione."
    1798-9 **These . . . life**] Cf. *Pandosto*, p. 637. HUDSON (ed. 1880): "The Prince
alludes to the floral trimmings, which make Perdita seem a kind of multitudinous
flower; all the adornings taking fresh life from her, and only diffusing the grace which
they strive to eclipse, as if they were the proper outgrowth of her being." WILSON
(ed. 1931): "Florizel is not paying a compliment merely, he is telling the audience
what the costume signifies; and it appears from [1807-8] that he had designed it."

Other eds. are less sure of this; e.g., KERMODE (ed. 1963): "Perdita's costume may have resembled that of the Roman goddess." See n. 1798. For more on the costumes, see n. 2557-8.

THORNE (1968, p. 38): "Perdita is the embodiment of the fertility ideal and . . . is beauty's summer, effecting the healing and re-creation of the mind. Perdita and the whole country setting . . . represent physical fertility and the creative power of nature; she, as Queen of the High Summer Feast, is presented in opposition to the forces of age and destruction which are set in motion by Leontes, who has become a representative of winter." LAROQUE (1974, p. 10): There is "a significant reversal of the roles. . . . This is one of the chief patterns of festive behaviour which can be traced back to the well-known Roman custom of slave and master exchanging roles during the feast of Saturnalia."

1798 **vnvsuall weeds**] COLES (1676, Wede): "A Garment" (*OED*, *sb.*² 1). In *Pandosto* Fawnia wears her best clothes, and her head is adorned with a garland (see p. 638). Eds. assume, no doubt correctly, that Perdita is similarly attired, since she is no shepherdess but Flora herself, although she speaks of being "Vildely bound vp" (1822) in "borrowed Flaunts" (1823).

1799 **Do's**] FURNESS (ed. 1898): "A singular by attraction from 'each part'" (ABBOTT §412).

life] SCHMIDT (1874): "Vivacity, animation, spirit."

1799-1802 **no . . . on't**] SHERMAN (1902, p. 143) finds here reason to think that Florizel "is a very proper young man, free wholly from the vice incident to courts, but a little flighty and pedantic in some conceptions of common things."

1799 **Shepherdesse**] WAIN (1964, p. 217) finds us taken "back to the world of *As You Like It*."

Flora] DOUCE (1807, 2:454): "The queen of the May is the legitimate representative of the Goddess Flora in the Roman festival," the Floralia, celebrated from 28 Apr. to 3 May. As one may see in Botticelli's *Spring*, she was favored by Zephyrus, the west wind, who "filled her garden with noble flowers and said, 'Goddess, be queen of flowers'" (see n. 1800). ARMSTRONG (1969, p. 68): "Flora's associations are with spring, flowers, and wanton erotic love." COLIE (1974, p. 274): Perdita's "disguise . . . represents her essence rather than covers or discovers her true self." HERFORD (ed. 1916-): Greene compares "his heroine in her festal garb to Flora" (see *Pandosto*, p. 636), and WHITE (ed. 1857) observes that Sh. mentions Flora only here. MUIR (1957, p. 248): "The name of Sabie's heroine may have suggested Florizel's lines," his allusion being to *Flora's Fortune*, for which see p. 675. PETERSON (*Time*, 1973, p. 212, n. 14): "When Perdita dons the robe of Flora the connotations evoked by the goddess' shady reputation in Renaissance England would hardly have been missed by the play's seventeenth-century audiences." Because of the excesses of the Floralia, she could seem unsavory. PETERSON quotes E. K.'s gloss on Spenser's March eclogue: Flora was "the Goddesse of flowres, but indede (as saith Tacitus) a famous harlot, which with the abuse of her body hauing gotten great riches, made the people of Rome her heyre: who in remembraunce of so great beneficence, appointed a yearely feste for the memoriall of her . . . making her the Goddesse of all floures" (ed. Osgood & Lotspeich, *Minor Poems*, 1943, 1:33). As the commentators on the eclogue point out, Tacitus did not say this, but Boccaccio and other Renaissance writers, most specifically COOPER (1565), did. A similar description of Flora is given by PHILLIPS (1658). Nevertheless, Perdita becomes Flora because she takes the winds of March, and the other months, with beauty. As HERFORD noticed, Greene's Fawnia "seemed to bee the Goddesse *Flora* her selfe for Beauty" (see below, p. 636), and Fawnia is not a girl to wade so deep that she slip over her shoes (p. 638). The Flora of *Flora's Fortune*, though mad for her Cassander's love, is similarly virtuous (see below, p. 676). BATE (1993, p. 229) thinks that "for [Florizel] to call Perdita Flora is to stake a claim for her by grafting his own name to her."

Peering in Aprils front. This your sheepe-shearing,   1800
Is as a meeting of the petty Gods,
And you the Queene on't.
    Perd. Sir: my gracious Lord,
To chide at your extreames, it not becomes me:

1800 Peering] 'Pearing WH2
1801 Is . . . meeting] Is as a merry meeting F2-ROWE2; Is a merry meeting ROWE3
1803 Sir] Sure COL2, COL3

1800 **Peering . . . front**] *OED* (Peer, *v*.² 3, citing this line): "To show [itself]";
cf. n. 1669. SCHMIDT (1874, Front): "Beginning" (cf. "summers front," *Son.* 102.7).
DEIGHTON (ed. 1889): "With the idea of Flora as a goddess stepping forth attended
by April, the months being her handmaidens." SIMPSON (1955, p. 40): These lines are
based on bits of Ovid's *Fasti* 5: *incipis Aprili, transis in tempora Mai*— "thou [Flora]
dost begin in April and passeth into the time of May" (185); *vere fruor semper*— "I
[Flora] enjoy perpetual spring" (207); and *arbitrium tu, dea, floris habe*— "Goddess, be queen of flowers" (trans. Frazer, 212). GARBER (1974, p. 175) discovers some
strained parallels: "Flora is described in Ovid (*Fasti* 5.231 ff.) as possessing a magical
flower which, given to Juno, makes her pregnant; . . . Perdita will herself enact this
role, giving flowers to the assemblage at the sheep-shearing and both directly and
symbolically encouraging fertility and fruition. 'April's front' is of course an image of
the shyness of early spring flowers; it is succeeded . . . by the full blossoming of
summer: [quotes 'the . . . winter,' 1887–9]."
    sheepe-shearing] F. W. CLARKE (ed. 1908, p. xiii n.): "That there was a more
serious side to these festivals, and that they formed occasions for more than innocent
mirth-making, is indicated in the old shepherd's speech [1501–9]. [Phillip] Stubbes
in his *Anatomy of Abuses* [1583; ed. Furnivall (CLARKE's collaborator in *WT* ed. 1908),
1877–82] has a very vigorous invective against May-games and kindred festivities for
this reason; while more than half-a-century later a book called *Funebria Florae* [1660],
by Thomas Hall, was devoted to the setting forth of the prophaneness, stealing, drinking, whoring, etc., which disfigured the celebrations of those rustic rites." There may
have been license after the sheep were shorn, of course, but CLARKE's evidence is
poor. Stubbes and Hall were Puritan zealots who found perdition everywhere but in
their own pulpits. The aging Shepherd complains about untamed youth (1501 ff.),
but so do many old men. For more on sheepshearing, see n. 1706.
    1801 **petty Gods**] FURNESS (ed. 1898): "The classical *Dii minores* [lesser gods],"
which include fauns, satyrs, nymphs, and other semidivine beings.
    1802 **the Queene on't**] BETHELL (1947, p. 93): Perdita, "being of royal birth and
yet of country nurture, is the . . . symbol of . . . union of court and country."
Actually, she is hardly countrified at all; she is usually perceived as royal. She is dressed
here as the Queen of the May, and see 1962, 1976–8, 1980–1, and 2843–4. EVANS
(1960, p. 300): "It is a brilliant new use of an old device: the masquerader unknowingly masquerading as what she is in fact." Yet TREWIN (1978, p. 266): "To the end,
the girl's voice should hint at her rustic youth," but no actresses are known to have
taken his advice. And compare, for example, n. 1804.
    on't] See n. 785–6.
    1803 **Sir . . . Lord**] COLLIER emends probably because the two terms of address
seem redundant, but cf. 416 and 2997 as well as "Sir, my Liege" in *Tmp.* 5.1.245
(2236).
    1804 **To . . . me**] BETHELL (ed. 1956): "This distorted word-order and the com-
pressed and metaphorical language that follows, sufficiently prove that energetic

336

(Oh pardon, that I name them:) your high selfe   1805
The gracious marke o'th'Land, you haue obscur'd
With a Swaines wearing: and me (poore lowly Maide)
Most Goddesse-like prank'd vp: But that our Feasts

---

rhythm, obscurity, &c. are not specially characteristic of the jealous Leontes but extend even to the healthy simplicity of Perdita. In fact, the verse of this play does not
normally reflect character but complexity of meaning."

   extreames] JOHNSON (ed. 1765): "Your *excesses*, the *extravagence* [sic] of your
praises" (*OED*, *sb*. 5, citing this line). MASON (1785, p. 133): Not extravagant praises
but extravagant conduct, which she specifies in 1805-7 as his disguise and her prank-
ing-up. The CLARKES (ed. 1865) find both meanings. HUNTER (ed. 1872), however, is
probably wrong that Perdita means "the extreme contrasts in your apparel."

   it . . . me] PARRY (ed. 1982): It "is not a fitting thing for me to do. (Nonetheless, she repeatedly shows her uneasiness about the element of 'art' involved in
dressing things up in this scene.)" For the omission of *does* in this expression, see
ABBOTT §305 and cf. n. 2005. BROOK (1976, p. 76, citing FRANZ §301) explains the
construction differently: "When [an infinitive] is the subject of a sentence, it is sometimes reinforced by the pronoun *it*."

   1805 **selfe**] For *self* as a noun, see ABBOTT §20.

   1806 **The . . . o'th'Land**] JOHNSON (ed. 1765): "The *object* of all men's *notice*
and expectation." SCHMIDT (1875, Mark): "An object looked to for guidance" or
"desired" (*OED*, *sb*.[1] 8). MAXWELL (ed. 1956): "Ornament" (not in *OED*).

   1807 **Swaines wearing**] For the kind of person Florizel might represent, see n.
1811-12. At 1990, however, he is spoken of as "faire Swaine." *OED* (Swain, *sb*. 4):
"A country or farm labourer, *freq*. a shepherd." PYLE (1969, p. 81): "Clearly Florizel's
costume . . . is stylized, for it makes Autolycus pass for a gentleman even among
gentlemen," in 5.2. They exchange clothes at 2520 approximately. PARRY (ed. 1982),
however, suggests that his disguise is "a smock over his courtier's shirt and breeches."
HOLLAND (1964, p. 44): It indicates "in a way [that] he is leaving his former self
behind." Perdita's disguise certainly does not indicate anything like this, however,
not to mention Polixenes's and Camillo's. See the next n.

   poore lowly Maide] MARTIN (1891, p. 24): "In her soft voice, her words, her
mien, there is something that speaks unmistakably of the royal blood within her. This
it is left to the impersonator of Perdita to suggest." EVANS (1960, p. 299), comparing
the heroines of Sh.'s other comedies: "Their identities were [their] best secrets: [they]
held a leverage that meant, in varying degrees, control of their worlds.
. . . Perdita . . . is ignorant that she masquerades at all." He speaks of Perdita the
shepherdess, not Perdita as Flora.

   1808 **Most**] The CLARKES (1879, p. 310): I.e., you have most.

   prank'd vp] KERSEY (1702, Prank up): "*Trim, deck*, or *set out*." JOHNSON
(1755): "To decorate; to dress . . . to ostentation." PAFFORD (ed. 1963): "It is usually
assumed that 'you have' is to be understood after 'maid'; i.e. that Florizel has in some
way dressed her up—it was one of his 'extremes'." But see n. 1798-9. ORGEL (ed.
1996): "It is Florizel, therefore, who has dressed her as Flora."

   1808-10 **But . . . Custome**] SCHANZER (ed. 1969, But that): "Were it not that."
BETHELL (ed. 1956): "I.e. there is always foolishness at feasts and the feasters 'swallow'
it because it is traditional." ORGEL (ed. 1996): "Either 'foolish antics accompany every
dish' or 'every group of diners includes some who behave foolishly'. Most editors cite
[313] in support of the latter paraphrase, with 'mess' meaning [four eating together,
as in 313]." See the next n. TILLEY C934 finds an application of the proverb "Custom

In euery Messe, haue folly; and the Feeders
Digest with a Custome, I should blush   1810
To see you so attyr'd: sworne I thinke,
To shew my selfe a glasse.
   Flo. I blesse the time
When my good Falcon, made her flight a-crosse

1810 Digest] Disgest F2, F3
    with] it with F2+
    a Custome] accustom CAM3 *conj.*, PEN2
1811 sworne] swoon MTBY2 *conj.*, THEOBALD (1729) *conj. in* NICHOLS (1817, 2:
363), HAN, CAP, RANN, SING2, DYCE, STAU, DEL, OXF1, BUL, CAM3, ALEX, PEL1, ARD2,
SIG, K&R, PEN2, OXF2, BEV4; so worn JACKSON (1819, pp. 142-3) *conj.*, COL2, COL3,
COL4; more INGLEBY (1853) *conj.* (& more), HUD2
1812 shew . . . a] see . . . i'the THEOBALD (1729) *conj. in* NICHOLS (1817, 2:
363), HUD2
1814 a-crosse] *Om.* v1785

---

makes sin no sin,'' and C. G. SMITH (1963, no. 49) finds a parallel in Leonard Culman,
Sententiae Pueriles.
    1809 euery Messe] HUNTER (ed. 1872): "In every grade of life." SCHMIDT (1875)
defines *mess* as "a dish" (*OED, sb.* 1); LOBBAN (ed. 1910) follows with "course."
DEIGHTON (ed. 1889) observes, however, that "though *digest* [1810] may contain an
allusion to *mess* in the sense of *dish* . . . , the primary meaning . . . is probably
one of the many parties into which feasters were divided." See n. 313 for "lower
messes," as well as *LLL* 4.3.203 (1551).
    folly] Perhaps influenced by SCHMIDT's gloss on 1056, HENLEY (ed. 1902): "*I.e.*
'larks.'" But Perdita, more serious than this, may mean "perversity of judgment, absurdity" (SCHMIDT, 1874, *Folly* 1). LEE (ed. 1907), however: "Strange frolics."
    Feeders] Some commentators take the word literally. The CLARKES (ed. 1865):
"'Eaters', and . . . 'graziers', or 'sheep-feeders.'" JERVIS (1868, Feeder): "A servant."
But Perdita means those who feed on folly.
    1810 Digest . . . Custome] CALDECOTT (MS 1813-33): "Reconcile themselves
to it under the plea of long established usage." HUDSON (ed. 1880): "Take it as natural,
or think nothing of it, because they are used to it." CORSON (1889, p. 369): Because
Sh. "wrote by ear [he] omitted to represent to the eye certain elements that are more
or less altogether absorbed in pronunciation." Thus *digest* = "Digest it," to which
all eds. nevertheless emend, and at 1965 *peepes* possibly = "peeps so." WILSON (ed.
1931), asserting that eds. quote no parallels for "with a Custome," considers emending, "'accustom' being an obs[olete] word meaning 'usage, tradition.'" "With custome of fell deeds," however, is found in *JC* 3.1.269 (1497). PAFFORD (ed. 1963)
discovers a pun on *digest*—(1) "assimilation by the system" (*OED, v.* 4) and (2)
"brook, endure" (*v.* 6). KELLETT (1923, p. 67), admitting that the word is "closely
allied to paronomasia": "*Digest* does *not* precisely give us a pun. It rather presents
us with one of Shakspere's so-called 'mixed metaphors', in which . . . his mind has
rushed so rapidly from one metaphor to the other that *our* minds, like panting Time,
toil after him in vain."
    blush] SPURGEON (1935, p. 59): "Life and feeling are continually conveyed by
these touches of colour coming and going on the speakers' faces." Cf. n. 2458 and
lines 1859, 1865, 1872, 1965, and 1980.
    1811-12 sworne . . . glasse] WARBURTON (ed. 1747): "*I.e.* one would think
that in putting on this habit of a shepherd, you had sworn to put me out of counte-

nance; for in this, as in a glass, you shew me how much below yourself you must descend before you can get upon a level with me." MALONE (ed. 1790): "The prince, by the *rustick* habit that he wears, seems as if he had sworn to shew her a glass, in which she might behold how she *ought* to be attired." He cites F1 *2H4* 2.3.31-2 (989-90): "He was the Marke, and Glasse, Coppy, and Booke, That fashion'd others." MALONE's explanation is essentially repeated by INGLEBY (1853, p. 379) and by WHITE (1854, p. 295), the latter saying that Florizel has "sworn to shew her, a swain's daughter, a reflex of her own condition, as if in a mirror, and, consequently, the difference between her actual position and his." CALDECOTT (MS 1813-33), on the other hand, believes that *sworne* pertains to Perdita: "Bound as I think myself by an obligation sacred as an oath, to shew myself a mirror, & all things faithfully to reflect." He seems to detect here the same dislike of falsity many find in 1912 ff.

DYCE (ed. 1857, 1:cciii) finds that "sworn . . . to show myself a glass" is impossible — "the word '*myself*' at once refutes it." He believes (1859, p. 83) that the word would have to be *me*, but, according to *OED* (3), *myself* "is often substituted for ME as the object of a verb [here an infinitive]." THIRLBY (MS 1747-53): Perdita "might see the greatest part of the change [in her appearance] without a glass." He wonders, "Had she any thing like a crown on?" The answer is, perhaps. In Campion's *Lord Hay's Masque* (1607; ed. Stephen Orgel and Roy Strong, *Inigo Jones*, 1:116) Flora wears a crown of flowers, and in Dekker's *London's Tempe* (1629; lines 296-7) as Queen of Flowers she wears flowers garlands on her head. PORTER & CLARKE (ed. 1908): "This mumming in *unusuall weeds*, which they have both done and are both commenting upon, is to his discredit, and, therefore, to her discredit, too, as she sees her action mirrored in his." To SISSON (1961, 1:199-200), it "is Florizel who is *sworn*, not Perdita, and she is referring back to her earlier contrast ['your . . . vp' (1805-8)]." He paraphrases: "I should blush to see you dressed up like me (though it is a custom at our feasts and so there is excuse); for indeed you seem (*I think*) to have taken upon yourself the duty of showing me, in your swain's dress, how I really ought to be dressed to suit my true station."

The emendation *swoon* yields "faint if I were to see myself in a mirror" (EVANS) or "swoon to recognize in you a mirror of myself" (ORGEL). MALONE (in STEEVENS, ed. 1793) opposes the change, because the word *swoon* "in the old copies of these plays is always written *sound* or *swound*." As DYCE (1859, p. 83) observes, however, *swoon(e)* occurs in *AYL* 4.3.158 (2312), *R3* 4.1.35 (2514), and its variants *swowne* in *3H6* 5.5.45 (3024) and *swoune* in *MND* 2.2.154 (809). *Swound* is even more common, and, as SINGER (1853, p. 77) says, *swound* "might easily be mistaken in manuscript for *sworne*." The only other instance of this word in *WT* is "swownded" (3098). Some eds., although dissatisfied with *sworne*, nevertheless think *swoon* an inappropriate word for Perdita (for other emendations, see the textual notes and p. 580). PIERCE (ed. 1918), for example, finds swooning "not very well in harmony with Perdita's healthful life and courageous character." WILSON (ed. 1931): Perhaps Perdita would not really swoon, "but she might say she would, to a lover. Furthermore, she is evidently in great agitation." PAFFORD (ed. 1963): "The expression would be normal from any girl even from one not of the swooning kind. . . . 'I'm sure I'd faint if I saw myself in a glass.'" WELLS (in WELLS & TAYLOR, 1987): "The physiological connection between blushing and swooning may support the emendation."

MALONE (ed. 1790, 1.1.xxxv) asserts that in *Mac.* 1.7.58 (537) *sworn* is disyllabic, but the line is hypermetrical even with the word as a monosyllable. HARDINGE (1801, p. 24), attempting the two-syllable pronunciation here, thinks it absurd.

1812 **To . . . glasse**] HERFORD (ed. 1916-): "I.e. if she saw herself in one."

1813-15 **I . . . ground**] MALONE (ed. 1790): "Taken from the novel." See p. 637.

1814 **her**] FRANZ §212: Sh. regards falcons, as well as, e.g., eagles, swans, nightingales, and spiders, as feminine.

339

Thy Fathers ground.   1815
   Perd. Now Ioue affoord you cause:
To me the difference forges dread (your Greatnesse
Hath not beene vs'd to feare:) euen now I tremble   (2▮
To thinke your Father, by some accident
Should passe this way, as you did: Oh the Fates,   1820
How would he looke, to see his worke, so noble,
Vildely bound vp? What would he say? Or how
Should I (in these my borrowed Flaunts) behold
The sternnesse of his presence?
   Flo. Apprehend   1825
Nothing but iollity: the Goddes themselues
(Humbling their Deities to loue) haue taken

1823 borrowed] borrow'd ROWE1-DYCE1, COL3-BUL, ARD1

1816 **affoord you cause**] KITTREDGE & RIBNER (ed. 1967): "Give you good reason (to 'bless the time')."

1817 **To . . . dread**] LERNER (1972, p. 129): "Perdita expresses fear but no guilt: she is troubled only by the thought that Polixenes will prevent their marriage, not by the thought that she isn't a fit mate for Florizel [because of her low social rank]." The difference in rank, however, underlies 1806–7 and 1817–20.

    difference] MASON (1785, p. 134): "Between his rank and hers." Cf. *MND* 1.1.135 (145).

    forges] SCHMIDT (1874): "Frames." ROLFE (ed. 1879): "Produces." HAPPÉ (1969): "Metaphorically, creates chains of."

1822 **Vildely bound vp?**] RANN (ed. 1787): "Thus coarsely clad." The metaphor has generated some pointless comment. JOHNSON (ed. 1765), heavily jocose, finds it more appropriate to Sh.'s profession than to Perdita's. KENRICK (1765, p. 91) argues that *bound up* suits the character because the term is used in husbandry and because the coarse garments of a swain would be tied with strings. BARCLAY (1766, pp. 63–4) thinks of the thongs of book covers, as also, he believes, in *Rom.* 3.2.83–4 (1735–6), where thongs are unmentioned. STEEVENS (ed. 1773) more appropriately cites the lover as book in *Rom.* 1.3.81 ff. (427 ff.). HUNTER (ed. 1872): "Engaged to one as lowly as myself. The metaphor is taken from a good book in a bad binding."

1823 **borrowed**] F's affix seems clearly intended to be elided, as ROWE and other early eds. indicate by -'d. WHITE (ed. 1857), however, restores -*ed* because it yields "a finer flow of the line," a strange alexandrine evidently. Modern eds., beginning with NEILSON (1908), print -*ed* because F does. The flaunts are borrowed, according to BETHELL (ed. 1956), because they "imply a rank not truly mine"; or, according to KITTREDGE & RIBNER (ed. 1967), because "I do not normally wear" them.

    Flaunts] JOHNSON (1755 and 1773), mistakenly: "Any thing loose and airy." CAPELL (1783 [1774], 1:glos.): "Gay Attire, Finery, Things that Girls flaunt in" (*OED*, *sb.* 2, citing this line).

1825–36 **Apprehend . . . Faith**] CRUTTWELL (1955, pp. 70–1): "These lines, . . . picking up, as they do, the words which come at [1800–2] . . . tell us that Florizel and Perdita are more than just a nice young couple in love with each other, and the sheep-shearing feast is more than just a rustic revel. Their love, with what it will bring about, has something akin to the divine, and the union of divine with human and lower than human; for this love will redeem the suffering which Leontes' jealousy caused and bring together the opposing worlds of country and court. The material of classical myth here serves a function deeper than decoration, more varied and dynamic than lyrical beauty." WATSON (1984, p. 257), in a different mood: "The speech is laden with Freudian slips, most prominently the entire comparison of his disguise to those of various gods who descended from higher stature only long enough to seduce or rape maidens and then abandoned them. Perdita should think carefully about her own image of the marigold, which is left weeping after the sun takes her to bed." This image is yet to be introduced (see n. 1918–19), and Florizel explicitly renounces Olympian lechery in 1832–6.

1825–6 **Apprehend . . . iollity**] MARSH (1962; 1969, p. 144): "Florizel, who believes that love will solve all their problems, hardly appears, in fact, to recognize that problems exist. He is in something like the state of unthinking innocence that Leontes and Polixenes once shared."

1825 **Apprehend**] The CLARKES (ed. 1865): "Used in its sense of 'fear', 'dread' [*OED* 11], as refers to the preceding speech; and in its sense of 'conceive' [*OED* 9] . . . as refers to the word 'jollity.'" RIDLEY (ed. 1935): "Imagine."

1826–36 **the . . . Faith**] LENNOX (1753, 2:81): "*Dorastus* speaks almost the same Words in" *Pandosto* (see pp. 639, 643). LENNOX conflates two passages from the novel that are given correctly by MALONE (ed. 1790): "The Gods aboue disdain not to loue women beneath. *Phoebus* liked *Sibilla*, *Iupiter Io*, and why not I then *Fawnia*, one something inferiour to these in birth, but farre superiour to them in beautie, borne to be a Shepheard, but worthy to be a Goddesse" and "And yet *Dorastus* shame not at thy shepheards weede: the heauenly Godes haue sometime earthly thoughtes: *Neptune* became a Ram, *Iupiter* a Bul, *Apollo* a shepheard: they Gods, and yet in loue: and thou a man appointed to loue." SCHANZER (ed. 1969): "No lines illustrate better Shakespeare's power of transmuting the lead he borrows into gold." For the echo in these lines of Francis Sabie's *Fissher-mans Tale*, see p. 677. MUIR (1957, p. 246): "Shakespeare, anxious to avoid the insipidities of pastoral, inserts . . . a few touches of rather grotesque realism." CRAIG (1948, p. 336) is not enthralled: "Florizel, enjoying his rôle as fairy prince, makes some condescending speeches out of Greene to the effect that he is like Jupiter." RUSHTON (1872) believes that Sh. "adopted or remembered literally the passage in [Lyly's *Gallathea*, in *Works*, ed. Fairholt, 1892, 1.1], where Tyterus says:— 'To gaine love, the gods have taken the shape of beasts.'"

Other critics find a philosophical import. KERMODE (1954, p. lvii): "Nature is always fertile; the better nature, however, is under magical restraint; and virginity is immemorially associated with magic power. . . . *The Tempest* makes much of this, and also of the contrast between the unchastity of the natural man . . . and the man of better nature," represented here by Florizel. J. H. S. ARMSTRONG (1969, pp. 65–6): Sh. "draws on the idea of the boundless versatility of the gods and invokes the legends of their metamorphoses, so that we glimpse for a moment a vista in which all possible developments seem open." TURNER (1971, pp. 157–8): "The reconciliation of the temporal and eternal worlds is symbolized . . . by the image of the gods incarnate in animal form. . . . The animal imagery reinforces the impression we have of the young lovers, of that innocence and consistency that animals possess." But bulls and rams are powerfully sexed, as are gods in their guises (see the next n.), which is why Florizel differentiates himself from them in 1832–6. KNOWLES (privately) finds all these opinions "quite impertinent to Sh.'s intent. Florizel is making an argument why she should not be embarrassed at his costume; the words *Goddes* and *Beasts* are emphatic: 'For love, the very *gods* (who are far more gracious than I) assumed the shapes of very *beasts* (who are far less gracious than a swain); therefore what I am doing is hardly so extreme as to make you blush.'"

The shapes of Beasts vpon them. Iupiter,
Became a Bull, and bellow'd: the greene Neptune
A Ram, and bleated: and the Fire-roab'd-God   1830
Golden Apollo, a poore humble Swaine,
As I seeme now. Their transformations,

1828-32 **Iupiter . . . now**] SIMPSON (1955, pp. 39-40) believes that the first two allusions derive from Ovid: *Iuppiter Europen . . . dilexit, tauro dissimulante deum*—"Europa . . . was loved of Jove; a bull's form disguised the god" (*Heroides* 4.55-6, trans. Showerman) and *aries Bisaltida fallis*—"as a ram [thou, Neptune] deceivedst Bisaltis [i.e., Theophane, daughter of Bisaltes]" (*Met.* 6.117, trans. Anderson). *OCD* (Europa): "Zeus loved her, and so turned himself into, or sent, a beautiful bull, which swam to the sea-shore where she was playing and enticed her by its mildness to climb on its back. Once there, she was carried away to sea, and landed in Crete. There she bore Zeus two or three children." *NCCH*, Theophane: Poseidon (Neptune) "carried her off to the island of Crumissa. When her other suitors followed, he transformed her into a ewe and himself into a ram. . . . He married Theophane and she bore him the ram with the golden fleece." With the Neptune passage THOMSON (1952, p. 132) compares Hyginus, *Fables*, 188 (ed. 1535, pp. 51-2), and with the allusion to Apollo he compares Ovid, *illud erat tempus, quo te pastoria pellis texit, onusque fuit baculum silvestre sinistrae* — "That was the time when you were covered by a pastoral skin and your left hand was weighed with a staff from the wood" (*Met.* 2.680-1, trans. Miller). Apollo, for a killing exiled from heaven and required to serve a mortal, kept the flocks of King Admetus and helped Admetus win Alcestis. BERGGREN (1985, p. 289) objects, however: "This attribution breaks the pattern [of beastly seductions] set by Jupiter and Neptune and indeed contradicts Florizel's own disavowal of all the gods' designs." She quite reasonably believes the source to be "In likenesse of a Countrie cloyne [clown] was *Phebus* pictured there [in Arachne's web]. . . . And how he in a shepeherdes shape was practising a wile The daughter of one *Macarie* dame *Issa* to beguile" (*Met.* 6.152-5, trans. Golding). BETHELL (ed. 1956): "Cf. *Pandosto*, p. 643. . . . Shakespeare seems to ridicule the passage—perhaps also the pastoral mode, and perhaps the pagan gods—by adding the comically realistic phrases 'and bellow'd', 'and bleated.'" ROOT (1903, p. 37): Only here does Sh. connect Apollo with the sun; he ordinarily regards the god as "patron of music and of learning." The connection may be made for contrast with watery green Neptune, for whom see n. 2911. GARBER (1974, p. 176): "Jupiter the king, Neptune the sea-god, and Apollo the poet and giver of inspiration are the three gods regnant in the play as a whole."

1831-2 **a . . . now**] For the confusion arising from Florizel's appearance, see nn. 2511-12 and 2557-8.

1832-6 **Their . . . Faith**] HARBAGE (1952, pp. 192-5): "In Shakespearean drama . . . youth is not lecherous. . . . Romeo is 'stainless' [3.2.13 (1657)] as Orsino is 'stainless' [*TN* 1.5.259 (552)]. The very 'ice of chastity' is in the kiss of Orlando [*AYL* 3.4.17 (1727)]. Young Malcolm affirms that he is 'unknown to woman' [*Mac.* 4.3.21 (1954)]. . . . Ferdinand has 'cold virgin snow' upon his heart [*Tmp.* 4.1.55 (1712)], and his intentions are as honorable as his hopes 'for quiet days, fair issue, and long life' [4.1.24 (1676)]. . . . The terrible bitterness of the husbands who think themselves betrayed . . . is partly owing to their knowledge that they themselves have been constant." TRAVERSI (1955, p. 142): "The gods, originally quoted to justify Florizel's own behaviour, are implicitly rebuked for the inferior purity of their mo-

Were neuer for a peece of beauty, rarer,
Nor in a way so chaste: since my desires
Run not before mine honor: nor my Lusts   1835
Burne hotter then my Faith.
    Perd. O but Sir,
Your resolution cannot hold, when 'tis

1834 in a] any RITSON (1783, p. 70) *conj.*, COL2
1836-7 *One verse line* mCAP2, v1793+
1836 Faith] faith does KEIGHTLEY *conj. in* CAM1, KTLY
1837 Sir] deere sir F2-v1813 (−MAL), SING1

---

tives." BATE (1993, p. 230), thinking of Apollo's amours, disagrees: "The language in
which he tries to differentiate himself from the rapacious divinities is not entirely
convincing. . . . The faith is all very well, but the lusts still burn hot. Shakespeare
shares with Ovid the conviction that . . . male desire always speaks the language of
sexual conquest." Here Florizel speaks of sexual conquest to disclaim it; see n. 1834.

    1833 **peece . . . rarer]** CALDECOTT (MS 1813-33, Piece): "Specimen." OED
(*sb*. 8c): "Applied to persons in whom some quality is realized." See 2265-6, where
Perdita is perceived as another kind of piece altogether, and for other significances,
see nn. 2561, 2562, 3115, 3229, and 3247-50. For the phrase, BETHELL (ed. 1956):
"For the sake of a more beautiful woman." For *peece*, KERMODE (ed. 1963): "Work
of art" (*OED, sb*. 17), as in 3103.

    1834 **in . . . chaste]** A. C. (in MALONE, ed. 1790, 10:605): "The transformations
of Gods were generally for illicit amours; and consequently were not 'in a way so
chaste' as that of Florizel, whose object was to marry Perdita." SCHMIDT (1875, Way):
"Manner, mode." HERFORD (ed. 1904): "Aim." EVANS (ed. 1974): "Purpose."

    1834-6 **since . . . Faith]** KITTREDGE & RIBNER (ed. 1967, Run not): "Do not
outstrip." SCHANZER (ed. 1969, Faith): "Pledge, promise (to marry her)," SCHMIDT's
gloss for 2329. For these and other meanings, see n. 672. With "this somewhat strange
remark of Florizel's," WILSON (ed. 1931) compares 3004, *Tmp.* 4.1.14-23 (1666-
75), and 4.1.51-6 (1707-13). BARBER (1985, p. 48): During the 17th c., "it becomes
rarer for *honour* in the sense of 'chastity' to be used of men, at any rate seriously,"
though the word does occur in *Cym.* 1.3.30 (299) and *Tmp.* 4.1.28 (1681).

    1836-7 **Burne . . . Sir]** Rather than F2's *deere* to regularize the meter, MALONE
proposed to reline (see p. 580), but in his ed. 1790 he suggests instead that "Burne"
be given two syllables. CHEDWORTH (1805, p. 125) and everyone else think this impossible.

    1836 **Faith]** SCHMIDT (1874): "Faithfulness in love," a gloss that PARRY (ed. 1982)
extends to "my promise (to marry you)." The word means the same in 2329; for
other meanings, see nn. 544-5, 672, 1193, and 2307.

    1838-42 **Your . . . life]** HARDINGE (1818, 3:74): "She tells him (for she has
much better sense than *he* has, though she is quite as much in love) that if his father
should oppose, he *must* give her up, or *she* must give up her life." ROLFE (ed. 1879),
for "Or . . . life": "I must exchange my life for death"; *change* means "exchange,"
as in 131. FURNESS (ed. 1898): "I doubt that her despondency went quite so far. She
was convinced that, if Florizel persisted in his purpose, the king would certainly
separate them by forcing Florizel to return to his home, and thus leave her to weep
out the rest of her days—a changed 'life' indeed for her." HERFORD (ed. 1916-)
disagrees: "Her life will be forfeited. The two 'necessities' are alternatives, one of

343

Oppos'd (as it must be) by th'powre of the King:
One of these two must be necessities,   1840
Which then will speake, that you must change this purpose,
Or I my life.
    Flo. Thou deer'st *Perdita,*
With these forc'd thoughts, I prethee darken not

1840 must be necessities] most be necessities F4; necessities must be HAN, KTLY

---

which will be realized, but not both. FURNESS's explanation . . . is therefore wrong, since this [changing her way of life] would be a consequence, not an alternative, of Florizel's giving up his claim to her hand." Some later eds.— EVANS (ed. 1974), for example — follow FURNESS nevertheless. CHARLTON (ed. 1916) agrees that Perdita foresees her death, "but merely as stating a fact, namely, that he will be deprived of her and so will be caused pain." WILSON (ed. 1931), however: She refers "to death alone. That she might well fear it, is clear from [2278-85] below." See further in nn. 1840-2 and 1841-2.

    1839 **must be**] Despite F's contractions, LETTSOM (MS 1840-65) notes that "the emphasis is on *must* not on *be.*" Hence *as it* rather than *th'powre* should be contracted.

    1840-2 **One . . . life**] *OED* (Necessity, *sb.* 6c, citing this line): "Something unavoidable." SCHANZER (ed. 1969): "The sentence apparently contains a zeugma: 'Either you will have to give up your resolution to marry me or, should you adhere to it, I shall lose my life.'" PAFFORD (ed. 1963): "Or at least some violent change such as imprisonment." The zeugma springs from *change purpose* and *change life;* see n. 1841-2. ORGEL (ed. 1996) glosses *One of these* as "each of these." Agreeing that a zeugma is involved, he disagrees "that Perdita is anticipating a death sentence. . . . The only evidence for this . . . is proleptic, Polixenes' threats at [2265-70]," which come as a surprise. Presumably, then, the change in Perdita's life will be her elevation from shepherdess to princess, but it is difficult to see why Florizel would regard this as a forced thought (see n. 1844).

    1840 **necessities**] Plural because of *two* or in anticipation of the options.

    1841 **speake**] Probably SCHMIDT's (1875) "make itself felt and call up to action" is relevant, though Schmidt does not cite this passage.

    1841-2 **change . . . life**] The CLARKES (ed. 1865, Change): "Used in the sense of 'alter' as regards 'purpose', and in the sense of 'exchange for death' as regards 'life.'" PAFFORD (ed. 1963): "The remark prepares for the exposure and the threats of Polixenes." LEE (ed. 1907), with whom TRAVERSI (1955, p. 143) agrees, interprets *Or . . . life* as "Or I must convert my life or rank of rusticity into one of gentility," which thwarts the purpose perceived by PAFFORD. LEE's interpretation is supported by SANDERS (1987, p. 79), however: "You'd expect her to say, '*And* I my life'— the 'change' . . . being the desolating return to pastoral singleness, as a consequence of Florizel's changing *his* purpose under royal pressure. But her 'Or' shows . . . that she does not believe she has yet changed her life at all. 'Or' [indicates] that Florizel's resolution *can* hold; in which case she must change her life far more radically." That is, she must become a princess, but it is impossible she should think so.

    1843 **deer'st**] To regularize the line, WALKER (1854, p. 144) wants to pronounce this word *deär'st.*

    1844 **forc'd**] MASON (1785, p. 134): "Far-fetched." CALDECOTT (MS 1813-33):

The Mirth o'th'Feast: Or Ile be thine (my Faire)   1845
Or not my Fathers. For I cannot be
Mine owne, nor any thing to any, if
I be not thine. To this I am most constant,
Though destiny say no. Be merry (Gentle)
Strangle such thoughts as these, with any thing   1850
That you behold the while. Your guests are comming:
Lift vp your countenance, as it were the day
Of celebration of that nuptiall, which
We two haue sworne shall come.
     Perd. O Lady Fortune,   1855
Stand you auspicious.

1847 nor] or COL3; not BEV
1849 Gentle] gentlest HAN; girl COL2, COL3, COL4
1852 your] you F4-ROWE2

"Not naturally growing out of what is before us," with which most eds. agree (glossing "strained"). The CLARKES (ed. 1865, citing 996): "False." See n. 995–6 for other instances. KERMODE (ed. 1963) adds "fearful."

1845–9 **Or . . . no**] PYLE (1969, p. 85): He makes "the loss of individuality through love necessary to attain the ideal of 'knowing oneself.'" VAN LAAN (1978, p. 233): "Florizel . . . pursues Perdita in order to *realize* his identity, including those elements of it deriving from his position as Polixenes' son."

1845 **Or**] FRANZ §586: Either.

1846 **Fathers**] DEIGHTON (ed. 1889): "Father's son."

1846–8 **For . . . thine**] PAFFORD (ed. 1963): "For I can be of no good to myself or to anyone if I lose you." LEWES (1894, p. 306): "Full of manly resolution is the Prince's answer." ARTHOS (1971, p. 153) finds a lover's similar affirmation of truth to self in *Err.* 3.2.37–8 (761–2): "Against my soules pure truth, why labour you, To make it wander in an vnknowne field?" Cf. *Tro.* 4.4.102–8 (2495–2501).

1849 **Gentle**] STAUNTON (ed. 1859): "Gentle one." SCHANZER (ed. 1969): "Somewhat like 'dearest.'" *Gentle* is also used substantively in *Ant.* 4.15.47 (3058) and *MM* 1.4.24 (374).

1850–1 **any . . . while**] DEIGHTON (ed. 1889): "The sights around you." HAPPÉ (1969): "The pleasures of the Feast."

1852 **Lift . . . countenance**] CALDECOTT (MS 1813–33) on 2987, "Take courage," with which SCHMIDT (1874) agrees. KITTREDGE & RIBNER (ed. 1967): "Look cheerfully." Cf. nn. 2331 and 2987.

1853 **nuptiall**] CRAIK (1859, §746): *Nuptials* is found only in *Per.* 5.3.80 (2334) and Q1 *Oth.* 2.2.7 (1104). In 20 other instances the word is sans -*s*, as at 2230. *OED*'s two earliest citations of the singular form are of *MND* and *WT*.

1855–6 **O . . . auspicious**] MACKINNON (1988, p. 143): "The weakness of her prayer suggests a frailty in the goddess." It is not clear why. Similar exclamations occur elsewhere (141, 686, 1395, 2359) with no implication of weakness.

1855 **Lady Fortune**] Fortune is also a lady in *Tmp.* 1.2.178–9 (289–90), *Per.* 4.4.48 (1771), *AYL* 2.7.16 (989), and *TNK* 3.1.15. Elsewhere she is a dame, a mother, a huswife, a whore, a strumpet with secret parts, a goddess, and a giglet.

Flo. See, your Guests approach,
Addresse your selfe to entertaine them sprightly,
And let's be red with mirth.
Shep. Fy (daughter) when my old wife liu'd: vpon　　　　　1860

1857 SCENE V. POPE, HAN, WARB, JOHN
　　　Enter All. F2-F4; *Enter Shepherd, Clown*, Mopsa, Dorcas, *Servants; with* Polixenes *and* Camillo *disguis'd.* ROWE1-CLN2, SIG+ (*subst.*); [the same] *come forward* ARD2

1857 **approach**] As a part of the disguise mentioned by eds. in the SD supplied here, SCOTT (1963, p. 412) notices that Polixenes and Camillo should have white beards, because of 2241. That line does not allude to Camillo's beard, however.
　　1858 **Addresse**] RANN (ed. 1787): "Prepare" (*OED, v.* 3).
　　entertaine] SCHMIDT (1874): "Amuse" (*OED, v.* 10). KITTREDGE & RIBNER (ed. 1967), probably more accurately: "Welcome" (*v.* 13).
　　sprightly] JOHNSON (1755), for the adjective: "Gay . . . vivacious."
　　1859 **let's . . . mirth**] WILSON (ed. 1931): "The injunction suggests that Perdita is pale with agitation." BETHELL (ed. 1956, Red): "Flushed." ORGEL (ed. 1996) adds "as the sign of excitement and a healthy complexion." Cf. nn. 1810, 2458.
　　1860-2005 **Fy . . . of**] DELIUS (1870, p. 251): The lovers lift their surroundings into a higher sphere, so that the clowns, disavowing their true, rougher nature, speak as well and as elegantly as the others in blank verse (until the Servant enters at 2005). BERRY (1988, p. 176): "He is subtly raised by the context, which is a seasonal celebration, and by the other speakers." KAUL (1987, p. 98): "To the extent to which the speech goes beyond the comparison between the dead wife and Perdita, and points to the larger contrast between the Shepherd and his wife on the one hand, and Leontes and Hermione on the other, the contrast would be between two social settings or two modes of life, the pastoral and the courtly. . . . The simple values necessary for human relationships . . . are perverted among the sophisticated but still practiced and preserved among the simple."
　　1860-7 **when . . . sip**] With this portrait of a person not in the drama, HERFORD (ed. 1916-) compares the Bastard's depiction of the Traveller (*Jn.* 1.1.189-204 [199-214]) and Hotspur's of the courtier on the battlefield (*1H4* 1.3.30-64 [352-86]). The wife's "robust geniality sets off with exquisite effect Perdita's shy and reticent grace" (p. xvii). CLARK (1930, p. 174): "There can be no doubt but that these details are facts, drawn from life. The Playwright must have known that jolly old wife; indeed many such." This is no doubt the impression Sh. hoped to create. BETHELL (1947, p. 43): "Another aspect of the contrast between older and younger generations; the old Shepherd presumably suspects Perdita of scorning the menial tasks which his 'old wife' had been content to perform." MARSH (1962; 1969, p. 144), differently: "She is now dead, and her position, with its duties as well as its delights, has passed in the natural order of things to Perdita. There is a good deal of dignity in the calmness with which the shepherd and Perdita accept this change as part of life." NEELY (1978, p. 189): "The shepherd's praise of his wife resembles Florizel's more formal praise of Perdita [1951-62, presumably], in its rhythms, its repetitions, its emphasis on particular and multiple actions, and its reference to singing and dancing." BERRY (1965, p. 94): "The bold and active life of these . . . lines is achieved with the help of only a single adjective 'old'; the rest is all nouns, verbs denoting being and doing, and adverbs — 'now heere', 'now'. It is the concentration of these nouns and verbs and the

This day, she was both Pantler, Butler, Cooke,
Both Dame and Seruant: Welcom'd all: seru'd all,
Would sing her song, and dance her turne: now heere
At vpper end o'th Table; now, i'th middle:
On his shoulder, and his: her face o'fire   1865
With labour, and the thing she tooke to quench it
She would to each one sip. You are retyred,

1865 and] and on KEIGHTLEY *conj. in* CAM1, KTLY
        o'fire] afire OXF2, BEV4
1866 thing] things F4-POPE1, HAN
        it$_\wedge$] ~ ; F4, CAM1, GLO, OXF1, SIG, PEN2

---

near-total absence of the adjective that gives the picture its realistic force: that and the rhythms which enact in movements of sound the pictorial constituents." MAC-KINNON (1988, pp. 143–4): "Shakespeare removes a potential emotional complica-tion by killing the Shepherd's wife (Perdita's feelings must be free to flow towards Hermione)."

1860 **liu'd:**] SIMPSON (1911, pp. 67–9): "It is the function of the colon to mark an emphatic pause." Here it follows an introductory clause, after which an emphatic pause would not be wanted. Crane frequently used a colon where other marks of punctuation were preferred by others (see p. 594).

1861 **both**] As LETTSOM (MS 1840–65) also notices, the CLARKES (ed. 1865): "Shakespeare . . . used 'both' for more than two objects named." See SCHMIDT (1874) and FRANZ §589.

Pantler] KERSEY (1702): "He that keeps the bread, in a noble-man's house." *OED* (Panter[1]): He "had charge of the pantry." *OED* speculates that the *l* was added by analogy with *butler*. HERFORD (ed. 1904) thinks that KERSEY's *he* could be a *she*.

Butler] *OED* (1): Dispenser of liquor.

1862 **Dame**] MINSHEU (1617): "Mistresse" (*OED* 2, citing this line). DEIGHTON (ed. 1889): "Lady of the feast."

1865 **On . . . and his**] ROLFE (ed. 1879): "Leaning over to serve them." For *on*, KERMODE (ed. 1963): "At." DEIGHTON (ed. 1889), less probably: "Dancing first with one partner and then with another."

her face o'fire] See nn. 1810 and 2458.

1866 **labour, . . . it$_\wedge$**] GRINDON (1930, p. 92): "One is afraid she is a toper!" Most eds. follow or adapt F's punctuation, evidently agreeing with ROLFE (ed. 1879) that "the shepherd does not mean that his wife drank so much as to increase the fire in her face; but that even when taking a draught to cool herself she did not forget her duty to her guests," by toasting each in turn, one supposes. SYMONS (in IRVING & MARSHALL, ed. 1890): The alteration of punctuation in F4 "take[s] away the poor woman's character. . . . No gentleman can hesitate which reading to adopt." SCHAN-ZER (ed. 1969), undeterred, favors the F punctuation as creating a more Shn. reading: "*The thing she took to quench* the fire had the effect of inflaming it all the more." He compares *Ant.* 2.2.207–9 (915–17).

1867 **She . . . sip**] ORGEL (ed. 1996): "More likely 'she would drink to each in turn' than 'she would give one sip to each of her guests.'"

retyred] *OED* (*ppl.a.* 3, citing this line): "Withdrawn into oneself."

347

As if you were a feasted one: and not
The Hostesse of the meeting: Pray you bid
These vnknowne friends to's welcome, for it is   1870
A way to make vs better Friends, more knowne.
Come, quench your blushes, and present your selfe
That which you are, Mistris o'th'Feast. Come on,
And bid vs welcome to your sheepe-shearing,
As your good flocke shall prosper.   1875
    Perd. Sir, welcome:
It is my Fathers will, I should take on mee
The Hostesseship o'th'day: you're welcome sir.
Giue me those Flowres there (*Dorcas.*) Reuerend Sirs,
For you, there's Rosemary, and Rue, these keepe   1880
Seeming, and sauour all the Winter long:
Grace, and Remembrance be to you both,

1876 Sir, welcome] Sirs, welcome ROWE1-THEO2, WARB-JOHN2; Sirs, you're welcome HAN; Welcome, sir CAP, v1793-SING1, HAL, HUD2; Sir, you're welcome mTYR
conj., KTLY
    1878 you're welcome sir,] *Change of address marked* CAP; *to* Cam. MAL+
        sir] Sirs ROWE1-JOHN2, v1773
    1882 to] unto POPE1-v1785 (−CAP)

1868 **feasted one**] HENLEY (ed. 1902): "Passive guest."
    1869-70 **bid . . . welcome**] WALKER (1860, 1:161) lists *vnknowne friends to's*
as a peculiar construction, with the adjective out of the normal order (*friends unknown to us*). Cf. ABBOTT §419a and §325. MOORMAN (ed. 1912), however, interprets
the construction to mean "bid them welcome to us."
    1871 **more knowne**] SCHANZER (ed. 1969): "Better acquainted."
    1872-3 **present . . . are**] KITTREDGE & RIBNER (ed. 1967): "Reveal yourself as
what you really are."
    1873 **Mistris o'th'Feast**] MALONE (ed. 1790): "From the novel." See p. 637.
ERICKSON (1982, p. 824): "As 'mistress o' th' feast' Perdita is quickly educated into
the role of a maternal feeder with a never-ending supply of goods and attentiveness."
That may have been the Shepherd's intention, but Perdita's main activities in the rest
of the scene are gillyvor rejection and dancing.
    1873-5 **Come . . . prosper**] PAFFORD (ed. 1963): "Perhaps this passage was
intended for Polixenes or Camillo rather than the Shepherd [an idea that also occurred
to THEOBALD; see p. 580]. In transcribing the *Come* of [1873] the copyist may have
glanced at the *Come* of [1872] and so omitted the speaker's name." The *us* is the
problem, but eds. seem to think that the Shepherd speaks to her as "Hostesse of the
meeting" and its presiding spirit.
    1875 **As . . . prosper**] The Shepherd remembers the festival's function as ritual;
merriment and good fellowship will induce new growth to replace the fleece being
harvested.
    As] "So" (ABBOTT §110). Cf. n. 3266.
    1876 **welcome**] LETTSOM (MS 1840-65): "The second syllable is accented." He
suggests that the word be rendered as two, *well come.*

1879-1930 Giue . . . growing] DRAPER (1985, p. 32): "By making them [her allusions to the flowers] appropriate to the maturity of the recipients she reinforces the dramatic substance of the scene, which includes characters of all ages, and recapitulates the thematic variety of the play through all the seasons (for instance, winter [1880-1]; autumn [1887-90]; summer [1917-19]; spring [1927])."

1879 Reuerend] BOORMAN (ed. 1964): "Both are disguised with beards." One cannot be sure about Camillo, although he may have had one sixteen years ago (see 1092). Polixenes has a white one, whether real or fake; see 2241.

1880-2 Rosemary . . . Remembrance] Perhaps inspired by THIRLBY (MS 1725-33?), THEOBALD (MS -1729?) compares Ophelia's speech in *Ham.* 4.5.175-82 (2927-34): "There's Rosemary, thats for remembrance. . . . There's Rewe . . . we may call it herbe of Grace a Sundaies" because, according to JOHNSON (1755), "holy water was sprinkled with it" or—perhaps the same idea—because it was used in exorcisms (Johnson's *Dictionary*, rev. H. J. TODD, 2nd ed., 1827, quoting Jeremy Taylor) or because *rue* also means "repentance" (*OED*, Herb-grace). HENLEY (in STEEVENS, ed. 1785): "The qualities of retaining *seeming* and *savour*, appear to be the reason why these plants were considered as emblematical of *grace* and *remembrance*." BEISLY (1864, p. 77): Rosemary retains seeming and savor (fair appearance as well as taste and smell) because it is green in winter; from William Coles's *Adam in Eden* he quotes (p. 78), "Rue maketh chaste and eke preserveth sight, Infuseth wit, and fleas doth put to flight." GERARD (1597, p. 1110): The flowers of rosemary "drie the braine, quicken the senses and memory." DYER (1889, p. 154): "In the bridal crown, the rosemary often had a distinguished place, [and] at the ceremony itself." CARRUTHERS (1879, p. 206): "At a funeral the sprigs were thrown on the coffin in the grave." In "The Rosemarie branch" Herrick writes: "Grow for two ends, it matters not at all, Be't for my *Bridall*, or my *Buriall*" (*Works*, ed. L. C. Martin, [1956], p. 232). BETHELL (ed. 1956): "It is fitting that she who symbolizes the new life of Leontes . . . should begin her flower-distribution with the symbols of remembrance and Our Lady, penitence and grace." For more on the two plants, see SEAGER (1896, pp. 262-6) and LEVER (1952, pp. 126-7). See also the next two nn.

1881 Seeming] JOHNSON (1755): "Fair appearance." WILSON (ed. 1931): "Colour." Perdita probably is speaking more generally, however; ELLACOMBE (1896, p. 273) speaks of the rosemary's leaves and scent remaining so long after picking that they "were almost considered everlasting."

sauour] MINSHEU (1617): "Taste . . . or smell."

1882 Grace . . . both] JOHNSON (ed. 1765): "*May you, old Gentlemen, be* good, *and may your* memories *be honoured*." PARRY (ed. 1982), more explicitly: "She hopes [they] will find divine grace (through repentance) at their deaths and be well remembered." For this and other meanings of *grace*, see n. 146. ELLACOMBE (1896, p. 276): "It was a natural thing to say that a plant which was so bitter, and had always borne the name of *Rue* or *Ruth*, must be connected with repentance. It was, therefore, the Herb of Repentance, and this was soon transformed into the Herb of Grace . . ., repentance being the chief sign of grace." On p. 273, ELLACOMBE quotes Sir Thomas More: "As for Rosemarine . . . tis the herb sacred to remembrance, and therefore to friendship." MARSH (1962; 1980, p. 145): "Grace and remembrance . . . remind them [the old] of the value of life, even when for them it is coming to its close; the grace of acceptance, and the memory of its goodness. The great seasonal cycle is again stressed." SCOTT (1963, p. 412) tries to link the gift of flowers explicitly to the action, an effort complicated by uncertainty whether both visitors are given both flowers or each a different one and, if so, which: "Polixenes would do well to repent in advance of his plans to sever the lovers . . . and remembrance of his former idyllic relations with Leontes . . . would prepare well for the marriage which will unite the two kingdoms and join country and court in full harmony. Or [if the king gets rue and the counselor rosemary] that Polixenes needs the

And welcome to our Shearing.
   Pol. Shepherdesse,   (2B2
(A faire one are you:) well you fit our ages   1885
With flowres of Winter.
   Perd. Sir, the yeare growing ancient,
Not yet on summers death, nor on the birth
Of trembling winter, the fayrest flowres o'th season
Are our Carnations, and streak'd Gilly-vors,   1890
(Which some call Natures bastards) of that kind

1888 Not] Nor ROWE1-POPE2, HAN
1889 flowres] flower CLN2
1890, 1910 Gilly-vors] Gillyflowers ROWE1-SING1, COL, HUD1, HAL

---

grace to repent of what he is about to do and Camillo should remember his homeland where Perdita and Polixenes must return . . . to heal all rifts." See further at n. 1903-6.

    Remembrance] TYRWHITT (in BOSWELL, ed. 1821, 4:138): Four syllables—*re-mém-be-ránce*. WALKER (1854, p. 9) and ABBOTT §477 agree. See also KÖKERITZ (1953, p. 293).

    1885-6 **well . . . Winter**] As HUNT ("Three Seasons," 1984, p. 304) notes, she initially gives them flowers symbolizing old age, because Polixenes at least wears a white beard (see nn. 1857 and 1879).

    1885 **our ages**] PYLE (1969, p. 85): "Polixenes' disguise makes him seem as old as Camillo . . . so that age and youth are sharply contrasted." Nothing indicates that Camillo is antiquated, however; he should not doddle into Paulina's arms at the end of the play.

    1887-1981 **Sir . . . Creame**] The style of this passage is analyzed by LUDWIG (1974, pp. 385-91).

    1887-1916 **the . . . me**] GRIFFITH (1775, p. 111): This passage "vindicates the rights of Nature, even over those arts that seem to vie and cooperate with her; for her *general laws* can never be controlled but by *bye ones* [i.e., bylaws accessory to the general laws] of her own making." Cf. 1901-3. (Regarding the art, GRIFFITH notes, "I have been told that different coloured silk thread, inserted in the roots, would have this effect.") KERMODE (1963, pp. 3-67): "The topic of their discussion is . . . a commonplace in the literature of the period. . . . Polixenes has the more favoured case to put, yet even so late as half a century later Marvell could argue Perdita's case in 'The Mower against Gardens'. . . . Perdita herself is in fact the product of long and careful cultivation; and it is this concealed truth that really gives the passage its full irony and justifies her refusal to act as Polixenes says she ought. She turns the analogy from horticulture to cosmetics ('the gillyvors are like painted women'), and so averts an unjust analogy between herself and the 'bark of baser kind.'"

    1887 **the . . . ancient**] THIRLBY (MS 1747-53): "Is this the time of sheepshearing any where[?]" He points out that "flowres Of middle summer" (1919-20) have blossomed. DYER (1884, p. 317): "*Sheep-shearing time* commences as soon as the warm weather is so far settled that the sheep may, without danger, lay aside their winter clothing." HUNTER (1845, 1:421): "This sheep-shearing is represented to be in autumn." HOLBROOK (1964, p. 170): "There is a significant compression or fusion of the seasons now, as in memory. [This scene] is in late autumn . . . but yet the

Festival is like a 'Whitsun Festival' at which Perdita is a May Queen or vegetation goddess." HUNTER adds: "Perdita, perceiving that she might have reminded them unpleasantly of their advanced period of life, says that she should not have presented them with the 'flowers of winter' were not the garden barren of such flowers as belonged to the period of life which precedes age, the gillivers." For speculations about the kings' ages, see n. 234. SCHANZER (1964, p. 74 n.): "Perdita is not saying that it is *now* autumn, but that the fairest flowers of autumn are carnations, etc." Although Autolycus's song (1669 ff.) sets the scene for spring, sheepshearing usually takes place in late June, and flowers of middle summer should be available then; Midsummer Day is 24 June. See n. 1706. WALLER (1970, p. 134) is right, however, that "so strong and complex are the temporal suggestions of the scene, that the impression is that all seasons and all hours of the day come to bear upon the action. The effect is of a paradoxical world, both timeless and yet deeply affected by time, with reminders of high summer, autumn, winter, and the spring of the lovers themselves." MACKINNON (1988, p. 145): "The flickering uncertainty about when exactly the sheep-shearing festival is taking place emphasizes its incandescent brevity." ORGEL (ed. 1996) glosses the line as "when autumn comes," avoiding the implication that it has already done so.

1889 **trembling winter**] DEIGHTON (ed. 1889): "The epithet . . . applies to the effect produced by winter," a metonymy.

fayrest] Trying for a pentameter, WALKER (1854, p. 169) suggests *fair'st*, but that does not help greatly. Cf. n. 156.

o'th] Usually *of the*, but PARRY (ed. 1982) interprets this instance as *of that*.

1890 **Carnations**] Like the gillyflower, a species of *Dianthus*, distinguished from the gillyflower by larger size and greater showiness. See RYDÉN (1978, p. 71).

1890-8 **streak'd . . . creating-Nature**] The word *Gilly-vor* occurs again at 1910 but not elsewhere in Sh. According to SMITH (1874, p. 13), Sh. was referring to "the wallflower [*Cheiranthus cheiri*]; and that is what the people of Stratford-upon-Avon and its neighborhood understand by the word gilliflower today." PRIOR (1863, p. 92) says that the name has "been transferred of late years to several cruciferous plants," among which he includes stocks and wallflowers (see *OED*, Gillyflower 2). Actually, GERARD (1597, pp. 371-7) also applies the name to several plants: "Wall flowers, or yellow stocke Gilloflowers" (*Viola lutea*), "Stocke Gilloflowers" (*Leucorum album, purpureum, violaceum,* and *sylvestre*), and "Dames Violets, or Queenes Gilloflowers" (*Viola matronalis*). DODOENS (1619) associates the name with nearly a dozen—yellow gillofers, feathered gillofers, rogues gillofers, etc. Most authorities, however, say the flower intended here is the *Dianthus caryophyllus; OED* (Clove-gillyflower 2) identifies it as "a clove-scented species of Pink . . . , the original of the carnation," which is called the English gillyflower (Gillyflower 3). *OED* derives the word from French *clou de girosle (girofre, gilofre)*. Like Perdita, GERARD (p. 472) and PARKINSON (1629, p. 306) distinguish between carnations and clove gillyflowers as two of the many varieties of *caryophyllus*. See SEAGER (1896, p. 126) and RYDÉN (1978, pp. 71-2). NAITO (1982, p. 157): "Streaked gillyvors are most probably artificial hybrids." SANDERS (1987, p. 86): "I don't want to join the horticultural litigation that has plagued the annotation of these lines." The litigation continues below, however.

1891 **bastards**] CROFT (1810, p. 11): "Those [flowers] that run from their colours, are, in the gardeners' phrase, called bastards." Since this meaning is not exactly supported by *OED*, though *bastard* is used in the names of certain plants resembling members of other species (*a.* 5b), the usage here is probably figurative: "Debased, adulterated, corrupt" (*a.* 4). MOORMAN (ed. 1912): "The meaning is that the streaked 'gillyvor' is as much the result of artificial breeding as of the creative force of Nature." HERFORD (ed. 1916-) "She means . . . that the gillyvors are not a spontaneous natural growth, but have been artificially crossed, the 'streaks' being the result of the

Our rusticke Gardens barren, and I care not
To get slips of them.
    Pol. Wherefore (gentle Maiden)
Do you neglect them.   1895
    Perd. For I haue heard it said,
There is an Art, which in their pidenesse shares
With great creating-Nature.
    Pol. Say there be:
Yet Nature is made better by no meane,   1900

1896 haue] *Om.* COL3

---

crossing." For the streaks as cosmetics, see n. 1887–1916. GREER (1986, p. 92):
"Shakespeare probably knew something of the greater vigour of hybrids." GREER
connects Perdita's remark with Edmund in *Lr.*, also Nature's bastard, a natural son.
See further in n. 1897–8. BOORMAN (ed. 1964): "Perdita's father called her a bastard
at her birth [990, 992, etc.]," and when he finds her the Shepherd assumes she is
some illegimate piece of work (1514–16). HEIMS (1988, p. 7), however: In an "eerie
irony, . . . Perdita is echoing her father's words. . . . The same attitude, set in differing contexts, resonates with varying luminosity."

1893 **slips**] BOORMAN (ed. 1964): "Cuttings. As 'carnations' and 'gillivors' had an
association . . . with 'loose women' [see n. 1897–8], there may be a play on 'slips'
('moral faults')," a reading that seems unlikely.

1897–8 **There . . . creating-Nature**] EVANS (ed. 1974, Art),: "I.e. the gardener's skill in cross-breeding." WAIN (1964, p. 220), more broadly: To Sh., *art* was
"everything that was not 'nature', including not only the arts of imagination but the
experimental sciences and an empirical skill like horticulture." JOHNSON (1755, Piedness): "Variegation; diversity of colour." On this subject, DYER (1916, 1:514) quotes
Bacon, *Sylva Sylvarum (Works*, ed. Spedding et al., 2[1859]:504): "Take gilly-flower
seed, of one kind of gilly-flower . . . and sow it; and there will come up gilly-flowers,
some of one colour, and some of another, casually, as the seed meeteth with nour-
ishment in the earth . . . as purple, carnation of several stripes: the cause is (no
doubt) that in the earth . . . there are very several [different] juices; and as the seed
doth casually meet with them, so it cometh forth." However, SINGER (ed. 1856):
Perdita means "producing by art particular varieties of colour on flowers, especially
on carnations." BEISLY (1864, pp. 83–4): "The streaked . . . are produced by the
flowers of one kind being impregnated by the pollen of another kind, and this art (or
law) in nature, Shakspere alludes to . . . as well as to the practice of increasing the
plants by slips." Since what occurs by chance is not artful, Perdita could not object
to natural variation (as may occur when bees or the wind carries the pollen). Hence
CHAMBERS (1931, p. 260): "The gardening books of the time . . . tell of the practice
of putting vermilion or cinnabar, azure or verdigris between the rind and the small
heads growing about the root, to modify the colour. And so Perdita does not care to
get slips of these flowers because . . . [t]hey are artificial, therefore illegitimate,
therefore bastards."

    GARDNER (1959, p. 300) finds a technique that seems even more reprehensible.
In connection with grafting, Bacon writes: "Divers seeds, put into a clout and laid in
earth well dunged, will put out plants contiguous; which afterwards being bound in,
their shoots will incorporate. The like is said of kernals put into a bottle with a narrow

mouth, filled with earth" (2:493). SCOTT (1963, p. 413 n.) finds in Jacques Bellot, *The Posye or Nosegay of Loue*, added to *The Englishe Scholemaister* (1580, sig. G1), that carnations of various hues signify love of various types (e.g., constant, sudden, impatient); sparckle (speckled) signifies inconstant or variable love. Gillyflowers are not included. Other critics believe that Perdita's objection has a different basis. Remembering "flurt gills" in *Rom*. 2.4.161 (1251), STEEVENS (ed. 1778) suspects that the flower's name connotes wantonness. In William Rowley's *A New Wonder, a Woman Never Vexed* (c. 1611), STEEVENS finds "a lover . . . behaving with freedom to his mistress as they are going into a garden, and after she has alluded to the quality of many herbs, he adds: 'You have fair roses, have you not?' 'Yes, sir, (says she) [Roses] but no *gilly-flowers*' [ed. Cheatham, 1993, 3.1.237-8]. Meaning perhaps that she would not be treated like a *gill-flirt*, i.e. a wanton [*OED*]. . . . I suppose *gill-flirt* to be derived, or rather corrupted, from *gilliflower*." STEEVENS is wrong about the derivation, which *OED* finds to be from *gill*, "a familiar or contemptuous term applied to a woman." DOUCE (1807, 1:356): A gillyflower streaked with white and red would be "a proper emblem of a *painted* or immodest woman; . . . she [Perdita] connects the gardener's *art* of varying the colours of . . . flowers with the art of painting the face."

FURNESS (ed. 1898) rejects this explanation; finding in CROOKE (1631, 1:223 for 235) that the "lappe [pudendum] or priuity may be likened to the great Cloue Gillyflower when it is moderately blown," he holds that Perdita's idea is "a fancied anatomical resemblance akin to those supposed to exist in other flowers to which 'liberal shepherds give a grosser name' [*Ham*. 4.7.170 [3162]." CROOKE's metaphor may be casual, yet GERARD (1597, p. 373) plainly alludes to sexual impropriety; regarding stock gillyflowers, he says, "They are not vsed in physicke, except amongst certaine Empericks [quacks] and Quacksaluers, about loue and lust matters, which for modestie I omit." PARKINSON (1629, p. 624), however, in describing the virtues of "stocke gilloflowers," says the juice "will helpe to strengthen and restore any member growne weake, loose, or out of joynt." WILSON (ed. 1931): In Spenser's *Shepheardes Calender* (April, 138), carnations and sops-in-wine (gillyflowers) are said to be worn of paramours, but these may be merely sweethearts (*OED*, *sb*. 2c), not illicit lovers (3); and the assertion that *gillyflower* means "light woman"—as in LEGOUIS (ed. 1936), BETHELL (ed. 1956), and LINDEN (1979)—gets flimsy support from *OED* (2b), which dates its first citation *ante* 1797. But see n. 1912-16.

1898 **Nature**] *OED* (*sb*. 11): "The creative and regulative physical power which is conceived of as operating in the material world and as the immediate cause of all its phenomena."

1900-8 **Yet . . . Nature**] PETERSON (*Time*, 1973, pp. 176-8) associates 1891-3 with the "maiden gardens" (virgin wombs) of *Son*. 16 and argues that Polixenes, testing Perdita in 1899-1908, "provides her with what seems to be a perfectly rational justification for her having children by Florizel. . . . She rejects [this] suggestion because she is thinking of her own 'maiden garden'. What may be natural in the breeding of flowers is unnatural in the breeding of men." TAYLER (1964, p. 135) disagrees: "The horticultural reasoning [may be] a trap, . . . a device by which Polixenes hopes to expose Perdita as a scheming wench who is after 'bud of nobler race', Florizel. But it is Perdita who first commits herself against 'nature's bastards', and Polixenes' tone, now deliberate, now authoritative, does not appear to support such an interpretation. The King seems pretty clearly to be reasoning in earnest." NAITO (1982, p. 158): "What he is ostensibly doing is not to assert the superiority of art by disparaging nature but to vindicate art in the name of nature and, finally, to establish a kind of happy union of art and nature." BERRY (1988, p. 177): "Polixenes is progressive with flowers, conservative with Florizel. But of course Shakespeare has it both ways, since Florizel's instinct is to mate with one of his own rank." MARX (1964, p. 67): "The context, it is generally conceded, lends Shakespeare's support to

But Nature makes that Meane: so ouer that Art,
(Which you say addes to Nature) is an Art
That Nature makes: you see (sweet Maid) we marry
A gentler Sien, to the wildest Stocke,
And make conceyue a barke of baser kinde   1905
By bud of Nobler race. This is an Art
Which do's mend Nature: change it rather, but
The Art it selfe, is Nature.

1901 ouer] even mTBY2 *and* CRAIK (1857, p. 23) *conj.*, HUD2

Polixenes' view of the matter: the artificial is but a special, human category of the natural. Mind and nature are in essence one. Nature is all." Polixenes's reasoning is often detached from the play to comment on such aesthetic or philosophical problems as the relationship of fact to fancy or reason to imagination. SHAW (1976, p. 21), for example: "Common in poetic criticism of the [Victorian] age is the quotation of [these] lines." He cites several instances.

1900-1 **meane . . . Meane**] SCHMIDT (1875): "That which is used to effect a purpose," often in the singular in Sh. (*OED, sb.*[2] 10a, citing this line). JOHNSON (1755): "Instrument." MAXWELL (ed. 1956): "Method." LOVEJOY & BOAS (1935, p. 207) regard this passage as a "devastating comment on the primitivism of Montaigne."

1901-3 **ouer . . . makes**] FURNESS (ed. 1898): "Over those arts which change Nature there rule laws that Nature makes. We may by our art or skill apply vermilion to the roots of a plant, but it would remain inert were it not that by Nature's law it is absorbed and driven by an unknown force into the petals of the flower. We may marry a gentler scion to the wildest stock, and there our art ends. But by Nature's higher over-ruling laws the scion is adopted, and converts the wild sap which feeds it into beneficient fruits." KITTREDGE & RIBNER (ed. 1967): "Thus art itself, which is the creation of man, is actually the creation of nature by which man himself is made." TAYLOR (1926, p. 193) finds the idea reiterated in *Tim.* 1.1.37 (51) and in *Paradise Regained* 2:296. See n. 1908.

1903-6 **you . . . race**] SMITH (1874, p. 14): "Here we have the whole theory of grafting clearly put by the pen of experience." SPURGEON (1935, p. 306): "In language which today we might apply to eugenics." BARBER (1976, p. 164): "The key words can apply both to plants and to human families (*marry, scion, stock, conceive, race*)." MAHOOD (1957, pp. 147-8) alleges that this passage is anticipated by 25-6 (see n.). MERCHANT (1959, p. 10): The metaphor Sh. "might easily have borrowed from [Thomas] Wilson's *Art of Rhetoric.*" MERCHANT may have in mind WILSON (1553; 1982, pp. 30-1): "For though many by nature without art, have proved worthie menne, yet is arte a surer guide than nature," though the resemblance, if there is one, escaped CRAIG ("Wilson's *Arte*," 1931). FURNESS (ed. 1898): "Polixenes . . . by his simile of marrying the gentler scion to the wildest stock has been stating the relative positions of his royal son and the shepherd's daughter." MOORMAN (ed. 1912) comments on the irony: "Before the scene is over, we witness the ungovernable fury of Polixenes that the 'gentler scion [shoot or slip]' that has sprung from his own loins should marry the 'wildest stock' that has grown up in the home of the shepherd." BERRY (1978, pp. 2-3): "Polixenes believes himself to be using a metaphor: the human term of 'gentler scion' is applied to a plant. But his own son, the 'gentler scion' Florizel, is wooing the shepherdess Perdita. The metaphor therefore picks up the actuality of the drama." This is topsy-turvy. *Scion* was a term in plant biology sometimes used metaphorically—e.g., as *OED* points out, in Thomas Lodge's *Rosalynde* (1590, sig. A4ᵛ; see KNOWLES ed., *AYL*, 1977, p. 390). Polixenes is using the word literally, and it is we who recognize that the natural principle applies to the union of prince and shepherdess.

SCOTT (1963, p. 413): "Polixenes' arguing a position which ironically should undermine his own opposition to the 'grafting' of Florizel and Perdita is of a piece with his accepting the flowers of grace and remembrance which also ought to affect his actions." Cf. n. 1882, but what should he remember? NELSON (1972, p. 64) sees the future marriage of the scion (Florizel) and the stock (Perdita) as "indicating a binding union between the workings of the natural world with the workings of man's learning and art." LERNER (1972, p. 129): "Whatever we think of Perdita's opinions, the fact of her existence fits his theory rather than hers. . . . [After] we remember the birth of Perdita . . . we realize that the whole debate was unnecessary, since there is no question of wilder stock. Instead of an enriching irony, we have a reassurance that they are only talking about flowers." EDWARDS (1976, p. 54) believes that the speech is uttered "in the spirit, perhaps, of the king who has amused himself," and NEELY (1985, p. 195), that Polixenes's "generalized distaste for women [is] pompously implicit in his discussion of grafting." For a parallel with *Mucedorus*, see p. 696.

1904 **gentler Sien**] SCHMIDT (1874, Gentle): "Noble." For *Sien*, see n. 1903-6. HONIGMANN (1965, p. 118) identifies *Sien* as a Shn. spelling; *syen* is found in Q1 *Oth.* 1.3.332 (684), *Syens* in F1 *H5* 3.5.7 (1386). Cf. n. 512.

1905 **make . . . kinde**] HUNTER (ed. 1872): "And make a bark of baser kind to conceive." DEIGHTON (ed. 1889): "*Bark*, part for the whole, but with an allusion to the process of grafting by cutting into the bark." This process will, as KITTREDGE & RIBNER (ed. 1967) say, "cause the wild stock to bring forth the cultivated flower."

1906-8 **This . . . Nature**] NICHOLL (1980, p. 27): "Resonant of alchemy."

1907 **mend**] SCHMIDT (1874): "Improve." Cf. 1983-4.

1908 **The . . . Nature**] A famous commonplace, although, as PAFFORD (ed. 1963) remarks, sometimes treated as a brilliantly original insight of Sh.'s. HUDSON (ed. 1852) quotes Bacon (*Works*, ed. Spedding et al., 1[1858]:496): "Libenter autem *Historiam Artium*, ut Historiæ Naturalis speciem constituímus; quia inveteravit prorsus opinio, ac si aliud quippiam esset ars a natura, artificialis a naturalibus" [We are rather induced to assign the History of Arts as a branch of Natural History, because an opinion hath long time gone current, as if *art* were some different thing from *nature*, and *artificial* from *natural*]; HUDSON also quotes Browne (*Works*, ed. Keynes, 1:26): "Nature is not at variance with art, nor art with nature; they being both the servants of his providence: Art is the perfection of Nature: Were the world now as it was the sixt day, there were yet a Chaos: Nature hath made one world, and Art another. In brief, all things are artificiall, for Nature is the Art of God." Contrasting Sh. with Bacon on art and nature, BOUTROUX (1916, p. 385) quotes from the third aphorism beginning *The Novum Organum* (*Works*, 1:157): "Natura [enim] non nisi parendo vincitur" [Nature to be commanded must be obeyed]. WILSON (1941, p. 432), who finds some 40 meanings ascribed to *nature* in Renaissance literary theory, selects "that which appoints and controls the 'laws' of literary art (as of all else) according to its own purpose, process, or form," a sense in which Petrarch and Daniel also use the word. WILSON (1943) provides other instances of the affinity between nature and art in classical and Renaissance thought, and LOVEJOY & BOAS (1935, pp. 166-9) discuss Plato's handling of the subject. WHITAKER (1953, pp. 120-1, 324) finds it mentioned in *Ven.* 289-94, *Luc.* 1373-9, *Tim.* 1.1.35-8 (49-53), and *Lr.* 4.6.86 (2533); BRYANT (1963, p. 392) in Peele's *Arraignment of Paris* (ed. Benbow, *Works*, 3:69, line 129), where Flora also appears.

KNOWLTON (1936, p. 734): "The problem is not a rivalry between Nature and Art, for man is a part of Nature, and in his art he must use Nature's material and her

Perd. So it is.

Pol. Then make you Garden rich in Gilly'vors,   1910
And do not call them bastards.

Perd. Ile not put
The Dible in earth, to set one slip of them:
No more then were I painted, I would wish

1910 you] your F2+

---

principles of growth or design, her 'ideas.' . . . [Polixenes expresses] a conception
of Nature somewhat devious and complex yet deeper and more basic than hers [Per-
dita's in 1912 ff.]. His idea, the more inclusive and sympathetic, appears to be that of
Shakespeare." KNOWLTON alludes to Jonson's praise of Shakespeare in the commen-
datory poem to F1 (sig. A4ᵛ), which says, in part: "For though the *Poets* matter Nature
be, His Art doth giue the fashion." REESE (1953; 1980, pp. 349-50): "Art, as the
interpreter of Nature's laws and therefore a means by which man might fulfil his
proper function, often improved Nature by elucidating mysteries which life itself left
dark." MILWARD (1964, p. 41): "This idea of Nature, . . . which would include all
works of human art without discrimination, is not the idea of Perdita, who rather
stands for Nature in its perfect condition, unspoilt by the lust or cunning of man and
adorned with divine grace." WAAGE (1980, p. 73) disagrees: "That art can 'change'
nature . . . is a totally new perception for Shakespeare. . . . So Perdita becomes
herself to Florizel and to us when experienced as a wave of the sea" (1956-7). EGAN
(1975, p. 68): "A creature of nature reformed and shaped by art is no less natural, . . . nature having originally created the artist." To account for its rejection by
Perdita, however, other critics treat Polixenes's argument as fallacious or morally
suspect. See n. 1912-16 and pp. 668, 696. FELPERIN (1972, p. 245 and n.) reports
that Herman Melville noted in his copy of Sh. "A world here."

   it selfe, is] WILSON (ed. 1931) finds that the "comma emphasises the 'is.'"

   1909 **So it is**] FURNESS (ed. 1898): "Perdita, true to her charming feminine nature,
instantly makes a personal application of what Polixenes has been saying, . . . and
this 'So it is' is uttered with a swift, furtive, smiling glance at Florizel. That it is no
real assent to the philosophy she has just heard is evident from her next words."
SCHANZER (ed. 1969): "It may be merely polite assent without real conviction. The
dramatic irony of the whole debate is heightened if both disputants are oblivious
throughout of its apparent relevance to the intended marriage of the young lovers.
Behind it lies the further irony that, unknown to them all, the debate possesses in
fact no true relevance to their situation." WILLIAMS (1967, p. 24): "Neither view is
wrong; pure nobility of Nature and the grace of Art will eventually merge in the statue
of Hermione."

   1910-13 **Then . . . them**] GRINDON (1930, p. 18) detects the flare-up of two
regal tempers: "The disguised king, not accustomed to having his advice rejected,
drops his 'gentle maiden' [1894] and 'sweet maid' [1903] and takes upon himself to
instruct her—to give orders and somewhat to reprove. . . . Then is our young princess, shepherdess though she appears, up in arms! . . . She drops the 'reverend sir'
[1879]. . . . The explosion is soon over, but what a bubbling over of her own father's hasty temper it has been. Quickly recovering, however, she tries to propitiate
him with [1916-21]. But Polixenes makes no reply, indeed he never speaks to her
again until he says:—'I'll have thy beauty scratched with briars' [2269]." J. SMITH

(1974, p. 151) finds that *Ile . . . them* "borders on the contemptuous." KNOWLES (privately): "It is misleading to suggest that because he doesn't speak to her for a while he is miffed; he praises her extravagantly in 1975-8, and again briefly at 2001. Her remark hardly need be contemptuous; it could be a pert and charming introduction to a final witty argument."

1910-11 **Then . . . bastards**] PORTER & CLARKE (ed. 1908): "That the assent of Polixenes to his own philosophy does not go very deep . . . in practical application, is part of the humor of this *Gilly'vor* episode."

1910 **you**] MCMANAWAY (1965, p. 188) holds that *you* for "yourself" is "a perfectly good reading," but with it an *a* or a *your* is needed. PAFFORD (ed. 1963): "Possibly . . . *yon*, the *u* being a turned *n*." It may be; *u* and turned *n* can barely be distinguished in the F font if at all (the roman *n* may be slightly narrower than the *u*). *Yon*, however, does not go as well as *your* with the pronoun of "Our rusticke Gardens barren" (1892) or with Perdita's pronouns (1912-21).

1912-16 **Ile . . . me**] The critics' tasks are to explain why Polixenes so adroitly justifies just what he is violently opposed to, the marriage of Florizel and Perdita, and why Perdita, having at 1909 acceded to Polixenes's argument, apparently contradicts herself and rejects her future happiness. CHAMBERS (1931, p. 261): "Polixenes has cornered Perdita: if she denies that this [the union of the scion and the stock] is a true marriage, she will be condemning herself; for she believes herself to be a shepherdess, and yet hopes to be married to Florizel, whom she knows to be the Prince." GRIFFITH (1775, p. 112): "Though she confess the truth of Polixenes' position, yet is she so jealous of the honour of our great parent [Nature], that even the appearance of a violation against her rights offends her." JAMESON (1889, p. 145): "Perdita does not attempt to answer the reasoning of Polixenes: she gives up the argument, but, woman-like, retains her own opinion, or, rather, her sense of right, unshaken by his sophistry," which his argument is not. HUDSON (ed. 1852): "Perdita is too guileless to take the force of Polixenes' reasoning; she therefore assents to it, yet goes on to act as though there were nothing in it: her assent, indeed, is merely to get rid of the perplexity it causes her; for it clashes with and disturbs her moral feelings and associations." To STOLL (1935; 1937, p. 103) her words are the product of "a pretty and feminine petulance. . . . She, a true woman, is of her own opinion still." CUTTS (1968, pp. 74-5): "Perdita's words vigorously oppose Polixenes' . . . but her actions and compliance with Florizel confute her words every bit as much as Polixenes' actions confute his."

HUNTER (1845, 1:421) finds her opinion of crossbreeding supported by PARKINSON (1656, p. 24), who strongly objects to false coloring, forcing, and other forms of interference with the natural culture of flowers—"if any man can form plants at his will and pleasure, he can do as much as God himself that created them." LEECH (1950, p. 134) discovers "the puritanic tinge of Shakespeare's latest phase" (see p. 717). TRAVERSI (1959, p. 24): "Natural in itself, a proper expression of her youthful innocence, this negation cannot be the last word in a play where youth and innocence are to find integration in the context of a wider experience." MARSH (1962; 1980, p. 146): "Her revulsion is violent, but her analogy is false, for the point of the argument is not that things should seem to be better than what they are, but that they can be changed for the better. Yet her point is valid in the sense that if she is not what she seems to be, she is tainted stock, and, as she directly says, not worth breeding from."

TAYLER (1964, p. 136): "Perdita's uneasiness in her 'borrowed flaunts' [1823], her modest conviction that she is, 'poor lowly maid, Most goddess-like prank'd up' [1807-8], has culminated in her final identification of Art with deceit, with false imitation, with 'painted' womanhood—a kind of Art morally and otherwise inferior to Nature." LIVINGSTON (1969, p. 341), with attribution to Lawrence J. Ross, similarly: "Perdita agrees with Polixenes' defense of art as natural; but being uniquely perfect in this world which does need to be changed, she again rejects artifice, although it may create 'the fairest flowers o' th' season' [1889]. . . . She objects not to Florizel's desire to 'breed by' her, but to the idea that his appetites might be stirred by her painted face. In keeping with traditional objections to art, she argues that the art which conceals reality and directs attention to appearances may pervert the imagination and move men to act for wrong reasons." EDWARDS (1968, p. 149) adds: "Perdita's refusal to accept the 'art of grafting' takes us further into the concept of the play. For the play itself is a story of grafting; of reinvigorating the old stock by the freshness of unsullied youth and love. And this story is the work of art, not a report of what great creating nature has done. The uncertainty in the debate leads to uncertainty on whether (dramatic) art is the refinement or the distortion of nature."

Other critics pursue the implications of "were I painted." SCHOTZ (1980, p. 52): "In rejecting the hybrid 'gillyvors', she rejects, too, an artificial femininity." DOLAN (1993, pp. 227-8): "Perdita will not regard nature — or, by extension, herself . . . as in need of improvement. In her view, the art that produces the gillyflower does not embellish nature but competes with and effaces it. . . . Aligning great creating nature with her own ability to breed, Perdita disdains those who prefer the gillyflower and the painted face, denouncing their taste as corrupt and insulting to nature, here symbolized by the body of a woman who asserts that she will not be improved on." DUSINBERRE (1975, p. 70): "Her chastity dictates a fastidious rejection of art, reminding the audience of the innocence of her own birth," a reading that seems unlikely.

Other recent explanations have taken a somewhat different turn. LOVEJOY (1948, p. 238) connects this passage with one in Montaigne's "Of Cannibals": "There is no reason, art should gaine the point of honour of our great and puissant mother Nature. We have so much by our inventions surcharged the beauties and riches of her workes, that we have altogether overchoaked her" (*Essais*, trans. John Florio, 1603; 1933, p. 163). LOVEJOY calls this "the *locus classicus* of primitivism in modern literature" and notes that Sh.'s "extreme antipathy to the passage is shown by the fact that he wrote two replies to it—a humorous one in *The Tempest*, a serious and profound one in *The Winter's Tale*." The connection between Montaigne and *Tmp.* is discussed by KERMODE (*Tmp.*, ed. 1954, pp. xxxiv-xxxviii) and the connection between Montaigne and *WT* by PAFFORD (ed. 1963, pp. 169-70). SCHANZER (ed. 1969) summarizes: Sh. "makes Perdita uphold [Montaigne's] primitivist point of view [, which] asserts the superiority of so-called 'savages' to civilized men, and, by analogy, of wild to cultivated fruits. . . . Montaigne uses the word 'bastardized' of cultivated fruits. . . . The argument put forward by Polixenes—that the art by means of which man improves the products of Nature is itself a creation of Nature—was equally familiar." That Sh. is antipathetic to the passage, as LOVEJOY thinks, is debatable; the argument is a standoff.

1913 **Dible**] MINSHEU (1617): "*Dibble or dubble to set herbes in a garden. . . . The right* dibble *is a* two-forked *toole.*" OED (Dibble, *sb.*, citing this line): "In its simplest form, a stout pointed cylindrical stick [but it may] be forked at the point." WALKER (1854, pp. 64-8): The word is "contracted into one syllable, or placed in a monosyllabic [position] of the line." Cf. n. 612.

1914-16 **No . . . me**] SCHANZER (ed. 1969): "Perdita's distaste for this is all of a piece with her revulsion against being *Most goddess-like pranked up* [1808]." She is, of course, so pranked at this moment. DENT (1971, p. 33): This "conclusion would seem to make even the admired Perdita seem pert and forward." WATSON (1984, p. 259): "Cosmetics, revealingly popular with the women of the Sicilian court [596-602], may represent an ethical danger analogous to the other Sicilian excesses." For the excesses, see, for example, n. 48.

1914 **were I painted**] HANKINS (1978, p. 197), oddly, finds it unclear whether the paint is on her skin or on canvas.

This youth should say 'twer well: and onely therefore   1915
Desire to breed by me. Here's flowres for you:
Hot Lauender, Mints, Sauory, Mariorum,

1917 Sauory,] ~ ∧ mCOL2 *conj.*, HAL

1915-16 **and . . . me**] EMPSON (1964; 1986, p. 234): "The word *breed* used coolly by a young virgin . . . would sound shameless if she were no less fiercely virtuous; but somehow the effect of being so farmyard is to appear very aristocratic."

1915 **therefore**] KITTREDGE & RIBNER (ed. 1967): "Because of that artificial appearance of beauty."

1916-74 **Here's . . . for 'em**] PAFFORD (ed. 1963): "The beauty and charm of Perdita, which are such a powerful force in the play, are here shown at their height. The previous talk with Polixenes, showing Perdita the resolute peasant girl, leads up to this important and memorable passage where Perdita's beauty, grace, and charm of person, of movement, and of language make their profound and permanent impression."

1916-21 **Here's . . . welcome**] BRANDES (1898, 2:286) finds Perdita's distribution of blossoms anticipated by Marina's "strewing flowers on the grave of her dead nurse just before Dionyza sends her away to be murdered" in *Per.* 4.1. CAPELL (1783, 2.4:175): "The address is to a different part of this numerous company, and the '*welcome*' . . . is to that part separately." PAFFORD (ed. 1963) and PARRY (ed. 1982) think he could be right, but SCHANZER (ed. 1969), following SCOTT (see n. 1882), is surely right that CAPELL is wrong: "Perdita is trying to make amends for her previous indiscretion (in giving Polixenes and Camillo flowers of winter) by now giving them flowers of summer, thus suggesting that she considers them to be 'men of middle age.'" PORTER & CLARKE (ed. 1908): "Take them to be addressed to Camillo, who responds to them."

1917-41 **Hot . . . one**] ORGEL (ed. 1996): "Perdita's list of flowers descends from a long tradition of flower catalogues. Both Theocritus (Idyll 11.45, 56-7) and Virgil (Eclogue 2.45-50) offer the beloved gifts of flowers; Bion's *Lament for Adonis* (75-6) decks the subject's bier with them, and Moschus' *Lament for Bion* (5-7) calls on the rose, hyacinth, and other flowers to mourn for him—compare Florizel's assumption in [1944] that Perdita is thinking of him as a corpse. The numerous Renaissance examples include Marot's elegy on the death of Louis of Savoy (225-40), Castiglione's *Alcon* (142-50), Spenser's April eclogue of the *Shepheardes Calender* (60-3, 136-44) and *Lay of Clorinda* (70-2)."

1917 **Hot**] Evidently modifies all five nouns. KITTREDGE & RIBNER (ed. 1967) disagree, however: "Certain varieties of lavender were hot, others cold. Perdita seems to be indicating which she has." It is true that French lavender (stechados or stickadove), for example, is cold; but see the following nn.

Lauender] Usually identified as *Lavandula spica*, called "lauander spike" by GERARD (1597, pp. 467-8), who describes it as "hot and drie." BEISLY (1864, p. 79): "Lavender was considered as an emblem of affection"; he quotes Drayton's "Ninth Eglogue" (ed. Buxton, 1:67): "He from his lasse him lavander hath sent, Shewing her love, and doth requitall crave." CARRUTHERS (1879, p. 191), however, believes it signifies distrust. DEIGHTON (ed. 1889) thinks *hot* means "strongly smelling," aromatic

The Mary-gold, that goes to bed with'Sun,
And with him rises, weeping: These are flowres
Of middle summer, and I thinke they are giuen   1920
To men of middle age. Y'are very welcome.
     Cam. I should leaue grasing, were I of your flocke,
And onely liue by gazing.

1921 Y'are] F1-JOHN2, WH1, BUL, CAM3-SIS, CLN2, ARD2, PEN2, BEV3; Ye're DYCE,
STAU, HUD2; You're CAP *etc.*
       very] *Om.* F4-POPE2

---

presumably, but FURNESS (ed. 1898): "Its smell is no stronger than 'mint'; in fact, it
is not as strong. . . .   Lavender was the flower for an ardent lover." He quotes from
"A Nosegaie," in Clement Robinson et al., *A Handful of Pleasant Delights* (1584; ed.
Hyder E. Rollins, 1925, p. 3): "*Lauander* is for louers true, . . . when they obtained
haue, the loue that they require, . . . quenched is the fire." Cf. 181. CHARLTON (ed.
1916) agrees but wonders whether "*ardent* lavender is suitable as a gift to . . .
'men of middle age.'" WILSON (ed. 1931) wonders the same, and finding no support
in *OED* for *hot* as "aromatic" or "ardent," considers emending; see p. 580. But *hot*
does mean "ardent"(*OED, a.* 6b), and the gift, which some might consider perfectly
appropriate, may to others have been intended as inspirational. DENT (1971, p. 67)
favors "pungent, acrid" (*OED, a.* 5). SAVAGE (1923, p. 273): Lavender is mentioned
by Sh. only here; the plant, introduced into England only about 1568, was not yet
widely grown.
       Mints] CHITTENDEN & SYNGE (1965-9): "Four species of Mentha have been
grown in British kitchen gardens." This one is usually identified as *Mentha spicata*—
also hot and dry, according to GERARD (1597, p. 553). To refer to the plant, Sh. uses
mints here and, in *LLL* 5.2.655 (2610), *mint*. Both the singular and the plural forms
were acceptable (*OED, sb.*[2] 1). GERARD (p. 552), for example, labels his illustration
of *M. sativa rubris* "Red Garden Mints" yet speaks, on the same page, of "another
sort of Mint." CLARK (1930, p. 175), taking the word as plural: "The mints were,
probably, spearmint [*M. viridis*] and peppermint [*M. piperita*]." *Webster's Third New
International Dictionary* (1971), however, identifies spearmint as *M. spicata.*
       Sauory] An herb similar to thyme. According to ELLACOMBE (1896, p. 292) and
SINGLETON (1933, p. 242), either winter savory (*Satureia montana*) or summer (*S.
hortensis*) may be meant. GERARD (1597, pp. 461-2): "Winter Sauorie is of temper-
ature hot and drie in the third degree. . . . Sommer Sauorie is not full so hot." SAV-
AGE (1923, p. 293): "Introduced into England about the year 1562 . . . used both
fresh and dried for seasoning purposes." VAN DAM (1900, p. 53): Pronounced *sa-v'ry*;
for other syncopations of *o*, see nn. 455, 1949, and 2233.
       Mariorum] ELLACOMBE (1896, p. 168): "Several species of Marjoram were
grown, especially the Common Marjoram (*Origanum vulgare*), a British plant, the
Sweet Marjoram (*O. Marjorana*) . . . and the Winter Marjoram (*O. Heracleoti-
cum*)." GERARD (1597, p. 540): "They are hot and drie in the second degree, after
some copies [authorities], hot and drie in the third degree."
       1918-19 **The . . . weeping**] DODOENS (1578, p. 163): Marigolds "do close, at
the setting downe of the Sunne, and do spread and open againe, at the Sunne rising."
Many allusions to this characteristic of the flower occur; see, for example, Marlowe,
Hero and Leander 5:464-8; Nashe, *The Unfortunate Traveller* (ed. McKerrow, 2:

218); Greene, *Menaphon* (6:94-5); Douce (1807, 1:357); Nicholson (1873); C. A. W. (1873); W. F. F. (1873); and Seager (1896, p. 199). Webb (1989): "The buds (and flowerheads) are sometimes suggestive of the sexual organs," by analogy with their opening and closing. Nicholson (1873, p. 284) holds that the marigold rises weeping because the flower "is a remembrance of her who rose early [Mary Magdalen], and, weeping, first saw the risen Lord." Bethell (ed. 1956), however: "Associated with Our Lady by witty derivation (Mary-gold)." Hunter (1845, 1:422), on the authority of Higgins (1585, p. 126), identifies the marigold as the sunflower. Higgins actually says: "Some take it [*Heliotropium*] for Marigold: some for Turnesol [heliotrope]"; for *Calendula* he gives "the Marigold." Gerard (1597, pp. 599-604) also assigns marigolds to the genus *Calendula*. Beisly (1864, p. 79) disagrees: "*Marigold* (Chrysanthemum segetum), is the field marigold [or corn marigold]. The C. Coronarium garden marigold is the flower alluded to by Shakspere, as he describes its *habit of closing its petals or florets at sunset, and opening them at sunrise*. The field marigold has not this habit. . . . When the flower is covered with dew in the morning, it does in truth rise or open its florets *weeping*. . . . In *Cymbeline*, [2.3.24 (986)], these flowers are called *winking* [closed] *marybuds*." Despite this conjecture, recent authorities, such as De Bray (1982, p. 110), identify Perdita's flower as the calendula. See also *Son.* 25.5-6 and *Luc.* 397. Although, in *WT*, Perdita calls them flowers (1916, 1919), Bethell (ed. 1956) asserts that these plants are actually herbs and that "significantly, the only flowers Perdita has are marigolds," which symbolize, he believes, marriage and the virtue of obedience. Peterson (*Time*, 1973, p. 178): "Probably alludes to the sorrows attendant upon the physical satisfaction of unsanctioned love." Watson (1984, p. 256): "Her wording fairly drips with overtones of human seduction and subsequent regrets."

1918 **with'Sun**] For the apostrophe's significance, see nn. 600 and 2594.

1920 **they are giuen**] Hunter (1845, 1:419-20): "The word *given* is here heraldic [*OED, v.* 24b]. . . . The old heralds had various systems of blazoning, each colour and metal being designated by a planet, a precious stone, an age of man, a flower. . . . Thus an association was formed between certain flowers and certain ages of the life of man." The examples he cites of the equation of men's ages and flowers, however, do not accord very well with Perdita's distribution. Deighton (ed. 1889), more reasonably: "It is the custom to give them." Or "I have given."

1921 **middle age**] Orgel (ed. 1996): "Perdita rectifies the implication of the 'flowers of winter' [1886] that Polixenes and Camillo are elderly."

Y'are very welcome] Siemon (1974, p. 10): "The debate is finally inconclusive. Polixenes' civilized theories are never brought to the test (although his commitment to them is exposed as a sham), and by the revelation of her true identity, Perdita is saved from the implications of her purist doctrine for a shepherdess in love with a prince. . . . Polixenes acts more on Perdita's theory than on his own, and Perdita's actions are consistent with her own theory only as an expression of some deeply and powerfully felt sense of her own nobility. . . . Perdita herself, according to Leontes, is one of nature's bastards, and he will no more have her in his court than she will have 'streak'd gillyvors' in her garden. . . . If anything, the action of the play vindicates both Leontes' and Perdita's purist theories; what it condemns is any attempt to act upon those theories without regard to the ambiguities of appearance and the complexities of reality."

1922-3 **I . . . gazing**] Deighton (ed. 1889, Grasing): "Used transitively or causally, grazing my sheep." He is mistaken; Camillo playfully imagines himself a sheep. Parry (ed. 1982): "The sight of your beauty would be food enough for me."

grasing . . . gazing] Miriam Joseph (1947, pp. 166-70): In paranomasia, words nearly but not precisely alike in sound are repeated. Sh. puts the figure to comic and, as here, to serious use.

Perd. Out alas:
You'ld be so leane, that blasts of Ianuary   1925
Would blow you through and through. Now (my fairst Friend,
I would I had some Flowres o'th Spring, that might
Become your time of day: and yours, and yours,
That weare vpon your Virgin-branches yet
Your Maiden-heads growing: O *Proserpina*,   1930
For the Flowres now, that (frighted) thou let'st fall
From *Dysses* Waggon: Daffadils,
That come before the Swallow dares, and take

1926 my] *Om.* HAN
    Friend] Friends F4, ROWE1-POPE2
1930 Maiden-heads] maidenhoods HUD2
1932 Daffadils] early daffadils HAN, CAP; yellow daffadils KEIGHTLEY *conj. in* CAM1,
KTLY; golden daffadils COLERIDGE (1813?; 1960, 1:108) *conj.*, HUD2

1924 **Out**] HALLIWELL (ed. 1859): "An intensity of expression of the word, *alas!*"
(*OED, int.* 2). That is, *out* makes *alas* more emphatic. COLLINS (ed. 1904-24?): Perdita
"punctures any attempt at hyperbole. Her poetry is organic and will not tolerate . . . artifice." This notion is belied by 1926 ff.

1926-47 **Now . . . armes**] According to HERFORD (ed. 1916-), Perdita's
speech "is redolent of her maiden passion. This is the clue to the sometimes daring
beauty of the epithets." STUDING (1970, p. 71), following LONG (1961, pp. 75-6),
finds it very redolent: She "is transformed from dignified goddess and rural hostess
to the 'loose' May queen. . . . Perdita's overt display of aggressive sensuality seduces
Florizel completely and, [at 1951-62], he expresses his desire to freeze his May queen
in this moment of ecstatic sensuality forever." So much for Perdita's "charming feminine nature" (see n. 1909).

1926-32 **Now . . . Waggon**] LINDENBAUM (1972, p. 16): "There is a strong note
of melancholy here and of regret over the fact that she cannot really bring spring
back to the earth. In handing out her flowers, Perdita is very conscious of the limitations placed on man's life by time's movement." GOLDMAN (1972, p. 135), similarly:
"We have a sense, with the daffodils (as with Perdita herself and her appearance after
three acts of Sicilian tragedy), of natural wonder braving the tragic world of winter
and storm. Yet it is a world full of tragic possibilities for the individual. The marigolds . . . the poor sheep . . . the pale primroses remind us of the pathetic characters who have not survived (Mamillius, Antigonus, and, at this point, Hermione)."
The note of melancholy seems dubious, however. The flowers of spring may be gone
for the time, but she and Florizel and the other young people wear upon their virgin
branches their maidenheads growing; and in the future is the flowery bank where
love will lie and play.

1926 **Friend**] SCHMIDT (1874) does not gloss this instance specifically; BETHELL
(ed. 1956) believes that Perdita means "lover," obviously in an innocent sense. He
may be right because of 1945 ff., yet here the word may represent only "one joined
to another in benevolence and intimacy" (SCHMIDT).

1927 **Flowres o'th Spring**] SIMS (1971) compares the "vernal flowers" in Milton's *Lycidas* 142-51.

1928 **Become . . . day**] DEIGHTON (ed. 1889): "Be suitable to your age; she is
addressing a young girl." Or Florizel.

1929-30 **That . . . growing**] THIRLBY (MS 1747-53, Branches): "Stalks," not exactly paralleled in *OED*. More likely "limb of a tree" (*sb*. 1), the *maidenheads* (= "maidenhoods") being equated with blossoms, a witty reversal of *deflowering* in the sexual sense.

1930 **growing**] *OED* (Growing, *vbl. sb.*. 3b, citing this line): "Advance, progress." As KNOWLES (privately) points out, this interpretation makes *Maiden-heads* possessive, but *growing* could as well be a participle and *Maiden-heads* nominative.

1930-43 **O . . . ore**] STEEVENS (ed. 1773) and later authorities find these lines indebted to Ovid: *quo dum Proserpina luco ludit et aut violas aut candida lilia carpit, . . . paene simul visa est dilectaque raptaque Diti: . . . ut summa vestrem laniarat ab ora, collecti flores tunicis cecidere remissis—* "Within this grove Proserpina was playing, and gathering violets or white lilies. . . . Almost in one act did Pluto see and love and carry her away. . . . Since she had torn her garment at its upper edge, the flowers which she had gathered fell out of her loosened tunic" (*Met.* 5.391-9, trans. Miller). GOLDING's (1567; 1965, 5.491-500) translation of the same passage is "While in this garden Proserpine was taking hir pastime, In gathering eyther Violets blew, or Lillies white as Lime, . . . Dis spide hir: lovde hir: caught hir up: and all at once well nere, . . . And as she from the upper part hir garment would have rent, By chaunce she let hir lap slip downe, and out hir flowres went." Sh. knew GOLDING's translation of the *Metamorphoses* (see ROUSE 1961, p. v). WIGSTON (1884, p. 5): "Now what are the leading features of this myth? First, a lost maiden, and the earth mother mourning for her. This mother is the sleeping earth during winter. With the recovery of Persephone, the earth ceases to be dead, for with the spring it puts on fresh life and beauty. The myth of Demeter *is therefore a Winter's Tale.*"

Although FRIPP (1930, pp. 102-3) had thought otherwise, SCHANZER (ed. 1969, 4.4.116-18 n.) assumes that Sh. used the translation, and MAHON (1984) finds in GOLDING two passages— "Hir mother stoode as starke as stone" (5.632) and "A collup of mine owne flesh" (5.651; cf. *WT* 213)—that reinforce the idea. Like ROOT (1903, p. 103), THOMSON (1952, p. 132) cites *Fasti*, 4.442 ff., and THOMSON adds Claudian's *Rape of Proserpine*. BALDWIN (1944, 2:465-8) detects the influence of Vergil. GREY (1754, 1:262) compares 1930-2 with Ceres's complaint of the rape of her daughter by dusky Dis in *Tmp.* 4.1.99 (1748). FREY (*Vast Romance*, 1980, p. 99): "In constructing his version of a re-creative world, Shakespeare could draw upon a variety of minor motifs and major models." He mentions Peele's *Arraignment of Paris* 1.3 (ed. Benbow, *Works*, 3:67-70), Beaumont and Fletcher's *Philaster* (1.2.113-35), and Lyly's *Endimion* (1.2.9-26). For other possible debts to Peele, see n. 627 and EDWARDS ("Seeing," 1986, pp. 79 ff.).

MUIR (*Last Periods*, 1961, pp. 48-9): "Proserpine is the spring goddess. The Whitsun Pastorals [see 1949] were May games [see n. 1948-50], celebrating the rebirth of the year; and Flora, whom she is now representing, is the Roman equivalent of the Queen of the May. Perdita, therefore, symbolizes the spring. . . . This symbolism is particularly appropriate to *The Winter's Tale*, in which the apparent death of Hermione is succeeded by her apparent resurrection and restoration; in which Perdita, the lost one, is found again and restored to her parents; and in which the love of the children atones for the tragic discord which estranges the parents." KAMACHI (1979, p. 30): Proserpina "has traditionally been regarded as an incarnation of the corn, which remains in the earth during the winter and grows out into the world with the coming of spring." She was so regarded, although COOPER (1565) says, "she is taken sometyme for the Moone." HOENIGER (1950, p. 22) finds "almost a conscious tradition linking the figure of the lost maiden . . . Perdita . . . to the pagan myth of Persephone on the one hand, and to Dante's Matilda or Milton's unfallen Eve on the other." GARBER (1974, p. 176), similarly: "The story of Proserpina and Ceres is of course the pattern of the story of Perdita and Hermione, the cycle of death and rebirth." H. SMITH (1974, p. 1564), also observing the "relation between the plot of the lost flower girl and the classical story of Proserpina," thinks it accounts for Sh.'s switching Greene's Sicilia and Bohemia, for "Proserpina's legend was of course set in Sicily." EDWARDS (1968, p. 148): "The strongest argument against taking Perdita as Proserpine, Hermione as Ceres, and the whole play as a re-enactment of the spring fertility-myth, is that Perdita so pointedly speaks of her non-identity with Proserpine." FRYE (1986, p. 161), however, alluding to Ceres's search for her abducted daughter: "Hermione doesn't search, but she doesn't come to life either (or whatever she does) until Perdita . . . is said to be found." And HORWITZ (1988, p. 12) reverses EDWARDS's nonidentity: "Perdita links herself explicitly with the regenerative myth of Proserpina, evoking not only the plenty of natural profusion associated with the goddess, but also the perpetual blight that can be cast by tyranny. . . . The effect of this imaginative effort is to generate life out of death," as in 1944-7. MAHOOD (1957, p. 159): "The . . . passage is full of what Herrick calls 'cleanly wantonness': the violets are as sweet as the breath of Venus, the primroses lovesick, the oxlip inviting, and the daffodils *take* the air."

RUSKIN (1846; 1903, 4:255-6), on Sh.'s language: "The imagination in these . . . lines goes into the very inmost soul of every flower, after having touched them all at first with that heavenly timidity, the shadow of Proserpina's, and gilded them with celestial gathering, and never stops on their spots or their bodily shape." ALEXANDER (1927, pp. 257-63): "When in [these] exquisite words she deplores that she has not spring flowers . . . she forgets that the actual flowers she would give for the most part are and do none of the things she says they are and do. She has given away her case against the gillyvors, and unknown to herself turned artist, while upholding nature. . . . Perhaps nature is beautiful to us only if we see it with the artist's eye." VAN DOREN (1939, p. 320) hears a note of sadness: "It [the speech] is homesick for blossoms which an older generation will never see again in their original innocence. . . . Both of them [Perdita and Florizel] will laugh in many springs; but their special charm resides for us in the fact that they stand adoring each other in the sunset of the year, in a glow whose depth they are too young to measure." PETERSON (*Time*, 1973, pp. 179-80): "A personal lamentation of unfulfilled womanhood. . . . [1936-9] almost certainly alludes to . . . Florizel [as] 'Golden Apollo' [1831]." WEINSTEIN (1971, p. 98): "The power of these lines comes from the juxtaposition of robust and fragile images: brave daffodils and bold oxlips are silhouetted by dim violets and pale primroses, and the short-lived frailty of the latter is curiously described as a sexual shyness or failure. In like terms Florizel is demonstrably a quick and ardent lover, but—like those ['Prime-roses' in 1936]—he is for a moment glimpsed not as a vigorous young man but as a short-lived one, a corpse strewn with flowers." MATHEW (1922, p. 48) links these lines with the flower lists in *Per.* 4.1.13-17 (1437-40) and *Cym.* 4.2.218-24 (2528-34). "The model for all these had been set . . . in Marlowe's *Dido*": "Amongst greene brakes Ile lay *Ascanius*, And strewe him with sweete smelling Violets, Blushing Roses, purple *Hyacinthe*: These milke white Doves shall be his Centronels" (2.1.317-20). GRENE (1967, p. 69): Bohemian Perdita praises English flowers.

1930-2 O . . . **Waggon**] STEARNS (1882, pp. 254-5): "This figure so directly calls to mind the style of fresco painting that adorns the ceiling of many Italian buildings, that it seems possible the Poet may have seen them with his own eyes."

1932 **From**] HUDSON (ed. 1852): "Because of the approach of" (*OED* 14). But probably "from the wagon as it carried you away."

Dysses] RANN (ed. 1787): "Pluto's." The name *Pluto* does not appear in Ovid's *Metamorphoses;* the god there is always *Dis.*

Waggon] DYCE (1853, p. 79): "Chariot." From Barnabe Barnes, *The Devil's Charter* (1607; ed. Pogue, 1980, 1.3550), he quotes "the wagon of blacke *Dis.*" HUDSON (ed. 1880) recalls Mercutio's mention of the small, gray-coated gnat as Queen Mab's waggoner (*Rom.* 1.4.67 [518]), "where later usage would require *charioteer.*" See also *Tit.* 5.2.48-51 (2334-7) and *AWW* 4.4.34 (2478).

1932-41 **Daffadils . . . Flowre-de-Luce**] WISE (1861, p. 65): "Every flower is mentioned in the order it grows." PULC (1971): "Each of the flowers Perdita mentions is symbolic of the quality of her love": daffodils, oxlips, and crown imperial = its radiant happiness; violets = modesty; lilies = purity and dignity; primroses = sensual pleasure. "Oxlips are hybrids [see n. 1939]. Perdita's mention of them seems to echo [1903-6 and] be a pointed allusion to the 'piedness' that would result from" the union of a shepherdess and a prince. "Yet the 'piedness' so suggested is of a noble kind, for the 'bold oxlips' are linked with the crown imperial. . . . At the same time, both 'crown imperial' and 'flower-de-luce' . . . hint at the imminent unmasking of Perdita."

1932-6 **Daffadils . . . breath**] BAGEHOT (1853; n.d., 1:119): "A perfectly poetic appreciation of nature contains two elements,—a knowledge of facts, and a sensibility to charms. . . . [These lines] seem to show that he [Sh.] knew those feelings of youth, to which beauty is more than a religion." STOLL (1935; 1937, p. 102): "The yellow flower flaunting in the winds is a little minx or hussy who has ventured foremost into the sunshine to captivate them and revel in their caresses." HALLIDAY (1954, p. 180), enraptured: "*Daffodils*, like a bow drawn at the end of the short line, followed by the leaping swallow flight and the breathless *beauty*; the shy withdrawal of *violets dim*, suggested by the sudden drop to the monosyllable and thin vowel; the whole bound together by the interplay of the short and long *i*'s, by the assonance of *flowers, swallow, sweeter, sweet friend, strew him*, and by the more prolonged echo of phrases, 'take . . . March', 'lack . . . garlands.'" EDWARDS (*Progress*, 1986, p. 171), in a different vein: "Perdita, if she refuses to create gillyflowers by grafting, has the power (when wearing a costume which she fears 'does change my disposition' [1950]) to bring into being a whole springtime of flowers. . . . In spite of herself Perdita demonstrates the power of art to create life." DENT's (1971, p. 45) "Critical comment is hushed to silence" is not quite right. For daffodils, see n. 1669.

1933 **come . . . dares**] GREY (1754, 1:262): "The swallows appear about the *vernal equinox,*" approximately 21 Mar. on the modern calendar. DYER (1884, p. 155): They are generally honored as harbingers of spring. DENT (1973, p. 139), however: "Of summer rather than of spring." *OED* (*sb.*[1] 1, citing this line) agrees with Dyer.

take] THEOBALD (MS -1729?): "Arrest [i.e., charm]." SCHMIDT (1875): "To touch; to strike in a beneficial or pernicious manner." PECK (1740, p. 227) believes the idea derived from Jth. 16:9 ("her beautie toke his minde prisoner"), and he finds similar passages in *Ado* 1.1.324 (314) and *Cym.* 1.6.103-4 (715-16). The captivating power of beauty is a commonplace, however. RIDLEY (ed. 1935): "The winds of March are not only captivated; they are quelled." See nn. 97 and 1211. HAPPÉ (1969) alone finds "to take sexual possession of" suggested.

The windes of March with beauty: Violets (dim,
But sweeter then the lids of *Iuno's* eyes,   1935
Or *Cytherea's* breath) pale Prime-roses,
That dye vnmarried, ere they can behold
Bright Phœbus in his strength (a Maladie

1934-9 **Violets . . . Maids**] ARMSTRONG (1963, p. 78): In Sh.'s imagination, "violets are closely associated with breath." ARMSTRONG compares "the sweet sound, That breathes upon a bank of violets, Stealing and giving odour!" (*TN* 1.1.5-7 [9-11]). TAYLOR (1972, pp. 52-3): "The placing of 'violets dim' and 'pale primroses' as strong nominatives prevents their being overwhelmed by the ardour of Cytherea's breath, Juno's eye-lids and 'Bright Phoebus in his strength', descriptions which manifest both subtle eroticism and passion. A pale primrose herself, in some ways, Perdita also is not dominated by her knowledge of erotic lore; her innocence is simply enlivened and made more valuable by her Ovidian sophistication."

1934-6 **(dim . . . breath)**] SIMPSON (1911, p. 91): "Brackets were useful in making a construction clear to the eye. They were frequently employed with adjectives or adjective phrases which follow a noun."

1934 **dim**] RUSKIN (1882; 1906, 25:393): "Perdita . . . calls it dim, at that moment, in thinking of her own love, and the hidden passion of it, unspeakable." LITTLEDALE (*TNK* ed. 1876, 1:111): "The sweetness of the violet's smell is contrasted with radiant beauty of the daffodils . . . , *dim* serving to subordinate the colour to the perfume, and perhaps meaning 'half-hidden from the eye', retiring, modest." He properly objects to SCHMIDT's (1874) "wanting beauty; homely" as prosy (or simply wrong). HENLEY (ed. 1902): "Dusky" (*OED*, *a.* 3, citing this line). MOORMAN (ed. 1912): "It may be that the white violet is referred to." CHARLTON (ed. 1916): "The idea is that they are of so subdued a colour that by the side of daffodils they are hardly seen." PAFFORD (ed. 1963), differently: "Because the hanging head is also usually concealed or partly concealed."

1935-6 **sweeter . . . breath**] JOHNSON (ed. 1765): Sh. "mistakes *Juno* for *Pallas*, who was the *goddess of blue eyes*. Sweeter than an *eyelid* is an odd image: but perhaps he uses *sweet* in the general sense, for *delightful*." MASON (1785, p. 135): Because the breath of Cytherea [Aphrodite, Venus; see next n.] is part of the comparison, Sh. "does not allude to the colour but to the fragrance of violets." Thus CHARLTON (ed. 1916): The idea is twofold, "more pleasing in appearance than the lids of Juno's eyes, and in perfume than Cytherea's breath." BECKET's (1815, 1:364) notion that *lids* means "lashes" is unsupported by *OED*. HUDSON (ed. 1852) thinks that *violets dim* suggests the violet-colored cosmetic, "which was doubtless perfumed," used by Grecian ladies to shade their eyelids. The CLARKES (ed. 1865) dislike the literalism of these remarks; they miss the poetry's "finest aroma of signification." Some of that aroma is "in the word 'lids' . . . which suggests lips resting upon the eyes and inhaling fragrance while caressing them," a splendid synesthesia. PARRY (ed. 1982): "More delicate (in their effect on one's senses)." PAFFORD (ed. 1963) gives instances of beautiful eyelids in *Per.* 5.1.110-11 (2091-2), Spenser's *Amoretti* 40 and *Faerie Queene* 2.3.25, and Sidney's *Arcadia* (ed. Evans, p. 63). As far as Juno is concerned, perhaps the lids are Sh.'s version of Homer's epithet for Hera, "ox-eyed."

1936 **Cytherea's**] Cytherea is an epithet for Aphrodite, because the goddess rose from the foam of the sea near Cythera (Cerigo), an Ionian island. Conventionally, Sh. several times uses Cytherea or Venus as a type of beauty; see ROOT (1903, p. 115).

1936-40 **pale . . . Imperiall**] HORWITZ (1988, p. 12): "The 'pale primroses . . .' are linked to the sexuality of the 'bold oxlips and / The crown imperial' . . . to provide an all-incorporating vision that does not deny loss and death, but includes it."

1936-8 **Prime-roses . . . strength**] GERARD (1597, p. 637): "They [primroses] are commonly called *Primulæ veris* [of the Spring], because they are the first among those plants that do flower in the spring." RYDÉN (1978, p. 72) and DE BRAY (1982, p. 14) identify this flower with the oxlip; their primrose is *P. vulgaris*. BEISLY (1864, p. 81): "They . . . are mostly sulphur-coloured, but some are occasionally found of paler hue, approaching to white." DE BRAY calls them "a unique shade of pale green-ish yellow — the colour of watery spring sunlight." On their marital status, MALONE (ed. 1790, 10:605) quotes WARTON's n. (ed. 1785) on Milton's line "the rathe [early] Primrose that forsaken dies" (*Lycidas* line 142 [*The Works of John Milton*, ed. Pat-terson, 1931-8, 1.1.81]). WARTON writes, "The general texture and sentiment of this [Milton's] line is from [this passage in *WT*]. Especially as he had first written UNWED-DED for *forsaken*. . . . It dies *unmarried* . . . because it grows in the shade, un-cherished or unseen by the sun, who was supposed to be in love with some sorts of flowers." BEISLY (pp. 81-2) disagrees: "The pale primroses that *die unmarried* must, I consider, be those which do not arrive at maturity by *producing seed*. . . . The pale primrose does not grow in the shade more than other primroses." These flowers do not produce seed, SAVAGE (1923, p. 61) explains, because, being very early, they expire before insects come to life to fertilize them. As HUNTER (ed. 1872) notes, they "die before the sun attains his summer vigour." PARRY (ed. 1982): "It is thus not a flower that 'marries' the sun as the marigold does (compare line [1918])." HAPPÉ (1969), somewhat differently: "The primrose cannot stand the full force of Phoebus, the summer sun, and so it symbolizes early and unfruitful death." In C. M. Skinner, *Myths and Legends of Flowers* (1911, p. 229), PAFFORD (1954) finds "that a certain Paralisos, son of Flora and Priapus, died because his betrothed had died, and was changed by the gods into a primrose." Skinner was unable to locate the source of the legend. To CHARLTON (ed. 1916), "the image has in it the suggestion of the sanctity and retiredness of a nunnery" (but see n. 1938-9). Further primrose lore may be found in ELLACOMBE (1896, pp. 239-45) and in LITTLEDALE (*TNK* ed. 1876, p. 110).

According to GRINDON (1930, p. 19), the early primrose does not set seed either. Although he does not cite this passage, for *die* COLMAN (1974) has "detumescence following orgasm, in male or female." Thus SANDERS (1987, p. 81) thinks the maids "are deplorably likely to 'die' before properly married," a witticism, if it is one, far from Perdita's style.

1938 **Phœbus**] COOPER (1565): "Apollo, the sonne of Jupiter and Latona, and is taken for the sonne [sun]." Perhaps the name is not italicized because the compositor understood it as that of a flower, like "Prime-roses." TILLYARD (1938, p. 46): "Apollo is the dominant god in *The Winter's Tale*. . . . He appears as the bridegroom, whom the pale primroses never know, but who visits the other flowers. . . . Perdita should be associated with them, as symbol both of the creative powers of nature, physical fertility, and of healing and re-creation of the mind." SITWELL (1948, p. 204) associates Apollo, "the Sun, that brings all to life," with the gold left with Perdita (1560 ff.), "a property of, and part of, the Sun." When the Clown is robbed, his purse turns cold (1786-7).

1938-9 **Maladie . . . Maids**] CAPELL (1783, 2.4:175): I.e., "paleness," and to the line from Milton that MALONE refers to (see n. 1936-8), STEEVENS (ed. 1803) adds the line "originally subjoined": "colouring the pale cheeke of uninjoyd love" (*Works* [1931-8], 1.2.470). The same association is found in Herrick's "The Primrose" (*Works*, ed. L. C. Martin, p. 208): "Ask me why this flower do's show So yellow-green, and sickly too?" — that is, manifesting symptoms of greensickness, or chlorosis (which is actually caused by a deficiency of iron rather than of love). See also "How Primroses came green" (p. 64). BUCKNILL (1860, p. 131), Victorianly: "Consumption, a malady to which persons of the age and sex are peculiarly liable." BETHELL (ed. 1956): "Per-

Most incident to Maids:) bold Oxlips, and
The Crowne Imperiall: Lillies of all kinds,   1940
(The Flowre-de-Luce being one.) O, these I lacke,
To make you Garlands of) and my sweet friend,
To strew him o're, and ore.
    Flo. What? like a Coarse?
    Perd. No, like a banke, for Loue to lye, and play on: 1945
Not like a Coarse: or if: not to be buried,
But quicke, and in mine armes. Come, take your flours,

1939 bold] gold mTBY3 *conj.*, HAN, WARB, JOHN, v1773
    1946 if:∧] Ff; ~ ,∧ ROWE1-POPE2, HAN, CAM1, GLO, IRV-BUL, ARD1, PEL1, SIG, PEN2, BEV; ~ . . . ∧ KTLY, CAM3; ~ ,— *or* ~ — ∧ THEO1 *etc.*

---

dita, who has recently had misgivings about the future course of her own love, thinks of herself as she adds [these words]." For more about greensickness and primroses in Sh. and other writers, see PAFFORD (ed. 1963, pp. 170-2).
    1939 bold Oxlips] Opposing THIRLBY's emendation, STEEVENS (ed. 1778): "The oxlip has not a weak flexible stalk . . . but erects itself boldly in the face of the sun." GRINDON (1883, pp. 116-18) asserts that this plant is not the true oxlip, *Primula elatior*, but the one GERARD (1597, p. 635) calls the "Field Oxelip, *Primula pratensis inodora lutea*." RYDÉN (1978, pp. 72-3), however, classifies the plant as *P. veris* X *vulgaris*; he adds, "His [Sh.'s] epithet here merely refers to the height of the oxlip as compared with the low primrose" (see also RYDÉN, p. 25). DE BRAY (1982, p. 38) comes full circle by classifying his oxlip as *P. elatior*, with which *OED*, citing this line, agrees. Earlier, CALDECOTT (MS 1813-33) identifies the oxlip as the greater cowslip; according to GERARD, the two plants, both primulas, are very similar; and according to *OED*, the oxlip is "now ascertained to be a natural hybrid between the cowslip and primrose." *OED* does not consider that *bold* means "striking to the eye" (*a.* 8) but, figuratively, "daring, fearless" (*a.* 1, citing this line). However, Perdita might characterize oxlips as bold because primulas "are the first among those plants that do flower in the spring, or . . . they flower with the first" (GERARD, p. 639). HAPPÉ (1969) contrasts *bold* with *pale* (1936).
    1940 Crowne Imperiall] ELLACOMBE (1896, p. 65): "A Fritillary (*F. imperialis*)." A showy plant, it was much admired; ELLACOMBE quotes Chapman ("Emperor of Flowers") and George Herbert ("A gallant flower"). According to DYER (1916, 1:513 n.), the plant was a novelty, "first described from Belgian gardens by [Matthias] Lobel [*stirpium adversaria nova*] in 1576." SAVAGE (1923, p. 57): It and the oxlip "blossom at the same time."
    1941 Flowre-de-Luce] The fleur-de-lis. GERARD (1597, pp. 45 ff.), describing some 20 varieties, identifies the flower as the iris; in this he agrees with COOPER (1565), SKINNER (1671), and other early botanists and is followed by modern authorities, including CHITTENDEN & SYNGE (1965-9) and DE BRAY (1982, p. 84). That Sh. calls it a lily is evident, however, and BEISLY (1864, p. 84) does too: "The white *lily* (Lilium album)." ELLACOMBE (1896, p. 101): "Shakespeare meant the Iris as the flower given by Perdita, and we need not be surprised at his classing it among the Lilies. Botanical classification was not very accurate in his day, and long after his time two such celebrated men as Redouté and De Candolle did not hesitate to include in the 'Liliaceæ', not only Irises, but Daffodils, Tulips, Fritillaries, and even Orchids." RYDÉN (1973, p. 194) gives a current opinion: *Flower-de-luce* (from the French *fleur de Louis*) is an Iris type (and, accordingly, no kind of lily in the botanical sense), perhaps

the common I. pseudacorus. . . . This is GERARD's "bastard Flower deluce," "called in Latin *Iris palustris lutea, Pseudoacorus,* and *Acorus Palustris*" (p. 46). Shakespeare also . . . may have meant the cultivated Iris germanica (most likely Lyte's "Iris Germanica" or GERARD's "Iris vulgaris") but the possible species/varieties are many [in Swedish].

1941-3 **O . . . ore**] FURNESS (ed. 1898): "A change of construction due to change of thought. . . . Perdita begins by wishing for enough flowers to make garlands of for all her companions and for Florizel, at the mere thought of whom the wish springs up not only for enough to make garlands for him, but to strew him o'er and o'er." The lonely parenthesis in line 1942 suggests, rather, that some text is missing. HAPPÉ (1969, Strew): "The word is appropriate to the action of putting flowers on a grave (cf. [*Ham.* 5.1.246 (3438) and *Cym.* 4.2.285 (2606)])." It is even more appropriate as "to cover (. . . any surface) with something loosely scattered or sprinkled" (*OED, v.* 2b, citing this line).

1941 **O, these**] FURNESS (ed. 1898): "'O', which we perceive to be almost meaningless . . . , GARRICK [in his *Florizel and Perdita* (1758, p. 21)] reads as an abbreviation of *of* [o'these], which I incline to think is the true reading."

1942 **you**] PARRY (ed. 1982): "The shepherdesses."

1944-7 **What . . . armes**] TRAVERSI (1969, pp. 312-13), missing the point: "The previous references to 'maladies' and unconsummated fading [1936-9] find their natural climax in Florizel's pathetically romantic evocation of the idea of death." But Florizel is teasing. TRAVERSI is right, however, about "the spontaneous warmth and confidence of Perdita's reply." BATTENHOUSE (1980, pp. 125-6) observes parallels in Canticles, but they seem remote. For example: "This confession of love . . . is like the shepherd-maiden's in the Song of Solomon who pictured her lover amid lilies (vi, 2) and spoke of his left hand under her head and his right hand embracing her (ii, 6)." VOSS (ed. 1829) has a better parallel in *TN* 2.4.59-60 (948), although the passage asks that a lover's corpse not be strewn with flowers. COOPER (1977, p. 177): "The love she imagines is open, joyous and unashamed. . . . Her associations are all with life, fertility, 'creating Nature.'" BARBER & WHEELER (1986, p. 300): "Holiday liberty moves young people away from family ties, out of the aegis of the older generation, freeing impulse from inhibition in the process of forming new ties in a new generation. Everyday decorum gives way to holiday liberty."

1945 **banke**] MURRY (1936, p. 384) is uncertain "whether these banks [this one, one in *TN* 1.1.6 (10), and one in *Tmp.* 4.1.64 (1722)] are the banks of lanes or rivers." THIRLBY (MS 1747-53), however: "Of flowers." BARBER (1959, p. 136 n.): "A recurrent feature of the type of pastoral which begins with something like 'As I walked forth one morn in May' is a bank of flowers. . . . This motif appears in the 'bank where the wild thyme blows' where Titania sleeps 'lull'd in these flowers by dances and delight' (*MND* 2.1.254 [635]). In such references there is a magical suggestion that love is infused with nature's vitality by contact."

Loue] SCHANZER (ed. 1969): "Cupid," but if he is the bank, she would be Love. FRYE (*Natural Perspective,* 1965, pp. 154-5), on love and death in Sh.'s comedies, discovers Eros (Love) identified here with Adonis, from whose blood a purple flower sprang (*Ven.* 1167-70).

play] HAPPÉ (1969): "She approaches sexuality with tact and reticence, and yet there is a frank acceptance of it. . . . The emotional associations . . . here are totally different from those aroused by Leontes' similar pun [269-70])."

1946-7 **Not . . . armes**] SCHMIDT (1874, Corse): Florizel's *Coarse* (1944) means "dead body," like the *corps* of 2794, and Perdita's means "a body in general" (*OED*, Corpse, *sb.* 1). HOLLAND (1964, p. 298) discovers an allusion to Perdita as Proserpina (see n. 2915), "the goddess of death, Mother Earth." SMITH (1966, p. 51), on the contrary: "Perdita is herself the lost Proserpina who will bring back spring to the court of Sicily and the heart of her mother." With some adjustments to the text,

Me thinkes I play as I haue seene them do
In Whitson-Pastorals: Sure this Robe of mine
Do's change my disposition: 1950 (2▌
    Flo. What you do,
Still betters what is done. When you speake (Sweet)
I'ld haue you do it euer: When you sing,

1952 betters] better F4
1953, 1954 I'ld] I'le F4-ROWE3

MENDILOW (1967, pp. 263-4) considers several interpretations possible and possibly coexisting, principally "not like a corpse <= dead body>; or if like a corpse <= body, whether dead or living>, then not like a dead one to be buried, but a living one to be embraced." This explanation is also found in BETHELL (ed. 1956), who comments on the supposed resemblance of the idea to Bellario's as she lies upon a flowery bank: "you sweete ones all [flowers], Let me unworthy presse you: I could wish I rather were a Course strewd 'ore with you, Then quicke above you" (Beaumont and Fletcher, *Philaster* [1609], 4.6.3-6). BETHELL notes, "If Shakespeare had the passage in mind, he has completely reversed the original thought, turning a melancholic desire for death into a triumphant assertion of love and life." Discussing the possible influence of Beaumont and Fletcher upon Sh., MUIR (1957, p. 239) mentions these lines inconclusively, but he leads MAXWELL (1958, p. 316) to remark that "it looks as if *Philaster*, where the lines are much less organic, were the debtor." PAFFORD (ed. 1963): "The lines seem organic in *Philaster* which is almost certainly earlier." See p. 613.

    1947 **But quicke**] MINSHEU (1617, Quicke): "Aliue." HUNTER (ed. 1872): "Unless buried alive." MARSH (1962; 1980, p. 149): "*Quick* suggests not only life as opposed to death, but also in its connotation of rapid movement, the passion and physical joy and the beauty of being young and in love. It is . . . the supreme affirmation of life, which can contemplate death steadily, and yet affirm that despite the inevitable end, life is supremely worth living." DAVIES (1986, p. 159): "It connotes haste, her passion's delighted urgency; and . . . the 'quick' life of the unborn child moving in the body of the mother," an association that perhaps would have surprised Perdita.

    Come . . . flours] THIRLBY (MS 1725-33?): "To Florizel." HERFORD (ed. 1916-): "She breaks off suddenly, conscious of the daring frankness into which her ardour has betrayed her, and excuses it as 'acting.'" See n. 1926-47. BARBER (1959, p. 127): "Her recovery is as exquisite as her impulse toward surrender: she comes back to herself by seeing her gesture as the expression of the occasion. She makes the festive clothes she wears mean its transforming power." PARRY (ed. 1982): "Presumably she gives Florizel some 'flowers of middle summer' too . . . since she has none 'of the spring.'"

    1948-50 **I play . . . disposition**] BASKERVILLE (1929, p. 9): "Indications are that summer games with pastoral features prevailed in the Cotswold region at least from the latter part of the sixteenth century till the middle of the seventeenth." THIRLBY (MS 1747-53) quotes *TGV* 4.4.158-61 (1977-80): "At *Pentecost* [Whitsunday, the seventh Sunday after Easter], When all our Pageants of delight were plaid [etc.]." Since Easter falls between 22 Mar. and 25 Apr., Pentecost may be as early as the second week of May and as late as the second week of June. MOORMAN (ed. 1912) thinks, rather, that "the reference is probably to the English morris-dances which were frequently performed at Whitsuntide." See n. 1988. FURNESS (ed. 1898): "It would be hardly fitting that Perdita should compare her speech and actions to anything less refined than a Pastoral, and it was only at Whitsuntide that she would be likely to see any theatrical performances at all." CHAMBERS (1903, 1:173 n.), however: "The May-game is probably intended," that being May Day festivities presided over by a May king and queen. WILSON (ed. 1931) follows CHAMBERS: "Perdita seems rather to have in mind some kind of flower-dance, perhaps with herself playing Maid Marian to Florizel's Robin, and it should be noted that mad Ophelia, who goes through much the same action with flowers as Perdita does, is given the snatch, clearly from some folk-song, 'For bonny sweet Robin is all my joy'" (*Ham.* 4.5.187 [2938]). EVANS (ed. 1974): "Perdita thinks of them [May games and dances] as somewhat indecent and is surprised at herself, a modest girl, for talking in their vein."

MACDONALD (1883, pp. 153-4): "She does not mean this [that her disposition has changed] seriously. But the robe has more to do with it than she thinks. . . . It is the robe that opens the door of her speech, and, by elevating her consciousness of herself, betrays her into what is only natural to her, but seems to her, on reflection, inconsistent with her low birth and poor education." CHARLTON (ed. 1916): "Perdita has none of the effusiveness of the general heroine of romance. This semi-apology for her rapturous confession of love adds as much dignity to her character as Hamlet's 'Something too much of this' [3.2.74 (1925)] does to his." BETHELL (ed. 1956) finds the Whitsunday association complexly significant: Sh. "links a late-summer sheep-shearing [see n. 1887] with spring festivities, suggesting the whole range of nature's development from first growth to fruition, and further links the natural order in its pagan expression (references to pagan deities [Flora, for example; see n. 1799]) with the Christian supernatural (Whitsun). . . . [Here] a boy actor plays a princess, thought to be a shepherdess, playing a queen's part at a festival and comparing herself to one who plays another queen's part at another festival!" STYAN (1975, p. 215): "The lines warn us that there is another Perdita to come. Polixenes . . . has watched the celebration from the periphery: when he stops it, reality returns. But the final movement of the play is coloured now by the ideal picture of the role she played in the inner play, and the theme of fulfilment is carried in the mind's eye as an image of Perdita 'the queen of curds and cream' to match the harmony of the fifth act." JONAS (1918, pp. 402-3) finds other theatrical allusions at 269-71, 1210-11, 1764-5, 2467-9, 2533-4, 3088-9, and 3365-9, and see n. 269-72.

1949-50 **Sure . . . disposition**] TAYLOR (1973, pp. 342-3): "To the onlookers, Perdita's royalty becomes outwardly recognizable, in the ceremonious gift-giving and the gorgeousness of her person and demeanour. But Perdita acknowledges a deep internal change — her word 'disposition' means 'nature' or 'temperament', not just whim. She cannot see how beautiful she is, but she seems to feel royalty in herself, as if in the play of her muscles, the flow of her language, and the largeness of her emotion. It is as if royalty were a great passion which, at this moment, she feels for the first time." CALDERWOOD (1987, p. 71), similarly: "Clothing is a kind of cultural second nature that confirms the natural status of the wearer. The trick, of course, is that the clothing must fit, which means that it must be tailored not just to the outward anatomy but to the inward parts as well. . . . The robe that makes her [Perdita] queen of the sheep-shearing festival . . . only confirms her natural status as a princess by concealing her seemingly natural status as a peasant. This enhancement of nature is familiarly glossed by Polixenes when he explains that gillyflowers . . . are improved by an art that 'is Nature'" (see 1908 and n.).

1949 **Robe**] LINTHICUM (1936, p. 213): "A generic term for clothes in general."

1951-62 **What . . . Queenes**] MOUNT ("Sidney," 1893) finds the origin of the speech in Sidney's *Arcadia*: "The force of love . . . doth so enchain the lover's judgement upon her that holds the reins of his mind that whatsoever she doth is ever in his eyes best. And that best, being by the continual motion of our changing life turned by her into any other thing, that thing again becometh best. . . . If she sit still, that is best. . . . If she walk, no doubt that is best. . . . If she be silent, that without comparison is best; since by that means the untroubled eye most freely may devour the sweetness of his object. But if she speak, he will take it upon his death that is best; the quintessence of each word being distilled down into his affected soul" (ed. Evans, 1977, p. 682). The similarity of the speeches is striking, despite the difference in the actions and their order; see ANDREWS (1972, p. 200) for more detail. HUDSON (ed. 1880): "Perdita does everything so charmingly, that her latest doing always seems the best. Thus each later deed of hers is aptly said to *crown* what went before; and all her acts are made queens in virtue of this coronation." WILSON (ed. 1931): "The fact that she is Queen of the Feast adds point." MUIR (*Last Periods*, 1961, p. 50): "By the consecration of her grace and beauty Perdita transforms the most mundane occupations into phases of enchantment." GOLDMAN (1972, p. 131): "He [Sh.] is describing a secular version of grace; Perdita betters her own nature in every act."

BETHELL (1947, p. 24): "The first six lines introduce the serious world of buying and selling, praying and giving alms into a lover's fancy and so strengthen it into more than fancy; an ideal attitude which is capable of application to the real. . . . The last three and a half lines restate more carefully what is said in the first two[, which] may be taken as meaning: 'Whatever you do is done the better because it is you who do it' (i.e., 'you bring a new grace to every action') . . . : 'Each of your acts is better than the preceding'; or again, straining the meaning a little: 'Your performance of any action is better than that of others'. Correspondingly, the last three and a half lines may mean: 'Now, in your present actions (i.e., 'in the present deeds'), everything you do, uniquely good in each detail, lends distinction to ('crowns') the deed itself ('what you are doing'), so that all your acts are pre-eminent' — the deed, itself indifferent, is dignified by the performer. Or we may perhaps say: 'Your performance of it ('each your doing'), uniquely good in each detail, makes superior ('crowns') whatever you may be doing *at present* ('in the present deeds'), so that all your acts are (successively) pre-eminent'. In this interpretation the lover sees his mistress' deeds as a scale of rising perfections. Thirdly . . . 'Your performance of it, uniquely good in each detail, renders superior what *you* are doing, among the deeds of all present ('present deeds' being now understood as a reference to place and not time), so that all your acts are pre-eminent.'"

EDWARDS ("Seeing," 1986, pp. 88-9): "What . . . done" (1951-2) "is often misunderstood to mean 'is an improvement on what you last did'. The ending of the speech [1959-62] explains the beginning. . . . As Dr Johnson [ed. 1765] put it, 'Your manner in each act crowns the act'. 'What you do / Still *betters* what is done'. That is to say, whatever you do always improves, or raises in value, the thing that is done. . . . For Florizel, the acted presentation of the spring is as beautiful and real as anything else that Perdita has done; her role as [Flora] as beautiful and real as anything else that Perdita has been. . . . 'What the imagination seizes as beauty must be truth. . . .' That is really the import of Florizel's speech, and it is the underlying meaning not only of Perdita's impersonation of the spring-goddess but of the whole play." MIRIAM JOSEPH (1947, pp. 149-50) uses lines 1959-62 to illustrate "auxesis . . . a figure which advances from less to greater by arranging words or clauses in a sequence of increasing force." For the importance of beautiful speech to a lover, see MEADER (1954, pp. 69-71); VICKERS (1971, pp. 97-8) uses this passage to illustrate Sh.'s mastery of the formal schemes of rhetoric.

EWBANK (1964, pp. 94-5): "Florizel's adoration is formulated as a desire to arrest time, to achieve permanence outside the flux of time. . . . The thinking is not naive, it is wishful, and consciously so." WALLER (1970, p. 136), similarly: "Florizel's idealization of his love and desire to have Perdita's beauty incarnated in all experience is expressed through terms implying a continual and restless temporal movement and a constant change of activity. . . . And yet . . . Florizel can express his desire for permanence only in terms provoking a greater sense of transience, in that he wants

I'ld haue you buy, and sell so: so giue Almes,
Pray so: and for the ord'ring your Affayres,   1955
To sing them too. When you do dance, I wish you
A waue o'th Sea, that you might euer do
Nothing but that: moue still, still so:
And owne no other Function. Each your doing,

1958 moue] but so move KEIGHTLEY *conj. in* CAM1, KTLY
   so] so, my fair CAP
1958-9 *Verse lines ending* own . . . doing, MAL-KNT1 (−v1821), HUD, SING2, HAL
   1959 doing] doing is HUD2

---

to resist any change to Perdita's beauty." NEELY (1975, p. 331): "He calls attention not to her conventional looks or abstract virtues, but to her particular *actions*: singing, speaking, buying, selling, praying. Aware of the 'singular' grace of each action . . . he merely points to her 'doing.'" LANGMAN (1976, p. 198): "This is no attempt either to exclude the mundane or to elevate it: rather, it is to accept the ordinariness of life, in an acceptance irradiated by the presence of the beloved. . . . She turns each moment of existence into delight, delight at all she is." DRAPER (1985, p. 31): "That such a response is not merely the dazzled effect of love is confirmed by [Polixenes at 1976–8] and [Camillo at 1980–1]."

   For other appreciative analyses, see KERMODE (ed. 1963, p. xxiv) and KNIGHTS (1976, pp. 603–4). LINDENBAUM (1972, p. 17), however: "If Shakespeare had wanted us to accept these sentiments without qualification, he probably would not have had Perdita object to them."

   1952 **Still betters**] DEIGHTON (ed. 1889): "Ever improves." For the part of speech of *betters*, see ABBOTT §290.

   1952-3 **When . . . euer**] The CLARKES (1879, p. 697): "The exigencies of the dramatic dialogue and situation, as well as the eloquent power in the words themselves, have forced upon the author the necessity of not only commenting upon his own phrases, but of commending them."

   1953-9 **When . . . Function**] WELLS ("Romance," 1966, pp. 67–8): "We remember Polixenes' description of the time when he and Leontes, the fathers of this pair, were 'Two lads that thought there was no more behind But such a day to-morrow as to-day, And to be boy eternal' [125–7]. The lines look forward too to the illusion created by the last scene, that time the conqueror has been conquered: an illusion created partly by the presence of this same Perdita."

   1955 **ord'ring**] DEIGHTON (ed. 1889): "Arranging, disposing, of."

   1956 **sing them too**] MARSH (1962; 1980, p. 149): "There is just a touch of irony . . . in the idea of Perdita's doing everything in song, though . . . the suggestion of harmony is not ironical. There is a touch of absurdity in the idea of singing the ordering of her affairs; clearly she must progress, and each succeeding thing 'betters what is done.'"

   1956-62 **When . . . Queenes**] HALE (1985, p. 149): "The speech is in character, for it has all the youthfulness which Aristotle found in hyperbole as such [*Rhetoric* 3.11.16]." The passage in Aristotle is translated by Rhys Roberts as "Hyperboles are for young men to use," but by Lawson-Tancred as "Exaggerations are also puerile."

   1956-9 **When . . . Function**] SMITH (1966, p. 50): "The paradox is concentrated in the image of the ever-changing wave of the changeless sea and in the am-

(So singular, in each particular)   1960
Crownes what you are doing, in the present deeds,
That all your Actes, are Queenes.
 Perd. O *Doricles*,
Your praises are too large: but that your youth
And the true blood which peepes fairely through't,   1965
Do plainly giue you out an vnstain'd Shepherd

1961 Crownes . . . are doing] Crowning . . . have done HUD2
 deeds] deed mTBY4 *conj.*, SPEDDING *conj. in* CAM1, GLO, HUD2, WH2, OXF1,
KIT1, PEL1
 1962 Queenes] queen's SING2, KTLY
 1965 peepes fairely through't] peeps forth fairly through it ROWE1-JOHN2, v1773;
peeps so fairly through't mLONG *conj.*, CAP, COL2, WH1, COL3, DYCE2, COL4, HUD2,
NLSN, KIT1, PEL1, OXF2; peeps fairly through it v1778-MAL, v1821, COL1, SING2, DYCE1,
HAL, STAU, DEL, OXF1; fairly peeps through it v1793-v1813, SING1, HUD1, KTLY; peep-
eth fairly through't mTBY4 *conj.*, GLO, WH2, CAM3; fairly peeps through't PEN1
 1966-7 Shepherd∧ . . . wisedome,] ~ , . . . ~ , ROWE; ~ , . . . ~ ∧ POPE1+

---

biguity of 'still' as associated with it. Florizel desires to control Time, to preserve each
of his humble mistress's queenly actions forever. But to keep each graceful gesture
'still' in the sense of keeping it always is to make it 'still' by robbing it of its essence,
which is movement, the evidence of life. It . . . turns the beloved to stone." Which
probably takes a lover's hyperbole too literally. TURNER (1971, p. 157): "A wave
moves, while the water itself is still. Perdita's beauty is the reconciliation of time and
eternity: of movement and stillness." BERRY (1981, pp. 124-5), comparing *Son.* 60:
"'Wave' is in Shakespeare the metaphor for rhythmic movement, and thus the principle of life itself. . . . 'Move still, still so' conveys the steady momentum of the
waves, apparently unchanging in themselves and in their relation to each other, yet
always in motion." BERRY also considers (pp. 125-7) the thematic importance of the
"alternative term" *dance* and the dances at 1988-9 and 2164. BRISSENDEN (1981, p.
89): "The sea is a major force in the play, and [this] phrase . . . contains the idea of
movement which remains nevertheless in one place: a wave rising then slipping back,
a dancer swaying to and fro." ESTRIN (1985, p. 120): "When Perdita moves, she
inspires Florizel to imagine the stillness (eternity) of her reproductive powers."
 1958 **Nothing . . . so**] ABBOTT (§509): Four accents; cf. 428. However, "here
still, which means 'always', is remarkably emphatic, and may, perhaps, be pronounced as a quasi-disyllable."
 moue . . . so] The CLARKES (ed. 1865): The words suggest "the to-and-fro
undulation of the water—the swing of the wave." ORGEL (ed. 1996): "Both perpetual
movement and stillness." BETHELL (1947, p. 24): A wave "with the two 'stills' upon
the crest. The unconscious effect of this . . . is to associate not only Perdita's dancing but the whole spring festival with the sea, so that Perdita in her dual relationship
to the sea and the spring season grows poetically into a symbol of life and creative
energy—a compound of Flora . . . with an Aphrodite chastened by prayer and alms-
giving." For other iterations, see 75, 1323, 1387, 1545, and 2807.
 1959 **owne**] The CLARKES (ed. 1865): To mean "possess," Sh. "generally employs
'owe.'" SCHMIDT (1875) gives only one other instance of *own* in this sense, *Cor.* 1.8.3
(727), which, like *WT*, is thought to derive from a scribal transcript. *OED*, citing this

line, gives "to have as one's function" (*v.* 2b) rather than "possess" (2a), but the CLARKES' observation remains valid.

Function] HUNTER (ed. 1872): "Faculty of motion." DEIGHTON (ed. 1889): "Occupation." PARRY (ed. 1982): incorporates both: "Have nothing else to do (but dance)."

1959-62 **Each . . . Queenes**] ZESMER (1976, p. 430): "His chief metaphor is chosen from royalty, although neither he nor Perdita as yet knows that what he says is literally true. . . . Polixenes senses that Perdita's bearing 'smacks of something greater than herself' [1977], and Camillo compresses her refinement and rusticity into an incisive image, 'the queen of curds and cream' [1981]."

1960 **singular**] On the one hand, the CLARKES (ed. 1865): "'Singularly excellent', 'select'" and SCHMIDT (1875): "Unparalleled." On the other, PORTER & CLARKE (ed. 1908): "Individual" and NEILSON & HILL (ed. 1942): "Distinctly yours."

particular] SCHMIDT (1875): "Single thing."

1961 **Crownes**] SCHMIDT (1874): "To top, to cover as with a crown."

in . . . deeds] FURNESS (ed. 1898): "Florizel is referring to Perdita's present distribution of flowers and to her bearing toward her guests." BETHELL (ed. 1956) disagrees: "The passage beginning 'each your doing' forms a concluding statement . . . and we should expect it to summarize what has gone before and to echo the opening proposition. . . . 'Each your doing' most naturally means *each of the activities just named*, i.e. speaking, singing, dancing. . . . 'The present deeds' must mean . . . *the time when the activity . . . is taking place.* . . . Each activity or 'doing' is thought of as involving many contributory 'deeds'—the 'particulars' of [1960]."

1962 **That**] So that. See n. 17.

all . . . Queenes] SINGER (ed. 1856): "*I.e.*, the acts of a queen." But nearly all readers consider the noun in the nominative plural, as does the *OED* (*sb.* 6b). CALDECOTT (MS 1813-33) paraphrases as "all your acts . . . have in female perfection as it were a royal supremacy," and the CLARKES (ed. 1865) as "the grace with which you perform every act . . . renders all your acts queens."

1963 ***Doricles***] Florizel's assumed name; see n. 3382 above.

1964 **large**] SCHMIDT (1874): "Extensive" (*OED, a.* 6). HERFORD (ed. 1904): "Unreserved" (*a.* 13). PIERCE (ed. 1918): "Extravagant" (*a.* 13 also).

1964-6 **your . . . Shepherd**] J. SMITH (1974, p. 156), who is not enchanted by the lovers: "Assurances of [this] sort are common form with spellbound young women; still less confidence is commanded by the assurance proclaimed by Florizel himself [in 1834-6]."

1965 **And . . . through't**] MALONE (ed. 1790) compares Chapman, *Hero and Leander* (1598, 3:39-40): "Through whose white skin, softer than soundest sleep, With damaske eyes, the rubie blood doth peep." *OED* (Peep, *v.*² 2c, citing this line): "To show itself a little unintendedly." DEIGHTON (ed. 1889): "The blush of ingenuousness which shows itself in your youthful countenance." HERFORD (ed. 1916-), however, thinks that "Perdita [is] referring to the natural ruddiness of a healthy body"; KITTREDGE & RIBNER (ed. 1967), to his "royal blood and rearing." Regarding flushing, see nn. 1810 and 2458. CORSON (1889, p. 369), anticipated by WALKER (1860, 2:260): *Peepes* = "peeps so," to which some eds. emend. Like WALKER, FURNESS (ed. 1898) thinks *so* is absorbed by *peepes*; see n. 1810. SYMONS (in IRVING & MARSHALL, ed. 1890): "Read with a strong accent on the word *true*, a lesser accent having been laid on the first word of the line." He adds, however, "Perhaps there is some corruption in the text." SCHANZER's (ed. 1969) solution is to pronounce *blood* with two syllables, which seems grotesque.

blood] PAFFORD (ed. 1963): "Birth and breeding."

1966 **giue you out**] ROLFE (ed. 1879): "Show you." See 2831 for another meaning, although PORTER & CLARKE (ed. c. 1903) believe that it applies here.

With wisedome, I might feare (my *Doricles*)
You woo'd me the false way.
   Flo. I thinke you haue
As little skill to feare, as I haue purpose   1970
To put you to't. But come, our dance I pray,
Your hand (my *Perdita:*) so Turtles paire
That neuer meane to part.
   Perd. Ile sweare for 'em.
   Pol. This is the prettiest Low-borne Lasse, that euer   1975

1970 to] in HAN
1974 'em] one MTBY2 *conj.*, THEOBALD (1729) *conj. in* NICHOLS (1817, 2:364),
RANN
     Musick. Dance forming. CAP
1975 prettiest] pettiest POPE1

    1966-7 **Shepherd**∧ **With wisedome**] POPE's alteration of the punctuation, COR-
SON (1876) objects, connects "With wisdom" and "I might fear," "but it is properly
connected with 'unstain'd', the meaning being 'a shepherd unstain'd with wisdom',
that is, an unsophisticated shepherd, who . . . says what he thinks, frankly and without reserve, and also without flattery." CORSON cites ABBOTT §419 on adjectival
phrases transposed, but he alone thinks this is one.
    1967 **With wisedome**] LEE (ed. 1907): "On consideration."
    1968 **woo'd . . . way**] BETHELL (ed. 1956): Were "trying to seduce me by flat-
tery."
    1969-71 **I . . . to't**] HEATH (1765, p. 216): "I have given you so little occasion
to fear . . . that you as little know how to begin to fear me, as I am far from giving
you any just ground for doing it." WARBURTON (ed. 1747) more accurately glosses
skill as "reason" (*OED, sb.*[1] 3, citing this line). Cf. n. 782. HUNTER (ed. 1872) glosses
the word as "cunning; artfulness" (possibly *sb.*[1] 6). HUDSON (ed. 1880): "'To *put* you
to't' is to *give* you *cause* or *occasion for* it." See SCHMIDT (1875, Put 3, with *to*) and
n. 67-8. GOTCH (1900, p. 330), following HUNTER, paraphrases the lines as "You
have as little knowledge of fear as I have purpose of deceit," but most commentators
prefer WARBURTON's "reason."
    1971-3 **But . . . part**] LEIMBERG (1987, p. 131) thinks these lines allude to "the
'married chastity' of the Phoenix and the Turtle whose love is of that kind which,
being 'love in twain', yet has 'the essence but in one' [*PhT* 25-6]" and "the dance
of the graces as part of the cosmic dance of world-harmony." For more on hand
giving and hand holding, see n. 172-201 and line 2170.
    1972 **Turtles**] I.e., turtledoves. HOLME (1688, 2.305): "The emblem of conjugal
love, and betoke[n]th matrimonial chastity. For if one of the pair dye, the other pineth
away, and dieth for grief." Cf. TILLEY T624. HARTING (1871, pp. 191-2) cites *1H6*
2.2.30 (801) and *Tro.* 3.2.178 (1811) as well as this passage. See also SEAGER (1896,
pp. 320-1) and cf. n. 3345-8.
    paire] *OED* (*v.*[1] 4b, citing this line): "Couple or mate."
    1974 **Ile . . . 'em**] DOUCE (1807, 1:358): "A common phrase of acquiescence
[meaning] 'I'll *warrant* you'" (*OED, v.* 14, citing this line). DEIGHTON (ed. 1889): "If
this is the true reading, it probably means, 'I will answer for the constancy of turtles
like ourselves,'" the meaning of *sweare for* found in SCHMIDT (1875). PAFFORD (ed.

Ran on the greene-sord: Nothing she do's, or seemes
But smackes of something greater then her selfe,
Too Noble for this place.

   Cam. He tels her something
That makes her blood looke on't: Good sooth she is   1980

1976 seemes] says mTBY2 *conj.*, COL2, WH1, COL3, COL4
1978–9 *One verse line* mCAP2, VALPY, COL, DYCE, DEL, CAM1-KTLY, HUD2+
1980 makes . . . looke] wakes her blood:— look COL2, COL3
     on't] out mTBY2 *and* mTHEO1 *conj.*, POPE2-PEN2 (−COL1, COL2, WH1, COL3,
HAL, KTLY, SIS), OXF2, BEV4

1963): "'I'll be sworn they do.' Typical of Perdita's downright country speech." A
few think the reading is not true (see the textual notes and p. 581), but most eds.
retain it and gloss much as DEIGHTON does. TENNYSON (1897; 1905, 2:290): "He [Lord
Tennyson] would say, 'There are three repartees in Shakespeare which always bring
tears to my eyes from their simplicity,'" this line being one.

   1975–8 **This . . . place**] HERFORD (ed. 1916–): "Shakespeare is a firm believer
in the manifestation, by indelible symptoms, of royal race." HUSSEY (1992, p. 227): It
is a "romance convention [that] if the characters are noble-born, their nobility shows
through their humble surroundings." COLIE (1974, p. 273): "He . . . expresses his
delight in her loveliness in narrowly social terms, professing himself unable to believe
that anyone so beautiful could possibly spring from peasant stock." BARBER (1964, p.
238): "A typical bit of Jacobean having-it-both ways: having the rustic virtues without
forfeiting the qualities thought to have come from high birth." SCHANZER (ed. 1969,
p. 43) rightly disagrees: "Perdita is in no way presented as an exemplar of rustic
virtues. What is emphasized . . . is the fact that she is so utterly different from what
her country upbringing would lead one to expect. . . . She has not become another
Mopsa and Dorcas." He compares the princes in *Cym.* For other intimations of Perdita's royalty, see n. 1959–62. SCOTT (1963, p. 414): "He assumes despite the evidence of his senses that Perdita is low-born just as Leontes had assumed from a mis-
interpretation of what he had heard and seen that Hermione was unfaithful," a
far-fetched analogy. NEELY (1985, p. 177): "He becomes a kind of rival of his son for
the affections of the 'low-born lass' he had . . . praised here." He actually does not
speak to her again until "Ile haue thy beauty scratcht with briers" (2269).

   1976 **greene-sord**] DYCE (1853, p. 80): *Sord* is an old form of *sward*. Sh. uses
the word only here. *Greensward* is grassy turf.

   Nothing . . . seemes] HARBOTTLE (1853, p. 96): "Nothing either in her acts
or her carriage [bearing, deportment]." The CLARKES (1879, p. 589, Seems): "Appears
to be, looks."

   1977 **smackes**] MINSHEU (1617): "Taste[s]." SCHMIDT (1875): Has "a taste or tincture." BOORMAN (ed. 1964): "Strongly suggests."

   greater] MAXWELL (ed. 1956): "Of gentler blood."

   1980 **That . . . on't**] Reading *out*, THEOBALD (1726, p. 114) paraphrases as "that
calls the Blood up into her Cheeks, and makes her blush." He adduces 1964–6 as
parallel. To these lines DEIGHTON (ed. 1889) adds "her wanton spirits looke out At
euery ioynt and motiue of her body" (*Tro.* 4.5.56–7 [2613–14]), where *looke out*
means "betray or reveal themselves." PAFFORD (ed. 1963): "The main objection to
reading *out* is the apostrophe. In *F* the *n* of *on't* is directly under the last letter in
[1979]. If the MS were similarly spaced, a comma placed rather below the line after

The Queene of Curds and Creame.

Clo.   Come on: strike vp.

Dorcas.   *Mopsa* must be your Mistris: marry Garlick
to mend her kissing with.

Mop.   Now in good time.   1985

Clo.   Not a word, a word, we stand vpon our manners,
Come, strike vp.

*Heere a Daunce of Shepheards and
Shephearddesses.*

1981-91 *As* F1 *except* 1986-7 *prose* POPE, THEO, WARB, JOHN; 1981-5 *verse lines
ending* up. . . . garlick . . . time., 1986-7 *prose*, 1990-1 *verse lines ending* this
. . . daughter? HAN; 1981-5 *as* HAN, 1986-91 *verse lines ending* manners.— . . .
what . . . daughter? CAP; 1981-5 *as* HAN, 1986-91 *verse lines ending* manners.—
. . . up. . . . what . . . daughter? v1793-v1813, SING, HAL; 1981-5 *as* HAN, 1986-
91 *verse lines ending* manners; . . . up. . . . this, . . . daughter? v1773, v1821,
KNT1-COL2, DYCE1-COL3, DEL2-CLN2, SIG, EVNS, BEV; 1981 *as* F1, 1982-7 *prose*, 1990-
1 *as* F1 ARD2, PEN2; 1981-2 *one verse line*, 1983-5 *prose*, 1986-91 *as* F1 OXF2
    1987 vp] up, pipers CAP
    Musick. MAL+

---

something—and a comma before a relative *that* is common—would almost certainly
cause *out* to be read *on't*. The same mistake is found in [*TN* 3.4.202 (1719), and *Cym.*
2.3.43 (1005)]. Cf. also note to II iv.76 [1236] in *N[ew] C[ambridge] Cym.*, ed. J. C.
Maxwell." The readings in *TN* and *Cym.*, however, are not universally regarded as
mistakes, and MAXWELL's n. argues for a confusion of *out* and *on't* that no one accepts.
PAFFORD is right about the position of the apostrophe, but of the relative *that*s on
this page of F1 (Bb2ᵛ; Compositor B), those at 1929, 1933, 1937, and 1962 are preceded by commas; those at 1973, 2003, and 2004 are not. There is nothing wrong
with *look on*, moreover. *OED* (Look, *v.* 1): "The usual prep. introducing the object
of vision is now *at*; the older *to look on, to look upon*, are in the literal sense either
arch[aic], or include a mixture of the notion of mental watching or contemplation."
SCHMIDT (1874) considers *look on* simply the equivalent of modern *look at*. COLLIER
(ed. 1842): "Florizell tells Perdita something that makes his blood come into her
cheeks 'to look *on it*,'" which HARBOTTLE (1853, p. 96) makes "look out upon it."
The antecedent of *it* is the thing said. Thus F. W. CLARKE (in FURNIVALL, ed. 1908),
reading *on't*: "The blood comes to the window, the surface, to look on the words."
For other instances, see nn. 1810 and 2458.
    Good sooth] See n. 71.
    1981 **The . . . Creame**] WILSON (ed. 1931) refers to DOUCE (1807, 2:457 and
n.), who mentions that the queen in western May games was called a whitepot queen.
Cf. n. 1948-50. DOUCE adds, "What these ladies exactly were is not easy to comprehend. *Whitepot* . . . was a kind of custard," made of "milk or cream boiled with
various ingredients, as eggs, flour, raisins, sugar, spices, etc." (*OED*). Perhaps among
her other duties the queen served the whitepot. WILSON connects whitepot with this
epithet, and BETHELL (ed. 1956) finds the linkage (i.e., monarch, milk) to be a symbol
of "the proper relation of court and country." PARRY (ed. 1982): What Camillo means
is that "Perdita's blush makes her exceptional beauty even more apparent." HAPPÉ

(1969): "The line reminds us that Perdita has a symbolic role in the feast." BRISSENDEN (1981, p. 45): "Perdita, a princess in reality but unknown as such to everyone on the stage, dresses up as royalty . . . and then is called [this] by Camillo." For other intimations of Perdita's station, see n. 1959-62. Considering that such a queen would be a milkmaid rather than a shepherdess, KNOWLES (privately) suggests that Sh. may have had in mind the description of Margaret's "princely huswifery" in Greene's *Friar Bacon and Friar Bungay*: "She turned her smock over her lily arms And dived them into milk to run her cheese; But, whiter than the milk, her chrystal skin, Checked with lines of azure, made her blush That art or nature durst bring for compare" (ed. Lavin, 1969, 1.1.76-81).

    Curds] *OED* (*sb.* 1, citing this line): "The coagulated substance formed from milk."

    1982-7 **Come . . . vp**] PAFFORD (ed. 1963): "This passage . . . is almost certainly meant to be prose for these characters do not speak verse. . . . The fact that the lines can be treated as blank verse probably illustrates a writer's difficulty in changing to a short passage of prose."

    1983 **Mistris**] BETHELL (ed. 1956): "'Partner' for the dance." For partners' kissing, see the next n.

    1983-4 **marry . . . with**] FURNESS (ed. 1898): *Marry* "is the common expletive" — expressing "asseveration, surprise, indignation, etc." (*OED, int.*). For *Garlick*, HUNTER (ed. 1872), strangely: "You will be garlic," and DYER (1884, pp. 538-9) finds a veiled allusion to the kiss as "the recognized fee of a lady's partner" in a dance. GOTCH (1900, p. 330) unconvincingly suggests that "Dorcas offers him [the Clown] something in imitation of Perdita's recent distribution of flowers and calls it garlic." DEIGHTON (ed. 1889): "You will need to fill your mouth with garlic to endure her strong breath when you kiss her," but Dorcas is speaking to Mopsa, not to the Clown. PAFFORD (ed. 1963): "Give her some garlic, it will make her kissing more fragrant"; this, as CALDECOTT (MS 1813-33) had noted, would be "a strong cure." KITTREDGE & RIBNER (ed. 1967): "[S]he is joking, of course," but one doubts it.

    1985 **in good time**] RANN (ed. 1787): "I'll assure you," sarcastically. PORTER & CLARKE (ed. 1908): "Mopsa is stirred up, but being weak in repartee only gets in [this] rustic exclamation." SCHMIDT (1875): "The French *à la bonne heure*, used . . . to express . . . astonishment and indignation" (*OED*, Time 42c). WILSON (ed. 1931): "Well, I never!" BETHELL (ed. 1956): "What (will you say) next?" HAPPÉ (1969): "Much depends upon the tone in which this is said. Mopsa might express indignation at the suggestion that her breath is offensive, or at the attempt to pair her with the Clown: or she may acquiesce with apparent reluctance."

    1986 **Not a word**] HERFORD (ed. 1904): "The clown checks Mopsa's angry retort in the presence of strangers."

    we . . . manners] JOHNSON (ed. 1765): "We are now on our [best] behaviour." For *stand vpon*, CALDECOTT (MS 1813-33): "Make a point of" (*OED*, Stand, *v.* 78g). SCHANZER (ed. 1969): "Value, set store by" (78j).

    1988 ***Daunce***] SORELL (1957, p. 381): A brawl, "a kind of French dance resembling a cotillon" (*OED, sb.*[3]), which in France was performed by young ladies and gentlemen disguised as peasants and shepherds. BROWN (1962, p. 225): "It is a ceremonious dance which . . . is an imitation of the pristine *order* of all created things, or of matrimony." Cf. n. 2164 and see p. 859. LONG (1961, pp. 78-9): Perhaps a roundel, used "to symbolize the union of the lovers."

    STUDING (1970, p. 71): "In actuality, an antimasque dance. . . . A pre-nuptial dance in the spirit of pagan ritual; . . . also the grand climax of Perdita's highly sexual rhetoric and seduction of the prince," for which see n. 1926-47. BRISSENDEN (1981, pp. 93-4) reverses this: "The love between Perdita and Florizel is wonderfully affirmed, leading to the dance of shepherds and shepherdesses, equivalent to the

Pol. Pray good Shepheard, what faire Swaine is this,   1990
Which dances with your daughter?
Shep. They call him *Doricles*, and boasts himselfe
To haue a worthy Feeding; but I haue it
Vpon his owne report, and I beleeue it:

1990 Pray] I pray mTBY2 *conj.*, HAN; Pray you WALKER (1860, 3:105) *conj.*, KTLY, HUD2
    this,] ~ . JOHN
1991 Which] Who POPE1-JOHN2, v1773
1992 and] and he ROWE1-JOHN2, v1773-v1813, SING1, HUD1, KTLY; he CAP
1993 Feeding] breeding WARBURTON *conj. in* HAN2, HAN, WARB, COL2
    but . . . it] I have it but HUNTER (1845, 1:423) *conj.*, SING2, KTLY; I but have it mTBY2 *conj.*, SEYMOUR (1805, 1:168) *conj.*, DYCE2, COL4, HUD2, BUL

---

masquers' dance — as indeed it is, since Florizel is disguised . . . and Perdita is wearing the 'borrowed flaunts' of her festival costume, as well as bearing her unknown identity as Leontes' daughter." CALDWELL (1984, p. 282): This "masque dance celebrates the future nuptials of Florizel and Perdita and confirms their verbally exchanged vows: the second antimasque dance of satyrs [at 2164] adumbrates Polixenes' disruption of banquet and betrothal." KING (1992, p. 93): "There is an interval of 175 lines between the Dance of Shepherds and Shepherdesses . . . and the Dance of Twelve Satyrs [1989 to 2164]; this allows time for six men who play Shepherds and six boys who play Shepherdesses to double as the twelve Satyrs." For more on antimasque, see n. 2164. CALDWELL finds other resemblances to the masque in this scene, but they are tenuous. BERRY (1988, p. 177): The dance "is an image of social harmony, with royalty and commoners moving in concert."

    1991 **Which**] For this use of the relative, see n. 572.

      daughter] WALKER (1854, p. 206), citing *Ham.* 1.3.117 (583) and other instances: "A trisyllable."

    1992 **and boasts**] For omission of the pronoun, see n. 299-300. Although *OED* offers no parallel, *boasts* may be used with reduced force — "speaking favorably of himself, he says." SCHANZER (ed. 1969): "Probably 'and, they say, he boasts himself . . .' is to be understood, setting off what others say about Doricles from what he himself has told the Shepherd."

    1993 **worthy Feeding**] THIRLBY (MS 1733-47?) equating "bounds of feede" (*AYL* 2.4.83 [868]): "Range of pasture land" (*OED*, Feed, *sb.* 2a). JOHNSON (ed. 1765): "A track of pasturage not inconsiderable, not unworthy of my daughter's fortune" (see *OED*, Feeding, *vbl. sb.* 3). CAPELL (1783, 2.4:175): "Maintenance, and income equal to it." ANON. (MS 1790-) MS4's "Good bringing up" is echoed by COLLIER (ed. 1858, 6:glos.), but *OED*'s latest record of *feed* in this sense is dated c. 1400. DELIUS (ed. 1860), incidentally: *Feeder* in *AYL* 2.4.99 (886), which some eds. adduce to explain *feeding* here, does not mean "shepherd" but "menial."

      but I] DYCE (ed. 1864) justifies the transposition of these words by reference to WALKER (1860, 2:246), who collects examples of this error in Sh.'s texts; many, like this one, are questionably erroneous. See the next n.

    1993-4 **but . . . report**] Eds. retaining the F reading explain it, when they do, with some strain. WHITE (ed. 1857), for example, devises an etymology for *but* that makes it "nearly equivalent to 'and.'" ABBOTT (§128): "*But* perhaps means 'only' . . . *i.e.* 'I have it *merely* on his own report, and I believe it too.'" See n. 711

He lookes like sooth: he sayes he loues my daughter,   1995
I thinke so too; for neuer gaz'd the Moone
Vpon the water, as hee'l stand and reade
As 'twere my daughters eyes: and to be plaine,
I thinke there is not halfe a kisse to choose
Who loues another best.   2000
    Pol. She dances featly.
    Shep. So she do's any thing, though I report it
That should be silent: If yong *Doricles*

1995 sooth:] ~ ? THEO3, THEO4
2000 Who] Which HAN
     another] the other HAN, RANN
2002 So] *Om*. WARB

---

for *but* more clearly in this sense. ROLFE (ed. 1879): Perhaps "one of those cases in which an intermediate thought is 'understood' but not expressed: he boasts of his farm; <a mere boast, you may say> *but* I have his word for it." ROLFE compares the use of *but* in 1657. FURNESS (ed. 1898) considers "the clause: 'boasts . . . feeding' as an indirect quotation, a continuation, in fact, of the common report which gave him the name Doricles[.] 'They call him Doricles and (they say) boasts . . .' etc."

    1995 **lookes like sooth**] CALDECOTT (MS 1813–33): "Carries a face of truth & honesty." Cf. n. 71.

    1996–8 **for . . . eyes**] SPURGEON (1935, p. 306): "The great natural movements seem the normal mode of expression and comparison" in *WT*, as here and also at 2908–9 and 2975. PETERSON (*Time*, 1973, p.182), alone: "The comparison seems innocent enough; but the moon is often associated with inconstancy and lawlessness." EGGERS (1979, p. 467) finds other instances of incapacitating exchanges of eyes, in *WT* 3021–2, *Cym.* 5.5.393–8 (3713–19), and *Tmp.* 1.2.487–93 (653–8).

    1997 **as**] PAFFORD (ed. 1963): "In such a manner as." HAPPÉ (1969): "So intensely as."

    1997–8 **hee'l . . . eyes**] Cited by WHITER (1794; 1967, pp. 101–2) to illustrate the association of "the *book* and the *eye of beauty*" in Sh.'s imagination. ARMSTRONG (1963, pp. 171–2) cites a dozen more instances of "the remarkable association between love and books."

    1997 **reade**] OED (*v*. 3c, citing this line): "Peruse," used figuratively. For a similar use, see n. 1514. KITTREDGE & RIBNER (ed. 1967), ignoring the metaphor: "Gaze into."

    1999 **halfe . . . choose**] OED (Choose, *v*. 12, citing this line): "No ground of preference," as in "not a pin (or the like) to choose between them."

    2000 **another**] CALDECOTT (MS 1813–33): "The other." See n. 1462.

    2001 **featly**] JOHNSON (1755): "Neatly; nimbly" (*OED, adv*. 2b, citing this line). CALDECOTT (MS 1813–33): "Elegantly" (*OED* 1). BETHELL (ed. 1956): "Ably," the sense in which "the Shepherd understands the word." *OED*'s nearest approximations are "aptly" (1) and "skilfully" (2). KNOWLES (privately): "With a pun; cf. *Tmp*. 1.2.380 (524)."

    2002–3 **though . . . silent**] DEIGHTON (ed. 1889): "I who, as her father, ought not to sing her praises." The general idea is proverbial; DENT compares TILLEY S114.

Do light vpon her, she shall bring him that
Which he not dreames of.   *Enter Seruant.* 2005
   Ser. O Master: if you did but heare the Pedler at the
doore, you would neuer dance againe after a Tabor and
Pipe: no, the Bag-pipe could not moue you: hee singes
seuerall Tunes, faster then you'l tell money: hee vtters
them as he had eaten ballads, and all mens eares grew to   2010
his Tunes.
   Clo. He could neuer come better: hee shall come in:
I loue a ballad but euen too well, if it be dolefull matter
merrily set downe: or a very pleasant thing indeede, and
sung lamentably.   2015
   Ser. He hath songs for man, or woman, of all sizes: (2)

2005 SCENE VI. POPE, HAN, WARB, JOHN
2010 grew] grow ROWE3-POPE2, HAN, HUD2, KIT1
2013 be] be a COL4

2004 **light vpon**] SCHMIDT (1874): "Fall to the share of." BOORMAN (ed. 1964):
"I.e. choose." PETERSON (*Time*, 1973, p. 183) alone finds a sexual double meaning.
   2004-5 **she . . . of**] HARDINGE (1818, 3:77): "Referring . . . to her bundle and
the jewels [i.e., the jewel about the neck of Hermione's mantle — 3043]." DEIGHTON
(ed. 1889): "Unexpected wealth."
   2005 **not dreames**] For the omission of *do* before *not*, see ABBOTT §305. ROLFE
(ed. 1879) compares 2250, 2322.
   Enter Seruant.] BOORMAN (ed. 1964): "Note the suspense of the half-divulged
secret, interrupted by the servant."
   2006-11 **O . . . Tunes**] The peddler, the bagpipe, and the (printed) ballads obviously belong to Sh.'s England and not to the Bohemia of some indefinite time. The
dramatic function of Sh.'s impropriety is discussed by MUIR (1951). Here, as BLUE-
STONE (1974, pp. 235-6) says, these allusions "render Bohemia as familiar as Paul's
Walk."
   2006-7 **at the doore**] SCHANZER (ed. 1969): "This and the reference in [2163]
show that Shakespeare imagined an indoor setting for the scene." Called for, however,
are eleven named characters, at least a dozen dancers, and probably some musicians,
as well as herbs and flowers. Rather than a door to a mammoth cottage, Sh. may be
thinking of the doors of his own stage.
   2007 **after**] DEIGHTON (ed. 1889): "To the music of."
   2007-8 **Tabor . . . you**] NAYLOR (1965, pp. 79-80): "The tabor . . . was a
small drum, which was used as accompaniment to the pipe, a large whistle with three
holes, but with a compass of eighteen notes . . . probably . . . about eighteen
inches long. . . . The bagpipe was very similar to the instruments of that name
which still exist." VOSS (ed. 1829): The bagpipe was preferred by country folk over
all other instruments. He is borne out by *OED*: "Formerly a favourite rural English
musical instrument."

2009 **seuerall**] PAFFORD (ed. 1963): "Different" (*OED, a.* 1b), as in 554. SCHAN-ZER (ed. 1969): "A good many" (*a.* 4). PARRY (ed. 1982): "A varied lot of" (*a.* 2c), as in 312.

tell] MINSHEU (1617): "Number" (i.e., count).

vtters] *OED* (*v.*[1] 1): "Sell." (6): "Speak, say, or pronounce" ("sing," in this instance). BOORMAN's (ed. 1964) suggested pun on *utter* as "to issue money" would be pointless. See n. 2144.

2010 **as**] SCHMIDT (1874): "As if."

eaten] *OED* (*v.* 1d, citing this line): "To treasure up, 'feed upon' (thoughts, words, etc.)."

ballads] BETHELL (ed. 1956): "Doggerel verses describing some startling con-temporary event, a murder, a hanging, or the birth of a two-headed calf." FIRTH (1916, 2:513): "Ballads multiplied exceedingly as the reign of Elizabeth drew to a close. To write them or sing them became a profitable trade." HARRISON (ed. 1947): They "were usually printed on a single large sheet of paper, surmounted with an ancient woodcut illustration. . . . Ballads were of all kinds, a fair proportion being doggerel accounts of recent sensational events, especially miraculous."

eares grew] RANN (ed. 1787): "Were rivetted as by a spell." BETHELL (ed. 1956): May "be meant to imply that their possessors became asses." ORGEL (ed. 1996): "Alluding to the story of Midas, who grew asses' ears as a punishment for preferring the sensual music of Pan to the rational music of Apollo (Ovid, *Metamorphoses*, 11.146 ff.)."

2012 **better**] SCHMIDT (1874): "More welcome." HERFORD (ed. 1904): "More op-portunely."

2013 **but euen**] SCHMIDT (1874, Even 4) regards *euen* in this usage (that is, when *but* is not a conjunction) as an intensifier. DEIGHTON (ed. 1889) thinks *but euen* redundant, although it and *euen but* are common. For examples in addition to SCHMIDT's, see *LLL* 5.2.433 (2367), *MV* 1.1.35 (39) and 5.1.272 (2699), *AYL* 2.7.3 (975), *Ham.* 1.1.81 (98), and *Lr.* 1.1.216 (235) and 3.2.65 (1719), among others.

2013–14 **dolefull . . . downe**] STEEVENS (ed. 1778): A "stroke aimed at the title page of [Thomas] Preston's *Cambises*" (1569), which describes that play as "A la-mentable tragedy *mixt ful of pleasant mirth*." A specific allusion is doubtful. FURNESS (ed. 1898) nevertheless quotes *MND* 5.1.57 (1854): "Very tragicall mirth," and ORGEL (ed. 1996) finds "a generic relevance to the play as a whole."

2014 **pleasant**] SCHMIDT (1875): "Merry, facetious."

2015 **lamentably**] *OED* (*adv.* 1, citing this line): "Dolefully." But with a pun on *adv.* 2: "Deplorably."

2016 **He . . . sizes**] PAFFORD (ed. 1963), referring to Étienne de Maisonneuve, *2 Gerileon of England* (trans. A. M[undy], 1592): "The stationers who printed and sold ballads employed vagabonds . . . as agents to sell them up and down the coun-try." PATTISON (1948, p. 17): "He [the ballad seller] studied his audience and had something for everybody. . . . It was a genuine form of early journalism with all the vigour and vices inseparable ever since from that public utility."

sizes] DEIGHTON (ed. 1889): "Kinds or sorts, as though he were talking of fitting a person with a garment." BETHELL (ed. 1956): "He is thinking of the gloves to which he is about to compare them." The word may not be entirely absurd, how-ever; *OED* (*sb.* 12) quotes "an answeare [to a letter] of the largest size" (Spenser) and "clamours of all size both high and low" (*LC* 21). *OED*'s gloss does restrict the word in this sense to immaterial things. The phrase is an absurdity in its modification, of course.

No Milliner can so fit his customers with Gloues: he has
the prettiest Loue-songs for Maids, so without bawdrie
(which is strange,) with such delicate burthens of Dildo's and Fadings: Iump-her, and thump-her; and where   2020
some stretch-mouth'd Rascall, would (as it were) meane
mischeefe, and breake a fowle gap into the Matter, hee
makes the maid to answere, *Whoop, doe me no harme good*
man: put's him off, slights him, with *Whoop, doe mee no*
harme good man.   2025
    Pol.   This is a braue fellow.
    Clo.   Beleeue mee, thou talkest of an admirable con-
ceited fellow, has he any vnbraided Wares?

2019-20 Dildo's and Fadings] *As a quotation* KNT, WH1; *all but* and *quoted*
JOHN1-SING1, COL1-DYCE1, COL3-STAU, KTLY, DYCE2, DEL4-HUD2, BUL
        Dildo's] *didle-dos* JOHN
    2020 Fadings] Fapings ROWE3-POPE2
    Iump-her, and thump-her] *As a quotation* JOHN1+ (−SIS, ARD2, PEN2)
    2022 gap into] jape in COL2; jape into SING2, WH1, COL3, DYCE2, COL4-WH2, BUL
    2028 vnbraided] embroided COL2, COL3, COL4, HUD2

2017 **Milliner**] KERSEY (1702): "That sells ribbons, gloves, &c." *OED* (citing this
line) adds, "Esp. such as were originally of Milan manufacture." As the pronoun
indicates, the milliner is a man, a haberdasher.
    2018 **so without bawdrie**] *OED* (Bawdry[1] 3, citing this line): "Lewdness in
speech or writing." CHARLTON (ed. 1916): Since "all the songs and ballads alluded to
in this scene are licentious [this description is] part of the joke, as Perdita realized."
See 2038-9.
    2019 **which is strange**] BETHELL (ed. 1956): "A reflection on the usual wares of
the pedlar. The comic effect is extended when it appears . . . that Autolycus' ballads
do not deserve this commendation."
    burthens] HUNTER (ed. 1872): Refrains.
    2019-20 **Dildo's and Fadings**] THEOBALD (1729, in NICHOLS, 1817, 2:364): "The
burthens of some songs of those times. . . . [*Fading*] was, I presume, the burthen
of some so prevailing a ditty, that a dance was composed to the tune." He cites
Beaumont, *The Knight of the Burning Pestle* 3. Interlude 8-9: "I will have him dance
Fading; *Fading* is a fine Jigge." Critics beginning with THIRLBY (MS 1725-33?) pursued the idea, incidental here, of *fading* as a dance; their findings are summed up by
BOSWELL (ed. 1821). *OED* (*sb.*, quoting this passage): "'With a fading' was the refrain
of a popular song of an indecent character." PARTRIDGE (1969), misunderstanding,
thinks *fading*, rather than being a refrain, is actually said to signify "refrain"; his
notion that commentators tautologically mean "'burdens of dildoes and burdens (or
refrains)'" is wrong. CHAPPELL (1859; 1965, 1:235-6), in fact, prints songs having
With a fading as a nonsense burden. Anticipated by FURNESS (ed. 1898), PARTRIDGE
is right, however, that "the pairing of *fading* with *dildo* is suggestive, especially in
conjunction with the next pairing of energetically erotic terms ['Iump-her, and thump-
her']. . . . *Fading* = *fading-away*, an orgasm-'death.'" Something similar seems to
have struck WHITE (1854, p. 296), who remarks that dildoes and fadings are "better

known perhaps to city debauchees than simple rustics," as though simple rustics were never simply debauched. STEEVENS (ed. 1785): "'With a hie, dildo dill' is the burden of the *Batchelors Feast*" (*A Book of Roxburghe Ballads*, ed. Collier, 1847, pp. 249 ff.); CHAPPELL (1:234–5) and PAFFORD (ed. 1963) add other examples. In tiny type *OED* defines *dildo* as "a name of the penis . . . or a figure thereof." Further dildo lore may be found in WEBB (1989), who, despite *OED* (citing this line) and PARTRIDGE, does not find *fading* to be an indelicate word, and in RUBINSTEIN (1984).

2021 **stretch-mouth'd**] SCHMIDT (1875): "Open-mouthed," which SCHANZER (ed. 1969) makes "wide-mouthed" and PARRY (ed. 1982) "leering." Differently, ROLFE (ed. 1879): "Broad-spoken"; according to LEE (ed. 1907), "foul-mouthed." HAPPÉ (1969): "Perhaps . . . a suggestive leer during the *gap* [2022]."

2022 **fowle gap**] There is no evidence for WHITE's (ed. 1857) assertion that "gap" is a form of *jape*. HUNTER (ed. 1872) defines the term as " a gross interpolation"; HARRISON (ed. 1947) says it is a "dirty crack." BETHELL (ed. 1956): "'Patter' spoken between parts of the song." STAUNTON (ed. 1859) cites Puttenham, *The Arte of English Poesie* (1589, p. 141), who describes a long parenthesis as making "a great gappe in the tale." SCHMIDT (1874), however, gives "a defect, a flaw" (*OED, sb.*[1] 6). If the gap is a gross interpolation and so a flaw, it need not be verbal; thus the CLARKES (ed. 1865) may also be right in glossing "stop or halt"—the halt in the matter providing occasion for suggestive behavior. HERFORD (ed. 1904): "Make a foul parenthesis in the song (by violence)." PAFFORD (ed. 1963): "The ballad is cleverly made to lead up to the probability of something bawdy which is then just as cleverly avoided" by the girl's intervention. He carefully reviews the case for emending to *jape*, although he (and subsequent eds.) retain *gap*.

2023–4, 2024–5 **Whoop . . . man**] FARMER(n STEEVENS, ed. 1773, 10:Pp5): A ballad to the tune of "Oh! do me no harm good man" appears in *The Famous History of Friar Bacon* (1st ed. 1625? [*STC* 1182.7]; ed. Dorothy Senior, *Some Old English Worthies*, 1912, p. 212). This lyric is adapted to the Bacon story; another to the same tune, perhaps more like Autolycus's delicate ballad, is given by FRY (1814, pp. 21–3). It begins: "There was an old lad Rode on an old pad [horse], Vnto an old punke, a wooing; He layed this old punke Vpon an old trunke, And there was good old doing." ANDERS (1904, p. 181): "*Whope do me no harme good Woman*" is said or sung by Secco in Ford's *The Fancies, Chast and Noble* (1638; ed. Hart, 1985, 3.3.138). RITSON (in STEEVENS, ed. 1793) finds the tune in William Corkine, *Ayres, to Sing and Play to the Lute and Basse Violl* (1610, sig. F1ᵛ). See p. 861. KERMODE (ed. 1963): "The joke . . . lies in the servant's praising Autolycus for the decency of his songs, and simultaneously betraying the fact of their indecency."

2024 **slights him**] SCHMIDT (1875, Slight): "To treat as insignificant." Virtually a repetition of *put's him off*.

2026 **This . . . fellow**] Because Polixenes speaks verse in this scene, WALKER (1854, p. 86) believes this to be a short verse line and that "this is" should be elided. Cf. nn. 2857 and 3363–4.

braue] KERSEY (1708): "Skilful, Excellent." JOHNSON (1755): "It is an indeterminate word, used to express the superabundance of any valuable quality in men or things." Ironical here but used straightforwardly in 2891. See also n. 3093.

2027–8 **an . . . fellow**] KERSEY (1708, Admirable): "That deserves to be admired, wonderful; excellent; rare." ABBOTT (p. 14): "A clever person." Cf. nn. 2489, 3021. For *admirable conceited*, MOORMAN (ed. 1912): "Wonderfully ingenious."

2028 **vnbraided**] HANMER (ed. 1743–4, 6:glos.): "Unfaded, fresh" (*OED, ppl. a.* 1, citing this line only, but see Braided, *ppl. a.* b). STEEVENS (ed. 1773), who, like JOHNSON (ed. 1765), took *braided* to mean "interwoven" (*OED, ppl. a.* a), nevertheless comments: "The drift of the Clown's question, is either to know whether Autolycus has any thing . . . worthy to be presented to his mistress: or, as probably, by

385

Ser. Hee hath Ribbons of all the colours i'th Rainebow; Points, more then all the Lawyers in *Bohemia*, can　　　　2030
learnedly handle, though they come to him by th' grosse:
Inckles, Caddysses, Cambrickes, Lawnes: why he sings
em ouer, as they were Gods, or Goddesses: you would
thinke a Smocke were a shee-Angell, he so chauntes to
the sleeue-hand, and the worke about the square on't.　　　　2035

Clo. Pre'thee bring him in, and let him approach singing.

Perd. Forewarne him, that he vse no scurrilous words
in's tunes.

2033 or] and POPE2-v1773 (−HAN, CAP); on KTLY
2035 sleeue-hand] sleeve-band HAN, WARB, JOHN1-v1773, RANN, COL2, COL3
2038 words] word WH1
2039 *Exit* Servant. CAP, DYCE, STAU, CAM1, GLO, DEL4, HUD2-EVNS (−CAM3), OXF2;
The Servant goes to the door. BEV

---

enquiring for something pedlars usually have not, to escape laying out his money at
all.'' The first of these alternatives is implied by recent glosses, which follow HANMER.
PAFFORD (ed. 1963), for example: "New, not shopworn." STEEVENS (ed. 1778) finds
"braided ware" in Middleton and Webster's *Anything for a Quiet Life* (ed. Lucas,
Webster, 1927, 3.2.179) and HUDSON (ed. 1852) notes the term in Marston's *The
Scourge of Villanie* (ed. Davenport, 1961, 5.73). Both instances indicate inferiority,
as is also the case in Thomas Deloney's *The Gentle Craft*, pt. 2 (ed. F. O. Mann, 1912,
p. 158), which HULME (1962, p. 299) notices. Lucas's gloss for *brayded* is "tarnished,
soiled."

　　Other senses have been suggested, but they are probably incorrect. MASON'S
(1785, p. 136) "not ornamented with braid" is elaborated by MALONE (ed. 1790):
"The clown is perhaps inquiring not for better than common, but for smooth, plain
goods . . . [such as] ribands, cambricks, and lawns [see n. 2032]," an idea that goes
in the wrong direction. JERVIS (1868) thinks the word is an intentional blunder for
embroidered; WHITE (ed. 1883), an unintentional one for the same word, so that the
Clown asks for unbraided wares by *embroidered*, that is, braided. The CLARKES (in
FURNIVALL, ed. 1908): "Genuine," because of the "braide" (plaited or deceitful)
Frenchmen of *AWW* 4.2.73 (2102). HULME (pp. 299–300) argues that *braid* as "an
adroit turn; a trick or subtilty" (*OED*, *sb.* 3) is also involved and that the word "refers
not only forward to the 'Ribbons' but backward and forward to the songs." "The
clown would have his love-songs without these evasions [i.e., subtleties], and with a
countryman's alertness . . . he asks directly for what he wants." This seems unlikely
in one who prefers maids with manners and secrets kept secret (2066–70). PORTER
& CLARKE (ed. 1908): "He is using the word in an affected tone of the Pedler while
conversing with his father's distinguished guest," another unlikely idea.

　　2029–35 **Hee . . . on't**] GOLDMAN (1972, pp. 132–3): "Autolycus is peddling
devices designed to add beauty to natural beauty, and he is selling works of art,

ballads . . . about freaks of fertility in nature and . . . taken as true by the wondering shepherds—whose healthy appetite for the impossibly creative and restorative
is as great as our own—or as Leontes' at the end of the play [quotes 3319-20]."

2029-30 **all . . . Rainebow**] Proverbial (TILLEY C519).

2030 **Points**] JOHNSON (1755): "String[s] with a tag," used rather than buttons
to fasten clothing (*OED, sb.*[1] B. 5). PORTER & CLARKE (ed. 1908), however, find in
HOLME (1688) "small wiers made round, through which the breeches hooks are put."
MALONE (ed. 1790) recognizes the pun on "single article, item, or clause," as in a
legal document (A. 5). FURNESS (ed. 1898): "Points of an argument." Further information on points of law may be found in WHITE (1913, p. 187).

2031 **by th' grosse**] SCHMIDT (1874): "In a body." PAFFORD (ed. 1963): "I.e.
wholesale," SCHMIDT's gloss for the phrase as it is used in *LLL* 5.2.319 (2244). KER-
MODE (ed. 1963) finds "reference to clerkly 'engrossing', the lawyer's fair copying,"
and ORGEL (ed. 1996) to "twelve dozen [*OED, sb.*[3]]; hence, in huge quantities."

2032 **Inckles, Caddysses**] MALONE (ed. 1790): "*Inkle* is a kind of [linen] tape"
(*OED, sb.*[1]). Costard mentions an "yncle" as an item that may be purchased with
remuneration (*LLL* 3.1.139 [905]). For *caddis*, HANMER (ed. 1743-4, 6:glos.): "A Gal-
loon [narrow ornamental braid] or Binding made of Worsted" (*OED* 2c, citing this
line: "used for garters, etc."). Cf. *1H4* 2.4.79 (1032).

Cambrickes] KERSEY (1702): "Fine linnen-cloth, made at *Cambray*, in the low-
Countries."

Lawnes] KERSEY (1708): "A[nother] sort of fine Linnen-cloth." Their whiteness
is praised at 2044. PIERCE (ed. 1918), wrongly: "Fine silks" (cf. *OED, sb.*[1] 4).

2032-3 **sings em ouer**] DEIGHTON (ed. 1889): "Describes them in song."

2034 **Smocke**] LINTHICUM (1936, p. 189): "A shirt-like garment worn as under-
wear [by women], and as a sleeping gown."

shee-Angell] ALEXANDER (1945, p. 76): "Angels in Shakespeare are usually
feminine."

chauntes to] BETHELL (ed. 1956): "Sings the praises of."

2035 **sleeue-hand . . . on't**] TOLLET (in STEEVENS, ed. 1778) quotes several instances of *sleeve-hand*, including COTGRAVE's (1611) trans. of *poignet de la chemise*
as "the wrist-band, or gathering at the sleeue-hand, of a shirt" (*OED*, Sleeve, *sb.* 8b,
citing this line, "cuff"). LINTHICUM (1936, p. 175), however: "It was not a separate
cuff, or even a wrist-band . . . but . . . the part of the sleeve nearest the
hand . . . as suggested by Cotgrave's definition." TOLLET glosses "worke . . . on't"
as "embroidering about the bosom part of a shift" (*OED*, Square, *sb.* 10a: "the breast-
piece of a dress"). For further details, see LINTHICUM, pp. 190-1, and for *on't* as "of
it," see n. 785-6.

2036 **bring . . . in**] SCHMIDT (1874): "To bear or carry [here to escort] from
without to within a certain precinct." An interior setting is not implied.

2038-9 **Forewarne . . . tunes**] THIRLBY (MS 1747-53, Scurrilous): "Obscene." *OED* (citing this line): "Characterized by coarseness or indecency." Although,
as TILLEY (1916, p. 77) points out, her warning is a sign of her modesty (cf. n. 375-
6), Perdita is not being prudish. As FRYE (1986, p. 166) puts it, "the primary meaning
is that she is a fastidious girl who dislikes obscenity, [but] her motives are magical as
well as moral: a festive occasion should not be spoiled by words of ill omen." According to FIRTH (1916, 2:516-17), "a large portion of these [popular ballads] consisted of amatory ditties. . . . Many . . . were immoral and indecent," and the Stationers' Company disciplined several of its members who were guilty of publishing
them. HOLBROOK (1964, p. 184): Autolycus's "all turn out to be filthy, in the end, by
double entendu."

Clow. You haue of these Pedlers, that haue more in   2040
them, then youl'd thinke (Sister.)
Perd. I, good brother, or go about to thinke.

Enter Autolicus singing.

Lawne as white as driuen Snow,
Cypresse blacke as ere was Crow,   2045
Gloues as sweete as Damaske Roses,
Maskes for faces, and for noses:
Bugle-bracelet, Necke-lace Amber,
Perfume for a Ladies Chamber:
Golden Quoifes, and Stomachers   2050
For my Lads, to giue their deers:
Pins, and poaking-stickes of steele.

2048 *bracelet*] Bracelets F4-JOHN2, v1773
     Necke-lace Amber] F1-MAL, CAM1, GLO, WH2, IRV, NLSN-PEL1, ARD2, EVNS+;
necklace-amber WARTON (1785, p. 238) *conj.*, v1793 *etc.*
     2052-3 *steele.* . . . *heele:*] ~ , . . . ~ : ROWE1-SIG, EVNS, BEV3; ~ , . . . ~ ,
BEV4

2040 **You haue of**] CALDECOTT (MS 1813-33): Is *of* "amongst" or "in the qualities they possess"? The former, according to the CLARKES (ed. 1865): "There
are . . . among." FURNESS (ed. 1898): *Of* = "some of," a partitive genitive; see AB-
BOTT §177. Thus NEILSON & HILL (ed. 1942): "There are some."
     2042 **go about**] HUDSON (ed. 1880): "*Wish* or *care*," the equivalent of *OED*'s
(About A. 10) "to form designs" and SCHMIDT's (1874, About 6) "to be going, to have
in hand, to make it one's task." NEILSON & HILL (ed. 1942): "Intend." Cf. n. 2584.
PAFFORD (ed. 1963): "The modern idiom would be 'have any intention of thinking,
have any desire to think.'"
     2043 *Autolicus*] EVANS (ed. 1974): "He is disguised with a beard (see [2596-7],
where he removes it)." He has also changed clothes. FURNIVALL (1879) finds Autolycus's spiel and his singing anticipated in *The Pedlers Prophecie* (1595; MSR 954-
61, 990).
     2044-55 *Lawne . . . buy*] For *lawn*, see n. 2032. For *WT*'s songs, see n. 1669-
80 and p. 853. This one, says DRAPER (1985, p. 33), is "the perfect ad-man's song."
WISE (1861, pp. 101-2) finds a pedlar's song in Munday, *The Downfall of Robert,
Earl of Huntingdon* (1601; ed. Meagher, 1980, lines 1556-65) that mentions some
of the same items—pins, gloves, masks, and poking sticks. NOBLE (1923, p. 97):
"Autolycus advances . . . as he sings, and consequently he has sung quite four lines
by the time he reaches his stand and is in position to display his wares as he sings
them over. Thereafter he requires pauses to enable him to dwell upon the merits of
his various goods." According to SALGADO (1977, p. 136), however, Autolycus "is
here clearly supplying the feminine luxury trade, with wares which he has, as likely
as not, come by honestly. It was not unusual . . . for the upright man [chief vagabond and thief] to unload his booty onto a pedlar." But how honest is it to receive
stolen goods? Moreover, it is doubtful that Autolycus has any of the goods mentioned;

most are appropriate to upper-class women, not to Mopsas and Dorcases. What he sells is the trumpery mentioned at 2474–6. For further information, see p. 862.

2044 *Lawne*] LINTHICUM (1936, p. 98): "Linen of such fineness that it was often called 'cobweb lawn.'"

as white . . . Snow] Proverbial (TILLEY S591). Cf. n. 2187.

2045 *Cypresse*] MINSHEU (1617, Cipres): "A fine curled [crepe] linenn." LINTHICUM (1936, pp. 118–19): "A light, transparent material. . . . The black was used for mourning." *OED* (Cypress³ 1c, citing this line): "Originally imported from or through Cyprus." *OED* Cypress¹ is cypress wood, to which Sh. also refers, certainly at *Shr.* 2.1.351 (1233) and probably at *TN* 2.4.52 (942).

blacke . . . Crow] Proverbial (TILLEY C844).

2046 *Gloues . . . Roses*] I.e., perfumed gloves (*OED*, Sweet, *a.* 2b, citing this line); see also 2073. According to LINTHICUM (1936, p. 269), sweet gloves were made in England by 1580, though those from Spain were thought the best. As for value, CUNNINGTON & CUNNINGTON (1970, p. 182): In 1592, a pair of new sweet gloves was exchanged for a pig; "they were often given as presents" and "were worn, carried, or tucked into the belt" (1972, p. 76). In *Ado* (3.4.62–3 [1558–9]), Claudio has sent Hero gloves that are an excellent perfume. The *damask rose* is frequently mentioned by Sh. GRINDON (1883, p. 154): "The damask or Damascus rose [is] noted for its fine crimson hue. . . . This species had (as to the present day) a white variety, and another that was particoloured," referred to in *AYL* 3.5.123 (1897). GERARD (1597, p. 1077) speaks of the "flagrant and odoriferous smell" of roses generally and (p. 1080) of the common damask rose as having "a more pleasant smell" than the white rose. Roses are proverbial paragons of sweetness (TILLEY R178).

2047 *Maskes . . . noses*] MACQUOID (1916, 2:97): Masks "were of various colours, and were much worn by ladies of quality when riding. The eyeholes were at times filled with glass." LINTHICUM (1936, p. 272): "The smaller mask [of velvet or other silk] which covered only the nose and part of the cheeks was used for concealing the identity of the wearer; the larger ones were protective [of a lady's complexion from the sun]."

2048 *Bugle*] KERSEY (1708): "A kind of Glass-beads." *OED* (Bugle, *sb.*³ 1): "Tube-shaped . . . usually black." For (2), *OED*, citing this line: "Made of, adorned with, or resembling bugles."

Necke-lace Amber] THIRLBY (MS 1733–47?): "Amber in beads fit for necklaces." WARTON (in STEEVENS, ed. 1785, p. 238): "*Perfume . . . Chamber*" (2049) modifies "*Amber*." He could be right. *OED* (*sb.*¹ 3) provides quotations showing that the resin was used both as a perfume and for ornaments.

2050 *Quoifes*] LINTHICUM (1936, p. 223): "A coif was a small cap covering the back and sides of the head, worn as an indoor head-dress." A *golden coif* was "embroidered in gold and trimmed with gold lace."

Stomachers] LINTHICUM (1936, p. 191): "The stomacher or placard, originating in a piece of armour to protect the chest, never lost its stiffness, though it became an ornamental, detachable shield worn over the abdomen under the doublet or kirtle body to fill the front opening in these garments."

2050–1 *Stomachers . . . deers*] ELLIS (1871, 3:964) finds similar rhymes, including *characters-tears-bears* in *LC* 16–18 and *ne'er-Jupiter* in *Tmp.* 4.1.76–7 (1734–5).

2052–3 *Pins . . . heele*] NEELY (1985, p. 203): "Phallic aggression and female passivity are trivialized."

2052 *poaking-stickes of steele*] STEEVENS (ed. 1773): They "were heated in the fire, and made use of to adjust the plaits of ruffs" (*OED*, Poking, *vbl. sb.* 2, citing this line). KNIGHT (ed. 1841) quotes Howes's continuation of STOW (1631, p. 1038): About the years 1573–4 "began the making of steele poking-stickes [which could be heated], and vntill that time all Lawnderesses vsed setting-stickes, made of wood or bone."

>   *What Maids lacke from head to heele:*
>   *Come buy of me, come: come buy, come buy,*
>   *Buy Lads, or else your Lasses cry: Come buy.*   2055

Clo. If I were not in loue with *Mopsa*, thou shouldst take no money of me, but being enthrall'd as I am, it will also be the bondage of certaine Ribbons and Gloues.

Mop. I was promis'd them against the Feast, but they come not too late now.   2060

Dor. He hath promis'd you more then that, or there be lyars.

Mop. He hath paid you all he promis'd you: 'May be he has paid you more, which will shame you to giue him againe.   2065

Clo. Is there no manners left among maids? Will they weare their plackets, where they should bear their faces? Is there not milking-time? When you are going to bed? Or kill-hole? To whistle of these secrets, but you must

---

2054 *come:*] *come buy;* KEIGHTLEY *conj. in* CAM1, KTLY
        come buy,] *Om.* v1785
2055 *buy.*] *buy,* &c. THEO1-v1821 (−HAN, CAP), SING, HAL
2067 bear] wear THEO2-v1773 (−HAN, CAP)
2068 not] not a HARN, HAL
2069 whistle] whisper mTBY2 *conj.*, COL2
        of] off HAN1, HAN2, CAP+ (−HAN3, KNT, ARD2, SIG, OXF2, BEV4)

DELIUS (ed. 1860) cites "your ruff must stand in print [precisely]; and for that purpose, get poking-sticks with fair and long handles, lest they scorch your lily sweating hands" (Dekker(?), *Blurt, Master-Constable*, ed. Bullen, 1885 1:64). WEBB (1989): In other contexts "the shape, and the action of its use (and possibly the heat) provide an analogue of the penis, while 'ruff' = vagina. . . . Bawdy in Autolycus' song is not certainly present. If the play director so decides, actors 'business'—pause and expressive gesture—may interpret" the expression as ribald. RUBINSTEIN (1984, Pin) has no doubt about the ribaldry since Autolycus sells dildos (2019-20) and *pin* means "penis" and pins and poking sticks are what maids lack.

2053 **What . . . heele:**] LIVINGSTON (1969, p. 346), relentlessly pursuing a theme: Autolycus's goods "are precisely the kind of ornamentation Perdita rejects [at 1914-16]. The promise to supply all a maid lacks comically challenges Polixenes' argument that 'nature is made better by no mean / But nature makes that mean' [1900-1]. Both the ornamental trifles and the ballads represent the 'unnatural' art which Perdita condemns, the art which competes with and exploits nature." BASS (1977, p. 20), in contrast: "The love tokens, the frippery, he sells are a spring kind of restorative to life, and Florizel and Perdita borrow his clothing to disguise themselves when they flee from Bohemia. . . . Guile is the means whereby grace returns to the kingdom [of Sicilia]." With *head to heele* DENT compares TILLEY T436; and cf. 2618. SCHANZER (ed. 1969) omits F's colon, finding it intrusive. ORGEL (ed. 1996), agreeing: "Most editors replace [it] with a period or an exclamation point. But a colon is not the end of a sentence." Actually, modern eds. sometimes treat the Elizabethan colon as terminal punctuation; consider, for example, EVANS's (ed. 1974) periods at *Ham.* 3.4.2 (2375), *Mac.* 3.1.137 (1144), and *WT* 1.1.21 (25), where F has colons.

2056-7 **If . . . me**] BOORMAN (ed. 1964): "Ironic."

2057 **it**] PARRY (ed. 1982): "My love for Mopsa."

2058 **bondage**] CALDECOTT (MS 1813-33): "I.e. impounding." SCHMIDT (1874): "Servitude." Playing upon *enthrall'd* (captivated by love), the Clown says he will buy the ribbons and gloves and enslave them to Mopsa. PAFFORD's (ed. 1963) "parcelled up," derived from *OED* (2c), seems inappropriate, but BOORMAN's (ed. 1964) "the ribbons would certainly be bound" catches a probable pun.

Gloues] WEBB (1989): "A gew-gaw, often perfumed [see 2073], desired by maidens from lovers." They may be more significant, however, for LINTHICUM (1936, pp. 267-8) points out that gloves were presented by a fiancé to his fiancée. See n. 2046.

2059 **against the Feast**] JOHNSON (1755, Against): "In provision for; in expectation of." GOTCH (1900, p. 330) suggests the feast is the parish festival held in honor of the saint for whom the church is named (cf. 1845, 1873, etc.), but Mopsa means this very celebration. WILSON (ed. 1931): "There is a streak of meanness in the Clown." He alone thinks so; see nn. 1550-1, 1709. PAFFORD (ed. 1963): "The country peasant is usually, and naturally, careful with his money." The Clown, however, is as generous as he can afford to be (see 1745-6). Mopsa's comment, which sets up 2061-2, is not acrimonious.

2061-2 **He . . . lyars**] A catty remark, exactly what he has promised her being left to the imagination. EVANS (ed. 1974) thinks she means "the rumor is that he has promised to marry you," but one doubts it. LINDENBAUM (1972, p. 19): He "has evidently tripped with several and has not yet retired from the field," but one doubts that too. ABARTIS (1977, p. 108): "The pregnancy and unfaithfulness that were such serious and ominous issues in Sicilia are here transformed into feeble insults." She understands (p. 109) the rivalry of the girls for the Clown's affection as "a comic variation on the tragic love triangle . . . in the first half of the play."

2064-5 **to . . . againe**] MAXWELL (ed. 1956): "Into giving back to him," which misses or avoids the point. KERMODE (ed. 1963): "Perhaps he has made you pregnant." An insult, but Dorcas started it (2061-2). PROUDFOOT (1976, p. 68): Dorcas's "horror at the thought of marrying a usurer [2090] tends to support the allegation," but it more likely supports her distaste for carbonado'd toads [2087].

2066-7 **Will . . . faces?**] JOHNSON (1755, Placket): "Petticoat." STEEVENS (ed. 1778, 4:405), more exactly: "The opening in a woman's petticoat." COLMAN (1974): "By extension, the female pudendum itself." JERVIS (1868), too delicately: "A woman's pocket." GOULD (1884, p. 22): "Probably a metaphrasis for secrets." See n. 2486. For the expression, SCHMIDT (1875): "Will they openly show to strangers what they ought to keep for their friends?" More likely it is "Will they egregiously expose private matters?" (PAFFORD, ed. 1963, suggests that *bear* may be "bare," but this is probably not the case; see n. 406.) For more on plackets, see n. 2486; and for odd examples of "interchangeability or displacement, where the female organ transposes to the face," see WEBB (1989).

2069 **kill-hole**] CAPELL (1783 [1774], 1:glos.): "Properly *Kiln-hole* . . . the Mouth of an Oven." STEEVENS (in REED, ed. 1803): "The place into which coals are put under a stove, a copper, or a *kiln* in which lime, &c. are to be dried or burned" (*OED*, Kiln 2). OED: "In M[iddle] E[nglish] the final *-n* became silent in most districts), hence the frequent spelling *kill* [as in *Wiv.* 4.2.58 (1949), the only other instance in Sh.]." HARRIS (in REED, ed. 1803): "Generally means the fire-place used in making malt; . . . still a noted gossiping place."

whistle of] SCHMIDT (1875): The Clown "meant to say *whisper*, but in his

be tittle-tatling before all our guests? 'Tis well they are   2070
whispring: clamor your tongues, and not a word more.

 Mop. I haue done; Come you promis'd me a tawdry-
lace, and a paire of sweet Gloues.

 Clo. Haue I not told thee how I was cozen'd by the
way, and lost all my money.   2075

 Aut. And indeed Sir, there are Cozeners abroad, therfore it behooues men to be wary.

 Clo. Feare not thou man, thou shalt lose nothing here.

 Aut. I hope so sir, for I haue about me many parcels
of charge.   2080

 Clo. What hast heere? Ballads?   (2]

 Mop. Pray now buy some: I loue a ballet in print, a
life, for then we are sure they are true.

2071 clamor] charm HAN, COL2, WH, COL3, KIT1; Clammer KEIGHTLEY *conj. in*
CAM1, HUD2, CAM3, ALEX, SIG, OXF2; Clam a' SIS

 2082 print, a] F1-ROWE2, ARD1, PEN1-ARD2; Print, or a ROWE3-v1773; print o'- COL,
WH, CAM, GLO, DEL4, OXF1, NLSN, SIS; print a- TYRWHITT *conj. in* v1773 (10:2M2^v),
v1778 *etc.*

---

blunder says more than he intended," but SCHMIDT does not reveal what that is. *OED*
(Whistle, *v.* 10, citing this line): "To speak, tell, or utter secretly, to 'whisper.'" Eds.
who print *off* may be influenced by *whistle off* as a hawking term (7b): "To send or
dismiss by whistling," although DEIGHTON (ed. 1889) glosses the phrase as "give vent
to."

 2070 **they**] PARRY (ed. 1982): Polixenes, Camillo, and the Shepherd are talking in
the background.

 2071 **clamor**] Much debated. WARBURTON (ed. 1747): "When bells are at the
height, in order to cease them, the repetition of the strokes becomes much quicker
than before; this is called *clamouring* them." JOHNSON (ed. 1765) quotes this gloss,
but — as WARNER (1768, p. 80) complains — in his *Dictionary* (1755) he defines the
words as "to make outcries; to exclaim; to vociferate," citing this line as well as *Mac.*
2.3.60 (809), where "cried out" is clearly required. GREY (1754, 1:263-4, citing *Ado*
5.2.82-3 [2499-2500]), is of similar mind: "When applied to bells, . . . not . . . a
ceasing, but a continued ringing." BECKET (1815, 1:366): WARBURTON means "ring
out your peal at once" and then "be silent," and NARES (1876; 1905) describes the
clamour or clam as "a general crash." *OED* cites this line as the first of two instances
under *Clamour*, v.^{2} 2 — "To stop from noise, to silence" — and equates *Clam*, v.^{2} 2 —
"To put an end to (din); to silence, hush." Like HERFORD (ed. 1904), eds. today gloss
as "constrain, repress" or something similar.

 Earlier, HUNTER (1845, 1:424) finds "Clamor the Promulgation of your tongues"
in John Taylor the Water Poet, *Sir Gregory Nonsense* (1622; *Workes*, 1630, Aa2);
KEIGHTLEY (1857, p. 86) thinks the verb means "press or squeeze" and the expression
means "hold your tongue." CROSBY (in HUDSON, ed. 1880): "*Choke up*, to stick or
fasten together." SCHMIDT (1874): "Strange expression. . . . If not a misprint, . . . it may be a misapplication of the word for 'charm,'" and proponents of
this emendation, such as WHITE (ed. 1857), note that tongues are charmed in *Shr.*
4.2.58 (1909), *2H6* 4.1.64 (2232), *3H6* 5.5.31 (3006), and *Oth.* 5.2.183-4 (3465-6).

NICHOLSON (1882), finding a Cumberland word, *clammers*, "a yoke for the neck of a cow to prevent her leaping hedges" (see *EDD*), has the Clown say "Clammer [i.e., put clammers on] your tongues, and let them not be unruly." BOORMAN's (ed. 1964) "surely the confusion is the Clown's" may reiterate TILLEY's (1930, p. 117 n.) idea that the Clown, meaning "silence," uses the opposite word. JOHNSON's (ed. 1765) n. on *Oth.* 5.2.183 (3465)—"to *clam* a bell is to cover the clapper with felt"— seems without basis. PORTER & CLARKE's (ed. c. 1903) "Make noise without sense" does not work with "not a word more."

2072-3 **tawdry-lace**] WARTON (in JOHNSON, ed. 1765, 8:Ii4) refers to SKINNER (1671): Ties, fringes, or bands bought at the church fair honoring St. Audrey, of whose title and name *tawdry* is a corruption. *OED* (citing this line), which gives a fuller account of the word's origin: "A silk 'lace' or necktie." HARNESS (ed. 1825) refers to the tradition that the tumor on the neck of which St. Audrey (Etheldreda) died was a judgment upon her vanity in having once worn necklaces. For *tawdry*, CALDECOTT (MS 1813-33): "Particoloured & smart enough for a holiday dress," but all *OED*'s instances of the adjective are pejorative. MACKAY (1884, p. 62) tries to find an antecedent Celtic word.

2073 **sweet Gloues**] See nn. 2046 and 2058.

2074-5 **Haue . . . money**] See n. 1743-4. COLLINS (ed. 1904-24?): "The Clown has evidently got some more money . . . as he buys many ballads afterwards [e.g., 2136-7]. His present words are a mere excuse."

by the way] *OED* (By, *prep*. 12, citing this line): "In passing along."

2076 **Cozeners**] *OED* (Cozener, citing this line): "Deceiver, cheat, imposter."

2076-7 **therfore . . . wary**] FURNESS (ed. 1898): "Autolycus, under the pretense of looking for cozeners, casts furtive glances about him to be sure of his company. If we were not in 'stage-land' we might wonder that Autolycus did not recognise Prince Florizel quite as easily as Polixenes recognised him." Polixenes knew Florizel was there, of course; Autolycus did not.

2077 **behooues**] MINSHEU (1617, it Behoueth): "It is requisite."

2079 **I hope so**] PAFFORD (ed. 1963): I.e., I hope not. Cf. *Cym.* 2.3.148 (1130). EVANS (ed. 1974): I "hope you are right."

parcels] MINSHEU (1617): "Small portion" (*OED*, *sb*. 4). SCHMIDT (1875): "A bundle, a package [*sb*. 7] . . . (or articles, items? [not in *OED*])."

2080 **charge**] MINSHEU (1617): "Cost." The CLARKES (ed. 1865): "Importance [*OED*, *sb*. 9] . . . momentous value." BOORMAN (ed. 1964): "Here Autolycus might slyly show the audience the Clown's purse, stolen [at 1743]." It would be empty if he had used its contents to buy the gewgaws he offers for sale here. See n. 1788.

2081 **hast heere?**] For the omission of *thou*, see ABBOTT §241.

2082-3 **Pray . . . true**] Regarding the special significance of their being in print, FURNIVALL (1886) quotes William Bullen, *A Dialogue* (1573, p. 90): "Our Iohns booke shal confounde your talke, for I did see it in writtying, and that whiche is written: I will beleue." MCMURTRY (1989, p. 132), similarly: "Mopsa [is] in awe of the authority of the [printed] page." BRYANT (1963, p. 397): "Mopsa's gullibility is no more grotesque and certainly less consequential than Leontes', who believed something worse upon less provocation." FELPERIN ("Tongue-Tied," 1985, p. 15): "Autolycus's ballads re-enact in a comic or surrealistic form not only Leontes' opening fantasies of illicit pregnancy and condign punishment, but his—and our—eagerness for verification, for grounding what must forever remain linguistic and poetic possibility in historical fact or empirical truth."

2082 **ballet**] BROOK (1976, p. 151): "Final *d* is sometimes unvoiced to *t* after *n*." He cites this word as an example, although it is *n*-less. Presumably the Clown says "Ballads" (2081), because the *d* is not final.

2082-3 **a life**] CALDECOTT (MS 1813-33), followed by JERVIS (1868), ABBOTT (§24), and SCHMIDT (1874): "On my life, *of* all things." *OED*, *adv*.¹, however: "[Prob.

Aut. Here's one, to a very dolefull tune, how a Vsu-
rers wife was brought to bed of twenty money baggs at   2085
a burthen, and how she long'd to eate Adders heads, and
Toads carbonado'd.

Mop. Is it true, thinke you?

Aut. Very true, and but a moneth old.

Dor. Blesse me from marrying a Vsurer.   2090

Aut. Here's the Midwiues name to't: one Mist. *Tale-
Porter*, and fiue or six honest Wiues, that were present.
Why should I carry lyes abroad?

Mop. 'Pray you now buy it.

Clo. Come-on, lay it by: and let's first see moe Bal-   2095
lads: Wee'l buy the other things anon.

Aut. Here's another ballad of a Fish, that appeared
vpon the coast, on wensday the fourescore of April, fortie

2084–7 how . . . carbonado'd] *As a title* CAP-DYCE1, HAL-DEL2, KTLY-KNT3,
HUD2, BUL, CAM3

2085 of] with F3-MAL (−CAP)

2092 Wiues] wives' v1778-OXF1 (−MAL, KNT, WH, CAM1, GLO, IRV), OXF2

2094–5 *Mop.* 'Pray . . . *Clo.* Come] *Mop.* Come v1785

2097–100 of . . . maids] *As a title* CAP, v1778-KNT2, DYCE, HAL, STAU, KNT3,
HUD2, BUL

---

formed on *lief* dear. . . .] . . . *To love alife*: to love dearly." If *OED* is right, then
TOLLET's (in STEEVENS, ed. 1778) supposition that *a* is short for "at" is mistaken; so
is BECKET's (1815, 1:36), that the *a* is Fr. *à* and that the meaning is "to the Life"; and
so are HALLIWELL's (ed. 1859) gloss, "as my life," and MOORMAN's (ed. 1912), "by
my life." PORTER & CLARKE (ed. 1908): "Or does she mean a personal account of
marvels, or travels, frequent at the time?"

2084–2103 **Here's . . . true]** KNIGHT (1947; 1965, p. 109): "Though the words
may not be scurrilous, the songs are ribald enough. . . . They are little burlesques
of our main fertility-myth, stuck in as gargoyles on a cathedral, and the two girls'
anxious enquiries as to whether the stories are true, with Autolycus' firm reassurances, serve to complete the parody." PAFFORD (ed. 1963): "In the usurer's wife and
the maid turned fish, Shakespeare is outdoing contemporary extravagances common
in street ballads and broadsides. . . . Ballad-makers deal in wonders ([3034–5]) but
Autolycus' accounts are so openly extravagant . . . that the audience will be moved
to laughter both by the ridiculous extravagances themselves and by the ridiculous
credulity of the peasants."

2086 **burthen]** JOHNSON (1755, Burden): "A birth: now obsolete."

Adders heads] Translating Vergil's *Georgics*, TOPSELL (1658, p. 628) calls them
"fearful." BOORMAN (ed. 1964) finds a pointless pun on *adder* as "'one who adds',
linking with 'usurer'."

2087 **Toads**] TOPSELL (1658, p. 726): "The most noble kinde of Frog, most venomous and remarkable for courage and strength."

carbonado'd] MINSHEU (1617, A Carbonádo): Scored "meate broiled on the coales" (*OED, v. arch.* 1, citing this line). JOHNSON (1755, To Carbonado): "To cut, or hack."

2090 **Blesse me**] OED (*v.*[1] 3b): "To guard oneself (with God's help) *from*." SCHMIDT (1874) cites instances of *God, Lord* (etc.) *bless* meaning "God preserve," as well as several occurrences, including this, of *bless* "without the word *God* or *heaven*."

2091 **Midwiues**] As "one Mist. *Tale-Porter*" indicates, the case and number of this word are possessive singular.

to't] BETHELL (ed. 1956): "To vouch for it." BOORMAN (ed. 1964): "Signed as a witness."

2091-2 ***Tale-Porter***] ORGEL (ed. 1996): "The name means tale-bearer, gossip." DEIGHTON (ed. 1889) compares "some carry tale," *LLL* 5.2.463 (2402). The same expression occurs in *Ven.* 657. COX (1969, p. 284): "The attester to the truth of the ballad . . . is appropriately named. . . . He [Sh.] not only reminds us that tales are made of the unreal [618-19], but he also reminds us that his story is a tale [1593-4]." As a midwife, she may also be a tail-porter.

2092 **honest**] See n. 381.

Wiues] CARRINGTON (1956): "Women" (*OED, sb.* 1). CLARK & WRIGHT (ed. 1863): To be consistent, eds. adding an apostrophe to this word ought to do the same to "Iustices" (2105). None does.

2093 **Why . . . abroad?**] MALONE (ed. 1790) has the unlikely notion that this line was inspired by "Theis things did auncient men report of credit verie good. For why there was no cause why they should lye" in GOLDING's Ovid (1567; 1965, 8.905-6). BOORMAN (ed. 1964, Abroad): "About, out in the country."

2095 **lay it by**] Following SCHMIDT (1874), DEIGHTON (ed. 1889): "Put it aside for me."

moe] See n. 57.

2096 **anon**] Immediately. See n. 1468.

2097-2103 **Here's . . . true**] Regarding extraordinary occurrences as subjects of ballads, STEEVENS (ed. 1778) compares 3033-5. MALONE (ed. 1790) records an entry in the Stationers' Register, 2 Apr. 1604, given by ARBER (1875-94, 3:107b) as "*The most true and strange report of A monstruous fishe that appeared in forme of A woman from the wa[i]st vpward Seene in the Sea.*" MALONE adds, "To this it is highly probable that Shakspeare alludes." COLLIER (ed. 1842) rejects such a notion, because he thinks it unlikely the "*strange report*" was a ballad and because Sh. does not "refer to any one production of the kind, but to the whole class." VOSS (ed. 1829) compares Trinculo's pennycatching painting of the strange fish in *Tmp.* 2.1.27-30 (1066-8). FURNESS (ed. 1898): "Halliwell [ed. 1859] devotes five folio pages and a full-page illustration to these ballads on fishes and on monstrosities."

2098 **wensday**] For the suppression of the first *d* in *Wednesday*, see FRANZ §60. BROOK (1976, p. 151, citing this instance): "*d* often disappears after *n*." But here it disappears before.

fourescore of April] With this phrase WALKER (1860, 3:106) compares "In this my fourscore summer," from *The Second Maiden's Tragedy* (ed. Lancashire, 1977, 2.1.29), but that is a conventional usage. What Autolycus says is "the 80th of April."

thousand fadom aboue water, & sung this ballad against
the hard hearts of maids: it was thought she was a Wo-   2100
man, and was turn'd into a cold fish, for she wold not exchange flesh with one that lou'd her: The Ballad is very
pittifull, and as true.

    Dor. Is it true too, thinke you.

    Autol. Fiue Iustices hands at it, and witnesses more   2105
then my packe will hold.

    Clo. Lay it by too; another.

    Aut. This is a merry ballad, but a very pretty one.

    Mop. Let's haue some merry ones.

    Aut. Why this is a passing merry one, and goes to the   2110
tune of two maids wooing a man: there's scarse a Maide
westward but she sings it: 'tis in request, I can tell you.

    Mop. We can both sing it: if thou'lt beare a part, thou
shalt heare, 'tis in three parts.

    Dor. We had the tune on't, a month agoe.   2115

    Aut. I can beare my part, you must know 'tis my oc-
cupation: Haue at it with you:

2104 too] *Om.* SING1, HUD1, OXF1
2116 know_∧] ~ ; JOHN

2099 **fadom**] I.e., fathom. SCHMIDT (1874): "A measure of length containing six
feet, used to measure deeps." Autolycus's fish would thus be 240,000 feet, or 45.5
miles, above sea level (cf. *OED*, Water, *sb*. 12).

2101 **cold fish**] RANN (ed. 1787): "The torpedo, or electrical eel." As synonyms
for *torpedo*, *OED* gives *cramp-fish* and *numb-fish* but not *cold fish*. Its earliest record
of *cold fish* as "emotionless person," seemingly an obvious significance in this context, is dated 1941. KNOWLES (privately) recalls that Angelo in *MM* was cold because
he "vvas begot betweene two Stock-fishes (*MM* 3.2.17 [1597])" and that Falstaff
attributes Prince John's cold blood to thin drink and eating fish (*2H4* 4.3.98–9
[2327–8]).

    for] MALONE (1780, 1:145): "Because."

2101–2 **exchange flesh**] *OED* (Exchange, *v.* 2, citing this line): "To give and
receive reciprocally." *OED* (Flesh, *sb*. 1g, citing this line): "In euphemistic phrases
with reference to sexual intercourse." WILLIAMS (1994, p. 507) glosses *flesh* here as
"vagina."

2103 **as true**] I.e., as true as it is pitiful, which is probably true, or as true as the
ballad of the Usurer's Wife, which is also probably true.

2104 **too**] BOORMAN (ed. 1964): "Indeed," but *too* does not have this meaning. Dorcas probably asks, incredulously, "Is it true as well as pitiful?"

2105 **Fiue . . . it**] The CLARKES (ed. 1865): "It is attested by the signatures of five justices."

witnesses] SCHMIDT (1875): "A thing which . . . bears testimony."

2108 **merry ballad, but**] BOORMAN (ed. 1964): "The 'but' suggests that 'merry' here means 'saucy' (requiring some apology)." The ballad may also be mirthful and brisk.

2110 **passing**] JOHNSON (1755): "Exceeding."

2110-11 **goes . . . man**] WILSON (ed. 1931): "[Alfred T.] Roffe [*The Handbook of Shakespeare Music* (1878)] mentions a song with this title, set to music by Dr Boyce, in 1759." PAFFORD (ed. 1963): "Roffe does not mention any setting entitled 'Two maids wooing a man'. It must be concluded either that a ballad of this title did exist but is lost—at any rate under that title; or else that Autolycus merely invented a plausible title." The tune has never been found. For "goes . . . of," the CLARKES (1879, p. 365): "'Is set to the tune', 'is adapted to the tune'." PARRY (ed. 1982), incorrectly: "Along the lines of."

2112 **westward**] DEIGHTON (ed. 1889): "In the west country, *i.e.* the west of England, for Shakespeare is thinking of his own country and its customs." MAXWELL (ed. 1969): "In England the 'unspoiled' country."

2113-17 **We . . . you**] BETHELL (ed. 1956): "Mopsa and Dorcas are going to read the words at sight, and the tune, which they 'had a month ago', they have presumably learned from the music." He does not extend this evidence to the vexed question of the Clown and his market list (see n. 1715). PAFFORD (ed. 1963): "The text does not justify the assumption that they could sight-read music," because they "may have picked up the tune a month ago although they had not learned the words." SCHANZER (ed. 1969): "The words of this song are clearly those of 'Two maids wooing a man', not those of Autolycus's *merry ballad*, which are sung to the same tune. When Mopsa says [2113-14,] she evidently means not only the tune but also the words of 'Two maids wooing a man'. There is therefore no indication that she and Dorcas can read either words or music. . . . Like Autolycus, they sing the song from memory." If she cannot read, Mopsa would have to "loue a ballet in print" (2082) only because of the authority print confers. See n. 2082-3.

2113 **part**] SQUIRE (1916, 2:43): "The melody assigned to a particular voice or instrument in concerted music."

2115 **on't**] See n. 785-6.

2116-17 **'tis my occupation**] DEIGHTON (ed. 1889): "Part of my occupation as a pedlar is to be able to join in singing catches." BROWN ("Laughter," 1966, pp. 113-14): "A clown's extra-dramatic statement about his own interests and a glancing jest at the expense of puritans whose accustomed phrase this was." With *part*, the expression is also salacious; *occupation* = "copulation." See COLMAN (1974, Occupy) and HENKE (1979, Occupied).

2117 **Haue . . . you**] The CLARKES (ed. 1865): "Implying readiness to undertake something proposed." SCHMIDT (1874): "I'll sing it with you"; for *have at it* he gives "begin." Hence ROLFE (ed. 1879): "I'll begin it, or try it." WRIGHT & LAMAR (ed. 1966): "Let's get on with it."

Song	*Get you hence, for I must goe*	
Aut.	*Where it fits not you to know.*	
Dor.	*Whether?*	2120
Mop.	*O whether?*	
Dor.	*Whether?*	
Mop.	*It becomes thy oath full well,*	
	Thou to me thy secrets tell.	
Dor:	*Me too: Let me go thether:*	2125
Mop:	*Or thou goest to th' Grange, or Mill,*	
Dor:	*If to either thou dost ill,*	
Aut:	*Neither.*	
Dor:	*What neither?*	
Aut:	*Neither:*	2130
Dor:	*Thou hast sworne my Loue to be,*	
Mop:	*Thou hast sworne it more to mee.*	
	Then whether goest? Say whether?	

Clo. Wee'l haue this song out anon by our selues: My
Father, and the Gent. are in sad talke, & wee'll not trouble   2135
them: Come bring away thy pack after me, Wenches Ile
buy for you both: Pedler let's haue the first choice; folow
me girles.   *Aut.* And you shall pay well for 'em.

Song.	*Will you buy any Tape, or Lace for your Cape?*	
	My dainty Ducke, my deere-a?	2140
	Any Silke, any Thred, any Toyes for your head	

2118–19 Song . . . Aut.] F1-F3; Song *after* 2117, *SP on* 2119 F4; *om.* Song, *SP*
on 2118 JOHN, OXF1; *Song. after* 2117, *om.* SP PEN1; *om.* Song *and SP* CLN2; SONG.
after 2117, *SP on* 2118 ROWE1 *etc.* (*subst.*)
      2119 *Where it*] *Where* F4-ROWE2; *Whither* COL2, COL3
      2135 Gent.] Gentlemen ROWE1+
      2138 *Exeunt Clown,* DORCAS, *and* MOPSA, [*after* girles.] COL2, DYCE, STAU-GLO
(−DEL2), HUD2-KIT1, ALEX+ (*subst.*); *Exit.* [*after* girles.] COL4; *Exit Clown, Dorcas*
and Mopsa. [*after* 'em.] PEN1
           And . . . 'em.] *Marked as aside* JOHN1-HAL, DEL2, KTLY, KNT3, DEL4, COL4
      2139 *Cape*] *cap* BLAIR
      2141 *Any Silke, any*] *And silk, and* THEO1-v1773 (−HAN, CAP)
           any Toyes] *And toys* BEV

2118–33 *Get . . . whether?*] For *WT*'s songs, see n. 1669–80 and p. 853. CA-
PELL (1783, 2.4:175–6): "A song of pure trochees," 2120–2 and 2128–30 excepted.
ARMSTRONG (1969, pp. 73–4) waxes philosophical: "He articulates for them in a song
about a mysterious journey their acute longing that the foreseeably uneventful progression of their days may somehow break into the unknown. . . . And this is momentarily to elude the oppression of a cyclical mode of life, of an inexorable arche-

typal pattern that has obtained from the beginning." DRAPER (1985, p. 33): The ballad "of gawdy sexual rivalry . . . matches the dramatic situation . . . between these two girls and the Clown," to which the tune (2111) is also appropriate. For an un-explained reason, the tune and the subjects of the two ballads—the usurer's wife (2084-7) and the cold fish (2097-2102)—remind DREW (1989, p. 99) of "Leontes' earlier interest in Hermione's supposed sexual dalliance with Polixenes." DREW attempts to prove that Autolycus is "a tragicomic microcosm of the broader concerns of the play."

The song makes remote sense. Although the man has made advances to both women, he asserts his independence by leaving and by keeping his destination a secret. Neither the grange nor the mill seems to have special significance; Mopsa guesses at two appropriate destinations, and Dorcas asserts that both are "ill," because no matter where he goes, he will leave her behind. The last line probably as much means "what are your intentions?" as "where are you going?"

2119 *it fits not*] PARRY (ed. 1982): "It is not suitable for."

2120 *Whether?*] For the rhyme of *whether-thether-neither*, see CERCIGNANI (1981, p. 51).

2123 *It . . . well*] PARRY (ed. 1982): "It's only proper, in the light of what you have sworn to me."

2124 *Thou*] COLLINS (ed. 1904-24?): "*I.e.* that thou."

2126 *Or thou goest*] HUNTER (ed. 1872): "Thou goest either" (FRANZ §586). *Or* probably means "whether," however; see SCHMIDT (1875), although he does not list this occurrence.

Grange] MINSHEU (1617): "A house or building, not only where corne is laid vp, as barnes be, but also where there be stables for horses, stalles for oxen, and other cattell, sties for hogges, and other things necessary for husbandrie." *OED* (*sb.* 1), however: "Barn." SCHMIDT (1874): "A solitary farm-house" (*sb.* 3).

2134 *haue . . . out*] CALDECOTT (MS 1813-33, Out): "Throughout, to the end of it." DEIGHTON (ed. 1889): "Sing it right through." Or, as CUTTS ("Setting," 1956, p. 88) says, "There was more to the song than is presented here." For another stanza, see p. 866.

anon] Immediately. See n. 1468.

2134-5 *My . . . talke*] BOORMAN (ed. 1964): "Another stage direction in the text." Cf. nn. 1412-13, 2190, and 2634-5. For the idea, in LONG (1961, pp. 75-8), that this conversation leads through several steps to Polixenes's savage denunciation of Perdita [2265-70], see p. 797.

2135 *sad*] MINSHEU (1617): "Pensive." HANMER (ed. 1743-4, 6:glos.): "Grave, sober, serious" (*OED, a.* 4). Cf. n. 616, 618.

2136-7 *Wenches . . . both*] CANFIELD (1989, p. 56): The Clown "embod[ies] the problem of the promiscuous sex urge of youth his father earlier laments [at 1501-5]. Is Florizel similarly just sowing his wild oats?"

2139-44 *Will . . . ware-a*] For *WT*'s songs, see n. 1669-80 and p. 853.

2139 *Lace*] BETHELL (ed. 1956): "Probably for tying the cape."

2140 *My . . . deere-a?*] KNOWLES (privately): "So Pyramus sings" in *MND* 5.1.286 (2080).

Ducke] JOHNSON (1755, citing this line): "A word of endearment, or fondness." Dainty ducks are proverbial; see DENT D630.1.

2140-4 *deere-a . . . weare-a . . . ware-a*] For the rhymes, see n. 1669-71.

2141 *Toyes*] MINSHEU (1617, Toies): See "Trifles." JOHNSON (1755): "A pretty commodity." *OED* (*sb.* 10), however: "A close cap or head-dress, of linen or wool, with flaps coming down to the shoulders, formerly worn by women in Scotland." *OED* adds that the use of the word here perhaps suggests its origin and that the sense here may be MINSHEU's. Toys (in the sense of "idle fancies" or "whims") in the head are proverbial (DENT T456.1).

Of the news't, and fins't, fins't weare-a.
Come to the Pedler, Money's a medler,
That doth vtter all mens ware-a.   *Exit*

Seruant. Mayster, there is three Carters, three Shep-   2145
herds, three Neat-herds, three Swine-herds y[t] haue made
themselues all men of haire, they cal themselues Saltiers,   (2B
and they haue a Dance, which the Wenches say is a gal-
ly-maufrey of Gambols, because they are not in't: but

2144 *ware-a.*] ~ *?* HUD2
    Exit] *Exit Clown*, Autolicus, Dorcas, *and* Mopsa. ROWE1-HUD1, SING2, WH1-
HAL, DEL2, KTLY, KNT3, DEL4 (*subst.*); *Exeunt* AUTOLYCUS, DORCAS, *and* MOPSA. COL4
2145 SCENE VII. POPE, HAN, WARB, JOHN
    Enter a Servant. ROWE1+ (*subst.*)
    is] are ROWE1-RANN (−CAP)
    Carters] goat-herds MTBY1 *conj.*, THEO1-CAP (−WARB), RANN, HUD2
2146 Neat-herds,] neat-herds, and ROWE1-v1773 (−CAP)

2142 *news't, and fins't, fins't*] NOBLE (1923, p. 97): The elisions "may be intended to mimic a salesman. . . . Shopkeepers had . . . their peculiar little man-
nerisms." They are actually intended to reduce two-syllable words to one syllable.
    weare-a] *OED* (*sb.* 3, citing this line): "What one wears or should wear."
    2143 *medler*] MINSHEU (1617): "Busie bodie, Iack of all sides." For *to meddle* he
gives "make, or haue to doe in this and that, to haue an oare in euery man's boate."
SCHMIDT (1875) agrees essentially that the word is used here in an unfavorable sense;
he too glosses it "busybody." The CLARKES (ed. 1865), neutrally: "Dealer." LEE (ed.
1907): "An agent that puts into circulation; . . . used in a good sense." BETHELL (ed.
1956): "Intermediary, means of exchange." CHARLTON (ed. 1916): "It [money] has a
share in all men do, prompting them to all and in all their exchangings and buyings
and sellings." NELSON (1972, p. 65) discovers "materialistic cynicism."
    2144 *vtter*] MINSHEU (1617, Vtterance): "Sale." REED (in MALONE, ed. 1790):
"Vend by retail" (*OED, v.*[1] 1). HUNTER (ed. 1872) finds a pun, for *utter* may also mean
"reveal" (*v.*[1] 7). HUDSON (ed. 1880): "*Publish*, to *offer for sale*, or to *make current* . . . used . . . in the sense of causing things to pass from hand to hand." SKEAT
(1882): "Keep on putting out." BOORMAN's (ed. 1964) "All men's wear shows that"
is not supported by *OED*. BOORMAN suggests the same pun on *vtter* that he found in
2009.
    ware-a] SCHMIDT (1875): "Merchandize."
    2145 **is**] For the singular verb, see n. 2638.
    Carters] Because the dancers are "foure-threes of Heardsmen" at 2157, THEO-
BALD (1729, in NICHOLS, 1817, 2:364) emends this word to *goat-heards*, thereby
encompassing "the four species of cattle, usually tended by herdsmen." Regarding
2157, CALDECOTT (MS 1813-33): "At a sheepshearing feast, if no one else, a sovereign
might well be allowed to reckon a *Carter* as such." The CLARKES (ed. 1865) also
defend F: "The farm-servant knows precisely what are the several callings of the
rustics . . . and designates them specially; but the king, hearing the repetition
words, *shepherds, neat-herds* [i.e., cowherds], and *swine-herds*, speaks of the whole
twelve as 'these four threes of *herdsmen*.'" CLARK (1930, p. 175): "This speech gives

us the number and purpose of the hands then employed about a substantial farm."

2146 Neat-herds] KITTREDGE & RIBNER (ed. 1967): "Tenders of cows."

2147 men of haire . . . Saltiers] COCKERAM (1623, Saults): "Leaps, iumpes" (*OED, sb.*²). ANON. (MS 1733-, Saltiers): "Dancers, jumpers," with which CAPELL (1783 [1774], 1:glos.) essentially agrees. WARBURTON (ed. 1747): "The phrase is taken from *tennis-balls*, which were stuffed with hair." He quotes *H5* 3.7.13-14 (1638-9): the Dauphin's courser "bounds . . . as if his entrayles were hayres." THIRLBY (MS 1747-53): "Thou simpleton," although FURNESS (ed. 1898) thinks WARBURTON right. EDWARDS (1748, p. 39): They are men "who have made themselves all over hairy (probably with goat-skins)[;] they call themselves *satyrs*," Saltiers being the Servant's approximation of this word. SCHMIDT (1875) and ONIONS (1986) concur. As DOUCE (1807, 1:361) points out, a "*Satyres* Daunce" is found in Thomas Ravenscroft, *A Briefe Discourse of . . . Charact'ring the Degrees* (1614; "Hunting and Hawking," C2ᵛ-4). WALKER (1860, 3:106): "Pronounced *sautiers*; whence the play on *satyrs.*" He and FURNESS find silent *l*'s in Elizabethan and later pronunciation of several words, including "Water" for *Walter* in Middleton's *Michaelmas Term* (ed. Levin, 1966, 1.1.145) and *2H6* 4.1.31-3 (2200-2). CERCIGNANI (1981, pp. 354-5), who agrees that *l* could be lost in *Walter*, nevertheless sides with the malapropists concerning *saltier*, adding that "the heraldic term *saltire* [a St. Andrew's cross]" is involved, though he does not say how. WARNER (1768, p. 29) thinks the word is Fr. *saulteur*, jumper or dancer, corrupted, and COLLIER (ed. 1842) considers Fr. *saultiers*, vaulters, because of the jumping in 2160. Neither explains why the Servant should know French, but PAFFORD (ed. 1963) believes that Sh. "probably intended *Saltiers* to suggest the dancers' two chief attributes — they are clad as *satyrs* and they are skilled *jumpers*: the word *sault, salt = jump* was in current use." It was (*OED, sb.*²), but not by Sh. According to BETHELL (ed. 1956), the Servant, mishearing *satyrs*, makes a "happy mistake."

As for their appearance as "men of haire," PAFFORD (ed. 1963): "They may have been adorned as were the satyrs in" Ben Jonson's masque *Oberon* (1611); the observation is no great help, because Jonson's satyrs are never described. Their principal entrance, however, is gambolic: "*they came running forth seuerally . . . leaping, and making antique action, and gestures*" (lines 29-31). BRISSENDEN (1981, p. 90): "In the . . . entertainments of the period in which they appear satyrs are almost invariably associated with disorder." For more on the connection of this scene with the masque, see n. 2164.

BRISSENDEN (1981, p. 91), considering 2159-60, wonders whether "professional tumblers or dancers may have been hired for both masque and play. [This scene] has at least eleven speaking characters, perhaps twelve [i.e., ten, perhaps eleven, depending on whether the Servants at 2005 and 2145 are one and the same], and there were probably some others, as shepherds and shepherdesses. It is also the only scene in Shakespeare in which the number of dancers is specified. When the satyrs enter, [there] are at least twenty-three people on the stage [including them]. This is a very large number. . . . The implication of the Servant's remark that 'one three' . . . had danced before the king [2158-9], then, could be that three of the satyrs were members of the company (£15 for 'Players' was included in the miscellaneous expenses of the masque) and that the other nine were brought in for the play's performance in the theatre."

2148-9 gally-maufrey of Gambols] For *gally-maufrey*, COCKERAM (1623): "A confused heape of things together." For *Gambols*, MINSHEU (1617): "Trickes played with the legs"; the CLARKES (ed.1865): "Hoppings" (*OED, sb.* 2, citing this line). Thus HARRISON (ed. 1947): "A jumble, or mix-up of dances." FREY (*Vast Romance*, 1980, pp. 16-17 n.): "There are indications (particularly in the mention of dancing before the King [2159]) that Shakespeare was alluding to Jonson's masques," which may have led to Jonson's apparently uncomplimentary remarks about *WT*. See nn. 0 and 1440.

they themselues are o'th'minde (if it bee not too rough   2150
for some, that know little but bowling) it will please
plentifully.
  Shep. Away: Wee'l none on't; heere has beene too
much homely foolery already. I know (Sir) wee wearie you.   2155
  Pol. You wearie those that refresh vs: pray let's see
these foure-threes of Heardsmen.
  Ser. One three of them, by their owne report (Sir,)
hath danc'd before the King: and not the worst of the
three, but iumpes twelue foote and a halfe by th'squire.   2160
  Shep. Leaue your prating, since these good men are
pleas'd, let them come in: but quickly now.
  Ser. Why, they stay at doore Sir.

Heere a Dance of twelue Satyres.

2154 homely] humble v1803, v1813
2160 a] *Om.* F4-POPE2, HAN
    squire] square ROWE1-RANN, ARD2, K&R, PEN2, OXF2, BEV4; squire CAPN
2163 *Om.* ROWE1-JOHN2
2163–4 Sir. *Heere . . . Satyres.*] sir. [*Exit.*| *Enter twelue Rusticks, presenting
Satyrs. Company seat themselves. Dance, and Exeunt Rusticks.* CAP, DYCE, SIS
(*subst.*); sir. [*Exit.*| *Re-enter* Servant, *with twelue rusticks habited like Satyrs. They
dance, and then exeunt.* MAL-DEL2, KTLY, KNT3-HUD2, OXF1 (*subst.*); sir. [*Exit.*| *Here
. . . Satyrs.* CAM1, GLO, WH2, IRV, BUL-ARD1, ALEX, PEL1, SIG, EVNS (*subst.*); sir. [*he
lets the herdsmen in* | *Here . . . Satyrs* CAM3, CLN2, PEN2, BEV (*subst.*)
2164 *After* 2165 HAN

2150 **are o'th'minde**] BETHELL (ed. 1956): "Are under the impression (that)."
  2151 **know . . . bowling**] JOHNSON (ed. 1765), incorrectly for *bowling*: "A
dance of smooth motion without great exertion of agility." Perhaps he is thinking of
the brawl, and to him the game was *bowls*, though *OED* (citing this line) has *bowling*
in the sporting sense from the year 1535. MASON (1785, p. 136) first connects the
word with lawn bowling, a gentle rather than a boisterous activity like the Saltiers'
dance. The intensity of physical activity in bowling and hence the Servant's meaning
have been disputed—WHITE (ed.1883), for example, says, "Bowls was a rough
game"—but neither STRUTT (1898, pp. 359–62) nor SIEVEKING (1916, 2:463–5) characterizes it as anything but a rather easy exercise, though bowling alleys could be
scenes of dissolute behavior. HUNTER (ed. 1872) seems to catch the Servant's point:
"More used to the game of bowling than to rustic dancing." Hence, *OED* (Bowl, *v.*[1]
3, citing this line): "To move like a bowl or hoop along the ground, to move by
revolution." RANN's (ed. 1787) "can only dance upon a bowling green" takes MASON
too literally.
  2153 **on't**] See n. 785–6.
  2154 **homely**] See n. 1651. DEIGHTON (ed. 1889): The Shepherd "is afraid that
Polixenes, who . . . he sees is some one of higher rank than the rest of his guests,
may be offended."

2154–6 **wearie . . . vs**] SCHMIDT (1875, Weary): "Harass by something irksome . . . tire." ROLFE (ed. 1879): "You tire these people who exert themselves for our amusement." CALDECOTT MS's (1813–33) "make uncomfortable" for the second *wearie* is unsupported by *OED*.

2156–7 **You . . . Heardsmen**] HERFORD (ed.1916–) compares Theseus's reply to the suggestion that homely foolery is not for him (*MND* 5.1.81–4 [1879–81]).

2157 **Heardsmen**] See n. 2145.

2158 **One three**] MAXWELL (ed. 1956): "One group of three."

2159 **danc'd . . . King**] WELSFORD (1927; 1962, p. 284): In an antimasque, "borrowed by Shakespeare from Ben Jonson." KERMODE (ed. 1963): "The performer of this dance had certainly done so, perhaps in this very dance." He alludes to the production of Jonson's *Masque of Oberon* on New Year's Day 1611; see p. 608. BRADBROOK ("Dramatic Romance," 1976, p. 82): "Actors from the King's Company regularly provided the antimasques at a royal performance; so two years later the same procedure was to be repeated when *Two Noble Kinsmen* embodied the Morris Dance of Country People, the second antimasque of Beaumont's *Masque of the Inner Temple and Gray's Inn*, performed for the marriage of the Princess Elizabeth" on 20 Feb. 1613. In this masque, incidentally, metallic statues also dance. BRADBROOK ("Open Form," 1976, p. 207) suggests that these dancers are the "nest of *Antiques*" Jonson alludes to in the Induction to *Bartholomew Fair* (line 128), but see n. 2164.

2160 **but**] CALDECOTT (MS 1813–33): "I.e. who does not."

th'squire] CAPELL (1783, 2.4:176–7) points out that COTGRAVE (1611) glosses *esquierre*, which some eds. translate as "foot-rule," as "Rule, or Squire." The latter is an early form of *square*, "an implement . . . for determining . . . right angles" (*OED, sb.* 1). *By the square* means "precisely, exactly" (1b). The expression is also found in *LLL* 5.2.474 (2413) and *1H4* 2.2.13 (748).

2161 **prating**] MINSHEU (1617, Prate): See "*to* Cackle, & *to* Babble."

2163 **at doore**] ABBOTT (§90): "*The* is . . . omitted after prepositions in adverbial phrases." Cf. 2594 and 2896. FURNESS (ed. 1898) considers the articles to be absorbed rather than omitted, a fine distinction. PAFFORD (ed. 1963): *At door* occurs often in Sh. but *at the door* even more often. For the significance of the door, see n. 2006–7.

2164 **Heere . . . Satyres**] Perhaps following WHALLEY (1756, 3:282), MALONE (in STEEVENS, ed. 1778, 4:288) quotes from the Induction to Jonson's *Bartholomew Fair* (127–30): "If there bee neuer a *Seruant-monster* i'the *Fayre;* who can helpe it? he sayes; nor a nest of *Antiques?* Hee is loth to make Nature afraid . . . like those that beget *Tales, Tempests*, and such like *Drolleries.*" MALONE identifies the twelve satyrs as the nest of antiques. See nn. 0 and 2147. A *drollery* is "a comic play or entertainment; a puppet-show" (*OED* 2); Sh.'s use of the word in *Tmp.* 3.3.21 (1543) may be part of the joke. THORNDIKE (1901, pp. 33–4): "While satyrs were not altogether uncommon on the Elizabethan stage, a dance of satyrs . . . was certainly an innovation in 1611. Such anti-masques were only introduced about 1608, and such a dance of satyrs is not found in any court masque before, or for that matter after, 1611. . . . Either Jonson must have borrowed from the public stage the idea . . . for his court masque [*Oberon, the Faery Prince*, performed 1 Jan. 1611], or Shakspere must have borrowed from the court masque this new and popular stage device. . . . The second alternative is far more probable because of the great importance of the court masques and the desire for novelty in them, and because the public may naturally be supposed to have been anxious to see a reproduction of a popular anti-masque." In *Oberon* the satyrs sing a song to the moon. "*The song ended: They fell sodainely into an antique dance, full of gesture, and swift motion*" (10: 351). WILSON (ed. 1931): "Almost certainly a morris dance." He no doubt means merely a fantastic or grotesque performance ("antique," or antic), not the morris in which the Robin Hood figures and the hobby horse appear.

In Marlowe's *Edward II*, as SORELL (1957, p. 380) notes, Gaveston arranges a plan to charm the pliant king: "men like Satyres grazing on the lawnes, Shall with their Goate feete daunce an antick hay" (1.1.59–60). The antic hay is a type of reel, and when Hamlet puts his antic disposition on, his behavior will seem "strange or odd" (1.5.170–2 [866–8]). COOPER (1977, p. 177): *Satyre* "is probably a Jacobean standardization of the 'salvage man', the wild man or wodwose who had figured in pageants in the country and at court for centuries, long before the satyr proper and his accompanying nymphs and shepherds became fashionable." Most eds., however, gloss as HAPPÉ (1969) does: "Woodland gods, classical in origin, reputedly lustful: they had animal form; ape's body, horse's tail, and two goat's feet."

In *Oberon* the comic or grotesque figures in the antimasque would have been impersonated by professionals rather than by gentlemen. (See further in n. 1500.) Financial records pertaining to the masque do show payment to "Players" but do not show who these performers were or the name of their company or companies (*Ben Jonson*, 10:521). It may be significant that three of the dancers have appeared before the king (2158–9), an observation said to be pointless were it not true (cf. PROUD-FOOT, 1966, p. 241). But this detail too turns out to be ambiguous (see p. 608). For another possible connection between the masque and *WT*, see n. 1500, and for 2164 as an antimasque dance, n. 1988. NICOLL (1958, pp. 56–7), having observed that the dance awkwardly prolongs the sad talk of Polixenes and Camillo: "There seems good reason for supposing that the Servant's announcement and the dance were an interpolation [possibly] inserted for the court performance of *The Winter's Tale* which took place on 5 November 1611. Thus, we need not necessarily assume that here in his original conception and handling of his theme Shakespeare was being directly influenced by the masque." IOPPOLO (1991, pp. 85–6): "It seems unlikely that Forman [see p. 606] saw but simply failed to note the dance of the satyrs in 4.4 of *The Winter's Tale* and the Hecate scene in *Macbeth* in his otherwise extremely detailed and precise summaries of the scenes of both plays. . . . The dance of the satyrs may then have been added sometime after the original performance of *The Winter's Tale*." Forman, however, also failed to note Hermione's resurrection, and the commentator who forgot that could forget anything. If NICOLL is right, however, the date of *WT* need not be later than 1 Jan. 1611, and the attempts of critics like CUTTS and BROWN (see below) to connect the satyrs with other elements of the play become nugatory.

FRYE (1962, p. 236): Perhaps the dance represents "a vision of nature demonstrating its creative power throughout the entire year." CUTTS (1968, p. 79), taking an opposing view: "The pastoral setting in which he [the satyr] is found may look harmless, but his very presence there spells goatish dispositions. No wonder Polixenes suggests it is time to part Florizel and Perdita, and that the matter may already have gone too far." BROWN (1962, p. 226): "This dance is a meaningful contrast, an antimasque to the first [dance; see n. 1988], being full of great 'jumps' and representing the antics of men without 'order', without control over their 'blood'. . . . It is the possibility of such disorder that alarms Polixenes and over against which Florizel and Perdita assert the mutual order . . . of their love." FOAKES (1971, p. 132): "Instead of the usual climax of a masque, in some form of beauty and virtue dispelling ugliness and evil, this masque-like sequence ends with the dance of goat-feet as anger and distress dispel gaiety and peace." BRISSENDEN (1981, p. 94): It "is followed by Polixenes' decision to separate the lovers, his doing so, and the overthrow of order. The satyrs' dance is the culminating preparation for Polixenes' action." Contrasting this dance with the earlier one (1988–9), HOLLAND (1964, p. 301): "The first one, coming after Perdita's great speech about the flowers, about nature, about Proserpina [1924–43], is a dance of shepherds and shepherdesses. The second . . . is a dance of satyrs, classic symbols for lust. Associated with woman we have the mating of man and woman, the act of procreation: associated with man alone we have only animal

Pol. O Father, you'l know more of that heereafter: 2165
Is it not too farre gone? 'Tis time to part them,
He's simple, and tels much. How now (faire shepheard)
Your heart is full of something, that do's take
Your minde from feasting. Sooth, when I was yong,

2165-6 *Pol.* O . . . Is] *Flo.* O . . . *Pol.* Is HAN
2165-7 O . . . much.] *Marked as aside* JOHN, v1773-v1785
2165 *rising from beside the Shepherd.* CAP
2166-7 Is . . . much.] F1-JOHN2, v1773-v1785; *marked as aside* CAP, RANN-DEL2,
KTLY, KNT3, DEL4; *To Cam.* CAM1 *etc.*
2168 do's] doth THEO2, WARB-RANN (−CAP)

---

lust." The man in question here, however, has an honor that burns hotter than desire
(1835-6).
    RHODES (1923, p. 100): "This SD could only have been added by one who knew
that the 'men of haire' that call themselves 'Saltiers' [2147] should have called themselves 'Satyres.'" That person, RHODES thinks, assembled a text of the play from
actors' parts (see n. 1500 and p. 591), but he could have been Crane or Sh. himself.
    2165 **O . . . heereafter**] WARBURTON (ed. 1747): "Replied by the king in an-
swer to the shepherd's saying *since . . . pleased* [2161-2]." CAPELL (1783, 2.4:177),
on the other hand: "The shepherd had been telling him, he saw it must be a match;
for the soliloquy following ['much.' (2167)] shews that matters relating to the young
couple had been their subject." RITSON (1783, p. 71) offers a third possibility: "The
line . . . seems to be in reply to some unexpressed [inaudible] question from the
old shepherd." Eds. generally agree with CAPELL; the CLARKES (ed. 1865), for example:
"The king has been cross-questioning the old shepherd as he proposed [at 1659-62],
and with the success he has anticipated." The CLARKES elsewhere (1879, p. 1) use
this speech to illustrate a principle: Sh. "sometimes allows his speakers to make abrupt
reference to some subject that has been talked of apart by two or more persons while
others are occupied more prominently on the scene." Cf. 628-9 and 2496-7. They
also point out that Camillo's private conversation with the lovers during Autolycus's
soliloquy becomes audible in much this way at 2496. PARRY (ed. 1982), who thinks
the dialogue leading to the dance of the satyrs and the dance itself "may be a topical
insertion," suggests that "this line was first meant to follow on directly (and rather
more suitably) after Autolycus' exit [at 2144]."
    Father] SCHMIDT (1874): "Appellation given to any old man."
    2166 **Is . . . gone?**] DEIGHTON (ed. 1889): "Have we not already allowed things
to go further than we should?" BETHELL (ed. 1956): The "question is rhetorical: he
has already made up his mind that the love of Florizel and Perdita has gone too far."
    farre gone] KNOWLES (privately): "Leontes's words at 303."
    2167 **He's . . . much**] COLLINS (ed. 1904-24?): "I.e. the old shepherd." See
1661-2.
    simple] SCHMIDT (1875): "Silly, witless," his definition 5, which he also applies
to the word in 2473, where Autolycus describes Trust, the sworn brother of Honesty.
BEVINGTON (ed. 1992) prefers "guileless," which is SCHMIDT 4.
    How now] See n. 201.
    2169 **Sooth**] See n. 71.

And handed loue, as you do; I was wont   2170
To load my Shee with knackes: I would haue ransackt
The Pedlers silken Treasury, and haue powr'd it
To her acceptance: you haue let him go,
And nothing marted with him. If your Lasse
Interpretation should abuse, and call this   2175
Your lacke of loue, or bounty, you were straited
For a reply at least, if you make a care
Of happie holding her.
   Flo. Old Sir, I know
She prizes not such trifles as these are: 2180
The gifts she lookes from me, are packt and lockt
Vp in my heart, which I haue giuen already,
But not deliuer'd. O heare me breath my life
Before this ancient Sir, whom (it should seeme)
Hath sometime lou'd: I take thy hand, this hand,   2185

2170 handed] handled MTBY4 *and* MCOL1 *conj.*, COL2, WH1, COL4, HUD2
2177 reply﹏] F1-POPE2, HAN; ~ ; HUD1, DYCE, WH1, CAM1, GLO, COL4+; ~ ,
THEO1 *etc.*
    a care] care THEO1-CAP (−HAN), DYCE2, HUD2, BUL
2180 She] Such ROWE2
2183 life] Love MTBY2 *conj.*, THEO1-JOHN2 (−HAN)
2184 whom] who F2+ (−PEN1, ALEX, CLN2, PEN2, EVNS)
2185 sometime] sometimes DODD (1780), COL2

2170 **handed**] CAPELL (1783 [1774], 1:glos.) uses THIRLBY's emendation as a definition: "Handle." SEYMOUR (1805, 1:167): "Kept fair terms with it [love], *bore it in
hand* [i.e., engaged in it]." SCHMIDT (1874): "To be hand and hand with, to devote
one's self to"; the CLARKES (ed. 1865) think Florizel has held Perdita's hand since line
1972. *OED* (*v.* 1), however, cites 977 for the literal meaning of *hand* and this line for
the figurative—"to deal with, treat of." LEE (ed. 1907) has it both ways: "Touched
or treated," and MAXWELL (ed. 1956) thinks of betrothal: "Pledged by hand," for
which see n. 2185-8. Most recent eds. follow *OED*, but see SELTZER in n. 188-91.
   wont] JOHNSON (1755): "Accustomed."
2171 **Shee**] The CLARKES (ed. 1865): Used "substantively to express the woman
especially beloved" *(OED* 7, citing this line). WILSON (ed. 1931): "Mistress, love." See
ABBOTT §224 and n. 100-1.
   knackes] JOHNSON (1755, Knack, citing this line): "A pretty contrivance; a
toy." HARNESS (ed. 1825): "Trifles," as at 2180. See 2272 for the word in another
context.
2172 **silken Treasury**] BETHELL (ed. 1956): "Collection of silks."
2172-3 **powr'd . . . acceptance**] CALDECOTT (MS 1813-33): "I.e. . . .
emptied it to her hand." KITTREDGE & RIBNER (ed. 1967): "So that she might choose
what she wished."
2174 **nothing . . . him**] JOHNSON (1755, Mart): "To traffick; to buy or sell."
RANN (ed. 1787): "And made no purchase of him."
2175 **Interpretation should abuse**] SEYMOUR (1805, 1:168): "Should miscon-

ceive your conduct." KERMODE (ed. 1963): "Choose to misunderstand," but later eds. do not make the abuse deliberate. BEVINGTON (ed. 1992), for example: "Should interpret wrongly."

2176-8 **you . . . her**] COLLINS (1904-24?): "You would be at a loss how to answer, at least if you take any thought for possessing her happily." PARRY (ed. 1982): "Polixenes is deliberately 'drawing out' his son, here."

2176 **straited**] JOHNSON (1755): "Put to difficulties." SCHANZER (ed. 1969): "At a loss." For the part of speech, see n. 2344.

2177-8 **make . . . her**] CALDECOTT (MS 1813-33): "Feel your happiness deeply interested in retaining her."

2177-8 **make . . . Of**] MAXWELL (ed. 1956, Care): "Serious wish." HUNTER (ed. 1872): "Feel interested in." MOORMAN (ed. 1912): "Care for."

2178 **happie holding her**] SCHMIDT (1874): "Seeing her happy." However, for *happie*, CHARLTON (ed. 1916): "Happily." For *holding*, BEVINGTON (ed. 1992): "Keeping."

2180-2 **She . . . heart**] The CLARKES (ed. 1865): "The proof here given that Florizel thoroughly appreciates the singleness [singularity?] of Perdita's character, proves him to be worthy of her." DUSINBERRE (1975, p. 124): "Perdita scorns the courtship of bribery." Unlike Florizel's mother, who was loaded with knacks (2171).

2181 **lookes**] For the omission of *for*, see ABBOTT §200.

2182-3 **which . . . deliuer'd**] SCHMIDT (1874, Deliver): "To speak, to communicate," punning on "transfer." BETHELL (ed. 1956): "'Which' refers to 'heart', thought of as a package of gifts; 'given . . . deliver'd' means that he loves her but has not yet made a formal declaration—they are not yet espoused. There is a pun on *deliver'd* as goods and *deliver'd* = *spoken*." BOORMAN (ed. 1964) finds the two senses to be "handed over" and "given legally." SCHANZER (ed. 1969) agrees: "Florizel is distinguishing between the free gift of his heart and the formal handing over of it, 'delivery' as a legal term being 'the formal transfer of a deed by the grantor' [*OED* 4b (*b*)]. The attempted marriage contract that follows is to be this 'delivery.'"

2183 **breath my life**] BETHELL (ed. 1956): "Make vows of lifelong love." CHARLTON (ed. 1916): "Florizel is somewhat sentimental; his breathing of his life . . . is soon 'put out' by [Polixenes's] prosaic remark [2189]." SCHMIDT (1874, Life): "Inmost part, essence."

2184 **Before . . . Sir**] MEADER (1954, p. 154): The betrothal has to this point been secret and "no more binding than the fidelity of the lovers makes it." It has, however, been confirmed by oath (MEADER, p. 190; see lines 1854, 2345). Florizel now "attempts to perform a public spousal," which, "because witnessed [2194 ff.], would be more binding," For *Sir*, see n. 295.

whom] For the form, see n. 1207.

it should seeme] Because of these words, FURNESS (ed. 1898) thinks the "ancient Sir" is Camillo. "Of the two, Camillo had been less able than Polixenes to conceal his admiration of Perdita [cites 1922-3, 1980-1, *Queene* as contrasting with *Lowborne* (1975)]. The lover's eyes have detected an old man's adoration." Despite this, the "ancient Sir" is the "Old Sir" of 2179, Polixenes.

2185 **sometime lou'd**] KITTREDGE & RIBNER (ed. 1967): "Once been a lover himself."

2185-8 **I . . . ore**] GREY (1754, 1:267) notes the similar passage in *MND* 3.2.142-8 (1162-8); HERFORD (ed. 1916-), in *Tmp*. 4.1.23-32 (1676-86); and PAFFORD (ed. 1963), in several other Shn. works. MIRIAM JOSEPH (1947, p. 154): The rhetorical device is "Exergasia, or expolitio, [which] augments by repeating the same thought in many figures." BETHELL (1947, p. 23): "There is no need to ascribe any intellectual subtlety to Florizel, yet his love-making has even more intellectual complexity than the jealousy of Leontes. A mere description of his mistress' hand [as here] produces a surprising collocation of images."

407

As soft as Doues-downe, and as white as it,
Or Ethyopians tooth, or the fan'd snow, that's bolted
By th'Northerne blasts, twice ore.
   Pol. What followes this?
How prettily th'yong Swaine seemes to wash   2190
The hand, was faire before? I haue put you out,
But to your protestation: Let me heare
What you professe.
   Flo. Do, and be witnesse too't.
   Pol. And this my neighbour too?   2195
   Flo. And he, and more
Then he, and men: the earth, the heauens, and all;
That were I crown'd the most Imperiall Monarch
Thereof most worthy: were I the fayrest youth
That euer made eye swerue, had force and knowledge   2200
More then was euer mans, I would not prize them
Without her Loue; for her, employ them all,

2187-9 *Three verse lines ending* snow, . . . ore. . . . this? F2-v1813, SING, KNT,
WH1, HAL, STAU, DEL, KTLY, OXF1; *two, ending* bolted . . . this?— COL, HUD, DYCE,
CAM, GLO, WH2, IRV, BUL-ARD1, KIT1+
2187 Ethyopians] Ethiop's DYCE1 *conj.*, DYCE2, HUD2
2188 blasts] blast F2-JOHN2
2197 the heauens] and heavens F4-v1773 (−CAP)
2200 force] sense COL2, COL4

2186 **As . . . it**] Doves are proverbially white (DENT D573.2), their down proverbially soft (D576.1). WEBB (1989): White is "the admired hue of the female (sometimes male) body and its parts."
    Doues-downe] WALKER (1854, pp. 234-5): Pronounced as a single word, with
the accent on the first syllable— i.e., *Dóues-dun.* FURNESS (ed. 1898): "A spondee."
    2187 **Or . . . bolted**] Rather than as an alexandrine, ABBOTT (§501) classifies
this line as a trimeter couplet, for he believes (§493) that "a proper Alexandrine . . . is seldom found in Shakespeare." That is true, of course, if most of the
lines with six accents are called something else. See nn. 77, 185, 190, 499, and 1264-
5. To ELLIS (1871, 3:944), ABBOTT's trimeter couplets are "an entirely new conception, whereby normal Alexandrines are made to be no Alexandrines at all."
    Ethyopians] COLLINS (ed. 1904-24?): "'Negro'; Ethiopia was an ancient name
of Africa." SUGDEN (1925): "Used vaguely for the whole of Africa S. of Egypt and the
Sahara desert."
    2187-8 **fan'd . . . ore**] HALE (1985, p. 149): "Does not Florizel's
tongue . . . remind us at the very height of the idyll of a coldness in things, in love's
course? If so, . . . Shakespeare maintains our subliminal connection with . . . his
tale of winter."

2187 **fan'd snow**] SCHMIDT (1874, Fan): "Blow as with a fan." Snow is also fanned in *MND* 3.2.141-2 (1166-7), and driven (blown, drifted) snow is proverbially white (TILLEY S591).

   bolted] HANMER (ed. 1743-4, 6:glos.): "Sift, as they do Meal thro' a sieve" (*OED, v.*¹ b. *trans.* and *fig.*, citing this line). RANN (ed. 1787): "Purified." Since flour is "the finer portion of meal . . . which is separated by bolting" (*OED*), the twice-bolted snow becomes extraordinarily white. Cf. n. 2044. BETHELL (1947, p. 23): "'Bolted' introduces a metaphor into the simile and supplies the further image of 'wheaten flour'; the snow is made purer by being twice sifted as wheaten flour is sifted of its impurities."

   2189 **What followes this?**] DEIGHTON (ed. 1889): "To what declaration is this a prelude?"

   2190-1 **How . . . before?**] Some eds. believe that Polixenes begins his assault upon the young couple as early as this speech. BETHELL (ed. 1956): "A note of irony." PARRY (ed. 1982): "This laconic comment, rather discourteously interrupting the flow of Florizel's ardent 'protestation', is perhaps the first hint of anger."

   2190 **seemes to wash**] BOORMAN (ed. 1964): "Strokes and presses, as if washing." Cf. nn. 1412-13, 2134-5, and 2634-5. KITTREDGE & RIBNER (ed. 1967): "Make more pure and beautiful."

   2191 **hand, was**] I.e., hand that was. ABBOTT (§244): "The relative is frequently omitted, especially where the antecedent clause is emphatic and evidently incomplete." Cf. 2355, 2754-5. PAFFORD (ed. 1963): "The comma . . . may be a misplaced apostrophe denoting an omission." Perhaps; cf. 13 and n.

   put . . . out] SCHMIDT (1875): "To make to forget one's part, to embarrass, to puzzle."

   2195 **And . . . too?**] FURNESS (ed. 1898): "Polixenes in his secret soul sympathised with his boy's adoration of Perdita, and hoped that this protestation would be one, which by referring to Florizel's tie to his father, should be heard by him alone. And it was this consciousness that had he been in his boy's place he would have been as steadfast to his love as his boy is, which lent an exaggeration to his anger when he revealed himself." Polixenes's question more likely concerns whether there will be an additional witness to Florizel's profession, the presence of whom would make it all the more binding. The neighbor is Camillo. See n. 2213-23 for more on troth plighting.

   2197 **men**] DEIGHTON (ed. 1889): "All mankind."

   2198-2202 **That . . . Loue**] WEINSTEIN (1971, p. 103): "Although Florizel's ardor is praiseworthy, is there not something fatuous about his exaltation?" PILGRIM (1983, p. 41): "This might seem, in itself, excessive and rhetorical, but . . . Florizel has said no more than he has meant."

   2199 **Thereof most worthy**] HUNTER (ed. 1872): "And most worthy of being so crowned."

   2200 **That . . . swerue**] CALDECOTT (MS 1813-33, Swerve): "Rove." DEIGHTON (ed. 1889): "That ever caused women . . . to look at him; possibly with the secondary sense of being inconstant." NEILSON & HILL (ed. 1942): "Attracted notice." BEVINGTON (ed. 1992) thinks the swerving occurs "out of awe and respect," but *fayrest* means "handsomest."

   force] SCHMIDT (1874): "Strength, vigour." The CLARKES (1879, p. 554): "'Influence' and 'virtuous excellence.'"

   2201 **not prize**] *OED* (*v.*¹ 3b, citing this line): "Care nothing for."

   2202 **employ**] The CLARKES (ed. 1865): *Would* is understood.

Commend them, and condemne them to her seruice,
Or to their owne perdition.

    Pol. Fairely offer'd.   2205

    Cam. This shewes a sound affection.

    Shep. But my daughter,
Say you the like to him.

    Per. I cannot speake
So well, (nothing so well) no, nor meane better   2210
By th'patterne of mine owne thoughts, I cut out
The puritie of his.

    Shep. Take hands, a bargaine;   (2
And friends vnknowne, you shall beare witnesse to't:
I giue my daughter to him, and will make   2215
Her Portion, equall his.

    Flo. O, that must bee
I'th Vertue of your daughter: One being dead,

2208 him.] ~ ? ROWE1+
2210 better‸] ~ , F3, F4; ~ . ROWE1+
2211 mine] my SING, HUD1, KTLY
      owne] *Om.* SING2

2203-4 **Commend . . . perdition**] HUDSON (ed. 1880): "*Commit* them to her service, or condemn them to their own *destruction*." For *commend* as "commit," cf. n. 1114 and line 1354. For the construction, cf. nn. 1246 and 1348-50. BETHELL (ed. 1956): "There may be a play on words: Perdita or perdition are the alternatives before him." TOLIVER (1989, p. 170): "An affiliation with the wit of the earlier comedies." J. SMITH (1974, p. 155), alone: *Condemne* "admits the wrongheadedness with which danger is defied."

2205 **Fairely offer'd**] CHARLTON (ed. 1916): "If we regard Polixenes as knowing what line of action he was to take, we cannot but regard this playing as cruel indifference and harsh cynicism. But that would be unjust. Polixenes is obviously troubled at his son's actions, and obviously does not approve of some elements in them. Yet he is charmed by Perdita's presence, and his dallying with and encouraging the lovers is not deliberate cruelty. His harshness is drawn out later, and by something of which as yet there has been no sign."

2206 **affection**] Probably "love" (*OED, sb.* 6); possibly "disposition" (4). Cf. nn. 26, 214, 2332-3, 3046, 3110.

2208 **him.**] Regarding ROWE's question mark, BOORMAN (ed. 1964): "This may well be the Shepherd's suggestion, not question, to his 'daughter.'"

2209-12 **I . . . his**] HERFORD (ed. 1916-): "Florizel has expressed an ideal of married life as high as her own, and though she cannot put it into words, she uses her own pure intentions to interpret his." PYLE (1969, p. 83): "Consciously she sees her royal lover's abilities as greatly exceeding her own, and finds equality only in the assumption that his love is as pure as hers is. . . . So her conservative nature reconciles itself with the strongest romantic impulses." EDWARDS (1980, pp. 43-4): "The immediate import . . . is of course depreciation of herself and praise of Florizel; his eloquence is far beyond hers and she cannot surpass his love. The implication of her words goes quite another way. Their true burden is that Florizel's speech, by itself, is nothing. 'I . . . better.' There is a clear inference that although speech has meaning, people have meanings too; the meanings of the heart do not depend on speech and can exist without it. . . . Though Florizel spoke well he might [theoretically] have 'meant' ill. . . . Neither the quality of her love nor her recognition of Florizel's has anything to do with a formal declaration in words, such as Florizel rather pretentiously makes."

2210 **nothing**] See n. 849.

2211 **By . . . out**] *OED* (Cut, *v.* 56k and Pattern, *sb.* 2 *fig.*, both citing this line): "Form, fashion, shape" and "design, pattern, outline." DEIGHTON (ed. 1889): I.e., "estimate . . . [,which is] a metaphor from shaping garments." COLLINS (ed. 1904–24?): "I.e. reason from the greatness of my love to that of his, as one copies a pattern in cutting out a dress." PAFFORD (ed. 1963): "She thinks that he must feel towards her as she does towards him." BEVINGTON (ed. 1992): "Not patterned on hers but rather perceived by her to be a model for her own." FURNESS (ed. 1898): "A woman's simile." Or a tailor's. He compares Imogen as "a garment out of fashion" (*Cym.* 3.4.51–3 [1722–4]).

2212 **puritie**] SINGER (ed. 1856): "Sincerity." Not exactly. "Freedom from moral corruption, from . . . sexual uncleanness, or pollution" (*OED* 3). BETHELL (ed. 1956): "She means that his intentions must be like hers."

2213–23 **Take . . . yours**] KNIGHT (ed. 1838–43, 8:213–14): "The troth-plight was exchanged without the presence of a priest, but . . . witnesses were essential to the ceremony. . . . Here . . . in the publicity of a village [sic] festival, the hand of the loved one is solemnly taken by her 'servant'; he breathes his life before the ancient stranger who is accidentally present. The stranger is called to be witness to the protestation; and so is the neighbour who has come with him [Camillo]." COOK (1991, p. 34): Marina (*Per.*), Perdita, and Miranda (*Tmp.*) are "scarcely past childhood. Part of the appeal to audiences may well derive from the distance between such a heroine and an eligible, flesh-and-blood English female. . . . [Their] extreme youth . . . makes an essential contribution to the atmosphere of fantasy engendered by the romances." Perdita's age is not much emphasized, however. Polixenes speaks of her beauty and natural nobility (1975–8), not her youth, and the Shepherd clearly regards her as marriageable (e.g., at 2003–5).

2213 **Take . . . bargaine**] Proverbial (DENT H109.1) and cf. n. 175.

2216 **Portion**] PHILLIPS (1706): "That Estate or Sum of Money, which a Woman brings to her Husband in Marriage."

2217–20 **that . . . wonder**] WRIGHT & LaMAR (ed. 1966): "I.e., her virtue in itself can match his portion, but the shepherd cannot possibly offer a dowry in money that would do."

The King's attitude, to this point, has been gently inquisitive if not sympathetic; cf. TAYLOR (1973, pp. 336–7). BROOKE (1905; 1913, p. 276): "This [statement] accounts for the violence of [Polixenes's] anger. On hearing it, Polixenes, after an attempt to control himself by reasoning with Florizel, breaks out into such a fury with every one that it almost seems as if Shakespeare, having represented in Leontes jealousy overwhelming reason, intended in Polixenes here to represent a swift storm of anger in which all reasonableness is destroyed." MARSH (1962; 1969, p. 151): "The violence of the opposition is so great, and finds expression in such cruelty, that it is impossible to avoid the assumption that this is a sort of sexual bitterness and jealousy, felt by a man who is growing old, and feels himself being pushed out." MARSH finds the jealousy expressed in 2278–85. Surprisingly few critics comment on how offensive Florizel's words are. TAYLOR calls them "shocking"; SUMMERS (1984, p. 35), "truly careless, if not callous." PORTER & CLARKE (ed. 1908): "This is what hurts Polixenes . . . like King Henry when Hal took the crown [*2H4* 4.5.21 (2543) ff.]."

411

I shall haue more then you can dreame of yet,
Enough then for your wonder: but come-on,   2220
Contract vs fore these Witnesses.
    Shep. Come, your hand:
And daughter, yours.
    Pol. Soft Swaine a-while, beseech you,
Haue you a Father?   2225
    Flo. I haue: but what of him?
    Pol. Knowes he of this?
    Flo. He neither do's, nor shall.
    Pol. Me-thinkes a Father,
Is at the Nuptiall of his sonne, a guest   2230
That best becomes the Table: Pray you once more
Is not your Father growne incapeable
Of reasonable affayres? Is he not stupid
With Age, and altring Rheumes? Can he speake? heare?
Know man, from man? Dispute his owne estate?   2235
Lies he not bed-rid? And againe, do's nothing
But what he did, being childish?

    2224 a-while, beseech you,] ∼ : ∼ ∼ , F2-JOHN2, v1773; ∼ , ∼ ∼ ; CAP, v1778+ (−CLN2, SIG)
    2225-6 *One verse line* v1793-BEV3
    2227-8 *One verse line* v1793-EVNS
    2228-9 *One verse line* mTBY2 *conj.*, mCAP2, BEV3
    2228 nor] or DEL
    2235 Dispute] dispose mTBY3 *and* mWARB *conj.*, COL2, COL4

    2219 yet] STAUNTON (ed. 1859): "*Now*," a meaning "indispensable to the antithesis" created by *Enough then*. LETTSOM (MS 1840-65): "I.e. *as yet*." HUNTER (ed. 1872): "One day," but for this meaning (*OED, adv.* 5) to operate, the order should be *I shall yet haue*. BOORMAN (ed. 1964), wrongly: "When that happens."
    2220 **Enough . . . wonder**] DEIGHTON (ed. 1889): "I will not at present say more to add to your wonder." But KERMODE (ed. 1963): "Enough to amaze you when you know of it."
    2221 **Contract . . . Witnesses**] ORGEL (ed. 1996): "Either a promise to marry or a declaration of marriage in the presence of witnesses constituted a legally binding contract. The first was a betrothal, and could be abrogated under certain conditions, but the second was a valid marriage subject to the matrimonial law. Since the proceeding is interrupted, it is not clear which sort of contract Florizel is about to propose. Leontes describes Florizel as both 'troth-plight' to Perdita and as his son-in-law in [3363-5]; but at [2974] Florizel denies that they are married."
    2224 **Soft**] SCHMIDT (1875): "Hold, stop" (*OED, adv.* 8a, citing this line).
    beseech] For the omission of the nominative, see ABBOTT §399.

2225-9 **Haue . . . Father**] SIMPSON (1955, p. 75) uses this cluster to illustrate Sh.'s fondness for short lines at the beginning of speeches, specifically 2229.

2225 **Haue . . . Father?**] MEADER (1954, p. 169): For betrothal, "the consent of a parent is not necessary. . . . In Shakespeare, as in the popular dramas generally, the young people marry their own choices without regard to parental wishes." In none of Sh.'s plays, however, does a prince marry without consent if his father is known to be alive.

2228 **He . . . shall**] TRAVERSI (1959, p. 27): "Florizel's emphatic denial . . . implies his readiness to accept a relationship essentially incomplete, incapable of attaining full consummation," in that it lacks the father's blessing.

2230 **Nuptiall**] For the singular form, see n. 1853.

2232-7 **Is . . . childish?**] HOLBROOK (1964, p. 185): "Polixenes speaks from age and maturity [yet] the mounting condemnation of Florizel begins to savour . . . of Leontes' envy." Despite our sense of Florizel's intuitive rightness, his apparent disregard of filial responsibility may seem adolescent self-indulgence until Polixenes loses his temper at 2260.

2232 **Is not**] DEIGHTON (ed. 1889): "The form of the question, 'is *not* your father', etc., 'is he *not*', etc., indicates surprise; surely he must be, etc., or you would not act in this way."

incapeable] KERSEY (1702): "*Unable*, or *unfit*."

2233 **reasonable**] OED (*a.* 2b, citing this line) only as a nonce use: "Requiring the use of reason." VAN DAM (1900, p. 53): Pronounced *rea-s'na-ble*; for other syncopations of *o*, see nn. 455 and 1917 and line 1949.

2234 **altring Rheumes**] PHILLIPS (1706, Rheuma): "A flowing down of Humours from the Head upon the lower Parts." DEIGHTON (ed. 1889): "Rheumatic affections [maladies] which have changed and disabled him," or, as Polixenes says, made him stupid. FURNESS (ed. 1898), however, quotes BARTHOLOMAEUS (1582, p. 71): "In these olde folke kinde [natural] heate is quenched . . . and humour is dissolued and wasted." FURNESS concludes "that the phrase does not mean . . . the 'Rheumes' which alter the man, but the Rheumes which are themselves altered." Later eds. generally side with Deighton; for example, LOBBAN (ed. 1910, Altering): "disfiguring" and MOORMAN (ed. 1912): "weakening." WILSON (ed. 1931), however: "I.e. changing the physical processes either (by disease) for the bad or (by medicine) for the good." He cites OED (Altering, *ppl. a.* 1), which quotes this line. Cf. n. 2444.

As for *rheum*, in *MM* it keeps company with the gout and serpigo, a disfiguring skin disease (3.3.31 [1234]). COLLINS's (ed. 1904-24?) and RIDLEY's (ed. 1935) gloss, "rheumatism," may be misleading. OED cites one early instance (1601) of this word as meaning a "defluxion of rheum"; *rheumatism* as the painful inflammation of the joints is found first in 1688, and HOENIGER (1992, p. 217) diagnoses the malady as "chronic rheumatism resulting from gradual bone decay." BETHELL's (ed. 1956) "weakening chills" seems inexact.

2235 **Dispute . . . estate?**] JOHNSON (ed. 1765): "Talk over his affairs," the meaning generally accepted. CHAMIER (in JOHNSON, ed. 1765, 8:Ii4ᵛ): "Allude[s] to the next heir sueing for the estate in cases of imbecillity, lunacy, &c." MALONE (1783, p. 22): "Can he maintain his right to his own property?" The same expression occurs in *Rom.* 3.3.63 (1866), where it has JOHNSON's meaning rather than the legal one. COLLINS (ed. 1904-24?) prefers "reason about his own state," because if *estate* means "affairs," 2232-3 would be repeated.

2237 **being childish?**] DEIGHTON (ed. 1889): "When he was a child." BETHELL (ed. 1956): I.e., "Is he in his second childhood?"

Flo. No good Sir:

He has his health, and ampler strength indeede

Then most haue of his age.   2240

Pol. By my white beard,

You offer him (if this be so) a wrong

Something vnfilliall: Reason my sonne

2243 Reason∧ my sonne∧] ~ , ~ ~ ∧ THEO1-SING1 (−HAN), KNT2-SING2, COL3-DEL2, KNT3; ~ , ~ ~ , VALPY, KNT1

2239 **ampler**] *OED* (Ample, *a.* 3, citing this line): "Extensive, abundant."

2240 **his age**] PYE (1807, p. 116): "This would imply that Polixenes though hearty was very old, but it appears from [234; see n.], that . . . he must be under forty-five at this time." WILSON (ed. 1931) makes his age 30 in Act 1, hence 46 now; PAFFORD (ed. 1963), who guesses Mamillius to be about 10, would have Leontes the same age as Pandosto, "who is about 50 when Fawnia is 16" (see pp. 635, 650). "It is a common fault in the comic drama to give the fathers of the younger characters the costume of grandfathers." At 2881 ff., Florizel resembles his father as Leontes remembers him when Leontes himself (and Polixenes too) was 21. See n. 2881–3.

2241–7 **By . . . businesse**] PYLE (1969, p. 86): "Polixenes is mild, reasonable and touching in his appeal to his headstrong son . . . to heighten the surprise of his sudden fury."

2241 **By . . . beard**] DYER (1884, p. 487): "It seems to have been customary to swear by the beard." Other instances are found in *AYL* 1.2.72–4 (239–40), *Tro.* 4.5.209 (2776), and *TGV* 4.1.10 (1556).

2242–7 **You . . . businesse**] WHITE (1854, p. 296): Punctuation after *sonne* "makes *Polixenes* say, 'My son, Reason should choose himself a wife'. Whereas he means to say, 'It is reasonable that my son should choose himself a wife[;] but it is quite as reasonable that the father should have something to say in the affair.'" For *Reason,* WHITE glosses "There is reason" (*OED, sb.*[1] 14). With the ellipsis here, ROLFE (ed. 1879) compares *Jn.* 5.2.130 (2384). Possibly, however, *Reason* is a personification and *my sonne* a nominative of address; if so, Polixenes says, "Young man, whoever chooses himself a wife should be Reason itself." Considering the passage, CHARLTON (ed. 1916): "Like Leontes, Polixenes himself is making a mess of things in the vital matter of the joy of a father and of fatherhood, 'all whose joy is nothing else but fair posterity'. And the fact that Polixenes, of whose goodness we are assured, makes such, if a much less harsh mistake, does by its similarity and its contrast suggest a little possible extenuation in the case of Leontes." But why should the issue of a peasant girl be regarded by a king as fair posterity?

2242–3 **You . . . vnfilliall**] HART (1894): "Can one not see the gathering wrath in the old father . . . the indignation in the words[?]" PAFFORD (ed. 1963) compares *Tmp.* 5.1.190–1 (2168–9), where "Ferdinand emphasizes that he chose Miranda when 'I could not ask my father for his advice.'" *OED* cites 2243 as its first instance of *unfilial.*

2243 **Something**] Somewhat. See n. 224.

Reason] SCHMIDT's (1875) gloss of the word here and in 2244 as "equity,

Should choose himselfe a wife, but as good reason
The Father (all whose ioy is nothing else   2245
But faire posterity) should hold some counsaile
In such a businesse.
   Flo. I yeeld all this;
But for some other reasons (my graue Sir)
Which 'tis not fit you know, I not acquaint   2250
My Father of this businesse.
   Pol. Let him know't.
   Flo. He shall not.
   Pol. Prethee let him.
   Flo. No, he must not.   2255
   Shep. Let him (my sonne) he shall not need to greeue
At knowing of thy choice.
   Flo. Come, come, he must not:
Marke our Contract.

---

fairness, justice" seems inappropriate. ORGEL (ed. 1996), comparing *Jn.* 5.2.130
(2384): "It is reasonable that."

   my sonne] BETHELL (ed. 1956): "'My son' has not slipped out unguardedly:
Polixenes speaks as of a hypothetical case." BEVINGTON (ed. 1992): "But of course
the application to Florizel is direct."

   2244 **as good reason**] BOORMAN (ed. 1964): "Equally reasonably."

   2245-6 **all . . . posterity**] TRAVERSI (1954, p. 158), oddly: "Polixenes . . . is
clinging in effect to the nearest available experience that recalls his own lost youth."
What he clings to is his hope for grandchildren.

   2246 **hold some counsaile**] BOORMAN (ed. 1964): "Be consulted." He adds,
improbably, "Shakespeare's audience would know that the marriage of a King's son
required the holding of a council." Sh.'s audience would more probably know that
the father's disapproval could prevent the marriage. See STONE (1977, pp. 180-93)
and MCMURTRY (1989, p. 118).

   2248 **yeeld**] BAILEY (1721): "Grant" (*OED, v.* 18c, citing this line).

   2249 **my graue Sir**] FURNESS (ed. 1898): "The reflex of the father's earnest
tones."

   2250 **not acquaint**] MAXWELL (ed. 1969): "I.e. can not." As to the omission of
do, see n. 2005, although PAFFORD (ed. 1963) suggests "transposition of the negative
and verb."

   2252-4 **Let . . . him**] HAPPÉ (1969): "Polixenes seems anxious to avoid a clash
at the last moment."

   2258 **Come, come**] PORTER & CLARKE (ed. 1908), metaphors uninhibited: "Florizel's temper and peremptory words are the last straw to kindle more such angry
arrogance from the old king."

   2259 **Contract**] ABBOTT (§490): Accented *con-tráct.* For the significance of the
contract, see n. 3363-5.

Pol. Marke your diuorce (yong sir)   2260
Whom sonne I dare not call: Thou art too base
To be acknowledge. Thou a Scepters heire,
That thus affects a sheepe-hooke? Thou, old Traitor,
I am sorry, that by hanging thee, I can
But shorten thy life one weeke. And thou, fresh peece   2265
Of excellent Witchcraft, whom of force must know
The royall Foole thou coap'st with.
  Shep. Oh my heart.
  Pol. Ile haue thy beauty scratcht with briers & made
More homely then thy state. For thee (fond boy)   2270

2262 acknowledge] acknowledg'd F2+
2263 affects] affect'st POPE1-DEL2, GLO-OXF1, PEL1
2264-5 *Verse lines ending* but . . . piece THEO1-SING1 (−HAN), HUD, SING2,
HAL, DEL, KTLY, DYCE2, IRV, BUL, KIT1-SIS, OXF2
2266 whom] who F2+ (−EVNS)
2267 Foole] food KNT
      coap'st] cop'dst mTBY2 *conj.*, CAP
2268 *Shep.*] *Per.* THEOBALD (1729) *conj. in* NICHOLS (1817, 2:364-5), COL2
2270 fond] found F4

2260-85 **Marke . . . to't**] MOULTON (1903, p. 74): "The explosion of royal
wrath comes as a harmless thunder." He alone thinks so. LLOYD (in SINGER, ed. 1856,
4:135): "The happiness of Perdita is as suddenly overcast as was that of her mother,
and the outburst of the irascible Polixenes is as sudden and violent as the jealousy of
Leontes." Cf. n. 2217-20. CHARLTON (ed. 1916): "Polixenes' fury appears to be an
intensified petulance into which he was goaded, not so much by the fact of Florizel's
courtship of Perdita, as by his refusal after entreaty to consult his father. Only thus is
his conduct justifiable at all." VAN DOREN (1939, p. 321): "This is some hairy god
more ancient than Jove and ten times more terrible in his caprice." The CLARKES
(1879, p. 617): "Perdita's reticent dignity of soul (inherited from her mother) as well
as her innate love of truth and candid nature are well indicated by her maintaining
silence while Polixenes rebukes his son and reproaches her, and again when Leontes
receives her and Florizel [2908 ff.]." KNIGHT (1947; 1965, pp. 110-11): "We recall
Capulet, Egeus, York, Polonius, Lear: Shakespeare's fathers are normally tyrannical
and Polixenes has, according to his lights, cause. His threats, as excessive as Capulet's,
drive home a contrast of social tyranny with rustic health." SCHANZER (1964, p. 77
n.) objects to his supposed resemblance to elderly fathers, because he is too young
(see n. 2240 for his age); BONJOUR (1969, p. 207) objects, too, because the present
Polixenes is in good physical condition [2239-40].
    Longing for symmetry, some critics attribute Polixenes's attack to a sexual envy
paralleling Leontes's jealousy. TRAVERSI (1959, p. 27): "Both [his behavior and Leontes's] proceed finally from aged impotence, both are inspired by resentment at the
irrevocable loss of youth, and both will have . . . to be replaced by repentance." If
he is right, Polixenes's repentance is to be inferred; it is not depicted. Rather than by
impotence, Polixenes may be inspired by the egregious violation of order and degree.
Once Perdita's identity is known, the offense vanishes. GRENE (1967, p. 72): "The
tyrannical acts of the first king spring from an altogether personal and peculiar char-

acter, those of the second are the conventional cruelties of an angry father." CUTTS (1968, p. 80): "In his condemnation of his son, . . . he [Polixenes] is re-enacting Leontes' role in the death of Mamillius." In his treatment of Perdita, "he is re-enacting Leontes' role in the calumniation and denigration of Hermione. . . . The bullying of the old shepherd . . . would seem to echo Leontes' treatment of Antigonus." ORNSTEIN (1986, p. 229), however, is not overwhelmed by the gravity of his threat in 2269-70: "It associates royal tyranny with the other calamities that spoil picnics . . . : poison ivy, ants, thistles, and bad weather." FOWLER (1978, p. 37): "Leontes' jealousy of a wife is expressed tyrannously, against the opinion of his court; Polixenes' jealousy of a son takes a more disguised, perhaps more socially acceptable, form." STOCKHOLDER (1987, p. 192): "Our knowledge that Polixenes' anger is inappropriate to the 'true' circumstances creates a parallel between him and Leontes, for both figures discern evil where there is none." Polixenes does not discern evil but royal folly.

2260 **diuorce**] SCHMIDT (1874): "Any separation of love." WEXLER (1988, p. 112): "Although he uses the word to denote the rupture between father and son, the more usual use of the term to separate husband from wife draws a parallel between Leontes and Polixenes through a pun." But Polixenes probably means "Mark your divorce from Perdita."

2260-3 **yong . . . sheepe-hooke?**] BONJOUR (1969, p. 208): "Polixenes' sore disappointment is all the greater owing to his deep fatherly affection [quotes 246-9]."

2261 **dare not**] DEIGHTON (ed. 1889): "Am ashamed to."

2262 **acknowledge**] WALKER (1860, 2:63): A confusion of final *e* with *d*. See n. 100-1.

2262-5 **Thou . . . weeke**] HUNTER (1845, 1:424): This whole speech "ought not to have been introduced at all in a scene to which it is so exquisitely incongruous." He finds these lines especially offensive.

2263 **affects**] MINSHEU (1617, Affect): "Affectionate [the verb] or desire" (*OED*, *v.*[1] 2). BOORMAN (ed. 1964) adds "aspires to" (*v.*[1] 1), which, if relevant at all, would be ironical. LETTSOM (MS 1840-65) objects that the unpronounceable *affect'st*, POPE's form adopted by some modern eds., causes the verb to refer to *Scepters heir* rather than to *Thou*. ABBOTT (§340), however: "In verbs ending with *-t*, *-test* final in the second person sing. often becomes *-ts* for euphony." *Thou* is thus the subject of *affects* despite the verb's apparent third-person ending.

   sheepe-hooke] DEIGHTON (ed. 1889): I.e., "the daughter of a shepherd." GOTCH (1900, p. 330), who evidently takes *affects* to mean "adopt artificially": "This is not metaphorical only. In 'Pandosto' it is expressly stated that the disguised Prince carries an actual sheep-hook." He does (see p. 639) (and so does Fawnia—see p. 643), but it is probably not alluded to here.

2263-70 **Thou . . . state**] BARBER (1964, p. 240): The element of irrational passion in this is nicely pointed up by the fact that [at 1903-6] he has argued to Perdita the importance of mixed marriages for the renewal of the nobility." PYLE (1969, pp. 86-7): "These sentences may seem fantastic—and no less so the sudden unsolicited suspension of their enforcement [2277-8]—so extravagant that we can hardly take them seriously; and that is one aspect of the situation. . . . The other is that this is tyranny and injustice at their worst." SCHANZER (ed. 1969, p. 34): "Autolycus gives what amounts to a *reductio ad absurdum* of this outburst in his talk with the Clown [at 2665-72]. . . . It takes our mind back to Paulina's outcry [at 1362-4]."

2265 **one weeke**] JERVIS (1868): "A short period; time indefinitely" (*OED*, *sb.* 2d). PORTER & CLARKE (ed. 1908): "An extravagant allusion to the trembling old grandsire's feeble age, which his abject fear of the king exaggerates."

2265-70 **And . . . state**] GOURLAY (1975, pp. 386-7): Sh. "borrows the attack of father upon daughter from his source and assigns it instead to Polixenes. Shake-

If I may euer know thou dost but sigh,
That thou no more shalt neuer see this knacke (as neuer
I meane thou shalt) wee'l barre thee from succession,
Not hold thee of our blood, no not our Kin,
Farre then *Deucalion* off: (marke thou my words)   2275
Follow vs to the Court. Thou Churle, for this time
(Though full of our displeasure) yet we free thee
From the dead blow of it. And you Enchantment,

2272 shalt neuer] shalt ROWE1-CAP, v1793-v1813, DYCE1 (*errata*), CAM1, GLO,
DYCE2, DEL4+
2275 Farre] Far F4-THEO2, WARB-CAP; Less HAN
then] as mTHEO1 *and* JOHN1 *conj.*, CAP
2278 you] your F3, F4

---

speare makes Polixenes' misogyny as savage as Pandosto's." NEELY (1978, p. 184):
"His vicious suggestive attack on Perdita (whom up to this point he had admired)
reveals nakedly the distaste for women wittily apparent in his tales of boyhood [124-
45] and pompously implicit in his discussion of grafting [1903-8]." KNOWLES (privately): "Making her homely is much milder than making the Shepherd dead. From
the evidence, he hates men worse."

2265-6 **fresh . . . Witchcraft**] PAFFORD (ed. 1963): "Young girl excelling in
witchcraft." Polixenes may be grudgingly or inadvertently complimentary: *fresh* is
"youthful . . . in the prime of life" (SCHMIDT, 1874), a meaning consonant with
"excellent." The adjective is again applied to Perdita in 2416; see that n. On the other
hand, FARMER & HENLEY (1890-1904; 1970) find that *fresh* in *Jn.* 3.4.145 (1530)
means "Inexperienced, but conceited and presumptuous," and if a similar meaning
obtains here, "excellent Witchcraft" could be an ironical oxymoron. DEIGHTON (ed.
1889) finds *fresh* [young] . . . *Witchcraft* "opposed to 'old traitor'; . . . *witchcraft*
has here the double sense of that which is enchanting, bewitching, and that which
exercises the evil influence ascribed to witches." EVANS (ed. 1974): "In [2278] *enchantment* has precisely the same duality of meaning." PAFFORD: "*Piece* could mean
a man or a woman and was not at this time normally used in a derogatory sense of a
girl." He cites *OED* (Piece, *sb*. 9a and b). ORGEL (ed. 1996): "Prototype, masterpiece."
For other uses of the word, see n. 1833. RUBINSTEIN (1984) suggests that *fresh* is
"sexually shameless" and *witchcraft* (because of Latin *ars magica*), "arse magic."

2266 **excellent**] WALKER (1860, 2:48): Two syllables.

whom] For the form, see n. 1207.

force] PHILLIPS (1706): "Necessity."

2267 **coap'st**] JOHNSON (1755, citing this line): "Encounter; to exchange kindness
or sentiments." SCHMIDT (1874): "Have to do with." PORTER & CLARKE (ed. c. 1903):
"Meetest, unitest with," which may approach RUBINSTEIN's (1984) "Copulated."

2268 **Oh my heart**] BLISSETT (1971, pp. 60-2), citing many examples, argues
that "near the heart of the play is the image of the heart and the heart's blood." He
interprets this line as a "comic parody of Leontes' *tremor cordis* [183]." KNOWLES
(privately) believes that no audience would find such a meaning in this commonplace.

2270 **homely . . . state**] EVANS (ed. 1974): *Homely* (see n. 1651) means "ugly
(with reference to *beauty*); . . . humble (with reference to *state*)." JOHNSON (1755,
State): "Rank; condition; quality."

fond] JOHNSON (1755): "1. Foolish; silly; indiscreet; imprudent; injudicious. . . . 3. Foolishly tender; injudiciously indulgent." Cf. n. 1597.

2271 **may**] DEIGHTON (ed. 1889): "Should."

2272 **That**] CARRINGTON (1956): "Because."

    no . . . neuer] KNIGHT (ed. 1841) is right that "the double negative . . . is characteristic of Shakspere's Time"; see ABBOTT (§406) and n. 1229-32. But this line may not be one. Although he follows F in eds. 1773-85, STEEVENS decides in ed. 1793 that *neuer* is an "absurd redundancy." STAUNTON (ed. 1859), agreeing, thinks the compositor's "eye caught it from the end of the line." Or perhaps Crane's did. CLARK & WRIGHT (ed. 1863) add other reasons for the omission: "The meter is improved by the change. . . . The sense is improved. Polixenes would rather make light of his son's sighs than dwell so emphatically on their cause."

    knacke] B. E. (1699): "A petty Artifice [*OED, sb.*² 1] . . . Toies [3]." Cf. 2171. EVANS (ed. 1974): "Crafty contriver."

    2273 **wee'l . . . succession**] BERGERON (1985, p. 163): "Polixenes . . . disinherits the son, leaving himself and the kingdom without an heir." He threatens to do so, but actually goes no further, although Florizel is said to have fled from his hopes when he fled from his father (2947).

    2275 **Farre . . . off**] THIRLBY (MS 1725-33?) glosses *than* as "as." HEATH (1765, p. 217): "Unless it [kinship] be as far off as Deucalion, or, as we should express it, as Noah's Ark." Deucalion, a legendary king of Thessaly, was the Noah of Greek mythology (see Ovid, *Metamorphoses*, ed. Miller, 1.312 ff.). Actually, as the CLARKES (ed. 1865) observe, Polixenes means "not even kindred farther back removed in period and consanguinity than between Deucalion and mankind will [he] hold to exist between his son and himself." BETHELL (ed. 1956): "As Deucalion is . . . the common ancestor of all, the statement is strictly nonsense. It is, of course, hyperbole intended to express his indignation." PORTER & CLARKE's (ed. 1908) far-fetched view: "Shakespeare's mention of Deucalion here suggests the possibility that he was led to think of applying the device of the statue coming to life by the account in Golding's 'Ovid', Bk. I. [ed. Nims, 451 ff.] of the repeopling of the earth after the flood by Deucalion and Pyrrha, out of . . . the stones of Mother Earth, which came to life as they threw them behind them."

    Commenting on JOHNSON's "far as," TYRWHITT (in STEEVENS, ed. 1773) explains F's "Farre" as a form of "the ancient comparative of *ferr* for *ferrer*" [*farrer* or *farther*], an opinion borne out by ABBOTT (§478) and *OED* (*adv.* Forms). In the textual notes, no record is kept of eds. after 1773 reading *far*, for, as many indicate, the word was generally known to mean "farther." Even WARBURTON may have been representing the comparative by his *Far*. PAFFORD (ed. 1963): "Other possible uses [of *farre* to mean 'farther' rather than 'far'] are at [182, 303, and 3355]. But *farre* is also the normal spelling of *far* in *F* even when the positive is certainly intended, e.g. [1450, etc.]." He also notes the spellings *starre* [50 etc.], *barre* [2273], and *marre* [2331, 3284]. BRADLEY (1916, 2:556) finds this Sh.'s only instance of comparative *farre*.

    2276-8 **Thou . . . it**] BETHELL (ed. 1956): "Polixenes has relented since [2264-5]."

    2276 **Churle**] B. E. (1699): "A selfish, sordid Clown." ANON. (MS 1733-): "Countryman, labourer." GOTCH (1900, p. 330): "The churl here is Florizel 'in swain's wearing,' not the Shepherd, who remains under the ban already pronounced." GOTCH alone thinks so, but the idea does make it unnecessary to assume that the reprieve is forgotten by both the Shepherd and Camillo. See n. 2297.

    2277 **(Though . . . displeasure)**] DEIGHTON (ed. 1889): Modifies *we*. *Churle* is also possible.

    free] Absolve. Cf. n. 1290.

    2278 **dead**] SCHMIDT (1874): "Deadly" (*OED, a.* 9, citing this line). See 2264-5. PAFFORD (ed. 1963) detects "something of the sense of 'unmitigated', 'unrelieved' [*a.* V.]."

Worthy enough a Heardsman: yea him too,   (2▮
That makes himselfe (but for our Honor therein)   2280
Vnworthy thee. If euer henceforth, thou
These rurall Latches, to his entrance open,
Or hope his body more, with thy embraces,
I will deuise a death, as cruell for thee
As thou art tender to't.   *Exit.*   2285

2283 hope] hoope mTBY1 *conj.*, POPE1+

2278-85 **And . . . to't**] For these lines as an expression of sexual jealousy, see
n. 2217-20.
2278 **Enchantment**] SCHMIDT (1875, p. 1422a): "Enchanter," the abstract for
the concrete, a kind of metonymy. Cf. nn. 1504, 2642. The CLARKES (ed. 1865): From
this word and from "fresh peece Of excellent Witchcraft" (2265-6), we "feel the
spell which [Perdita's] artless fascinations exercise over the king; all the more forcible
in its [sic] effect from being thus reluctantly acknowledged — as if in spite of himself."
See n. 2265-6. PAFFORD (ed. 1963) says the word has "a bad sense (witch . . .) and
a good sense (in appreciation of her beauty)."
2279-81 **yea . . . thee**] DEIGHTON (ed. 1889): "Yea, worthy too of him who (if
the honour of my family were not concerned) shows himself unworthy of you."
MOUNT ("*Winter's*," 1893): "But in what possible sense was he (Florizel) making
himself unworthy of her? He meant no ill; in fact his purpose of marriage was the
very thing that drove his father furious; and if he had made himself unworthy, how
could 'our honour therein' diminish or affect the unworthiness?" INGLEBY (1894)
replies: "Polixenes, admitting the enchanting sweetness of Perdita, allows her to be
worthy any one of her own position; and indeed even worthy him who by his base
filial conduct has made himself unworthy her; but, not to give himself away, he in-
terpolates the saving clause of his own honour, which puts the balance against her."
ADAMS (1894) replies that *but* does not mean "except," as MOUNT thinks, but "only,"
and *for* means "because of." HART (1894) paraphrases: "You are worthy even of this
young prince, who, by his present course of unfilial conduct, shows himself to be
unworthy of your beauty — except for our honour centered in him [i.e., his royalty]."
GOTCH (1900, p. 330) alone believes that their clothes are the point: Florizel is in the
garb of a shepherd; Perdita is pranked up as a goddess. SCHANZER (ed. 1969): "Prob-

ably Polixenes is using the plural of majesty, *honour* here having the rare meaning of 'exalted position': '. . . if my exalted position were not involved.'" *Our* may well be a form of the royal *we*, but *OED* (*sb.* 4) does not distinguish "exalted position" from "dignity, distinction," a sense SCHMIDT (1875) finds frequently in Sh. INGLEBY and recent eds. explain the passage much as HART does, sometimes adding to Florizel's unworthiness his neglect of a prince's duty to marry a woman of his rank.

2281 **thee.**] See n. 1598.

2281-5 **If . . . to't**] MARSH (1962; 1980, p. 152): "The sadistic pleasure he [Polixenes] takes in the thought of marring the beauty he cannot enjoy, suggests the torment of mind of a man who feels that life is slipping away from him. . . . The sexual basis of the imagery gives the clue to the feeling that inspires it. This is the challenge of evil that Perdita and Florizel have to face, just as Hermione had to face it sixteen years before." STUDING (1982, p. 225), similarly: "His bawdy language surely echoes Leontes' jealous speeches." The sadistic pleasure is gratuitous, and Polixenes is probably not old enough to feel much vital slippage (see n. 2240). The imagery may be sexual, but a mutual sexual attraction is an important element in the contract that Polixenes cannot help but regard as disastrous. His anger and Leontes's jealousy seem very different.

2282 **Latches**] BOORMAN (ed. 1964): "Clasps [i.e., 'fastening for a door or gate' (*OED, sb.*[1] 2)]. . . . Also . . . 'snare, trap' [*sb.*[1] 1], which adds to Polixenes' savage attack." WRIGHT & LaMAR (ed. 1966) take the word metaphorically: "Embraces."

2283 **hope**] I.e., hoop (*OED, sb.*[1] Forms). JOHNSON (1755): "Encircle; to clasp." BOORMAN (ed. 1964): "There may be a play on 'hoop' and 'hope' (hope for), which were pronounced alike." According to CERCIGNANI (1981, p. 182), *hope* had the vowel sound of modern *scope*; he does not discuss *hoop*, but (p. 184) *proof, behoof,* and *aloof* have the modern vowel sound. For the part of speech, see n. 2344. As for the hooping, PORTER & CLARKE (ed. 1908) think "Perdita stands thus embracing Florizel, comforting him in the shock of Polixenes' disclosure of himself and throughout the fierceness of his onslaught."

2285 **As . . . to't**] For *tender,* KITTREDGE & RIBNER (ed. 1967): "Gentle" and MAXWELL (ed. 1969): "Vulnerable." For *to't*, the CLARKEs (ed. 1865): "Compared with it." For the entire line, CALDECOTT (MS 1813-33): "In the degree that thou art tender to undergo it." DEIGHTON (ed. 1889): "As thou art unfit from your tender age to suffer such a fate."

Exit] HARDINGE (1818, 3:42): "He [Polixenes] takes at the impulse of momentary anger the worst course imaginable,—after bouncing to the son, and with some cruelty insulting the girl, *he leaves them together!* he leaves *Camillo* of the party, conceiving, perhaps, that *he* would be a kind of bail for the re-appearance of the lover at court in his proper element. We *now* see how artfully and how ably the Poet had made *Camillo* solicit his own departure for *Sicily* [1617-22]."

Perd. Euen heere vndone:
I was not much a-fear'd: for once, or twice
I was about to speake, and tell him plainely,
The selfe-same Sun, that shines vpon his Court,
Hides not his visage from our Cottage, but   2290
Lookes on alike. Wilt please you (Sir) be gone?
I told you what would come of this: Beseech you
Of your owne state take care: This dreame of mine
Being now awake, Ile Queene it no inch farther,
But milke my Ewes, and weepe.   2295

2286 SCENE VIII. POPE, HAN, WARB, JOHN
   heere∧ vndone:] ~ , ~ , JOHN, CAM3
2289 his] this THEO2
2291 on] on all MAL *conj. (withdrawn* 10:606), HUNTER (1845, 1:425) *conj.,*
SING2; on it MTBY3 *conj.* (on't), KTLY; on's ANON. *conj. in* CAM1, HUD2
2293 This . . . mine] from this my dream HAN
   mine∧∧] ~ ,∧THEO, WARB; ~ ,— JOHN1+ (−SIG, EVNS, OXF2)

2286-95 **Euen . . . weepe**] HARDINGE (1818, 3:40): "It [this speech] marks a
noble spirit of honest pride in the girl struggling with modesty and gentleness of
nature—as we know who she is, it affects us the more." LOBBAN (ed. 1910, p. xiii):
She acts "with all the courage and dignity of her undreamed-of royal blood." CHARL-
TON (ed. 1916) notes "(1) her absolute self-assurance without conceit, for she mentions the sun and her cottage, not herself, when she is protesting against the indignity
the King had thrown on her; (2) her utter unselfishness in immediately offering to
release Florizel; at the same time showing her clearer vision of the results of her
defiance; (3) her ready self-resignation and self-adaptation, 'I'll queen it no inch farther.'" RIDLEY (1937, p. 209), finding that she speaks with her mother's spirit, confesses to "a very subtle touch of puzzlement as to whence she derived the spirit."
BETHELL (ed. 1956) would have her speak "in a reminiscent wonder at herself." BAR-
BER (1964, p. 240): "Polixenes' violent pride in birth is nicely put in its
place. . . . The sun image suggests the equality of souls before God; so it asserts the
essential brotherhood of man." TAYLER (1964, p. 131), similarly: "This satiric cut—
it is in no sense 'democratic'—is of the kind common in pastoral."
   Some critics interpret these lines as indications of Perdita's courage and innate
royalty, yet her response may also seem typical of a bitterly disappointed young girl.
She was "not much" afraid, but "not much" is not the same as "not at all," despite
RIDLEY (n. 2287). She was about to say, pointlessly (see n. 2289-91), that king and
peasant are equals under the sun, but she never did, as LERNER (1972, p. 129) notices.
To acknowledge this much, however, is not to share the opinion of J. SMITH (1974,
p. 151) that "Perdita carries herself with the somewhat stolid, because unimaginative,
steadfastness of her mother."As COLERIDGE recognizes (see n. 2291-5), she informs
Florizel that she told him so. See 2325 as well. Despite her fears, she dreamed of
marrying a prince, and she is heartbroken to be awakened. WEINSTEIN (1971, p. 103)
adds, "Yet this dream of her love and her queenship, while only a fantasy to her, will
be revealed in Act V to be true." Cf. FURNESS (n. 2291-5) and TRAVERSI (1954, p.
159). WRIGHT (1979, p. 150) goes too far in speaking of the young people's "cowardice in the face of Polixenes' rage."

2286 **Euen heere**] SCHMIDT (1874) interprets *euen* as "precisely, exactly," which may cause Perdita to say "undone here and now, before our marriage or the realization of other hopes for the future." HERFORD (ed. 1904), however: "I.e. without waiting for the threatened doom."

vndone] BAILEY (1721, Undoe): "Ruin." THIRLBY (MS 1733-47?): "Note her name Perdita." Regarding punctuation, STAUNTON (ed. 1859), who follows F in putting a heavy stop after this word (STAUNTON, like CAPELL, makes it an exclamation point), nevertheless observes "that the passage would be more in harmony with the high-born spirit by which Perdita is unconsciously sustained . . . if it were read . . . 'undone,'." He was anticipated in this by JOHNSON and followed by WILSON (ed. 1931), who finds the exclamation pointless. He thinks "the F. colon perhaps marks the pause of agitation."

2287 **a-fear'd**] *OED* (Afeard, *ppl. a.*): "Used more than 30 times by Shakspere, but rare in literature after 1700, having been supplanted by AFRAID. It survives everywhere in the popular speech." At 2311, set, like this line, by Compositor B, the form is *affear'd*. RIDLEY (ed. 1935): "She feels that she naturally should have been *afeard* before the king—she has been true to her blood, and felt, to her own surprise, like a king's daughter." See n. 2286-95, however. BULLOUGH (1975, 8:196): Cf. Fawnia's courage (p. 653).

2289-91 **The . . . alike**] COLLINS (ed. 1904-24?): The sun "is a looker-on in both cases; *on* is adverbial." The ubiquity and egalitarianism of the sun are biblical (Ps. 19:6, Eccles. 42:16, Matt. 5:45) and proverbial (TILLEY S985: "The Sun shines upon all alike"). THEOBALD (MS -1729?) compares "That Sun that warmes you heere, shall shine on me" (*R2* 1.3.146 [438]). The proverb appears in other forms, in *H5* 4 Prol. 43-5 (1832-4), *Tro.* 1.3.89-94 (548-52), and *Cym.* 3.4.139 (1823); and critics quote many non-Shn. parallels, for which see WHITING (1968, S893) and WILSON (1970). FRIPP (1938, 2:739): "Love knows not distinction of rank or occupation. . . . Nor is Perdita ashamed to be a shepherd's daughter." TRAVERSI (1954, p. 159), however: "The equality of 'court' and 'cottage' is a commonplace of pastoral, the expression of a convention rather than the reflection of any deep reality." THOMPSON (1971, p. 157): "Imagine what havoc it would make of this romance if Perdita were insisted upon as truly a shepherd's daughter whose merit shone in her proud assurance that her love was as good as that of any princess." BARBER (1964, p. 240), however, thinks the "brotherhood of man" is the point; see n. 3144-53. For another biblical allusion in this pagan atmosphere, see n. 533.

2291 **Lookes on alike**] DODD (1752, 1:148): "Looks alike on the court and cottage." MALONE, who previously (1780, 1:145) believed a word omitted after *on*, in STEEVENS (ed. 1793): "To *look upon* [i.e., *on*], without any substantive annexed . . . appears to have been legitimate." He cites *Tro.* 5.6.10 (3440) and *3H6* 2.3.27 (1087), passages, says DYCE (ed. 1864), not akin to this one. STEEVENS (ed. 1793): "To look *on*, i.e. to be a mere idle spectator" (*OED*, Look, *v.* 39). This is the meaning of *looke vpon* at 3308, but here SCHMIDT's (1874) "regards both with the same eye" is more suitable. Cf. CORSON (1889, p. 369): *On alike* = on all alike [i.e., indifferently] and n. 1810. HUNTER (1845, 1:425) inserts *all* because "in such a connection [it] might easily be lost"; he convinces SINGER only, though a few other eds. mention the possibility. PAFFORD (ed. 1963) adds *'s* [i.e., on's] to the possible omissions. "But the metre is against an omission."

2291-5 **Wilt . . . weepe**] COLERIDGE (1813; 1960, 1:109): "Noble pride and grief [vent] themselves in a momentary peevishness of resentment toward Florizell." FURNESS (ed. 1898): "I can see no trace of *peevishness* here. Perdita was heart-broken; she knew that Florizell must go, and the sooner the parting was over the better." ENRIGHT (1970, p. 194), similarly: "Admirable . . . and impressively adult. . . . Florizel's rather belated expression of resoluteness of purpose [2311-14] is schoolboyish in comparison."

Cam. Why how now Father,
Speake ere thou dyest.
　　Shep. I cannot speake, nor thinke,
Nor dare to know, that which I know: O Sir,
You haue vndone a man of fourescore three, 　　　　　　　2300
That thought to fill his graue in quiet: yea,
To dye vpon the bed my father dy'de,
To lye close by his honest bones; but now
Some Hangman must put on my shrowd, and lay me
Where no Priest shouels-in dust. Oh cursed wretch, 　　　　2305
That knew'st this was the Prince, and wouldst aduenture
To mingle faith with him. Vndone, vndone:
If I might dye within this houre, I haue liu'd
To die when I desire. 　　　　　　　　　　　　　　*Exit.*

2302 dy'de] died on SEYMOUR (1805, 1:169) *conj.*, KTLY
2309-10 *One verse line* mCAP2, v1793+ (−BEV)
2309 *Exit.*] *Om.* CAM3

2292 **Beseech**] For the omission of the nominative, see ABBOTT §399.
　　2293 **state**] JOHNSON (1755): "Rank." PAFFORD (ed. 1963): Perhaps "condition" as well. HAPPÉ (1969): "Prospect of succession to the throne."
　　　　This] CAPELL (1783, 2.4:177): Preceded by *As for*, understood. Like most eds. he puts a dash after "mine" to indicate that the speech is broken off.
　　2294 **Queene it**] *OED* (*v.*, citing this line as its first example): "To act . . . as a queen." CHARLTON (ed. 1916) adds, "Or affianced bride of the king to be." For *it* used indefinitely, see ABBOTT §226 and BROOK (1976, pp. 75-6). PAFFORD (ed. 1963): Perhaps she also means "I'll cease from being queen of this feast." WILSON (ed. 1931): "She no doubt removes from her head the floral garland" (see THIRLBY's question in n. 1811-12).
　　2295 **milke my Ewes**] CLARK (1935, p. 142): "Ewe's milk was also a common drink [of country folk]. Tea . . . was unknown to the Elizabethans."
　　2296 **how now**] See n. 201.
　　2297 **Speake . . . dyest**] PAFFORD (ed. 1963): "Apparently a reminder of the sentence at [2264-5] although this had been revoked at [2277-8]. It seems that neither Camillo nor the Shepherd had appreciated the reprieve." But Camillo may say this only because the Shepherd seems terminally distraught or, as BEVINGTON (ed. 1992) suggests, grief stricken. PYLE (1969, p. 89) calls the line "unseasonable bluff heartiness." ORGEL (ed. 1996): "Does 'for this time' [2276] merely imply a brief reprieve?" PORTER & CLARKE (ed. 1908): An "implicit stage direction for the actor to show the extreme feebleness and collapse of the old man."
　　2298-9 **I . . . I know**] TAYLOR (1972, p. 52): "The Shepherd echoes the words of Camillo's predicament" at 482.

2299 **Nor . . . I know**] Critics disagree on what knowledge he means. The CLARKES (ed. 1865) think Sh. teaches that "had the old Shepherd had moral courage to speak out that which he knows [about Perdita] . . . he would have been spared the fears he here expresses." That he does not is in character, however, and permits the evolution of the plot. PARRY (ed. 1982): The Shepherd expresses here his inability "to face the fact of the death sentence" pronounced at 2263–5; he describes his feelings at 2300 ff. BETHELL (ed. 1956): "He dare not admit his knowledge to himself— dare not think about it." PAFFORD (ed. 1963), improbably: "Cf. [483–6]. This is dramatic comparison between the bearing of Polixenes and that of Leontes when he also considered himself outraged. Polixenes also threatens, but withdraws his threats. If Shakespeare had the parallel in mind, Camillo's words at [482] might also have recurred to him." KNOWLES (privately): "He means 'I'm scared out of my wits.' He cannot talk, or reason, or even call to mind or attend to ideas he already knows."

2299–2309 **O . . . desire**] HUDSON (ed. 1852): "Some of the critics have been rather hard on the old Shepherd, for what they call his characteristic selfishness in thinking so much of his own life, though he be fourscore and three, and showing so little concern for Perdita and Florizell [see p. 797]. But it is the thought, not so much of dying, as of dying like a felon, that troubles and engrosses his mind. His unselfish noble honesty in the treatment of his precious foundling is quite apparent throughout. The Poet was wiser than to tempt nature overmuch, by making the innate qualities of his heroine triumphant over the influences of a selfish father."

2302 **dy'de**] HUNTER (ed. 1872): "For *died on*." For the omission of the preposition, see n. 742. HERFORD (ed. 1916–): "A parallel construction to (e.g.) 'the day my father died', 'where' being understood, as there 'when.'"

2303 **honest**] KITTREDGE & RIBNER (ed. 1967): "Honourable." BERKELEY & KARIMIPOUR (1985, p. 94), however: "The Shepherd reveals his class origins by referring to his father as 'honest', a word that . . . sometimes imports condescension," as in *Ado* 3.5.1 (1596) and 3.5.12 (1607). The word is condescending only when used by a superior to an inferior (*OED, a.* 1c).

2304–5 **Some . . . dust**] GREY (1754, 1:268): "Meaning, that he should be buried under the gallows [in unconsecrated ground], without the burial service," like a felon. GREY alludes to the rubric in the 1549 Book of Common Prayer directing the priest to cast earth upon the corpse; in 1552 and later versions, a bystander does this. DOUCE (1807, 1:361): "A whimsical anachronism[, since] the old shepherd was a Pagan." CALDECOTT (MS 1813–33): "Malefactors were probably then, as now in Ireland, executed in shrowds." Regarding *shouels-in*, WALKER (1860, 3:114): "Pronounce *shools-in*," which HENLEY (ed. 1902) prints.

2304 **Some . . . shrowd**] SCHMIDT (1875): "Some hangman must put my shroud on me."

2305 **shouels-in**] Neither DOBSON (1968) nor CERCIGNANI (1981) comments.

2306 **aduenture**] Dare. See n. 95.

2307 **mingle faith with**] DEIGHTON (ed. 1889): "Plight . . . to." For a related meaning of *mingle*, see n. 182.

　　faith] SCHMIDT (1874): "Vow of love." For other meanings, see nn. 544–5, 672, 1193, and 1836.

　　Vndone, vndone] BETHELL (ed. 1956): "Presumably the Shepherd was too agitated to realize that Polixenes had pardoned him [2276–8]."

2308–9 **If . . . desire**] PAFFORD (ed. 1963) compares *Mac.* 2.3.91–2 (852–3).

Flo. Why looke you so vpon me?   2310
I am but sorry, not affear'd: delaid,
But nothing altred: What I was, I am:
More straining on, for plucking backe; not following
My leash vnwillingly.
    Cam. Gracious my Lord,   2315
You know my Fathers temper: at this time
He will allow no speech: (which I do ghesse
You do not purpose to him:) and as hardly
Will he endure your sight, as yet I feare;
Then till the fury of his Highnesse settle   2320
Come not before him.
    Flo. I not purpose it:
I thinke *Camillo*.
    Cam. Euen he, my Lord.
    Per. How often haue I told you 'twould be thus?   2325
How often said my dignity would last
But till 'twer knowne?

2310 SCENE IX. POPE, HAN, WARB, JOHN
2316 my] your F2+
2319 sight, as yet$_\wedge$] $\sim$ $_\wedge$ $\sim$ $\sim$, mTBY2 *conj.*, HAN, JOHN1+
2320 Highnesse] highness CAP+ (−KTLY, PEN, SIG)
2323 thinke$_\wedge$] $\sim$, ROWE1-CAM3 (−DYCE, HUD2, BUL), SIS, CLN2-SIG, OXF2
    Camillo.$_\wedge$] $\sim$?$_\wedge$ ROWE3, COL, HUD, DYCE, STAU-GLO, DEL4, WH2+; $\sim$ —
THEO1, THEO2, WARB; $\sim$?— THEO3, JOHN, v1773

2310 **you**] BETHELL (ed. 1956): "Perdita (?)." Probably. Polixenes and the Shepherd have exited, and the speech would be inappropriate to Camillo, because a prince
would not acknowledge a subject's implicit doubt or criticism. PORTER & CLARKE (ed.
1908), however: "It is to Camillo. . . . He has addressed the old man. He turns
now . . . to regard the young Prince, intently, to see what mettle is in him after this
disaster."
    2311-13 **I . . . backe**] MIRIAM JOSEPH (1947, pp. 115-16) cites this passage as
an example of restrictio, "a figure whereby after making a general statement one
excepts a part."

2311 **affear'd**] See n. 2287.

delaid] The CLARKES (ed. 1865): "Besides . . . 'deferred or postponed in my intentions', means 'temporarily checked . . . or frustrated in them.'" SCHMIDT (1874), however, gives only one appropriate definition of the verb used intransitively, "to retard." Cf. *OED* (*v.*¹ 3).

2312 **But nothing altred**] PAFFORD (ed. 1963): "Both his love and his purpose are constant."

What . . . am:] GENTLEMAN (ed. 1774), alone: "Throws open his shepherd's vest, and discovers his rich garment."

2313-14 **More . . . vnwillingly**] MADDEN (1897, pp. 173-4): The source of the metaphor is coursing with greyhounds. Thus DEIGHTON (ed. 1889): "Like a greyhound who has caught sight of the hare but is held back . . . , I only struggle the harder to get free from the leash." None of *OED*'s illustrations of the expression (Leash, *sb.* 4, citing this line) mentions greyhounds, although a hound of some kind is clearly implied. SCHMIDT (1875, p. 1418b) uses *plucking back* to illustrate the gerund employed in a passive sense—i.e., being plucked back. For *pluck* he gives "to pull, to tug, to tear." WILSON (ed. 1931), for *not . . . vnwillingly*: "I.e. not being dragged along against my will." COLLINS (ed. 1904-24?): "I.e. *even* unwillingly."

2315 **Gracious my Lord**] For the transposition, see n. 390.

2316 **my**] PAFFORD (ed. 1963): "Probably caught from the line above." PORTER & CLARKE (ed. 1908) try wildly to justify *my* by supposing Camillo not yet to have put off his disguise, which they groundlessly suppose to be that of a young man. Polixenes has revealed himself; and where he is, Camillo is not far behind.

temper] SCHMIDT (1875): "Temperament" (*OED*, *sb.* 9, citing this line).

2318 **purpose to him**] MINSHEU (1617, Purpose): See "Intend." HAPPÉ (1969): "Intend to offer him."

2320 **his Highnesse**] DELIUS (ed. 1860): Not merely the royal title but the majesty of Polixenes, which has been offended by Florizel's love affair. The lower-case *h* adopted by CAPELL (ed. 1768) and most later eds. may indicate they have the same idea, and the same ambiguity may be present in 2388. BOORMAN (ed. 1964) prefers "pride or anger." The first of these senses is recognized by *OED* (*sb.* 3) but the second is not; neither is found by SCHMIDT (1874), or ONIONS (1986) to occur in Sh.

2322 **not purpose**] As to the position of *not*, see n. 2005.

2323 **I thinke *Camillo***] HARRISON (ed. 1947): "Florizel recognizes Camillo through his disguise." BETHELL (ed. 1956): "Camillo probably removes it as he replies." Perhaps, but 2315-21 are a giveaway.

2325 **How . . . thus?**] The CLARKES (ed. 1865): This speech "marks the noble indignation of Perdita at the king's charge that she has sought to win Florizel [2278-85]." PORTER & CLARKE (ed. 1908): It indicates "that she was anew impressed by [the] disclosure of the rank and dignity of the second guest." She actually recalls her fear of discovery (1817-24).

2326 **dignity**] JOHNSON (1755): "Advancement; preferment." MAXWELL (ed. 1969): "I.e. honor of being the Prince's betrothed." BEVINGTON (ed. 1992): "I.e., the new status this marriage would have offered." Cf. nn. 28, 2946, and 3088.

2327 **But . . . knowne?**] DEIGHTON (ed. 1889): "Only till it became known what our relations to each other were."

Flo. It cannot faile, but by
The violation of my faith, and then
Let Nature crush the sides o'th earth together,   2330
And marre the seeds within. Lift vp thy lookes:
From my succession wipe me (Father) I
Am heyre to my affection.

2332 my] thy CAP, RANN

2328-33 **It . . . affection**] COLIE (1974, p. 276): "Florizel, a prince disguised as
a lordling-shepherd, accepts the shepherd's ideals of democracy and love, which he
recognizes as based on notions of natural rightness if not of natural right." The idea
of the shepherd's democracy derives from 2286-95, which has been called "in no
sense 'democratic'" (see the n.), and rather than the shepherd's love Florizel seems
to be speaking only of his own, for which he is willing to sweep aside everything.
This certifies him to be a hero of romance rather than a champion of the rights of
man. TAYLOR (1973, p. 339): The speech "epitomizes both his recklessness and the
easy abruptness with which he shrugs off the tie of blood." BERGERON (1985, p. 167):
"He wants to impress Perdita with the depth of his love for her, but he seems a bit
foolish — perhaps even selfish." BERNARD (1979, p. 222), for the defense: "For one
possessed of such a constant vision of the abiding order of things, even 'fantasy'
['fancie'] is trustworthy."
    2329 **faith**] SCHMIDT (1874): "Vow of love." See n. 1834-6.
    then] EVANS (ed. 1974): "I.e. when that happens."
    2330-1 **Let . . . within**] SITWELL (1948, p. 205): "At the thought of violation of
faith," Florizel speaks these words because "the creative processes of Nature, healing
and re-making all, overcoming the winter death, — these rule the play." NOBLE (1935,
p. 248): "Sides of the earth" occurs in Jer. 6:22; *sides of the world* appears in *Ant.*
1.2.192 (292) and *Cym.* 3.1.50 (1428). THEOBALD (MS -1729?) compares *Mac.*
4.1.58-60 (1588-90) and *Lr.* 3.2.6-9 (1661-4). BETHELL (ed. 1956): "These seeds
['germens' in *Mac.* and *Lr.*] are . . . the sources of life and growth in the created
world. Their destruction would be the end of all things." WHITAKER (1953, p. 324)
notices the seeds of things to come in *2H4* 3.1.84 (1501). BARBER (1964, p. 241): Sh.
previously used similar images "for the universal disorder that follows from the violation of Degree: but Florizel says that disorder will follow if he *fails* to violate Degree
(by disobeying his father and marrying out of his class)." ANON. (1930) rather pointlessly thinks the seeds are "fossils, then supposed to originate in the rocks under the
influence of the stars."
    2331 **Lift . . . lookes**] STEEVENS (ed. 1793) compares Ps. 4:6: "Lift vp the light
of thy countenance." Cf. nn. 1852 and 2987.
    2332-46 **From . . . belou'd**] MIRIAM JOSEPH (1947, p. 105): An example of eus-
tathia, a pledge of constancy, "Florizel's undismayed response when threatened with
disinheritance of a kingdom, should he persist in loving Perdita."
    2332-3 **I . . . affection**] DEIGHTON (ed. 1889): "All the inheritance I covet is
that of my love" or, as PIERCE (ed. 1918) puts it, I "have an inheritance in my love"
(*OED*, Affection, *sb.* 6). PARRY (ed. 1982), somewhat differently: "Nothing can take
away my right to my love for you." *Affection* may also mean "feeling as opposed to
reason" (*sb.* 3, which, however, includes "lust," inappropriate here but see *Luc.* 271).
ORGEL (ed. 1996): "Passionate love." For other senses, see nn. 26, 214, 2206, 3046,
and 3110.

Cam. Be aduis'd.

Flo. I am: and by my fancie, if my Reason   2335
Will thereto be obedient: I haue reason:
If not, my sences better pleas'd with madnesse,
Do bid it welcome.

Cam. This is desperate (sir.)

Flo. So call it: but it do's fulfill my vow: 2340

2336 obedient:] ~ , ROWE1+
2337 ⋀pleas'd with madnesse,] (~ ~ ~) F2-F4

2334 **Be aduis'd**] YOUNG & MOSELEY (ed. 1965): "Be cautious [*OED, ppl. a.* 2]. Florizel in his answer takes the word in its sense of 'counselled' [*ppl. a.* 6]."

2335-8 **I . . . welcome**] CHARLTON (ed. 1916): "Florizel is somewhat reckless; but his passion and ardour are of the right sort, and, moreover, they do not prevent his thinking of his father [as shown by 2346 ff.]." FRYE (1962, pp. 236-7): His "is a state of mind above reason. . . . Leontes' jealousy is a fantasy below reason, and hence a parody of Florizel's state. Camillo, who represents a kind of middle level in the play, is opposed to both, calling one diseased [391] and the other desperate [2339]. . . . When Leontes has returned to his proper state of mind, he echoes Florizel [at 3272-3]." WEINSTEIN (1971, p. 104) nevertheless finds here "an uncanny resemblance to Leontes," as do BRADBROOK ("Dramatic Romance,"1976, p. 89) and NICHOLS (1981, p. 186). ORGEL (ed. 1996): "In making reason subservient to fancy, Florizel is inverting the ethical hierarchy of the faculties."

2335 **fancie**] Florizel uses this word as a synonym for "affection" (2333). MINSHEU (1617) equates it with *Fantasie*, which he glosses with the Latin *Phantasia*. THOMAS (1587): "Phantasia . . . *imagination.*" JOHNSON (1755): "Inclination; liking; fondness" (*OED, sb.* 8). JOHNSON (ed. 1765): "Love" (8.b). SCHMIDT (1874) agrees, although *affection, love, imagination*, and *fantasy* were not sharply distinguished. See nn. 1046 and 3256. BETHELL (ed. 1956): "There is a play upon *fancy = imagination* (in our modern sense) and *fancy = love*; but there is a real relationship between the meanings, since love arises in the fancy, whence it *ought* to be submitted to the judgement of reason. . . . Shakespeare seems . . . to question this orthodox view of things: *reason* comes to have rather the sense of *worldly wisdom*, and there is a hint that something akin to 'intuition' (which the Elizabethans would have included under 'reason', as its highest operation) is alone to be trusted." "For the psychology involved," KERMODE (ed. 1963) compares *MND* 5.1.2 ff. (1794 ff.): Theseus on the lunatic, the lover, and the poet. The context here narrows the range, however, for what Florizel fancies is simply to marry Perdita; the betrothal at 2259 would have been the decisive step.

2335-6 **if . . . reason**] WRIGHT & LAMAR (ed. 1966): "If I can make my reason serve my love (make possible its realization), I shall be sane."

2338 **it**] MOORMAN (ed. 1912): "Madness." DRAPER (1985, p. 35): "Commitment that may look like 'madness' is to be preferred to more realistically rational behaviour; and this is accepted by the audience as a superior form of rationality . . . because . . . Perdita justifies such commitment."

2340 **but it**] STAUNTON (ed. 1859): "*As*, is understood, — 'but *as* it.'" DELIUS (ed. 1860): "But only it." HUNTER (ed. 1872): "If it does but." To STAUNTON's interpretation, FURNESS (ed. 1898) prefers "the tone of calm assurance, free from any limitation," such as the condition that his madness is justified by his vow.

I needs must thinke it honesty. *Camillo*,
Not for *Bohemia*, nor the pompe that may
Be thereat gleaned: for all the Sun sees, or
The close earth wombes, or the profound seas, hides
In vnknowne fadomes, will I breake my oath   2345   (2
To this my faire belou'd: Therefore, I pray you,
As you haue euer bin my Fathers honour'd friend,
When he shall misse me, as (in faith I meane not
To see him any more) cast your good counsailes
Vpon his passion: Let my selfe, and Fortune   2350
Tug for the time to come. This you may know,
And so deliuer, I am put to Sea
With her, who heere I cannot hold on shore:
And most opportune to her neede, I haue
A Vessell rides fast by, but not prepar'd   2355
For this designe. What course I meane to hold

2343 thereat] thereout HAN
        all] all that F2-ROWE
2344 seas, hides] F1; seas hides IRV, NLSN, ALEX, CLN2, ARD2, K&R, PEN2+; sea
hides MTBY4 *conj.*, CAP, V1778, RANN, CAM1, GLO, DYCE2, HUD2, WH2, OXF1, KIT1;
seas hide F2 *etc.*
2347 honour'd] *Om.* F2-RANN
2348 ∧as (in] (~ ∧ ~ ROWE1+
2353 who] whom F2-CAM3 (−DYCE, IRV, BUL, NLSN), PEL1-SIG
2354 her] F1-POPE2, KNT1-HUD1, IRV, BUL, ALEX, SIS, SIG, EVNS, OXF2; the CAP; our
MTBY2 *conj.*, THEOBALD (1729) *conj. in* NICHOLS (1817, 2:365), THEO1 *etc.*

2341 **needs must**] PARRY (ed. 1982): "Am obliged to."
        honesty] WRIGHT & LAMAR (ed. 1966): "Honest behavior."
2341–6 *Camillo . . . belou'd*] BETHELL (ed. 1956): "Florizel uses large cosmic
references as did Leontes (see [n. 708]), but to swear his faith, not his unfaith. In his
love he is the exact opposite of Leontes in his jealousy and so helps to symbolize the
'new life.'" MCFARLAND (1972, p. 138): "The resonant dignity of his language seems
all-encompassing in its affirmation of trust, loyalty, and coming together; in its rejection of the divisiveness of authoritarian rage." KNIGHTS (1976, p. 608): "It is only
with this, the assertion of a love that, very credibly, is not Time's fool, that we can
pass to the final image of integration in the last act."
2342–3 **the . . . gleaned**] BOORMAN (ed. 1964): "The vain glory that may be
got from it."
2343 **thereat**] SCHMIDT (1875): "At or in possessing it [Bohemia]." DEIGHTON
(ed. 1889) thinks the word equivalent to *therein*.
        for] CARRINGTON (1956): "*I.e. not* for."
2344 **close**] SCHMIDT (1874): "Shut fast . . . tight." DEIGHTON (ed. 1889), however: "Secret, as if unwilling to give up her treasures."

wombes] JOHNSON (1755): "To inclose; to breed in secret," an instance of the Elizabethan conversion of nouns into verbs (ABBOTT §290). For other conversions, see the next n.

hides] ABBOTT (§333): A third-person plural in *-s* rather than in *-st*. PAFFORD (ed. 1963), alternatively: "*Seas* may be treated as a collective, parallel with *earth*." In either case, COLLINS (ed. 1904–24?): "The assonance helps the emphasis." HAPPÉ (1969), has another idea: "*Seas* may have been caught from *sees* [2343]." For F2's alteration, see n. 30.

2345 **vnknowne fadomes**] KITTREDGE & RIBNER (ed. 1967): "Depths never probed."

2347 **As . . . friend**] Eds. following RANN (ed. 1787) print this line as does F, where it may be a hexameter or, by the elision of "you haue" and "euer," a pentameter. Following DYCE (ed. 1864), SCHANZER (ed. 1969) prints the elisions. WALKER (1860, 1:81) wishes to contract "you haue euer" to *y'have e'er*.

2348 **misse**] SCHMIDT (1875): "Feel the want of." DEIGHTON (ed. 1889), however: "Find I have gone away."

faith] SCHMIDT (1874): "In sooth, indeed." See nn. 544–5, 672, 1193, 1836, and 2307 for other meanings.

2349–50 **cast . . . passion**] BETHELL (ed. 1956): "Metaphor from casting water on a fire."

2350 **passion**] CARRINGTON (1956): "Anger."

2351 **Tug . . . come**] JOHNSON (1755, Tug, citing this line): "To labour; to contend; to struggle." LEE (ed. 1907): "Fight it out henceforth." PAFFORD (ed. 1963), rather oddly, finds "the spirit . . . a little reminiscent of Autolycus" because of his "life to come" (1698).

you may know] HUNTER (ed. 1872): "You are at liberty to say you know."

2352 **deliuer**] SCHMIDT (1874): "To speak, to communicate."

2353 **who**] For the form, see n. 827.

2354 **most . . . neede**] BOSWELL (ed. 1821): "'The need we have of her', i.e. the vessel." FURNESS (ed. 1898): "Herein KNIGHT [ed. 1841] is his solitary adherent." DYCE (ed. 1857) believes that the change to *our* is justified because of "your neede" at 2361, but SYMONS (in IRVING & MARSHALL, ed. 1890) defends F: "Florizel's main thought is of Perdita, and by saying '*her* need' he shows how completely she has absorbed his thoughts even to the exclusion of himself." PAFFORD (ed. 1963): If *her* is wrong, it may have been carried down from 2353. If not, "the mistake would more probably occur from mishearing than misreading." Mishearing as a source of error in this text is very unlikely; see p. 590. PROUDFOOT (in WELLS & TAYLOR, 1987): "Graphically, 'your' (written 'yʳ') is a likelier source of the error." His opinion arises from the fact that the Elizabethan manuscript "h" had a tail rather like that of the "y"; the interpretation is implausible, however, because *your* makes no sense, since Florizel and Camillo have not yet joined forces.

opportune to] OED (Opportune, *a.* 2, citing this line): "Fitting . . . seasonable." KITTREDGE & RIBNER (ed. 1967): "Fortunately for." CAPELL (1783, 2.4: 229): Accented *oppórtune*. See ABBOTT §490.

2355 **Vessell rides**] I.e., at anchor. For the omission of the relative, see n. 2191.

2355–6 **not . . . designe**] DEIGHTON (ed. 1889, Design): "A purpose, an intention, a contriving." BOORMAN (ed. 1964): "Shakespeare is perhaps stressing the absolute innocence of Florizel (as previously in this scene)." Florizel's plans, beyond marrying Perdita, are unknown (the implication that he had none may be right), but since he did not expect to be discovered, he would not have had a ship ready for flight.

Shall nothing benefit your knowledge, nor
Concerne me the reporting.
    Cam. O my Lord,
I would your spirit were easier for aduice,   2360
Or stronger for your neede.
    Flo. Hearke *Perdita*,
Ile heare you by and by.
    Cam. Hee's irremoueable,
Resolu'd for flight: Now were I happy if   2365
His going, I could frame to serue my turne,
Saue him from danger, do him loue and honor,
Purchase the sight againe of deere Sicillia,
And that vnhappy King, my Master, whom
I so much thirst to see.   2370
    Flo. Now good *Camillo*,
I am so fraught with curious businesse, that
I leaue out ceremony.
    Cam. Sir, I thinke
You haue heard of my poore seruices, i'th loue   2375
That I haue borne your Father?

2364 irremoueable,] ~ ‸ STAU, DEL
2372 curious] serious mTBY3 *conj.*, COL2, COL4, HUD2
2373 *going.* MAL-DEL2, KTLY, DEL4, COL4
2375 i'th] o'th' JOHN

2357-8 **Shall . . . reporting**] SCHMIDT (1874, Concern): "To be of importance
to, to interest." DEIGHTON (ed. 1889): "It will not do you any good to know, nor do
I care to tell you." HAPPÉ (1969): "Florizel is not anticipating help from Camillo at
this point."

2357 **benefit**] *OED* (*v.* 1, citing this line): "Improve, help forward."

2360 **easier for**] ROLFE (ed. 1879): "More inclined to take." ORGEL (ed. 1996):
"More at ease with."

2362 **Hearke *Perdita***] The CLARKES (ed. 1865): "He sees that she stands silently—as it were irresponsively and unassentingly by . . . [;] he hastens
to . . . convince her of his unswerved faith, and persuade her to his views; [his
taking her aside] affords opportunity for Camillo's soliloquy." BETHELL (ed. 1956):
"This crude device . . . to permit another character to . . . make a 'direct address' . . . is repeated at [2472 and 2543]. Shakespeare is concerned in this part of
the scene principally with managing his plot, and so, now the tension is lowered, he
has the opportunity of detaching the audience (who will have been concerned over

Florizel and Perdita) and renewing for them the atmosphere of 'an old tale' by telling it in an 'old' way." COGHILL (1958, p. 37) suggests that Perdita, who has been silent, sympathizes "with the caution of Camillo, [and] makes some impulsive gesture towards him at [2361], to show her feelings." This gesture provokes Florizel to take her aside "for a brief private colloquy, to divulge the plan he is keeping so secret from Camillo." But Florizel has no plan.

2363 **by and by**] JOHNSON (1755): "In a short time."

2364 **irremoueable**] JOHNSON (1755): "Not to be changed." STAUNTON (ed. 1859): "Employed adverbially." He compares *damnable* earlier (see n. 1373–4) and here omits F's comma. DELIUS alone follows him, though the possibility of adverbial use is sometimes mentioned. The CLARKES (ed. 1865): "If we take it as an adjective, we must understand 'he's' as repeated before 'resolv'd.'" *OED* (*a*. 2, citing this line) evidently finds no difficulty in this understanding.

2365–8 **Now . . . Sicillia**] WATSON (1984, p. 262), comparing Camillo's reason for fleeing Sicilia (460–4): "Camillo is given a soliloquy on both occasions to weigh his choices, and each time his decision to flee to the other kingdom is based on a perfect balance of principled Sicilian philanthropy and pragmatic Bohemian self-serving."

2365–6 **Now . . . turne**] FOAKES (1971, p. 135), who does not care for him: "Camillo abandoned one master, Leontes, in Act I, and now is disloyal to a second, Polixenes." Cf. n. 464–5.

2367 **do . . . honor**] ABBOTT (§303): "The verb [*do*] was sometimes used transitively with an objective noun."

2368 **Purchase**] Possibly *OED* (*v*. 6b): "To acquire by toil, suffering, danger or the like." HERFORD (ed. 1904): "Win." MOORMAN (ed. 1912): "Obtain" (4a).

2369 **vnhappy**] Unfortunate.

2371–3 ***Camillo*, . . . ceremony**] CAPELL (1783, 2.4:178): "Meant as taking leave; the reply . . . tends to detain him." MALONE (ed. 1790) accordingly adds the SD, which survives until 1878. CLARK & WRIGHT (ed. 1863) argue that instead of going, Florizel "apologises to Camillo for talking apart to Perdita in his presence." Some eds. subsequently adopt their semicolon, causing Florizel to say, "I am now ready to hear you." Others evidently think that without the SD, F's comma implies the same.

2372 **fraught**] JOHNSON (1755, citing this line): "Filled; stored; thronged." ROLFE (ed. 1879): "Charged, burdened."

curious] The CLARKES (ed. 1865): "Requiring special care." MOORMAN (ed. 1912): "Either, business requiring anxious [*OED*, *a*. 1b] care, or, particular business." The latter alternative may misunderstand *OED*, which, regarding *curious*, uses *particular* to mean "exact, precise." ORGEL (ed. 1996): "Complex" (*OED* 10b: "Intricate"). SCHMIDT (1874): "Embarrassing" (i.e., hampering).

2373 **I . . . ceremony**] ORGEL (ed. 1996): "I omit the courtesy due you." PORTER & CLARKE (ed. 1908): "To apologize for keeping the councillor waiting on him while he confers privately with Perdita."

2375 **seruices**] FURNESS (ed. 1898): "From what Camillo foretells about the reception of Florizel by Leontes, it is evident that Florizel knew of the special service which Camillo had rendered in aiding the escape of [Polixenes] from Sicily." DEIGHTON (ed. 1889): "He perhaps refers rather to [the] escape . . . than to services rendered since, though Florizel in his answer acknowledges these also."

Flo. Very nobly
Haue you deseru'd: It is my Fathers Musicke
To speake your deeds: not little of his care
To haue them recompenc'd, as thought on.   2380
   Cam. Well (my Lord)
If you may please to thinke I loue the King,
And through him, what's neerest to him, which is
Your gracious selfe; embrace but my direction,
If your more ponderous and setled proiect   2385
May suffer alteration. On mine honor,
Ile point you where you shall haue such receiuing
As shall become your Highnesse, where you may
Enioy your Mistris; from the whom, I see
There's no disiunction to be made, but by   2390
(As heauens forefend) your ruine: Marry her,
And with my best endeuours, in your absence,

2383 what's] what is mTBY2 *conj.*, HAN, v1773-KNT2, HUD, DYCE, HAL, CAM1-KTLY, KNT3, WH2, IRV, ARD1, CAM3, KIT1, PEL1
     neerest] near'st mTBY3 *and* WALKER (1854, p. 169) *conj.*, HAL, DYCE2, HUD2
2384-6 selfe; . . . direction, . . . alteration.] Ff, ROWE, HAN, ARD1-KIT1, SIS, CLN2, EVNS+; ~ , . . . ~ , . . . ~ , POPE, KNT, HUD, SING2, DYCE, WH1, CAM1, IRV, OXF1, BUL; ~ ; . . . ~ , . . . ~) CAP, v1778-SING1, HAL; ~ , . . . ~ ; . . . ~ ,) THEO1 *etc.*
2389 from] for BEV3
2392 And∧ with . . . endeuours, . . . absence,] ~ , ~ . . . ~ , . . . ~ , CAP; ~ (~ . . . ~ ∧ . . . ~) v1785-IRV, BUL-CAM3, PEN2; ~ ∧ ~ . . . ~ ∧ . . . ~ ∧ OXF1, ALEX, CLN2, ARD2, OXF2; ~ ∧ ~ . . . ~ ∧ . . . ~ , EVNS

2378 **Musicke**] Anticipated by CALDECOTT (MS 1813-33), JERVIS (1868): "Delight; happiness" (*OED, sb.* 2c *fig.*, citing this line).
2380 **recompenc'd . . . on**] The CLARKES (ed. 1865): "Recompensed as highly as they are estimated." For *as*, CHARLTON (ed. 1916): "'As often as' or 'as soon as.'" Eds. generally prefer the CLARKES.
2382 **If . . . please**] WALKER (1860, 1:206): "*Si tibi placeat* [if it be pleasing to you]." ABBOTT (§309): "*May* . . . is a modest way of stating what ought to be well known" (see also BLAKE [1983, p. 92]). DEIGHTON (ed. 1889) adds: "'May' is extremely deferential."
2383 **And . . . is**] Rather than eliding *what is*, as F does, WALKER (1854, p. 169) prefers *what is near'st*, because the *e* in superlatives is often suppressed.

2384 **selfe;**] SIMPSON (1911, p. 57-8): "The semicolon is used to mark off a dependent clause at the beginning of a sentence, especially if the comma is used in the immediate context. The only modern equivalent, which would not be suitable in all cases, is the dash."

embrace . . . direction] DEIGHTON (ed. 1889): "Accept the advice I give you." Camillo is being deferential, as he is in 2385-6; he knows Florizel has no project.

2385 **ponderous**] JOHNSON (1755, citing this line): "Important; momentous." PAFFORD (ed. 1963): "In 'more ponderous' Camillo is tactfully and deferentially referring to Florizel's 'project' as being weightier and of greater importance than his own 'direction.'" WRIGHT & LAMAR (ed. 1966) find him "tactful but ironic in so describing Florizel's sketchy plan."

setled] SCHMIDT (1875): "Fixed." Cf. 3272.

2386 **suffer**] SCHMIDT (1875): "Allow."

2387 **Ile . . . receiuing**] YOUNG & MOSELEY (ed. 1965): "I'll direct [*OED*, Point, *v.* 12a] you to where you will have such a reception."

2388 **Highnesse**] See n. 2320 for the ambiguity.

2389 **Enioy**] MINSHEU (1617): "Haue the possession of." Camillo, like Leontes at 2986, probably means "marry." See that n.

the whom,] Whereas *which* or *the which* in similar constructions is common (see nn. 415, 736, and 2428.), ABBOTT (§270) finds that *the* is not similarly attached to *who*, the construction here being "perhaps, unique in Shakespeare." It may have been adopted for meter. SIMPSON (1911, pp. 51-3) finds that a comma is placed after a relative only when the relative follows a preposition. "This is necessarily detached from the verb, and the comma is inserted partly [as an] enclosing comma . . . , partly because the arrangement of the words suggests an inversion."

2390 **disiunction**] JOHNSON (1755, citing this line): "Separation."

2391 **forefend**] KERSEY (1708): "Forbid." HANMER (ed. 1743-4, 6:glos.) adds "prevent" (*OED*, Forfend, *v.* 2).

2392 **And∧ with . . . endeuours, . . . absence,**] SCHANZER (ed. 1969) states the alternatives as "and where, together with my best endeavours in your absence, you may strive to appease your angry father" and "and with my best endeavours in your absence I *shall* strive to appease your angry father." He prefers the former. As the textual notes indicate, however, early eds. attempted to improve F by emending 2393 to *I'll strive*, which implies that Camillo plans to influence Polixenes. The idea of making "with . . . absence" parenthetical, which obviates the need of emendation and which suggests that Florizel will make the peace, may first have been CAPELL's; it is made evident by the parentheses introduced by STEEVENS (ed. 1785). HERFORD (ed. 1904), however: "By a change of construction, refers to Camillo." HERFORD (ed. 1916-): "The absent Florizel can do nothing to 'qualify' his father's anger; this is to be the work of Camillo, who will use his 'best endeavors' for that end." According to BETHELL (ed. 1956), the reader may bring "Ile" down from 2387 to go with "striue." KNOWLES (privately), citing ABBOTT (§399), calls the construction "a simple (and common) omission of the nominative." PARRY (ed. 1982), on the other hand: "Camillo expects Florizel to be able to win Leontes' support for putting his case to Polixenes."

Your discontenting Father, striue to qualifie
And bring him vp to liking.
   Flo. How *Camillo*   2395
May this (almost a miracle) be done?
That I may call thee something more then man,
And after that trust to thee.
   Cam. Haue you thought on
A place whereto you'l go?   2400
   Flo. Not any yet:
But as th'vnthought-on accident is guiltie
To what we wildely do, so we professe

2393-5 *Three verse lines ending* strive . . . liking. . . . *Camillo*, HAN, v1773;
two, ending qualify, . . . Camillo, mCAP2, v1793+
    2393 discontenting] discontented ROWE1-JOHN2
         striue] I'll strive ROWE3-THEO2, WARB-CAP, v1778-RANN; I will strive HAN,
v1773
    2394 him vp] *Om.* ROWE
    2403 To] Of ROWE1-THEO2, WARB-JOHN2; Towards HAN

    2393 **discontenting**] CAPELL (1783, 2.4:178): "With whom you have cause to be
discontented" (*OED, ppl. a.* 1) MALONE's (ed. 1790) "discontented" probably means
"feeling or showing discontent" (*OED, ppl. a.* 2, citing this line); BOSWELL (ed. 1821,
1:583) classifies the word as an active participle used for the passive. See FRANZ §664;
ABBOTT (§372) suggests that this form "may perhaps be explained by the use of the
verb 'content you'; 'I discontent (me)' meaning 'I am discontented.'" HERFORD (ed.
1904): "Indignant." PORTER & CLARKE (ed. 1908): "Suggests a continuing state of
fuming discontent." PAFFORD (ed. 1963) finds parallels in "'all-obeying breath' (*Ant.*
3.13.77 [2244]), i.e. 'obeyed by all'; and 'his unrecalling crime' (*Luc.* 993), i.e. 'un-
recalled crime'. Contrast 'grim-look'd' i.e. 'grim-looking' (*MND* 5.1.169 [1972])."
    2393-4 **qualifie . . . liking**] CALDECOTT (MS 1813-33): "Temper & assuage
[*OED* 8] . . . & work him up [*OED, v.* 27, citing this line] to assent & approbation."
The CLARKES (ed. 1865): "Pacify, and bring him round to approving the marriage."
For *qualify*, see n. 720. DEIGHTON (ed. 1889): "The idea is probably that of screwing
an instrument up to certain pitch." BOORMAN (ed. 1964) suggests that *qualifie*, in
addition to "appease," may mean "dilute" (actually "modify" [*OED* 11]), which yields
"Your father is lacking in contents, so I will water him down and bring him to your
liking or taste." In all these glosses, Camillo is assumed to be the actor. MALONE's (ed.
1790) reading, however— "And where you may, by letters, entreaties, &c. endeavour
to soften your incensed father, and reconcile him to the match; to effect which, my
best services shall not be wanting during your absence"— makes Florizel the actor.
ORGEL (ed. 1996): "Since Camillo's projected abilities in the matter are called miraculous and more than human [2396-7], it looks as if Florizel, at least, understands
Camillo to be offering to deal with Polixenes himself."
    2396 **(almost a miracle)**] SIMPSON (1911, p. 93): "Adjectives are enclosed within
brackets where we should employ the hyphen if we used any punctuation at all."
TRAVERSI (1955, p. 161): "The phrase, indicating that there is about Camillo himself
at this stage 'something more than man', suggests the presence of the divine working
behind his project." ENRIGHT (1970, p. 195): "To the cooler judgment . . . it will

appear that at the best Camillo is planning to exploit Leontes' remorse on the subject of Polixenes by implying an untruth about Florizel's relations with his father, and the worst that he is simply serving his own turn." Camillo's plan is no doubt faulty (for example, Florizel could not have carried off for long the pretense of being his father's ambassador), but TRAVERSI is right at least that feeble human actions are forwarding the will of Apollo.

2398 **after that**] DEIGHTON (ed. 1889): "Besides that." But LOBBAN's (ed. 1910) "in that character" is favored by most later eds. HAPPÉ (1969): "Because of that, i.e. his supernatural goodness." BEVINGTON (ed. 1992, After): "Ever after."

2402–5 **But . . . blowes**] RABKIN (1971, p. 36) is reminded of the winds that blow metaphorically or actually elsewhere in the play (see 63–4, 1084, 1498–9, and 1542–3). "We recognize that . . . the winds of the world and the winds of human passion are identical." PETERSON ("Barks," 1973, pp. 97–8), however, discovers the emblem of the tempest-tossed bark, a commonplace in Sh. (as in *3H6* 5.4.1–38 [2884–2921]) and in 16th-c. literature generally (e.g., "Christian resolution, that saileth in the frail bark of the flesh through the waves of the world," in Bacon, "Of Adversity," *Essayes*, 1625).

2402 **th'vnthought-on accident**] MASON (1785, p. 137): Polixenes's "unexpected discovery." FURNESS (ed. 1898): "This may be so, but the whole phrase is nevertheless a general truth." RUSHTON (1907, pp. 42–4), who finds Sh. so conversant with legal matters that he "must have been, for some time, a student-at-law" (p. 61), explains that one who acts unlawfully ("wildely") is guilty of chance consequences (if A, meaning to murder B, accidentally kills C, then A has murdered C). See also nn. 112 and 1304–10. ABBOTT (§431) on *vnthought-on*: "The preposition usually attached to a certain verb [here *think*] is sometimes appended to the participle of the verb in order to make an adjective." See the n. following.

2402–3 **guiltie . . . do**] *OED* (Guilty, *a*. 3) uses this passage to illustrate *guilty to* meaning "culpably responsible for (a result)." ABBOTT (§188) agrees: "Chance is said to be 'responsible *to*' rashness (personified)"; yet he asks, "Or is *to* 'as *to*', *i.e.* as regards?" MALONE (ed. 1790) compares *Err.* 3.2.163 (953), but, as FURNESS (ed. 1898) notes, the expression there is not parallel. GOTCH (1900, p. 330) groundlessly thinks *guilty to* means "'guilty towards' some future action, whereas 'guilty of' would refer to the past"; *OED* does not make the distinction. Sh. does use *guilty to* elsewhere to mean *guilty of* (e.g., *Err.* 3.2.163 [953]) but prefers *guilty of* (some 30 instances). MAXWELL (ed. 1956), for the expression: "His unforeseen discovery by his father is to blame for what he rashly does." CUNNINGHAM (1951, pp. 34–6) finds that a distinction is drawn between causal and casual actions. "For example, if a man gets drunk and in that state 'unintentionally' kills another, he is not directly guilty of homicide spiritually, whatever he may be legally, for the result is beyond his intention. But . . . he is guilty of such a degree of irrational drunkenness as rendered the homicide possible, or even probable. The substance of his sin, then, lay in the choice by which he came into the condition of 'wildly doing'. . . . The initial choice of going off with Perdita is within Florizel's power, and he will make it, for he has embraced the condition of 'wildly doing'. . . . Hence what follows, as particularly the place whereto they'll go, will be accidental and the result of chance."

2403 **we . . . we**] COLLINS (ed. 1904–24?): "The second *we* . . . is the 'royal plural' [cf. 2463], the first is probably general." KNOWLES (privately): "Both could be general."

wildely] See nn. 800 and 2435. *OED* (*adv.* 1, citing this line): "In disorder or confusion."

2403–5 **so . . . blowes**] JOHNSON (ed. 1765): "As *chance* has driven me to these extremities, so I commit myself to *chance* to be conducted through them." WEINSTEIN (1971, p. 104): "He ominously echoes Leontes' 'I am a Feather for each

Our selues to be the slaues of chance, and flyes
Of euery winde that blowes.   2405
    Cam. Then list to me:
This followes, if you will not change your purpose
But vndergo this flight; make for Sicillia,
And there present your selfe, and your fayre Princesse,
(For so I see she must be) 'fore *Leontes*;   2410
She shall be habited, as it becomes   (2▌
The partner of your Bed. Me thinkes I see
Leontes opening his free Armes, and weeping
His Welcomes forth: asks thee there Sonne forgiuenesse,
As 'twere i'th'Fathers person: kisses the hands   2415

2404 chance] Chances ROWE1, ROWE2
2407-8 followes, . . . flight; . . . Sicillia,] Ff, ROWE, POPE, HAN, ARD1-ALEX,
CLN2+; ~ . . . . ~ , . . . ~ ; JOHN, v1773, COL, DEL, HUD2, OXF1, NLSN, PEL1; ~ ,
. . . ~ , . . . ~ ; THEO1 *etc.*
2409 your fayre] fair ROWE2
2414 there] the F3-PEN2 (−ALEX, ARD2)
    Sonne forgiuenesse,] *As a quotation* ALEX, ARD2, OXF2, BEV4

Wind that blows'" (1084). But in 2406 ff., Camillo manages "to perfect symbolically
the Prince's passion by gracing it with rational reflection."

    2404-5 flyes . . . blowes] ANON. (MS 1733-) imaginatively connects *flyes*
with the fly of a compass, defined by PHILLIPS (1658) as "that part . . . where the
32 points of the winds are described," i.e., the compass card. The sense does not
accord with the construction, however, and SCHMIDT (1874) is no doubt right that
"the insect Musca" (*OED, sb.*[1] 1b) is meant. HAPPÉ (1969): "Flies that are unable to
protect themselves from the wind." ORGEL (ed. 1996) thinks Florizel means moths,
not flies (*OED* 1a: "Any winged insect").

    2406 list] Listen. BOORMAN (ed. 1964) suggests "a possible sense of 'lean over
[*OED, v.*[5]] in the wind' . . . : i.e. incline yourself to my advice."

    2408 vndergo] Undertake. See n. 1095-6.

    make for Sicillia] MINCOFF (1941, p. 10), commenting on motivation: "Flor-
izel . . . is recommended to seek the shelter of Leontes' court . . . while Greene
had merely conjured up a storm that drove the unwilling Dorastus onto the coast of
Bohemia." See p. 649.

    2409-12 and . . . Bed] FELPERIN (1972, p. 240): Camillo's "art forces the anti-
artificial Perdita to take on still another disguise as a princess which is really no
disguise at all — 'the art itself is nature.'"

    2410 For . . . be] BOORMAN (ed. 1964): "The suggestion is 'must pretend to
be.'" KNOWLES (privately): "Or 'is destined to be,' repeating the idea of 2389-91 and
anticipating 2416." Cf. n. 2416.

    'fore] FURNESS (ed. 1898): "The omission . . . of *be-* . . . is not here the
ordinary omission authorised by poetic license, but is due to the 'be' immediately
preceding it." Furness compares 600, though it contains an omission of another type.

2411 **habited**] Dressed. For the noun, CAWDREY (1604, Habite): "Apparell." BUL-
LOKAR (1616): "The outward attire of the bodie, whereby one person may be distinguished from another; as the habit of a Gentleman, is different from the habit of a
merchant."

2412–15 **Me . . . person**] SIEMON (1974, p. 12): "Florizel . . . occupies Mam-
illius' place in the pattern of loss and recovery as a son restored to a father. . . .
Leontes is in the father's person, and the language cannot be other than intentional."
More obviously, Leontes will ask Polixenes's forgiveness in the person of Florizel.

2413 *Leontes . . . weeping*] SAINTSBURY (1923, 2:36–7): "In *The Winter's Tale*
we have blank verse of the very latest kind. . . . The writer not only indulges in the
redundant syllable [i.e., an eleventh] freely, but is particularly fond of making his
coupling foot with the next line redundant," as the *-ing* of *weeping* is here. . . .
There might be some reason for thinking *The Winter's Tale* Shakespeare's first experiment in very free redundance and overlapping [enjambment] combined: perhaps
one made very much earlier than is usually thought, and kept back." SAINTSBURY's
idea that *WT* is an early play has long been abandoned; see p. 602.

free] JERVIS (1868): "Eager, ready." MOORMAN (ed. 1912): "Gracious, willing."
MAXWELL (ed. 1956): "Hospitable." PAFFORD (ed. 1963): "Generous, liberal." SCHAN-
ZER (ed. 1969): "Noble." For additional adjectival senses, see nn. 185, 355, 812, 871,
and 2811. HAPPÉ (1969): "A reminder that Leontes is now recovering his true nobility."

2414 **asks**] ROLFE (ed. 1879): "An ellipsis of the nominative [ABBOTT §399; cf. n.
299–300], with a change of construction [ABBOTT §415; cf. n. 3092–4]."

2414–15 **asks . . . person**] FURNIVALL & CLARKE (ed. 1908) treat *there* as an
adverb of place and introduce quotation marks and exclamation points—"Sonne!
Forgiuenesse!" As for the place, PORTER & CLARKE (ed. 1908): He "sees the prince
in Leontes' arms," which Camillo imagines Leontes to have opened at 2413. PAFFORD
(ed. 1963): "Retention of 'there' suggests the visualizing of the scene (cf. Malvolio's
'Toby approaches; curtsies there to me' [*TN* 2.5.60–1 (1077)]), and 'Son', impossible
from Camillo addressing Florizel, is not out of place from Leontes." Sh. does use *son*
as "a term of affectionate address to a man or boy by an older person or by one in a
superior (esp. ecclesiastical) relation" (*OED, sb.* 3) but, unless a cleric is speaking,
very rarely (Menenius calls Coriolanus "son" at *Cor.* 5.2.68 [3306]). Leontes will never
have seen Florizel. Moreover, SYMONS (in IRVING & MARSHALL, ed. 1890): "I do not
think . . . Shakespeare could have written so jerky a line as this makes, or used so
curious a construction as *asks* with an exclamatory sentence depending on it." And
F1's *there* might be a mistake of "yʳ" for "yᵉ," though "yʳ" is the harder reading.
Paraphrasing F3's version, DEIGHTON (ed. 1889): "Asks of thee forgiveness, as though
he were asking your father (of whom it was needed)." HAPPÉ (1969): "*There* suggests
that Camillo sees the reconciliation vividly in his mind's eye."

2416 **fresh**] Perdita is *fresh* at 2265, here, and at 2443. Of the first two, the
CLARKES (ed. 1865) rhapsodize: The word "serves to set her in her clear-complex-
ioned, clear-souled purity and brightness before us, with the bloom of a country
maiden's cheek, and the white temples of a born princess." This is dubious for 2265;
see n. 2265–6. Here and at 2443 the word means "blooming, looking healthy or
youthful" (*OED, a.* 9b). ORGEL (ed. 1996) adds "newly-created." TRAVERSI (1954, p.
162) thinks "the adjective is full of the suggestion of life spontaneously reborn."

Princesse] HAPPÉ (1969): "Camillo sees the reunion in dramatic terms—but
not as the audience foresees it since he does not know who Perdita is. The audience
may anticipate here the full reunion of Perdita and Leontes."

Of your fresh Princesse; ore and ore diuides him,
'Twixt his vnkindnesse, and his Kindnesse: th'one
He chides to Hell, and bids the other grow
Faster then Thought, or Time.
    Flo. Worthy *Camillo*,   2420
What colour for my Visitation, shall I
Hold vp before him?
    Cam. Sent by the King your Father
To greet him, and to giue him comforts. Sir,
The manner of your bearing towards him, with   2425
What you (as from your Father) shall deliuer,
Things knowne betwixt vs three, Ile write you downe,
The which shall point you forth at euery sitting
What you must say: that he shall not perceiue,
But that you haue your Fathers Bosome there,   2430
And speake his very Heart.
    Flo. I am bound to you:
There is some sappe in this.

2419 or] of PEL1
2424 comforts] comfort mTBY3 *conj.*, COL4, HUD2
2428 sitting] fitting THEO, CAP, v1778-RANN

2416-19 **diuides . . . Time**] *OED* (Divide, *v.* 8e, citing this line): "To distribute (attention, etc.) between different objects." ABBOTT (§223, Him): "Himself." BETHELL (ed. 1956, Divides): "A rhetorical term. He keeps referring to both subjects, his former unkindness and his present kindness, putting them in separate categories—condemning the one and wishing the other to grow more quickly than a thought comes to mind or time passes." YOUNG & MOSELEY (ed. 1965, Unkindness): "Unnaturalness as a father (in exposing Perdita)." ROLFE (ed. 1879): "*Kindness* seems to combine the ideas of good-will and tenderness." DEIGHTON (ed. 1889) amplifies to "the kindness he now feels towards him and you." ORGEL (ed. 1996): "Family feeling in the largest sense, a natural affection deriving from a sense of shared humanity."

    2417 **th'one**] WALKER (1860, 2:91): Pronounced *thun*. FURNESS (ed. 1898) prefers *thown*, for which see CERCIGNANI (1981, p. 130).

    2418 **chides**] PAFFORD (ed. 1963): "Consigns with sorrow and anger." SCHMIDT (1874): "Coming near the sense of to curse."

    2418-19 **grow . . . Time**] SCHMIDT (ed. 1870, p. 284): *Faster* has both its meanings, "more rapid" as well as "more secure." Thus SCHMIDT (1875, p. 1421a): "Take a firmer root than thought or time, which are proverbially fast, that is swift" (TILLEY T240 and T327). Regarding their firmness, FURNESS (ed. 1898), however: "Of all elements utterly lacking stability, 'thought' and 'time' are almost the archetypes."

2421 **colour**] HUNTER (ed. 1872): "Pretext" (*OED*, *sb*. 12). DEIGHTON (ed. 1889), improbably: "There may be an idea of a ship hoisting its colours as a signal."

Visitation] See n. 9.

2422 **Hold vp before**] BEVINGTON (ed. 1992): "Present to."

2423-31 **Sent . . . Heart**] SEYMOUR (1805, 1:169): "It is not very suitable to the character of either the good Camillo, or the princely Florizel to propose or adopt an imposition like this."

2423 **Sent**] The CLARKES (1879, p. 303): I.e., that you are sent. See ABBOTT §413.

2424 **comforts**] MINSHEU (1617, Comfort): "Consolation, solace." Cf. n. 967. DEIGHTON (ed. 1889): "Comfortable assurances." PAFFORD (ed. 1963): "Reassurances of friendship." Differently, PORTER & CLARKE (ed. c. 1903): "Assistance." HAPPÉ (1969): "Relief from feelings of guilt towards Polixenes by a friendly approach."

2424-31 **Sir, . . . Heart**] CHARLTON (ed. 1916): "Camillo is unscrupulous in his Polonius-like use of 'windlaces and assays of bias'; he not only suggests deliberate falsification to Florizel, but in the very act of doing so is deceiving him: and that under the pretence of being secret with him. Yet this is a romance, not a tragedy; and moreover Camillo has a greater heart than has Polonius: so he is not in the end struck dead . . . — he is married to Paulina."

2426 **deliuer**] Communicate. See n. 2352.

2427 **betwixt vs three**] As ROLFE (ed. 1879) previously noticed, DEIGHTON (ed. 1889): "'Betwixt' should properly refer to two persons or parties only," and Sh. thus uses the word everywhere but here. *OED* (2), however, recognizes the meaning "among . . . in reference to more than two." The three are Leontes, Polixenes, and Camillo.

2428 **The which**] See nn. 415, 736, and 2389.

point you forth] ROLFE (ed. 1879): "Point out the way before you." MAXWELL (ed. 1956): "Guide."

sitting] THEOBALD (ed. 1733) paraphrases his emendation as "ev'ry convenient Opportunity; every Juncture, when it is *fit* to speak of such, or such, a Point." WARBURTON (ed. 1747): "Audience . . . of the King and Council . . . Council-days." HEATH (1765, p. 215), less grandly: "Conference," with which SCHMIDT (1875) agrees. PORTER & CLARKE (ed. 1908) seem confused: "Every time he sits down to write his father Camillo will forewarn him what . . . it will be best for him to say." Camillo and Florizel will be seas apart.

2429 **that**] So that (ABBOTT §283).

2430 **But that**] "Except" or "otherwise than" (ABBOTT §122).

haue . . . Bosome] ROLFE (ed. 1879): "Are intrusted with his inmost thoughts and feelings." MAXWELL (ed. 1956, Bosome): "Confidence." For other meanings, see n. 327.

2432 **bound**] JOHNSON (1755, Bind): "Oblige by kindness."

2433 **sappe**] RANN (ed. 1787): "Relish." More likely, "vitality"; see *OED* (*sb.*[1] 1b) and *Ant.* 3.13.191 (2379), which STEEVENS (ed. 1793) compares. EVANS (ed. 1974): "I.e. promise of success."

    Cam. A Course more promising,
Then a wild dedication of your selues   2435
To vnpath'd Waters, vndream'd Shores; most certaine,
To Miseries enough: no hope to helpe you,
But as you shake off one, to take another:
Nothing so certaine, as your Anchors, who
Doe their best office, if they can but stay you,   2440
Where you'le be loth to be: besides you know,
Prosperitie's the very bond of Loue,
Whose fresh complexion, and whose heart together,
Affliction alters.
    Perd. One of these is true: 2445
I thinke Affliction may subdue the Cheeke,
But not take-in the Mind.
    Cam. Yea? say you so?
There shall not, at your Fathers House, these seuen yeeres
Be borne another such.   2450

2434 Course] cause GLO, WH2, NLSN
2439 who] which HAN
2449-50 *to Florizel* CAM3

2434-6 **A . . . Shores**] MAXWELL (in PAFFORD, ed. 1963) compares *Cor.* 4.1.35-7 (2474-6).
    2434 **Course**] MINSHEU (1617): "A way or meanes." The metaphorical meaning may be "the action of running, as a *shippe* at sea."
    2435 **wild dedication**] BETHELL (ed. 1956): "Thoughtless handing-over." For *wild*, see nn. 800 and 2403.
    2436 **vnpath'd**] JOHNSON (1755, citing this instance): "Untracked; unmarked by passage."
    vndream'd] KITTREDGE & RIBNER (ed. 1967): "Never visited, even in dreams," i.e., unimagined.
    2438 **But . . . another**] STEEVENS (ed. 1793) quotes "To shift his being, Is to exchange one misery with another" (*Cym.* 1.5.54-5 [554-5]). DEIGHTON (ed. 1889): "In 'shake off' and 'take' the metaphor is from diseases."
    2439 **Nothing so certaine**] PAFFORD (ed. 1963): "'Nothing' has the Elizabethan adverbial sense of 'by no means', 'In no way.'" PARRY (ed. 1982), taking the word as a noun: "Sure of nothing but."
    your] PAFFORD (ed. 1963): "Has the Elizabethan sense of 'these [anchors] so well known to us all' or '[anchors] for example'" (ABBOTT §221).
    Anchors] THIRLBY (MS 1733-47?) sees the anchor here, "firm & stedfast," as the emblem of the hope of 2437. These anchors, however, "stay you, Where you'le be loth to be" (2440-1), hopelessly.
    2439-41 **who . . . be**] The CLARKES (ed. 1865, Who): "Which." ABBOTT (§264): "*Who* . . . is used of inanimate objects regarded as persons." WILSON (ed. 1931): "I.e. even the most detestable country would seem preferable to putting out again to sea."
    2440 **Doe . . . office**] JOHNSON (1755, Office): "Agency; peculiar use." For

other senses, see nn. 857, 1121, and 2820. For the phrase, KITTREDGE & RIBNER (ed. 1967): "Serve you best." KNOWLES (privately, Best): "Best under the circumstances; not ideally the best use."

2442-4 **Prosperitie's . . . alters**] BETHELL (ed. 1956): "Camillo utters the worldly wisdom of his years and profession." DENT compares, in addition to "Prosperity gets friends but adversity tries them" (TILLEY P611), "In Time of prosperity friends will be plenty, in time of adversity not one among twenty" (TILLEY T301). C. G. SMITH (1963, no. 244) finds parallels in Publilius Syrus, *Sententiae*.

2442 **bond**] BOORMAN (ed. 1964): "Either 'the binding force' [*OED, sb.*[1] 7] or 'the essential condition' [which Boorman says is 'the legal sense' but which is not in *OED*]."

2443 **fresh**] See n. 2416.

complexion] SCHMIDT (1874): "The colour of the skin, particularly of the face," the meaning, according to SCHMIDT, being somewhat narrower here than in 487. DEIGHTON (ed. 1889): Perdita at 2446 "applies the word . . . literally to the cheek." To the sentiment DEIGHTON applies the proverb "When poverty comes in the door, love flies out the window" (TILLEY P531).

2444 **alters**] CHARLTON (ed. 1916): "*I.e.* changes for the worse." KITTREDGE & RIBNER (ed. 1967): "Cease loving." Cf. n. 2234.

2446-7 **I . . . Mind**] COSGROVE (1977, pp. 178-9): "Perdita is insisting that there is a value in love which escapes the calumny of time." KNOWLES (privately) compares *Son.* 116.9-10.

2446 **subdue**] NEILSON & HILL (ed. 1942): "I.e., with tears." The word probably means "prevail over" here (*OED, v.* 2); affliction not only covers the cheek with tears but robs it of color.

2447 **take-in**] STEEVENS (ed. 1778), comparing *Ant.* 3.7.24 (1886): "Conquer, . . . get the better of" (*OED,* Take, *v.* 84h). PAFFORD (ed. 1963): "The regular term for capturing a town or province." HENLEY (in STEEVENS, ed. 1793): "*Include or comprehend*" (841, first citation 1677). RANN's (ed. 1787) "reach, affect" is not exactly supported by *OED*.

Mind] PAFFORD (ed. 1963): "Used for 'the spiritual part of the human being, the soul' [*OED, sb.* 17]." This is probably right; SCHMIDT (1875), who does not cite this passage (nor does ONIONS [1986]), nevertheless recognizes this definition (1). Yet SCHMIDT (2) — "sentiments, disposition" — may also be possible.

2448-50 **Yea? . . . such**] WALKER (1854, pp. 23-4): "He is struck . . . with the unexpected wisdom of the remark [Perdita's]." Recalling Camillo's unromantic sentiments at 2442-4, ALEXANDER (1938, pp. 204-5): "The old man is surprised into confessing a faith he has concealed even from himself. . . . Shakespeare now sees the daily beauty in the life of . . . a Perdita as a conquest of the world that reveals a power comparable to that in the tragic power of an Antony or a Coriolanus." KERNAN (1975, 3:450), differently: "Camillo's dry response . . . contains sad knowledge of what happens to love supported by nothing but natural desire when beauty dies and adversity comes on." WRIGHT (1979, p. 156), similarly: "While he finds her opinion charming and nicely expressed, he is not persuaded by her argument." But his next words, whatever their exact meaning (see n. 2449), clearly express his approbation.

2449 **your Fathers House**] KITTREDGE & RIBNER (ed. 1967): "Whether Camillo is addressing Florizel or Perdita is not clear." BETHELL (ed. 1956), believing he speaks to Perdita: "There will not be any more pretty—and wise—maidens at home like Perdita—with dramatic irony, because the audience know that (*a*) she is not born where Camillo thinks, and there cannot be any more like her born in a shepherd's cottage, and (*b*) Leontes will live without an heir until Perdita is found." WILSON (ed. 1931), however: "Camillo is addressing Florizel." EVANS (ed. 1974) agrees: "Even in the royal palace people of Perdita's quality are not often born."

these seuen yeeres] SCHMIDT (ed. 1870): "An indefinite, considerable time" (*OED,* Seven, *a.* 1d, citing this line). See TILLEY Y25. SCHANZER (ed. 1969): *Seuen* is monosyllabic here.

Flo. My good *Camillo*,
She's as forward, of her Breeding, as
She is i'th' reare'our Birth.
   Cam. I cannot say, 'tis pitty
She lacks Instructions, for she seemes a Mistresse   2455
To most that teach.
   Perd. Your pardon Sir, for this,
Ile blush you Thanks.
   Flo. My prettiest *Perdita*.
But O, the Thornes we stand vpon: (*Camillo*)   2460
Preseruer of my Father, now of me,
The Medicine of our House: how shall we doe?
We are not furnish'd like *Bohemia's* Sonne,
Nor shall appeare in *Sicilia*.

2452-4 *Verse lines ending* as . . . pity mCAP2, v1793-OXF1, ALEX, PEL1-EVNS,
OXF2; *ending* is . . . pity SPENCE (1890) *conj.*, BUL, SIS, BEV4; *ending* as . . . birth.
. . . pity BEV3
   2452 She's] She is POPE1-PEN2 (−SING2, BUL, SIS)
   2453 She is] *Om.* HAN, CAP, RANN, v1793-v1813, HUD2
          'our] Ff, DYCE, IRV, CAM3, KIT1, PEL1, BEV; o'her ROWE1, ROWE2, CAM2, BUL,
ARD1; o'our ROWE3-THEO2, WARB, THEO4, COL3, CAM1, NLSN, ALEX, SIS; of HAN, JOHN1-
v1813, COL2; of our KNT, SING2, STAU, KTLY, OXF1; 'f our WH; our v1821 *etc.*
   2454 'tis] 'tis a WH1
   2455 Instructions] instruction WH1
   2457 Sir, for this,] Ff, SIS; ~ , ~ ~ : ROWE1-THEO2, WARB-v1785, MAL-KNT2, DYCE,
WH1, HAL, KNT3, BUL; ~ ; ~ ~ ∧ mTBY3 *conj.*, HAN1 *etc.*
   2458-9 *One verse line* mCAP2, VALPY, KNT2+ (−SING2, HAL, KNT3)
   2462 Medicine] medicin (i.e., Fr. *médecin*) TBY2, THEOBALD (1729) *conj. in*
NICHOLS (1817, 2:365), CAP (*errata*), v1778, RANN-v1813
   2464 appeare] appear't COL2, COL3, COL4; appear SO STAU *and* LETTSOM *in*
WALKER (1860, 1:232) *conj.*, HUD2, OXF2
          Sicilia] *Sicily* F2-v1813, COL2
          Sicilia.] ~ — ROWE1-COL1, COL2, HAL, KTLY, COL4

2452-3 **She's . . . Birth**] MALONE (ed. 1790), like HANMER presumably, thinks
that *She is* was erroneously repeated from 2452; without it, 2453 links with 2454 as
a pentameter. SEYMOUR (1805, 1:169), interpreting HANMER's emendation: "Her accomplishments are as conspicuous as her birth is obscure." BETHELL (ed. 1956), with
a different reading, "That 'breeding' means *upbringing*, not *accomplishments*, is
confirmed by [3047]." See also n. 2601. OED (*vbl. sb.* 4): "The results of training as
shown in personal manners and behavior," which might be considered "accomplishments"; it adds, however, "generally used for 'good breeding', good or proper manners." For *forward of*, HUNTER (ed. 1872): "In advance of, superior to." PAFFORD
(ed. 1963): "For . . . 'in the rear' with the sense of 'lagging behind', cf. *Ham.* [1.3.34
(497)]."
   To COLLIER (ed. 1858) the apostrophe in *reare'our* "sufficiently proves that *o'*,

very commonly used for *of*, had dropped out"; CORSON (1889, p. 369) thinks *of* absorbed, an idea that seems to have occurred earlier to ANON. (MS4, 1790-). The dropping out could have been Crane's; as HOWARD-HILL (1972, p. 129) remarks, *WT*'s apostrophes "are used many times to denote omission of . . . notional words" (see p. 594). ABBOTT (§202), however, lists this and several similar expressions in which *of* is simply omitted—e.g., "Fastned our selues at eyther end the mast" (*Err.* 1.1.85 [88]). See n. 1810 for a possible parallel. SPENCE (1890) paraphrases: "She is as much before (or above) us in breeding as she is behind (or below) us in birth."

Many eds., nevertheless, prefer *her* to *our*. HERFORD (ed. 1916-): "This is a necessary correction of Folio *'our*, which destroys the balance of the thought. Florizel is not comparing Perdita with himself either in birth or breeding, but saying that she has the quality of the high-bred with the status of the low-born." CHARLTON (ed. 1916): "Such a personal contrast between Perdita's and Florizel's state as *'our* would imply, would be intolerable patronage in Florizel's mouth at this point." WILSON (ed. 1931), however, in favor of *'our*: "But surely what Florizel intends to express is his wonder that her breeding should be as much above the education of a shepherd's cottage (cf. [2455, 'She lacks Instructions']) as her birth is below that of a princess (cf. [2449, 'at your Fathers House']). The F. reading is the essential link between Camillo's two speeches, and neither Elizabethans nor Jacobeans would find anything patronizing in Florizel speaking of her lowly birth at this point."

2455 Instructions] MAXWELL (ed. 1956): "Schooling." See n. 2452-3.

2455-6 she . . . teach] *OED* (Mistress, *sb.* 9, citing this line): "A woman who has mastered any art, craft, or branch of study." BOORMAN (ed. 1964): "She seems fit to instruct most teachers." For this as Sh.'s self-congratulation, see n. 1952-3.

2456 To] BETHELL (ed. 1956): "Compared with."

2457 Your . . . this] PORTER & CLARKE (ed. 1908): "Camillo implies [2454-6] that she has corrected him, justly, . . . and feeling this implication she craves pardon." BOORMAN (ed. 1964): "Perdita apologizes for not speaking her thanks."

2458 Ile . . . Thanks] SPURGEON (1935, p. 307): "The ebb and flow of emotion [is] exquisitely mirrored in the ebb and flow of blood in the face, obeying, as it does, the same laws, and responding to the same inner stimulus." Cf. n. 1810 and lines 1859, 1865, 1872, 1965, and 1980.

2460 the . . . vpon] APPERSON (1929, p. 627): "*To sit or stand upon thorns* = To be impatient." See TILLEY T239.

2461 Preseruer . . . me] TRAVERSI (1959, p. 29): This "apostrophe . . . binds the past action yet again to a future anticipated in the present, giving each its due place in the play's continuous line of living development."

2462 Medicine] MINSHEU (1617): "Physician." CALDECOTT (MS 1813-33): "Healing spirit." MOORMAN (ed. 1912) favors "physician" because of "Meet we the Med'cine of the sickly Weale, And with *him* poure . . ." (*Mac.* 5.2.27 [2207]). SCHMIDT (1875) agrees, but BETHELL (ed. 1956), who evidently prefers "healing substance," says that MINSHEU's definition is "quite unnecessary here." Later eds. do not agree. As physician of the royal house, Camillo becomes aligned with Paulina (cf. 965).

House] SCHMIDT (1874): "Family."

how . . . doe?] DEIGHTON (ed. 1889): "'What shall we do?' or, 'How shall we act?'"

2463 furnish'd] SCHMIDT (1874, Furnish): "Equip, fit out." Cf. "appointed" (2468).

2464 appeare in *Sicilia.*] Objecting to ROWE's dash, DYCE (1844, p. 84) argues that the sense is complete: "'Nor shall appear [like Bohemia's son] in Sicilia.'"

Sicilia] Because of meter, VAN DAM (1900, p. 89) believes that Sh. wrote *Sicily*, as at 256.

Cam. My Lord,   2465
Feare none of this: I thinke you know my fortunes
Doe all lye there: it shall be so my care,
To haue you royally appointed, as if
The Scene you play, were mine. For instance Sir,
That you may know you shall not want: one word.   2470

Enter Autolicus.

Aut. Ha, ha, what a Foole Honestie is? and Trust (his
sworne brother) a very simple Gentleman. I haue sold
all my Tromperie: not a counterfeit Stone, not a Ribbon,
Glasse, Pomander, Browch, Table-booke, Ballad, Knife,   2475
Tape, Gloue, Shooe-tye, Bracelet, Horne-Ring, to keepe
my Pack from fasting: they throng who should buy first,   (2

2466 thinke∧ you know∧] ~ , ~ ~ , THEO1-COL2 (−HAN, KNT2, HUD1), COL3,
HAL, DEL, KNT3; ~ ∧ ~ ~ , SING2
    2469 play] play'd LETTSOM *conj. in* DYCE2, HUD2
        mine] true COL2
    2471 SCENE X. POPE, HAN, WARB, JOHN
        ad. *laughing* EVNS
    2474 Stone, not] Stone, nor ROWE2
    2475 Table-booke] table-hook WH1
    2477 fasting] fastning F2-POPE2
        throng] thronged MTBY3 *conj.*, COL2, COL3, HUD2

2466 **fortunes**] SCHMIDT (1874): "Wealth."
    2468 **royally appointed**] JOHNSON (1755, To Appoint): "To equip; to supply
with all things necessary." CAPELL (1783 [1774], 1:glos.): "Dress or fit out." PAFFORD
(ed. 1963): "Camillo in fact fails to get this done. It is one of the trivial loose ends of
the play."
    as if] WALKER (1860, 3:114–15): Pronounce *ás if*, "since *'s if* seems hardly
imaginable." It is quite imaginable, as LETTSOM (MS 1840–65) points out.
    2468-9 **as . . . mine**] HARBOTTLE (1853, p. 96): "As if *he* [Camillo] were the
party interested in" the scene. EGAN (1975, p. 58): Camillo instead imagines himself
mounting a play that he has composed, will costume, and is now directing (see n.
2533–4). HAPPÉ (1969): He "is now the puppet-master; a role shared with Autolycus
and Time." BETHELL (ed. 1956) alone thinks "this is rather patronizing on Camillo's
part." JONAS (1918, pp. 402–3) finds other theatrical allusions at 269–71, 1210–11,
1764–5, 1948–9, 2533–4, 3088–9, and 3365–9, and see n. 269–72.
    2469 **instance**] HERFORD (ed. 1904): "Proof."
    2470 **want:**] COGHILL (1958, p. 38): The colon "indicate[s] a sudden pause.
. . . Camillo . . . has *heard* the approach of Autolycus . . . and draws his companions aside."

2471-2 **Enter . . . is?**] For the technique of the talk aside, see n. 2362. TRAVERSI
(1954, pp. 163-4): "The purpose [of this scene] is to introduce a note of relativity
into the action, a sense that even the most serious of the novelties we have just
witnessed are not to be regarded as final in their validity. . . . The spirit of Autolycus . . . is a necessary background to the main theme." DEAN (1979, p. 292 n.)
suggests that the comment is supposed to reflect ironically on Florizel's words at
2341, but a specific connection seems pointless. BASKERVILLE (1929, p. 289 n.) lists
a dozen plays in which characters similar to Autolycus appear. JORGENSEN (1962, p.
9) comments on the personification of Honesty in other plays, a vestige of the morality
play tradition, and (p. 19) on Honesty as a fool, as in *Oth.* 3.3.382 (2027).

2472-95 **Ha . . . Army**] For other depictions of the robbery of those distracted
by ballads, PAFFORD (ed. 1963) refers to Robert Greene, *The Thirde and Last Part of
Conny-catching* (1592; ed. Harrison, 1923, pp. 26-9) and "the co-operative work of
Edgworth and Nightingale" in Jonson, *Bartholomew Fair*—e.g., in 3.5.

2472-3 **what . . . brother**] Proverbial (DENT H539.1).

2473 **sworne brother**] DEIGHTON (ed. 1889) compares 247.

simple] Dumb. See n. 2167 for other meanings.

2474 **Tromperie**] MINSHEU (1617): "Old baggage." KERSEY (1702): "Paltry stuff"
(*OED*, *sb.* 2a, citing this line).

2475 **Glasse**] THIRLBY (MS 1733-47?): "Looking glass."

Pomander] PHILLIPS (1658): "A little round ball made of several fragrant per-
fumes to smell to, or hang about the wrist." GREY (1754, 1:269): "Worn in the pocket,
or about the neck, to prevent infection in times of plague." MACQUOID (1916, 2:116):
Autolycus's pomanders "would have been the common wax perfume balls moulded
into shapes and impregnated with scent." LINTHICUM (1936, p. 276), however: *Pomander* could mean either the substance or the container, "a hollow metal ball,"
which she believes is alluded to here.

Browch] MINSHEU (1617): "Bágue qu'on pend au cól." PHILLIPS (1658): "*Ouch*,
a collar of Gold, a Jewel or Tablet [a flat ornament]; it is also caled [sic] a brooch."
HANMER (ed. 1743-4, 6:glos.): "Worn . . . sometimes about the Arm."

Table-booke] HALLIWELL (ed. 1859): Memorandum book (*OED*). Those described by HALLIWELL have leaves of parchment or vellum coated with a composition
such as gypsum, upon which one writes with a fine stylus. HUNTER (ed. 1872) adds
that they were "often made of slips of ivory."

2476 **Shooe-tye**] Shoe string (*OED*, Shoe, *sb.* 6c, citing this line), probably ornamented.

Horne-Ring] Little seems to be known about horn rings; *OED* (Horn, *sb.* 28)
says simply "made of horn" and quotes this instance as its only example. PAFFORD's
(ed. 1963) observation that "horn was often a constituent of rings alleged to have
magic qualities" seems inappropriate; these rings could be merely ornaments made
of a readily available, cheap material.

2477 **from fasting**] BETHELL (ed. 1956): "I.e. he has sold everything and there is
nothing to feed his pack with, to put into it" (cf. *OED*, Fast, *v.²* 2, citing this line).
SCHANZER (ed. 1969): From "being empty."

throng] DYCE (ed. 1864) questions whether this is a form of the past tense. If
so, *OED* does not record it. The CLARKES (1879, pp. 73-4): A deviation in tense,
"which imparts a spirited effect to the description."

as if my Trinkets had beene hallowed, and brought a benediction to the buyer: by which meanes, I saw whose
Purse was best in Picture; and what I saw, to my good   2480
vse, I remembred. My Clowne (who wants but some-
thing to be a reasonable man) grew so in loue with the
Wenches Song, that hee would not stirre his Petty-toes,
till he had both Tune and Words, which so drew the rest
of the Heard to me, that all their other Sences stucke in   2485
Eares: you might haue pinch'd a Placket, it was sence-
lesse; 'twas nothing to gueld a Cod-peece of a Purse: I
would haue fill'd Keyes of that hung in Chaynes: no
hearing, no feeling, but my Sirs Song, and admiring the

2481 remembred] remember F4
      My] My good ROWE1-JOHN2
2486 Eares] their ears mTBY2 *and* MASON (1785, p. 137) *conj.*, RANN
2488 would] could mLONG *conj.*, GLO, WH2, PEL1, BEV, OXF2

2478–9 **as . . . benediction**] MILWARD (1973, p. 26): "Old Catholic customs,
such as . . . hallowing 'trinkets' with the sign of the cross, . . . seem to come spontaneously to the dramatist's mind without any necessary link with their context." An
object may be hallowed, however, without the sign of the cross; see *OED* (Hallow,
v. 2, citing this line) and SCHMIDT (1874). *OED* (Benediction 2, citing this line): "Bless-
edness." JOHNSON (ed. 1765): "This alludes to beads often sold by the Romanists, as
made particularly efficacious by the touch of some relick." HARRISON (ed. 1947, Hallowed): "Blessed by the Pope." KITTREDGE & RIBNER (ed. 1967), questionably: "Autolycus is thus associated with the pardoners of the Middle Ages." Autolycus is merely
making an amusingly exaggerated comparison.
    2480 **best in Picture**] Interpretations vary. RANN (ed. 1787): "Had most coin in
it." The picture would be of the face of the monarch on a piece of money, as in
Donne's "the King's reall, or his stamped face Contemplate" ("The Canonization,"
ed. Patrides, 1985, lines 7–8). See PARTRIDGE (1967), s.v. Queen's picture, and cf.
"these will serue to picke the pictures out o' your pockets" (Jonson, *Bartholomew
Fair*, 3.5.53–4). PORTER & CLARKE (ed. 1908), mistakenly: "He had the group spread
out before him with all its possibilities as to valuables quietly exhibited as if in a
picture or chart." LOBBAN (ed. 1910), more generally: "Best to look at, i.e., the fat-
test." That is, fat with coin. WHITE (ed. 1857), probably too cleverly: "Is 'picture'
used in the sense of 'seeming', and . . . a pun upon 'pick'?" WILSON (ed. 1931),
similarly: "Possibly . . . a cant term meaning 'for picking,'" but no such term has
been documented. For *in picture*, BOORMAN's (ed. 1964) "in the picture," "in evidence" is similar to HAPPÉ's (1969) "in appearance."
    2480–1 **good vse**] HAPPÉ (1969): "Financial advantage."
    2481–2 **but something**] DEIGHTON (ed. 1889): "*I.e.* wits." HAPPÉ (1969): "A
great deal." ORGEL (ed. 1996): "Only one thing," but the one thing is a great deal.
    2483 **Petty-toes**] Literally, "Pigs Feet sous'd" (KERSEY, 1708). MOORMAN (ed.
1912): "Thence applied to those of a child." CHARLTON (ed. 1916): "A diminutive of
contempt."

2485-6 **all . . . Eares**] HUNTER (ed. 1872): "They were all ear." BETHELL (ed. 1956): Their senses "became hearing, so that they had no sense but that." He quotes Chapman, *Hero and Leander* (5:88): "All their sences climbd into their eares." MOORMAN (ed. 1912), literally: The other senses "were fixed on to their ears." ORGEL (ed. 1996): They were "stopped with hearing."

2486-7 **you . . . Purse**] HARTWIG (1978, p. 101), alone: "The suggestions of castration and sterility in both situations are the result of unreasonable fascination with sexual aberrations."

2486 **pinch'd**] PARTRIDGE (1969): "In ordinary sense, but with a sexual connotation . . . with a pun on *pinch*, 'to steal.'"

Placket] Also at 2067, where the Clown's "plackets" for *faces* expresses incongruity and inappropriateness. Here, however, the allusion is to "the opening in a petticoat or skirt, at the crotch. By extension, the female pudendum itself; by further extension, the whole woman" (COLMAN, 1974). STEEVENS (ed. 1793) finds placket pinching illuminated by GUILPIN (1598 [1974], Epi. 32): "But she which longs to tast of pleasures cup, In nipping [pinching] would her petticoate weare [wear or were] vp." Alternatively, because FLORIO (1611) for *Thorace* gives "a placket, a stomacher, or a breast plate for the body," HUDSON (ed. 1852) understands *placket* and *stomacher* to be synonymous. FLORIO's definition is derived from the nearly identical gloss of THOMAS (1587), whom HUDSON also cites. In both FLORIO and THOMAS, *placket* seems to mean either "apron" or "petticoat," but the garment, by extension again, also signifies the woman who wears it (*OED* 2). Cf. n. 2066-7. MOORMAN (ed. 1912) takes the phrase more straightforwardly—"stolen a petticoat." PARRY (ed. 1982), for the expression: "You could have squeezed a girl's private parts without her feeling a thing."

2486-7 **sencelesse**] PHILLIPS (1706): "That has no Sense or Feeling." PARTRIDGE (1969): Punning on "idiotic; insensible," but "idiotic" does not seem to work.

2487 **nothing**] HAPPÉ (1969): "Triviality; and pun on 'noting' of the tune." He compares *Ado* 2.3.57 (893). See also n. 2490.

gueld] RUBINSTEIN (1984, Cut) finds a pun on *gulled*.

Cod-peece] LINTHICUM (1936, p. 204): "A bag-like appendage attached by points [laces] to the front" of the breeches. The device accommodated the genitals, for which form-fitting hose left no room. It could be large enough to be used as a pocket; in *The Duchess of Malfi* (ed. J. R. Brown, 1964, 2.2.39-41) a Switzer is said to have hidden a pistol in his great codpiece, an idea Webster found in Nashe. In the present instance, to *gueld* means to "slit the pocket" (= the scrotum) to remove the purse (= the testicle), although for *purse*, PARTRIDGE (1969) gives "scrotum." See RUBINSTEIN (1984, Yield) for more on *hanging, geld*, and *gelding*.

2487-8 **I would**] HUDSON (ed. 1880), comparing *Tmp.* 2.1.185 (863) and 287 (986): "Our present usage requires *should*. . . . The auxiliaries were often used indiscriminately." ABBOTT (§331), however, rather vehemently denies that *would* was used for *should*. FURNESS (ed. 1898): "I would . . . had I wanted to." Recent eds. emend.

2488 **fill'd Keyes of**] I.e., filed keys off.

Keyes] FARMER & HENLEY (1890-1904; 1970, Key): "The *penis*." Their citation is dated 1772.

2489 **my Sirs**] HERFORD (ed. 1904): "The clown's." McPEEK (1969, p. 245) imagines that the offstage song was sung by Autolycus, who "was able to entrance his listeners and cut their purses at the same time." But it was the Clown who sang, probably accompanied by the girls (see 2134).

admiring] CAWDREY (1604, Admire): "Maruell at." Cf. nn. 2027-8, 3021, and 3232.

Nothing of it. So that in this time of Lethargie, I pickd   2490
and cut most of their Festiuall Purses: And had not the
old-man come in with a Whoo-bub against his Daughter, and the Kings Sonne, and scar'd my Chowghes from
the Chaffe, I had not left a Purse aliue in the whole
Army.   2495

2490 Nothing] noting ANON. *conj. in* CAM1, WH2

2490 **Nothing**] STAUNTON (ed. 1859) considers that this word is actually an old
spelling of *noting* (see *OED*, Note, *v.²*, Forms); *OED* (Nothing, *sb*. 7, citing this line),
however, defines it as "Nothingness." Rather than an old spelling of *noting*, the
CLARKES (ed. 1865) find a pun on the word, which was similarly pronounced (see n.
2487 and CERCIGNANI, 1981, p. 137). The CLARKES compare *Ado* 2.3.57 (893), where
play on several senses occurs, including "notes of music." These senses probably do
not include "singing," the gloss by BOORMAN (ed. 1964), for *note* meaning "sing" is
scantily documented by *OED* (*v.²* 8). ELLIS's (1871, 3:971) opinion that the word is
actually a misprint of *noting* probably influenced WHITE's (ed. 1883) emendation.
WILSON (ed. 1931) glosses *Nothing* as "nonsense" but also recognizes the pun. JOR-
GENSEN (1962, p. 32): "Autolycus uses the word to describe both the vacuity and the
technique of [the] song." PAFFORD (ed. 1963): "Triviality." CANFIELD (1989, p. 54)
thinks that "Autolycus's 'nothing' picks up Leontes's [at 377–89] and redefines it:
there really *is* no truth, just appearances."

    Lethargie] SCHMIDT (1874): "Unconsciousness." DEIGHTON (ed. 1889): "*I.e.*
of all their senses except that of hearing."

    2491 **cut . . . Purses**] COLLIER (ed. 1858, 6:glos.) for *cut a purse* gives "pick a
pocket," the modern equivalent, though the Elizabethan underworld recognized both
specialties.

    Festiuall] SCHANZER (ed. 1969): "(Adjective) brought for the feast." ORGEL
(ed. 1996): "Full." DEIGHTON (ed. 1889) finds the expression sarcastic.

    2492 **Whoo-bub**] KERSEY (1708, Hubbub): "A great Tumult, or Uproar." *OED*
adds, "Esp. the confused shouting of a battle cry or 'hue and cry' by wild and savage
races." HUDSON (ed. 1852) finds the terms connected in Barnabe Rich's title *The Irish
Hubbub or, The English Hue and Cry* (1617).

    2493–4 **scar'd . . . Chaffe**] Possibly adapted from the proverb "Old Birds are
not caught with chaff" (TILLEY B396). SCHMIDT (1874, Chaff): "The husks of corn
separated by thrashing," worthless stuff, in which choughs search for the grain.

    2493 **Chowghes**] KERSEY (1702): "Country-clown." *OED* (Chuff, *sb.¹*): "<In 17th
c. sometimes spelt *chough* by confusion with, or play on, the name of the bird.>
1. A rustic, . . . churl. 2. Generally applied opprobriously . . . to any person dis-
liked." The avian chough, HANMER (ed. 1743–4, 6:glos.) says, "is most like to a Jack-
daw, but bigger." ORGEL (ed. 1996): "Birds easily attracted and caught." BOORMAN
(ed. 1964) thinks that *choughs* and *chaff* were pronounced alike, but DOBSON (1968)
gives examples of the former with a long *o*, as in German *Sohn* (p. 507), and the latter
with the *a* of "*amoeba*" (p. 431).

    2495 **Army**] DEIGHTON (ed. 1889): "Used for the sake of the word 'alive' as ap-
plied to 'purse.'" BETHELL (ed. 1956): "Autolycus' theft becomes a military enterprise
against an army of purses. It is the more apt that he is not strictly a pickpocket but a
cutpurse and uses cold steel" (2490–1).

Cam. Nay, but my Letters by this meanes being there
So soone as you arriue, shall cleare that doubt.
    Flo. And those that you'le procure from King *Leontes*?
    Cam. Shall satisfie your Father.
    Perd. Happy be you: 2500
All that you speake, shewes faire.
    Cam. Who haue we here?
Wee'le make an Instrument of this: omit
Nothing may giue vs aide.
    Aut. If they haue ouer-heard me now: why hanging.   2505
    Cam. How now (good Fellow)
Why shak'st thou so? Feare not (man)
Here's no harme intended to thee.
    Aut. I am a poore Fellow, Sir.
    Cam. Why, be so still: here's no body will steale that   2510

2496-7 *Prose* POPE
2502 Who] Whom COL, HUD1, DEL2, OXF1
2506-8 *Verse lines ending* so? . . . thee. HAN, CAP-RANN, CAM1, COL4, BUL, PEL1,
SIG, EVNS+; *prose* MAL-DEL2, GLO-DEL4, HUD2-OXF1, NLSN-SIS, CLN2, ARD2, PEN2 (*some
eds. doubtful*)
2506-7 Fellow) Why] fellow, come, why HAN; fellow? Wherefore CAP
2509-24 2509 *and* Why . . . still: [2510] *as one verse line*, Here's [2510] . . .
it. [2523] *prose*, 2524 *as* F1 HAN; *thirteen verse lines ending* still; . . . yet, . . .
must . . . instantly,— . . . change . . . pennyworth, . . . boot. . . . enough.
. . . gentleman . . . sir?— . . . pr'ythee. . . . cannot . . . unbuckle.— CAP

2497 **that doubt**] The CLARKES (ed. 1865): "Referring to one supposed to be
expressed by the prince during their conference apart." Cf. nn. 628-9 and 2165 for
a similar situation.
    2500 **Happy**] MINSHEU (1617) compares "Blessed, Prosperous."
    2502 **Who . . . here?**] A conventional expression. See DENT W280.2.
    Who] For the form, see n. 827.
    2503 **Instrument**] KITTREDGE & RIBNER (ed. 1967): "Servant, agent."
    this] HERFORD (ed. 1904): "This fellow."
    2505 **hanging**] UNDERHILL (1916, 2:398): "All felonies, except petty larceny (i.e.
the theft of goods under the value of twelve pence), were punishable with death."
PORTER & CLARKE (ed. 1908) quote from Hugh Jackson, *A Diamonde Most Precious*
(1577), to the same effect. DEIGHTON (ed. 1889): "That is the mildest punishment I
can expect." BETHELL (ed. 1956): "Clearly Autolycus *did* fear for his earthly future."
    2506-8 **How . . . thee**] For *how now*, see n. 201. PAFFORD (ed. 1963): "Camillo
is speaking prose to an inferior." As the textual notes show, however, some eds.
disagree. BROWN (1967, p. 100): "Camillo supplies a spoken stage-direction in case
the actor [of Autolycus] does not see the cue for yet another transformation."
    2509 **I . . . Fellow**] PAFFORD (ed. 1963) compares the poor fellows in *MM*
2.1.223 (669) and *AWW* 1.3.14 (339-40).
    2510 **that**] DEIGHTON (ed. 1889): "*I.e.* your poverty."

from thee: yet for the out-side of thy pouertie, we must
make an exchange; therefore dis-case thee instantly (thou
must thinke there's a necessitie in't) and change Garments
with this Gentleman: Though the penny-worth (on his
side) be the worst, yet hold thee, there's some boot.   2515

 Aut. I am a poore Fellow, Sir: (I know ye well
enough.)

 Cam. Nay prethee dispatch: the Gentleman is halfe
fled already.

 Aut. Are you in earnest, Sir? (I smell the trick on't.)   2520

 Flo. Dispatch, I prethee.

 Aut. Indeed I haue had Earnest, but I cannot with
conscience take it.

 Cam. Vnbuckle, vnbuckle.

Fortunate Mistresse (let my prophecie   2525
Come home to ye:) you must retire your selfe
Into some Couert; take your sweet-hearts Hat
And pluck it ore your Browes, muffle your face,
Dis-mantle you, and (as you can) disliken

2513 a] *Om.* THEO2-KNT1 (−HAN, CAP), HAL
2518 prethee dispatch] pr'ythee now, dispatch CAP
2519 already] ready ROWE2, ROWE3
2520 on't] of it CAP-SING1, COL1-COL2, COL3, HAL, DEL
2522-3 *Marked as aside* CAP
2526 ye] you CAP-HAL (−WH1), DEL, KTLY, KNT3, COL4
2528 your Browes] thy brows v1821

2511 **out-side . . . pouertie**] MAXWELL (ed. 1956): "Thy rags."

2511-12 **we . . . exchange**] COX (1969, p. 291): "The clothes exchange itself
appears superfluous. Camillo apparently decides that a disguise is necessary for Florizel's safe journey to the ship. . . . Yet Florizel is already in a disguise. . . . We may
assume that Camillo believes that Florizel needs another disguise, since the 'swain's
wearing' is rich enough for the rustics to believe it is the dress of a courtier [2631]
and since Florizel's disguise as a swain has been revealed for what it is to a number
of country folk. . . . But since Polixenes has returned to Court, Florizel's ship 'rides
fast by', and no later reference is made to a result of Florizel's disguising himself as a
peddler, the focus of the clothes exchange is on Autolycus."

2512 **dis-case**] JOHNSON (1755): "To strip; to undress." Sh. uses the word only
here and in *Tmp.* 5.1.85 (2041). *Uncase* also occurs twice. *Case* here is "the skin or
hide of an animal" (*OED, sb.*[2] 4), "applied to clothes or garments" (4b). Cf. nn. 2519,
2695. For *Pandosto*'s uncasing, see p. 645.

2513 **thinke**] SCHANZER (ed. 1969): "Realize."

2514-15 **Though . . . worst**] SCHMIDT (1875): "Though he have the worst of
the bargain."

2515 **boot**] MINSHEU (1617): "Advantage. . . . So we say, . . . *What boots will you give me?*" JOHNSON (ed. 1765): "*Something over and above*, or, as we now say, *something to boot*" (*OED*, *sb.*¹ 1). See n. 2557-8. The distinction BECKET (1815, 1: 366) makes between this meaning and "compensation, reward" (*sb.*¹ 9) is not supported by SCHMIDT (1874), who agrees with JOHNSON—that is, that Camillo tips Autolycus (ostensibly to equalize the exchange). BOORMAN (ed. 1964) believes the pun on the word is obvious, but perhaps it does not even exist.

2516-17 (**I . . . enough.**)] According to DENT K171.1, these words are usually addressed "to supposed knaves, villains," so the comic point here evidently is the reversal. The expression, with variations, occurs a half-dozen times in Sh., sometimes ironically (e.g., Beatrice to the masked Benedict, *Ado* 2.1.133 [539]). WELLS & TAYLOR (1987, p. 601): Here and at 2520, "Crane appears to use parentheses to mark passages spoken aside," which the early eds. probably also understood, although HANMER (ed. 1743) was the first formally to mark them.

2519 **fled**] THEOBALD (MS -1729?): "Flay'd," of which *fled* is a variant form. MALONE (ed. 1790, 10:607): "Half stripped" (*OED*, *v*. 3b, citing this line only, as a humorous nonce use). MALONE adds, "Half covered with vermin already, or half excoriated by their bite," but that meaning is inappropriate to the gentleman. The CLARKES (ed. 1865): "Playing on the word 'discase', used [at 2512]; 'case' being an old word for 'skin.'" See nn. 2512, 2695. One may be half stripped from top to bottom (or vice versa) or from outside to inside; BOORMAN (ed. 1964) has it both ways: "I.e. with the top clothes removed."

2520 (**I . . . on't.**)] PAFFORD (ed. 1963): "He tumbles to the reason why they want his clothes." For the parentheses, see n. 2516-17.

     smell] SCHMIDT (1875): "Perceive." Cf. TILLEY S558.

     on't] See n. 785-6.

2522 **Earnest**] CAPELL (1783, 2.4: 179): "Some rich thing which he finds about the garments that Florizel reaches to him, which his '*conscience*' makes him return; . . . playing upon [*earnest* in 2520]." He has, rather, shifted the meaning of that word to "the money which is given in token that a bargain is ratified" (JOHNSON [1755]), the meaning here. As FURNESS (ed. 1898) indicates, Autolycus would never return anything. The same pun occurs in *Err.* 2.2.23 (419). MOORMAN (ed. 1912): "The allusion is not quite clear: it may be that Florizel offers him money [at 2521], or it may be that he has already received something from Camillo." He has; WILSON (ed. 1931): "I.e. the 'boot' [2515]." PORTER & CLARKE (ed. 1908): "Autolicus is playing the honest and trusty part now."

2525-6 **Fortunate . . . ye**] According to the CLARKES (ed. 1865), *prophesie* alludes "to his having said, '*Your* fair *princess* (for so, I see, she must be)' [2409-10]." HUDSON (ed. 1880), more plausibly: "May my use of the word *fortunate* be prophetic, and come home to you as such [i.e., prove true]!" PARRY (ed. 1982) adds: "May the way I have imagined you arriving at Leontes' court [2413 ff.] come about."

2526 **retire**] KERSEY (1702, Retire): "Withdraw."

2527 **Couert**] SCHMIDT (1874): "Thicket," probably correctly, because the word in this sense is a hunting term, appropriate to the speaker. Some eds. define *covert* more generally, as "shelter" or "hiding place." THIRLBY (MS 1725-33?), differently, suggests that instead of being meant literally (retire "to undress & disguise"), *covert* may refer to "the disguise it self," into which Perdita would retire. His interpretation is not impossible; see *OED* (Covert, *a*. 2 and *sb*. 2c).

2528 **Browes**] Forehead, as in 222.

2529 **Dis-mantle**] PHILLIPS (1658): "To take off a cloak or mantle" (*OED*, *v*., citing this line). Florizel refers to Perdita's unusual weeds (1798), "under which she would presumably have her peasant's blouse and skirt" (BETHELL, ed. 1956).

     as you can] The CLARKES (1879, p. 305): I.e., "as well as you can."

     disliken] JOHNSON (1755): "To make unlike" (*OED*, citing this line only). JERVIS (1868): "To disguise; to conceal," with which SCHMIDT (1874) agrees.

The truth of your owne seeming, that you may   2530
(For I doe feare eyes ouer) to Ship-boord
Get vndescry'd.
   Perd. I see the Play so lyes,
That I must beare a part.
   Cam. No remedie: 2535
Haue you done there?
   Flo. Should I now meet my Father,
He would not call me Sonne.
   Cam. Nay, you shall haue no Hat:
Come Lady, come: Farewell (my friend.)   2540
   Aut. Adieu, Sir.
   Flo. O *Perdita*: what haue we twaine forgot?
'Pray you a word.   (2B
   Cam. What I doe next, shall be to tell the King

2530 your] their THEO3, THEO4

2530-1 may$_\wedge$ . . . eyes$_\wedge$ ouer)] $\sim$ — . . . $\sim$ — $\sim$ $_\wedge$ SCHMIDT (1875, Over,
adv. 1) *conj.*, ARD1, OXF2

2531 ouer] over you ROWE1-KNT2, HAL, DEL, KTLY, KNT3, OXF1; ever mCOL1 *conj.*,
COL, HUD1; over 's mLET *conj.*, DYCE2, HUD2

2538-41 *Three verse lines ending* have . . . friend. . . . Sir. HAN, v1793-v1813,
SING1, KNT1, KNT3; *ending* hat:— . . . friend. . . . sir. SING2, HAL; *two, ending*
hat:— . . . sir. mCAP2, v1821, KNT2-COL2, DYCE1-COL3, STAU-DYCE2, DEL4-EVNS,
OXF2; *four, ending* son. . . . hat. . . . friend. . . . sir. BEV3; *three, ending* son.
. . . hat. . . . sir. BEV4

2539 *giving it to* Perdita. CAP, COL2, DYCE, CAM1, GLO, HUD2+ (*subst.*)

2544 be] be next ROWE1, ROWE2

2530 **truth . . . seeming**] CALDECOTT (MS 1813-33, Seeming): "Present appearance." Struck by the ambiguity in dislikening the truth of seeming, he points out
that it arises because the verb "has less direct connection with one of the subject
matters viz. with *truth*, than it has with the other [*seeming*]." KERMODE (ed. 1963)
suggests that the complicated expression "may indicate Shakespeare's obsessive interest in problems related to 'truth' and 'seeming.'" The complexity of the situation
is substantial. Because she wears unusual weeds, Perdita's seeming, or appearance, is
that of hostess of the festival and of Flora, queen of a meeting of the petty gods (1798-
1802); and because she is royal, the seeming is not far from being. When she dis-
mantles, she presumably becomes a shepherdess again, an appearance less true to
her true being than the illusion. As BARTON (1980, p. 148) notes: "Camillo's counsel . . . not only brings truth and falsehood into a linguistically dizzying relationship . . . ; it expresses a truth beyond Camillo's ken."

   2531 **eyes ouer**] SINGER (ed. 1856): "Over-eying" (i.e., observation). See *OED*
(Over-eye, *v.*), which cites "I . . . wretched fooles secrets heedfully ore eye" (*LLL*
4.3.77-8 [1413-14]); see also "ouer-eying of his odde behauior" (*Shr.* Induction 1.95
[105]). The CLARKES (ed. 1865): At 1648-9, "Polixenes has said to Camillo, 'I have
eyes under my service, which look upon his removedness'; therefore, 'eyes over' [may
mean] 'spying eyes.'" CORSON (1889, p. 370) thinks *ouer* = "'overt', open or watch-

ful," the *t* having been absorbed. He compares "ouer Test" in *Oth.* 1.3.107 (449), usually emended to *overt*. See n. 1810. ROLFE (ed. 1879), however: "Elliptical for 'over us', if the text is right." MOORMAN (ed. 1912), finding the explanations of F "highly fanciful," adopts SCHMIDT's emendation, but eds. generally accept the CLARKES' explanation.

2532 **vndescry'd**] SCHMIDT (1875): "Undiscovered."

2533-4 **I . . . part**] The CLARKES (ed. 1865) understand Perdita's reluctance to be an expression of her "lily rectitude," but this lily, though under compulsion, does disliken the truth of her seeming. For *lie*, SCHMIDT (1874) gives "to be in a place or state"; hence, Perdita says, "I see the drama we are acting out has reached the point at which I must play my part." BETHELL (ed. 1956): "Continues the stage metaphor, which is persistent while this rather theatrical escape is carried out and old-fashioned stage-technique is employed." Cf. n. 2468-9. PAFFORD (ed. 1963): "Not an attempt to be jocular—that was not in Perdita's character—but said with resignation." EGAN (1975, p. 59): "Every element in Camillo's dramatic vision does in fact become literal reality: Perdita *is* the daughter of a king . . . , the betrothal of the lovers is blessed by all, and the two kings . . . are joyfully reunited. Moreover, Leontes' heir restored, the way is paved for the culminating reunion of Leontes and Hermione." For other theatrical allusions, see at 269-71, 1210-11, 1764-5, 1948-9, 2467-9, 3088-9, and 3365-9. BOORMAN (ed. 1964) believes that the metaphor may pertain as well to gambling.

2539 **you . . . Hat**] HUNTER (ed. 1872): "No one will [off-]cap to you," because you will not be recognized as the prince. More likely, Camillo says these words as he takes Autolycus's hat from Florizel and hands it to Perdita.

2540 **Lady**] The CLARKES (ed. 1865): Calling Perdita "Lady" is "not only a spontaneous homage to her native refinement" but also a characteristic act of the veteran courtier. Seeing that she will marry the heir apparent, he "almost unconsciously gives her a title befitting her prospective rank." They may be right about the title, but his impatience is more to the point. Perdita probably looks at the hat with revulsion.

2541 **Adieu, Sir**] As BROWN (*Shakespeare's Plays*, 1966, p. 101) implies, the French farewell is not typical of Autolycus the vagabond. "He is ready for his new role . . . : comically he is *just* ready, for he is still wearing his pedlar's false beard (cf. [2596-7])."

2542 **what . . . forgot?**] STEEVENS (in REED, ed. 1803): One of Sh.'s "dramatic expedients to introduce a conversation apart, introduce a sudden exit, &c." PAFFORD (ed. 1963): If F's ? stands for !, "the line may mean: 'What, Perdita! Have you and I forgotten our vows, our resolution to stand by each other!' . . . This may be another 'Lift up thy looks' to Perdita [2331 and 2987]." On the whole, however, he agrees with STEEVENS. PILGRIM (1983, p. 65) believes that Florizel's "Fortune speed vs" (2550) indicates that during Camillo's soliloquy, Florizel and Perdita have been praying.

2543 **'Pray . . . word**] For the technique of the talk aside, see n. 2362. COGHILL (1958, p. 38): "Addressed . . . to Autolycus, so as to draw him away as well, and leave Camillo isolated for his direct address. Therefore what they have forgotten concerns Autolycus too." They seem to have moved away from Autolycus at 2540-1, however.

2544-9 **What . . . Longing**] BETHELL (ed. 1956): "This is not meant as a betrayal. Camillo expects the young couple to be married before Polixenes and he can reach Sicilia." MOWAT (1976, pp. 25-6), however, finds it "the treachery of a seemingly helpful Camillo, who . . . frames the entire business to serve his own ends, and gives no thought to the fate of the young couple." VAN LAAN (1978, p. 235): "Camillo . . . acts primarily for selfish reasons, but he nonetheless makes possible not only the permanent union of the lovers but also the reconciliation of [the kings] and the reunion of Leontes and his daughter." Sh., however, probably gives Camillo a motive for immediate plausibility only, or perhaps to show how individual desires

Of this escape, and whither they are bound;   2545
Wherein, my hope is, I shall so preuaile,
To force him after: in whose company
I shall re-view *Sicilia*; for whose sight,
I haue a Womans Longing.
    Flo. Fortune speed vs: 2550
Thus we set on (*Camillo*) to th'Sea-side.
    Cam. The swifter speed, the better.   *Exit.*
    Aut. I vnderstand the businesse, I heare it: to haue an
open eare, a quick eye, and a nimble hand, is necessary for
a Cut-purse; a good Nose is requisite also, to smell out   2555
worke for th'other Sences. I see this is the time that the
vniust man doth thriue. What an exchange had this been,
without boot? What a boot is here, with this exchange?
Sure the Gods doe this yeere conniue at vs, and we may
doe any thing extempore. The Prince himselfe is about   2560
a peece of Iniquitie (stealing away from his Father, with

2551 *Exit* Flo. & Per. ROWE1-JOHN2, v1773 (*subst.*)

2552 *Exit.*] *Om.* ROWE1-JOHN2, v1773; *Exeunt* Florizel, Perdita, *and* Camillo. CAP, v1778+ (*subst.*)

2553 SCENE XI. POPE, HAN, WARB, JOHN
    heare] heard HAN

2558 *strikes his leg* [*before* What] CAM3
    with] without mTBY4 *conj.*, GENT

---

unwittingly contribute to the execution of Apollo's will. A selfish man would not last long with Paulina.

2547 **To**] For *to* as "with a view to" or "for an end," see ABBOTT §186. For the omission of *as* in relatival constructions, see ABBOTT §281.

    force him after] KITTREDGE & RIBNER (ed. 1967): "Make him pursue them."

2548 *Sicilia*] ERICKSON (1982, p. 824): "King as well as country."

2549 **I . . . Longing**] DELIUS (ed. 1860) compares the same words in *Tro.* 3.3.237 (2094), and see DENT L421.1. DEIGHTON (ed. 1889): "That eager desire which pregnant women feel for different kinds of food." NOVY (1984, p. 171): "Men in the romances are not only more interested in young children than are the tragic heroes, but they are also more apt to apply to themselves imagery of women's close biological relationship with children." This line is her sole example.

2555 **a good Nose**] BETHELL (ed. 1956): "To 'smell out' or discover the most likely purses for cutting."

2556-7 **that the . . . thriue**] WILSON (ed. 1931) compares Ps. 37:35: "I haue sene the wicked strong, & spreading him self like a grene baye tre." PAFFORD (ed. 1963)'adds Ps. 73:3, Job 21:7, and Jer. 12:1. BOORMAN (ed. 1964): "Autolycus stresses 'un-.'" TRAVERSI (1954, p. 164): "Clearly no part of the prevailing spirit of the play. Autolycus . . . moves throughout on the margin of the action." That is true, but GODDARD (1951, p. 656) notes, "the rogue Autolycus is transmuted into a gentleman by exchange of clothing with the prince." There is perhaps something to this, for Autolycus is accepted as an equal by the gentlemen in 5.2. See n. 2595–6, however.

2557–8 **What . . . exchange?**] BEVINGTON (ed. 1992, Boot): "Added payment" and "profit." Pedringano puns similarly in Kyd, *The Spanish Tragedy*, 3.6.47–8. Referring to 2631–2, THIRLBY (MS 1725–33?) recalls that Florizel is disguised as a shepherd, as does CHEDWORTH (1805, pp. 126–7) in a n. on 2631. There actually should be little boot in the exchange, although WILSON's (ed. 1931) SD supposes that *boot* is not only "advantage" but also princely footware. SHATTUCK (1974, 9:*WT* ii): "If Florizel actually did 'obscure' himself in the garments of a shepherd swain, as appears in [1806–7, 1821–2, etc.], then there is not much point to his exchange of costume with Autolycus [see n. 2511–12]. . . . Kemble disposed of the problem by adopting Garrick's commonsensical solution: the *exchange* of costume is simply omitted, and presently Autolycus explains in a soliloquy that he got the elegant garments he is wearing by stealing them off a 'silken gamester' whom he found drunk and asleep under a hawthorne tree. This may not be Shakespeare, but it is efficient."

HERFORD (ed. 1916–): "No doubt [Florizel's garb] would be the swain's 'Sunday best', matching the festal dress of Perdita; but that is not enough to account for the Shepherd's remark [at 2631–2]." WILSON (ed. 1931, at line 1798): As a complement to Perdita's elegant costume, Florizel had designed "for himself a becoming swain's attire to match, which though Perdita complains of it [1805–7 and 1810–11] was rich enough to suggest the court to Autolycus and the two shepherds. . . . When [Granville-Barker] produced the play in 1912 the lovers both wore 'fancy-dress.'" A 'Swaines wearing' that brings a blush of embarrassment does not sound much like fancy dress; however, Autolycus's exchanged wardrobe does impress the Clown and the Shepherd (2631–4). Perhaps it is merely a matter of degree, anything much better than homespun seeming grand to country folk. LOBBAN (ed. 1910): "One suggestion is that he was only outwardly disguised [i.e., by a cloak] and that Autolycus was wearing also the fine clothes that had been concealed." FOSS (1932, p. 139) would have Autolycus pick up the cloak and hat discarded by Polixenes at 2260, "to make the shepherd's dress more courtier-like". For more on the "clothing crux," see pp. 845–6 and n. 0 for GERVINUS's opinion that the "error" may have been deliberate. GERVINUS does not say how the discrepancy should be resolved in production. PORTER & CLARKE (ed. 1908), on another tack: "Or does he find in the pocket of the prince's suit a purse he had left there?"

2559 **conniue**] SCHMIDT (1874): "To close the eyes upon a fault" (*OED*, *v*. 3, citing this line).

2560 **extempore**] RANN (ed. 1787): "With a wet finger [i.e., readily]." LOBBAN (ed. 1910): "On the spur of the moment and without a thought." ORGEL (ed. 1996): "And by implication, without consequences." BOORMAN (ed. 1964): "This theatrical term [cf. *1H4* 2.4.280 (1234–5)] would cause a laugh on the stage in this context," but one doubts it, because the word was used in many contexts other than the theatrical.

2560–5 **The . . . Profession**] TAYLOR (1973, p. 353): "This is double-talk, but its paradoxical combination of opportunism and gratuitousness captures his [Autolycus's] character perfectly."

2560–2 **The . . . heeles**] FOAKES (1971, p. 135): "Autolycus gives us a different perspective on what we see."

2560 **about**] SCHMIDT (1874): "Engaged in, or intent on."

2561 **peece**] CHARLTON (ed. 1916), without exact support of *OED*: "Used in a general sense for and as 'thing': here its meaning is a little more particular, 'act.'" SCHMIDT (1875): "A part considered by itself and taken as a whole . . . used in a periphrastical way" (*OED*, Piece, *sb*. 8). For other uses of the word, see n. 1833.

his Clog at his heeles:) if I thought it were a peece of honestie to acquaint the King withall, I would not do't: I
hold it the more knauerie to conceale it; and therein am
I constant to my Profession.   2565

Enter Clowne and Shepheard.

Aside, aside, here is more matter for a hot braine: Euery
Lanes end, euery Shop, Church, Session, Hanging, yeelds
a carefull man worke.

Clowne. See, see: what a man you are now? there is no   2570
other way, but to tell the King she's a Changeling, and
none of your flesh and blood.

Shep. Nay, but heare me.

Clow. Nay; but heare me.

Shep. Goe too then.   2575

Clow. She being none of your flesh and blood, your
flesh and blood ha's not offended the King, and so your
flesh and blood is not to be punish'd by him. Shew those
things you found about her (those secret things, all but

2562-3 it were . . . would not do't] it were not . . . would do't WARBURTON
conj. in HAN2, HAN, WARB, JOHN, v1773-v1813 (−MAL), DYCE2, HUD2, BUL; not it were
. . . would do't CAP, RANN, SING2
  2565 I] *Om.* ROWE2
  2566 *After* 2569 STAU, DEL, OXF1
  2578 those] these THEO1

2562 **Clog . . . heeles**] Proverbial (DENT C426.1).
  Clog] "Impediment, encumbrance, hindrance" (*OED, sb.* 3), punning on "a
block or heavy piece of wood . . . attached to the leg or neck of a man . . . to
prevent escape" (2) and "a shoe with a thick wooden sole" (6). Helena is Bertram's
clog in *AWW* 2.5.53 (1324). HENLEY's (ed. 1902) "(Slang) wife" is not borne out by
FARMER & HENLEY (1890−1904; 1970), though that is what Helena is. KNOWLES (privately): "The joke is that the 'stealing' prince is already wearing a prisoner's gyves."
  2562-5 **if . . . Profession**] MALONE (ed. 1790): "The prince, says he [Autoly-
cus], is about a bad action, he is stealing away from his father: If I thought it were a
piece of honesty to acquaint the king, I would not do it, because that would be
inconsistent with my profession of a knave; *but I know that the betraying the prince
to the king would be a piece of knavery with respect to the* prince, *and therefore I
might, consistently with my character, reveal that matter to the king,* though *a
piece of honesty to him*: however, I hold it a *greater* knavery to conceal the prince's
scheme from the king, than to betray the prince; and therefore, in concealing it, I am
still constant to my profession." COLLIER (ed. 1842), more succinctly: "I would not
acquaint the king with what I know, because it would be a piece of honesty, and
inconsistent with my profession. I hold it the more knavery to conceal it." The
CLARKES (ed. 1865): "There is an effect of antithesis between 'a piece of honesty' and
'more knavery'; but it is really a comparison between two knavish acts." BETHELL (ed.
1956): "Consider Autolycus as hesitating, and so teasing the audience, who are on

the side of Florizel and Perdita. 'If I thought it was honest, I shouldn't do it', he says, implying that, as it would be knavery, he will do it. Then a pause and . . . he changes his mind: it is greater knavery to keep silent. The speech is, of course, a witty self-justification: he will keep constant to his profession of knave." MARSH (1962; 1980, p. 154): "Reluctant to be caught out in an honest or disinterested action, he pretends that what he decides to do is the greater villainy, yet he does the right thing, and conceals the flight. . . . The contrast between his ebullience, and the fundamentally evil cruelty of Polixenes, is very marked."

2562 **if**] ORGEL (ed. 1996): "I.e. even if."

peece] HERFORD (ed. 1904): "Work, act." For other uses of the word, see n. 1833.

2563 **withall**] SCHMIDT (1875): "With it." Cf. n. 766 for the word in another sense.

2565 **Profession**] JOHNSON (1755): "Calling; vocation [*OED* 6]," the meaning SCHMIDT (1875) finds here and at 1767. SCHANZER (ed. 1969): "Avowed practice" (*OED* 4). BROWN (*Shakespeare's Plays*, 1966, p. 101): He speaks for the actor who plays the part as well as for Autolycus.

2567 **Aside**] BETHELL (ed. 1956): "Let me step aside."

matter . . . braine] CALDECOTT (MS 1813-33, Hot): "Busy, working"; SCHMIDT (1874, Hot 2): "Ardent, fiery"; SCHANZER (ed. 1969): "Keen." YOUNG & MOSELEY (ed. 1965): "Business for an active man. There may be a play on 'matter' and 'hot brain', referring to the suppuration of inflamed areas," but that is unlikely.

2567-9 **Euery . . . worke**] Some eds. quote GREENE (*Second Pt.*, 1592; 1922, pp. 33-4): "Let this suffice, at any great presse of people or meeting: There the foist [pickpocket or cheat] and the Nip [cutpurse] is in his kingdome."

2568 **Session**] See n. 1138.

2569 **carefull**] SCHMIDT (1874): "Attentive, provident." BROWN (1967, p. 101), ironically: "Indulging a clown's customary transference of values."

2570-2 **See . . . blood**] The CLARKES (ed. 1865): "Most true to Shakespeare's philosophy of 'good in everything,'" the Clown perceives "that in their present strait honesty is the best policy." More likely he is frightened enough to recommend that the silence (about the changeling and the "secret things" [2579]) enjoined by the Shepherd at 1563-5 be broken in order to placate the king. CHARLTON (ed. 1916) makes a different point: "Autolycus overhears this, though the Clown does not know him in his new gear. But by hearing it, Autolycus sees a motive for carrying the Shepherd and the Clown to Florizel, a circumstance which is purely a thing of chance in *Pandosto*. Unconsciously, too, Autolycus is thus to become an instrument in the final *dénouement*."

2570 **what . . . now?**] Interpretations vary. DEIGHTON (ed. 1889): "How absurd you are." BOORMAN (ed. 1964): "What an obstinate man you are!" PARRY (ed. 1982): "I.e. a condemned one." The last seems on the right track; perhaps, "What a fix you're in."

2571 **Changeling**] See n. 1558.

2572 **flesh and blood**] Proverbial (TILLEY F366).

2574 **Nay . . . me**] The CLARKES (1879, p. 326): Emphasizing *me*. See n. 1060.

2575 **Goe too**] FURNESS (ed. 1898): "Generally deprecatory . . . as in [264; see n.] but here it means, 'Go on.'"

2576-8 **She . . . him**] MIRIAM JOSEPH (1947, p. 177) cites this as one of Sh.'s few fully stated syllogisms. More common is the figure syllogismus, for which see n. 1526-8.

2579 **things . . . her**] THIRLBY (MS 1747-53): The expression "Those secret things" was "sought for the sake of the silly bawdy joke that follows but [certainly] not forc'd."

2579-80 **all . . . her**] SCHANZER (ed. 1969): "Hermione's jewel," which Perdita

what she ha's with her:) This being done, let the Law goe   2580
whistle: I warrant you.

   Shep. I will tell the King all, euery word, yea, and his
Sonnes prancks too; who, I may say, is no honest man,
neither to his Father, nor to me, to goe about to make me
the Kings Brother in Law.   2585

   Clow. Indeed Brother in Law was the farthest off you
could haue beene to him, and then your Blood had beene
the dearer, by I know how much an ounce.

   Aut. Very wisely (Puppies.)

   Shep. Well: let vs to the King: there is that in this   2590
Farthell, will make him scratch his Beard.

   Aut. I know not what impediment this Complaint
may be to the flight of my Master.

   Clo. 'Pray heartily he be at' Pallace.

   Aut. Though I am not naturally honest, I am so some-   2595
times by chance: Let me pocket vp my Pedlers excre-

   2588 know] know not MTBY2 *conj.*, HAN, CAP, RANN, KTLY, DYCE2, COL4, HUD2, OXF1, BUL, CAM3, KIT1, SIG, PEN2, OXF2, BEV4

   2594 at' Pallace] F1 (*possibly* at ' Pallace), DYCE1, WH2, ARD, CAM3, KIT1, CLN2, EVNS+; at the Palace ROWE3-JOHN2, v1773, DYCE2, HUD2, PEL1; at Pallace F2 *etc.*

"has put on for the feast." KNOWLES (privately): "And no one noticed a shepherd girl wearing a royal jewel?" The phrase is merely a part of the silly bawdy joke.

   2580–1 **goe whistle**] SCHMIDT (1875): "I.e. you are beyond its reach." *OED* (Whistle, *v.* 9, citing this line): "Unceremonious or contemptuous dismissal." PAFFORD (ed. 1963): "Proverbial for 'any effort will be futile' [TILLEY W313]."

   2581 **warrant**] SCHMIDT (1875): "Assure."

   2582–5 **I . . . Law**] BETHELL (ed. 1956): "There is a good deal of alteration of character for local purposes in the treatment of the Shepherd. When he is with the serious characters he is himself of some dignity, but with the Clown he becomes predominantly comic, though still retaining the integrity and feudal feeling of his generation. He is as much outraged as Polixenes at the way in which Florizel and Perdita would flout 'degree' in their marriage."

   2584 **goe about to**] DEIGHTON (ed. 1889): "Have the intention of" (*OED*, Go, *v.* 49b). Cf. n. 2042.

   2585 **Brother in Law**] *OED* (b, citing this as its only example): "*Humorously.* The father of one's daughter-in-law or son-in-law."

   2586–7 **Brother . . . him**] PARRY (ed. 1982): "You couldn't have been any more distant relation than brother-in-law to him."

   2587 **Blood**] BOORMAN (ed. 1964): "The usual sense and that of 'relative' (the Clown himself)." According to SCHMIDT (1874), Sh. does use the word to "denote relation and consanguinity," though SCHMIDT does not cite this instance.

   2588 **dearer**] MAXWELL (ed. 1956): "Of greater worth." PARRY (ed. 1982): "The Clown supposes that his father's blood would *literally* improve in quality if he were to become one of the royal family."

by . . . ounce] CALDECOTT (MS 1813-33): "I.e. not at all"; he praises "this arch affection of a sagacity & wisdom." Against emending, the CLARKES (ed. 1865) believe that Sh. creates "a humorous effect; by giving the form of a commonly known phrase, yet varying a word or so, and thus producing the impression of the usual phrase itself." The CLARKES (1879, p. 505): "By omitting the 'not' . . . our dramatist, besides giving the effect of characteristically blundering phraseology to the rustic speaker, also affords opportunity for Autolycus's sly rejoinder." DEIGHTON (ed. 1889) observes that the positive statement nevertheless has a negative implication. He compares "What mightst thou do, that honour would thee do, Were all thy children kinde and naturall" (*H5* 2 Prol. 18 [480-1]), where the sense is "thou not do." FURNESS (ed. 1898) wants the Clown to accompany these words "with a knowing wink," which BETHELL (ed. 1956) likes because the "assertion . . . would fit . . . with Autolycus' 'Very wisely' [2589]." WILSON (ed. 1931), on the emended reading: "The Clown's head is much bothered by these arithmetical problems; cf. [1701 ff.]."

2589 **Puppies**] JOHNSON (1755, Puppy): "A name of contemptuous reproach to a man."

2590 **let vs to**] BROOK (1976, p. 112): "A verb of motion is often omitted after . . . *let* . . . when followed by . . . a prepositional phrase."

2591 **Farthell**] COTGRAVE (1611, Pacquet): "A small bundle, or fardel" (*OED*, Fardel, *sb.* 1, citing 2638). The word also occurs at 2600, 2636, 3013, and 3124. HANMER (ed. 1743-4, 6:glos.) adds: "A pack" (Ital. *fardello*).

make . . . Beard] BOORMAN (ed. 1964): "Make him think."

2592-3 **what . . . be**] CALDECOTT (MS 1813-33): "In the language of proceedings in equity, suit, or humble petition of *Complainants*." He compares 2718-19. SCHMIDT (1874, Complaint): "Accusation."

2593 **my Master**] DEIGHTON (ed. 1889): "*I.e.* Florizel, whom he has of his own accord adopted as his master." "Of his own accord" is suppositious. We know only that Autolycus indicates, at 1681, 2516-17, 2715, and here, that he has known Florizel as his master. Florizel never recognizes him, however, even when they are together at sea, and at the end of the play there is no question of Autolycus's reentering Florizel's service. The anomaly arises because Sh. did not fully transform Greene's Capnio into Autolycus. See pp. 646 ff. HASTINGS (1940) reports that KITTREDGE believed Autolycus's autobiography to be self-contradictory; a petty thief's son would not have served the prince or worn three-pile (1681-2) and a gentleman would not have been whipped out of court (1757-8) or have looked out of place in good clothes (2630-1). "The fun of all this is of course the transparency of Autolycus's attempt to deceive." See n. 2556-7, however.

2594 **at' Pallace**] CLARK & WRIGHT (ed. 1863): "The apostrophe, if it be not a misprint, point[s] either to the omission of the article or its absorption in rapid pronunciation, as in [1918]. Perhaps the Clown speaks of the King being 'at palace' as he would have spoken of an ordinary man being 'at home.'" For *at*, see n. 2896, however, and for the omission of *the*, n. 2163.

2595-6 **Though . . . chance**] Sometimes I blunder into honesty (as now). PAFFORD (ed. 1963): "He will now do something to help the fugitives (i.e. be honest) because he senses that there is chance of further personal gain. He already has Florizel's clothes and something to boot [2515] and his quick nose for further booty will sense that there is something to be got out of the rustics and maybe more from the prince [2712-16]. But he is a rogue by inclination and on the whole does good to them against his will [3132]."

2595 **naturally**] *OED* (*adv.* 1b, citing this line, and 2): "In respect of natural constitution."

2596-7 **excrement**] COCKERAM (1623): "Any thing which naturally growes in the body, which may bee taken away without any harme thereto." THEOBALD (1726, p. 48): "*Hair* and *Nails* are *excrementitious*." THIRLBY (MS 1725-33?): "Beard with

461

ment. How now (Rustiques) whither are you bound?

Shep. To th ' Pallace (and it like your Worship.)

Aut. Your Affaires there? what? with whom? the
Condition of that Farthell? the place of your dwelling?   2600
your names? your ages? of what hauing? breeding, and
any thing that is fitting to be knowne, discouer?

Clo. We are but plaine fellowes, Sir.

Aut. A Lye; you are rough, and hayrie: Let me haue
no lying; it becomes none but Trades-men, and they of-   2605
ten giue vs (Souldiers) the Lye, but wee pay them for it
with stamped Coyne, not stabbing Steele, therefore they
doe not giue vs the Lye.

Clo. Your Worship had like to haue giuen vs one, if   (2
you had not taken your selfe with the manner.   2610

2601 ages] Age ROWE2-v1773 (−CAP)
2602 to] for to ROWE1-v1773 (−CAP)
2608 not] *Om.* WARBURTON *conj. in* HAN2, HAN, WARB
2610 manner] manour HAN

---

which he had disguis'd himself." KENRICK (1765, p. 92) notes the occurrence of the
word in *LLL* 5.1.109-10 (1836-8): "with his royall finger thus dallie with my excrement, with my mustachie." Sh. uses *excrement* neutrally as "bodily outgrowths" in
Ham. 3.4.121 (2502) and *MV* 3.2.87 (1433) and perhaps neutrally as "hair" in *Err.*
2.2.79 (472); however, because the word also meant "ordure" (MINSHEU, 1617), he
seems to have intended an off-color suggestion in *LLL* and perhaps here too—the
polite sense was rather high-toned for Autolycus. AS YOU LIKE IT (1789, p. 712)
wrongly thinks Autolycus refers to "the pedler's manners, which I have lately been
practising." KREIDER (1941, p. 18 n.): "How long Autolycus has been wearing the
beard is not clear from the text. In his first appearance he cozens the clown, and yet
in the second he faces his victim without being recognized. Perhaps his prophecy
[1786-90] . . . that he will see the clown again . . . should be considered implied
preparation for the disguise." Since the beard is "Pedlers excrement" (2596-7), however, he must have adopted it after 1794 and before his entry at 2043.

2597 **How . . . bound?**] For *how now*, see n. 201. PARRY (ed. 1982): "Having
taken off the false beard, he now puts on a false voice." What he does is to play the
courtier as the courtier appears from the peasant's point of view. The performance
could include a bad imitation of upper-class accent.

2598 **To . . . Worship.)**] BOORMAN (ed. 1964): "Although Autolycus has removed his pedlar's disguise, the Clown does not recognize the rogue who robbed
him in [4.3]."

and it like] ROLFE (ed. 1879): "If it please"; as SCHMIDT (1874) says, "a phrase
of courtesy." Cf. n. 2611.

2599 **what? with whom?**] KERMODE (ed. 1963): "Parodying a form of legal questioning to terrify the rustics."

2600 **Condition . . . Farthell?**] RANN (ed. 1787): "Contents of that bundle."
For *condition*, CALDECOTT (MS 1813-33) gives "nature" (*OED, sb.* 12) and SCHMIDT
(1874), "quality" (also 12). See n. 2591.

2601 **hauing**] HANMER (ed. 1743-4, 6:glos.): "A possession in any thing." MA-LONE (ed. 1790): "Fortune, estate" (*OED, vbl. sb.*). STEEVENS (ed. 1793) compares *Wiv.* 3.2.72 (1331-2), and FURNESS (ed. 1898), *AYL* 3.3.377 (1561-2).

breeding] SCHMIDT (1874) favors "descent, extraction" [*OED, vbl. sb.* 1b] but considers "education" [3] possible. Cf. n. 2452-3.

2602 **discouer**] Reveal. See n. 1170.

2603 **plaine**] See n. 2604 for the pun.

2604-8 **A . . . Lye**] CHARLTON (ed. 1916): "Autolycus . . . makes great game of logic and plays on words. He confuses the clowns by his display of intellectual jugglery, and at the same time impresses them with the dignity of soldiership and of men of his quality."

2604 **rough, and hayrie**] RANN (ed. 1787): "Clad in skins." He may be confusing 2147. BOORMAN (ed. 1964): "Playing on 'plain' (as meaning 'smooth')." ROWSE (1980, pp. 48-9): A similar pun is found in *Err.* 2.2.72 ff. (466 ff.), written 1592-4. "It refers to Jacob and Esau; the Geneva Bible [ed. 1560, Gen. 27:11] tells us that Jacob was 'a plain man', and Esau 'rough', for which the BISHOPS' Bible [ed. 1569] has the word 'hairy'. . . . It is fascinating to observe this combination of the Bishops' with the Geneva Bible, and reappearing over such a long span." Actually, Geneva calls Jacob "smothe" and Esau "rough," and Bishops' describes Jacob as "smoothe" and Esau as "heary," but ROWSE's point may still be valid.

2606 **giue . . . Lye**] RANN (ed. 1787): "Cheat, impose upon us [e.g., with shoddy wares]." Awareness by eds. that Autolycus is punning develops later; see n. 2607-8.

2607-8 **they . . . Lye**] THIRLBY (MS 1725-33?): "I.e. because they are paid for it." HUDSON (ed. 1880), on the other hand, thinks Autolycus is "punning on the phrase, using it in the sense of dealing in lies, or cheating by means of falsehood, as he himself has often done in selling his wares. Giving the lie in this sense is paid with money, and not with stabbing, as it is in the other sense. And in lying his customers out of their cash, Autolycus has had his lies well *paid for*; therefore he did not *give* them the lie." Autolycus's logic has been questioned by P. A. DANIEL (see p. 583) and by DEIGHTON (ed. 1889): "It looks . . . as if the words 'stamped coin' and 'stabbing steel' had been transposed. There is little point in Autolycus' saying that the payment was made in 'stamped coin' not 'stabbing steel', whereas in his assumed character there would be a point in the boast that tradesmen were reimbursed by 'us soldiers' not in the ordinary way, but by being run through with the sword. Further, 'stamped coin' as an antithesis to stabbing steel seems in itself more likely" than the opposite. FURNESS (ed. 1898) surrenders: "Autolycus was not the man to waste logic on 'puppies' if by puzzling their poor brains he could impress them with his importance." TILLEY (1930, p. 121), however, believes that Autolycus intentionally reverses the positions of "stamped Coyne" and "stabbing Steele" to express "covertly his sympathy with his fellow 'tradesmen' at a time when the soldier's part he is simulating demands that he say the opposite." WILSON (ed. 1931), differently: "'To give the lie' has the obvious meaning of 'to accuse one of falsehood to his face', the soldier's retort to which is 'stabbing steel'; but tradesmen 'give the lie' in another sense, i.e. they palm off short measure, or inferior goods, or even false coin (v. [*OED*, Lie, *sb.*] 1c]) upon simple customers like soldiers, who pay for it in honest money, so that the tradesmen do not 'give the lie', they *sell* it."

2609 **had like to**] DEIGHTON (ed. 1889): "Were likely to." PORTER & CLARKE (ed. c. 1903): "Had almost."

2610 **with the manner**] HANMER (ed. 1743-4, 6:glos.): "Manour or Mainour or Maynour, an old Law-term . . . signifies the thing which a thief takes away or steals: and to be taken with the *manour* or *mainour* is to be taken with the thing stolen about him or doing an unlawful act, . . . as we say, *in the fact*" (*OED*, Mainour, manner 2). TILLEY M633: "Sinful act." This idea is found in MACKAY (1884, p. 61),

Shep. Are you a Courtier, and't like you Sir?

Aut. Whether it like me, or no, I am a Courtier. Seest
thou not the ayre of the Court, in these enfoldings? Hath
not my gate in it, the measure of the Court? Receiues not
thy Nose Court-Odour from me? Reflect I not on thy   2615
Basenesse, Court-Contempt? Think'st thou, for that I
insinuate, at toaze from thee thy Businesse, I am therefore no Courtier? I am Courtier *Cap-a-pe*; and one that
will eyther push-on, or pluck-back, thy Businesse there:
whereupon I command thee to open thy Affaire.   2620

2611 Are you] Are yon F2, F3
      and't] and' F4; and ROWE1-JOHN2 (−HAN)
2616 Basenesse, Court-Contempt?] baseness?— court-contempt. JOHN
2617 at] F1; to mGREY *conj.*, CAP, CAM3, PEN2, OXF2, BEV4; and MAL; that ALEX,
EVNS; or F2 *etc.*
      toaze] toze POPE1-KNT2, DYCE1, HAL-DEL2, KNT3, DEL4; touze COL, HUD1,
SING2, WH1, KTLY, IRV; touse DYCE2, HUD2, WH2, NLSN
2619 pluck] push ROWE3-POPE2, HAN
2620 I] *Om.* ROWE3

---

who connects it with sheep-stealing, and in WHITE (1913, p. 187). MALONE (ed. 1790)
compares Costard's "The manner of it is, I was taken with the manner" (*LLL* 1.1.204–
5 [214]). Anticipated by CALDECOTT (MS 1813–33), DEIGHTON (ed. 1889), however:
The Clown "would scarcely dare to charge Autolycus with having been about to lie
to them if he had not caught himself in the act. 'To have given us one' must therefore
mean 'to have charged us with lying', and 'if you . . . manner' *may* mean, 'if you
had not arrested yourself in the act of doing so, and taken the sting out of the "lie
direct" by the remainder of your speech.'" PORTER & CLARKE (ed. 1908): "A phrase
for retracting what was said." Perhaps the Clown, however, by using a term he does
not fully understand, insults the supposed courtier without meaning to do so. CHARL-
TON (ed. 1916): "Probably the Clown is trying somewhat blunderingly to compliment
Autolycus: he says, in effect, 'You told us that tradesmen often give you soldiers the
lie, and we were believing it to be so, though it is certainly a lie: and so you caught
yourself in the act of giving us this very wrong impression, and then so finely demonstrated that tradesmen dare not give you soldiers the lie.'" TILLEY (1930, p. 117):
"The Clown intended to explain that Autolycus had misunderstood his earlier words,
'We are but plain fellows sir'. However, his confusion of 'taken' for 'mistaken' . . . gives his words a meaning far from the propitiatory meaning he intended," which is "Your worship had like to have given us the lie, if you had not
mistaken yourself with the manner (or meaning of my words)." WILSON (ed. 1931),
oppositely: "'Your worship was about to give us a false coin (as a tip), had you not
taken yourself in the act', i.e. had not your meanness restrained you." Later critics do
not agree; BOORMAN (ed. 1964), for example: "Autolycus seemed about to 'give them
both the lie' (call them liars, at [2604], and fight over it), but stopped himself in the
very act (took himself 'with the manner'). There may be a reference to some such
by-play here, at [3137–9]," but that seems unlikely.

2611 **Are . . . Courtier**] WILSON (ed. 1931): "Florizel's 'swain's wearing' [1807] is evidently a pretty costume." But see n. 1811-12.

and't like you] DEIGHTON (ed. 1889): "If you please to tell us." Cf. n. 2598.

2612-20 **Whether . . . Affaire**] HERFORD (ed. 1916-): "Autolycus's quick wit at once sees the superior opportunities of the 'courtier' rôle, suggested by the Shepherd's simple question, and instantly changes over into the appropriate style and vocabulary. Compare Falstaff's parody of the courtly style [*1H4* 4.2.398 ff. (1357 ff.)]." BRYANT (1963, p. 391): "Autolycus . . . captures the superficiality of the courtier's vain affectations."

2613 **ayre**] *OED* (13, citing this line): "Manner, look, style." But 2615 proves that Autolycus puns on 6: "Odour, redolence."

enfoldings] JERVIS (1868): "Garments" — as DEIGHTON (ed. 1889) remarks, an affectation. This instance of the word is the only one in Sh. with an *e*. The usual form (4 times) is *infold*, which *OED* calls an obsolete variant of *enfold*.

2614 **measure . . . Court?**] MALONE (ed. 1790, 10:607): "The stately tread of courtiers." MALONE may allude to the dance called the measure, which is described as "grave and stately" (*OED, sb.* 20).

2615 **Court-Odour**] WILSON (ed. 1931) compares "The Courtiers hands are perfum'd with Ciuet" (*AYL* 3.2.64 [1260-1]).

2615-16 **Reflect . . . Court-Contempt?**] KITTREDGE & RIBNER (ed. 1967): "Do I not look down upon your lowly positions with the contempt of a courtier?"

2616 **for that**] The CLARKES (ed. 1865): "Because."

2617 **insinuate**] Glosses are affected by emendations of "at," generally recognized as wrong. MALONE (in STEEVENS, ed. 1778), reading "and": "Cajole, to talk with condescension and humility" (*OED, v.* 2b). SCHMIDT (1874): "Intermeddle," which SCHANZER (ed. 1969), reading "to," expands to "make my way in a sinuous or subtle manner." *Toaze* may contrast with this word or restate its meaning. See below.

at] HULME (1962, p. 209) believes "at" reproduces a pronunciation variant of *or*, but she gives no other examples. Emended according to eds.' understanding of what *toaze* means.

toaze] MINSHEU (1617, to Touse): "To Pulle, to Hale, to Tugge" — as MALONE (in STEEVENS, ed. 1778) points out, the sense of *MM* 5.1.313 (2690) and a contrast with *insinuate*. HANMER (ed. 1743-4, 6:glos., Toze, reading "or") agrees that this is the literal meaning but adds, "Figuratively, by artful insinuations to draw out the secrets of a man's thoughts" (*OED*, Toze, *v.*[1] c., equating the word with TEASE *v.*[1] 1 and citing this line), a meaning that amplifies *insinuate*. STEEVENS (ed. 1778, reading "or"): "To disentangle wool or flax," a word Autolycus adopts because the Clown would not understand *insinuate*. HENLEY (in STEEVENS, ed. 1793), however: "To *insinuate*, and to *tease*, or *toaze*, are opposites. The former signifies to introduce itself obliquely into a thing, and the latter to get something out that was knotted up in it." He receives some support from ANON. (MS 1733-): "Extort by violence," but this may be merely a guess. *OED* does not bear HENLEY out, nor does it support MAXWELL's (ed. 1956, "or") "tear." CLARK & WRIGHT (ed. 1863): "It is not improbable . . . that Autolycus may have coined a word to puzzle the clowns, which afterwards puzzled the printers." BEVINGTON (ed. 1992, "to") for the expression: "Pry [insinuate] in order to tease, draw out, comb out."

2618 *Cap-a-pe*] BLOUNT (1656): "From head to foot," as in 2053. The CLARKES (1879, p. 736): "Originally employed to express clad in a complete suit of armour." See TILLEY T436 and C864. KERMODE (ed. 1963): I.e., "thorough, complete."

2620 **whereupon**] *OED* (*adv.* 3b, citing this line): "(with clause as antecedent.) On which account . . . wherefore."

open] SCHMIDT (1875): "Disclose."

Shep. My Businesse, Sir, is to the King.

Aut. What Aduocate ha'st thou to him?

Shep. I know not (and't like you.)

Clo. Aduocate's the Court-word for a Pheazant: say
you haue none.   2625

Shep. None, Sir: I haue no Pheazant Cock, nor Hen.

Aut. How blessed are we, that are not simple men?
Yet Nature might haue made me as these are,
Therefore I will not disdaine.

Clo. This cannot be but a great Courtier.   2630

Shep. His Garments are rich, but he weares them not
handsomely.

Clo. He seemes to be the more Noble, in being fantasticall: A great man, Ile warrant; I know by the picking
on's Teeth.   2635

2624 Pheazant] present KENRICK (1765, p. 93) *conj.*, DYCE2, KNT3, COL4, ARD1
2626 Pheazant_∧] ~ , mTBY2 *conj.*, CAP+ (−EVNS)
2627-9 *Prose* ARD1, BEV3
2630 be but] but be HAN, COL2, CAM3

2622 **Aduocate**] SCHMIDT (1874): "One who pleads the cause of another," the
same sense the word has in 865 and 2993. VICKERS (1968, p. 415), unaccountably:
"Autolycus over-reaches himself in his new style, falling into a malapropism."

2623 **and't like**] If it please. See n. 2598.

2624 **Aduocate's . . . Pheazant**] WARBURTON (ed. 1747): "Satire, on the bribery of courts." WILSON (ed. 1931): "The Clown's line of thought is clear enough. He
is confusing the two kinds of 'court' and has in mind [bribery by bird]." The Clown
also takes *advocate* to mean a thing rather than a person. REED (ed. 1803) refers to
a parliamentary debate in D'EWES (1682) that alludes to "the inferiour sort of Justice
[of the peace], commonly called Basket Justices," and to justices "that for a half Dozen
of Chickens will dispense with a dozen of penal Statutes." DENT (1973, p. 109): "A
brace of pheasants continues to this day to be a court-word for advocate in some
country circles." Only WHITE (ed. 1883) finds "here a jingling play on pheasant,
peasant, and present." For more on birds and the law, see *AYL* (ed. KNOWLES, 1977,
n. 1133), and cf. the Clown in *Tit.*, who hopes to have justice in exchange for two
pigeons (4.3.88 ff. [1955 ff.]). For an opinion of this kind of humor, see n. 3135-6.
BOORMAN (ed. 1964), impossibly: "A play . . . on 'pheasant'– 'fees (-ant)', with a
hit at advocates (lawyers)."

BARTON (1929, p. 55) has a more attractive explanation: "There was a notable
family of advocates of the name of Phesant who were conspicuous at Gray's Inn and
in the Courts." In 1611, when *WT* was acted, "the elder [Peter] Phesant had died
recently and the younger [Peter] Phesant was a junior member of the bar. The father's
name was familiar to the public and the son was following him in the advocate's

profession. . . . Thus the collocation of the words 'advocate' and 'pheasant' is explainable." Records of the Fesants (or Phesants) are in WILLIAM RALPH DOUTHWAITE, *Gray's Inn: Its History and Associations* (1886, pp. 58 and 68), but the idea that Sh. alludes to them is not generally accepted. COOPER (1977, p. 59, citing this instance) has another explanation: "Almost every way of presenting the shepherd [in pastoral] has two sides to it, the comic and the idyllic, mocking the rustic or criticizing the courtly; and sometimes both can happen at once."

2626-9 **None . . . disdaine**] FURNIVALL (1878, on meter): Lines 2626-7 make a pentameter couplet, though he concludes that Sh. "probably intended [2626] to be prose." WILSON (ed. 1931) disagrees; 2630 "indicates that verse was intended" and 2626-7 rhyme. WHIBLEY (1916, 2:505): Autolycus "takes a noble pride in his own superiority," but others detect irony. PAFFORD (ed. 1963): "Autolycus is a temporary gentleman speaking [verse] grandiloquently." SCHANZER (ed. 1969): "A parody of the language of the court." BETHELL (ed. 1956): "This comic 'elevation' in a prose context produces the Clown's admiring comment" (2630).

2627-9 **How . . . disdaine**] NOBLE (1935, p. 248): "Probably the Parable of the Pharisee and Publican was sufficiently familiar to the audience to make this assumption of superiority by Autolycus amusing. *Cf.* Luke xviii.XI: 'God, I thanke thee, that I am not as other men are.'" STAUFFER (1949, p. 300): "It is difficult to tell whether he is laughing at the shepherds, or whether he is laughing at himself, or whether Shakespeare is laughing at him, or whether both together are laughing at all of us who, but for the grace of God, would go like simpletons." WAIN (1964, p. 224): "Autolycus has his own parody of the Nature *versus* Art debate, as he preeningly reflects on his own superiority to the countrymen. . . . Like Perdita, he owes his superiority to a more generous endowment by Nature, yet he chooses to appear before them as a courtier, owing his attainments to upbringing, politeness, and Art generally." BERRY (1988, p. 178): "With a lyric swoop into blank verse, surely Autolycus . . . addresses the audience directly."

2629 **disdaine**] JOHNSON (1755): "Scorn."

2630 **be but**] PAFFORD (ed. 1963), asserting that this "usage . . . was not uncommon," finds an example in *Pandosto* (see p. 634).

2631-2 **His . . . handsomely**] GRIFFITH (1775, p. 113): "There is a good ridicule, here, on the affectations of persons of rank, in the description of the manners by which the vulgar often distinguish their *betters*—perhaps their *superiors* only." The CLARKES (ed. 1865): An instance of "the shrewd instinct that frequently distinguishes unlettered men." PARRY (ed. 1982): "Probably Florizel's clothes are not Autolycus' size." On Florizel's clothes (now on Autolycus), see nn. 2557-8 and 2633-4.

2633-4 **fantasticall**] SCHMIDT (1874): "Indulging the vagaries of the imagination, capricious, whimsical." The clothes may seem handsome, but Autolycus wears them crazily.

2634-5 **the . . . Teeth**] NEILSON & HILL (ed. 1942): "The way he picks his teeth." JOHNSON (ed. 1765, citing *Jn.* 1.1.190 [200]): "To pick the teeth was . . . a mark of some pretension to greatness or elegance." GILDEMEISTER (ed. 1870): In Sh.'s time, toothpicks were a novelty imported from the Continent. FURNESS (ed. 1898): "The mark of a traveller, wherein consisted the elegance." BOORMAN (ed. 1964): "Another stage direction in the text." See nn. 1412-13, 2134-5, and 2190. The CLARKES (1879, pp. 680-1) list this and other "fantastical styles in dress, and fanatical adoption of foreign modes."

Aut. The Farthell there? What's i'th' Farthell?
Wherefore that Box?

Shep. Sir, there lyes such Secrets in this Farthell and
Box, which none must know but the King, and which hee
shall know within this houre, if I may come to th' speech   2640
of him.

Aut. Age, thou hast lost thy labour.

Shep. Why Sir?

Aut. The King is not at the Pallace, he is gone aboord
a new Ship, to purge Melancholy, and ayre himselfe: for   2645
if thou bee'st capable of things serious, thou must know
the King is full of griefe.

Shep. So 'tis said (Sir:) about his Sonne, that should
haue marryed a Shepheards Daughter.

Aut. If that Shepheard be not in hand-fast, let him   2650
flye; the Curses he shall haue, the Tortures he shall feele,
will breake the back of Man, the heart of Monster.

Clo. Thinke you so, Sir?

Aut. Not hee alone shall suffer what Wit can make
heauie, and Vengeance bitter; but those that are Iermaine   2655
to him (though remou'd fiftie times) shall all come vnder
the Hang-man: which, though it be great pitty, yet it is
necessarie. An old Sheepe-whistling Rogue, a Ram-ten-
der, to offer to haue his Daughter come into grace? Some
say hee shall be ston'd: but that death is too soft for him   2660

2638 lyes] lie COL2
2641 of] with PEN1
2650 not] not now OXF1
2651 Tortures] torture OXF1

2636-7 **The . . . Box?**] For *farthell*, see n. 2591. SCHANZER (ed. 1969): "The
fardel consists of the garments worn by the infant Perdita when found; the *box*
contains presumably the remainder of the gold and the scroll left with her by Antigonus (see [1556-61] and [3042-5])."

2638 **there . . . Secrets**] ABBOTT (§335): *Lyes* is singular because it precedes
the plural subject, the number of which "is as yet future and, as it were, unsettled."
Confusion of number often occurs with *there*. Cf. 3152-3.

2638-9 **such . . . which hee**] For the construction, see n. 27.

2640-1 **come . . . him**] KITTREDGE & RIBNER (ed. 1967): "Come to where I
can speak with him."

2642-5 **Age . . . himselfe**] See *Pandosto*, p. 647.

2642 **Age**] SCHMIDT (1875, p. 1422a): "Old man," the abstract for the concrete,
a kind of metonymy. See nn. 1504, 2278.

lost thy labour] To lose labor (labor in vain) is proverbial (TILLEY L9 and V5).

2644-7 **The . . . griefe**] PARRY (ed. 1982): "At this point he [Autolycus] may or may not have formed the intention of taking the Clown and Shepherd to Florizel, but he has certainly decided to go by [2677]."

2645 **a new Ship**] STEARNS (1882, p. 153): "Because the air in a new ship is much purer than in an old one; as the bilge-water is less fouled by accumulated sediment." GOTCH (1900, p. 330), hopelessly: "Speaking to a shepherd and the son of a shepherd, he [Autolycus] rests assured they will hear his words as 'an ewe sheep.'" Sh. does commit a *ship-sheep* pun in *Err.* 4.1.93-4 (1082-3), but not here.

purge Melancholy] KITTREDGE & RIBNER (ed. 1967): "Cure his melancholy by taking a purge." Or perhaps by a change of air and scene; see BURTON (1628; 1989-90, 2:64-7). HANKINS (1978, p. 129), discussing choler as an antecedent to melancholy, believes Polixenes's depression to be brought on by "his choleric outburst against Florizel and Perdita" (2260 ff.). But since the king is not aboard the ship, he may not be full of grief either.

Melancholy] SCHMIDT (1875): "Depression of spirits." BETHELL (ed. 1956): One of the "four 'humours' or temperaments."

ayre] RUBINSTEIN (1984) finds a pun on *heir*. Polixenes is melancholy because Florizel is missing.

2646 **capable**] MINSHEU (1617): "Fit to receiue." JOHNSON (1755): "Able to understand." EVANS (ed. 1974): "Know anything about."

2648 **should**] ABBOTT (§324):list see emphs sort a "Was to." BLAKE (1983, p. 96) adds "ought to have."

2650 **in hand-fast**] RANN (ed. 1787): In "hold, custody" (*OED*, Handfast, *sb*. 1b, citing this line only). STAUNTON's (ed. 1859) insistence that the word means "*main-prize*, . . . to be at large only on security given" is unsupported by *OED*. According to BARTON (1929, p. 103), by Sh.'s time the word "had become quite non-technical." Followed by BEVINGTON (ed. 1992), PORTER & CLARKE (ed. 1908): "If she be not betrothed securely."

2654 **Wit**] Usually, "ingenuity." The CLARKES (ed. 1865): "Here . . . 'skill in cruelty', 'barbarous invention.'"

2655 **heauie**] Probably SCHMIDT (1874, 2a): "Grievous, hard, severe," although this instance is not cited.

Iermaine] JOHNSON (1755, German, citing this line): "Related." CARRINGTON (1956): He "is still talking in the 'grand style.'"

2656 **remou'd**] *OED* (*ppl. a.* 1, citing this line): "Properly denoting a degree in descent, as *first cousin once removed* = a cousin's child; but in later use freq. employed in vague designations of distant relationship." BOORMAN (ed. 1964) thinks there is a pun, which he does not explain.

2658-9 **An . . . grace?**] RUBINSTEIN (1984, Whistle): "Autolycus compares the shepherd to Abraham, who asked by God to 'offer' his child 'took the ram and offered him up for a burnt offering' (Gen. 22:13-22). The shepherd offered his child (Perdita), not to come into *God*'s grace, but into grace, i.e. favor and royal title."

2658 **Sheepe-whistling**] SCHMIDT (1875): "Whistling for sheep, tending sheep." DEIGHTON (ed. 1889): "It is the dogs not the sheep that obey the call of the whistle," but that detail may be beneath Autolycus's notice.

2659 **offer**] SCHMIDT (1875): "Attempt, (sometimes almost = to dare)."

come into grace] ROLFE (ed. 1879): "Marry the prince." DEIGHTON (ed. 1889): Autolycus may also have in mind that royal persons were addressed as *your Grace* [as at 355]. LEE (ed. 1907): "Get into good society." For other meanings of *grace*, see n. 146. BOORMAN (ed. 1964) finds a pun on *grease*, that "being associated with the trade of shepherd."

2660 **ston'd . . . soft**] BOORMAN (ed. 1964): "A play on . . . words."

(say I:) Draw our Throne into a Sheep-Coat? all deaths
are too few, the sharpest too easie.
   Clo. Ha's the old-man ere a Sonne Sir (doe you heare)
and't like you, Sir?
   Aut. Hee ha's a Sonne: who shall be flayd aliue, then   2665
'noynted ouer with Honey, set on the head of a Waspes

2663 Sir] *Om.* KNT3

   2661 Draw our Throne] MOORMAN (ed. 1912): "Autolycus pretends to be quoting the very words of the king," but he may pretend to speak merely as a patriotic
Bohemian. BOORMAN (ed. 1964, Draw): "Entice" (*OED* 26) and "reduce" (not exactly
supported).
      Sheep-Coat] JOHNSON (1755, citing this line): "A little inclosure for *sheep*"
(*OED*: "A slight building"). SCHMIDT (1875), wrongly: "The cottage of a shepherd."
   2664 and't like] See n. 2598.
   2665-72 Hee . . . death.)] RHODES (1980, p. 10): "What is funny, apart from
the dramatic situation, is the casual elaboration of these atrocities, the jocular 'three
quarters and a dram dead'; yet the punishments themselves, considered for what they
are, are unthinkably horrifying. This unsettling technique, which drags the reader's
feelings in opposite directions at once, is the most conspicuous effect of the grotesque." For a comparison with Polixenes's outburst at the festival, see n. 2263-70.
BERRY (1981, pp. 134-5), reminded of Paulina at 1362-5 and Polixenes at 2269-70
and 2284-5: "The Tyrant's tortures are real, if verbal, possibilities. Autolycus exor-
cizes them, makes them vain gestures, objects of derision."
   2665-7 flayd . . . dead] REED (ed. 1793) finds in Henri Estienne, *The Stage of
Popish Toyes* (1581, p. 33), "a book which Shakspeare might have seen," that the
Count of Gilderland, smeared with honey and fly-bitten, died after a miserable confinement in an iron cage. HERFORD (ed. 1904), more relevantly: "The . . .
description follows with little variation that which Shakespeare had read in Boccaccio's story of Ambrogiuolo (*Decameron*, 2:9), the immediate source of the wager
story in *Cymbeline*." The passage is "Then the Soldane strictly commaunded, that on
some high and eminent place of the Citie, Ambrogiuolo should be bound and impaled
on a stake, having his naked body nointed all over with hony, and never to bee taken
off, untill (of it selfe) it fell in peeces, which, according to the sentence, was presently
performed" (BULLOUGH, 1975, 8:62). ALEXANDER (1938, p. 207) takes Sh.'s use of it
as proof that he read Italian, for no version existed in English. As ANDERS (1926, p.
173) notes, Boccaccio borrowed his execution from Lucius Apuleius, *The Golden
Asse* (see pp. 684-5). THEOBALD (1909, p. 78) thinks that Sh. went directly to Apuleius. ROGERS (1916, 1:184-5) says it was commonly known that Spaniards, their
hearts hardened by the Inquisition, "did these very things" to captive Englishmen as
well as to Indians and Africans. MAXWELL (in PAFFORD, ed. 1963) notes "that the
torture is mentioned in William of Malmesbury's *Historiae Novellae*. . . . The Latin
text of this was printed by Sir Henry Savile in *Rerum Anglicarum Scriptores*, 1596
(f. 105v, ll. 2-3), reissued in 1601 (p. 186, ll. 18-19)." Sh. is not known to have been
acquainted with this work.
   2665-9 then . . . then . . . then . . . then] VICKERS (1968, p. 416): "A
gloating *anaphora* [repetition]."
   2666 'noynted] ABBOTT (§460): A spelling indicating that a syllable that is now
pronounced was then omitted. Cf. n. 1282.
      head] SCHMIDT (1874): "Top."

Nest, then stand till he be three quarters and a dram dead:
then recouer'd againe with Aquavite, or some other hot
Infusion: then, raw as he is (and in the hotest day Prognostication proclaymes) shall he be set against a Brick-wall,   2670
(the Sunne looking with a South-ward eye vpon him;
where hee is to behold him, with Flyes blown to death.)
But what talke we of these Traitorly-Rascals, whose miseries are to be smil'd at, their offences being so capitall?

2667 then] there CAP, COL2, DYCE2, HUD2
2670 he] *Om.* HARN

2667 **dram**] One-sixteenth ounce avoirdupois, or one-eighth fluid ounce. Figuratively, "and a little more," as in 748. BETHELL (ed. 1956): "Comic, since it implies
that 'three quarters' refers to weight or bulk."
    2668–9 **Aquavite . . . Infusion**] MINSHEU (1617, Aqua vite): "Burnd wine."
KERSEY (1708): "A sort of Cordial Water, made of brew'd Beer strongly hopp'd, and
well fermented." Subtle may refer to this when he accuses Face of having sold "the
dole-beere to *aqua-vitæ*-men" (Jonson, *The Alchemist*, 1.1.53). In popular use, as
WARNER (1768, p. 104) says, the word meant "any kind of strong water," such "as
brandy, spirits, etc." (*OED* 2). The point here, however, is that Autolycus treats aquavite as another hot infusion, whereas, according to PHILLIPS (1658), *infusion* "is used
in Physick, for a steeping of roots or leaves, or any kind of medicine, in some liquid
substance for a certain time, till the chiefest of their virtue be drawn out." But neither
aquavite nor a hot infusion would be welcome to a hot man on a hot day. SCHMIDT
(1874, Hot 6): "Heating, spirituous."
    2669–70 **Prognostication proclaymes**] JOHNSON (ed. 1765): "Foretold in the
Almanack." MALONE (ed. 1790, 10:607): "Almanacks were . . . published under this
title." *OED* (Prognostication 2): "An astrological or astrometeorological forecast for
the year, published in (or as) an almanac, hence an almanac containing this." *STC*
385.3–532.11 provides many examples.
    2671 **South-ward**] *OED* (*a.*, citing this line): "Facing . . . towards the south."
    2672 **hee**] HAPPÉ (1969): "The sun." ORGEL (ed. 1996): "Or the Clown's father."
    Flyes] SCHANZER (ed. 1969): "Any winged insect" (*OED*, *sb.*[1] 1) but, according
to SCHMIDT (1874), "subst[antially] the insect Musca" (1b).
    blown] JOHNSON (1755, To Blow v. a.): "To infect with the eggs of flies."
Swelling results. In *Tmp.*, Ferdinand mentions fly-blowing at 3.1.63 (1309) and Trinculo at 5.1.284 (2281); so does Cleopatra in *Ant.* 5.2.59–60 (3268–9). SCHANZER (ed.
1969), asserting that filling him up with eggs is "a very improbable way of killing a
man," thinks the word means "puffed up, swollen." But that definition amounts to
the same thing as JOHNSON's, since swelling would accompany infection.
    2673 **what**] ABBOTT (§253): "'For what', 'why' (quid)."
    Traitorly-Rascals] ABBOTT (§447): "The *-ly* represents 'like', of which it is a cor-
ruption." *OED*'s first citation of *traitorly* as an adjective is dated c. 1586; its last, 1668.
    2674 **capitall**] MINSHEU (1617): "Deadly." JOHNSON (1755): "Criminal in the
highest degree, so as to touch life." BOORMAN (ed. 1964): "The modern pun is possible," by which he may mean "punishable by death" (*OED*, *a.* 2b) and "important,
first-class" (6e) or "excellent, 'first rate'" (7), though neither of the latter is cited
before the 18th c. and both seem inapplicable anyhow.

Tell me (for you seeme to be honest plaine men) what you
haue to the King: being something gently consider'd, Ile
bring you where he is aboord, tender your persons to his
presence, whisper him in your behalfes; and if it be in
man, besides the King, to effect your Suites, here is man
shall doe it.

    Clow. He seemes to be of great authoritie: close with
him, giue him Gold; and though Authoritie be a stub-
borne Beare, yet hee is oft led by the Nose with Gold:
shew the in-side of your Purse to the out-side of his
hand, and no more adoe. Remember ston'd, and flay'd
aliue.

    Shep. And't please you (Sir) to vndertake the Businesse
for vs, here is that Gold I haue: Ile make it as much
more, and leaue this young man in pawne, till I bring it
you.

    Aut. After I haue done what I promised?

    Shep. I Sir.

    Aut. Well, giue me the Moitie: Are you a partie in
this Businesse?

    Clow. In some sort, Sir: but though my case be a pit-
tifull one, I hope I shall not be flayd out of it.

    Aut. Oh, that's the case of the Shepheards Sonne:
hang him, hee'le be made an example.

    Clow. Comfort, good comfort: We must to the King,
and shew our strange sights: he must know 'tis none of
your Daughter, nor my Sister: wee are gone else. Sir, I
will giue you as much as this old man do's, when the Businesse is performed, and remaine (as he sayes) your pawne
till it be brought you.

2675 (2.
2680
2685
2690
2695
2700

2677 aboord] abroad CLN2
2678 behalfes] behalf F4-JOHN2
2679 man, . . . King,] ~ ∧ . . . ~ ∧ DYCE, CAM1, HUD2-NLSN, ALEX, PEL1, CLN2,
SIG, EVNS, BEV
    is man] is a man F3-v1785 (−CAP, v1778), OXF1, PEN1; is man a HAL; is the
man mLONG *conj.*, KTLY
2682 and] an WALKER (1860, 2:157, 246) *conj.*, DYCE2, HUD2
2688 that] the ROWE1, ROWE2
2691 promised] have promised COL3, OXF1
2693 partie] parting F4-ROWE2

2675-6 **what . . . to**] BETHELL (ed. 1956): "What is your business with."
2676 **something**] Somewhat. See n. 224. *OED* (*adv.* 2c) cites this line.
    gently consider'd] JOHNSON (ed. 1765): "I who am regarded as a gentleman."

STEEVENS (ed. 1773), more to Autolycus's point: *"I having a gentlemanlike consideration given me*, i.e. a bribe." In ed. 1778, STEEVENS adds examples from Robert Wilson, *The Three Ladies of London* (1584; ed. H. S. D. Mithal, 1988, lines 460-1) and John Day, *The Isle of Gulls* (1606; ed. Raymond S. Burns, 1980, 4.1.59-60). HERFORD (ed. 1904): "For a small consideration." To STEEVENS's gloss, PAFFORD (ed. 1963) adds, "Being had [held?] somewhat in regard as a man of noble rank (i.e. and so having influence)." HAPPÉ (1969) adds, "being quite highly regarded." But ORGEL (ed. 1996) points out that "the Shepherd duly offers Autolycus the bribe at [2688]."

2677 **he**] PAFFORD (ed. 1963): "To the rustics 'he' must mean the king. But Autolycus refers to the prince. From this point Autolycus begins to work out the plan of getting them on board on the pretext that he is taking them to the king." Thus *besides* in 2679 must mean "who is near to" as well as "other than." However, because *King* is the obvious antecedent of *he*, PAFFORD's interpretation seems unnecessarily complicated. And Autolycus is lying in any case.

tender] MINSHEU (1617): "Carefully to offer" (possibly *OED, v.*[1] 2, the term being misused of persons rather than things). SCHMIDT (1875): "Show, or introduce?" HAPPÉ (1969): "Conduct." Autolycus may lose some control of the high style he has adopted.

2678 **presence**] MINSHEU (1617): "The Chamber of *Presence* in a Princes Court. . . . The gentlemen waiters must there be *present* to giue their attendance at the *Kings* or *Princes* presence and pleasure." But by *his presence*, Autolycus means no more than "him."

whisper him] For the omission of the preposition, see ABBOTT §200.

2678-9 **in man**] KITTREDGE & RIBNER (ed. 1967): "In any man's power."

2679 **besides the King**] MOORMAN (ed. 1912) thinks that within commas the phrase means "to say nothing of the fact that it is the king." PAFFORD (ed. 1963), however: "Who is near to" or "other than." See n. 2677.

effect] JOHNSON (1755): "Attempt with success."

2679-80 **man shall**] WHITE (ed. 1857): "Man that shall" (ABBOTT §244).

2681-2 **close with him**] SCHMIDT (1874, Close): "Come to an agreement." HARRISON (ed. 1947): "Accept his offer."

2682 **and**] ABBOTT (§105): "Even."

2683 **hee is**] WALKER (1860, 2:246): "I think the English of Shakespeare's time requires *is he*." FURNESS (ed. 1898): "Which is possibly why the Clown uses 'he is.'"

led . . . Nose] As bears are, but playing upon the more general sense "govern" (FARMER & HENLEY [1890-1904; 1970]). PAFFORD (ed. 1963): "Led in docile manner." TILLEY N233, however, quotes FLORIO (1611), s.v. *Menár per il náso*: "To lead by the nose, that is, to make a foole of one," which would also be appropriate here.

2689 **in pawne**] RIDLEY (ed. 1935): As a "hostage."

2693 **Moitie**] Half, the other half being the "as much more" of 2688-9. See n. 1213 for other meanings. CHARLTON (ed. 1916): "Autolycus wants immediate possession."

2695 **In some sort**] BOORMAN (ed. 1964): "In a way."

case] RANN (ed. 1787, glos.): Situation, but with a pun on "skin, hide." HENN (1972, p. 52), more exactly: "The 'term of art' for a fox's skin." See nn. 2512, 2519. DELIUS (ed. 1860) compares the similar wordplay in *Rom.* 4.5.99-100 (2678-9).

2699 **Comfort, good comfort**] OED (*sb.* 9, citing this line): "Take comfort, cheer up." DEIGHTON (ed. 1889), however: "May we have good comfort. . . . Perhaps also . . . it is a pretty kind of comfort that Autolycus offers."

We must to] For the omission of the verb, see FRANZ §621 and *WT* 3360.

2700 **'tis none of**] BOORMAN (ed. 1964): "It is not a question of." KITTREDGE & RIBNER (ed. 1967), preferred by later eds.: "She is not."

2701 **gone**] PAFFORD (ed. 1963): "Undone." Cf. 1500.

Aut. I will trust you. Walke before toward the Sea-   2705
side, goe on the right hand, I will but looke vpon the
Hedge, and follow you.

Clow. We are bless'd, in this man: as I may say, euen
bless'd.

Shep. Let's before, as he bids vs: he was prouided to   2710
doe vs good.

Aut. If I had a mind to be honest, I see *Fortune* would
not suffer mee: shee drops Booties in my mouth. I am
courted now with a double occasion: (Gold, and a means

2711 *Exeunt.* F3-ROWE1; *Exeunt Shep. and Clown.* ROWE2+ (*subst.*)

2705 **before**] KITTREDGE & RIBNER (ed. 1967): "Ahead of me."

2706-7 **I . . . Hedge**] THIRLBY (MS 1733-47?): "Does he mean piss?" He compares RAY (1737, p. 70): "*To make Water*, &c. . . . To look upon the wall." BETHELL
(ed. 1956): A device to get the Clown and Shepherd off the stage so that Autolycus
may speak directly to the audience in 2712 ff. ADAMS (1989, p. 106): "Urinate [is
what] Autolycus presumably does onstage, as he soliloquizes, with a degree of dis-
creetness that's up to the actor."

2708 **euen**] DEIGHTON (ed. 1889): "*I.e.* that is not too strong a word to use."

2710-11 **prouided . . . good**] PYLE (1969, p. 95): "This seems laughably
ironic, but not in the long run."

2710 **prouided**] KITTREDGE & RIBNER (ed. 1967): "Sent by divine Providence,"
which links with the Clown's "bless'd . . . euen bless'd."

2712-13 **If . . . mouth**] HUGHES (1940, p. 221): "The eternal confidence man
gloats over his eternally imbecile victim."

2713 **suffer**] SCHMIDT (1875): "Allow."

Booties . . . mouth] JOHNSON (1755, Booty, citing this line): "Things gotten
by robbery" (*OED, sb.* 3, "a prize," citing this line). PAFFORD (ed. 1963) adds, "Something extra and unexpected." He finds in Greene, *A Disputation between a Hee
Conny-catcher and a Shee Conny-catcher*: Careless people invite thievery, "for who
loues wyne so ill, that he will not eate grapes if they fall into his mouth" (1592; ed.
HARRISON, 1922?, p. 14).

2714 **courted . . . with**] MAXWELL (ed. 1956): "Tempted . . . by."

occasion] SCHMIDT (1875): "Anything occurring incidentally, accident, good
or bad fortune." MOORMAN (ed. 1912), however: "Almost equivalent to 'motive',
which is one of the meanings of the Latin *occasio*." CARRINGTON (1956): "Opportunity."

2715 **the . . . Master**] See n. 2593.

which] CARRINGTON (1956): "Refers to the second 'occasion.'"

2715-16 **who . . . aduancement?**] HARBOTTLE (1853, p. 97): "Who knows but
my availing myself of the means to do the prince my master a service, may come back
in the shape of some advancement?" FURNESS (ed. 1898): "Autolycus has two ventures
on hand: Gold from the Shepherd, and an experiment on the Prince. Of the issue of
the former he is certain; but as to the shape for good or for ill, in which the result of

to doe the Prince my Master good; which, who knowes   2715
how that may turne backe to my aduancement?) I will
bring these two Moales, these blind-ones, aboord him. If
he thinke it fit to shoare them againe, and that the Complaint they haue to the King, concernes him nothing, let
him call me Rogue, for being so farre officious, for I am   2720
proofe against that Title, and what shame else belongs
to't: To him will I present them, there may be matter in
it.
                                            Exeunt.

2716 how . . . backe] but luck may turn LETTSOM *conj. in* WALKER (1860, 1:xliv),
HUD2

       backe] luck COL2, COL3, COL4
2722 will I] I will SING1, HUD1, COL2
2723 *Exeunt.*] *Exit.* ROWE1+ (*subst.*)

---

the experiment on the Prince will come back to him, he is doubtful." He paraphrases:
"As to which, who knows how that may recoil [*OED*, Turn, *v.* 70b: 'To send or give
back'] to my advancement?" Rather than doubtful as to good or ill, however, Autolycus may be uncertain only of the size of the reward, since no ill should come of
doing the Prince good: "Who knows how substantially that may return?" DEIGHTON
(ed. 1889): *Turne backe* "is used for the sake of the antithesis with 'advancement.'"
WILSON (ed. 1931): It is equivalent to "turn out." PARRY (ed. 1982, Advancement):
"A better station in life."

    2717 **Moales, these blind-ones**] ONIONS (1916, 1:482): "The eye of the mole,
which . . . is so minute that it always has been and still is, popularly, supposed to
be non-existent; to this belief there are no less than three references [this, *Tmp.*
4.1.194 (1870), and *Per.* 1.1.100 (146)]."

    him] SCHMIDT (1874): "His ship." Cf. "aboord the Prince" (3123).

    2718 **shoare**] JOHNSON (1755, citing this line only): "Set on shore. Not in use."
OED (*v.*[4] 2) finds the same sense in Chapman's *Odyssey* (1611, 16.98). ABBOTT (§290):
"Any noun or adjective could be converted into a verb." According to YOUNG &
MOSELEY (ed. 1965), Autolycus means "dismiss them as of no importance."

    2718-19 **Complaint**] DEIGHTON (ed. 1889): "*I.e.* of Florizel having resisted
them." See n. 2592-3.

    2719 **concernes him nothing**] DEIGHTON (ed. 1889): "Is of no importance to
him."

    2720-1 **I . . . Title**] JOHNSON (1755, Proof): "Hardened." HERFORD (ed. 1904):
"He may be called a rogue by way of abuse, but is secure against legal arrest and
punishment as a 'rogue and vagabond.'" HERFORD alludes to *An Acte concernyng
punysshement of Beggers & Vacabundes* (22 Hen. VIII, c. 12), for which see CHAM-
BERS (1923, 4:260). More likely, he has been called "rogue" so often that he has
become indifferent to the insult.

    2722-3 **there . . . it**] SCHMIDT (1875): "Something may be made of it." *OED*
(Matter, *sb.*[1] 11c, citing this line): "Some importance attaches to it."

Actus Quintus. Scena Prima.   **5.1**

2724 ***Actus . . . Prima.***] DANIEL (1879, p. 179): An interval for the journey, after which commences the eighth and last day represented. CLAPP (1885, p. 403) agrees that the three scenes of Act 5 "occupy but a single day" and that "though the multiform incidents of the Winter's Tale are spread over a period of sixteen years, the time consumed by their action within the play is in the aggregate only about a week." HERFORD (ed. 1916-): "The action returns to the Sicilian court. Little attempt is made to provide evidence of the passage there of the sixteen years requisitioned by the dramatist to enable Perdita to grow up in Bohemia. Leontes reappears, indistinguishable from the penitent king who had retired at the close of [3.2]. Paulina is her old self, sleepless champion of his slandered wife, and not a whit mellowed by the years of his 'saint-like sorrow'. But the court has begun to hint discreetly at the need of an heir, and therefore of a second marriage. Paulina meets this with brilliant diplomatic skill, first pointing to the oracle's declaration that Leontes would not have an heir, and then guiding him tactfully, step by step, into the trap which is also to be the solution of the whole trouble — his consent to take, should he marry, only a wife whom she would provide. The climax of the Leontes-Hermione story appears to be in sight. But the situation thus successfully arranged is disturbed . . . by two events, equally startling to the persons on the stage, and of romantically contrasted import, — the arrival of Florizel and Perdita, unattended, and the reported arrival of Polixenes and Camillo. With his usual delicate instinct Shakespeare transforms a repulsive trait in Greene's narrative at this point into an added beauty. Greene had made the king openly and persistently court his unknown daughter [see p. 651]; Leontes feels the charm of her beauty, and his admiring gaze alarms for a moment the ever suspicious Paulina. But his words to Florizel [2995-6] are a playful jest, and his reply to Paulina [3001-2] hints at incipient recognition that it is Hermione's daughter that stands before him." CHARLTON (ed. 1916) finds "Leontes so purified that he is spiritually fitted for the return of Hermione." LAWLOR (1962, p. 103): "In the space of [this] one scene . . . we [travel] all the way from a sadly penitent Leontes to a magnanimous host, taking the part of the young against the old." YOUNG & MOSELEY (ed. 1965) also do not agree with HERFORD that the 16-years-older king has remained the same: "Leontes' grief is as extreme as was his jealousy. His verse too has changed; gone are the tumbled imagery and violent cadences of his early speeches; now we have a gentle, reflective simplicity, akin to that of the chastened Lear. . . . Passions have been purged, and Shakespeare can use his new Leontes to build up to the climax of Hermione's return."

Regarding the locale, SEWELL (1945, p. 211): "Some kind of unity (however inadequate) is given to *The Winter's Tale* by the return to Sicily at the end of the play." Regarding the season, WALLER (1970, p. 134): "The . . . act appears to take place in autumn, the time of the harvest, and so the seasonal movement of the second half of the play is from winter to autumn." HARRISON (ed. 1947): Regarding "how and why Paulina has concealed Hermione for sixteen years[:] 'How' is unanswerable: but the reason is plain. Apollo has shown very definitely by his Oracle that he is dominant in the affairs of Sicilia. The only way to prevent Hermione from presenting Leontes with an heir is to pretend that she is dead." BATE (1993, p. 53): "The final act . . . is exceptional in its way of reworking the Pygmalion story without any implication of beastliness or, in Paulina's term, unlawfulness [3302]."

Enter Leontes, Cleomines, Dion, Paulina, Seruants: 2725
Florizel, Perdita.

Cleo. Sir, you haue done enough, and haue perform'd

2725   *Changes to* Sicilia. POPE1+ (−PEL1, CLN2, PEN2, OXF2) (*subst.*)
       A Room in Leontes' *Palace.* CAP, MAL+ (−PEL1, CLN2, PEN2, OXF2) (*subst.*)
       Seruants:] *Om.* KIT1, OXF2
2726   *Florizel, Perdita*] *Om.* ROWE1+
2727   *Cleo.*] *Om.* v1773

SPENCER (1940, p. 369): "Structurally, the only serious blemish [in the whole play] is the tedious preparation of the fifth act for its one great scene. For a while the play moves much too slowly, especially in Scene ii, the expository conversation of the walking [?] gentlemen." WEBSTER (1942, p. 275) agrees: "The end of Act IV and the first two scenes of Act V move at a snail's pace." PARRY (ed. 1982), however: "The act is really one 'movement', . . . and its keynote is wonder." As to the material, GODDARD (1951, pp. 657-8): "Shakespeare finds himself . . . with two heroines on his hands. [He] has prepared for several highly dramatic recognition scenes: one between the father and his lost daughter, another between the husband and his 'dead' wife, a third between the mother and the lost daughter, and a fourth between the other King and his prospective daughter-in-law, not to mention the reunion between the two Kings themselves which involves another type of recognition. . . . He sacrifices the daughter to the mother dramatically by narrating instead of presenting the reunion of daughter and father (and incidentally the meeting of the two Kings). . . . The highlight [is made] the scene in which Hermione . . . returns to life and is reunited with her husband and her daughter." LUDWIG (1974, p. 368): "When Camillo, Polixenes, and Perdita arrive at Leontes' court . . . , they are returning both to the place where we the audience first saw them and to the original identities which the play gave them, Camillo as friend and counselor to Leontes, Polixenes as 'brother' to him, and Perdita as his daughter. . . . Just before Florizel arrives, Paulina mentions that . . . Mamillius . . . would have 'paired Well' with [him]. . . . Leontes betroths Camillo to Paulina, thereby filling the gap created by Antigonus' death."

HIRST (1984, p. 32): "Shakespeare's art is not one of grafting, but of juxtaposition. The last act brings these oppositions together—father and child, old friend and enemy, Bohemia and Sicily, country and court, death and rebirth, suffering and reconciliation."

2727-32 **Sir . . . selfe**] HAMMERSMITH (1981, p. 172) views this soliloquy as "clearly a response to something Leontes has already said, which is probably represented in . . . 2733-9." MARTZ (1980, p. 129): *Saint-like, fault, redeem'd, penitence, trespas, euill,* and *forgiue* "provide a much stronger tinge of Christian reference than anything found earlier in the play. They begin to shift the balance away from things Greek or pagan toward things Christian." NOBLE (1935, pp. 81-2): "Inspired by the rendering of Ezekiel xviii. 21-2, prefixed to the daily offices. . . . It is difficult not to associate ['At . . . euill'] with 'I wil put al his wickednes out of my remembraunce sayeth the Lord' [Ezek. 18, before the Order for Morning Prayer in the 1559 Book of Common Prayer]." He compares *TGV* 5.4.79-81 (2205-7). R. M. FRYE (1963, p. 243), however: "Cleomenes' words are essentially un-Christian. Luther teaches that no one should claim 'to have sufficient contrition. Such an attitude is presumptuous and fabricated, for no one has sufficient contrition for his sin' [from

A Saint-like Sorrow: No fault could you make,
Which you haue not redeem'd; indeed pay'd downe
More penitence, then done trespas: At the last   2730
Doe, as the Heauens haue done; forget your euill,
With them, forgiue your selfe.
    Leo. Whilest I remember
Her, and her Vertues, I cannot forget
My blemishes in them, and so still thinke of   2735 (2l
The wrong I did my selfe: which was so much,
That Heire-lesse it hath made my Kingdome, and
Destroy'd the sweet'st Companion, that ere man
Bred his hopes out of, true.
    Paul. Too true (my Lord:)   2740
If one by one, you wedded all the World,

2735 of] *Om.* OXF1
2739-40 of, true. | *Paul.* Too true] of. | *Pau.* True, too true MTBY2 *conj.*, THEO1-
KNT2, DYCE1-BEV3 (−COL3); of: true− | *Paul.* Too true SING2; of. True? | PAULINA.
Too true DEY (1906) *conj.*, OXF2, BEV4

'The Sacrament of Penance']. According to Luther, such views are essentially heathen," and so, FRYE points out, is the world of *WT*. Yet NOBLE recognizes that "By
Penitence th'Eternalls wrath's appeas'd" (*TGV* 5.4.81 [2207]), and, as ROWSE (1963,
p. 131) says, the "doctrine of the absolute value of repentance, and the moral obligation to accept the repentant, appears again and again in the plays." Hence WALLER
(1970, p. 137): "Leontes' renewed happiness is based on an inner change of life, and
it is a process that has both needed and wasted sixteen years." On a more worldly
note, J. SMITH (1974, p. 130): "Against any such project [as Cleomines's] . . . Paulina
stoutly protests, and so appears to sing yet another tune. By now however she is
laying a plot of her own, for a purpose to be revealed at the close of Act V." On one
level, she cannot be plotting. As she points out (2772-3), Leontes cannot have an
heir until the lost child be found, and she cannot know if or when that will occur.
    2728 **fault . . . make**] PARRY (ed. 1982): "There is not a single fault which you
even *might* have committed." For the construction, see 151 and 1407.
    2729-30 **pay'd . . . trespas**] *OED* (Pay, *v.*[1] 5b): "*Pay down*: to lay down money
in payment" (7a, citing this line): "To give, render (something that is owed . . .).""
PARRY (ed. 1982): "You have done more penance than is required by your offences."
    2730 **penitence**] SCHMIDT (1875): "Repentance" (*OED* 2). SCHANZER (ed. 1969):
"Penance" (1). *OED* comments, however, that sense 1 usually includes sense 2. VAN
DAM (1900, p. 67): Pronounced *pen'tence*.
    At the last] BOORMAN (ed. 1964): "Now at last."
    2731-2 **forget . . . selfe**] DANBY (1952, p. 89): Helicanus tells Pericles "To
beare with patience such griefes as you your selfe doe lay vpon your selfe" (*Per.*
1.2.65-6 [290-1]).
    2731 **euill**] MAXWELL (ed. 1969): "Sin."
    2732 **With them**] DEIGHTON (ed. 1889): "Like them."
    2733-49 **Whilest . . . seldome**] GRIFFITH (1775, p. 110): "Leontes manifests
the same humiliation and contrition for his crime, that he did before [e.g., at 1403–

5]: but as an interval of sixteen years, spent in sorrow and repentance, had passed between these two æras, he . . . shews an uneasiness at the reproach, and entreats to be relieved from it for the future; but in a manner . . . gentle and submissive." LUDWIG (1974, p. 397), similarly: "His worthiness for forgiveness is defined precisely by his contrary, opposite insistence that he is not worthy and will never be worthy of being forgiven." HOROWITZ (1965, pp. 75-7), comparing "When hee shall heare she died vpon his words, Th Idæa of her life shall sweetly creepe, Into his study of imagination" (*Ado* 4.1.223-5 [1886-8]): "The double knowledge that this study of imagination is designed to bring, self-knowledge and knowledge of what's lost, is . . . the content of Leontes' exercise. . . . [His] wintry contemplation is more than a mere study, however. It is a penance, a spiritual exercise that tempers his being, disciplines his hot summer blood, purges the pitiless spirit that committed his child to destruction and severed all the lifelines of his 'gracious' queen, and it looks towards a greater birth." PARTRIDGE (1982, p. 4): "Leontes speaks gracious verse, to mark his release from the earlier incoherent passion."

2735 **My . . . them**] DEIGHTON (ed. 1889): "My faults in regard to them." See ABBOTT §162.

2737 **Heire-lesse . . . Kingdome**] TINKLER (1937, p. 347): "The prince becomes almost a projection of the father [quotes 205-6] and through him the 'wrong' of Leontes makes of the kingdom a Waste Land." See n. 2757-61.

2738-9 **ere . . . of**] BETHELL (ed. 1956): "Ever gave man hopes for a happy future." DEIGHTON (ed. 1889) thinks *bred* not used primarily of the begetting of children, "though there may be an allusion to the word [*Heire-lesse*, 2738]." BOORMAN (ed. 1964), on the contrary: "With the suggestion of children as the 'hopes' of a father."

2739-40 **of, true. | Paul. Too**] CALDECOTT (MS 1813-33), glossing *true* as "with truth or truly; or it may be, being true, in respect of her being a pattern of fidelity," notes that the word is reiterated "with something of a new modification of its meaning" in 2879. COLLIER (ed. 1842): "Leontes, in grief and remorse, states a fact, and adds mournfully 'true'; to which Paulina naturally adds that it is 'too true.'" Eds. who adopt THIRLBY's emendation probably agree with HALLIWELL (ed. 1859) that F is "extremely forced and unnatural." PORTER & CLARKE (ed. 1908), however: "The one verb most needed to sum up with, at this dramatic juncture, is . . . that out of her he had *bred . . . true*. For this declaration is Perdita's patent of good fortune." HAMMERSMITH (1981, pp. 172-3), differently: "Leontes, speaking directly to Cleomenes (and by no means ruefully), stops him, perhaps by pointing a finger as well, as he firmly says, 'true'—meaning 'I'll hear no more to the contrary'. Paulina, seeing that Cleomenes is disposed to press his point with some spirit, then interrupts . . . with her further elaboration of the point (2740-4). . . . Leontes' self-affirming 'true' is but a clipped form of . . . 'I say <or speak, or tell (you)> true'."

2740-4 **Too . . . vnparallell'd**] FURNESS (ed. 1898): "Paulina had to contend, single-handed, against the influence of the whole court, and, peradventure, for aught she knew, against the king's own secret inclinations. Not only must Leontes be hindered from marrying again, but his repentance must be kept free from the influence of 'time's strong hours', and the past be kept ever-present to him,—to effect this, no speech can be too cutting, and no stab go too deep." MELCHIORI (1960, p. 63): "Leontes' mourning for his dead wife has become a habit, needing the constant stimulation of Paulina to keep it alive." BAMBER (1982, p. 179) also finds something mechanical: "Leontes [who might have listened to Cleomenes] chooses to listen instead to Paulina, who keeps open a wound that might have healed. And Paulina at this point is much less compelling than she is both earlier and later in the play. Her sharpness toward Leontes has become routine and her praises of Hermione are both tired and excessive. . . . Cleomenes speaks for mental health: surely the time for self-forgiveness has come. Paulina urges Leontes to hang on to his desire beyond all reason." But that surely is the point; the miracles wrought by romance require dedication beyond all

Or from the All that are, tooke something good,
To make a perfect Woman; she you kill'd,
Would be vnparallell'd.
    Leo. I thinke so. Kill'd?   2745
She I kill'd? I did so: but thou strik'st me
Sorely, to say I did: it is as bitter
Vpon thy Tongue, as in my Thought. Now, good now,
Say so but seldome.
    Cleo. Not at all, good Lady: 2750
You might haue spoken a thousand things, that would
Haue done the time more benefit, and grac'd
Your kindnesse better.
    Paul. You are one of those
Would haue him wed againe.   2755
    Dio. If you would not so,
You pitty not the State, nor the Remembrance
Of his most Soueraigne Name: Consider little,
What Dangers, by his Highnesse faile of Issue,
May drop vpon his Kingdome, and deuoure   2760
Incertaine lookers on. What were more holy,

2746 She] Kill'd? she mTBY2 *conj.,* THEOBALD (1729) *conj. in* NICHOLS (1817, 2: 366), THEO1-JOHN2 (−HAN), DYCE2, HUD2
    2748 thy] my CAM1
        good_∧] ~ , DYCE2 (*errata*), WH2, NLSN
    2751 spoken] spoke POPE1-RANN, DYCE2, HUD2, OXF2
    2754 one] none F4
    2756 so] *Om.* HAN
    2758 Name] dame v1803-SING1, KNT1 (*text;* name *in* Postscript, 6:viii), KNT3

---

reason. PARTRIDGE (1982, p. 4): "Paulina insists that a second wife should possess all the noble qualities of the first; and this should suggest that she has something to disclose." If so, the suggestion fails to reach Leontes.
    2742-3 **from . . . Woman**] KITTREDGE & RIBNER (ed. 1967): "Took one good quality from each of the women in the world and combined them all in one perfect woman." "This is a favorite thought," JOHNSON (ed. 1765) remarks, citing *AYL* 3.2.157-8 (1347-8) and *Tmp.* 3.1.6-8 (1290-2). SULLIVAN (in GUAZZO, 1925, 1: xxxviii): Indebted to GUAZZO. See n. 498-505, however, for another effort to link Sh. and this Italian author. From Sh. and other writers, PAFFORD (ed. 1963) adds a half-dozen more expressions of the same idea.
    2746 **strik'st**] For other occurrences of *strike,* see n. 283.
    2747 **Sorely**] OED (*adv.* 2, citing this line): "Severely."
    to say] ABBOTT (§356): "In saying." For the indefinite or gerundial use of the infinitive, see n. 704 and cf. 886, 1560, and 2853.
    as bitter] PARRY (ed. 1982), wrongly: "As bitter to my taste." Leontes refers to the bitterness of Paulina's "kill'd."
    2748 **Now, good now**] WHITE (ed. 1857) compares *Tmp.* 1.1.15 (23), where *good* alone as an appellative means "good fellow." OED (Good now, citing this line),

however: "An interjectional expression denoting acquiescence, entreaty, expostulation, or surprise." ABBOTT (§13) illustrates this usage by citing *Ham.* 1.1.70 (86), but since neither Q2 nor F punctuates that reading, it may be interpreted either way. For *WT*, most eds. follow *OED* and punctuate after *good now*, including HERFORD (ed. 1916-), who glosses "a persuasive mode of address, often accompanying a merely courteous request." COLLINS (ed. 1904-24?), differently: *Good* "probably qualifies *now* for emphasis, as in *Hamlet*, I.i.70 [86]. . . . It is also possible to take it as a vocative, 'good lady.'" WRIGHT & LAMAR (ed. 1966): "If you will be so good now," but HERFORD seems to be right that the words do not have a specific meaning. ORGEL (ed. 1996) finds another instance in *Ant.* 1.3.78 (394).

2750 **Not at all**] HUNTER (ed. 1872): "Do not say it at all."

2752 **done . . . benefit**] PIERCE (ed. 1918): "Suited the occasion better." BETHELL (ed. 1956): "Been more valuable at this time."

grac'd] SCHMIDT (1874): "To set off . . . to exalt" (*OED, v.* 4). MAXWELL (ed. 1956): "Befitted."

2754-5 **those Would**] For the omission of the relative, see n. 2191.

2756-66 **If . . . to't?**] TRAVERSI (1955, p. 168): "For Dion Leontes is a king as well as a husband and his duty to the state justifies a line of conduct which, as an individual, he would not necessarily be required to follow."

2757-61 **You . . . on**] TINKLER (1937, p. 346): "As a personal, tragic figure he [Leontes] does not impress: it is only when one becomes aware of the immense importance of his role for the effect on, the part played in, other people, that he becomes interesting." See n. 2737. TINKLER adds, "The burden of Scapegoat and Tragic Hero is shifted from Leontes to his son," a point that has only formal significance, if any. SANDERS (1987, p. 106): "This rather masculine version of moral responsibility, in which personal preference and emotional fitness must give way to the common good, is encountered head on by Paulina's antithetical female version [2767-8 'There . . . gone:)']."

2757 **pitty . . . Remembrance**] FURNESS (ed. 1898): "A zeugma, 'You pity not the state, nor [regard] the remembrance,' etc."

pitty] Feel compassion for (*OED, v.* 1).

2757-8 **Remembrance . . . Name**] COLLIER (ed. 1842): I.e., "the preservation of the *name* of Leontes by marrying again, and having issue to succeed to the throne." BETHELL (ed. 1956): Cf. "Royalties repayre" (2763). FURNESS (ed. 1898): Ed. 1803's "dame," probably a typographical error, stood for nearly 40 years before KNIGHT corrected it.

2758 **Consider little**] FURNESS (ed. 1898): "You little consider."

2759 **Dangers . . . Issue**] HARRISON (ed. 1947) suggests an allusion to "the perpetual anxiety throughout Queen Elizabeth's reign that chaos would follow at her death because there was no certain heir to the throne."

faile of Issue] BOORMAN (ed. 1964): "Lack of an heir." See n. 1102 and, for the part of speech, n. 2931.

2760 **drop . . . deuoure**] DEIGHTON (ed. 1889): "Like a pestilence." Like a bird of prey seems more likely.

2761 **Incertaine lookers on**] Variously interpreted. CAPELL (1783, 2.4:179): Innocent persons uncertain of the rightful heir "in a contest about succession." CALDECOTT (MS 1813-33), however, interprets *Incertain* as "unadvised & unprepared"; SCHMIDT (1874), as "indifferent, not taking measures to prevent the calamity"; and NEILSON & HILL (ed. 1942), as "wavering." KNOWLES (privately): "In doubt, troubled, apprehensive about the event." *OED* (citing this line) agrees with CAPELL on "uncertain" (cf. 1354). For the phrase, HERFORD (ed. 1904): "Irresolute counsellors who have foreseen the danger without guarding against it"; PORTER & CLARKE (ed. 1908): "Weak-kneed subjects always ready . . . to be the prey of their own fears"; PAFFORD (ed. 1963): "Those needing guidance and rule."

Then to reioyce the former Queene is well?
What holyer, then for Royalties repayre,
For present comfort, and for future good,
To blesse the Bed of Maiestie againe   2765
With a sweet Fellow to't?
    Paul. There is none worthy,
(Respecting her that's gone:) besides the Gods
Will haue fulfill'd their secret purposes:
For ha's not the Diuine *Apollo* said?   2770
Is't not the tenor of his Oracle,
That King *Leontes* shall not haue an Heire,
Till his lost Child be found? Which, that it shall,
Is all as monstrous to our humane reason,
As my *Antigonus* to breake his Graue,   2775
And come againe to me: who, on my life,
Did perish with the Infant. 'Tis your councell,
My Lord should to the Heauens be contrary,
Oppose against their wills. Care not for Issue,

2762-3 Then . . . then] Than . . . than F4+
2762 Queene is well?] Queen? This will. WARBURTON *conj. in* HAN2, HAN, WARB,
CAP
    2773 Which, . . . shall,] ~ ∧ . . . ~ ∧ DYCE, CAM1, HUD2-NLSN, KIT1, ALEX,
PEL1, PEN2, BEV3+; ~ ∧ . . . ~ , SIS, CLN2, SIG, EVNS
    2779 *To the King.* [*before* Care] THEO1+ (*subst.*)

2761-2 **What . . . well?**] CHARLTON (ed. 1916): "This mention of the rejoicing
that might be if the queen were alive, alludes to such an event as entirely suppositious.
Still, the mere mention helps to create the suitable atmosphere." CHARLTON misses
the point, however; see the next n.
    2762 **is well**] MALONE (1780, 1:146): "At rest; dead." HENLEY (in STEEVENS, ed.
1793) thinks the expression was adopted from 2 Kings 4:26. *Well*, however, is the
word of the KING JAMES (1611) rather than the Geneva version, and the expression
appears in *Rom.* 4.5.76 (2656), written in 1594-5. Sh. uses the euphemism often—
e.g., *Ant.* 2.5.33 (1064), *Mac.* 4.3.179 (2019), *2H4* 5.2.3 (2882)—and it is proverbial
(TILLEY H347).
    2763-4 **Royalties . . . good**] JOHNSON (1755, Repair): "Restoration." CAPELL
(1783, 2.4:179-80): "Repair [of] the broken succession." He thinks the "present
comfort" is the king's and the "future good" is the state's, but the terms may as
readily be general. KITTREDGE & RIBNER (ed. 1967), however: "Restoration of the
King to health." BOORMAN (ed. 1964): "Someone whom the King can frequent" and
"something for the King's well-being." CAPELL is surely right in the main.
    2767-80 **There . . . Heire**] Although he cites 3337-40, SEMON (1974, p. 97)
believes that Paulina "has not understood the oracle." But see n. 3337-40. PETERSON
(*Time*, 1973, p. 192): "*Paulina*'s refutation draws together the acts of remembering
Hermione and of obeying the oracle. The latter follows as a consequence of the
former. To forget Hermione and marry is to oppose the will of the gods. To remember
is to obey and . . . to trust that the heavens will provide the throne with an heir."

2768 **Respecting**] MINSHEU (1617, Respect): See "Regard, Consideration," words that may mean "look (back) at" or "think carefully about." Some eds. choose one, some the other, some both. COLLINS (ed. 1904-24?): "In comparison with."

2768-77 **besides . . . Infant**] CHARLTON (ed. 1916): "The threads of the plot are being drawn together. One thing now mentioned as monstrous to human reason we . . . know to be about to be revealed as fact: and so we are gradually being prepared to accept an even greater monstrosity of reason." ASP (1978, p. 155): "She refutes them by her steadfast belief in the will of the gods. . . . Paulina reinforces [their] belief in the transcendent meaning of events, i.e., that action is . . . a pattern of meaningful occurrences ordained by the benevolent decrees of divine reason."

2768-9 **Gods . . . secret purposes**] PAFFORD (ed. 1963): "Will see to it that their secret purposes are fulfilled." WALLER (1970, p. 137): "Terms used by Shakespeare to describe a mysterious dimension of human experience; not forces influencing men from outside but a determining pressure acting from within the very conditions of being human." MACKINNON (1988, pp. 150-1): "Obedience to the Oracle is the same as obedience to whatever happens, an acceptance of the world. What Paulina counsels Leontes against is the renewed exercise of the will."

2769 **Will . . . purposes**] HUNTER (ed. 1872): "Will have their secret purposes to be fulfilled." BETHELL (ed. 1956): *Will* = "must." CARRINGTON (1956): *Will* = "have determined to." BOORMAN (ed. 1964): *Will* = "demand."

2771 **tenor**] MINSHEU (1617): "Effect, or purport." KITTREDGE & RIBNER (ed. 1967): "Intent, meaning."

2772-3 **King . . . found?**] THIRLBY (MS 1733-47?): See 1315-16.

2773 **Till**] ALMASY (1981, p. 126): "She moves beyond grief to hope in believing the Oracle offers a promise that Perdita will be found. . . . Significantly she has changed the wording of the Oracle" from *if* to *till*.

2773-9 **Which . . . wills**] MIKO (1989, p. 267): "Paulina doesn't know anything about Antigonus's death or the fate of Perdita, oracles are notoriously ambiguous, and the heavens' will is hardly obvious to anyone. Her human reason isn't, in itself, much more impressive than Leontes' in Act I. Of course, she has other (real) reasons to talk this way, as she soon begins to hint."

2773-6 **Which . . . me**] PYLE (1969, p. 103): "The suggestion that a dead man should return from the grave . . . is of obvious dramatic importance; and it is supported by the hypothesis . . . that Hermione herself might appear as a ghost [2793-4, 2801-5, 2822-4]."

2773 **Which**] COLLINS (ed. 1904-24?): "Referring to the words *be found*. It is possible to keep the comma of the Folio after *which*, thus making *which* refer to the whole sentence, with *that it shall* as an explanatory parenthesis."

2774 **monstrous**] RANN (ed. 1787): "Impossible." MAXWELL (ed. 1956): "Incredible." BETHELL (ed. 1956): "Unnatural."

humane] For the spelling, see n. 1203.

2775 **my . . . breake**] For the construction, see n. 1405.

2777-9 **'Tis . . . wills**] PYLE (1969, p. 102): "This argument is unanswerable. We remember what happened when Leontes opposed the heavens' wills [at 1321-2]." For these lines as evidence of Sh.'s religious views, see n. 324-8.

2778 **contrary**] SCHMIDT (1874): "Adverse." He accents *contráry*, as does PAFFORD (ed. 1963), who observes that the word is similarly accented in *Tim.* 4.3.145 (1759). ROLFE (ed. 1879), however, prefers *cóntrary*, as in 478 and 831.

2779 **Oppose against**] JERVIS (1868): "Resist." The same redundancy is found in *Tim.* 3.4.79 (1211), *Lr.* 4.2.74 (2318) and 4.7.31 (2783), and elsewhere in Sh.

2779-81 **Care . . . Worthiest**] PAFFORD (ed. 1963) believes Sh. here reminds his audiences "that although many representations had been made to Elizabeth that she should marry, she . . . died without an heir, but . . . there had been a happy succession to the throne."

The Crowne will find an Heire. Great *Alexander*   2780
Left his to th' Worthiest: so his Successor
Was like to be the best.
    Leo. Good *Paulina*,
Who hast the memorie of *Hermione*
I know in honor: O, that euer I   2785
Had squar'd me to thy councell: then, euen now,
I might haue look'd vpon my Queenes full eyes,
Haue taken Treasure from her Lippes.
    Paul. And left them
More rich, for what they yeelded.   2790
    Leo. Thou speak'st truth:
No more such Wiues, therefore no Wife: one worse,

2783 Good] Ah! good HAN; Thou good CAP, HUD2; My good KEIGHTLEY *conj. in*
CAM1, KTLY

2780 **The . . . Heire**] TENNENHOUSE (1986, p. 183): "Shakespeare prevents Perdita's return from being understood simply as a daughter's reunion with her natural
father when, in the most explicit terms possible, he represents Perdita and Leontes
in terms of the crown and its heir." See n. 1315. The relationship is reiterated in 3039,
and in 3192 the "Heires" are Perdita, heiress to the Sicilian crown, and Florizel, heir
to that of Bohemia.
    2780-2 **Great . . . best**] THOMSON (1952, p. 133): "Evidently from Justin [*His-
tory*], 12.15. 'cum deficere eum amici viderent, quaerunt, quem imperii faciat here-
dem: respondit, Dignissimum [When his friends saw that his strength was leaving
him, they asked whom he made heir of his authority, he answered "The worthiest."
Trans. THOMSON].'" PAFFORD (ed. 1963), however, finds similar words in Quintus
Curtius, *The Acts of . . . Alexander. Translated . . . by Iohn Brende* (1602, ff. 295,
300°), as well as in Arrian, *Anabasis of Alexander* (7:26), a work apparently not
translated into English by 1611. "This particular passage can be taken as a compliment
to [King] James. . . . But perhaps [it] merely echoes the sentiment in Quintus Curtius."
    2781 **Successor**] SCHANZER (ed. 1969): *Súccessor*.
    2783-2809 **Good . . . Paulina**] MARSH (1962; 1980, p. 155): "For Leontes, the
calmness and control of whose utterance shows how far he has progressed in command of himself since the death of Hermione, this is in a sense a test. To the best of
his knowledge Hermione is dead." Leontes's vision of his haunting by Hermione,
sainted yet soul-vexed, and his murder of any new wife, seem far from controlled,
however.
    2785-90 **O . . . yeelded**] DUSINBERRE (1975, pp. 120-1) uses these lines to
argue that Sh. "freed himself from the concept of sex in marriage as an act of power
and possession. . . . The generosity of sexual love in marriage permeates the last
plays. . . . If sex has nothing to do with property, then there is no loss involved in
sexual love."
    2786 **squar'd me to**] Followed. See n. 1483.
    2787 **full eyes**] CALDECOTT (MS 1813-33): "Matronlike, dignified, as those of
Juno, the Queen of the Gods." SCHMIDT (1874): "Not sunk, hollow, and dim, but

lively and bright." WRIGHT & LAMAR (ed. 1966): "I.e., instead of imagining them closed in death." Probably, however, "large, . . . protuberant" (*OED, a.* 10, which quotes "a full black Eye" from the year 1688). PORTER & CLARKE (ed. 1908) alone suggest that Leontes means "look'd full in the eyes of my Queen."

2788 **Treasure**] PARRY (ed. 1982): "I.e. the sweetness (of her kiss)."

2790 **More . . . yeelded**] CALDECOTT (MS 1813–33): "As having afforded additional proof of true conjugal affection."

2791 **Thou speak'st truth**] DEIGHTON (ed. 1889): "In what she said in [2767–82]."

2792 **No . . . Wiues**] DEIGHTON (ed. 1889): "There are no more wives like her to be found."

2792–6 **one . . . me?**] See the textual notes. HENLEY (in STEEVENS, ed. 1793) believes "the sense [of the lines] to be sufficiently clear" if a second *appear* is understood, presumably before "Soule-vext" (2795). The CLARKES (ed. 1865): "The word 'appear', while forming part of the parenthesis, has the effect of being understood in conjunction with the previous and succeeding context; and though not absolutely being one of the verbs to which 'sainted spirit' is the nominative, yet, from its position, giving that impression to hearers of the whole sentence." Cf. n. 359–65. SPENCE (1890) concurs: *appeare* "must be understood as repeated, thus:— . . . (Where we offenders now appear) *appear* soul-vext." If so, lines 2792–6 may be paraphrased: "Using a worse wife better than Hermione would make Hermione's sainted spirit enter her body again, and on this stage (the here and now) where we who have offended (in general and against her in particular) appear, being angered to her very soul, begin to remonstrate: 'Why is this insult offered to me?'" Thus, although the passage is strained, it is not impossible as it stands, but few eds. have been satisfied with it. One of these is CHARLTON (ed. 1916), who nevertheless finds a "somewhat harsh ellipsis of one occurrence" of *appear*.

THEOBALD (ed. 1733), however, explaining his emendation *offend Her*: "The [F] Grammar is defective. . . . The King [should] say, that *Paulina* and He offended his dead Wife's Ghost with the Subject of a second Match; rather than in general Terms to call themselves *Offenders, Sinners*." THIRLBY (MS 1733–47?) objects: "He had said nothing for it & Paulina is strong against it." KNIGHT (ed. 1841): Making "Where . . . now" the parenthesis causes "Spirit" to become the subject of "appeare." An understood *are* follows "we."

WILSON (ed. 1931), who adopts DELIUS's reading, asserts that "'move' might very easily be misread as 'nowe' in Shakespeare's hand." The error apparently never occurred; the word *now* is emended in no other Shn. texts. PAFFORD (ed. 1963) prefers HEATH's emendation, which "seems to arise naturally from the preceding lines and requires little alteration to the text. Leontes is saying that it would indeed be a crime to take a new wife and that if he did so (were he such an offender) it would be enough to make Hermione's spirit appear and reproach him." TAYLOR explains his emendation (in WELLS & TAYLOR, 1987): "F. 'Morne' (i.e. 'mourne') could be misread 'nowe'; the usage is paralleled in *Sir Thomas More* [Add. II.D.136–7 in the Oxford Original-Sp. ed. 1987], 'the king . . . is clement yf thoffendor moorne'. 'Morne' links offenders with 'stage' as 'scaffold' (*OED*, sb. 4e); the image 'relates to the final scene, when Leontes is taken to a new wife, whom he *will* use better, at which point Hermione *does* again possess her corpse, and appear on a *stage* (not only the theatrical one, but a step or raised platform on which the 'statue' appears), where Leontes the offender *mourns* (the sight of the statue is *piercing to* his soul, [3225])." WELLS continues, "As the punctuation is almost certainly Crane's, there is no difficulty in making 'spirit', rather than 'Offendors', the antecedent of 'appeare.'" There may be no difficulty about that, but while "Moone" appears for *morn(e)* in *Tit.* 2.2.1 (701) and "morning" for *mourning* (a spelling variant), no form of *mourn* appears as "now(e)." ORGEL (ed. 1996): "The problem is not grammatical, it is why Leontes

485

And better vs'd, would make her Sainted Spirit
Againe possesse her Corps, and on this Stage
(Where we Offendors now appeare) Soule-vext,   2795
And begin, why to me?
    Paul. Had she such power,
She had iust such cause.
    Leo. She had, and would incense me
To murther her I marryed.   2800
    Paul. I should so: (2B
Were I the Ghost that walk'd, Il'd bid you marke
Her eye, and tell me for what dull part in't
You chose her: then Il'd shrieke, that euen your eares
Should rift to heare me, and the words that follow'd,   2805
Should be, Remember mine.
    Leo. Starres, Starres,

2795 (Where . . . appeare) Soule-vext,] (Where we offendors now appear) Soul-
vext. F3; (Where we offend Her now) appear soul-vext, mTBY2 *conj.*, THEOBALD
(1729) *conj. in* NICHOLS (1817, 2:366), THEO, WARB, JOHN, v1773-v1785, DYCE, KTLY,
COL4, HUD2, BUL, ALEX; (Where we offended anew) appear soul-vext, HAN; (Were we
offenders now) appear soul-vext, HEATH (1765, pp. 218-19) *conj.*, RANN, ARD2;
(Where we offenders now,) appear, soul-vexed, KNT, WH1, STAU, DEL, CAM1, KIT1,
PEL1, EVNS; Where we're offenders now, appear soul-vex'd, MITFORD (1844, p. 128)
conj., GLO, WH2-OXF1, BEV; Where we offenders move, appear soul-vex'd, mTBY3 *and*
DEL2 *conj.*, ARD1, CAM3, PEN2; Where we offend as now, appear soul-vexed, SIS;
Where we offenders mourn, appear soul-vexed OXF2
  2796 And . . . me] Begin, *And why to me* mLONG *conj.*, CAP, MAL-SING1, COL1-
SING2, COL3, HAL, NLSN, CLN2; And begin, *why? to me* MASON (1785, p. 137) *conj.*,
RANN
       me?∧] ~ ; F2, F3; ~ . F4; ~ ?— THEO, WARB, JOHN, v1773, v1778, NLSN;
~ ? . . . KTLY; ~ —? KIT1, N&H, EVNS; ~ — ALEX
  2798 such] *Om.* F3-CAP (−THEO1, THEO2), v1785, RANN, MAL+ (−RID)
  2802 walk'd] wak'd ROWE2, ROWE3
  2803 for] of RID
  2806-7 *One verse line* mCAP2, v1793+
  2807 Starres, Starres] Stars, very stars HAN, CAP v1793-v1813

---

should refer to himself, his court, and especially Paulina, as 'offenders'. If the Folio
reading is correct, this may be a simple acknowledgement that, in contrast with the
saintliness of Hermione's spirit, we are all sinners. Alternatively, it may imply that we
offend her memory by merely discussing the question of remarriage. Or it may express
Leontes' conviction that our continued life constitutes a continuing affront to her
offended spirit. The argument against the Folio reading, that Hermione's spirit would
not take offence since the idea of remarriage is being rejected, and that Paulina is in
any case not at fault, is scarcely relevant: this is a play in which reproach is so generalized that every major character is at some point declared criminally guilty of something. . . . There is, in short, no reason to emend."

Advocating *why? to me*, MASON (1785, p. 137): "To call me to account." MALONE (ed. 1790): "Why to me *did you prefer one less worthy*, Leontes insinuates would be the purport of Hermione's speech." BOSWELL (ed. 1821): "Why such treatment to me? when a worse wife is better used." Most eds. gloss similarly—MOORMAN (ed. 1912), for example, "[why] this humiliation?"

WRIGHT (ed. 1891): "Ben Jonson begins his Execration upon Vulcan with the words 'And why to me this?', which may perhaps be a reminiscence of the present passage."

2794 **possesse**] KITTREDGE & RIBNER (ed. 1967): "Take possession of (as a ghost)."

Corps] See n. 1946-7 for several meanings of *corps*. MAXWELL (1956, p. 55): According to Renaissance theorists, to reappear "a departed spirit . . . would assume a body of air. The one thing that no theorists admitted was that the [dead] man's very body, animated by his very soul, could return from the grave. Yet nothing less than that will do for Leontes here." MAXWELL further notices that when the possibility of Antigonus's return to life is mentioned, he will "breake his Graue" (2775) and that "when Hermione moves, one must at least entertain the notion of a literal rising from the dead." That the spirit could repossess the body was a folk belief which Sh. made use of. PAFFORD (ed. 1963, p. 138 n.) holds that the ghost of Hamlet's father is incorporeal, but MAXWELL notes that Hamlet addresses him as "dead corse" (3.3.52 [637]).

2796 **why to me?**] PORTER & CLARKE (ed. 1908): The words suggest "the open-mouthed look of reproach, dumb, but eloquent."

2797 **Had . . . power**] PORTER & CLARKE (ed. 1908): "That is, if souls have power to visit earth as ghosts. This reflects, besides, Paulina's own secret consciousness that Hermione has not such power, because she is not yet dead."

2798 **such**] In favor of F3's omission, CAPELL (1783, 2.4:180) argues that this word was erroneously carried down from 2797. CALDECOTT (MS 1813-33), retaining it: "Exactly *that* cause . . . that very ground for reappearing." CLARKE (in FURNIVALL, ed. 1908), similarly: "Even such."

2799-2800 **She . . . marryed**] ABRAMS (1986, p. 159): "If ever he were to marry, Leontes fantasizes, Hermione's spirit would 'possess her corpse' [2794] and return to the world seeking explanations; the ghost, possessing him [to commit this murder]. This new phase of madness then . . . inverts his earlier jealousy *of* Hermione."

2799 **had**] BOORMAN (ed. 1964): "I.e. would have."

incense] MINSHEU (1617): "Moue . . . Prouoke."

2801 **should so**] BEVINGTON (ed. 1992): "Would similarly incite you."

2803 **tell . . . part**] For parallel phrasing, PAFFORD (ed. 1963) compares *Ado* 5.2.60-5 (2478-83).

dull] SCHMIDT (1874, 7): "Dim, clouded," though (2) "spiritless, lifeless" also seem possible. KITTREDGE & RIBNER (ed. 1967): "Unattractive." DEIGHTON (ed. 1889): "Compared to mine."

2804 **that**] So that. See n. 17.

2805 **rift**] JOHNSON (1755): "To cleave; to split" (*OED*, $v.^1$ 1, citing this line).

2806 **Remember mine**] DEIGHTON (ed. 1889): "*I.e.* my eye." PAFFORD (ed. 1963): "Recalls the Ghost's exit words 'Remember me' in *Ham*. [1.5.91 (776)]." BROOKS (in PAFFORD, ed. 1963): "Paulina's comparison of the first wife with any second has resemblance with Hamlet's indignant comparison of Gertrude's first husband with her second ('Hyperion to a satyr' [1.2.140 (323)])."

2807 **Starres, Starres**] The CLARKES (1879, p. 424): Iteration used "to express passionate regret and anguish." For other uses, see 75, 1323, 1387, 1545, and 1958.

And all eyes else, dead coales: feare thou no Wife;
Ile haue no Wife, *Paulina.*
   Paul. Will you sweare   2810
Neuer to marry, but by my free leaue?
   Leo. Neuer (*Paulina*) so be bless'd my Spirit.
   Paul. Then good my Lords, beare witnesse to his Oath.
   Cleo. You tempt him ouer-much.
   Paul. Vnlesse another,   ·   2815
As like *Hermione*, as is her Picture,
Affront his eye.
   Cleo. Good Madame, I haue done.
   Paul. Yet if my Lord will marry: if you will, Sir;
No remedie but you will: Giue me the Office   2820
To chuse you a Queene: she shall not be so young
As was your former, but she shall be such
As (walk'd your first Queenes Ghost) it should take ioy
To see her in your armes.
   Leo. My true *Paulina*,   2825
We shall not marry, till thou bidst vs.

2818–19 Good . . . Yet] Good madam, — | *Pau*. I have done. | Yet mTBY2 *conj.*,
CAP, RANN, MAL-v1821, SING, DYCE, STAU-KTLY, DEL4+ (−COL4, OXF2)
    2818 I] pray ROWE1-JOHN2, v1773
    2819 Sir] Sirs F4; *om.* KNT
    2821 you a] your mTBY4 *conj.*, HUD2 (*attrib. to* WALKER), OXF2

    2808 **all eyes else**] KITTREDGE & RIBNER (ed. 1967): "All other eyes."
    coales] *OED* (*sb.* 2, citing this line): "Charred remnant."
    feare . . . Wife] CHARLTON (ed. 1916): "Paulina's insistence on Leontes'
swearing not to marry again assures us of one moral change in Leontes' spiritual
regeneration by showing us his susceptibility to persuasion and argument . . . , and,
moreover, it focuses attention on Paulina and her mysterious actions and motives."
    2810–11 **Will . . . leaue**] SNIDER (c. 1890, p. 495): "Here begins the little in-
trigue of this part [of *WT*], which will be solved by the reappearance of Hermione."
LAWLOR (1962, p. 102): "The first indication that this settled course [of mourning]
will have an end." HELLENGA (1976, p. 16): "In obtaining from Leontes a promise
never to marry without her consent she is not testing him, or demonstrating to the
audience that he is morally fit — he has already been certified — but manoeuvering
him into position, ensuring the success of the cosmic plan." See p. 739.
    2811 **free**] SCHMIDT (1874): "Unconstrained." For other adjectival senses, see nn.
185, 355, 812, 871, 2413.
    2813 **good my Lords**] For the transposition, see n. 390.
    2814 **tempt**] SCHMIDT (1875): "Provoke." MAXWELL (ed. 1956): "Urge." BETHELL
(ed. 1956): "Try, test."
    ouer-much] Cf. "ouer-fond" (3125).
    2816 **Picture**] The picture of Hermione does "affront" Leontes (see next n.), and
it is a perfect likeness. See 3181 and 3203–12.

2817 **Affront**] MINSHEU (1617): "Come face to face . . . Incounter." HANMER (ed. 1743–4, 6:glos.) adds "confront." PORTER & CLARKE (ed. c. 1903): "Come before." Sh. uses *affront* on three other occasions, always in this sense. *Confront* is somewhat more frequent.

2818–19 **Good . . . Yet**] Defending F against THIRLBY's alteration, KNIGHT (ed. 1841): "The vehemence of Paulina overbears the interruption of Cleomenes, and he says, 'I have done.'" She would not say these words because "she is evidently going on, perfectly regardless of any opposition." SINGER (ed. 1856) in favor of reassigning "I haue done": "Paulina gives way to his [Cleomenes's] expostulation, and *has done* with the point she was urging; she only continues speaking to hint a possible concession." DYCE (ed. 1857) agrees, because of another supposed misassignment; at 2739–40 "a word, which undoubtedly belongs to Paulina, is in the folio made a portion of the preceding speech." The word ("true") does not quite undoubtedly belong to her, however; see the textual note. HAMMERSMITH (1981, pp. 173–4): "What Capell [or THIRLBY] and those who follow him ignore . . . is the obvious fact that Cleomenes so clearly *does* have done—he never speaks again in the play—while Paulina so equally plainly does *not* have done. . . . The comma after 'Madame' is equivalent to a dash." WELLS (in WELLS & TAYLOR, 1987), who follows F, replies to SINGER's point: "Paulina's concession from a position of strength [achieved by Cleomenes's capitulation] is no less effective [than her retreating with 'I haue done'], and is consistent with the comedy in her presentation." The comedy perhaps lies in the sudden precariousness of her 16-year plan and in the vigor of her defense of it.

2819–29 **Yet . . . then**] LLOYD (in SINGER, ed. 1856, 4:128–9): "Perhaps there is a slight hint in the earlier acts [quotes 'if . . . eye,' 1392–3] that Hermione may not be dead after all, [yet] it is only at the commencement of the last act [here presumably] that [one] can be expected to gather . . . that Hermione still lives." Most critics disagree; for instance, EDWARDS (*Progress*, 1986, p. 172): "If they [the original audience] knew Greene's story [they] would assume that the queen had indeed died—an assumption that Shakespeare drops no hint to discredit, keeping a major turn of the plot secret from his audience for the first time in his career." KNOWLES (privately) recalls Aemilia in *Err.*, but perhaps her reappearance as the Abbess does not qualify as a major turn. ORNSTEIN (1986, p. 232): "Knowing that Perdita lives, we are ready to believe in possibilities that seem monstrous to human reason. If the oracle is true, then Paulina's prophecy may be no less true; there may be another woman as like Hermione as her ghost." ORNSTEIN seems to forget that the new queen "shall not be so young As was your former." HARTWIG (1972, p. 115 n.): "There is a submerged insistence in this speech and in others which Paulina makes in this scene that Hermione remains, even in death, a vital figure. This is one of the subtle ways by which the audience is prepared, against its 'factual' knowledge, for the ultimate revelation that Hermione lives." Stressing the importance of traditional roles and situations in *WT* (see n. 1012–36), HARTWIG (p. 116) asserts that Paulina "has forced Leontes to allow her yet another role with which to rule him—now she is his procuress," but 2820–4 do not sound like ordinary procuring. PARRY (ed. 1982): "Paulina is, as it were, beginning to bring home to Leontes the 'possibility' of Hermione. *He* takes the conversation to be ironically confirming the sheer impossibility of bringing her back."

2820 **No remedie**] HAPPÉ (1969): "If there is no other way."

Office] JOHNSON (1755): "A publick charge or employment." For other senses, see nn. 857, 1121, and 2440.

2823 (**walk'd . . . Ghost**)] ROLFE (ed. 1879): "That is, *if* it walked; the inversion being like that still common with *have*, *be*, etc. Cf. [2858]."

Paul. That
Shall be when your first Queene's againe in breath:
Neuer till then.

Enter a Seruant.   2830

Ser. One that giues out himselfe Prince *Florizell*,
Sonne of *Polixenes*, with his Princesse (she
The fairest I haue yet beheld) desires accesse
To your high presence.

Leo. What with him? he comes not   2835
Like to his Fathers Greatnesse: his approach
(So out of circumstance, and suddaine) tells vs,
'Tis not a Visitation fram'd, but forc'd
By need, and accident. What Trayne?

Ser. But few,   2840
And those but meane.

Leo. His Princesse (say you) with him?

Ser. I: the most peerelesse peece of Earth, I thinke,
That ere the Sunne shone bright on.

Paul. Oh *Hermione*,   2845
As euery present Time doth boast it selfe
Aboue a better, gone; so must thy Graue
Giue way to what's seene now. Sir, you your selfe

2830 SCENE II. POPE, HAN, WARB, JOHN
   Seruant] *Gentleman* THEO1-PEN2 (−NLSN, KIT1, PEL1, ARD2, SIG) (*and so in*
SPs)
   2831 out himselfe] himself out POPE, HAN
   2833-5 *Three verse lines ending* desires . . . presence. . . . not JOHN, v1773-
MAL; *two, ending* access . . . not mCAP2, v1793+
   2835 What$_\wedge$] ~ ! COL2
   2843 I:] Yes; ROWE1-JOHN2
   2846 euery] ever F4

2827-9 **That . . . then**] MARTIN (1891, pp. 30-1): "The first hint is given that
Hermione is still alive." MARTIN invents a long account of Paulina's detecting signs of
life in the unconscious Hermione, having her secretly taken to her own home, and
having an empty coffin sent to the grave. Gradually Hermione comes to herself and
is comforted with expectation that the oracle will be fulfilled. "The name of Leontes
is not mentioned. . . . Her heart is dead towards him. . . . [Yet] seeing the genuine
contrition of Leontes, Paulina would not abandon the hope that Hermione might in
time be reconciled to him" (p. 31). ENGLAND (1982, p. 77): "This hint . . . is designed to nurture emerging hope in Leontes and in us." NEWTON (1986, p. 149):
"Paulina's authority over Leontes . . . has its basis in a belief that only she is convinced of, that the oracle's forecast [1315-16] means that the king's daughter will be
rediscovered."

490

2828 **againe in breath**] PORTER & CLARKE (ed. 1908): "This is the most open clew to the sequel." *Breath* here means, as usual, "respiration," but *OED* gives this as its only instance of the phrase.

2830 *Seruant*] COLLIER (ed. 1842) favors *Gentleman*, because "it is obvious from what he says, and what is said to him [e.g., 2848-53], that he is above the rank of 'a servant.'" COLLIER is so taken with this idea that in his ed. 1858, he reports that the Old Corrector—he himself—changed *Seruant* to *Servant-poet*, "as if he were a poet retained in the service and pay of Leontes," although this reading does not appear in his ed. 1853. HUNTER (1954, p. 130): "This poet must, on a normal computation, be an old man. It would be more in the order of things, if he had become, like Paulina, fixed in loyalty to the old days. But he is credible. If there is less life in him, there is still a great deal of the love of life." PAFFORD (ed. 1963): "Some official is intended, lower in status than the courtier-Gentlemen of v.ii or the Lord of [2940 ff.]." SCHANZER (ed. 1969): "A gentleman in the king's service could be . . . described" simply as *Seruant*. MAHOOD (1992, p. 230, n. 4): Possibly the First Gentleman of 5.2.

2831 **giues out**] SCHMIDT (1874): "Declare[s]." See n. 1966 for another meaning.

2832-3 **she The fairest**] I.e., the fairest she. For *she* meaning "woman," see ABBOTT §224.

2833 **The . . . accesse**] For scansion, see n. 156. ABBOTT (§490): *Accesse* is accented *accéss*.

2835 **What with him?**] DEIGHTON (ed. 1889): "What brings him here?" SCHANZER (ed. 1969), more accurately: "'What are those with him?' (The question is repeated in [2839] in *What train?*)"

2836 **Like to**] BETHELL (ed. 1956): "In a manner appropriate to."

approach] MAXWELL (ed. 1956): "Coming."

2837 **out of**] JERVIS (1868): "Without."

circumstance] CALDECOTT (MS 1813-33): "All usual forms & ceremonies" (*OED*, *sb*. 7, citing this line). FURNESS (ed. 1898): "Everything which should precede and accompany a Royal Progress [which this is not], avant couriers, heralds, military displays, etc." For related meanings, see nn. 796, 1192, and 3041.

2838 **Visitation**] Visit. See n. 9.

fram'd] KERSEY (1708, Frame): "To contrive." JOHNSON (1755): "To plan."

2839 **need, and accident**] For the possible hendiadys, see n. 904-5.

Trayne] MINSHEU (1617): "Companie of seruants, attending vpon anie prince."

2841 **meane**] SCHMIDT (1875): "Humble, poor."

2843-4 **the . . . on**] PARRY (ed. 1982): "The most beautiful human creature in the world." KITTREDGE & RIBNER (ed. 1967): "The human body, being composed of the same four elements as the physical earth, was often treated as analogous to it." BETHELL (ed. 1956): "Carries on the image of fertility, &c., used in [3.1] for the divine creativeness and so links up Perdita with the good Providence signified by the oracle." For the various meanings of *peece*, see n. 3229. DENT P289.1 finds "peece peerelesse" in John Heywood's *Dialogue* (1546).

2844-5 **That . . . Hermione**] For scansion, see n. 1220.

2846-8 **As . . . now**] ALEXANDER (1979, p. 242): "Paulina feels that Hermione's beauty, celebrated in its time, is being implicitly slighted; she deplores man's capacity to forget."

2847 **Aboue . . . gone**] DEIGHTON (ed. 1889): "As being superior to a better time that is past."

Graue] WARBURTON (ed. 1747): "Epitaph." EDWARDS (1750, p. 87): "Thy beauties, which are buried in the grave; the continent for the contents." The CLARKES (ed. 1865): "It forms a corresponding image with . . . 'piece of *earth* [2843]'; it affords befitting antecedent to 'colder than that theme [2850]' . . . and impress[es] upon Paulina's hearers . . . that Hermione's remains repose in the 'grave.'" For the clause, DEIGHTON (ed. 1889): "So must you, now that you are dead, endure to be depreciated in comparison with what is living."

Haue said, and writ so; but your writing now
Is colder then that Theame: she had not beene,   2850
Nor was not to be equall'd, thus your Verse
Flow'd with her Beautie once; 'tis shrewdly ebb'd,
To say you haue seene a better.
   Ser. Pardon, Madame:
The one, I haue almost forgot (your pardon:)   2855
The other, when she ha's obtayn'd your Eye,
Will haue your Tongue too. This is a Creature,
Would she begin a Sect, might quench the zeale
Of all Professors else; make Proselytes
Of who she but bid follow.   2860
   Paul. How? not women?
   Ser. Women will loue her, that she is a Woman
More worth then any Man: Men, that she is
The rarest of all Women.
   Leo. Goe *Cleomines*,   2865

2847 Graue] graces HAN; grace mTBY4 *conj.*, COLLIER (1841, p. 15) *conj.*, COL, HUD1, SING2, KTLY

2849 but] that HAN

2850 then] on HAN

2850-1 Theame: . . . equall'd,] ~ , . . . ~ ; F4, JOHN, v1773, MAL-ARD1, KIT1, CLN2-ARD2, EVNS, BEV3; ~ ; . . . ~ ; ROWE1-WARB

2851 not] she POPE1-JOHN2, v1773

2857 a Creature] such a creature HAN, v1793-v1813, HUD2; a creature, who KEIGH-TLEY *conj. in* CAM1, KTLY

2860 who] whom mFLV. a.80 *conj.*, HAN, COL, HUD, DEL

   bid] did COL1, COL2, DEL2, COL4

2849-50 **but . . . Theame**] RANN (ed. 1787): "Though your zeal on that subject is somewhat abated." MALONE (ed. 1790): "I.e. than the lifeless body of Hermione, the *theme* or *subject* of your writing." BETHELL (ed. 1956): "Hermione is alive, as Paulina knows."

2850-1 **Theame: . . . equall'd,**] JOHNSON (ed. 1765), and some later eds., consider "she . . . equall'd" a line of the Servant's verse (*thus* = "in this way"). Others consider it a statement of his theme (*thus* = "consequently"). The former seems truer to F; the latter perhaps makes better sense. SCHANZER (ed. 1969) objects to the former because the tenses are wrong ("what the Gentleman must have written is 'she has not been, nor is not to be, equalled'"), but Paulina may recast the tenses to emphasize the deadness of the past. ROWE's noncommittal semicolons came into being because F4's comma after "Theame" has a fleck over it.

2850-3 **she . . . better**] EWBANK (1964, p. 96 n.) compares 1591-3. Regarding the poem, WATSON (1984, p. 267): "A typical piece of Sicilian art, emptily flattering the royal family with the illusion that it could overcome time."

2852 **Flow'd . . . ebb'd**] BETHELL (ed. 1956): "The metaphor . . . is taken from a flowing stream" and changed "from stream to sea." Rather, it is tidal—*OED* (Flow, *v.* 10): "Of the sea, a tidal river, etc.: To rise and advance."

'tis] Anticipated by COLLINS (ed. 1904-24?), BETHELL (ed. 1956): "Paulina, as usual, speaks vehemently and inaccurately. ''Tis' refers to 'verse' [2851] but the gentleman has written no verse about Perdita: the reference changes 'written poetry' [2851] to 'poetic ability' [2852]." KNOWLES (privately): "''*Tis* refers to 'Beautie', which once swelled in his verse but now has ebbed, since he can depreciate it."

shrewdly] SCHMIDT (1875), misleadingly, since the ebb of the tide is the subject: "In a high and mischievous degree." ROLFE (ed. 1879): "Combining the ideas of *much* and *badly.*" EVANS (ed. 1974) does that: "Grievously."

2853 **To say**] For the indefinite or gerundial use of the infinitive, see n. 704 and cf. 886, 1560, and 2747.

2855 **The . . . forgot**] MAHOOD (1992, p. 73): "This implies he is old enough to have been in Leontes' train in the earlier part of the play, and it is tempting to identify him with the attendant . . . whom Leontes sends . . . to enquire after Mamillius [at 919], and who may reappear [at 1126] to announce the return of Leontes' emissaries from Delos. The advantage . . . is that it associates the lost Mamillius with the new-found Perdita and both with the Oracle."

one] HAPPÉ (1969): "Hermione."

2857 **Will . . . Creature**] To regularize the line, WALKER (1854, p. 84) elides *this is* and gives *creature* three syllables. Cf. nn. 2026, 3363-4.

Tongue] BETHELL (ed. 1956): "Praise."

Creature] HENLEY (ed. 1902): "Trisyllable."

2858 **Sect**] HAPPÉ (1969): "A new type of religion."

2858-9 **quench . . . else**] HUDSON (ed. 1880): "Put them [adherents of other religious faiths] out of heart and hope by surpassing them."

2859 **all Professors else**] COLLINS (ed. 1904-24?): "Of all who profess other sects." KERMODE (ed. 1963): "Especially Puritans." PAFFORD (ed. 1963, Professor): "Professor of Christianity," because in *H8* 3.1.115 (1747) the word has that meaning. So it does also in *1H6* 5.1.14 (2347). MARTZ (1980, p. 130): The word "is bound to recall such sixteenth-century phrases as 'professors of Christ's name and doctrine', or 'the professors of God's truth in England.'"

Proselytes] *OED* (*sb.* 1, citing this line): "Convert[s]."

2860 **who**] MOORMAN (ed. 1912): "Those whom." ABBOTT (§274): "Not the object of the preposition," the clause being the object. For the form, see n. 827.

2861 **How? not women?**] MACDONALD (1882, p. 158): "Paulina . . . is a thorough partisan, siding with women against men, and strengthened in this by the treatment her mistress had received from her husband! Having received assurances that 'women will love her' [2862], she has no more to say." FURNESS (ed. 1898): Since the speech "is not a question but an assertion," it should be followed by an exclamation point [which F's *?* may represent] or a period. Thus CARRINGTON (1956): "Paulina implies that women will not love one more beautiful than themselves."

2863 **worth**] *OED* (*a.* 2b) labels this usage archaic but gives many other examples, most of them earlier than the 19th c.

2864-5 **The . . . *Cleomines***] For scansion, see n. 1220.

Your selfe (assisted with your honor'd Friends)
Bring them to our embracement. Still 'tis strange,   (2)
He thus should steale vpon vs.   *Exit.*

    Paul. Had our Prince
(Iewell of Children) seene this houre, he had payr'd   2870
Well with this Lord; there was not full a moneth
Betweene their births.

    Leo. 'Prethee no more; cease: thou know'st
He dyes to me againe, when talk'd-of: sure
When I shall see this Gentleman, thy speeches   2875
Will bring me to consider that, which may
Vnfurnish me of Reason. They are come.

     Enter Florizell, Perdita, Cleomines, and others.

Your Mother was most true to Wedlock, Prince,
For she did print your Royall Father off,   2880
Conceiuing you. Were I but twentie one,
Your Fathers Image is so hit in you,
(His very ayre) that I should call you Brother,
As I did him, and speake of something wildly
By vs perform'd before. Most dearely welcome,   2885
And your faire Princesse (Goddesse) oh: alas,

    2868 thus should] should thus THEO3, THEO4, SIG
       Exit.] Ff; *Exit* Cleo. ROWE1-JOHN2, v1773-RANN, KIT1, OXF2 (*subst.*); *Exeunt*
CLEOMENES, *Lords, and Gentleman.* CAP, MAL-DEL2, KTLY, KNT3-COL4, OXF1, CLN2
(*subst.*); *Exeunt Cleomenes and others.* CAM1 *etc.*
    2871 full a] a full F3-POPE2, HAN
    2872-3 *One verse line* mCAP2, v1793-v1813, SING, KNT2, WH1, HAL, KTLY, DYCE2,
HUD2, BUL, PEL1, ARD2, PEN2, OXF2
    2873 cease] *Om.* HAN, v1793-v1813, SING1, HUD2
    2878 SCENE III. POPE, HAN, WARB, JOHN
       and others] *Om.* STAU
    2886 And] As THEO1-v1773 (−HAN, CAP), MAL
       your] you mTBY4 *conj.*, v1821, OXF1
       she unveils [*after* princess] CAM3
       Princesse (Goddesse)] princess-goddess WALKER (1860, 1:24) *conj.*, DYCE2,
HUD2, BUL

    2866 **assisted with**] MOORMAN (ed. 1912): "Accompanied by." See nn. 3072,
3266.
    2867 **embracement**] JOHNSON (1755): "Hug." PARRY (ed. 1982): "Welcome,"
possibly *OED* 4.
    2868 **steale vpon vs**] MAXWELL (ed. 1969): "I.e. Come unannounced."

2869-71 **Had . . . Lord**] PAFFORD (ed. 1963): Sh. "clearly wishes us to match Florizel with Mamillius." PYLE (1969, p. 105): "Prepared to meet his past, he [Leontes] sees in Florizel not Mamillius but Polixenes, the occasion indeed of self-reproach [2889-91, 2904-6, 2931-3], but also of happy memory and hope for the future [2883-5, 2891-3]."

2870 **payr'd**] *OED* (Pair, *v.*¹ 2, citing this line): "To 'go' with, so as to match."

2873 **'Prethee . . . cease**] STEEVENS (ed. 1793): *Cease* is a marginal gloss on "Prethee no more" that "crept into the text." LETTSOM (in DYCE, ed. 1864) thinks the passage "an evident jumble of two genuine readings, one the correction of the other"; see p. 584. Few eds. agree with either opinion.

2874 **dyes . . . againe**] PAFFORD (ed. 1963): "Proverbially the revealing of griefs is a renewing of sorrow (Tilley, R89)." C. G. SMITH (1963, no. 248) finds a parallel in Publilius Syrus, *Sententiae*.

2875 **thy speeches**] DEIGHTON (ed. 1889): "Your comparison between him and my dead son."

2877 **Vnfurnish**] JOHNSON (1755, citing this line): "Deprive." ABBOTT (§166): *Of* is used "with verbs that signify, either literally or metaphorically, depriving."

They are come] PARRY (ed. 1982): "The entry of Florizel and Perdita introduces a long, still and speechless pause . . . as the young couple stand 'begetting wonder' [2888]." For Perdita as a reproduction of Mamillius, see n. 1796.

2879-93 **Your . . . him**] TOLIVER (1989, p. 177): Perdita's "likeness to Hermione extracts from Leontes a mixture of affection and surprise and lifts the dialogue of host and diplomat to the verge of lyric."

2879-81 **Your . . . you**] WATSON (1984, p. 265): "Precisely what Leontes refused to believe . . . at Perdita's birth."

2879 **true**] See n. 2739-40.

Wedlock] *OED* (*sb.* 1, citing this line): "The marriage vow or obligation."

2880-1 **For . . . you**] For the printing metaphor, see n. 1021-5.

2881-3 **Were . . . Brother**] The implication is that Florizel is now about 21, and since 16 years have passed since 1.1, Mamillius would then have been 5. DODDS (1939), taking Mamillius and Florizel to be the same age and Mamillius to have been 6 or 7, adds 16 to make Florizel now 22 or 23. If Mamillius was 10, as PAFFORD supposes, Florizel would now be 26, not impossibly old for Perdita. See n. 2240.

2882 **hit**] *OED* (*v.* 14, citing this line): "To obtain an exact . . . representation of." DEIGHTON (ed. 1889): "The metaphor is of hitting a mark." BETHELL (ed. 1956): "Cf. a 'striking' likeness. The metaphor is from a stamp or seal."

2883 **ayre**] KERSEY (1708): "Looks, Countenance, Carriage" (*OED* 14, citing this line).

2884-5 **something . . . before**] Cf. "my Lords Tricks, and yours, when you were Boyes" (122). For *wildly, OED* (*adv.* 2b, citing this line): "In freedom from control, at one's own will." NEILSON & HILL (ed. 1942): "Boisterously"; KITTREDGE & RIBNER (ed. 1967): "Without thought"; EVANS (ed. 1974): "Madly, exuberantly."

2886 **And**] THEOBALD (ed. 1733) paraphrases his emendation: "He had lost a pair of Children, who might have stood the Wonder of two Worlds, the Objects of Admiration to Gods and Men; as this young Prince and his Princess did, in his Opinion."

Princesse (Goddesse)] WALKER (1860, 1:21-4) considers this a "double substantive . . . resolved into two simple epithets" and would read *Princess-goddess*. FURNESS (ed. 1898) objects: "'Goddess' is a climax." BETHELL (ed. 1956): "This combines the suggestions of [4.4], the 'queen' references and 'Flora.'"

oh:] WILSON (ed. 1931): "The colon . . . implies . . . that the exclamation goes with 'goddess!' to express Leontes' amazement as Perdita first unveils herself before him. Cf. [3001-2]."

I lost a couple, that 'twixt Heauen and Earth
Might thus haue stood, begetting wonder, as
You (gracious Couple) doe: and then I lost
(All mine owne Folly) the Societie,   2890
Amitie too of your braue Father, whom
(Though bearing Miserie) I desire my life
Once more to looke on him.
   Flo. By his command
Haue I here touch'd *Sicilia*, and from him   2895
Giue you all greetings, that a King (at friend)

2888 thus haue] have thus IRV, RLTR
2893 on him] on THEO1-RANN; upon v1793-v1813
2894 By] Sir, by THEO1-RANN
2896 at] as F2-POPE2, HAN, JOHN2, MAL, COL, HUD1; and mTBY2 *conj.*, GENT, HARN

   2887 'twixt . . . Earth] BETHELL (ed. 1956): This expression "has no clear meaning after 'wonder' or 'begetting'; it must be taken with 'stood.'" HAPPÉ (1969), however: "By their earthly and heavenly qualities."
   2888 begetting wonder] KITTREDGE & RIBNER (ed. 1967): "Causing onlookers to be amazed at their beauty."
   2891 braue] Worthy, noble. See n. 2026.
   2891-3 whom . . . him] HUNTER (ed. 1872): "To look on whom once more, I, though bearing misery, desire continuance of my life." HUDSON (ed. 1880) is clearer: "Whom I desire to live to see again, though life is a misery to me." HERFORD (ed. 1904): *Him* is "an idiomatic repetition of the object already expressed in the relative 'whom,'" or as the CLARKES (1879, p. 609) say, a pleonasm.
   2892 my life] SCHMIDT (1874): "In my life." MOORMAN (ed. 1912): "An adverbial phrase— . . . before I die." BETHELL (ed. 1956): It is, rather, the object of *desire*. "Leontes, though life is a misery to him, yet desires to live to see Polixenes again."
   2894-2939 By . . . you?] HARDINGE (1818, 3:40): "The two lovers offer themselves to *Leontes* with a lie, in which the young Prince (to do him justice) appears to feel no embarrassment, is a most promising adept, and is quite at home. During the whole of that [this] scene *Perdita* is mute—but she looks volumes—we may naturally suppose her like her mother." Perdita speaks at 2970, after the "scene" has ended. PARRY (ed. 1982), questionably: "The lie feels, and works, like truth—not only as it affects Leontes, but also as it affects the audience."
   2896 Giue] OED: "To deliver (a message, etc.)," with this line as its first citation.
   at friend] RANN (ed. 1787): "Upon friendly terms, living at friendship with another." OED (Friend, *sb.* 6b, citing this line): "On one's side." MALONE (ed. 1790): *At* should be *and*, these words having previously been confused in *WT*. MALONE is perhaps thinking of 2617, where only he emends to *and*. STEEVENS (ed. 1793): "Perhaps . . . *at friendship*." ABBOTT (§§140, 143), however, explains *at* as a reconstruction of Anglo-Saxon *on* or *an*, which had become *a* (as *on live* and *on foot* had become *alive* and *afoot*). This *a-* "was becoming unintelligible and vulgar in Shakespeare's time, and he generally uses *at* instead." Cf. "the wind at helpe" (*Ham.* 4.3.44 [2705]). For the omission of *the*, see n. 2163. STAUNTON (ed. 1859): In *Cym.* 1.4.106 (420) and *JC* 3.1.143 (1362) the expression is *to friend*.

Can send his Brother: and but Infirmitie
(Which waits vpon worne times) hath something seiz'd
His wish'd Abilitie, he had himselfe
The Lands and Waters, 'twixt your Throne and his,   2900
Measur'd, to looke vpon you; whom he loues
(He bad me say so) more then all the Scepters,
And those that beare them, liuing.
   Leo. Oh my Brother,
(Good Gentleman) the wrongs I haue done thee, stirre   2905
Afresh within me: and these thy offices
(So rarely kind) are as Interpreters
Of my behind-hand slacknesse. Welcome hither,
As is the Spring to th'Earth. And hath he too

2900 Lands] land OXF1, CLN2

2897–9 **but . . . Abilitie**] PIERCE (ed. 1918): "But that the infirmity which comes with age has somewhat stolen from him (seized) the traveling ability which he wishes for." For *but* as "except," see ABBOTT §120, and for *something* as "somewhat," see n. 224. WILSON (ed. 1931, Seiz'd): "Arrested." SCHANZER (ed. 1969): "Taken prisoner."

2898 **waits vpon**] *OED* (*sb.* 14n, citing this line): "To attend as a concomitant or consequence." Cf. 163.

    worne] *OED* (*ppl. a.* 3, citing this line): "Of time . . .: Past, spent." HAPPÉ (1969), however: "The wearing out of age."

2899 **wish'd Abilitie**] HAPPÉ (1969): "The strength he would like still to enjoy."

2901 **Measur'd**] SCHMIDT (1875): "Pass over." Shn. travel also measures territory in, for example, *LLL* 5.2.184 ff. (2082 ff.), *Tmp.* 2.1.259 (955), and *Son.* 50.4.

2902–3 **Scepters . . . liuing**] KITTREDGE & RIBNER (ed. 1967): "Those living kings who bear them (sceptres)." The CLARKES (ed. 1865): "Shakespeare . . . impersonates 'sceptres' here, as royal rulers, yet veils the impersonation by the words 'those . . . them.'"

2906 **offices**] See n. 1121. SCHMIDT (1875), similarly: "An act of good will, a kind service." MOORMAN (ed. 1912): "Words of good-will."

2907 **rarely kind**] HAPPÉ (1969): "Since few others are capable of such kindness." SCHMIDT (1875, Rarely): "Extraordinarily, excellently."

2907–8 **are . . . slacknesse**] Anticipated by COLLINS (ed. 1904–24?), MAXWELL (ed. 1956): "Emphasize my tardy, inadequate action." For *behindhand* as "tardy," *OED* cites this instance only. KERMODE (ed. 1963): "Put into words feelings I've been too slow in expressing." For *interpreters*, WRIGHT & LAMAR (ed. 1966) give "reminders"; SCHMIDT (1874), more exactly, "expounders."

2908–9 **Welcome . . . th'Earth**] For the imagery, see n. 1996–8, and for Perdita's silence, n. 2260–85. MUIR (*Last Periods*, 1961, p. 49): "It is almost as though Perdita had become the goddess whose part she had assumed." BROCKBANK (1966, p. 200): "Moral growth is presented as a seasonal process, enabling Leontes to greet Perdita, when innocence returns to Sicilia," with these words. THORNE (1968, p. 41): "Their arrival has a rejuvenating effect upon Leontes, who is experiencing the autumn

Expos'd this Paragon to th'fearefull vsage   2910
(At least vngentle) of the dreadfull *Neptune*,
To greet a man, not worth her paines; much lesse,
Th'aduenture of her person?
    Flo. Good my Lord,
She came from *Libia*.   2915
    Leo. Where the Warlike *Smalus*,
That Noble honor'd Lord, is fear'd, and lou'd?
    Flo. Most Royall Sir,
From thence: from him, whose Daughter
His Teares proclaym'd his parting with her: thence   2920
(A prosperous South-wind friendly) we haue cross'd,
To execute the Charge my Father gaue me,
For visiting your Highnesse: My best Traine
I haue from your *Sicilian* Shores dismiss'd;
Who for *Bohemia* bend, to signifie   2925
Not onely my successe in *Libia* (Sir)
But my arriuall, and my Wifes, in safetie
Here, where we are.
    Leo. The blessed Gods
Purge all Infection from our Ayre, whilest you   2930

2911 least] best mTBY4 *conj.*, WH2
2918-19 *One verse line* HAN, CAP+
2920 his] his, HAN, CAP-GLO, DYCE2+; her, mTBY2 *and* JOHN1 *conj.*, KTLY
2928-9 *One verse line* mCAP2, v1793+
2928 we are] we happily are HAN, CAP

---

of the body, and turns his sorrow into joy and his penance into health." According
to IWASAKI (1973, p. 262), Perdita's reception by Leontes is "the realization of Antigonus' prayer at his leaving the infant Perdita on the Bohemian shore, believing it to
be fathered by Polixenes [1485-8]." ORGEL (ed. 1996): "A variation on the proverbial
'welcome as flowers in May' (DENT F390)."

    2909-13 **And . . . person?**] PORTER & CLARKE (ed. 1908): He himself had com-
mitted her to Neptune's "fearefull vsage" "when as a babe he sent Antigonus away
with her."

    2910 **Paragon**] CAWDREY (1604): "Patterne, example" (*OED*, *sb*. 1). BULLOKAR
(1616): "A beautifull peece, a louely creature" (1a).

    2911 **vngentle**] See n. 1476.

    Neptune] ROOT (1903, p. 90): Used by Sh. "not [as] a divinity but a personi-
fication, more or less vivid, of the sea." An exception seems to occur at 1829-30,
which refers to Neptune's seduction of Theophane, but that allusion comes from
Pandosto. See n. 1828-32.

    2913 **aduenture**] Risk. See n. 95.

    2914 **Good my Lord**] For the construction, see n. 390.

2915 **Libia**] COOPER (1565): "Amonge the Greekes, the generall name of all Africa: . . . of the Romaines . . . from Aegypte to the west Ocean. . . . The Spaniardes do commonly call them all Moores." THIRLBY (MS 1725-33?): "Does Libya breed such fair women?" He suggests *Lydia* (see p. 584). PORTER & CLARKE (ed. 1908): "Shakespeare chose *Libia* [rather than Greene's Padua (*Pandosto*, p. 650)] because it might seem to give her loftier birth and be farther from detection." HOLLAND (1964, p. 297): "A kind of underworld, a dark, African world like the underworld from which Proserpina [with whom we identify Perdita because of 1930] . . . emerges to bring the spring, as indeed she [Perdita] does bring the spring to Sicily, which has been a Waste Land these past sixteen years." KITTREDGE & RIBNER (ed. 1967): "Florizel is telling the story he was told to tell by Camillo." Because of the extra syllable, VAN DAM (1900, p. 89) believes that Sh.'s form of this word was *Liby*, and that *Libia* was supplied by editors, that is, Crane or Compositor A.

2916 **Smalus**] Naturally he has attracted little attention. STOKES (1924) thinks his name may perhaps be a corruption of Ismael; PAFFORD (ed. 1963) more plausibly suggests a corruption of *Synalus*, the name of a suitably warlike figure in Plutarch's Life of Dion §25. *Synalus* has too many syllables but may be elided. For Smalus's place in the play, see n. 1299.

2917 **Noble honor'd**] The CLARKES (1879, p. 79): "Shakespeare occasionally uses more than one epithet descriptive of an object [or person]; generally for the sake of giving emphatic effect."

2920 **his parting**] Following HANMER in reading *his, parting*, RANN (ed. 1787): "To be his indeed." MALONE (ed. 1790), similarly: "At parting."

2921 **A . . . friendly**] Speaking of the repetition, in this part, of "many of the motifs of the first movement," SMITH (1966, p. 51): "Again there is a sea voyage, this time with no storm . . . which brings all estrangements and oppositions to reunion, restoration, and reconciliation." But the south wind is Florizel's invention; the lovers have actually sailed to Sicilia through "extremitie of Weather" (3127), which made them both seasick.

prosperous] SCHMIDT (1875): "Favourable."

friendly] Being friendly or favorable. See ABBOTT §§380-1.

2922 **execute the Charge**] KITTREDGE & RIBNER (ed. 1967): "Carry out the command."

2923-4 **My . . . dismiss'd**] His explanation for their inadequate attendance. See 2840-1.

2923 **My best Traine**] DEIGHTON (ed. 1889): "The best part of my retinue."

2925 **bend**] JOHNSON (1755): "Direct to a certain point." JERVIS (1868): "Make for" (*OED, v.* 20a).

2926 **my successe**] KITTREDGE & RIBNER (ed. 1967): "How I have fared."

Libia] See n. 2915.

2928-9 **Here . . . Gods**] Most eds. leave this line metrically short. The emendation *happily*, says MITFORD (1844, p. 128), HANMER "must have picked up from some suburban couple arrived at their own door from a journey to town to lay in their stock of tea and sugar."

2928 **Here, where**] MALONE (ed. 1790): "Dissyllables," to make 2928-9 a pentameter, an idea in which STEEVENS (ed. 1793) has "not the smallest degree of faith."

2929-39 **The . . . you?**] MORO & WILLEMS (1982, p. 45): "When Leontes . . . discovers that they are fugitives, he helps to turn their lie into truth by welcoming them like princes at his court. Their version of reality fulfills his deepest wish to be reconciled with Bohemia."

2929-30 **The . . . Ayre**] BETHELL (ed. 1956): "Reminiscent of the island of Delphos [quotes 1146]."

Doe Clymate here: you haue a holy Father,
A gracefull Gentleman, against whose person
(So sacred as it is) I haue done sinne,
For which, the Heauens (taking angry note)
Haue left me Issue-lesse: and your Father's bless'd   2935
(As he from Heauen merits it) with you,
Worthy his goodnesse. What might I haue been,
Might I a Sonne and Daughter now haue look'd on,
Such goodly things as you?

                Enter a Lord.   2940

    Lord. Most Noble Sir,
That which I shall report, will beare no credit,
Were not the proofe so nigh. Please you (great Sir)
Bohemia greets you from himselfe, by me:
Desires you to attach his Sonne, who ha's   2945

2931 holy] noble COL2
2940 SCENE IV. POPE, HAN, WARB, JOHN
2943 nigh] high THEO2, WARB-JOHN2, V1773

2931 **Clymate**] JOHNSON (1755): "To inhabit. A word only in *Shakespeare*." OED agrees, citing this line only. PORTER & CLARKE (ed. c. 1903): "Visit, sojourn." For the conversion of nouns to verbs, see n. 2344, and for other "parts of speech diversely used" by Sh., see the CLARKES (1879, pp. 492-9).
    holy] SINGER (1853, p. 80), comparing "holy *Gonzallo*" (*Tmp.* 5.1.62 [2018]): "Reverend" (*OED, a.* 3c). The CLARKES (ed. 1865): "Virtuous, righteous" (SCHMIDT [1874]; not in *OED*).
    2932 **gracefull**] MINSHEU (1617): "Gracious." *OED* (*a.* 1, citing this line): "Holy." COLLINS (ed. 1904-24?): "Chosen for its connection with *holy* and *sacred*." MAHOOD (1957, p. 160): Ironical. "In fact, Polixenes, in breaking the match between Florizel and Perdita, has shown a lack of that imaginative vision . . . which Leontes has now acquired and which makes him the lovers' advocate."
    2933 **sacred**] HERFORD (ed. 1904): "I.e. in virtue of his royalty, the epithet being currently applied to all sovereigns as such."
    2934 **note**] For other instances of noting, see n. 298.
    2935 **Haue . . . Issue-lesse**] CHARLTON (ed. 1916): "Perdita . . . is actually before him. . . . Generally called Dramatic Irony."
    and] PAFFORD (ed. 1963): "On the other hand."
    2938 **Sonne and Daughter**] PAFFORD (ed. 1963): "Since in Elizabethan English 'son' is normal also for 'son-in-law' Leontes is in fact looking on his son-to-be, as well as on his daughter. Cf. [2978-80]." HAPPÉ (1969): "A piece of dramatic anticipation characteristic of this play."
    2942 **will**] For *will* rather than *would*, see ABBOTT §371.
    credit] COLES (1676): "Belief, trust."
    2944 **from himselfe**] THIRLBY (MS 1733-47?): "How knew you yᵗ the Prince brought pretended greetings from his father?"
    2945 **attach**] CAWDREY (1604): "Sease vpon, [ar]rest, or hold."

(His Dignitie, and Dutie both cast off)
Fled from his Father, from his Hopes, and with
A Shepheards Daughter.
    Leo. Where's *Bohemia*? speake.
    Lord. Here, in your Citie: I now came from him.   2950
I speake amazedly, and it becomes
My meruaile, and my Message. To your Court
Whiles he was hastning (in the Chase, it seemes,
Of this faire Couple) meetes he on the way
The Father of this seeming Lady, and   2955
Her Brother, hauing both their Countrey quitted,
With this young Prince.
    Flo. Camillo ha's betray'd me;
Whose honor, and whose honestie till now,
Endur'd all Weathers.   2960
    Lord. Lay't so to his charge:
He's with the King your Father.
    Leo. Who? *Camillo*?
    Lord. Camillo (Sir:) I spake with him: who now

2950 your] the MTBY4 *conj.*, v1803-SING1
    came] come OXF1
2953 Whiles] Whilst ROWE1-v1773 (−CAP); While SIS

2946 **Dignitie, and Dutie**] SCHANZER (ed. 1969): "His dignity as a prince and his duty as a son."
    Dignitie] SCHMIDT (1874): "Grandeur." *OED* (2, citing this line): "Honourable or high estate, position, or estimation." Cf. nn. 28, 2326, and 3088.
    2947 **Hopes**] DEIGHTON (ed. 1889): I.e., "of coming to the throne."
    2951 **amazedly**] HUNTER (ed. 1872): "Confusedly."
    2951-2 **it . . . Message**] DEIGHTON (ed. 1889): My confused speech "is in keeping with the astonishment I feel ['My meruaile'], and the message I bring." WRIGHT (1981, p. 190) considers "meruaile . . . Message" a hendiadys, "my astonishing message." See n. 904-5 for more on hendiadys in *WT*.
    2953 **Whiles**] See n. 279.
    hastning] VAN DAM (1900, p. 47) notices the syncopation of the *e* in *hastening*. For other syncopations of *e*, see nn. 222, 313, 381, 692, 813, and 1302.
    2955 **seeming**] CALDECOTT (MS 1813-33): "Of false pretense & exterior." He compares Angelo as a seemer in *MM* 1.3.54 (346). YOUNG & MOSELEY (ed. 1965): "Counterfeit."
    2958-60 ***Camillo* . . . Weathers**] MIKO (1989, p. 269): "And Camillo has. Apparently honor and honesty don't mean just one thing, as the naive Florizel thinks."
    2960 **Endur'd all Weathers**] DEIGHTON (ed. 1889): "Been proof against all attacks." Or "vicissitudes." For a similar expression, see *TN* 1.5.238 (529).
    2961 **Lay't . . . charge**] BETHELL (ed. 1956): "You may rightly accuse him of that." PARRY (ed. 1982): "Accuse him in person."

Ha's these poore men in question. Neuer saw I   2965
Wretches so quake: they kneele, they kisse the Earth;
Forsweare themselues as often as they speake:
Bohemia stops his eares, and threatens them
With diuers deaths, in death.
   Perd. Oh my poore Father: 2970
The Heauen sets Spyes vpon vs, will not haue
Our Contract celebrated.
   Leo. You are marryed?
   Flo. We are not (Sir) nor are we like to be:
The Starres (I see) will kisse the Valleyes first: 2975
The oddes for high and low's alike.
   Leo. My Lord,
Is this the Daughter of a King?
   Flo. She is,
When once she is my Wife.   2980
   Leo. That once (I see) by your good Fathers speed,
Will come-on very slowly. I am sorry
(Most sorry) you haue broken from his liking,
Where you were ty'd in dutie: and as sorry,
Your Choise is not so rich in Worth, as Beautie,   2985
That you might well enioy her.

2971 Heauen . . . vpon] heav'n which sets spies on POPE, HAN; heaven sits spies
upon HARN; heavens set spies upon mTBY2 *conj.*, STAU; heaven set spies upon BUL
2984 as] so HARN
2985 Worth] Birth WARBURTON *conj. in* THEO1, HAN, WARB

2965 **question**] Talk. See n. 1660 and *OED, sb.* 2. DELIUS (ed. 1860): Legal examination, trial, which, FURNESS (ed. 1898) observes, is "a needless amplification of
the ordinary meaning of 'question.'" Some later critics, such as COLLINS (ed. 1904-
24?), nevertheless agree with DELIUS; HERFORD (ed. 1916-) glosses "examination (by
torture) [*OED, sb.* 2b]." This exercise has not actually taken place but is threatened;
see 2968-9.
   2965-7 **Neuer . . . speake**] BEVINGTON (1984, p. 89): "We trust the reliability
of this report because we have already seen the Clowns reacting [at 2650-74]."
   2966 **they . . . Earth**] Proverbial (TILLEY D651). EVANS (ed. 1974): "I.e. abase
themselves on the ground."
   2967 **Forsweare**] MINSHEU (1617, Foresworne): "Puriured." KERMODE (ed.
1963): "Deny on oath."
   2969 **With . . . death**] DEIGHTON (ed. 1889): "With all manner of tortures, each
sufficient to cause death." COLLINS (ed. 1904-24?): "With the pain of death constantly
repeated," or, as HAPPÉ (1969) puts it, with "many deaths in one."
   2970 **Oh . . . Father**] PILGRIM (1983, p. 83, n. 1): "Perdita's *first* thought is not
of the ruin of her own hopes."

2971 – 2 **The . . . celebrated**] Perdita's participation in the deception of Leontes causes critics some embarrassment. The CLARKES (ed. 1865): This sentence "shows she feels how little the clandestine course they have pursued, together with the false-hoods it involves, are likely to be blessed by Heaven's sanctioning their union." ROLFE (ed. 1879, pp. 21 – 2): "In the strait in which they are placed, she cannot deny the story which Florizel relates [at 2894 ff.] — she will not confirm it. Her silence, in spite of all the compliments and greetings of Leontes, has a peculiar and characteristic grace; and at the conclusion of the scene, when they are betrayed, the truth bursts from her as if instinctively."

2971 **Heauen sets Spyes**] In his note on *Lr.* 5.3.17 (2957), JOHNSON (ed. 1765) glosses *spies* as "angels commissioned [by God] to survey and report the lives of men." PARROTT (1953, p. 431) argues that the omniscient Christian God needs no spies; "heathen deities, on the contrary, at times need human informers," and it is to these that Perdita must refer. PAFFORD (ed. 1963): "It is unlikely, however, that Shake-speare had in mind any distinction of this kind."

2972 **Our Contract celebrated**] ROLFE (ed. 1879): "Our betrothal consummated by marriage."

2975 **The . . . first**] For the imagery, see n. 1996 – 8.

2976 **The . . . alike**] CAPELL (1783, 2.4:181): "An application of his preceding comparison; that the difficulties ['oddes'] of high and low's meeting . . . were hardly less than that of the vallies and stars' meeting." As FURNESS (ed. 1898) remarks, CAPELL probably refers to social rank; cf. *OED* (High, *sb.*[2] 17d): "(People) of all conditions." SINGER (ed. 1856), slightly differently: "Fortune is as unfavorable to us as Prince and Princess, as when we were Shepherd and Shepherdess." DEIGHTON (ed. 1889) and later eds.: "The chances of good luck are the same for the high-born as for the humble, *i.e.* the fact of my being a king's son does not necessarily cause fortune to favour me." DOUCE (in STEEVENS, ed. 1793), however, contends that *high and low* refers to false dice, as in *Wiv.* 1.3.86 (377), the die being loaded to show either a high or a low number. WILSON (ed. 1931), consequently: "Fortune is a cheater who beguiles princes and shepherds alike with his false dice." BETHELL (ed. 1956) objects that "if 'high' and 'low' signify (*a*) the dice and (*b*) princes and shepherds, the passage cannot mean that princes and shepherds (meaning (*b*)) are cheated by false dice (meaning (*a*)). It must mean simply, 'The chances for "high" and "low" are 'equal', 'high' and 'low' signifying *at the same time* dice and social classes. Moreover, the reference cannot be to *false* dice: it is only with *true* dice that the chances would be equal." He also believes that the stars signify the highborn Florizel and the valleys, the lowborn Per-dita.

2978 – 80 **Daughter . . . Wife**] PAFFORD (ed. 1963): "Play on the Elizabethan 'daughter' and 'daughter' = 'daughter-in-law.'" Cf. n. 2938.

2983 **broken . . . liking**] SCHMIDT (1874, Liking): "Contentedness." HAPPÉ (1969): "Approval." WRIGHT & LAMAR (ed. 1966), for the phrase: "Displeased him."

2984 **ty'd**] PAFFORD (ed. 1963): "Bound."

2985 **Worth**] Because Leontes, "so far from disparaging . . . her [Perdita's] Worth . . . rather esteems her a Treasure," WARBURTON (in THEOBALD, ed. 1733) changes to "Birth." THEOBALD (ed. 1733) retains "Worth," since Sh. may mean "the Royalty of her Dower." MALONE (ed. 1790) follows doubtfully: Since Sh. "often uses *worth* for *wealth*," that sense too may be present. JOHNSON (ed. 1765): "*Worth* signifies any kind of *worthiness*, and among others that of high descent. The King means that he is sorry the Prince's choice is not in other respects as worthy of him as in beauty." The CLARKES (1879, p. 603), similarly: "Worldly position or estimation."

2986 **well enioy her**] DEIGHTON (ed. 1889): "With all propriety take her to wife." SCHMIDT (1874) glosses the word, as used here, as "obtain or possess with pleasure," and sexual pleasure is presumably implicit. For the word in erotic contexts, see PAR-TRIDGE (1969). Cf. n. 2389.

Flo. Deare, looke vp:
Though *Fortune*, visible an Enemie,
Should chase vs, with my Father; powre no iot
Hath she to change our Loues. Beseech you (Sir)   2990
Remember, since you ow'd no more to Time
Then I doe now: with thought of such Affections,
Step forth mine Aduocate: at your request,
My Father will graunt precious things, as Trifles.
Leo. Would he doe so, I'ld beg your precious Mistris,   2995

2988 *Fortune*, visible$_\wedge$] $\sim$ $_\wedge$ $\sim$, HAN
    visible] visibly COL4
2992 Affections,] $\sim$. WARB

2987 **looke vp**] *OED* (Look, *v.* 45c) finds this expression, meaning "cheer up, take heart," only in Sh. For other occurrences, see DENT L431.1. Cf. nn. 1852 and 2331.

2988 **visible an Enemie**] The CLARKES (ed. 1865): "'Appearing as a visible enemy', or 'appearing visibly as an enemy.'" Probably the latter, for "Adjectives are freely used as Adverbs" (ABBOTT §1). DEIGHTON (ed. 1889), agreeing: "Who is clearly hostile to us."

2989 **chase**] SCHMIDT (1874): "Pursue [*OED*, *v.*¹ 1b]." WILSON (ed. 1931): "Harass [*OED*, *v.*¹ 2c, citing this line] (with a quibble upon the military sense [2])."

with] HUNTER (ed. 1872): "By means of." DEIGHTON (ed. 1889): "Together with, as well as."

iot] ORGEL (ed. 1996): "Smallest bit. From *iota*, the smallest letter in the Greek alphabet."

2990 **change our Loues**] KITTREDGE & RIBNER (ed. 1967): "Affect our love for one another."

2991-2 **since . . . now**] RANN (ed. 1787): "When your love was coeval with mine." MALONE (ed. 1790), more plainly: "When you were of my age." For *since* as "when," see ABBOTT §132.

2992 **with . . . Affections**] ROLFE (ed. 1879): "Recalling what your feelings then were." EVANS (ed. 1974): "How it felt to be in love."

2993 **mine Aduocate**] KITTREDGE & RIBNER (ed. 1967): "As a pleader in my behalf." For Paulina as advocate, see n. 865.

2994 **as**] KITTREDGE & RIBNER (ed. 1967): "As though they were."

2995 **I'ld . . . Mistris**] HALLIWELL (ed. 1859): Sh. recalls "the revolting incident of the original novel [*Pandosto*], where the King attempts the seduction of Fawnia [see p. 651]. It is true that, in the text, there is merely the evidence of great kindness, yet the prose tale has probably exerted an influence on the direction of the dialogue." RANK (1912; 1992, p. 311) detects a clear instance of the incest motif, a "fantasy of marriage with the unrecognized daughter." Like other followers of RANK, DEAN (1979, p. 202): *Pandosto*'s "clear case of an attempted father-daughter incest . . . surfaces momentarily" here, and at 2998 ff. "Paulina jumps to the attack and sharply corrects Leontes' wandering desires." Some further developments of this idea are summarized by HOLLAND (1966, pp. 310-11). BETHELL (ed. 1956), however: "Shakespeare . . . makes of this [the revolting incident], first, a harmless sally of wit, and then [3001-2] a deeply pathetic touch of dramatic irony, as Leontes shows himself to be drawn to Perdita because she reminds him of Hermione." Both ideas are

Which he counts but a Trifle.

   Paul. Sir (my Liege)
Your eye hath too much youth in't: not a moneth
'Fore your Queene dy'd, she was more worth such gazes,   (2B6[vb])
Then what you looke on now.   3000

   Leo. I thought of her,
Euen in these Lookes I made. But your Petition
Is yet vn-answer'd: I will to your Father:
Your Honor not o're-throwne by your desires,

---

expressed earlier by SACHS (1923, pp. 79-80), who adds (p. 80): "Leontes' daughter appears to him to be, as it were, his wife who has *remained young*. She is a picture of the object of his love at the time of his greatest desire, which she re-awakens in him against his will" and (p. 81) "Shakespeare softened the theme [of father-daughter incest] but did not erase it, and its psychological roots remained [as in *Pandosto*] in the father's preference of the young daughter to the aged wife." At this point Leontes does not know he has an aged wife. For further comment, see nn. 2724 and 3217-18.

   2996 **Trifle**] Probably *OED* (*sb.* 3) — "A small article of little intrinsic value; a toy, trinket, bauble, knickknack" — used figuratively, rather than (2c) — "A worthless person; a trifler."

   2997 **Sir (my Liege)**] For terms of address similarly repeated, see 416 and 1803.

   2998 **Your . . . in't**] DEIGHTON (ed. 1889): "You look upon her too much with the admiration of youth, without that judgment you should have at your time of life." ENRIGHT (1970, p. 197), rather differently: "The process of regeneration hasn't quite finished him off. There must be something left for Hermione to come back to." HARP (1978, pp. 304-5), also differently: "Paulina does not yet realize that Leontes no longer lusts to make reality conform to his desires, but is content to admire the surprises which it presents to him. . . . One can see . . . how radically Shakespeare has departed from . . . *Pandosto* [in which the king] decides to throw Dorastus into prison so that he may attempt the immediate seduction of Fawnia." See p. 650.

   3001-2 **I . . . made**] HUDSON (ed. 1880): "Leontes takes so quickly and so strongly to Perdita . . . because he instinctively and unconsciously recognises in her a new edition, as it were, of Hermione." HOENIGER (1950, p. 19): "The close degree of resemblance, symbolizing a degree of identity, between the children and both Leontes and Hermione forms a significant fact in this play. However, a strange similarity between Leontes and Polixenes is also hinted at quite clearly [in 130-1]. . . . Parents are depicted as on the one side closely resembling, on the other side as hostile to their children." WILSON (1984, p. 351): The words are "reminiscent of Admetus' partial recognition of the veiled Alcestis."

   3003-5 **I . . . you**] WEINSTEIN (1971, p. 108): "In this moment of regeneration he symbolically redeems his past inconstancy." BASS (1977, p. 21): "Florizel is like enough to his father for Leontes to recover his old friendship and trust of Polixenes. . . . Leontes is willing to match that image with Perdita, who is the image of Hermione. . . . He even presses for the young couple's marriage because Perdita, not yet known for who she really is, reminds him so much of Hermione." For another interpretation, see the next n.

   3004 **Your . . . desires**] PAFFORD (ed. 1963): "Provided your wishes prove not to be incompatible with your honour." WRIGHT & LAMAR (ed. 1966): "Provided that your desires have been honorably restrained, or are being sought by honorable means." Cf. n. 1834-6. For the participle to express a condition, see ABBOTT §377.

I am friend to them, and you: Vpon which Errand   3005
I now goe toward him: therefore follow me,
And marke what way I make: Come good my Lord.

Exeunt.

Scœna Secunda.   5.2

3005 friend] a friend v1803-SING1, COL, HUD1, WH1, PEL1
3009 SCENE V. POPE, HAN, WARB, JOHN
          SCENE, *near the Court in* Sicily. THEO1+ (−HAN, PEL1, CLN2, PEN2, OXF2)
(subst.)

KNOWLES (privately), however: "Not *provided* but *since*. If Leontes were in doubt, he would not already have decided to help Florizel (3003). Both Perdita and Florizel have expressed honorable wishes for marriage (2972, 2980, 2993–4), as Leontes clearly understands; he would not seek out Polixenes to promote anything else." GIRARD (1987, pp. 51–2), alone: Leontes's friendship to Florizel's desires suggests that the king shares the prince's desire for Perdita. Having said so, he adds *and you*, "uttered perhaps with a sigh of regret," to indicate that he will not pursue his desire.

     3005–7 **Vpon . . . make**] PILGRIM (1983, p. 37): "He gives a lively, almost brisk, consent . . . and *strides* off . . . to put it into effect. Here is the complete restoration of Leontes." For the exit cue, see n. 3182.

     3006 **toward**] OED (*prep.* 1c, citing this line as its last example): Of motion "with implication of reaching." The equivalent of *towards* in 1781.

     3007 **marke . . . make**] THIRLBY (MS 1747–53, Way): "Progress," with which SCHMIDT (1875, Make way) concurs: "Advance successfully." For the phrase, DEIGHTON (ed. 1889): "See what effect my pleading may have upon him and act accordingly." BOORMAN (ed. 1964): "Ambiguous (*a*) 'Note the way I go' and (*b*) 'See what progress I make.'" Gloss *a* presumably means "see how I go about it."

     Come good my Lord] For the transposition, see n. 390.

     3009 *Scœna Secunda*] PYLE (1969, p. 110): "The scene does not take place 'Before Leontes' palace' as [some] editors unaccountably have it, but in one of the waiting-rooms where gentlemen in waiting chat and gossip endlessly, constantly on the look out for news to relieve the tedium." The unaccountable eds. are restating THEOBALD. Some critics admire the scene; others find it a gross violation of dramatic propriety, the worst mistake in a far from perfect play. GILDON (1710, p. 336), in favor: "The Narration of the Discovery . . . is not only entertaining but moving, and he [Sh.] seems accidentally to have hit on something like the Ancients whose *Catastrophes* were generally in Narration." GERVINUS (1877, p. 815): "The poet has wisely placed this event [the meeting of Leontes and Perdita] behind the scenes, otherwise the play would have been too full of powerful scenes." QUILLER-COUCH (1917, pp. 305–6), responding: "If we choose to tread foot with Gervinus . . . ; if, having been promised a mighty thrill, in the great master's fashion, we really prefer two or three innominate gentlemen entering and saying, 'Have you heard?' 'You don't tell me!' . . . —I say, if we really prefer this sort of thing, . . . then Heaven must be our aid." HARRISON (1927, pp. 40–1): "But Gervinus—and Shakespeare—are right. Had these events been shown, not only would the final explanations have been prolonged, but the emotion of the audience would have been dribbled away before the great climax." VON GREYERZ (1965, pp. 43–4): "The dramatist succeeds in disclosing, by the courtiers' report, their deep emotion at the marvellous reconciliation, and thereby prepares us for the miracle of Hermione's 'resurrection'. Thus, the reported scene achieves dramatic economy in two ways: it avoids direct performance [while] retaining the dramatic aspects and simultaneously presents the event combined with its evaluation." PITT (1981, p. 129), also in favor, but oddly: Perdita's "reunion with her father and his reconciliation with Polixenes take place off-stage, thus avoiding the sort of tedium the audience had to suffer in Act V of *Cymbeline*."

LAWLOR (1962, p. 108): The gentlemen "are the living proof of what Camillo and Archidamus had told us [in 1.1]: that 'a gallant child' 'makes old hearts fresh'; and that life and death are lesser things beside the restoration of a succession to the kingdom. It is a sound instinct that prompts the producer to make these courtiers old, even very old, men." Comparing Queen Gertrude's description of Ophelia's death (*Ham.* 4.7.166–83 [3157–74]), Jaques's [i.e., the Lord's] description of the dying deer (*AYL* 2.1.29–43 [632–50]), and the Gentleman's description of Cordelia's reception of the news of Lear's state (*Lr.* 4.3.11–32 [2347+11–+33]), SPENS (1922, p. 18): The events are narrated rather than depicted "to eke out the scanty resources of his [Sh.'s] stage and actors." Elsewhere (pp. 23–4) she strangely "suspects that such a curiously undramatic scene . . . may be the reading version of what was acted in dumb show in the theatre." BLUESTONE (1974, p. 139): "His reason . . . is probably that between the Bohemian sheepshearing scene of IV.iv and the Sicilian scene of V.iii, a great many changes of costume occur." Since the King's Men did not wear elaborate costumes, the changes probably would not have been an important factor. BRADBROOK (1932, p. 57) thinks the dumb show, which "had structural possibilities in the vivid presentation of matters relevant to the plot but not requiring much stress to be laid upon them," would have been superior to this conversation and might have been used here "if the rather too similar device of Hermione as the living statue had not been so close." Even so, she adds (pp. 118–19): "No playwright nowadays would stage Ophelia's first interview with Hamlet 'off', or Leontes' recognition of Perdita; the audience would want to see it, and the actor to act it. But a piece of descriptive verse was as satisfactory to Shakespeare's company as a strong scene. The feeling was there, in the verse, just the same."

Feeling notwithstanding, DRAPER (1985, p. 361): "If there is any clear *scène à faire* [big scene] in the play, the disclosure of Perdita's identity is it, since, in fulfilling the oracle's prophecy, it gives Leontes an heir, Florizel a wife, and Perdita a royal family. . . . We want the scene to be a dramatic present, not deflected into a narrative past." VAN DOREN (1939, p. 321): Perhaps Sh. "was weary of a plot which already had complicated itself beyond comfort; or that a recognition scene appeared in his mind more due to Hermione. . . . Perhaps he could not imagine . . . what Leontes would say."

HARNESS (ed. 1825), however, had already found an explanation for the scene with which many later critics agree: "Probably the event is given in the narrative that the paramount interest of the play may rest, as it ought to do, with restoration of Hermione." ORNSTEIN (1986, p. 232): "If Shakespeare conceived of [*WT*] as a play in which the innocence of youth redeems the sins and suffering of age, the arrival of Florizel and Perdita at Leontes' court would provide a satisfying conclusion. . . . By reporting this discovery scene, not staging it, Shakespeare signals that the ultimate resolution of his play is yet to come." FURNESS (ed. 1898): Sh., mindful of the extravagance of its action and emotion, had the scene reported to avoid the danger of its toppling over into comedy or even farce.

BETHELL (ed. 1956) introduces another issue: "This report of Perdita's discovery is comic—another instance of Shakespeare's capacity for making the serious comic by altering the . . . point of view. Yet, as in the previous discovery of Perdita, as an infant [3.3], the comic dialogue is shot through with phrases of deep significance. . . . Throughout the dialogue of the courtiers we have the wit of the period made ridiculous by excess or inappropriateness [as at 3021-2, for example]." HERFORD (ed. 1916-): Although there is no satirical intent, the narrative is conspicuously affected. The most pathetic moments are, in fact, conveyed in phrases most calculated to banish pathos (cf. [3081-4, with which he compares *Ham.* 1.2.11 ff. (188 ff.)]). The affectation much displeases J. SMITH (1974, p. 134): "Who, without previous knowledge of the play, could feel confident that reunion between Perdita and Leontes had actually taken place, depending as he must on what he overhears of the courtiers' effusions?" CHARLTON (ed. 1916), more favorably: "The scene . . . is in prose, as being less intense than verse . . . and the interest is diversified by the introduction of such subsidiary appeals as the courtier's euphuistic mode of speech and the humour of Autolycus, the Clown, and the Shepherd. All these forbid a concentration of interest on Florizel and Perdita." Instead of euphuism, DRAPER (1985, p. 39) is reminded of the "'wit' of Metaphysical poetry."

WHITE (1981, p. 108), acknowledging the humor, supports HARNESS: "Leontes is presented as overwhelmingly guilty, and his daughter is a continuing sign of his past guilt, and a further enforcement of grief, since it does not affect the kind of suffering which he has been undergoing. For this reason, the reconciliation . . . is presented in a mode very close to parody, for the language of the Gentlemen is self-regarding and euphuistically old-fashioned. Shakespeare is not simply 'saving up' his climax. He is recognising that this incident, although essential for the completion of the plot, is potentially emotionally distracting, and he is carefully skirting the problem." HUSSEY (1992, p. 160) refers to it as "the curious scene in prose (where verse might normally be expected). . . . Probably the prose here is meant simply to convey information in a play whose verse syntax is notoriously difficult." KNIGHT (1947; 1965, p. 116): "The scene is preparatory to the greater miracle and its style well-considered. . . . It strikes a realistic and contemporary note, using the well-known trick of laying solid foundations before an unbelievable event: we are being habituated to impossible reunions." His idea is reiterated by RICHMAN (1990, p. 113): The "narrators instruct the spectators how they should react to the miracle that is to come." See n. 3131 for further preparation. For more opinions of the conception and the style of the scene, see DELIUS (1870, p. 251), MUIR (1969, pp. 87-9), and FOAKES (1971, p. 141).

As for the personnel, FOSS (1932, pp. 136-7): They include "three new characters in whom it is difficult to be interested. As one of them was Paulina's Steward, and as he appears to have been allowed to remain in the King's presence longer than the other two, it seems they could not have been of very high rank, but merely gentlemen's gentlemen, or flunkeys, which would account a little for Autolycus being present and allowed to listen." FOSS is wrong at least about *steward*, defined as "an official who controls the domestic affairs of a household, supervising the service of his master's table, directing the domestics, and regulating household expenditure" (*OED, sb.* 1), like Antonio in Webster's *Duchess of Malfi.* FOSS himself points out (p. 143) that Malvolio, the Countess Olivia's steward, is a gentleman (*TN* 4.2.82 [2067]). There is no reason not to believe the SDs' designation of *Gentleman.* FOSS may also be wrong about Autolycus, who once wore fine clothes and served the Prince and could conceivably be a fallen gentleman, or, as WHITE (1939, p. 158) suggests, "a gentleman servingman, like Fabyan in *Twelfth Night.*" PARTRIDGE (1982, p. 3): "His dress should therefore have an air of distinction; and he should be presented as a stage-pilferer, rather than a thief." See nn. 1681-2 and 2593.

Enter *Autolicus, and a Gentleman.*   3010

Aut. Beseech you (Sir) were you present at this Relation?

*Gent.*1. I was by at the opening of the Farthell, heard
the old Shepheard deliuer the manner how he found it:
Whereupon (after a little amazednesse) we were all com-   3015
manded out of the Chamber: onely this (me thought) I
heard the Shepheard say, he found the Child.

Aut. I would most gladly know the issue of it.

*Gent.*1. I make a broken deliuerie of the Businesse;
but the changes I perceiued in the King, and *Camillo*, were   3020
very Notes of admiration: they seem'd almost, with sta-

3016 this (me thought)] Ff; ～ , ～ ～ , ROWE1-v1793, SING, KIT1, EVNS, BEV4;
～ ∧ ～ ～ ∧ CAM1,   GLO,   WH2-OXF1,   NLSN-CAM3,   SIS-CLN2,   PEN2,   BEV3;
～ , ～ ～ ∧ v1803 *etc.*
3019 make] made PEN1

3010 *Gentleman*] For a possible earlier appearance, see n. 2830.

3011 **Beseech**] For the omission of the nominative, see ABBOTT §399.

3011-12 **this Relation**] DEIGHTON (ed. 1889): "The narration of this story."

3013 **Farthell**] I.e., fardel or bundle. See n. 2591.

3014 **deliuer**] Tell. See n. 2352.

3015 **after . . . amazednesse**] DEIGHTON (ed. 1889): "*I.e.* at first the king and
Camillo were so amazed at the story that no notice was taken of us." MOORMAN (ed.
1912): When they "had recovered from their first shock of amazement."

3018 **issue**] Outcome (*OED, sb.* 10). PARRY (ed. 1982): "What happened next,"
which is unsupported by *OED*.

3019-53 **I . . . of**] SUMMERS (1984, p. 39): The Gentlemen "use a great many
words to describe how far the events and the emotions aroused by them went beyond
words."

3019 **broken deliuerie**] SCHMIDT (1874): "A fragmentary report, having many
gaps in it." ORGEL (ed. 1996): "Disjointed report." BOORMAN (ed. 1964): Also "a
halting way of speaking." Cf. n. 2352.

3020-6 **the changes . . . them**] DONAWERTH (1984, p. 82): "The Renaissance
thought especially worthy of picturing in painting or poetry . . . the expressions
and gestures, the 'changes' or motions of the affections [by which] we interpret the
inner man by the outer."

3021 **very . . . admiration**] JOHNSON (1755, Note *and* Admiration): True tokens (*OED, sb.*[2] 7, as in 380) of wonder. MOORMAN (ed. 1912), however: "Exclamations of wonder; literally, notes of exclamation (!)" (*sb.*[2] 10, citing this line). CHARL-
TON (ed. 1916): "'The changes in the king and Camillo marked their amazement as
plainly and as fully as the mark of exclamation denotes the spirit of the words it
follows.'" COLLINS (ed. 1904-24?) rejects the reference to the exclamation point
because it "was not in general use in Shakespeare's time," but it does appear in the
printed texts of the period. For other instances of noting, see n. 298, and for *wonder*,
see n. 2027-8, 2489.

ring on one another, to teare the Cases of their Eyes.
There was speech in their dumbnesse, Language in their
very gesture: they look'd as they had heard of a World
ransom'd, or one destroyed: a notable passion of Won-   3025
der appeared in them: but the wisest beholder, that knew
no more but seeing, could not say, if th'importance were
Ioy, or Sorrow; but in the extremitie of the one, it must
needs be.   *Enter another Gentleman.*
Here comes a Gentleman, that happily knowes more: 3030
The Newes, *Rogero.*
     *Gent.*2. Nothing but Bon-fires: the Oracle is fulfill'd:
the Kings Daughter is found: such a deale of wonder is
broken out within this houre, that Ballad-makers cannot
be able to expresse it.   *Enter another Gentleman.* 3035
Here comes the Lady *Paulina's* Steward, hee can deliuer
you more. How goes it now (Sir.) This Newes (which

3023 speech] a speech HARN
3024 as] as if ROWE1-POPE2, HAN
3031 *Rogero*] Ruggiero OXF2

3022 **Cases**] JOHNSON (1755): "Covering." SCHMIDT (1874): "The eyelids, and
sockets of the eyes," though here, FURNESS (ed. 1898) thinks, only the first meaning
is appropriate. According to BETHELL (ed. 1956), however, the violation of propriety
is the point. CALDECOTT (MS 1813-33) compares *Per.* 3.2.98 (1298-9).
     3023-5 **There . . . destroyed**] GRIFFITH (1775, p. 115): The allusion is "to the
two principal articles in the Old and New Testament, the fall of man, and his redemption." KNIGHT (1947; 1965, p. 117): "Notice the apocalyptic suggestion of 'ransomed' and 'destroyed': is the miracle a transfiguration of nature or wholly transcendental? Certainly it strikes 'wonder.'" He later answers his own question; see n. 3319-
20. VICKERS (1968, p. 422): "These antitheses become resolved into the basic
opposition . . . , that between . . . joy and woe." Cf. 3059 ff. MUIR (1969, p. 100):
"Beneath the artificial language, we can see careful preparation for the final scene
and hints of the symbolical meaning of the play. This [passage] links up with the
language of redemption in the last scene." PARTRIDGE (1982, p. 1): "The theme of
redemption is implied, but not explicitly stated in Christian terms. In Acts III and IV,
Shakespeare, in fact, preserves a note of salutary Hellenic paganism." KERNAN (1975,
3:454), also thinking of the play's end, finds here the "familiar mixture of tears and
smiles with which life in the Shakespearian world is felt in the moments when it is
experienced fully and truly." Regarding the dichotomy of the world ransomed or
destroyed, NEVO (1987, p. 97): In *WT*, "tragedy will not absorb or synthesize comedy,
nor comedy tragedy."
     3025-9 **a . . . be**] SANDERS (1987, p. 111): "The best way of honouring the
emotion of the participants is to recognize that we can't begin to know what it is."
     3025 **notable**] For other instances of noting, see n. 298.
          passion] SCHMIDT (1875): "Any disposition or affection ruling the mind."
     3026-8 **the . . . Sorrow**] JOHNSON (1755, Importance, citing this line): "Mat-
ter; subject" (*OED* 4: "Import"). STAUNTON (ed. 1859): "A mere spectator could

never have said whether their emotions were of joyful or sorrowing significance." The CLARKES (1879, p. 560): "Occasioning cause." On the basis of "important outrage" in *The Faerie Queene* 2.6.29.2, COLLIER (ed. 1842) connects Sh.'s word with Fr. *emporter*, "to be carried away." His *FQ* reading, however, is an error in the poem's 1596 ed.; 1590 and other early eds. read "importune."

3027 but seeing] CHARLTON (ed. 1916): "Than what could be seen." MAXWELL (ed. 1956): But "what he saw."

importance] SCHMIDT (1874): "Import, meaning." ORGEL (ed. 1996): "Implications."

3028 extremitie] MINSHEU (1617): "Vttermost of any thing."

of the one] ROLFE (ed. 1879): "That is, of the one or the other."

3030 happily] MINSHEU (1617): "*By* Happe, *or* chaunce." SCHMIDT (1874): "Perhaps." See ABBOTT §42.

3031 *Rogero*] PAFFORD (ed. 1963): "This is unlike the Plutarchian names of the other male characters [see nn. 3371 ff., above]. It was the name of a popular tune." For the tune, see CHAPPELL (1859; 1965, 1:93-5); further information may be found in ROLLINS (1922, p. 176). THOMAS (1922), who is generally skeptical of Sh.'s indebtedness to such Spanish sources as the *Amadis* romances of Feliciano de Silva (but see n. 3382 above, and p. 680), nevertheless is struck by the fact that one of Feliciano's heroes is named Rogel de Grecia; THOMAS implies that Sh. could have imitated this name in the atypical *Rogero*. Before *WT*, however, *Rogero* had been used in *The First Part of Jeronimo* (1600-5) and *The Insatiate Countess* (1607-8); Sh. did not have to go to Spain to find the name. Or possibly a Shn. *R*-name from Plutarch was transformed to *Rogero* by Crane or Compositor A. DUFFIN (1994, pp. 23-4) thinks Sh. deliberately adopted the name to allude to a ballad entitled "The torment of a Jealious minde," which was sung to a tune called "Rogero" (*The Shirburn Ballads*, ed. Andrew Clark [Oxford, 1907], no. 44). In the song the unjustly suspected wife dies. Thus the misled audience would experience a heightened joy when Hermione's survival is revealed.

3032 Bon-fires] It is not clear why THEOBALD (MS - 1729?) should mark this word "Anachron[ism?]." *OED* (*sb.*) shows it in use in THEOBALD's time to mean a large open-air fire "on some festive occasion" (4b), though the spelling was commonly *bone-fire*. WHITER (1794; 1967, pp. 214-15) cites this instance of the common association of bonfires with "scenes of Public rejoicing." See *Pandosto*, pp. 621, 655.

3033-5 such . . . it] For the deal of wonders expressed by ballad makers, see the subjects of Autolycus's ballads, 2097-2102. WILSON (ed. 1931): "The ballad-maker was the popular journalist of the age, always on the look-out for a fresh 'sensation.'" HARTWIG (1972, p. 131) finds much more to it: "The gentlemen's narrative provides an artificial modulation between the pastoral world, where ballads celebrate an event, and the actualized dream of the tragicomic world, where wonder is enacted onstage. The narrative marks out a step in the transition from an art form which farcically abstracts events from life (Autolycus' ballads [2097-2102]) to the statue scene, which infuses art into life."

3034 broken out] KITTREDGE & RIBNER (ed. 1967): "Revealed."

that] BOORMAN (ed. 1964): "I.e. that even."

3035 *another Gentleman*] MAHOOD (1992, p. 11): "In 1912 Nigel Playfair, having been killed off in the middle of another London play, stepped nightly across to the Savoy to play the Third Gentleman in Granville Barker's production" of *WT*.

3036 deliuer] See n. 2352.

3037 How goes it] The CLARKES (1879, p. 365): "What is going on?"

3037-9 This . . . suspition] BOORMAN (ed. 1964): "Here Shakespeare anticipates and disarms criticism of his far-fetched plot." For *old tale*, RANN (ed. 1787): "A romance." The expression, with some variation, occurs also at 618, 1593, 3070, and 3328. BETHELL (1947, p. 53): "Such internal comments upon the nature of a story

is call'd true) is so like an old Tale, that the veritie of it is
in strong suspition: Ha's the King found his Heire?

    *Gent.*3. Most true, if euer Truth were pregnant by   3040
Circumstance: That which you heare, you'le sweare
you see, there is such vnitie in the proofes. The Mantle
of Queene *Hermiones*: her Iewell about the Neck of it:
the Letters of *Antigonus* found with it, which they know
to be his Character: the Maiestie of the Creature, in re-   3045
semblance of the Mother: the Affection of Noblenesse,
which Nature shewes aboue her Breeding, and many o-
ther Euidences, proclayme her, with all certaintie, to be
the Kings Daughter. Did you see the meeting of the
two Kings?   3050

    *Gent.*2. No.

    *Gent.*3. Then haue you lost a Sight which was to bee
seene, cannot bee spoken of. There might you haue beheld one Ioy crowne another, so and in such manner, that
it seem'd Sorrow wept to take leaue of them: for their   3055

3041 Circumstance] circumstances CAP (*text*; circumstance *in errata*)

3043 *Hermiones*] *Hermione* ROWE1-COL3 (−CAP, MAL, WH1), DEL, KTLY, KNT3, COL4, OXF1, SIG

3048 all] *Om.* HARN

3052 haue you] you have COL, WH1, DEL, OXF1

---

always remind us of its unreality. . . . They combine with the deliberately old-fashioned technique to insist that it is after all only a dramatic performance." MUIR (1969,
p. 101), however: "The continual references in *The Winter's Tale* to the incredible
nature of the story have the paradoxical effect of undercutting . . . scepticism."
GODDARD (1951, p. 649) thinks that "we are more inclined to accept an impossible
story if the teller frankly confesses his awareness of the strain to which he is subjecting
our credulity," but it seems more likely that Sh. invokes a romantic order of truth
different from the naturalistic. See n. 181-92. LAROQUE (1982, p. 28) finds an echo
of "And their words seemed to them as idle tales" (Luke 24:11). This is the language
of the King James Version (1611); the Geneva Bible has "as a fained thing." More
appropriate is THOMAS (1907, p. xv): The words "seem like Shakespeare's direct
reference to his original," *Pandosto.*

    3039 **Heire**] For Perdita as heir, see nn. 1315 and 2780.

    3040 **pregnant**] RANN (ed. 1787): "Confirm'd." SCHMIDT (1875): "Clear, evi-
dent." DEIGHTON (ed. 1889): This gloss "does not give the full force of the metaphor,
i.e. if ever truth was with child by reality; possibly with reference to the words 'he
can *deliver* you more' [3036-7], the steward acting in this matter as midwife."
WRIGHT & LAMAR (ed. 1966): "Enlarged."

    3041 **Circumstance**] SCHMIDT (1874): "Facts from which a certain presumption
arises, which give evidence of some truth." For related meanings, see nn. 796, 1192,
and 2837.

    3041-2 **That . . . proofes**] BOORMAN (ed. 1964) finds "a hint of apology that
this scene is merely reported."

3042 **vnitie**] MINSHEU (1617, Vnion): "Agreement."

proofes] I.e., the mantle, the jewel, the letters, etc. MUELLER (1971, p. 228): "In his chapter on Recognitions Aristotle writes: 'As to its different kinds, the first, least artistic, but most frequently used through lack of talent, is recognition by token or signs' (*Poetics*, 16.54b20–21)." MUELLER believes that this convention contributes to *WT*'s "consciously ostentatious and antiquated stage technique," described by BETHELL (see p. 716).

3043 **Iewell**] SCHMIDT (1874): "Any personal ornament of gold or precious stones."

3044 **Letters**] SCHANZER (ed. 1969): "What has been written" (*OED, sb.*[1] 3b).

3045 **his Character**] At 1489, Antigonus leaves with the infant Perdita "thy character"; see n. 1489. The word here means "the fashion of a Letter" (CAWDREY, 1604) or "handwriting" (*OED, sb.* 4c). Her character is thus confirmed by his character.

Creature] SCHMIDT (1874): "Living being." The CLARKES (ed. 1865): Also "offspring" (*OED* 4).

3046 **Affection of Noblenesse**] Like MALONE (ed. 1790, 2:245 and 10:607), SCHMIDT (1874, Affection): "Bent of mind, disposition" (*OED, sb.* 4). HUNTER (ed. 1872): "Proclivity towards nobleness." For other senses, see nn. 26, 214, 2206, 2332–3, and 3110. RANN (ed. 1787): "Air of nobility, noble carriage" (*OED, sb.* 12; first citation, 1636).

3047 **Breeding**] Upbringing. See nn. 2452–3, 2601.

3048 **proclayme**] *OED* (*v.* 4 *fig.*, citing this line): "Prove."

3052-3 **Then . . . of**] WATKINS (1950, p. 227): Despite this declaration, he "proceeds to speak of it so graphically that we do indeed see the occasion."

Sight . . . seene] Which *sights* intrinsically are, but here the sight must be heard. BERRY (1965, p. 74): By the time he wrote *WT*, Sh. "was easily able . . . to endow the dramatic mode with an Inset power [an Inset is a descriptive episode 'where the imagined spectacle', the reunion, 'is at odds with the actual spectacle' (p. 3)] by positioning it in the background and to endow the narrative mode with dramatic immediacy by placing it in the foreground." EGGERS (1979, p. 468): "The 'reversal' enhances the wonder of the event described. The audience [here] identifies with characters who are made to credit an incredible . . . story."

3053 **spoken of**] HUNTER (ed. 1872): "Described."

3053-67 **There . . . doe it**] HASLER (1983, p. 210): "One is struck by the contrast between the highly demonstrative self-abandonment described [here] and the remarkable, controlled restraint shown in 5.3. It seems that for very good reasons Shakespeare entrusted the 'wading in tears' to our imaginations rather than a concrete enactment by real actors. . . . The emotions stirred up in 5.3 are of the kind that is beyond words, his [Leontes's] silence therefore is the best and most adequate response."

3053-6 **There . . . teares**] COLLINS (1880, p. 739) finds this sentence and 3090-2 "very good specimen[s]" of the "modified euphuism" derived by Sh. from John Lyly. Commenting on 3090-2, MOORMAN (ed. 1912): "Shakespeare liked nothing better than to make gentlemen of the court indulge in affected, euphuistic language. He discards the stilted utterance of Greene's *Pandosto* except where, in this scene, the speakers are courtiers." BETHELL (ed. 1956): "They were weeping because their sorrow had been turned to joy, so the ingenious Third Gent. personifies sorrow and makes her weep at parting from them. It is not a helpful figure." TRAVERSI (1955, p. 185) agrees: "The artificiality of elaboration seems to be insufficiently integrated into a true artistic effect."

3054 **crowne**] *OED* (*v.*[1] 9, citing this line): "Add the finishing touch to."

so . . . manner] RITSON (in STEEVENS, ed. 1793): "The technical language of conveyancers [who draw up deeds, leases, etc.]." DEIGHTON (ed. 1889): "As if."

Ioy waded in teares. There was casting vp of Eyes, holding vp of Hands, with Countenance of such distraction,
that they were to be knowne by Garment, not by Fauor.
Our King being ready to leape out of himselfe, for ioy of   (2(
his found Daughter; as if that Ioy were now become a   3060
Losse, cryes, Oh, thy Mother, thy Mother: then askes
Bohemia forgiuenesse, then embraces his Sonne-in-Law:
then againe worryes he his Daughter, with clipping her.
Now he thanks the old Shepheard (which stands by, like
a Weather-bitten Conduit, of many Kings Reignes.) I   3065
neuer heard of such another Encounter; which lames Re-
port to follow it, and vndo's description to doe it.

    *Gent.*2.   What, 'pray you, became of *Antigonus*, that
carryed hence the Child?

3057 Countenance] countenances mTBY4 *conj.*, GLO, WH2, OXF1, NLSN
3064 which] who ROWE1-JOHN2, v1773
3065 bitten] beaten F3-RANN, COL2, COL3
3067 doe it] draw it HAN; show it COL2, COL3, COL4; do it justice SING2 *conj.*,
KTLY

3056-8 **There . . . Fauor**] J. SMITH (1974, p. 137), disapprovingly: "A statement that, at moments of deep and violent disturbance, not only human feelings but
human beings are to be recognized only by their physical accompaniments." HAPPÉ
(1969): "Implies a degree of detachment from the events described. It is part of the
delicate machinery of this scene whereby the reunion of Leontes and Perdita is kept
at a distance (cf. the partial anticipation by Camillo [2412-19])."
    3057 **Countenance**] SCHMIDT (1874): "Appearance, deportment." DEIGHTON
(ed. 1889): "It may either be taken as in reality plural [countenances], there being
other examples in Shakespeare of nouns in -*ce* having such forms for their plural [see
ABBOTT §471]; or as the abstract for the concrete." COLLINS (ed. 1904-24?): Possibly
singular because of "Garment" and "Fauor" (3058).
    distraction] *OED* 4: "Violent perturbation . . . approaching to temporary
madness"; cf. 227. DEIGHTON (ed. 1889): "Ecstasy." COLLINS (ed. 1904-24?): Bewilderment. BOORMAN (ed. 1964): "Violently mixed feelings." PAFFORD (ed. 1963, citing
H8 3.1.112 [1743]): "Distortion."
    3058 **were . . . knowne**] BETHELL (ed. 1956): "Could be recognized only."
    by . . . Fauor] JOHNSON (1755, Favour): "Countenance." RANN (ed. 1787):
"Rather by their dress, than their features."
    3059 **leape . . . himselfe**] *OED* (*v.* 2b, citing this line): "An expression of
delight." Proverbial (TILLEY S507).
    ioy of] *OED* (*prep.* 14b, citing this line): "Supplied [today] by *on account of,
for, at.*"
    3060-4 **now . . . Now**] The CLARKES (1879, p. 77): "Our poet occasionally uses
the word 'now' when referring to a past time; thereby giving wonderfully spirited
effect to passages of narration."
    3061 **thy . . . Mother**] LANGMAN (1976, p. 202): "In *Pandosto* at this juncture

the king embraces the girl, crying 'my daughter Fawnia! ah sweet Fawnia! I am thy father Fawnia' [see p. 655]." LENZ (1986, p. 112): Perdita's "reunion with her father is joyful, but it is counterbalanced by the loss of Hermione."

3063 **worryes**] SCHMIDT (1875, Worry): "To tear, to lacerate, to pull to pieces." *OED* (*v.* 3c, citing this line only): "To kiss or hug vehemently." J. SMITH (1974, p. 138), who dislikes the expression: "As a dog might worry a bone."

worryes he] The *he* may have been added to give weight to the clause or in anticipation of the next sentence.

clipping] JOHNSON (1755, Clip): "To embrace, by throwing the arms round."

3064 **which**] For this use of the relative, see n. 572. FURNESS (ed. 1898), however: Possibly "used proleptically in reference to the conduit, in which simile, by the way, we see the 'gentlemanlike tears' whereof the Clown afterward boasted [3152-3]."

3065 **a . . . Reignes**] BARBER (1964, pp. 248-9), perhaps overingeniously: "The shepherd here becomes a type of the continuity of rural life, with its toughness ('weather-bitten'), its life-giving qualities, and its channelling of tradition (both suggested by *conduit*, which presumably carries water). . . . Kings may come and go, but the conduit and the old shepherd remain." KNIGHTS (1976, p. 610): "The simile suggests a succession of generations that, in the forms of culture, stretches far beyond the span of father and mother and child." PORTER & CLARKE (ed. 1908) find puns on *wether*, a castrated sheep, and *rains*.

Weather-bitten] STEEVENS (ed. 1778), quoting "The air bites shrewdly" (*Ham.* 1.4.1 [604]) and "when it [the wind] bites and blows" (*AYL* 2.1.8 [614]): "Corroded by the weather" (*OED*, citing this line as its first instance). The word is not a form of *weather-beaten*.

Conduit] HENLEY (in MALONE, 1780, 2:704), quoting *Rom.* 3.5.130-1 (2168-9): "Conduits [fountains] representing a human figure, were heretofore not uncommon." HARRISON (ed. 1947): "Water for domestic use in the City of London was drawn by water carriers from conduits at various places. . . . The dripping conduit is a natural poetic image for tears." PAFFORD (ed. 1963): Conduits "were frequently in the form of an old man's head. The image is of the old shepherd weeping."

of] BEVINGTON (ed. 1992): "During."

3066 **Encounter**] SCHMIDT (1874): "A seeing or finding each other."

3066-7 **which . . . doe it**] THIRLBY (MS 1733-47?): "She will outstrip all praise and make it halt behind her" (*Tmp.* 4.1.10-11 [1661-2]). Rather than "praise" (for *report*), SCHMIDT (1875) gives "a telling or speaking of something." BETHELL (ed. 1956): "It is impossible to recount fully." PARTRIDGE (1982, p. 1): Here and at 3328, "Shakespeare owned that *The Winter's Tale* might overstrain credulity. Rational coherence was not, however, his intention." Nevertheless, as MIKO (1989, p. 270) says, "they describe it [the reunion] very adequately."

3067 **vndo's . . . it**] The CLARKES (ed. 1865): "'Description' immediately preceding 'do' causes the latter to stand for 'describe', while there is a kind of play between the words 'undoes' and 'do' maintained by using 'do' instead of 'describe'. . . . The latter of the two 'its' . . . , while referring to 'encounter', *also* refers to 'description.'" The CLARKES (1879, p. 517) are less opaque: "Ruins description in attempting to describe it." DEIGHTON (ed. 1889): "Beggars description to portray it." WILSON (ed. 1931), however: "I.e. discharge it, deliver it. The expression 'do a message' is frequent in Shakespeare [e.g., *TGV* 4.4.88 (1909) and *Tro.* 1.3.219 (679)]." Regarding the statement, TREWIN (1978, p. 267): "Whereupon he undoes description." BEVINGTON (1984, p. 19): "Shakespeare does not stage the 'sight' for us. . . . He chooses instead to assert the impossibility of conveying through words what the combined joy and sorrow of the reunion was like. . . . The reunion itself was characterized by wordlessness [quotes 3056-8]. So too with the reunion after so many years of Leontes and Camillo [quotes 3021-2]."

*Gent.*3.   Like an old Tale still, which will haue matter   3070
to rehearse, though Credit be asleepe, and not an eare o-
pen; he was torne to pieces with a Beare: This auouches
the Shepheards Sonne; who ha's not onely his Innocence
(which seemes much) to iustifie him, but a Hand-kerchief
and Rings of his, that *Paulina* knowes.   3075
   *Gent.*1.   What became of his Barke, and his Followers?
   *Gent.*3.   Wrackt the same instant of their Masters
death, and in the view of the Shepheard: so that all the
Instruments which ayded to expose the Child, were euen   3080
then lost, when it was found. But oh the Noble Combat,
that 'twixt Ioy and Sorrow was fought in *Paulina.* Shee
had one Eye declin'd for the losse of her Husband, another eleuated, that the Oracle was fulfill'd: Shee lifted the
Princesse from the Earth, and so locks her in embracing,   3085
as if shee would pin her to her heart, that shee might no
more be in danger of loosing.
   *Gent.*1.   The Dignitie of this Act was worth the audience of Kings and Princes, for by such was it acted.

3070 matter] matters F4-MAL (−CAP)
3072 to] in HAN3
3073-4 Innocence (which . . . much)] ∼ , ∼ . . . ∼ ∧ THEO2, WARB-v1773
(−CAP)
3085 locks] lock'd mTBY3 *conj.*, HAN
3087 loosing] losing her COL2, COL3, KTLY, HUD2

3070 **old Tale**] HERFORD (ed. 1916-): "Emphasizing its *Märchen* character." Cf.
nn. 181-92 and 3037-9, as well as lines 615-18, 1593, 3038, and 3328.
   still] DEIGHTON (ed. 1889): "Referring to the former strange story."
   matter] JOHNSON (1755): "Subject; thing treated."
   3071 **rehearse**] SCHMIDT (1875): "Recite . . . tell." Taking the dramatic sense,
BOORMAN (ed. 1964) discovers "a sly hit at the contemporary theatre, and his own
extraordinary plot."
   Credit] MINSHEU (1617): "Trust." SCHMIDT (1874): "Belief, faith."
   3071-2 **not . . . open**] COLLINS (ed. 1904-24?): "Though no one believes it."
   3072 **with**] ABBOTT (§193): "Often used to express the juxtaposition of cause and
effect." See nn. 2866, 3266.
   3072-3 **This . . . Sonne**] PAFFORD (ed. 1963): "This the shepherd's son
avouches." SCHMIDT (1874, Avouch): "Assert, maintain" (*OED, v.* 7). LEE (ed. 1907):
"Corroborates" (*v.* 4). Cf. nn. 1690 and 3359.
   3073 **Innocence**] SCHMIDT (1874): "Plainness and artlessness bordering on silli-
ness" (*OED* 3, citing this line). WRIGHT & LAMAR (ed. 1966): "Simple-mindedness."
BEVINGTON (ed. 1992) adds: "Such that he would be unable to invent such a story."
   3074 **iustifie him**] SCHMIDT (1874): "Confirm what he declares."

516

3078 Wrackt] Shipwrecked. MINSHEU (1617) does not distinguish between *wrack* and *wreck*. A "WRECK *is where* a ship is perished at the Sea, *and* no man escapeth aliue out of the Ship" (*OED*, Wrack, *v.*² 2).

3079 in . . . Shepheard] THIRLBY (MS 1733-47?): "Not so but of his son." He cites 1525 ff. and 3072-3. But the shepherd's son was also a shepherd.

3080 Instruments which] BETHELL (ed. 1956): "Agents who."

expose] *OED* (*v.* 2, citing this line): "To abandon (an infant)."

3082-4 Shee . . . eleuated] MAXWELL (ed. 1969, Declined): "Cast down in sorrow." Like DELIUS (ed. 1860), FURNESS (ed. 1898) compares *Ham.* 1.2.11 (188), which, being emblematic rather than descriptive, BETHELL (ed. 1956) finds no parallel. BETHELL comments, "The remarkable behaviour of Paulina's eyes should be enough to warn us that the Third Gent. is not a wholly serious character. . . . He speaks as if describing Paulina physically, and uses terms . . . [that] can signify directions as well as states of mind." Fastening only upon the directions, J. SMITH (1974, p. 138): "The poor lady appears to undergo a punishment like that of the rack, or of a rending asunder by horses." The expression is proverbial (TILLEY E248); it is sometimes applied ironically ("The wepying of an heire is dissembled laughyng, yea he reioyceth though he wepe") but in other forms (e.g., L92a) expresses a genuine mixture of contradictory emotions: "So weeping, smiling greete I thee my earth" (*R2* 3.2.110 [1370]). See also *Lr.* 4.3.11-24 (2347+10- +24). As PAFFORD (ed. 1963) argues, Paulina's mingled emotions are not feigned, and the Gentleman's description of their noble combat, though artful, is not less than serious. The image is discussed more fully in WHITE (1959).

3083-4 another] The other. See ABBOTT §88.

3085 locks] *OED* (*v.*¹ 6e, citing this line as its earliest instance): "Embrace closely." CARRINGTON (1956): "The present tense makes the description more dramatic." BLUESTONE (1974, p. 139): "The Third Gentleman reporting this action ordinarily imitates in gesture the locked embrace against his own body."

3087 loosing] LETTSOM (MS 1840-65): "Being lost"; hence, the second *shee* in 3086 is Perdita. PAFFORD (ed. 1963): "But 'loosing', carrying on the sense of 'pin', may be right: 'that she might no longer be in danger of being physically separated from her'. Probably both senses are present."

3088-89 The . . . acted] EDWARDS ("Seeing," 1986, pp. 86-7): This "assertion of the First Gentleman (who wasn't a witness) . . . only emphasises the cheapness given to the momentous events by the prattle of the Third Gentleman, who is overarticulate." DEATON (1936, p. 55) asks why this scene is reported rather than depicted. For answers, see n. 3009.

3088 Dignitie] *OED* (1): "Worthiness, worth, nobleness, excellence." For another use of the word, see nn. 28, 2326, and 2946.

3088-9 Act . . . audience . . . acted] HUNTER (1926, pp. 305-6 n.) finds this passage one of ten in Sh. in which the word *act* occurs in conjunction with other theatrical terms. He uses the information to argue that Sh. espoused a five-act structure, a question still debated (see Bernard Beckerman, "Shakespeare's Dramatic Methods," *William Shakespeare: His World, His Work, His Influence*, ed. John F. Andrews, New York, 1985, 2:405-6). The collocation is nevertheless a fact. SCHANZER (ed. 1969): "The primary meaning [of 'Act'] is evidently 'that which took place'. . . . But the further, obsolete, meaning of 'performance of part of a play' [*OED* 7, not marked *Obs.*] is also present, and is responsible for the playhouse-metaphors in the rest of the sentence." JONAS (1918, pp. 402-3) finds other theatrical allusions at 269-71, 1210-11, 1764-5, 1948-9, 2467-9, 2533-4, and 3365-9. LAWRENCE (1937, p. 11) is reminded of "You . . . That are but mutes, or audience to this act" (*Ham.* 5.2.334-5 [3818-19]), and BARTON (1986, p. 40) of "*A Kingdome for a Stage, Princes to Act, And Monarchs to behold the swelling Scene*" (*H5* 1.0. 3-4).

*Gent.*3. One of the prettyest touches of all, and that   3090
which angl'd for mine Eyes (caught the Water, though
not the Fish) was, when at the Relation of the Queenes
death (with the manner how shee came to't, brauely confess'd, and lamented by the King) how attentiuenesse
wounded his Daughter, till (from one signe of dolour to   3095
another) shee did (with an *Alas*) I would faine say, bleed

3091-2 (caught . . . Fish)] *Om.* HAN, WARB
3091 caught] and caught KEIGHTLEY *conj. in* CAM1, KTLY
3093 brauely] heavily COL2, COL3, COL4

3090-3100 **One . . . vniuersall**] HALE (1985, p. 156): "The roundabout syntax . . . tinges the first sentence with absurdity. The extremism of the conceits, too,
makes us aware of the preciosity of the manner of the utterance. . . . Since
. . . Perdita, the subject, [is] neither roundabout nor precious . . . the Gentleman
and his manner [deflect] onto himself any ridicule and disbelief. . . . His final sentence . . . insinuates the key-image of the finale, the changing of marble to colour."
        3090-2 **that . . . Fish**] J. SMITH (1974, p. 137): "The well-bred joke . . . aims
at geniality, relieving without discrediting seriousness." CALDECOTT (MS 1813-33),
for *caught . . . Fish*: "Drew from them the moisture of their eyes . . . tho I don't
tell you, that it extracted their *orbs*." STRUTT (in SEYMOUR, 1805, 1:171): "What most
claimed my observation; but which *bedimming* with tears my sight, prevented my
beholding it." HUNTER (ed. 1872): "Drew tears from me, but not my eyes [i.e., I did
not cry my eyes out]." BETHELL (ed. 1956) literal-mindedly complains: "What are 'the
fish'? They cannot mean his eyes (i.e. his attention), as they should, for that was caught
or he would not have wept. The image *looks* clever but fails to 'work out.'" For more
on the style, see n. 3053-6 and for more on angling, n. 1658.
        3092-4 **when . . . how**] ABBOTT (§415): A "construction changed by change
of thought. . . . The narrator first intends to narrate the point of time, then diverges
into the manner, of the action." ABBOTT appears to be mistaken. The pretty touch is
the way in which her attentiveness wounded Perdita when she heard the account.
        3093 **brauely**] WHITE (ed. 1857): "Implying candor and courage." For the more
general sense, see n. 2026.
        3094-7 **how . . . Teares**] DEIGHTON (ed. 1889, Attentiveness): Listening atten-
tively. WILSON (ed. 1931), more accurately: "I.e. 'the hearing of it.'" BETHELL (ed.
1956): "Wounded by Attention (personified) she bleeds tears." COGHILL (1958, p.
39): "Could Donne have found a better hyperbole than 'wounded', or Crashaw a
more felicitous conceit for eyes and tears?" MUIR (1969, pp. 99-100): COGHILL "is
wrong to compare the conceits to those of the metaphysicals. . . . The style of this
scene is purely Arcadian [i.e., after Sir Philip Sidney]. . . . It is significant that in the
one play which used *Arcadia* as a source, *King Lear*, Shakespeare should write in
the Arcadian style [as at 4.3.16-24 (2347+16-+24)]." DELIUS (ed. 1860), however,
compares the "wonder wounded hearers" of *Ham.* 5.1.257 (3452).
        3095-6 **from . . . another**] DEIGHTON (ed. 1889): "Passing from one manifes-
tation of grief to another."
        3096 *Alas*] For the part of speech, see n. 2931.
        faine say] DEIGHTON (ed. 1889): "Literally gladly say, here, I might almost say."

Teares; for I am sure, my heart wept blood. Who was
most Marble, there changed colour: some swownded, all
sorrowed: if all the World could haue seen't, the Woe
had beene vniuersall.   3100

  *Gent.*1. Are they returned to the Court?

  *Gent.*3. No: The Princesse hearing of her Mothers
Statue (which is in the keeping of *Paulina*) a Peece many
yeeres in doing, and now newly perform'd, by that rare
Italian Master, *Iulio Romano*, who (had he himselfe Eter-   3105

3098 Marble, there∧] F1, F2, THEO, WARB, JOHN, CAM3, SIS, ARD2; ~ ∧ ~ , F4,
ROWE, CAP-v1821, HAL, DEL; ~ ∧ ~ ∧ F3 *etc.*

3105 he] *Om.* ROWE1, ROWE2

3096-7 **bleed . . . blood**] *OED* (Bleed, *v.* 7b) cites this as its first instance of
the word in a transferred sense. PARRY (ed. 1982): The weeping was "profoundly
heartfelt." PAFFORD (ed. 1963): "Perhaps suggested by the belief that sighs did cost
the heart blood."

3097-8 **Who . . . colour**] BETHELL (ed. 1956): "This has the appearance of paradox, for marble cannot change colour: but 'marble' is used metaphorically (petrified
with wonder, rigid with attentiveness—or, perhaps, hard-hearted), while 'changed
colour' is literal." The pun on *marble* was detected by early editors. STEEVENS (ed.
1778) had glossed it "petrified with wonder," whereas to MALONE (1780, 1:146) it
meant "hard-hearted, unfeeling" (*OED, sb.* 7b, citing this line). MOORMAN (ed. 1912)
compares "I am Marble constant" (*Ant.* 5.2.40 [3490]), where *marble* implies firmness of resolution, an idea inappropriate here; more to the point is that hard hearts
are proverbially stone, flint, or marble (TILLEY H311). McPEEK (1969, p. 250): "All
were transformed. And we might well be ready for the final shape-shifting, the story
of the statue of Hermione." GARBER (1987, p. 139): "The intimation is the more
pointed because of the specific moment at which it occurs in the narrative—'the
relation of the Queen's death' [3092-3]—and it sets up, in dramatic terms, the mysterious finale."

3098 **swownded**] Swooned. *OED* describes *swound* as a "later form of swoune,
SWOON with excrescent *d.*" Since he set "*sounds*" in *2H6* 3.2.32 (1728) and
"swoone" at *R3* 4.1.35 (2514), Compositor A seems to have had no preference as to
form, so *swounded* may have stood in his copy here. *Swounds* occurs in *MM* 2.4.24
(1027), another play printed from a Crane transcript.

3102 **hearing**] BOORMAN (ed. 1964): "I.e. . . . had heard (the sentence, as it
stands, is unfinished)." Or elliptical.

3102-3 **Mothers Statue**] CRAIG (1948, p. 339): "The device of the statue was
introduced into Greene's story in order to mitigate the tragedy. It may have been
introduced into the play during the process of composition, since its effect is that of
an afterthought."

3103 **Peece**] For the various significances, see n. 3229.

3104 **in doing**] The CLARKES (1879, p. 356): "In course of execution."

3104-5 **newly . . . Romano**] HERFORD (1927, pp. 280-1): "The solitary mention, in all Shakespeare, of the name of any artist whatever." THEOBALD (ed. 1733):
Giulio "was born in the Year 1492 [i.e., c. 1498], . . . and dy'd Eighteen Years before

the Latter [Sh.] was born [i.e., 1546]. . . . It was a strange Absurdity, sure, to thrust it [a tribute to Giulio] into a Tale, the Action of which is suppos'd within the Period of Heathenism, and whilst the Oracles of *Apollo* were consulted." WARBURTON (ed. 1747) too is miffed: "He [Sh.] makes of this famous painter, a *Statuary* [sculptor] . . . but, what is worst of all, a *painter of statues,*" i.e., Sh.'s Romano first created the statue, then colored it. Hence TOLLET (in STEEVENS, ed. 1778): "I wish we could understand this passage, as if *Julio Romano* had only painted the statue carved by another." This understanding is possible, for *perform* may mean "to complete by the addition of ornament" (*OED, v.* 2b; see also n. 3104). To show that in Sh.'s time marble statues were painted, TOLLET refers to Jonson, *The Magnetic Lady* 5.7.90-2, and to Sir Henry Wotton, *The Elements of Architecture* (1624, p. 89), and adds "unless [it] were painted, there could be no ruddiness upon her lip [3283], nor could the veins 'verily seem to bear blood' [3261-2]." CHEW (1947, p. 11) similarly: "The allusion to the painter's share of the work is dramatically necessary because, being Hermione herself, the supposed statue must appear to Leontes in such colours."

THORP (1931, p. 686) finds little difference in the distinction between sculpting and painting: "The sixteenth century interchanged the technical terms of the two arts. A statue was a picture; a statue was painted— . . . both statues and pictures were counterfeits and shadows of life." SMITH (1985, p. 21) describes an engraving depicting a "winged figure that poses inside a darkened niche in Julio's design of Victory . . . not a living creature but a statue." Earlier, ELZE (1873; 1874, pp. 286-9) had attempted a different explanation: Since Sh. could not himself have seen Giulio's paintings and then identified him as a sculptor, he must instead have relied upon two epigraphs quoted by Vasari (*Le vite de' più eccellenti pittori, scultori, ed architettori,* in *Le opere di Giorgio Vasari,* ed. Gaetano Milanesi, Firenze, 1906, 5:557):

> *Romanus moriens secum tres Julius arteis*
> *Abstulit (haud mirum), quatuor unus erat*

> [No wonder Giulio Romano in dying took away
> three arts; four was one]

and

> *Videbat Juppiter corpora sculpta pictaque*
> *Spirare, et aedes mortalium aequarier Coelo,*
> *Iulii virtute Romani.*

> [Jupiter saw sculpted and painted bodies
> breathe, and the dwellings of mortals made
> equal to those in heaven by the skill of
> Giulio Romano]

The *tres artes* would include sculpture and that Romano "could put Breath into his work" seems inspired by *videbat Juppiter corpora spirare.* "Either Shakespeare must have studied Vasari [in Italian, as his *Lives* had not yet been translated], or he had been in Mantua and had there seen Romano's works and read his epitaphs." The first of these suppositions may not be utterly out of the question. On indirect evidence, GRILLO (1949, p. 125) concludes that Sh. "must somehow or other have learned enough Italian to read and understand" Italian writers, and MUIR (1957, p. 7) notes that he "seems to have read parts of Giraldi's *Hecatommithi* and several Italian plays in the original." ZIEGLER (1985, p. 208) also raises the possibility. Cf. n. 2665-7 and see the discussions of Sh.'s supposed use of Cinthio Giraldi for *MM* (ed. Eccles, 1980, pp. 301-5) and *Oth.* (ed. Sanders, 1984, pp. 2-3).

As to the second supposition, DE MONTMORENCY (1913, p. 739): "These various pictures [the breathing statues of the second epigraph, apparently] seem some evidence of an early visit to Italy [by Sh.] with a company of actors." He points out (p. 740) that Mantua, where Romano spent most of his career, is the locale of *TGV*, *Shr.*, and *Rom*. JUSSERAND (in LEE, ed. 1907, p. xiv), facetiously: "If we accept this conclusion, we must also accept the belief that, at the time of Shakespeare's visit, Mantua was by the sea and north of Milan," as in *TGV* (see n. 1440). Sh. seems to have confused Mantua with Padua in *MV* 3.4.49 (1775). BETHELL (ed. 1956): "The description in Shakespeare's text is *not* a criticism especially appropriate to Romano but a commonplace eulogy such as was applied to any painter or sculptor . . . though his associating Romano with sculpture, and the fact that the text needs some wresting to make him merely the colourist of the statue, would render it likely that he was in some way acquainted with the statement of the epitaph, which is the only known authority for Romano as *sculptor*." GREEN (1870, p. 111) finds another assumption more attractive: "As there were 'sixteen [paintings] by Julio Romano' in the fine collections at Whitehall, made, or, rather, increased by Charles I., of which Henry VIII. had formed the nucleus, it is very probable there were in England some by that master so early as the writing of the *Winter's Tale*, or even before. . . . It may therefore be reasonably conjectured that in the statue of Hermione Shakespeare has accurately described some figure which he had seen in one of Julio Romano's paintings." KÜNSTLER (1956) argues that the Italian princess Giovanna d'Arragona was this figure.

It is at least true that Romano's name and reputation were known to Sh.'s contemporaries. Jonson mentions him in *Underwood* LXXVII and *Discoveries* line 1584, in both instances in lists of famous Renaissance painters. FAIRCHILD (1937, p. 75): Giulio's "acknowledged skill would account for the lifelike appearance of Hermione." BRANDES (1898, 1:139), however: "Giulio Romano, with his crude superficiality, could not possibly have aroused his [Sh.'s] admiration had he known his work." This harsh judgment is mitigated by the better informed views of HARTT (1958), who nevertheless makes it clear that Giulio's achievements were in painting, decoration, and architecture. HARTT's own idea (1:193-4, n. 1) about the creator of the supposed statue is that there were two Giulio Romanos, the other one being a maker of painted stucco reliefs and hence conceivably a sculptor. HOY (1973, pp. 65-6, n. 1): Romano "was a master of painted but seemingly statuary forms set forth in equivocal surroundings. His frescos in the *Sala di Costantino* in the Vatican . . . are virtuoso examples of art imitating not only nature but other forms of art. Painted to simulate tapestry, the figures in the frescos are remarkable for their sculptured shapes. . . . The words [of the] Third Gentleman . . . are entirely in accord with his [Romano's] contemporary reputation." MARTINET (1975), who also discusses his trompe l'oeil works, finds thematic links between Romano and Sh., and SALINGAR (1984, pp. 16-17) agrees, adding (p. 17) that Romano's "genuine but generic-sounding name, Julius the Roman, contributes to that sleight-of-hand or flickering ambiguity between actuality and impossibility characteristic of this romance."

To MATCHETT (1969, p. 103), the origin of Romano's name is "less important than why it has been brought in at all. Surely it is here as part of the general insistence that we not suspect the statue of being anything more than a statue." Responses differ. NEVO (1987, p. 127): "We really see what Leontes sees. . . . It is a mirror-image of Romano's illusionist skill. Romano's craft made statues so real-seeming that they seemed real persons. Paulina has made a real person so statuesque as to seem a statue." BARKAN (1981, p. 657): "The most important link between Shakespeare's lines and Vasari's appears in the references to the whole combative spirit of the *paragone* [comparison]. . . . To a reader of Vasari—especially one who had never seen any of the artist's work—Giulio Romano would appear as a great and godlike creator, master of many arts and worthy opponent of Nature herself as a creator. . . . Shakespeare required such a figure with whom he could credit the creation of a work of art that was . . . both sculpted and painted and which finally proves to be not a work of art at all." BARTON (1990, pp. 86-7): "Most of the members of Shakespeare's audience, at least at Blackfriars, would have recognized Romano's name, and probably have known something about his work. Not, however, until the play was over could they possibly have puzzled out why Shakespeare had, so startlingly, introduced him. The recovery of Hermione from a death of sixteen years is something so delicate and emotionally fraught . . . that it required a palisade of safeguards, of which Julio Romano, a tangible Renaissance figure, is one. It is under the aegis of this Italian artist's demonstrable reality that what is arguably the most implausible event in the entire Shakespeare canon comes safely home." ZIEGLER (1985) argues on indirect evidence that Sh. would have known an Italian conduct book by Giovanni Michele Bruto, translated as *The Necessarie, Fit, and Convenient Education of a yong Gentlewoman* by W. P. and published by Adam Islip in 1598. It mentions Julio Romano (sig.C4ᵛ), but as a painter, not a sculptor.

KNIGHT (ed. 1841, Comedies 2:340): Romano "stands as the abstract personification of excellence in art," the artist himself not being intended. BETHELL (1947, p. 36): "So-called anachronism also helps to produce an impression of timeless universality. . . . There would be no point in this [the allusion] if Shakespeare had not assumed that Romano would be known . . . as either a great sculptor or a sculptor of life-like portraits. Yet, if the audience knew so much, they would presumably be aware that he belonged to the Renaissance, not to the Graeco-Roman period. . . . Anachronism such as this is clearly not due to the writer's ignorance; in a sense it is quite deliberate." Whether Romano was known to Sh.'s audience is not the question, according to FRYE (1962, p. 241): "The entire reference to Romano seems pointless. We do not need this kind of art when we have the real Hermione, and here again, whatever Romano's merits, neither he nor the kind of realism he represents seems to be very central to the play itself." HARTWIG (1972, p. 133) thinks "the anachronism of the work's having been 'perfected' by a Renaissance artist . . . is a signal for the audience to be alert for the revelation." FARRELL (1975, p. 235, n. 25) takes it as "Shakespeare's joke [adding] liberating and complex comedy to a complexly solemn rebirth of love."

It seems quite a complex irony that Hermione's statue was begotten by the creator of the *posizioni* that inspired Aretino's pornographic sonnets. Aretino's erotica were known to Sh.'s contemporaries (Jonson, for example, alludes to obscene Aretine in *Volpone* 3.4.80, 3.4.96, and 3.7.60 and *The Alchemist* 2.2.44). GURR (1982, p. 60) argues that "the art which restores Hermione . . . needs the kind of magic which that rare Italian pornographer alone could give it: the art of giving life to a picture, indicated by a name associated with pictures and statuesque postures of such a kind of naturalness that art itself is not called in question." The pictures of Aretino's postures are, however, monumentally gymnastic, anything but natural. SPENCER (1977, p. 43) forbears from suggesting that those who caught the allusion to the pornographic postures "would snigger again at the allusion to Hermione's 'naturall Posture' [3212]."

Another explanation altogether is that of BAUGHAN (1937): Sh. confused Julio Romano with Johnchristopher Romano, a sculptor, who appears in Castiglione's *Book of the Courtier* (Tudor Trans. 23, 1900, pp. 93 ff.). Sir Thomas Hoby's translation, published in 1561 and often thereafter, was widely read. According to SCOTT (1901), Sh. may also have been indebted to Castiglione for the merry war of Beatrice and Benedick in *Ado*. ZIEGLER (1985, p. 204, n. 2): "We know from Vasari [ed. Milanesi, 5:533], however, that the *painter* Giulio Romano, was also a friend of Castiglione's." Other Julios are found by SPENCER (pp. 48-9), who proposes the following "editor's note": "The name 'Giulio Romano' for a skilled Italian artificer is theatrically effective. No sculptor of this name is known, but Shakespeare may have had memories of the painter and architect Giulio Romano (Giulio Pippi, 1499-1546) or the musician Giulio Romano (Giulio Caccini, *c.* 1545-1618). The latter was still alive at the time of the composition of *The Winter's Tale* and his work was known in England. Shakespeare's eye may have caught the name in Robert Dowland's recently published volume of lute-songs, *A Musicall Banquet.* . . . (London, 1610). This was compiled from 'the rarest and most judicious Maisters' ('To the Reader'), and Nos XVIII and XIX are ascribed to *Giulio Caccini detto Romano*. The attribution of the supposed statue to an Italian, the emphasis on the extreme realism of his work, and the details used in describing it in the chapel in [5.3], may be due to Shakespeare's having heard something of recent developments in Italian sculpture. In the hill-towns of Piedmont and Lombardy (Orta, Varallo, and elsewhere), where they were likely to be seen by travellers arriving over the Alps and to provide them with first impressions of Italian artistry, life-size, painted, terra-cotta statues, of startling realism, were from the 1590s onwards being placed in a series of hill-side chapels (forming a 'Sacro Monte')."

DUFFIN (1994, p. 22) also believes that the allusion is to Giulio Caccini and that Sh.'s linking the name of the Italian musician to the sculptor and painter of Hermione's statue "could well have been a sign that Hermione's statue was not a statue, that the 3rd Gentleman who delivered that speech was deliberately being obscure and ironic." For a possible connection with the story of Pygmalion, see p. 694.

Because of his connection with the name Doricles (see n. 3382, above), Sh.'s indebtedness to Marston for the idea of a statue that comes to life may deserve more attention than it has received, although Marston's lubricious poem bears no other similarity to *WT*. FAIRCHILD (1937, p. 73) agrees that Sh. adapts the Pygmalion story; "as artist, he becomes Romano; as lover and husband, he becomes Leontes." LAROQUE (1984, pp. 216–17) believes Sh. "more indebted to the story of Deucalion and Pyrrha" in Golding's Ovid than to Pygmalion, but his verbal parallels are not persuasive. LOTHIAN (1930, p. 424) alone thinks that Sh.'s "careless reading" of a passage in Aretino's *Marescalco* 5.3 led to the impression that Romano was a sculptor who rivaled nature. See p. 685.

Stories of other living statues may be found in BAUM (1919) and in LANCASTER (1932), who believes that Sh. was inspired by any one of several French plays of the 17th c. in which the motif is found (see p. 694). TAYLOR's (1938) idea that Bandello's "Timbreo and Fenicia" (Novella 22), a source of *Ado*, "may . . . explain the statue coming to life" has won no support, chiefly because "Timbreo" has no statue. NEELY (1978, p. 187) suggests that in addition to the Pygmalion story, Sh. may have been inspired by GOLDING's 1567 trans. of Ovid's account of Persephone's rape (*Met.* 5.632): "Hir mother stoode as starke as stone, when she these newes did heare."

Several BBC listeners comment on ISAACS's ("400 Years," 1966, p. 684) talk on Sh.'s 400th birthday. According to ISAACS, Sh. "knew nothing about art[;] . . . he did not know that Julio Romano was not a sculptor, though where he came across that name Lord only knows." PARES (1966, p. 775) refers to the Vasari epigraphs given above, but HETHERINGTON (1966) points out that Vasari's "sculpture was apparently only gesso in high relief, and a portrait-statue of Hermione would be out of character." ISAACS ("Shakespeare," 1966, p. 895) replies that "Vasari was very scrupulous about the labels he placed on his artists. . . . Whenever an artist is also a sculptor as well as a painter he says so," and he does not so identify Romano. But as is indicated above and as PARES (1966, p. 930) points out, the first edition of Vasari (1550) clearly does say that Romano was a sculptor. KENNET (1966) adds that Sh. needed no specific source for his knowledge of Giulio, because he "was very famous throughout Europe." As for Romano as a sculptor, he imagines that "Shakespeare went to Nonsuch [the royal palace in Surrey] and there he asked . . . for the history of the stucco figures and the famous carved slate surrounds. He was told they were the work of Nicholas Moden (Nicolo da Modena) and that Moden had told the English craftsmen who worked under him that he had learned his general style from Julius the Roman."

nitie, and could put Breath into his Worke) would beguile Nature of her Custome, so perfectly he is her Ape:
He so neere to *Hermione*, hath done *Hermione*, that they
say one would speake to her, and stand in hope of answer.
Thither (with all greedinesse of affection) are they gone,   3110
and there they intend to Sup.

    *Gent.*2. I thought she had some great matter there in

3106 put] but F3-ROWE2
3107 he is] is he CAP
3112 *Gent.*2.] 1 *Gent.* v1821, COL1, COL4

3104 **perform'd**] SCHMIDT (1875, Perform): "To execute." The CLARKES (1879,
p. 576): "Completed, achieved" (*OED, v.* 1), an idea reiterated by CHEW (1947, p.
11). BARKAN (1981, pp. 657–8): "Giulio's *performance* of the statue, while in a literal
sense suggesting its completion, can hardly fail to remind us of both the character of
Hermione's performance and of Shakespeare's own medium of art." At this point we
know nothing of Hermione's performance.

3105–7 **who . . . Ape**] THIRLBY (MS 1725–33?): "He breathed into his nostrils
the breath of life. The meaning of the whole is If he were immortal & c^d make his
statues live, [he] w^d get Nature's trade from her, working as well as she." Similarly,
HEATH (1765, p. 220): "Were Julio Romano as immortal as Nature, and could, like
her, put breath into his works, he would be so generally preferred as to beguile [rob]
her of her custom." JOHNSON's (ed. 1765) version is "if *Julio* could always continue
his labours, he would mimick nature," by being her ape, or imitator. HARRISON (ed.
1947) has an interesting variation: He "would cheat Nature by creating living creatures." PAFFORD (ed. 1963): "The strife of art with nature . . . is related to the grafting talk of Perdita / Polixenes, [1894–1916]."

3107 **Custome**] PORTER & CLARKE (ed. c. 1903): "Trade."

3108–9 **He . . . answer**] Sh. does not want us to remember that no one has as
yet seen the statue of Hermione. Regarding the speaking, BARTON (1986, p. 37):
"Perdita, in fact, will do just this, while her father stands torn between his rational
knowledge . . . and a delirious persuasion that he may be right in supposing that 'it
breath'd' [3261]."

3109 **would**] DEIGHTON (ed. 1889): "Would be likely."

3110 **greedinesse**] SCHMIDT (1874): "Eagerness."

    affection] Desire (*OED, sb.* 5: "disposition towards, bent"). For other senses,
see nn. 26, 214, 2206, 2332–3, and 3046. For the phrase, CHARLTON (ed. 1916):
"Hunger of love" and SCHANZER (ed. 1969): "Eager desire."

3111 **Sup**] WRIGHT & LAMAR (ed. 1966): "I.e., feed their emotion." EVANS (ed.
1974): "Perhaps concluding the figure in *greediness* — satisfy their hunger to see it."
BEVINGTON (ed. 1992): "Or, perhaps, have a commemorative banquet."

3112–14 **I . . . House**] BONJOUR (1952, p. 200): "This will serve very aptly,
once we know of Hermione's revival, as a retrospective explanation of the way her
seclusion was effected. But at the present juncture, the comment is also intended to
make the spectator wonder whether the making of a statue was enough to account
for Paulina's visit to a lonely house for no less than sixteen years, at the rate of two
or three times a day." One wonders if any spectator ever so wondered. BOORMAN
(ed. 1964): "The Second Gentleman seems to know more about Paulina than her
steward, the Third Gentleman."

hand, for shee hath priuately, twice or thrice a day, euer
since the death of *Hermione*, visited that remoued House.
Shall wee thither, and with our companie peece the Re-   3115
ioycing?

    *Gent.*1. Who would be thence, that ha's the benefit
of Accesse? euery winke of an Eye, some new Grace
will be borne: our Absence makes vs vnthriftie to our
Knowledge. Let's along.   *Exit.* 3120

    Aut. Now (had I not the dash of my former life in
me) would Preferment drop on my head. I brought the

3119 vs] it OXF1
3120 *Exit*] *Exeunt* ROWE1 + (*subst.*)
3121 I not] not I ROWE2-THEO1, HAN

    3112 **there**] Exasperated by this unlocated locative, and presumably as well by "thither" and "there" in 3110-11, THIRLBY (MS 1725-33?) asks, "Where Willy? *There* shd look backwards in this place, not forwards."

    3113-14 **shee . . . House**] BETHELL (ed. 1956): "Shakespeare dodges the awkwardness of Hermione's survival. . . . Here is just a hint of Paulina's activity in the matter."

    3113 **priuately**] OED (*adv.* 2, citing this line): "Quietly." SCHMIDT (1875): "Alone, by one's self."

    3114 **remoued**] MALONE (ed. 1790): "Remote; retired."

    3115 **peece**] JOHNSON (1755): "Enlarge by the addition of a piece." For other uses of the word, see n. 1833.

    3117-18 **benefit of Accesse**] PIERCE (ed. 1918): "Privilege of admittance."

    3118-19 **euery . . . borne**] BATTENHOUSE (1980, p. 126): "The biblical idea of being led from grace to grace is here being echoed." He finds other gratuitous parallels—e.g., the three courtiers and the wise men.

    3118 **Grace**] SCHMIDT (1874): "Happiness, blessedness." WRIGHT & LAMAR (ed. 1966): "Miracle." For other meanings of *grace*, see n. 146.

    3119-20 **vnthriftie . . . Knowledge**] JOHNSON (1755, Unthrifty, citing this line): "Prodigal . . . wasteful." SCHMIDT (1875, Unthrifty): "Not intent on increasing, and hence not increasing, our knowledge." DEIGHTON (ed. 1889): "Carelessly omitting to store up what we might." BETHELL (ed. 1956): "I.e. we'll be missing the news."

    3121-30 **Now . . . discredits**] To GRIFFITH (1775, p. 115) alone, Autolycus's soliloquy demonstrates that *"honesty is the best policy"* and *"character . . . the immediate jewel of the soul."*

    3121-2 **Now . . . head**] PYLE (1969, p. 116) thinks Autolycus means that he has just picked someone's pocket.

    3121 **dash**] RANN (ed. 1787): "Smatch, spice, tincture" (OED, *sb*[1] 5b, citing this line). SCHMIDT (1874): "Mark of infamy." BETHELL (ed. 1956): "A witty understatement on the part of Autolycus." HAPPÉ (1969), however: "A trace or stain left by his former life of stealing. . . . He appears much more reflective [than in Act 4] and perhaps regretful." PARRY (ed. 1982) thinks he means "taste for."

    3122 **Preferment**] PARRY (ed. 1982): "Presumably . . . a post at court again."

old man and his Sonne aboord the Prince; told him, I
heard them talke of a Farthell, and I know not what: but
he at that time ouer-fond of the Shepheards Daughter (so   3125   (20
he then tooke her to be) who began to be much Sea-sick,
and himselfe little better, extremitie of Weather continuing, this Mysterie remained vndiscouer'd. But 'tis all
one to me: for had I beene the finder-out of this Secret,
it would not haue rellish'd among my other discredits.   3130

Enter Shepheard and Clowne.

Here come those I haue done good to against my will,
and alreadie appearing in the blossomes of their Fortune.
      Shep.   Come Boy, I am past moe Children: but thy   3135
Sonnes and Daughters will be all Gentlemen borne.
      Clow.   You are well met (Sir:) you deny'd to fight
with mee this other day, because I was no Gentleman

3124 them] him v1803, v1813
3127 better,] better, and KEIGHTLEY *conj. in* CAM1, KTLY
3131 SCENE VI. POPE, HAN, WARB, JOHN
3132 come] comes VALPY, RID
3138 this] the HAN

3123 **aboord the Prince**] SCHMIDT (1874): I.e., aboard the prince's ship. YOUNG
& MOSELEY (ed. 1965, Aboard): "Into the presence of," unsupported by *OED* or
SCHMIDT.
      3124 **Farthell**] See n. 2591.
      3125 **ouer-fond**] *OED* (*a.*, citing this line): "Having too great an affection." Cf.
"ouer-kind" (24) and "ouer-much" (2814).
      so] CHARLTON (ed. 1916): "As."
      3126 **Sea-sick**] PORTER & CLARKE (ed. 1908): "Shakespeare's invention to account
for the secret of Perdita's birth not being made known before, while yet making use
of Autolicus to bring the shepherd and his son to Sicilia." Comparing Lyly, *Euphues
and his England* (ed. Bond, 2:29, 33), where Philautus is similarly afflicted, PAFFORD
(ed. 1963) finds a common "touch of realism." PARRY (ed. 1982), however: "A make-
shift explanation of why the 'mystery' of Perdita's true identity remained unsuspected
by Florizel during the voyage." PARRY alleges that few people worry about such
things, though it is evident that Sh. did.
      3128 **vndiscouer'd**] WRIGHT & LAMAR (ed. 1966): "Unexplored."
      3128-9 **all one**] BEVINGTON (ed. 1992): "All the same."
      3130 **not . . . discredits**] KERSEY (1702, Relish): "To have a good savour; to
approve of." *OED* (*v.*[1] 6, citing this line): "To find acceptance or favour." FURNESS

(ed. 1898): "Would not have been relished by the kings and Florizel." LOBBAN (ed. 1910) extends the meaning to "not have harmonized" and MOORMAN (ed. 1912) to "found acceptance." BETHELL (ed. 1956): "I.e. made me acceptable in spite of the things [counted against me]." ROLFE (ed. 1879) thinks the line may mean "it would have counted as nothing in comparison with my discredits, would not have served to give them even a 'relish of salvation'" (*Ham.* 3.1.92 [2367]), an unlikely interpretation. For another sense, see 783. Comparing him favorably with Parolles in *AWW*, BROOKS (in PAFFORD, ed. 1963) finds that Autolycus has an admirably "discreet estimate of himself and his place in life." FOSS (1932, p. 139), however: "He appears to be in a pretty abject state. . . . It seems that he has had poetic justice meted out to him between the Acts and been beaten, starved, and deprived of all his money"—an assertion for which there is no evidence.

discredits] MINSHEU (1617): See "Dishonour, Infamie, & Ignomie." JERVIS (1868): "Offence; misdeed."

3131 *Enter . . . Clowne*] DELIUS (1870, p. 251): In the plain prose of the two Clowns, with their wonderful naïveté over their newborn nobility, we have an amusing contrast with the ceremonious and artistic prose of the earlier part of the scene. RICHMAN (1990, pp. 113–14): "The colloquy . . . is sandwiched between the account of Perdita's restoration and the unveiling of her mother's statue, providing the relief of laughter. It insures that the audience will come to the final scene with high expectation, acute judgment, and refreshed emotion."

3132 **done . . . will**] PARRY (ed. 1982): "Autolycus' intention when he introduced the Shepherd and Clown to Florizel was to do a good turn to *himself*, not to them! . . . They have been raised to the rank of gentleman. . . . The Clown, who . . . may be drunk (see [3155–6]), tries to talk in gentlemanly style." The Clown's rhetorical adventures need not be inspired by alcohol, however; see n. 3155–6.

3133–4 **blossomes . . . Fortune**] DEIGHTON (ed. 1889): "Their [elegant] dress."

3135 **moe**] See n. 57 for the distinction between *moe* and *more*.

3135–6 **thy . . . borne**] SEGAR (1590, p. 36): "In saying a Gentleman borne, we meane he must be descended from three degrees of gentry, both on the mothers and fathers side." See also n. 3139–40. Thus the Shepherd is not exactly right, but, unlike the Clown, he knows in general what the term means. BROOK (1976, pp. 186–7): "A fairly frequent comic situation arises when a character fails to understand the words used by himself or someone else," as is the case in the lines following. The Clown's misunderstanding of *advocate* (2624–5) is another example. BROOK adds (p. 187): "This type of humour is old." WEDGWOOD (1964, p. 181): "Shakespeare depicts the sudden rise in fortune of two humble folk," which WEDGWOOD finds analogous to the rise in social rank enjoyed by many "humble folk" during the Jacobean period. BERRY (1988, p. 179): "Shakespeare had been a 'gentleman born' for over ten years by the time of *The Winter's Tale*. One wonders if it was a company injoke." On his father's side, however, Sh. was only a second-generation gentleman.

3137–40 **you . . . borne**] BETHELL (ed. 1956): "According to the Clown, the two notes of a gentleman are his clothes and his quarrelsomeness." He further notes that in 3167–82, the Clown adds swearing, lying, admiration of "toughness," and patronizing of the undeserving.

3137 **deny'd**] MINSHEU (1617, To Denie): "Say no." The CLARKES (ed. 1865): "Refused" (*OED*, *v.* 8). BOORMAN (ed. 1964) thinks Autolycus had begun to pick a fight but backed down (see n. 2610); PARRY (ed. 1982) says that, if the Clown is not drunkenly inventing, "a snub . . . has occurred since the end of [Act 4]."

3138 **this other**] I.e., the other. FRANZ (§316): Quite recently.

borne. See you these Clothes? say you see them not,
and thinke me still no Gentleman borne: You were best   3140
say these Robes are not Gentlemen borne. Giue me the
Lye: doe: and try whether I am not now a Gentleman
borne.

   Aut. I know you are now (Sir) a Gentleman borne.

   Clow. I, and haue been so any time these foure houres.   3145

   Shep. And so haue I, Boy.

   Clow. So you haue: but I was a Gentleman borne before my Father: for the Kings Sonne tooke me by the
hand, and call'd mee Brother: and then the two Kings
call'd my Father Brother: and then the Prince (my Bro-   3150
ther) and the Princesse (my Sister) call'd my Father, Father;
and so wee wept: and there was the first Gentleman-like
teares that euer we shed.

   Shep. We may liue (Sonne) to shed many more.

   Clow. I: or else 'twere hard luck, being in so preposte-   3155
rous estate as we are.

   Aut. I humbly beseech you (Sir) to pardon me all the
faults I haue committed to your Worship, and to giue
me your good report to the Prince my Master.

   Shep. 'Prethee Sonne doe: for we must be gentle, now   3160
we are Gentlemen.

3139 Clothes] cloths CAP, HAN3
3141 Gentlemen] gentleman BLAIR, SING, HUD1, OXF1, CLN2, ARD2
3142 a] *Om.* OXF1, CLN2, SIG

3139-43 **See . . . borne**] DUSINBERRE (1975, p. 236): "The despised Jacobean
creation of new peers, the mushroom knights who had sprung up overnight, gave an
edge to" these lines.

  3139-40 **See . . . borne**] DENT compares "Fine clothes make not a gentleman"
(TILLEY S451) and "It takes three Generations to make a gentleman" (DENT G58.1).
Regarding the latter, cf. n. 3135-6. DRAPER (1985, p. 40), who finds the "second half
of [5.2] something like a burlesque anti-masque to [the] courtly extravaganza" of the
first half: "The paradox of primitive emotion in sophisticated guise, which is the
hallmark of the first part of the scene, is parodied in the luxurious clothes which turn
the Clown into 'a gentleman born'; and the marvelling over close family ties which
have been rediscovered and renewed, is travestied in the royal kinship he can now
boast of [in 3147-53]."

  3140-1 **were best say**] MAXWELL (ed. 1969): "Might as well say." For the construction, see ABBOTT §§230, 352.

  3141-2 **Giue . . . Lye**] HARRISON (ed. 1947): "I.e. insult me now and see
whether I'll fight. The clown here gets his own back for Autolicus' former condescending behaviour: see [2597 ff.]." SIEVEKING (1916, 2:402): "Giving the lie [calling
one a liar] in some form or other was the final and irrevocable provocation, the
dishonour of which bloodshed alone could wipe out."

3144-53 **I . . . shed**] BARBER (1964, p. 245): "This of course is farce, but all the same it presents a situation which the play accepts with good humour and equanimity—the yeoman rising to be a gentleman; and the comically reiterated terms of relationship underline the brotherhood of humanity already suggested by Perdita's sun shining on court and cottage alike [2289-90]."

3144 **I . . . borne**] PARRY (ed. 1982): "Autolycus prudently takes the line of least resistance."

now] KNOWLES (privately): "With a joke—just now."

3145 **any . . . houres**] DEIGHTON (ed. 1889): "For the last four hours at least." ELZE (1876, pp. 290-4): *Four*, as well as *forty* and *forty thousand*, is used to denote an indefinite number. ELZE cites a number of examples from Sh. and other Elizabethans. He is supported by BROOK (1976): In Sh., "the numeral *four* is sometimes used vaguely with *hours* and *days* to denote fairly long periods of time." BROOK cites *Ham.* 2.2.160 (1192) and *Cor.* 1.2.6 (320).

3147-53 **I . . . shed**] PYLE (1969, p. 117): An "unconscious parody of the meeting of the two kings." BISWAS (1979, p. 93) finds that "the new gentry [of 16th-c. England] is caricatured," while BERGERON (1985, p. 164) calls the acceptance of the Shepherd and the Clown "a marvelous redefining of the royal family." MIRIAM JOSEPH (1947, p. 193): "In the fallacy of amphibology the ambiguity lies, not in a word, but in the grammatical construction. . . . In [3136-44] *gentleman born* had been used repeatedly as a phrase meaning *born a gentleman*, but here *born* links itself to *before*, making the remark ludicrous." BOORMAN (ed. 1964) suggests a pause after "Gentleman" to emphasize the linkage. For these lines as parody of the first part of the scene, see n. 3139-40.

3148-9 **tooke . . . hand**] SLATER (1982, p. 52): "It is the gesture of relationship." Hands are taken or urged to be taken a dozen times in *WT*, most significantly near the end (3164, 3238, 3293, 3315, 3358) as a symbol of the reunion of Hermione and Leontes.

3152-3 **there . . . teares**] For *was*, see n. 2638.

3155-6 **preposterous**] THIRLBY (MS 1733-47?): To be read *prosperous*, correcting the Clown's blunder, as SCHMIDT (1875) says, or, as LOBBAN (ed. 1910) puts it, a "happy variation." HUDSON (ed. 1880) thinks the blunder may be intentional, but that seems doubtful; as TILLEY (1930, p. 111) says, "mistaking the word is a stock device repeatedly used" by Sh.'s clowns. HERFORD (ed. 1916-): It "has unconscious irony as suggesting the absurd inversion of his real and his apparent status." BOORMAN (ed. 1964) thinks the word "in its original sense ('reversed, cart-before-the-horse') . . . could well apply to their change of fortune."

3156 **estate**] MINSHEU (1617): "Condition."

3157-9 **I . . . Master**] PARRY (ed. 1982): "This extravagantly respectful tone is thoroughly tongue-in-cheek, though . . . Autolycus has *some* serious intent."

3158 **your Worship**] CARRINGTON (1956), who seems less sure of the tongue in the cheek: "Now the tables are turned. The last time this phrase was used it was by the Clown to Autolycus [at 2609]."

3159 **me**] BEVINGTON (ed. 1992): "On my behalf." An ethical dative, for which see n. 1598.

3160-1 **for . . . Gentlemen**] ROLFE (ed. 1879): "The shepherd's expression of 'Noblesse oblige.'" ROLFE compares the Shepherd's resolve to do good deeds as a proper response to his good fortune (1576-7). PAFFORD (ed. 1963): To be gentle is to "act with dignity, as befitting someone who is well born." BARBER (1964, p. 245), however: "The double meaning of *gentle* is used to suggest that the achieving of the social status will lead to the achieving of the appropriate moral qualities." SCHANZER (ed. 1969) finds a different double meaning: "For the Clown the chief marks of the gentleman are his fine clothes and his readiness to fight and swear, for the old Shepherd they are generosity and courtesy." KNIGHTS (1976, pp. 610-11): "Natural good

Clow. Thou wilt amend thy life?

Aut. I, and it like your good Worship.

Clow. Giue me thy hand: I will sweare to the Prince,
thou art as honest a true Fellow as any is in *Bohemia.*   3165

Shep. You may say it, but not sweare it.

Clow. Not sweare it, now I am a Gentleman? Let
Boores and Francklins say it, Ile sweare it.

Shep. How if it be false (Sonne?)

Clow. If it be ne're so false, a true Gentleman may   3170
sweare it, in the behalfe of his Friend: And Ile sweare to
the Prince, thou art a tall Fellow of thy hands, and that
thou wilt not be drunke: but I know thou art no tall Fellow of thy hands, and that thou wilt be drunke: but Ile
sweare it, and I would thou would'st be a tall Fellow of   3175
thy hands.

Aut. I will proue so (Sir) to my power.

Clow. I, by any meanes proue a tall Fellow: if I do not
wonder, how thou dar'st venture to be drunke, not being
a tall Fellow, trust me not. Harke, the Kings and the Prin-   3180
ces (our Kindred) are going to see the Queenes Picture.
Come, follow vs: wee'le be thy good Masters.   *Exeunt.*

3164 thy] your OXF1
3170 ne're] near JOHN1
3173 know thou] know that thou KNT3
3178 proue] to prove THEO1
3180 *Trumpets. [before* Harke!] COL2, COL3, DYCE2, COL4, HUD2, BUL, OXF2
(*subst.*)
3182 Masters] Master F2-ROWE3

---

breeding." KNOWLES (privately): "After *pardon* (3157), *gentle* must mean "mild, forgiving." DRAPER (1985, p. 40): Autolycus's "courtly self becomes dependent on that
innate goodness of the rustics which originally enabled him to dupe them."

3162-8 **Thou . . . it**] SULLIVAN (1925, 1:lxxxviii): Indebted to GUAZZO. See n.
498-505, however.

3162-3 **Thou . . . Worship**] "Amend your lives, for the kingdom of God is at
hand" is one of the sentences with which Morning Prayer begins. DRAPER (1985, p.
40): "Autolycus's promise . . . is . . . a parody of Leontes' repentance."

3162 **amend**] MINSHEU (1617): "To take away the fault or blemish."

3163 **and it like**] See n. 2598.

3165 **as . . . Bohemia**] Possibly ironical, although Bohemians seem decent
enough. Cf. n. 2556-7.

   honest] EVANS (ed. 1974): "Worthy."

   true] KERMODE (ed. 1963): "Honest (as opposed to thieving)."

3166 **say . . . sweare**] PAFFORD (ed. 1963): A distinction between saying and
swearing is also drawn at 92-3 and at 663-4. C. G. SMITH (1963, no. 282) finds a
parallel in Leonard Culman, *Sententiae Pueriles.*

3167 **Not . . . Gentleman?**] The CLARKES (1879, p. 685): Sh. "satirises the assumption of its being an aristocratic privilege to swear."

3168 **Boores and Francklins**] HOLME (1688, 3.72): "A BOOR or SWAIN is a Country Man that hath neither Breeding or Manners, one that lives in the countrey Villages, and knows nothing at all of Civil Behaviour." JOHNSON (1755, Boor): "A lout; a clown," like the speaker not very long ago. GILDON (1710, p. lxix, Franklin): "A Freeman, or Gentleman, &c." JOHNSON (ed. 1765), however: "A *freebolder*, or *yeoman*, a man above a *villain*, but not a *gentleman* [OED 2]." The point is that a franklin—gentleman or not—would resent being linked so casually with a boor.

3172, 3173-4, 3175-6 **tall . . . hands**] For the principal meaning, FURNESS (ed. 1898) quotes COTGRAVE (1611, *Main, homme à la*): "A man of execution or valour," or, as OED (Tall, *a.* 4) has it, "Ready, active" or "Stout of arm, formidable with weapons." PAFFORD (ed. 1963): "The use of 'a tall man' in this sense was new in the 1590's." See TILLEY M163 for dated citations. RUSHTON (1868, p. 31) finds in PUTTENHAM (1589, p. 184) that the expression is also used "of an arrant ruffian" "to excuse a fault, & to make an offense seeme lesse than it is." The Clown and some critics unintentionally, and Autolycus intentionally, may understand other senses. HANMER (ed. 1743-4, 6:glos.): "Eminent, notable, considerable." JOHNSON (1755, Tall, citing 3172): "Sturdy; lusty." STEEVENS (ed. 1778) adds for *man of his hands*: "A fellow skilful in thievery" (OED: "deft, skilful with <his> hands"), the sense Autolycus probably understands privately at 3177. HALLIWELL (ed. 1859) owlishly rejects this interpretation, "for the Clown knew for certain that Autolycus was a thief, and there would, therefore, be no humour in such an equivoque," but the Clown has no inkling of what subsidiary meaning his fire-new fashionable phrase may have. MASON (1785, p. 138), mistakenly: "a stout fellow for your size," because horses are measured in hands. NARES (1876; 1905, Hand, at any hand), however, also thinks both "bold" and "high" may be meant. BOORMAN (ed. 1964) would like Autolycus to be played by a short actor.

3175 **I . . . would'st**] BOORMAN (ed. 1964): "I hope you may."

3177 **to my power**] ROLFE (ed. 1879): "To the best of my ability." SCHANZER (ed. 1969): "Secretly making his promise refer to his valiant use of his hands as a cut-purse and pick-pocket."

3178, 3180 **tall**] See n. 3172, etc.

3180 **trust me not**] A fashionable expression; see DENT T558.1.

Harke] COLLIER may be right that a flourish has sounded, although most eds. evidently think that the Clown means "listen to me."

3180-1 **the Kings . . . Kindred**] TRAVERSI (1955, p. 187): His "pretentiousness . . . is absurd, comic, but not entirely devoid of pathos. His attitude stands out alike against the spirit of the main court action and against . . . the constant scepticism of Autolycus." COLIE (1974, p. 277): "The playwright . . . has it both ways, as Perdita's rediscovered condition confirms the gentility she always displayed, and the members of her family remind us of the loss incurred in giving up country matters [!] for city behavior, their artless simplicity for the artifice and lying of sophisticated society."

Princes] BOORMAN (ed. 1964): "Both Florizel and Perdita ('Prince' could be used for both males and females)."

3181 **Picture**] KERSEY (1702): "*Painting, image*, or *representation*." OED (*sb.* 2d): "A statue or monumental effigy." Cf. 2816.

3182 **Come, follow vs**] Discussing exit cues, SMITH (1962, p. 887) observes that "masters normally precede their inferiors off the stage," which is hardly surprising. Cf. 814 and 3006.

good Masters] WHALLEY (in STEEVENS, ed. 1785): "The Clown conceits himself already a man of consequence at court. . . . An inferior, or suitor, . . . [would] beg of the great man . . . that he would be *good master* to him," become his benefactor and afford him protection. SCHMIDT (1875): "Patron." The main point, of course, is

Scæna Tertia.   **5.3**

3183 *Scæna Tertia*] SCENE VII. POPE, HAN, WARB, JOHN
Paulina's *House*. POPE1+ (−PEL1, CLN2, PEN2, OXF2) (*subst.*)

that upon his promise to amend his life, the shepherds, however illogically, accept
Autolycus. ABARTIS (1977, p. 107) believes that he "becomes part of the pattern of
release; if Autolycus can receive mercy, we are prepared to wish mercy for Leontes."

3183 *Scæna Tertia*] FISHER (1931, p. 157): "The end of *The Winter's Tale* is, as
it were, forced upward, but it does not rise enough to overcome the weight either
of the scene which precedes it or the sad death of Mamillius and the heavy, ridiculous
jealousy of Leontes." HONIGMANN (1955, p. 37 n.): "That the statue-scene was in
Shakespeare's mind from the start appears from the seemingly inconsequential whim-
sicality that 'they that went on crutches ere he was born desire yet their life to see
him a man' [41–2], anticipating 'I . . . have preserv'd/Myself to see the issue' [3339–
40]; and from the references to people almost dead being revived [2667–8]; from
the references to 'breaking the grave' [2775], and to 'marble' persons [3097–8]."
DRAPER (1985, p. 40): "The very fact that this is an ensemble scene, with almost the
entire cast on the stage, is . . . a signal that the plot is nearing culmination." STYAN
(1967, p. 134): "This scene [is] designed to provide graduations of Hermione's return
to life." For a thought that may be its origin, see n. 712–22. HERFORD (ed. 1916–):
It "effects the reunions and recognitions which normally closed the 'Romance' comedies, but in a way . . . entirely original. . . . When Hermione is at length recognized, it is her union with Perdita, not with Leontes, upon which the whole emotional
stress is laid. She embraces him [3322], but does not once address him, and he only
once, at the close, addresses her. . . . On the other hand, the reunion of mother and
daughter touches a chord of emotion all but unexampled elsewhere in Shakespeare."

BETHELL (ed. 1956) believes that the scene hints at "what Shakespeare felt about
the life of Christian devotion, here and hereafter. . . . He conveys this very indirectly." FRYE (1957, p. 184): "The closing scene . . . makes us think, not simply of
a cyclical movement from tragedy and absence to happiness and return, but of bodily
metamorphosis and transformation from one kind of life to another. The materials of
the *cognitio* . . . are so stock that they would be 'hooted at like an old tale', yet
they seem both far-fetched and inevitably right, outraging reality and at the same time
introducing us to a world of childlike innocence which has always made more sense
than reality." EWBANK (1964, p. 97): "The whole scene has about it a sense of the
fulness of time." YOUNG & MOSELEY (ed. 1965): "This scene is the second (main)
climax of the play, as the Trial Scene [3.2] was the first. In both, Hermione, the vehicle
of 'grace', is dominant—in the Trial Scene by her contrast to Leontes, in this by being
physically set apart. There is an almost religious solemnity about the grouping around
her statue (note that Paulina [i.e., Perdita] kneels [see 3236]), about Leontes's reca-
pitulation of his sin in his wonderment; even the speeches take on an almost antiph-
onal quality. The use of music at the crucial moment of Hermione's descent from the
pedestal heightens this feeling." WAITH (1982, p. 118): "In only one other scene of
the play is there so religious an atmosphere—in the description of the Delphic Oracle

Enter Leontes, Polixenes, Florizell, Perdita, Camillo,
Paulina: Hermione (like a Statue:) Lords, &c.　　　3185

 Leo. O graue and good *Paulina*, the great comfort
That I haue had of thee?
 Paul. What (Soueraigne Sir)
I did not well, I meant well: all my Seruices　　　(2C1ᵛᵃ)

3185 *Hermione . . . Statue:*] *Om.* ROWE1+ *(subst.)*

[at 1149—54]." LEECH (1978, p. 53), on masque similarities or dissimilarities: "We . . . have the coming to life of the apparent statue of Hermione, and her descending to pay homage to her lord Leontes. . . . There is a reversal, for the sovereign is the one who comes with his court, the disguised figure the one who accepts (and reciprocates) his devotion. Incidentally, Paulina is clearly the 'presenter' in this echo of the masque." CALDWELL (1984, p. 284): "The awakening of faith in this scene follows the three stages of formal meditation . . . which correspond to the acts of memory, understanding, and will." PARRY (ed. 1982): "The play is shaped to make us believe, with Leontes, that Hermione has indeed died in [3.2]. . . . Her coming alive only really happens as an act of willed imagination. A faith . . . is what makes it work."

 3185 **like a Statue**] SAUNDERS (1960, pp. 413-14): "In 29 of [39 plays produced at the Globe between 1599 and 1613] a stage-arras is necessary for the action: a prominent feature, then, of Globe productions. . . . In several plays a simple traverse across the rear of the Platform will suffice as concealment," as here. LLOYD (in SINGER, ed. 1856, 4:156): "The self-collected dignity of the entire character of Hermione is in harmony with her appearance as a statue. . . . She is . . . not more statuesque than in the trial scene, and in both combines the beauty of repose with that of the sensitiveness of life." PITT (1981, pp. 128-9), who finds Hermione "a remote and passionless figure," thinks the statue a masterstroke because it makes visual her personality, which is "an image of perfect fidelity." MACK (1962, p. 290): The play "finds its summing up and resolution in a figure . . . that is *both* Nature and Art."

 Lords, &c.] Although their intentions seem to be the same, some eds. follow F1, some expand *Lords, &c.* to "Lords, and Attendants," and a few translate it to "and Others." PROUDFOOT (1976, p. 77 n.): "The final &c may mean no more than the '*attendants*' to which editors generally expand it, but could plausibly be extended to include all six characters from [5.2], who leave the stage with the evident intention of being present at the unveiling of 'the Queenes Picture' [3181]. The presence, in the background, of the Shepherd and the Clown might even add force to Paulina's" lines at 3342-3. Apparently &c. is not used in any other Shn. SDs to indicate important characters, however. In *R2* Q1597, &c. at 2.1.68 (710-11) represents a half-dozen members of the royal train who are named in F; in *Wiv.* 3.2.50 (1311) it represents several characters whose names are omitted from a SP for want of space. Otherwise, &c. means "Others," a category too general to signify Perdita's foster family.

 3186 **graue**] SCHMIDT (1874): "Worthy, reverend, venerable" (*OED, a.*¹ 3), as in 1152 and 2249. SCHANZER (ed. 1969) prefers "having weight and importance" (1).

 comfort] *OED* (*sb.* 5, citing this line): "Relief or support in mental distress or affliction."

You haue pay'd home. But that you haue vouchsaf'd   3190
(With your Crown'd Brother, and these your contracted
Heires of your Kingdomes) my poore House to visit;
It is a surplus of your Grace, which neuer
My life may last to answere.
    Leo. O *Paulina*,   3195
We honor you with trouble: but we came
To see the Statue of our Queene. Your Gallerie
Haue we pass'd through, not without much content
In many singularities; but we saw not
That which my Daughter came to looke vpon,   3200
The Statue of her Mother.
    Paul. As she liu'd peerelesse,
So her dead likenesse I doe well beleeue
Excells what euer yet you look'd vpon,
Or hand of Man hath done: therefore I keepe it   3205
Louely, apart. But here it is: prepare

3191 these your] these STAU *conj.*, CAM3; these young OXF2
3196 came] come WH1
3206 Louely] Lonely mTBY2 *conj.*, HAN, CAP+ (−RLTR, CLN2)

3190 **pay'd home**] Anticipated by CALDECOTT (MS 1813-33), ROLFE (ed. 1879): Paid "in full." DEIGHTON (ed. 1889): "'Home' is an adverb" (*OED, adv.* 5). *OED* considers this idiom to be *in malam partem*, but ONIONS (1986) records the neutral sense. See DENT H535.1.

3191 **your . . . your**] Because of meter, STAUNTON (ed. 1859) thinks the second *your* "to be an interpolation of the compositor."
    contracted] For the contract, see 2221, 2259, and 2972.

3192 **Heires**] See nn. 1315 and 2780.

3193 **surplus**] SCHMIDT (1875): "Overplus" (*OED, sb.* 1, citing this line).
    Grace] See n. 1221.

3194 **answere**] JERVIS (1868): "Pay for." *OED* (*v.* 25): "Give back in kind." PARRY (ed. 1982): "She feels deeply honoured to have [royalty] as her guests."

3195-3201 **O . . . Mother**] TAYLOR (1973, pp. 337-8): "Leontes' address is poised and ceremonious; 'many singularities' is the language of dispassionate connoisseurship, not wild anticipation, and 'my daughter' indicates his focus of interest. . . . Leontes doesn't expect to have the experience he suffers when Paulina draws the curtain [at 3208], with its quick changes from silent wonder to remorse to a mad transport of hope."

3196 **We . . . trouble**] HUDSON (ed. 1880): "*Trouble*, and not *honour*, is the emphatic word here. 'The honour we are doing you puts you to trouble.'" SCHMIDT (1875, Trouble): "Molestation," but *OED* (*sb.* 3) "care, toil" seems more likely. FURNESS (ed. 1898) compares *Mac.* 1.6.12-14 (444-6).

3198 **content**] *OED* (*sb.*²): "Satisfaction, pleasure." SCHMIDT (1874): Hence "applause, delight."

3199 **singularities**] MINSHEU (1617): See "Excellencie" (*OED* 6). PHILLIPS (1706): "Rarity" (so in SCHMIDT [1875]). JOHNSON (1755, citing this line): "Curiosity" (*OED* 9b). KERMODE (ed. 1963): "Varieties" (not in *OED*).

3202 **peerelesse**] BERNARD (1979, p. 223): An "awful pun," presumably on *incomparable* and *without looking upon* during her seclusion, which is awful.

3203-5 **So . . . done**] WATSON (1984, p. 269): Paulina's "beautifully equivocal clue . . . encourages and then forbids him to view the statue as a superhuman creation of human art; it forbids and then encourages him to view it as the divinely created woman he has known."

3203 **dead**] BOORMAN (ed. 1964) suggests "exact" as a double meaning (*OED* 31b), but SCHMIDT (1874) does not list the word in this sense.

3206 **Louely**] WARBURTON (ed. 1747): "Charily, with more than ordinary regard and tenderness." Not in *OED*. JOHNSON (ed. 1765): "I am yet inclined to *lonely*, which in the old angular writing cannot be distinguished from *lovely*. To say, that *I keep it alone, separate from the rest*, is a pleonasm which scarcely any nicety declines." MALONE (ed. 1790): F's reading could have been produced by the "inversion of the letter *n*." He finds *u* for *n* in F1 at *R3* 4.4.323 (3108), *AWW* 1.3.177 (498), and *Wiv.* 4.6.39 (2382). BOORMAN (ed. 1964) suggests that the word was affected by "liuely" in 3207. HALLIWELL (ed. 1859) incorrectly reports that F1 reads *lonely*; CLARK & WRIGHT (ed. 1863) observe that CAPELL's F1 and the copy of N. M. Ferrers (see n. 1572-3) read *lowely*, their misprint for "Louely," corrected by WRIGHT (ed. 1891). BETHELL (ed. 1956), in favor of the F1 reading: "'Lonely' produces a tautology . . . ; 'lovely, apart' [expresses] the cloistered beauty of Hermione." DRAPER (1985, p. 41): "With loving care." PAFFORD (ed. 1963): *Lonely* = "isolated." "Leontes has just asked why they have not yet seen the statue, and Paulina tells him—because the statue is kept apart and by itself."

3206-10 **But . . . wonder**] BARBER (1969, p. 59): "The scene on one side is like a medieval miracle where a saint's statue moves, a statue, say, of the Holy Mother. Hermione finally speaks after Perdita has kneeled to her in prayer." FARRELL (1975, pp. 52-3): "Paulina stages a sort of play-within-a-play" in benign contrast to the (p. 53) "ruthless, simplistic plot" in which Leontes "casts Hermione as the lascivious wife, and Polixenes as the treacherous friend."

3206 **here it is**] Having passed through the gallery (3197), they are now in the chapel (3290). COWLING (1926; 1927, pp. 177-8): "The initial direction [at 3184-5] suggests that Hermione, draped as a statue, was brought on the platform with the rest, absurd though this would have been. But Paulina's lines . . . suggest almost to conviction that Hermione was 'apart' behind the arras, and Leontes' plea [3255] coupled with Paulina's playful threat [3267-9] are clear proof that Hermione was discovered." HOSLEY (1971, p. 32): On the Elizabethan stage, the statue would be located in "the discovery-space . . . generally an open tiring-house doorway within which curtains . . . , or in front of which hangings . . . had been fitted up." The curtain in ROWE's SD is mandated by 3255.

WICKHAM (*Heritage*, 1969, p. 264): "It was surely Shakespeare's intention (made explicit by the fact that the statue is in the chapel . . .) that this particular statue should resemble the effigies which normally graced the tombs of the gentry . . . — painted effigies modelled from the death masks and actual clothes of the deceased." Uninformed spectators would surely take the figure for a statue. According to WILSON (ed. 1931), "that it cannot be [so taken] by us is one of the many disabilities we suffer from knowing Shakespeare so well." Hence RICHMAN (1990, p. 114): "The audience's admiration for the actress disguised as a statue should equal the characters' admiration for the statue itself." PARRY (ed. 1982): Hermione's posture "has to be both dignified and demure, no doubt with eyes cast down—a pose that makes being a statue easier for the actress." SPEAIGHT (1973, p. 40): Sarah Siddons picked up "a hint from the Egyptian statues in Lansdowne House for the right attitude—arms held close to the sides and hands clenched—to express intensity of feeling." MARTIN (1891, pp. 32-3), however, speaking of her own performances: "You may imagine how difficult it must be to stand in one position, with a full light thrown upon you, without moving

To see the Life as liuely mock'd, as euer
Still Sleepe mock'd Death: behold, and say 'tis well.
I like your silence, it the more shewes-off
Your wonder: but yet speake, first you (my Liege)   3210
Comes it not something neere?
    Leo. Her naturall Posture.
Chide me (deare Stone) that I may say indeed
Thou art *Hermione*; or rather, thou art she,
In thy not chiding: for she was as tender   3215
As Infancie, and Grace. But yet (*Paulina*)

3208 Paulina *draws a Curtain, and discovers* Hermione, *standing like a Statue.*
ROWE1+ (*subst.*)

---

an eyelid for so long a time. . . . I prepared myself by picturing what Hermione's feelings would be when she heard Leontes' voice. . . . Her heart hitherto has been full only of her lost children. She has thought every other feeling dead, but she finds herself forgetting all but the tones of the voice, once so loved, now broken with the accents of repentence. . . . Of the sorrow she had . . . wished for him [at 731-2] she is now a witness, and it all but unnerves her. Paulina had, it seemed to me, besought Hermione to play the part of her own statue, in order that she might hear herself apostrophised, and be a silent witness of the remorse and unbated love of Leontes before her existence became known to him, and so be moved to that forgiveness, which, without such proof, she might possibly be slow to yield. [When Lady Martin played opposite Macready] there was a dead awe-struck silence, when the curtains were gradually drawn by Paulina. She has to encourage Leontes to speak [at 3210]."

VENEZKY (*Pageantry*, 1951, p. 128) compares the disclosure of the living Hermione with that of Ferdinand and Miranda in *Tmp.* 5.1.171.1-2 (2141-2). "Shakespeare uses the disclosure not for an effect of horror [as, for example, Marston does in *Antonio's Revenge* 1.3.129, ed. Gair, 1978], but rather for one of beauty or magic." HUNTER (1965, p. 202): Sh. "could . . . have revived Mamillius too. There was nothing, except artistic conscience, to prevent him from having the renowned Julio Romano create a mother-son group." HUNTER's point is that a balanced estimate of the play must include Mamillius's death as well as Hermione's miraculous revival. STUDING (1971, p. 24): "The entire stylized stagecraft, with its positioned, awe-struck characters gathered magnetically around the central symbol of the drama, emblematically, as well as symbolically, mocks the supposed work of art; and, indeed, the characters, like the 'statue' itself, are . . . truly brought to life and awakened to a higher reality."

3207-8 **Life . . . Death**] PAFFORD (ed. 1963): "'Life imitated as closely as ever sleep imitated death'. That sleep is the image of death is proverbial (TILLEY, S527)." DELIUS (ed. 1860) had previously found *mock* as "imitate" in *Tim.* 1.1.35 (49). JOHNSON (1755, Still): "1. Silent. . . . It is well observed by *Junius* [Sir Philip Francis?], that *st* is the sound commanding silence. . . . 2. Quiet; calm. . . . 3. Motionless." CHARLTON (ed. 1916): The spondees create an "appropriate slowness." BETHELL (ed. 1956) notices the pun on *Life* and *liuely* (JOHNSON, 1755: "With strong resemblance of life"). There is probably another, on *mock'd*, at 3207 = "mimicked" (SCHMIDT [1875]) or "parodied" (DRAPER, 1985, p. 41) and at 3208 = "derided" (SCHMIDT).

OED (*v.* 4, citing this line) seems, however, to conflate these senses: "To ridicule by imitation. . . . Hence to imitate." C. G. SMITH (1963, no. 271) finds parallels in Homer, Cato, Vergil, Ovid, and Leonard Culman, *Sententiae Pueriles*.

Having examined the use of *mock* and the concept of mockery in *WT* and in Sh.'s other plays, BEREK (1978, pp. 300-1) concludes that "the statue imitates life as sleep imitates death. . . . As sleep is preferable to death, so the statue is preferable to life," since there are flaws in living beings that may be perfected by art. His idea is partly repeated by FREY (1988, p. 44): "Shakespeare takes pains to suggest that the statue is in some sense more alive than its beholders. In the strange analogy of Paulina, it imitates life as sleep imitates death. Beyond the stone veil of the statue lies a superior life." DRAPER (p. 41): Sleep, "though it 'mocks' death by seeming indistinguishable from it, also hints at a suspension of life which is restorative rather than mortal." PARRY (ed. 1982) believes that Paulina has, "perhaps at the back of her mind," the image of "the way she herself was 'mocked' . . . by Hermione's death-like swoon in court—see [1332]." One doubts it. HALE (1985, p. 157): "Paulina is blurring the distinction between living and dead; by conceits she is unsettling her listeners' hold on what they thought they knew."

3208 **behold . . . well**] *OED* (Well, *a.* 9a, citing this line): "Of good or satisfactory appearance."

3209-10 **I . . . wonder**] SELTZER (1967, p. 163): "Shakespeare writes into the moment of revelation one of his rare stage pauses, to mark the solemnity of the moment." PARRY (ed. 1982): "The 'life' in the statue makes statues of the beholders, for a while." SAHEL (1984, p. 359): As if she were a disciple of Julio Romano, master of the trompe l'oeil, . . . she will ask, as soon as the curtain is drawn, for a critical evaluation (in Fr.). DRAPER (1985, p. 41): "The audience on the stage in effect guides the response of the audience in the actual theatre."

3209 **shewes-off**] CALDECOTT (MS 1813-33): "Displays, denotes." *OED* (Show, *v.* 12b): "To display in relief or by contrast; to set off, enhance in appearance." This is the only instance listed by SCHMIDT (1875) or *OED* of *shows off* in this sense.

3211 **Comes . . . neere?**] DEIGHTON (ed. 1889): "Is it not a fairly good likeness?" PARRY (ed. 1982): "I.e. close to real life." For *something* as "somewhat," see n. 224; and for *it not*, see n. 1804.

3212 **Posture**] JOHNSON (1755): "Voluntary collocation of the parts of the body with respect to each other."

3213-14 **Chide . . . Hermione**] BERGERON (1978, p. 130): "When the curtain is drawn and Leontes, seeing the statue, remarks [these words], the dramatic irony is not felt either on the stage or in the audience." BELLETTE (1978, p. 74): "He now turns to Hermione as if for the first time, and asks *her* to speak that *he* might. It is the reverse in every way of the trial scene and represents the final, accurate location of truth, not in plots, trials or even divine pronouncements, but in a natural posture and a figure now aged and wrinkled." HUNT ("Standing," 1984, p. 31): "That art was outstanding, according to Renaissance theorists, that was so life-like that it chided life for failing to be as vital."

3214 **Thou . . . she**] For scansion, see n. 1220. Here ABBOTT accents *art, mi, rath, thou,* and *she*; his scheme accords two syllables to *Hermione*. SCHANZER (ed. 1969) reduces *Hermione* here and at 3217 to three, "the 'o' being scarcely sounded."

3216 **Infancie, and Grace**] WAIN (1964, p. 223): He "links the memory of Hermione with the memory of that Eden from which he and his friend [Polixenes] were expelled by the mere fact of growing up and developing adult passions [130-8]; but he adds . . . 'grace', to the softness of infancy." GARBER (1984, p. 38): *Infancie* reminds "the audience of the earlier scene in which an actual infant appeared" (928 ff.). GARBER does not say what purpose is served thereby. SCHMIDT (1874, Grace): Probably "any excellence which conciliates love or makes well pleasing." For other meanings of *grace*, see n. 146. KAMACHI (1983, p. 68): "Graceful infant."

Hermione was not so much wrinckled, nothing
So aged as this seemes.
   Pol. Oh, not by much.
   Paul. So much the more our Caruers excellence,   3220
Which lets goe-by some sixteene yeeres, and makes her
As she liu'd now.
   Leo. As now she might haue done,
So much to my good comfort, as it is
Now piercing to my Soule. Oh, thus she stood,   3225
Euen with such Life of Maiestie (warme Life,
As now it coldly stands) when first I woo'd her.
I am asham'd: Do's not the Stone rebuke me,
For being more Stone then it? Oh Royall Peece:
There's Magick in thy Maiestie, which ha's   3230
My Euils coniur'd to remembrance; and
From thy admiring Daughter tooke the Spirits,
Standing like Stone with thee.

3223 As] And OXF1
3232 thy] my THEO1-v1773 (−CAP)
     Spirits] Spirit ROWE1, ROWE2

3217-18 **Hermione . . . seemes**] SEYMOUR (1805, 1:171) objects that Hermione "was not wrinkled at all." No one else has thought her so flawless. Indeed,
MELCHIORI (1960, p. 64): "Hermione is . . . a little the worse for wear." SACHS
(1923, p. 80): The "tender and erotically-tinged attitude of the father towards his
daughter [see 2995 and n.] accords well with the refusal to acknowledge old age: the
wish that the wife remain forever young, ever the same, like a picture or
statue. . . . It is . . . completely comprehensible as the representation of a wish-
fulfillment." MARSH (1962; 1980, p. 158): "The final note of the play, its last honesty,
that nothing can bring back the time that has been wasted." MAVEETY (1966, p. 277):
"It was quite unnecessary for Shakespeare to point out that Hermione has aged; yet
he does. . . . Hermione is alive and forgives her husband; yet the fading of her
beauty, is a sober reminder that sixteen years have elapsed and cannot be recalled."
BRADBROOK ("Dramatic Romance," 1976, p. 87), similarly: "Hermione reappears as
what Time and Leontes have made her; her funeral effigy . . . perpetuates what he
had inflicted upon the living woman." SIDER (1973, p. 9): "The family is reunited,
but much of their life together has been lost, as Leontes reminds us. . . . This bit-
tersweet resolution strikes a stronger sympathetic note than the perfect sweetness
and light . . . of the earlier serious comedies." COLIE (1974, p. 282), vastly: "Of
Hermione's wrinkles the playwright has made a symbol for all the failures of art to
match reality. . . . Wrinkles are the anti-romantic attribute of mature life: if Hermione is to be restored to Leontes with any significance to that restoration, she must
return at time's full cost, her loss made calculable and conscious. The wrinkles are
signs that suffering really *means*." HATTORI (1982, p. 85): "Meant not for a touch of
bathos but as a reward for the king's own mellowing age. . . . It is primarily a play
about a moment of happiness."

3217 **Hermione**] See n. 3214 for suggested pronunciations.

nothing] JOHNSON (1755): "Not at all." For *nothing* as an adverb, see ABBOTT §55.

3218 **So . . . seemes**] LLOYD EVANS (1982, p. 368): "Ironically ageing is irrelevant to what, now, Leontes realizes with all his heart—that he loves Hermione and, after sixteen years the 'spirit' of her love shines through what he takes to be stone." What he speaks of, however, is furrows, not the spirit of love.

3220-2 **So . . . now**] FOWLER (1978, p. 53): "The wrinkles are . . . an occasion of comedy: Leontes' noticing them obliges Paulina to think on her feet."

3221 **lets goe-by**] MAXWELL (ed. 1969): "Indicates the passage."

3221-2 **makes . . . now**] The CLARKES (ed. 1865): "Makes her as she would have looked had she lived now." According to ABBOTT (§107), the *as* only appears to be used for *as if*; the *if* actually is implied by the subjunctive (*liu'd*).

3224 **it**] I.e., the statue or possibly her death.

3225 **piercing . . . Soule**] WARD (1987, p. 550) compares "And a sworde shal pearce through thy soule" (Luke 2:35).

3225-7 **Oh . . . her**] For another recollection of his wooing, see 172-6.

3226-64 **warme . . . warme**] JAMESON (1833; 1889, p. 192): "The expressions used here by Leontes . . . and by Polixenes . . . appear strangely applied to a statue. . . . [The] effect . . . at the same moment is and is *not* illusion— . . . the conviction of death and the impression of life, the idea of a deception and the feeling of a reality."

3228-9 **Do's . . . it?**] NOBLE (1935, p. 248): "The figure of the stone rebuking from the wall is not unknown in the Bible." He cites Hab. 2:10-11. MIRIAM JOSEPH (1947, p. 85): The rhetorical figure is *ploce*, "employed . . . in the later plays, often to express intense feeling." Ploce is word repetition for emphasis.

3229 **Stone**] BOORMAN (ed. 1964): "Unfeeling." For "hearts of stone," see TILLEY H311 and Ezek. 36:26.

Peece] SCHMIDT (1875): "Applied to persons sometimes in contempt: [2265-6]. . . . Oftener to denote a person of supreme excellence: . . . [1833, 2843]." It may also mean "a work of art, a painting or statue," as at 3103. Here SCHMIDT thinks the last significance applies, but WHITE (ed. 1883) and PAFFORD (ed. 1963) name the second. For other uses of the word, see n. 1833.

3230-3 **There's . . . thee**] MINSHEU (1617, Spirit): "Life of man." SCHMIDT (1875): "Vital power" (*OED, sb.* 1). BETHELL (ed. 1956): "The image here extends to a brief allegory: the *magic conjures* his past sins up again (like evil spirits) and takes away the *spirits*, or *life* of Perdita, making her like a marble statue. The theme of 'black' and 'white' magic runs through the scene [see 3293-5 (which BETHELL does not mention), 3302-3, 3312-13]." The spirits, according to YOUNG & MOSELEY (ed. 1965), are "the 'animal spirits', which were regarded as the source of motion; . . . they mediated between the body and the soul." DAVIES (1986, p. 162): "The watchers of the mystery turn to stone; they seem to die while the apparently insentient and inanimate stone of the statue, warm and breathing, comes out of its veil. The dimensions cross."

3231 **My . . . remembrance**] CHAMPION (1970, p. 169): "Paulina dramatically forces Leontes to recreate the experience of his repentance."

coniur'd] SCHMIDT (1874): "To influence by magic," in a transferred sense. EVANS (ed. 1974): "Summoned up (as a magician summons up evil spirits)." For another meaning, see n. 509.

3232-3 **From . . . thee**] To turn to stone from wonder is proverbial (DENT S893.1). RICHMAN (1990, p. 114): The description "may be taken as a stage direction."

3232 **admiring**] Wondering. See nn. 2027-8, 2489.

3233 **Standing . . . thee**] DEIGHTON (ed. 1889): "Now herself more like stone than flesh and blood."

Perd. And giue me leaue,
And doe not say 'tis Superstition, that   3235
I kneele, and then implore her Blessing. Lady,
Deere Queene, that ended when I but began,
Giue me that hand of yours, to kisse.
　　Paul. O, patience:
The Statue is but newly fix'd; the Colour's   3240
Not dry.
　　Cam. My Lord, your Sorrow was too sore lay'd-on,
Which sixteene Winters cannot blow away,
So many Summers dry: scarce any Ioy
Did euer so long liue; no Sorrow,   3245
But kill'd it selfe much sooner.
　　Pol. Deere my Brother,
Let him, that was the cause of this, haue powre

3236 then] thus mCAP2, COL2, COL3
3240 Colour's] colours mTBY2 *conj.*, WALKER (1860, 3:116) *conj.*, HUD2
3243 sixteene Winters cannot] cannot sixteen winters v1785
3245-7 *Verse lines ending* sorrow, . . . brother, mCAP2, v1793-COL4, WH2+;
but . . . brother, mTBY2 *and* WALKER (1854, p. 28) *conj.*, HUD2
3245-6 Sorrow, But] sorrow, sir, But CAP; sorrow ever But KTLY; sorrow but It
WALKER (1854, p. 28) *conj.*, HUD2
3247 Deere∧] ~ , F4, ROWE

3234-6 **And . . . Blessing**] SMITH (1985, p. 19): "Paulina's 'poor house' [3192]
is referred to by Leontes as a 'gallery' [3197], but in the crucial moments just before
the statue awakes Paulina herself calls it a 'chapel' [3290]." The first, however, is
politely depreciatory; the second alludes to one portion of the house; the third alludes
to another or perhaps a separate building. For these lines as evidence of Sh.'s religious
views, see n. 324-8.
　　3235 **Superstition**] BOORMAN (ed. 1964): "Superstitious Popery." CRUTTWELL
(1955, p. 82) finds "both Catholic sentiment and Protestant apologizing for it . . . in
Perdita's response to what she believes is the statue." MAXWELL (ed. 1969): "An
allusion to the Protestant attack upon kneeling before images of the Virgin." Perdita's
denial of superstition, however, calls the superstition to mind.
　　3237-8 **Deere . . . kisse**] CALDECOTT (MS 1813-33) compares *Per.* 5.1.211-
12 (Q2187-8). LEIMBERG (1987, p. 131): "From the very first she [Perdita] behaves
as if she did not accept Paulina's subterfuge. To her the statue is her mother, the
queen." Yet Perdita clearly believes her mother to be dead (3237, where *ended
. . . began* means "died when I hardly began to live").
　　3239 **O, patience**] JOHNSON (ed. 1765): "Stay a while, be not so eager." Perdita's
touch would, of course, reveal that the stone is flesh. PARRY (ed. 1982): This "would
defeat the purpose of Paulina's 'art', which is to change Leontes' feelings about his
wife from remorse to yearning." DELIUS (ed. 1860) believes that *patience* is "pardon,"
as in "by your patience."

3240-1 The . . . dry] Influenced no doubt by the semicolon after *fix'd* and the apostrophe of *Colour's*, all eds. but HUDSON think the line a sentence with two independent clauses. The alternative is to discount the semicolon and to take *Colour's* as nominative plural, the construction being an elliptical clause with the verb *are* omitted. THIRLBY (MS 1725-33?) reads *colours* but then seems to change his mind: "If he [Sh.] had meant *ut hic* [as this] he wd have wrote *colour*." WALKER (1860, 3: 116), citing this as an instance of the apostrophe in the plural, says merely "*Colours*, surely." For the painting of the statue, see n. 3104-5.

3240 fix'd] SCHMIDT (1874, Fix): "To set, to place in general" (*OED, ppl. a.* 1). FAIRCHILD (1937, p. 74): "Rendered hard or non-volatile" (4a), or as HAPPÉ (1969) explains, "'applied' but not 'set.'" This meaning, however, postdates Sh. Thus Paulina seems to mean "The statue was only recently put in place. After that it was painted, and the paint has not dried."

3242-6 My . . . sooner] RICHMAN (1990, p. 166): "The differences between the portrayed penances of Posthumus [in *Cym.*] and Leontes and those of Bertram [in *AWW*] and Angelo [in *MM*] may suggest that Shakespeare was not himself wholly satisfied with the endings to the so-called problem comedies."

3242 too sore lay'd-on] WRIGHT & LAMAR (ed. 1966): "Felt so grievously"; the adverb is SCHMIDT's gloss. HAPPÉ (1969): "Painfully acquired. The metaphor is from painting," but paint is not sorely applied. BEVINGTON (ed. 1992) gives "heavily"; *heavy* is one of SCHMIDT's synonyms for *sore* as an adjective. SCHMIDT (1874, Lay 11): "To apply as a colour . . . (Leontes' sorrow being compared with the colouring of Hermione's statue)." KNOWLES (privately): "More likely, 'lay on a burden' or 'inflict a punishment.'"

3244 So . . . dry] CHARLTON (ed. 1916): "'Which so many summers cannot dry.'"

3245 Did . . . Sorrow] For the scansion, see n. 1353 and ABBOTT §508. Here the vacant syllable falls between *liue* and *no*. Some critics, however, emend the line; see, in addition to the textual notes, p. 585.

3245-6 no . . . sooner] LEE (ed. 1907) compares "If the liuing be the enemie to the greefe, the excesse makes it soone mortall" (*AWW* 1.1.57-8 [59-60]), which he glosses "excessive indulgence in grief puts an end to it." Comparing 1430-2, PARRY (ed. 1982) seems to think that Camillo chides Leontes for "an overdone expression of [his] feelings." It is more likely that he calls attention to the king's extraordinarily long immersion in grief.

3247-50 Deere . . . himselfe] DEIGHTON (ed. 1899): "Let him (*i.e.* myself) who was, though unintentionally, the cause of this, have the power by his sympathy to divert upon himself so much of this grief as he may justly make his own." PAFFORD (ed. 1963): Polixenes's "magnanimity is typical of ideal friendship. . . . The heavens are continuing the love between the two friends [26, 35-6]. . . . Polixenes . . . exaggerates his responsibility for Hermione's 'death' and, in sympathy for the overpowering remorse in which Leontes is lost, further exaggerates it in order to help his friend." PAFFORD compares Valentine's forgiving Proteus (*TGV* 5.4.82-3 [2208-9]), *JC* 4.3.86 (2064), *Son.* 88.13-14, and *TNK* 2.2.79 (184-5) and refers to the description of the friendship cult in MILLS (1937). JOHNSON (1755, Piece, citing this line): "To join; to coalesce; to be compacted." WRIGHT & LAMAR (ed. 1966, Piece up): "Make up for"; SCHMIDT (1875) prefers "hoard up, so as to have his fill." HAPPÉ (1969): "Assume." For other uses of the word, see n. 1833.

3247 Deere my] For the reversal, see n. 390.

To take-off so much griefe from you, as he
Will peece vp in himselfe.   3250
   Paul. Indeed my Lord,
If I had thought the sight of my poore Image
Would thus haue wrought you (for the Stone is mine)
Il'd not haue shew'd it.   (2❛
   Leo. Doe not draw the Curtaine.   3255
   Paul. No longer shall you gaze on't, least your Fancie
May thinke anon, it moues.
   Leo. Let be, let be:
Would I were dead, but that me thinkes alreadie.
(What was he that did make it?) See (my Lord)   3260
Would you not deeme it breath'd? and that those veines
Did verily beare blood?
   Pol. 'Masterly done:
The very Life seemes warme vpon her Lippe.

3250 vp in] upon WH1
3254 Il'd] I'll v1821
    shew'd] you shevv'd F3; shew'd you F4-POPE2, HAN
3257 moues] move POPE1-JOHN2
3259 alreadie.] Ff, OXF2; already | I am but dead, stone looking upon stone.—
COL2, COL3, COL4; already— ROWE1 *etc.*

3251-4 **Indeed . . . it**] GRENE (1967, p. 85): "We wonder here, though perhaps
not very much, what sort of woman Paulina is that takes such evident pleasure in
making Leontes suffer."
   3253 **wrought**] STEEVENS (ed. 1793): "Worked, agitated." NEILSON & HILL (ed.
1942): "Moved."
   for . . . mine] DEIGHTON (ed. 1889): "I say *my* statue, for it is *mine*." The
parenthesis may have been added to show that "my poore Image" alludes to the
statue rather than to Paulina herself.
   3255 **Doe . . . Curtaine**] STYAN (1967, p. 135): "Intent upon stirring feeling in
Leontes, she [thrice; here, 3267, and 3285] teases him by moving close to the curtain."
PROUDFOOT (1976, p. 77): Her offers "allow for the possibility that it is 'truly' a statue,
while the responses of Leontes [3260-2] and Polixenes [3263-4] encourage the hope
that this . . . is indeed Hermione."
   3256-7 **No . . . moues**] CHARLTON (ed. 1916): "Skilfully and gradually, by suggestion, the atmosphere of expectation is created: we are made to expect the impossible." PETERSON (*Time*, 1973, pp. 202-3): "The destructive action . . . began when
a violent passion, awakened by an act of memory [172-6], led Leontes to charge
Hermione with infidelity. . . . Once again intense feelings inspired by an act of remembering stir the fancy." YUNE (1973, pp. 60-1): "Gradually Leontes sees the mo-

tion of life beyond the stillness of art. The two pieces, the statue and the image in his mind, art and nature[,] become one. Through his love of Hermione the image of her in his mind comes to reality." PARRY (ed. 1982): "From now on his [Leontes's] imagination ('fancy') repeatedly urges him to see that Hermione really is alive, until she really does stir. At the same time, it is a statement that 'explains' — as the beholder's 'fancy' — any slight but perceptible movement that the actress . . . may involuntarily make" up to 3311. The latter idea seems doubtful.

3256 **Fancie**] SCHMIDT (1874): "Imagination." See nn. 1046 and 2335 for related meanings. HAPPÉ (1969): "There may also be a suggestion of 'madness' here."

3257 **anon**] Immediately. See n. 1468.

3259 **Would . . . alreadie**] WARBURTON (ed. 1747): "The sentence compleated is, . . . *already I converse with the dead*. But there his passion made him break off." HEATH (1765, p. 221): Sh. means the opposite — "methinks, she is already on the point of moving." TIECK (ed. 1825-33, 9:357) interprets the line: "Would I were dead" — if I could thereby reanimate Hermione — "but that, methinks, already — " but even as I wish this, there are signs of life in the statue (in Ger.). KNIGHT (ed. 1841): "The abrupt breaking off is one of those touches of nature with which Shakspere knew how to give passion an eloquence beyond words." LETTSOM ("New Readings," 1853, p. 202): "The train of emotion is evidently this: — Would I were dead, but *that* methinks already (he is about to add) I am, when the life-like appearance of the statue forcibly impresses his senses, whereupon he checks himself and exclaims, 'What was *he* that did make it' — a god or a mere man, &c." STAUNTON (ed. 1859) interprets "Would . . . dead" not as "I wish I were dead" but as "an imprecation, equivalent to — '*Would I may die*,'" as in *TGV* 4.4.171 (1992); Leontes thus says, "May I die, if I do not think it moves *already*." FURNESS (ed. 1898) believes that this reading "carries conviction" and so does BETHELL (ed. 1956), but not all critics are persuaded.

The CLARKES (ed. 1865) paraphrase: "Would I were dead with her, but that methinks already she moves and breathes, and lives again to me." They add, "He is wholly possessed by the growing conviction that what he looks upon moves, breathes, exists." LETTSOM (MS 1840-65) thinks *that* refers "to the supposed motion of the statue hinted at in [3256-7]. There should be a full stop after already. . . . It is evident from [3256-7], that Hermione could no longer maintain the death-like immobility of a statue, and that a suspicion of the truth is in a manner dawning on the mind of Leontes." It is uncertain whether this interpretation precedes or follows the more conventional one of 1853 given above, but it may derive from Macready's performance. MARTIN (1891, p. 34) reports that when Macready broke off after *alreadie*, the question "Has he seen something that makes him think the statue lives?" suggested itself. PORTER & CLARKE (ed. 1908): "Leontes wishes he were dead, so stirred is his spirit with desire to join hers, but thinks he is already dead so joined with her he feels."

3260 **What . . . it?**] BETHELL (ed. 1956) paraphrases: "What sort of person? (— a magician?)," but *What* may = "who." See ABBOTT §254.

3262 **verily**] BARTON (1986, p. 38): This "uncommon and arresting adverb . . . suggest[s] what is special and extraordinary about a stone image which, by laying claim to motion and speech, is about to break through the barrier dividing even the most realistic sculpture from life." The adverb is not so uncommon; Sh. uses it 14 times (7 in *WT*), the King James Bible about 100 times.

3263 **'Masterly**] DEIGHTON (ed. 1889): "In a masterly manner" (*OED, adv.*, citing this line). See ABBOTT §447. The apostrophe presumably represents *It is*.

Leo. The fixure of her Eye ha's motion in't,   3265
As we are mock'd with Art.
   Paul. Ile draw the Curtaine:
My Lord's almost so farre transported, that
Hee'le thinke anon it liues.
   Leo. Oh sweet *Paulina*,   3270
Make me to thinke so twentie yeeres together:
No setled Sences of the World can match
The pleasure of that madnesse. Let't alone.
   Paul. I am sorry (Sir) I haue thus farre stir'd you: but
I could afflict you farther.   3275
   Leo. Doe *Paulina*:
For this Affliction ha's a taste as sweet
As any Cordiall comfort. Still me thinkes
There is an ayre comes from her. What fine Chizzell
Could euer yet cut breath? Let no man mock me,   3280
For I will kisse her.

3265 fixure] fissure WARB *conj.* (*withdrawn* mWARB), BLAIR
3266 As] And CAP, HUD2; So MASON (1785, p. 138) *conj.*, RANN
    we are] are we RANN
    are] were ROWE3-v1778 (−CAP)
3273 Let't] Let's F3, F4, ROWE2; Let JOHN
3274-5 *Prose (but* 3276 *indented*) IRV

3265 **The . . . in't**] JOHNSON (1755, Fixure): "Position," to which JERVIS (1868) adds "Stability; firmness" (*OED*, citing this line and *Tro.* 1.3.101 [560], the one other occurrence of the word in Sh.). EDWARDS (1748, p. 15): "Though the eye be fixed . . . yet it seems to have motion in it, that tremulous motion which is perceptible in the eye of a living person how much soever one endeavours to fix it." The CLARKES (ed. 1865): "The immobility of eye proper to a statue seems to have the motion of a living eye." For *fixure of her Eye* NARES (1876; 1905), oddly, thinks "the attachment of the eye, that by which it is fixed into the head, has motion; as a string, or some such contrivance." SCHMIDT (1874): "Direction," but directions have no motion. KITTREDGE & RIBNER (ed. 1967): "The way the eye has been created (in its colour as well as its position)." HAPPÉ (1969) returns to JOHNSON: "Fixed position (as a statue). The word is meant to clash as a paradox with *motion.*"

3266 **As . . . Art**] For *as*, MALONE (1783, p. 22): "As if," but SINGER (ed. 1856): "So that" (ABBOTT §110). Cf. n. 1875. For *with*, STEEVENS (ed. 1793): "By," as in 2866 and 3072. Hence LEE (ed. 1907): "For so we are mocked by art"; BEVINGTON (ed. 1992): "In such a way that we are fooled by artistic illusion." WAITH (1982, p. 119) describes what follows as "the capstone to the much-discussed treatment of the theme of art and nature running through the play." According to HUDSON (ed. 1852), the statue and the on-stage viewers begin to change places: "The illusion is all on the understandings, not on the feelings of the spectators: they *think* it to be a statue, yet *feel* as if it were the living original; seem to discern the *power* without the *fact* of motion; have a *sense* of mobility in a *vision* of fixedness. And the effect spreads through them into us; insomuch that we almost fancy them turning into marble, as they fancy the marble turning into flesh." Perhaps confused by HUDSON, HUNTER (ed. 1872), oddly: "As if the motion of our eyes were mocked by art." HERFORD (ed. 1916-): "Leontes believes that he is looking at a real work of art, and that he is really 'mocked' by its life-like character, as he might be by any work of similar realism." EDWARDS (1986, p. 92, n. 12): "A brilliant double-cross by Shakespeare, for Leontes is mistaken; it is not a triumph of art that Leontes is beholding, but Hermione herself. It is in that 'Hermione herself' that the mockery lies, for Hermione is a boy-actor pretending to be Hermione pretending to be a statue." PETERSON (*Time*, 1973, pp. 203-5): The art that has in fact contributed to the restoration of Hermione is the art of memory as rigorously exercised by Leontes under Paulina's scrupulous supervision. BOORMAN (ed. 1964): There are "two possible meanings (*a*) 'for thus we are deceived by the artist's skill' and (*b*) 'as if we are deceived by magic.'" For art as magic, see 3319. COLLINS (1982, p. 59): "The meaning of 'mock'd' which first comes to mind is that of 'imitation'. . . . [Yet] 'mock'd' takes on a second meaning, that of 'deceived', and perhaps a third, that of 'ridiculed.'"

3267 **Ile . . . Curtaine**] The CLARKES (ed. 1865): "Paulina's anxiety on this point serves to manifest her dread lest Hermione's firmness should fail her during this agitating scene; while all that she else says helps gradually to lead Leontes towards the fact that his wife indeed lives." The latter part of this statement seems right, the former doubtful, for Paulina seems perfectly in control, and her suggestion that Leontes be parted from the statue is a step in her psychological manipulation of him. See n. 3255.

3268 **transported**] PHILLIPS (1658, Transport): "A sudden trance, or rapture of mind." HAPPÉ (1969): "Carried away." For a related meaning, see n. 1343.

3269 **anon**] Immediately. See n. 1468.

3272 **setled . . . World**] For *setled*, KITTREDGE & RIBNER (ed. 1967): "Calm, untroubled by emotion"; see also n. 2385. For *sences*, OED (10 *pl.*): "The mental faculties in their normal condition of sanity; one's 'reason' or 'wits.'" For *of the world*, OED (World, *sb.* 20b, citing this line): "In the world." BETHELL (ed. 1956): "Sanity as the world regards it." PARRY (ed. 1982): "Commonly held and scientifically endorsed views of what reality is." LAWLOR (1962, p. 103): "The statue awakens an impossible longing; and the illusion that it lives is preferable to reality." BROOKS (in PAFFORD, ed. 1963) finds a parallel with Florizel at 2335-8: "Florizel in his love of Perdita and Leontes in his love of Hermione each recognizes something stronger than the rational." The same may be said of all lovers in Sh., if not everywhere.

3275 **afflict**] WARBURTON (ed. 1747): Used "in the sense of *affect*." EDWARDS (1750, p. 65): "Grieve, trouble" (*OED*, *v.* 3).

3277 **Affliction**] HEATH (1765, p. 221), continuing EDWARDS's interpretation of 3275: "Remorse."

3278 **Cordiall**] MINSHEU (1617): "A generall name giuen to those medicines which purge not, but only comfort the heart and the bodie decaied, as most conserves" (*OED*, *a.* 2b, citing this line). See nn. 40-1, 415.

3279 **There . . . her**] OED (Air 9, citing this line): "Breath." LETTSOM (MS 1840-65) compares 3261.

3279-80 **What . . . breath?**] NEELY (1975, p. 336): "He first marvels that art could be so lifelike, and then, with a significant change in emphasis, that anything so lifelike could be art." FELPERIN (*Deconstruction*, 1985, p. 175): "Combining catachresis [misuse of words] and onomatopoeia . . . , he [Sh.] has fixed our sense of wonder on a succession of monosyllables composed of short vowels chopped off by dental stops, and by so doing, has imitated in language the sharp clicks of a chisel tapping through its medium."

3279 **fine**] OED (*v.* 8, citing this line): "Sharp-pointed, keen-edged; sharp."

3280-1 **Let . . . her**] PARRY (ed. 1982), comparing 3234-8: "She [Perdita] saw her mother as a living saint, then. Now Leontes sees his wife as a living woman. And she *is* both." NEELY (1985, p. 206): "His determination to kiss the statue signals Paulina that he is ready for reunion with the woman Hermione."

Paul. Good my Lord, forbeare:
The ruddinesse vpon her Lippe, is wet:
You'le marre it, if you kisse it; stayne your owne
With Oyly Painting: shall I draw the Curtaine.   3285
    Leo. No: not these twentie yeeres.
    Perd. So long could I
Stand-by, a looker-on.
    Paul. Either forbeare,
Quit presently the Chappell, or resolue you   3290
For more amazement: if you can behold it,
Ile make the Statue moue indeed; descend,
And take you by the hand: but then you'le thinke
(Which I protest against) I am assisted
By wicked Powers.   3295
    Leo. What you can make her doe,
I am content to looke on: what to speake,
I am content to heare: for 'tis as easie
To make her speake, as moue.
    Paul. It is requir'd   3300
You doe awake your Faith: then, all stand still:
On: those that thinke it is vnlawfull Businesse
I am about, let them depart.
    Leo. Proceed:
No foot shall stirre.   3305

3292 moue∧ indeed;] ∼ ; ∼ , STAU
3296 you can] can you KNT3
3302 On:] F1-ROWE3, KNT, COL1, COL2, CAM1, GLO, WH2, IRV, ARD1, SIS, CLN2,
EVNS, BEV; And∧ POPE1-THEO2, WARB-JOHN2; Or∧ HAN1 *etc.*

3282 **Good my Lord**] For the transposition, see n. 390.
    forbeare] SCHMIDT (1874): "Abstain from doing what was purposed" (*OED*,
v. 5). I.e., Stop! The word occurs again at 3289.
    3283-4 **The . . . kisse it**] See n. 3104-5. CAMDEN (1952, p. 189): Sh. here "was
as usual writing for the ages," for Elizabethan lip rouge, like today's, "was far from
being permanent." Paulina is speaking of the wet paint on the statue, however.
    3285 **shall . . . Curtaine**] See n. 3255.
    3289-93 **Either . . . hand**] DRAPER (1985, p. 42): "Paulina is given words
which screw the already heightened tension a notch higher."
    3289 **forbeare**] See n. 3282 for the usual meaning, which Paulina seems to repeat.
SCHMIDT's (1874) "leave a place" is not exactly supported by *OED*. SCHMIDT takes
Quit . . . Chappell as appositive to "forbeare," but the clause could be a second
imperative, with *and* omitted.
    3290 **presently**] Now. See n. 874.
    Chappell] ARMSTRONG (1969, p. 75): "A building whose atmosphere is deter-
mined by those rites through which we commit our dead to the timeless, yet keep

them folded within a human and institutional continuity, a shrine largely given over to that ancestral world which persistently asserts itself in *The Winter's Tale.*" He compares 2300-3. This chapel is, of course, not the one of 1431, in which Hermione and Mamillius lie buried. FRYE (1978, p. 37): "We notice how frequently the 'higher' place in the romances is represented by an inner one: the cave of Belarius in *Cymbeline*, [this], Prospero's cell in *The Tempest.*"

resolue] KERSEY (1702): "Determine"; SCHMIDT (1875): "Prepare" (both evidently equivalent to "make up one's mind" [*OED, v.* 19a]). Thus LEE (ed. 1907) glosses "Either . . . you" as "Either abstain from touching, and at once quit the chapel, or make up your mind."

3291 **behold it**] DEIGHTON (ed. 1889): "Endure to behold it."

3292 **Ile . . . indeed**] ENGEL (1980, p. 3): "The statue that comes to life to take part in dramatic action was a stock, sensational device in Renaissance English drama." Examples are the Brazen Head in Greene's *Friar Bacon and Friar Bungay*, "the statue of Pompey and the dreamed statue of Caesar" in *JC*, and the statue of Fortune in Jonson's *Sejanus His Fall.*

indeed] SCHMIDT (1874): "Really, in fact."

3295 **By wicked Powers**] PAFFORD (ed. 1963): "Shakespeare is careful to emphasize that black magic is not being used, as also in [3319-20]."

3296-9 **What . . . moue**] SANDERS (1987, p. 112): "What can he know any more, about the possible and the impossible, when what was lost has begun to be found?"

3300-1 **It . . . Faith**] MELDRUM (1968, p. 57) is reminded of "For as the bodie without the spirit is dead, euen so the faith without workes is dead" (Jas. 2:26). DRAPER (1985, p. 11): "Shakespeare seems to show awareness of the possibility of a sceptical response, and yet builds his reckoning of it into the text in such a way that it can be interpreted as either an attempt to lift the audience on to a level of suprarational understanding [as here] or a tacit recognition of the inevitable fragility of the illusion that is being created, shared and conspiratorially enjoyed with the audience [as at 3279-80]." BEVINGTON (1985, 2:328): "Paulina's role in this restoration resembles that of the dramatist, for she deals in the illusion of death and rebirth." O'CONNELL (1985, p. 305): "The effect on an audience is analogous to religious experience: an act of faith is required for the enactment of the seeming miracle."

3301 **Faith**] Belief. See n. 544-5.

all stand still] KAMACHI (1979, p. 37): "They stand like statues, in perfect silence and stillness, watching the statue of Hermione."

3302 **On**] KNIGHT (ed. 1841): "Let us go on. The king immediately adds 'proceed.'" MOORMAN (ed. 1912): "Let us go forward in our work," or, as CARRINGTON (1956) puts it, "let what I am about to do go on." COLLIER (ed. 1842), less aptly: "Let those *go on*, and depart, who think it is unlawful business I am about." PORTER & CLARKE (ed. 1908): "Possibly it was a signal, given with a gesture, to the musicians that they were to place themselves ready to begin when she gave the word." Although sense obviously can be found in *on*, many recent eds. think *or* the better reading; WILSON (ed. 1931): It "seems certain. The F. colon need not disturb us, since once the compositor had set up 'On', he or his corrector would be almost bound to insert a colon to make some kind of sense." PAFFORD (ed. 1963) paraphrases the emendation: "Stand still or <rather as an afterthought as she changes her mind> those who have any doubts, let them go."

vnlawfull Businesse] HUDSON (ed. 1880): "Practising magic . . . was regarded as conspiring with 'wicked powers', and so was punished as a capital crime." MACDONALD (1985, 1:185): "Parliament made conjuring evil spirits a secular crime punishable by death in 1563 and added necromancy to the roll of capital offenses in the second witchcraft statute of 1604." Cf. *AYL* (ed. Knowles, 1977, n. 2470).

  Paul. Musick; awake her: Strike: 3306
'Tis time: descend: be Stone no more: approach:
Strike all that looke vpon with meruaile: Come:
Ile fill your Graue vp: stirre: nay, come away:

3306 Musick;] ~ , HUD, DYCE, WH, STAU, DEL, CAM1, GLO, IRV-ARD1, ALEX, CLN2, ARD2, SIG, PEN2, BEV; ~ᴧ COL
3308 vpon] on you HAN; upon you KEIGHTLEY *conj. in* CAM1, KTLY

3306-17 **Musick . . . Suitor?**] COGHILL (1958, p. 40): "Against all the invoca-
tions of Paulina, [Sh.] piles up colons . . . his deliberate contrivance for this special
effect; only at the end of the long, pausing entreaty, when the suspense of her mo-
tionlessness has been continued until it must seem unendurable, is Hermione allowed
to move." The effect is the same whether the colons are Sh.'s or Crane's. LONG (1961,
p. 90): "The punctuation of these lines indicates that the awakening . . . is a gradual
one. Paulina's commands are seemingly spoken between rather long pauses during
which mysterious music could be heard with great effect. . . . The command 'Strike'
was usually associated with string instruments." See the next n. and, for other instances, n. 283.
   3306-11 **Musick . . . you)**] JONES (1971, p. 30): "Her words assume a charged
formulaic brevity. . . . There are here eleven pauses in four lines [3306-9]. But the
entire scene has been conducted at a measured tempo: only by carefully marked stages
and finally as if step by step are we led to the moment of highest feeling when the
statue moves. The essential beauty of [recognition] scenes lies in their deployment
of time; they are entirely a matter of fulfilled expectations." GARBER (1987, p. 139):
"A trope familiar from lyric 'comes to life,' as it were in drama, and there occurs a
double uncanniness. As the statue . . . moves and speaks, the figure of prosopopeia
[the attribution of human qualities to subhuman things] likewise comes alive."
   HUNTER (1965, p. 135): An earlier play in which an apparent statue revives is *The
Trial of Chivalry* (1599-1604). However, DESAI (1952, p. 85), among others, asserts
that "the death of the heroine and her rebirth as a different person, and her being
recognised," are repeated here from the supposed death of Hero in *Ado*. FRYE (1978,
p. 36): "A similar image of resurrection is employed when Pericles is roused from his
stupor by Marina [*Per.* 5.1], and when Imogen recovers from the narcotic drug
[*Cym.* 4.2.291 (2613)]." SMITH (1985, p. 16): "Two separate scenes in *Pericles*
are . . . fused to form the statue scene. . . . Thaisa, to all appearances dead in childbirth like Hermione, is miraculously brought back to life [in 3.2]." For the second
instance, SMITH reasonably assumes that in *Per.* 5.2-3, the Temple of Diana would
have been furnished with an image of the goddess. Hermione, incidentally, seems to
die of shock, not the rigors of childbirth (1332-3). BOLTE ("Schlussscene," 1891)
describes Hendrik de Graeff's 17th-c. Dutch play, *Alcinea, of stantvastige Kuysheydt*
(*Alcinea, or Steadfast Chastity*) (Amsterdam, 1671), in which a character corresponding to Paulina stands like a statue and a wronged wife appears to return from the
dead. BOLTE rather pointlessly questions whether *WT* and *Alcinea* might not have a
common source other than Greene. PARROTT (1949, p. 386): "The transformation of
a statue into a living woman goes back to the legend of Pygmalion and Galatea: the
story had been told again and again since Ovid, but never with such dramatic effect.
Yet we may well recognize in this *coup-de-théâtre* Shakespeare's ingenious adaptation

of one of the devices of the Court Masque where a transformation scene discloses a group of statue-like and silent figures, who later come forward to take part in the action." QUENNELL (1963, p. 323): "Here is a stratagem that must have appealed to the Jacobean stage-designer, with his liking for dumb-shows, transparencies, and other ingenious scenic whims. The spectacle of Hermione, first statuesque and immobile, then slowly coming to life, would have given the designer just the pretext he needed."

EWBANK (1964, p. 98): "In tone and phrasing [Paulina's words are] very like a presenter's call for the chief figure of the masque to appear." EWBANK's single example is "the call for Neptune" in the masque in Beaumont and Fletcher's *The Maid's Tragedy* (1.2.164-7), and the resemblance is slight. She also points out that "in fact no masque-writer had used [living statues] before *The Winter's Tale* was first performed [in 1610-11]. Soon after[,] . . . however, both Campion and Beaumont in their respective masques for the Princess Elizabeth's wedding, made use of statues coming alive." Campion's *The Lords' Masque*, performed on 14 Feb. 1613, introduces two groups of four statues that are brought to life and dance with masquers (ed. Sabol, 1991, pp. 153-86); his *Earl of Somerset's Masque*, performed on 26 Dec. 1613, restores twelve knights who have been transformed into pillars of gold (ed. Vivian, 1900?, pp. 153-4). Beaumont's *Masque of the Inner Temple and Gray's Inn*, performed on 20 Feb. 1613, introduces an unspecified number of statues (probably four), who dance with each other (lines 165-80). As EWBANK observes, Bacon, who sponsored Beaumont's masque, includes "Statua's Moving" among the figures commonly found in antimasques (*Essays*, ed. Kiernan, 1985, p. 118).

A difference, perhaps significant, between the living statues of the masques and that of *WT* is that the former are strangely costumed and made up—some are metallic—whereas if we did not know the figure of Hermione to be a statue, we would take her for a woman, for she has been naturalistically painted. MATCHETT (1969, p. 102): "The statue . . . reminds us immediately of the dramatic medium. We no sooner see the statue than we recognize the actress—or in Elizabethan times the actor—in the costume of Hermione. . . . How else would we stage a statue but to have it represented by the actor who played the character the statue itself represents?" MORO & WILLEMS (1982, p. 45): "Artifice in this case is used to promote rebirth. This is brought into relief by the structural parallelism existing between the trial-scene [3.2] that ends in Hermione's pretended death and the statue-scene that ends in her pretended resurrection." NOVY (1984, p. 16): "The comparison of control to stone and emotion to flesh—an image Shakespeare has used since the sonnets—becomes part of the visual imagery of the play, as the figure of Hermione moves, in the imagination of the audience offstage and on, from statue to live human being."

EDWARDS (*Progress*, 1986, p. 54): "Shakespeare's plays are full of people stepping outside their proper personalities and deceiving others in order to bring about desired ends both good and bad. The good deceivers include . . . Paulina." GREEN (1890, pp. 34-5): "'Tis now Paulina's hour of triumph. For this moment she has given her soul's devotion through the emptied years. Seeing the way is prepared, the hour ripe with a promised fruition, she now awakens to life the statue-like Hermione, and her words, from their electric power, seem to give the vital spark to the marble form." BETHELL (ed. 1956): Lady MARTIN's explanation (see n. 3206-10) "is as good a way as any of accounting for Hermione's submitting to the theatricality of the statue pose, except that she would doubtless have forgiven Leontes from the beginning: her withdrawal was not in anger but to fulfill the oracle. It is more likely that she would need proof of his love in order to gain courage to return to him who had once rejected her. It is unlikely, however, that Shakespeare troubled to give himself a psychologically consistent account of the matter." ALEXANDER (1938, p. 211): "What might have proved the somewhat stagey device of the descent from the pedestal is carried beyond the merely theatrical by a powerful current of feeling; for Leontes gives life to the statue before him like another Pygmalion, animating it . . . by the passionate recollection of the past." MINCOFF (1941, p. 13), however, feels no powerful current: "If the protests against Hermione's reappearance . . . are no greater than they are, it is chiefly because Hermione and Leontes have already dropped out of the picture . . . : Hermione's position has been taken by Perdita[;] she has become a supernumary whose fate cannot seriously affect the structure of the drama." GARNER (1989, pp. 144-5): "A man's idealization of his beloved dooms their relationship to failure. The woman who must be, or is, killed is the woman on a pedestal. . . . Hermione's return as a statue that comes to life symbolizes that meaning. . . . 'descend . . . more' mainly describes not her action but rather a movement in Leontes, a change in the male psyche. [He] has had to face the possibility of [her] infidelity, in other words, to accept her as a human woman, who may . . . fall. . . . Time blunts his sexual fears since Hermione returns only when she is past childbearing age."

MUIR (1965, p. 91), comparing critical disapproval with theatrical success, concludes: "The actors taught the critics that the statue scene, far from being absurd, could be overwhelmingly effective on the stage. . . . But, of course, a scene could be immensely effective on the stage without being satisfying to the reader, and without being great drama." LÜTHI (1957, p. 304): The romance makes the impossible possible. Hermione's "resurrection" is the dramatic, theatrical expression of the possibility of the impossible (in Ger.). ADELMAN (1973, p. 167), similarly: In the romances "the impossible is no longer a matter of poetic assertion: it actually takes place on the stage. When Hermione steps down from her pedestal . . . , the impossible has been achieved. . . . No one would think of questioning Hermione about her perverse sadomasochistic desire to torment Leontes by remaining hidden until Perdita is found or about her living arrangements during that period; nor in fact do we take the rationalization that she has remained hidden very seriously. We know that she has come back to life. We do not, that is to say, seek to explain the impossible away. Instead, we gladly accept the impossibility for the sake of the symbolic pattern: she must remain hidden until her daughter has grown up and returned; only thus can the validity of the natural process of regeneration be asserted." MARSHALL (1986, pp. 300-1): "The locus of dramatic concern falls less on Hermione herself than on the charged reactions of those around her. Their experience, which is also the experience of the audience, is one of death followed by miraculous reunion. . . . The play insists that Hermione is dead, then restores her to life by a theatrical miracle." McIVER (1979, p. 350): "The audience of kings and princes stand in relation to the unveiling of the statue as the audience . . . stands in relation to the scene as a whole. Leontes, Polixenes, Perdita, and Paulina are almost wholly reacting to the statue; they are not really acting. The audience analogously is reacting to the scene as a whole. The responses of the stage audience to every step of the unveiling infect the responses of the larger audience, so that we feel ourselves both in and outside the play world simultaneously." ORNSTEIN (1967, p. 46): "Although great creating Nature may reincarnate some of the rareness of Hermione in Perdita, the true miracle of *The Winter's Tale* is Paulina's art, which preserves and enriches the wonder of Hermione herself."

PARROTT (1949, p. 381): "The unveiling of the statue was evidently planned for the indoor theatre [i.e., Blackfriars] where the possibility of brilliant lighting on the inner stage of a darkened house would make the discovery most effective." NICOLL (1958, p. 54) responds: "There was no brilliant lighting in the early theatres: the sole means of illumination was by candle-light." Comparing this scene with *Per.* 5.1.222-9 (Q2196-2202), COWLING (1913, pp. 72-3): "The idea underlying both scenes is the power of music to restore the dead to life." He is overwhelmed by neither. "According to modern notions, both scenes are weak; and one wonders what the author's motive really was. Did the music betoken a miraculous event, or was it used simply to enhance the emotion of the scene?'' There is no reason, of course, why both could not obtain. SCHOLES (1916, pp. 3-6): Since the stage could not be darkened and limelight did not exist "to carry with him [Sh.] his audience in scenes of the 'supernatural' he made use not of varied lights and shades of colour, but of tones. . . . Here something more than a word of command to the statue was needed. Such a word would have given the whole affair the flavour of a conjuring trick. Probably the music should continue for a little time, growing gradually louder, the 'statue' seeming to come little by little to life, until . . . no statue but a living woman steps down to embrace her husband.'' HIRST (1984, p. 70) also seems to respond to COWLING: "Music, by heightening the excitement and pathos of the action, helped the audience to suspend their disbelief and be drawn into the world of romance. Shakespeare employed music . . . nowhere more effectively than in the moments of reawakening and rebirth" in *Per.*, *WT*, and *Tmp.* SHIRLEY (1963, p. 18): Because viols "aided in reviving Thaisa after the shipwreck" (*Per.* 3.2.90), they "probably were employed for . . . Hermione's statue scene." Recent eds. of *Per.*, however, do not read "viol" at the crucial place but "vial," the small medicine bottle. STYAN (1975, p. 53), dubiously: "The mock-magic of Paulina's comedy priestess is delightfully enhanced by the music which punctuates the clipped phrases with which she awakens the 'dead' Hermione. The more awesome the sound, the better the jest, since the audience guesses more than Leontes that the statue lives by a pre-arranged miracle to test his repentance, and so assumes Paulina's careful mysticism to enjoy the role of magician itself.'' INGRAM (1966, p. 245): "The music is not only the quintessence of the general musical atmosphere of the second part of the play, but it is natural to the particular mood of Leontes. . . . It is music . . . for the reuniting of the lovers. . . . The emotional control exercised by the music is vital to the effect of this moving and dangerous scene.''

3306 **Musick . . . Strike**] Like COLLIER, LETTSOM (MS 1840-65) wants to omit punctuation after "Musick" so that the meaning is "Let Music &c."

Strike] SCHMIDT (1875): Strike up, sound.

3308 **all . . . vpon**] RANN (ed. 1787): All that "look on you" (ABBOTT §192). Cf. n. 2291. HERFORD (ed. 1904), however: "Look on," merely.

meruaile] MINSHEU (1617, Maruaile): "Wonder.''

3309 **Ile . . . vp**] *OED* (Fill up, s.v. Fill, *v.* 17h, citing this line): "To do away with (a hole) by filling." BETHELL (ed. 1956): "Presumably Paulina means that, by summoning Hermione to move, she is making it impossible for her to return to the 'grave' of her retirement." Or, more simply, "I cancel your death." PAFFORD (ed. 1963): "Paulina emphasizes that Hermione has returned as from the grave to actual life. When it comes to be learnt . . . that Hermione never has died then the very thought of Hermione's 'grave' will be obliterated from men's minds.'' PYLE (1969, p. 122), improbably: "It seems not unlikely that the words have been preserved from a stage in the writing in which Hermione stood as a statue on her own tomb." BOORMAN (ed. 1964) thinks she means merely "I'll draw the curtains behind you." At the other extreme, DAVIES (1986, p. 141): "The blending of Hermetic and Eleusinian material in the person of Paulina issues in the unprecedented concept of the magus as a woman, calling out the life from her likeness, as naturally and as 'lawfully' as in giving physical birth.''

Bequeath to Death your numnesse: (for from him,   3310
Deare Life redeemes you) you perceiue she stirres:
Start not: her Actions shall be holy, as
You heare my Spell is lawfull: doe not shun her,
Vntill you see her dye againe; for then
You kill her double: Nay, present your Hand: 3315
When she was young, you woo'd her: now, in age,
Is she become the Suitor?
    Leo. Oh, she's warme:
If this be Magick, let it be an Art
Lawfull as Eating.   3320   (2

3311 redeemes] redeem HARN
3317 Suitor?] ~ . ROWE3-DEL2 (−CAP, KNT1, COL1, COL2), KTLY-BUL (−COL4, IRV)
3320-1 *One verse line* MTBY2 *conj.*, v1793+ (−OXF2, BEV4)

3310-11 **Bequeath . . . you)**] *OED* (Bequeath, *v.* 4a, citing this line): "Hand over . . . assign." RUSHTON (1869, pp. 14-23) examines *bequeath* in connection with the suggestion that Sh. may have drawn his own will. BETHELL (ed. 1956), in quite a different vein, finds an allusion to baptism; FARRELL (1989, p. 54) sees the Virgin's exaltation evoked and the New Testament's promise of eternal life echoed.

3310 **numnesse**] JOHNSON (1755, Numb): "Torpid; . . . chill; motionless."

3311 **Deare . . . you)**] THIRLBY alone (MS 1725-33?) wonders, "Does she mean Perdita's being alive?"

she stirres] For the possibility that the dead Hermione has again been possessed by her spirit, see n. 2794. HAPPÉ (1969): "Until Hermione does move, the audience does not know that she is alive." STYAN (1967, p. 135): "Nature and art unite in the human sphere. This coming to life is prolonged with intensity for almost five minutes . . . , a slow miracle exactly traced by the author for a mood of ritual and magic. Especially remarkable is the way in which Paulina hints at life in the statue little by little before the consummation, so that if the audience does not believe in the cold stone, she at least compels it to share Leontes' experience with him." GRIVELET (1980, p. 183) suggests that when the statue moves, it is Leontes who comes to life. BARKAN (1986, pp. 286-7): "In the midst of the confusions between mimesis and metamorphosis life turns to art and art turns to life. . . . What is true for plant husbandry is also true for the statue/Hermione: 'The art itself is nature [1908].'" SIMROCK (1831; 1850, p. 103): "The preservation of [Hermione] reminds us of the preservation and subsequent discovery of Lucina, in 'Apollonius of Tyre', which Shakespeare had previously made use of [in *Per.*]."

3312 **her . . . holy**] KITTREDGE & RIBNER (ed. 1967): A reminder "that Paulina is not using black magic; Hermione is not to be regarded as a ghost or demonic spirit."

3313 **my . . . lawfull**] SIEMON (1974, p. 16 n.): Paulina "denies that she is assisted by 'wicked powers' [3293-5]. . . . Paulina seems to distinguish between two kinds of magic, not between the real thing and a parlor-game imitation of it." BLISSETT (1971, p. 55) remembers that "the possessed Leontes" called Paulina "A mankinde Witch" (982).

3314 **for then**] BETHELL (ed. 1956): "If you do (shun her before she die)." He evidently means "if you ever shun her." SCHANZER (ed. 1969): "If you shun her now."

3315 **double**] SCHMIDT (1874): "To twice the degree." DEIGHTON (ed. 1889), more probably: "A second time." PAFFORD (ed. 1963): "Even at this stage Paulina reminds Leontes of his crime." ABRAMS (1986, p. 160), in an ingenious spiritualist interpretation, offers a "dark other meaning." She may be a doppelgänger. "Is this Hermione's double . . . not Hermione herself, whom Leontes will now install in his heart of hearts?"

present your Hand] BELLETTE (1978, p. 74): "The counterpart of Hermione's earlier gesture to Polixenes" (at 180 approximately). NEELY (1985, p. 207): "Leontes' acceptance of her new autonomy, his abandonment of possessiveness, is embodied in his presentation of his hand." As YOUNG (1992, p. 184) notes, she "apparently has offered her hand before he gives his." VISWANATHAN (1987, p. 50), who examines hand giving and hand taking throughout the play (32, 174, 188 and 201, 564, perhaps 766, 1863 [in the dance], 1956 and 1988-9 [dancing again], 2164 ["the antimasque of the dance"], 2185 and 2213 [handfasting], 2415 [hand kissing], 3148-9, 3164, 3238 [almost], 3293 [in anticipation] and 3315, and 3358), finds this "a second handfasting, echoing the echo in [174] . . . ; the handfasting now makes the reunion a true re-marriage." LEIMBERG (1987, pp. 131-3): "When the final taking of hands is effected, the spectator thinks of the giving of hands, remembered as well as performed in [172-201] when all the mischief began. . . . [The gesture] is part of the magic, . . . no longer black but white. The visual arts, poetry and music are at its command, and it is healing and life-giving."

3317 **Is . . . Suitor?**] *?* could indicate either a question or an exclamation, although no ed. has introduced the latter mark. DYCE (1844, p. 85), however: "Assuredly no question is asked. Paulina means, 'you formerly wooed her, and now she wooes you'. The original compositor put an interrogation-point, because 'Is she' sounded like a question." ROLFE (ed. 1879) prefers F: "Paulina says in substance: Do not be afraid of her, but give her your hand; you wooed her once, is she become the suitor now? This does not imply that Hermione makes no advances, but rather indicates surprise that he who once wooed her should now 'shun' her when she approaches him and let her do *all* the wooing." BETHELL (ed. 1956) agrees: "Paulina [is] urging Leontes out of his amazed stupor and conscience-stricken shyness." FARRELL (1983, p. 77): "Restored to life, Hermione possesses a new spiritual power sufficient to awe her once-dominating husband and king," but Leontes seems more likely to be stunned by his own surprise.

3318 **Oh, she's warme**] MATCHETT (1969, p. 105): "It is Hermione who comes to Leontes. He has only one brief exclamation when they touch . . . and Hermione says not one word. . . . Her forgiveness is clear in her coming to Leontes and their reunion is clear in their embrace." SIEMON (1974, p. 11): "Hermione's reaction as she grasps the implication of his [Leontes's] jealous rage—stunned disbelief yielding to wonder—is precisely Leontes' when she steps down from her pedestal. These are things to be wondered at." One could as easily argue that the reactions are precisely different—Leontes's, a wondrous joy; Hermione's, an "honorable Griefe . . . which burnes Worse then Teares drowne" (718-19). SIMPSON (1955, p. 37) believes that this line is indebted to a detail in Ovid's account of Pygmalion: *Incumbensque toro dedit oscula: visa tepere est*—"And bending over the couch he kissed her. She seemed warm to his touch" (*Met.* 10.281, trans. Miller). The resemblance seems slight. CAPELL (1783, 3:423) finds "Stay, she is warme" in Beaumont, Fletcher, and Massinger, *Thierry and Theodoret* 5.2.168.

3319-20 **If . . . Eating**] See n. 3295. KNIGHT (1947; 1965, p. 125): "Hermione's restoration not only has nothing to do with black magic; it is not even transcendental. It exists in warm human actuality . . . : hence our earlier emphases on warmth [see nn. 3226-64, 3318] and breath [lines 3261, 3280]; and now on 'eating' too." BYLES (1979, p. 91), by contrast: "For Leontes, the statue of Hermione is an erotic object that he would like to devour." CAVELL (1987, p. 216): "Leontes' words suggest that

Pol. She embraces him.

Cam. She hangs about his necke,
If she pertaine to life, let her speake too.

Pol. I, and make it manifest where she ha's liu'd,
Or how stolne from the dead?   3325

Paul. That she is liuing,
Were it but told you, should be hooted at
Like an old Tale: but it appeares she liues,

3324 it] *Om.* HAN
     where] that OXF1

---

there is an unlawful as well as a lawful eating. . . . *Coriolanus* . . . was in part
built from the idea there is an unlawful, or prelawful, eating, a cannibalism." FARRELL
(1989, p. 175) also finds sublimated cannibalistic impulses, Leontes being "passionately starved," but Michael TAYLOR (1982, p. 241) observes "something of the mysterious authority of the conjunction between art and nature that the play dramatizes."
NEVO (1987, p. 128) discovers "primal oral fantasies . . . in the tragic phase" of the
play (e.g., the spidery cup, the bear, the devouring sea). "Now at last . . . is hunger
legitimized."

3321-3 **She . . . too**] The CLARKES (1879, p. 616): Hermione "is exactly the
woman to give no other than mute token of reconciliation when she throws herself
into her husband's arms, and forgives him the injustice he once did her. Her reticence
is thus marked, by the comment of others." BROWN (*Performance*, 1967, p. 43):
"Silence is often used by Shakespeare to accentuate a reaction that can only be expressed physically. . . . Joy [may be] expressed by an inarticulate response, identified in the comments of bystanders." EWBANK ("Poetry," 1971, p. 104): "He shows
his awareness . . . of realities which language cannot get at." STYAN (1975, pp. 208-
9): The tableau "summarizes the action and allows time to the audience to evaluate
its impact at a crucial point; meanwhile speech focuses exclusively on what the eye
has gathered generally." SANDERS (1987, pp. 116-17) compares the silence between
Penelope and the returned Odysseus: "I cannot find a word to say to him; I cannot
ask him anything at all; I cannot even look him in the face" [*Od.* 23.105-7]. Another
embrace was long ago falsely imagined by Leontes; see 404-5 and n. RICHMOND
(1977-8, p. 341): "There is no forgiveness because there was never animosity on
Hermione's part."

    Several critics have questioned the propriety of the reconciliation. H. COLERIDGE
(1851, 2:149): "Is it possible that one who had once fallen thus [as Leontes has done]
could ever again be worthy of a restoration to happiness?" SCHELLING (1908, 2:201-
2) concurs: "Nowhere in Shakespeare are the ethical sensibilities of the modern
reader so disturbed as in the forgiveness and reconciliation to his steadfast and incomparable queen of unreasoning and headstrong Leontes, jealous-mad with the foul
images of his own making. In the just code of the land of romance happiness and
tender mercy are not for such as Leontes; but in this imperfect world of ours we
know that such precious forgiveness as that of Hermione and Imogen [in *Cym.*] often
waits on the unworthy, and that remorse and atonement may be not less heroic than
death." Surely remorse and atonement, as well as Hermione's unshaken love for her
husband, no longer possessed by the foul images, have justified forgiveness. MAT-
THEWS (1913, p. 338), however, believes that Hermione's forgiving Leontes "without

one word of reproach" is "frankly unfeminine," and SQUIRE (1935, p. 85) says that "the end of *The Winter's Tale* is forced and flat. Hermione has to be brought round. From a woman full of character and eloquence she becomes a docile stick, simply for Shakespeare's convenience." WEXLER (1988, p. 116), deconstructively: "Since these two observations [at 3321 and 3322-3] are the only textual evidence that Hermione forgives Leontes, the scene could also be performed to keep forgiveness in question. The embrace . . . could be limited to a perfunctory, wifely response to Leontes' tardy and reluctant kiss. Then she would turn from him to her daughter." GARNER (1989, p. 147): "Behind the . . . forgiveness . . . is the working out of a male fantasy . . . that a woman will always forgive a man no matter how terribly he wrongs her. Shakespeare's solution is always a variation on the story of patient Griselda. When that resolution strains credulity, many read it as illustrating Christian forgiveness, an example to which we might all aspire."

More traditional is HERFORD (ed. 1916-, p. xxii): "The solution [here] superficially resembles that in *Much Ado*, where Hero . . . is restored to Claudio in the person, as he supposes, of her cousin. . . . We forget it [the restoration] a moment later. . . . In the early and middle comedies the reunion of kin, or of husband and wife, where it occurs at all, has rarely any emotional significance. . . . It is only in the latest group of comedies that these meetings of separated kin or estranged companions are drawn with pathos; and here the pathos is sometimes, as in the meeting of Posthumus and Imogen [in *Cym*.], and in the present scene, of an overpowering intensity." FARRELL (1989, p. 21): "The resurrected Hermione is so idealized that her autonomy can be consummated in a mute identification with authority as she embraces the king . . ., while her potentially threatening aspect — her uncompromising individuality — is displaced onto the outspoken Paulina." But the embrace must signify that she is no longer autonomous, and the outspoken Paulina no longer has cause to be so. KAHN (1980, p. 240): "At the cost of great suffering, Leontes wins the fullest acceptance of woman, and *The Winter's Tale* presents the richest vision of male identity defined within the family."

3323 **pertaine to life**] *OED* (Pertain, *v*. 1, citing this line): "Belong." KITTREDGE & RIBNER (ed. 1967): "Belongs among the living, is truly alive."

3324 **make it manifest**] KITTREDGE & RIBNER (ed. 1967): "Explain."

3328 **Like . . . Tale**] HERFORD (ed. 1916-): Cf. 615-18, 1593, 3038, and 3070. See also nn. 0 and 181-92. KNIGHT (1947; 1965, p. 125): "The poet carefully refuses to elucidate the mystery on the plane of plot-realism. . . . Paulina merely observes that she [Hermione] *is* living [3326]." BETHELL (ed. 1956): "Shakespeare allows that the tale is thin, and yet coolly closes the scene without answering the questions which begin to trouble the characters and no doubt occur to the audience. Paulina in her forthright way points out [3341-3] that such explanations are inappropriate to the occasion. . . . Factual completeness would merely distract . . . from symbolic significance." BROOKS (in PAFFORD, ed. 1963) is metadramatic: "On one level this contributes to the sense of actuality: 'this is like an old tale, therefore it is not one'; but on a deeper level to the sense of various planes of reality . . . by a comment that reminds us that the action is itself enacted story." He compares *Ant*. 5.2.218-21 (3461-4), *TN* 3.4.127-8 (1648-9), *1H4* 2.4.395-6 (1354-5), and *Cym*. 5.5.228 (3511). See n. 3066-7 for another admission of *WT*'s incredibility. GOLDMAN (1972, p. 134): "We remember . . . that Mamillius began a tale and left it unfinished before he disappeared from the story to die. . . . His was a winter's tale, a sad tale [and] by an act of art the winter's tale has become a summer's tale. We are likely, however, to think of Mamillius at the play's end, and we certainly think of Antigonus when a new husband is found for Paulina." Mamillius and especially Antigonus are history, however, for most playgoers probably submerged in present wonder.

appeares] SCHMIDT (1874): Is evident.

Though yet she speake not. Marke a little while:
Please you to interpose (faire Madam) kneele,   3330
And pray your Mothers blessing: turne good Lady,
Our *Perdita* is found.
 Her. You Gods looke downe,
And from your sacred Viols poure your graces
Vpon my daughters head: Tell me (mine owne)   3335
Where hast thou bin preseru'd? Where liu'd? How found
Thy Fathers Court? For thou shalt heare that I
Knowing by *Paulina*, that the Oracle

3329 **Though . . . not**] Lyons (1962, p. 269): "it is almost as though Shakespeare explicitly emphasizes Hermione's silence [at 3323 and here] in order that he may commit this climactic moment to a stage image, to a moving tableau."

3330 **interpose**] Schmidt (1874): "Step in between" (*OED, v.* 4b, citing this line). Happé (1969): "Come forward, and cause Hermione to speak."

 Madam] Deighton (ed. 1889), incorrectly: "Generally and more properly used of a married woman." As Minsheu (1617) says, it is "a title giuen to a Ladie," to which *OED* (*sb.* 1) adds "of high rank." Bevington (ed. 1992): "Addressed to Perdita as Princess and affianced to be married."

3331 **your Mothers**] Herford (ed. 1916-, p. xxi): The restoration of mother to daughter and vice versa is rare in Sh., for "almost all his heroines, for excellent dramatic reasons, are without a living mother." Juliet is an exception. In *Ado* Q1, Leonato, Hero's father, enters at 1.1.0.1 with "*Innogen his wife*," but she is never again heard of.

3331-2 **turne . . . found**] Pyle (1969, p. 119): "Hermione's attention has to be drawn to Perdita . . . so wholehearted has been her spontaneous welcome for Leontes."

3332 **Our . . . found**] Harrison (ed. 1947): "This is the high moment of the last scene. It is notable that the three characters which stand out are all women." Meldrum (1968, p. 57) finds them symbols of Faith, Hope, and Charity, "parts of a greater whole — sanctifying grace." Frye (*Perspective*, 1965, p. 112): "Hermione . . . begins to speak as soon as Paulina pronounces [these] magic words . . . and thus announces the fulfilling of Apollo's oracle." Styan (1967, p. 136): "In one silent gesture must be felt the happiness of bringing to an end the torment of waiting and hoping. Spectacle, characterization and theme are fused in these last moments." Happé (1969): "This succinct line, with the contrast in meaning between *Perdita* (she who was lost) and *found* marks the fulfillment of the Oracle." Wilson (1984, p. 352), locating, a parallel scene: "Euripides' Alcestis upon her return from death never speaks a word to Admetus," her husband.

3333-40 **You . . . yssue**] Granville-Barker (1912; 1974, p. 22) admires the "perfect sufficiency of Hermione's eight lines (oh, how a lesser dramatist might have overdone it with Noble Forgiveness and what not!)." Cutts (1968, p. 82): "There is no doubt that Hermione preserved herself, not so much for Leontes, but because the oracle gave hope that Perdita was alive." Hardman (1985, pp. 234-5): "Whether or not Leontes deserves an alleviation of suffering, no direct connection is made between his condition and what happens." Traub (1988, p. 230) finds no very happy ending: Hermione's "silence toward Leontes bespeaks a submissiveness most unlike her previous animation. Rather than being a victory for the wronged heroine, the final scene works as wish fulfillment for Leontes, who not only regains his virtuous wife and loses his burden of guilt, but also reassumes his kingly command of all social relations, represented by his deft matchmaking and integration of . . . Paulina and Camillo. . . . The conflicts ostensibly resolved by the 'new marriage' still lurk in the background." HAPPÉ (1969), earlier, had found no submissiveness: "The restrained tone of this her only speech [in the scene] contributes much to the credibility of this moment."

3333-5 **You . . . head**] BETHELL (ed. 1956): "In her first words Hermione prays for 'graces'. . . . See [n. 177]." ORGEL (ed. 1996) compares "Gonzalo's invocation of grace upon Ferdinand and Miranda," in *Tmp.* 5.1.201-2 (2182-3). According to FOWLER (1978, p. 52), these lines show that "the softened Hermione is weeping."

3334-5 **from . . . head**] CHEDWORTH (1805, p. 128): "Pouring a phial of oil on the head of a person anointed king." EATON (1860, p. 172) thinks of Rev. 5:8, in which the four and twenty elders are equipped with "golden viales full of odours, w^c are the prayers of the Saintes." FRIPP (1938, 2:741), improbably: "Shakespeare's audience would recognize the allusion." HALLIWELL (ed. 1859) thinks the allusion is also to Isa. 45:8: "Ye heauens, send the dewe from aboue & let ye cloudes drop downe." HEILBRUN (1973, pp. 32-3) misquotes Hermione in trying to show that "the recognition of the daughter as a true inheritor . . . is part of the androgynous vision." RYLANDS (1928, p. 221) notices that the passage is paralleled in *Tmp.* 5.1.201-2 (2182-3): "looke downe you gods And on this couple drop a blessed crowne" and is similar to *Cym.* 5.5.350-1 (3662-3): "The benediction of these couering Heauens Fall on their heads like dew." According to *OED* (*sb.* b), the allusion is that identified by MALONE (1780, 1:146-7), the pouring out, in Rev. 16:1, of the seven golden vials of the wrath of God mentioned in Rev. 15:7, the contents now being graces. MARSH (1962; 1980, p. 160): "Perdita receives a formal blessing because she is the incarnation of new life." YOUNG (1992, pp. 186-7) invokes parental blessings found in Peter Erondell, *The French Garden* (1605), but the similarity is faint. He seems right, however, that the scene gains power from the "common experience for many of the play's first viewers" of formal parental blessings and from Leontes's violent refusal to bless the infant Perdita (980-3).

3334 **graces**] See n. 730.

3337 **Thy Fathers Court?**] BROOKE (1905; 1913, p. 283): "In [this phrase] is contained the pardon of Leontes."

3337-40 **For . . . yssue**] ADAMS (1989, pp. 103-4): "The wonderful here melts into the inexplicable; the story does not end, it dissolves. Hermione has lived as in a tomb for sixteen years, during which her passionately repentant husband has daily visited her grave, yearning to have her back; yet she has remained silent, unmoved. Why? Better not ask. It's a mystery, veiled and irrational as a dream, and as little to be questioned." Raising her own questions in 3335-7, Hermione here anticipates Perdita's and ours. She remained silent so that which was lost could be found, not only Perdita but Leontes as well, whose regeneration is a major part of the triumph of time. See the n. following.

3338-40 **Knowing . . . yssue**] THIRLBY (MS 1733-47?): "She [Hermione] was in court when the oracle was read & heard it [1313 ff.]." Sh. forgot this. PYLE (1969, p. 128), replying to COLERIDGE's criticism of the oracle (see n. 1313-16): "Only Paulina saw its implication until she explained it to Hermione. . . . Paulina understood . . . *if that which is lost be not found* to mean . . . *Till his lost child be found.* That is to say, she saw in the condition 'if that which is lost be not found' a statement of the possibility of its own fulfilment." RIEMER (1980, p. 141): "Her plans and designs could not have reached fruition had she not faith . . . in an impersonal pattern of benevolence manifesting itself in the apparently purposeless and random events of the play. She put her trust, that is, in a natural providence." PARRY (ed. 1982): Sh. "is suggesting that Paulina made a further private consultation—in which the oracle gave a more definite hint ('hope') of Perdita's survival," a baseless idea.

3338 **Knowing**] Contracted by WALKER (1854, p. 120) to one syllable.

Gaue hope thou wast in being, haue preseru'd
My selfe, to see the yssue.   3340
    Paul. There's time enough for that,
Least they desire (vpon this push) to trouble
Your ioyes, with like Relation. Go together
You precious winners all: your exultation
Partake to euery one: I (an old Turtle)   3345 (2
Will wing me to some wither'd bough, and there
My Mate (that's neuer to be found againe)
Lament, till I am lost.
    Leo. O peace *Paulina*:

3339-41 *Verse lines ending* myself, . . . *that*; v1793, v1803; *ending* preserv'd
. . . *that*; mCAP2, v1813+ (−BEV)
3342 Least] Lest F3-PEN2, OXF2

3339 **in being**] KERMODE (ed. 1963): "Alive."
3340 **yssue**] WRIGHT & LaMAR (ed. 1966): "Outcome." CAVELL (1987, p. 218) amplifies: "The issue of the oracle." PARRY (ed. 1982): Also "my child." MARSH (1962; 1980, p. 160): "Hermione does not speak again, for if she were to turn to any practical discussion, the religious mood of her restoration would be shattered."
3341-3 **There's . . . Relation**] RANN (ed. 1787): "Desist from these enquiries now, lest the company should wish to interrupt you, at this juncture ['push'; see n. 3342], with their curiosity." DELIUS (ed. 1860), similarly: Were Perdita to give a full report, all the others would wish to make and answer similar inquiries. EVANS (ed. 1974): "The last thing they want, at this critical moment [push], is to trouble your happiness with such an account." BEVINGTON (ed. 1980), who prints *least* in preference to *lest*, the usual modernization: "The last thing they desire at this dramatic moment is to interrupt your joys with a narrative of that sort." His ed. 1992, however, prints *lest*. PARRY (ed. 1982): "Paulina emphasises that . . . of prime importance now is feeling joy . . . , not the seeking of explanations." Her consideration obviates explanation of how Hermione has spent the last sixteen years, and it also prevents Perdita's reply to Hermione's questions. Regarding the former, MARSH (1962; 1980, p. 159): "In the solemnity of this moment . . . no member of the audience can possibly be concerned with the practical consideration of how Paulina could have kept the living Hermione hidden for so long." Regarding the latter, REESE (1953; 1980, p. 180) tentatively suggests that if the same boy played Hermione and Perdita, a silent substitute for Perdita would have been provided here, which was done in the productions of Anderson and of Allen (see p. 804).

3342 **push**] JOHNSON (1755, citing this line): "A sudden emergence [unforeseen occasion]." SCHMIDT (1875), after DELIUS (ed. 1860): "An impulse given, a setting in motion." HARRISON (ed. 1947), improbably: "Moment of excitement."

3343 **with like Relation**] CALDECOTT (MS 1813-33, Like): "Such like," presumably their own stories. CHARLTON (ed. 1916): "*I.e.* with your (Hermione's) tale."

3344-8 **You . . . lost**] JOHNSON (ed. 1765): "You who by this discovery have *gained* what you desired may join in festivity, in which I, who have lost what can never be recovered, can have no part." For *precious winners*, HERFORD (ed. 1904), following the CLARKES (1879, p. 316): "Winners of what you prize." For *lost*, LEE (ed. 1907) has "given up (to death)." DRAPER (1985, p. 44): "Paulina is snatched from her sentimental—and decidedly out-of-character—intention of withdrawing from society, and paired off . . . with Camillo."

3345 **Partake**] CAPELL (1783, 2.4:183): "Participate [i.e., impart]" or, as VALPY (ed. 1833) has it, "communicate" (*OED*, Partake 2, citing this line). The CLARKES (1879, p. 574): "Mutually share." They consider (p. 806) the verb to be intransitive, although *OED* gives many examples of its transitive use.

to euery one] RANN (ed. 1787): "Among you."

3345-8 **I . . . lost**] THIRLBY (MS 1733-47?) cites RAY (1674, p. 203): "As true as a Turtle to her mate" (TILLEY T624). MALONE (in STEEVENS, ed. 1778) finds another turtle on a leafless tree in Lodge's *Rosalynde*, the source of *AYL* (ed. Knowles, 1977, p. 448); ANDERS (1904, p. 107) believes that image is echoed here. Cf. n. 1972. PAFFORD (ed. 1963) compares Thaisa's lament, *Per.* 3.4.8-11 (1360-3), and see 1972. BATTENHOUSE (1980, p. 137): "The dove of the Song of Solomon"; the avian progression accords with the alteration of the woman who was once Dame Partlet (992). SCHMIDT (ed. 1870, p. 285) finds the turtledove as a symbol of widowhood in the pre-14th-c. *Gesta Romanorum*.

3346 **wing me**] KITTREDGE & RIBNER (ed. 1967): "The ethical dative." Or perhaps a reflexive. *OED* cites this instance as its first in the sense "take flight, fly."

3347-8 **My . . . lost**] HARDINGE (1818, 3:48): "A *turn* upon *lost* and *found*: that *I* may lament the mate *I* have *lost*, and cannot *find* again till *I* am *lost*, and *for ever.*"

3347 **My Mate**] HARDINGE (1818, 3:47): "You recollect that *Antigonus*, the mouthful of the bear, was her husband." FURNESS (ed. 1898): "It is well that the martyr, Antigonus, should be remembered,—but where is the little Mamillius? Possibly the omission was intentional. Any allusion to him might have proved too much for Hermione's self-control."

3348 **lost**] ONIONS (1986): "Brought to destruction or death."

3349-69 **O . . . away**] HAPPÉ (1969) remarks upon "the calm and dignified style of Leontes' speech, contrasting with the disjointed and distorted movement of his speeches in [1.2]." TAYLOR (1972, p. 55), similarly: "The play's closing lines . . . are a model of ease and simplicity, a generation separating them from the tortured syntax of Leontes' jealousy. . . . Such a transformation measures in rhetorical terms the difference between radically different ways of apprehending reality; speaking in innocence and then from knowledge is like speaking . . . 'from the ends of opposed winds' [33]."

3349 **O peace *Paulina***] SUMMERS (1984, p. 43): "A sentiment . . . long delayed . . . and much desired."

Thou shouldst a husband take by my consent,   3350
As I by thine a Wife. This is a Match,
And made betweene's by Vowes. Thou hast found mine,
But how, is to be question'd: for I saw her
(As I thought) dead: and haue (in vaine) said many
A prayer vpon her graue. Ile not seeke farre   3355
(For him, I partly know his minde) to finde thee
An honourable husband. Come *Camillo*,

3350-1 **Thou . . . Wife**] Critics explain this unexpected pairing with some difficulty. JAIN (1948, p. 34): "We cannot be sure whether she really marries again. These
words are . . . just to console her." LENNOX (1753, 2:75), however: "The good old
Paulina is rewarded with another husband, in the Room of her lost *Antigonus*."
More romantically, MOULTON (1903, p. 75): "If Paulina is still left in lonely sorrow
for her mate irremediably lost, a comforter is at hand in Camillo; the autumn idyl that
unites these two—the main contrivers of the disentanglement—is the final note in
the restoration, and the oracle of lost and found stands complete." NELSON (1972, p.
62) discovers "continued fecundity" rather than an autumn idyll. THALER (1927, p.
758): "With the re-establishment of the Queen, Paulina's occupation's gone, and Camillo has long been homesick, which—being interpreted by Leontes [at 3356; see n.]—
means that he is not disinclined to the match." PYLE (1969, p. 129): "A piece of pure
comedy routine. The old stagers are silently happy to be paired off by order and
without warning." SCOTT (1920, p. 155): "Possibly to rid himself finally of her reproaches, Leontes insists that she should marry Camillo—a somewhat ambiguous
reward for his fidelity." HARTWIG (1972, p. 134): "The final note of reconciliation is
appropriately the resumption of Leontes' control over his most unruly subject, Paulina." CARRINGTON (1956, p. 12) finds it an artistic mistake: "The marriage . . . is
superfluous. The only marriage in which we are interested is that of Florizel and
Perdita." MATCHETT (1969, p. 106): "A coldly symbolic arrangement." PITT (1981,
p. 132): "Too abrupt and mechanical." WELLS ("Happy Endings," 1966, pp. 121-3):
"There are mitigating circumstances. We know that Camillo is truly worthy; Leontes
seems at least to have made enquiries of Camillo [3356]; but . . . the lady's acquiescence is taken for granted. Perhaps it was enough that her husband came with the
recommendation of two kings. . . . Perhaps it is unreasonable to expect psychological realism at the ends of his [Sh.'s] comedies. . . . The play cocks a snook at itself,
assisting the audience's return to the world of actuality." NEELY (1978, p. 182): "A
startling reversal of the convention of old tales," the reward of the triumphant hero
with a bride. BOOTH (1979, p. 120), observing that the parts may be doubled: "The
pairing . . . would have seemed less arbitrary, less an act of mere authorial tidiness,
to an audience that saw one actor play Antigonus in Acts II and III and Camillo in the
other three acts." RABKIN (1981, p. 137): "The conventions of a miracle turned back
into mere comedy require that . . . she marry Camillo." TOLIVER (1989, p. 173):
"The play is finally not much interested in grief, either in Leontes' over Hermione or
Paulina's over Antigonus. Restored to a sense of proportion, feeling an obligation to
make his subjects happy, the magistrate shuts off the latter with" this matchmaking.
See further in n. 3355-7.

3350 Thou shouldst] DEIGHTON (ed. 1889): "You are bound to." SCHMIDT (1875) points out, however, that *should* may be "used of subjective as well as absolute obligation"—that is, as "ought to" rather than as "must."

3351 Match] SCHMIDT (1875): "Agreement." BOORMAN (ed. 1964): Also "a marriage match."

3352 made . . . Vowes] THIRLBY (MS 1725–33?): See 2810–11 and 2826. Either Leontes's memory is inaccurate (he swore "Neuer to marry, but by [Paulina's] free leaue" [2811], but she made no corresponding promise) or he means "since I put you in charge of my marriage, you should allow me to take charge of yours."

3353 is . . . question'd] DEIGHTON (ed. 1889): "Is what I must extract from you by question." KITTREDGE & RIBNER (ed. 1967, Questioned): "Further examined." SIDER (1973, p. 9): "We cannot frame the question till we find the Queen alive. . . . Leontes refers in passing to the mystery [here], but he is content to let it remain a mystery for the moment. And in a moment the play is over."

3353–5 for . . . graue] Cf. n. 1426–32 for Leontes's resolution to do these things.

3354 (As . . . dead] PORTER & CLARKE (ed. 1908): Hermione "was shown to the king as if dead, after the trial scene [3.2]." Not necessarily. After Hermione's collapse, Paulina specifically reports that she is dying (1332–3); Leontes's prediction of her recovery (1335) seems only wishful thinking.

3354–5 many A] ABBOTT (§85) suggests that the meaning of *many* here is "often," which justifies its separation from *A* by the line break. BLAKE (1983, p. 78) agrees on the meaning.

3355 A prayer] In F1 a space type prints between these words.

3355–7 Ile . . . husband] GERVINUS (1877, p. 814): The union of "Camillo, the medicine of both houses, preserver of both parents and children . . . with the other preserver, Paulina, has . . . a suitable sense, notwithstanding her age, which is unsuitable for marriage." If she were 30 in the early part of the play, she would now be a decrepit 46. See nn. 819 and 3379. Discussing the vindication of morality at the end of many Elizabethan plays, CREIZENACH (1909; 1916, p. 269): "In some case the rewarding of the noble characters appears to be rather overdone, . . . even . . . the betrothal of Paulina and Camillo." STOPES (1916, p. 38), however: "Leontes . . . finds a consoler and a husband for her in the good Camillo. Shakespeare thus completes his portrait of the only *Woman-friend* that Stage Kings had ever had, the sole example which even he gives of Platonic affection in a Court." Not all critics—e.g., GREEN (1890, p. 36)—are convinced that the marriage occurs, but SNIDER (c. 1890, p. 498) believes "we may suppose [Camillo] to be more congenial to her nature than Antigonus . . . ; the male and the female mediatorial characters, both royal and subordinate, belong together." BATTENHOUSE (1980, p. 137) too is heartened: "Her second marriage, to a diplomat of more faith and courage than Antigonus, holds promise of being more rewarding than her first."

3355 farre] PAFFORD (ed. 1963): "Perhaps the comparative [farther]. Cf. [2275]."

3356 For . . . minde] A justification perhaps not to be taken very seriously. PORTER & CLARKE (ed. 1908), however: "This gives room for a guess that Camillo had been long a faithful lover of Paulina, a youthful suitor perhaps, too worthy of her to succeed before, when Antigonus married her." THALER (1927, p. 758) thinks Leontes has inferred a desire for Paulina from Camillo's homesickness; see n. 3350–1.

For] PAFFORD (ed. 1963): "As for."

And take her by the hand: whose worth, and honesty
Is richly noted: and heere iustified
By Vs, a paire of Kings. Let's from this place.   3360
What? looke vpon my Brother: both your pardons,
That ere I put betweene your holy lookes
My ill suspition: This your Son-in-law,
And Sonne vnto the King, whom heauens directing
Is troth-plight to your daughter. Good *Paulina*,   3365
Leade vs from hence, where we may leysurely

3358 by the] *Om.* COL2, COL3
3359 Is] It v1821; Are HAL
3361 What? . . . Brother:] ∼ , . . . ∼ ? CAP; ∼ ? . . . ∼ ? v1773-v1785; ∼ !
. . . ∼ : SING, COL, HUD, DYCE, WH, STAU, CAM1, GLO, IRV-ARD1, KIT1, ALEX, PEL1-
PEN2; ∼ , . . . ∼ . OXF2
3363 suspition] suspicions SIS
          This] This' WALKER (1854, p. 81) *conj.*, DYCE2, DEL4, OXF1, CAM3, KIT1,
CLN2, PEN2+; This is mTBY2 *and* WALKER (1854, p. 81) *conj.*, KTLY, HUD2, WH2, IRV
3364 whom] from HAN; who mTBY2 *conj.*, CAP-RANN, GLO, KTLY, HUD2, WH2, IRV

3358 **whose**] THEOBALD (MS - 1729?): "Camillo's." HERFORD (ed. 1916-): "Probably Paulina's." Strictly speaking, THEOBALD is right, for Polixenes, one of the "paire
of Kings" (3360), could not attest to Paulina's character. But the words may be spoken
with some justifiable license, and ORGEL (ed. 1996) points out that the antecedent is
her.
          honesty] See n. 381.
3359 **richly noted**] HERFORD (ed. 1904): "Highly reputed." BETHELL (ed. 1956):
"Widely known." BOORMAN (ed. 1964): "Well-known to be precious." For other
instances of noting, see n. 298.
          iustified] JOHNSON (1755): "Maintain" (*OED* 5b: "Maintain as true"). SCHMIDT
(1874): "To ratify," but *OED*'s first citation for the word in this sense is dated 1682.
See n. 12 for another meaning. ROLFE (ed. 1879, citing 3072-4): "Avouched."
3360 **Let's from**] For omission of the verb after *let* followed by a preposition, see
FRANZ §621.
3361 **What? . . . Brother**] HARRISON (ed. 1947): "Everything has been happily
explained and reconciled except for Polixenes' reunion with Hermione." Yet at this
final juncture, what Leontes says is a little uncertain; since few comment, it is difficult
to know exactly what eds. want to imply by their alterations to the punctuation of
this line. In F1-4, the question mark after *What* could signify either a query or an
exclamation. From ROWE (ed. 1709) on, though, it implies an inquiry, perhaps "what
are you doing?" or "why do you ignore him?" STAUNTON (ed. 1859): "Remembering
how . . . her innocent freedoms with Polixenes had been misconstrued, . . . she

[Hermione] now turns from him . . . with feelings of mingled modesty and apprehension." WILSON (ed. 1931), regarding *What?*: "Uttered as he suddenly catches sight of Polixenes, and forgets [remembers] he has been leaving him out of it." RIDLEY (ed. 1935), however: "The point is surely much sharper and more ironic than that. . . . Hermione is rather consciously *not* looking at Polixenes. [See HUNTER below.] Leontes gives her, but in a very different spirit, as direct a command as his [83]." CAPELL's (ed. 1768) moving the question mark to follow *Brother* suggests that Hermione already looks at Polixenes (CAPELL's idea alone). The exclamation point, says HUNTER (ed. 1872), "refers to Hermione fearing to look upon Polixenes." It may suggest surprise or perhaps an admonition of the gentlest sort. Presumably the comma of WELLS & TAYLOR's Oxford ed. (1986) means about the same, but even less emphatically. PARRY (ed. 1982), completely differently: "Leontes notices that Polixenes is gazing in admiration at Hermione," and now the two can share admiration without arousing his suspicion. For *upon* as "on," see ABBOTT §192.

3361–3 **both . . . suspition**] HOLBROOK (1945, p. 178), no admirer of Leontes: "The slightness of his nature is shown by his almost perfunctory amends when all is said and done." BYLES (1979, p. 91), similarly: "His apology is quite superficial."

3362 **holy lookes**] SCHMIDT (1874, Holy): "Virtuous." Cf. n. 2931. BETHELL (ed. 1956): "Contrast the 'practis'd smiles' of [189]."

3363–5 **This . . . daughter**] The contract Florizel speaks of at 2221 and 2259 is the betrothal or troth plight. That it had virtually the force of marriage is indicated by Polixenes's speaking of it as a nuptial (2230) and by the rank name of the "Flax-Wench" who "puts to Before her troth-plight" (369–70), the implication being that her putting to afterward would be condoned. Here Florizel is Hermione's son-in-law, although the solemnization of the marriage is still to come. Ceremonies of betrothal are also referred to in *TN* 4.3.22–8 (2137–43) and 5.1.156–61 (2318–23) and *MM* 4.1.71–2 (1850–1).

3363–4 **This . . . directing**] LEE (ed. 1907): "A gesture might well supply *is* after *this*, and *whom heaven's directing* (*i.e.*, who under heaven's direction) is a grammatical solecism of a kind which is *familiar* in Shakespeare's work." With WALKER's (1854, p. 81) interpretation of *this* as a contraction, cf. nn. 2026 and 2857. MOORMAN (ed. 1912): "This is your son-in-law and the son of Polixenes; under the guidance of heaven he is pledged to marry your daughter." For the confused construction, see ABBOTT §410.

3364 **whom heauens directing**] MALONE (ed. 1790): "In the absolute case," signifying "*him* heavens directing." ROLFE (ed. 1879), who reads *This is*: "It seems awkward to make the leading sentence 'This your son-in-law is troth-plight to your daughter' — the assertion being already implied in the subject — and to make 'whom heavens directing' merely parenthetical. . . . 'Whom heavens directing' is a 'confusion of construction' [ABBOTT §410; see also §415] for 'Who, heavens directing him,'" as MALONE had said. HERFORD (ed. 1904) explains: "'Who', the subject of *is*, is made the object of 'heavens directing.'" In his ed. 1916–, he tries again: "'Whom', the subject of 'is troth-plight', [is] governed by 'directing' — 'who, by heavens' direction.'" As for the significance, BETHELL (ed. 1956): "This states a doctrine which governs the whole action of the play."

3366 **Leade . . . hence**] WAYNE (1985, p. 182): "It is a small gesture, but kings in Shakespeare's plays do not usually allow their subjects, especially their female subjects, to lead them on or off the stage."

Each one demand, and answere to his part
Perform'd in this wide gap of Time, since first
We were disseuer'd: Hastily lead away.   *Exeunt.* 3369
                                            FINIS.   3389

3369 We] *Om.* F3, F4

3367-8 **part Perform'd**] The culmination of the play's theatrical imagery (see nn. 269-71, 1210-11, 1764-5, 1948-9, 2467-9, 2533-5, and 3088-9), which BETHELL (ed. 1956) construes in religious terms: "The actors on the stage and the actors on the stage of life have a certain freedom of will to 'interpret' their parts, but there is a script they must adhere to." Both stage and world are "mere spectacle," reality being with God. UPHAUS (1970, p. 42) instead finds the theatrical imagery "another aspect of ceremony," a theme beginning with the royal attorneying of the kings' encounters at 29-31.

3368 **gap of Time**] PAFFORD (ed. 1963), comparing *Ant.* 1.5.5 (527) and *Cym.* 3.2.62-3 (1530-1): The expression's "use here reminds us of Time and his promise to present what we have now seen completed." See 1586. HOY (1964, p. 273): Although it "has 'dissever'd' husbands and wives, parents and children [the gap] is closed at last, and thanks are offered where they are due: to heaven."

3368-9 **first . . . away**] The CLARKES (1879, p. 676): *WT* "is the only one of Shakespeare's plays which does not afford an instance of the dialogue in a scene ending with a rhyming couplet."

3369 **disseuer'd**] SCHMIDT (1874, Dissever): "Separate." WATSON (1981, p. 13): "Leontes uses [this word] to describe the entire process of his separation from and reunion with his wife and friends—as if to underscore the central motif of spiritual growth through pruning." He catalogs the play's references to cutting (e.g., "cut my lace," 1359), but no other critics have found pruning to be a significant theme.

Hastily lead away] PALMER (1887, p. 271) finds other "directions to some or all of the actors as to the manner or object of their leaving the stage or their destination" in the final lines of *Ado* ("Strike up, pipers" 5.3.130-1 [2684]), as well as a dozen other Shn. plays. VAN DAM (1900, p. 50, Hastily): Pronounced *hast'-ly*, the idea, as well, of WALKER (1854, p. 189). For other syncopations of *i*, see nn. 162, 313, and 942. EDWARDS (*Progress*, 1986, p. 172): "Even during Shakespeare's great triumph in this statue-scene, he insists on hinting at explanations and narrations which would surely destroy everything if they were permitted—the absurdity, or the immorality, of Hermione's sixteen-year deception of her husband." Critics differ on this and other emanations of the past that modify the play's final effect. Some neither forget nor forgive. DAVIES (1986, pp. 156-8): "We recollect the death of Mamillius and Antigonus, perceive the ageing of Hermione, the broken life of Leontes, and know the characters move by the graveside. . . . [*WT*] remains a tale of winter, Mamillius's tale." KERNAN (1975, 3:454): "Hermione returns to life, but her face is aged and wrinkled; in her joy at the return of Perdita, Paulina remembers that her husband Antigonus dies in saving the child; Mamillius still lies in the grave, a delicate flower of early spring that died before it could 'behold Bright Phoebus in his strength' [1937-8]." DRAPER (1985, p. 367): Mamillius's "absence leaves the reunited family vaguely incomplete."

On the other hand, BARTON (1980, p. 149): "Leontes does not get back exactly what he threw away. Still, he gets back far more than men can realistically expect. *The Winter's Tale* admits something that Shakespeare's Elizabethan Comedies had

tried to deny: happy endings are a fiction. A fiction, but not quite a fairy-tale." ERICK-
SON (1982, p. 822): "Because Hermione lives, Leontes [sic] can eventually take the
place of the son who has been sacrificed for the father's sacrilege against maternity."
ERICKSON (1990, p. 187): The ending of *WT* "restores to Leontes his central position
as paternal authority. . . . [It] does not say 'no' to the fathers but concentrates on
reforming patriarchy and assimilating women with a boundless capacity to forgive
into the revised image of benign patriarchy." Hermione's boundless capacity is to be
assumed from her embrace; she does not speak to Leontes. That patriarchy is reformed may be inferred from the acceptance of the new order by Leontes and Polixenes, and that women are assimilated into it is suggested by the unexpected marriage
of Paulina to Camillo. MCMANUS (1988): "A new valuing of women [is] demonstrated
by the proposed marriage of Paulina and Camillo, advisors and friends whose importance to the security of the kingdom establishes them as equals." FRYE (1986, p. 170),
on Leontes's words: "There is no time to be lost, once one has found it again." HALL
(in BERRY, 1989, p. 212): "Why does he want to go hastily? Why does he, as the king,
ask others to lead? Also it's not a rhyming couplet. It is a suspended end." KNOWLES
(privately) on *hastily*: "Because he is eager to hear, in a place more conducive to
leisure, the stories that each will tell." Leontes does not ask others to lead; he asks
Paulina, in whose house he is a guest, to do so. And the lack of a final couplet may
suspend the end; among the comedies, *TGV, LLL, Ado*, and *Tmp*. are left similarly
hanging.

3370–88 For notes on these lines, see pp. 4 ff.

APPENDIX

Irregular, Doubtful, and Emended Accidentals in F1

For an explanation of the contents of this list, see page ix. In the notes, the lemma is the reading of this edition's text. For emendations, the lemma is followed by the siglum of the edition from which the emendation is drawn and then by the rejected F1 reading and the sigla of the 17th-c. editions reading differently from the lemma. If no source is given for the emendation, the reading adopted is to be found in none of the folios. Doubtful and irregular readings are merely listed. (|) indicates that the reading is found in a full line; (?) indicates dubiety or an alternative to the reading adopted, although not a correct one in the judgment of the editor. In notes pertaining to variants in punctuation, a swung dash (~) shows that a word in the lemma is replaced in substantially the same form, and an inferior caret (ᴧ) calls attention to a lack of punctuation.

```
 42  life,] F2; ~ . F1
100  o'th' Clock] o'th'Clock F1
107  seek] F1 (|); seeke elsewhere
     Stars] F1 (|); starres elsewhere
166  th'Goale] th' Goale F1 (?)
227  look] F1 (|); looke elsewhere except 1332 Look
423  Leo.] F2; ~ ᴧ F1
453  wil] F1 (|); will elsewhere
613  stirs] F1 (|); stirre(s) elsewhere except 3274 stir'd
628  Leon.] F1 (|); Leo. elsewhere
696  withᴧher] F2; ~ . ~ F1
724  Highnes] F1 (|); Highnesse elsewhere
800  haue] F2 (have); hane F1
845  gracious] F2; gtacious F1
854  you.] F3; ~ , F1, F2
870  Your] F2; your F1
874  presently] F2; presenrly F1
882  good.] F2; ~ , F1
```

902 o'th'cause] *second apostrophe indistinct in* F1
914 Mother.] F2; ⁓ .' F1
959 me.] ⁓ : F1–F4
988 honest.] F2; ⁓ : F1
1131 th'Court] th' Court F1 (?)
1160 successefull] F2; snccessefull F1
1204 then, but] F2; then,but F1 (?)
1284 i'th' open] i'th'open F1 (?)
1304 shal] F1 (|); shall *elsewhere*
1311 *Cleo.*] F2; ⁓ ∧ F1
1313 *chast*] F1 (|); chaste *elsewhere*
1331 strike] F2; r *inverted* F1
1332 Look] F1 (|); looke *elsewhere except* 227 look
1374 much,] ⁓ . F1–F4
1388 sweet'st,] F2; ⁓ . F1 (?)
1471 Thrower] F2; Thower F1
1502 sleep] F1 (|); sleepe *elsewhere*
1508–9 Mai- | ster] F1; master *elsewhere except* 2145 Mayster
1512 verie] F1 (|); very *elsewhere*
     prettie] F1 (|); pretty *elsewhere*
1548, 1559 olde] F1 (|); old *elsewhere*
1560 Golde] F1 (|); gold *elsewhere*
1577 on't.] F2; ⁓ ∧ F1
1592 th'freshest] F2; th'sreshest F1
1606 daughter] daugh- | (ter (*turnunder*) F1
1621 allay (or] F2; ⁓, ⁓ F1
1634 punnishes] F1 (|); punish('d) *elsewhere*
1638 son] F1 (|); sonne *elsewhere*
1656 cottage.] F2; ⁓ ∧ F1 (|)
1662 'Prethe] F1 (|); prethee *elsewhere*
1663 busines] F1 (|); businesse(s) *elsewhere*
1673 *bleaching*] F2; *bleachiug* F1
1690 *auouch*] F2; *auoueh* F1
1730 detestable] F2; derestable F1
1745 Doest] F1 (|); dost *elsewhere*
     mony . . . mony] F1 (|); money *elsewhere*
1749 anie] F1 (|); any *elsewhere*
1815 ground.] F2; ⁓ . F1 (?)
1841 purpose,] pur- | (pose, (*turnunder*) F1
1860 Fy] F1 (|); fie *elsewhere*
1926 fairst Friend,] fairst | (Friend, (*turnover*) F1
1947 flours] F1 (|); flowres *elsewhere*
1966 Shepherd] F2; Sphepherd F1
2017 customers] F2; cnstomers F1
2027 Beleeue] F2 (Beleeve); Beleeee F1
2061 then] F2; rhen F1
2067 bear] F1 (|); beare *elsewhere*
2072 promis'd] F2; ptomis'd F1
2076–7 ther- | fore] F1; therefore *elsewhere*
2078 here.] F2; ⁓ ∧ F1 (|)
2096 things] F2; rhings F1
2121 Mop.] F2; ⁓ ∧ F1
2125 *Let*] F2; *Le*▪ F1 (*foot of type prints*)

2126, 2132 Mop:] F2 (~ .); ~ ∧ F1
2135 wee'll] F1 (|); wee'l *or* wee'le *elsewhere*
2137 folow] F1 (|); follow *elsewhere*
2138 *Aut.*] F2; ~ : F1
2139 *Cape*] F2; *Crpe* F1
2145 Mayster] F1 (|); master *elsewhere except* 1508 maister
2147 cal] F1 (|); call *elsewhere*
2191 you out] F2; youout F1
2199 Thereof] F2; The reof F1
2253, 2255 *Flo.*] F2; ~ ∧ F1 (?)
2265 But] F2; but F1
2406 *Cam.*] F2; ~ , F1
2453 reare'our] reare' our F1 (?)
2612 like] F2; lke F1
2619 eyther] F1 (|); either *elsewhere*
2658 whistling] F2; whistiing F1
2714 means] F1 (|); meanes *elsewhere*
2717 him. If] ~ . if F1; ~ , if F2–F4
2949 speake.] F3; ~ : F1, F2
3109 answer] F1 (|); answere *elsewhere*
3220 excellence,] F2; ~ . F1 (?)
3274 stir'd] F1 (|); stirre(s) *elsewhere except* 613 stirs
3338 the] F2; rhe F1 (?)
3341 time] F2; ttme F1

Unadopted Conjectures

3381 *Bohemia*] Illyria (*throughout*) BERKENHOUT (1790)
4–10 *Eight verse lines ending* visit . . . occasion . . . foot; . . . difference . . . *Sicilia.* . . . of . . . *Bohemia* . . . him. mTBY4
6 shall] will mF2FL21
11 Wherein] where if GOULD (1887, p. 69)
16 will] must mTBY3
17–18 insufficience] insufficiency mFLV.a.80
26 there] then mTBY3 (*and withdrawn*)
27 which] as mF2FL21
30 attornyed] atourned [with splendid retinue] BECKET (1815, 1:349)
32 shooke] shake mTBY4
33 embrac'd] embrace mTBY4
49 *Mamillius*] To line 192 PARRY (1979, p. 57)
51 haue left] did leave SEYMOUR (1805, 1:157)
63 Or] To mTBY4
63–4 blow No . . . to] grow To . . . and CARTWRIGHT (1866, p. 14); blow In . . . to STAUNTON (1874, p. 461)
63 blow∧] ~ , [blow = blossom] LAMBRECHTS (1965, p. 956)
64 No sneaping] Nose-nipping mCOL3 (*attrib. to* Col. Curwin?)
65 This is] These are HUD2
74 ('beseech you) so] so I beseech you mFLV.a.80

569

75 none, none] no none mFLV.a.80

76 So . . . me] could win me so soone as yours mFLV.a.80

82 Farewell (our Brother.)] Brother farewell mF2FL21

our] deare mFLV.a.80

91 tell] tell's mTBY3

92 *Om.* mTBY4

98 let] diet *or* list mTBY3; sit KEIGHTLEY (1867, pp. 197–8)

behind] beyond mTBY3, HEATH (1765, pp. 202–3; *in error?*)

Gest] just THEO1; les [time] BECKET (1815, 1:349–50); longest COLERIDGE (1813?; 1960, 1:107)

99 (good-deed)] good mTBY3

101 Lady] loving KELLNER (1925, p. 140)

she] else mTBY3

103–5 *One verse line* mCAP2

105 Verely?] *Om.* mF2FL21

107 would seek] should think mFLV.a.80

114 your] our GOULD (1884, p. 22)

120 Gaoler] harsh gaoler mSTAU

127 Boy] boys mTBY3

133 ill-doing] ill-doingness BULLOCH (1878, pp. 115–16)

nor] neither SPEDDING *in* CAM1

dream'd] dream'd then mSTAU; dream'd we even KEIGHTLEY (1867, p. 198)

136 blood] food GOULD (1887, p. 69)

137–8 Imposition clear'd, Hereditarie] inquisition clear'd, Heaven would be GOULD (1884, p. 22)

146 Grace] Heaven's grace STAUNTON (1874, p. 461)

boot] both HEATH (1765, p. 203)

151 fault] faulty LAMBRECHTS (1965, p. 957)

162 deed] *Om.* ANON. ("Discovery," 1853, p. 255)

164 Our] Your mLET

166 With] Wi'th' mTBY2

we heat an Acre.] the heat, an acre NICHOLS (1861, p. 20)

heat] tread mTBY3; beat mTBY4, CARTWRIGHT (1866, p. 14); hoop mTBY4; hent SCHMIDT (1875, p. 1452); head [advance] GOULD (1887, p. 69)

167 was] was then mTAY

175 A] Or OXF2

177 'Tis] That was LETTSOM *in* DYCE2

180 Friend] royal friend mTAY

185 free] fair mTBY2

186 Bountie] bounties mLONG

Bountie, fertile Bosome] bounty: — fertile become JACKSON (1819, pp. 131–2)

190 Looking-Glasse] glass WALKER (1860, 3:91, *and withdrawn*)

sigh] sing mTBY4

197–200 Come . . . Neat.] *Om.* mCOL2

198 but] not mBRAE

200 all] all alike LETTSOM *in* DYCE2; *or* virginalling still mLET

Still] Still, still STAUNTON (1874, p. 461)

204 pash] bush [tail] BECKET (1815, 1:350–1); patch JERVIS (1868)

208 o're-dy'd] oft dyed STAU

213 Most] My mTBY4

Dam, may't be] Dam', may't be? [apostrophe indicating suspension?] mTYR

214–22 Affection . . . Browes.)] *Om.* COLNE

214 Intention] Intension [i.e., intensity] TANNENBAUM (1928, p. 360)

215 do'st . . . things] makest impossible things *or* dost make things impossible mTBY3; dost make impossible things mTBY4

216 with] by mTBY4

218 credent] evident mTBY2

220 (And . . . it,] *Om.* CAPN

221 (And that] Find it LETTSOM *in* DYCE2

224–6 *Her.* He . . . vnsetled. *Pol.* How? my Lord? *Leo.* What . . . Brother?] He . . . unsettled. *Her.* How? My lord! *Pol.* What . . . brother? NICHOLSON *in* CAM2

225–6 How . . . cheere?] *Continued to Hermione* DEY (1900)

225 How?] How i'st mLONG

226–9 *Four verse lines ending* you, . . . brow . . . lord? . . . earnest. WALKER (1860, 3: 91)

227 Brow] thought mTBY4

233 requoyle] recall GREY (1754, 1:246)

240 Egges for Money] ayes for money BECKET (1815, 1:351–2); aches from any BULLOCH (1878, p. 116)

253–5 We . . . welcome] *Her.* We . . . lord, | And . . . steps. *Leo.* How thou | Lovest . . . welcome DEY (1907)

256 deare] dears't mTBY4

267 allowing] all-owing mTBY3

270 whose issue] who sees't mSTAU

277–80 And . . . will.] *Om.* mCOL2

281 tenth] tenth part mF1FL10

282 Physick] Why, Physick mLET

there's] there is YOUNG (1928, p. 214)

285–9 From . . . not.] *Om.* mCOL2

290 you] you you COL1

291–2 *One verse line* WALKER (1860, 3:91)

292 What? *Camillo*] What Camillo, art STAUNTON (1874, p. 461)

294 thou'rt . . . man:] to Camillo mTBY2 (*and withdrawn*)

296 his] this mTBY3

303 a so-forth] and so forth MAL; a sea-froth JACKSON (1819, pp. 132–3)

308 so] as mTBY4

310 is] in GREY (1754, 1:246)

312 Seueralls] Severall mCOL2

313 Messes] nesses [ignorants] BECKET (1815, 1:352)

316–19 *Verse lines ending* ha? . . . why? mCAP2

317–19 *One verse line* WALKER (1860, 2:145)

317 Ha?] Ha? Ha? STAUNTON (1874, p. 461)

318 longer] longer, sir STAUNTON (1874, p. 461)

319 why?] why, but why? WALKER (1860, 2:145); why? why stays? STAUNTON (1874, p. 461)

327 from thee departed] have departed from thee WALKER (1860, 3:92)

330 seemes] seem'd mTBY4

334 restrayning] restraining it mTBY3, STAUNTON (1874, p. 863)

335–7 *Marked* "out" m1778BL

338 home] false GOULD (1887, p. 69)

343–5 But . . . forth] *Om.* mCOL2

349 euer fearefull] over-fearful mTBY4

352 non-performance] now-performance HEATH (1765, p. 205)

363–4 Cogitation Resides] vegetation Rides mTBY3

364 thinke)] think so *or* think$_\wedge$ mTBY2

369 puts to] puts Toe [tow] mTBY2; buts [twists] tow JACKSON (1818)

373 My] A mLET

376 that] black mSTAU

378 meating] meting [measuring] JOHN1 (*attrib. to* Thirlby)

379 Cariere] Course mLET

381 Honestie] modesty (?) mF2FL48 (trimmed; *the reading incorrectly attrib. to* Pope)

383 Noone] noon-day *or* high noon ANON. *in* CAM1

388 haue] are LETTSOM *in* DYCE2

400 my Wiues] her mFLV.a.80

400-1 Liuer . . . life] life . . . liver DANIEL (1870, p. 44)

401 as] as is mFLV.a.80

would] could mTBY4

419 Maliciously] Suspiciously ANON. ("Discovery," 1853, p. 255)

421 (So . . . ∧being Honorable.)] ∧ ~ . . . (~ ~ ∧) MAL

421-3 *Verse lines ending* have . . . rot. SPEDDING *in* CAM1

421-2 *One verse line* WALKER (1860, 3:92)

being Honorable.) I] being honourable, Sir, | I STAUNTON (1874, p. 863); benign, and honourably To BULLOCH (1878, pp. 116-18)

422-3 I haue . . . *Leo.* Make] *Leo.* Have I . . . Make mLONG

I . . . rot] *Leo.* I've lov'd thee. Mark this question, and go do't HEATH (1765, pp. 205-6)

423-4 *Verse lines ending* think . . . unsettled, WALKER (1854, p. 7)

423 rot] do't JACKSON (1819, pp. 135-6)

428 Is] Is full of mTAY

Nettles,] nettles, vipers WALKER (1860, 2:16); nettles, pismires ANON. *in* CAM1; stinging nettles STAUNTON (1874, p. 863)

of] of bees of mTBY4

432 man] any man mLONG

blench] flinch mTOOK

437 thereby] thereto mTBY4

for sealing] for seeling m1768FL

442-3 *One verse line* WALKER (1854, p. 66)

442 to] t' WALKER (1854, p. 66)

449 all] well mTBY2

466 Starre] stars mTBY4

480-1 breeding, That . . . Manners.] breeding. What . . . manners. mTBY2

482 not] not, do not mF2FL27

483 doe not?] *Om.* mLONG

483-4 doe you . . . not? . . . me,] you do . . . not . . . me? mTBY2

and dare not? . . . me,] and dare not be intelligent?—To me mTBY3

488 for] sir mTBY2

489 A partie] answered mTBY3

493 name the] name't mLET

502 gentle] *gentile or gentil* [*Fr.*] BECKET (1815, 1:353)

520 vtter it] utter 't WALKER (1854, p. 102)

523 am appointed him] am appointed for *or* sir mTBY2; appointed am mF2FL48 (*and withdrawn*), ANON. *in* HAL

529 vice] advise STEEVENS (v1778); vice [advice *or* advise] mPER

531 my] let my mFLV.a.80

533 Best] blest LAMBRECHTS (1965, p. 957)

534 freshest] *Om.* mFLV.a.80

536 shun'd] fear'd mFLV.a.80

539 his thought] this thrice mTBY2; your thought mTBY4; this oath LETTSOM *in* DYCE2

ouer] over! JACKSON (1819, pp. 136-7); erres GOULD (1887, p. 69); error FISHER (1985, p. 21)

541 Influences] influence WH1 (5:388 and 1:*xlvii*)

544 his] this mTBY4

546–9 *Four verse lines ending* body. . . . sure, . . . question . . . born. WALKER (1860, 3:95)

561–2 condemnd . . . his] condemned; . . . is AS YOU LIKE IT (1789, p. 711)

561 mouth:] mouth, & WALKER (1860, 3:95)

562 Thereon] Thereto mTBY4

his] the *or* swift mTBY4

565 places] paces mWARB, MALONE (1783); paces [*It.* "comforts"] *or* peaces BECKET (1815, 1:354)

567 hence departure] hence-departure mTBY4

568–71 *Four verse lines ending* for . . . it . . . it . . . conceive mTBY2

568 Iealousie] his jealousy WALKER (1860, 2:257, *and withdrawn*); jealousy, Camillo CARTWRIGHT (1866, p. 14)

570, 571 Must it] It must SEYMOUR (1805, 1:160)

573 him: why his] him honour, why's mSTAU; love him, why's STAUNTON (1874, p. 864)

574–6 me . . . but] my Good expedition. Be my friend, . . . theme; but say *or* me; With expedition go my friend, &c. mTAY

575–7 *Lined* 576–7, 575 (*with* consort *for* comfort) BULLOCH (1878, pp. 118–19)

575–6 friend, and comfort∧ . . . Queene,] ~ ∧ ~ ~ , . . . ~ ∧ BECKET (1815, 1:354–5)

comfort . . . Theame] consort . . . throne JACKSON (1819, pp. 137–8); God comfort . . . theme SING2; conserve . . . throne WHITE (1854); comfort . . . shame TANNENBAUM (1928, p. 362)

comfort . . . nothing] God comfort The gracious queen; and pardon his crime, but offspring LLOYD (1892); comfort! The gracious queen, part of his theme, wot nothing ADAMS (1892)

576 Queene, part] Queen's; [*a line lost*] part JOHN1

Queene, . . . nothing] queen (part of his theme 'bout nothing) MOREHEAD (1814, p. 28); queen's part of this theme, but noting SPENCE (1890)

but nothing] not noting SING1; by his noting ORGER (1890, p. 65)

579 my . . . hence:] me alive off. Hence, mTBY4

582 Come] *Pol.* Come mLONG

593–4 *Verse lines ending* still. . . . lord? WALKER (1860, 3:97)

594 Lord] good Lord mTBY4

595–600 *Five verse lines ending* yet . . . best; . . . hair there, . . . moon . . . this? mTBY4

598 in] like *or* as mTBY4

605 not her] never mTBY4

608 seruices] service mLET

615–20 *Three verse lines ending* be? . . . winter: . . . sir: mCAP2

626 Crickets] giglets mTBY4

628 his Traine?] *Om.* mTBY4

630 Behind] Beyond mTBY4

631–2 them Euen to] them Even unto *or* Them even to mTBY2

633 blest] blessed then STEEVENS (v1793)

637 drinke; depart] drinke deep mLONG; drink deep o't STAU; drain it deep JERVIS (1860; *withdrawn* 1861); drink, repeat it *or* drink a draught CARTWRIGHT (1866, p. 14); drink deep on't mLET

642 Hefts] hests [heats, violent actions] BECKET (1815, 1:355)

645 is] was mTBY3, LETTSOM *in* DYCE2, KEIGHTLEY (1867, p. 200)

648 pinch'd Thing] pinchin [one who is to be played upon] *or* pinc'd thing [one who is mocked] BECKET (1815, 1:355); perch'd thing JACKSON (1819, pp. 138–9)

649 at will] withall mTBY2
650-1 easily . . . his] easy ope? By's a KELLNER (1925, p. 171)
653 command] commandement [three syllables] WALKER (1854, p. 127)
654 know't] know it but mTBY4
    too well] too well, too well ANON. *in* CAM1
658 this?] ~ ∧ mTBY3
661 big-with] big MAXWELL *in* ARD2
663 *Her*. But] *Ant.* KELLNER (1925, p. 43)
    Il'd] I'll *or* I mTBY4
    had] has KEIGHTLEY (1867, p. 200)
664 would] will *or* do mTBY4
665 Nay-ward] wayward mTBY4
679 grieue . . . be] grieve't should be so mTBY4
687 Ile] Ild CAM3
689 a like] alike mTBY3
690 out] off mTBY4
694-7 *Four verse lines ending* her . . . know . . . principal . . . those mTAY
694-5 *Verse lines ending* one . . . herself, WALKER (1860, 3:98)
694 Federarie] federate KEIGHTLEY (1867, p. 200)
    and] ay, and WALKER (1860, 3:98)
    one] one too mTBY4
695-7 *Three verse lines ending* with . . . principal; . . . those mTBY2
695 What] She is what mTAY
    her selfe] herself with none ANON. *in* CAM1
696 that] *Om.* mTBY2
710 is . . . guiltie] afar off [barely insinuates], is guilty BECKET (1815, 1:355); has a share
of guilt mSTAU; is so far guilty DYCE2; is a fere [accomplice] of guilt KELLNER (1925, p. 31)
711 But] By DANIEL *in* CAM2
714 Good] *Om.* SEYMOUR (1805, 1:161)
739 (Sir)] so, mTBY4
741 I meane] ye clean mSTAU
744 my Stables] my stabler *or* my stablers CAM1 (*withdrawn* CAM2); me shackles BULLOCH
(1878, pp. 119-20); constables KINNEAR (1883, p. 179; me constables 1885, pp. 259-60); my
shackles GOULD (1887, p. 69)
746 farther∧] further, mTBY2
755 I . . . him:] And I would damn him; *or* And I would—damn him;— MITFORD (1844,
p. 127); I'd geld and damn him KINNEAR (1883, pp. 179-80); I would—Lord, damn him! SCHMIDT
(ed. 1870, p. 281)
    Land-damne him: be] hang him. But be CARTWRIGHT (1866, p. 14)
    Land-damne] half-damn HEATH (1765, pp. 208-9); land-dam [bury] MALONE (1783); lau-
danum FARMER *in* v1793 (KNIGHT, ed. 1841: "A joke"); langue dam [stop his tongue] BECKET
(1815, 1:355-6); live-damn WALKER (1860, 3:99); Lent-damn NICHOLSON *in* CAM1 (3:430; *withdrawn* 1867, p. 435); hand-damn BROWNE *in* CAM2; land-ram NICHOLSON (1867, p. 435, *and
withdrawn*); lambaste KEIGHTLEY (1867, pp. 200-1); land-drum BULLOCH (1878, pp. 120-1);
lam— damn ["lamback" broken off] PLATT (1906); loud-damn BURTON (1970, p. 228)
757 and . . . some] nine, the third is yet but *or* . . . yet some mTBY2
759 gell'd] kill mTBY4
760 co-heyres] my heirs mTBY4
761 glib] geld mTBY3; lib GREY (1754, 1:250); unsib HEATH (1765, p. 209); glib them ARD2
766-7 *Om.* mCOL2
766 withall] with all mF2FL48
    touches the forehead of Antigonus with his fore and middle fingers in imitation of a
SNAIL'S HORNS HENLEY *in* v1793

767–8 that . . . so] of that you feel. *Ant.* If so HEATH (1765, pp. 209–10)

767 feele] work mSTAU

770 the . . . sweeten] to sweeten the face mFLV.a.80

773 *Lord*] *Antigonus* THEOBALD (1729) *in* NICHOLS (1817, 2:360)

lacke] lack it *or* lack't mTBY3

780 Cals] Lacks mTBY2

783 a truth, like vs:] as truth; like us, mTBY2

785–7 *Verse lines ending* is . . . liege, mSTAU

785 ord'ring on't] ordering of it mTBY2

786 all] *Om.* mSTAU

787 wish] do wish mLET (*withdrawn*)

800 wilde] wide mTBY2

805 well?] well? Say. mSTAU

810 credulitie] incredulity mTBY3

816 vs] our mTBY4

820 *At the Gate of a Prison.* FURNESS (v1898)

827–45 *Thirteen verse lines ending* then, . . . contrary . . . ado, . . . from . . . lawful, . . . them? . . . apart . . . forth. . . . madam, . . . conference. . . . make . . . colouring. . . . lady? BAYFIELD (1920, pp. 348–9)

829–45 *Fourteen* [?] *verse lines ending* Queen. . . . contrary . . . ado . . . from *then as* F *until* 842–5, *which end* a-do, . . . colouring. . . . lady? mTBY2

853 poore] pure mTBY3

856 Lunes] loons *or* lowns mTBY2

871 free] fair mTBY4

876 hammered] murmured mWRAY

877 not tempt] n't attempt mTBY4

903 She] She, she mLET

th'Adultresse] th' adultresse lives GOULD (1887, p. 69)

904 Arme] aim mTBY3, FIELD (1847, p. 138)

905 braine] aime GOULD (1887, p. 69)

plot-proofe] shot proof mTBY3, WH1 (*if* aim *in* 904)

908–15 *Five verse lines ending* lord. . . . night; . . . see . . . dishonour . . . deeply; mTBY3

910–12 *Verse lines ending* to-night; . . . discharg'd. mTBY2

912–15 *Three verse lines ending* see . . . dishonour . . . deeply, WALKER (1854, p. 23)

915 deeply] heavily *or* deadlily mTBY4; deeply in mSTAU

917 Spirit] sport mTBY4

922 Alliance] allies mTBY4

928 *Enter Paulina*] *Enter Paulina, Antigonus and others following* after 945 [929–44 *within*] TANNENBAUM (1928, p. 366)

930 Lords] lord mTBY3

second] seconds YOUNG & MOSELEY (ed. 1965)

935 hath] has mTBY4

945 Who] Ho mTBY3; Whose ARD2

953 on] of mTBY4

964–5 me . . . My] one . . . Her mSTAU

967 comforting] combating mTBY4

973 her] it mTBY3, HEATH (1765, p. 210)

her good so] it good too mLET, DANIEL (1870, p. 45)

982 mankinde] vampire mWRAY

990–2 Bastard, . . . thou$_\wedge$ art woman-tyr'd: . . . heere.] ~ — . . . ~ , ~ ~ ? . . . ~ ? mTYR

991 tyr'd] rid mTBY4, mWRAY

995 hands] hand WALKER (1860, 1:252–3)
996 forced] forged mTBY3; forg'd mTBY4; falsed COL3
 basenesse] base name mTBY3
1004 But . . . heere] That's here but one mTBY2
1007 Swords] sword mTBY4
1013 beat] bait mPER
1017 them] it CAPN (V.R.)
1021 Matter] mappe [type] mSTAU
1022 And] A TANNENBAUM (1928, p. 363)
1024 Chin, and] *Om.* RITSON (1792)
 Smiles] Smile TANNENBAUM (1928, p. 359 n.)
1029 No] Put no mTBY2
1030 Her] *Om.* AS YOU LIKE IT (1789, p. 711)
1034–6 *Spoken aside* ANON. *in* CAM1
1054 *Ioue*] God ANON. *in* CAM1
 her] him HEATH (1765, p. 210)
1056 o're] o' ANON. *in* FURNESS (v1898)
1074 my] *First Lord. My* ANON. *in* CAM1
1079 of . . . on] us: on ANON. *in* CAM2
1083 We] *Lords. We* ANON. *in* CAM1
1090 Mid-wife] mad wife mTBY2
1092 this] his [Antigonus's] THEOBALD (1729) *in* NICHOLS (1817, 2:360); your mCOL2
1093 this] the [?] mTBY3
1104 lewd-tongu'd] loud-tongued mTBY2
1123 this] his RODERICK (1758, p. 213)
1127 Posts] post mTBY4
1129 An houre since:] *Om.* mTBY3
1130 are∧] ∼ , FURNESS (v1898)
1135–6 fore-tells The] for't tells That mTBY3; it foretells The KEIGHTLEY (1867, p. 201)
1146–72 *Om.* COLNE
1156 eare] near mTBY4
1168 end the] end her mTBY4
1177 Euen] Ever ANON. *in* CAM1
1182 the . . . the] her . . . her mTBY2
 Purgation:] ∼ — FURNESS (v1898)
1190 *with*] with him and *or* with him and with mTBY3
1191 *pretence*] practise WALKER (1860, 2:245)
1215 prate] plead KEIGHTLEY *in* CAM1
1217 Griefe] speech *or* breath DANIEL (1870, p. 45); gifts KELLNER (1925, p. 58)
1223 encounter] a counter mTBY4
1223–4 vncurrant . . . strayn'd] uncurrent have I Been staind JOHN1; uncredent, have I
Been stain'd BECKET (1815, 1:357–8); occurrent I Have strain'd WH1
1224 t'appeare] to appare [i.e., appair, make worse or weaken] mSTAU
 thus;] ∼ — FURNESS (v1898)
1230 bolder] bold mTBY4
 wanted] vented BAILEY (1866, p. 369)
1236 Mistresse of] Mistresse of that mLONG; misreport *or* misprision ANON. *in* CAM1; mistress
of [*a line om.*] ANON. *in* CAM1; my distress DANIEL (1870, p. 45); 'm [*or* I'm] mistress ANON. *in*
PERRING (1885); my stress of fortune ANON. *in* CAM2; my share is KELLNER (1925, p. 137)
1237 Which] That SEYMOUR (1805, 1:165)
1243 So] Such mTBY2
1247 Euen] Ever mTBY2
1254–6 *Verse lines ending* what you . . . Sir, BAYFIELD (1920, p. 349)

1263 your] the (*written* yᶜ) mLET
  Fact] Sect mLONG, FARMER *in* v1773 (10:Pp5); Pack JOHN1; pact ANON. *in* CAM1
1274 giue] hold mWRAY
1283 Lastly] Hastily BUCKNILL (1860, p. 130)
1285 limit] limb JOHN1
1291 proofes] proof mTBY4
1293 Your] Mine mF2FL27
1298 his] the mTBY4
1300 here₍ₐ₎] ~ , mTBY4, TANNENBAUM (1928, p. 365)
1302 flatnesse] blackness mWRAY
1319 truth] true mTBY4, JERVIS (1860, p. 13)
1320 Lord] good Lord mLET
1350 being done] doing mTBY4
1352 quit] quits mLUSH
1353 knew] knew to be ANON. *in* CAM1; know mLET
  great)] great and growing mTBY3
  hazard] fearful hazard MALONE *in* v1785; doubtful hazard MAL; hazarding ANON. *in*
CAM1
1356 Pietie] purity mTBY3
1363 Racks? Fires? What] what racks, what fires, what *or* what racks, what fires mTBY3
  flaying?] flaying, tearing WALKER (1860, 2:13)
1366 To] The mTBY4
1371 of] to mCOL2
1372 *Polixenes*, 'twas] *Polixenes* was mCOL2
1373 of] for mTBY2; *om.* mTBY4
1374 damnable] damnably mLONG
1382 the] thy OXF2
1385 no] now mTBY3
1393 her eye] or eye mTBY3
1395 would] *Om.* mTBY2
1399 naked] crooked mTBY2
1401 In] And mTBY3
1413 What's . . . what's] She's . . . so mTBY4
  and] as mTBY2
1414-15 receiue . . . petition] revive affliction By repetition LETTSOM *in* DYCE1 (1:cciv);
receive affliction At my monition CARTWRIGHT (1866, p. 14); receive affliction At my mad passion
or revive [*withdrawn*] affliction At my perdition mSTAU
1415 At] By LETTSOM *in* DYCE1 (*errata*)
  petition] relation SINGER (1853, p. 75)
1422-4 (Who . . . well] *Verse lines ending* and . . . well, WALKER (1860, 3:102)
1422 take] take but mLET
  you] you and mLET [*withdrawn*]
1434-5 I . . . sorrowes.] I . . . Come my Lds, | And . . . sorrows. mTBY2
1435 these] these untimely mLET
1444 heauens] Gods mTBY3
1447 Ile] 'twill mTBY4
1459 thing] things mTBY4
1462 some] sometimes mLONG
  another] on other ANON. *in* CAM1
1463-4 vessell . . . fill'd] vestal . . . veil'd BROWNE *in* CAM2
1464 fill'd] still CARTWRIGHT (1866, p. 14)
  becomming] o'er-brimming DANIEL (1870, p. 45); become it KINNEAR (1883, p. 183);
beteeming ARD1

1467 gasping] gaping *or* gaping as mTBY3

1468 the] their mTBY4, TANNENBAUM (1928, p. 365)

1472 babe] baby mTBY2

1474 weepe] land CARTWRIGHT (1866, p. 14); bear't GOULD (1884, p. 22); wrap DEIGHTON (1898); meve [move] KELLNER (1925, pp. 92, 119)

1481 so] sooth WARB

1490 pretty] pity GOULD (1884, p. 22)

1499 Chace] waye *or* trace mTBY4

1501 ten] 19 mTBY4, mF2FL27, GILDEMEISTER (1870, pp. 114–15)

1502 youth] our youth mTBY4

1505–6 boylde-braines] broild brains mWARB

1506 of] between mTBY3
         and two] to two mTBY3

1512 Childe] girl child mSTAU

1513 bookish] book-wise mTBY4

1514 the] this mTBY2

1515 staire-worke] stairs-work [stair-foot *and* stair-head *withdrawn*] mTBY2

1523 talke . . . art] talk on, when I am *or* be talk'd on, when thou art mMAL1 (p. 34)

1525–8 *Four verse lines ending* land; . . . sea, . . . firmament . . . point. mTBY2

1531 takes] tears CARTWRIGHT (1866, p. 15)

1533 not] some not mTBY2; sometimes not mTBY4

1534 Moone] sun mTBY3

1535 you'ld] you should mTBY3

1541, 1547 Gentleman] old gentleman mSTAU

1547 Gentleman] old gentleman MAL

1548 the] tho' [though] JACKSON (1819, pp. 141–2)

1550 would] would not THEOBALD (1729) *in* NICHOLS (1817, 2:362)

1556 take . . . take] takt . . . takt TANNENBAUM (1928; take't 1933)

1580 try] tire mTBY3

1583 it not a] it not as *or* it not as a *or* not as a mTBY4

1585 vntride] untold mTBY3, GOULD (1887, p. 69)

1588 ore-whelme] root up mLET

1595 my Scene] the scenes mTBY4

1596–8 betweene: *Leontes* leauing∧ ∧Th'effects . . . iealousies, . . . himselfe.] ~ ∧ ~ ~ , (~ . . . ~ ∧ . . . ~) mTYR

1597 iealousies,] jealousie mTBY4

1598–9 me . . . I] we . . . we mTBY3; we . . . you JOHN1

1599 I] we mTBY2

1601 I mentioned] we mentioned *or* I mention'd ere mTBY2; I mention'd here *or* we mentioned ere mTBY3; Mentioned LETTSOM *in* DYCE2

1604 wond'ring] worth mSTAU

1605 prophesie] t'prophesie mTBY4

1608 of Time] o'th' time mTBY4

1610 that] then *or* this mTBY4; then KEIGHTLEY (1867, p. 201)

1617 Countrey:] country and mTBY4

1620 feeling] killing mTBY4

1623 rest] list mTBY4

1632 my] thy mLONG
         the] thy mTBY3

1636 losse] losses mLET

1638 Kings] Fathers mF2FL27

1643 are] is mTBY2

1644 missingly] wissenly [attentively] BECKET (1815, 1:360); wittingly TANNENBAUM (1928, p. 365)

1645 frequent] fervent mTBY4

1647 considered] observed mTBY4

1648 eyes] spies mTBY4

1657 but] that mLET

1665 willingly] will willingly mTBY4

1668 *Autolicus*] AUTOLYCUS *very ragged* WH1 (*attrib. to* F1)

1669 *to peere*] t' appear mTBY4, TANNENBAUM (1928, p. 365); to 'pear TANNENBAUM (1928, p. 365)

1670 *Doxy*] daisies m1733FL4

1672 *raigns . . . winters*] runs . . . winter *or* vein . . . winter's mTBY3; runs . . . winters MASON (1785)

      in] o'er m1733FL4

1673 *sheete*] shift mTBY2, mF4TCC

1675 *pugging*] tugging mF4TCC

1678 *heigh*] heigh ho WALKER (1860, 3:104); hey! the finch KINNEAR (1883, p. 185)

      the Iay] heigh, the Jay FURNESS (v1898)

1679 *Are*] Her *or* Their mTBY2

      songs] songsters mTBY4

1680 *in*] on mTBY4

1682 seruice] suit and service mTBY2

1691 sheetes] ballads WALKER (1860, 3:104)

1695 this] my mCOL2

      silly] shy mF2FL27

1697 Beating and hanging] hanging and beating COL3

1698 thought] thoughts mTBY4

1701 Leauen-weather toddes] — living wether tods — [*blanks indicating numbers not supplied*] MALONE (1783; *withdrawn* MAL 10:604)

      toddes] todde mTYR

1711 three-man] They're men, *or* They're main *or* thrum-men [weavers] THEOBALD (1729) *in* NICHOLS (1817, 2:208–9)

      but] but that mTBY4

1715 none] no *or* no, no mTBY3

1719 me] the— [beginning to invoke the Trinity] THEOBALD (1729) *in* NICHOLS (1817, 2:363); *om.* JOHN1

1725 are] were mTBY2

1740 softly,] softly, softly! mTBY3

1761 but] bit mSTAU; jot *or* whit *or* bit PERRING (1885)

      abide] away mTBY3

1762 this] the mTBY4

1764 (a Bayliffe)] to a bailiff CAM1

      compast] compos'd mLONG

1767 knauish] other knavish mF2FL27

      onely in] in only mTBY4

1769 for . . . Prig] on . . . a prig mTBY4

1789 vnrold] unrogued LETTSOM (1853)

1792 *bent*] hand mTBY4; bend SCOTT (1815, ch. 22)

1792-4 *Stile-a . . . Mile-a*] stile, o . . . mile, o PLAYFORD (1651); stil-e . . . mil-e LEWIS *in* CAM1

1799 a] new mTHEO1

1805-13 your . . . I] 1808-10 But . . . blush, *then* Nay, swoon, I think, to see you so attired. *then* 1805-7 your . . . wearing; *then* and the poor lowly maid, Most goddess-like, prank'd up. *Flor.* A glass to shew thyself. I BECKET (1815, 1:362-3)

1810-11 I . . . thinke,] (sworne I think) To see you so attired, I should blush STEEVENS (v1773)

1811-12 sworne . . . glasse] sorely shrink . . . i' th' glass BAILEY (1862, 1:211); swoon . . . myself. *Flo.* Ah! lass DANIEL (1870, p. 46)

1811 sworne] scorn MITFORD (1844, p. 127); frown *or* more BAILEY (1862, 1:210); 'tis worn mTAY

1812 glasse] face HUDSON *in* CAM2

1815 ground] grounds mTBY4

1822 Vildely] So vildly mTBY2

1829 the] sea ANON. *in* CAM1
greene] great mTBY4

1833 neuer] neither mTBY2

1836-8 *Verse lines ending* your . . . 'tis MALONE *in* v1785; *withdrawn* MAL

1840 must be] must-be mSTAU
be necessities,] be, necessity mTBY3; be necessarily *or* of necessity mTBY4

1841 then will] will then *or* then you'll mTBY4

1842 I] I forfeit mWARB

1843 Thou deer'st] My dearest *or* Thou dreamest *or* Hearest thou mTBY2

1851 behold] be bold GOULD (1884, p. 22)

1873 Come] *Pol.* Come mTHEO1; *Pol.* or *Cam.* Come ARD2

1876 welcome] welcome hither *or* welcome to us KEIGHTLEY (1867, p. 203)

1885 well] Will STAU
ages] age mTBY4

1887 growing] now growing mFLV.a.80

1890 our] your mBRAE

1893 get] set mTBY2

1901 ouer] ever *or* e'er ANON. *in* CAM1

1904 wildest] wilder ANON. *in* CAM1

1906 Nobler] noble mTBY4

1908 Nature] nature's mTBY2

1910 you] yon ARD2

1914 I would] you would mTBY4

1917 Hot] gote [goat] CAM3
Mints] mint mTBY2, WALKER (1860, 1:246, *and withdrawn*)

1925 that] the mTBY4

1930 growing] blowing mWARB

1932-4 *Three verse lines ending* come . . . winds . . . dim, mTBY2

1932 From] From dusky mTBY4; *illegible n. in* mTBY3 *on possible insert before* daffadils
Daffadils] brighter *or* brightest *or* glorious daffadils COLERIDGE (1813?; 1960, 1:108)

1935-6 the . . . Or] *Om.* mFLV.a.80

1946 if: not$_\wedge$] $\sim$ $_\wedge$ $\sim$: MENDILOW (1967, p. 264)

1956 them] that mTBY4

1958 still, still] still-still mSTAU
so:] so, my love *or* so, my dear'st mSTAU; so again: mLET

1959 owne] owe mTBY4
doing] *A word and line or two om.* WALKER (1860, 1:74); doing [present Exalts your doings past; each past, remember'd] mLET

1961 are] were mSTAU

1965 which peepes] the which *or* pee-pes YOUNG (1928, p. 215)
peepes fairely through't] through it fairely peeps STAU

1970 skill] call DANIEL (1870, p. 46)

1974-5 *Perd. . . . Pol.*] *Pol.* (*aside*) JOHN1
1974 Ile sweare] Elsewhere JACKSON (1819, p. 143)
    'em] me MASON (1785)
1976-7 or . . . But] but . . . Or DANIEL (1870, pp. 46-7)
1976 seemes] deems ANON. *in* CAM1
1983-7 *Four verse lines ending* garlick . . . time. . . . word, a word, . . . up. mTBY2
1986-7 *Verse lines ending* word, a word; . . . up. WALKER (1860, 3:105)
1990-1 *Verse lines ending* swain . . . daughter? WALKER (1854, p. 206)
1991 dances] danced mTBY3
1992 They call] He calls mTBY2
    and] 'a MALONE (1783)
1994 and] but mTBY3
2010 grew] grew hungry mSTAU
2021 stretch] stretch'd mTBY2
2022 gap] jest ARD2
2024 slights] flings mTBY4
2026 *Verse* WALKER (1854, p. 86)
    Pol.] *Mop.* or *Dor.* mTBY3
2027 Beleeue] Beshrew mTBY4
2028 vnbraided] braided JOHN1; embraided HARBOTTLE (1853, p. 96)
2032 Caddysses] cadizes [Cadiz goods] BECKET (1815, 1:365)
2033 em ouer] over them mTBY4
2035 sleeue-hand] Silesia *or* sleasie holland PECK (1740, p. 241)
2042 thinke] hear mSTAU
2048 *Amber*] *of amber* mTBY3
2054 *come:*] *come: lads* or *come: come* mTBY3
2057 it] I mTBY4
2064 will] I will mTBY4
2071 clamor] clamme [stop, coagulate] DOUCE (1807, 1:359-60); clam [cover a bell's clapper with felt] CROFT (1810, p. 11; *from* MAL); chamber JACKSON (1819, p. 144); chommer [cease, hold] CORNISH (1852); clam, clem, *or* clammer [press, squeeze] KEIGHTLEY (1853, pp. 44, 615, and 1857, p. 86); chaumbre [restrain] ARROWSMITH (1853, p. 567); clemmer [clem] KEIGHTLEY (1867, p. 205); shame o' PERRING (1885, p. 141); slaken mWRAY; charm a ARD2
2082-3 a life] as I love life *or* as I love my life mTBY3
2085 twenty] twin mTBY2
2086 burthen] birth ANON. *in* CAM1
2098 fourescore] first mTBY4
2101 cold] cod mF2FL27
2104 it] that mTBY4
2113-14 thou shalt heare] they shall hear it mTBY4
2142-4 *news't, and fins't, fins't* . . . *doth vtter*] *newest, and finest* . . . *utters* mF2FL21
2147 Saltiers] Satiers mCOL2
2151 bowling] howling mSTAU
2156 You] We mTBY4
2157 Heardsmen] hairy men mTBY3; hair-men mTBY4
2163 they . . . doore Sir] sir, they . . . door KEIGHTLEY (1867, p. 205)
2170 handed] hended [dallied with] mWARB; bandied mSTAU
2172 Treasury] treasure mTBY3
2176 straited] straiten'd mTBY4
2177 a reply] reply mSTAU
2186 it] milk mTBY4
2187 Ethyopians] Ethiop LETTSOM *in* WALKER (1860, 3:108)
2188 ore.] ~ — FURNESS (v1898)

2193 professe] protest mTBY3
2197 and men] all men mTBY4
2200 had] with mTBY4
2203 and] or mTBY2
2212 puritie] parity SING2
2220 come-on] come, on mTBY3
2221 Witnesses] Witness mLET
2224 Swaine] stay mTBY4
2225-7 *Verse lines ending* father? . . . this? mTBY2, mCAP2
2234 altring] aking GOULD (1884, p. 22)
2235-7 Dispute . . . againe, . . . he did] Manage . . . in pain . . . he's bid GOULD
(1884, p. 22)
2235 Dispute] compute JOHN1; dispense ANON. *in* CAM1; discern mLET
2240 of] at mTBY3
2243 my] the mTBY3, DYCE2; that the *or* good my mTBY3; 'tis my mLET; any CRAIK *in* OXF2
2250 I] I'le mF2FL27
2259 Marke] Make mTBY4
2265 shorten] short WALKER (1860, 3:109-13)
2272 no more] *Om.* mLET
2275 *Deucalion*] Noah mTBY4
2278 dead] dread mTBY2, CLN2
      you] thou ANON. *in* CAM1
2283 hope] clip mTHEO1 (*and withdrawn*); cope mTHEO1
2286 vndone:] ~ , STAU
2290-1 Cottage, . . . on] Cottages, | But . . . on all mLET
2291 on] on both mTBY3, MALONE (1780; *withdrawn* MAL 10:606)
2302 dy'de] did mTBY3
2310 vpon me] *Om.* STEEVENS (v1793)
2314 vnwillingly] willingly m1768FL
2328 faile] fall ANON. *in* CAM1
2330 together] *Om.* mFLV.a.80
2337 sences] fancy mTBY4
2340 but] but as mTBY3, mTAY
2343 for] not for mFLV.a.80
      or] *Om.* mLONG
2344 wombes] enwombes mFLV.a.80
2345 my] mine mFLV.a.80
2354 her] y^r [your] PROUDFOOT *in* OXF2
2358 Concerne] concerns mTBY4
2362 Hearke] Deare GOULD (1887, p. 69)
2364 irremoueable] irremoveably mTBY2; immoveable ANON. *in* CAM1
2372 curious] anxious GOULD (1884, p. 58)
2380 thought on] they ought *or* well as thought on mTBY2; they ought. On mTBY4
2383 through] thorough mTBY2
2389 whom] who *or* which mTBY3
2392 And] I'll mLONG
      absence,] absence) I'll DANIEL *in* CAM2
2393 striue] thus strive mTBY2
2394 liking] like it mTBY4
2402 th'vnthought-on] th'unthinking *or* the innocent mTBY4
      guiltie] guide mTBY4
2404-5 flyes Of] flies To *or* flies For *or* feathers for mTBY4; fly with m1768FL
2414-16 asks . . . kisses . . . diuides] ask . . . kisse . . . divide mLONG

2414 thee there] there the RITSON *in* v1793

2416 Princesse; ore and ore∧] ~ ∧ ~ ~ ~ , mTBY4

2424 comforts. Sir,] ~ , ~ . mTBY4

2428 sitting] sifting mTBY2, JACKSON (1819, pp. 144-5)

2436 vndream'd] undeemed [untried] mWARB

2443 heart] heat mTBY4

2453 is i'th' reare'our] is i'th' rear i' her mTBY3; is, I fear, of BULLOCH (1878, pp. 121-2)

2455 lacks] lack'd mTBY4

2457 this] this my lack of speech mSTAU

2468 if] *Om.* LETTSOM *in* DYCE2

2472 Trust] Truth mTBY3

2477 fasting] failing [breaking] mTBY4

2480 Picture] pictures [cards] mTBY3; pasture ANON. *in* CAM1; posture FURNESS (v1898)

2485-6 that∧ . . . Eares:] ~ , . . . ~ , mTBY4

2487 a Cod-peece] the codpiece mTBY4

2489 hearing, no feeling,] feeling, no hearing, *or* hearing, no feeling, nothing mTBY2
      my Sirs] mysers [usurer's] GOULD (1887, p. 69)

2494 the Chaffe] their chaff mTBY4

2498-9 *Flo.* . . . you'le . . . *Cam.*] *Om.* . . . I'll . . . *om.* mTBY3

2519 fled] shed WH1

2524 Vnbuckle, vnbuckle] Unbutton, unbutton mTBY4; Come, unbuckle, unbuckle CAPN

2531 ouer] overt JERVIS (1860, p. 13; *om. from* 1861); oversharp LAMBRECHTS (1965, p. 957)

2547 whose] his ANON. *in* CAM1

2560 extempore] with impunity *or* hoc tempore *or* in tempore mTBY4

2562-3 honestie . . . would not] dishonesty . . . would mTBY3

2563 would not] would—not mSTAU

2570 See, see] Shee, shee [pshaw] mTBY2; sessa [meaning uncertain; cf. *Shr.* Ind.1.6] mTBY3

2579 found] sought mTBY4

2584 neither∧] ~ , mTBY4

2591 Beard] head mTBY4

2599 Affaires] affair mTBY4

2604 A] You *or* Ye mTBY2

2607 with . . . not] not with . . . but DANIEL (1870, p. 47)
      stamped . . . Steele] stabbing steel, not stamped coin DEIGHTON (ed. 1889, p. 179)
      not stabbing] note-stabbing [wound-impressing] mTHEO1

2609 vs] your self mTBY2

2617 at toaze] or tease mLONG; as to axe [ask] BULLOCH (1878, pp. 122-3); to learne GOULD
      (1887, p. 69); or ease SPENCE (1890); or coax mPER; to toaze ("in order to tease") PEN2

2633 be] me WALKER (1860, 3:115)

2635 on's] of's CAPN (V.R.)

2650 hand-fast,] band, fast, WH1

2651 Curses] lashes mTBY4

2655 heauie . . . bitter] bitter . . . heavy m1768FL

2658-9 Ram-tender] ram-pander mTBY4

2672 him] his Death mCOLE

2677 where . . . aboord] aboard where he is mTBY4
      is∧] ~ , mTBY4

2682 and] for DANIEL (1870, p. 47)

2683 hee is] is he WALKER (1860, 2:246)

2684 out-side] inside mTBY2

2693 Moitie] money mTBY4

2695 sort] case mTBY2

2706 looke] leeke [piss] mTHEO1

2716 how that . . . backe] both . . . belike BAILEY (1866, pp. 241-2); but . . . back KIN-
NEAR (1883, p. 188)

     backe] Turke mSTAU

2720 so farre] over mTBY2

2739-40 true. *Paul.*] *Paul.* True, mTHEO1; *Paul.* 'Tis true mLONG

2742 the] them mTBY4

2752 time] king GOULD (1884, p. 58)

2756 so] too mTBY3

2758 little] a little HEATH (1765, p. 218)

2760 his] this mTBY4

2769 secret] sacred mTBY2

2779 Oppose] Oppos'd mTBY4

2794-6 and . . . me?] (and . . . appear soul-vex'd,) And begin, why to me? MAL

2795 (Where . . . appeare) Soule-vext,] (Where we offenders now appear, soul-vex'd)
STEEVENS (v1773); (Where we offended,) now appear JACKSON (1819, pp. 145-6); (Where we
offend her) new appear soul-vex'd, SPEDDING *in* CAM1; Where we offenders show, appear soul-
vext, ORGER (1890, pp. 64-5); (Where we offenders move) appear HERFORD (ed. 1916-); Where
we offended, new-appear soul-vex'd, A. WALKER *in* ARD2

     Offendors . . . appeare)] offended,) now appear, JACKSON (1819, p. 146)

2795-6 now . . . me?] move) appeare, Soul vext At my sin, to eye me. RASHBROOK (1947)

2796 And . . . me?] Appear in white to me mTBY2; Beginning, "Why to me?" mLET; And
beckon to me 'Why?' BULLOCH (1878, pp. 123-4); And bellow 'Why to me?' KINNEAR (1883,
pp. 188-9); And beg*in* 'why?' to me. SPENCE (1890); Demanding, Why to me? ORGER (1890, p.
65); And begging 'Why' to me. A. WALKER *in* ARD2

     why] woe mTBY2, mPER

2798 iust such] such just GOULD (1884, p. 22)

2807 Starres, Starres] Starres, living [*or* sparkling *or* heavenly] Starres mLET

2826 bidst] Bridest mGREY

2829-31 *Verse lines ending* himselfe . . . *Florizell.* mTBY2

2830 *Seruant*] *Servant-poet* mCOL2

2835 What] What Trayne mTHEO1

2849 so;] she— mTBY4

2857 This is] This' WALKER (1854, pp. 84-5)

2860 who] them SEYMOUR (1805, 1:170)

     but bid] bid but mFLV.a.80

     follow] follow me mTBY4

2873 'Prethee . . . cease] Prithee no more *or* I prithee, cease LETTSOM *in* DYCE2
     'Prethee] Pray WALKER (1860, 3:116)

2886 Princesse (Goddesse)] priceless Goddess mSTAU

2895 touch'd$_\Lambda$] ~ , mTBY2

2896 at] a mWARB, STEEVENS (v1793); to ANON. *in* DYCE2
     friend] friends SEYMOUR (1805, 1:170)

2898 times . . . seiz'd] limbs . . . stay'd GOULD (1884, p. 22)
     times] time mLET

2915, 2926 *Libia*] Lydia mTBY2; Lycia DOUCE (1807, 1:362-3)

2916 *Smalus*] Synalus ARD2

2920 his] at mWARB, HEATH (1765, p. 219)

2921 friendly] friending mTBY2

2929 The blessed] The ever-blessed MAL; Oh! [*or* And] may the Blessed MITFORD (1844, p.
128)

2930 whilest] while mFLV.a.80

2932 Gentleman] gentle man mCAP2

2934 For] Of mTBY2

2935 and] *Om.* TANNENBAUM (1928, p. 363)

2961 so] sir mTBY4

2973 You are] Then you are not mTBY3

2974 *Flo.*] *Per.* mF2FL27, GOTCH (1900)

2976 *Given to* Leo. *or* Lord mTBY3

2986 That] Then mTBY3

2988 visible an] visibly our *or* visible as *or* visible and mTBY4

2991 since] when KTLY (2:513)

3002 these] those CAPN (V.R.)

3011-12 Relation] revolution mTBY3

3020-9 the changes . . . be.] *Om.* mCOL2

3024 very] every ANON. *in* CAM1

3027 seeing] by seeing mWARB

3045 in] and mTBY2

3046 Affection] Affectation mTHEO1

3049-3100 Did . . . vniuersall.] *Om.* mCOL2

3052 was] wants mTBY4

3053 of] oft mTBY4

3054 crowne] drown mTBY4

3072 with] of CAPN (V.R.)

3117-20 *Four verse lines ending* benefit . . . eye . . . us . . . along. WALKER (1860, 1: 13)

3117 thence] from hence mFLV.a.80

3118 winke] winking WALKER (1860, 1:13)

3125 he at] being at *or* he being mTBY4

3127-8 continuing] commencing mTBY4

3152 there was] these was m1768FL; these were RANN

3178 proue] do prove mTBY3

3189 Seruices] Seruice mLET

3193 Grace] favour mFLV.a.80

3194 may] can mFLV.a.80

3204 you] you've ANON. *in* CAM1

3206 apart] aperte [*L.* "on purpose"] BECKET (1815, 1:367-8)

3217 much] *Om.* mTBY4, SEYMOUR (1805, 1:171)

3221 lets . . . makes] let . . . made mTBY4

3235 And] A [Ah!] KELLNER (1925, p. 128)

3242 Sorrow was] sorrow's [the color of Leontes's sorrow] mTBY2

3245 no] nor ever ANON. *in* CAM2

3246 But] But it mLET

3253 Would . . . mine)] For the stone is mine, would thus have wrought you mWARB
    (for . . . mine)] For the stone i'th'mine TYRWHITT (1766, pp. 26-7); For a stone o'th' mine AS YOU LIKE IT (1789, p. 712)

3259 I . . . thinkes] 'twere alive, but that methinks t's mTBY3
    alreadie.] already | I am in heaven, and looking on an angel. ANON. *in* SINGER (1853, p. 81)

3262 beare] beat mTBY3

3301-2 still: On] still On't NICHOLSON *in* CAM2

3302 On:] All mCOL2; But GOULD (1884, p. 22); Oh! TANNENBAUM (1928, p. 364)

3308 vpon] upon't ANON. *in* CAM1

3310 numnesse] dumbness GOULD (1884, p. 22)

3315 kill her double] kill her doubly mTBY2; double kill her mTBY4

3321-2 *One verse line* mCAP2

3322-3 *Verse lines ending* pertain . . . too. mTBY2, WALKER (1860, 3:116)

3322-4 She . . . I] *Verse lines ending* pertain . . . Ay mLET
3346 bough] bower mTBY1
3358 worth, and honesty] honesty and worth mTBY2
3361 What? . . . vpon$_\wedge$ . . . Brother:] $\sim$ $_\wedge$ . . . $\sim$, . . . $\sim$? [What do you look upon, my brother?] mWARB
    my] me m1768FL
3363 This your Son-in-law] *Addressed to Shepherd* mWARB
3364 heauens] heaven m1768FL
3367 one] other mTBY4
3369 disseuer'd: Hastily$_\wedge$] $\sim$ $_\wedge$ $\sim$: mSTAU

The Text

Authenticity

That Sh. was not the author of the entirety of *WT* was casually suggested by POPE (ed. 1725, 1:xx): "I make no doubt to declare that those wretched plays [such as *Pericles*, added to the canon in F3], cannot be admitted as his. And I should conjecture of some of the others, (particularly *Love's Labour Lost*, *The Winter's Tale*, and *Titus Andronicus*) that only some characters, single scenes, or perhaps a few particular passages, were of his hand." ROBERTSON (1930, pp. 133-4), a more dedicated disintegrator, also finds *WT* unworthy. Time's prologue (lines 1579-1611) "has quite an un-Shakespearean aspect. The 'I mentioned' [1601], further, implies a previous prologue, which has been dropped. Perhaps the clearest ground for suspecting a non-Shakespearean hand is the rhyming of 'after' with 'daughter', a thing unexampled in Shakespeare's serious work, but emphatically of a kind of perverse rhyming much affected by Chapman." (For the rhyme, see n. 1606-7.) "The chief æsthetic difficulty of the play," Leontes's sudden jealousy, "is not 'like' [*134*] Shakespeare. . . . It would be a more satisfying solution if . . . the unnaturally rapid action had been imposed by a previous constructor, of whom we seem to find plain traces."

The critical problems ROBERTSON discovers have concerned others (see n. 181-92 for Leontes's jealousy, for example), but no one else attributes the apparent disparities to a previous constructor. *WT* is generally regarded as authentically Sh.'s. Some critics who accept this opinion believe, nevertheless, that the play as it stands is a revision of a version in which Hermione really dies. See, for example, CRAIG (*Revisions*, 1931, pp. 347-8) and, for a more recent expression of the idea, MUELLER (1971).

The 1623 Version of The Winter's Tale

The printing of the First Folio (1623), in which *WT* was originally published, has been analyzed by WILLOUGHBY (1932), by SHROEDER (1956), and, most thoroughly and expertly, by HINMAN (1963), on whose work much of this account is based. On 8 November 1623, close to the publication date of *Mr. William Shakespeares Comedies, Histories, & Tragedies,* sixteen of the plays were entered in the Stationers' Register to Edward Blount and Isaac Jaggard (ARBER, 1875–94, 4:69). Blount, a publisher and bookseller, was the leading member of the syndicate sponsoring publication of the First Folio. Isaac Jaggard, a printer, publisher, and bookseller, had replaced his late father, William, as a principal member of the syndicate. WILSON (1925) believes that because of William's blindness and failing health in 1622–3, Isaac was the chief overseer of the printing of the collection. The entry covers "soe manie of the said Copies as are not formerly entred to other men" and lists, according to their order in the Folio, eight comedies, two histories, and six tragedies.

WT is the last of the comedies named in the entry; it is also the last play in the first section of F1 (the Comedies), where it occupies sigs. Aa1–Cc2 (pages 277–303); gathering Cc is a single sheet. The play is preceded by *AWW* (sigs. V1^v–Y1^v) and *TN* (Y2–Z6). The text of *WT*, which concludes in the top third of Cc2, is followed by "The Names of the Actors." Sixteen characters are identified by name, and *"Other Lords, and Gentlemen, and Seruants. Shepheards, and Shephearddesses"* covers the rest (see p. 4). Among the Comedies, the first, second, and fourth plays — *Tmp.*, *TGV*, and *MM* — are equipped with similar dramatis personae, and all were probably typeset from manuscripts in the hand of the scribe Ralph Crane, of whom more below. He may have compiled these lists, although ECCLES (ed. *MM*, 1980, p. 3, n. 2940) points out that in the case of a work by Webster, Crane "is more likely to have copied than to have originated the list printed in [*The Duchess of Malfi*] in 1623 [from another Crane transcript], since it names . . . actors . . . who had died in 1614, and . . . in 1619." *Wiv.*, the third play in the Comedies section and probably another Crane copy, lacks space for such a list.

Beneath "The Names of the Actors" in *WT* is the satyr tailpiece, in which a small defect acquired during the course of the F1 printing shows that the last page of *Jn.* (b5^v) was printed before the last page of *TN* (Z6) and the last page of *WT* (HINMAN, 1:179–80). Sig. Cc2^v is blank. Since the play following *WT* in the Folio is *Jn.*, the first of the history plays, the blank may seem to have been left so that the Histories section of the book could begin on a recto. This nicety, however, was actually compelled by the fact that *Jn.* and part of *R2*, which follows *Jn.*, had been printed before the typesetting of *WT* began (HINMAN, 1:37). It is more extraordinary that the first page of *WT* is preceded by blank Z6^v. HUNTER (1845, 1:417) suggests that there was "some danger of losing this play. In the folio collection there is a blank page following *Twelfth Night*, as if there the collection of comedies ended, and the histories were about to begin: and my copy of the first folio actually wants the *Winter's Tale*." POLLARD (1909, p. 135) thought there had been simply a miscalculation of the space required for *TN*, but the anomaly seems to arise from another and more complicated cause.

As HINMAN (2:521) explains — repeating to some extent the conclusions of WIL-LOUGHBY (1932, pp. 34–43) — when *AWW* was nearly completed, Compositor B, who had been working alone on that play, skipped to the Histories. With Compositor C

he set all of *Jn.*, which begins at sig. a1, and then two pages of *R2*, b6–6ᵛ. B at that
point returned to the Comedies. By himself he finished *AWW* and *TN*, which concluded on Z6. He then set two more pages of *R2* and, after an interruption for work
on another book, with Compositor A set ten more pages of *R2* and proceeded to *WT*.
The blank Z6ᵛ is thus a legacy of the excursions from the Comedies into the Histories
and back again, sheet Z having been printed before copy for *WT* was available. (SHROE-
DER, p. 42, notices another minor consequence: In the first sheet of *Jn.* to be printed,
sig. a3 is designated Aa3, in the style of the signature alphabet to be used later for
WT.) HINMAN continues: "For some reason the copy for *Twelfth Night* was not readily
available when quire X was finished (though it evidently became so soon afterward),
and . . . the copy for *The Winter's Tale* was in like manner unavailable when quire
Z was finished (though on this occasion the want was made good even more quickly
than before). . . . No difficulty over copyright can be supposed — only some short-
lived trouble over the copy itself." He thus puts to rest several earlier speculations,
such as that of WHITE (ed. 1857, 5:275): "It is possible that in gathering the plays
together Heminge and Condell forgot this one [*WT*] until the folio was nearly in type;
but it is more probable that, finding it no more tragical [i.e., less so] in its course or
its catastrophe than *Cymbeline*, they first intended to class it with the Tragedies [as
Cym. is], and after it was ready to be struck off restored it to its proper place among
the Comedies." Equally groundless is the explanation of FURNESS (ed. 1898, p. vii)
that "inasmuch as the sheets were printed off . . . at different presses [he seems to
be referring, incorrectly, to printing houses], it was undoubtedly easier to leave a
whole page blank at the end of a signature than to transfer a single page of *The
Winter's Tale* to the press that was striking off *Twelfth Night*."

According to HINMAN (2:496–503), the formes of quires Aa through Cc were set
by Compositors A and B in the following sequence:

A B	A B	A A	A A	A A	A B	B B
Aa3ᵛ:4	Aa3:4ᵛ	Aa2ᵛ:5	Aa2:5ᵛ	Aa1ᵛ:6	Aa1:6ᵛ	Bb3ᵛ:4

B A	B A	B A	B A	B A	A -	A B
Bb3:4ᵛ	Bb2ᵛ:5	Bb2:5ᵛ	Bb1ᵛ:6	Bb1:6ᵛ	Cc1:2ᵛ	Cc1ᵛ:2

His compositor attributions agree with the earlier allocation by PAFFORD (1961,
p. 173) and the later allocation by WELLS & TAYLOR (1987, p. 150). For HOWARD-HILL
(1973, pp. 84–7), however, it is uncertain that "the A of the early comedies and the
A of *WT* and the histories [are] the same compositor. . . . The compositor of *WT*
prefers 'indeed', 'mistresse', [and in elisions] 'x'th', and 'x'le' whereas in A's pages
of *Tmp.*, *TGV*, *Wiv.*, *MM* and *MV* the corresponding preferences are 'indeede', 'mistris', 'x'th/xth', and 'x'll'." HOWARD-HILL also finds (p. 85) that, with respect to *chuse*
(two instances in *WT*) / *choose* (0), *deare* (2) / *deere* (2), *deuil(l)* (2) / *diuell* (0),
graunt (1) / *grant* (0), *grief(ue)* (8) / *greef(ue)* (0), *Heauen* (11) / *heauen* (0), *howre*
(0) / *houre* (1), *indeed* (10) / *indeede* (0), *mistresse* (7) / *mistris* (2), *scarce* (1) /
scarse (0), *suddaine* (1) / *sodaine* (0), *yeere* (7) / *yeare* (0), and *young* (8) / *yong*
(0), Compositor A of *R2* and *WT* preferred the first form and Compositor A of the

earlier Comedies the second. As the figures indicate, though, not all of these preferences are expressed powerfully or even at all in *WT* alone.

HOWARD-HILL explains his differentiation between the two Compositors A
(pp. 86–7): "Whereas the comedies compositor would quite often space a fair number of internal commas, occasionally more than were left without spaces, the practice
of the [87] histories A is much more pronounced and never, in the plays . . .
examined, is there a greater number of spaced commas to unspaced commas. . . .
Also, before *WT*, the compositor A [of the Comedies] was indifferent to whether he
set the first word of the speech together with the speech-prefix in a catchword, or
the speech-prefix alone, but in the histories his invariable practice was to supply the
first word of the dialogue with which the next page started." In *WT*, catchwords
consisting of speech prefix and a word of dialogue are found on Aa3, Aa5^v, Bb5^v, and
Cc1, all attributed to A, whereas abbreviated speech prefixes only are found on Aa4,
Bb1^v, Bb2, and Bb2^v, all attributed to B. The Compositor A of *WT* thus appears to be
the Compositor A of the Histories, not the Compositor A of the earlier Comedies. The
latter was designated F by HOWARD-HILL (1973, p. 87). But WERSTINE (1984, p. 92),
noticing that in the text assigned to Compositor F, portions of prose speeches that
"mark a change of address or of topic" may be given a new line, a characteristic of
Compositor D, wonders whether "any distinction can be made between the two
workmen." (The subject awaits further investigation.) Moreover, the validity of spacing as a compositorial discriminant has been questioned by MCKENZIE (1984). He
found that its apparent testimony in early books printed at the Cambridge University
Press does not accord with the work records kept.

The signatures of *WT* translate into line numbers as follows:

Compositor A: (Aa3^v) 623–754, (Aa3) 497–622, (Aa2^v) 365–496, (Aa5) 1005–1136, (Aa2)
233–364, (Aa5^v) 1137–1255, (Aa1^v) 101–232, (Aa6) 1256–1387, (Aa1) 1–100, (Bb4^v–
Cc1^v) 2411–3319

Compositor B: (Aa4–4^v) 755–1004, (Aa6^v) 1388–1513, (Bb3^v–4) 2147–2410, (Bb3)
2016–2146, (Bb2^v) 1884–2015, (Bb2) 1759–1883, (Bb1^v) 1635–1758, (Bb1) 1514–1634,
(Cc2) 3320–3369.

And they translate into sequentially ordered signatures and line numbers as follows:

Compositor A: (Aa1–3^v) 1–754, (Aa5–6) 1005–1387, (Bb4^v–Cc1^v) 2411–3319

Compositor B: (Aa4–4^v) 755–1004, (Aa6^v–Bb4) 1388–2410, (Cc2) 3320–3369.

About the order of composition there is little different from the regular procedure
for typesetting F1. The manuscript text would be cast off—that is, before typesetting
began, the words of the manuscript would be allotted to specific type pages—so that
the two compositors could work more or less simultaneously. Both started with the
innermost forme; and then one of them usually worked backward through the page
sequence of each quire and the other forward. Since much of the text is regular verse,
its casting off amounted to little more than counting the number of verse lines needed
to fill the two columns of each page. Even on pages largely of prose (e.g., Bb1–2),

white lines left above and below stage directions and scene heads permitted expansion or contraction, so that the typeset words could be fitted into the estimated space. Nothing shows what B did while A set Aa1ᵛ- 2ᵛ, 5ᵛ- 6 by himself.

The few irregularities are minor. On Aa1, the first page of the play but the last of the Aa gathering set by Compositor A, the white space preceding and following *Scœna Secunda*, near the foot of column a, is reduced, to allow plenty of room for the ornament, head title, and initial entrance direction at the top of the page and to avoid having the scene head or the initial SD stand alone at the foot of the column. At 467 (Aa2ᵛb), perhaps to gain a couple of lines, an entrance direction, rather than being centered, is set on the same line as the conclusion of a speech—or, if the direction had been overlooked earlier, it could have been inserted there after the column was in type. SDs similarly placed are found at 2005 (Compositor B) and at 3029 (Compositor A). On Bb3a there are about two lines of white space above and below Autolycus's song (2044- 55), but on Bb3b his second song in the scene (2139- 44) is crowded into the text: A one-line speech has been run into the concluding line of another speech (2138); the logotype "yᵗ" is used (2146, its only appearance in *WT*, although "yᵉ" is found at 1672); and probably line 2080 has been moved from the head of column b to the foot of column a̧, where it now occupies the direction line, normally blank in column a. Lines 2145- 6 may have been reset. PAFFORD (1961, p. 173) suspects "some mistake in the casting off or else some later insertion, perhaps the song." The latter seems likely, and if the song was overlooked, it may have been written on a piece of paper not a part of the main MS. PAFFORD suggests, too, that the typesetting of Bb3 was done by Compositor E, supposed to be an apprentice, but HINMAN and HOWARD-HILL disagree. PAFFORD's opinion, however, is shared by CAIRNCROSS (1972, p. 382).

HARRISON (1948, p. 242) argues that "in his later plays not only did Shakespeare abandon blank verse in conversation, but in the longer speeches he often substituted for the normal pattern of five feet . . . a much freer short line verse." This opinion is reiterated by BERTRAM (1981), who urges modern editors to forgo relining as iambic pentameter the apparently irregular verse of the early eds. In doing so, he says, they obscure Sh.'s rhetorical instructions to the actors, instructions that are embodied in the lineation of the early texts. WERSTINE (1984), investigating whether the line division in the Folio is Sh.'s or the F compositors', finds that in the late plays, including *WT*, departures from iambic pentameter are usually caused by the compositors' need to create or waste space to make cast-off copy fit its typographical allocation. The irregular lineation has nothing to do with rhetorical instructions.

The F1 Copy

According to GREG (1957, 3:1111), "There is external evidence of trouble over the copy for this play [*WT*], for on 19 Aug. 1623 the Master of the Revels relicensed the piece since 'the allowed booke was missing[e]' [see p. 604], though by that time the play must have been already printed." And it probably was; HINMAN (1:357) believes that the work on quires c and Aa–Cc "may well have" taken place in December 1622. (Earlier scholarship, summarized by GREG, 1955, p. 461, arrived at nearly the same date, late November.) Even though the manuscript of *WT* bearing the original license had been lost, however, at least one other copy existed to provide a basis both for the production with which the Master of the Revels, Sir Henry Herbert, was concerned and for F1 printer's copy. WILLOUGHBY (in J. D. WILSON, ed. 1931, p. 113 n.) suggests that what Herbert actually saw was the printed sheets of *WT*. This is possible, of course; as GREG (1955, p. 417 n.) points out, though, "they would have needed a lot of editing [presumably the addition of bookkeeper's notes for control of the performance and perhaps the cutting of dialogue] and have provided very little room for it." KNOWLES (privately) suggests that "the company may have retrieved from Jaggard the Crane transcript." That is also a possibility. Manuscript returned by modern letterpress printers may be too marked up and inky for theatrical use, but the copy for the 1591 English translation of *Orlando Furioso*, as described by GREG (1924), is quite neat. In that case, however, it may have made a difference that the manuscript was being received by Sir John Harington, the translator. Because the F1 text has no theatrical stigmata, there is no support for the opinion, voiced by LEE (1902, p. xxvi), that "after being represented on the stage," the MS version of the play licensed by Herbert "was sent to press."

In his *TGV*, WILSON (ed. 1921, p. 78) had argued that "the 'copy' for *The Two Gentlemen* was made up by stringing together players' parts and arranging them in acts and scenes by the aid of a 'plot.'" A *plot* in this sense was an outline of the action of a play, recording entrances and exits, properties, noises, and other details of performance of which the prompter wanted to be reminded (for further information, see GREG, 1922). WILSON's idea was quickly adapted to *WT*. Because, in his opinion, *WT* has "no stage-directions, or very few," RHODES (1922, pp. 59–60) asserts that the text cannot "have been set up by the printer from the prompt-book." It was, instead, (p. 60) "assembled" from the players' parts, "complete with cue, dialogue, and certain directions, and . . . a detailed extract from the stage-directions to serve as his [the prompter's] remembrancer" — that is, the plot. The plot would furnish a "guide for sorting the players' parts and keeping them in order whilst pasting them together into one continuous text," which would, however, "inevitably lack many directions." RHODES finds that *WT* "bears all the stigmata of an 'assembled' text. The entrances of the players are not, as usual, distributed in the places where they are due to appear, but each scene is headed by a list of characters. . . . In all the five acts there are not more than a dozen incidental entrances and exits, and those are mostly of minor characters."

The same idea is expressed more fully by RHODES (1923, pp. 98–100), and, after it receives favorable mention by POLLARD (1923, p. 8), is reiterated by J. D. WILSON (1924, pp. 72–6). This view, reflecting JOHNSON's (1756; 1968, 7:52) opinion that Sh.'s plays were "printed . . . from compilations made by chance or by stealth out of the separate parts written for the theatre," was obviously influenced by *TGV*'s and *WT*'s massed entries (that is, the lists at the head of a scene not only of the characters who appear at its beginning but also of those who enter later). *WT* has massed entries at 2.1, 2.2, 2.3, 3.2, 3.3, 4.4, 5.1, and 5.3. The characters are listed according to social rank or importance in the drama in 2.1 (in two groups) and 5.3 but in the approximate order of their speaking in 2.2, 2.3, 3.2, 3.3, and 4.4. In 5.1, those present at the beginning are in order of rank; Florizel and Perdita, named last, enter later. Plays in the Ben Jonson folio (1616) also have massed entries, as do the quartos from which the folio texts derive. In Webster's *Duchess of Malfi* (1623), according to BALD (1931–2, pp. 244–6), occasionally a character named in a massed entry fails to appear in the scene; and GREG (1931–2) reports that in Massinger's autograph MS of *Believe as you List*, a massed entry includes characters who enter later. In these instances, players' parts cannot have been involved unless, as in the case of *BAYL*, the point of entry was specified in another direction or could be deduced from another feature of the text. In any event, parts do not seem to have been involved in *WT*.

Although it was endorsed by J. D. WILSON in his 1931 ed. of *WT* (p. 122), the theory of assembled texts was to collapse under its impracticalities. (For a history of its career, see GREG, 1955, pp. 156–8.) Speculation about the fate of *WT*'s allowed book continued, however. ADAMS (1917, p. 25, n. 2) guesses that the MS was "misplaced by the printer" of F1. Such an eventuality would be possible if the allowed book was printer's copy, for *WT* probably was printed in December 1622, and the entry in Herbert's office book was dated 19 Aug. 1623 (see p. 590). In the decade following ADAMS's study, though, *WT*'s textual history began to be understood differently. GREG (1926, p. 154) found that the manuscripts of Fletcher and Massinger's *Barnavelt* and Middleton's *The Witch* (see below, p. 600) were in the same handwriting, and F. P. WILSON (1926–7) proved that the hand was that of Ralph Crane, a scrivener associated with the King's Men, who had signed his name to his transcript of Fletcher's *Demetrius and Enanthe; or, The Humorous Lieutenant* (see below, p. 600). To this signed document, Crane's other surviving work, some also signed, is linked by distinctive and recurrent stylistic features. WILSON's attribution of the Folio copy of *WT* to Crane was attacked unsuccessfuly by TANNENBAUM (1933, pp. 75–86), who mistakenly thought the MS was "quite possibly Shakespeare's own manuscript."

F. P. WILSON (1926–7, pp. 211–14) describes "some general characteristics of [Crane's] work. 1. A publisher who came by one of Crane's transcripts might reasonably expect from the printer an accurate text. . . . 2. All Crane's transcripts are carefully divided into acts and scenes. . . . [*212*] 3. Those stage-directions in *Barnavelt* which are in Crane's handwriting give little information apart from mere statements of exits and entrances [Fletcher and Massinger's *Barnavelt* is preserved in British Library MS Add. 18653; see Fredson Bowers, ed., in *The Dramatic Works in the Beaumont and Fletcher Canon*, 8:485–501]. . . . In Crane's other transcripts the directions never smack of the theatre. . . . [*214*] Statements of entrances are massed together at the head of each scene." CHAMBERS (1930, 1:488–9) finds that the SDs in *WT* consist of "little more than entries and exits, and the latter are often omitted. The entries are normally given in [4.3] and [5.2], but for the other scenes all the characters taking part, whether they are present from the beginning or not, are grouped in the initial entry. This follows the order of their appearance, and in

[2.1, 3.2, 5.1, and 5.3], but not elsewhere, the successively appearing characters or [489] groups of characters are marked off by colons in the stage-directions." HOWARD-HILL (1972, p. 130) points out that the massed directions with colons were typeset by Compositor A, those without by Compositor B, who "was apparently unwilling to print the colons from copy."

The entrance directions are of four types. The first, reflecting English tradition, marks entrances as the characters appear (4.3 and 5.2). The second, reflecting neo-classical tradition, includes some of the massed entries discussed earlier (p. 591). In this type, all the characters appearing in the scene are named in the initial SD, although some actually enter later; their entrances are unmarked (2.1, 2.2, and 3.2; the SD for 3.2 omits Paulina, unless she is included among the Ladies, and the Servant who enters at 1323). The third is neutral: all characters who appear in the scene are present from the beginning (1.1, 1.2, 3.1, 4.1, 4.2, and 5.3). The fourth is hybrid: all who appear in the scene are named in the initial entry but some actually enter later, and their entrance is marked (2.3, 3.3 [except for the Shepherd who enters at 1501], 4.4 [except for the Servant who enters at 2145], and 5.1 [except for the Lord who enters at 2940]). Since the stage directions in all the Shn. texts thought to be printed from foul papers are in the English style and since there is no reason to think that Jaggard would have introduced the neoclassical, Crane must be its source and the source of the inconsistencies as well.

Only a few SDs add anything to the bare entrances and exits: *as to her Triall* (1174-5), *pursued by a Beare* (1500), *the Chorus* (1579), *singing* (1668 and 2043), *Heere a Da(u)nce of* (1988 and 2164), and *like a Statue* (3185). Of these, *singing* is common, of course. *As to* is unusual; it occurs in only two other Shn. SDs (*Trumpets sound as to a charge* [*TNK* 5.3.55.1]; *Enter as to the Parliament* [*R2* 4.1.0.1 (1921)] and there in F only, not in Q). *WT*'s *pursued by* is unique in Sh. *Like* is sometimes preceded by a participle—for example, *habited like Shepheards* (*H8* 1.4.63 [753]) or *drest like Vincentio* (*Shr.* 4.4.0 [2180])—but more often in Sh. it is not—*Enter Ariel like a water-Nymph* (*Tmp.* 1.2.316 [453-4]) and *like a Harpey* (3.3.52 [1583]), *like Gentlemen* (*MM*, DP [2946]), and *like himselfe* (*Tim.* 1.2.0 [341]). Similar SDs appear in *AYL*—*like Forresters* (2.1.0 [606]) and *like Out-lawes* (2.7.0 [972]); in *Tit.*—*like a Cooke* (5.3.25 [2525]); and in *Cym.*—*like a poore Souldier* (5.2.0.4 [2894]). These texts were printed from a variety of sources, according to WELLS & TAYLOR (pp. 145-7), who represent a recent, although not universally shared, opinion: *Tmp.* from a Crane transcript possibly of foul papers, *MM* from a Crane transcript of what we now call a promptbook, *Tim.* from foul papers (Middleton's and Sh.'s), *AYL* from a transcript or a promptbook, *Tit.* from foul papers, and *Cym.* from a transcript "probably by Crane, of a manuscript in two hands." The SDs in *WT* obviously contribute nothing to our knowledge of Crane's copy.

Punctuation marks, especially parentheses and apostrophes, provide another approach to the study of the F1 version of *WT*. THORNDIKE (1934), having assiduously counted the parentheses in the F1 texts thought not to have been printed from quartos, finds the greatest number in *WT* (369, 2 short of the number given by a later critic—see below, p. 594), *2H4* (259), *Wiv.* (219), *Cym.* (158), and *TGV* (129). The printer's copy for all but *2H4* is now believed, with more or less conviction, to have been Crane transcripts. THORNDIKE also notices that *TGV, Wiv.*, and *WT* have collective entries of the type found in Crane's (MS Malone 25) transcript of Thomas Middleton's *A Game at Chess*. PAFFORD (1961, pp. 175-7) notes that, in *WT*, apostrophes mark—in addition to omitted vowels (as in *'d* preterits)—parts of words (*cam't* for *came it, le't* for *let it*) and entire words before exclamations or appeals (*'Beseech you*) or in the middle of a phrase (*Who taught 'this*). "The apostrophe is also used where apparently nothing has been dropped. . . . E.g., *has*—the verb, not a contraction of *he has*—is usually printed *ha's*. . . . [*176*] The apostrophe was sometimes perhaps used vaguely, to indicate that writer or compositor realized that a word was abbreviated but did not know how to show it; e.g. *Gillyvors*, presumably for *gillyflowers* . . . is first spelt *Gilly-vors* [line 1890] and then *Gilly'vors* [1910]. In contrast there are cases where something is dropped but no apostrophe used." Instances include *Ile* (73, 95, 97, 121, etc.), *th* for *the* (1408, 1450, 2375), *tane* (1730), *ha* (1743), and *fore* (2221). HOWARD-HILL (1972, p. 129) also finds "many possessive singulars of nouns with apostrophes after vowels [e.g., *Camillo's* (792), *Cytherea's* (1936)], 'it's' with the apostrophe [for *its*—e.g., 231, 236, 357, 1488], 'it' for the possessive [e.g., 1110, 1279]." To the suggestion by PAFFORD (p. 176) that the colons punctuating many SDs might be traceable to Edward Knight, at one time bookkeeper to the King's Men, HOWARD-HILL (1966) objects that Crane's MS Malone 25 uses colons in massed entries to separate characters who enter later from those with whom the scene begins, whereas Knight did not use colons for this purpose.

The fundamental study of Crane's work is HOWARD-HILL (1972), which superseded such earlier studies as that of SOMER (1962). A summary of HOWARD-HILL's and other research on Crane is provided by HAAS (1989). Eight of Crane's dramatic manuscripts survive, three being of Middleton's *A Game at Chess*. Three additional MS copies of this play, one in Middleton's hand, also exist, and comparison of Crane's versions with Middleton's affords an unusual opportunity to isolate many details attributable to the scribe rather than to the copy from which he worked. Eight non-dramatic transcripts in Crane's hand have also survived, and comparison of these and the dramatic transcripts permits more characteristics of Crane's work to be identified. Those evident in *WT* include The Names of the Actors (3370-88) and the massed entrances mentioned above; division of the text into acts and scenes; descriptive stage directions (see p. 593); some characteristic spellings (the very common '*em*; see below for many more); the Jonsonian elision at 109 (*Verely'is*); numerous hyphens linking, for example, prepositions and objects, prefixes and stems, adverbs and adjectives, adjectives and substantives, and stems and suffixes (6, 17, 24, 30, 50, 73, 79, etc.); and, according to HOWARD-HILL (p. 82), huge quantities of colons and parentheses, 839 of the former and 371 of the latter. He points out (p. 87) that "of the possible situations where parentheses [to enclose vocatives] could have been used," 39% of the vocatives in *WT* have them. WELLS & TAYLOR (p. 601) add "parentheses to mark passages spoken aside" at 2516-17 and 2520. Crane may not be entirely responsible for the text's numerous hyphens, however; MCKENZIE (1959, p. 81) finds that in setting *MV* Q2 (1619), "Compositor B" hyphenated such words as *bed-fellow* and *me-thinks* 25 times and deleted the hyphen in his copy only 9 times. (While John F. Andrews found that *me-thinks* was hyphenated only by "Compositor B"'s fellow-workman on *MV* [1619] and the other Pavier quartos ["The Pavier Quartos of 1619 — Evidence for Two Compositors" (Vanderbilt diss., 1970)], nonetheless it remains true that "Compositor B" did introduce hyphens into many words he set in these quartos. There is reason to doubt, however, that Compositor B worked on the Pavier quartos: see R. KNOWLES, *SB* 35 [1982], 202.)

A great many of Crane's characteristic spellings appear in *WT*, although, as one might expect, there are some exceptions. HOWARD-HILL's summary (pp. 64–8) includes, but is not limited to, the following:

-ei-, never *-ie-* (all such spellings in *WT* accord with modern convention — e.g., *perceiue* [263] and *Heire* [1315])

-lly, never *-ly* (the same — e.g., *naturally* [2595])

-ing, never *-eing* (the same — e.g., *mouing* [431])

-nck (e.g., *prancks* [2583] and *wrinckled* [3217], although these are far outnumbered by such *-nk* forms as *ranke* [369] and *Winke* [414])

-ll, never *-l* (*Royall* [28], *wooll* [1703], but *wil* [453] and *shal* [1304], both full lines)

-s, never *-es*, for plurals of nouns with short vowels (e.g., *Gifts* [31], *things* [2939])

-es, never *-s*, for plurals of nouns ending in *-th/sh/ch* (*Oathes* [85], *blushes* [1872], *Wenches* [2136])

-ings, never *inges*, for words ending in *-ing* (*Fadings* [2020] but *singes* [2008], a full line; the spelling is not found elsewhere)

-s or *-sse*, never *-ss* (e.g., *killes* [1750], *Presse* [74], *kisse* [3284], but also *Princess* [2832])

b is not doubled before *-'d* or *-ed* (e.g., *rob'd* [past tense of *rob*; 1729], but *crabbed* [173]); it is doubled before *-ing* after short vowels (e.g., *stabbing* [2607])

d is not doubled before *-s* or *-es* (but *toddes* [1701], *Goddes* [1826], *addes* [1902], *oddes* [2976]), before *-ing* (but *bidding* [733, 1100, and 1143]); or before *-er* (e.g., *hinder* [79])

g is not doubled before *-ing*, *-er*, *-es*, but is probably doubled after an unvoiced short vowel (e.g., *Egges* [206], *Dagger* [235], *pugging* [1675])

Doubled consonants are retained before *-ed*, but one *-l* may be dropped before *-d* (e.g., *crabbed* [173], *spotted* [427], *Added* [793], *muzzel'd* [235], and *Il'd* [462]). An exception to the doubling of *l* before *-ed* is *(vn)setled* (this word only) (224, 424, 1767, 2385, and 3272)

m is doubled medially only after short vowels (e.g., *(be)comming* [8 and 1464], *Commission* [97], and *command* [1665]) but not before *-es* or *-s* (e.g., *lames* [3066] and *redeemes* [3311], plurals in which the vowels are long)

n is doubled medially after short vowels (e.g., *Sonne(s)* [46 and 3136], *manner* [3093], and *winners* [3344]) but not after long vowels or before *-s* (e.g., *finer* [312] and *begins* [469])

p is generally not doubled medially, but there are exceptions (e.g., *Coppy* [197], *slipperie* [365], *Lippe* [479], *Appollo's* [801])

r is doubled after short vowels (e.g., *Starre* [50], *morrow* [61], and *Iarre* [100])

s is doubled after short vowels (e.g., *Hostesse* [121], *Kisse* [165 and 3284], and *Glasse* [402])

t is doubled after short vowels and before *-ing* (e.g., *pitty* [670] and *committing* [1189]) *w* is always single

z is always single (reversed in *WT*: *muzzel'd* [235] and *Chizzell* [3279]).

Other Crane preferences are for *w* in such words as *sowr'd* (173), *Lowt* (397), *scowre* (631), *lowd'st* (865), *Perswades* (868), *powre* (927 and 1586), and *howre* (1587); for internal *a* in *roab'd* (1830), *Coarse* (1944, 1946), *poaking* (2052), and *coap'st* (2267); for *-que* in *Basilisque* (496), *publique* (815), and *Heretique* (1042); for internal *-y-* in *prayse* (18), *trayn'd* (25), and *tyre* (66); for *blood* (20 times; no other spelling occurs). He was elsewhere indifferent to the termination *ance/aunce*, but in *WT aunce* is found only in *daunce(s)* (183 and 1988), whereas *dance* occurs eight times, once at 1991 — two lines from *Daunce*. Among spellings preferred by Crane and not likely to have been altered to justify lines of type, HOWARD-HILL (pp. 100–2) lists, for *WT*, *Councels* (326; plural noun), *Physick* (282), *powrefull* (284, 622), and *wayting* (163).

Those that also may signify Crane are *councell* (singular nouns: 2777, 2786), *extreames* (1804), *flowre(s)* (1879, 1886, 1889, 1916, 1919, 1927, 1931, 1941), *graunt* (187, 2994; but also *grant* [1616]), *howre* (1587), *moneth(s)* (98, 173, 2089, 2871, 2998), *powr'd* (2172), and *publique* (815). And to these HOWARD-HILL adds (pp. 171–2) Crane spellings adopted by Compositor B against his preference: *Angell* (2034), *answere* (2023), *approach* (1465, 1857, 2036), *choice* (2137, 2257), *daylie* (1434 as *dayly*), *deed* (797, 1571), *extreames* (1804), *forth* (837, 979, 1606), *happie* (2178), *howre* (1587), *mightie* (921, 1725), *moneth* (2089), *need* (1722, 2256; *neede*, 6 times), *old* (1860, 2089, 2179, 2263, 3328, 3345; *olde*, twice), *powre* (927, 1586, 1839), *son* (1638, 3363; *sonne*, 39 times), *sun* (1717, 1918), *wee'll* (2135; *wee'l* 5 times), *yeere(s)* (1585, 1617, 1671; *yeare(s)* [1399, 1887]).

Spellings in Crane's transcripts that ECCLES (ed. *MM*, 1980) discovered in *MM* also appear in *WT*: *beleeue* (12 times), *Coyne* (2607), *deere* (10 times; *deare* 11 times), *(vn)easie* (118, 1661, 2662, 3298), *medler* (2143), *meere* (901, 1322, 1326), *mistris* (6 times; *mistresse*, 7 times), *neere* (8 times), *peece* (11 times; *pieces* once), *practise/practis'd* (189, 1352), *sence* (8 times), *thether* (1662, 2125; *thither*, 3 times), *vertue* (7 times), and *yong* (5 times; *young*, 9 times). Of all these spellings, KABLE (1968, pp. 157–9) found *extreames* (1804), *howre* (1587), and *moneth* (2089) to be contrary to Compositor B's preference, hence his copy spellings. KABLE's opinion, however, is compromised by R. KNOWLES's finding that the work was not Compositor B's (see p. 595).

The two plays also display some similarities in punctuation. In *WT* as in *MM*, colons are preferred to semicolons, although more strongly (1 per 29 words, as opposed to 1 per 140 in *MM*). The exclamation point does not appear. Sometimes the question mark is exclamatory (at 265, for example), but in many instances its exclamatory function cannot be distinguished clearly from its interrogative one. One difference from *MM* and the transcripts is that the suffix is nearly always *-nesse* in *WT*; only one *-nes* is found, in 1663, a full line.

HOWARD-HILL (pp. 66–8) separately categorizes Crane's spellings of "words that have been used to identify the stints of Jaggard's compositors." His tabulation may be compared with the occurrence of the spellings in *WT* (see table). Ignoring counts

	Crane Transcripts		WT A		WT B	
	NO.	%	NO.	%	NO.	%
ancient	3	21	—	—	3	75
auncient	11	79	—	—	1	25
been	0		15	52	0	
beene	0		14	48	4	50
ben	5	5			—	—
bin	1	—			4	50
byn	108	95			—	—
blood (only)	89		16		4	
dear(e)	3	5	10	77	1	12
deer(e)	53	95	3	23	7	88
do	35	9	2	3	35	95
doe	345	90	61	97	2	5
doo	2	1	—	—	—	—
n/either	51	100	3	75	9	100
eyther	—	—	1	25	—	—
goe	130	100	24	100	3	15
go	—	—	—	—	17	85
greef(e)(ue)	1	—	1	12	3	100
greif(ue)	41	91	—	—	—	—
grief(ue)	3	7	7	88	—	—
heire (only)		10	5		2	
here	229	96	29	100	2	11
heere	9	4	—		17	89
here's	48	100	2	100	6	86
heeres	0		—		1	14
houre	1	2	8	100	1	50
howre	61	98	—		1	50
Ile	39	14	33	100	32	100
I'll	247	86	—		—	
indeed	46	100	11	100	2	40
indeede	—		—		3	60
mistris	22	85	1	13	5	100
mistresse	3	12	7	87	—	
mistrisse	1	3	—		—	
note (only)	27		8		3	
o	67	27	17	52	15	60
oh	179	73	16	48	10	40
shew	11	13	11	100	4	100
show	71	87	—		—	
traitor	17	89	1	34	3	100
traytor	2	11	2	66	—	
yeare	30	41	—		2	40
yeere	43	59	7	100	3	60
yong	47	98	—		5	100
young	1	2	9	100	—	

597

below 3, one finds that Compositor A agrees with Crane in preferring *blood, doe, n/ either, goe, heire, indeed*, and *note* but disagrees in preferring *beene, dear, grief, houre, Ile, mistresse, o, shew, yeere*, and *young*; and that Compositor B agrees in preferring *blood, n/either, here's, traitor, yeere*, and *yong* but disagrees in preferring *ancient, beene/bin, do, go, greef, heere, Ile, indeede, mistris, o*, and *shew*. HINMAN's (1:180) observation that "the spellings in the First Folio . . . are unquestionably printing-house spellings in the main — the spellings of the compositors who set them into type" is confirmed by the saving grace of "in the main."

Crane's Copy

Because Crane exerted such a strong influence on the form of the texts he transcribed, it is not surprising that critics find it difficult to penetrate his version of *WT* as it is represented in F1. GREG (1955, pp. 416–17) believes that *WT* was late reaching the printer only because of the time required to make for Jaggard a transcript of the foul papers, an opinion with which EVANS (ed. 1974, p. 1604) agrees. HOWARD-HILL (1965, p. 340), having protested against too facile an acceptance of numerous parentheses as indicative of Crane's transcription, suggests, nevertheless, that the number in *WT* may indicate that the play was printed from a Crane transcript of his own earlier transcript, an idea developed further by HOWARD-HILL a year later (1966, p. 140). When, according to HOWARD-HILL, "copy was being gathered for the Folio, Crane was given foul papers for *Winter's Tale* with instructions to prepare also the prompt-book for playhouse use. Crane prepared the promptbook first before making the transcript for the printer for by so doing he would release the foul papers in the shortest possible time to return to the security of the players' collection of manu-scripts. Had he prepared the Folio copy before the promptbook, we should not have the clean and sophisticated text, showing an unusually large number of parentheses, that we find in the Folio. On the same evidence, Crane apparently retained the promptbook, but probably returned the foul papers, so that he would avoid having to make both transcripts from foul papers. . . . He chose, therefore, to delay delivery of the Folio copy, perhaps thinking, or indeed knowing, that the printers had enough to go on with. [HOWARD-HILL (1992, p. 128) conjectures that the delay arose from Crane's occupation with his transcript of Webster's *Duchess of Malfi*.] From this order of events, we get a good, clean, literary text, with an unusually high number of pa-rentheses consistent with other Crane transcripts from his own earlier papers, and, of course, a delay which affected the printing of *Winter's Tale* in the First Folio." In his major work on Crane, HOWARD-HILL (1972, p. 131) adds, "The massed entries [appearing in F1 and deriving from the printer's copy] would have been out of place in a copy made for a promptbook but [they] easily could have been compiled from a transcript with conventional entries. Why he [Crane] should choose massed entries when he had a clean manuscript available is not readily explained, but the variety of the directions argues that the copy was prepared in some haste, under conditions which did not allow the scribe to adopt the massed convention completely."

The idea that the *WT* copy was a transcript of a transcript had appeared earlier in HOWARD-HILL (1965, pp. 337-8). The number of *WT*'s parentheses (371, 268), the article indicates, is substantially greater than that in the other Folio Comedies believed to have been set from Crane manuscripts—*Tmp.* 98 (115), *TGV* 128 (150), *Wiv.* 218 (241), and *MM* 75 (78); the first figure is the actual incidence and the second, the actual adjusted for the length of the plays. Since the Folio compositors did not have an identical fondness for parentheses, the figures adjusted for length become, when further adjusted to allow for Compositor A's preference, *Tmp.* 116, *TGV* 131, *Wiv.* 308, and *MM* 62, in contrast to *WT*'s 415. Moreover, Crane's several transcripts of *A Game at Chess* indicate that every time Crane recopied a text, he "tended to reproduce the parentheses of his copy, but added to them, and . . . added more parentheses when he was transcribing from his own copy" (p. 336). The *WT* transcript, HOWARD-HILL (1972, p. 70) observes, "must have been made after any other transcripts he made for the Folio. Therefore the scribe's habits would have been influenced both by the character of the copy before him, and by his increasing familiarity with the kind of material he had to work from."

A question about this theory arises from the massed entries. If they were undesirable in a promptbook, as HOWARD-HILL says, and if the *WT* promptbook was created before the printer's copy, would Crane, having copied in the first transcript the entrances where the play's action required them, have then taken the trouble to extract and compile these entries for each of the play's eight scenes they head? The compilation is incomplete, moreover (4.3 and 5.2, which might have been massed, are not), and the style of the massed entries differs (see p. 592). Crane's motive would have been professional pride or a classical preference (massed stage directions serve no essential literary or dramatic purpose), which he indulged even though, as noted above, "the copy was prepared in some haste, under conditions which did not allow the scribe to adopt the massed convention completely" (HOWARD-HILL, 1972, p. 131). In response, WELLS & TAYLOR (p. 601) state that "as the Folio had been printed [*WT* in Dec. 1622] long before Herbert saw the new prompt-book [on 19 Aug. 1623], this [HOWARD-HILL's explanation] seems unlikely. The original prompt-book might even have been lost as a result of being copied by Crane for the Folio." They also allude to THORNDIKE's idea that the dance of satyrs at 2164 was taken from Jonson's *Oberon* (see n. 2164): "The passage introducing this dance could be omitted without disturbing the dialogue; no one comments upon the dance afterwards; moreover, the Clown's comment that 'My Father, and the Gent. are in sad talke' [2134-5] would be naturally followed, after the exit of Autolycus and his clients, by Polixenes' 'O Father, you'l know more of that heereafter' [2165], which indicates that they have been carrying on a conversation which we have not heard. Polixenes' comment is not nearly so natural after the satyr dance, since it suggests that he had been talking to the Old Shepherd rather than attending to the dance he had himself insisted upon witnessing [2156-7]. There is no reason to doubt Shakespeare's authorship of the passage introducing the dance, but it could be a late addition; if so, Crane was copying a prompt-book, and the original composition was earlier than January 1611." (See p. 608.) Regarding the supposed unnaturalness of 2165, however, not one of the acting editions collated for this edition cuts it (see p. 819). Since there are no other traces of Crane's having copied *WT*'s promptbook, the apparent anomaly probably arises from an aberration in foul papers, toward which the clothing crux may also point (see n. 2557-8 and p. 845).

The foul papers of one of Sh.'s compositions— 147 lines of *Sir Thomas More*, a play of uncertain date originally by Anthony Munday and Henry Chettle—may have survived. Having been heavily censored by the Master of the Revels for political reasons, the play was parceled out to several playwrights for salvage. The 147 lines are indeed foul—punctuation lacking, SDs absent or incomplete, SPs mistaken or vague, words omitted, and verse mislined—but they have perhaps created too strong an impression of Sh.'s scribal carelessness. It may be true that Jaggard's "initial editorial policy called for scribal transcripts to be given to the printer if quartos were not available" (ECCLES, ed. *MM*, 1980, p. 293). Nevertheless, recent critical opinion, as represented by WELLS & TAYLOR (pp. 145-7), is that foul papers more or less certainly were the initial printer's copy for as many as 17 of the 35 plays included in F1. If this opinion is correct, the foul papers of *WT* could have served as Crane's copy as well.

Crane's Reliability

In about 1625, Crane transcribed Thomas Middleton's *The Witch* for a presentation by the author (see GREG, 1941-2). Three of the songs in this transcript are preserved in other versions. In 1625, Crane made a private transcript of Fletcher's *Demetrius and Enanthe, or the Humorous Lieutenant*, which may be compared with the independent text of the play published in the Beaumont and Fletcher folio of 1647, a version representing the play as cut for production (see Cyrus Hoy, ed., in *The Dramatic Works in the Beaumont and Fletcher Canon*, 5:293). NOSWORTHY (1965, p. 221), having examined these sources, concludes: "It is clear that Crane, though an elegant scribe, was at times an extraordinarily perfunctory one. Carelessness, combined with strange orthography, occasionally results in misreadings which would have baffled any compositor. . . . That he was, like many another scribe, occasionally guilty of sins of omission is a ready inference. . . . [Sh.] Folio texts based on Crane transcripts must obviously be viewed with suspicion. He was doubtless responsible for the sprinkling of apparent nonce-words which defy emendation, and there are often grounds for suspecting small omissions." HOWARD-HILL (1972, p. 133) differs, however: "Even when he [Crane] may be suspected of error, the reading of his transcript is at the least plausible. If his sophistication of the texts he transcribed had been less, more could be discovered of the nature of his copy. The 'goodness' of . . . *WT* means little more than that the printer's copy was free from obvious error. The general level of Crane's accuracy was high, but he was not reluctant to interfere with his text, consciously or unconsciously, when its meaning was obscure to him." That the F1 text of *WT* is not considered word-perfect is evident from the long history of its emendation recorded in this edition's textual notes; for a contrast of the repairs made by two recent eds., see p. 601 below.

The Printer's Reliability

There is almost no evidence of proofreading. As PAFFORD (1961, p. 178 n.) notes, "Some copies of F1 may have *a Bears*. [at 1500], but apparently in most it is *a Beare*." This possible press variant is not mentioned in his ed. 1963, however. HINMAN (1: 264) reports that page number 281 (sig. Aa3) is 285 in one copy (Folger 24) and that in about a third of the more than fifty copies he collated, a mark appears between the first *e* and the long *s* of *these* in 1880. One cannot be at all exact in judging the accuracy of the compositors, for their errors may have been corrected in an earlier stage of proof than the one that has survived, or they may have faithfully transmitted incorrect readings introduced by Crane. Nevertheless, it is interesting to observe that in a conservatively edited version of the play and a more radically edited version, the rate of error is similar. EVANS (ed. 1974) makes twenty substantive emendations:

> Compositor A: 175, 237, 290, 368, 1185, 1207, 2617, 2739–40, 2798, 2818–19, 3206
> Compositor B: 945, 1559, 1678, 1810, 1910, 2262, 2272, 2316, 3363

The Oxford editors (1986) emend in nineteen of these instances (2818–19 excepted) and nineteen more:

> Compositor A: 11, 213, 1353, 2464, 2488, 2530–1, 2588, 2751, 2795, 2821, 3191, 3302
> Compositor B: 896, 1617, 1811, 1965, 1980, 2184, 2266

Compositor A set 2,046 lines, or 61% of the text; Compositor B, 1,323 lines, or 39%. In EVANS's judgment, 55% of the play's substantive errors are found in A's work; in the Oxford editors', 57%. Compositor A may thus seem to have performed slightly more reliably than B in typesetting *WT*, but this estimate takes no account of errors made by Crane or resident in the MS he copied.

Subsequent Early Editions

The later history of *WT* in the 17th c. is told primarily by the entries in the Stationers' Register, quoted and annotated by GREG (1957, 3:1113–21). After the publication of F1, Isaac Jaggard's widow transferred "her parte in Shackspheere playes" to Thomas and Richard Cotes on 19(?) June 1627, and on 16 Nov. 1630 Edward Blount transferred his right to sixteen plays, including *WT*, to Robert Allot. The publication of F2 (1632) ensued; the work was printed by Thomas Cotes for Allot and four other stationers. This edition was twice reissued. Because Allot's widow was about to marry Philip Chetwind—who was a clothworker rather than a stationer—she was forced to give up her copies (on 7 November 1636; the Stationers' Register entry is dated 1 July 1637). Chetwind recovered the copyrights, however, and became the publisher of the two issues of F3 (1663–4), in the manufacture of which three printers participated. Yet the Stationers' Company continued to regard the copyrights as the property of Richard Cotes, and on 6 August 1674 transferred them (including the right to *WT*) to John Martin and Henry Herringman; these rights were again transferred by Martin's widow to Robert Scott, on 21 August 1683. F4 followed in 1685, its three sections (Comedies, Histories, and Tragedies) evidently having been printed simultaneously by three printers. Textual changes made in *WT* in the three derivative folios and in the principal later versions may be found in the notes of this edition. None of these changes has independent textual authority.

The Date of Composition

External Evidence

Early attempts to date *WT* were influenced by the opinion that so irregular a play must have been the work of an inexperienced playwright and by the entry dated 22 May 1594 in the Stationers' Register of "a booke entituled *a Wynters nightes pastime*" (ARBER, 1875–94, 2:650), which was taken to be *WT*. ULRICI (1839; trans. 1846, p. 269) wrote, for example, that "this is probably the same drama as we now have, which, upon its revision, received a name more suited to its altered form." The equation was not unreasonable, for the Accounts of the Revels at Court record a performance by the King's Men on 5 November 1611 of "A play called ye winters nightes Tayle" (see CUNNINGHAM, 1842, p. 210, and STREITBERGER, 1986, p. 48); CHAMBERS (1923, 4:125) identifies this later wintry amusement as *WT*.

Overly imaginative discoveries of allusions also interfered. WALPOLE (1768, 2: 114–16) thought that *WT* "was certainly intended (in compliment to queen Elizabeth) as an indirect apology for her mother Anne Boleyn. . . . [*115*] The unreasonable jealousy of Leontes, and his violent conduct in consequence, form a true portrait of Henry the Eighth, who generally made the law the engine of his boisterous passions. . . . Several passages . . . touch the real history nearer than the fable. Hermione on her trial says, ['For Honor, 'Tis a deriuatiue from me to mine, And onely that I stand for' (1217–19)]. This seems to be taken from the very letter of Anne Boleyn to the king before her execution, where she pleads for the infant princess his daughter." Adding several similar details, WALPOLE concludes (*116*): "The Winter Evening's Tale was therefore in reality a second part of Henry the Eighth." For the compliment to have point, Queen Elizabeth must have been alive to receive it; hence, in WALPOLE's view, *WT* preceded her demise, in 1603. The letter to which WALPOLE alludes is found in *The Harleian Miscellany* (1808, 1:201–2). According to *DNB* (s.v. ANNE), the letter is "a manifest fabrication of the time of Queen Elizabeth"; nevertheless, it speaks with pathetic dignity of the foul blots on the most dutiful wife and on the infant princess. A modernized text is in BLACK (1933, pp. 46–7).

Far-fetched notions abound. CAPELL (1783, 2.4:176) finds several absurd reasons to think that at the time he wrote *WT*, Sh. had his mind on a country matter, his retirement (e.g., the mention of "*th'Grange, or Mill*" at 2126). The play is "a writing *for* Stratford, or a writing at it." CAPELL dates the play 1613, after *H8* and before *Tmp.* (1614). Ironically, CAPELL is nearer current opinion than the more judicious MALONE (in STEEVENS, ed. 1778, 1:285). Influenced by the entry of *A Winter Night's Pastime*, "which might have been the same play," MALONE assigns *WT* to 1594, although his respect for WALPOLE, the silence of Francis Meres's *Palladis Tamia: Wit's Treasury* (1598), which mentions a dozen other Shn. titles, and the paucity of couplets in *WT* (characteristic of Sh.'s early style) make him "doubt whether it ought not to be ascribed to the year 1601, or 1602." By the time of his own edition of *WT* (MALONE, ed. 1790), he was convinced that *A Winter Night's Pastime* was not *WT*, and its removal from consideration made WALPOLE's conjecture "extremely plausible" (1.1: 350). Meanwhile, BLACKSTONE (in STEEVENS, ed. 1785) discovered in the lines "If I could find example Of thousand's that had struck anoynted Kings, And flourish'd after, Il'd not do't: But since Nor Brasse, nor Stone, nor Parchment beares not one, Let Villanie it selfe forswear't" (460–4) "an allusion to the death of the queen of Scots. The play therefore was written in king James's time." His argument is that an allusion to Mary, Queen of Scots, King James's mother, could never have been made before Queen Elizabeth's death, for Queen Elizabeth, however reluctantly, had consented to Queen Mary's execution. Trapped, MALONE (1.1:351) attempted to have it both ways: Sh. "lay'd the scheme of the play in the very year in which the queen died [1603], and finished it in the next." He discovers, however, in the Stationers' Register, 2 April 1604, the entry of *The Strange Report of a Monstruous Fishe* (see n. 2097– 2103), to which, he believes, Autolycus alludes, and he also finds the Puritan who sings psalms to hornpipes (1712–13) a corroborating detail, because (1.1:352) "the precise manners of the puritans was at this time much ridiculed by protestants." As for style, the meter is "less easy and flowing" than is usual in Sh.'s plays and the phraseology "more involved and parenthetical. . . . In this harshness of diction and involution of sentences it [*WT*] strongly resembles" *Tro.* and *H8*. The latter play is now dated 1612–13, not long after *WT*, but *Tro.* some ten years earlier. Nevertheless, MALONE knew that Jonson had alluded to *WT*, as well as to *Tmp.*, in the Induction to *Bartholomew Fair*, first produced in 1614 (see n. 0), and so again changed his mind (1.2:286): Jonson "joined these plays in the same censure, in consequence of their having been produced at no great distance of time from each other; and . . . *The Winter's Tale* ought to have been ascribed to the year 1613."

HURDIS (1792, pp. 22–3), is unconvinced: "The faults of its [*WT*'s] metre and its language are so numerous, that it must be ranked with [*Ant., H8, Cor.*, and *Cym.*], . . . the earliest efforts of our poet's muse." The "anointed kings" passage, HURDIS believes (p. 23), was inserted later. "The compliment he has paid to the Queen in the fable of the play . . . affords a strong proof that it was written during her lifetime. For it is not likely that he [Sh.] would endeavour to exculpate Anne Bullen in the reign of James." CHALMERS (1799, pp. 396–401)—whom F. W. CLARKE (in FUR-

NIVALL, ed. 1908, p. ix) calls "the Sir Politick-Would-Be of Shakespearean criticism" — observes several historical allusions in *WT* but not BLACKSTONE's, for, CHALMERS says, BLACKSTONE's mind was "not very amply stored with historical knowledge" of the Elizabethan period. He believes that the lines BLACKSTONE cited — "If I could find example Of thousand's that had struck anoynted Kings" (460- 1) — reflect the public prayers offered for the queen after the failure of Essex's rebellion; an allusion such as "Heire-lesse it hath made my Kingdome" (2737) would have been inappropriate in King James's time, for he had heirs. Thus, CHALMERS concludes, *WT* was written in 1601. Also rejecting BLACKSTONE and his use of the execution of the Queen of Scots as evidence, DOUCE (1807, 1:347) notes: "The perpetrator of that atrocious murder *did flourish* many years afterwards." DOUCE therefore thinks the allusion in lines 460- 4 is to King James's escape from the Gowrie conspiracy (1582), "an event often brought to the people's recollection during his reign."

Opposition to such fanciful guessing was bound to arise. BOSWELL (ed. 1821, 14: 234- 5), for example: "I confess I am very sceptical as to these supposed allusions by [235] Shakspeare to the history of his own time. If the plots of his plays had been of his own invention, he might possibly have framed them with a view of that kind; but this was unquestionably not the case with the play before us; and if any one had intended a courtly defence of Queen Elizabeth's mother, it must have been Greene, and not Shakspeare. Garinter, the Mamillius of our poet, dies under the same circum-stances, in the novel [see p. 632]; nor is it, as Mr. Walpole seemed to suppose, an unnecessary incident, because it fulfils the declaration of the oracle, 'that if the child which was lost could not be found, the king would die without an heir' [1315- 16]. To say that a child resembles her father is surely not so uncommon a remark as to make it evident that it had reference to a particular individual; nor is there any thing very courtly or complimentary in Paulina's angry allusion to the old proverb."

Moreover, MALONE had already found the clue needed to begin working through the early speculations, although he did not immediately recognize its value. In his "Historical Account of the Rise and Progress of the English Stage" (ed. 1790, 1.2:1- 284), MALONE first makes use of a document that has since disappeared, the office book of Sir Henry Herbert, Master of the Revels to King James. As CHAMBERS (1930, 2:347) explains, the "*Office Book* of Sir Henry Herbert, Master of the Revels, . . . is now lost, but in 1790 was in the house of Francis Ingram at Ribbesford, Worcester-shire, which had belonged to Herbert." MALONE (1.2:226) quotes Herbert's memo-randum: "For the king's players. An olde playe called *Winters Tale*, formerly allowed of by Sir George Bucke, and likewyse by mee on Mr. Hemmings his worde that there was nothing prophane added or reformed, thogh the allowed booke was missinge; and therefore I returned itt without a fee, this 19 of August, 1623." *Book* in this context is probably the technical term for the prompt copy of the play on which the license to act was inscribed (see GREG, 1931, 1:192- 3), although POLLARD (1920, p. 67) had thought that the term "possibly [referred to] the original manuscript." Bucke, or Buc, was Master of the Revels from 1610 to 1622; Hemmings, or Heminge, was an actor with, and the business manager of, the King's Men.

George Buc had served as deputy Master from 1603, however, and CHALMERS

(1799, pp. 200 ff.) prints extracts from the Stationers' Registers showing Buc as licenser for the printing of plays as early as 1606. MALONE may or may not be right that Buc did not license plays for performance before he became Master (see ECCLES, 1933, p. 458). Thus critics like ROLFE (ed. 1879, p. 10 n.), who asserts that "the *Stationers' Registers* show . . . that he [Buc] had practically the control of the office from the year 1607," are saying more than the entries in the Registers prove. The same applies to critics like WICKHAM (1973, p. 96 n.); they maintain that until his official installation as Master, Buc licensed for printing only. ALBRIGHT (1927, p. 246), incidentally, asserts that *WT* was relicensed to prevent its being "taken over by another company because it was in print," but GREG (1928, p. 96) points out the obvious—that Buc acted not for ALBRIGHT's reason "but because the authorised copy had been lost." That copy was apparently on hand when the play was acted at court on 7 April 1618 and perhaps in 1619 as well (see below, p. 798); as BALDWIN (*Division*, 1965, p. 51) notes, its absence may have been discovered when the company began to prepare for the court performance of 18 January 1624 (see p. 798). GREG (1954, p. 150): "*The Winter's Tale* is peculiar in that it may have been a late addition to the folio, and that a new prompt-book was licensed by Herbert in August 1623. . . . These facts are probably related, but it is not clear that they have any bearing on the nature of the text."

DRAKE (1817, 1:504–5), convinced that *Tmp.* "was written towards the close of 1611," argues (1:497) that *WT* was written "towards the close of 1610" and was "*licensed* and *performed* during the succeeding year." The order of the two plays is assumed to be that in which they were named by Jonson. Without mentioning DRAKE, MALONE (in BOSWELL, ed. 1821, 2:463) states: "I . . . suppose The Winter's Tale to have been originally licensed by him [Buc] in the latter part of that year [1610] or the beginning of the next." He therefore assigns the play to 1611. Although DUTTON (1991, p. 151) finds "no cogent evidence that Buc was involved . . . in the censoring of plays *for performance*, prior to Tilney's death," critics by and large have accepted MALONE's *terminus a quo*. According to HALLIWELL (ed. 1859, 8:40), for example, "In the absence of any direct evidence to the contrary, it seems . . . unnecessary to suggest that the Winter's Tale may have been one of the dramas that passed under Buck's review during the tenancy of Tylney in the office; and it may fairly, at present, be taken for granted that the comedy was not produced until after the month of August, 1610." HUNTER (1845, 1:416) believes that prior to 1610, Buc licensed both for performance and for printing; on the basis of a supposed affinity of *WT* with *TN*, he dates *WT* "not later than 1601 or 1602"—or, if licensing by Buc must be taken into account, 1606, the year after the Gunpowder Plot, because of the "anointed kings" passage (see n. 460–4). As for the absence of the allowed copy, MALONE suggests that it was destroyed in the Globe fire of 1613, but CHAMBERS (1930, 1:488) disagrees, pointing out that there was a performance in 1618 and "probably another about 1619." The former is attested by CUNNINGHAM (1842, p. xlv): "To John Heminges &c upon a warrant dated 20 April 1618 for presenting two severall Playes before his Ma^{ty}. on Easter Monday Twelfte night the play soe called and on Easter Tuesday the Winter's Tale xx^{li}." The latter is inferred from the appearance of "The Winters

Tale" on a piece of waste paper from the Revels Office (see MARCHAM, 1925, pp. 7, 13).

Important new evidence of *WT*'s date came to light with the discovery of a passage in Simon Forman's "Bocke of Plaies" (Bodleian Library MS Ashmole 208, fols. 201ᵛ-202). As PAFFORD ("Forman," 1959, pp. 289-90) remarks, "W. H. Black began to catalogue the Ashmole manuscripts in 1830 or 1831, and there is a note by Black on a proof-sheet of the catalogue against [*290*] the entry of the 'Bocke of Plaies' which reads 'I made a transcript of this curious article, in 1832, for my friend J. P. Collier.'" The so-called Book of Plays consists of memoranda made in 1611 by Forman after seeing four plays at the Globe — *Macbeth, Cymbeline, Richard II* (not Sh.'s), and *WT*. Of *WT* he wrote:

> IN the Winters Talle at the glob 1611 the 15 of maye ☿ [Wednesday]
> Obserue ther howe Lyontes the kinge of Cicillia was overcom wᵗʰ Ielosy of his wife with the kinge of Bohemia his frind that came to see him. and howe he Contriued his death and wold haue had his cup berer to haue poisoned. who gaue the king of bohemia warning therof & fled with him to bohemia/Remēber also howe he sent to the Orakell of appollo & the Aunswer of apollo. that she was giltles. and that the king was Ielouse &c and howe Except the child was found Again that was loste the kinge should die wᵗʰout yssue. for the child was caried into bohemia & ther laid in a forrest & brought vp by a sheppard And the kinge of bohemiā his sonn maried that wentch & howe they fled into Cicillia to Leontes. and the sheppard hauing showed the letter of the noble man by whom Leontes sent a was [away? it was?] that child and the Iewells found about her. she was knowen to be leontes daughter and was then 16 yers old
> Remember also the Rog that cam in all tottered like coll pixci /. and howe he feyned him sicke & to haue bin Robbed of all that he had and howe he cosoned the por man of all his money. and after cam to the shep sher with a pedlers packe & ther cosoned them Again of all ther money And howe he changed apparrell wᵗʰ the kinge of bomia his sonn. and then howe he turned Courtiar &c / beware of trustinge feined beggars or fawninge fellouse.

This transcription appears in EVANS (ed. 1974, p. 1842). It agrees in all but a few insignificant details with those given by PAFFORD (ed. 1963, pp. xxi-xxii) and by CHAMBERS (1930, 2:340-1). *Coll pixci*, or *Colt-pixie*, means "a mischievous sprite or fairy" (*OED*); QUILLER-COUCH (ed. 1931, p. viii) gives "a shaggy goblin-horse" (GROSE, 1787). About the memorandum, QUILLER-COUCH observes: "If we may draw the inference, Forman's rather elaborate description of the plot seems to indicate that *The Winter's Tale* was in May 1611 a new play." The *WT* summary is actually no more elaborate than the summaries of *Mac.* (1606) and *Cym.* (1609-10?). BULLOUGH (1975, 8:118), commenting on whether there might have been an earlier version of *WT*: "Forman's summary of what he saw omits the statue, but since his account of *Cymbeline* omits the dénouement no argument can be drawn that on 15 May 1611 the play lacked the climactic scene."

Forman's notes were first published by COLLIER (1836, p. 20), in a somewhat modernized version. As COLLIER's forgeries and impostures were revealed, Forman's

Book of Plays also fell under suspicion, but W. H. Black's note proves it genuine. Further authentication became available with the publication by CUNNINGHAM (1842) of extracts from the Revels Accounts, in which the performance of *WT* on 5 November 1611, mentioned above, is recorded. COLLIER (ed. 1842, 3:425–6), however: "'The Tempest' and 'The Winter's Tale' were both acted at Whitehall, and included in Sir George Buc's account of the expenses of the Revels from October, 1611, to October, 1612. How much older 'The Tempest' might be than 'The Winter's Tale', we have no means of determining; but there is a circumstance which shows that the composition of 'The Tempest' was anterior to that of 'The Winter's Tale'. . . . [*426*] There is . . . one remarkable variation [between *Pandosto* and *WT*]; in the former the infant Fawnia is put into a boat ['to be carried into the midst of the sea, and there left to the wind and wave']. Shakespeare . . . describes the way in which the infant [Perdita] was exposed very differently, and probably for this reason:—that in 'The Tempest' he had previously (perhaps not long before) represented Prospero and Miranda turned adrift at sea in the same manner [as Fawnia]. When, therefore, Shakespeare came to write 'The Winter's Tale' . . . he varied from the original narrative, in order to avoid an objectionable similarity of incident in his two dramas." Although COLLIER may be mistaken that *Tmp.* is the earlier play, his opinion carried some weight; it is quoted with approval later, by HUDSON (ed. 1852, 4:6), for example, and it reappears in MUIR (1957, p. 243): "Possibly the first version of *The Tempest* had been written before *The Winter's Tale*, so that Shakespeare could not easily repeat the incident of the babe adrift in a boat." That there was more than one version of *Tmp.* is a supposition, however, that disappears from MUIR (1977). Nevertheless, it is possible that *Tmp.* antedates *WT*. According to ORGEL (ed. *Tmp.*, 1987, pp. 63–4), "There is . . . not . . . any way of determining chronological priority between *The Tempest* and *The Winter's Tale*. . . . [*64*] The most we can say is that the evidence supports a date of late 1610 to mid-1611 [for *Tmp.*], and that Shakespeare was writing the play just after, or just before, or at the same time as *The Winter's Tale*." HALLIWELL (ed. 1859, 8:44): "With equal probability, it might be conjectured that Shakespeare, having omitted the incident in the construction of the Winter's Tale, introduced it in the Tempest as one especially suited to a romantic drama of that description."

Another approach is represented by PROCTER (1844, 1:x–xi), who finds *WT* too badly written to be a late play: "As a general principle, . . . I would say, that the plays in which signs of imitation (particularly imitation of style) are manifest, should be accounted the earliest; and that those wherein the poetry is redundant and far exceeds the necessities and purposes of the story, should be held to have preceded, in point of time, the great and substantial dramas, in which the business of the play is skilfully wrought out, and where the poetry springs out of the passion or humour of the characters, and serves to illustrate and not to oppress them. In conformity with this view, I think that the [*xi*] 'WINTER'S TALE', although perhaps not actually performed until the year 1611, can never have been the last work of Shakspere. It is far more like the labour of his youth," an idea to be revived seventy-five years later on supposedly scientific as well as impressionistic evidence (see p. 610). Nevertheless, by the time of HUDSON (ed. 1852, 4:6), the composition of *WT* was assigned to "the winter of 1610-11." The later limit is 15 May 1611, when Forman saw the play. The earlier limit, THORNDIKE (1900, pp. 116-17) argues, was shortly after 1 January 1611, the date of the performance at court of Ben Jonson's *Oberon*, the action of which opens upon Silenus, a shaggy old forest god, and at least five of the satyrs over whom he presides (the number who speak). For the probable reappearance of three of these satyrs in *WT*, see n. 2164 and p. 855. The "shortly" arises from the assumption that the three saltiers who danced before the king (2158-9) must have done so recently in order for the audience, or at least the members of it who knew about courtly amusements, to grasp the allusion and perhaps also in order for the men still to be available to perform in *WT*. Yet the line is spoken in modern performances, its significance having become that the three will unknowingly dance before the king once more—that is, King Polixenes. It possibly never meant more than this. Moreover, as NICOLL suggests (see n. 2164), the satyr dance could be an interpolation. Thus *WT* may have no precise anterior limit, but, as WELLS & TAYLOR (1987, p. 601) point out, if the Crane transcript from which the F text was typeset derived from the promptbook, "the original composition predates January 1611" (see p. 599).

Two attempts to prove *WT* an occasional play were made by WICKHAM (*"The Winter's Tale*," 1969, and "Investiture," 1969), in the second of which the first is summarized: "Critical discussion of *The Winter's Tale* has centred on the sixteen-year gap dividing the Sicilian court scenes from the Bohemian pastoral scenes bridged only by *Time* as Chorus. . . . This odd structural pattern may have stemmed from a deliberate emblematic purpose. Since the skeleton of the plot is the fusing of seemingly irreconcilable opposites, and as nowhere in contemporary politics were such opposites more glaringly apparent than in Anglo-Scottish relations . . . Shakespeare deliberately reworked (and altered) . . . *Pandosto* at a narrative level in order to reflect emblematically the reunion of the British Isles under his master, James I. The datum point was the legend of the division of Britain by King Brutus among his three sons and Merlin's prophecy of eventual reunion under a descendant of King Arthur. Henry VII had seen himself as that descendant and James viewed his own claim to the crowns of Scotland and England through Henry's daughter Margaret (James's great-great-grandmother) as the fulfillment of the prophecy." WICKHAM continues: "*The Winter's Tale* may be regarded not only as a figurative compliment to James I, but also Shakespeare's contribution to the investiture of Henry, Prince of Wales and Heir Apparent, in 1610. The evidence is drawn from two pageants by Anthony Munday, two masques by Ben Jonson, a poem and a masque by Samuel Daniel, three of James I's own speeches and two statues," the memorial effigies of Queen Elizabeth and Mary, Queen of Scots, commissioned by King James and placed on the queens' tombs in Westminster Abbey. Examination of this evidence "combines to designate *The Winter's Tale* as written for performance in the autumn of 1610 before the King and the Heir Apparent . . . ; to reveal it as [figuring] the mystical marriage of Prince Henry (Florizel) to the three kingdoms whose original unity was lost but has been found (Perdita) thanks to 'Time' and King James' own 'piaculous action'; and finally to show that, by substituting for the dead Queen of Greene's novel the living statue of Hermione . . . , Shakespeare created a work of art which was as effective an emblem for his court audience as it was enjoyable dramatic romance for his wider public in the city." EVERETT (1970) supports WICKHAM's parallel of Hermione and Mary, Queen of Scots: "Hermione's blend of royal dignity and pathos . . . [is] expressed in *The Winter's Tale* by a few phrases so like echoes of Mary's words [as given by Antonia Fraser in *Mary, Queen of Scots,* 1969] as to suggest the possibility of a real connexion. Mary told the deputation of lords who came to announce her trial: 'I am myself a Queen, the daughter of a King'. Hermione refers to herself during her trial as 'a great king's daughter' [1213], and later . . . says, 'The Emperor of Russia was my father' [1299]." Having cited several similar parallels, EVERETT concludes, "There is, in short, enough dignity and pathos in the Jacobean (as distinct from the Elizabethan) image of Mary Stuart, to give an added interest to Shakespeare's creation of Hermione, perhaps his queenliest heroine."

Apart from EVERETT, however, WICKHAM's topicality seems to have attracted no supporters. Regarding the statues of the two dead queens, SMITH (1972, pp. 217-18) observes: If either "had anything to do with *The Winter's Tale*, it would seem to be Mary's, not Elizabeth's; Mary could in some sense be thought to be resurrected by the investiture of her grandson as Prince of Wales. The trouble is that Mary's statue was not finished until 1612 . . . and by this time *The Winter's Tale* had been on the stage for two years. But Wickham, undismayed, says [in "Heritage," 1969] the sculptors lived in Southwark . . . and Shakespeare could have dropped in at their studio any time from 1606 to 1610 to see [*218*] how the statue was coming. On this frail evidence we are asked to believe that Florizel represents Prince Henry." Nevertheless, these ideas are reiterated and further developed in WICKHAM (1973). BULLOUGH (1975, 8:117) objects, though: "It is going too far to suggest that the play 'figures the mystical marriage of Prince Henry (Florizel) to the three kingdoms whose original unity was lost but had been found (Perdita).' . . . If there was such an allegorical intention why did not Shakespeare make Florizel (like Greene's Dorastus) rule over two kingdoms at the end of the play?" To which it might be replied that Florizel, as Perdita's consort and Mamillius reborn, will reign over two kingdoms, although that fact will hardly save WICKHAM's case.

Internal Evidence

As FURNESS (ed. 1898, p. 316) says, RODERICK (1758, p. 225) was apparently the first to observe that the verse lines of *H8* more frequently than those of other plays "end in a redundant syllable." MALONE (in STEEVENS, ed. 1778, 1:280 n.) adds that a mixture of rhyming lines and blank verse is "a circumstance which seems to characterize and distinguish our poet's earliest performance." From these beginnings developed a close study of Sh.'s style to determine, more exactly than external evidence allows, when he wrote his works.

The earliest critic to divide Sh.'s career into four periods distinguished by stylistic differences was BATHURST (1857). By the third quarter of the 19th c., one of the internal tests of chronology given by WARD (1875, 1:359-63) was versification, subdivided as follows: (a) Rhyme: "Progress from more to less rhyme may be held to accompany the general progress of Shakspere as a dramatic writer." (b) Stopped and unstopped lines: "A 'stopped' line is one in which the sentence, or clause of the sentence, concludes with the line; but it is not always possible to determine what is to be regarded as the clause of the sentence, whether *e.g. and* is to be regarded . . . as beginning a new clause. The stopping of the sense is . . . often of more importance than the 'stopping' of the sentence." (c) Feminine endings, or line endings with an eleventh, unaccented, syllable: "While it is certain that Shakspere employed the feminine endings sparingly in many of his plays . . . regarded as early, it is certain that in those plays which on other grounds may be regarded as . . . late . . . he employed these endings largely." WARD's examples, supplied by FLEAY, include *Shr.* (now dated 1593-4), line 260, and *WT* 639, but also *R3* (1592-3), line 570. The tabulations are not adjusted for the length of the plays or the proportions in them of verse and prose. And (d) Other verse tests, such as irregularities in the trimeter couplets of the early plays and, in the late plays, such carelessness as the failure to mark the caesura.

FLEAY himself (1876) divides Sh.'s career into periods characterized by more or less distinct metrical features. In the last period (pp. 70-1), doggerel, alternately rhyming lines, and couplets are absent; alexandrines, with considerable variation in the position of the caesura, increase; and so do feminine endings; and so do "lines of less than five measures." FLEAY assigns *WT* (p. 136), along with *Cym., Cor., Ant.,* and *Tmp.*, to Sh.'s fourth (and last) period, but in a postscript (p. 138) creates a fifth period for *Tmp.* and *WT* alone. The actual date he assigns to *WT* is 1610-11 (p. 54) or 1611 (p. 130), 1611? having earlier been proposed by FURNIVALL (1874, p. xlv). Later, FLEAY (1886, p. 65) decides that *WT* "was certainly produced early this year [1610], before Jonson's *Alchemist*, which was acted and entered S[tationers'] R[egister] October 3." FLEAY's techniques and conclusions raised questions immediately (see the discussion following the reading of his paper before the New Shakspere Society on 13 Mar. 1874, in FLEAY, 1874), and he changed his mind as his investigations continued. In any event, his date for *WT* was not affected; in the 1886 work (p. 247) as in the 1874 volume (p. 10), it is 1610. By introducing this type of analysis, FLEAY hoped to apply a scientific technique to the problems of Shn. chronology, but his followers proved capable of wild variations in method and conclusions, and he himself could not count.

The predilection for Shn. statistics, however, extends to BATHER's "Table of Plays, According to Number of Puns" (1887, p. 74), which shows a decrease in the number of puns per 100 lines from 3.97 in *LLL* to 0.26 in *WT*. As a technique for dating, the scheme is demolished by the fact that *Tit.* contains only 0.15 and *3H6* only 0.14. BAYFIELD's (1920, pp. 402-3) verse analysis reveals that *WT* "must have been written some years before the generally received date 1610. . . . It suggests that the performance at the Globe theatre on May 15, 1611 . . . must refer to a revival. . . . [*403*] [*WT*'s] versification is in fact of a quite different period [from that of the late plays. *WT* was written] near *Troilus and Cressida, The Taming of the Shrew*, and *Timon*.'' On the other hand, impressionistic critics who did not conduct verse tests could also reach strange conclusions. SPENS (1922, p. 92), for example, ''suspects that all the Romances . . . were written originally by Shakespeare at the very beginning of his career, and that they were for the most part one or two act pieces forming part of a series.'' MATHEW (1922, p. 41) agrees in part: ''These Plays were written first when Shakespeare was young and revised when he was mature.''

The testimony of internal evidence is usually linked to the historical and practical facts of Sh.'s career, the latter being, for instance, that Sh. could not write more than a certain amount in a certain period, about two plays a year when his known work is distributed over the period during which he is believed to have been active. The distribution may also be colored by assumptions, not necessarily wrong, about Sh.'s development as a man and an artist. As DOWDEN (1877, pp. 37–41) puts it, ''We need no scientific test to make us aware that, in passing from *Love's Labour's Lost* to *Hamlet*, and from *Hamlet* to *The Tempest*, we pass from youth to manhood, and again from a manhood of trial and sorrow to a riper manhood of attainment and of calm.'' Affected by the transitions are (*a*) style and diction. ''In the earliest plays . . . the idea is at times hardly sufficient to fill out the language in which it is put; in the middle plays . . . there seems a perfect balance and equality between the thought and its expression[; in the latest] this balance is disturbed by the preponderance or excess of the ideas over the means of giving them utterance. . . . (*b*) The growth of Shakspere's taste and judgment. . . . [*38*] (*c*) In the structure of the play and grouping of characters there is, in some of the early plays, a tendency to formal symmetry, an artificial setting of character over against character, and group against group. . . . Afterwards the outline of the play is drawn with a freer because a firmer hand. (*d*) . . . By degrees the characterisation becomes profound and refined. . . . (*e*) The entire reflective power deepens. . . . (*f*) The imagination . . . becomes passionately energetic, of daring and all-comprehensive power, as in *King Lear*, or lofty and sustained, with noble ideality, as in *The Tempest*. (*g*) The sympathy with human passion and the power of conceiving and dramatically rendering it in its most massive and most intense [*39*] forms increases. (*h*) . . . The humour of the dramatist . . . becomes full of grave significance, and works in conjunction with his (*i*) Deepening pathos. . . . (*j*) Finally, in moral reach, in true justice, in charity, in self-control, in all that indicate fortitude of will, the writings of the mature Shakspere excel, in an extraordinary degree, those of his younger self.'' These characteristics obviously cannot be quantified, but the alteration in Sh.'s verse can be. ''At first Shakspere has his breaks and pauses at the end of the line—the verse is 'end-stopt'; gradually he more and more [carries] on the sense from one line to another without a pause at the end of the line [but] in some part of the line other than the end.'' Light and weak endings increase. The first group, in DOWDEN's classification, encompasses words on which (p. 41) ''the voice can to a small extent dwell'' (*am, are, be, can, could;* the auxiliaries *do, does, has, had; I, they, thou*). The weak endings are "more fugitive and evanescent . . . , including such words as *and, for, from, if, in, of, or.* Now weak endings hardly appear in Shakspere's early or middle plays. . . . Nor do they come in by slow degrees at a later period. . . . In *Macbeth* light endings appear for the first time in considerable numbers; weak endings in considerable numbers for the first time in *Antony and Cleopatra.* This test serves perfectly to pick out the plays which form the group belonging to Shakspere's last period of dramatic authorship; and within that period it probably serves to indicate nearly the precise order in which the plays were written." DOWDEN reproduces part of a table devised by INGRAM (1874, p. 450) showing percentages of light and weak endings, from *Mac.* through *H8*, in a sequence that does not quite bear DOWDEN out, in that it places *Tmp.* earlier than *Cym.* and *WT.* Similarly, DOWDEN reproduces a table he attributes to HERTZBERG; it shows the percentage of double, or feminine, endings increasing from *LLL* (4) through *Tmp.* and puts *WT* (31.09) before *Cym.* (32) by a whisker. Actually, the table HERTZBERG published (1878, p. 252) reverses the sequence (*WT* 32.5), but in neither accounting is the difference great enough to establish priority. (Similar data from which similar conclusions were drawn persisted; see, for example, NEILSON & THORN-DIKE, c. 1913, pp. 69–75.)

The history of stylistic analysis and the efforts of other contributors to it are described in detail by CHAMBERS (1930, 1:242–74). As a prelude to his own assignment of dates, he provides a thorough discussion of the problem of chronology, an evaluation of the evidence of dates, and (in 2:397–408) his own metrical tables, several of them corrected versions of FLEAY's. He believes (1:489) that "the style and metre group *Winter's Tale* with *Cymbeline* and *Tempest*, and it may reasonably be placed between them. A date early in 1611 is suggested by the probability that the bear of iii.3 and the dance of satyrs at [2164] were both inspired by Jonson's mask of *Oberon* on 1 January 1611." For the bear, see n. 1500, and for the satyrs, n. 2164. GRAY (1931, p. 148) averages "the percentages of double [i.e., feminine] endings, run-on lines, and speeches ending with the line" and discovers that the results for *WT, Tmp.,* and *Cym.,* though close to those for *Cor.* on the earlier side and *H8* on the later, are also close to each other. Having related independent clauses to verse lines, LANGWORTHY (1931, p. 748) gets similar results for the same plays, although his data order them as *Tmp., Cym.,* and *WT.* LAW (1936, pp. 50–1) tabulates the dates assigned by ADAMS (1923), ALDEN (1925), CHAMBERS (1930), CRAIG (ed. 1931), CAMPBELL (1932), PARROTT (1934), and BROOKE (ed. 1935). All give 1610 or 1610–11. So does REINHOLD (1942, p. 87); like ORAS (see below), REINHOLD calculates split lines (pentameters shared by two or more speakers) as a percentage of the total lines in each play to show that their number generally increases with time. In an early statistical study, YARDI (1946) uses multiple measurements of metrical data for the discrimination of groups; the results place *WT* with *Cym.* and *Tmp.* but do not provide actual dates. BRAINERD's (1980) statistical study of Shn. chronology has no bearing, for *WT,* dated 1610.5, is a member of the test set, plays for the most part unambiguously dated.

A few recent critics dissent. WENTERSDORF (1951, p. 178), combining such stylistic features as split lines, extra syllables within and at the end of lines, feminine endings, and alexandrines into a metrical index for each play, finds the three last to have been written in CHAMBERS'S (1930) order, but he moves each work back by a year, *WT* to 1609-10. As *Tmp.* was performed at court on 1 November 1611, it would have been acted publicly "at least by the summer of 1611," since public success presumably preceded the selection of any play for presentation at court. If the dance of satyrs in *WT* derives from Jonson's *Oberon*, *WT* may nevertheless have been in existence prior to January 1611, when the masque was performed, and the satyrs subsequently added. "It has also been suggested that the bear scene in Act iii was borrowed from . . . 'Mucedorus', which was revived by the King's Men shortly before 1610. If this was the case (as the bear episode is not in Shakespeare's source for *WT*), it points to an upward [i.e., anterior] time limit late in 1609. . . . Finally, the reference at [461] is sufficiently motivated by the story and in any case too general to warrant interpretation to the murder of Henri IV on 14 May 1610" (see CHAMBERS, 1930, 2:489). Having assigned *Per.* to 1607-8 and *Tmp.* to 1610-11, WENTERSDORF accordingly dates *Cym.* and *WT* 1608-9 and 1609-10, respectively. Also dissenting is ORAS (1960), who studies three types of pauses in the verse of Sh. and a number of other early writers, under three heads: all pauses indicated by the internal punctuation of the earliest eds. (A-patterns); strong pauses indicated by punctuation heavier than commas (B-patterns); and lines shared by two or more speakers — split lines — (C-patterns). That the punctuation may be scribal or compositorial is recognized, but it is still considered a valid marker because its source is contemporaneous. The data are presented numerically and graphically, and although no actual dates are assigned, the patterns of *Cym.* and *WT* resemble each other more strongly than they resemble the patterns of the other works studied.

ALEXANDER (ed. 1951, p. xv), wisely declining to be pinned down to more than "an approximate order of composition," places *WT*, along with *Per.*, *Cym.*, *Tmp.*, and *H8*, between 1608 and 1613. MAXWELL (ed. *Cym.*, 1960, p. xi), commenting on 1609-10 and 1610-11 for the dates of *Cym.* and *WT*, respectively: "It is reasonable to associate the greater artistic assurance of *The Winter's Tale* with a later date [than *Cym.*'s], which is also supported by the fact that Shakespeare undoubtedly knew the Boccaccio source of *Cymbeline* when he wrote *The Winter's Tale*. I think [the 1610-11] date for *The Winter's Tale* may well be a year too late. There is a fairly close verbal parallel between *The Winter's Tale* [1941-7] and *Philaster* [4.6.2-8], which seems to me most easily explained as an echo of the former by the latter; and *Philaster* is not later than 8 October 1610 [see CHAMBERS, 1923, 3:223]." To TILLYARD (1938, pp. 9-10), however, the echoes seem reversed: Sh. is improving Fletcher (see n. 1941-7). In any case, as PAFFORD (ed. 1963, p. 97 n.) remarks, the strewing of corpses as well as bridal beds with flowers is a common idea.

As for the presence of *Cym.*'s source in *WT*, the story in question is the ninth novel of the second day of Boccaccio's *Decameron*. MUIR (1977, pp. 262-3) summarizes it: "Some Italian merchants at an inn in Paris deride the idea of a female chastity and Bernabo of Genoa is provoked by Ambrogiuolo to bet on the chastity of his wife, Ginevra. On going to Genoa, Ambrogiuolo realizes that he cannot seduce Ginevra. Concealed in a chest, he is able to observe the pictures of her bedroom, to steal a ring and other belongings, and to observe a mole on the lady's breast. Bernabo is convinced that he has lost the wager and he orders his servant to murder Ginevra. The servant, convinced of her innocence, spares her. She dresses in his clothes and takes service with the Soldan. One day she sees her purse and girdle in a stall in the market-place. When the truth comes to light, Ginevra reveals herself to her husband and forgives him. The villain is tortured to death:

> the verie same day that hee was impaled on the stake, annointed with honey, and fixed
> in the place appointed, to his no meane tormente: he not onely died, but likewise was
> deuoured to the bare [263] bones, by Flies, Waspes, and Hornets, whereof the Countrey
> notoriously aboundeth.

As Iachimo is forgiven, this torture is not used in *Cymbeline*; but in *The Winter's Tale* Autolycus tells the Clown [2665–72]." SMITH (1972, p. 216) holds that "it is generally agreed . . . that *The Winter's Tale* is the later of the two [because] the use of the leftover passage about the punishment of the villain . . . suggests that *The Winter's Tale* followed *Cymbeline*."

Earlier, however, NOSWORTHY (ed. *Cym.*, 1955, pp. xvi–xvii), instead of drawing this conclusion, recognizes "the possibility that Shakespeare owed the name 'Belarius' [in *Cym.*] to the Bellaria of Greene's *Pandosto* . . . so that the evidence can point either way. My own guess is that the composition of the two plays was more or less simultaneous or, at any rate, that both had been written, revised and prepared for the stage before either was actually performed, with consequent cross-fertilisation. This view . . . tallies with the attractive theory, put forward by [BENTLEY, 1948], that the impending acquisition of the Blackfriars private theatre led, in the Spring and Summer of 1608, to discussions among the King's Players as a result of which Shakespeare was henceforth to write with the Blackfriars in mind, and not the Globe, and that [*Cym.*, *WT*, and *Tmp.*,] in that [xvii] order, were the fruits of that decision. BENTLEY says nothing about their respective dates, but the application of his theory would . . . suggest 1608 for the first play of the series." Recalling that it was at the public theater that Forman saw *WT*, NOSWORTHY demurs at "and not the Globe," preferring to think that after his company acquired the Blackfriars theater in 1608, Sh. wrote dual-purpose plays, "for such, most emphatically and triumphantly, the Romances are." If *Cym.*, the first play of the series, was composed in 1608, 1608–9 would presumably be the date of *WT*. Although PAFFORD (ed. 1963, p. xxiii) does not deal explicitly with NOSWORTHY's idea, he comments: "The language, style, and spirit of the play all point to a late date. The tangled speech, the packed sentences, speeches which begin and end in the middle of a line, and the high percentage of light and weak endings are all marks of Shakespeare's writing at the end of his career. But of more importance than verse tests is the similarity of the last plays in spirit and themes. . . . Practically all authorities . . . accept, with minor variations, the approximate dates given by Chambers [i.e., 1610-11]." Those who do not follow CHAMBERS may instead favor WENTERSDORF—for example, FITCH (1981, p. 300), who, in a revival of sense-pause investigation, decides on 1609-10.

Summary

A comprehensive reexamination of the internal evidence of *WT*'s date is made by TAYLOR (in WELLS & TAYLOR, 1987, pp. 93-109). Among the data included are the percentage of rhyme to verse and to prose; colloquialisms in verse (e.g., *i'th'*, *'em*, *'ll*, *I'm*), which show "that Shakespeare's reversion to an antiquated dramatic form [the romance] apparently coincides with some backsliding toward a less colloquial poetry" (p. 101); and a revision of WENTERSDORF's metrical indices and ORAS's pause patterns. TAYLOR concludes (p. 107) that "although minor ambiguities remain about the order of particular plays, we can be reasonably confident about the shape of the canon after about 1597." Nevertheless, recent eds. differ to some extent, as the following comparison shows (see table).

CHAMBERS (1930) is included because his chronology was accepted by many eds. until recently; all his dates given here are reiterated by McMANAWAY (1950). *Lr.* is present because TAYLOR holds that the text of that play included in F1 is a revision of the text that first appeared in the quarto of 1608 substantial enough to constitute a new creation. *Cardenio* is a play based on a story in *Don Quixote* and thought to be by Shakespeare and Fletcher (as are *H8* and *TNK*). As CHAMBERS (1930, 1:539) notes: "A play of *Cardenno* or *Cardenna* was given by the King's men at court in the winter of 1612-13." It was acted in 1727 under the title *Double Falsehood* and printed in 1728 as "Written Originally by W. Shakespeare; And now Revised and Adapted to the Stage by Mr. Theobald." BEVINGTON's *WT* range is an innovation for him; his previous editions of the *Works* (1973 and 1980) substantially agree with CHAMBERS and with EVANS (c. 1610-11). He appears to have extended these dates on the chance that TAYLOR may be right, a question that critics of *Lr.* will have to decide. As it now stands, however, c. 1610-11 is as close as one can come to the date of *WT*.

A Comparison of Four Chronologies

	CHAMBERS 1930	EVANS ed. 1974	TAYLOR 1987	BEVINGTON ed. 1992
Per.	1608-9	1607-8	1607	1606-8
Cym.	1609-10	1609-10	1610	c. 1608-10
WT	1610-11	1610-11	1609	c. 1609-11
Lr. rev.			1610	
Tmp.	1611-12	1611	1611	c. 1611
H8	1612-13	1612-13	1612-13	—
Cardenio	—	1612-13	1612-13	—
TNK	1612-13	1613	1613-14	1613-16

Sources

Primary Source

PANDOSTO

The first ed. of *WT* to quote extensively from *Pandosto* to illustrate Sh.'s dependence was MALONE (ed. 1790). Recognition of *WT*'s source preceded MALONE by a century, however. LANGBAINE (1691, p. 466): "The Plot of this Play may be read in a little Stitch-pamphlet, which is call'd, as I remember, *The Delectable History of* Dorastus *and* Fawnia," otherwise *Pandosto*, by Robert Greene. ROWE (ed. 1709, 1:xxvii-xxviii): "*The Winter's Tale* . . . contains the space of sixteen or seventeen Years, and the Scene [*xxviii*] is sometimes laid in *Bohemia*, and sometimes in *Sicily*, according to the original Order of the Story." GILDON (1710, p. 336): "Whence I suppose the Absurdities are copyed, and the making *Bohemia* of an Inland, a maritime Country." The opinion of GREY (1754, 1:244) "that *Dorastus* and *Faunia* is of a more modern date [than *WT*], and borrow'd from *Shakespeare*" was refuted by FARMER (in STEEVENS, ed. 1778). FARMER reported a copy of *Pandosto* with a publication date of 1588, considerably before any date proposed for Sh.'s play.

On 1 July 1588, "A booke intitled *the complaint of tyme*" was entered in the Register of the Company of Stationers to Thomas Orwin (ARBER, 1875-94, 2:493). *Pandosto. The Triumph of Time* was printed by Orwin for the stationer Thomas Cadman (*RSTC* [3:277] 12285); *The Historie of Dorastus and Fawnia* is its head title. The discrepancy between the title as given in the Register and the title as published creates some uncertainty that the entry pertains to the novel (see WELLS, 1988, pp. xxx-xxxi); even so, there is no reason to doubt that the novel appeared in 1588. It was frequently reprinted—in 1592, 1595, 1600 (*RSTC* 12287.5, a single copy in the Biblioteka Gdanska), 1607, 1609, 1614, 1619, 1621 (a single copy in the Vienna National Library, located by WELLS; not in *RSTC*), 1629, 1632, 1632-6 (date cropped; see WELLS, p. xxxviii), 1636, and c. 1640 (date cropped; see ALLISON, 1975, no. 84). WELLS (pp. xl-xlii) identifies eleven more editions of *Pandosto*, including an abridgment, published from 1648 to the end of the century and seven or eight more complete eds. and abridgments from about 1700 to 1735; uncertainties in the tabulation arise from difficulties in distinguishing the eds. and in dating them. The title pages of eds. 1588 through 1632 carry as a subtitle *The Triumph of Time*; in eds. 1636 and following, the earlier title and subtitle are replaced by *The Pleasant Historie of Dorastus and Fawnia*, the title LANGBAINE was thinking of.

JUSSERAND (1890; 1966, p. 155): The novel "had an immense success, much greater according to appearances than the exquisite drama of a 'Winter's Tale', that Shakespeare drew from it." COLLIER (1836, p. 19 n.) alleges that the 1609 ed. "is probably the very one used by our great Dramatist." In a subsequent work, COLLIER (ed. 1842, 3:476 n.) declares that in eds. of *Pandosto* published after 1588, the oracle's words are "the king shall live without an heire," whereas in 1588 the word is "die." He settled on 1609 rather than an earlier ed. because it is the one that most immediately preceded the writing of *WT*. The actual situation, according to WELLS (1988, p. 128), is that the eds. of 1588, 1592, and 1595 read "liue," as Sh. does (*WT* 1315), whereas 1609 and subsequent eds. read "die." MUIR (1957, p. 240) asserts that Sh. used the 1588 ed., but, as WELLS remarks, MUIR evidently did not know that the 1592 and 1595 eds. existed. Since Sh. did not reproduce a unique feature of any of these eds., the specific one he consulted cannot be ascertained. Moreover, COGGINS (1980) argues that there seems to have been a 1584 ed., no copies of which are known to have survived.

Later versions of *Pandosto* are found in LENNOX (1753), a paraphrase; COLLIER, *Shakespeare's Library*, vol. 1 (1843; 1875); *NUC* lists an ed. from the 1840s, possibly a separate issue of the COLLIER text, which seems not to be noticed elsewhere; an ed. of 1858, according to S. A. Tannenbaum & D. A. Tannenbaum, *Elizabethan Bibliographies: Robert Greene* [1939], possibly the version in HALLIWELL (ed. 1859); A. B. Grosart, *The Life and Complete Works of Robert Greene*, vol. 4 (188?); MORLEY (ed. 1887), an abridgment; Anon., Pandosto, or The Historie of Dorastus and Fawnia, *by Robert Greene* (New Rochelle, 1902); THOMAS (ed. *Pandosto*, 1907); James Winny, *The Descent of Euphues* (Cambridge, 1957); BULLOUGH (1975); and WELLS (ed. *Pandosto*, 1988, but finished in 1962). Eds. of *WT* containing *Pandosto* include those of HALLIWELL, MORLEY (1887), FURNESS (ed. 1898), and PAFFORD (1963).

According to BOLTE ("Schlussscene," 1891, p. 90), the novel provided material for a French play and a Dutch play: Jean Puget de La Serre's *Pandoste ou la Princesse malheureuse, en deux journées* (Paris, 1631), which was performed at the Hôtel de Bourgogne in 1631; and Meynert Voskuyl's *Dorastus en Fauniaas* (Amsterdam, 1637). The *British Library Catalogue* also lists Voskuyl's *Bellaria en Pandostos* (Amstrelredam, 1637). THOMAS (1907, p. xix) reports that a French version by Alexandre Hardy, who wrote several pastoral plays, is now lost. JUSSERAND (in LEE, ed. 1907, pp. xxviii–xxix) gives further details: "The first translation was printed at Paris, 'chez Guillaume Marette', in 1615, under the title of 'Histoire tragique de Pandosto roy de Bohême et de Bellaria sa femme. Ensemble les amours de Dorastus et de Faunia. . . . [xxix] Le tout traduit premièrement en Anglois de la langue Bohême, et de nouveau mis en françois par L. Regnault'. . . . The translation [takes] a good many liberties . . . with the text (some voluntary, others not). . . . To the supposed 'Bohemian' original there is no further allusion." One adaptation, *Le roman d'Albanie et de Sycile par le Sr du Bail gentil-homme Poict[evin]*, appeared in 1626, and another, *Histoire de Pandolphe, roy de Bohême et de Cellaria sa femme,* in 1722. JUSSERAND also supplies (pp. xxxvi–xxxix) "the sketches made by the stage decorator [xxxvii] Mahelot for the scenery used in the performance" of Hardy's dramatic version.

A derivative in blank verse, Francis Sabie's *The Fissher-mans Tale* (*RSTC* 21535), appeared in 1595, some copies being issued as a part of Sabie's *Pans Pipe*, three eclogues in hexameters; and *The Fissher-mans Tale* was followed by a second part, *Flora's Fortune* (*RSTC* 21536), also in 1595. These poems were reprinted by HALLIWELL (ed. 1859, 8:127–60)—possibly from a defective copy, since the "extracts," as he calls his text, run from line 632 of *The Fissher-mans Tale* to the end of *Flora's Fortune*.

Pandosto of 1588 collates A-G⁴. The one surviving copy, located in the British Library, lacks the four leaves of sig. B; the missing text is supplied here by the edition of 1592, Folger Shakespeare Library. In the following reprint, the black letter of these eds. is rendered as roman and the roman as italic. "The Epitaph" (p. 633) is italic in ed. 1588. Most ornaments are ignored. Macrons and abbreviations of *the*, *and*, *that*, and *with* have been expanded. The two- and three-line initials beginning certain paragraphs are reduced to regular capitals, turned letters are returned, and the white space preceding and following some lines of dialogue has been removed. Footnotes show the origin of emendations of the 1588 and 1592 texts; the spelling of the emendations has been altered occasionally to accord with that of the copy-text. Asterisks in the text call attention to the footnotes. In the notes, a wavy dash in the variant reading repeats the word of the lemma in the corresponding position; the caret indicates absence of punctuation.

Important points of comparison and contrast between Greene's novel and Sh.'s play, and representative commentary on them, may be found in the following notes: 3370, 3371, 3378, 3379, 3381, 3382, 3388, 14-16, 50-1, 121-3, 181-92, 234, 269-72, 285-8, 288, 410, 450-1, 455-66, 461, 468-81, 565, 582, 583, 648, 715-19, 798-805, 800, 938-41, 980, 1016-17, 1062, 1111-15, 1133, 1147, 1173, 1191-5, 1202-6, 1219-21, 1222-4, 1263, 1280, 1293, 1299, 1347-8, 1366-85, 1437, 1440, 1486, 1507, 1509-10, 1512, 1559, 1596-8, 1691-2, 1795, 1798-9, 1798, 1799, 1826-36, 1828-32, 2240, 2263, 2408, 2512, 2630, 2724, 2915, 2926, 2995, 2998, 3032, 3061. Passages of the novel referred to in these commentary notes are here preceded by bracketed TLN numbers of those notes, inserted into the text. In addition, TLN numbers for some other lines in *WT*, which correspond to passages in *Pandosto* but are not discussed in the notes, are likewise inserted here into the text before the corresponding passages of the novel.

PANDOSTO.
¶The Triumph
of Time.

WHEREIN IS DISCOVERED
by a pleasant Historie, that although by the meanes
of sinister fortune Truth may be concea-
led, yet by Time in spight of fortune it
is most manifestly reuealed.

Pleasant for age to auoyde drowsie thoughtes,
profitable for youth to eschue other wanton
pastimes, and bringing to both a de-
sired content.

Temporis filia veritas.

¶*By Robert Greene* Maister of Artes
in *Cambridge.*

Omne tulit punctum qui miscuit vtile dulci.

[ornament]

Imprinted at London by *Thomas Orwin* for *Thomas
Cadman*, dwelling at the Signe of the *Bible*, neere
vnto the North doore of Paules,
1588.

TO THE GENTLEMEN REA-
DERS HEALTH.

The paultring Poet *Aphranius* being blamed for troublinge the Emperor *Traian*
with so many doting *Poems*: aduentured notwithstanding, stil to present him with
rude and homely verses, excusing himselfe* with the courtesie of the Emperour,
which did as friendly accept, as he fondly offerd. So Gentlemen, if any condemne my
rashnesse for troubling your eares with so many vnlearned Pamphlets: I will straight
shroud my selfe vnder the shadowe of your courtesies, and with *Aphranius* lay the
blame on you aswell for frendly reading them, as on my selfe for fondly penning them:
Hoping though fond curious, or rather currish backbiters breathe out slaunderous
speeches: yet the courteous Readers (whom I feare to offend) wil requite my trauell,
at the least with silence: and in this hope I rest: wishing you health and happines.

Robert Greene.

TO THE RIGHT HO-
norable George Clifford Earle of Cumber-
land, Robert Greene wisheth increase
of honour and vertue.

The Rascians (right honorable) when by long gazing against the Sunne, they
become halfe blinde, recouer their sightes by looking on the blacke Loade stone.
Vnicornes being glutted with brousing on roots of Licquoris, sharpen their stomacks
with crushing bitter grasse.
Alexander vouchsafed as well to smile at the croked picture of Vulcan, as to
wonder at the curious counterfeite of Venus. The minde is sometimes delighted as

---

*himselfe] 1595; himfelfe 1588

much with small trifles as with sumptuous triumphs, and as wel pleased with hearing of Pans homely fancies, as of Hercules renowmed laboures.

Syllie Baucis could not serue Iupiter in a siluer plate, but in a woodden dish. Al that honour Esculapius, decke not his shrine with Iewels. Apollo giues Oracles as wel to the poore man for his mite, as to the rich man for his treasure. The stone Echites is not so much liked for the colour, as for vertue, and giftes are not to be measured by the worth, but by the will. *Mison* that vnskilfull Painter of Greece, aduentured to giue vnto *Darius* the shielde of Pallas, so roughlie shadowed, as he smiled more at the follie of the man, then at the imperfection of his arte. So I present vnto your honour the triumph of time, so rudelie finished, as I feare your honour wil rather frowne at my impudencie, then laugh at my ignorancie: But I hope my willing minde shal excuse my slender skill, and your honours curtesie shadowe my rashnes.

[A2ᵛ] They which feare the biting of vipers doe carie in their hands the plumes of a Phœnix. Phydias drewe Vulcan sitting in a chaire of Iuory. Caesars Crow durst neuer cry, *Aue*, but when she was pearked on the Capitoll. And I seeke to shroude this imperfect Pamphlet vnder your honours patronage, doubting the dint of such inuenomed vipers, as seeke with their slaunderous* reproches to carpe at al, being oftentims, most vnlearned of all: and assure my selfe, that your honours renowmed valure, and vertuous disposition shall be a sufficient defence to protect me from the Poysoned tongues of such scorning Sycophants, hoping that as Iupiter vouchsafed to lodge in Philemons thatched Cotage: and Phillip of Macedon, to take a bunche of grapes of a country pesant: so I hope your honour, measuring my worke by my will, and wayghing more the mind than the matter, will when you haue cast a glaunce at this toy, with Minerua, vnder your golden Target couer a deformed Owle. And in this hope I rest, wishing vnto you, and the vertuous Countesse your wife: such happy successe as your honours can desire, or I imagine.

Your Lordships most duetifully to com-
maunde: Robert Greene.

THE HISTORIE OF
DORASTUS AND
FAWNIA.

Among al the Passions wherewith humane mindes are perplexed, there is none that so galleth with restlesse despight, as that infectious soare of Iealousie: for all other griefes are eyther to bee appeased with sensible perswasions, to be cured with wholesome counsel, to be relieued in want, or by tract of time to be worne out, (Iealousie only excepted) which is so sawsed with suspitious doubtes, and pinching mistrust, that whoso seekes by friendly counsaile to rase out this hellish passion, it foorthwith suspecteth that he geueth this aduise to couer his owne guiltinesse. Yea,

---

*slaunderous] 1592; slaunderours 1588

who so is payned with this restlesse torment doubteth all, dystrusteth him-selfe, is alwayes frosen with feare, and fired with suspition, hauing that wherein consisteth all his ioy, to be the breeder of his miserie. Yea, it is such a heauy enemy to that holy estate of matrimony, sowing betweene the married couple* such deadly seedes of secret hatred, as Loue being once rased out by spightful distrust, there oft ensueth bloudy reuenge, as this ensuing Hystorie manifestly prooueth: wherein *Pandosto* (furiously incensed by causelesse Iealousie) procured the death of his most louing and loyall wife, and his owne endlesse sorrow and misery.

In the Countrey of *Bohemia* there raygned a King called *Pandosto*, whose fortunate successe in warres against his foes, and bountifull curtesie towardes his friendes in peace, made him to be greatly feared and loued of all men. This *Pandosto* had to Wife a Ladie called *Bellaria*, by birth royall, learned by education, faire by nature, by vertues famous, so that it was hard to iudge whether her beautie, fortune, or vertue, wanne the greatest [A3ᵛ] commendations. These two lincked together in perfect loue, led their liues with such fortunate content, that their Subiects greatly reioyced to see their quiet disposition. They had not beene married long, but Fortune (willing to increase their happines) lent them a sonne, so adorned with the gifts of nature, as the perfection of the Childe greatly augmented the loue of the parentes, and the ioy of their commons: in so much that the *Bohemians*, to shewe their inward ioyes by outwarde actions, made [TLN 3032] Bonefires and triumphs throughout all the Kingdome, appointing Iustes and Turneyes for the honour of their young Prince: whether resorted not only his Nobles, but also diuers Kings and Princes which were his neighbours, willing to shewe their friendship they ought to *Pandosto*, and to win fame and glory by their prowesse and valour. *Pandosto*, whose minde was fraught with princely liberality, entertayned the Kings, Princes, and noble men with such submisse curtesie, and magnifical bounty, that they all sawe how willing he was to gratifie their good wils, making a generall feast for his Subiects, which continued by the space of twentie dayes: all which time the Iustes and Turneys were kept to the great content both of the Lordes and Ladies there present. This solemne tryumph being once ended, the assembly taking their leaue of *Pandosto* and *Bellaria*: the young sonne (who was called [see n. 3382] *Garinter*) was nursed vp in the house, to the great ioy and content of the parents. Fortune enuious of such happy successe, willing to shewe some signe of her inconstancie, turned her wheele, and darkned their bright sun of prosperitie, with the mistie cloudes of mishap and misery. For it so happened that *Egistus* King of *Sycilia*, [TLN 25–7] who in his youth had bene brought vp with *Pandosto*, desirous to shewe that [TLN 27–33] neither tracte of time, nor distance of place could diminish their former friendship, prouided a nauie of ships, and [TLN 50, 1147, 1440] sayled into *Bohemia* to visite his old friend and companion, who hearing of his arriuall, went himselfe in person, and his wife *Bellaria*, accompanied with a great traine of Lords and Ladies, to meet *Egistus*: and

---

*couple] WELLS (1988); couples 1588

espying him, alighted from his horse, embraced him very louingly, protesting that nothing in the world could haue happened more acceptable to him then his comming, [TLN 1238–40] wishing his wife to welcome his olde friend and acquaintance: who (to shewe how she liked him whom her husband loued) inter-[A4]tayned him with such familiar curtesie, as *Egistus* perceiued himselfe to bee verie well welcome. After they had thus saluted and embraced eche other, they mounted againe on horsbacke, and [TLN 121–3] rode toward the Citie, deuising and recounting, howe being children they had passed their youth in friendely pastimes: where, by the meanes of the Citizens, *Egistus* was receyued with triumphs and showes in such sort, that he maruelled how on so small a warning they coulde make such preparation. Passing the streetes thus with such rare sightes, they rode on to the Pallace, where [TLN 14–16] *Pandosto* entertained *Egistus* and his *Sycilians* with such banqueting and sumptuous cheare, so royally, as they all had cause to commend his princely liberality, yea, the verie basest slaue that was knowne to come from *Sycilia* was used with such curtesie, that *Egistus* might easily perceiue how both hee and his were honored for his friendes sake. [TLN 181–92] *Bellaria* (who in her time was the flower of curtesie)* willing to show how unfaynedly shee looued her husband by his friends intertainement, used him likewise so familiarly, that her countenance bewraied how her minde was affected towardes him: oftentimes comming her selfe into his bed chamber, to see that nothing should be amis to mislike him. This honest familiarity increased dayly more and more betwixt them; for *Bellaria* noting in *Egistus* a princely and bountifull minde, adorned with sundrie and excellent qualities, and *Egistus*, finding in her a vertuous and curteous disposition, there grew such a secret vniting of their affections, that the one could not well be without the company of the other: in so much that when *Pandosto* was busied with such vrgent affaires, that hee could not bee present with his friend *Egistus*, [TLN 260] *Bellaria* would walke with him into the Garden, where they two in priuat and pleasant deuises would passe away the time to both their contents. This custome still continuing betwixt them, a certaine [TLN 181–92] melancholy passion entring the minde of *Pandosto*, draue him into sundry and doubtfull thoughts. First, he called to minde the beauty of his wife *Bellaria*, the comelines and brauerie of his friend *Egistus*, thinking that Loue was aboue all Lawes, and therefore to be staied with no Law: that it was hard to put fire and flaxe together without burning: that their open pleasures might breede his secrete displeasures. He considered with himselfe that *Egistus* was a man, and must needes loue: that his wife was a woman, [A4ᵛ] and therfore subiect vnto loue, and that where fancy forced, friendship was of no force. These and such like doubtfull thoughtes a long time smoothering in his stomacke, beganne at last to kindle in his minde a secret mistrust, which increased by suspition, grewe at last to a flaming Iealousie, that so tormented him as [TLN 900] he could take no rest. He then began to measure all their actions, and to misconstrue of their too priuate familiaritie, iudging that it was not for honest affection, but for disordinate fancy, so that hee began to watch them more narrowely, to see if hee could gette any true or certaine proofe to confirme his doubtfull suspition.

---

*curtesie)] 1595; ~ , 1588

While thus he noted their lookes and gestures, and suspected their thoughts and meaninges, they two seely soules who doubted nothing of this his treacherous intent, frequented daily eache others companie, which draue him into such a franticke passion, that he beganne to beare a secret hate to *Egistus*, and a lowring countenaunce to *Bellaria*, [TLN 227] who marueiling at such vnaccustomed frowns, began to cast beeyond the Moone, and to enter into a thousand sundrie thoughtes, which way she should offend her husband: but finding in her selfe a cleare conscience, ceassed to muse, vntil such time as she might find fit opportunitie to demaund the cause of his dumps. In the meane time *Pandostoes* minde was so farre charged with Iealousy, that he did no longer doubt, but was assured (as he thought) that his Friend *Egistus* had entered a wrong pointe in his tables, and so had [TLN 269-72] played him false play: wherupon desirous to reuenge so great an iniury, he thought best to dissemble the grudge with a faire and friendly countenance: and so vnder the shape of a friend, to shew him the tricke of a foe. Deuising with himself a long time how he might best put away *Egistus* without suspition of treacherous murder, hee concluded at last to poyson him: which opinion pleasing his humour, he became resolute in his determination, and the better to bring the matter to passe he called vnto him [TLN 446] his cupbearer, with whom in secret he brake the matter: promising to him for the performance thereof, to geue him a thowsande crownes of yearely reuenues: his cupbearer eyther being of a good conscience, or willing for fashion sake, to deny such a bloudy request, began with great reasons to perswade *Pandosto* from his determinate mischief: shewing him what an offence murther was to the Gods: how such vnnaturall actions did more displease the heauens, than [B1, 1592] men: and that causeles crueltie did seldome or neuer escape without reuenge: he layd before his face, that *Egistus* was his friend, [TLN 461] a king, and one that was come into his kingdome, to confirme a league of perpetuall amitie betwixt them, that he had and did shew him a most friendly countenaunce, how *Egistus* was not onely honored of his owne people by obedience, but also loued of the *Bohemians* for his curtesie. And that if now he should without any iust or manifest cause, poyson him, it would not only be a great dishonor to his Maiesty, and a meanes to sow perpetuall enmitie betweene the *Sycilians* and the *Bohemians*, but also his owne subiectes would repine at such trecherous crueltie. These and such like perswasions of [TLN 410] *Franion* (for so was his cupbearer called) [TLN 371-432] could no whit preuaile to disswade him from his deuilish enterprise, but remaining resolute in his determination, his furie so fiered with rage, as it could not be appeased with reason: he began with bitter taunts to take vp his man, and to lay before him two baytes: preferment, and death: saying that if he would poyson *Egistus*, he should [TLN 459-60] aduaunce him to high dignities: [TLN 450-1] if he refused to do it of an obstinate minde, no torture should be to great to requite his disobedience. *Franion* seeing, that to perswade *Pandosto* any more, was but to striue against the streame: [TLN 433-52] consented as soone as oportunity would giue him leaue to dispatch *Egistus*, wherewith *Pandosto* remained somwhat satisfied, hoping now he should be fully reuenged of such mistrusted iniuries, intending also [TLN 440-2] assoone as *Egistus* was dead, to giue his wife a sop of the same sawce, and so be rid of those which were the cause of his restles sorrow. While thus he liued in this hope, *Franion* beeing secret in his chamber, began to meditate with himselfe in these termes.

Ah *Franion*, treason is loued of many, but the traitor hated of all: vniust offences may for a time escape without danger, but neuer without reuenge, thou art seruant to a king, and must obey at commaund: yet *Franion*, against law and conscience, it is not good to resist a tyrant with armes, nor to please an vniust king with obedience. What shalt thou do? Folly refuseth* [B1ᵛ, 1592] gold, and frensie preferment, wisedome seeketh after dignitie, and counsel looketh for gayne. *Egistus* is a stranger, to thee, and *Pandosto* thy soueraigne: thou hast little cause to respect the one, and oughtest to haue great care to obey the other. Thinke this *Franion*, that a pound of gold is worth a tunne of lead, great gifts are little Gods, and preferment to a meane man, is a whetstone to courage: there is nothing sweeter than promotion, nor lighter than report: care not then though most count thee a traytor, so all cal thee rich. Dignitie (*Franion*) aduaunceth thy posteritie, and euill report can hurt but thy selfe. Know this, where Eagles build, Faulcons may pray: where Lyons haunt, Foxes may steale. Kings are knowen to commaunde, seruaunts are blamelesse to consent: feare not thou then to lift at *Egistus, Pandosto* shall beare the burthen. Yea but *Franion*, conscience is a worme that euer biteth, but neuer ceaseth: that which is rubbed with the stone *Galactites* will neuer be hot. Flesh dipped in the sea *Ægeum*, will neuer be sweete: the hearbe *Tragion*, being once bit with an *Aspis* neuer groweth, and conscience once stayned with innocent bloud, is alwayes tyed to a guiltie remorse. Preferre thy content before riches, and a cleare mind before dignitie: so being poore thou shalt haue rich peace, or els rich, thou shalt enioy disquiet.

Franion hauing muttered out these or such like words, seeing either he must dye with a cleare minde, or liue with a spotted conscience: he was so [TLN 455–66] combered with diuers cogitations that hee could take no rest, vntill at last he determined to breake the matter to *Egistus*, but fearing that the king should either suspect or heare of such matters, he concealed the deuise till oportunitie would permit him to reueale it. Lingring thus in doubtfull feare, in an euening he went to *Egistus* lodging, and desirous to breake with him of certaine affaires that touched the king, after all were commaunded out of the chamber: *Franion* made manifest the whole conspiracie, which *Pandosto* had deuised against him, desiring *Egistus* not to accompt him a traytor for bewraying his maisters counsell, but to thinke that he did it for conscience, hoping that although his maister inflamed with rage, or incensed by some sinister reportes, or slaunderous [B2, 1592] speaches, had imagined such causelesse mischief: yet when time should pacifie his anger, and trie those talebearers but flattering Parasites, then he would count him as a faithfull seruaunt, that with such care had kept his maisters credit. *Egistus* had not fully heard *Franion* tell forth his tale, but [TLN 574] a quaking feare possessed all his limmes, thinking that there was some treason wrought, and that *Franion* did but shadow his craft with these false colours: wherefore he began to waxe in choler, and sayd that [TLN 468–81] he doubted not *Pandosto*, sith he was his friend, and there had neuer as yet bene any breach of

---

*refuseth] WELLS (1988); refused 1592

amitie: he had not sought to inuade his lands, to conspire with his enemies, to dis-swade his subiectes from their allegance: but in word and thought he rested his at all times: he knew not therfore any cause that should moue *Pandosto* to seeke his death, but suspected it to be a compacted knauery of the *Bohemians*, to bring the king and him at oddes. *Franion* staying him in the midst of his talke, told him that to dally with Princes was with the swannes to sing agaynst their death, and that if the *Bohemians* had intended any such secret mischief, it might haue bene better brought to passe then by reuealing the conspiracie: therefore his Maiestie did ill to misconstrue of his good meaning, sith his intent was to hinder treason, not to become a traytor and to confirme his premises, if it please his Maiestie to flee into *Sycilia* for the safegard of his life, he would goe with him: and if then he found not such a practise to be pretended, let his imagined trecherie be repayed with most monstrous torments. *Egistus* hearing the solemne protestation of *Franion*: began to consider, that in loue and kingdomes, neither faith, nor law is to bee respected: doubting that *Pandosto* thought by his death to destroy his men, and with speedy warre to inuade *Sycilia*: these and such doubtes throughly weighed, he gaue great thankes to *Franion*, promising if he might with life returne to *Syracusa*, that he would create him a Duke in *Sycilia*: crauing his counsell how he might escape out of the countrey. *Franion*, who hauing [TLN 565] some small skill in Nauigation, was well acquainted with the Portes and Hauens, and knew euery daunger in the Sea, ioyning in counsell with the Maister of *Egistus* Nauie, rigged all their [B2ᵛ, 1592] ships, and setting them a floate let them lye at anker, to be in the more readinesse when time and wind should serue. Fortune although blind, yet by chance fauoring this iust cause, sent them [TLN 582] within 6. dayes a good gale of wind, which *Franion* seeing fit for their purpose, to put *Pandosto** out of suspition, the night before they should saile, he went to him and prom-ised, that the next day he would put the deuise in practise, for he had got such a forcible poyson as the very smell thereof should procure sodaine death. *Pandosto** was ioyfull to heare this good newes and thought euery houre a day till he might be glutted with bloudy reuenge, but his suite had but ill successe: for *Egistus* fearing that delay might breede daunger, and willing that the grasse should not be cut from vnder his feete, taking [TLN 285-8, 288] bagge and baggage with the helpe of *Franion*, [TLN 554-5, 649-53] conueyed himself and his men out of a posterne gate of the Citie so secretly, and speedely, that without any suspition they got to the sea shoare, where, with many a bitter curse taking their leaue of *Bohemia*, they went aboord, weighing their Ancres: and hoysting sayle, they passed as fast as winde and sea would permit towardes *Sycilia*; *Egistus* being a ioyfull man, that he had safely past such trecherous perils. But as they were quietly floating* on the sea, so *Pandosto* and his Citizens were in an vprore: for seeing that the *Sycilians* without taking their leaue were fled away by night, the *Bohemians* feared some treason, and [TLN 628-32] the king thought that without question his suspition was true, seeing his cup-

---

*Pandosto] 1595; *Pandasto* 1592
*Pandosto] 1607; *Pandasto* 1592
*floating] 1607; flouting 1592

bearer had bewrayed the summe of his secret pretence: whereupon [TLN 643-9, 693-4] he began to imagine, that *Franion* and his wife *Bellaria* had conspired with *Egistus*, and that the feruent affection she bare him, was the onely meanes of his secret departure, in so much that incensed with rage, he commaunded that his wife should be carried to straight prison, untill they heard further of his pleasure. The guarde vnwilling to lay their hands on such a vertuous Princesse, and yet fearing the kings furie, went very sorrowfully to fulfill their charge, [TLN 583] comming to the Queenes lodging, they found her playing with her young sonne *Garinter*, vnto whom with teares doing the message: *Bellaria* astonished at such a hard censure, and finding her cleare conscience a sure aduocate to pleade in her case, went to the prison most willingly: where [TLN 715-19] with sighs and teares, [B3, 1592] she past away the time till she might come to her triall.

But *Pandosto*, whose reason was suppressed with rage, and whose vnbridled folly was incensed with furie: seeing *Franion* had bewrayed his secrets, and that *Egistus* might wel be rayled on, but not reuenged: [TLN 901-8] determined to wreake all his wrath on poore *Bellaria*, he therfore caused a generall Proclamation to be made through all his Realme, that the Queene and *Egistus* had by the helpe of *Franion* not only committed most incestuous adulterie, but also had conspired the Kings death: Wherupon the Traitor *Franion* was fled away with *Egistus*, and *Bellaria* was most iustly imprisoned. This Proclamation being once [TLN 1280] blazed through the countrey [TLN 1164-5], although the vertuous disposition of the Queene did halfe discredit the contents: yet [TLN 583] the sodaine and speedie passage of *Egistus*, and the secret departure of *Franion* induced them (the circumstances throughly considered) to thinke that both the Proclamation was true, and the King greatly iniured: yet [TLN 734-71] they pitied her case, as sorowful that so good a Ladie should be crossed with such aduerse Fortune. But the King, whose restlesse rage would admit no pity, thought that although he might sufficiently requite his wiues falshood with the bitter plague of [TLN 648] pinching penurie, yet his minde should neuer be glutted with reuenge, till he might haue fit time and oportunitie to repay the treacherie of* *Egistus* with a fatall iniurie. But a curst Cow hath oft times short hornes, and a willing mind, but a weake arme: for *Pandosto* although he felt, that reuenge was a spurre to warre, and that enuie alwayes proffereth steele, yet he saw, that *Egistus* was not onely of great puissance, and prowesse to withstand him, but [TLN 921-2] had also many Kings of his alliance to ayde him, if neede should serue: for [TLN 1299] he married the Emperours* daughter of *Russia*. These and such like considerations something daunted *Pandosto* his courage, so, that he was content rather to put vp a manifest iniurie with peace, than hunt after reuenge with dishonor and losse: determining since *Egistus* had escaped scotfree, that *Bellaria* should pay for all at an vnreasonable price.

Remaining thus resolute in this determination, *Bellaria* continuing still in prison, and hearing the contents of the Proclamation, knowing that her mind was neuer touched with [B3ᵛ, 1592] such affection, nor that *Egistus* had euer offered her such

---

*of] 1607; *om.* 1592
*Emperours] 1595; Emperous 1592

discurtesie, would gladly haue come to her answer, that both she might haue knowne her vniust accusers, and cleared her selfe of that guiltlesse crime.

But *Pandosto* was so enflamed with rage, and infected with Iealousie as he would not vouchsafe to heare her nor admit any iust excuse, so that she was faine to make a vertue of her neede, and with patience to beare these heauie iniuries. As thus she lay crossed with calamities (a great cause to increase her griefe) she found her selfe quicke with childe: which assoone as she felt stir in her bodie, she burst foorth into bitter teares, exclaiming against fortune in these tearmes.

Alas *Bellaria*, how infortunate art thou because fortunat, better hadst thou bene borne a begger than a Prince: so shouldest thou haue bridled Fortune with want, where now she sporteth her selfe with thy plentie. Ah happy life where poore thoughts, and meane desires liue in secure content, not fearing Fortune because too low for* fortune, thou seest now *Bellaria*, that care is a companion to honor, not to pouertie, that high *Cædars* are frushed [broken, snapped] with tempests, when low shrubs are not toucht with the wind: precious Diamonds are cut with the file, when despised peables lie safe in the sand: *Delphos* is sought to by Princes, not beggers: and Fortunes altars smoke with Kings presents, not with poore mens gifts. Happy are such *Bellaria*, that curse Fortune for contempt, not feare, and may wish they were, not sorrow they haue bene. Thou art a Princesse, *Bellaria*, and yet a prisoner, borne to the one by discent, assigned to the other by despite, accused without cause, and therefore oughtest to die without care: for patience is a shield against Fortune, and a guiltlesse mind yeeldeth not to sorow. Ah, but Infamie galleth vnto death, and liueth after death: Report is plumed with Times feathers, and Enuie oftentimes soundeth Fames trumpet: thy suspected adulterie shall fly in the aire, and thy knowne vertues shall ly hid in the earth: one Moale stayneth a whole face, and what is once spotted with Infamy can hardly be worne out with time. Die then *Bellaria*, *Bellaria* die: for if the Gods should say thou art guiltlesse, [B4, 1592] yet enuie would heare the Gods, but neuer beleeue the Gods. Ah haplesse wretch, cease these tearmes: desperat thoughts are fit for them that feare shame, not for such as hope for credite. *Pandosto* hath darkned thy fame, but shal neuer discredit thy vertues. Suspition may enter a false action, but proofe shall neuer put in his plea: care not then for enuie, sith report hath a blister on her tongue: and let sorrow bite them which offend, not touch thee that art faultlesse. But alas poore soule, howe canst thou but sorrow? Thou art with child, and by him that in steed of kind pitie pincheth thee in cold prison. And with that such gasping sighes so stopped her breath, that she could not vtter any mo words, but wringing her hands, and gushing foorth streames of teares, she passed away the time with bitter complaints.

The Iaylor pitying these her heauy passions, thinking that if the king knew she were with child, he would somwhat appease his furie, and release her from prison went in all hast, and certified *Pandosto* what the effect of *Bellarias* complaint was: who no sooner heard the Iaylour say she was with child, but as one possessed with

---

*low for] COLLIER (1843); low. For 1592

a phrensie, he rose vp in a rage, swearing that she and the bastard brat she was withal, should dy, if the gods themselues said no: thinking assuredly by computation of time, that *Egistus*, and not he, was father to the child. This suspitious thought galled a fresh this halfe healed sore, in so much as he could take no rest, vntil he might mitigate his choler with a iust reuenge, which happened presently after. For *Bellaria* was brought to bed of a faire and beautiful daughter, which no sooner *Pandosto* heard, but [TLN 1016- 17, 1062] he determined that both *Bellaria* and the yong infant should be burnt with fire. [TLN 1077-83] His Nobles hearing of the Kings cruel sentence, sought by perswasions to diuert him from this bloody determination: [TLN 980] laying before his face the innocencie of the child, and the vertuous disposition of his wife, how she had continually loued and honored him so tenderly, that without due proof he could not, nor ought not to appeach her of that crime. And if she had faulted, yet it were more honorable to pardon with mercy, then to punish with extremity, and more Kingly, to be commended of pity, than accused of [TLN 1293] rigor. And as [B4ᵛ, 1592] for the child, if he should punish it for the mothers offence, it were to striue against nature and iustice: and that vnnaturall actions do more offend the Gods then men: how causelesse crueltie, nor innocent bloud neuer scapes without reuenge. These and such like reasons could not appease his rage, but he rested resolute in this, that *Bellaria* being an adulteresse, the child was a bastard, and he would not suffer that such an infamous brat should call him father. [TLN 1084- 1115] Yet at last (seeing his noble men were importunate vpon him) he was content to spare the childs life, and yet to put it to a worser death. For he found out this deuise, that [TLN 1111- 15] seeing (as he thought) it came by Fortune, so he would commit it to the charge of Fortune, and therfore he caused a little cock-boate to be prouided, wherein he meant to put the babe, and then send it to the mercie of the seas, and the destinies. From this, his Peeres in no wise could persuade him, but that he sent presently* two of his Gard to fetch the child, who being come to the prison, and with weeping teares recounting their maisters message: *Bellaria* no sooner heard the rigorous resolution of her mercilesse husband, but she fell againe downe in a sound, so that all thought she had bin dead, yet at last being come to her selfe, she cried and scriched out in this wise.

Alas sweete infortunate babe, scarse borne before enuied by fortune: would the day of thy birth had bin the tearme of thy life, then shouldest thou haue made an end to care, and preuented thy fathers rigor. Thy faults cannot yet deserue such hatefull reuenge, thy dayes are too short for so sharpe a doome, but thy vntimely death must pay thy mothers debtes, and her guiltlesse crime must be thy gastly curse. And shalt thou sweete babe be committed to fortune? When thou art alreadie spighted by fortune: shall the seas be thy harbour, and the hard boate thy cradle? Shall thy tender mouth in steede of sweete kisses, be nipped with bitter stormes? Shalt thou haue [TLN 1496- 7] the whistling winds for thy Lullabie, and the salt sea fome in steed of [TLN 1277- 80] sweet milke? Alas, what destinies would assigne such hard hap? What

---

*presently] 1595; presenty 1592

father would be so cruell? Or what gods wil not reuenge such rigor? Let me kisse thy lips (sweet infant) and wet thy tender cheekes with my teares, and put this chaine [C1, 1592] about thy litle necke, that if fortune saue thee, it may helpe to succour thee. Thus, since thou must go to surge in the gastfull seas, with a sorrowfull kisse I bid thee farewell, and I pray the Gods thou mayst fare well. Such, and so great was her griefe, that her vital spirits being suppressed with sorrow, she fell downe in a traunce, hauing her sences so sotted with care, that after she was reuiued, yet she lost her memorie, and lay for a great time without mouing as one in a traunce. The gard left her in this perplexitie, and caried the child to the king, who quite [C1, 1588] deuoide of pity, commanded that without delay it should bee put in the boat, hauing neither saile nor other to guid it, and so to bee carried into the midst of the sea, and there left to the wind and waue as [TLN 1115] the destinies please to appoint. The very shipmen seeing the sweete countenance of the yong babe, began to accuse the King of rigor, and to pity the childs hard fortune: but feare constrayned them to that which their nature did abhorre: so that they placed it in one of the ends of the boat, and with a few greene bows made a homely cabben to shroud it as they could from wind and weather: hauing thus trimmed the boat they tied it to a ship, and so haled it into the mayne Sea, and then cut in sunder the coarde, which they had no sooner done, but there arose a mighty tempest, which tossed the little Boate so vehemently in the waues, that the shipmen thought it coulde not continue longe without sincking, yea the storme grewe so great, that with much labour and perill they got to the shoare. But leauing the Childe to her fortunes. Againe to *Pandosto*, who not yet glutted with sufficient reuenge, deuised which way he should best increase his Wiues calamitie. But first assembling his Nobles and Counsellors, [TLN 1173] hee called her for the more reproch into open Court, where it was obiected against her, that she had committed adulterie with *Egistus*, and conspired with *Franion* to poyson *Pandosto* her husband, but [TLN 1191-5] their pretence being partely spyed, shee counselled them to flie away by night for their better safety. *Bellaria*, who standing like a prisoner at the Barre, feeling in her selfe a cleare Conscience to withstand her false accusers: seeing that no lesse then death could pacifie her husbands wrath, waxed bolde, and desired that she might haue Lawe and Iustice, for mercy shee neyther craued nor hoped for, and that those periured wretches, which had falsly accused her to the King, might be brought before her face, to giue in euidence. But *Pandosto*, whose rage and Iealousie was such, as no reason, nor equitie could appease: tolde her, that for her accusers they were of such credite, as their wordes were sufficient witnesse, and that the sodaine and secret flight of *Egistus*, and *Franion* confirmed that which they had confessed: and as for her, it was her parte to deny such a monstrus crime, and to be impudent in forswearing the [TLN 1263] fact, since [TLN 1229-32] shee had past all shame in committing the fault: but her stale countenaunce should stand for no coyne, for as the Bastard which [C1ᵛ] she bare was serued, so she should with some cruell death be requited. *Bellaria* no whit dismayed with this rough reply, [TLN 1196-1228] tolde her Husband *Pandosto*, that he spake vpon choller, and not conscience: for [TLN 1207-9] her vertuous life had beene euer such, as no spot of suspition could euer staine. And if she had borne a frendly countenaunce* to *Egistus*, it was in respect he was his friende, and not for any lusting affection: therefore if she were condemned without any further proofe, [TLN 1293] it was rigour, and not Law. The noble men which sate in iudgement, said that *Bellaria* spake reason, and intreated the king that the accusers might be openly examined, and sworne, and if then the euidence were such, as the Iury might finde her guilty (for seeing she was a Prince,* she ought to be tryed by her peeres)* then let her haue such punishment as the extremitie of the Law will assigne to such malefactors. The king presently made an-swere, that in this case he might, and would dispence with the Law, and that the Iury being once panneld, they should take his word for sufficient euidence, otherwise he would make the proudest of them repent it. The noble men seeing the king in choler were all whist, but *Bellaria*, whose life then hung in the ballaunce, [TLN 1288-90] fearing more perpetuall infamie, then momentarie death, tolde the king, if his furie might stand for a Law, that it were vaine to haue the Iury yeeld their verdit, and therefore she fell downe vpon her knees, and desired the king that for the loue he bare* to his young sonne *Garinter*, whome she brought into the world, that hee woulde graunt her [TLN 583, 798-805, 800] a request, which was this, that it would please his maiestie to send sixe of his noble men whome he best trusted, to the [TLN 1147] Isle of *Delphos*, there to enquire of the Oracle of *Apollo*, whether she had committed adultery with *Egistus*, or conspired to poyson him with *Franion*: and if the God *Apollo*, who by his deuine essence knew al secrets, gaue answere that she was guiltie, she were content to suffer any torment, were it neuer so terrible. [TLN 1293-8] The request was so reasonable, that *Pandosto* could not for shame deny it, vnlesse he woulde bee counted of all his subiects more wilfull then wise, he therefore agreed, that with as much speede as might be there should be certaine Embassadores dispatched to the Ile of *Delphos*: and in the meane season [TLN 811-14] he* com-manded that his wife should be kept in close prison. *Bellaria* hauing obtained this graunt, was now more [C2] carefull for her little babe that floated on the Seas, then sorrowfull for her owne mishap. For of that she doubted: of her selfe shee was as-sured, knowing if *Apollo* should giue Oracle according to the thoughts of the hart, yet the sentence should goe one her side, such was the clearenes of her minde in this case. But *Pandosto* (whose suspitious head still remained in one song) chose out six of his Nobility, whom hee knew were scarse indifferent men in the Queenes behalfe, and prouiding all things fit for their iourney, sent them to *Delphos*: they willing to fulfill the Kinges commaund, and desirous to see the situation and custome of the Iland, dispatched their affaires with as much speede as might be, and embarked them-selues to this voyage, which (the wind and weather seruing fit for their purpose) was

---

*countenaunce] 1592; countedaunce 1588
*Prince,] 1629; ⁓) 1588
*peeres)] 1607; ⁓ , 1588
*bare] 1592; hare 1588
*he] 1592; be 1588

soone ended. For [TLN 1133, 1134] within three weekes they arriued at *Delphos*, where they were no sooner set on lande, but with great deuotion they went to the Temple of *Apollo*, and [TLN 1152-8] there offring sacrifice to the GOD, and giftes to the Priest, as the custome was, they humbly craued an aunswere of their demaund: they had not long kneeled at the Altar, but *Apollo* with a loude voice saide: *Bohemians*, what you finde behinde the Alter take, and depart. They forthwith obeying the Oracle founde a scroule of parchment, wherein was written these words in letters of Golde.

The Oracle.

Suspition is no proofe: Iealousie is an vnequall iudge: Bellaria is chast: Egistus blameless: Franion a true subiect: Pandosto treacherous: his babe an innocent, and the King shal liue without an heire: if [TLN 1313-16, 3378] *that which is lost be not founde.*

As soone as they had taken out this scroule, the Priest of the God commaunded them that [TLN 1168-70, 1304-10] they should not presume to read it, before they came in the presence of *Pandosto*: vnlesse they would incurre the displeasure of *Apollo*. The *Bohemian* Lords carefully obeying his commaund, taking their leaue of the Priest, with great reuerence departed out of the Temple, and went to their ships, and assoone as wind would permit them, sailed toward [C2ᵛ] [TLN 1147] *Bohemia*, whither in short time they safely arriued, and with great tryumph issuing out of their Ships, went to the Kinges pallace, whom they found in his chamber accompanied with other Noble men: *Pandosto* no sooner saw them, but with a merrie countenaunce he welcomed them home, asking what newes: they tolde his Maiestie that they had receiued an aunswere of the God written in a scroule, but with this charge, that they should not read the contents before they came in the presence of the King, and with that they deliuered him the parchment: but his Noble men intreated him that sith therein was contayned either the safetie of his Wiues life, and honesty, or her death, and perpetuall infamy, that he would haue his Nobles and Commons assembled in the iudgement Hall, where the Queene brought in as prysoner, should heare the contents: if shee were found guilty by the Oracle of the God, then all should haue cause to thinke his rigour proceeded of due desert: if her Grace were found faultlesse, then shee should bee cleared before all, sith she had bene accused openly. This pleased the King so, that he appointed the day, and assembled al his Lords and Commons, and [TLN 1173] caused the Queene to be brought in before the Iudgement seate, commaunding that the inditement shoulde bee read, wherein she was accused of [TLN 1187] adultery with *Egistus*, and of conspiracy with *Franion*: *Bellaria* hearing the contentes, was no whit astonished, but made this chearefull aunswer.

[TLN 1202-6] If the deuine powers bee priuy to humane actions (as no doubt they are) I hope my patience shall make fortune blushe, and my vnspotted life shall staine spightfull* discredit. For although lying Report hath sought to appeach mine

---

*spightfull] 1607; spightfully 1588

honor, and Suspition hath intended to soyle my credit with infamie: yet where Vertue keepeth the Forte, Report and suspition may assayle, but neuer sack: [TLN 1219-21] how I haue led my life before *Egistus* comming, I appeale *Pandosto* to the Gods, and to thy conscience. [TLN 1240] What hath passed betwixt him and me, the Gods onely know, and I hope will presently reueale: [TLN 1238-43] that I loued *Egistus* I can not denie, that I honored him I shame not to confesse: to the one I was forced by his vertues: to the other for his dignities. But as touching lasciuious lust, I say *Egistus* is honest, and hope my selfe to be found without spot: for *Franion*, I can neither accuse him, nor excuse him: for [TLN 1254-7] I was not [C3] priuie to his departure, and that this is true which I haue heere rehearsed, [TLN 1294] I referre my self to the deuine Oracle.

Bellaria had no sooner sayd, but the King commaunded that one of his Dukes should reade the contentes of the scroule: which after the commons had heard, they gaue a great showt, reioysing and clapping their hands that the Queene was cleare of that false accusation: but [cf. the contrasting TLN 1321-2] the King whose conscience was a witnesse against him of his witlesse furie, and false suspected Iealousie, was so ashamed of his rashe folly, that he intreated his nobles to perswade *Bellaria* to forgiue, and forget these iniuries: promising not onely to shew himselfe a loyall and louing husband, but also to reconcile himselfe to *Egistus*, and *Franion*: reuealing then before them all the cause of their secrete flighte, and how treacherously hee thought to haue practised his death, [cf. TLN 1347-8] if the good minde of his Cupbearer had not preuented his purpose. As thus he was relating the whole matter, [TLN 1326-7] there was worde brought him that his young sonne *Garinter* was sodainly dead, which newes so soone as *Bellaria* heard, surcharged before with* extreame ioy, and now suppressed with heauie sorrowe, her vitall spirites were so stopped, that [TLN 1332-3, 1388] she fell downe presently dead, and could be neuer reuiued. This sodaine sight so appalled the Kinges Sences, that he sanck from his seate in a sound so as he was fayne to be carried by his nobles to his Pallace, where hee lay by the space of three dayes without speache: his commons were as men in dispaire, so diuersely distressed: there was nothing but mourning and lamentation to be heard throughout al *Bohemia*: their young Prince dead, their vertuous Queene bereaued of her life, and their King and Soueraigne in great hazard: this tragicall discourse of fortune so daunted them, as [TLN 938-41] they went like shadowes, not men: yet somewhat to comfort their heauie hearts, they heard that *Pandosto* was come to himselfe, and had recouered his speache, who as in a fury brayed out these bitter speaches.

[TLN 1366-85] O miserable *Pandosto*, what surer witnesse then conscience? What thoughts more sower then suspition? What plague more bad then Iealousie? Vnnaturall actions offend the Gods, more than men, and causelesse crueltie neuer scapes without re-[C3ᵛ]uenge: I haue committed such a bloudy fact, as repent I may, but recall I cannot. Ah Iealousie, a hell to the minde, and a horror to the conscience,

---

*with] 1595; whith 1588

suppressing reason, and inciting rage: a worse passion then phrensie, a greater plague than madnesse. Are the Gods iust? Then let them reuenge such brutishe crueltie: my innocent Babe I haue drowned in the Seas: my louing wife I haue slaine with slaunderous suspition: my trusty friend I haue sought to betray, and yet the Gods are slacke to plague such offences. Ah vniust *Apollo, Pandosto* is the man that hath committed the faulte: why should *Garinter,* seely childe, abide the paine? Well sith the Gods meane to prolong my dayes, to increase my dolour, I will offer my guiltie bloud a sacrifice to those sackles soules, whose liues are lost by my rigorous folly. And with that he reached at a Rapier, to haue murdered himselfe, but his Peeres being present, stayed him from such a bloudy acte: perswading him to think, that the Commonwealth consisted on his safetie, and that those sheepe could not but perish, that wanted a sheepheard: wishing, that if hee would not liue for himselfe, yet he should haue care of his subiects, and to put such fancies out of his minde, sith [TLN 1413–14] in sores past help, salues doe not heale, but hurt: and in thinges past cure, care is a corrasiue: with these and such like perswasions the Kinge was ouercome, and began somewhat to quiet his minde: so that assoone as hee could goe abroad, hee caused his wife to bee embalmed, and wrapt in lead [TLN 1428] with her young sonne *Garinter:* erecting a rich and famous Sepulchre, wherein hee intombed them both, making such sollemne obsequies at her funeral, as al *Bohemia* might perceiue he did greatly repent him of his forepassed folly: [TLN 1428–30] causing this Epitaph to be ingrauen on her Tombe in letters of Golde:

¶The Epitaph.

Here lyes entombde Bellaria faire,
   Falsly accused to be vnchaste:
Cleared by Apollos sacred doome,
   Yet slaine by Iealousie at last.

What ere thou be, that passest by,
Cursse him that causde this Queene to die.

[C4] This Epitaph being ingrauen, [TLN 1430–5] *Pandosto* would once a day repaire to the Tombe, and there with watry plaintes bewaile his misfortune: coueting no other companion but sorrowe, nor no other harmonie, but repentance. But [TLN 1596–8] leauing him to his dolorous passions, at last let vs come to shewe the tragicall discourse of the young infant.

Who being tossed with Winde, and Waue, floated two whole daies without succour, readie at euery puffe to bee drowned in the Sea, till at last [TLN 1443–5, 1491, 1525–36] the Tempest ceassed, and the little boate was driuen with the tyde [TLN 1437, 1440] into the Coast of *Sycilia,* where sticking vppon the sandes, it rested. [TLN 1486] Fortune minding to be wanton, willing to shewe that as she hath wrinckles on her browes: so shee hath dimples in her cheekes: thought after so many sower lookes, to lend a fayned smile, and after a puffing storme, to bring a pretty calme: shee began thus to dally. It fortuned a poore mercenary Sheepheard, that dwelled in *Sycilia,* who got his liuing by other mens flockes, missed [TLN 1507] one of his sheepe, and thinking it had strayed into the couert, that was hard by, sought very diligently to find that which he could not see, fearing either that [TLN 1508] the Wolues, or Eagles had vndone him (for hee was so poore, as a sheepe was halfe his substaunce) wandered downe toward the Sea cliffes, to see if perchaunce the sheepe was browsing on [TLN 1509-10] the sea Iuy, whereon they greatly doe feede, but not finding her there, as he was ready to returne to his flocke, hee heard a childe crie: but knowing there was no house nere, he thought he had mistaken the sound, and that it was the bleatyng of his Sheepe. Wherefore looking more narrowely, as he cast his eye to the Sea, he spyed a little boate, from whence as he attentiuely listened, he might heare the cry to come: standing a good while in a maze, at last he went to the shoare, and wading to the boate, as he looked in, he saw the little babe lying al alone, ready to die for hunger and colde, wrapped in a Mantle of Scarlet, richely imbrodered with Golde, and hauing a chayne about the necke. The Sheepeheard, who before had neuer seene so faire a Babe, nor so [TLN 3043] riche Iewels, [TLN 1512] thought assuredly, that it was some little God, and began with great deuocion to knock on his breast. The Babe, who wrythed with the head, to seeke for the pap, began againe to cry a fresh, whereby the poore man knew that it [C4ᵛ] was a Childe, which by some sinister meanes was driuen thither by distresse of weather: maruailing how such a seely infant, which by the Mantle, and the Chayne, could not [TLN 2630] be but borne of Noble Parentage, should be so hardly crossed with deadly mishap. The poore sheepheard perplexed thus with diuers thoughts, tooke pity of the childe, and determined with himselfe to carry it to the King, that there it might be brought vp, according to the worthinesse of birth: for his ability coulde not afforde to foster it, though his good minde was willing to further it. Taking therefore the Chylde in his armes, as he foulded the mantle together, the better to defend it from colde, there fell downe at his foote a very faire and riche purse, wherein he founde [TLN 1560-1] a great summe of golde: which sight so reuiued the shepheards spirits, as he was greatly rauished with ioy, and daunted with feare: Ioyfull to see such a summe in his power, and feareful if it should be knowne, that it might breede his further daunger. [TLN 455-66] Necessitie wisht him at the least, to retaine the Golde, though he would not keepe the childe: the simplicity of* his conscience feared him from such deceiptfull briberie. Thus was the poore manne perplexed with a doubtfull *Dilemma*, vntil at the last the couetousnesse of the coyne ouercame him: for what will not the greedy desire of Golde cause a man to doe? So that he was resolued in himselfe to foster the child, and with the summe to relieue his want: resting thus resolute in this point, he left seeking of his sheepe, and as couertly, and secretly as he coulde, went by a by-way to his house, least any of his neighbours should perceaue his carriage: assoone as he was got home, entring in at the doore, the childe began to crie, which his wife hearing, and seeing her husband with a yong babe in armes, began to bee somewhat ielousse, yet marueiling that her husband should be so wanton abroad, sith he was so quiet at home: but as women are naturally giuen to beleeue the worste, so his wife thinking it was some

---

*of] 1592; if 1588

bastard: beganne to crow against her goodman, and taking vp a cudgel (for the most maister went breechles) sware solemnly that shee would make clubs trumps, if hee brought any bastard brat within her dores. The goodman seeing his wife in her maiestie with her mace in her hand, thought it was time to bowe for feare of blowes, and desired her to be quiet, for there was non such matter: but if she could holde her peace, they were [TLN 1559] made for euer: and with [D1] that he told her the whole matter, how he had found the childe in a little boat, without any succour, wrapped in that costly mantle, and hauing that rich chaine about the neck: but at last when he shewed her the purse full of gold, she began to simper something sweetely, and taking her husband about the neck, kissed him after her homely fashion: saying that she hoped God had seene their want, and now ment to relieeue their pouerty, and seeing they could get no children, had sent them this little babe to be their heire. Take heede in any case (quoth the shepherd) that you be secret, and blabbe it not out when you meete with your gossippes, for if you doe, we are like not only to loose the Golde and Iewels, but our other goodes and liues. Tush (quoth his wife) profit is a good hatch before the doore: feare not, I haue other things to talke of then of this: but I pray you let vs lay vp the money surely, and the Iewels, least by any mishap it be spied. After that they had set all things in order, the shepheard went to his sheepe with a merry note, and the good wife learned to sing lullaby at home with her yong babe, wrapping it in a homely blanket in sted of a rich mantle: nourishing it so clenly and carefully as it began to be a iolly girle, in so much that they began both of them to be very fond of it, seeing, as it waxed in age, so it increased in beauty. The shepheard euery night at his comming home, would sing and daunce it on his knee, and prattle, that in a short time it began to speake and call him Dad, and her Mam: at last when it grew to ripe yeeres, that it was about seuen yeares olde, the shepheard left keeping of other mens sheepe, and with the money he found in the purse, he bought him the lease of a pretty farme, and got a smal flocke of sheepe, which when *Fawnia* (for so they named the child) came to the age of ten yeres, hee set her to keepe, and shee with such diligence performed her charge as the sheepe prospered marueilously vnder her hand. *Fawnia* thought *Porrus* had ben her father, and [TLN 3388] *Mopsa* her mother, (for so was the shepheard and his wife called) and* honoured and obeyed them with such reuerence, that all the neighbours praised the duetifull obedience of the child. [TLN 1651-3] *Porrus* grewe in short time to bee a man of some wealth, and credite: for fortune so fauoured him in hauing no charge but *Fawnia*, [D1ᵛ] that he began to purchase land, intending after his death to* giue it to his daughter: so that diuerse rich farmers sonnes came as woers to his house: for *Fawnia* was something clenly attired, beeing of such singular beautie and excellent witte, that whoso sawe her, would haue thought shee had bene some heauenly nymph, and not a mortal creature: in so much, that when she came to the age of [TLN 1585, 2240, 3221, 3243] sixteene yeeres, shee so increased with exquisite perfection both of body and minde, as [TLN 1976-8] her natural disposition did bewray that she was borne of some high

---

*and] 1609; *om.* 1588
*death to] 1592; 1588 *damaged*

parentage: but the people thinking she was daughter to the shephard *Porrus*; rested only amazed at hir beauty and wit: yea she won such fauour and commendations in euery mans eye, as her beautie was not onely praysed in the countrey, but also spoken of in the Court: yet such was her submisse modestie, that although her praise daily increased, her mind was no whit puffed vp with pride, but humbled her selfe as became a country mayde and the daughter of a poore sheepheard. Euery day she went forth with her sheepe to the field, keeping them with such care and diligence, as al men thought she was verie painfull, defending her face from the heat of the sunne with no other vale, but with a garland made of bowes and flowers: which atire became her so gallantly, as [TLN 1799] shee seemed to bee the Goddesse *Flora* her selfe for Beauty. Fortune, who al this while had shewed a frendly face, began now to turne her back, and to shewe a lowring countenance, intending as she had giuen *Fawnia* a slender checke, so she woulde giue her a harder mate: to bring which to passe, she layd her traine on this wise. *Egistus* had but one only son called *Dorastus*, about the age of twenty yeeres: a Prince so decked and adorned with the gifts of nature: so fraught with beauty and vertuous qualities, as not onely his father ioyed to haue so good a sonne, and al his commons reioyed that God had lent them such [TLN 1806] a noble Prince to succeede in the Kingdom. *Egistus* placing all his ioy in the perfection of his sonne: seeing that hee was now mariage-able, sent Embassadors to the King of *Denmarke*, to intreate a mariage betweene him and his daughter, who willingly consenting, made answer, that the next spring, if it please *Egistus* with his sonne to come into *Denmarke*, hee doubted [D2] not, but they shoulde agree vpon reasonable conditions. *Egistus* resting satisfied with this friendly answer, thought con-uenient in the meane time to breake with his sonne: finding therfore on a day fit oportunity he spake to him in these fatherly tearmes.

Dorastus, thy youth warneth me to preuent the worst, and mine age to prouide the best. Oportunities neglected, are signes of folly: actions measured by time, are seldome bitten with repentance: thou art young, and I olde: age hath taught me that, which thy youth cannot yet conceiue.

I therefore will counsell thee as a father, hoping thou wilt obey as a childe. Thou seest my white hayres are blossomes for the graue, and thy freshe colour fruite for time and fortune, so that it behooueth me to thinke how to dye, and for thee to care how to liue. My crowne I must leaue by death, and thou enioy my Kingdome by succession, wherein I hope thy vertue and prowesse shall bee such, as though my subiectes want my person, yet they shall see in thee my perfection. That nothing either may faile to satisfie thy minde, or increase thy dignities: the onely care I haue, is to see thee well marryed before I die, and thou become olde.

Dorastus who from his infancy, delighted rather to die with *Mars* in the Fielde, then to dally with *Venus* in the Chamber: fearing to displease his father, and yet not willing to be wed, made him this reuerent answere.

Sir, there is no greater bond than duetie, nor no straiter law then nature: disobe-dience in youth is often galled with despight in age. The commaund of the father ought to be a constraint to the childe: so parentes willes are laws, so they passe not all lawes: may it please your Grace therefore to appoint whome I shall loue, rather then by deniall I should be appeached of disobedience: I rest content to loue, though it bee the only thing I hate.

Egistus hearing his sonne to flie so farre from the marke, began to be somewhat chollericke, and therefore made him his hasty aunswere.

[D2ᵛ] What *Dorastus* canst thou not loue? Commeth this cynicall passion of prone desires, or peeuish frowardnesse?* What doest thou thinke thy selfe to good for all, or none good inough for thee?* I tell thee, *Dorastus*, there is nothing sweeter then youth, nor swifter decreasing, while it is increasing. Time past with folly may bee repented, but not recalled. If thou marrie in age, thy wiues freshe couloures will breede in thee dead thoughtes and suspition, and thy white hayres her lothesomnesse and sorrowe. For *Venus* affections are not fed with Kingdomes, or treasures, but with youthfull conceits and sweete amours. *Vulcan* was allotted to shake the tree, but *Mars* allowed to reape the fruit. Yeelde *Dorastus* to thy Fathers perswasions, which may preuent thy perils. I haue chosen thee a Wife, faire by nature, royall by birth, by vertues famous, learned by education, and rich by possessions, so that it is hard to iudge whether her bounty, or fortune, her beauty, or vertue, bee of greater force: I meane, *Dorastus*, *Euphania* Daughter and heire to the King of *Denmarke*.

Egistus pausing here a while, looking when his son should make him answere, and seeing that he stoode still as one in a trance, he shooke him vp thus sharply.

Well *Dorastus* take heede, the tree Alpya wasteth not with fire, but withereth with the dewe: that which loue nourisheth not, perisheth with hate: if thou like *Euphania*, thou breedest my content, and in louing her thou shalt haue my loue, otherwise; and with that hee flung from his sonne in a rage, leauing him a sorrowfull man, in that he had by deniall displeased his Father, and halfe angrie with him selfe that hee coulde not yeelde to that passion, whereto both reason and his Father perswaded him: but see how fortune is plumed with times feathers, and how shee can minister strange causes to breede straunge effectes.

It happened not long after this, that there was [TLN 1795] a meeting of all the Farmers Daughters in *Sycilia*, whither *Fawnia* was also bidden as the [TLN 1709, 1802, 1873] mistres of the feast, who hauing attired [D3] her selfe [TLN 1798-9] in her best garments, went among the rest of her companions to the merry meeting: there spending the day in such homely pastimes as shepheards vse. As the euening grew on, and their sportes ceased, ech taking their leaue at other, *Fawnia* desiring one of her companions to beare her companie, went home by the flocke, to see if they were well folded, and as they returned, it fortuned that *Dorastus* (who all that daye [TLN 1813-15] had bene hawking, and kilde store of game) incountred by the

---

*frowardnesse?] 1607; ~. 1588
*thee?] 1607; ~ . 1588

way these two mayds, and casting his eye sodenly on *Fawnia*, he was halfe afraid, fearing that with *Acteon* he had seene *Diana*: for hee thought such exquisite perfection could not be founde in any mortall creature. As thus he stoode in a maze, one of his Pages told him, that the maide with [TLN 1798] the garland on her heade was *Fawnia* the faire shepheard, whose beauty was so much talked of in the Court. *Dorastus* desirous to see if nature had adorned her minde with any inward qualities, as she had decked her body with outward shape, began to question with her whose daughter she was, of what age and how she had bin trained vp, who answered him with such modest reuerence and sharpnesse of witte, that *Dorastus* thought her outward beautie was but a counterfait to darken her inward qualities, [TLN 2451-3] wondring how so courtly behauiour could be found in so simple a cottage, and cursing fortune that had shadowed wit and beauty with such hard fortune. As thus he held her a long while with chat, Beauty seeing him at discouert, thought not to lose the vantage, but strooke him so deepely with an inuenomed shafte, as he wholy lost his libertie, and became a slaue to Loue, which before contemned Loue, glad now to gaze on a poore shepheard, who before refused the offer of a riche Princesse: for the perfection of *Fawnia* had so fixed his fancie as he felt his mind greatly chaunged, and his affections altered, cursing Loue that had wrought such a chaunge, and blaming the basenesse of his mind that would make such a choice: but thinking these were but passionat toies that might be thrust out at pleasure, to auoid the *Syren* that inchaunted him, he put spurs to his horse, and bad this faire shepheard farwell.

Fawnia (who all this while had marked the princely ges-[D3ᵛ]ture of *Dorastus*) seeing his face so wel featured, and each lim so perfectly framed, began greatly to praise his perfection, commending him so long, till she found her selfe faultie, [TLN 1799] and perceiued that if she waded but a little further, she might slippe ouer her shooes: shee therefore seeking to quench that fire which neuer was put out, went home, and faining her selfe not well at ease, got her to bed: where casting a thousand thoughts in her head, she could take no rest: for if she waked, she began to call to minde his beautie, and thinking to beguile such thoughts with sleepe, she then dreamed of his perfection: pestred thus with these vnacquainted passions, she passed the night as she could in short slumbers.

Dorastus (who all this while rode with a flea in his eare) coulde not by any meanes forget the sweete fauour of *Fawnia*, but rested so bewitched with her wit and beauty, as hee could take no rest. He felt fancy to giue the assault, and his wounded mind readie to yeeld as vanquished: yet he began with diuers considerations to suppresse this frantick affection, calling to minde, that *Fawnia* was a shepheard, one not worthy to bee looked at of a Prince, much lesse to bee loued of such a potentate, thinking what a discredite it were to himself, and what a griefe it would be to his father, blaming fortune and accusing his owne follie, that shoulde bee so fond as but once to cast a glaunce at such a country slut. As thus he was raging against him selfe, Loue, fearing if shee dallied long, to loose her champion, stept more nigh, and gaue him such a fresh wounde as it pearst him at the heart, that he was faine to yeeld, maugre his face, and to forsake the companie and gette him to his chamber: where being solemnly set, hee burst into these passionate tearmes.

Ah *Dorastus*, art thou alone? No not alone, while thou art tired with these vnacquainted passions. Yeld to fancy, thou canst not by thy fathers counsaile, but in a
frenzie thou art by iust destinies. Thy father were content, if thou couldest loue, and
thou therefore discontent, because thou doest loue. O deuine Loue, feared of men
because honoured of the Gods, not to be suppressed by wisdome, because not to be
comprehen-[D4]ded by reason: without Lawe, and therefore aboue all Law.

How now *Dorastus*, why doest thou blaze that with praises, which thou hast
cause to blaspheme with curses? Yet why should they curse Loue, that are in Loue?

Blush *Dorastus* at thy fortune, thy choice, thy loue: thy thoughts cannot be
vttered without shame, nor thy affections without discredit. Ah *Fawnia*, sweete
Fawnia, thy beautie *Fawnia*. Shamest not thou *Dorastus* to name one vnfitte for thy
birth, thy dignities, thy Kingdomes? Dye *Dorastus, Dorastus* die, better hadst thou
perish with high desires, then liue in base thoughts. Yea but, beautie must be obeyed,
because it is beauty, yet framed of the Gods to feede the eye, not to fetter the heart.

Ah but he that striueth against Loue, shooteth with them of *Scyrum* against the
winde, and with the Cockeatrice pecketh against the steele. I will therefore obey,
because I must obey, *Fawnia*, yea *Fawnia* shal be my fortune, in spight of fortune.
[TLN 1826–36] The Gods aboue disdain not to loue women beneath. *Phoebus* liked
Sibilla, Iupiter Io, and why not I then *Fawnia*, one something inferiour to these in
birth, but farre superiour to them in beautie, borne to be a Shepheard, but worthy to
be a Goddesse.

Ah *Dorastus*, wilt thou so forget thy selfe as to suffer affection to supresse
wisedome, and Loue to violate thine honour?* How sower will thy choice be to thy
Father, sorrowfull to thy Subiects, to thy friends a griefe, most gladsome to thy foes?
Subdue then thy affections, and cease to loue her whome thou couldst not loue,
vnlesse blinded with too much loue. Tushe I talke to the wind, and in seeking to
preuent the causes, I further the effectes. I will yet praise *Fawnia*, honour, yea and
loue *Fawnia*, and at this day followe content, not counsaile. Doo *Dorastus*, thou
canst but repent: and with that his Page came into the chamber, whereupon hee
ceased from his complaints, hoping that time would weare out that which fortune
had wrought. As thus he was pained, so poore *Fawnia* was diuersly perplexed: for
the next morning getting vp very earely, shee went to her sheepe, thinking with [D4ᵛ]
hard labours to passe away her new conceiued amours, beginning very busily to driue
them to the field, and then to shift the foldes, at last (wearied with toile) she sate her
down, where (poore soule) she was more tryed with fond affections: for loue beganne
to assault her, in so much that as she sate vpon the side of a hill, she began to accuse
her owne folly in these tearmes.

Infortunate *Fawnia*, and therefore infortunate because *Fawnia*, thy [TLN 2263]
shepherds hooke sheweth thy poore state, thy proud desires an aspiring mind: the
one declareth thy want, the other thy pride. No bastard hauke must soare so hie as

---

*honour] 1592; hononour 1588

the Hobbie, no Fowle gaze against the Sunne but the Eagle, actions wrought against nature reape despight, and thoughts aboue Fortune disdaine.

Fawnia, thou art a shepheard, daughter to poore *Porrus*: if thou rest content with this, thou art like to stande, if thou climbe thou art sure to fal. The Herb *Anita* growing higher then sixe ynches becommeth a weede. *Nylus* flowing more then twelue cubits procureth a dearth. Daring affections that passe measure, are cut shorte by time or fortune: suppresse then *Fawnia* those thoughts which thou mayest shame to expresse. But ah *Fawnia*, loue is a Lord, who will commaund by power, and constraine by force.

Dorastus, ah *Dorastus* is the man I loue, the woorse is thy hap, and the lesse cause hast thou to hope. Will Eagles catch at flyes, will Cedars stoupe to brambles, or mighty Princes looke at such homely trulles. No, no, thinke this, *Dorastus* disdaine is greater then thy desire, hee is a Prince respecting his honor, thou a beggars brat forgetting thy calling. Cease then onely to say, but to thinke to loue *Dorastus*, and dissemble thy loue *Fawnia*, for better it were to dye with griefe, then to liue with shame: yet in despight of loue I will sigh, to see if I can sigh out loue. *Fawnia* somewhat appeasing her griefes with these pithie perswasions, began after her wonted maner to walke about her sheepe, and to keepe them from straying into the corne, suppressing her affection with the due consideration of her base estate, and with the impossibilities of her loue, thinking it were frenzy, not fancy, to couet that which [E1] the very destinies did deny her to obteine.

But *Dorastus* was more impatient in his passions: for loue so fiercely assayled him, that neither companie, nor musicke could mittigate his martirdome, but did rather far the more increase his maladie: shame would not let him craue counsaile in this case, nor feare of his Fathers displeasure reueyle it to any secrete friend: but hee was faine to make a Secretarie of himselfe, and to participate his thoughtes with his owne troubled mind. Lingring thus awhile in doubtfull suspence, at last stealing secretely from the court without either men or Page, hee went to see if hee coulde espie *Fawnia* walking abroade in the field: but as one hauing a great deale more skill to retriue the partridge with his spaniels, then to hunt after such a straunge pray, he sought, but was little the better: which crosse lucke draue him into a great choler, that he began both to accuse loue and fortune. But as he was readie to retire, he sawe *Fawnia* sitting all alone vnder the side of a hill, making a garland of such homely flowers as the fields did afoord. This sight so reuiued his spirites that he drewe nigh, with more iudgement to take a view of her singular perfection, which hee found to bee such, as in that countrey attyre shee stained al the courtlie Dames of *Sicilia*. While thus he stoode gazing with pearcing lookes on her surpassing beautie, *Fawnia* cast her eye aside, and spyed *Dorastus*, which* sudden sight made the poore girl to blush, and to die her christal cheeks with a vermilion red: which gaue her such a grace, as she seemed farre more beautiful. And with that she rose vp, saluting the Prince with such modest curtesies, as he wondred how a country maid could afoord such courtly

---

behauiour. *Dorastus*, repaying her curtesie with a smiling countenance, began to parlie with her on this manner.

Faire maide (quoth he) either your want is great, or a shepheards life very sweete, that your delight is in such country labors. I can not conceiue what pleasure you should take, vnlesse you meane to imitate the nymphes, being your selfe* so like a Nymph. To put me out of this doubt, shew me what is to be commended in a shep-herdes life, and what [E1ᵛ] pleasures you haue to counteruaile these drudging la-boures. *Fawnia* with blushing face made him this ready aunswere.

Sir, what richer state then content, or what sweeter life then quiet, we shep-heards are not borne to honor, nor beholding vnto beautie, the lesse care we haue to feare fame or fortune: we count our attire braue inough if warme inough, and our foode* dainty, if to suffice nature: our greatest enemie is the wolfe: our only care in safe keeping our flock: in stead of courtly ditties we spend the daies with cuntry songs: our amorous conceites are homely thoughtes: delighting as much to talke of *Pan* and his cuntrey prankes, as Ladies to tell of *Venus* and her wanton toyes. Our toyle is in shifting the fouldes, and looking to the Lambes,* easie labours: oft singing and telling tales, homely pleasures: our greatest welth not to couet, our honor not to climbe, our quiet not to care. Enuie looketh not so lowe as shepheards: Shepheards gaze not so high as ambition: we are rich in that we are poore with content, and proud onely in this that we haue no cause to be proud.

This wittie answer of *Fawnia* so inflamed *Dorastus* fancy, as he commended him selfe for making so good a choyce, thinking, [TLN 2449-53] if her birth were aunswerable to her wit and beauty, that she were a fitte mate for the most famous Prince in the worlde. He therefore beganne to sifte her more narrowely on this manner.

Fawnia, I see thou art content with Country labours, because thou knowest not Courtly pleasures: I commend thy wit, and pitty thy want: but wilt thou leaue thy Fathers Cottage, and serue a Courtlie Mistresse.

Sir (quoth she) beggers ought not to striue against fortune, nor to gaze after honour, least either their fall be greater, or they become blinde. I am borne to toile for the Court, not in the Court, my nature vnfit for their nurture, better liue then in meane degree, than in high disdaine.

Well saide, *Fawnia* (quoth *Dorastus*) I gesse at thy thoughtes, thou art in loue with some Countrey Shep-[E2]hearde.

---

*your selfe] 1592; you,selfe 1588
*foode] 1592; fdode 1588
*Lambes,] 1614; ~ ∧ 1588

No sir (quoth she) shepheards cannot loue, that are so simple, and maides may not loue that are so young.

Nay therefore (quoth *Dorastus*) maides must loue, because they are young, for *Cupid* is a child, and *Venus*, though olde, is painted with fresh coloures.

I graunt (quoth she) age may be painted with new shadowes, and youth may haue imperfect affections: but what arte concealeth in one, ignorance reuealeth in the other. *Dorastus* seeing *Fawnia* helde him so harde, thought it was vaine so long to beate about the bush: therefore he thought to haue giuen her a fresh charge: but he was so preuented by certaine of his men, who missing their maister, came posting to seeke him: seeing that he was gone foorth all alone, yet before they drewe so nie that they might heare their talke, he vsed these speeches.

Why *Fawnia*, perhappes I loue thee, and then thou must needes yeelde, for thou knowest I can commaunde and constraine. Trueth sir (quoth she) but not to loue: for constrained loue is force, not loue: and know this sir, mine honesty is such, as I hadde rather dye then be a *Concubine* euen to a King, and my birth is so base as I am vnfitte to bee a wife to a poore farmer. Why then (quoth he) thou canst not loue *Dorastus*? Yes saide *Fawnia*, when *Dorastus* becomes a shepheard, and with that the presence of his men broke off their parle, so that he went with them to the palace, and left *Fawnia* sitting still on the hill side, who seeing that the night drewe on, shifted her fouldes, and busied her selfe about other worke to driue away such fond fancies as began to trouble her braine. But all this could not preuaile, for the beautie of *Dorastus* had made such a deepe impression in her heart, as it could not be worne out without cracking, so that she was forced to blame her owne folly in this wise.

Ah *Fawnia*, why doest thou gaze against the Sunne, or catch at the Winde: starres are to be looked at with the eye, not reacht at with the hande: thoughts are to be measured by Fortunes, not by desires: falles come not by sitting low, but by climing too hie: what then shall al feare to fal, because some [E2ᵛ] happe to fall? No,* lucke commeth by lot, and fortune windeth those threedes which the destinies spin. Thou art fauored *Fawnia* of a prince, and yet thou art so fond to reiect desired fauours: thou hast deniall at thy tonges end, and desire at thy hearts bottome: a womans fault, to spurne at that with her foote, which she greedily catcheth at with her hand. Thou louest *Dorastus, Fawnia*, and yet seemest to lower. Take heede, if hee retire, thou wilt repent: for vnles hee loue, thou canst but dye. Dye then *Fawnia*: for *Dorastus* doth but iest: the Lyon neuer prayeth on the mouse, nor Faulcons stoupe not to dead stales [*OED, sb.*³ 1: "A decoy-bird"]. Sit downe then in sorrow, ceasse to loue, and content thy selfe, that *Dorastus* will vouchsafe to flatter *Fawnia*, though not to fancy *Fawnia*. Heigh ho: Ah foole, it were seemelier for thee to whistle as a Shepheard, then to sigh as a louer, and with that she ceassed from these perplexed passions, folding her sheepe, and hying home to her poore Cottage. But such was the incessant sorrow of *Dorastus* to thinke on the witte and beautie of *Fawnia*, and to see how

---

*No,] 1595; ~ ∧ 1588

fond hee was being a Prince: and how froward she was being a beggar, that* he began to loose his wonted appetite, to looke pale and wan: in stead of mirth, to feede on melancholy: for courtly daunces to vse cold dumpes: in so much that not onely his owne men, but his father and all the court began to maruaile at his sudden change, thinking that some lingring sickenes had brought him into this state: wherefore he caused Phisitions to come, but *Dorastus* neither would let them minister, nor so much as suffer them to see his vrine: but remained stil so oppressed with these passions, as he feared in him selfe a farther inconuenience. His honor wished him to ceasse from such folly, but Loue forced him to follow fancy: yea and in despight of honour, loue wonne the conquest, so that his hot desires caused him to find new deuises, for hee presently made himselfe a shepheards coate, that he might goe vnknowne, and with the lesse suspition to prattle with *Fawnia*, and conueied it secretly into a thick groue hard ioyning to the Pallace, whether finding fit time, and oportunity, he went all alone, and putting off his princely apparel, got on those shepheards roabes, and taking [TLN 2263] a great hooke in his hand (which he had also gotten) he went very an-[E3]ciently [BULLOUGH (1975, 8:184): "like an old man . . . 'anxiously' perhaps"] to finde out the mistres of his affection: but as he went by the way, seeing himselfe clad in such vnseemely ragges, he began to smile at his owne folly, and to reproue his fondnesse in these tearmes.

Well said *Dorastus*, thou keepest a right *decorum*, base desires and homely attires: thy thoughtes are fit for none but a shepheard, and thy apparell such as only become a shepheard. A strang change from a Prince to a pesant? What is it? thy wretched fortune or thy wilful folly? Is it thy cursed destinies? Or thy crooked desires, that appointeth thee this penance? Ah *Dorastus* thou canst but loue, and vnlesse thou loue, thou art like to perish for loue. Yet fond foole, choose flowers, not weedes: Diamondes, not peables: Ladies which may honour thee, not shepheards which may disgrace thee. *Venus* is painted in silkes, not in ragges: and *Cupid* treadeth on disdaine, when he reacheth at dignitie. [TLN 1826–36] And yet *Dorastus* shame not at thy shepheards weede: the heauenly Godes haue sometime earthly thoughtes: [TLN 1828–32] *Neptune* became a Ram, *Iupiter* a Bul, *Apollo* a shepheard: they Gods, and yet in loue: and thou a man appointed to loue.

Deuising thus with himselfe, hee drew nigh to the place where *Fawnia* was keeping her shepe, who casting her eye aside, and seeing such a manerly shepheard, perfectly limmed, and comming with so good a pace, she began halfe to forget *Dorastus*, and to fauor this prety shepheard, whom she thought shee might both loue and obtaine: but as shee was in these thoughts, she perceiued then, it was the yong prince *Dorastus*, wherfore she rose vp, and reuerently saluted him. *Dorastus* taking her by the hand, repaied her curtesie with a sweete kisse, and praying her to sit downe by him, he began thus to lay the batterie.

If thou maruell *Fawnia* at my strange attyre, thou wouldest more muse at my

---

*that] 1607; then 1588

vnaccustomed thoughtes: the one disgraceth but my outward shape, the other dis-
turbeth my inward sences. I loue *Fawnia*, and therefore what loue liketh I cannot
mislike. *Fawnia* thou hast promised to loue, and I [E3ᵛ] hope thou wilt performe no
lesse: I haue fulfilled thy request, and now thou canst but graunt my desire. Thou
wert content to loue *Dorastus* when he ceast to be a Prince, and graunted* to become
a shepheard, and see I haue made the change, and therefore hope* not to misse of
my choice.

Trueth, quoth *Fawnia*, but all that weare Cooles [cowls] are not Monkes: painted
Eagles are pictures, not Eagles, *Zeusis* Grapes were like Grapes, yet shadowes: rich
clothing make not princes: nor homely attyre beggers: shepheards are not called
shepheardes, because they were [wear] hookes and bagges: but that they are borne
poore, and liue to keepe sheepe, so this attire hath not made *Dorastus* a shepherd,
but to seeme like a shepherd.*

Well *Fawnia*, answered *Dorastus*: were I a shepherd, I could not but like thee,
and being a prince I am forst to loue thee. Take heed *Fawnia*, be not proud of beauties
painting, for it is a flower that fadeth in the blossome. Those which disdayne in youth
are despised in age: Beauties shadowes are trickt vp with times colours, which being
set to drie in the sunne are stained with the sunne, scarce pleasing the sight ere they
beginne not to be worth the sight, not much vnlike the herbe *Ephemeron*, which
flourisheth in the morning and is withered before the sunne setting: if my desire were
against lawe, thou mightest iustly deny me by reason, but I loue thee *Fawnia*, not to
misuse thee as a Concubine, but to vse thee as my wife: I can promise no more, and
meane to performe no lesse.

Fawnia hearing this solemne protestation of *Dorastus*, could no longer withstand the assault, but yeelded vp the forte in these friendly tearmes.

Ah *Dorastus*, I shame to expresse that thou forcest me with thy sugred speeche
to confesse: my base birth causeth the one, and thy high dignities the other. Beggars
thoughts ought not to reach so far as Kings, and yet my desires reach as high as
Princes, I dare not say *Dorastus*, I loue thee, be-[E4]cause I am a shepherd, but the
Gods know I haue honored *Dorastus* (pardon if I say amisse) yea and loued *Dorastus*
with such dutiful affection as *Fawnia* can performe, or *Dorastus* desire: I yeeld, not
ouercome with prayers, but with loue, resting *Dorastus* handmaid ready to obey his
wil, if no preiudice at all to his honour, nor to my credit.

Dorastus hearing this freendly conclusion of *Fawnia* embraced her in his armes,
swearing that neither distance, time, nor aduerse fortune should diminish his affection: but that in despight of the destinies he would remaine loyall vnto death. Hauing

---

*graunted] WELLS (1988); *om.* 1588
*hope] WELLS (1988); *om.* 1588
*shepherd] 1592; shephherd 1588

thus plight their troath each to other, seeing they could not haue the full fruition of their loue in *Sycilia* for that [TLN 1817-20, 1838-49] *Egistus* consent woulde neuer bee graunted to so meane a match, *Dorastus* determined assone as time and oportunitie would giue them leaue, to prouide a great masse of money, and many rich and costly iewels, for the easier cariage, and then [TLN 2351 ff.] to transporte them selues and their treasure into Italy, where they should leade a contented life, vntil such time as either he could be reconciled to his Father, or els by succession* come to the Kingdome. This deuise was greatly praysed of *Fawnia*, for she feared if the King his father should but heare of the contract, that his furie would be such as no lesse then death would stand for payment: she therefore told him, that delay bred daunger: that many mishaps did fall out betweene the cup and the lip, and that to auoid danger, it were best with as much speed as might be to pass out of *Sycilia*, least fortune might preuent their pretence with some newe despight: *Dorastus*, whom loue pricked forward with desire, promised to dispatch his affaires with as great hast, as either time or oportunitie would geue him leaue: and so resting vpon this point, after many imbracings and sweete kisses they departed. *Dorastus* hauing taken his leaue of his best beloued *Fawnia*, went to the Groue where hee had his rich apparel, and there [TLN 2512] vncasing himself as secretly as might be, hiding vp his shepheards attire, till occasion should serue againe to vse it: hee went to the pallace, shewing by his merrie countenaunce, that either the state of his body was amended, or the case of his minde [E4ᵛ] greatly redressed: *Fawnia* poore soule was no less ioyful, that being a shepheard, fortune had fauoured her so, as to reward her with the loue of a Prince, hoping in time to be aduaunced from the daughter of a poore farmer to be the wife of a riche King: so that she thought euery houre a yeere, till by their departure they might preuent danger, not ceasing still to goe euery daye to her sheepe, not so much for the care of her flock, as for the desire she had to see her loue and Lord *Dorastus*: who oftentimes, when oportunitie would serrue, repaired thither to feede his fancy with the sweet content of *Fawnias** presence: and although he neuer went to visit her, but in his shepheards ragges, yet his ofte repaire made him not onely suspected, but knowne to diuers of their neighbours: who for the good will they bare to old *Porrus*, tould him secretly of the matter, wishing him to keepe his daughter at home, least she went so oft to the field that she brought him home a yong sonne: for they feared that *Fawnia* being so beautifull, the yong prince would allure her to folly. *Porrus* was striken into a dump at these newes, so that thanking his neighboures for their good will hee hyed him home to his wife, and calling her aside, wringing his handes and shedding foorth teares, he brake the matter to her in these tearmes.

I am afraid wife, that my daughter *Fawnia* hath made her selfe so fine, that she will buy repentance too deare. I heare newes, which if they be true, some will wish they had not proued true. It is tould me by my neighbours, that *Dorastus* the Kinges sonne begins to looke at our daughter *Fawnia*: which if it be so, I will not geue her a halfepeny* for her honestie at* the yeeres end. I tell thee wife, nowadaies beauty is a great stale to trap yong men, and faire wordes and sweete promises are two great enemies to a maydens honestie: and thou knowest where poore men intreate, and cannot obtaine, there Princes may commaund, and wil obtaine. Though Kings sonnes daunce in nettes, they may not be seene: but poore mens faultes are spied at a little hole: Well, it is a hard case where Kinges lustes are lawes, and that they should binde poore men to that, which they themselues wilfully breake.

[F1] Peace husband (quoth his wife) take heede what you say: speake no more then you should, least you heare what you would not: great streames are to be stopped by sleight, not by force: and princes to be perswaded by submission, not by rigor: doe what you can, but no more than you may, least in sauing *Fawnia*s mayden-head, you loose your owne head. Take heede I say, it is ill iesting with edged tooles, and bad sporting with Kinges. The Wolfe had his skinne puld ouer his eares for but looking into the Lions den. Tush wife (quoth he) thou speakest like a foole. If the King should knowe that *Dorastus* had begotten our daughter with childe (as I feare it will fall out little better) the Kings furie would be such as no doubt we should both loose our goodes and liues: necessitie therefore hath no lawe, and I will preuent this mischiefe with a newe deuise that is come into my head, which shall neither offend the King, nor displease *Dorastus*. I meane to take the chaine and the iewels that I found with *Fawnia*, and carrie them to the King, letting him then to vnderstand how she is none of my daughter, but that I found her beaten vp with the water alone in a little boate wrapped in a rich Mantle, wherein was inclosed this treasure. By this meanes I hope the King will take *Fawnia* into his seruice, and we whatsoeuer chaunceth shal be blamelesse. This deuice pleased the good wife very well, so that they determined assoone as they might know the King at leisure, to make him priuie to this case. In the meane time *Dorastus* was not slacke in his affaires, but applyed his matters with such diligence, that he prouided all thinges fitte for their iourney. Treasure and Iewels he had gotten great store, thincking there was no better friend than money in a strange countrey: rich attire he had prouided for *Fawnia*, and, because he could not bring the matter to passe without the helpe and aduice of some one, he made an old seruant of his called *Capnio*, who had serued him from his childhood, priuie to his affaires: who seeing no perswasions could preuaile to diuert him from his setled determination, gaue his consent and dealt so secretly in the cause, that within short space, hee had gotten a ship ready for their passage: the Mariners seeing a fit gale of winde for their purpose, wished *Capnio* to make no delayes, [F1ᵛ] least if they pretermitted this good weather, they might stay long ere they had such a fayre winde. *Capnio* fearing that his negligence should hinder the iourney, in the night time conueyed the trunckes full of treasure into the shippe, and by secrete meanes let *Fawnia* vnderstand, that the next morning they meant to depart: she vpon this newes slept verie little that

---

*halfepeny] 1592; halfepenp 1588
*honestie at] 1592; honestiect 1588

night, but gotte vp very early, and wente to her sheepe, looking euery minute when she should see *Dorastus*, who taried not long, for fear delay might breede daunger, but came as fast as he could gallop, and without any great circumstance tooke *Fawnia* vp behinde him and rode to the hauen, where the shippe lay, which was not three quarters of a mile distant from that place. He no sooner came there, but the Marriners were readie with their Cockboate to set them aboard, where being coucht together in a Cabben they past away the time in recounting their old loues, til their man *Capnio* should come. *Porrus* who had heard that this morning the King would go abroad to take the ayre, called in haste to his wife to bring him his holyday hose and his best Iacket, that he might goe like an honest substantiall man to tell his tale. His wife, a good cleanly wenche, brought him all things fitte, and spungd him vp very handsomlie, giuing him the chaines and Iewels in a little boxe, which *Porrus* for the more safety put in his bosom. Hauing thus all his trinkets in a readines, taking his staffe in his hand he bad his wife kisse him for good lucke, and so hee went towards the Pallace. But as he was going, fortune (who meant to showe him a little false play) preuented his purpose in this wise.

He met by chaunce in his way *Capnio*, who trudging as fast as he could with a little coffer vnder his arme to the ship, and spying *Porrus* whome he knewe to be *Fawnia*s Father, going towardes the Pallace, being a wylie fellow, began to doubt the worst, and therefore crost him the way, and askt him whither he was going so earely this morning.

Porrus (who knew by his face that he was one of the Court) meaning simply, told him that the Kings son *Dorastus* dealt hardly with him; for he had but one Daughter who was a little beautifull, and that his neighboures told him the young [F2] Prince had allured her to folly, he went therefore now to complaine to the King how greatly he was abused.

Capnio (who straight way smelt the whole matter) began to soothe him in his talke, and said, that *Dorastus* dealt not like a Prince to spoyle any poore manes daughter in that sort: he therefore would doe the best for him he could, because he knew he was an honest man. But (quoth *Capnio*) you lose your labour in going to the Pallace, for [TLN 2642–5] the King meanes this day to take the aire of the Sea, and to goe aboord of a shippe that lies in the hauen. I am going before, you see, to prouide all things in redinesse, and if you will follow my counsaile, turne back with me to the hauen, where I will set you in such a fitte place as you may speake to the King at your pleasure. *Porrus* giuing credit to *Capnio*s smooth tale, gaue him a thousand thanks for his friendly aduise, and went with him to the hauen, making all the way his complaintes of *Dorastus*, yet concealing secretlie the chaine and the Iewels. Assone as they were come to the Sea side, the marriners seeing *Capnio*, came a land with their cockboate, who still dissembling the matter, demaunded of *Porrus* if he would go see the ship? who vnwilling and fearing the worst, because he was not well acquainted with *Capnio*, made his excuse that he could not brooke the Sea, therefore would not trouble him.

Capnio seeing that by faire meanes hee could not get him aboord, commaunded the mariners that by violence they should carrie him into the shippe, who like sturdy knaues hoisted the poore shepheard on their backes, and bearing him to the boate, lanched from the land.

Porrus seeing himselfe so cunningly betraied durst not crie out, for hee sawe it would not preuaile, but began to intreate *Capnio* and the mariners to be good to him, and to pittie his estate, hee was but a poore man that liued by his labour: they laughing to see the shepheard so afraide, made as much haste as they could, and set him aboorde. *Porrus* was no sooner in the shippe, but he saw *Dorastus* walking with *Fawnia*, yet he scarse knew her: for she had attired her selfe in riche apparell, which* so increased her beauty, that shee resembled rather an Angell than a mortall creature.

[F2ᵛ] *Dorastus* and *Fawnia*, were halfe astonished to see the olde shepherd, maruailing greatly what wind had brought him thither, til *Capnio** told them al the whole discourse: how *Porrus* was going to make his complaint to the King, if by pollicie he had not preuented him, and therefore now sith he was aboord, for the auoiding of further danger it were best to carrie him into *Italy*.

Dorastus praised greatly his mans deuise, and allowed of his counsaile; but *Fawnia*, (who stil feared *Porrus*, as her father) began to blush for shame, that by her meanes he should either incure daunger or displeasure.

The old shephard hearing this hard sentence, that he should on such a sodaine be caried from his Wife, his country, and kinsfolke, into a forraine Lande amongst straungers, began with bitter teares to make his complaint, and on his knees to intreate *Dorastus*, that pardoning his vnaduised folly he would giue him leaue to goe home: swearing that hee would keepe all thinges as secret as they could wish. But these protestations could not preuaile, although *Fawnia* intreated *Dorastus* very earnestly, but the mariners hoisting their maine sailes waied ankers, and hailed into the deepe, where we leaue them to the fauour of the wind and seas, and returne to *Egistus*.

Who hauing appointed this day to hunt in one of his Forrests, called for his sonne *Dorastus* to go sport himselfe, because hee saw that of late hee began to loure; but his men made answer that hee was gone abroade none knew whither, except he were gone to the groue to walke all alone, as his custome was to doe euery day.

The King willing to waken him out of his dumpes, sent one of his men to goe seeke him, but in vaine, for at last he returned, but finde him he could not, so that the King went himselfe to goe see the sport; where passing away the day, returning at night from hunting, hee asked for his sonne, but he could not be heard of, which draue the King into a great choler: whereupon most of his Noblemen and other Courtiers poasted abroad to seek him, but they could not heare of him through all *Sicilia*, onely they missed *Capnio* his man which againe [F3] made the King suspect that hee was not gone farre.

Two or three daies being passed, and no newes heard of *Dorastus*, *Egistus* began to feare that he was deuoured with some wilde beastes, and vpon that made out a

---

*which∧] 1607; ⁓, 1588
*Capnio] 1592; *Capino* 1588

great troupe of men to go seeke him; who coasted through all the Country, and searched in euerie daungerous and secrete place, vntill at last they mette with a Fisherman that was sitting in a little couert hard by the sea side mending his nettes, when *Dorastus* and *Fawnia* tooke shipping: who being examined if he either knewe or heard where the Kings Sonne was, without any secrecie at all reuealed the whole matter, how he was sayled two dayes past, had in his company his man *Capnio*, *Porrus* and his faire Daughter *Fawnia*. This heauie newes was presently caryed to the King, who halfe dead for sorrow commaunded *Porrus* wife to be sent for: she being come to the Pallace, after due examination, confessed that her neighbours had oft told her that the Kings Sonne was too familier with *Fawnia*, her Daughter: where-uppon, her husband fearing the worst, about two dayes past (hearing the King should goe an hunting) rose earely in the morning and went to make his complaint, but since she neither hearde of him, nor saw him. *Egistus* perceiuing the womans vnfeyned simplicity, let her depart without incurring further displeasure, conceiuing* such se-cret greefe for his Sonnes recklesse follie, that he had so forgotten his honour and parentage, by so base a choise to dishonor his father, and discredit himselfe, that with very care and thought he fel into a quartan feuer, which was so vnfit for his aged yeeres and complexion, that he became so weake, as the Phisitions would graunt him no life.

But his sonne *Dorastus* little regarded either father, countrie, or Kingdome in respect of his Lady *Fawnia*, for fortune smyling on this young nouice, lent him so lucky a gale of winde, for the space of a day and a night, that the maryners lay and slept vpon the hatches; but on the next morning about the breake of the day, the aire began to be ouercast, the winds to rise, the seas to swel, yea presently [TLN 2408] there arose such a fearfull tempest, as the ship was in danger to be swallowed vp with euery sea, the maine mast with the violence of the wind was thrown [F3ᵛ] ouer boord, the sayles were torne, the tacklings went in sunder, the storme raging still so furiously that poore *Fawnia* was almost dead for feare, but that she was greatly comforted with the presence of *Dorastus*. The tempest continued three dayes, al which time the Mariners euerie minute looked for death, and the aire was so darkned with cloudes that the Maister could not tell by his compasse in what Coast they were. But vpon the fourth day about ten of the clocke, the wind began to cease, the sea to waxe calme, and the sky to be cleare, and the Mariners descryed the coast of *Bohe-mia*, shooting of their ordnance for ioy that they had escaped such a fearefull tempest.

Dorastus hearing that they were arriued at some harbour, sweetly kissed *Fawnia*, and bad her be of good cheare: when they tolde him that the port belonged vnto the cheife Cittie of *Bohemia* where *Pandosto* kept his Court, *Dorastus* began to be sad, knowing that his Father hated no man so much as *Pandosto*, and that the King himself had sought secretly to betray *Egistus*: this considered, he was halfe afraid to goe on land, but that *Capnio* counselled him to chaunge his name and his countrey, vntil such time as they could get some other barke to transport them into *Italy*.

---

*conceiuing] 1614; conceiling 1588

Dorastus liking this deuise made his case priuy to the Marriners, rewarding them bountifully for their paines, and charging them to saye that he was a Gentleman of *Trapalonia* called *Meleagrus*. The shipmen willing to shew what friendship they could to *Dorastus*, promised to be as secret as they could, or hee might wish, and vppon this they landed in a little village a mile distant from the Citie, where after they had rested a day, thinking to make prouision for their mariage, the fame of *Fawnias* beauty was spread throughout all the Citie, so that it came to the eares of *Pandosto*, who then [TLN 2240] being about the age of fifty, had notwithstanding yong and freshe affections: so that he desired greatly to see *Fawnia*, and to bring this matter the better to passe, hearing they had but one man, and how they rested at a very homely house, he caused them to be apprehended as spies, and sent a dozen of his garde to take them: who being come to their lodging, tolde them the Kings message. *Dorastus* no [F4] whit dismayed, accompanied with *Fawnia* and *Capnio*, went to the court (for they left *Porrus* to keepe the stuffe) who being admitted to the Kings presence,* *Dorastus* and *Fawnia* with humble obeysance saluted his maiestie.

Pandosto amased at the singular perfection of *Fawnia*, stood halfe astonished, viewing her beauty, so that he had almost forgot himselfe what hee had to doe: at last with stearne countenance he demaunded their names, and of what countrey they were, and what caused them to land in *Bohemia*. Sir (quoth *Dorastus*) know that my name *Meleagrus* is,* a Knight borne and brought vp in Trapalonia, and this gentle-woman, whom I meane to take to my wife is an Italian [TLN 2915, 2926] borne in Padua, from whence I haue now brought her. The cause I haue so small a trayne with me is for that, her friends vnwilling to consent, I intended secretly to conuey her into Trapalonia; whither as I was sailing, by distresse of weather I was driuen into these coasts: thus haue you heard my name, my country, and the cause of my voiage. *Pandosto* starting from his seat as one in choller, made this rough reply.

Meleagrus, I feare this smooth tale hath but small trueth, and that thou couerest a foule skin with faire paintings. No doubt this Ladie by her grace and beauty is of her degree more meete for a mighty Prince, then for a simple knight, and thou like a periured traitour hast bereft her of her parents, to their present griefe, and her insuing sorrow. Till therefore I heare more of her parentage and of thy calling, I wil stay you both here in *Bohemia*.

Dorastus, in whome rested nothing but Kingly valor, was not able to suffer the reproches of *Pandosto*, but that he made him this answer.

It is not meete for a King, without due proofe to appeach any man of ill be-hauiour, nor vpon suspition to inferre beleefe: straungers ought to bee entertained with courtesie, not to bee intreated with crueltie, least being forced by want to put vp iniuries, the Gods reuenge their cause with rigor.

Pandosto hearing *Dorastus* vtter these wordes, [TLN 2998] commaunded that

---

*presence,] 1592; ⁓. 1588
*is,] ⁓ ∧ 1588-95; *reading differs* 1601+

he should straight be committed to prison, vntill such [F4ᵛ] time as they heard further of his pleasure, but as for *Fawnia*, he charged that she should be entertained in the Cohrt, with such curtesie as belonged to a straunger and her calling. The rest of the shipmen he put into the Dungeon.

Hauing thus hardly handled the supposed Trapalonians, [TLN 2724] *Pandosto* contrarie to his aged yeares* began to be somewhat tickled with the beauty of *Fawnia*, in so much that hee could take no rest, but cast in his old head a thousand new deuises: at last he fell into these thoughtes.

How art thou pestred *Pandosto* with fresh affections, and vnfitte fancies, wishing to possesse with an vnwilling mynde, and in* a hot desire troubled with a could disdaine! Shall thy mynde yeeld in age to that thou hast resisted in youth? Peace *Pandosto*, blabbe not out that which thou maiest be ashamed to reueale to thy self. Ah, *Fawnia* is beautifull, and it is not for thine honour (fond foole) to name her that is thy Captiue, and an other mans Concubine. Alas, I reach at that with my hand which my hart would faine refuse: playing like the bird *Ibys* in Egipt, which hateth Serpents, yet feedeth on their egges.

Tush, hot desires turne oftentimes to colde disdaine: Loue is brittle, where appetite, not reason, beares the sway. Kinges thoughtes ought not to climbe so high as the heauens, but to looke no lower then honour: better it is to pecke at the starres with the young Eagles, then to prey on dead carkasses with the Vulture: tis more honourable for *Pandosto* to dye by concealing Loue, then to enioy such vnfitte Loue. Dooth *Pandosto* then loue? Yea. Whome? A maid vnknowne, yea and perhapps, immodest, stragled out of her owne countrie: beautifull, but not therefore chast: comely in bodie, but perhappes crooked in minde. Cease then *Pandosto*, to looke at *Fawnia*, much lesse to loue her: be not ouertaken with a womans beauty, whose eyes are framed by arte to inamour, whose hearte is framed by nature to inchaunt, whose false teares knowe their true times, and whose sweete wordes pearce deeper then sharpe swordes. Here *Pandosto* ceased from his talke, but not from his loue: for although he sought by reason, and wisedome [G1] to suppresse this franticke affection, yet he could take no rest, the beautie of *Fawnia* had made such a deepe impression in his heart. But on a day, walking; abroad into a Parke which was hard adioyning to his house, he sent by one of his seruants for *Fawnia*, [see n. 2995] vnto whome he vttered these wordes.

Fawnia, I commend thy beauty and wit, and now pittie thy distresse and want: but if you wilt forsake Sir *Meleagrus*, whose pouerty, though a Knight, is not able to maintaine an estate aunswerable to thy beauty, and yeld thy consent to *Pandosto*, I wil both increase thee with dignities and riches. No sir, answered *Fawnia*: *Meleagrus* is a knight that hath wonne me by loue, and none but he shal [TLN 404] weare me:

---

*yeares] 1592; yeaxes 1588
*in] WELLS (1988); *om.* 1588

his sinister mischance shall not diminishe my affection, but rather increase my good will. Thinke not though your Grace hath imprisoned him without cause, that feare shall make mee yeeld my consent: I had rather be *Meleagrus* wife, and a beggar, then liue in plenty, and be *Pandosto*s Concubine. *Pandosto*, hearing the assured aunswere of *Fawnia*, would, notwithstanding, prosecute his suite to the vttermost: seeking with faire words and great promises to scale the fort of her chastitie, swearing that if she would graunt to his desire, *Meleagrus* should not only be set at libertie, but honored in his courte amongst his Nobles: but these alluring baytes could not intise her minde from the loue of her newe betrothed mate *Meleagrus*: which *Pandosto* seeing, he left her alone for that time to consider more of the demaund. *Fawnia*, being alone by her selfe, began to enter into these solitarie meditations.

Ah, infortunate *Fawnia*, thou seest to desire aboue fortune is to striue against the Gods and Fortune. Who gazeth at the sunne weakeneth his sight: they which stare at the skie, fall oft into deepe pits: haddest thou rested content to haue been a shepheard, thou neededst not to haue feared mischaunce. Better had it bene for thee, by sitting lowe, to haue had quiet, then by climing high to haue fallen into miserie. But alas, I feare not mine owne daunger, but *Dorastus* displeasure. Ah sweete *Dorastus*, thou art a Prince, but now a prisoner, by too much [G1ᵛ] loue procuring thine owne losse. Haddest thou not loued *Fawnia* thou haddest bene fortunate. Shall I then bee false to him that hath forsaken Kingdomes for my cause? No; would my death might deliuer him, so mine honor might be preserued. With that, fetching a deepe sigh, she ceased from her complaints, and went againe to the Pallace, inioying a libertie without content, and profered pleasure with smal ioy. But poore *Dorastus* lay all this while in close prison, being pinched with a hard restraint, and pained with the burden of colde, and heauie Irons, sorrowing sometimes that his fond affection had procured him this mishappe, that by the disobedience of his parentes, he had wrought his owne despight: an other while cursing the Gods and fortune, that they should crosse him with such sinister chaunce: vttering at last his passions in these words.

Ah vnfortunate wretch, borne to mishappe, now thy folly hath his desert: Art thou not worthie for thy base minde to haue bad fortune? could the destinies fauour thee, which hast forgot thine honor and dignities? Wil not the Gods plague him with despight that payneth his father with disobedience? Oh Gods, if any fauour or iustice be left, plague me, but fauour poore *Fawnia*, and shrowd her from the tirannies of wretched *Pandosto*, but let my death free her from mishap, and then, welcome death! *Dorastus* payned with these heauie passions, sorrowed and sighed, but in vaine, for which he vsed the more patience. But againe to *Pandosto*, who broyling at the heat of vnlawfull lust coulde take no rest but still felte his minde disquieted with his new loue, so that his nobles and subiectes marueyled greatly at this sudaine alteration, not being able to coniecture the cause of this his continued care. *Pandosto*, thinking euery hower a yeare til he had talked once againe with *Fawnia*, sent for her secretly into his chamber, whither though *Fawnia* vnwillingly comming, *Pandosto* entertained her very courteously, vsing these familiar speaches, which *Fawnia* answered as shortly in this wise.

Pandosto

[G2] *Fawnia*, are you become lesse wilfull and more wise, to preferre the loue of a King before the liking of a poore Knight? I thinke ere this you thinke it is better to be fauoured of a King then of a subiect.

Fawnia

Pandosto, [TLN 2446–7] the body is subiect to victories, but the mind not to be subdued by conquest: honesty is to be preferred before honour, and a dramme of faith weigheth downe a tunne of gold. I haue promised *Meleagrus* to loue, and will performe no lesse.

Pandosto

Fawnia, I know thou art not so vnwise in thy choice, as to refuse the offer of a King, nor so ingrateful as to dispise a good turne: thou art now in that place where I may commaunde, and yet thou seest I intreate. My power is such as I may compell by force, and yet I sue by prayers: Yeelde *Fawnia* thy loue to him which burneth in thy loue. *Meleagrus* shall be set free, thy countrymen discharged: and thou both loued and honoured.

Fawnia

I see, *Pandosto*, where lust ruleth it is a miserable thing to be a virgin, but know this, that I will alwaies preferre fame before life, and rather choose death then dishonour.

Pandosto seeing that there was in *Fawnia* a determinate courage to loue *Meleagrus*, and a resolution without feare to hate him, flong away from her in a rage: swearing if in shorte time she would not be wonne with reason: he would forget all courtesie, and compel her to graunt by rigour: but [TLN 2287] these threatning wordes no whit dismayed *Fawnia*; but that she still both dispighted and dispised *Pandosto*. While thus these two louers stroue, the one to winne loue the other to liue in hate: *Egistus* heard certaine newes by Merchauntes of *Bohemia*, [G2ᵛ] that his sonne *Dorastus* was imprisoned by *Pandosto*, which made him feare greatly that his sonne should be but hardly intreated: yet considering that *Bellaria* and hee was cleared by the Oracle of *Apollo* from that crime wherewith *Pandosto* had vniustly charged them, hee thought best to send with all speed to *Pandosto*, that he should set free his sonne *Dorastus*, and put to death *Fawnia* and her father *Porrus*: finding this by the aduise of Counsaile the speediest remedy to release his sonne, he caused presently two of his shippes to be rigged, and thoroughly furnished with prouision of men and victuals, and sent diuers of his nobles Embassadoures into *Bohemia*; who willing to obey their King, and relieue their yong Prince: made no delayes, for feare of danger, but with as much speed as might be, sailed towards *Bohemia*: the winde and seas fauored them greatly, which made them hope of some good happe, for within three daies they were landed: which *Pandosto* no soner heard of their arriuall, but [TLN 3006] hee in person went to meete them, intreating them with such sumptuous and familiar courtesie, that they might well perceiue how sory he was for the former iniuries hee had offered to their King, and how willing (if it might be) to make amendes. As *Pandosto* made report to them, how one *Meleagrus*, a Knight of Trapolonia, was lately ariued with a Lady called *Fawnia* in his land, comming very suspitiously, accompanied onely with one seruant, and an olde shepheard. The Embassadours perceiued by the halfe, what the whole tale ment, and began to coniecture, that it was *Dorastus*, who for feare to bee knowne, had chaunged his name: but dissembling the matter, they shortly ariued at the Court, where after they had bin verie solemnly and sumptuously feasted, the noble men of *Sicilia* being gathered togither, they made reporte of their Embassage: where they certified *Pandosto* that *Meleagrus* was sonne and heire to the King *Egistus*, and that his name was *Dorastus*: how contrarie to the Kings minde he had priuily conuaied away that *Fawnia*, intending to marrie her, being but daughter to that poore shepheard *Porrus*: wherevpon* [TLN 2943–8] the Kings request was that *Capnio*, *Fawnia*, and *Porrus*, might bee murthered and put to death, and that his sonne *Dorastus* might be sent home in sa-[G3]fetie. *Pandosto* hauing attentiuely and with great meruaile heard their Embassage, willing to reconcile himselfe to *Egistus*, and to shew him how greatly he esteemed his fauour:* although loue and fancy forbad him to hurt *Fawnia*, yet in despight of loue hee determined to execute *Egistus* will without mercy; and therefore he presently sent for *Dorastus* out of prison, who meruailing at this vnlooked for curtesie, found at his comming to the Kings presence, that which he least doubted of, his fathers Embassadours: who no sooner sawe him, but with great reuerence they honored him: and *Pandosto* embracing *Dorastus*, set him by him very louingly in a chaire of estate. *Dorastus* ashamed that his follie was bewraied, sate a long time as one in a muse, til *Pandosto* told him the summe of his Fathers embassage: which he had no sooner heard, but he was toucht at the quicke, for the cruell sentence that was pronounced against *Fawnia*: but neither could his sorrow nor perswasions preuaile, for *Pandosto* commaunded that *Fawnia*, *Porrus*, and *Capnio*, should bee brought to his presence; who were no sooner come, but *Pandosto* hauing his former loue turned to a disdainfull hate, began to rage against *Fawnia* in these tearmes.

Thou disdainfull vassal, thou [TLN 1691–2] currish kite, assigned by the destinies to base fortune, and yet with an aspiring minde gazing after honour: [TLN 2265–70, 2278–85] how durst thou presume, being a beggar, to match with a Prince? By thy alluring lookes to inchant the sonne of a King to leaue his owne countrie to fulfill thy disordinate lusts? O despightfull minde, a proud heart in a beggar is not vnlike to a great fire in a smal cottage, which warmeth not the house, but burneth it: assure thy selfe that thou shalt die, and [TLN 2263–5] thou old doating foole, whose follie hath bene such, as to suffer thy daughter to reach aboue thy fortune, looke for no other meede, but the like punishment. But *Capnio*, thou which hast betrayed the King, and

---

*wherevpon] 1592 (?); where vpon 1588
*fauour] 1607; labour 1588

has consented to the vnlawfull lust of thy Lord and maister, I know not how iustly I may plague thee: death is too easie a punishment for thy falsehood, and to liue (if not in extreme miserie) were not to shew thee equitie. I therefore award that thou shall haue thine eyes put out, and [G3ᵛ] continually while thou diest, grinde in a mil like a brute beast. The feare of death brought a sorrowfull silence vpon *Fawnia* and *Capnio*, but *Porrus* seeing no hope of life, burst forth into these speeches.

Pandosto, and ye noble Embassadours* of *Sicilia*, seeing without cause I am condemned to die; I am yet glad I haue opportunitie to disburden my conscience before my death: I will tel you as much as I know, and yet no more than is true: whereas I am accused that I haue bene a supporter of *Fawnias* pride, and shee disdained as a vilde begger, so it is that I am neither Father vnto her, nor she daughter vnto me.

For so it happened that I being a poore shepheard in *Sicilia*, liuing by keeping other* mens flockes: one of my sheepe straying downe to the sea side, as I went to seeke her, I saw a little boat driuen vpon the shoare, wherein I found a babe of sixe daies olde, wrapped in a mantle of skarlet, hauing about the necke this chaine: I pittying the child, and desirous of the treasure, carried it home to my wife, who with great care nursed it vp, and set it to keepe sheepe. Here is the chaine and the Iewels, and this *Fawnia* is the childe whome I found in the boate. What shee is, or of what parentage, I knowe not, but this I am assured that she is none of mine.

Pandosto would scarce suffer him to tell out his tale, but that he enquired the time of the yeere, the manner of the boate, and other circumstaunces, which when he found agreeing to his count, he sodainelie leapt from his seate, and kissed *Fawnia*, wetting her tender cheeks with his teares, and crying [TLN 3061] my daughter *Fawnia*, ah sweete* *Fawnia*, I am thy Father, *Fawnia*. This sodaine passion of the King draue them all into a maze, especially *Fawnia* and *Dorastus*. But when the King had breathed himselfe a while in this newe ioy, [TLN 3039–49] he rehearsed before the Embassadours the whole matter, how he hadde entreated his wife *Bellaria* for iealousie, and that this was the childe whome hee sent to float in the seas.

Fawnia was not more ioyfull that she had found such a Father, then *Dorastus* was glad he should get such a wife. The [G4] Embassadors reioyced that their yong prince had made such a choice, that those Kingdomes which through enmitie had long time bin disseuered, should now through perpetual amitie be vnited and reconciled. The Citizens and subiects of *Bohemia* (hearing that the King had found againe his Daughter, which was supposed dead, ioyfull that there was an heire apparent to his Kingdome) made [TLN 3032] Bonfires and showes throughout the Cittie. The Courtiers and Knights appointed Iusts and Turneis to signifie their willing mindes in gratifying the Kings hap.

Eighteene daies being past in these princely sports, *Pandosto*, willing to re-

---

*Embassadours] 1592; Emabassadours 1588
*other] 1592; others 1588
*sweete] 1592; swtete 1588

compence old *Porrus*, of a shepheard made him a Knight: which done, prouiding a sufficient Nauie to receiue him and his retinue, accompanied with *Dorastus, Fawnia*, and the *Sicilian* Embassadours, he sailed towards *Sicilia*, where he was most princelie entertained by *Egistus*; who hearing this comicall euent, reioyced greatly at his sonnes good happe, and without delay (to the perpetuall ioy of the two yong Louers) cele-brated the marriage: which was no sooner ended, but *Pandosto* (calling to mind how first he betraied his friend *Egistus*, how his iealousie was the cause of *Bellarias* death, that contrarie to the law of nature hee had lusted after his owne Daughter) moued with these desperate thoughts, he fell into a melancholie fit, and to close vp the Comedie with a Tragicall stratageme, hee slewe himselfe, whose death being many daies bewailed of *Fawnia, Dorastus*, and his deere friend *Egistus*, *Dorastus* taking his leaue of his father, went with his wife and the dead corps into *Bohemia*, where after they were sumptuouslie intombed,* *Dorastus* ended his daies in contented quiet.

FINIS

SHAKESPEARE'S USE OF *PANDOSTO*

General Indebtedness

GOLLANCZ (ed. 1894, 41:viii) summarizes the "notable refinements due to the dram-atist[:] . . . (i.) in the novel Hermione's prototype actually dies upon hearing of the death of her son; (ii.) her husband destroys himself, after becoming enamoured of his unknown daughter; (iii.) the characters of Paulina, Autolycus, and Antigonus are en-tirely Shakespeare's; (iv.) Hermione's character is ennobled throughout; Shakespeare admits no 'incautiousness' on her part, no unqueenly condescension in meeting the charge [of infidelity]; (v.) Bohemia takes the place of Sicily, and *vice versa* . . . ; finally, (vi.) the names are changed throughout." To vi., Mopsa is an exception.

UPTON (1746, pp. 40-1) finds Sh. culpable for the major error of basing a play on *Pandosto* and for minor errors of execution. To explain, he invokes the Aristotelian defects of poetry—one "arises from itself, <per se,> the other is accidental: <*per accidens*:> for if it chuses subjects for imitation, out of its power and reach, the fault is from itself; <per se,> but when it chooses ignorantly, the fault is accidental." The defect per se is "the [*41*] making choice of such a story as the *Winter's Tale*, &c. . . . The [defect *per accidens*] is where Shakespeare, not heeding geography, calls Delphi an isle." WARBURTON (ed. 1747, 3:277) despises the source but praises the play: it is "written in the very spirit of its author. . . . This was necessary to observe in mere justice to the Play, as the meanness of the fable, and the extravagant conduct of it, had misled some of great name [Dryden and Pope] into a wrong judgment of its merit; which, as far as it regards sentiment and character, is scarce inferior to any in the whole collection."

LENNOX (1753, 2:75-87), however, is of just the opposite opinion: "If we com-

---

*intombed] 1592; 1588 *damaged*

pare the Conduct of the Incidents in the Play with the paltry Story on which it is founded, we shall find the Original much less absurd and ridiculous. . . . The King's Jealousy is the Foundation of all the Adventures that followed, but extravagant as its Consequences are in both, yet the Rise and Progress of this terrible Passion is better accounted for in the Novel than the Play." She recounts the incidents in *Pandosto* leading to the onset of the King's jealousy, concluding (p. 76): "This Account . . . does not absolutely clash with Probability." She summarizes the action of *WT* to line 116 approximately. (P. 77): "*Polixenes* complies at her [Hermione's] Request [to extend his visit], and certainly he must be a very ill bred Monarch had he done otherwise.

"All [their] Conversation passes in the Presence of *Leontes*, who from hence takes Occasion to be jealous, and passes in an Instant from the greatest Confidence, Security, and Friendship imaginable, to the last Extremity of Jealousy and Rage. What wonderful Contrivance is here?" To the play's disadvantage, a comparison of a half dozen more incidents follows, concluding with (p. 85) "The Novel makes the Wife of the jealous King die through Affliction for the Loss of her Son; *Shakespear* seems to have preserved her alive for the sake of her representing her own Statue in the last Scene; a mean and absurd Contrivance; for how can it be imagined that *Hermione*, a virtuous and affectionate Wife, would conceal herself during sixteen Years in a solitary House, though she was sensible that her repentant Husband was all that Time con-[86]suming away with Grief and Remorse for her Death; . . . how ridiculous also in a great Queen, on so interresting [sic] an Occasion, to submit to such Buffoonery as standing on a Pedestal, motionless, her Eyes fixed, and at last to be conjured down by this magical Command of *Paulina* [quotes 3306–11]. . . . [87] His *Winter's Tale* is greatly inferior to the old paltry Story that furnished him with the Subject of it."

CAPELL (1783, 3:233–4) disagrees with LENNOX, as one might expect: "This miserable story [*Pandosto*] — writ in the days of Euphuism, as appears from the style of it — is not so exactly followed by SHAKESPEARE as some have conceited; *Bellaria* (his [Greene's] *Hermione*) does not come to life again, but dies in good earnest when her son dies; and *Pandosto*, (his *Leontes*) when all is over, his daughter found again, and marry'd to her lover, falls into a melancholy, and kills himself. These are the principal differences between him and the story-writer with respect to the fable: the language it is dress'd in, (some expressions excepted, which [234] are of small importance) the characters, the sentiments, are all his own; and he has also enrich'd it with the following additional characters, — *Antigonus*, and his wife *Paulina*; the shepherd's son, & his mistresses; *Autolicus*, and some others. For the rest, — the story he chose to follow is adher'd to a little too closely, and (namely) without sufficient attention to one capital absurdity respecting the scene of it: some excuse may be made for him, that will be found in another place [see n. 1440]." Among others disagreeing with LENNOX is ESCHENBURG (ed. 1801, 5:210), who defends Sh.'s depiction of the quirks of human nature; the playwright, he says, demonstrates quite profoundly how easily the ember of jealousy may burst into an all-consuming flame.

A more detailed analysis of Sh.'s debt is made by SKOTTOWE (1824, 2:290–300).

"The novel marks the growth of this passion [jealousy] in the king; in the play it is instantaneous and uncontrollable. . . . With the forlorn hope of saving the infant's [Perdita's] life, Anti-[*291*]gonus . . . consents to carry it to a desert place . . . and there leave it. . . . In the novel, the king exposes the child in an open boat to the mercy of the wind and waves. . . . Greene's tyrant resolves to burn both the mother and the child; but the queen's demand for an open trial is warmly seconded by the nobility, and the king prudently consents to send six of his nobility to the *Isle* of Delphos. . . . In [*WT*], the embassy originates with Leontes himself. . . . [*299*] If not a more natural, Shakspeare has certainly substituted a more agreeable conclusion to his drama. Indeed, few scenes of greater interest, and none managed with a more consummate knowledge of stage effect, are to be met with [*300*] than that which closes the Winter's Tale. With the exception of this striking scene, Shakspeare has done little towards the improvement of the story he worked from; but he was more successful in his delineation of its principal characters."

Other critics also regard the novel somewhat more favorably than CAPELL had done. DYCE (ed. *Dramatic Works of Greene*, 1831, 1:liii), for example: "To those who may read the novel for the first time, having a previous acquaintance with the play of Shakespeare . . . the former will appear cold and uninteresting on a recollection of the marvellous truth and reality of the latter. But *Pandosto* is far from a contemptible production: if portions of it are disfigured by bad taste and coarseness of feeling, there are also portions composed in a very pleasing and affecting manner."

ULRICI (1839; tr. 1846, p. 265), however: "Shakspeare has contrived out of a tasteless, affected romance, of at most passing interest, to make a truthful and immortal drama." COLLIER ([1843], 1:i–iii), similarly: "Let any person well acquainted with The Winter's Tale read the novel of 'Pandosto', . . . and he will be struck at once with the vast pre-eminence of Shakespeare, and with the admirable manner in which he has converted materials supplied by another to his own use. The bare outline of the story (with the exception of Shakespeare's miraculous conclusion) is nearly the same in both; but this is all they have in common, and Shakspeare may be said to have scarcely adopted a single hint for his descriptions, [*ii*] or a line for his dialogue; while in point of passion and sentiment Greene is cold, formal, and artificial: the very opposite of every thing in Shakespeare. . . . [*iii*] Nothing can well be more lame, unsatisfactory, and even offensive than the winding up of Greene's novel, where he makes Pandosto first fall desperately and grossly in love with his own daughter, and then, without any adequate motive, commit suicide. . . . Shakespeare . . . saw at once how the preceding incidents might be converted to a great dramatic and moral purpose, the most pathetic and the most beautiful."

KNIGHT (ed. 1841, 2:337–9): In *Pandosto* "the story of the preservation of the deserted infant is prettily told [quotes 'It fortuned . . . necke' (C4)]. Although the circumstances of the child's exposure are different, Shakspere adopts the shepherd's discovery pretty literally. . . . The infant in the novel is taken to the shepherd's home, and is brought up by his wife and himself under the name of Fawnia. In a narrative the lapse of sixteen years may occur without any violation of propriety. The shepherd of Greene . . . would sing to the child and dance it on his knee; then, a few lines onward, the little Fawnia is seven years old; and, very shortly, [quotes 'when she came . . . parentage' p. 635]. These changes, we see, are gradual. But in a drama, whose action depends upon a manifest lapse of time, there must be a sudden transition. Shakspere is perfectly aware of the difficulty; and he diminishes it by the introduction of Time as a Chorus. . . .

[338] "Shakspere has exhibited his consummate art in opening the fourth act with Polixenes and Camillo, of whom we have lost sight since the end of the first. Had . . . he brought Autolycus, and Florizel, and Perdita, at once upon the scene . . . the continuity of action would have been destroyed; and the commencement of the fourth act would have appeared as the commencement of a new play. . . . Autolycus and the Clown prepare us for Perdita. . . . There perhaps never was such a union of perfect simplicity and perfect grace as in the character of Perdita. What an exquisite idea of her mere personal appearance is presented in Florizel's [1956-8]. Greene, in describing the beauties of his shepherdess, deals only in generalities [quotes 'It happened . . . hard fortune' (p. 637)]. But Greene was unequal to conceive the grace of mind which distinguishes Perdita:— [339; quotes 1803-7]. Contrast this with Greene [quotes '*Fawnia* poore soule . . . King' (p. 645), stressing 'hoping in time to be aduaunced']. Here we see a vulgar ambition, rather than a deep affection. Fawnia, in the hour of discovery and danger, was quite incapable of exhibiting the feminine dignity of Perdita [quotes 2287-95]. This is something higher than the sentiment of a 'queen of curds and cream'.

"In the novel we have no trace of the interruption by the father of the princely lover, in the disguise of a guest at the shepherd's cottage [2260 ff.]. Dorastus and Fawnia flee from the country without the knowledge of the king. The ship in which they embark is thrown by a storm upon the coast of Bohemia. Messengers are despatched in search of the lovers; and they arrive in Bohemia with the request of Egistus that the companions in the flight of Dorastus shall be put to death. The secret of Fawnia's birth is discovered by the shepherd; and her father recognises her. But the previous circumstances exhibit as much grossness of conception on the part of the novelist [KNIGHT probably alludes to Pandosto's attraction to Fawnia, p. 650.], as the different management of the catastrophe shows the matchless skill and taste of the dramatist. We forgive Leontes for his early folly and wickedness; for during sixteen years has his remorse been bitter and his affection constant."

As SKOTTOWE had noticed, Greene sets the infant Fawnia adrift in an open boat, whereas Sh. employs Antigonus to abandon Perdita in Bohemia. COLLIER (ed. 1842, 3:426) offers an ingenious, although defective, explanation of the change: In " 'The Tempest' he [Sh.] had previously . . . represented Prospero and Miranda turned adrift at sea in the same manner as Greene had stated his heroine to be disposed of [and so] Shakespeare . . . varied from the original narrative, in order to avoid an objectionable similarity." The defect is that *WT* was written before *Tmp.* (see p. 602), although the idea that *Tmp.* in some form may have antedated *WT* also occurs to MUIR (1957, p. 241; see below). WHITE (ed. 1857, 5:270), alternatively: "Shakespeare knew—none better—that the dramatic value of an impression produced upon the eye is much greater than that of one produced upon the ear; and on his stage Greene's disposition of the royal babe could not be represented, while that adopted by him could."

HUDSON (ed. 1852, 4:6-13): "Greene . . . had indeed much more of learning than of judgment in the use and application thereof; it having been seemingly impossible for him to write without overloading his pages with classical allusion, or [7] to hit upon any thought so trite and commonplace but that he must run it through a series of aphoristic sentences twisted out of Greek and Roman lore. . . . Like all the surviving works of Greene, Pandosto is greatly charged with learned impertinence, and in the annoyance thence resulting one is apt to overlook the real merit of the performance. It is better than Lodge's Rosalynd [the source of *AYL*] for this reason, if for no other, that it is shorter. . . . [*13*] In the novel Paulina and the Clown are wanting altogether, and Capnio yields but a slight hint, if indeed it be so much, towards the part of Autolycus. And, besides the great addition of life and matter in these persons, the play has several other judicious departures from the novel. In Leontes all the revolting features of Pandosto, save his jealousy and the headstrong insolence and tyranny consequent thereon, are purged away; so that while the latter has neither intellect nor generosity to redeem his character, jealousy being the least of his faults, the other has a liberal stock of both. And in Bellaria the Poet had little more than a bare framework of incident wherein to set the noble, lofty womanhood of Hermione, — a conception far, far above the reach of such a mind as Greene's. In the matter of the painted statue Shakespeare, so far as we know, was altogether without a model. . . . Hermione's character . . . is the shaping and informing power of the whole drama . . . the prolific germ out of which the entire work is evolved."

WHITE (ed. 1857, 5:271-2), in comparing the two characters, agrees with LENNOX (p. 656): "Greene gives *Pandosto* more cause for his jealousy than Shakespeare gives to *Leontes*. For in the tale *Bellaria*, though entirely innocent, uses *Egistus* 'so familiarly, that her countenance bewraied how her minde was affected towardes him: oftentimes comming her selfe into his bed chamber, to see that nothing should be amis to mislike him' [p. 622]; and also 'there grew such a secret vniting of their affections, that the one could not well be without the company of the other' [p. 622]. It [*272*] may possibly have been Shakespeare's intention to make its sudden birth and its extravagance characteristic traits of *Leontes*' jealousy; but this difference between the play and the novel seems rather due to a necessity for the compression of the latter."

GERVINUS (1863, 2:467-8): "Shakespeare has done with this narrative, as he usually did with his bad originals, he has done away with some indelicacy in the matter, and some unnatural things in the form; he has given a better foundation to the characters and course of events; but to impart an intrinsic value to the subject as a whole, to bring a double action into unity, and to give the play the character of a regular drama by mere arrangements of matter and alteration of motive, was not possible. The wildness of the fiction, the improbability and contingency of the events, the gap in the time . . . could not be repaired by any art. Shakespeare, therefore, began upon his theme in quite an opposite direction. He increased still more the marvellous and miraculous in the given subject, he disregarded more and more the requirements of the real and probable, and treated time, place, and circumstances with the utmost arbitrariness. . . . [*468*] The scenic effect, the excellent character- ization of certain personages, the beauty of the language of the play were acknowl- edged [by early critics], but the poet was continually upbraided for those very marvels, which we think he did not introduce as any thing else."

WIGSTON (1884, p. 3): "In borrowing Greene's story, he [Sh.] took it on account of its title [see p. 618], in relation to its subject matter, — disharmony and separation, followed by reconciliation and heavenly harmony as in Cymbeline and Pericles, — the exposure of an infant and its re-discovery through time."

MORLEY (ed. 1887, pp. 8-9): "To change a real to a supposed death, required invention of means of concealment, and this requirement was met by the creation of the character of Paulina. . . . Shakespeare gives . . . a husband to Paulina, Antigo- nus, who is of gentle heart, though he obeys the evil bidding of the king, and the infant is committed to the waves, surrounded by the tenderest care until the hour of its exposure upon a coast not found by chance, but chosen at the bidding of a dream. This done, the poet gets rid of the men who are no longer wanted in the story, and who would be in the way if they lived and returned to Sicily. He gives emphasis at the same time to the peril of the child by destroying the ship and its crew in a storm at sea, and giving Antigonus to a wild beast on land, 'so that all the instruments which aided to expose the child were [*9*] even then lost when it was found' [3079-81]. In the following scenes dramatic life could not have been put into the telling of the tale without the addition of the shepherd's son. His wife, who is in Greene's tale, could not have been used for the purposes served by Shakespeare's invention of the clown- ish son and of the rogue Autolycus. Greene uses the shepherd's wife as a means for bringing about the solution of the plot, and had the shepherd carried off by force upon the ship of the offended king. Shakespeare removes several improbabilities, and gets rid of incidents that mar the grace of the tale, including Pandosto's animal love for his unrecognised daughter. His changes in the manner of bringing about the so- lution of the plot, as far as concerns Florizel and Perdita, are mainly produced by his invention of Autolycus, the merry rogue — a cashiered courtier — who sings his songs at the sheep-shearing, fleeces the rustics, and half in hope to recover favour with the prince, sends the witnesses who can untie the knot of the tale on board the prince's ship to Sicily. It is enough to suggest playfully that Florizel and Perdita were too full of their affairs to ask many questions of other people, and that they were sea-sick as well as love-sick. The reader who follows attentively Shakespeare's use of Autolycus as a means of putting dramatic life into the solution of the plot without spoiling the pastoral grace and playfulness of that part of the story, will see that but for his trick in sending the bearers of the fardel to the Prince's ship instead of to the King, Perdita must have been identified before the persons of the story were about Leontes in the close."

SNIDER (c. 1890, pp. 502-3): "The central fact is that Shakespeare turns Greene's novel, which is tragic, into a comedy or mediated drama. Both Hermione (Bellaria) and Leontes (Pandosto) perish in the novel; the world of mediation is essentially unknown to Greene. The wife breaks down under her trials, when her boy Garinter (Mamillius) dies; she has not sufferance, which saves herself, her husband, her world. Still, the novelist dwells upon her purity, nay, he speaks of her patience, but it bears no fruit in his work, it is not the triumphant patience of the Poet. In like manner Leontes shows repentance in Greene's book, but it is not that complete undoing of guilt which bridges the great chasm and brings restoration of wife, child, and world. Through these two ideas—the repentance of the husband and the long-suffering of the wife—the whole play is changed into a purgatorial discipline, with the outlook of salvation; the two characters are me-[503]diated and brought back even into their secular existence."

NEILSON (ed. 1906, p. 419): "The superb dignity of Hermione which almost lifts her above pity, the plain-spoken loyalty of Paulina, the peculiar poetic charm of the pastoral scenes of which Perdita is the centre, the humor of the rogue and the rustics, the elements, in short, which make the play delightful, are all Shakespeare's. To Greene belongs the credit of framing an interesting romantic story, the improbabilities and surprises of which Shakespeare seems to have taken no pains to abate, but which, on the contrary, he capped by devising a closing situation, theatrically effective, indeed, but more defiant of likelihood than anything in his source."

THOMAS (ed. *Pandosto*, 1907, pp. xi–xiii): "Greene's style is, of course, characteristic of himself, and his pleasant conceits find no place in Shakespeare's mature drama. The curious moralizations from natural history, the familiar use of proverbial lore, the dissertations on abstract themes, and the laboured style abounding in antithesis and alliteration combine to place *Dorastus* in the long line of euphuistic novels, of which Lyly was the originator. Greene is often coarse, but he has that Elizabethan gift of sweetness, which is unmistakable. The pathetic scene, in which [*xii*] Bellaria laments over the loss of her child ['Alas . . . fare well' (pp. 628–9)], appealed to Shakespeare, and the lines [1496–7] are reminiscent of Greene's words ['Shalt . . . milke?' (p. 628)].

"[Sh.'s] changes . . . are due in the main to the exigencies of dramatic form. . . . Long-winded speeches and dreary monologues . . . are either omitted altogether, shortened, or converted into dialogue. . . . Action is concentrated [for] dramatic unity. . . . To dramatic causes, likewise, we owe the creation of Antigonus, Paulina, and Autolycus, in whom respectively are concentrated the nobles, ladies, and clowns of the novel. At other times, Shakespeare enlarges from a brief hint given by Greene. There is no counterpart in the novel of the pathetic scene in *The Winter's Tale*, in which the [*xiii*] character of young Mamillius is developed. . . . In the same way, Greene's reference to the storm at sea is expanded into Act III. sc. iii of *The Winter's Tale*."

PORTER & CLARKE (ed. 1908, pp. 124–5): "There are events in Greene's plot which Shakespeare altogether discards: The refusal of the prince to marry a Danish princess to suit his father, before he meets the shepherdess; the fear of the shepherd and his wife . . . lest the prince will bring shame upon their daughter. This fear is very important in Greene's plot, for it causes them,—gossip as to the prince's familiarity with their foster-daughter being brought to their ears,—to decide to tell the king that she is not their own child. It will be noticed that Shakespeare not only discards this, he invents the king's presence at the betrothal in its stead, and this in the play frightens the shepherd and his son (who takes the place of the wife in Greene's story) into confession.

"Autolicus is not in Greene; but in Greene's plot a servant of the prince, named Capnio, plays soberly the part which Autolicus plays humorously in Shakespeare's plot by intercepting the shepherd on his way to confess to the king, and enticing him on shipboard.

"In Act V. the restoration of the castaway daughter and the union of the young lovers are based on the same events as in Greene's plot, but they are brought about by so different a manipulation of the incidents that there is scarcely anything in common save the arrival in port, in the country of the jealous king, of the eloping lovers and the old shepherd.

"All that Camillo and Paulina effect in Act V. is not in Greene. Shakespeare discards an important incident in Greene's story; *i.e.*, the tyranny of the king on the [*125*] arrival of the lovers, which causes him to imprison the prince and try to make the shepherdess his concubine, until an embassy arrives from the prince's father demanding that he free his son and kill the shepherdess and her father. The confession of the old shepherd then following, the king, ashamed of his action toward his own daughter, kills himself.

"All that defeats such misery as this, which in Greene's plot so mars his union of the young lovers, is due to Shakespeare."

According to STOPES (1916, pp. 32–8), the playwright reverses Greene's emotional geography, sending the hot-blooded Leontes to Sicily, the cooler Polixenes to Bohemia: (p. 33) "Shakespeare evolves the character of Antigonus out of one of the Chief Lords" . . . (p. 35) but "does not allow Antigonus to cast the babe away in a small boat, to find Bohemia. He knew that an infant could not live so long without food. So he makes Antigonus take it in a ship, where, it is to be supposed, he saw the child fed."

PIERCE (ed. 1918, p. 129) similarly: "By interchanging throughout the parts of Bohemia and Sicily he [Sh.] probably meant to veil the extent of his debt to a book that was still popular, although he may have believed that the suddenness of Leontes' jealousy would seem truer to life in a hot-blooded Sicilian than in a native of Central Europe."

KITTREDGE (ed. 1936, p. 432): "Some significant variations [from *Pandosto*] may be noted[:] Apollo is consulted at the request of the queen. The king does not blaspheme when the oracle is read in court; he repents instantly and is making public confession when word is brought that his son is dead. This news is fatal to the queen. . . . The baby is not left on the shore; it is abandoned at sea (like Prospero and Miranda in *The Tempest*) in a boat without sail or rudder, which comes safe to land by good fortune after a mighty storm. Antigonus and Paulina have no prototypes in the novel and Shakespeare's Camillo combines the rôles of two of Greene's characters. The old shepherd comes from the novel, but his son and Dorcas and Mopsa and Autolycus are all new characters. Rustic revels are mentioned in the tale, but not described. . . . The novel has a happy ending, so far as the young people are concerned, but Pandosto . . . is a tragic personage throughout. After years of mourning for his dead wife, he falls in love with Fawnia . . . , whom of course he supposes to be the shepherd's daughter. When he learns that she is his own child . . . he is overjoyed; but after her marriage he is smitten with remorse for all his sins, falls once more 'into a melancholie fit' [p. 656], and kills himself."

PRUVOST (1938, p. 573): Among these [Greene's romances] his *Pandosto* seems to occupy a place apart because it offers one of the first uses in England, if not the first, of a theme in which the love of children comes to restore the concord and harmony destroyed by the discords and the defects of parents. It is precisely the theme that Shakespeare handled several times toward the end of his career. Would he have done so if Greene had not written his *Pandosto*? It is not impossible. But since in *The Winter's Tale* he dramatized Greene's romance, one does not in the least exaggerate the influence of Greene in saying that he furnished Shakespeare the very special formula of the last plays (in Fr.).

MUIR (1957, p. 241): "Shakespeare follows the earlier part of the source fairly closely. Greene described how the guard was sent to arrest Bellaria [quotes 'comming . . . sonne' (p. 626)]. On this hint Shakespeare constructed the scene . . . in which Mamillius begins his interrupted tale [2.1]. But Leontes himself, not merely the guard, comes in to order Hermione's arrest. . . . [*Pandosto*'s] order of events is quite satisfactory in a prose narrative, but it lacks dramatic tension. Shakespeare realized that he would spoil Hermione's speech at the trial, in which she appeals to the oracle, if he allowed her to appeal to the oracle in a previous scene [as Bellaria does]; so he made Leontes himself decide to send a deputation to Apollo's temple at Delphos in order to satisfy other people. The substance of the oracle is not known until it is read out at the trial, and the King immediately declares that there is no truth in it. News is brought that Mamillius has died, and we assume, as Leontes himself does, that this is a judgement from Apollo on account of his blasphemy. Hermione faints, and Pauline [sic] brings word that she is dead. Bellaria is indeed dead; but Hermione recovers, unknown to Leontes.

"The only substantial passage in the novel which Shakespeare borrows with comparatively little alteration is Bellaria's speech at the trial [quotes 'If the deuine . . . Oracle' (p. 631)]."

WELLS ("Romance," 1966, pp. 64–5, 69–70): "*Pandosto* is a collection of clichés, the well-worn themes and stock situations of pastoral romance. . . . [65] During the play we are reminded of the old-fashioned nature of the story we are watching. By a sort of alienation technique Shakespeare draws our attention to the nature of the fiction [as at 1590–4, 3070, and 3327–8]. . . . It appears not only that Shakespeare was fully aware of the unrealities of the story, but that he deliberately played upon the audience's awareness too, inviting them to recall similar situations—even perhaps their memories of the source story itself, and also the centuries of tradition that lie behind it.

"Shakespeare's handling of *Pandosto* is characterized at once by extreme freedom and by a remarkable willingness to turn to account even minute details of the original. He both takes over the episodic structure and draws attention to it in the long speech of Time as chorus [1580-1611]. This emphasis seems designed to stress the romantic nature of the tale: in the non-dramatic romances, time is commonly the ally of chance and fortune in bringing about the changes of the actions. Time's speech is pivotal to the play. Shakespeare may have got the idea for it from Greene's subtitle, which is *The Triumph of Time*; and Greene's title-page bears the tag 'temporis filia veritas' [truth is the daughter of time]. Certainly Shakespeare makes of the time element a poetic complex that helps in giving the play a richness of harmony without parallel in the novel. Showing how human beings can achieve at least the illusion of having triumphed over time, Shakespeare creates that illusion for us. . . .

"[69] In *The Winter's Tale* there are no macrocosmic implications. Emphasis is placed not on the group but on individuals whose suffering we have closely followed. . . . [Leontes's closing (3366-9)] is not in fact a high romantic climax. The emphasis is not on the lovers, but on the older generation. . . . [70] In his adaptation of *Pandosto* Shakespeare has produced a work that is far more powerful as a human document . . . not by denying the romance elements in Greene's book but by readjusting them—sometimes adding to them, sometimes toning them down with a modified realism, and always investing them with a poetic rather than a mundane reality."

COLIE (1974, p. 278 n.): "Though the statue is not in Greene's *Pandosto*, there may be some hints in the source nevertheless." She quotes: "painted Eagles are pictures, not Eagles, *Zeusis* Grapes were like Grapes, yet shadowes: rich clothing make not princes: nor homely attyre beggers: shepheards are not called shepheardes, because they were [wear] hookes and bagges: but that they are borne poore, and liue to keepe sheepe, so this attire hath not made *Dorastus* a shepherd, but to seeme like a shepherd" (p. 644).

FREY (*Vast Romance*, 1980, pp. 56-60): "Whereas Greene couches his opening in euphuistic terms and suggests slyly that his potential critics are 'oftentimes most unlearned of all', Shakespeare seconds no such attitude, choosing instead to develop through Archidamus, [57] who represents pastoral Bohemia, the hints in his source about the superiority of rude but willing minds and art." FREY continues with comparisons of the two authors' handling of the mission to Delphos and of the love exchanges—(p. 59) "Perdita is much less pert and pithy in her speech than is Fawnia. But Shakespeare expands upon Greene's hints to suggest her deeply instinctual commitment to the natural as opposed to the artificial way in all things." He concludes, (p. 60) "An aspect of Shakespeare's method, then, is to seize upon certain parts of *Pandosto*—professed authorial goals, various scenes, particular characters—and to enlarge upon them, challenging from various angles their stereotypic artfulness."

PILGRIM (1983, pp. 9-10): "The great scene, in which Paulina brings the baby princess in her arms from the [10] prison to Leontes in the vain attempt to soften his jealous madness [2.3], is developed from Greene's short mention of the jailor's pity for Bellaria . . . and hope of securing her release from prison by going to the king and telling him she was with child. Still less was it necessary for Shakespeare to make Paulina not only the fearless accuser of Leontes in his jealousy but also the guide of his actions and keeper of his conscience during the period of remorse. Never, perhaps, in drama has there been so grand an extension of the 'confidente's' [sic] role." PILGRIM also describes the development of Camillo from Greene's Franion and of Leontes from Pandosto.

DONAWERTH (1984, pp. 124–39): In *Pandosto* "the oracle, an exception to the general rule, means simply what it seems to mean, and only the Princess is found. Shakespeare closely follows the wording of the oracle, except for the names; but he does change the story, with the result that the same words, unambiguous in *Pandosto*, are richly ambiguous in *The Winter's Tale*. . . . [*139*] In Greene's romance . . . [t]he oracle is fulfilled in one sense only: the lost daughter is found."

BULLOUGH (1975, 8:123–32): "Shakespeare's main departures from Greene are as follows: names and settings are changed; the king's jealousy is speeded up, with consequent loss of probability; Leontes himself sends to consult the Oracle before his wife's trial, and does not, like Pandosto, do so only when his wife demands it; unlike Pandosto Leontes rejects the Oracle's verdict, and his im-[*124*]mediate bereavements are seen as punishments for blasphemy. Paulina is a new character and her continuing part is original; the child is not cast adrift in a boat but taken to Bohemia by Antigonus, another new character. Shakespeare introduces a bear to kill him, and a storm to sink the ship. Polixenes is present at the shearing-feast, which, with the entertainment offered there, is also new; likewise Autolycus and his tricks. *Pandosto* lacks the broad humour of *The Winter's Tale*, and also the discussion of ethical topics. The emotional intensity and poetic feeling of the piece are of course Shakespeare's own. . . . [*132*] The repentance of Pandosto [for his wife's death] is noted by Greene but not emphasized, and nothing is made of it when he meets his unknown daughter after sixteen years. Instead, he keeps her lover in prison, and tries to seduce her, then, being refused, is willing to have her killed to please Egistus. Leontes, however, aided by that embodied conscience Paulina . . . is made to suffer the torments of remorse until the last moments of the play, and, looking back over the dialogue, it is obvious that from the moment when Paulina brought news of Hermione's supposed death [1358 ff.] the intention was to bring her back.

"Shakespeare's reasons for this drastic departure from his source were complex. He had already [dealt with recognitions in *Per.* and reconciliations in *Cym.*]. If the new play was to have such an ending [as *Cym.*] it would be impossible to take over Greene's backsliding Pandosto . . . and to have him mar his daughter's marriage either by living on or committing suicide. On the other hand, to leave Leontes in penitential misery without any recompense would be both harsh and undramatic. Above all, Shakespeare [wanted not mere entertainment] but a thought-provoking piece with strong ethical and religious overtones. . . . He now invents a variant on [the restoration of Hero in *Ado*], the 'living statue' of the desired woman."

MACKINNON (1988, p. 139): "The last significant action of Greene's *Pandosto* . . . is committed by Pandosto himself, who 'calling to mind' all the evil he has done ['fell into a melancholie fit, and to close vp the Comedie with a Tragicall stratageme, hee slew himself'] [p. 656]. We could not ask for a clearer statement of generic purpose. However, Greene's syntax is significantly uncertain. We are left in doubt whether the intention of the 'tragical stratagem' is the author's, who would here interpolate this clause as a breezy aside to his audience, or Pandosto's, who would then assume an attitude of frozen self-regard. Such unclarity is richly suggestive, for it invites us to speculate on Pandosto's feelings, but must finally leave us uneasy. If Greene himself is confessing to a 'stratagem', how tawdry his work must seem. It is also an error of taste to have Pandosto kill himself because the comic reconciliation the subtitle . . . promises is left incomplete. Shakespeare reverses Greene's direction here, and closes up his tragical drama with a comical stratagem.''

ADAMS (1989, pp. 109–10): ''Though king Leontes' abrupt, unmotivated rage in the first act of *WT* has been amply criticized as a deficiency in the play, not so much attention has been paid to the abrupt, unmotivated rage of king Polixenes in Act IV. In fact, *Pandosto* provides both monarchs with ample motivation. Bellaria . . . comes close to playing fast and loose with her royal guest; Greene slyly tempts us into thinking it likely. And Egistus' fury with his son Dorastus flares up for reasons that Elizabethans would have found instantly familiar; the father had arranged a marriage for his son . . . and was not going to see it disrupted by an affair with a common shepherdess. But Shakespeare made no effort to provide credible motives for Leontes/Pandosto, and discarded the motive that Greene had already provided for Polixenes/Egistus. Lacking the sort of specific motivation that would distinguish them, the two [kings] meld practically indistinguishably into identical mechanisms of suspicion, sullen repression, and abrupt fury burst-[*110*]ing out into fantastic threats of burning, mutilation, and bloody execution.

''If the kings are twin bogeys, setting the two halves of the plot into motion, they play little part in the reconciliation. In the course of Act V, Leontes never addresses to his daughter a word that the audience can hear, nor does Polixenes say a word to his son; in fact, Leontes addresses only a brief sentence to Bohemia, perfunctorily begging pardon for his scandalous suspicions and his efforts to murder a sacred guest as well as a dear friend. [ADAMS apparently alludes to 3361–3. Leontes's earlier and presumably more copious apology is reported at 3061–2.] Thus . . . the true climax of that last scene rises from the reunion of mother and daughter.''

As mentioned above, most critics think that Sh. greatly improved Greene's romance. The opinion of many is summed up by SACHS (1923, p. 84): ''One can put one's finger on the difference between commonplace talent and genius. [*Pandosto*] is logically correct but nevertheless leaves the reader cold. In [Sh.'s] play, however, the plot is logically absurd and yet we are deeply moved by it because it is built up on deep psychological truth.'' Like LENNOX (see p. 656), though, a few seem less enthusiastic about his changes. BOAS (1896, pp. 519–20): Sh.'s ''ending is far more satisfactory to our moral sense [than Greene's], and the scene where the living statue steps down from the pedestal into her husband's arms is one of the most beautiful in the dramatist's writings. Yet the change is not altogether an artistic improvement. . . . The jealousy of Pandosto towards his queen had been the prologue to the main narrative, of which Fawnia is the centre. In the course of her tangled love-romance, the girl not only secures happiness for herself, but is made by destiny, who is the presiding genius of the story, the instrument of vengeance for her mother's wrongs.

This effective bond between the opening incidents of the tale and its later stages is lost in Shakspere's version, where the relations between the jealous king and his wife are [*520*] lifted into the foreground of the action, and the fortunes of their daughter become a subordinate and almost entirely detached episode." CHAMPION (1970, pp. 164–5): "The general alterations from . . . *Pandosto* . . . heighten the fictional tone. Bellaria, for example, is a more credible character than Hermione; her reaction to her husband's unfounded jealousy is forthright and vocal, and their alienation builds more slowly and predictably. Then, too, the transfer of the action from one kingdom to another is less contrived in Greene." In CHAMPION's view, Capnio is better motivated than Camillo to accompany the lovers, the conversation of 1.1 sounds hyperbolic, and (p. 165) "one device after another confirms [*WT*'s] fictional tone."

BISWAS (1971, pp. 154–65), similarly: "Shakespeare has modified the source-story . . . with the result that the story becomes sensational but the action lacks adequate motivation. For example, Leontes' jealousy is unplausible, and the incidents of Antigonus being eaten up by a bear and of Hermione's revival . . . are characteristic of romance and tragi-comedy. Even the character of Autolycus, for which Shakespeare may have derived hints from realistic portraits of London rascals, [*155*] is an item in this fantasia, for he tells absurd stories of fishes that sing ballads, while relieving the rustics of their purses, and his thievery is less a crime than the inspiration of a knavish god. . . . [*160*] He [Sh.] has introduced the love affair of Perdita and Florizel much later than the corresponding episode in Greene and it is also subordinate to the main story, with which it is imperfectly blended. Shakespeare has not borrowed the horrible suggestion of incest. . . . But he has had to pay a price for this omission, for the two parts of the play fall apart and are less well-knit than Greene's story. . . . [*165*] Shakespeare's manipulation of the source materials in The Sheep-shearing Scene [4.4] confirms the impression that he used the source as merely a starting point for something different . . . the opposition between Fortune and Nature, Nature and Nurture."

Genre

SMITH (1897, p. 378 n.): In *WT* "the pastoral element borrowed from Greene's *Pandosto* is so completely subordinated that we can hardly say it exists at all. Who would ever speak of Perdita as an Arcadian? In all probability Shakespeare realized how little dramatic power existed in the pastoral theme, and was too wise to risk the experiment of writing a true pastoral drama." GREG (1906, p. 411) agrees: "The shepherd scenes of that play [*WT*] . . . owe nothing of their treatment to pastoral tradition, nothing to convention, nothing to aught save life as it mirrored itself in the magic glass of the poet's imagination."

GREENLAW (1916, pp. 145–7) does not: "Greene's story is [*146*] much farther removed from true pastoral than Shakespeare's; what has really happened is that Shakespeare has transformed a romance of adventure which patronizes the 'homely pastimes' of shepherds . . . into the most exquisite and satisfying pastoral in Elizabethan literature. . . . Fawnia is a Pamela of the Richardsonian type, concerned about her virtue, ambitious yet suspecting the intent of the Prince; her reputed father, a worthy predecessor of Pamela's father, is wholly different from the old shepherd of *The Winter's Tale*, for he suspects that the prince has designs upon his daughter's virtue. . . . [*147*] Dorastus does not go to live among the shepherds in order to woo his lady, he merely puts on a shepherd's coat when he pays his visits, changing back to his 'riche apparel' when the call is over. We are not surprised that after the betrothal Fawnia's chief thought is joy to have won 'the love of a Prince, hoping in time to be advaunced from the daughter of a poore farmer to be the wife of a riche King' [p. 645]. . . . How completely all this is changed by Shakespeare needs no illustration."

HERFORD (ed. 1904, 4:265–9): Greene's "execution was evidently controlled by the purest spirit of romance, according to the Sidneian and Lylyan model fashionable in 1588. The *Arcadia* served as model for the matter, the [*266*] *Euphues* for the speech. In the tragic story he framed a pastoral idyll, even outbidding Sidney's pseudo-classic *mise-en-scène* by permitting his injured Bohemian queen to appeal, with success, to the oracle of Delphi; while the personages throughout express their passions and their hesitancies with an oppressive appetency, like Lyly's, for the symmetries of speech and the analogies of nature. . . . [*269*] It is plain that Shakespeare did not attempt to efface the marks of the 'old tale' in his [source] materials; at certain points he even heightens them. He repeats with perfect gravity Greene's geographical and historical eccentricities, and caps the oracle of Delphos and the coast of Bohemia with a sculptor, Giulio Romano"; see n. 3104–5. On HERFORD's last point, HARP (1978, p. 296), however: " 'Old tales' in Shakespeare generally means old wives' tales, that is, lies. . . . But . . . some of the characters . . . are also aware of the improbability of the events in which they participate, and it is this very improbability that forces them to the astonishing conclusion that old tales may . . . help reveal the true nature of experience." For more on the credibility of old tales, see n. 3037–9.

MOORMAN (ed. 1912, p. xxvii): "The pastoral convention, to which Sidney and Spenser had in their day rendered full and frequent obeisance, and to which even such robust intellects as those of Ben Jonson and Cervantes paid loyal homage, had always seemed an unreal and artificial thing in the eyes of Shakespeare." He refers to Sh.'s transformation of Thomas Lodge's pastoral *Rosalynde* into *AYL*; see KNOWLES (ed. *AYL*, 1977, pp. 490–4 and 511–27).

BETHELL (1947, pp. 34–5): "Greene insisted on Bohemia's coastline to emphasise the fact that his Bohemia was not the Bohemia of contemporary diplomatic reports but a romantic Ruritania or Arcadia where the strangest things might happen. And Shakespeare, who rejected so much of Greene's story in adapting it to his purpose, deliberately preserved the sea-coast of Bohemia because he was especially anxious to liberate [*35*] himself from the localisation of his play world in the contemporary map of Europe."

PARROTT (1949, pp. 383–4): "Shakespeare changes the whole tone of the story. It is not clear that Greene knew very well what he was doing; all he wanted was to write a romantic tale packed with situations giving occasion for his favorite long and euphuistic soliloquies. Shakespeare knew better than to 'close up a [sic] comedy with a tragical stratagem' [p. 656]; in fact he seems to have planned to convert Greene's story into a tragi-comedy where a near tragic beginning should be brought to a happy close. He retains the general outline of the novel, but he eliminates its most tragic incidents, the death of the Queen, Pandosto's unnatural passion for his daughter, and his final suicide. . . . In [*384*] the second part of the play, to give a realistic background to a romantic tale he brings in certain comic characters, the stupid Clown, Perdita's foster-brother, with his rustic sweethearts, and the rogue, Autolycus. There is no place for such characters in Greene's artificial pastoral, but they are quite at home in an English rustic festival."

Characters

Autolycus

WHITE (1892, p. 55): "The 'Winter's Tale' probably explains why Shakespeare was called the English Terence in 'The Scourge of Folly', [c.] 1611." White alludes to the collection of epigrams by John Davies of Hereford (1565?–1618); one is addressed "To our English Terence, Mr. Will. Shake-speare." After summarizing Terence's *Andria*, however, White concludes that the plays have virtually nothing in common except a generic resemblance shared by Autolycus and *Andria*'s servant, Davus. NEILSON (ed. 1906, p. 419): "For [Autolycus], and for his song in IV.iii.1 ff. [1669 ff.,] hints may have been derived from Tom Beggar in Robert Wilson's *Three Ladies of London* (1584)."

Camillo

BONJOUR (1952, p. 197): In 4.4, "the double arrival of the lovers and Polixenes . . . is natural and convincing. The fact that so human a sentiment as Camillo's longing for his native country is so deftly used to motivate the whole proceeding is not the least of Shakespeare's accomplishments in that matter. Moreover, there is not the slightest doubt that this rôle of Camillo's, entirely missing in Greene, provides yet another effective link between the two centres of interest in the drama, owing to the conspicuous part he now plays in both stories, of which he is no mean *agent de liaison*. . . . Shakespeare's preservation of Hermione, together with his creation of Camillo's part in the last acts, are two main factors which give the play a unity of theme altogether lacking in Greene's novel."

Leontes

SCHELLING (1928, pp. 410–11): "Shakespeare's King Leontes, when his un-[*411*] reasonable jealousy and his wicked defiance of the oracle have lost him his wife and children, spends years, we are led to infer, in repentance and remains true to the memory of his unparalleled queen. This makes possible the reconciliation in the end and the joy and hope that springs from the restoration of the lost ones and Perdita's marriage to her Prince Florizel. But it is not only in these and in several minor changes that Shakespeare betters Greene's plot for dramatic use, but the invention and introduction of new characters. Antigonus, incomparable Paulina, Mopsa, Dorcas, the clown, and above all Autolycus—all these are Shakespeare's invention."

LAWRENCE (1960; 1969, pp. 176-7): Sh. "altered his source in making the king's jealousy break forth abruptly, in the midst of gay and playful conversation, but he has left some indecision as to how far these suspicions had already been smouldering beneath the surface. . . . Had Leontes been represented as suspicious from the start, a false idea of the affection of Polixenes and Hermione might well have been created, which it would have been difficult to efface. . . . [*177*] Sudden and unjustified suspicions were . . . common in popular story-telling. . . . Greene's novel . . . is set in a framework of romantic commonplaces. Archaic details of the old and widespread Accused Queen motive were occasionally retained by both Shakespeare and by Greene. . . . Sudden and baseless rages are common in romance, and easily became a convention in romantic drama. We are not told why the Usurping Duke [in *AYL*] suddenly breaks in on Rosalind . . . and incontinently banishes her, nor why Old Capulet [in *Rom.*] treats his only child . . . with such violently cruel harshness, which even a crossing of his wishes does not seem to explain."

ARMSTRONG (1969, pp. 60-1): "Nowhere else does he [Sh.] follow one source throughout, but [*61*] exchange its quite straightforward central motivation for one so improbable that it has exercised readers ever since. In Greene's *Pandosto* . . . Pandosto . . . is provoked to jealousy in the most direct way imaginable: [quotes '*Bellaria* . . . thoughtes' (p. 623)]. Under these circumstances, it would have needed all the explanatory resources of depth psychology if Pandosto had *not* felt angry and jealous."

SCHANZER (ed. 1969, p. 25): "In the first half of the play Leontes still bears some resemblance to his counterpart in the novel. In the second half the two characters cease to have anything in common. [Pandosto imprisons Dorastus and tries to seduce Fawnia.] When he finds her firm against all promises and threats, his love for her turns to hatred, so that he is quite ready . . . to have her put to death. Nothing could be more of a contrast with Leontes, who, after sixteen years of penance for his crimes, is shown to be all goodness, humility, and courtesy. While Pandosto's re-enactment of it sixteen years later makes his cruel behaviour towards his queen seem something rooted in his nature, that of Leontes is made to seem a unique and short-lived aberration, a solitary fit of insane delusion during which he becomes utterly transformed, a stranger to his true self."

MOWAT (1976, pp. 9-12), a minority view: "Instead of emphasizing the love between Leontes and Hermione, he [Sh.] passes over Greene's account of 'these two, linked together in perfect love' [p. 621], and has Leontes summarize his courtship in the curt lines: 'Three crabbed months had sour'd themselves to death / Ere I could make thee open thy white hand / And clap thyself my love' ([173-5]). The sole references to their affection are Hermione's playful words: 'Yet, good-deed, Leontes, / I love thee not a jar o' th' clock behind / What lady she her lord' ([99-101]) and Leontes' declaration to the court that the defendant is 'one of us too much belov'd' [1178-9]. In several places [*10*] where references to their love would seem natural, Shakespeare omits them. In the introductory scene, for instance, the picture drawn of the fortunate Leontes includes no mention of a wife. Yet, in *Pandosto*, it is largely the ideal love between Pandosto and Bellaria that makes Fortune envious, and causes her to turn her wheel, and darken 'their bright sun of prosperity with the misty clouds of mishap and misery' [p. 621]. Again, in the trial scene, where Hermione is listing the joys of her past life, she speaks tenderly of her children, but, of Leontes, she recalls only that she once had his 'favor' [1273]. . . . Throughout the 'tragic' section of *The Winter's Tale*, Leontes' character is in keeping with the pettiness of his passion. . . . [12] Pandosto, before jealousy overtook him, was a courageous warrior and a generous lord. Leontes, in contrast, is a frightened man, afraid to take open revenge on Polixenes [quotes 921–2]. He will instead revenge himself on his helpless wife."

Perdita and Florizel

SCHANZER (ed. 1969, pp. 26–7): "The transformation of the novel's young lovers is less profound than that of Pandosto, but still far-reaching. . . . Dorastus is ashamed of his love for the shepherdess Fawnia and tries his utmost to resist it. Like his father (and Polixenes) he sees it as dishonourable, disgraceful, calamitous. Only because he finds his love stronger than his sense of 'honour' does he finally yield to it and, after Fawnia refuses to become his mistress, offer to make her his wife. Nothing could be further removed from Florizel's exaltation of Perdita above any princess, his total unconcern about her social station, his declaration that [quotes "I was . . . alike" (2287–91)].

"Fawnia's thoughts, when she finds herself in love with the Prince, also dwell mainly on the difference of rank between them. Where for Perdita 'the difference forges dread' [1817] because it threatens the continuance of their relationship, Fawnia sees her love for the Prince as a violation of the order of nature, and therefore likely to have dire consequences. As she is preoccupied with social [27] rank, what pleases her most about the projected marriage to Dorastus is the thought of one day becoming queen. Hence it does not come as a surprise that when, at the end of the novel, she discovers the man who has been treating her and her lover in the most villainous fashion to be her father, we are told (apparently without the least touch of irony): 'Fawnia was not more joyful that she had found such a father than Dorastus was glad he should get such a wife' [p. 655]. We are worlds away from Perdita. . . . Much as he has done with Leontes, Shakespeare has made the young lovers far more attractive and lovable than are their counterparts in *Pandosto*."

Other Sources

ROBERT GREENE'S CONY-CATCHING PAMPHLETS

Sh. drew details of Autolycus's bilking of the Clown (1718 ff.), and perhaps his picking and cutting of the festival purses under the cover of song (2481 ff.), from one, possibly two, of Robert Greene's cony-catching pamphlets. Sh. was clearly indebted to *The Second Part; The Thirde* may have provided some suggestions. See also nn. 1718 and 2567–9.

THE

SECOND

and last Part of Conny-catching.

R[obert] G[reene].

1592.

There walked in the midle walke [of St. Paul's] a plaine Country farmer, a man of good wealth, who had a well lined purse . . . which a crue of foists [pickpockets] hauing perceiued, their hearts were set on fire to haue it, & euery one had a fling at him, but all in vaine, for he kept his hand close in his pocket, and his purse fast in his fist. . . . At last one of the crue . . . walkt directly before him and next him three or foure turnes, at last standing still, he cried alas honest man helpe me, I am not well, & with that sunck downe suddenly in a sown, the pore Farmer seeing a proper yong Gentleman (as hee thought) fall dead afore him, stept to him, helde him in his armes, rubd him & chaft him: at this there gathered a great multitude of people about him, and the whilest the Foiste drewe the farmers purse and away: by that the other thought the feat was done, he began to come something to himselfe againe, and so halfe staggering, stumbled out of Paules, and went after the crue where they had appointed to meet, and their boasted of his wit and experience.

THE

THIRDE

and last Part of Conny-

catching.

By R[obert] G[reene].

1592.

. . . Com to Gracious street, wher this villanous pranke was performed. A roging mate, & such another with him, were there got vpon a stal singing of balets which belike was som pretty toy, for very many gathered about to heare it, & diuers buying, as their affections serued, drew to their purses & paid the singers for them. The slye mate and his fellowes, who were dispersed among them that stoode to heare the songes: well noted where euerie man that bought, put vp his purse againe, and to such as would not buy, counterfeit warning was sundrie times giuen by the rogue and his associate, to beware of the cut pursse, and looke to their pursses, which made them often feel where their pursses were, either in sleeue, hose, or at girdle, to know whether they were safe or no. Thus the craftie copesmates were acquainted with what they most desired, and as they were scattered, by shouldering, thrusting, feigning to let fall something, and other wilie tricks fit for their purpose: heere one lost his purse, there another had his pocket pickt, and to say all in briefe, at one instant, vpon the complaint of one or two that sawe their pursses were gone, eight more in the same companie, found themselues in like predicament.

FRANCIS SABIE'S POEMS

That Sh. may also have been indebted to an offspring of *Pandosto* was suggested and more or less dismissed by CHAMBERS (1930, 1:489–90): "There is not much to suggest that Shakespeare used a derivative from Greene in Francis Sabie's *Fisherman's Tale* (1595)." Sabie actually wrote two poems based on Greene's work, *The Fissher-mans Tale* and a second part, *Flora's Fortune*. The first was entered, on 21 November 1594, to the stationer Richard Jones as "a booke intituled, *the fisher mans tale conteyninge the storye of* CASSANDER *a Gretian knight*" (ARBER, 1875–94, 2:666). The second part, although it has new signatures and an entirely reset title page, does not seem to have been entered; Jones perhaps trusted that one fee would cover both parts. Also in 1595, Jones entered and published *Pans Pipe, three pastorall eglogues*, to which "The printer hath annexed the Fisher-mans tale." Although *Flora's Fortune* is unmentioned, *RSTC* believes the two parts "were intended to be issued" as sections of *Pans Pipe*.

The stories told by these poems may be summarized as follows.

The Fissher-mans Tale

Driven ashore by a storm, a fisherman discovers a small stone building strangely decorated with pictures of sea gods; it is evidently a mysterious temple. An apparently aged man, who seems more divine than mortal, welcomes him, and in response to the fisherman's inquiry, tells his tale. He is Cassander, also a fisherman. He is of noble birth, however, and once sought fame through deeds of arms. After distinguishing himself in the Holy Land and elsewhere, he served the ruler of Bohemia, who led forty thousand men against the Turkish lord who had abducted Bohemia's beautiful daughter. Cassander's extraordinary deeds in battle win the day and the daughter, but Cassander modestly declines grateful Bohemia's offer of his crown and her hand. He departs, having demonstrated that neither wealth nor station interests him.

After many adventures Cassander comes at last to Arcadia, where, among a troop of fair shepherdesses, he sees one whose beauty exceeds Venus's and whose modesty Diana's. As she looks at him, she too is affected, and her color comes and goes. Modesty requires the entranced Cassander to depart, but he inquires about her of an aged herdsman. "She is," he replies, "supposed the daughter of old Thirsis, and she

674

herself doth know no less." Actually, however, the old man reveals, Thirsis found her as a baby, wrapped in a scarlet mantle and lying in a boat. Because of her astonishing beauty, many men now want her, but she rejects them all.

Cassander's attempts to persuade himself not to love her are fruitless. Can it be that Cassander the Grecian Conqueror is infatuated with a shepherd's trull? It can, for Apollo, Mars, and mighty Jove himself have been love's victims. So Cassander disposes of his steed and his weapons and buys country russet and a flock of sheep, content with his lowly estate if he can but see his love. Unknown to him, his love is equally infatuated and also despairing, for how could such a flock-attending drudge as she hope for a famous knight, one perhaps as false as he is fair?

They meet one day while tending their sheep. Mistaking him for a stranger shepherd, she is so attracted that she quite forgets her love for Cassander. He points out that if she grazes her flock alone, she exposes herself to lions and bears and wolves and many other hazards. He offers to marry her so that she can leave behind the dangers and discomforts of single life. When she demurs, he reveals that he is the knight she recently met who now has set aside his fame and dignity to woo her, because Love levels differences in rank. He is eloquent, and she gives him her hand and heart.

Thirsis, having discovered their intimacy, berates her for loving a stranger who will surely desert her when her beauty fades. Henceforth, he will graze the flock and she will remain at home, out of Cassander's sight. Cassander is frantic when, rather than Flora, a hostile and uncommunicative Thirsis appears in the fields. Disguised as a beggar, Cassander cries for alms at Thirsis's door, and Flora recognizes him. She needs immediate help; tomorrow she weds Coridon. Stripping off his disguise, Cassander hurries to the port and arranges passage to Greece. That night he comes for Flora and would have escaped with her undetected had not his horse neighed as they mounted. Awakened, Thirsis pursues them. They manage to board, and Thirsis rages from the shore until Cassander, fearing that his angry words will provoke intervention, forces him into the ship. What is about to happen suddenly strikes Thirsis: he will be taken away from his dear old wife, tossed about on the sea, and finally his bones will lie in some vicious foreign land. He begs to be let go, but the ship puts to sea with him aboard.

Envious Fortune frowns. A storm strikes, the wind and sea go mad, rigging snaps, sails are blown to shreds, the ship splits on the rocks. Cassander tries to rescue Flora, but only he reaches the rock upon which the stone temple stands. Here he has been ever since, sometimes believing that Flora and Thirsis survived, sometimes not, but if he could be reunited with her, his white hairs, bent limbs, and ashen complexion would vanish and his youth would return.

Flora's Fortune

Parted from Cassander, Flora and Thirsis are rescued by a passing ship. After visiting the isle of Delphos, they return to the Greek mainland, where they resume their former life.

The poem now looks backward to Flora's parents. King Palemon of Greece marries the beautiful Julina, a German princess. After the death of his father-in-law, Palemon goes to Germany to claim its crown; he leaves Julina in the care of Eristo, "a grave and senile man," whose integrity is undoubted. Before long, however, Eristo dotes upon the lovely queen and tries to seduce her. In a rage at her indignant refusal, he writes to Palemon that he has seen Julina playing Venus's games with Lord Alpinor and that they conspire to murder him and take the crown of Greece. Eristo has Alpinor jailed and murdered, reported a suicide.

Raging, Palemon returns to Greece and, on Eristo's testimony, condemns Julina to a pitchy dungeon until Apollo or Themis, the goddess of law and justice, confirms her treachery. By this time, Julina is great with child—Alpinor's, Palemon believes. Alone in her cell, she brings forth a daughter sweet, whom Palemon orders to be set adrift. The queen kisses her little girl, consigns her to the gods' mercy, and sends with her, wrapped in a robe and a scarlet mantle, a ring, a golden chain, and a purse of golden coins. The wherry boat is thrust off, and the babe floats upon the sea.

At Themis's temple the Greek peers sent to learn the goddess's judgment receive a sealed scroll, which they deliver to Palemon. Julina is brought to hear what Palemon is sure will be the goddess's condemnation of her. Instead the goddess proclaims her chaste and adds that if Destiny helps not, Palemon shall die issueless. The nobles unbind the queen, whom maltreatment has made a pale and grisly ghost, assuring her that Palemon repents. It is too late, however; exhausted with grief, she dies. Palemon's life becomes perpetual grief.

The baby's boat makes its way into the Humber, an Arcadian river, where it comes to rest in the bulrushes. Thirsis, a poor hired herdsman, finds the child and the rich things sent with her by the queen. His wife, Mopsa, delighted with their miraculous wealth, agrees to keep their discovery a secret lest the king come and take it all away. She pretends to her neighbors that the baby is her own. Thirsis buys a flock and soon grows rich; Flora, raised to be a shepherdess, grows in beauty and has many suitors, all of whom she scorns.

At this point the plot of *The Fissher-mans Tale* is summarized and then continued. Cassander lives upon his craggy rock, and Flora and Thirsis, from whom Cassander was separated by the storm, having visited Delos, resume their lives as shepherds in Greece, the land of Flora's father, Palemon. At length Cassander is rescued by a passing ship and brought to Greece also, where, all unknown to him, Flora has caught the eye of young Dryano, the son of the false Eristo who caused her mother's death. Thinking to command the love of the shepherd wench, Dryano sends his servant for her, but Flora scornfully rejects the proposition, not only because she is virtuous but also because she knows exactly who Dryano is and what his father did to Queen Julina. Perhaps she should have anticipated Dryano's response to her rejection of him: he has both Flora and Thirsis brought before the king on judgment day. His curiosity having prompted him also to be present, Cassander hears them accused of treason, condemned on Dryano's perjured testimony, and sentenced by Palemon to death. Although he does not recognize her, Cassander, heavyhearted, watches as Flora is bound to the stake and Thirsis is hauled to the gibbet. Expecting to die, Thirsis reveals everything—his finding Flora in the boat, the token with her, her elopement with Cassander, his pursuit, the shipwreck and separation from Cassander, their return to Greece. As he listens, Cassander's frosty locks become golden and his pallid face a healthy red. Palemon's heart leaps as he recognizes the tokens and his daughter, and on her prompting, he has the villains hanged "before sweet Flora's face." Cassander embraces Flora. Even Homer "with his quaint *Pernassus* verse" could not express half the joys of old Palemon and indeed all the company.

According to HONIGMANN (1955), CHAMBERS underestimated Sh.'s debt to Sabie, for some passages of *WT* are closer to *The Fissher-mans Tale* and to *Flora's Fortune* than to *Pandosto*. The resemblances are italicized:

(a) the heauenly Godes haue sometime earthly thoughtes: Neptune became a Ram, Iupiter a Bul, Apollo a shepheard: they Gods, and yet in loue: and thou a man appointed to loue. (*Pan.* sig. E3)

Loue conquers all things: it hath conquered
Apollo once, it made him be a *swaine*.
Yea mightie Mars in armes inuincible,
It forced hath to lay aside his speare,
Loue made the sea-god *take* a Wesils *shape*,
Yea mighty *Ioue*, whose rage makes earth to shake,
Loue made to *take the* snow-white *shape of* Bull:
(*FT* sigs. C4 – C4ᵛ)

the Goddes themselues
(Humbling their Deities to loue) haue *taken*
The shapes of Beasts vpon them. Iupiter,
Became a Bull, and bellow'd: the greene Neptune
A Ram, and bleated: and the Fire-roab'd-God
Golden Apollo, a poore humble *Swaine*
As I seeme now.
(*WT* 1826 – 32)

(b) the aire began to be ouercast, the winds to rise, the seas to swel, yea presently there arose such a fearfull tempest, as the ship was in danger to be swallowed vp with euery sea, the maine mast with the violence of the wind was thrown ouer boord, the sayles were torne, the tacklings went in sunder, the storme raging still so furiously that poore Fawnia was almost dead for feare, but that she was greatly comforted with the presence of Dorastus. The tempest continued three dayes, al which time the Mariners euerie minute looked for death, and the aire was so darkned with cloudes that the Maister could not tell by his compasse in what Coast they were. (*Pan.* sigs. F3 – F3ᵛ)

But see what chanc'd, a sudden storme arose,
Skies looked blacke, clouds ouerwhelmd the skies, . . .
                    . . . as once when *angrie Iuno*

Sude to the wind-god for Aeneas bane,
Seas sweld, ropes crackt, sayles rent, *shipmen cride out*,
Ay me, poore wretch, my little fleeting *barke*,
Leapt like a feather, tost with blastes of wind:
One while it seemde the loftie skies to touch,
Straightwaies I thought it went to Plutoes lake, . . . *(FT* sig. B2ᵛ)
. . . Feare not I say, these waues and *blustering* winds
. . . the *frothy* seas. *(FT* sig. B3ᵛ)

　　　　　　the skies looke grimly,
And threaten present *blusters*. In my conscience
The heauens with that we haue in hand, are *angry* . . .
Looke to thy *barke* . . .
Oh, the most pitteous *cry* of the poore soules, sometimes to see 'em, and not to see 'em:
Now *the Shippe boaring the Moone with her maine Mast*, and anon swallowed with
yest and *froth*. *(WT* 1442–1535)

(c) *Pandosto* lacks this passage.

He straightway charg'd him take the bastard brat,
Throw't in a boat, and let it flote on seas . . .
Thrise kist she her sweet babe, and *dew'd the face*
With her Chrystalline pearl-resembling teares,
Impatient, *thrise of sorrow she fel downe* . . . *(FF* sig. D4ᵛ)

The ruthfull mother when she saw it goe,
Cride out and *scrikt*, renting her yellow haire . . . *(FF* sig. E1)
Her eies which once like glittering Diamonds were,
Now bleared were with *fountaines of her teares. (FF* sig. E2ᵛ)

I neuer saw a vessell of like *sorrow*
So fill'd, and so becomming: in pure white Robes
Like very sanctity she did approach
My Cabine where I lay: *thrice bow'd before me,*
And (gasping to begin some speech) *her eyes*
Became two spouts; the furie spent, anon
Did this breake from her. Good Antigonus,
Since Fate (against thy better disposition)
Hath made thy person for the *Thrower-out*
Of my poore babe, according to thine oath,
Places remote enough are in Bohemia,
There weepe, and leaue it crying: and for the babe
Is counted lost for euer, Perdita
I prethee call't: For this vngentle businesse
Put on thee, by my Lord, thou ne're shalt see
Thy Wife Paulina more: and so, with *shriekes*
She melted into Ayre. *(WT* 1463–79)

(d) Apollo with a *loude voice* saide (*Pan.* sig. C2)

these *thundering voyces* sent *(FF* sig. B3)

> the burst
> And the eare-deaff'ning *Voyce* o'th'Oracle,
> *Kin to Ioues Thunder*, so surpriz'd my Sence,
> That I was nothing. (*WT* 1155–8)

(e) The following minor coincidences: Two messengers sent to Apollo's temple (*WT* 798–802, *FF* sig. D4ᵛ), six (*Pan.* sig. C2); the oracle is consulted before Perdita's birth in *WT* and *FF* but after in *Pan.*; "the title 'The Winter's *Tale'* reminds one of 'The Fisherman's Tale': indeed Sabie observes that he wrote his book to 'expell . . . the acoustomed tediousnes of colde winters nightes' [*FF* sig. A2ᵛ], an apology Shakespeare may echo in [618]" (HONIGMANN, 1955, p. 29).

(f) The following resemblances of *WT* to Sabie; there are no corresponding passages in *Pandosto*:

> (*i*) I should leaue grasing, were I of your flocke,
> And onely liue by gazing. (*WT* 1922–3)

> Good Lord, how long could I haue found in heart,
> T'aue gazed on her mind-reioycing shape.
> Whole dayes, whole yeares, my life I could haue spent
> In vewing her. *(FT* sig. C3ᵛ)

> (*ii*) Fy (daughter) when my old wife liu'd: vpon
> This day, she was both Pantler, Butler, Cooke,
> Both Dame and Seruant: Welcom'd all: seru'd all, . . .
>   her face o'fire
> With labour, and the thing she tooke to quench it
> She would to each one sip. You are retyred,
> As if you were a feasted one: and not
> The Hostesse of the meeting: . . . (*WT* 1860–9)

> My mother oft hath told me in a rage,
> That I liue like a Lady vnto her,
> I (saith she) care for all things which be done,
> I serue the Swine, I giue the Pulhens meat:
> I fret, I chide, I neuer am at rest,
> And thou doest nought but walke the pleasant fieldes . . . *(FT* sig. D2ᵛ)

> (*iii*)   I (an old Turtle)
> Will wing me to some wither'd bough, and there
> My Mate (that's neuer to be found againe)
> Lament, till I am lost. (*WT* 3345–8)

> And as a Turtle Doue, when she hath lost
> Her louing mate, so seem'd he to lament . . . *(FF* sig. C3ᵛ)

HONIGMANN (p. 30) concludes: "Some of the Sabie-Shakespeare parallels could be explained away as natural to their contexts and therefore independent inventions, e.g. (b), (c); others are drawn from different contexts in *The Fisherman's Tale* and *The Winter's Tale*, e.g. (b), (f, iii). Nevertheless, enough of these parallels can be traced to make it seem quite probable that Shakespeare had read [both parts of] *The Fisherman's Tale* — for, after all, they would have been equally natural to the context in *Pandosto*, where analogous material is lacking."

A few of the collocations apparently derived from Sabie could have come directly from *Pandosto*:

> (a) *taken The shapes of* resembles *vnder the shape of* (*Pan.* A4ᵛ).
> (b) *sky, barke,* and *maine mast* are closely associated (*Pan.* F3–F3ᵛ)
> (f,i) Dorastus is "glad now to gaze on a poore shepheard" (*Pan.* D3).

These instances are too sparse to impair HONIGMANN's argument. Hence, BULLOUGH (1975, 8:130): Sh. "may have been encouraged by *The Fisherman's Tale* to develop its vignettes of rustic life, for Cassander disguises himself as a real English shepherd, buys 'sheepe and cotes' [C4ᵛ], and sets up as a newcomer to the district before wooing the maiden. Later he disguises himself as a crippled beggar to visit Flora's house, and receives alms. Obviously Cassander enjoys his deceit. Is this the germ of Autolycus?"

Possible Sources, Analogues, and Imitations

AMADIS DE GRECIA AND OTHER ROMANCES

SOUTHEY (1807, 1:xliv–xlv): "One of the Spanish Romances has had the singular fortune to be imitated by the three greatest writers of Elizabeth's age. In Amadis of Greece [Feliciano de Silva's continuation of *Amadis of Gaul*] may be found the Zelmane of the Arcadia, the Masque of Cupid of the Faery [xlv] Queen, and the Florizel of the Winter's Tale. These resemblances are not imaginary (Florizel indeed is there with the same name) — any person who will examine will be convinced beyond a doubt that Sidney, Spenser, and Shakespere, each of them imitated this book." THOMAS (1922, pp. 21–2): "Southey had in mind those scenes in which Prince Florizel, 'obscured with a swain's wearing', woos Perdita, just as his namesake in *Amadis de Grecia* turns shepherd [22] to court the temporary shepherdess Silvia. . . . The pastoral scenes in question [were] taken over . . . from [*Pandosto*] but as in these scenes Greene was clearly inspired by Feliciano de Silva, Shakespeare incurs at least a second-hand indebtedness to *Amadis de Grecia*." O'CONNOR (1970, p. 214): "René Pruvost . . . believes that the story of Florisel and Silvie in Book IX of *Amadis* provided Greene with the nucleus for his tale: 'The books of *Amadis* gave him the theme of a little princess born in prison and brought up as a shepherdess, who later is wooed by a prince disguised as a shepherd' [PRUVOST (1938, p. 301)]. [This] might explain Shakespeare's use of the name Florizel and show Southey right once more." Note: "As Mary Patchell points out (*The Palmerin Romances in Elizabethan Prose Fiction*

[New York: Columbia UP, 1947], p. 114), Shakespeare may have derived the name directly from the *Amadis*."

BROWNE (1876): "As in 'As You Like It' there are traces of the Charlemagne romances [see KNOWLES ed. *AYL*, 1977, p. 501], so I think in this drama there are evidences of Shakespeare's familiarity with those of Amadis. Florizel, as Don Florisel, is the hero of the ninth book of the 'Amadis' series, believed to have been written by Don Feliciano de Silva, and originally published at Burgos in 1535. . . . No English version of it is known, but . . . there may be an abstract of his adventures in 'The Treasury of Amadis of Fraunce', London, 1567. [AMADIS, 1572?, is an anthology of orations, each preceded by a headnote describing the occasion and identifying the characters involved. Dom Florisell is mentioned several times (e.g., on 2E2 and 2E3).] . . . It is by no means improbable, however, that Shakespeare knew the story in the French version of Charles Colet, 'Champenois' (1564). . . . There is no mention of Don Florisel in Greene's book, but he has taken the name of one of his characters (Garinter) from it [*Amadis of Fraunce*, presumably]. . . . La bella Perdida [occurs in] the original Amadis." JUSSERAND (in LEE, ed. 1907, pp. xxiii–xxiv) believes that book 8 of *Amadis* also contributed: "Not only are the facts similar in the novel and the romance, but . . . the tone and manner (with an abundance of speeches, dialogues, and monologues, [*xxiv*] a conspicuous verbosity throughout) offer also striking resemblances."

An imprisoned princess, having given birth to a beautiful daughter, entrusts the child to a faithful servant and his wife, who take it to Alexandria. There she is raised to be a shepherdess; she is called Sylvia. Like Fawnia, she is wooed by rich suitors in whom she has no interest, but one day Prince Florizel sees her and falls in love. Because she will marry only a shepherd as she herself is, Florizel adopts shepherd's garb, in which he woos her. After this, the stories diverge.

HONIGMANN (1955, pp. 31–3): *WT* "may owe more to the novel than the name Florizel. Of particular interest are the similarities between the action connected with the statue of Hermione [5.3] and a story [*Amadis* 9:18–21, quoted from the ed. of Christophle Plantin, Anvers, 1561] of which I give a summary. . . .

"Manatiles, King of Epirus, had an only son, Arpilior, who loved Princess Galatée. Manatiles also fell in love with Galatée and killed his wife in order to be able to marry her. One day, finding that Arpilior and Galatée loved each other, Manatiles almost killed his son in his jealousy, father and son being parted by courtiers. There lived at that time 'vn fort sçauant homme,' a magician who, to calm the king and to save the lovers, 's'auisa de dresser vn ymage si bien ressemblant au jeune Prince, qu'il ne lui restoit que la parole' [decided to have an image made so much like the young prince that only speech was lacking; cf. *WT* 3108–9], and another 'image' [effigy, statue] of Galatée. These images were beheaded, the prince, the princess and the king coming at a different hour each day to visit the images, Manatiles thinking Arpilior and Galatée both dead, the prince and princess thinking each other dead, and all of them taking the images to be real corpses. Having paid their visits the prince and princess 's'en retournent chacun en leur prison, ou ils sont secretement nourris, & entent le sage homme que ceey se face tant que le Roi vivra' [each returned to his own prison, where they are secretly fed, and the wise man intends that this continue while the king lives].

"This story was told to Florisel and Silvie, who stole into the palace grounds and managed to see the images: 'contemplerent longuement les cors & les têtes d'icelles ymages, qui se montroyent aussi vermeilles comme si elles eussent été coupees tout fraichement' [for a long time they contemplated the bodies and the heads of those images, which appeared as ruddy as if they had just been cut off; cf. *WT* 3240–1]. When Manatiles later visited the images, Florisel and Silvie heard him soliloquise:

> O Dieu souverain, ou auoise-ie l'esprit, quand ie permis que telle cruauté fût executee en mon propre enfant. . . . Ah amour, que tu es cause de grandes malheurtés & infortunes, ne m'étoit-ce point assés d'auoir m'êchamment meudry ma femme tant preude & chaste, sans me souiller, [32] & contaminer mes mains de mon sang propre, priuant moy & ce tant riche Royaume de legitime heritier?

> [O sovereign Lord, where was my mind when I permitted such cruelty to be visited upon my own child. . . . Ah love, who are the cause of great unhappiness and adversity, was it not enough to have wickedly murdered my wife so modest and chaste, without staining myself and dirtying my hands with my own blood, depriving myself and this very rich realm of a legitimate heir? Cf. *WT* 2733–9 ff.]

Manatiles decided, however, that repentance was foolish, and thought that the 'execution' of the two lovers was an act of justice.

"When Galatée came to visit the image of Arpilior, Silvie told her that she had been enchanted, and convinced her that the image was not a real body. Florisel, Silvie and Galatée then waited for the real Arpilior to appear. When he arrived, Galatée ran to meet him,

> & se ietta à son col, le tenant long tems embrassé sans pouvoir faire autre chose que pleurer & soûpirer profondement de grand joye qu'elle auoyt [and threw her arms about his neck, holding him for a long time unable to do anything but weep and sigh profoundly because of the great joy she felt; cf. *WT* 3322].

Arpilior, however, stood bewildered, forcing Galatée to exclaim: 'ne soyés plus abusé d'vne statuë composee par art magique & deceptif, voyés la viue image de vôtre amye' [don't be deluded any longer by a statue made by deceptive magic; see the living image of your love]. But Arpilior 'pensoyt que ce fût quelque fantôme: parquoy demoura tout rauy, & ne sçauoit bonnement que dire ou faire' [thought that she was a ghost because she had indeed died, and he hardly knew what to say or do; cf. *WT* 3209–10]. — Then Galatée 'le print par la main . . . (et Arpilior) reconnoissant sa fidele amye, l'embrassa amyablement, & baisa par plusieurs fois' [took him by the hand . . . (and Arpilior) recognizing his faithful love, embraced her fervently, and kissed her again and again; cf. *WT* 3315–21]. Later Florisel killed Manatiles, Arpilior married Galatée, and the magician was rewarded for preserving them.

"Lastly the magician threw a spell on the garden in which the images had been kept, filling it with statues of the heroes and heroines of the Amadis stories. Florisel entered the magic garden and was overjoyed to see the statues

> & pensa par plusieurs fois monter sus le trône, pour les aller embrasser, estimant que ce n'étoyt faintise ni enchantement, ains chose vraye [and thought several times to mount the throne in order to embrace them, believing that this was neither fantasy nor enchantment but the real thing; cf. *WT* 3280–1].

"At first sight the resemblances to *The Winter's Tale* are not very startling. Manatiles, a jealous tyrant, kills his wife and tries to kill his only child and heir. The heir (Arpilior) is miraculously preserved by the friendly magician (who corresponds to Paulina in *Winter's Tale*); and so on. It is the magician's use of statues, and specifically Arpilior's reactions when he finds that Galatée is really alive, which seems to have the more immediate bearing on *The Winter's Tale*. The repetition that Paulina can make the statue move *by magic*— [3230, 3293–5, 3302–3, 3319]—could be partly due to the fact that Paulina's role may be modelled on that of the magician. Similarly the statement that Paulina ['hath priuately, twice or thrice a day, euer since the death of *Hermione*, visited that remoued House' (3113–14)], the 'house' being her own home [3192], seems less peculiar—why should the wife of a nobleman live in a 'removed house', and 'visit' her own home?—when we recall that the magician kept Arpilior and Galatée secretly in prisons. . . . *[33]* If Shakespeare took the name Florisel from [*Amadis* 9] there is some likelihood that he had met with Arpilior and Galatée.

"Besides the possibility that 'la bella Perdida' suggested 'Perdita' to Shakespeare, as Browne believed [see above, p. 681], a prophecy quoted in the chapter immediately following the end of Manatiles [9:22] could have had the same result:

> Quiconques cherchera Armide, peut entrer franchement, mais la saillie a deus extrêmes de la gaigner ou pedre, iusques à ce que les perdus soyent trouués par la perduë [Whoever will seek Armide may enter freely, but the undertaking has two extremes of gain or loss, until the lost things are found by the lost one].

Here there is an arresting resemblance to [1315–16], which Shakespeare transcribed from *Pandosto* [see p. 631]. In *The Winter's Tale* 'that which is lost' is Leontes' daughter: the allusion to 'la perduë' in a similar context in *Amadis* may have moved Shakespeare to give Leontes' daughter her name (la perduë = Perdita)."

HONIGMANN's argument may have been unknown to O'CONNOR (1970, p. 158): "There is not a shred of evidence that Shakespeare ever read so much as a book of *Amadis*"; any apparent influence was derived through *Pandosto* (see also O'CONNOR, p. 214).

BULLOUGH (1975, 8:119–22) believes that in addition to *Amadis*, Greene— hence Sh. indirectly—was influenced by another popular romance, *The Mirrour of Knighthood*. The complete *Mirrour* consists of four parts: part 1 (3 books) was written by Diego Ortuñez de Calahorra; part 2 (2 books), by Pedro de la Sierra; and parts

3 and 4 (2 books each), by Marcos Martinez. All were translated into English and published between 1578 and 1597. "The name of the young prince Garinter comes from the Ninth Book. . . . [*121*] Both the lost princess reared by shepherds and the amorous prince disguising himself as a shepherd appear in *The Second Part* . . . (1583). In Chapter XVI two newly born children are stolen by the Giant Galtenor from the chamber of the Empress Claridiana (f. 87ʳ), and suckled very healthily by a lady and a lioness. The boy is called Claridiano, the girl Rosalvira. At the age of six they are taken by the Giant on his travels in a chariot drawn by griffins. Rosalvira wanders off one day and is found by a shepherd, who (like [*122*] Greene's Porrus) consults his wife. . . . They bring up the child as a shepherdess. In Chapter XX Prince Claridiano, enamoured of an unknown Pastora (shepherdess) . . . goes among the King's shepherds, 'in his hands a shepheards crooke. Also he carried with him a little lute. . . . He attracts the fair Pastora by his music.' "

APULEIUS

According to STARNES (1945, pp. 1044-6), "for this bizarre incident [the death of Antigonus], Shakespeare seems to have been recalling part of a story in *The Golden Ass*" of Apuleius, book 7—from which, STARNES finds, Sh. also drew material for *TGV*. He summarizes as follows (p. 1045): "Shepherds, seeking a stray cow, find an ass, ridden by a stranger, and try to take the beast to the rightful owner—the cruel boy [who earlier had been appointed the ass's driver]. They find the boy's body 'rent and torne in peeces and his members dispersed in divers places', which, Lucius says, 'I well knew was done by the cruell Beare. . . . Then they gathered together the peeces of his body and buried them' [trans. Adlington, rev. Gaselee, Loeb Classical Lib., p. 339]." STARNES comments, "In both accounts [*WT*'s and *Asse*'s] are shepherds searching for a stray sheep (cow); they are surprised by finding what they are not looking for (an infant, an ass); then they discover the mangled body of a man, partly eaten by a bear; and they resolve to bury what remained of the body. The similarities in characters, in incident, in the bizarre quality of the episode, in the order of details, and in the feeling produced that Antigonus and the cruel boy met a deserved fate can hardly be explained as coincidence.

"Another scene in the play seems also to reflect Shakespeare's recollection of . . . Apuleius. . . . Autolycus, trying to frighten the shepherd, exclaims, 'the curses he shall have, the torture he shall feel, will break the back of man, the heart of monster' [2651-2]. For his own purposes, the rogue elaborates his description of the suffering which the shepherd and his son shall endure. (A) He has a son who shall be flayed alive; (B) then 'nointed over with honey, set on the head of a wasp's nest; then stand till he be three (C) quarters and a dram dead . . . then raw as he is, and in the hottest day prognostication proclaims, shall be set against a brick-wall, the sun looking [*1046*] with a southward eye upon him, where he is to behold him with flies blown to death [2665-72].' " With these details, STARNES compares the methods proposed by the thieves to torture Charite and the ass: "(A) 'the fourth said she should be flead alive' [6:143, and] (C) 'Then let us lay this stuffed ass upon a great stone against the broiling heate of the Sunne, so they shall both sustain all the punishments which you have ordained' [6:143, and] an account of a master's ingenious torture of his wicked servant— . . . (B) 'First, after that he (the master) had put off all his (the servant's) apparell, he annointed his body with honey, and then bound him sure to a fig-tree, where in a rotten stock a great number of Pismares . . . had builded their neasts,—the Pismares after they had felt the sweetnesse of the honey, came upon his body, and by little and little (in continuance of time) devoured all his flesh, in such sort, that there remained on the tree but his bare bones' " (8:190).

TOBIN (1984, pp. 151–2): "The description of the 'statue' of Hermione . . . is itself Apuleian and the attribution of it to Julio Romano additionally so. . . . The action of [5.3 follows] that of Lucius' meeting with his aunt, Byrrhena, in Book II.

"Lucius, newly arrived in Hipata, accidentally meets his aunt Byrrhena who invites him to her house where there is much sculpture so finely carved that 'Art (is) envying Nature.'" She shows him beautifully wrought pieces, and then "lectures Lucius on the dangers of witchcraft as practiced by Pamphile," an event that TOBIN believes is related to Paulina's "you'le thinke (Which I protest against) I am assisted By wicked Powers" (3293–5). TOBIN finds other thematic parallels of a similar type, as well as the appearance in both works of such words as *house, marble, marvel,* and *wicked.*

ARETINO

LOTHIAN (1930) tries "to show that Shakespeare was very probably familiar with the five comedies of Aretino" and "his one tragedy, the *Orazia,* either at first hand, through his own knowledge of Italian, or indirectly through some friendly interpreter." In 1588, four of the comedies—*Marescalco, Talanta, Cortigiana,* and *Hipocrito*—had been published in Italian in London. LOTHIAN finds the following resemblances to *WT*: First, "the use of Autolycus as a vendor of knick-knacks and ballads" (p. 419). *Cortigiana* 1.4 has a ballad-monger and *Marescalco* 3.1, a huckster (who is depicted as a Jew). They have in common with Autolycus only their professions and the crying of their wares, although Furfante in the former does sell *alle belle historie.* The second similarity is that the term *three-pile(d), de tertio pelo* in *Marescalco,* occurs in *WT* (1681–2), *LLL* 5.1.407 (2339), and *MM* 1.2.32 (128) [and *MM* 4.3.10 (2087)]. As for the third similarity (p. 424), "it seems . . . just possible that, in running rapidly through a somewhat uninteresting passage of *Marescalco,* Shakespeare's careless reading left him with the impression that Julio Romano was a sculptor and that he was, like Titian, 'emulus naturae.' " In the passage (5.3), which is in Italian, Romano and a marble monument are mentioned in adjoining sentences but not otherwise connected. According to LOTHIAN, the 1588 version is as follows:

> *Pedant.* Sì pittoribus, un Titiano emulus naturae. Immo magister, sarà certo fra Sebastiano de Venitia divinissimo. Et forse Julio Romano curie, et de lo Urbinate Raphaello allumno. Et ne la marmorarea facultate, che dovea dir prima (benchè non è anchora decisa la preminentia sua). Un mezo Michel Angelo, un Jacopo Sansavino speculum Florentie. (5.3, p. 40ᵛ).

In modern Italian (ed. G. B. De Sanctis):

> *Pedante.* Si pictoribus, un Tiziano emulus naturæ immo magister, sarà certo Fra Sebastiano de Venetia divinissimo. E forse Julio Romanæ curiæ, e de lo Urbinate Rafaello alumno. E ne la marmorea facultate, che dovea dir prima (benché non è ancora decisa la preminenzia sua), un mezzo Michel Angelo, un Jacopo Sansovino, speculum Florentiæ. [For more on Sh.'s knowledge of Italian, see nn. 2665–7 and 3104–5, as well as PRAZ (1958, pp. 164–7) and MUIR (1977, p. 6).]

In English (trans. Bruce Penman):

> *Pedant. Si pictoribus* [As for painters], well, in that case he will be a Titian *emulus naturae immo magister* [a rival of nature, or rather its master], he will certainly be a fra Sebastiano, the inspired painter of Venice. Or perhaps he'll be a Giulio Romano of the Pope's court, and the pupil of Raphael of Urbino. And in sculpture, which I should have mentioned first (though its preeminence is not yet fully decided), he may be half a Michelangelo, or a Jacopo Sansovino, *speculum Florentiae* [mirror of Florence].

THE BIBLE

FRIPP (1938, 2:741–3): In *WT* "we are in the puritan atmosphere of *Cymbeline* and *The Tempest*. There are references to Judas Iscariot [533], Jacob and Esau [2604], the Lord's Prayer ['trespas . . . euill . . . forgiue' (2730–2)], 'amendment of life' [as in Matt. 3:1 (3162)], and probably to Elijah [1118–19] and Christ before Pilate [867–8; cf. Matt. 27:12]. Biblical language and thought are frequent— 'hold my peace', 'verily' (repeated again and again), 'false as water', sin to strike an anointed king, slander 'sharper' than a 'sword', Jove's better 'guiding spirit' for a 'babe', 'commit adultery', 'one jot', 'harden the heart', 'first-fruits of the body', the 'sins of youth' forgiven, 'grow in grace', 'the life to come', 'pace softly', 'bring thee on thy way', 'name put in the Book of Virtue', 'a merry heart', 'lift up your countenance', 'flesh and blood', stoned to death, the Queen 'well' in death, 'Heaven's spies', a world ransomed or destroyed. Dorcas is a Biblical name. Once or twice there is a concession to Catholicism [326–7 and 3235–6]; and the Clown, after the manner of the foolish, gibes at the Puritan who 'sings psalms to hornpipes' [1713]."

Regarding lines 130–52, "the best, and only contemporary, commentary on this passage is Romans v.12 and 14, in the Geneva Version of 1587, with its marginalia: 'Wherefore as by one man sin entered into the world, and death by sin, and so death went over all men (*From Adam, in whom all have sinned, both guiltiness and death came upon all*), in whom all men have sinned (*By Sin is meant that disease which is ours by inheritance, and men commonly call it Original Sin*). Death reigned even over them also that sinned not (*The very infants, which neither could ever know nor transgress that natural law, are notwithstanding, dead as well as Adam*).' The last note replaces in the older editions: '*He meaneth young babes, which neither had the knowledge of the Law, of Nature, nor any motion of concupiscence.*' "

DAPHNIS AND CHLOE

WOLFF (1912, pp. 452–5) asserts that a predecessor of *Pandosto* may also have contributed to *WT*: "Shakespeare seems to have desired to employ . . . normal causation and human motive wherever possible, instead of chance. This desire would render him dissatisfied with Greene's easy fashion of letting mere Fortune cast the child on the coast of the very country where reigns the unjustly suspected friend of her father,—the country where that friend's son will afterward fall in love with this very child grown to girlhood. . . . For the purpose . . . of getting the child exposed in Bohemia and nowhere else, he [Sh.] invented Antigonus. Leontes commissions Antigonus to expose it somewhere [1105 ff.], and Antigonus's own belief in Hermione's guilt—together with the request of Hermione's phantom . . . —leads him to expose it in Bohemia, the country of the child's supposed father [1483–8]. . . . Once invented, however, Antigonus must be killed as soon as he has performed his task of exposing Perdita." Moreover, the Shepherd must be got to the beach to discover her. Sh. finds both problems solved in Longus's pastoral romance *Daphnis and Chloe*, translated from Jacques Amyot's French version by Angell Daye in 1587 (*RSTC* 6400). In that work, the noise of "the young Methymnaeans' hunting . . . frightens the sheep and goats from their upland pastures down to the shore." Sh., WOLFF says, "borrowed this hunt, and . . . used it both to send the bear that devours Antigonus, and at the same time to frighten the sheep away from the hills so that the shepherd must seek them along the shore and there find the child." In *Daphnis and Chloe*, however, neither a bear nor a character corresponding to Antigonus appears. Instead, to "the griefe of the *Methiniens*, . . . beeing at their sport, and hauing fastned their boat with a strong oziar [willow] band, the goates of *Daphnis* by their euill attendaunce and keeping has browzed the same in sunder" and set the boat adrift (F3ᵛ). No bear, no Antigonus, probably no influence.

JOHN DAY

BULLOUGH (1975, 8:131–2): "It is possible that Shakespeare took a hint for the presence of Polixenes at the feast [4.4] and his behaviour, at first kindly and then forbidding, from John Day's comedy *Humour out of Breath* played by the Children of the King's Revels in 1607 or 1608, and published in 1608. In this play Octavio Duke of Venice advises his sons Francisco and Hippolito to turn from war to love. . . . Accordingly they dress as shepherds. . . . Their father accompanies them in disguise. . . . He wants them to have experience but not to make bad matches. However, they woo daughters of Octavio's enemy the exiled Anthonio Duke of Mantua, Hermia and Lucida, [*132*] who are poorly dressed and fishing with rod and line. Both fathers are against their children marrying beneath them, but when Anthonio knows who the young men are he agrees. In IV.i Octavio throws off his disguise and forbids the marriages, rather like Polixenes."

ESMOREIT

Sh. did not know this Middle Dutch play, but SALINGAR (1974, p. 49) thinks Greene "knew some variant form" of it. IWASAKI (1984, pp. 23–7) treats it as an example of the Calumniated Wife story, to which type *WT* also belongs. In *Esmoreit* the Queen of Sicily is imprisoned for infanticide, the false charge being brought by her husband's ambitious cousin, who disposes of her baby by selling it to the astrologer of the King of Damascus. The astrologer hopes to forestall an astral prediction that the King's son of Sicily will be his master's bane if great care is not taken. The child is raised as a Saracen by the princess Damiette. Eighteen years later, the two are in love, but before they are betrothed, Esmoreit wants to discover who he is. Wearing his swaddling band about his forehead, he arrives in Sicily, where from her window the queen recognizes the cloth, for in her own needlework it bears her husband's arms. Her innocence is vindicated, Esmoreit is recognized by the king, Damiette and the astrologer arrive in time for the wedding, the villainous cousin is hanged, and the Saracens, including Esmoreit, are converted. The play's similarity to *WT*, as one can see, is not close.

EURIPIDES

LLOYD (in SINGER, ed. 1856, 4:131–3): "The Alcestis of Euripides, both in treatment and incident, has many points of analogy with The Winter's Tale. . . . [*132*] The ancient critics noted it [*Alcestis*] as partaking rather of comedy than tragedy, as it starts from trouble and misfortune, and concludes with general satisfaction; and having regard to the tenor of some portions, the proper effect of comedy was thought to approximate to the satirick tone. Admetus, fated to die, is by favour of Apollo permitted to prolong his life by furnishing Death with a voluntary substitute. He urges the duty upon his aged parents, who repudiate the proposal with very marked reflections on its unreasonableness, and on his coolness in the proposition, but they fail to bring home to him this view of his conduct; and when his wife Alcestis becomes the volunteer, he grieves her fate as he would at an inevitable blow, is inconsolable at his bereavement, would fain accompany her, but, wrapped up in blind selfishness, never once contrasts her conduct, which he so much admires, with his own. His position is placed before him most forcibly by his father, but he can only see his father's selfishness not his own, and drives on in dark obstinacy upon the path that must end in his being undeceived to humiliation the most degrading.

"No word of reproach passes the lips of Alcestis; but her parting appeal to him, to spare her children the unhappiness of a stepmother, speaks expressively. If she says a word to set forth her sacrifice and the contrast of her self-devotion to the coldness of others, it is to urge a claim to this consideration for those she leaves behind, and she places them solemnly in his hands upon formal declaration of the stipulation. There is no mistaking in the comparative coldness of her adieu to him, a sense of the forfeiture he has incurred of that respect without which love lives not. She dies on the stage like Hermione, and her sorrowing husband forthwith prepares her solemn funeral, rejecting his father's contribution, as he regards him as the impersonation of cowardice and selfishness. It is when he returns from the entombment, and stands before the doors of his widowed household, that his nobler heart recovers, and he passionately avows that too late he learns his wife has the nobler and better fate; he has forfeited happiness and fame together, his dwelling must henceforth be unbearable, and elsewhere he can only hope for the vituperation he utterly deserves. The Chorus comfort him, and urge the reparation of funeral honour. In the meanwhile Hercules brings back Alcestis veiled, rescued by his arm from the already closed clutches of Thanatos, hateful to God and man. Hercules pretends that his companion is a prize won in games, and offering to leave her with Admetus and even referring to renewed wedlock, draws from him expressions soothing to his [*133*] revived queen, as those that Paulina draws from the penitent Leontes. Yet, like Leontes gazing at the statue, he looks till the force of resemblance raises him to the highest pitch of agitation. At length, by gradation like that in Shakespeare's play, the form of his wife in unveiled, and he recognizes her and falls on her neck. But she stands speechless; the purifications due to the infernal gods must first be performed, and a three days' interval elapse before he may hear her voice; and thus in her silent presence the play concludes.

"The elevated dignity and majesty thus expressed in the figure of Alcestis, the vindication of the self-devoted womanhood from the selfish neglect of a stronger power but an inferior nature is admirably realized, and is parallel to the reparation accorded to Hermione, who suffers with dignity as well as patience, and preserves herself not from consideration for a husband who has forfeited his nobler title, but for the sake of a daughter lost, but promised by the oracle to be found. The silence of Alcestis is not more satisfactory and expressive than the circumstance that, in the single short speech of Hermione, her words recognize and address alone her recovered daughter. She extends her hand to Leontes, and when he embraces her in joyful astonishment, full forgiveness is sealed by her frank embrace and entire reconciliation. 'She hangs upon [sic] his neck' [*3322*]; but it is when the recovered Perdita kneels that her mother's voice is heard again, and then, as if in the same awe of the powers of death from whom Hermione and Perdita seem, like Alcestis, to have been recovered, the scene hastily closes and the play is at an end."

PORTER (1891, pp. 279-80): "In both stories [*WT* and Euripides's *Alcestis*], a likeness of the lamented wife . . . is proposed as a consolation [to the bereaved husband]. The suggestion of the body without the soul is plain. Leontes and Admetos, too, are both to be tempted to disregard an overweening sorrow for their wives, and the voice of accusing impurity they recognize is to be overwhelmed, so that they may love again . . . for the good of the state. . . . Paulina is the Herakles of 'The Winter's Tale', and she scourges Leontes to his honor, till he says [*2792-6, 2808-9*]. Then, since Paulina can work wonders as well as Herakles, and [*280*] since Leontes, too, can be faithful to the death, she can address him, as Herakles addresses Admetos, to 'the true eye, true body of the true live wife.'"

P.A.C. (1892, pp. 516-17): "In Greene and in Shakespeare the King wishes the Queen's death because he is uncomfortable so long as she lives, and he prefers his comfort to aught else, taking it as his conjugal right and royal prerogative. See [*900*,

1141-2]. The Queen, understanding this, says, [My Life stands in the leuell of your Dreames (1258)]. To [him] she says, [can Life be no commoditie] when love [The crowne and comfort of my Life] is gone [1272-4]. So Alkestis [would not live on, torn away from thee, . . . wherefore spared I not] to die for him [The gifts of youth still mine, wherein I joyed (ed. Way, 287-9)]. [*517*] Admetos' image of his wife, that he would have made by the cunning hands of artists [348-9] is possibly a prototype of the statue of the Queen. . . . Compare, also, Herakles' trial of Admetos [1008-1120?] with Paulina's trial of Leontes [5.1]; and Herakles' restoration of the unknown Alkestis to her husband [1121] with Paulina's bringing the statue of the Queen to life."

PORTER & CLARKE (ed. 1908, 34:120-1): "It is not known that any English adaptation . . . was at that time extant of the 'Alkestis'; but there is no need to suppose, if Shakespeare's creative instincts were bent, in the remodelling of this play, toward Euripides' treatment of the conquest of death, that he would be barred from getting all the suggestion he needed, even if there really were no English translation of it published, from the edition of Euripides published in 1602. . . . [*121*] [The plays] were all translated into Latin, with the Greek text opposite."

GOLLANCZ (ed. 1894, 41:viii): "The Greek element in Shakespeare's list of names [of *WT*'s characters] is striking, and should perhaps be considered in connexion with the Alcestis *motif* of the closing scene of the play." He provides the following translation:

> *Hercules.*   Toward her turn thine eyes,
> And say if she resembleth not thy wife.
> Rest happy now, and all thy pains forget.
>   *Admetus.* O ye immortal gods! what can I say
> At this unhoped, unlooked for miracle?
> Do I in truth behold my wife, or doth
> Some phantom of delight o'erpower my sense?
>   *Hercules.* This is no phantom but your own true wife.
>   *Admetus.* Art sure she is no ghost from the nether world?
>   *Hercules.* You did not think a sorcerer was your guest.

THOMAS (ed. *Pandosto*, 1907, pp. xvi-xvii): "It is in regard to the story of the queen that Shakespeare differs most from Greene, by introducing an Alcestis *motif*. . . . It is not impossible that Shakespeare read the play in a literal Latin version, such as [H.] Stephens' [*Tragœdiæ selectæ Æschyli . . . Sophoclis, Euripidis* (Geneva, 1567)]." Alcestis and Hermione have been several times compared (see VELZ, 1968), but there is no evidence that Sh. directly knew any version of Euripides's play. As THOMAS notes, however, the story of Admetus and Alcest is told in *A Petite Pallace of Pettie His Pleasure* (1576).

DRIVER (1960, pp. 197-8): "If Euripides thought Admetus possessed any internal guilt, he did not dramatize it. Instead, he dramatized the story of a man and wife bound by an external necessity, from which they are released only by an external benevolence. The only internalization is that of the feelings in a situation from which there seems to be no escape. The state of Admetus and Alcestis at the end is therefore not essentially different from that at the beginning. They are released *from* an imprisonment, but they are not reconciled *to* anything. This means there is an inherent balance in the [*198*] work, of which the highly theatrical *agons* with their frequent use of stichomythia are excellent expressions. . . . However much we may enjoy it technically or because of its emotion, it can never represent to us what the tragicomedies of Shakespeare do, which utilize the forms of the stage to body forth the images of man's internal history, with its furor, its disseverances, and its reconciliation."

NUTTALL (1972, p. 220): "The objective similarity of certain passages (especially *Alcestis*, 1121–50, and *The Winter's Tale*, [3030–3130]) is beyond dispute. The *Alcestis* is early Euripides (438 B.C.) but, with its comic episodes and solemn-happy ending, it anticipates the manner of the late romantic tragedies. And it is the manner which is important. There is a sense in which the correspondences between the *Alcestis* and *The Winter's Tale* are in any case the *less* striking in virtue of the fact that the story of the *Alcestis* is the story of *The Winter's Tale*. But the congruity of atmosphere between late Shakespeare and late Euripides has a more persistent, if less tangible, interest. If we read, not as source-hunters but as critics, we shall see that late Euripides is *like* Shakespeare as no other dramatist is."

COLLIER (1843, 1:8): Sh. "had also an eye to [George] Gascoigne's [and Francis Kinwelmershe's] paraphrase of the 'Phœnissæ' of Euripides, presented at Gray's Inn in 1566," and printed in Gascoigne's *Works*, 1573, 1575, 1587. In *Pandosto* the child is set adrift in a boat without sail or rudder, whereas in *Jocasta*, Gascoigne's version of *Phœnissæ*, the infant Oedipus, abandoned because of the prophecy that he will destroy his father, is rescued and raised by a shepherd. WELLS (1988, p. lix): "This is the full extent of the analog and the situation is of course commonplace."

FOLKTALES

BURTON (1988, pp. 176–9): "The separation of family members and their eventual reunion forms the basic pattern of events which, being shared by a distinct body of Middle English romances and *The Winter's Tale*, links them together. In each work the pattern unfolds in four distinct phases . . . : A woman is separated from the father of her child or children. [*177*] . . . The child or children are reared away from home. . . . A long time lapse ensues, during which the child or children grow up. . . . The family is reunited." Using the system of classification devised by Stith Thompson in *The Folktale* (1946), BURTON finds that (p. 178) "the principal motifs as they appear in *The Winter's Tale* are as follows. Hermione, a wife and mother, is persecuted (S410) by being slandered as an adultress (K2112). Her child, Perdita, is driven out by a hostile relative (S322) and abandoned (S301). She is reared by a herdsman (S351.2). The eventual reunion of father and daughter is accidental (N732)." BURTON also discovers (p. 179) a number of subordinate motifs: difference of social rank between lovers (T91.6); cruel fathers and husbands (S11; S62); episodes of trickery—Hermione's feigning death (K1860), Florizel's disguising himself as a

691

shepherd, and Polixenes's posing as a swain (K1816.6; K1816.9); tokens of royalty left with an abandoned child (S334); and prophecies (M300), including Antigonus's dream (D1812.3.3). "So, as the play itself acknowledges, *The Winter's Tale* is indeed like 'an old tale' [3038, 3070, 3328]."

EMANUEL FORD

THOMAS (ed. *Pandosto*, 1907, p. xviii): "Edward [i.e., Emanuel] Ford's long-forgotten romance, *The famous and pleasant History of Parismus, the valiant and renowned Prince of Bohemia* [1598], bears little enough resemblance to either *Dorastus* or *The Winter's Tale*, but it is interesting to discover therein certain of the motives employed by both Greene and Shakespeare. These include a royal child raised in the wilderness, a coastal Bohemia, and a bear with a taste for human flesh." A second part entitled *Parismenos* appeared in 1598, and both parts were reprinted several times. An ursine excerpt from the second part is printed by BULLOUGH (1975, 8:203–4).

THOMAS HEYWOOD

The Golden Age, the first of Thomas Heywood's five *Ages* plays, is dated 1609–11, thus possibly earlier than *WT*; SCHANZER (1960, p. 23), however, believes it likely that "Heywood was the borrower." SCHANZER describes (pp. 21–2) the material in question: "In the *Golden Age* there is one scene which it is difficult to read without being reminded of *The Winter's Tale*. . . . Saturn's mother, Vesta, comes to him to plead for the life of the child to which his wife, the Queen, has just given birth, and which he is bound by oath to destroy ([Pearson ed.] p. 13 ff.). Though there are few, if any, close verbal echoes, this scene brings forcibly to mind that in which Paulina visits Leontes with the new-born child to plead for its mother. It is above all a similarity of [22] dramatic situation and incident: the outspoken woman pleading with the King, accusing him of tyranny, his angry outbursts, his wavering mind [quotes 1084], his repentance, followed by his determination to lead a life of penance and sorrow. Among the more detailed resemblances one may compare the Queen's 'Sweet Lad, I would thy father saw thee smile, | Thy beauty and thy pretty Infancy, | Would molifie his heart wer't hew'd from flint' (p. 16) with Paulina's [865–6]; and Vesta's 'Tyrant, I will' (p. 15 . . .) with Paulina's [1362]. Contiguous with this scene, in the one case immediately preceding, in the other directly following upon it, we have in both plays the description of Apollo's oracle at Delphos. In the *Golden Age* we find 'After our *Ceremonious* Rites perform'd, | And *Sacrifice* ended with *reuerence*, | A murmuring *thunder* hurried through the *Temple*' (p. 13; [italics supplied]). That the italicized words also occur in the corresponding account in *The Winter's Tale* (III.i [1146–58]) means little by itself, for they are just the words one would expect in any description of the oracle. It is their juxtaposition with the scene discussed above which makes the resemblance significant."

GREENE'S *FRIAR BACON*

PARROTT (1949, p. 88): "The realism of the scene at Harlston Fair in *Friar Bacon* is a forerunner of the sheep-shearing feast in *The Winter's Tale*." See also n. 1981.

THE JEALOUS DUKE

This "sad doggrel" — which appears in Thomas Jordan, *A Royal Arbor of Loyal Poesie* [1663], pp. 46–51 (sigs. 2C3ᵛ–2D2) — was brought to light by COLLIER (1836, pp. 41–2) and printed in a modernized version by COLLIER (1866, 3:123–7). Although it probably condenses *Pandosto* or Sabie's poems (see p. 674), it could conceivably descend from *WT*. Here the shepherdess, actually the daughter of the Duke of Parma, meets the handsome prince.

The jealous Duke, and the injur'd Dutchess: A story.
Tune, *The Dream*.

7.

At sixteen years of age she was
  The prettiest Nimph
That trod on grass;
Once a day when she did keep
  (As she suppos'd) Her fathers sheep,
A Gentleman which her fair face lookt upon,
  Was strucken straight in love,
And 'twas the Duke of *Padua*'s Son;
Who from that hour would every day come to see
  His Mistress whom he lov'd like life,
Though of a low degree.

8.

Much love there was betwixt them both,
  Till they contracted were by oath,
Which when his father came to know,
  Then did begin
The Lovers woe;
For with extream outragious words he begun
  To bid him leave her,
Or he'd never own him as a son;
The Prince did vow his love he ne're would withdraw
  Although he lost his father,
And the Crown of *Padua*.

LIVING STATUES

As HALLIWELL (ed. 1859, 8:269) notes, a living statue is found in Richard Flecknoe's *Erminia* (1661) — a play that, according to LANGBAINE (1691, p. 201), was never acted. In 1.5 a prince assumes the *"form of Mars's Statue"* and speaks to the chaste heroine, whose resistance to his advances has turned him, he says, to frozen marble.

PORTER & CLARKE (ed. 1908, 34:121): "The statue scene as given in Lyly's 'Woman in the Moon [1.1]' was doubtless known to Shakespeare, and suggested to him his very different treatment. . . . Lyly's statue that came to life was made by Nature, attended by her handmaidens Concord and Discord, and she created it at the request of shepherds who craved a mate like themselves 'but of a purer mould.' " The eds. quote this stage direction: "They draw the Curtains from before NATURES shop, where stands an Image clad and some vnclad, they bring forth the cloathed image" (*Works*, ed. Bond, 3:243). Concord, a maiden accompanying Nature, embraces the image, which comes to life as Pandora.

MOORMAN (ed. 1912, pp. xxx-xxxi): "The famous Pygmalion and Galatea legend [in Ovid's *Metamorphoses*] presents a certain parallel. The story was, of course, well known in Elizabethan England, and as recently as 1598 it had been made the theme of a narrative poem by Marston, entitled *The Metamorphosis of Pygmalion's Image*." KITTREDGE (ed. 1936, p. 432): "A poet who wrote *Venus and Adonis* in 1593 (or earlier) did not need to ask Lyly or Marston in 1611 to lead him to the story of Pygmalion in Ovid's *Metamorphoses* (x, 243 ff.)." GREEN (1870, p. 109 n.) had previously observed that "the ivory statue changed into a woman, which Ovid describes, . . . is a description of kindred excellence to that of Shakespeare." BULLOUGH (1975, 8:232) calls attention to the desire of both Pygmalion and Leontes (3281) to kiss their images. For more on Ovid, see below (p. 696).

LANCASTER (1932) finds living statues in several French plays, including Durval's *Agarite* (1633 or 1634) and Alexandre Hardy's *Inceste supposé* (1595-1631), lost but known, to some extent, from the stage decorator's notebook and from a play by La Caze from what seems to be the same source, *L'Inceste supposé* (c. 1638). LANCASTER suggests that the presently unknown story underlying these plays also furnished Sh. with the idea of Hermione's statue.

Dismissing this notion with the brevity it perhaps deserves, TAYLOR (1938, pp. 82-5) argues that Sh. follows *Pandosto* to about the middle of the third act of *WT*, where he decides to let Hermione live rather than die as does Bellaria. "From this point . . . Greene's story can be of no use to Shakspere so far as the Hermione story is concerned. . . . The restoration to life of a [83] heroine who had been struck down under almost identically the same circumstances, and in almost identically the same way, he had already handled successfully in *Much Ado* with the aid of [its source,] the Bandello story ["Timbreo and Fenicia," Novella 22 in *La Prima Parte de la Novelle del Bandello* (Lucca, 1554)]. . . . Hence *Much Ado* . . . has to be thought of as a source of *The Winter's Tale*." He suggests, in addition, (p. 85) that Hermione's apparent resuscitation may derive from *A Larum for London, or The Siege of Antwerp* (c. 1594-1600), a play performed by the Lord Chamberlain's Men. "Either as actor in the play or producer or merely as one financially interested, Shakspere could hardly fail to be impressed by the remarkable device of the Duke of Alva, being carried as dead through the streets, but once inside the walls coming to life.

The other play of decided significance in this connection . . . is *The Tryall of Chevalerie*" (see below).

Medieval stories about living statues are surveyed by BAUM (1919).

EL MARMOL DE FELISARDO

MORLEY ed. (1887): "It has been said [by CARO (1879) and BOYLE (1885)] that it [*Pandosto*] was founded on a story of the treatment of his wife by a Duke Masovius *Zemovitus* [see "Siemowitsch," below] of which there is an account by Tcharikovski, Archbishop of Gnesen, in the second volume of Sommersberg's 'Rerum Silesiarum Scriptores'. It has been suggested also that some Latin version of that story had been seen by Lope de Vega as well as by Robert Greene, and that thus points of resemblance between Greene's 'Pandosto' and Lope de Vega's 'El Marmol de Felisardo' may have arisen." The suggestion was made by SCHACK (1854, 2:338): In its plot, *Marmol* clearly shows a relationship with *WT*; since the latter is descended primarily from *Dorastus and Fawnia*, it must be presumed that this novel too availed itself of an unknown older story from which Lope also drew (in Ger.).

FURNESS (ed. 1898, p. 323), adding that KLEIN (1874, 10:494) "affirms that there is a remarkable similarity between the two dramas," summarizes Lope's play: "Felisardo, who passes as the son of noble parents, and is a student, wins the love of Elisa, the daughter of an Alcalde, and, at last, the consent of her father to their marriage. It turns out, however, that Felisardo is a natural son of the king, who, by the death of his lawful heir, is obliged either to recall Felisardo or to die heirless. Accordingly the King sends an Admiral to bring the young man to Court. It now appears that Elisa has a twin brother, Celio; and the resemblance of these twins to each other is so exact that when the Alcalde wished to fit out Celio as a page to the Court, he takes Elisa by mistake, and dispatches her, dressed in boy's clothes, as a page to Felisardo. A marriage is arranged between Felisardo and the daughter of the Admiral, but the young prince will not listen to it, and, on the advice of his merry servant, Tristan, feigns himself in love with a marble statue in the garden, and to such an extreme did he carry this feigned fascination that at last, to save him from dropping into his tomb, the King consented that he should wed the statue. Of course, Elisa was dressed up as the statue; whereupon the King was obliged to keep his word and sanction the marriage." FURNESS adds, "In Johnsonian phrase, 'let us hear no more' of *El Marmol de Felisardo* as a source of *The Winter's Tale*."

MUCEDORUS

SPENS (1922, p. 87): "Mucedorus himself, a Prince disguised as a Shepherd, reminds us of Prince Florizel [and] has not Mouse the clown much in common both with the Clown . . . and with Autolycus?" This popular play was published in 1598 and reprinted in 1606; an augmented version appeared in 1610 and often thereafter. It features a bear that does a comic turn with a clown named Mouse. For more on this subject and dramatic bears in general, see n. 1500.

BULLOUGH (1975, 8:128): "A parallel use of imagery has been noted between *Mucedorus* [ed. Tucker Brooke, 1908] I.i.47, 'My minde is grafted on a humbler stocke', and *WT* [1903–4]. Shakespeare may have remembered the grafting-image and the ambiguous phrase in *Mucedorus* when working on the art-nature theme in relation to the Prince's love for the shepherdess Perdita. . . . Mouse . . . has much in common with the Clown [in *WT*]. Maybe the same actor played both parts."

OVID

LAMB (1989, pp. 70–2): "Autolycus's name, obtrusively Ovidian among traditional pastoral names like Dorcas and Mopsa, calls attention to itself and to its source. His description of himself as a 'snapper up of unconsidered trifles' because he was 'littered under Mercury' [1692–4] derives unmistakably from the moral commentaries on Ovid's Autolycus from book 11 of the *Metamorphoses*. Fathered by Mercury upon a mortal woman at almost the same time that Apollo engendered his 'twin' brother Philammon, Autolycus . . . appropriately represents [*71*] false art. While the art of his brother Philammon, who 'in musicke arte excelled farre all other, / As well in singing as in play' [GOLDING tr., *Ovid*, 1567; 1965, lines 365–6], delighted without deception as befitted the son of Apollo, Autolycus inherited his father's unscrupulous nature [quotes lines 360–3]." LAMB also finds Paulina connected with Ovid "[*72*] through the submerged myth of Pygmalion." For more on Autolycus and Ovid, see n. 3385 (p. 11).

GEORGE PEELE

EDWARDS (" 'Seeing,' " 1986, pp. 79–91), noting that "winter's tale" is mentioned twice in the induction to *The Old Wives Tale* (see nn. 0, 627), finds other resemblances: "the prominence of references to the passing of the seasons, the appearance of a figure representing Time in the middle of the play, . . . the theme of resurrection [and] more important . . . the sudden shifts of focus in presenting what is proclaimed to be a very unlikely story, and especially the movement between narration and performance." Additional connections with Peele are apparent, EDWARDS observes: in *The Arraignment of Paris* (ed. Benbow, 1.3), the goddess Flora prepares for the entry of Pallas, Juno, and Venus by creating a second flowery spring much in Perdita's manner; (p. 80) "framing techniques . . . to suggest different layers and levels in the fiction" occur in *The Arraignment, The Battle of Alcazar*, and *David and Bathsabe*. In *WT* (p. 86) "Time is the concealed presenter, . . . the tale-teller. Or rather, the tale-teller adopts the guise of Time. . . . He has two subordinates who do some tale-telling for him, the Clown and the Third Gentleman," the first inarticulate in describing the shipwreck and the death of Antigonus (1530–43), the second overarticulate in describing the meeting of the kings and the exchange of information that follows (as at 3090–3100). (P. 87): "The first episode is entirely new material . . . ; the second a re-working of Greene. . . . To create these incidents and to have them related in a particular way is a single act of free artistic choice.

"The arresting coincidence of the bear and the shipwreck is required in order to destroy all the evidence of witnesses to the abandoning of Perdita. . . . This destruction of witnesses is necessary only because Shakespeare has provided the witnesses. . . . Shakespeare seems to have set up the problem in order to produce its far-fetched solution. Similarly the pell-mell of greeting and discoveries [in 3056–63] is entirely Shakespeare's choice." The point is that Sh., in these instances and in others, emphasizes by narration the absurdity of the fiction at the same time that he makes convincing by performance incidents of equal or greater improbability. (P. 91) "The play consists basically of three extended actions: calumny and rejection; love in the younger generation; reunion and restoration. Each of these actions is brilliantly realised before us. But they are brought before us as make-believe, and their status insisted on by those parts of the story that are narrated rather than performed. They are moments in a most improbable tale, moments that a supreme dramatic artist has chosen to make real and convincing. It is not in any way a new thing for Shakespeare to demonstrate how 'we are mocked by art.' "

PLUTARCH

HALES (1876; 1884, p. 109) asserts that "all these [*WT*'s] names, except perhaps Dorcas and Leontes, are found in Plutarch's *Lives*." Plutarch actually contains quite a few of the names that appear in *WT*: Cleomines, Dion, Hermione (as the name of the city on the east coast of the Peloponnesus; see n. 3377 [p. 7] for the person), Leontes (see n. 3371), and Autolycus (see n. 3385). Polyxemus, Camillus, and Paulinius also occur in Plutarch.

THE PROSERPINA MYTH

That the myth of Proserpina or Persephone was on Sh.'s mind when he wrote *WT* is evident from 1930–2. As GOLDING's translation of Ovid's *Metamorphoses* (1567; 1965, 5:485–708) tells the story, Proserpina, the beautiful daughter of Jove and Ceres, is gathering flowers when Dis, god of the Underworld, spies her, loves her, and carries her off to his domain. As Ceres seeks her through land and sea, "the worlde did want," for famine fell upon it. Ceres at last learns that Proserpina, though "Not meerie [merry]," is nevertheless "a Queene, . . . of great God Dis the stately Feere [fere, consort]." She appeals to Jove. Although sympathetic, he points out that Dis, his brother and equal in power, is a son-in-law not to be despised. Nevertheless, Proserpina can be rescued if she has eaten nothing while in the Underworld, but this possibility vanishes when it is discovered that she has sucked the juice of seven pomegranate seeds. Even so, Jove effects a compromise: "And now the Goddesse Proserpine indifferently doth reigne Above and underneath the Earth, and so doth she remaine One halfe yeare with hir mother and the resdue with hir Feere" (701–3)—and thus summer and winter came into being.

For correspondences between the myth and *WT*, see n. 1930–43. HONIGMANN (1955, p. 35) quotes Leonard Digges's translation of Claudian's *Rape of Proserpine* (1617) on the significance of the myth: "By the person of *Ceres* is signified *Tillage*. By *Proserpine*, the seedes which are sowed, by *Pluto* [Dis], the earth that receiues

697

them. . . . By the sixe Moneths that *Proserpine* remained in Hell, are vnderstood, the sixe, in which the seede is vnderground . . . by the other sixe that shee is with her Mother, is set downe, when the corne is ripe." HONIGMANN adds (pp. 36–8) regarding 2416–19: "Kindness and unkindness are equivalents of summer and winter, as throughout the play, and unkindness is chidden to *hell* because hell stands for . . . the winter months of unkindness; while the verb *grow* continues the allusion. [At 2330–1] can we doubt that Perdita=Proserpine=the seed in the earth? . . . [*37*] When Hermione, who still loved Leontes when they were reunited [quotes 3322], declared, in her only speech after her 'return to life', that she preserved herself in order to see her daughter again, not mentioning any wish to see her husband, it seems that Shakespeare at this point was thinking of her primarily as Ceres (who had lost her daughter) rather than as Hermione (who loves her husband as well as her daughter). . . . [*38*] Perhaps . . . the switch [in *WT* of Greene's two countries and their kings] was not due to heedlessness and geographical ignorance but to the desire to reinforce the Proserpine-Perdita parallel with Ceres-Hermione a Queen of Sicily as in the myth."

ROGUE LITERATURE

As indicated above (p. 672), for the conceit of the foist performed at St. Paul's, Sh. relied mainly on Greene's *Second Part of Conny-catching*. HAZLITT (1875, 1:4:10), however: When he created Autolycus, Sh. may have "had in his recollection that extraordinarily curious production of Thomas Newberry, 'The Book of Dives Pragmaticus, 1563." In it, Dives, "the great Marchant man" (sig. A1), offers wares to all sorts of people, from popes, cardinals, and kings to reapers and mowers and players and minstrels; the purpose was to acquaint "Seruauntes and Chyldren" with a vocabulary of objects in common use. Dives has no connection with Autolycus, however, except that he, too, is a pedlar.

SIDNEY

BULLOUGH (1975, 8:125–6): "In Sidney's *Arcadia* (1590 version, from which Shakespeare took the Edmund–Gloster story in *Lear*) there are several resemblances to details in *The Winter's Tale*. Pyrocles, disguised as the Amazon Zelmane, finds his friend Musidorus disguised as a shepherd. . . . Zelmane is invited by King Basilius to watch some Pastorals enacted in a natural theatre (Ch. 19). Musidorus gets admission too, calling himself Dorus. Zelmane is just speaking to his beloved Philoclea, 'when sodainely there came out of a wood a monstrous Lion, with a she-Beare not far from him, of litle less fiercenes'. Zelmane cuts off the lion's head and presents it to Philoclea. Musidorus slays [*126*] the bear and presents one of its paws to his love, Pamela, who tells how he killed the beast and how the foolish Dametas played the coward most comically. After this they have Pastorals in the evening by torchlight, and Dametas acts as director. Analogous to *The Winter's Tale* are the mingling of a disguised prince with shepherds, the sudden appearance of a bear, arousing terror and laughter in quick succession, the Pastoral festivity with dancing and singing, its first sports including a leaping dance of shepherds in honour of Pan and his Satyrs.''

SHAKESPEARE'S PLAYS

Similarities between aspects of *WT* and Sh.'s earlier plays have frequently been noted—for example, by SCHANZER (ed. 1969, pp. 12–13): "In dramatizing the 'resurrection' of Hermione, he [Sh.] evidently drew on memories of two of his own previous plays, *Much Ado About Nothing* and *Pericles*. The plot-parallels between *The Winter's Tale* and *Much Ado About Nothing* are the more extensive: in both plays the husband (or bridegroom) publicly accuses his wife (or bride) of unchastity; she falls into a swoon and is believed to be dead by all who are present; but she recovers, and is secretly hidden away, while her husband (or bridegroom) continues to believe her to be dead. He discovers her innocence, repents of his actions, devises an epitaph for her tomb setting forth the cause of her death, and vows to visit that tomb as an act of penance (daily in *The Winter's Tale*, once a year in *Much Ado About Nothing*). He promises—and here Shakespeare drew on memories of Bandello's *novella* [22 (1554)], his source for *Much Ado About Nothing*, [13] rather than on the play itself—that when he marries again he will only take a wife chosen for him (by the slandered woman's father in the one case, her friend in the other). One further hint Shakespeare may have derived from the *novella*. Describing the slandered woman lying in her swoon, Bandello remarks that she resembled a marble statue rather than a live woman. This may have suggested the idea of making Hermione pose as her own statue. . . .

"In the shaping of the statue-scene memories of the finale of *Pericles* played a major part. In both plays a queen is believed to be dead. . . . But she returns to life and remains in seclusion for many years. . . . The final scene depicts her reunion, after this long gap of time, with husband and daughter, who had both firmly believed her to be dead. In both plays this scene breathes a similar atmosphere of ceremonious solemnity turning to wonder and joy; in both the daughter kneels before her mother, who calls her 'my own.' "

MACKAIL (1911, p. 215): Just as *Tmp.* is the by-product of *AYL* and *Mac.*, *WT* is the by-product of *Oth.* and *Ado*.

SIEMOWITSCH (OR SEMOVIT OR ZIEMOWIT)

HERFORD (ed. 1904, 4:265) summarizes the findings of CARO (1879) and BOYLE (1885): "The germ of the romance [*Pandosto*] was probably an actual incident in the fourteenth-century annals of Poland and Bohemia. A king, Siemowitsch, conceived suspicions of his wife, a lady of the Bohemian court, threw her into prison, where she bore a son, then caused her to be strangled, and the child sent away. The child was finally restored to Siemowitsch, who died, deeply repentant, in 1381—the year in which Anne of Bohemia, a kinswoman of the murdered wife, gave her hand to Richard II. The lively intercourse with Bohemia which ensued upon that marriage may well have set the tradition of this bit of criminal history afloat in England. . . . A faint trace of the original locality perhaps survives in Greene's Bohemian king and court." A more detailed summary of CARO's article is given by FURNESS (ed. 1898, pp. 322–3); see also *El Marmol de Felisardo*, above. CARO's study appears to be a continuation of an article published in the *Magazin für die Literatur des Auslandes* in 1863.

SPENSER

GREY (1754, 1:244–62): "Several things in this play seem to resemble *Spenser*'s story of *Melibee, Pastorella*, and Sir *Calidore*." He quotes *FQ* 6.12:3–9, the story of Sir Bellamour's marriage to Claribel, the birth of Pastorella, the baby's abandonment, and her discovery by the shepherd, whose honest wife nurses her. With Florizel's praise of Perdita (1798–1802), GREY compares Calidore's first meeting with Pastorella (6.9.9, 11); Perdita's allusion to Florizel's déclassé costume (1803–12) he likens to Calidore's shepherd's weed, adopted for the love of Pastorella (6.9.36). "*Perdita* imagined that the shepherd was her real father. Of the same opinion was *Pastorella*, with regard to the shepherd *Melibee*" (p. 261).

KERMODE (ed. 1963, pp. xxvi–xxvii): "For [the most important clue to the nature of *WT*] we should turn to the greatest works in prose and verse of the period, Sidney's *Arcadia* and Spenser's *Faerie Queene*. It is no reflection on Greene to say that his novel cannot live with such romances as these; for they are in intention and performance the profoundest and most serious art of the period. . . . They nevertheless use romantic themes. They are concerned less with psychological realism than with supernaturally sanctioned reality under human appearances. Shakespeare knew them both, and used them, especially Spenser. Marina is his Florimel, Perdita his Pastorella; in *The Winter's Tale* he transforms Fawnia, Greene's royal changeling, and does so to make her like Spenser's noble shepherdess. And insofar as *The Winter's Tale* is philosophical it is Spenserian too; like Spenser, Shakespeare is preoccupied by Time as destroyer and renewer, that which ruins the work of men but is the father of truth. Just as the sea appears to be aimlessly destructive, tearing apart father and child, husband and wife, [*xxvii*] but in the end is seen to be 'merciful' because it finally brings them together and restores their happiness, so Time only seems to change things because it must renew their truth."

BULLOUGH (1975, 8:126): "In [*FQ* 6.4] Calepine is out walking in the woodland 'To take the ayre, and heare the thrushes song' when he sees 'A cruell Beare, the which an infant bore / Betwixt his bloudie jawes, besprinckled all with gore' (17). Chasing the beast[,] Calepine forces it to lay down its spoil,

> Wherewith the beast, enrag'd to loose his pray,
> Upon him turned, and with greedie force
> And furie, to bee crossed in his way,
> Gaping full wyde, did thinke without remorse,
> To be aveng'd on him, and to devoure his corse. (20)

Calepine kills the bear by thrusting a stone down its throat and fighting it on the ground.

> Then tooke he up betwixt his armes twaine
> The litle babe, sweet relicke of his pray;
> Whom pitying to heare so sore complaine,
> From his soft eyes the teares he wypt away,
> And from his face the filth that did it ray.

He finds the child to be unharmed, and leaves him with the childless Matilda, wife of Sir Bruin, and the adopted boy becomes a famous knight.

"This passage, combining the discovery and cherishing of a baby with danger from a bear may have passed through Shakespeare's mind when planning the exposure of Perdita."

THE THRACIAN WONDER

This good-natured heroical-pastoral romance was first mentioned in a Stationers' Register entry dated 29 November (for December?) 1653. It was published in 1661 by the piratical Francis Kirkman; the quarto title page gives the authors as John Webster and William Rowley, an attribution rejected by HARBAGE et al. (1989). FLEAY (1890, p. 409; and 1891, 1:278) assigns the work to Thomas Heywood, asserting (1891, 2: 332) that "the plot is from *Curan and Argentile*, William Webster's poem, 1617, which was an enlargement of Warner's story in his *Albion's England*, 1586," and that the attribution to John Webster was made because "Kirkman confused the two Websters." That the source of *The Thracian Wonder* is actually Greene's *Menaphon*, however, was demonstrated almost simultaneously by BRERETON (1907) and ADAMS (1906), and its similarities to *WT* were accounted for by the similarities between *Menaphon* and *Pandosto*. The date was taken to be in the 1590s. HATCHER (1908), however, argues that, in addition to *Menaphon*, *The Thracian Wonder* was influenced by other works by Greene such as *Orlando Furioso* and *James the Fourth*; he finds that it (p. 19) "belong[s] . . . somewhere between 1600 and 1610." Still, HATCHER, like his predecessors, stops short of making it a source of *WT*. CRUPI (1971, p. 347), in fact, believes that *The Thracian Wonder* is indebted to *WT*, "which would place *The Thracian Wonder* after 1611."

MARKS (1908, pp. 48–9) summarizes the plot of *The Thracian Wonder*: "Ariadne, daughter to King Pheander, has clandestinely married Radagon, who is disguised as a menial at the court of Pheander, and is King of 'Scicillia'. When the marriage is disclosed, the maiden's father at once begins a course of the most tyrannical cruelty. He banishes Ariadne and the little son Eusanius, putting them to sea in a boat; he then proceeds to banish Radagon in the same fashion. Finally, he exiles his own brother Sophos for pleading the cause of Ariadne. As a punishment for the King's sins, a terrible plague attacks the court, an oracle revealing that until the monarch makes retribution, the country shall know neither peace nor prosperity. Overcome with remorse, Pheander goes out as a pilgrim seeking Ariadne. In the mean time the daughter and her little son and Radagon have [49] come to shore; Radagon and Ariadne, although mutually attracted, do not recognize each other. In the end a recognition takes place, they are discovered by Pheander, and all return happily homeward." She adds (pp. 49-50): "Some of the scenes bespeak at least a smattering of a knowledge of classical idyls [sic], for the pastoral quality is at times closely imitated. The [50] mythological ingredients are further borne out by the appearance of the Goddess Pithia and of a Chorus and 'Time'. Titterus and Pallemon and a Clown afford the merry element, and very merry and full of coarse jests they are. There is, too, a fisherman among the *dramatis personæ*, an interesting 'pastoral-piscatory' touch, and also the usual religious accompaniment of the pastoral play, *a priest*."

THE TRIAL OF CHIVALRY

KOEPPEL (1896) believes that Sh. borrowed the idea of Hermione's statue from *The History of the Trial of Chivalry* (1599-1604), an anonymous play published in 1605 as lately acted by the Earl of Derby's company. In it, the supposed alabaster statue of a kneeling man holding a prayer book is actually a disdained lover whose repentant lady will "dayly deck" his "tombe and statue with sweet flowers" (ed. Bullen, 3 [1884], 336). He is indeed a living statue, but beyond that he and Hermione have nothing in common. BULLOUGH (1975, 8:229-32), who prints excerpts, compares the lady's utterance "A certayne softe remorce Creeps to my heart" with Leontes's remorse at 3223-9, but the connection is insignificant. Nevertheless, VELIE (1972, p. 108) asserts: "*The Trial* was performed . . . only a half dozen years or so before Shakespeare wrote *The Winter's Tale*, and we are certain that Shakespeare was in London during that period. It seems probable, then, that in writing a play with strong elements of melodrama, he consciously borrowed from another Elizabethan melodrama." The date of *The Trial* is too uncertain, however, to permit certainty about Sh.'s whereabouts when it was acted.

Criticism

General Assessments

Despite the extraordinary regard usually expressed for Sh.'s work, the critical reception of *WT* reminds us that for particular plays the delight of one critic is often the displeasure of another.

A few critics voice outright disapproval. DRYDEN (1672; 1978, 11:206): The play is "either grounded on impossibilities, or at least, so meanly written, that the Comedy neither caus'd your mirth, nor the serious part your concernment." LENNOX (1753, 2:75): "If we compare the Conduct of the incidents in [*WT*] with the paltry Story on which it is founded, we shall find the Original much less absurd and ridiculous. If *Shakespear* had even improved the Story . . . yet he would still have been accountable for what remained." BRIDGES (1907, 10:331): "It may be that Shakespeare wished to portray this passion [jealousy] in odious nakedness without reason or rein, as might be proper in a low comedy, where its absurdity would have been ridiculed away: but if so, his scheme was artistically as bad as any third-rate melodrama of today: the admixture of tragic incident creates a situation from which recovery is impossible." QUILLER-COUCH (1917, pp. 260-8) lets pass the gap in time as an "honest failure" but refuses to absolve Sh. of "far less venial" flaws: the bungled presentation of Leontes' jealousy (p. 262); the lack of groundwork for Hermione's apparent death and real concealment; the exchange of clothes by Florizel and Autolycus, which does nothing to further the plot; that "naughty superfluity" — the bear (p. 264); the "scamping" of the recognition scene (p. 265). His final judgment (p. 268): "We must admit that the play never lodges in our minds as a whole." PETTET (1949, pp. 166-7): "Leontes and Hermione, Polixenes, Florizel and Perdita [are] but names, the names of puppets — speaking some magnificent verse, of course — who dance to the compulsive strings of an extravagant, highly coloured story. . . . Motivation, too, is often weak and thoroughly unplausible [e.g., Leontes' "monstrous and instantaneous jealousy"; his readiness to marry a wife of Paulina's choice; Hermione's concealment for "sixteen long years in order to punish a thoroughly chastened and repentant husband" (p. 167)]. . . . As the price that we pay for our far-fetched romantic stories we must accept behaviour and motives that are quite incredible and sometimes, as with Hermione, inconsistent with the disposition of the particular character concerned." HALLIDAY (1954, p. 174): "Shakespeare, after the tremendous strain of the tragedies, seems to have welcomed a less exacting dramatic form in which character was of secondary importance, and which afforded him the chance of writing the equivalent of the lyric poetry that he had renounced after *The Merchant of Venice*," though HALLIDAY calls the poetry of *WT* "abstract and colourless."

Others find little or nothing to criticize and much to admire. WARBURTON (ed. 1747, 3:277): "This play throughout is written in the very spirit of its author. . . . The meanness of the fable, and the extravagant conduct of it, had misled some of great name into a wrong judgment of its merit; which, as far as it regards sentiment and character, is scarce inferior to any in the whole collection." CLARKE (1863, p. 345): "The general plot and incidental circumstances of 'The Winter's Tale' are more varied, exciting, and sensuously appealing than perhaps any other of Shakespere's plays." DOWDEN (1875; 1877, pp. 403, 406): *WT* is a work of "his period of large, serene wisdom." The play, however "mellowed, refined, . . . exquisite," is "written with less of passionate concentration than the plays which immediately precede [it], but with more of a spirit of deep or exquisite recreation. . . . [*406*] His present temper demanded . . . [that] the dissonance must be resolved into a harmony. . . . While grievous errors of the heart are shown to us, and wrongs . . . as cruel as those of the great tragedies, at the end there is . . . reconciliation." IDEM (1875; 1890, p. 60): "It will be felt that the name which I have given to this last period — Shakspere having ascended out of the turmoil and trouble of action, out of the darkness and tragic mystery, the places haunted by terror and crime, and by love contending with these, to a pure and serene elevation — it will be felt that the name, *On the heights*, is neither inappropriate nor fanciful." SYMONS (in IRVING & MARSHALL, ed. 1890, 7: 320): "For sheer realism, for absolute insight into the most cobwebbed corners of our nature, Shakespeare has rarely surpassed this brief study. . . . We close The Winter's Tale with a feeling that life is a good thing, worth living." SWINBURNE (1905; 1909, pp. 52-3) praises "the tragedy, the comedy, the pastoral fusion of them both, the heavenly harmony of the close." Somehow ignoring *Oth.*, he adds: *WT* is "the only serious study of jealousy which Shakespeare ever deigned to take of so base a moral infirmity or vice. . . . [53] There is no such pastoral poetry, such pastoral drama, in the world." MASEFIELD (1912, pp. 228-30): *WT*, perhaps the "gentlest" of Sh.'s plays, "is done with a tenderer hand than [229] the other works," suggesting why "the sudden shocks and interruptions of life, which play so big a part in the action of [*Per., Cym., WT, Tmp.*], have full power here. [Mamillius's] winter's tale is interrupted. The rest of the play results from the interruption. . . . [230] [Leontes's] remorse gives to the last great scene" an intense beauty, "hardly endurable." GREENLAW (1916, p. 146): "Shakespeare has transformed a romance of adventure which patronizes the 'homely pastimes' of shepherds, 'shepheards ragges,' and the garlands woven of shepherds' 'homely flowers' into the most exquisite and satisfying pastoral in Elizabethan literature." SACHS (1923, p. 84): "One can put one's finger on the difference between commonplace talent and genius. [*Pandosto*] is logically correct but nevertheless leaves the reader cold. In [*WT*], however, the plot is logically absurd and yet we are deeply moved by it because it is built up on deep psychological truth." SCHELLING (1928, p. 411) attributes Sh.'s success to the "invention and introduction of new characters. . . . Antigonus, incomparable Paulina, Mopsa, Dorcas, the clown, and above all Autolycus."

TRAVERSI (1938; 1969, 2:320-1): The "pattern of reconciliation" — the embrace of Leontes and Hermione, Hermione's blessing of her daughter, and the "ratification of marriage for Paulina and Camillo by Leontes and Polixenes, newly rejoined in amity" — makes it "hard to find, even in Shakespeare, a more pro-[321]found purpose more consistently carried out to its proper artistic conclusion." IDEM (1954; 1965, p. 105) also praises the "poetic mastery so evident in this play, the extraordinary range of imagery and superb control of rhythm . . . consistently used to clarify character and motive [while] dramatic action [is] perfectly balanced in its several parts. Behind the repeated stress laid on the fact that we are following a fable . . . lies a consistent desire to make this action, this fable, the instrument for a harmonious reading of human experience." LEAVIS (1942, p. 341): In *WT*, the "relations between character, speech and the main themes of the drama are not such as to invite a psychologizing approach. . . . So large a part of the function of the words spoken by the characters is so plainly something other than to 'create' the speakers or to advance an action. . . . It is enough here to remind the reader of the way in which personal drama is made to move upon a complexity of larger rhythms — birth, maturity, death, birth. . . . This is a striking instance of Shakespeare's ability to transmute for serious ends what might have seemed irremediably romantic effects."

CRAIG (1948, pp. 328-9, 331) approves the play's "abundance of life and action . . . accompanied by very great clarity and very definite motivation. . . . The poetic beauty of *The Winter's Tale* is comprehensible, great and tangible, not subtle. . . . [*329*] [*WT*] has suspense throughout; its events follow in causal sequence. It is not a mere succession of striking single scenes. Its situations are of the greatest dramatic power. . . . [*331*] In spite of the great gap of time which elapses between the third and fourth acts, the play is a single tale and, in its way, a masterpiece of plot-making." NICOLL (1952, pp. 166-7): *WT* "may be esteemed one of [Sh.'s] most successful plays" because, despite a certain naïveté, its "characters are endowed with life while they retain an ability to shift their natures and indulge in wholly unmotivated actions. . . . The world of the dream and the vision remains still potent. . . . [*167*] Although [the poet] has become almost incapable of disassociating in his mind the dream from the reality, [he] yet preserves what can only be called a humorous attitude." SEN GUPTA (1961, p. 68): The play is "a bold experiment in form, a tour de force. Here Shakespeare is not interested in adequately motivating actions; rather he presents spectacular situations which derive their effectiveness from mutual contrast" (as in the reversal of "romantic friendship" to suddenly frenzied, causeless jealousy). ROWSE (1963, pp. 424-6) calls *WT* "a most beautiful and moving play. . . . [*425*] Though the style is compacted and full of matter . . . the writing is direct and forceful. No-one can say that the poetry is inferior. The play makes a tremendous impact, harmonious and integrated. . . . One is moved to tears. . . . [*426*] What Shakespeare did was to give it all his genius."

NUTTALL (1966, pp. 57-8): "Art is reasonable, life is capricious. In [*WT*] Shakespeare succeeded in giving his wildly improbable story the warmth of actual life; he succeeded in giving it realism. . . . [*58*] It is the realism . . . that makes it a miracle play; that is, a play about a miracle. . . . [*WT*] is not indeed like 'most of life'. . . . It is instead like something very rare and sweet. Most of us have never experienced anything so wonderful and never will, but Shakespeare shows us what it might be like if we did." THORNE (1968, pp. 34-6): "In no other Shakespearian comedy are the ritual 'death' and the kingly protagonists so real and yet so monumental. . . . [*35*] The unreality of the sixteen years of ritual penance undergone by [Leontes] . . . and the implausibility of the statue scene vanish in the emotional truth of the fairy tale quality of the play. . . . [*36*] The play is intensely serious; it is not indulgent in a romantic fairy-tale way to the necessities of an exotic plot." SCHANZER (ed. 1969, pp. 45-6): *WT*'s "construction is coming to be seen not as clumsy and artless but as entirely purposeful and carefully planned, the proper vehicle for the play's significances. . . . [*46*] Its intensely moving events, the rich variety of its characters and incidents, and above all, the splendour of its language, put it among [Sh.'s] most masterly creations."

FELPERIN (1972, p. 244): *WT* "illustrates no cold-blooded interest in dramatic craftsmanship . . . or absorption in play-making for its own sake. The motto for [*WT*] is not art for art's sake . . . but art for life's sake. In a play in which nearly every line is a comment on every other line, Shakespeare creates not only a glittering artifact but one of his most successful representations of this world." SIEMON (1972, p. 443):

"In its vision of the precarious balance between health and decay, good and evil; in its assertion, with the full realization of the possibilities for human misery, of the possibility for human happiness; in its insistence that evil is self-destructive and that good may come out of evil, not inevitably but through the co-operation of Divine Grace and human will, the play is perhaps Shakespeare's most profoundly optimistic statement of the human condition. Its success is owing to the full exposition of the human condition latent in the pattern of comedy." EGAN (1975, p. 56): *WT* represents Sh.'s "richest and most comprehensive use of the tragicomic romance form. . . . [Sh.] fully works out its form's pattern of movement from error, chaos, and separation toward repentance, regeneration, and reunion, elevating it to the level of an integral and far-reaching work of art." HARP (1978, p. 295): Renaissance thinkers, inheriting "the tradition of wonder from a long line of classical and medieval thinkers[,] . . . regarded wonder as both the origin and permanent companion of all rational inquiry. Wonder was not considered merely an inarticulate, emotional response . . . to the glories of nature . . . but was rather considered a truly rational movement of the mind towards fresh knowledge. . . . Wonder is nowhere more conspicuous in Renaissance literature than in Shakespeare's late romances, and of those most mysterious plays none is more suffused with wonder than [*WT*]."

JARRELL (1961; 1980, p. 328): *WT* is "the best of the plays that come after *Antony and Cleopatra*; the mastery and objective perfection of the writing remind one of— perhaps helped to produce—Milton's *Comus*." CALDER-MARSHALL (1982, 1:249), who acted Hermione: "The differences and varieties [of emotions in *WT*] are those of life itself"; the play also creates a "strong feeling for the goodness and power of youth and childhood, not just its wholeness, but its power to do good to older people." ADAMS (1989, pp. 118–19, 121): "Verbally, it's the most rarefied of the romances. . . . Imaginatively, it allows and elicits flights. . . . [*119*] The Play [is] an artful construct celebrating natural impulses. . . . Remote allusions [are] to be pursued by the individual fancy—intimations, not assertions. They may well be limitless. . . . The seacoast of Bohemia is an ancient joke that at a stroke renders the play's geography pretend. . . . This sense of airy vacancy in the play contributes to a lack of moral pressure that may well be one of the most precious things about it. . . . [*121*] The characters breathe the air of an unquestioning eclecticism, but it renders the commonplace luminous. . . . By spelling out little but suggesting much, [*WT*] manages to be both a very simple play and one on which meditation can linger long and spread widely." NEVO (1987, p. 95): "*The Winter's Tale* is safely ensconced among the masterpieces."

Nonetheless a number of critics say that the play is genuinely flawed because Sh.'s powers waned at the end of his career. WENDELL (1894, pp. 384, 386–7): "Tolerably effective in conception, the play is at once too compressed for full effect, and perceptibly less spontaneous, less simple, less plausible, less masterly than the greater work [*Oth.*] which it instantly recalls. . . . [*386*] Except in the great pastoral scene, this mastery lacks the final grace of unconscious spontaneity. . . . [*387*] Conscious deliberation means effort; effort means creative exhaustion . . . and the effort tells the final story,—Shakspere's old spontaneous power was fatally gone." BOAS (1896, pp. 517-18) cites incidents "inadequately motivated," as well as subordinate figures lacking in the "distinctive vitality of the minor characters in earlier plays. . . . [*518*] [*WT*] exhibits, beyond any work of Shakspere, the characteristic defects of Romantic drama, and it could not have been written at the period when he was working with energies strung to their highest intensity." STRACHEY (1904; 1922, p. 64): "With what perversity is the great pastoral scene in *The Winter's Tale* interspersed with long-winded intrigues, and disguises, and homilies? For these blemishes are not . . . interesting or delightful in themselves; they are merely necessary to explain the action, and they are sometimes purely irrelevant." BRANDES (ed. 1905, 4:xiii) wrongly (see lines 2869-74 and 2887) offers Mamillius's passing "entirely out of everyone's memory" at the end of the play as "another proof of . . . Shakespeare's negligent style of work in these last years of his working life" (though BRANDES recognizes "a certain unity of tone and feeling" in this "apparently disconnected plot").

JAMES (1937, p. 207): "The failure of Shakespeare's imagination to 'idealize and unify' the world of human experience . . . as he faced it in the tragedies" presaged that the last plays would not be among Sh.'s greatest work, "for the simple reason that they are not . . . of the order of imagination which is 'human and dramatic'— they are of the order of imagination which is 'enthusiastic and meditative.' . . . It is a platitude of criticism that the later plays are the writings of a man careless of what he is doing. . . . And it is not an accident that Shakespeare's last plays are tortured by a sense of inexpressiveness and failure." CHARLTON (1938, pp. 267-9): "In no sense are [the last plays] an answer . . . to the great tragedies [which give us Sh.'s] deepest insight into human destiny. . . . [*268*] The essential truth is that their view of life is less profound and less compelling than the view of it presented either in the tragedies or in the earlier and mature comedies. Though the romances are Shakespeare the man's last words on humanity and on destiny, they are not therefore his profoundest words. . . . There can scarcely be a shadow of doubt that, in the romances, Shakespeare the dramatist is declining in dramatic power. . . . [He loses] his intuitive sense of the essential stuff of [*269*] drama, of the impact of man on men and on the things which in the mass make that experience which we call life. . . . There could be no clearer evidence of the weakening of Shakespeare's dramatic genius." EVANS (1948; 1965, p. 63): *WT* has its own brilliance but lacks the "advancing command" of Sh.'s earlier achievement. SEWELL (1951, p. 137): "In Leontes we have very good evidence of the change—it amounts almost to an impairment—in Shakespeare's vision. . . . We might even feel in the early part of the play . . . that the writing is a little stale, because Shakespeare had done it, or something very like it, before. So much so that there is a certain morbidity in the representation of the state of jealousy, and the effect is one of pastiche."

Equally certain that Sh.'s powers remained unimpaired as the playwright composed *WT*, other critics praise it as a product of his mature genius. FURNIVALL (1877, p. xci) praises "the last complete play of Shakspere's as it is [but see p. 602], the golden glow of the sunset of his genius over it, the sweet country air all through it. . . . Of few, if any of his plays, is there a pleasanter picture in the memory than of *Winter's Tale*." BAYNES (1894, pp. 130-2): "In this [final] period of Shakespeare's dramatic career, years had evidently brought enlarged vision, wider thoughts, and deeper experiences . . . more intense moral struggles, larger and less joyous views of human life. . . . [*131*] The dramas of this period display an unrivalled power of . . . sounding the most tremendous and perplexing problems of human life and human destiny . . . [and] the great virtues of invincible fidelity and unwearied love. . . . [*132*] In the three dramas . . . which may be said to close [Sh.'s] dramatic career [*Cym.*, *WT*, *Tmp.*] . . . the deeper discords of life are not finally resolved. . . . The virtues of forgiveness and generosity, of forbearance and self-control, are largely illustrated." TEN BRINK (1895, pp. 97–9): In *WT*, Sh.'s "passion does not . . . reach the height it attained in the great tragedies; but in psychological truth, in poetical creative power, in profundity of thought," *WT* is not an inferior play. The earlier (p. 98) "brilliant comedies" (*AYL*, *Ado*, *TN*) anticipate *WT*, which appears "as the perfectly ripened fruit of a life rich in experience, like gold that emerges [*99*] tried and proved from the fire after a long process of refinement."

JUSSERAND (in LEE, ed. 1907, p. xvii): That Sh.'s genius "was in no way impaired by age (he was only forty-seven) is shown again and again" in *WT*. RALEIGH (1907, p. 209): "A pervading sense of quiet and happiness . . . seems to bear witness to a change in the mind of" Sh., so that in *WT*, "the forces of destruction do not prevail, and the end brings forgiveness and reunion. . . . This new-found happiness is a happiness wrung from experience. . . . An all-embracing tolerance and kindliness inspires these last plays." MASSON (1914, pp. 104–5): Sh. "persevered in dramatic production [nearly to the end of his life]. It may be seen also that his power was unabated . . . abundant and [*105*] complex intellectually, . . . exuberant, and at the same time . . . knotty and corrugated with sheer thought." SCHELLING (1923, p. 117): Sh., suffering an artistic deterioration under the influence of Fletcher, "reached in these latter days the calm of harbor; that the waves no longer heaved with the heavy unrest of tragedy nor danced with the delight of frolicsome comedy, takes nothing from the blue of his later ocean or the quiet depths of those pellucid waters."

SPENCER (1940, pp. 367–9): "This dramatic romance affords a delightful and comprehensive entertainment. . . . [*368*] It is a play of abundant energy, written toughly, and brilliant with unique characters. Shakespeare is not repeating himself, he is not played out, his invention is still peerless. Varied as the drama is, there is no lack of unity, for the tone throughout is one of mature confidence in human nature. Few plays offer such a galaxy of lovable personages. . . . Autolycus and the three women [Hermione, Perdita, and Paulina] are the best testimony that [*369*] Shakespeare is still at the full tide of his powers." WILSON (1945; 1946, pp. 128–9): Critics who feel that Sh. was "losing grip upon his theatre and upon his art" at the end of his career probably also believe that "any change from the high tragedy of a *King Lear* is a falling off. But there is no need to suppose that Shakespeare was losing grip." Sh.'s drama was not static; from the tragedies he was (p. 129) "moving on to an experiment in a new kind."

BRYANT (1963, p. 393): Sh. explores the nature of evil by converting "the stereotyped conventions of the pastoral drama into highly original instruments which combine to form one of the best of his last plays." WAIN (1964, pp. 217, 224) calls *WT*

"the first perfectly realized masterpiece among the final group [of plays]. . . . [*224*]
It is a profound lyrical meditation on the theme of forgiveness and renewal, full of
delicacy and beauty, yet always close to the earth and the human heart-beat. Shakespeare never wrote a more perfect work."

HARTWIG (1970; 1972, pp. 176–7): "Criticism which fails to distinguish between
Shakespeare's goals in the tragicomedies and those of his other plays falsifies his
achievement. Even in generic criticism, a preference for tragedy, for comedy, or for
chronicle plays may encourage the judgment that the late plays reveal a falling off in
Shakespeare's artistic control." SPENCER (1970, pp. 72, 77): *WT* is a product of Sh.'s
maturity, a work of "ripe accomplishment, beginning a new phase of his writing,
rather than the [work] of his balmy old age. . . . Shakespeare shows an audacity in
his theatrical representations which he had never, or rarely, shown before, or never
to such an extent within a single play. . . . [77] Shakespeare has succeeded in intensifying each moment of the play so that these apparent audacities of construction
increase the dramatic excitement rather than reduce our emotional involvement. This
success . . . indicates the full maturity of Shakespeare's art." VISWANATHAN (1987,
pp. 43–4) applauds the "abundant experimental vigour" of the later plays and Sh.'s
"remarkable response to, as well as full participation in, his theatrical milieu (neither
was he bored with things nor was there a decline in his powers). . . . In Shakespeare's late plays the virtuoso-like . . . juxtaposition or fusion of the naive and the
'marvellous' — or [*44*] of the realistic and the idealistic — has a way of evoking at once
an attention to (and admiration for) the art of the playwright and a feeling for the
human reality of the drama." MIKO (1989, p. 260): "Shakespeare in these last plays
is enjoying a freedom of experimentation, both with 'new' material and with dramatic
form, that presupposes most of his previous work. . . . His attitude . . . [is] not
merely experimental but playful, especially with the extremes which literary conventions exist to control: death, obsession, contrary or excessive emotional attitudes
and . . . [the] ineradicable wish to make the world fit our desires."

Another group of critics acknowledges *WT*'s blemishes but also notices its special
beauties. LEWES (1894, p. 309): "One thing is evident in all his works — the truth of
his character-drawing. . . . This truth, this presentation of character in harmony with
nature, is the mark of a great poet. Before this all other drawbacks and faults entirely
disappear." BULTHAUPT (1903, 2:378) finds intolerable Leontes's sudden mental conversion to madness and his rejection of the Delphic oracle in two lines (1321–2); he
finds the time gap merely unsettling. But the whole of Act 4 gives evidence of Sh.'s
sovereign genius, though the play suffers a relapse in a fifth act that creaks in all its
joints (in Ger.). MATTHEWS (1910, p. 153): The playwright "must expend his invention, and he must be as ingenious as may be in adroit devices to sustain the interest
of his story. On the characters who live and move inside this play, he must
. . . breathe life, so that they will exist for us long after we have lost our liking for
the kind of story in which they originally figured. . . . The plot of [*WT*] is a tissue of
absurdities, but the young loves of Perdita and Florizel . . . are eternally human."

HERFORD (1912, pp. 83, 85): The play is "full of beauty and charm" but it does
not "harrow nor, in the strict sense, greatly amuse; the pathos of Hermione . . . does

not approach that of Desdemona; the humour of Autolycus is a thin beverage compared to the rich wine of Falstaff. The characters, again, are slighter, the action less closely knit" than in the other plays, though in *WT* these (p. 85) "slighter profiles are exquisitely fine and true." BROOKE (1913, pp. 253-4): The play is "so varied in events and characters, and the characters play in and out of one another with such a charm of contrast, that the surprises of intellect and emotion are as numerous as they are pleasant. And these surprises are yet so mellowed by the temperance and beauty of the poetic tongue in which they are given, and so carefully [motivated], that they do not startle us more than noble art permits. . . . [*254*] [*WT* has] enough fantasy in it to charm the children, and enough passion to make the elders pensive. . . . Of course, the interval of sixteen years in the middle is awkward. . . . The unity of the action is too rudely broken. But there is, at the end, the impression of a spiritual unity." MACKENZIE (1924, pp. 428, 444): "Though [*WT*] is less satisfactory from the structural point of view than the middle comedies, it is written both carefully and beautifully, and its lapses are not due to heedlessness so much as to the sheer technical difficulty of arranging its action in a pattern suitable for dramatic representation in little more than two hours' time." As for character drawing (p. 444): "It is not ineffective, by any means, especially in the portrayal of the women. . . . They are drawn masterly, in a few clear lovely strokes that make them come alive, but neither they nor their experience are studied, analysed, *lived into*, as had been Shakespeare's custom: and the same is true even more of their accompanying men. They are . . . but symbols . . . seen in relation to something that matters more than themselves. It is as if he had ceased now to explore life . . . and had set himself simply to express what he had found it, in the long run."

Modifying his initial disapproval, WILSON (ed. 1931, pp. xxiv-xxvi): "On the whole . . . we must grant that the many critics who detect evidence of 'failing powers' in his later plays . . . say it with particular effect about [*xxv*] [*WT*]. . . . For in this play the tragedy and comedy are not woven. . . . This play never fits into our mind as a whole. . . . [*xxvi*] When *The Winter's Tale* comes to our mind, nine out of ten of us forget its shreds and patches, and think, with a glance at Autolycus, mainly of that Sicilian [sic] scene and Perdita. . . . The beauty of that setting, and of its language, must always redeem this play for the reader, as the slow descent of Hermione from her pedestal must ever hold the breath of a spectator. The one effect comes of sheer poetry, the other belongs to the art of the theatre: in both of which Shakespeare, spite of any drawback or difficulty, had learnt, with a careless ease, to excel." LEECH (1950, pp. 133, 135): Though Sh. was not "indifferent to the plays he was writing, we can admit that in certain places he relaxed visibly at his task." *WT* may have more vitality and joy than *Cym.* or *Tmp.*; Autolycus may be (p. 135) "the last of Shakespeare's comic figures to win our sympathy"; the sheep-shearing scene may be "in its lyrical kind unmatched." Yet *WT* has a "haphazard structure, exemplified notoriously in the convenient devouring of Antigonus, with the craftsmanship of individual scenes varying from the highest to almost the lowest, with lyrics and lyrical blank verse finer than ever before." COLIE (1974, pp. 266-7) sees a play "conspicuously ill-made, . . . in which our attention is withdrawn from verisimilitude; in which motivations are not to be inquired into; in which the marvelous, the incredible, the impossible are so insisted upon . . . that they force themselves to become subjects of critical consideration. . . . [This] truncated torso of a play pays no tribute to demands for classical [*267*] modulation. . . . Shakespeare's play simply forces us to face what is 'tragic' and what is 'comic' in life and in plays, forces questions of genre and decorum. . . . [The play] flaunts its artfulness and its sublime contempt for mere art."

Some critics assert that these blemishes go unnoticed in performance. H. COLE-RIDGE (1851, 2:150): "The progressive interest of the play, *malgré* the vast hiatus for which Shakspeare himself thought it necessary to apologise, is well sustained. . . . The whole is pleasing and effective on the stage." PRICE (1890, pp. 195–6, 207): The play "seems to lack all the marks of what is called artistic unity," defies dramatic law, and is a "mere medley of diversified effects. . . . [*196*] And yet, when the play was put upon the stage, well-mounted and well-acted, it became . . . the darling of the public. . . . [*207*] This play marks the final phase of [Sh.'s] skill in dramatic construction"; Sh. combines "a perfect tragedy with a perfect comedy." MATTHEWS (1913; 1970, p. 337): The story is "abnormal and far-fetched. . . . The hot jealousy of Leontes . . . impossible. . . . [*WT*] has the full flavor of the dramatic romance, yet its story is not so artificially involved. Its plot is simpler and clearer in the performance, and more appealing, in spite of the arbitrariness of the motiveless jealousy." RIDLEY (1937, p. 208): "The sudden frantic blazing up of Leontes' jealousy seems unnatural to the point of absurdity. . . . He seems not so much too bad as too silly to be true, and, as we read, his falsity tinges the whole of the first three acts with unreality. . . . But when we see the play on the stage the actor . . . can make Leontes credible . . . so that the play is no longer founded on an unreality, and our appreciation is greatly increased. . . . The first three acts take on a quite unexpected force." BROWN (1962; 1968, p. 235): "The most astonishing fact [during performance] is the subtlety of the audience's involvement: the audience responds to a widely and minutely considered dramatic world, and, because nothing is circumscribed by explicit statement or judgement, responds with ease, concern and delight. The theatrical life of *The Winter's Tale* . . . derives unity, subtlety, and force from a comprehensive attitude to personal relationships and society which is never stated yet always formative."

COGHILL (1958, p. 31): Despite the "critical commonplace" that *WT* is an "ill made play" or a "conscious return to a naïve and outmoded technique," Leontes's jealousy, the bear (a tour-de-force), Time's years-spanning speech, the recounting of Perdita's recovery and the statue scene are all "gripping and memorable" on stage. PURDOM (1963, pp. 180–2): The play does not have the "rationality of natural life," nor should that be expected. On the other hand, (p. 182) "the poetry is so delicious, yet much of it so complex and concentrated, that it asks for the perfection of art from the players; and the play's action is so thrilling, yet so touching, that it demands the most faithful devotion to the text from producers." COTTRELL (1964, pp. 71, 73): "*The Winter's Tale* is not an easy play to accept at first reading, though audiences viewing the work have always found it more acceptable as theatre. . . . [*73*] Especially may it be said of [*WT*] that the play in production is the thing. . . . [Sh.] used

711

some of his most intensified poetry to convey truths about human beings and to create believable people. And he evolved a structure which, though broken and widespread, offers firm support for the total meaning of the play. These are characteristics present in all of Shakespeare's best plays, but their presence in *The Winter's Tale* allows it to emerge as a fascinating, compelling, and strangely memorable work."

KERMODE (ed. 1963, p. xxxv): *WT* has "a natural energy that supports all it says about natural power; its scheme is deep-laid and its language fertile in suggestion. It will not be trapped by the historian [nor] caught in the net of allegory. . . . We value it not for some hidden truth, but for its power to show . . . something of life that could only be shown by the intense activity of intellect and imagination in the medium of a theatrical form. It is not a great allegory or a great argument, but a great play." IDEM (1963, p. 39): "The greatness of the play is self-evident; it does not need the prestige of covert meanings." NUTTALL (1966, p. 9): *WT* is less intelligent than *Ham.*, less profound than *Lr.*, less elegant than *LLL*, much more disturbing than *MND*, and not at all a "pretty play, of 'merely aesthetic' appeal. It does not so much charm the eye as pierce the viscera. It does not divert the spectator; it turns him inside out." GRENE (1967, pp. 68–9): "However one may judge the play most truly—as tragedy, ironic comedy, or fantasy—one knows firmly and immediately that it is entirely successful in producing its effect. . . . [69] It *is* intensely theatrical. . . . We seem to be seeing real life transformed into a fairy tale" that "exposes human roots." COLLINS (1982, p. 59): "Insofar as we are made aware that in Shakespeare's last plays it is the playwright who directs the action, we are also made aware that the power to arrange such happy endings in the midst of such threatening circumstances is confined to the playhouse. Our double awareness makes it quite clear that what appears to be is not; the illusion of an earthly paradise is at once granted and taken away. . . . What we feel will not be so much the purgation of melancholy as its accentuation." DAVISON (1982, pp. 65–6): "Possibly the idea of a winter's tale . . . provides the fundamental element of illusion which helps a company and an audience to come to terms with the play and to respond to it in its parts as a whole. . . . The manner in which Shakespeare holds over the various actions of the play so that the eventual fulfillment of each reflects one upon another in part [66] explains the success of the play in performance. . . . [*WT* is] a multi-faceted jewel which suddenly comes into our view."

As might be expected, however, some critics accept *WT* as better reading than acting material. GENTLEMAN (1774, 5:151) finds beauty "even in wildness; it [*WT*] is a parterre of poetical flowers sadly choked with weeds. . . . The present copy . . . studiously prun'd and regulated, by the ingenious Mr. *Hull, of Covent-Garden*, [is] certainly made much . . . more bearable than the author left it; however we think [the play will never] do great matters on the stage." INCHBALD (ed. 1808, 3:3): *WT* is "among those dramas that charm more in perusal than in representation. The long absence from the scene of the two most important characters, Leontes and his wife, and the introduction of various other persons to fill their places, divert, in some measure, the attention of an audience; and they do not so feelingly unite all they see and hear into a single story, as he who, with a book in his hand, and neither his eye nor ear distracted, combines, and enjoys the whole grand variety." LUSERKE (1957, p. 196): *WT* is the draft of a Shakespearean masterpiece, though it never became one onstage because the theatrical conventions, musical capabilities, stage shape, and actors of Sh.'s time held the playwright and his piece to a conservative realization; thus it remained a torso, unrealized in its full potential, because it had to effect a compromise with the audience and the latter's expectations (in Ger.).

One blemish that critics weigh against *WT*'s beauties is its neglect of the unities (surprisingly, of concern through the 19th century). HUDSON (1848, 1:319): "Winter's Tale outdoes all the rest of Shakspeare's fictions in disregard of the far-famed Unities of time and place. With geography and chronology [Sh.] plays the wildest tricks imaginable. . . . Notwithstanding which, the play is pervaded with the strictest unity of interest and purpose; the violations of local and chronological order being forgotten in the far higher order which is everywhere preserved." IDEM (1872; 1973, 1:453–4): The neglect of the unities is not troublesome "until one goes to viewing the parts of the work with reference to ends not contemplated in the use made of them here. . . . It is enough that the materials . . . agree in working out the issue proposed, the end thus regulating the use of [*454*] the means." H. COLERIDGE (1851, 2:148–9) praises this "wild drama" for its comedic excellence and "exquisite" pastoral; he cares as little for the (p. 149) "improbability of events . . . as for the violation of the unities and the outrages on geography." GERVINUS (1863, 2:485): Sh. "wished purposely to brave the narrow-minded upholders of the unities of time and place"; BOODLE ("Theory," 1885, p. 318): "A unity given by character-development is the principle of Shakespeare's art." LANG (1894, p. 710): "The topic and theme of *Winter's Tale* entirely lack unity. . . . [Sh.] was wholly indifferent to the unities of Aristotle." The CLARKES (1879, p. 107): Sh. ignores the classical conventions in favor of "an original and admirable system of Dramatic Time, which permits his adopting a story that demands scope of period to properly delineate its various incidents, to develop its different characters, and to depict the multiform emotions elicited by successive events and situations. This system is so ingenious in itself, and is put into operation with so masterly a skill, that it enables the reader or spectator to see a long course of time, or a limited space of time, or even a simultaneous progress of protracted time and current time both together, without a violation of probability or injury to naturalness of effect." BOAS (1882, p. 40): Sh. disregards the dramatic unities in *WT* because he sets about to demonstrate a higher law of art through an ennobling imitation of nature and the beautiful representation of truth with the aid of fantasy (in Ger.).

GOLLANCZ (ed. 1894, 41:x): *WT*, "with its interval of sixteen years between two acts, may be said, too, to mark the final overthrow of Time—the hallowed 'Unity of Time'—by its natural adversary, the Romantic Drama. The play recalls Sir Philip Sidney's criticism, in his *Apologie for Poetrie* [1581–3?], anent the crude romantic plays popular about 1580, . . . of the abuse of dramatic decorum by lawless playwrights, who . . . neglected both 'time and place.' [*WT*], perhaps the very last of Shakespeare's comedies, appropriately emphasises, as it were, the essential elements of the triumph of the New over the Old. Sidney could not foresee, in 1580, the glorious future in store for the despised Cinderella of the playhouses." BRANDES (1898, 2:60): "As if in defiance of those classically cultivated people who demanded unity of time and place, [Sh.] allowed sixteen years to elapse between two acts. In other words, he freely improvised . . . upon a given poetic theme . . . content with a general harmony of colour and unity of tone, without giving much thought to any ultimate meaning."

KILBOURNE (1906; 1973, p. 89): Modern audiences who "are not enslaved by the rules of pseudo-classicism and who accept the spirit and method of the romantic drama regard the lapse of time between acts as a perfectly legitimate dramatic convention. . . . In this case it was necessary to the dramatic purpose." CHAMBERS (ed. 1907, pp. 8–9): Sh. sets "the unities at nought in a way which it would be difficult not to regard as deliberate"; if he (p. 9) "'lacked art' in Ben Jonson's . . . sense, it is clear that the lack arose from no incomplete mastery, but from an effort, unintelligible to Ben's more rigid mind, after an unlimited freedom of technique." BETHELL (1947, p. 67): In *WT*, Sh. employs "not only a method of dramatic presentation but also a statement, complex and profound, of the nature of reality. This fusion of method and statement is the last degree of organic unity." TRAVERSI (1959, p. 20): "The successive stages of [*WT*] constitute a closely knit and homogenous development. Between the jealous obsession of Leontes, which the 'gods' expose and punish, and his final reconciliation to Hermione, the delicate beauty of the pastoral episode stands, not as an escape into make-believe, but as a perfectly-timed affirmation of rebirth, there and there only appropriate." When the Shepherd takes up the infant Perdita, he binds "the past to the future in a way highly characteristic of this beautifully constructed and unified play. The 'things dying' . . . belong to the past . . . ; the 'things new-born,' tangibly revealed in the person of the helpless child, look forward to the future, to the final restoration . . . of the values of life in fertility and 'grace.'" SCHANZER (1975, p. 61): Sh.'s "device of making Father Time himself disparage [the neoclassical demand for unity of time] as a passing fashion" (1583–8) is simply one of the "various ways in which, in the course of his dramatic career, Shakespeare expressed his sense of the absurdity" of the convention. HASSEL (1980, pp. 219–20) reviews the "preposterous" death of Antigonus, the quick leap from tragedy to comedy and the (p. 220) spanning of 16 years in 32 lines: "Only a playwright well-practiced in playing with the fragile, foolish conventions of his art would try so audacious a thing. Only a Shakespeare who has already discovered and exploited the humbling but joyous connections between the 'insubstantial pageants' of lovers and playwrights would risk such aesthetic folly. That it works again is eloquent testimony to the coherence of Shakespeare's dramatic vision." NICHOLS (1981, p. 178): Without sacrificing artistic unity, Sh. "violates the traditional dramatic unities in order to present a fuller vision of human life."

Many critics acknowledge but overlook—or justify—the anachronisms and other anomalies in *WT*. MUIR (1951, pp. 529, 532–3) defends them by claiming that Sh.'s "anachronisms were deliberate and calculated. . . . [532] Shakespeare made use of topical allusions and of ideas that were in the air . . . for the purpose of suggesting the abiding significance of his plays by infusing them with the spirit of the age." Thus the dramatic function of anachronism: "to show that beneath the changes of manners, customs, and institutions the people of a past century are not essentially different from ourselves" (p. 533).

DOUCE (1807, 1:364): "In point of fine writing [*WT*] may be ranked among Shakespeare's best efforts. The absurdities pointed at by Warburton, together with the whimsical anachronisms of Whitsun pastorals, Christian burial, an emperor of Russia, and an Italian painter of the fifteenth century, are no real drawbacks on the superlative merits of this charming drama." He neglects to mention the seacoast of Bohemia, but for a discussion of that, see n. 1440. SCHLEGEL (1808; 1846, p. 396): "The calculation of probabilities has nothing to do with such wonderful and fleeting adventures, ending at last in general joy; and accordingly Shakespeare has here taken the greatest liberties with anachronisms and geographical errors." HALLIWELL (1850; 1966, p. 102, n.2, 103): Some English critics "would smile at the idea of Shakespeare voluntarily falling into a geographical error," since (p. 103) the seacoast of Bohemia is an "error rather suited to the fabulous nature of the story, which runs into the region of fable and the age of poesy, better than the most accurate geographical definition." IDEM (ed. 1859, p. 37): Sh.'s "best defence, if any apology be desired for an error of detail in a legendary drama in which all exactitude in particulars of localities and manners are intentionally disregarded, consists in the comparative neglect of geographical education in his time."

LLOYD (in SINGER, ed. 1856, 4:2): "What parts of this drama could be attributed to any even of the most skilful of [Sh.'s] contemporaries? It was perhaps the descrepancies of the plot . . . and the anachronisms which made Dryden and Pope overlook the beauties of execution in this enchanting play." The CLARKES (ed. 1865, 1:721): "To those who perceive how the poet can adhere to the strictest accuracy where accuracy is needful to art-verity and can also make accuracy subservient to typical truth in productions purely romantic, there is no more violence offered to imaginative credence by assembling together in 'The Winter's Tale' Apollo's oracle, an allusion to Judas Iscariot, an Emperor of Russia, a Puritan who 'sings psalms to hornpipes', 'one Mistress Tale-Porter', 'Whitsun-pastorals', a baptismal 'bearing-cloth', Bohemia as a maritime country, Delphos as an island [for the idea that Delphos is not an anachronism at all, see n. 1147], and Julio Romano as flourishing in times when pagan gods were oracularly consulted, than by congregating in a poetical forest [in *AYL*] lions, goats, serpents, lambs, oaks, olives, palm-trees, osiers, &c., where all these things, each in their several introduction, serve the art-purpose of vividly idealising the subject treated." SNIDER (1875, p. 80): Sh. violates history, chronology, and geography "with an audacity which has often called forth the sneers and the ire of pedantic erudition." Scoffing at such criticism, SNIDER praises the play, suggesting that "probability, as a canon of Shakspearian criticism, is wholly meaningless and inapplicable; . . . it ought to be eschewed altogether." FURNIVALL (1877, p. xci): We "accept the medley and anachronisms of this play" and ignore its confusions because Sh.'s version of his source was "informed by a new spirit, instinct with a new life." LEWES (1894, p. 309) rejects the notion that "ignorance [was] the source of these historical and geographical blunders, or that Shakespeare really was not aware that he was mixing up time and place in such a manner. This hypothesis does not agree with the deep . . . knowledge and insight he shows."

LOUNSBURY (1901, pp. 105-6): Sh. mixes "ancient times and customs and countries with modern" in a way that (p. 106) "would tend to make the conventional classicist shudder. . . . The disgust which these violations of rules caused the professional critics prevented them from doing justice to the skill with which the whole piece had been constructed. . . . Whether well or ill done, [*WT*] was done as deliberately as it was audaciously. An examination of it leaves no doubt on that point. In his own mind the dramatist was clearly satisfied with the wisdom of his proceeding." KILBOURNE (1906; 1973, p. 90): "Even if he [Sh.] knew Greene to be wrong on these points [whether Bohemia had a seacoast or Delphos was an island], he probably thought it not worth while to correct them" for they are "far too trivial to raise such a pother about." BETHELL (1947, pp. 34-5, 37): "Greene insisted on Bohemia's coast-line to emphasise the fact that his Bohemia was not the Bohemia of contemporary diplomatic reports but a romantic Ruritania or Arcadia where the strangest things might happen. And Shakespeare, who rejected so much of Greene's story in adapting it to his purpose, deliberately preserved the sea-coast of Bohemia because he was especially anxious to liberate [35] himself from the localisation of his play world in the contemporary map of Europe. . . . [37] Anachronism such as [ascribing Hermione's statue to Julio Romano] is clearly not due to the writer's ignorance; in a sense it is quite deliberate. But it is not self-conscious, since there is no evidence that Shakespeare ever considered the alternative of writing in historical perspective." KNIGHT (1947; 1966, p. 128): *WT* "may seem a rambling, perhaps an untidy, play; its anachronisms are vivid, its geography disturbing. And yet Shakespeare offers nothing greater in tragic psychology, humour, pastoral, romance. . . . The more profound passages are . . . evidence of what is beating behind or within the creative genius at work. . . . A vague, numinous, sense of mighty powers, working through both the natural order and man's religious consciousness . . . to preserve, in spite of all appearance, the good [Life itself]." RUSEV (1982, pp. 59-60): Sh. showed such an accurate knowledge of geography in many plays (*TN, MM, Wiv., Oth.,* e.g.) that — considering the availability of Mercator's map of Europe and Ortelius' atlas and considering Sh.'s knowledge that (p. 60) "the Black Sea is one with no ebb and flow of the tide, a fact not generally known even today" — we cannot accept that Bohemia's seacoast is born of Sh.'s ignorance. Sh.'s creative purposes are served by "bestowing a sea-coast on Bohemia, even if that meant running counter to the facts of geography."

In summation, MARSH (1962; 1980, pp. 160-1): *WT* is a "serious poetic statement of the nature of good and evil, of life and death. It does provide what someone has said all great poetry should provide, a momentary clarification of life. Here Shakespeare is at grips with the ultimate problems of human existence; his conclusions are the play, and any attempt to boil them down into an easily assimilable 'philosophy of life' is sure to fail. But . . . certain generalizations can perhaps be advanced. . . . The value of life is that it is life, and not death, even if to be alive is to be exposed to countless dangers and pains. The problem of evil . . . [161] can only be opposed by a belief in qualities like love, honesty, justice [that] . . . have power to liberate the individual from the prison of self. . . . The play suggests that to live until one dies is the great affirmation that man is called upon to make, and that it carries its own reward."

Succinct overviews of criticism and critical theory are offered in OVERTON (1989, "An Introduction to the Variety of Criticism") and PAFFORD (ed. 1963, pp. xxxvii–xliv).

Genre

Critics discuss *WT*'s use of the features of one genre or another without actually placing it wholly in any, because it is a hybrid, borrowing from many genres without belonging primarily to one.

MÉZIÈRES (1860; 1882, p. 518): Although *WT* is not pastoral, comedy, or tragedy, Sh. "touches on all three genres, rather than fixing on one, [to produce] . . . a rapid sketch of three kinds, none of which is perfect." HALL (1871, p. 245), however: *WT* may "truly be termed a tragic-comic pastoral, for the oracle of Delphi decides the tragic catastrophe and prepares the reader for the happy conclusion of the piece." GERVINUS (1849–50; 1863, 2:469) agrees. Like RISTINE (1910, p. 113), ADAMS (1923, p. 417) calls *WT* a tragicomedy embodying, as its title suggests, the qualities of a romance. KERMODE (ed. *Tmp.*, 1954, p. lix): "The pastoral romance gave [Sh.] the opportunity for a very complex comparison between the worlds of Art and Nature; and the tragicomic form enabled him to concentrate the whole story of apparent disaster, penitence, and forgiveness into one happy misfortune, controlled by a divine Art." IDEM (1963, p. xxiv): The last plays "could well be called Romantic tragicomedies." BENTLEY (1964, p. 94) suggests romances, tragicomedies, "or simply the plays of the fourth period." To VELIE (1972, pp. 61, 91, 112–13), the combining of "the happy ending of comedy with the serious tone and action of tragedy" produces "elements of melodrama," which Sh. makes sophisticated through (p. 91) his rigorous psychological examination of Leontes and (p. 112) an ending that does not resurrect Antigonus and Mamillius. Sh. combines (p. 113) "psychological realism, complication comedy, and romance" to achieve a "dramatic form that is excellently suited to convey the theme of repentance." KRIER (1982, pp. 343–4), however: *WT* gives us "a complete and highly compressed tragedy, with deaths and a sea of blood," with "real evil, not the appearance of it only," and with "real, far-reaching and ruinous" consequences. *WT* "gives us enough tragic catastrophes in three acts . . . for a full tragedy. . . . [344] Yet it is precisely at this nadir that Shakespeare chooses to make a comedy of the play. . . . The switch in tone is certainly unexpected. . . . But comedy here is allowed to be as dominant a tone as tragedy is. . . . [Both] are sustained in the play as a paradox of two apparently incompatible genres . . . which do in reality exist together, unblended, each with its characteristic atmosphere."

A few critics offer singular notions of genre. HUGO (1868, 4:38): From its earliest publication this play has been the subject of a mistake; placed by the editors of [F1] in the list of Comedies, it has been accepted according to its label, and held to be . . . a light and fanciful improvisation. . . . [*WT*] is no comedy; it is a tragedy. . . . It is so by its general composition, by its impassioned tone, and by the ascending scale of its chief scenes (in Fr.). WILLIAMS (1967, p. 19): The "abstract form [of Time, the Chorus] harks back to the morality plays." WINCOR (1950, pp. 219–26) vacillates: *WT* may derive from "the old festival plays that celebrate the return of spring after a barren winter" in drama that grows (p. 220) "out of seasonal rites and worship. . . . [*226*] If Shakespeare did not conceive this as a festival play, he at least was conscious of working in terms of allegorical winter and spring." HOY (1973, pp. 64–5): *WT* "may be said to come into its own on the Jacobean stage with the advent of tragi-comedy, which is the mannerist dramatic form par excellence. . . . [65] The mannerist features of [*WT*] are particularly prominent. The process of temporal foreshortening, whereby Leontes' jealousy . . . is full grown within the space of some sixty lines, is as violent as any spatial foreshadowing in Tintoretto. The Chorus of Time . . . fulfills its purpose by the familiar mannerist device of directly signalling to the audience"; omitting Perdita's recognition scene (3010–3100) "has its analogy in the tendency in mannerist painting to relegate the principal scene or figure from the foreground or centre to the background or side," and the statue scene reveals the "mannerist fondness for securing bizarre and somewhat equivocal effects from mixing figures on pedestals with living figures."

THOMPSON (1971, pp. 154–5): *WT* "may be regarded as the final romanticization of revenge tragedy," in which the hero "searches for a cause and interprets all evidence in light of his own belief that his honor has been besmirched. He then fancies himself free to plot, threaten, devise punishments, and ensnare his enemies, all in the name of [*155*] his cherished honor." But (p. 156) tragedy is countered and revenge purged "by employing romantic conventions to unravel the plot." HARTWIG (in KAY & JACOBS, 1978, pp. 98–101): Sh. "experiment[s] with the possibilities of parody" by substituting an onstage Autolycus for the absent Leontes. The (p. 100) "false plea" Autolycus makes "as victim [1729–68] literalizes Leontes' false plea as cuckold. . . . Autolycus is both his own attacker and victim; so is Leontes. . . . [*101*] By containing disorder through comic inconsequence, he [Autolycus] provides an undersong which contrasts with and makes more credible Leontes' release from false illusion." PILKINGTON (1981, p. 79) anticipates NEVO (1987, pp. 18, 96), who finds the literary model for *WT* in fantasy—"a processing of symbolic elements and of episodes into ordered and coherent narratives, possessing purposive characters and consequential occurrences, beginnings, middles and teleological ends, but which are also capable of evoking the tremors, in consciousness, of unconscious pressures and desires enmeshed in a network of tentacular roots." Fantasy (p. 96) animates, unifies, and shapes *WT*, and from it the play "derives its power to move us," if the audience is "receptive to the resonances of deep-level fantasy" and willing to get beyond "traditional explications" of the play.

A number of critics associate *WT* with allegory or emblem. HARBAGE (1961, p. 442): The "exchange of banter [121–52]" between Hermione and Polixenes is, "through imagery and allusion, an allegory of the fall of Man, a commentary upon *Genesis*, 3:1-5"; though MUIR (1969, p. 101) asserts that Sh. "never indulged in allegory as such," he acknowledges allegorical and emblematic "undertones" in the play. HOENIGER (1950, pp. 13-15): The "whole tone of the play with its repeated allusion to supernatural forces and its at times unearthly serenity" suggests allegory, in which (p. 14) the precise meaning of words depends on speaker as well as listener. "It then follows that if the poet desires to convey a profound vision of reality, he will seek to break away from . . . words which have become chained. . . . [*15*] Therefore [allegory] is one of the most poetic forms of speech, for in it words are loaded with the greatest possible symbolic suggestion. It is not surprising, then, if a great poet resorts to allegory to express his vision." NUTTALL (1966, p. 38) calls Time an "unashamedly allegorical figure who has stepped out of an altogether older type of drama," while SALINGAR (1966, p. 3) notes Time's "emblematic function, bringing out the significance of the action he foreshadows." MAHOOD (1992, p. 35): Time is an "allegorical abstraction who is at once outside the action and, by his very nature, operative within it . . . [since] all events under the sun are the products of Time."

CLUBB (1972, pp. 24-6): "Traditionally, as a fact of natural history, as literary subject, and as simile, the bear, unformed [at birth, to be licked into shape by its mother], and therefore potentially tragic or comic, must have seemed almost emblematically appropriate" to *WT* in suggesting that (p. 26) "human nature [is] primitive but promising, somewhat amenable to refining influences" or, as HARDMAN (1985, p. 233) would have it, in suggesting the "superiority of art over nature." WICKHAM (1973, pp. 97-8): In "an emblem . . . both narrative and characters need do no more than reflect a particular situation. . . . [*WT*] reflects the surprising, if not miraculous, reunification of the British Isles in the person of the heir-apparent, Prince Henry" (see p. 608). The emblematic structure represents "Union . . . followed by . . . Disintegration or Discord, followed by Reunion and future happiness. . . . [*98*] There is now a strong case regarding the curious structure of [*WT*] as having been deliberately engineered to contain an emblematic device." FOWLER (1978, pp. 41-2, 49) finds in Leontes's sin "an allegory about harmony, with Hermione representing a state of mind lost and recovered; and an allegory about guilt's virtual death, with Hermione as the soul that dies. These meanings are not logically compatible. But then, [the play] is not [*42*] simple allegory. . . . [*49*] The last three acts of [*WT*] are allegorical romance . . . [and] in such a form, continuity sometimes depends entirely on the . . . allegory." GRANTLEY (1986, pp. 19-36): Emblematic characterization in *WT* devolves from the foregrounded "moral dichotomy producing choice and/or conflict" in medieval allegorical drama and its successor, the Tudor interlude. In Leontes we see (p. 21) "the corrupting process of life and the necessity for spiritual rebirth," in Paulina (p. 26), Leontes's conscience, and in Autolycus (p. 26), something of the Vice, though Sh. was attempting neither a (p. 36) "straightforward moral allegory" of the fall and redemption of man, nor a 17th-c. "version of earlier scriptural plays." Rather, he draws on themes central to the religious drama of his youth and "traditional images of enormous dramatic and mythic power . . . [which] effectively constitute the tradition of which [*WT*] can be regarded as part." DAVIDSON (1982, pp. 73-83), FABINY (1984, pp. 89-92), and IWASAKI (1984, pp. 68-71, 90) also consider the play emblematic.

Some critics see in *WT* the traits of fable, fairy tale, or folk tale. SNIDER ([c. 1890], p. 463): "All the characters are given up to the sport of circumstances; but over this realm of contingency hovers an order. . . . Life has some secret principle which controls Space and Time, controls what seems to be accident, controls even falsehood and wrong. This is, in literature, the domain of the Fairy Tale." PAFFORD (ed. 1963, pp. lxiii-lxiv): *WT* "inextricably" mingles realistic characters with fable and fairy story, but Sh. (p. lxiv) "has taken pains to turn improbabilities, even impossibilities, in the fable, into possibilities." HARTWIG (1970; 1972, p. 31) echoes both critics: "The deaths [of Mamillius and Antigonus] are . . . an encroachment of the actual upon the illusionary world of fairy tale. . . . Shakespeare did not want to create a world that could float free of actuality or escape from life's meaningful issues," yet his "choice of a fabulous plot increases the expectation that actions are under a control which operates beyond man's power." MILLS (1966, pp. 110-11) contends: "We do not look for psychological realism in . . . plays [like *WT*]. Instead, we expect to find whimsical and impulsive behavior on the part of the leading characters, sudden reversals and surprises in the action, and magical or supernatural forces shaping the outcome. . . . We must respect the *genres*. . . . [*111*] Perhaps one reason [Sh.] chose the 'fairy tale' genre was to spare himself the necessity of 'psychologizing.'" HAPPÉ (1969, p. 11): The fairy story is suggested by Perdita's miraculous rescue and growth into a "remarkably beautiful princess, whose distinction of manner reveals her true nobility, which is unknown to herself and to those around her." BULLOUGH (1975, 8:367): It is "surprising and significant . . . that so much of [Sh.'s] source-material contains strong folk-elements which anthropologists have traced in oral story and legend. Among these we may note: 'the long-lost child and/or wife' motif . . . 'the calumniated wife' . . . 'the prince and the shepherdess'." MAITRA (1960, p. 83) alludes to Sh.'s "prolific use of folklore," LAROQUE (1982, p. 25) to Sh.'s blending of "folk-custom" and other traditions.

Other critics find *WT* masque-like. WELSFORD (1927; 1962, pp. 288-9): "People demanded variety entertainments . . . which combined the attraction of masque and drama, [and Sh.] supplied them with romances in which even the darker aspects of life were [*289*] invested with an enigmatic beauty. . . . Underneath the incongruous medley, there runs a kind of enchanted tune . . . which atones for all the surface discords and inconsistencies. . . . The romantic tendencies in drama seem always to have been strengthened when the influence of the masque was particularly potent." LONG (1961, pp. 68-9): The "almost inexhaustible mine" of elements the Stuart masque provided for Sh. are primarily musical—(p. 69) declamations, dialogue songs, dance songs, choral songs, motets, and closing songs. LEECH (in KAY & JACOBS, 1978, pp. 40-1, 53) offers a list of features—a presenter's speech; the appearance of the masquers; the masquing dance; (p. 41) the "revels" ("taking into the masque persons of the opposite sex who had previously been among the audience"); a "withdrawal of the masquers from the great hall into which they had come as alleged strangers";

and the antimasque, which "commonly came right at the beginning or after the presenter's speech"—to suggest that (p. 53) "Shakespeare had the masque very much in mind when he wrote [*WT*]." STUDING (1970, pp. 56–60) points to the appearance of the goddess Flora, the floral beauty of the sheepshearing, the antimasque satyrs' dance, the transformation of Hermione in the statue scene and other "spectacular visual effects" as belonging to the "sphere of the masque. . . . [57] Aside from the obvious masque influence . . . the whole play is textured with sensational and spectacular elements—pageantry, ceremony, and ritual—which . . . [58] overwhelm us visually. . . . [59] Moreover . . . as the play progresses the visual and spectacular volume increases, along with, of course, dramatic tensions. . . . [60] Spectacular stagecraft is fused, dramatically and visually, with theme, character, plot, and symbol." JACQUOT (in LEECH & MARGESON, 1972, pp. 164–5) lists the "affinities between [*WT*] and the masque" as "recourse to the supernatural, and the happy ending after unbelievable adventures"; the fundamental difference is that *WT*'s reconciliations and reunions are obtained only after "the trial and repentance" of Leontes through long years in which "the force of evil has first to exhaust itself. . . . A number of masques, it is true, imply a reversal of condition, the breaking of a spell and the freeing of captives. But in [*WT*] the events leading to a happier state and a brighter vision are set in a much broader perspective." BRADBROOK (*Monument*, 1976, p. 210): The audience's foreknowledge of the secret of the statue scene is "in itself . . . in the tradition of the masque rather than the theatre, for in masques an element of shock and wonder was integral to the effect." FRYE (in KAY & JACOBS, 1978, p. 30): "The structure of the romance . . . approximates the complete polarity of the antimasque and masque. . . . In the romances, the blocking worlds are an intense contrast to the comic spirit, often forming tragic actions in themselves, as in [*WT*] particularly. Something in these worlds has to be condemned and annihilated, not simply reconciled or won over, before the festive conclusion can take place. What is annihilated is the state of mind [e.g. Leontes's jealousy] rather than the people in those states, though some of the people get annihilated too." SPENDER (1982, 1:235) also discusses the play's use of conventions of the masque.

Many critics accept F1's designation of *WT* as comedy, though comedy with a difference. MOWAT (1969, p. 46): The play offers an expansion of Sh.'s comic vision. The first half is "grotesque, rather warped comedy, issuing into purer comedy in the second half of the play. . . . By patterning the first part of this comedy along superficially tragic lines, Shakespeare offers us a view of man hardly to be achieved in more straightforward comedy." MOWAT (1976, p. 99) adds: *WT* offers a new "open form drama, specifically, in which cause-and-effect patterns are broken, generic conventions abandoned . . . and dramatic illusion repeatedly broken through narrative intrusion, spectacle, and other sudden disturbances of the aesthetic distance." CHAMPION (1971, p. 447): By "literally touching the emotional strings of tragedy," yet maintaining audience detachment or even disallowing "the spectator's total emotional commitment," Sh. produces "an art form which on occasion resembles tragedy in terms of narrative but is quite distinct from it in terms of the relationship between the character and the spectator. The result is . . . Shakespeare's most complex comedy." FOAKES (1971, pp. 94–5): Designations other than comedy are misleading "when in fact [the] drive to establish what [Giovanni Battista] Guarini called 'the comic order' is clear from the start. However, the dispassionate, primarily psychological treatment of character noticed in the [*95*] late tragedies feeds into the last plays, in which characters tend to be given, not explained or motivated." SIEMON (1972, p. 442): "The readjustment of comic form to accommodate a penetrating analysis of the nature of evil and of its effect on society reaches fruition" in *WT*'s efficient conflation of villain and hero in Leontes. LATIMER (1984, p. 127): Those surrounding him "take action to steer Leontes from his disastrous course. . . . That response, shared by all the members of the Sicilian court, but centered in Camillo, Paulina, Antigonus, and Hermione, is predominantly a comic one. They work to deflect Leontes' rage . . . from his intended victims and to prevent his potentially tragic action from becoming fully developed. They form a community which . . . protects him from his own worst deeds. . . . This comic action . . . begins the moment Leontes' suspicions are first aired and forms a continuous line of action that unifies the entire play."

Other critics are more interested in the play's pastoral elements. CHAMBERS (ed. 1907, pp. 10–11): Act 4 of *WT* marks the first time Sh. has "given himself up to any full indulgence" in the pastoral tradition—the "idealization of the shepherd's life which the imagination of the Renascence poets, first on the continent and then in England, had built up upon the eclogues of Theocritus and of Virgil, and upon certain chansons of love-adventure between knights and village maidens. . . . The poetry of the reaction from civilization . . . [exalts] the simplicity and content of the meadows above the pomps of mortal state," though the pastoral tradition is (p. 11) "never to be mistaken for a transcript of rustic life. Its significance resides, not in any fidelity to the fact of the peasant, but in its relation to the state of mind of the world-wearied courtier or scholar who writes it." BERNARD (1979, pp. 219–20), however: Failure to go beyond "the conventional bucolic features of the fourth act to explore the pastoralism of the play as a whole" results in a reading "not so much wrong as it is incomplete. . . . [*220*] [Sh.] fully appropriates the spirit of Renaissance pastoralism and embodies it in an organically, even definitively pastoral work." BRYANT (1963, pp. 387–93): Sh. uses conventions from the Greek pastoral eclogue (humor and realism), its Roman adaptation (satire of the court), the Greek romance (seeming disparities of birth between the male and female protagonists), and earlier Italian and English versions of these forms (Autolycus-like characters) to transform the conventions of the pastoral into an involved, subtle commentary on appearance and reality. He nonetheless writes (p. 393) "within a well-defined tradition and the material he used was chosen consciously from that tradition. . . . In [*WT*], the evil lies not in appearance itself but in the royal mind which insists that appearance is reality. To explore this premise, Shakespeare converts the stereotyped conventions of the pastoral drama into highly original instruments which combine to form one of the best of his last plays."

TINKLER (1937, pp. 349, 351–2): Sh. recognizes "the essential values of the pastoral life . . . and there is no attempt to falsify these by presenting them in a sentimental light. . . . [*351*] The limitations of the shepherd community are readily recognized, but they do not necessarily invalidate the essential values of that mode. . . . [*352*] Continual twisting of a seemingly simple attitude is achieved in an amazing variety of ways, as for example when the ballad singing is used, not only to reinforce the fertility aspect of the rural mode . . . but also to expose the credulity of the rustics." DORAN (1954, p. 215) agrees: Sh.'s "last three romances are all to some degree affected by pastoralism. . . . [*WT*], especially, is informed by the whole complex tradition. On the one hand, the charm of the Golden Age becomes the charm of youth and a restoration of hope and goodness to older people who have spoiled their lives with suspicion and discord; but, on the other hand, we are not allowed to grow sentimental over Perdita's sheepcote." COOPER (1977, pp. 175, 178): "The modern association of pastoral with the beauty of the natural world is given almost its first expression here" in an (p. 178) "affirmation of the golden world within the fallen, presented not as a piece of romantic optimism but as a counterweight to a tragic view of the human condition."

Some criticism focuses on pastoralism with a difference. SNIDER (1877, 2:71): "Bohemia . . . is a poor, mountainous, uncivilized region, inhabited by shepherds. But it is free from the strife and calamity of Sicilia; its people are simple and humble, yet at the same time they are joyous and humane. . . . Such a society is transitory. . . . It develops contradictions within itself by which it is destroyed. Its destiny is to return to Sicilia, which has passed through such difficulties and harmonized them," an idea he repeats (1890, p. 493). ROSENMEYER (1969, pp. 21, 24-5): The Hesiodic tradition is "activist, critical, and realistic," the Hesiodic "code of country living is one of discipline and foresight," and the British pastoral tradition, including *WT*, (p. 24) has some of the Hesiodic in it. The (p. 25) "grimness and absurdities of the Hesiodic world are emphasized in order to free the imagination for the perception of pastoral beauty and pastoral freedom. . . . The use of the Hesiodic strain as a deflector . . . often has the effect of putting the pastoral in a humorous light." LERNER (1970; 1972, pp. 128-9): Sh. seems to be "pushing his pastoral towards radicalism" by having Florizel fall in love with a shepherdess who (p. 129) "expresses fear but no guilt" over the possibility that she is an unfit mate for a prince. Though "this seems democratic, the catch . . . is so obvious that we can easily miss it: Perdita is not a shepherdess after all, but a king's daughter, as we have known all the time. . . . Shakespeare has shown the democratic implications of pastoral and then betrayed them" by offering a "glow of satisfaction at the brushing aside of degree and wealth, of delight that true worth and beauty can be recognised in a cottage" but, at the same time, setting up "a rule that quite clearly stops cottage lasses from getting ideas."

JARRELL (1980, p. 328): *WT* is "a sexual pastoral the real subject of which is the emotional connection between one generation and the next: the Oedipus complex. This deliberately improbable pastoral combines a concentrated, altogether incomparable treatment of jealousy with the most idealized and Arcadian of love affairs. The 'perilous stuff' with which *Hamlet* and so many other plays had been charged is no longer perilous" in *WT*. It is, "so to speak, neurosis recollected in tranquillity." STUDING (1982, pp. 218, 224-6): *WT* uses the pastoral mode "not as convention but, rather, as a vehicle to develop and forward the story. . . . Instead of pastoral

. . . conventions, we have pastoral *devices* that function to mirror courtly values and echo Leontes' sinful passion. Especially in [the] context of the first three acts of the play, the situations of pastoralism often cast a negative aura on country life": Polixenes succumbs to a Leontes-like passion; Perdita faces a king's wrath as her mother did; Florizel's escape parallels Mamillius's death; the shepherds succumb to the riches of the corrupt Sicilian court; (p. 224) the satyrs' dance, lusty and bawdy, is itself "a property of court values and entertainment. . . . [*226*] The country scenes counter the nature of pastoralism. Bohemia is not a refuge offering a serious value contrast to another society." See also LASCELLES (1959, pp. 85-6), WEINSTEIN (1971, pp. 97-9), and MCFARLAND (1972, pp. 123-4).

For one group of critics, *tragicomedy* is the term that best describes the play. SEMON (1974, p. 89): "It can . . . [make] a statement about the world which expresses neither an essentially comic nor . . . an essentially tragic point of view; tragicomedy is not subject to the common generic conceptions." HIRST (1984, pp. 26, 29): Sh. "came under the influence of Fletcher, and through him Guarini," and thus contributed to the tragicomic genre. The final plays, including *WT*, reveal (p. 29) "a struggle to find a theatrical form, a dramatic structure which could not only contain the diversity of genres he was treating, but give them unity, coherence and meaning." GREENBLATT (1988, p. 125): "The close of a tragicomedy frequently requires the audience to will imaginatively a miraculous turn of events, often against the evidence of its senses (as when . . . at the close of [*WT*] the audience accepts the fiction that Hermione is an unbreathing statue in order to experience the wonder of her resurrection)." A few critics suggest a mingling of tragicomedy and romance. THORNDIKE (1901; 1965, p. 163): "In its mixture of tragic and idyllic, in ingeniously dramatic situations and dénouement, in weakened characterization, and in a more dramatic style, [*WT*] belongs to the romance type of Beaumont and Fletcher." RISTINE (1910, p. 113) anticipates and ADAMS (1923, pp. 411, 417) and FRYE (1970, p. 123) follow HERFORD (ed. 1916-, p. vii) in putting *WT* in that "particular class of [tragicomedies] which have been known in England latterly as 'Romances', marked by . . . a deliberately unreal use of space and time." FRYE (p. 125) adds: "Young lovers share center stage with older generations," their problems are directly connected to the problems of mature love, and the play points to "a more encompassing reconciliation between generations within the total human community." ABARTIS (1977, pp. 44-7) acknowledges that certain tragicomic incidentals (e.g., "an ambiguous oracular pronouncement, one or more pastoral scenes, a disguised maiden, a lost child, an absolute villain or villainess, a perfect hero or heroine, a love which is threatened, and a heroine who is calumniated") derive from narrative romance. Sh. then adapts these elements "to a dramatic medium, the essentials of which are character and conflict." Along the way, he provides that which is (p. 46) specific to tragicomedy as a dramatic form— "the manipulation of surprises, reversals, recognitions, and the sine qua non, 'the happy change.'" Sh. also explores (p. 47) "serious moral issues. . . . The surprises and happy reversals have an ethical point." EDWARDS (*Progress*, 1986, pp. 161, 173): "Romance is a useful term in Shakespeare criticism, but it is not confined to the last comedies and it does not explain them. It is better to take the late 'romances' as a sub-group of particular importance within the wider category of tragicomedy," in the Shakespearean version of which (p. 173) the consequences of the tragic crisis are evaded through "extraordinary interventions which often seem to belong to another level or kind of drama."

Romance seems the most fitting designation to other critics. NUTTALL (1966, pp. 9-10) explains: *WT* is "closely associated, in time and in genre, with [*Per.*, *Cym.*, and *Tmp.*]; that is to say, . . . the group of plays which Coleridge termed the Romances [see COLERIDGE, 1960, 1:117-18]. These plays conform to a loose Elizabethan definition of comedy in that the principal persons of the drama, though they may fall into great distress, are ultimately spared for a happy ending in love and reunion. Thus it is perfectly fair to call them comedies. . . . The reason why most critics and commentators have been unwilling to rest content with the designation 'comedy' is that without being actually inaccurate it fails to convey any hint of what is distinctive about these plays [their pattern of loss and renewal, their special sense of myth]. . . . [*10*] A term was needed sufficiently comprehensive to cover all four plays, sufficiently narrow to exclude the rest of the comedies. 'Romance' . . . has proved useful." CHILDRESS (1974, pp. 45-7, 51-4) disagrees: Romance became a popular label "because of the breadth of interpretation it permits. It is not a generic term at all. . . . [*46*] The discrepancy between 'romance'—the medieval genre—and the modern meanings of 'romantic' is enormous; yet Northrop Frye, E. C. Pettet, R. G. Hunter, and others use it apparently as an adjective for . . . Shakespearean 'romance'. . . . [*47*] If we do not try to define romance too narrowly, then it is easy enough to apply the term to the later plays" despite unusual elements such as (p. 51) Sh.'s use of the grotesque, "alien to romance [but] especially effective in distancing the spectator from the action. . . . [*52*] Antigonus, by romance standards, is cowardly and unfeeling, and his loyalties are misplaced. But the punishment that follows his misdeed is too swift, too cruel and too comic. . . . His death is not tragic, nor comic, nor satiric: it is grotesque. The distance between romance and [*WT*] is greatest in this scene. . . . [*54*] Clearly a new terminology is needed. . . . We must recognize that . . . these final plays are something other than 'romances.'" He does not say what. ORGEL (ed. 1996, p. 3) also maintains that "notions of genre have changed radically since the Renaissance. Genres for us are exclusive and definitive, whereas for the Renaissance they tended to be inclusive and relational. . . . Attempts to move beyond the circularity of the definition, refine its terms, [and] establish the genre within a tradition, have revealed a good deal about the history of romance, but perhaps nothing so much as its ultimate inadequacy as a critical category for Shakespearean drama." Despite these arguments, many critics adopt the designation.

Among those who do, many focus on the play's classical associations. CHAMBERS (ed. 1907, pp. 5-6): What "Aristotle distinguished under the name of Anagnorisis, as a typical element of classical tragedy . . . in the process of time has generally borne a romantic handling, and has gathered about itself all the associations of romantic interest," found in specific elements like (p. 6) "truth that will out through disguises, wrongs that in the end become rights again, wanderings that lead homewards in the eventide." WILSON (ed. 1931, p. xv): "Oracles, shipwrecks, royal infants exposed on mountain-sides or cast adrift on perilous seas to be rescued by poor folk and nurtured as shepherd boys and cottage maids; pastoral love-making, daisy-chains, sheepfold prowled about by bear . . . search by desolated or repentant parents, rescue and recognition by the aid of tokens . . . all these belong to the outfit of 'classical' romance which the Renaissance brought back into fashion, superseding the romances of Chivalry." CRAIG (1948, p. 337), acknowledging the same constituents, suggests that the play combines "two sorts of Greek romance, the one full of adventure, passion, and danger; the other gentle and pastoral." SCHANZER (ed. 1969, pp. 12-16) suggests a combination of Greek Romance and Shn. comedy: The happy ending of *WT* "makes the plot conform not only to the conventions of Greek romance but also to those of Shakespeare's comedies. . . . None of [the comedies] includes the death of a central character who is a model of virtue. . . . The Queen had to be kept alive if the play was to conform to the pattern. . . . [*16*] The romance motif of a statue impersonated by a living woman believed dead, the sacrifice of psychological verisimilitude to theatrical effect[,] . . . the subordination of everything else to the rousing of a feeling of wonder—all this is characteristic of Greek romance." And though GESNER (1970, pp. 81-2) calls *WT* "an almost separate genre—a kind of special academic discipline within the Shakespearean canon, a romance genre which frequently disregards narrative or psychological reality and moves its way with sweeping metrical freedom from states of prosperity through tragic upheaval, loss, and destruction, to restored order and tranquillity"—she concludes that (p. 82) "this separate subdivision of the Shakespeare canon . . . belongs to the tradition of the Greek romances." DEAN (1979, pp. 11-13) also finds a "Hellenistic pattern" in these elements, noting that "the complexity itself stands out in the dramatic foreground as one of the most powerful impressions received by the audience from the romance experience. . . . [*13*] The complete work of romance will eventually unify disunified action by first creating the impression of disorder," then retrieving "our sense of an ordered universe" (through the recovery of "whomever was thought to be lost," for example).

Others emphasize the surprises and improbabilities of Romance. SYMONS (in IRVING & MARSHALL, ed. 1890, 7:318) calls *WT* "a typically romantic drama" because it is "constructed in defiance of probabilities, which it rides over happily. It has all the license and it has all the charm of a fairy tale; while the matters of which it treats are often serious enough, ready to become tragic at any moment." MATTHEWS (1913; 1970, pp. 336-7) specifically mentions *WT*'s time gap, lack of emotional unity, mingling of disparate scenes, use of extraneous spectacular effects (the bear, the dances), and (p. 337) the final series of discoveries and recognitions culminating in the shock of surprise at the statue scene. WENDELL (1894, p. 385): "One touch . . . [which] tends to show that Shakspere would deliberately guard against any impression of reality . . . [is his] wanton departure from geographic fact," thus placing the Romance "in no real world, but rather in such a world just beyond the limits of reality." CHAMBERS (1925, pp. 296-7): In *WT*, "the course of human affairs is swathed and interpreted by the enigmatic utterances of an oracle. . . . For the philosophy of the universe, that in Shakespeare's later moods lies behind and determines romance, the amazement is converted into the symbol and manifestation of an overruling force working by hidden ways to bring the ends of man to good. . . . [*297*] Romance, indeed, will not have you apply too searching a psychology. . . . But art may take its standpoint at more than one degree of remoteness from real life." MINCOFF (1941, pp. 14, 18): Sh. probably sacrificed his integrity deliberately, choosing, in "the new fashion of writing introduced by Beaumont and Fletcher," to exploit surprise "as a definite dramatic effect to be aimed at. . . . [*18*] [*WT*] belongs to the genre of romance or melodrama that was finally to establish the use of the unexpected on the stage." PETTET (1949, pp. 163–4) summarizes: The play's "mass of incident," its "vigour and excitement of narrative . . . [are] quite unhampered by considerations of verisimilitude. . . . The romances aim deliberately at the far-fetched, the astounding and the incredible. With realism jettisoned, extravagance becomes a virtue. . . . Strictures based on the criterion of realism are quite irrelevant . . . and they would certainly have meant nothing to Shakespeare, who was content to satisfy the tastes of an audience that had been conditioned by centuries of romantic verse and [*164*] prose to enjoy a story of fantastic make-believe." EDWARDS (1958, p. 15) and HOLLAND (1964, p. 285) also find the romances marked by the farfetched and the fantastic. (HOLLAND adds: "This can be fairly trashy stuff, all things considered.")

Other critics, like HUNTER (1965, pp. 137–8), accept the special atmosphere "in which miracle is constantly possible and finally occurs" but also maintain that the miraculous, such as Hermione's "statue" coming to life, (p. 138) "can usually be explained naturalistically." WELLS ("Romance," 1966, pp. 65, 70): Leontes's personal responsibility for the deaths and misfortunes of other characters in the play "diminishes to some extent the part played in the action by those typical romance agents, chance, fate, fortune, etc. Shakespeare is humanizing his source, giving it greater relevance to normal life, making it a story of human beings rather than of puppets. . . . [*70*] In [*WT*] there are no macrocosmic implications. . . . Shakespeare has produced a work that is far more powerful as a human document . . . not by denying the romance elements in Greene's book but by readjusting them—sometimes adding to them, sometimes toning them down with a modified realism, and always investing them with a poetic rather than a mundane reality." PETERSON (1973, pp. 153–4): *WT* "exploits the license of romance to focus upon a reality beyond the level of physical and psychological verisimilitude. . . . [*154*] Shakespeare's concerns here are not with realistic illusion. . . . He is concerned to 'rehearse' the ways in which the past may affect the present and shape the future." HATTORI (1982, p. 87): Sh. is "engaged in an almost overly conscientious application of realism. As if he feels indebted to his fabulous plot, he toils over lining every action of every character with realism."

WILLIAMS (1967, pp. 1–2, 38) espouses a critical viewpoint that centers on the human experience within the context of the Romance: "Shakespearean romance can be defined as a poetic solution to the metaphysical problem, in Elizabethan terms, of the place of Mutability and Nature in human life. . . . [*2*] Romance, then, involves both a special manipulation of natural law and a peculiar sort of experience in response to the workings of that law. . . . [*38*] While controlling the laws of his romantic universe from above . . . Shakespeare has avoided an abstract discussion of his philosophical point of view. His metaphysics are translated into human sensibilities." FELPERIN (1972, pp. 61, 66): "The natural and social orders are seen not as essentially good in the romances, but at best as not good enough. For in these plays . . . a recalcitrance to human desire [is] built into the universe itself." Yet the romances end with (p. 66) "the recovery of spiritual integrity as well as personal and social identity." RICHMOND (1977-8, pp. 339, 341): "In the Renaissance the romance was systematically attacked by humanists . . . because it distracted from proper masculine concerns. But the poets . . . did not reject the wisdom of romance. . . . Shakespeare evolves from the tragedy of Othello . . . to [*WT*], where he tells the same story with a happy ending because in the world of romance . . . everything is possible. The play is a triumph, but the values are traditionally more feminine than masculine. . . . [*341*] In Shakespeare, then, humanity's future lies in the feminine principle, for which his respect and admiration are so vast. . . . This is the ultimate feminism, though it is a variety shunned by most feminists."

Genre is also discussed by NICOLL (1958, p. 51), DRIVER (1960, pp. 179-80), CUTTS (1968, "Introduction"), LANGMAN (1976, p. 195), EGGERS (1979, p. 455), and HALE (1985, pp. 147-51).

Themes and Significance

TIME'S MUTABILITY

WIGSTON ([1884], p. 12) observes that Time as Chorus "points to something serious, and beyond the mere surface of the play"—nothing less, according to WALLER (1970, p. 135), than the "thematic justification of the play's intention and meaning. . . . Time is established as the medium of all human growth and fulfillment, and the play itself is now seen as the unfolding of events by Father Time himself." COSGROVE (1977, p. 178) also makes this point. EWBANK (1964, p. 84): Sh. "makes the Triumph of Time into a controlling theme of his tale; in doing so he transforms what the conventional motto suggests—a simple victory of Time, the Father of Truth—into a dramatic exploration of the manifold meanings of Time," one of which critics like KERMODE (ed. 1963, pp. xxvi-xxvii) find in the juxtaposition of "Time as destroyer and renewer, that which ruins the work of men but is the father of truth, . . . [and that which seems] aimlessly destructive . . . [*xxvii*] but is in the end seen to be 'merciful' because it finally . . . must renew truth." YOUNG (1972, p. 134) agrees: Sh. makes linear time the irrevocable "enemy to human aspirations," cyclical time a restorative "in harmony with man's hopes."

A number of critics find greater significance in the way Time connects the world of the audience to the world onstage. BETHELL (ed. 1956, p. 25) notes that one theme of the play juxtaposes "various 'planes of reality'"—the timeless imaginative world of the play as seen against the real world of time, for example. "Time tells us that even 'this present'—the *now* of the audience—will itself become an old tale: our own lives are given the same degree of reality or unreality as the tale of Leontes, and only Time is timeless." FELPERIN (1972, pp. 227, 230): "The natural cycles of birth, death, and rebirth . . . are existentially realized on stage. . . . The seasons change in the world of this play just as they do in the real world. . . . The imagery faithfully reflects not only the world outside the play but the world inside the play as well. . . . [*230*] By soliciting our imaginative cooperation in the dramatic process . . . the Chorus of Time also works to make us aware of the play as a play. . . . Time mediates between the worlds of life and art and plays upon our sense of their separateness and their continuity, their dissimilarity and their resemblance. He reminds us, that is, that his powers of destruction and recreation (his speech [1580–1611] is the apotheosis of the play's imagery of natural process) extend beyond the play world into the real world, and that the principals [of the play] are subject to the same laws as we." DEAN (1979, pp. 252–4) finds in Time's appearance "one of the most serious moments in the play—for *our* ruler is speaking, the ruler of nature and art. . . . We are entertained and informed by a power we are subject to in the very moment we watch its ingratiating performance. . . . [*253*] We are forced to recognize the ineluctable motions governing life, . . . the common process . . . in which both audience and actors grow fresh and wax stale. . . . [*254*] Time's appearance in [*WT*] brings out the idea of an entity which is both ruthless and ceaseless, pleasing and informative." GARNER (1985, pp. 347–50) concurs: "In drama, time is a theme by necessity, for in the medium of performance it stands as an inescapable backdrop to dramatic action, as well as a fundamental condition of theatrical life." Sh.'s (p. 349) investigation of the relationship between the present and its temporal contexts extends to (p. 350) "his audience's temporal experience of the play in performance."

Some critics think the theme of Time the destroyer predominates. TRAVERSI (1969, 2:300): "The action of time, as seen at this stage of the play [124–45], is a corrupting action; experience, as it enters into the life of innocence, destroys the foundations of spontaneous friendship." ORGEL (ed. 1996, p. 17) is less restrictive: *WT*'s "realities are not the facts of history but the terrifying truths of the inner life— the destructiveness of jealousy, the creations of sexual fear, the complexities of love, the imponderable unpredictability of family relationships and deep, long-lasting friendships, the divided loyalties inherent in even the most devoted service. The insistent theme is time; but a time removed from history and located within the family, time as defined by generations, by youth and age, by the relations between parents and children, and by the blood-brotherhood of male bonding starting in early childhood." Like HOLLAND (1964, p. 291), EDWARDS (1968, pp. 148–9) sees as meaningful Sh.'s suggestion of "the inevitable decay of whatever is fresh and new. If spring comes, can winter be far behind? When Time enters as Chorus, he is not only a device to bridge a long gap in the narrative [*149*] of the story: he is inexorable time, whose hand is upon Perdita and Florizel." Yet LINDENBAUM (1986, pp. 126–7) concludes: [*WT*] is "a celebration of life . . . [*127*] as it exists in . . . a world governed by time. It is Shakespeare's considerable achievement in this play . . . that he can bring us to accept the view of time as constantly moving forward and hence eroding and destructive, and to accept it not merely with resignation but with equanimity and even enthusiasm."

Other critics, including ARTHOS (1964, p. 161), assert that the main point of the play is "the power of time to redeem." SMITH (1966, p. 46): "Time changes all things, but it is the regenerative rather than the destructive aspects of mutability which are stressed. Without change and decay there can be no continuance of life." ANSARI (1979, p. 131) also calls attention to "the triumph of the choric Time over the tangle of events in the play." RUNDUS (1974, p. 123) regards Time's speech "as a tribute to the . . . dynamic force which will soon restore and sanctify, through the processes of regeneration (Perdita and Hermione) and unceasing penance (Leontes), a harmony and ethos earlier destroyed by . . . Leontes' jealousy." FOAKES (1971, p. 131), however, finds that Time is merely "an observer. . . . This figure of Time seems to claim his independence from human affairs. . . . He is not concerned to bring truth to light or vindicate innocence. . . . Time focuses our attention on events, and . . . remains, like providence, inscrutable." Additional discussion can be found in CHEW (1947, p. 90), NUTTALL (1966, p. 38), PETERSON (*Time*, 1973, pp. 155-7), KAMACHI (1979, pp. 28, 35), LLOYD EVANS (1982, pp. 367-74), EDWARDS ("Seeing," 1986, p. 86), LENZ (1986, pp. 102-5), WILDERS (1988, pp. 264-6), ADAMS (1989, p. 115).

NATURE (AND ART)

For a few critics—LEAVIS (1942, p. 345) is one—the Nature which gives "depth and richness of significance" to the play is equated with "nature at large," a force associated with "the concrete presence of time in its rhythmic processes" and all forms of "growth, decay and rebirth." HILLMAN (1979, pp. 16-17): Perdita's flowers symbolize "the richness and beauty of nature's creations, on the one hand, their fragility and transience on the other. . . . [17] She shows herself highly conscious of the changing seasons" (and mortality), but she counters "by affirming life and love . . . in a way which implies that death, too, is a part of nature and that love can flourish in its shadow." Some critics also recognize, with FRYE (1962, p. 246), that "nature is associated, not with the credible, but with the incredible: nature as an order is subordinated to the nature that yearly confronts us with the impossible miracle of renewed life," in the (IDEM, "Nature," 1965, p. 56) "world of higher nature which romance approaches," a world "not of time but of the fulfillment of time." KNIGHT (1947; 1966, pp. 90-1): "Nature rules our play" and is "responsible for the miraculous perpetuation and re-creation of worn and sinful man." The miraculous can have (p. 91) "Christian impact," though the "natural majesty explored is also in part Hellenic." In the play's descriptions of Nature, SEN GUPTA (1950, p. 223) discerns "the workings of a superhuman agency from whom proceed life and beauty"; BUSH (1956, pp. 130-2) sees a Nature that is "the source of life and love, a seen and unseen lesson in goodness, and a creator of innocence and bounty—a perfect image, undoubted, unconfined and unquestioned. . . . [132] Nature and art are gentle rivals in the creation of the beautiful and wonderful, but art can never match the miracle of natural things." For additional criticism, see SCHANZER (ed. 1969, pp. 36-8),

NICOLL (1952, pp. 171-2), HOLBROOK (1964, pp. 134-5), and WILLIAMS (1967, pp. 21-38).

Of more particular significance is the critics' identification of, first, the Perdita-Polixenes debate over gardening [1887-1921] and, second, the statue scene [3183 ff.] as the primary loci of *WT*'s juxtaposition of nature and art. Examining and taking up Perdita's side, COOPER (1977, p. 141) reminds us that since the demise of the "Golden Age . . . [the] life of pure Nature was damaged by the invention of arts, of building, of commerce." Thus when Perdita rejects grafting, "she is insisting on the integrity of Nature before the 'improving' influences of Art. Love itself must be simple and whole . . . and she will have as little to do with the art of make-up to attract Florizel as with the false breeding of flowers." DOLAN (1993, pp. 227-8): "Perdita rejects the conflation of nature and art . . . espoused in the play by Polixenes. Perdita will not regard nature — or, by extension, herself — as 'impotent and defective,' as in need of improvement. In her view, the art that produces the gillyflower does not embellish nature but competes with and effaces it. . . . [*228*] Aligning great creating nature with her own ability to breed, Perdita disdains those who prefer the gillyflower and the painted face, denouncing their taste as corrupt and insulting to nature."

Other critics assume a position that transcends both Perdita's and Polixenes's. KNIGHT (1947; 1966, p. 105): The speakers are "at cross purposes, since one is referring to art, the other to artificiality. . . . Human civilization, art and religion are clearly in one sense part of 'great creating nature', and so is everything else. But Perdita takes her stand on natural simplicity, growing from the unforced integrity of her own country up-bringing in opposition to the artificialities of . . . the court: she is horrified at dishonouring nature by human trickery. Observe that both alike reverence 'great creating nature', though differing in their conclusions." FRYE (1962, p. 244): "What happens in [*WT*] is the opposite of the art of the gardener as Polixenes describes it [the gardener (p. 241) "may help or change nature . . . but can do so only through nature's power"]. A society which is artificial in a limited sense at the beginning of the play becomes at the end still artificial, but natural as well. Nature provides the means for the regeneration of artifice. But still it is true that 'The art itself is nature' [1908]," a customary disclaimer, according to KERMODE (ed. 1963, pp. xxxiii-xxxiv), when "the art of the gardener in improving wild natural stocks was treated as a figure of the distinctive human power to improve and civilize the environment." Perdita, however, makes the case that the gardener is "not an improver of nature but a pander. . . . Shakespeare's purpose is not to identify himself with one or other side so much as to tell the audience that the great topic of the relations between art and nature are relevant to his purposes; to establish [*xxxiv*] . . . the 'better nature' of Perdita, and to prepare the way for a climactic [statue] scene in which . . . we shall see finally the incomparable work of 'great creating Nature.'"

Nonetheless critics attempt to establish which side of the art-nature antithesis Sh. takes. Most put him on the side of art, some making Julio Romano the representative figure of the artist. WAAGE (1980, pp. 65-6): *WT* owes something to "Italian Renaissance art theory as well as art practice." Sh. displays "a certain boldness" in citing Romano, whose "morally lascivious" illustrations of Aretino were well-known in England, as "the artist capable of rendering life beautifully enough to engender the miracle of divine (and connubial) love." More to the point, Sh.'s allusion (p. 66) "at a most solemn moment to a painter whose name had such unattractive connotations" might reveal that "this provocative use of a specific artist's name" illustrates a theme of *WT* and contemporary works—the power of art not merely to imitate nature but to "transcend and transform it." GURR (1982, pp. 57–60): "The only instance anywhere of Shakespeare referring to a real, known artist" suggests that Sh. "knew exactly what he was doing with the Romano reference. . . . That the reference is to the Romano who drew the erotic pictures for which Aretino wrote his *sonnetti lussuriosi* and which became known as Aretino's postures . . . [*58*] would certainly give a point, not merely to the otherwise pointless specification of this 'rare Italian master' . . . but also to the . . . exclamation with which Leontes greets the sight of the statue—'Her natural posture!' [3212]. . . . [*59*] Shakespeare in this final act of the play is emphasising the unnatural, nonrealistic nature of Leontes' redemption. . . . [*60*] If we see Hermione truly restored to life . . . we obscure the essential point that art is not life, and that restoration and redemption are functions of an art which, however lawful, is precisely unnatural." HOMAN (1973, p. 73), however, puts Sh. on the side of nature: the excellence of Romano's statue "results solely from the fact that a real-life woman has assumed a position on the pedestal. . . . This moment when [Sh.] supposedly reveals his deepest thoughts about art is actually a tribute to life rather than to art." (Comment on the relationship between art, nature, and the natural work of art may be found in n. 3104–5 on Julio Romano.)

More often, however, critics focus on Sh.'s commitment to his own art. FARRELL (1983, pp. 94–5) states the case generally: "Shakespeare's conspicuous humility as an artist disguises striving for autonomy. . . . The extremes of the artist's role parallel the ambivalent valuation of art in the Renaissance. . . . Like the artist, art is nothing and yet supreme. . . . Immediately self-effacing, the dramatist may nevertheless be 'godlike' in the larger transaction which is the play," since the communal experience of playwright, actor, and audience as sharers in the drama being played out onstage (p. 95) "allows the artist to achieve autonomy even as he honors the bonds of community." Of *WT* specifically, WIGSTON (1884, pp. 13, 16–17) says: The play may be "the self-reflecting portrait of Shakespeare's own art in conflict with Time"; he (p. 16) "reconciles not only the divorce and disharmony of his own art . . . but that of classical and present times also. . . . [*17*] Does Hermione represent Ceres, and by reflection Shakespeare's own art . . . ? Is Proserpina the lost unity of Shakespeare's art, and as summer, the full glory of its spiritual light?" FOAKES (1971, pp. 134, 143–4): The disguises assumed by Polixenes, Camillo, and Florizel say that "clothes seem to make the man, and art in this way conceals, alters, sometimes mends nature. . . . [Disguises] also indicate various possibilities for deceit and sharp practice. . . . It would be . . . a partial view that finds only a pattern of lies and deceptions, and of art affecting nature for the worse." Instead, *WT* (p. 143) focuses on the contradictions in the relation of art to nature, showing us "art as, at one end of the spectrum, artifice, trickery, deception, disguise, cheating. . . . At the other end of the spectrum,

. . . deception and [*144*] disguise may be used to bring about restoration and harmony." These ends lead WATSON (1981, p. 13) to cite cutting and pruning references (1359–60, 1903–6) in claiming that Leontes is "restored by Art. . . . Such cuttings have paradoxically healed rather than rent the flaws in not just one person, but the infected society that he leads. . . . Cutting abounds in the world . . . of nature and that of the play. When what is truly of noble stock, having fallen into disgrace in fortune and men's eyes, is restored to its rightful place through some kind of Art . . . everyone breathes easier." ALEXANDER (1979, p. 242): With the statue scene Sh. acknowledges that one way to "satisfy the longing to immortalize what is immediately perfect is through art." BARKAN (1981, p. 661): The scene gives us "a definition of the power of art," characteristically expressed by Sh. "in terms of mystery, madness, and inspiration." WHITE (1985, p. 155): "Shakespeare achieves a resurrection that art can bring on various levels." He retrieves Greene's story from obscurity by "placing its fable in a medium that demands performance by living people" and, in reviving Hermione, brings life "in a literal sense to a story which . . . had closed with death," but which now concludes every performance "on a note of hard-won hope." HONIGMANN (1982, pp. 112–14): "Where Jonson invoked Cicero's definition to condemn art that runs away from nature and truth, Shakespeare falls back on the customary Renaissance defence, that art is the agent of nature and operates within nature's domain." By Ciceronian definition, comedy should imitate life, be an "image of truth." But in *WT*, both Time and Polixenes argue that "nature must not be seen as unchangeable, — so why call it a crime when the dramatist adjusts custom and nature to suit his purposes? . . . [*113*] Shakespeare saw an opening [cites Mopsa, Dorcas, and Autolycus discussing "true" ballads, 2082–2106], and mercilessly derided those who insist on truth in literature. . . . [*114*] The play's questioning of Nature, Life and Truth climaxes in the statue-scene. . . . In a play in which Shakespeare defends the dramatist's right to disregard law and custom, it is surely no accident that everything converges upon a 'marvel' that defies all rational explanation."

A number of critics refashion the traditional Renaissance opposition of art to nature into an opposition of illusion to reality, putting Sh. and *WT* on the side of theatrical illusion and artificiality. As DRIVER (1960, p. 179) points out, the theme of truth opposed to illusion is natural in plays because theater itself is "based upon illusion and pretense as inherent properties in its form," but the "theme of truth and illusion is accentuated in tragi-comedy because . . . it relies so frankly on theatrical pretense." RABKIN (1967, p. 220) adds: "We find ourselves believing in imaginary characters as if they were real. . . . Much of the power of [*WT*] is generated by our sense of the elusive but compelling analogy between the art with which it imitates life and the life that it imitates." EGAN (1975, p. 1) agrees. GOLDMAN (1972, pp. 124–7): To understand the vision of Sh.'s last plays, we must understand that the "great destructive forces" of Time and Nature are "indifferently restorative, [but] restorative enough to keep growth happening." *WT* makes an effort "to find dramatic equivalents for this endless superhuman recreation . . . [*127*] by striking reminders of theatricality, by devices that make us specially conscious that as an audience we are partisans of the happy ending, that we admire the working out of intricate plots or the reunion of scattered families as we enjoy the recurrence of spring." ROSE (1972, pp. 169, 171): "Art itself becomes a dominant theme" of the play. But with the (p. 171) "figure of Time in the center of the play" as "the image of an artificer who is also a force of nature [and] thus an emblem of the play's central concern . . . we can perhaps understand why Sh. ascribes to 'great creating nature' the authorship of one of his most plainly artificial plays." COLLINS (1982, pp. 57-9): At "crucial points in the action when our connivance in the illusion of real life is most necessary if we are to be emotionally affected by the plight of the characters, we are reminded by the use of stage-metaphors [e.g., 2794-5]" that (p. 58) "we are in a theatre where the laws which ordinarily govern men's lives are conveniently suspended. . . . [59] Our emotional response will be qualified by the intellectual recognition that the 'delight' we experience is the result of illusion." TAYLER (1964, pp. 121-33), however, maintains that in the traditional art-nature antithesis, Sh. is associated with nature or life rather than art: The conjunction of traditional pastoral elements and Sh.'s "explicit interest in the philosophical problem of Nature versus Art" creates (p. 127) "a pattern . . . of harmony and alienation, of integration and disruption. . . . [133] In the cycle of disruption and integration the moments of . . . pastoral integrity provide . . . visions of ideal order. . . . Perdita's royal blood manifests itself despite her surroundings and not because of them. For Shakespeare, then, shepherds may serve as exemplars of virtue if they are royal shepherds, and Nature may do without the civilizing influence of Art if it is royal Nature." Others who discuss this opposition: FIEDLER (1949, p. 80), GRENE (1967, p. 68), HOLT (1969, pp. 47-50), ORTEGO (1970, pp. 31-2), CURTIS (1980, p. 436), LENZ (1986, p. 90).

Some critics interpret the play as resolving the dichotomy between art and nature that it presents. BETHELL (1947, p. 27): The "generalisation about Art and Nature is . . . put into the mouth of the most illustrious representative of the court [Polixenes]. Does it not, then, hint at the opposition of court and country . . . , suggesting that a worthy culture must consist in the marriage of urban and rural virtues and that that aspect of civilisation which 'mends' or improves our natural condition . . . is itself part of the natural order?" REESE (1953, p. 494) so affirms: "Shakespeare was insisting [1887-1908] that art, as the interpreter of Nature's laws and therefore a means whereby man may fulfil his proper function, often added to Nature by elucidating mysteries which life itself left dark. . . . The superiority of art over Nature would be dangerous doctrine . . . were it not safely qualified by the belief that art itself is of Nature's making." LUDWIG (1974, pp. 393-6): "The idea that art and nature can coalesce, be identical, figures importantly in the immediate context of the moment of Hermione's return. . . . [394] The statue is and is not Hermione. . . . [395] No theater, . . . no makeup expert, . . . no actor, however well-controlled, can [396] fool the members of an audience into believing that what they are seeing is a statue. . . . The audience must hold in its mind two contradictory ideas about what is going on in the play at the moment after the statue is unveiled. And the double attitude the audience must take is consonant with . . . the scene's insistence on the pattern of the merging of art and nature." IWASAKI (1984, p. 85) sees no merger, but only that Nature and Art, once "viewed as opposing each other, are reconciled and collaborate with each other'' by the end of *WT*. Hawkins (1976, p. 127): "Paulina's art, like Shakespeare's, so glorifies the wonder-working, life-giving power of nature that when the majestic but 'coldly' standing statue of Hermione is infused with 'warm life' one cannot but marvel at the miracle. . . . In Shakespeare the experience of human love . . . finally wins over life itself as the greatest wonder, the most high miracle, the final mystery." Holland (1964, pp. 292, 300–1) figures the dichotomy in terms of gender: In *WT*, woman is (p. 301) "the repository of nature, man the creator of art." To the Elizabethan, (p. 292) "the word 'art' meant all human activities . . . which added to or in some way went beyond natural processes." In the play, Sh. "sets off against . . . nature, all kinds of human contrivances. . . . [This] cluster of things [is] associated with ceremonies, with clothing, with words, with playacting, with all kinds of artificial formalities." On the other hand, Perdita's loss leaves Sicilia "wintry, infertile, despairing, without an heir, [but] she makes of Bohemia . . . a kind of 'green world'." In the play, (p. 300) men are associated with the superficial, women with (p. 301) "true grace."

Others regard any perceived resolution of the nature-art opposition as illusory and refuse to follow critical tradition in celebrating the function of art in the play. Newton (1986, p. 150): In the statue scene, "a ceremony which overcomes the divisions and distortions of the past is created by art, trickery and manipulation, yet it appears to all the participants that nature triumphs over art. But necessity for such a ceremony indicates that no fundamental change has taken place in the relations of husband and wife, king and state. . . . The only change that has been effected is a psychological one in which both ruler and ruled recover from the traumatic events of the past. . . . But nothing has happened to prevent the authority figure from acting as he has done in the past." Williamson (1986, p. 152) agrees: Hermione's forgiveness "once again signals . . . the acceptance by women of an asymmetrical relationship in the greater male privilege to err with impunity. Thus, with much relief," Leontes can immediately start ordering people about once again. *WT* "alerts the audience to the process . . . [of] art using nature to mythologize power. The more aware the audience becomes that it is watching a work of art, the more conscious it will be that what is made to seem natural and inevitable is really artifice conforming to human authority." Lamb (1989, pp. 69, 76–83): Through Autolycus (the artist who seeks self-amusement and financial reward) and Paulina (the artist who teaches lessons of moral worth), *WT* (p. 76) "examines the very problems surfacing in the debate over theater. . . . It explores the morality of the theater, especially as measured by its effect on an audience; it explores the kinds of 'truth' [77] available to the 'old tales' and dramatic performances; it explores the effect of perceiving language and reality solely in terms of literal rather than complex truth. . . . [83] Not only does [*WT*] refuse to resolve the contradictory views of the artist presented through Paulina and Autolycus, but the play further complicates each of the two attitudes towards Art." According to Riemer (1980, pp. 10–11), however, Sh.'s "detailed and sustained treatment of the function and nature of art" reveals art as [11] "essentially devoid of extractable meanings or significances," while Colie (1974, pp. 277–9) cites the "unnatural confluence" of the themes of art and nature, reality and imitation, to claim that the whole art-nature debate "turns out to have been totally irrelevant. . . . *[278]* The scene of Hermione's statue . . . similarly cheats our expectation" — since Hermione (p. 279) has been only figuratively turned to stone, her statue's "returning to life confers upon [Leontes] his full life again. The illusion here is not that art is an illusion but that life is."

Others discussing the nature-art dichotomy: WAIN (1964, p. 224), SALINGAR (1966, p. 30; 1984, pp. 2, 19), MUELLER (1971, pp. 232-8), RABKIN (1971, p. 39; 1981, pp. 118-40), HARTWIG (1972, pp. 5-6), YOUNG (1972, p. 121), KERNAN (1975, pp. 448-50), BEREK (1978, pp. 289-98), MCIVER (1979, pp. 342-50), ESTRIN (1985, pp. 178-9), RICO (1985, pp. 287-8), and BARKAN (1986, pp. 283-6).

The nature theme is further developed, according to KNIGHT (1947; 1966, p. 76), in the "strong suggestion throughout of season-myth, with a balance of summer against winter . . . [and] maturity and death . . . against birth and resurrection." MUIR (1974, pp. 37-9): "There is also, as critics have pointed out, a curious suggestion that underneath the conscious level of the play is a vegetation myth." ANSARI (1979, p. 141) is one of those critics: "The restorative and regenerative function of Perdita as a vegetation deity" is one crucial theme of the play, "inseparably intertwined" with a second, the "coalescence between art and nature." TINKLER (1937, p. 358) is another: "The significance of the tale begun by Mamillius is stressed by frequent reference to the pregnancy of the queen, and this association with ideas of vegetation myths and rites is reinforced . . . throughout the play. To one living in a vital agricultural community the association between the idea of a divine king and the rhythm of the seasons, which is indeed the larger rhythm of this play, is natural. The play opens just before winter . . . and passes through it to the spring festivities of the shepherds. Perdita and Florizel are almost vegetation deities (Mamillius, whose place they take, died at the beginning of Winter) and are 'welcome as the Spring to the earth' [2908-9]." FRYE (1957, p. 138) and SCOTT (1963) also belong to this group.

For many critics, the only nature myth to discuss involves Persephone and Demeter: MUIR (1969, p. 101), for one, has no doubt that Sh. is "attempting, among other things, to reinterpret the story"; DAVIES (1986, p. 154) believes that Sh. was giving us his "fullest exploration of the relationship between the Eleusinian myth and the shapes and meanings of human life." Obviously unaware of WIGSTON (1884, pp. 5, 13), CALDECOTT (1891, pp. 27 ff.) expresses surprise that no one has read the play as a "nature or solar myth" clearly referring to Demeter-Ceres and her sacred island, Sicily. But WIGSTON was already surprised that (p. 5) "no one has as yet called attention" to these parallels: "Hermione falls like Winter into her death-sleep, or art sleep, with the exposure of Perdita. Hermione is restored to life, through the restoration and re-discovery of Perdita. Perdita, like Persephone, is a lost child. . . . *[13]* The central Myth of the Eleusinian Mysteries, as typified in the wanderings of Ceres, . . . is the phenomenal one of the alternation of summer and winter, upon which was hung the doctrine of immortality of the soul, of light and darkness, of matter and mind, of conflict and reconciliation." "A mythological reading . . . entirely consistent with the principles of Renaissance mythopoeia" is pursued by GUJ (1983, pp. 6-20): The rites of Eleusis "were known to, and understood by, cultivated persons in

the sixteenth and seventeeth centuries. . . . [*8*] Shakespeare had in mind the Eleusinian mysteries, which are often alluded to in Renaissance mythographical manu-
als. . . . [*19*] The injunction to depart and the exclusion of the uninitiated from the
rituals were a characteristic feature of the Eleusinian mysteries [the courtiers are
commanded out of the chamber at the reunion of Leontes and Perdita (3013–17) and
the "command is repeated more forcefully in the last scene by Paulina"]. . . . [*20*]
Shakespeare, through the work of the mythographers, if not by a direct knowledge
of classical sources, knew of this important detail and used it to suggest that the
inspiration for his play rested on the myth of the Eleusinian . . . mysteries."

LEIMBERG (1988, pp. 130–1) adds details: "The name 'Hermione' is, in the non-
Homeric, chthonic [infernal] field of Greek mythology, the surname of Demeter as
well as, by analogy, of Persephone. 'Hermione' is also the name of the town where
the rape of Persephone is said to have happened. . . . Within the Homeric tradition,
Hermione is the daughter of Helen who, for her part, resembles an archaic fertility-
goddess as Persephone does. According to another tradition, Hermione was the
mother of the Graces, i.e., she is another Harmonia and called by that name. . . .
Hermione-Harmonia was a goddess of fertility and, consequently, a goddess of life as
well as a goddess of death. Her being raped by the god of the nether world sometimes
was followed by the story of her redemption, of the finding and home-coming of the
victim. . . . [*131*] Nearly all of these motifs or themes reappear in [*WT*]: pregnancy
denoting fertility, a happy marriage and its tragic destruction, or, contrary to both
marriage and fertility, the denial of marriage and children for the supposedly widowed
king; the allusion to Proserpina; the near identity of mother and daughter; the subject
of death and rebirth; the appearance of Autolycus as a deputy of his father Hermes;
the homonymity of Polixenes and Polyxenos (another name for Hades); the stress on
Hermione's sisterly relation with 'grace' [169]; a happy mother being tragically bereft
of her children; and, ultimately, the finding of her who was lost, the re-awakening of
her who had descended into the realm of death, and her redemption." ARNOLD (1953,
pp. 504–5) claims that not even Pluto is missing from the play: The "ravisher of the
spirit, the seducer of the body, the corrupter of virginal innocence, the Tempter," is
present in Sh's (p. 505) Autolycus, whose winter is "the season of forced, unwilling
chastity, summer the time he celebrates . . . earthy delights." MINCOFF (1992, p.
79) cautions that to convert the play into a nature myth results in "distorting and
impoverishing it. . . . Too much insistence on the supposed nature myth has tended
to obscure the traditional pastoral contrast between the confined life of the court,
which breeds such sophistications as destructive jealousy (and, as a parallel, social
restrictions in the second part) and the happy, uncomplicated life of the country,
where love follows its natural impulses and the blows that fall come only from the
sophisticated life outside." That view has not deterred WIGSTON (1888, p. 146),
KNIGHT (1936, p. 155), ARMSTRONG (1969, pp. 64–76), LAROQUE (1974, p. 12; 1982,
p. 26), ANSARI (1979, p. 136), FREY (*Vast Romance*, 1980, pp. 61–2), HONIGMANN
(1982, p. 117), NEELY (1985, p. 198), and BATE (1993, pp. 220–40) from associating
Perdita and Hermione with the myth of Ceres and Proserpine or with other mothers
and daughters of myth. The idea that *WT* reflects esoteric Renaissance knowledge of

mythology is further pursued by MUELLER (1971, p. 229), TAVERA (1974, p. 20; in Fr.), and GOURLAY (1975, pp. 376-95).

REPENTANCE AND RENEWAL

SNIDER ([c. 1890], pp. 463-4) says that *repentance* is the "controlling principle which holds [*WT*] together. . . . [*464*] The whole phenomenal world is brought into dependency upon repentance." VELIE (1972, p. 107) agrees: In *WT*, Sh. "makes a serious study of the mental processes of a man who sins and repents," because he was "vitally interested" in any doctrine that interested his contemporaries and, "as the principal means of thwarting eternal damnation, repentance was of major concern to the Elizabethans." HOROWITZ (1965, pp. 73-4): This concern is illustrated in Leontes's restoration to "humanity and reason," a "major movement" of the play achieved (p. 74) after the "elaborate purgatorial experience" that atones for those he has cast out or destroyed, though ADAMSON (1986, p. 63) says there is no possibility of "ever taking away Leontes' kind of guilt" for mad acts generated by the "doctrinally authoritative stigma on human sexuality." Other critics suggest only that Leontes's penitence is imperfect. SEWELL (1951, pp. 138-9) thinks Hermione's "forgiveness . . . has little compassion in it" because Leontes shows "remorse, but no humility. . . . [*139*] What has happened within the repentant spirit is made altogether subordinate to the mere fact of repentance." FRYE (*Perspective*, 1965, p. 111) agrees: The forgiveness is "structural, not moral," and Sh. gives the penitence a "technical emphasis rather than an oozing through of personal benevolence." Considering Leontes's reaction to Perdita (2995-3002), MELCHIORI (1960, p. 64) suggests that Leontes is not so much "redeemed through suffering, as . . . he has ceased to suffer." WRIGHT (1979, p. 149) has Sh. "slyly undercut the reformation theme": Leontes not only imagines himself "the murderer of a second, hypothetical wife" (2791-5, 2799-2800) but is "highly attracted" to Perdita (2995-3002). "There is something disconcerting about this penitent, in the full flush of his remorse, energetically contemplating both murder and incest," though HAPPÉ (1969, p. 18) finds the response innocent: Leontes merely "sees his wife in Perdita, who thus induces a feeling of tenderness which is the right basis for the reunion." SANDERS (1987, pp. 53-4) concludes: "The trouble with [Leontes's] penitence . . . is that it cannot alter what has been done. It is, in its essence, self-regarding and therefore, in the presence of the larger troubles it has [*54*] created, impertinent. . . . It is possible to find [Leontes's penitence] perfectly just, sincere, honest . . . yet still distasteful." DAVISON (1982, p. 66) speculates that what cannot be undone "is, perhaps, an attempt by Shakespeare to present his audience with the whole gamut of experience and emotion, so that we can realise that reconciliation is meaningless unless it comprehends not only real loss but the awful grotesquerie sometimes attendant upon death."

NOVY (1984, p. 178) instead stresses the "mutuality between repentance and forgiveness," a reminder that other critics, including TRAVERSI (1969, 2:314), have found that Sh.'s "intuition about the necessary relation between the mutability of life and the infinite value of human experience which it conditions but which is finally incommensurate with it" is integrated into the "wider framework of penitence and reconciliation." Similarly HOY (1964, pp. 270-1) seems to discern that *WT* "celebrates the mysterious and beatific wonders which patience under affliction and a hearty repentance for past sins can accomplish. It celebrates as well the human capacity to forgive all injuries and the wrongs which innocence might ever have been made to suffer at the hands of the guilty. . . . [*271*] A harsh and threatening actuality is miraculously transformed by . . . repentance, faith, and forbearance." MC-FARLAND (1972, p. 140) mentions the "exalted tone of wonder and renewed joy" evoked by the final reconciliations which, MUIR (1974, p. 43) says, "could not happen without positive virtuous action or repentance by the main characters. . . . The happy endings depend on repentance and forgiveness." ABARTIS (1977, p. 88) concurs: *WT* offers "the purest statement of the theme latent in tragicomedy—that after tragedy there is comedy, after error there is forgiveness and renewal." THALER (1927, p. 761), STAUFFER (1949, pp. 294-5), BONJOUR (1952, p. 208), DRIVER (1960, pp. 191-4), MENDL (1964, p. 200), JOSEPHS (1967, p. 20), BARBER & WHEELER (1986, p. 328), GREENBLATT (1988, pp. 132-3), and WEXLER (1988, pp. 116-17) also discuss repentance, forgiveness, and reconciliation.

To BARBER (1964, pp. 244-9), the key theme of the play is "clear enough. Shakespeare envisages a reconciliation . . . in which renewal will be brought to the court from below, while the inhabitants of the cottage will be refined by the influence of the court. . . . [*248*] The continuity of human history," the way "life goes on generation after generation despite all conflicts and disturbances," and the sense of (p. 249) "human generations stretching back and forward" are part of this theme. HOL-BROOK (1964, p. 156) agrees with KNIGHTS (1976, p. 611), who contends that the "renewal of life is the main theme of the play," and SACKS (1980, p. 87): "The single reality in the romances is the survival of humanity through generation." For MARSH (1962; 1980, p. 126), this point is made in the play's recognition that "life does not die, it goes on, passing from father to son"; for GAJDUSEK (1974, p. 151), in its emphasis on the "finding of the heir or successor who can rid the land of the curse or enchantment or spell of death"; for HAPPÉ (1969, p. 16), YOUNG (1992, p. 187), and THORNE (1982, pp. 91-2), in "the medicinal influence [the young] exert on the older generation." Youth is presented as (p. 92) "a renewer of life and antagonist to death"; the young are able to purge "King and country . . . of error, and sin, as the generations merge in significance." According to TRAVERSI (1955, pp. 125-6), Sh. demonstrates the importance of generation in "the function of new-born innocence as a healing power in redressing the excesses that [*126*] spring from the distortions of sexual feeling."

While HOY (1978, pp. 78, 84), Mark TAYLOR (1982, p. 51), and SCHOTZ (1980, p. 51) agree that "the rejuvenation of the King/Father . . . and the kingdom as a whole" depends on "the banished daughter" returned, perhaps because, as QUI-NONES (1972, p. 438) says, Perdita supplants Hermione "in the human chain of repeated birth," or as LINDENBAUM (1972, p. 14) suggests, Perdita "is the repository of Hermione's thoughts in the next generation." SCHOTZ (pp. 52-3) also stresses the importance of Leontes's embracing of "the female mysteries . . . essential to the renewal of the male. . . . [53] Leontes is the only Shn. male to embrace woman-as-mother in a life-enhancing way, and [*WT*] the only play in which the restoration of the mother-daughter cathexis [investment of libidinal energy] is perceived as necessary for male psychic health and welcomed in all of its power." HARDING (1979, p. 60): Although Leontes finds the statue more wrinkled than the Hermione he remembers, he retains the "capacity to respond to the mature woman as a development of the girl she had been. . . . His capacity to love her occurs simultaneously with the recovery of his effectiveness as a ruler and with the establishment of the succession." ENGEL (1980, p. 9) views Hermione's supposed statue as "the means by which Leontes and his generation may partake of the regeneration otherwise available only to the young. . . . Only with her restoration, unheralded and wholly unexpected, does Shakespeare allow a . . . renewal unparalleled in Renaissance drama." GARBER (1981, pp. 178–9) calls Leontes's "capacity to compare, contrast and discriminate" between the Hermione that was and her wrinkled statue (p. 179) "a trial or test, which marks the initiate as successful—or not—in his relationships . . . with history."

FREY (*Vast Romance*, 1980, p. 165) says: "The whole drama flows into the two climactic moments" of Hermione's reunion with Leontes and their joint reunion with Perdita. Earlier, he ("Interpreting," 1978, pp. 300–3) emphatically states: "The daughter's choice of a husband who is independent of her father's influence proves a catalyst, though a bitter one, for the changes necessary to a revitalization of the home society. . . . Only daughters are looked to for continuation of the central family," and even Florizel, the husband Perdita brings home, is meant (p. 303) "to teach or permit her father a newfound love and forgiveness made possible and believable amid the restored patriarchal security." FREY is anticipated by BETHELL (1947, pp. 94–5), who finds Perdita's marriage the assurance of social regeneration because Florizel and Perdita are (p. 95) "a younger generation, unsophisticated, and life-affirming; Leontes and Hermione are an older generation, sophisticated, and life-denying," and followed by ETTIN (1984, p. 80), for whom "Perdita's ease with the natural order of life," despite her firm belief in "the proper order of nature and society," promises a fresh start through "the fusion of natural and social values." BOOSE (1982, p. 338): Leontes "is punished by the . . . death of the son he imagines will carry his lineal posterity. Only when he comes to value 'that which has been lost'—the daughter Perdita, who is a matrilineal rather than a patrilineal extension—is Leontes allowed the partial restitution implicit in his adoption of Florizel. And even this compensation is made possible only through the return and affirmation of the hitherto unvalued daughter." FAAS (1984, p. 146), however: Sh., "while elaborating upon the rebirth theme, puts increasing emphasis on the continuance of death and suffering." ALMASY (1981, pp. 121, 124) objects to "those who slight the centrality of Leontes . . . by overemphasizing the importance of the younger generation. . . . It is Leontes' life that . . . affords the audience a focus to unite the various structural and thematic elements"; this is established when (p. 124) he reappears as the center of attention in the fifth act.

Discussion of generational renewal is also found in WILSON (ed. 1931, p. xix),

IDEM (1932, p. 140), TILLYARD (1938, pp. 44-6), SPENCER (1942, pp. 268-9), DESAI (1952, p. 84), BLAND (1953, pp. 42-3), TRAVERSI (1955, p. 174), LEECH (1958, p. 30), WILLIAMS (1967, pp. 12-15), EDWARDS (1968, p. 144), THORNE (1968, pp. 42-3), SWINDEN (1973, pp. 156-7), COLMAN (1974, p. 144), WHEELER (1980, pp. 163-6), TAYLOR (*Purpose*, 1982, p. 51), KASTAN (1982, pp. 126-8), and TRAUB (1987, pp. 228-30).

Religious renewal interests FURNIVALL (1877, p. xci), for whom Christian tenets underlie the whole of *WT*. PILGRIM (1983, pp. 27, 78) finds in Leontes's "spiritual progress, with its three stages of sin, repentance and restoration," the central theme of the play. Presented (p. 78) "in dramatic terms . . . whether consciously or unconsciously on the part of the author it is impossible to say, [is] the essential character of the doctrine of the Body of Christ." BARBER (1964, pp. 236-7) and BETHELL (1947, pp. 14, 38-9) also believe that "the interpretation of life that Shakespeare presents is . . . profoundly Christian. . . . [*38*] The play, in fact, has as many obviously Christian references as pagan. . . . [*39*] The importance attached to moral attitudes is especially Christian," even the hints of Leontes's and Polixenes's early reluctance to deal with their sinful natures at all, for, as LINDENBAUM (1972, p. 13) points out, the desire "to be Boy eternall [124-7]" suggests a yearning for a prelapsarian existence "which implies that sexual love could be no part of man's experience in his unfallen condition"; the latter point is also made by NEELY (1978, p. 183; 1985, pp. 194-5) and STOCKHOLDER (1987, p. 185). BASS (1977, pp. 16-17), however: If Polixenes imagines that, had he and Leontes continued as boys eternal, they might somehow (p. 17) "have been guiltless of original sin," he fails to recognize "the necessary role of grace after the Fall." WATSON (1984, p. 276) concludes: "Leontes is torn between the heritage of Adam, which makes him a sinner, and the heritage of God, which obliges him to purity. In learning to acknowledge the limiting father Adam, Leontes learns . . . through a penitent recognition of the natural grace that still inhabits the fallen world . . . [that he may gain] through the greatest humility . . . an identity at once filial and perfect."

Though SMITH (1964, p. 280) objects that "overt religious references in the play are predominantly pagan, and it takes considerable straining of the language, structure, and atmosphere of the play to make a specifically Christian doctrinal statement out of it," few critics have problems discussing the play's attention to spiritual renewal and the redeeming grace most often associated with Hermione, Perdita, or both. BRYANT (1955; 1961, pp. 209-10): "Only a very devious dialectician would ever attempt to disprove the connection between Hermione and . . . Christian grace. . . . [*210*] The manifestation of grace in her is so discernible as an imperfect realization of that quality which is perfectly manifested in the Son of God that we are led to see in her simple acts of forgiveness the pale but unmistakable reflection of His mercy and redeeming love." MENDILOW & SHALVI (1967, p. 252) affirm that for all its "pagan or classical or fairy-tale source, setting or theme, [*WT* is] essentially and triumphantly Christian in tone and philosophy. . . . [Its] Christianity seems to be even further emphasised by the fact that the instruments of salvation are none other than the people who have been sinned against." In MILWARD's (1964, pp. 31-2, 35) view these people include both Hermione, who "maintains, both in . . . words and in her later example, that women may . . . be the means of grace and redemption to men," and Perdita, whose "nature is shown as ordered to the grace which grows in her with the passing of Time." MILWARD (1973, p. 270) adds: "Mother and daughter may be said to represent two stages of grace for Leontes—before and after its loss by sin." Evidence of this grace for both McMANUS (1988) and ERICKSON (1985, p. 162) comes with the "miraculous change" in Leontes when he "relinquishes his view of women as degraded and learns to see them as sanctified."

MARSHALL (1986, pp. 294–302) offers an interesting, somewhat off-beat discussion of parallels between the play and the "vision of human destiny associated with mortalism, a widespread heresy in post-Reformation England," but for more traditional discussions of religious or moral renewal see KNIGHT (1933, pp. 124–5), MAHOOD (1957, pp. 150–1), MAVEETY (1966, pp. 273–9), MELDRUM (1968, p. 52), TRAVERSI (1969, 2:313), SIEMON (1972, pp. 442–3), SPEAIGHT (1977, pp. 349–50), KAHN (1980, pp. 219–35), BARBER & WHEELER (1986, p. 299), and SANDERS (1987, p. 40).

Drame à Clef

Some critics imply the play is a form of *drame à clef*. BENTLEY (1948, pp. 48–9): "The character of Shakespeare's last plays is in accord with the known facts of theatrical history; it accords with the biographical evidence of Shakespeare's long and close association with all the enterprises of the [49] Lord Chamberlain's–King's men for twenty years; it is in accord with his fabulously acute sense of the theatre and the problems of the actor. . . . The company was experienced and theatre-wise"—as was Sh. He could not fail to produce a play that reflected the theatrical circumstances of his life.

Thus ROWSE (1963, p. 278): The Sh. who wrote *WT* is "now fulfilled and successful, well off and in harbour," unlike the early Sh. who expressed "resentment against his profession" in Sonnet 111. HOLLAND (1964, p. 301): *WT* is Sh. "at the end of his career. He must have known that he was going to retire within a year or so, and he takes this chance to look back on his own art, an art of disguise" and fakery akin to the "ballads of Autolycus." HOLBROOK (1964, pp. 145, 175): *WT* reflects "Shakespeare's own life approaching winter. . . . [175] Time might be the composite figure Prospero-Shakespeare himself"—or, according to BATESON (1978, p. 74), the playwright confronting "dramatically the arrival of his own old man's age." WHITE (1985, p. 146) thinks Time speaks "explicitly [in] the voice of the dramatist himself"; ROSE (1972, p. 170) finds that idea "tempting." TURNER (1971, p. 150) adds that the role was "perhaps acted by Shakespeare" when *WT* was first performed. HARDY (1989, p. 25) concludes that the chorus "as a narrator-figure stand[s] closer to the author than the dramatic characters."

NUTTALL (1966, p. 39): "Those in the audience who recognised that Shakespeare himself was playing the part of Time" caught on to an "in-joke." WILES (1987, p. 156), however: Autolycus "conceals" the real "in-joke"; in the character who humbles himself to accept patronage from the Shepherd and Clown, we see Robert Armin, who "published a specimen of his own balladry in an apparent bid for court patronage. Armin's own multiple identities—as writer of ballads, tradesman, fool, King's servant, would-be courtier—are refracted through the assumed role or alias of Autolycus." ADAMS (1989, pp. 102–3), however, identifies Autolycus "with Shakespeare himself as a figure in and behind the playhouse. . . . In Autolycus we have an instance, exceptional mainly in its pointedness, of Shakespeare larking with his entire relation to the theater. . . . [103] In the person of Autolycus Shakespeare gives away the whole show to anyone witty enough to get his point."

STRACHEY (1906; 1922, pp. 64–5): Looking at *WT* and the other romances as the product of Sh.'s "retirement" years in Stratford, "it is difficult to resist the conclusion that he was getting bored. . . . Bored with people . . . with real life . . . with everything except poetry and poetical dreams. . . . [65] If we are to learn anything of his mind from his last works, it is surely this." But CHAMBERS (ed. 1907, pp. 13–14) warns against the "dangerous pastime" of tracing reflections of Sh.'s "personal circumstances upon the mirror of his art." Yet he succumbs to the approach himself: *WT* pictures (p. 14) "the surroundings, familiar to [Sh.] in boyhood, to which he had come back in all the freshness of recovered liberty and peace." KNIGHT (ed. 1843, 8: 71) associates the sheepshearing episode with "the keen and prying observation of a boy occupied and interested with such details," DOWDEN (1875; 1890, p. 151) with the mature poet "now returned to Stratford . . . [and] in a happy spirit renew[ing] his acquaintance" with his boyhood home. CLARK (1930, pp. 175–6) agrees with KNIGHT, BRINK (1895, p. 95) with DOWDEN. JUSSERAND (in LEE, ed. 1907, [15:] xix): "The whole play teem[s] with allusions to fondly remembered, and sometimes ironically recalled, experiences of boyhood," though the (IDEM, "*Winter's Tale*," 1925, p. 229) "quieting influence of resumed country life" leaves Sh. increasingly indifferent "to facts and probabilities. He had never cared much whether any Bohemia had any seashore; he cared even less now."

Critics also associate *WT* with members of Sh.'s family. KNIGHT (ed. 1843, 8:112) equates Mary Shakespeare with Hermione, William with Mamillius. FURNIVALL (ed. [1877], p. xcii): *WT* and Sh.'s part of *H8* make "us believe that this twice-repeated reunion of husband and wife, in their daughter, late in life, this twice repeated forgiveness of sinning husbands by sinned-against wives, have somewhat to do with Shakspere's reunion with his wife, and his renewed family life at Stratford." SWINBURNE (1880; ed. 1925, 11:222) finds in Mamillius the "suggestion that Shakespeare as he wrote had in mind his own dead little son still fresh and living at his heart." MASSON (1914, p. 118) also thinks that audiences seeing Leontes and Mamillius onstage will "see Sh. remembering his own fireside and his play and prattle there once with his dead boy Hamnet." JUSSERAND (in LEE, ed. 1907, [15]:xvii), however: Sh. found the inspiration for Mamillius in his granddaughter Elizabeth. HARRIS (1909, pp. 337–8): His health broken, Sh. writes *WT* when he is "too tired to invent or even to annex; his own story is the only one that interests him." Thus his daughter Judith becomes Perdita and Hermione is the result of Sh.'s speculative (p. 338) "what if"— what if the faithless Mary Fitton had been true?

SMEATON (1911, p. 505): The "whole scene of the sheepshearing festival is a picture of rural Warwickshire in the early seventeenth century. . . . In the flowers which Perdita scatters before the guests at the feast, we seem to catch a glimpse of some such scene, which had taken place . . . years before, when young William Shakespeare, then unmarried, had seen the beautiful Anne Hathaway as queen of the feast of that day, and had straightway fallen in love with her. So graphic a picture as is drawn in [*WT*] . . . must surely have been sketched from the life." SACHS (1923, p. 80): "It is not necessary to point out in detail how well [Leontes's disappointment with Hermione's aged and wrinkled statue (3217–18)] corresponds with the case of Shakespeare himself who on returning home would have to resume life together with his wife who was several years older than he." FRIPP (1938, 2:740, 436): Sh. "may have known a female Autolycus, one Avice Clarke, the inventory of whose belongings on her death in the summer of 1624 . . . bear a striking resemblance to those of Sh.'s delightful vagabond." FRIPP writes with more assurance that (p. 436) "Leontes suffers from a physical malady. A muscle or blood-vessel breaks and he is no longer himself. . . . This is medical, a matter which doubtless the Poet discussed with his son in law, Doctor Hall." WARD (1987, p. 547) too: "In his semi-retirement [Sh.] had the pleasure of many conversations with his son-in-law John Hall, the physician, and this may be one reason why [*WT*] is so full of references to physic, infection, disease, and cure."

Critics who do not see personal connections make court ones. INCHBALD (ed. 1808, 3:5) and BARBER (1964, p. 239): Sh. alludes to Anne Boleyn in the character of Hermione. Though FOSS (1932, p. 137) thinks so too, he believes Sh. tries to "cloak his design of writing a fanciful account of the scandal of his Sovereign's parents." (Also see p. 602.) MILWARD (1973, pp. 82–3): Leontes, who corresponds to Henry VIII, confesses "his former injustice to Polixenes. . . . Here it is enough to point out that . . . [*WT* seems] to look forward to a reconciliation between England and Rome, as expressed [*83*] in the reunion of Leontes with Polixenes." EVERETT (1970) and EDWARDS (1976, p. 52) identify Hermione with Mary Stuart. EDWARDS, however: That the identification is sympathetic is "almost beyond dispute." CHAMBERS (ed. 1907, p. 14): There is a "temptation to trace the lineaments of the gallant and too early lost Prince Henry" in Florizel. ALLEN (1936): Experiences in the lives of Lord and Lady Oxford—particularly Oxford's conviction that the Lady Elizabeth deVere was not his daughter—suggest that Lord and Lady Oxford are the models for Leontes and Hermione, their daughter Elizabeth for Perdita, the Duchess of Suffolk for Paulina, and Lady Mary Vere for Emilia. BETHELL (1947, p. 87) connects the dangers of an uncertain succession at the end of Elizabeth's long reign with Leontes's situation in *WT*.

HARRISON (ed. 1947, p. 133) sees parallels between the "circumstances of Paulina's entry to the Court" and the Gunpowder Plot, for complicity in which the Earl of Northumberland was condemned and imprisoned in the Tower in 1606. "His countess (notorious for her violent and forceful personality) gained access to the King and openly and violently accused the Earl of Salisbury of unjust dealing. She was so clamorous in her abuse of Salisbury that he was obliged to write to the Earl of Northumberland to ask him to restrain his wife's fury." KUHL (1952): Sh. has "in mind

England's plight, her lean years under a jealous king who, with the aid of Cecil, attempted to thwart the expansionist group led by Sandys, Southampton, and Pembroke. The entire play seems conceived in this spirit . . . [of] . . . concern over England's fate in a time of austerity." GREG (1955, p. 417): "It has . . . been suggested with some plausibility that the last act as we have it is not the original conclusion of the play. . . . The most likely occasion for the alteration would be the performance in connection with Princess Elizabeth's marriage festivities in the winter of 1612–13." STERNFELD (1956, p. 328): The sixteen-year-old Prince of Wales took an active part in discussions of his own possible Spanish or French alliance and more than once was in disagreement with his father and his father's counsellors. Moreover, the hand of fifteen-year-old Princess Elizabeth was sought by many candidates. Since that time the significance of the marriage of Florizel and Perdita . . . became obvious (in Fr.).

BERGERON (1978, p. 127): Civic pageants featuring Time speaking "doggerel," a developing taste for masques, Princess Elizabeth's wedding (14 February 1613) within two months of the funeral procession of Prince Henry (7 December 1612)—whose extremely life-like, flexible effigy was displayed both in the funeral chariot and in Westminster Abbey when the prince was buried—connect the play and the real world (the two latter items suggesting the shepherd's "things dying" and "new borne," 1553–4). IDEM (1985, p. 178): "Shakespeare opened the book of kings, the text of the Stuart royal family, read it, closed it, and opened his fiction to its interpenetrating presence. In the years immediately before [*WT*], the royal family had experienced domestic family strife, the . . . Gunpowder Plot, the births and deaths of two royal children, the coming to court of Princess Elizabeth, the investiture of Prince Henry, and marriage negotiations for the royal children. If not these precise events, then surely the general pattern of the intertwined nature of royal family and politics . . . finds its way into the intertextual nature of [*WT*]." WILLIAMSON (1986, p. 112): The last plays relate to "the political discourse of Jacobean England." BETHELL (ed. 1956, p. 257) and HOTINE (1983, pp. 129–30): A performance of WT occurred on 5 November 1611, the anniversary of the Gunpowder Plot.

See also HARRIS (1911, pp. 337–8), MURRY (1936, p. 408), WILLIAMS (1941, pp. 70–1), EDWARDS (1975, pp. 37–9), YATES (1975, p. 35).

Technique

STRUCTURE

Many critics think of the play as bipartite even while disagreeing on the purpose and effect of such a division.

LLOYD (1875; 1894, p. 157): The "peculiarity of [*WT*'s] composition . . . in the abstract appears like an experiment and a dangerous one; it is rare, if not unprecedented in any art, to find an effective whole resulting from the blank opposition of two precisely counterbalanced halves when not united by common reference to some declared third magnitude. Nor is such a uniting power wanting in the present instance. . . . The leading masses [the halves] are contrasted with a breadth and boldness that strain the very limits of coherence, but it [the structure] still holds . . . to the perfect and rounded conclusion." PRICE (1890, pp. 199, 203–6): "The play is . . . a genuine diptych in construction. . . . To bring the two parts into artistic union, the characters . . . [form] three symmetrical groups: . . . (9) characters that belong altogether to the tragedy; . . . (12) characters that belong altogether to the comedy; and . . . (7) characters that belong in common to tragedy and to comedy. . . . [203] The expiring movement of the tragedy is made the birth of the comedy [at 1500]. . . . [204] The climax of the comic action comes in its right place, [in 4.4]. . . . As the climax of the tragedy was the culmination of hatred in Leontes for Hermione, so the climax of the comedy is the culmination of love in Florizel for Perdita. . . . [205] At this point comes that feature of the double play which forms its chief divergence from dramatic usage. In general, after the climax there comes a catabasis [falling action] that is equal in number of stages to [or shorter than] the epitasis [the rising action or complication]. But here [in the comic half of the play, unlike the tragic half where they are equal] . . . the catabasis is carried on . . . to the enormous length of 800 lines [from Camillo's resolve to help the young lovers to Paulina's exhibition of Hermione's statue before Leontes]. . . . In length and in fulness of contrivance, it far transcends the norm of dramatic usage. . . . It carries on the action not only of Florizel's love but also of Leontes' [206] folly. . . . Hence, serving a double purpose, the catabasis is here carried . . . to a double length . . . ; and what seemed at first a careless blemish turns out to be a bold and original stroke of art."

HERFORD (ed. 1904, 4:269): "Two sharply-marked phases, each occupying almost exactly half the play . . . [create a] 'wasp-like' structure nowhere else in [Sh.] approached. The drama owes its beautiful harmony of effect very little to mechanical coherence of plot." MACKENZIE (1924, p. 429): The structure "suffers at times from the telescoping of the action made necessary by the fact that it [*WT*] is really two plays in one. But it is lucid, shapely, in its way even compact." VAN DOREN (1939; 1953, pp. 313, 319): "The time which goes unchronicled between the third and fourth acts might seem to give us two plays instead of one, but there is only one . . . dedicated to . . . the opposition between age and youth, cruelty and goodness, jealousy and faith. . . . [319] The play is one but its halves are two, and each of them underlines the other." CRAIG (1948, p. 328): The "very splitting of [the play] makes it easier to follow and, since events and motives are simple, makes its characters stand out more clearly." HEIMS (1988, p. 6): Two devices (one dramatic, the other narrative) create the "harmonious unity of the play. . . . Of the dramatic element, there are two components. . . . Perdita's presence in both parts of the play . . . helps to unify it [as does] the significance of her presence. The narrative device is the introduction of the playwright himself as the choral figure, Time."

Though JUSSERAND (1925, p. 229) thinks Sh. is indifferent "to an accurate joining of his story's several parts," other critics disagree and readily explain how he joins them. MINCOFF (1941, pp. 37-9): Since *WT*'s "two parts were divided in time . . . and the interest shifts to an entirely fresh set of characters who were not even in existence during the opening scenes, the join could only be effected by running the first part into the second as far as possible. For this purpose the figure of Camillo was retained as a link . . . [along with] the continued interest in the older generation." When the same characters appear in two consecutive scenes where locale or time clash with one another, Sh. seeks (p. 39) "to wedge the two scenes apart by some short interlude that did not necessarily form an integral part of the plot" (e.g. 1144-72, showing Cleomines and Dion returning from Delphos). PYLE (1969, p. 88): Sh. uses Polixenes's explosion of temper at Florizel, Perdita, and the Shepherd to "afford fleeting but impressive parallels with Leontes in the earlier part of the play, reminding us of his rage, his sudden cruelties, his vacillation. . . . Just as Leontes' rage and cruelty caused Polixenes and Camillo to run for their lives and his infant daughter to be cast out . . . so now both the kings' children will have to fly. . . . The parallelism produces a sense not only of unity in diversity but also of controlling purpose behind the seemingly haphazard and accidental." SIEMON (1974, p. 15): "Parallel actions enable Shakespeare to explore the possibilities for good and evil in society." In the first part, Leontes's community is "made sterile . . . through a mistaking of the appearance of truth for truth itself"; in the second part, Polixenes's community is threatened with death, loss of its heir, and the lovers' separation "through a mistaking of true value. . . . The values and dangers of each extend into the other and neither can be completed without bringing the other to completion."

KNIGHTS (1976, pp. 608-9): Acts 1-3 are "mainly given to creating a sense of Leontes' unbalanced self-enclosure. . . . The play's second movement has given us a state of being that offered the strongest possible contrast to the [*609*] state displayed by Leontes in the opening acts—a spring and summer opposed to Leontes' winter." DEAN (1979, p. 251) agrees: *WT* ultimately "succeeds as a romance drama because of its efficient balance of opposing personalities and themes. . . . [Sh.'s] creation of contrasting forces in [*WT*] does make for a wintry first half and a spring-like second half to the play. . . . [*WT*] is well-balanced in large proportions." SPENDER (1982, pp. 234-7): The two parts of the play are "deeply interwoven, perhaps musically and thematically rather [*235*] than by story-line or plot. . . . Although this play seems fragmented, threatening even to fall apart in the middle when considered as action or plot, it has a great symphonic unity. . . . [*237*] The second half of the play reflects back on the first like criticism of it." MALE (1984, pp. 7-8): The two parts of the play consist of a series of "sequences." In part one, the first sequence leads to Hermione's trial, the second covers the "rapid and overlapping events that follow the message from the oracle," and the final sequence concludes with Perdita's discovery by the Shepherd and Clown. Time's speech, a self-contained sequence, marks the conclusion of the tragic elements and initiates "a new, more hopeful phase. . . . It comes precisely at the centre of the play, although in the text it begins Act 4." The first sequence of part two introduces Autolycus to establish (p. 8) "a lively, light-hearted tone" and ends with "Polixenes throwing off his disguise and revealing his true identity." A new sequence begins "with the denunciation of Florizel and Perdita by Polixenes. . . .

The first part of Act 5 provides the next sequence," ending with Leontes's promise to intercede on behalf of the young lovers, and the "final sequence consists of a series of reunions and reconciliations culminating in the statue scene. . . . The formal pattern of this sequence is completed by the pairing of the two trusty councillors, Paulina and Camillo. . . . By tracing this sequence of scenes, a clear and logical dramatic pattern emerges: the first concerned with discord and separation and death, the second with love, reunion and reconciliation. The formal act and scene divisions have largely been ignored."

HOLBROOK (1964, p. 172) labels 3.3 (1436–1577) "the pivot of the play," as does FRYE (1970; 1982, p. 131): WT's "great structural problem . . . is solved by using as a hinge on which both parts of this tale can move in unison . . . [the] spectacular entrance and exit of the bear, followed by the Clown's spectacular description of how the bear ate the man and how the mariners drowned, [marking] finis to one portion of the plot . . . and [preparing] for a fresh development and progression in the last two acts." HIRSH (1981, pp. 201–4): "For a brief moment at the center of this central, pivotal scene, the stage is occupied only by the infant Perdita, who was falsely assumed by Leontes in the tragic first half of the play to be the product of his wife's adultery and who as an adult is restored and reconciled to her father in the comic second half. The segments following this moment strangely mirror the segments that precede it." Antigonus, (p. 202) believing the baby a bastard, abandons her while the Shepherd, "arriving at the same conclusion," takes her up, (p. 204) grateful for his "lucky day" (1575–6) even though he "decided to take care of the forsaken child before he discovered the gold, and the Clown intends to bury the remains of Antigonus despite the storm. . . . Antigonus and the Mariner have done their 'ungentle business' in an 'ill time' and have been punished. . . . The Shepherd and the Clown have done their 'good deeds'" and are rewarded. R. P. KNOWLES (1982, p. 274): WT "carries farther the movement in the last plays away from the intimation of providential control toward full identification with artistic control by employing Apollo, the god of, among other things, music, poetry, and the healing arts, as the presiding deity of the play, and by relegating the deity as deity to a more minor place in the story. The oracle, nevertheless, plays an important role in effecting the shift from the Dionysian first half of the play, with its confusion, noise, and pain, to the the Apollonian second half of harmony and healing."

WILLIAMS (1941, pp. 279–80), however: "Perhaps the most masterly use of prologue is . . . to knit together the two uneven parts of [WT]. . . . [280] Old Father Time is allowed his power, but his senile humour lightens the discourse and leads naturally into the rustic comedy scenes that follow." BERRY (1965, p. 93): "The purpose of 'Time, the Chorus' is copulative—to prevent one play becoming two plays. . . . If Time succeeds, and it is a critical point whether 'he' does, then an audience, which for all of three Acts has been experiencing a heady and violent here and now, thrusting towards its apparent satisfaction in tragedy, have [sic] to adjust the perspective and perceive the Bohemia scenes . . . through the lens of the tragedy-determined first half. If Time does succeed . . . the audience is confronted by a pastoral romance [4.4] in Bohemia which is judged in one way by the lovers and in a very different way by themselves." SMITH (1966, pp. 48-51): *WT* has two halves encompassing three movements. The first movement culminates with (p. 49) the Bohemian storm, the second begins with the appearance of the Clown and Shepherd. But the "ambiguous figure of Time . . . accentuates and bridges the division between the two halves of the play." The second movement (p. 50) culminates in Perdita's flower-speech (1876 ff). The two dances and the (p. 51) "interlude of the entrance of Autolycus" create an antimasque pattern which forms the "bridge to the third movement. In this, many of the motifs of the first movement are repeated. . . . All estrangements and oppositions [are brought] to a reunion, restoration, and reconciliation."

SCHANZER (ed. 1969, pp. 32-8): The creative, restorative second half of the play offers parallels and contrasts with the predominantly destructive first half. Sh. (p. 35) uses Time and his hourglass to mark the break but also our sense of the similarity of the two parts (see n. 1595, pp. 298-9). This parallelism or (p. 38) "pattern of repetition" increases "our sense of the fragility, the precariousness of human happiness." TURNER (1971, p. 148): "Time's speech comes at the pivot of the whole play, and must bring into relationship" the two extremes of "black tragedy" and "bucolic comedy"—the "widest range Shakespeare has ever attempted in one play." YOUNG (1972, pp. 116-18): By introducing Time, Sh. "emphatically" exposes the bifurcation to create (p. 117) a "deliberately naive structure" as a "joke on those who took their categories too seriously and who would not or could not question the rules." But the joke "has justifications that go to the heart of the play's vision," stressing the "arbitrary aspects of genre," the polarizing of "elements—good and evil, life and death, loss and restoration . . . youth and age," and throwing "the tradi-[*118*]tional pastoral oppositions—court and country . . . complexity and simplicity—into vivid relief." VAN LAAN (1978, pp. 223, 226, 232): The whole of *WT* is governed by the "internal dramatist"—a figure originating in the stage Machiavel or Vice. In the first part, Leontes is the (p. 226) "prominent internal dramatist." The second half of the play (p. 232) "is also governed by an internal dramatist, but this one is not a fallible human being; it is, instead, Time, who enters to mend the plot so that, despite Leontes, it can have a happy ending." KRIER (1982, pp. 346-9): Time "might be called 'the great hinge' on which the play and its paradoxes turn. . . . Clearly it [Time's speech] is the junction" between the first half of the play, in which (p. 347) "all has been rush, haste, pressure, clock time, frenzy" and (p. 349) the second, which "reverses the time sense, so that the dominant tone is leisurely, spacious, and seasonal, while the urgency of time's press is contained within it."

HARDMAN (1985, p. 235): "To express the passage of time through a speaking personification is a very obvious reminder that we are witnessing a stage performance," and thus the joint "between the two parts is forced upon our attention . . . by reference to dramatic theory, by use of traditional romance motif, and by emblem, by stagecraft, and by dramatic device. The change of mode is thus not naturalistic, but self-consciously literary and artful"; HARDY (1989, pp. 24-5) agrees, though he thinks "the self-conscious address serves dramatic form, telling the audience just enough, linking the past with present, and urging attention towards the future. . . . [25] Time's levity, profundity, thrilling seriousness and humour are also right for the two times and two tones of the play. . . . Time is authorial and authoritarian." But then, as MAHOOD (1992, p. 35) points out, since "all events under the sun are the products of Time, he can legitimately consider himself the originator of the entire action."

SMEATON (1911, p. 506) is not smitten with the divided plot: It "can scarcely be called a perfect technical success. The two parts, the Hermione and the Perdita, do not fit in very closely to one another." And though WILSON (1932; 1937, p. 140) finds the two worlds of the play, corresponding to London and Stratford, "brought together cunningly in the reconciliation scene of the living statue," he suggests the resolution did not satisfy Sh. himself: "Two separate worlds [one blessed, one bitter] even when reconciled in a finale do not make one world or one play. . . . The problem was both a technical and a spiritual one." CARRINGTON (1956, pp. 12–14): The lack of cohesion and unity in the play is a (p. 13) "major weakness" of overall construction even though "individual scenes in the two halves . . . [14] are well linked together." TAYLOR (1973, pp. 344–50): In the "tragic movement" of *WT*, the climax "must necessarily be delayed," stimulating our impatience. The second half (p. 348) "has nearly the opposite effect. . . . [349] We learn patience. . . . The movement . . . is spasmodic, . . . [350] the action has lost its greatness and urgency." The overall rhetorical structure of the play consists of "peaks and lulls."

Dissatisfaction with this structure leads HIEATT (1978, pp. 239–42) to declare: "The similarity between the first three and the fourth Acts suggests that a two-part view of the play accounts for only a portion of a larger, more complicated scheme. As for the alleged unifying function of parallel action, the linear development of [*WT*] denies that its structural segments are linked primarily by cross-reference. Events are arranged chronologically throughout and, unlike those of the double plot, bear not only a comparative but a sequential, cause-and-effect relationship. Thus, despite their disjunctive nature, the structural segments will cohere on the basis of an over-all shaping principle, while their parallel action will have the secondary function of underscoring and redefining this principle in terms of theme." In the first movement, (p. 242) a "king's passion runs its dreadful course"; young love is the subject of the second movement, "followed by a major shift in time and place, which in turn precipitates [the third] organic action ending with the return of Hermione[,] . . . each part having its separate setting and grouping of characters, its individual reversals of fortune and mood, its discrete increment of fictional time."

Other critics also declare the play a triptych. SNIDER (1877, 2:58–9): The play has "three grand movements or divisions. . . . The first portrays the guilt of the King of Sicilia; . . . [Sicilia] is the world of strife, contradiction, and wrong. . . . The second movement shows . . . the simple pastoral realm that is free from the tragic conflicts of Sicilia. But it, too, will ultimately develop a collision within itself. . . . The third movement is the penitent world, in which the King . . . sees those who were dispersed brought back, and those who were lost restored to himself. The logical thought of the action, therefore, is that guilt produces the second or pastoral world, and repentance the third or restoration. . . . All the special or mediated dramas [the

Romances] of Shakespeare, as distinguished from his tragedies and pure comedies, have three movements of a similar character. For [59] the guilt of man can be atoned for only by repentance; and Art, the representation of man, must employ the same instrumentality." PAFFORD (ed. 1963, pp. liv–lv): "It is better to give it three parts [1.1–3.2, 3.3–4.4, and 5]. . . . But [WT] is not [lv] a dramatic curiosity consisting of separate parts; it is a whole. . . . Not only does the middle part stir the mind and heart of itself, but by the contrast of its beauty, love, youth . . . and venial roguery, it intensifies the dramatic effect of the ugliness, the oppressive adult madness, hatred and murderous crime at court in the first part and the sober serenity of the last. It is so essential to the plot that, if it were removed, the last part also could not exist." KERMODE (ed. 1963, pp. xxvii, xxx) also divides the play in three parts, of which the ending is an "act of recognition . . . nowhere more daringly conceived" and the whole of the play as (p. xxx) "unorthodox structurally" as the final scene. SWINDEN (1973, p. 164): WT "is, in everything but its plotting, three separate works of art"; the first is an "almost complete tragic action in three acts"; Act 4 is "completely divorced from everything around it"; Act 5 is equally unconnected to the other segments.

HAPPÉ (1969, p. 13): "Destructive and fatal aspects" of WT are confined to Acts 1 and 2 and the first part of Act 3. A lengthy pastoral episode provides complete contrast. "Finally the play moves back to Sicilia where the effects of the pastoral are worked out. . . . The different aspects of the story are concentrated at length so that the contrast is massive, simple and powerful." NELSON (1972, pp. 58–9): The play features "two levels of experience" (the "apocalyptic vision" of Leontes's palace; the "idyllic vision" of the pastoral world) on which Sh. "constructs a cyclical structure which reinforces the prevailing theme of rebirth." To suggest the rebirth cycle, the three-part structure moves the action from Sicilia to Bohemia and back to Sicilia "for the final reordering of society." Sh. also "lends his ending an irrevocable unity through a skillful use of contrasts and parallels": two tyrannically unjust monarchs create disorder in their kingdoms, mother and daughter are "identified with perfection and reconciliatory powers, and two loyal servants help to bring about the final reconciliation." The (p. 59) cyclical action, parallels, and contrasts achieve "a sense of an all-inclusive harmony, where one generation is united with another, where man is in harmony with nature, where all levels of humanity are brought into social cohesion, and where all these actions are directed and reinforced by an artistic vision of spiritual inviolability at the end." LENZ (1986, pp. 93–6, 110) "divides [WT] into three distinct sections [part one consisting of acts 1–3, part two of act 4, part three of act 5], each associated with a specific genre" and with (p. 96) "a set formula" consisting of "a prophetic statement; a series of remarks, actions and events that substantiate the prophecy; and the ironic fulfillment of the original statement. This pattern . . . can be found in the play's plot skeleton. There is the oracle about finding that which is lost, the scenes devoted to the lost one, Perdita, and her eventual restoration to her father, each step corresponding to a section of the play as [LENZ has] divided it: prediction (Part One), substantiation (Part Two), fulfillment (Part Three)." With the final change of locale that brings the characters together in Sicilia, (p. 110) "we should

751

recognize the legitimacy of the three part division. . . . The play that begins as a tragedy . . . and turns to pastoral . . . finishes as a romance."

Critics occasionally discuss models for the triptych. MARTZ (1980, pp. 123–4, 131): *WT* is "a trilogy of redemption on the Aeschylean model." Though he is "not prepared to press this idea very hard," he finds the analogy useful in revealing the play's essential tripartite division of tragedy, comedy, and miracle. To accommodate this division, (p. 124) the "second play" begins not with Time (4.1) but with the change of scene from Sicilia to Bohemia (3.3), showing the movement from (p. 131) "the ancient tragedy of blood through the cyclical, pagan world of great creating nature, and on now to the present time when, in humanist terms, faith, nourished by art and grace, may witness a triumphant restoration of the world to goodness." COHEN (1982, p. 128): Sh.'s "entire theatrical career can be seen as one vast dialectical structure, in which the comedies engender their own antithesis in the subsequent tragedies, which are in turn negated and superseded by the synthetic vision of the romances. In the structure of each [romance] . . . Shakespeare internally recapitulates the general progression of two decades. Nowhere is this clearer than in [*WT*'s] self-consciously disjunctive structure."

TRAVERSI (1955, pp. 106–7) suggests a four-part division, a "beautifully balanced construction," analogous to four musical movements. The first "deals with the tragic breakdown of . . . unity"; the second is the "turning-point of the whole action" since it sets the destructive tempest [symbol of "divine displeasure"] against the Shepherd's discovery and rescue of the abandoned baby in a single episode that connects "the tragic past with the happy future in an anticipation of the final reconciliation." The third is an "evocation of spring" in the pastoral scene, which also exposes Perdita to "the maturing influence of adverse circumstances." The fourth (p. 107) shows "penitence as prelude to restoration" of harmony between Leontes and Polixenes, and Leontes and Hermione, at the last restored "in all her gracious perfection." LEECH (1958, pp. 25, 30) and VYVYAN (1960, p. 17): The play is Terentian. Each act corresponds to a phase of the story.

Several other unique views of structure are explored. DRIVER (1960, pp. 181–3): "The pattern is circular, with the pastoral scenes enveloped by those of court life. The idea of roundedness and enveloping is suggested early in the play by Hermione's pregnancy. . . . [*182*] The image of the pregnant circle comes in also through the idea of the blessed island . . . of Apollo [quotes 1146–8]. The earth itself is also imagined as a sphere in the center of other spheres [refers to 708–9]. Perhaps the most important occasion of the encircling idea, however, is in the famous speech which Polixenes delivers to Perdita [1899–1908]. . . . [*183*] The form of the play contains the meaning, yet the meaning is that which stands above and controls the form." GARBER (1974, p. 163): "The large structural units of the play are the four seasons of the year: winter in the opening 'jealousy' scene at Leontes' court; spring with the finding of the child in Bohemia; summer in the great pastoral scene of the sheepshearing; and autumn or harvest in the return to Sicilia and the restoration of the king's wife and child, assuring order and fertility. This cyclical movement is occasionally cut, or halted by moments of . . . [timelessness], when the world of dream and the irrational intersects with the ongoing world which surrounds it." HALE (1985, pp. 152-3): "A balancing of the effects of evil and good is an organizing principle of Shakespeare's treatment of romances . . . [*153*] bound up with its time-span of two generations, corroborated by its seasonal progression through winter to spring and onwards." BATTENHOUSE (1980, p. 133): The structure emerges as "a manifestation of faith balanced against the threefold manifestation of faithlessness in prodigal Leontes, Polixenes and Autolycus. Of the four guardians, the old Shepherd and his son are rustics while Camillo and Paulina are courtiers. But all four have shepherding roles which develop progressively in the drama's action." PEYRÉ (1984, p. 155): In the midst of the play there are several "tableaux" of a theatrical nature: the Polixenes/Hermione dumb show . . . ; the vision of Antigonus; the reunion of Leontes and Perdita . . . ; the statue of Hermione, the resurrection of which is . . . like "an old tale" [3328] and could not happen without the cooperation of the spectators [quotes "It . . . Faith" (3300-1)]. The play employs its own mirrors and sets onto the stage situations that reflect the theatrical situation itself (in Fr.).

Others who comment on structure: RISTINE (1910; 1963, p. 113), WELSFORD (1927; 1962, p. 288), GROSE & OXLEY (1965; 1969, p. 82), MUIR (1968, p. 14), BON-JOUR (1969, p. 209), BLISSETT (1971, pp. 53-6), JONES (1971, pp. 68, 85), REES (1971), EVANS (ed. 1974, p. 1564), PRESTON (1978, p. 422), UPHAUS (1981, p. 70), DRAPER (1985, p. 14), FRYE (1986), CASTROP (1987, p. 75), and TOLIVER (1989, p. 154).

LANGUAGE AND STYLE

KENNEDY (1942, p. 111): With Sh.'s maturity comes "an enriching in expression, an increasing ease with which an outline is worked out, and a subduing of outline in the attainment of the total ultimate effect." The language and style are vehicles of Sh.'s achievement, although his handling of them in *WT* is not universally admired.

The CLARKES (ed. 1865, 1:678, citing 777-86) think the "entirely confused con-structions" and "imperfectly expressed sentences" result in incoherent ideas "hud-dling one upon another; parenthetical and ill-sequent." LATHAM (1887-92, p. 424) also notes Leontes's "unclearness of style," an idea PYLE (1969, p. 21 n.) develops: "In framing the spectacle of Leontes' unsettlement in incoherent monologue [Sh.] makes the incoherence at least somewhat informative. . . . But incoherence it re-mains." WENDELL (1894, pp. 379-81): "In both substance and style the *Winter's Tale* is overcrowded . . . [*380*] obscure and crabbed. The verse is more licentiously free than ever before, and at the same time overpacked with [*381*] meaning. . . . He [Sh.] cares about substance rather than style. Thoughts crowd upon him. . . . He disdain-fully neglects both the amenity of regular form, and the capacity of human audiences. In [*WT*] Shakspere's style is surely more decadent than ever before." SNIDER (c. 1890, p. 459): "The versification of [*WT*], while not so fluent and harmonious as in his earlier works," nonetheless has a "sweep and flexibility, showing indeed an orchestral variety and strength." CARRINGTON (1956, p. 28, quoting 1347-50 through "done:") also has some reservations: "Dramatically such a style is inferior, as it is difficult to understand the thought at the speed at which it is spoken. But the *form* of Shakespeare's mature verse [makes] the dialogue more natural and more adapted to different characters" because of run-on lines, feminine endings, and rich, vivid imagery.

More often, however, critics praise the fluidity, the appropriateness of *WT*'s verse. HERFORD (ed. 1916–, p. vii) admires the "bold and often exceedingly beautiful subordination of the line to the sentence or the paragraph in verse-rhythm." CORSON (1889, pp. 75–7): "As the poet advances in dramatic identification, the metre of his blank verse yields more and more to the movement of the thought," a view BRINK (1895, p. 98) echoes enthusiastically: "His verse . . . has become an instrument which he treats with a royal arbitrariness . . . but which still resounds with the irresistible torrent of his thoughts." SAINTSBURY (1923, 2:36) explains: Sh. "not only indulges in the redundant syllable [an eleventh syllable added at the end of a pentameter] freely, but is particularly fond of making his coupling foot with the next line redundant [cites 2413–14 where -*ing* is redundant]. . . . So, too, he is also fond of fashioning this union out of the conjunction 'and' [as in 1939–40] — a perfectly justifiable thing . . . but . . . a dangerous one in unskilful hands." KERMODE (ed. 1963, p. xxii): The "turbulence both in the action and in the language" of *WT* is reflected in the verse, which "frequently registers not a gentle detachment but rather a remarkable activity of mind. Thus the jealousy of Leontes may . . . be a less complex matter than that of Othello; but it is less simply expressed." VICKERS (1971, p. 97): "What modern critics describe as the 'texture' of verse is in fact the product of a skilful use of rhetoric," especially such schemes of construction as parallelism, antithesis, anaphora, and epanalepsis, though McDONALD (1985, pp. 316, 328–9) stresses the periodic organization of Sh.'s verse: "Convoluted sentences or difficult speeches become coherent and meaningful only in their final clauses . . . [just as] the shape and meaning of events become apparent only in [*WT*'s] final moments. . . . [*328*] Correspondence of language, form, and dramatic universe suggests an identification among speaker, dramatist, and Providence that clarifies the meaning not only of the play in question but of the tragicomic universe as well. If Leontes' verse does not immediately make itself clear, neither does Sh.'s construction of events, nor does the divine architect's of events, nor . . . of man's experience. . . . [*329*] The grammatical delays and obstacles that temporarily obscure meaning in the middle of a protracted sentence are parts of a larger whole that is eventually elucidated. Something similar may be said of the particular happening in the action of [*WT*]."

BETHELL (1947, pp. 22–3) claims that Sh. makes little attempt "to indicate character by giving a particular type of verse permanently to a particular stage personage," that there is (p. 23) "less difference in the quality of the verse between Leontes and Perdita than between Leontes jealous and Leontes penitent," and that "to have differentiated character by means of the verse would have meant sacrificing complexity . . . and what [the characters] are is much less important than what they say." Many critics are convinced otherwise. KNIGHT (1947, p. 83) first issues a warning — "One must beware of regarding tormented rhythms as a poetical goal. Possibly we over-rate Shakespeare's rough-handling of language to correspond to the twists and jerks of psychic experience. . . . One can often approve a poet's disrespect to the tyrannies of rhythm and syntax; but there are dangers. . . . Such a crammed, often cramped . . . style is certainly most effective when expressing nightmare or disintegration. . . . Where no especial disorder . . . is concerned, the result can irritate.'' KNIGHT finally asserts: "With Leontes, however, the purpose has been patent; the disrupted style not merely fits, it explores and exposes, the anguish depicted.'' As SMITH (1968, p. 318) says: "It is not that Shakespeare is presenting his character purely in terms of language rather than action, but that in Leontes the language is very pertinent indeed.''

HARDINGE (1818, 3:50): "If you mark the *words* [in the opening dialogue between Leontes and Polixenes (50-82)], you will find how infinitely more *quaint* and *forced* are the *Sicilian* ones, which is the nature and genius of all counterfeited affections. They overshoot the object of their aim, by determining not to be short of it. The sentences of *Leontes* are short, and are evidently constrained,—those of *Polyxenes* natural and flowing, easy and careless.'' HUDSON (1848, 1:324, citing 181-92): Leontes's speech "seems to have caught the distemper of the character: crabbed, knotty, harsh, oblique, enigmatical, vague, full of violent jerks, and stops, and starts, and ending neither here nor there, it betrays at every turn the monster of the thought.'' TINKLER (1937, pp. 355, 361) says of the "complex disorganization'' of 377-83: Leontes's speech "rapidly becomes more inclusive and more suggestive. This acceleration is seen in the jerky movement, the telescoping of phrases which become more and more elliptical, and the progressive repetition. . . . [*361*] The deaths of his son and wife are 'purges' for the king and there is a sudden, daring modulation in the feeling. The crude coarseness and spasmodic movement give way to a calm resignation. The difference may be seen in comparing the verse of the Jealousy Speeches with that of the repentant ones [1338-57, 1424-35].'' THORNE (1971, pp. 56-63) describes Leontes's early incoherence as "highly idiosyncratic,'' his grammar revealing "unusual features not to be found . . . elsewhere in the play,'' including awkard syntax which (p. 57) "serves to underline the absurdity'' of Leontes's assertion that "To mingle friendship farre, is mingling bloods'' (182); the "use made of conjunction to turn his sentences into lists . . . of synonyms or near synonyms [e.g. 185-6, 188-91]''; (p. 58) the use of words from one sentence "expressing [Leontes's] morbid imaginings'' to suggest the words of the next (320-4), by which means he convinces himself that he is "dealing with a mass of objective evidence''; (p. 59) the use of semantically empty pronouns—those referring to other pronouns or lacking clear referents (283-5)—to suggest Leontes's "tragic capacity to take his own expressions of jealousy as reports of states of affairs actually existing in the outside world''; (p. 61) a reduction in connections between parts of sentences (328-30) that isolates the sentence from its context to make one part an ironic commentary on the other. To THORNE, the "compression and confusion of Leontes' style of speech'' convey the qualities of his mind, to FREY (*Vast Romance*, 1980, p. 124), his "isolation and constriction'' does so, and DRAPER (1985, p. 19) also notes this isolation: Leontes's language turns "inward, ceasing to be a means of communication,'' though Sh.'s deliberate obscurity is "highly effective'' in dramatic terms. KNIGHTS (1976, pp. 601-2): It is impossible to make Leontes's speech "conform to ordinary syntactical forms:

the point is its disjointedness. The marked caesuras and the frequent parentheses produce a panting, heaving movement which tells you what to think of the appearance of argument with which Leontes tries to establish his belief. . . . [*602*] Fissures in the deep structure of the sentences are used to express a distortion . . . in the preverbal levels" of Leontes's thought.

At this same level—a "pre-linguistic state of consciousness" where, according to NEELY (1975, p. 324), Leontes's emotions originate—the "inchoate emotion seeks shape and expression in words, and words in their turn give it substance and definition." Michael TAYLOR (1982, p. 233): Leontes "seems unable to prevent his words . . . from [becoming] acts of semantic treachery," possibly because, as HUNT ("Standing," 1984, pp. 20-1) says, Leontes believes his "autocratic words create their own private contexts for understanding. . . . In their 'truth', they need no accompanying contexts for interpretation. . . . [*21*] In Leontes's opinion, the act of speech fixes character forever." WEXLER (1988, pp. 109-10) agrees: "Leontes' accusations require no corroboration because he has the power of assertion. Language supplies all the proof he needs. . . . [*110*] Meaning is self-present in words" and his words, he believes, "correspond to external reality." HOLBROOK (1964, pp. 147, 151): Leontes's words are "coarse and inchoate. . . . Sensual imagery of coition mingled with disgust" push him into using (p. 151) "the crudely emotive language of the London street [359-70]." NUTTALL (1966, p. 26): Leontes indulges in equivocation and "sexual double-entendres . . . [in] such numbers that the conscientious annotator could fill pages with them [quotes 190-1, 197-8, 269-71]." KNIGHT (1947, p. 81): "The spasmodic jerks of his language reflect Leontes' unease: he is, as it were, being sick; ejecting a poison, which yet grows stronger; something he has failed to digest, assimilate. . . . Our most virulent speech of disgust involves the much-loathed spider [quotes 636-42]," the words of which, BARTON (1980, p. 133) states, "involuntarily but quite explicitly" inform us that Leontes has poisoned his own mind. MARSH (1962; 1980, pp. 128-30): "Because [Leontes's] concern is with [*129*] self there is even a note of grim enjoyment in 'my heart dances [183],' . . . [and] something akin to enjoyment in the realization of his own importance as a wronged husband. . . . [*130*] In words of the greatest crudity and bitterness he describes what appears to him as the absolute lack of virtue in the sexual relationship, which perpetuates life [quotes 274-86]." HUSSEY (1992, p. 232): Sh. lets Leontes play with the different sense of words, but Leontes "always chooses the worst sense," the "deliberately, revoltingly obscene" sense.

Also commenting on Leontes's language: LAWRENCE (1937, p. 46), GODDARD (1951, p. 651), EVANS (1952, p. 181), SMITH ("Affectio," 1963, p. 163), FOAKES (1971, p. 121), TROUSDALE (1976, pp. 31-2), BELLETTE (1978, pp. 67-8), DAVID (1978, p. 33), ANSARI (1979, p. 125), SPENDER (1982, p. 236), ORNSTEIN (1986, p. 221), SANDERS (1987, p. 24).

Some of Hermione's conversation with Polixenes, NATHAN (1968, p. 19) claims, is actually "provocative," while FRENCH (1972, pp. 138-42) says the lines she uses to get Polixenes to stay (104-15) are almost crude. The (p. 141) "obvious sexual connotations" and overtones of her dialogue, given Hermione's advanced pregnancy,

(p. 142) "must jangle in the ears of a man already thinking about married sexuality." FELPERIN ("Tongue-Tied," 1985, p. 9): The more carefully we look at Hermione's lines (149-80), the less conclusive of her innocence the verbal evidence is, since her language may be construed "either within or outside the bounds of royal hospitality and wifely decorum. Her emphasis on greater warmth in persuasion may signify flirtation; the indefinite antecedents of her royal pronouns, self-incrimination; her earthy wit, bawdry; and her rhetorical juxtapositions of 'husband' and 'friend,' a fatal identification of the two." Michael TAYLOR (1982, p. 232), however, maintains the opposite: Hermione "speaks a language everyone understands. . . . Guileless, exuberant, colloquial, varied in tone and structure, studded with exclamations and questions," her language, with its "innocent fervor" and wit, is that of "a good woman in a fallen world." FRIPP (1938, 2:745) thinks Hermione's "defence in the Court of Justice should be noted for . . . the 'broken metre' of a troubled speaker." KENNEDY (1942, p. 162), however, notes her skills — "Her forensic achieves the introduction of rhetoric in poetic according to the best classical tradition" — as does BELLETTE (1978, pp. 69-70): "The weight of the [trial] scene is carried by Hermione. . . . Her sense of occasion and her timing are impeccable. . . . [70] Her 'case' rests upon such plain and unadorned words as 'honour' [1215-17], 'love' [1241 etc.], 'free' [1290], 'friend' [1246]." PITT (1981, p. 128), however, suggests that her language "never seems to bring us close to her suffering. . . . The cadences of her long speeches contesting Leontes' indictment [1196-1295] are eloquent and measured, but their very logic and polish encourages us to approach Hermione intellectually rather than through the language of the heart."

Perdita's verse evokes a similar reaction. HUNTER (1954, p. 286): We see in her "unmistakably the quality of a princess" because Sh. "has written into her speech a most remarkable expression of her personality. It is delicate, dainty, maidenly speech, coy and sweet, and though spoken with the freshness of the springtime meadows, yet still girlishly precise and proper with the dignity of a princess to the manner born." PAFFORD (ed. 1963, p. lxxvii) does not find her quite so delicate: "Perdita is a shepherdess and her speech is frank and outspoken, like that of all Shakespeare's women. There is little spiritual and nothing sentimental in the expression of her love for Florizel," though HOBSON (1972, p. 204) praises her beautifully realized love-language (e.g., 1945-50). Like PAFFORD, SWINDEN (1973, p. 158) says Perdita's "language is full of references to breeding and bastards, impregnated with knowledge of the body, of sexuality, of the physicality of being. . . . Perdita's conversation with Polixenes is . . . full and frank," though "consistent with her undoubted spiritual and technical ignorance." PITT (1981, p. 129): Her language "sparkles with energy and colour, reflecting her close association with nature" and the fresh, warm innocence and "playful sexuality" of her relationship with Florizel.

Time's language and style get almost as much attention as Leontes's language does. Many critics find the speech (1580-1611) inferior. RIDLEY (1937, p. 208): "One hopes not Shakespeare's." WHITE (ed. 1857, 5:397): "There could hardly be a greater difference in style than that between Time's speech as Chorus and the rest of the verse in this play. The former is direct, simple, composed of the commonest words used in their commonest signification, but bald and tame, and in its versification very constrained and ungraceful: the latter is involved, parenthetical, having a vocabulary of its own, but rich in beauties of thought and expression, and entirely untrammelled by the form in which it is written. . . . The Chorus I believe not to have been written by Shakespeare." ROLFE (ed. 1879, p. 181) rejects it because "not only the style of the speech, but its being in rhyme, may lead us to doubt whether S. wrote it." HUDSON (ed. 1880, 7:282): "The authorship . . . is, to say the least, exceedingly doubt-ful. . . . The workmanship is at once clumsy, languid, and obscure. Shakespeare indeed is often obscure; but his obscurity almost always results from compression of thought, not from clumsiness of tongue or brain." WILSON (ed. 1931, p. 159): "The style of this Chorus, with its rhyming couplets, its forced rhymes, its jerky rhythms and its obscure emptiness, is exactly that of the verse in [*MM* and *AWW*] which I attribute to a collaborator."

GREG (1955, p. 417), however: "It is no great achievement . . . but not all readers will agree with [WILSON's] denigration of the style or refuse to find in it some Shakespearian turns of phrase." STAPFER (1879; 1880, p. 60) does: "It would be im-possible to speak in a quieter and prouder tone than this, and nothing is more striking in Time's speech than its dignified calmness and serenity." KITTREDGE (ed. 1936, p. 432): Time "should speak in character. And that is precisely how he does speak — as old Father Time — a doddering, toothless ancient, halting but fluent, senile but self-assured, ridiculous but triumphant [character]. . . . If the speech were better, it would not be so good." PAFFORD (ed. 1963, pp. lxxxvi–lxxxvii, 168): "The language of Time befits the character in its rather naive simplicity and befits the 'scene' as being an episode quite distinct from the course of the play. . . . [*lxxxvii*] This pageant language was probably as conventional as stage dialect and is precisely the language which an audience would expect from old Father Time," perhaps because it is (p. 168) "the conventional language used in contemporary Lord Mayor's pageants, and entirely befits the character of Time and the purpose of the speech. It acts as a bridge, gives information, and distinguishes Time from the other characters." TURNER (1971, pp. 147–9): "Time's speech *is* obscure. . . . It is very difficult to get anything of significance out of these short, ambiguous phrases. The words in the speech are impenetrable: generalized and impassive, very different from the concrete and partic-ular language Shakespeare seems to use even for his most universal philosophy. . . . Various points, however, should lead us to a realization of the importance of the speech of Time. First of all we note its dense and complex grammar, with the syn-tactical ambiguities which often appear when Shakespeare is bent on conveying dif-ficult and important ideas. . . . [*148*] The simplicity and impenetrability of the words are deliberate. . . . [*149*] It is enough to put Time on the stage, give him a speech of oracular obscurity, and let the play itself fill his words with particular meaning." LLOYD EVANS (1982, p. 369): "Despite the fact that [Time's] words are neither stirring, philosophical, memorable or lyrical, his actual intervention at this point has a pow-erful influence on our experience of the play. There is no other play which at any given point offers such a tremendous sense that what has happened prior to the point is not only literally in the past but, as it were, historically and dramatically so." LUDWIG

(1974, p. 380): The style of the speech "is perfectly suited to its description of time as a force which brings together in itself all kinds of opposites." Time's couplets contrast with patrician blank verse on the one hand and plebeian prose on the other.

TINKLER (1937, p. 350) takes note of an exception: "Unlike the other rustics, who all speak in prose, the Shepherd speaks in verse which is yet very close to prose: it has a remarkably concrete quality, which at one level might be discussed in terms of a realism which is concerned with the depiction of a precise visual impression in the style of Dutch paintings. . . . The movement of the verse enacts the gestures of the speaking peasant, slow heavy gesture — 'pantler, butler, cook . . . welcomed all, served all' [1861 - 2] — which are never quite clumsy, and seem to bring remarkable weight behind each point as if the whole body were speaking." COOPER (1977, pp. 141, 143): "When the Old Shepherd does speak in blank verse it is still in a naturalistic low style, not elevated beyond his rank [cites 1865 - 6]. . . . The integrity of pastoral life comes from its realism . . . and from the art that is rooted in nature. . . . [*143*] Moral value and linguistic simplicity are equated; the poetic theory reinforces the moral statement implicit in the world of pastoral."

In discussing the language of shepherds, clowns, and servants, however, critics are usually talking about Sh.'s prose, despite STEINER's (1961, p. 249) feeling that though the clown, the servants, and the shepherd "speak in prose, . . . poetry knocks at every door." DELIUS (1870, pp. 228 - 9, 250 - 1) assigns Sh.'s prose to three different levels: The lowest befits Sh.'s clowns, though not only clowns speak it. Direct, unadorned, syntactically simple, it is natural for dialogue, less natural for mono- logue. At a higher level is the conversational prose of characters from upper social strata, marked by (p. 229) structured expressions and fairly complicated syntax and serving as a vehicle for intentional, subtle humor and wit. The highest level — euphu- istic prose used in formal situations by the aristocrats and characterized by elegantly turned phrases and complicated metaphors and syntactic structures (antithesis es- pecially) — is employed in the last plays to report on specific events or to establish a festive, ceremonial tone. Both (p. 250) 1.1 and 4.2 are euphuistic; 3.3 uses levels one and two (the Clown's description of the shipwreck [1530 - 43] demonstrates Sh.'s virtuosity); (p. 251) 5.2 combines levels one and three (in Ger.).

CRANE (1951, p. 122) finds that the "use of prose in exposition-scenes suggests Shakespeare's desire to render his exposition more natural by introducing it into casual conversation," but CHAMPION (1970, p. 165) finds the exposition of lines 44 - 7 anything but natural: In describing "the entertainment . . . and the long-lived and powerful bond of friendship between the two kings," Camillo and Archidamus use "terms so extravagant as to suggest artificiality." FELPERIN (1972, p. 223) calls the idiom of these lines "perfectly colloquial" but adds: "To the extent that their figures of speech play on the impossible and conjure up the miraculous, their language is . . . oracular, reflective of the romantic nature of the play as a whole." FRENCH (1972, pp. 135 - 6) believes that the two courtiers, "more than half-aware of the ab- surdity" of their speech, themselves burlesque it, thus raising "implicit questions about what words the voice of true feeling could ever find in [Leontes's] court." TOLIVER (1989, p. 159): Camillo and Archidamus manage "to suggest an opera buffa"

with their attempts at urbanity and their use of unwieldy language to describe supposedly "powerful and enduring" sentiments. HARBAGE (1961, p. 444) insists, however, that Camillo's speech, "consistently straightforward and lucid," is the "'normal'
language of the play. It is wonderfully quick, compact, expressive," an expressiveness
also noted in his use of "the language of disease" (e.g., 353-4, 491-4) by MOULTON
(1903, p. 66) and CLEMEN (1951, p. 198). ADAMS (1989, pp. 93-4): Camillo exercises
greater "suavity and dexterity" in courtly compliment than Archidamus, whose "less
urbane diction and ruder [*94*] notions of entertainment" suggest that Sh. thought of
Bohemia as "a more natural and genuine society—less sophisticated than Italy but
more authentic."

Dissecting the language of the other inhabitants of Bohemia, BORINSKI (1955,
pp. 64-5) finds the prose of the Shepherd and Clown "basically . . . naturalistic
. . . because these clowns are real peasants. . . . Their images are of the homeliest
kind [cites "as you'ld thrust a Corke into a hogshead" (1535-6)]. Yet their speech is
nevertheless stylized. In such a passage as ["the men are not yet cold vnder water,
nor the Beare halfe din'd on the Gentleman: he's at it now" (1546-7)] the effect is
produced by means which might be deemed overdone in a purely realistic comedy;
here it is stylization with poetic overtones." VICKERS (1968, pp. 413, 420), "pleased
to discover more energy and invention in the lower medium [in *WT*] than in any of
the late comedies," notes that the Clown (p. 420), in promising to bury any scraps
of Antigonus left behind after the bear finishes feeding, refers to Antigonus as *it*
(1570), making "left-overs" of a human being and even further reducing Antigonus
"to a pronoun, and neuter at that. . . . By the clever manipulation of the sequence
of [the Clown's] speech and his use of imagery and rhetorical structure, Shakespeare
has succeeded in completely dehumanizing the sailors and Antigonus (no deaths move
us less), turning the potentially tragic into the comic. . . . This is surely the most
creative adaptation of prose in all the last plays." HARDY (1989, pp. 21-2) also calls
this "great comic narrative. . . . The naive Clown is used to mimic maladroit telling. . . . [*22*] This is a rare instance of present tense, or nearly present-tense, narrative . . . up-to-date and immediate. . . . Its presentness has a special comic grisly
vivacity. . . . The narration creates an emotional collision, comic and grotesque."

The pastoral world also has its scoundrel. BORINSKI (1955, p. 65): Autolycus is
also "differentiated from the peasants. . . . He is a clever rogue, and accordingly his
speech is more intellectual, with a higher proportion of nouns and abstracts, even
learned allusions and especially metaphors, always the surest sign of intellectuality.
He is full of irony, but his irony is different from Falstaff's; it is finer, gentler. . . .
There is poetry in his roguery."

TRAVERSI (1955, pp. 181-4): Another segment of "grave and involved prose
[3011-3182] is seen, on closer reading, not to be mere decoration, but to belong to
the spirit of the play, in forming which it plays its own distinctive part. . . . The
Gentleman's account of the finding of the child Perdita, as related by the Shepherd,
and the manner of the telling, far from being an excursion into literary artifice, is
admirably calculated both to maintain the necessary 'legendary' quality of the episode . . . and to further the symbolic unity of the whole. . . . [*183*] The prose, at

once carefully elaborated and finely evocative, is . . . a factor of primary importance. . . . The words of the Gentleman are charged with symbolic undertones [quotes 3053–6]. . . . [*184*] The apparently contrary emotions of joy and sorrow have become fused. . . . The wrapping of this description in carefully elaborated forms of expression, coupled with the stressing of its similarity to an old 'tale', contributes to removing the action from common modes of feeling, and thus to the creation of the necessary symbolic atmosphere."

Paradoxically, the conclusion (3184 ff.) interests critics not for its dialogue but for its silences. ADAMS (1989, p. 105) finds it chilling that "Leontes never addresses to his daughter a word that the audience can hear, nor does Polixenes say a word to his son; in fact, Leontes addresses only a brief sentence to Bohemia, perfunctorily begging pardon for his scandalous suspicions and his efforts to murder a sacred guest as well as a dear friend [3361–3]." MATCHETT (1969, p. 104): The statue scene, climaxing "not in a burst of impassioned verse, but in a silent embrace," suggests not just a curious circumstance but a reflection of the play's attention to the limitations of language. "Silence, then, becomes the final language, the language of love and forgiveness which all can understand, the wordless communion in which the exchange is most complete." DUSINBERRE (1975, p. 221): Words, especially those which "give shape to Leontes' imaginings, seem in the end suspect and inexpressive"; Hermione and Leontes, reunited "after sixteen years . . . embrace silently. The trial scene desecrated words between them."

Characters

Regarding *WT*'s characters, FELPERIN (1972, pp. 218–20): Sh. endows his "major characters with a life that extends beyond the confines of the immediate action, and of which we catch fleeting glimpses as they speak or are spoken of by others. . . . [*219*] It is a striking feature of [*WT*] that it reveals much more of the vital information concerning the principals than is, strictly speaking, required by the plot or usual even in a Shakespearean play [e.g., Hermione's recollection of her father, Polixenes's of his and Leontes's childhood, Leontes's of his courtship]. . . . The world of this play is populated with characters . . . who bear an extraordinary resemblance . . . to the men and women we know in the real world. . . . [*220*] [*WT*] presents the archetypal aspect of human experience, but it does so by making the part suggest the whole, the personal suggest the universal, the momentary self-revelation of a character evoke a complete offstage existence."

ANTIGONUS

Not all critics treat Antigonus kindly. CLARKE (1863, p. 357): "We scarcely regret his [Antigonus's] fate since he lent himself to the king's cruelty" by consenting to expose the infant Perdita. The CLARKES (ed. 1865, 1:677, n. 22): "In the very first words Antigonus utters" (735–6), he "admits the possibility that Hermione may be guilty [actually he uses "Iustice" ironically]. . . . Antigonus at once proclaims himself the courtier, the man who points out to his royal master the expediency and policy of what he is about to do as touches his own person, his consort, and his heir-apparent. . . . Antigonus, with his courtier pliancy and lack of earnest faith—having a glimpse of the better, yet following the worser path—becomes the agent for the king's cruelty to his infant daughter, and loses his own life in the unworthy act." FARRELL (1975, p. 215): When Camillo flees, Antigonus replaces him as counselor, however briefly. "Symbolically, Leontes' 'madness' drives out good counsel, leaving a henpecked and irresolute old man whose weakness mirrors the King's." FOWLER (1978, p. 45): "Antigonus has a conventional inclination to obey his sovereign right or wrong. . . . In a sense he is even accessory to Leontes' crimes. . . . Antigonus acts 'against generation'—and against faith in Hermione's innocence—when a vision convinces him of her guilt." Mark TAYLOR (1982, pp. 20-3): Antigonus harbors "nearly unspeakable incestuous desires" as he offers to geld his daughters if Hermione is adulterous (cites lines 758-60). When he swears to Leontes that he will do anything to prevent the immediate death of Perdita, Antigonus commits himself to the repugnant act of exposing the baby. On the journey, his dream of Hermione convinces him she was unchaste. He says so twice (quotes 1483-8, 1491-3) and seems to believe it. Since, on reaching Sicilia again, he could geld his daughters, "Antigonus's death is both punishment and prevention: he has acted against one innocent, and he would act against three more. . . . Incest (including mutilation as a symbol of incest) is an unimaginably severe threat to the moral order, and it is forestalled by Antigonus's death" (p. 23). TAYLOR alone seems to think so.

Other critics view Antigonus favorably. HAPPÉ (1969, pp. 20-1): Antigonus, like Paulina and Camillo, is a representative of the "forces of reconciliation and common [21] sense. . . . Each seeks to put right the wrongs done by Leontes. Paulina stands out for her sharp tongue, Camillo for his balanced judgment and resourcefulness and Antigonus for his loyalty to Hermione." SCHANZER (ed. 1969, p. 18): Antigonus does not die "for allowing himself to become an accessory to the crime [of exposing the infant]. . . . This is not how Shakespeare presents the matter. He depicts Antigonus as an entirely upright, humane, and honourable old courtier, who carries out the command in fulfillment of a solemn oath, and as an alternative to seeing the child 'instantly consumed with fire' [1062]. . . . Shakespeare could not have been more careful to keep Antigonus free from guilt in the exposure of the child." Whatever the case, BARTON (1980, p. 143) notes, Antigonus "pays heavily" for misinterpreting his dream about Hermione.

AUTOLYCUS

This skillfully created character, Sh.'s own invention, pleases many critics. JOHNSON (ed. 1765, 2:349), tersely: "*Autolycus* is very naturally conceived, and strongly represented." PRICE (1890, p. 204): The character took on a life of its own as Sh. developed it, and the "excessive length" of development simply mirrors Sh.'s own "delight in the character itself." HUDSON (1848, 1:336): "The most amiable and ingenious thieving rogue we shall anywhere find. . . . The sight, or smell, or suspicion of money, transforms him into an artist; and he cheats almost as divinely as those about him love. In [a]cuteness, he outyankees the Yankees altogether." CLARKE (1863, p. 361): "That inexhaustible wag of a pedlar. . . . What a zest, what intense relish he has in trickery! . . . With what a twinkle of the eye, and irrepressible drollery beneath all, he shows the humour of the thing." GILES (1868; 1887, pp. 199–200): "But for Autolycus, the ideal world would have wanted its most admirable rascal—the actual world . . . a type for characters that are like him in everything but his brilliancy. For he is a brilliant scapegrace; a knave of many faculties; of sparkling versatility of parts; with wit equal to his thievery; quick, sharp, and changeable. . . . He never loses his self-respect being detected, or by failure. . . . [*200*] Autolycus is the generic charlatan . . . consummate in . . . lying, fraud, and imposition."

HERFORD (ed. 1904, 4:271): Autolycus, "the source of almost all the humour in the play," is "conceived with the finest congruity to his surroundings. Instead of being a court-jester adrift . . . he is the embodiment of rustic knavery, shrewdness and gaiety." CHANDLER (1907, 1:237): The sprightly and witty Autolycus "excels all the beggar-book crew or the rogues of reality. . . . [He] can no more repent and reform than Falstaff." SMEATON (1911, p. 513): Autolycus, "the ancestor of all the glorious 'picaroons' that were to follow him, of the line and lineage of Gil Blas, . . . [is] unquestionably the most delightful of all Shakespeare's rogues. Gifted with a glib tongue, he is never at a loss for a plausible story." AYDELOTTE (1913, p. 33): Autolycus "is compounded of many simples and mellowed by a touch of poetry which magically transforms the realism of the picture into something still more real. . . . He has the carefree spirit of the real vagabond as he trudges gaily on his knavish road." MATTHEWS (1913; 1970, p. 338): Autolycus is unscrupulous, friendly, rascally, wily. But with his sense of humor, "all the scenes in which he appears ring true." CRAIG (1948, p. 340): The character is a unique creation whose appeal lies "not so much in the cleverness of his roguery as in its lack of malice and in its congeniality with poetry."

NUTTALL (1966, p. 40): "Autolycus, with all his cunning, is as free from real *sophistication* as his victims. His first song [1669–90] sets a tone which never needs to be modified [in its] . . . joy and rapacity. Autolycus is as innocent as a magpie or a kite . . . utterly innocent, and utterly dishonest. His type of innocence . . . is not amenable to sentimental treatment." SENG (1967, p. 231): "Autolycus is more than a clowning peddler, ballad-singer and rogue, and he is more than an incidental character in the play. . . . Time as a Chorus . . . may advance the action of the play sixteen years, but it is not until Autolycus bursts onto the stage with song at [1668] that the change in time—and mood—becomes believable. With his entrance the dark and tragic winter of Leontes' jealousy melts into a spring of promise and young love." FREY (*Vast Romance*, 1980, pp. 148–9): Autolycus "mediates humorously between the claims of Polixenes and those of Perdita and Florizel. He excites a laughter whose result is always to lessen the tension between opposing forces: age and youth, pretension and reality, greed and charity, wrath and forgiveness. . . . [*149*] The Autolycan scene . . . generates the energy of laughter and carries the action forward." TREWIN (1978, p. 265): Autolycus is not to be seen merely as "an expansive variety act. He may be a vagrant rich in ballads, songs, and snatches; but he is also a fellow sharp of mind and eye."

Autolycus's sharp practices, however, lead some critics to discuss his flaws — along with mitigation for them. ROFFE (1872, p. 14): Autolycus is morally indefensible but "must be allowed to have a grain of geniality about him, which . . . has made it possible for him to be . . . artistically fitted into his position in [*WT*]. . . . He is indeed a most roguish Pedlar, but he is also right willing to sing, even for singing's sake." SNIDER (1877, pp. 487–9): "Autolycus is . . . not wholly a product of shepherd life, but apparently of the court also. . . . He is, moreover, negative only to the honesty of the pastoral character, while he par-[*488*]ticipates in its free joyousness and sportive nature. He is one [of] Shakespeare's higher efforts in comic delineation. . . . He is a rogue not so much from malice as from pleasure; he takes delight in thievery for its own sake rather than for its gains. He is aware of his misdeeds, and laughs at them. . . : His cunning is a source of continuous chuckling to himself. . . . He . . . belongs to the class of consciously comic characters, who make fun and enact folly chiefly for themselves. He celebrates his vagabond life and thievish disposition in verse. . . . He will assist in [*489*] breaking up the pastoral world and transferring it to Sicilia, where he will repent."

KNIGHT (1947; 1966, pp. 100, 111–12): Autolycus, at first "a figure of absolute comedy[,] . . . Spring incarnate, carefree, unmoral, happy, . . . sets the note for a spring-like turn in our drama"; but he also serves (p. 111) "to elaborate the vein of court satire already suggested by Polixenes' behaviour [2665–74]; it is almost a parody of that behaviour. The pick-pocket pedlar, now himself disguised as 'a great courtier' [2630], becomes absurdly superior. . . . His elaborate description of torments is extremely cruel; but then the court—Polixenes' harshness fresh in our minds—is cruel. . . . [*112*] After donning courtier's clothes, his humour takes an unnecessarily cruel turn. . . . His vice becomes less amusing as he indulges his lust for power; as his egotism expands, a cruel strain . . . is revealed; and he is at once recognized as inferior to the society on which, as a happy-go-lucky ragamuffin, he formerly preyed for our amusement. . . . Autolycus's last entry . . . is peculiarly revealing: we see him now bowing and scraping to his former gull [the Clown]. . . . The romance is to survive; not so Autolycus, who is to lose dramatic dignity."

MARSH (1962; 1980, pp. 143–4): "Set against the chill of winter is the red blood [*144*] of vigorous life, and in the robustness of this life is perhaps the clue to the way Autolycus should be taken. He is clearly not wholly admirable, for he preys on the credulity of the simple country folk. On the other hand, his crimes are not crimes against life, in the sense that he is never guilty of the cruelties of Leontes or Polixenes, and he does serve a useful purpose in exposing pretension and vanity." PAFFORD (ed. 1963, pp. lxxx–lxxxi): As a thief, cheat, and pickpocket, Autolycus could be "unpleasant" but isn't, because his "crimes" are primarily tricks, while he is (p. lxxxi) "an intelligent rogue, a schemer of ability [who] excites admiration and provokes laughter at the same time." CAZAMIAN (1965, pp. 295–6): Autolycus's "daily sinning" is no more than "a round of cheats, lies, thefts, and every fleshly excess." Autolycus may be more cheeky than "many rogues in the English literature of the Renaissance;

but none [is] more convincing, more brazen, and tricky than [he]. . . . [*296*] Still, the main source of his appeal is conscious, sly roguery." VICKERS (1968, p. 414): Though we may admire the resourceful guller, Autolycus's attitudes and "especially his images reveal a boasting superiority which is less attractive. . . . He is a cross between Chaucer's Pardoner and Falstaff. . . . But although Autolycus has the dissembler's power to adopt styles and is therefore potentially evil, he remains within a comic frame. . . . We are sure that no harm will come to anyone." PYLE (1969, p. 78): Autolycus, who "bursts upon the play unannounced, altering its tone, its point of view, enlarging its scope, at least for a time," may be a scoundrel, but "his thievery is all the best of fun."

MCFARLAND (1972, p. 132): "Autolycus is not a cerebral critic of the pastoral world, but a kind of life-force . . . that prevents us from wholly forgetting the troubles that accompany remembrance of the past. Though benign, he is nonetheless a thief, which is not socially acceptable; so his role confirms the hint of malaise found in the conception of winter, rather than spring, as the pastoral matrix." However, ORNSTEIN (1986, p. 227): Autolycus is a "born entertainer . . . too cowardly to rob and not especially greedy; he is not, therefore, very dangerous to the commonweal."

SANDERS (1987, p. 95): "There are many reasons—and satisfying ones—why Autolycus is in this play: unimpeded by scruple, he [gives] us the amorality of the natural . . . de-romanticised . . . country life. . . . He is the ubiquitous spirit . . . at once parasitic and creative." BROWN (*Shakespeare's Plays*, 1966, pp. 104–5): Autolycus's actions evoke from the audience "laughter, connivance and appreciation, relaxation and admiration. . . . In a drama about the influences of time, he provides a timeless artistry and remains unchanged at the conclusion. He brings topicality to a fantastic tale, an escape from the consequences of knavery to a moral confrontation, and a grotesque embodiment of irresponsible fears and aggressions, of vigorous and sexual activity, to a shapely and often refined romance." Autolycus heightens the mirth of the sheepshearing by his (p. 105) "instinctive and irresponsible enjoyment" of it, and when he finally exits at 3182, the "audience's contentment at the invincible humour and roguery of Autolycus disposes it to accept the strange, severe and sweetened theatricality of the concluding scene."

FRIPP (1938, 2:739–40): Autolycus is the vehicle (or, to BETHELL, 1947, p. 41, the "chief instrument") for criticizing the court of James I. "Shakespeare cared for Autolycus infinitely more than for the corrupt official, and the costly, parasitic, often syphilitic young blood, who gathered from many parts about the King at Whitehall," for, intentionally or not, Autolycus (p. 740) "renders real service" to the prince. ARMSTRONG (1969, p. 73): "The great thieves of myth are felt to be godlike" and to have an important "poetic function to fulfill in relation to idyllic pastoral." Autolycus, as Sh.'s version of the type, "is everywhere the agent of anti-systematic change." KAULA (1976, p. 292), questionably: Autolycus's peddling of counterfeit goods and references to his *trumpery, wares,* and *hallowed trinkets* "appear to indicate that one of Autolycus' several roles is that of the cunning merchant of popish wares. . . . As this kind of merchant Autolycus would be a vehicle for satirizing the well-publicized activities of the missionary priests in England."

Critics look at the "work [Autolycus has] to do in the plot" (HARBAGE, 1961, p. 455) in order to discern qualities of his character. He introduces most of the songs. GOSSE (in GOLLANCZ, ed. 1916, p. 53): Autolycus's "rogue songs" ("Daffadils" [1669 ff.] and "Lawn" [2044 ff.]) are not merely "intensely human and pointedly Shakespearean, but . . . an integral part of the drama. They complete the revelation of the complex temperament of Autolycus . . . [including] his impish mendacity, his sudden sentimentality." NOBLE (1923, p. 94): Autolycus's entrance song is "used as a soliloquy, whereby the audience can have intimate information as to Autolycus's point of view, and never has any man been limned more tersely and vividly." TRAVERSI (1954; 1965, pp. 138-9): Autolycus's songs indicate an impatience with "all social restraint. . . . [*139*] In Autolycus the sense of freedom takes the form of an abandonment of all normal social forms and restraints, the positively valuable." MCPEEK (1969, pp. 238, 241-3): In him "all the ingredients of roguery and vagabondage blend except violence and malice. He is an amiable outlaw [and] . . . [*241*] ballad singer. . . . [*242*] Autolycus, like Hermes, has magical qualities as a musician; his songs penetrate to the 'bright mystery at the heart of all things' . . . [*243*] marvels in themselves."

The songs also introduce a sexual element sustained through the sheepshearing. RIEMER (1980, pp. 83, 179, 181, 185): The "astonishing Autolycus, in the artificial world of the pastoral," is both an "essential element in this 'philosophical' conceit of Platonic optimism . . . [and] an emblem, though an unruly and amoral one, of the freedom of pastoral." Renaissance Platonism found its (p. 179) "intellectual and emotional inspiration in images of the antique world"; thus when Autolycus (p. 181) "invades the play, with him comes an image of the antique world in its truly elemental, pagan quality." Beyond the "essentially *witty* allusion" to his namesake and to the "ancient image of misrule" (lines 1692-6), Sh. establishes Autolycus as "a priapic figure *par excellence*" with (p. 185) "some characteristics of the great god Pan." GARBER (1981, p. 158): "It is not until the arrival of Autolycus that sexual energies are fully acknowledged or accepted in the world of the sheepshearing feast." NEELY (1985, p. 204): Autolycus, the "parodic double of Leontes," transmutes "the conflicts and motives of the first three acts" into comedy: that is, Leontes's sexual revulsion is reversed by the cheerful comic "grotesqueries" of Autolycus's ballads.

He is also the criminal element in the second half of the play. FOAKES (1968, pp. 125-6): Autolycus "seems a figure from a real world, and stands out from the artificial pastoral world of romance to make an especially strong [*126*] impact on an audience by his very solidity; this affords a basis for giving some emphasis to what he is and does. . . . His roguery is itself substantial and . . . represents a real element of subversion. . . . He is a born rogue, whose ingrained habit is to be corrupt, and to seek to corrupt others." IDEM (1971, pp. 138, 140): "If he does no real harm, it is not altogether for want of trying. . . . [*140*] He is naturally addicted to the deceptions and disguises which others in Bohemia adopt for special purposes; but these others, Florizel, Camillo, Polixenes, even Perdita, are linked with him in practising arts which are natural to him . . . arts not in themselves good, and closely allied to vice." COX

(1969, pp. 286, 298), however: Sh. uses Autolycus as an agent of "a power for good," although "the agency is not necessary" since the revelations about Perdita's birth could take place without him. According to Cox (p. 298), "Shakespeare, then, through the agency of the rogue shows how Providence, working through falsehood and seeming falsehood, elicits truth and increases the store of good."

HARTWIG (1970; 1972, p. 120): Autolycus is "a corrupt version of the dramatic force that Apollo manifests in the first half of the play"; he is also (IDEM, 1978, pp. 98, 100) a parodic "onstage substitute" for the absent Leontes, since like the King, Autolycus is (p. 100) "both his own attacker and victim. . . . The difference between the original and the imitation is that Autolycus *knows* he is playing both parts. Leontes has to learn that he is." So too BATTENHOUSE (1980, pp. 127, 130–1): Autolycus mirrors, "with comic exaggeration," Polixenes's attitudes manifested in his treatment of Perdita; furthermore, an Autolycus "dressed in Florizel's garments while at heart still roguish is an emblem of the court's superficial concept." Autolycus provides (p. 130) "a comic version of the code of Leontes" and (p. 131) "several obvious points of analogy with a Leontes who wanders into communicating with dreams, makes a pack of scandals of his nothings, and hawks them for public approval." The self-victimization of Leontes is parodied by Autolycus's fiction of "having taken a beating from an outsider, who in fact is Autolycus's undivulged self."

FELPERIN (1972, p. 217): Autolycus is Sh's "most tempting rogue" next to Falstaff "and, in a phrase . . . 'a wondrous necessary man' in the action of romance. . . . [By] sowing confusion in pursuit of self-interest he ultimately promotes the interest and felicity of the principals." PETERSON (*Time*, 1973, pp. 183, 190): Autolycus is a "master of deception and exploiter of unsanctioned sensuality. . . . His role as Perdita's foil is unmistakable"; he is also an (p. 190) "extemporizer and opportunist" whose motives are as selfish as Camillo's are benevolent. Yet "in seeking to use time to his own advantage he unwittingly becomes an instrument of renewing time. . . . Autolycus' knavery serves the ends of renewal." ABARTIS (1977, pp. 105, 107): Autolycus focuses the audience on Leontes's "generically required release. . . . [*107*] Autolycus is the summer agent of an escape from punishment, of mercy, and he is never punished despite all his cheating, lying and stealing. Leontes' punishment occurs in the winter world of Paulina, but his salvation is brought along with Autolycus."

BARTON (1980, p. 148): Autolycus, genial mover of the plot, may first seem "a hypocrite and dissembler"; his "real association, however, is with fictions rather than with genuine evil. Certainly his decision not to take the obviously profitable step of [betraying Florizel to Polixenes] — because to do so would be an honest action, and Autolycus prefers to remain true to his own falsehood — is scarcely that of a man whose villainy we can take seriously." Since even the Clown, his chief victim, defends him, it is "impossible for us to regard him as anything but what he is: a creator of fictions who, by not betraying Florizel to Polixenes, and by inventing a tale which frightens the Old Shepherd and the Clown into Sicily with the all-important fardel, is in fact the agent of the happy ending."

However, LLOYD EVANS (1982, p. 373): Autolycus is Sh.'s "reminder to us that the world of commodity has not been and cannot be forgotten. In this respect, he may represent the extent of Shakespeare's sensitivity to audience-reaction, for only so much romance can be absorbed."

Nevertheless, some critics see little or no reason for Autolycus's presence in the play at all. WRIGHT ("Extraneous Song," 1927, p. 264): Autolycus's songs have "no dramatic value outside the clown scenes which are themselves extraneous." WILSON (ed. 1931, p. xx): "As a factor in the plot, though from the moment of his appearance [Autolycus] seems to be constantly and deliberately intriguing, in effect he does nothing at all. As a part of the story he is . . . negligible." SEN GUPTA (1950, p. 223): Autolycus is "unnecessary to the plot of the drama" but "organic to the play in a much deeper sense. The dreamland of [*WT*] becomes fully convincing only when we find that even its rogue and vagabond is an imaginative genius." FRYE (1962, p. 235): "In many comedies, though never in Sh., the *cognitio* is brought about through the ingenuity of a tricky servant. Autolycus has this role in [*WT*], for though 'out of service' he still regards Florizel as his master, and he has also the rascality and the complacent soliloquies about his own cleverness that go with the role. He gains possession of the secret of Perdita's birth, but somehow or other the denouement takes place without him, and he remains superfluous to the plot." SCHANZER (ed. 1969, pp. 19-20): Autolycus's part in advancing the plot (getting the Shepherd and the Clown aboard the ship to Sicilia) is so minimal that Sh. "could easily have devised some other means of getting them on to the ship. He wanted Autolycus above all as a purveyor of the laughter and songs which . . . serve as a contrast to the wintry gloom which the actions of Leontes have created at his court" — and for his attractive qualities of (p. 20) "sprightliness, volatility, a ready wit, a love of music, and an aptitude for commerce. . . . Autolycus is . . . one of Shakespeare's most vivid and entertaining creations." CHAMPION (1970, pp. 169-70): Autolycus, "the most conventionally comic character in the play," is, (p. 170) unlike Paulina, who is essential to the narrative, "entirely peripheral. But to the story as drama, the two serve the same function as comic pointers."

Others who comment on this character: FURNIVALL (1877, p. xcii), HASTINGS (1940), PARROTT (1949, pp. 81-91), MACNEICE (1967, p. 234), FARNHAM (1971, pp. 168-9), and PAULIN (1983, in Fr.).

CAMILLO

SLEETH (1936, pp. 97-8, 110-11) draws from sources of Sh.'s time (including Bacon and More) a description of the ideal Elizabethan counselor, applying to Camillo (but not to that other faithful servant, Paulina) the best qualities: noble blood, good name, prudence, wisdom, high standards of morality, concern for the common good, honesty, imperviousness to flattery, and so forth. Naturally, other critics debate whether Camillo measures up.

A few find him objectionably self-serving, especially in his flight to Bohemia. LENNOX (1753, 2:82): Camillo, a "treacher[ous] and self-interested" creature, insinuates himself into the service of Polixenes to avoid the wrath of Leontes, then betrays

Florizel's confidences when he wishes to end his exile. BIRCH (1848, p. 521): Camillo is guilty of "dissembling and falsehood," though his perfidies ultimately "lead to a happy issue and the fulfilment of the oracle." FOAKES (1971, p. 122): "He first protests, but then goes along with Leontes and accepts the task of poisoning Polixenes, and finally runs away, simply abandoning the loved master who had brought him 'from meaner form . . . to worship' (410–11)." ADAMS (1989, pp. 98–9): "Though consistently labelled 'honest,' and given to asserting things on his 'honor,' [Camillo] is not, in the moment of crisis, much of a paragon. After feigning docile obedience to Leontes, he easily moves to conniving at the escape of Polixenes, while barely considering the fate to which he is abandoning Hermione; after promising to help Florizel against [Polixenes's] bilious rage, he instantly goes back on his promise, and for the least loyal of reasons, his own desire to see Sicily again. . . . [99] Camillo, though a man of some rank and pretensions to honor, directly and unhesitatingly betrays his word given to Florizel."

Generally, however, Camillo is admired. HUDSON (1848, 1:335): A "venerable and amusing" character, "Camillo never deceives but when honesty requires it; and then he deceives to perfection. . . . He tries to do good or prevent evil by telling the truth, till he sees there is no hope, and then he effects his purpose by telling downright falsehoods . . . as if he were willing to be lost himself, provided he may thereby save others. . . . His integrity and wisdom [make] him a light to the councils and a guide to the footsteps of the greatest around him. . . . [Camillo is] the salt of society and the strength of government." LLOYD (1894, pp. 165–6): Camillo's "virtue, which is his character, is the very growth of the trying circumstances by which he is surrounded. He is frank and bold to the fullest extent that is consistent with prudence and usefulness; he carries prudence and management to the fullest extent that consists with self-respect and honour. In truth he is as virtuous and direct as a man can be who is fain to live among the hard conditions of a court. . . . We must approve and admire the sagacity with which he proves the strength of unreasoning prejudice, and hoodwinks and eludes [166] the power he can neither disabuse nor contend against."

TINKLER (1937, p. 356) notes "the integrated balance of Camillo, the sane man of good sense. The impression of the latter is produced in the first scene. . . . He never lets impulsive action lead him astray." HIBBARD (1964, pp. 110, 112–13): In the character of Camillo, Sh. creates a counselor and servant who "exercises a profound influence for good. . . . [112] The Elizabethan doctrine of the sanctity of Kingship, so prominent in the histories and the tragedies, has here been combined with the idea set out by Castiglione that the courtier should not commit [113] treason, even when commanded to do so by his lord. . . . It is fitting that at the end of the play Camillo should be married to Paulina, for she is his female counterpart and virtually takes over the office of good counsellor and plain speaker in Sicily" after Camillo leaves with Polixenes. PYLE (1969, pp. 25–6): Camillo is "a man of honour, good, wise, reliable, a perfect counsellor," perhaps because he (p. 26) "interprets duty in the spirit rather than the letter" of what is required of him. BATTENHOUSE (1980, p. 135): Camillo is a "diplomat of real courage . . . a gardener who uses art to mend nature" in Sicilia and Bohemia. Camillo advises Florizel to seek refuge in

Sicilia, putting into play a strategy that accords with his "love for Polixenes and Leontes alike."

Camillo's motivation and its results interest many critics. The CLARKES (ed. 1865, 1:677, n. 22): "Camillo is the faithful counsellor, the honest friend, the loyal servant, who strives to preserve the intrinsic honour of his king, rather than to maintain himself in his [king's] favour." He, who cannot violate his "honourable nature and integrity of purpose, becomes the ultimate bond of reconciliation and union between the two kings and their respective children." SNIDER (c. 1890, p. 491): Camillo's actions are guided by his "strongest wish . . . to be restored to his country, especially since that which separated him from it [Leontes's aberrant behavior] has been wholly removed. He is the great manager— he will find some means of accomplishing his end. . . . He expressly declares that the repentance of the King of Sicilia is what motives his return." BONJOUR (1952, p. 197): "So human a sentiment as Camillo's longing for his native country is . . . deftly used to motivate the whole proceeding [the return to Sicilia]. . . . Moreover, there is not the slightest doubt that this rôle of Camillo's . . . provides yet another effective link between the two centres of interest in the drama, owing to the conspicuous part he now plays in both stories, of which he is no mean *agent de liaison*." PAFFORD (ed. 1963, p. lxxvi): Camillo is brave, loyal, intelligent, understanding, able and devoted to the right rather than to persons. ARONSON (1972, pp. 284, 287): Any interpretation of *WT* begins with the "archetypal image of the physician," or healer, who suffers in spirit along with the "patient"; all healing is a "rebirth, a kind of incubation during which the physician remained in the background and the patient sought . . . 'to bring out the cure whose elements he bore within himself'"; in *WT*, the healer is Camillo, whose insight makes him (p. 287) "the first . . . to recognize the existence of the disease. It is also he alone who attempts to make the patient realize the perils to his soul should he refuse the remedy." However, Leontes's cure is not effected by Camillo. ROCKAS (1975, p. 3): Camillo, despite his many speeches and appearances, serves "primarily as an agent of the plot and the generalized ethos of the play: his 'character' is simply a composite of what keeps the play on its ethical track." Similarly TREWIN (1978, p. 263) thinks of Camillo as "merely a functionary of the plot." WHITE (1985, pp. 148, 150): Camillo "acts as an anchor of decency. . . . [He becomes] a quiet monitor for our responses. Through him especially we comprehend that a terrible injustice is being perpetrated by Leontes." Furthermore in Polixenes's court, he serves as (p. 150) "plotter when the story gets tangled [and] also as a firm guide for our moral sympathies."

FLORIZEL

One critic expresses dismay at Florizel's behavior. BIRCH (1848, p. 521): Florizel is "one of those sons who is made to look forward to his father's death, even in his hearing." Like Camillo, "the young man has no great regard for truth."

Others are resolute champions. INCHBALD (ed. 1808, 3:6): The idea that "Florizel should introduce himself to the court of Sicilia, by speaking arrant falsehoods" is a "disgraceful improbability"; she makes sure that it is by adopting Kemble's cuts of troublesome lines (see Text on the Stage, p. 837). HUDSON (1848, 1:333–4): "Unless he were willing to give up all the rest of the world for her," Florizel is not worthy of Perdita. But in fact, "the prince shows himself abundantly worthy of her in the sacrifices he makes, and the dangers he confronts for her sake. . . . Prizing his love before the crown . . . prizing truth and honour above all things . . . [334] Florizel is every way the peer of Perdita: none but the best of men could have felt the perfections of such a woman. . . . Alive and glowing with the fire of noble passions, himself the very sum and abstract of true manliness, of honour, purity, intelligence, and dignity, he seems at once the flower of princes, and the prince of gentlemen." PAFFORD (ed. 1963, p. lxxix): Florizel's lovemaking is "ardent, manly, and animated. . . . His resolution and courage are of vital importance in the play. . . . He will sacrifice everything for his love and can see no obstacle as insuperable." SCHANZER (ed. 1969, p. 26): Greene's Dorastus proposes marriage only after Fawnia refuses to become his mistress. "Nothing could be further removed from Florizel's exaltation of Perdita above any princess, his total unconcern about her social station." PILGRIM (1983, p. 40): "The splendour of Florizel lies in great part . . . in his confidence and in his fearlessness. He reminds us of a knight of chivalric romance."

HOLBROOK (1964, p. 156) suggests that Mamillius and Florizel are linked in the first scene, presumably by an allusion to Mamillius by Bohemian Archidamus (line 37), so that "while Mamillius is not reborn, it is Florizel who replaces him, as the promise of the inheritance restored." UPHAUS (1981, p. 73) agrees that Florizel replaces Mamillius.

HERMIONE

Not even Hermione earns uniform critical praise. For LENNOX's (1753, 2:75) opinion of the Queen's "ridiculous" posing as a statue, see p. 657. HARDINGE (1818, 3:45): Hermione's long concealment from her "thoroughly repentant" husband is neither "compassionate, nor just, or natural. . . . Nothing *will* or *can* justify the absurdity of it." SHERMAN (1902, p. 115): As Leontes urges Hermione and Polixenes to walk off together (254–8), "we have just been regretting the lengthening moments of her complaisance to Polyxenes, and now this seeming neglect [Hermione's failure to wipe Mamillius's "smutch'd" nose (196)] has palpable influence with us to her disadvantage. The doubts of Leontes, voiced openly concerning the lad's paternity, have by no means an idealising effect upon her wifehood." MATTHEWS (1913; 1970, p. 338): "Her noble eloquence in the trial scene does not proceed from the mouth of the same woman whose witty banter has enlivened the opening episodes. Frankly unfeminine also is the forgiveness of her husband without one word of reproach." DEAN (1979, p. 288): "The cause of Leontes' torture is not only his own guilt and the wilfulness of Paulina, but a strain of cruelty in the character of Hermione. She expresses the natural fury of a mother revenging a mortally wounded child, compounded with an excessively passionate 'Sicilian' nature [Sh., of course, tells us she is by birth Russian (1299)]. It is perhaps difficult for the reader to think of Hermione in negative terms, yet her cruel response to her husband's merciless actions attests to a dark kinship between the spirits of Leontes and his wife."

Most critics, however, countenance her behavior. JAMESON (1833; 1889, pp. 188, 190): "The character of Hermione is considered open to criticism on one point. . . . She secludes herself from the world for sixteen years . . . and is not won to relent from her resolve by [Leontes's] sorrow, his remorse, his constancy to her memory: such conduct, argues the critic, is unfeeling as it is inconceivable in a tender and virtuous woman. . . . [*190*] Would his repentance suffice to restore him at once to his place in her heart, to efface from her strong and reflecting mind the recollection of his miserable weakness? . . . Methinks that the want of feeling . . . and [lack of] consistency would lie in such an exhibition as this." HUDSON (1848, 1:326–8): As "afflictions thicken upon her, until she appears truly sublime," Hermione "evinces a most deep, intense feeling of the awful indignity put upon her, and a lofty self-respect that scorns alike to resent it and to succumb to it. . . . Her conscious innocence can thus sustain her against the world. . . . [*327*] The firmness with which she persists for sixteen years in hiding her life from the king . . . [*328*] is all in perfect keeping with her character." DOWDEN (1875; 1877, pp. 412–13): "From the first Hermione, whose clear-sightedness is equal to her courage, had perceived that her husband laboured under a delusion which was cruel and calamitous to himself. From the first she transcends all blind resentment, and has true pity for the man who wrongs her. But if she has fortitude for her own uses, she also is able to accept for her husband the inevitable pain which is needful to restore him to his better mind. She will not shorten the term of his suffering, because that suffering is beneficent. And at the last her silent embrace carries with it — and justly — a portion of that truth she had uttered long before: [quotes "how . . . mistake," 701–5]. [*413*] The calm and complete comprehension of the fact is a possession painful yet precious to Hermione, and it lifts her above all vulgar confusion of heart or temper, and above all unjust resentment." LLOYD (1894, pp. 159–60): "Our ancestors admired the conduct and character of patient Griselda," the married woman who would "cast away . . . and abdicate all self-respect and independence." But Hermione illustrates that "prudence in the face of overwhelming odds may not, with self-respect, be tame beyond a certain point, and submissiveness afterwards . . . is mere slavishness. . . . [*160*] The true theme of highest admiration is that tone and temper that touches the exact mean, . . . never too indulgent to tyranny on the one hand, nor too indignant at it on the other, simply because personal suffering is in question. . . . To give in to [such tyranny] is little less than to be an accomplice as well as a victim. Therefore Hermione, with nobleness of heart . . . asserts her innocence with firmness [as she] justly denounces the tyranny and lawless rigour of her accuser and judge" who, when he has "filled up the measure of his wrong[,] gives way to no weak and insufficient suggestions to relieve the penalty he justly suffers, until . . . a conjuncture of circumstances . . . invite and allow her to raise up the penitent guilty, without degrading her own dignity and injured innocence. . . . With clear and steady intellectual light [Hermione] illuminates every perversity in her husband's course." LEWES (1894, pp. 304–5): "Feminine tears and lamentations do not accord with this character. . . .

[Hermione] defends herself eloquently and gravely, in the full consciousness of her innocence. . . . She speaks not with anger or bitterness, but like a queen, who defends her children's honour in her own." She cannot be reproached for (p. 305) "allowing her husband and the world to believe her dead. . . . Her husband's momentary remorse is not enough to win back his lost place in her heart."

CLARK (1936, p. 76): "Hermione has . . . plenty of innate strength, courage, and endurance. . . . She possesses a quiet distinction and noble bearing which, allied to a saint-like patience, enable her to suffer stoically the cruel injustice of her husband. . . . [Her self-imposed seclusion] would, indeed, only be possible to the type of woman Shakespeare has purposely shown Hermione to be. . . . Her strong, reflective mind would not be able to efface the recollection of her husband's contemptible weakness. In what masterly fashion Shakespeare has portrayed the complete self-possession necessary to meet so extraordinary a situation!" PAFFORD (ed. 1963, pp. lxxiii–lxxiv): Hermione is beautiful, witty, spirited, happy, frank, and secure in Leontes's love "right to the moment when his jealousy is first made known to her. After that she can never be gay and vivacious again. . . . [*lxxiv*] In the final scene she speaks only to [Perdita] . . . [and] the only reason she gives to explain why she has remained apart from her husband is that the Oracle gave her hope that Perdita lived." GREER (1986, p. 112): Hermione "by a living death . . . expiates her husband's crimes of jealousy," yet she is not one of Sh.'s stereotypical redemptive women, passively upholding a double standard of sexual morality. "Hermione is not rejected by her husband, who repents when he learns of the oracle and of his son's death as foretold by it. Rather, she refuses to live by his side in a tainted union and chooses to be buried alive, as it were, for sixteen years."

A few critics find Hermione bland. DESAI (1952, p. 49): Compared with most of the women in Sh.'s comedies, Hermione is uninspiring, dull, and vapid. "Not all the defence of her character by Mrs. Jameson [see p. 774] can reconcile us to her, after she leaves the court and goes into oblivion from which, not she, but her wraith, a statue almost like her, seems to have been brought and palmed off as Hermione. She is what she is required to be—a mere statue, beautiful and well cut." CHAMPION (1970, pp. 162–3): Most of the characters surrounding Leontes are "highly stylized[,] . . . 'flat' or one-dimensional and, consequently, artificial"; Hermione is "perhaps the most striking illustration [of this]. . . . [*163*] Although a character of infinite dignity, [she] is frankly a passive pawn who is acted upon but who exerts no positive force." NORVELL (1984, pp. 8, 11): "So severe is Leontes in his sin that Hermione cannot be resigned to reunion with him even at the point of his confession and repentance. . . . So, if Hermione is not necessarily weak, she is forced to show her strength and express her cause in passive decorum. . . . [*11*] In the hierarchical decorum of [Sh.'s] day women were ideally passive and silent."

But critics usually heap praise on the character. INCHBALD (ed. 1808, 3:4): "This injured queen" ranks high in "virtue and every endearing quality. . . . The mad conduct of Leontes is . . . the occasion of such noble, yet such humble and forbearing demeanour on the part of his wife, that his phrenzy is rendered interesting by the sufferings it draws upon her: and the extravagance of the first is soon forgotten, through the deep impression made by the last." JAMESON (1833; 1889, pp. 182-4): "Hermione is most distinguished by her magnanimity and her fortitude. . . . [*183*] The most vivid impression of life and internal power . . . renders the character of Hermione one of [Sh.'s] masterpieces. . . . A grand and gracious simplicity, an easy, unforced, yet dignified self-possession, are in all her deportment and in every word she utters. . . . [*184*] The boundless devotion and respect of those around her, and their confidence in her goodness and innocence, are so many additional strokes in the portrait." CLARKE (1863, pp. 347, 350): Hermione is a worthy "heroine of a tragic drama . . . a perfectly regal woman. . . . Forgetting her own individual affliction . . . [she falls] senseless at the news of the death of her son, Mamillius." The CLARKES (ed. 1865, 1:687): Her "mute succumbence" when she hears of Mamillius's death is "profoundly true to character. . . . She is not a woman 'prone to weeping' [715], one who can so ease her heart of that which 'burns worse than tears drown' [718-19]: she can command her voice to utter that dignified defence of her honour, and bear the revulsion of thanksgiving at the divine intervention on her behalf with the single ejaculation of 'Praisèd!' [1318] but at the abrupt announcement of her boy's death she drops, without a word, stricken to the earth by the weight of her tearless woe." GREEN (1890, pp. 10-11): "Fair, beautiful, heroic queen! Would your spirit could be spread abroad, that every mother, wife and daughter might catch but a breath [*11*] and rejoice to claim you as their own. It is the feminine element in Shakespeare which, beyond all others, insures the immortality of his genius. For as woman is closer to nature than man, so a literature that would endure must combine the masculine and feminine."

THALER (1947; 1970, p. 21): "Shakspere's test and definition of what is feminine is not circumscribed by the bubbling vivacities, charming as they are, of Beatrice and Rosalind. . . . Queen Hermione's silence, far from being unfeminine, is surely a credit to her womanliness, her humanity, and to the artistry of Shakspere." NUTTALL (1966, pp. 24-5): "There is no doubt of Hermione's essential fidelity to her husband. The question is: does she *flirt* with Polixenes? It certainly looks as if she does. . . . [*25*] [Yet] to stress this aspect is to falsify; or at least to distort, since it transforms what is essentially background into foreground. . . . For, ultimately, it is Hermione's loving chastity which is dominant in the scene, not her flirtatiousness."

RICHMOND (1977-8, pp. 340-1): A being more poised than Hermione is hard to imagine; "firm but tactful, she knows that humanity cannot survive through the assertion of rights and prerogatives. . . . [*341*] There is no self-immolation in Hermione. . . . The 'passive' feminine role is here a creative one, infinitely superior to male assertiveness." DASH (1980, pp. 276-7): Hermione "does not, on her first appearance, impress the reader or auditor as an independent, strong, [*277*] self-confident person. She belongs to that race of human beings whose inner strength surfaces only during periods of trial. Thus, when we first meet her, she is happy, complacent, relaxed, and utterly womanly. . . . Large with child, . . . she expresses visually as well as in her words a dependent, sexist role. . . . Not until her life is challenged does Hermione reveal the core of strength that is to sustain her . . . through the trial, then through sixteen years in seclusion." SUMMERS (1984, pp. 29-30), however: In *WT*, Hermione is "the most clearly noble character." She "neither falters nor lapses into shrillness [quotes 701-5, 731-2]" when threatened but, (p. 30) "completely unafraid . . . , [she] firmly asserts her honour [and] denounces injustice." RICHMAN (1990, p. 115): Hermione "is all three of the things that she has seemed to be. As work of art, work of magic and work of nature, she embodies the principal elements that surprise and delight audiences. It is appropriate that the scene of which she is the center should be one of Shakespeare's most profoundly amazing."

Other critics discussing Hermione: HAZLITT (1817, p. 280), FURNIVALL (1877, p. xcii), WINTER (1892; 1893, p. 109), FOAKES (1971, p. 128), KAMACHI (1983, pp. 61-3), PILGRIM (1983, pp. 53-9).

LEONTES

GARDNER (1980, p. 63): "Leontes is not merely the central figure in the play's pattern of tragedy-and-reconciliation. We respond to him as a realized personality . . . a focus for, and an animating participant in, those values and meanings and fulfilments which gather in the final scenes."

Some critics, however, find him less rounded than this. SEN GUPTA (1950, p. 241): Leontes is merely a theatrical tool who "seems to be less a human being than a mechanical contrivance that sets the plot going." PAFFORD (ed. 1963, pp. lxxi ff.): Leontes is "primarily an agent to bring an evil force rapidly into play" rather than a character "to be examined closely as a man; he is more important as a vehicle. . . . He is not shown as achieving humility, and his 'growth' seems to be what may be described as an unavoidable minimum in the circumstances."

Many critics incline to this view, saying little about Leontes's abiding personal and ethical nature but much about the single, aberrant trait that dominates the character's development and behavior in the first segment of *WT*—the violent jealousy.

A few readers see it as innate. The CLARKES (ed. 1865, 1:665): He is "a susceptible, irritable, jealous-natured man. . . . With the injustice of a man naturally prone to jealousy, [he] urges his wife to entreat their guest, and then resents her success in prevailing with him; encourages and induces her to use persuasive language, and then pervertedly deems it a sinful allurement." SHERMAN (1902, p. 117): Leontes is jealous because he is "Sicilian, and exhibits somewhat of the intense and summary hatred peculiar to his race." MACKENZIE (1924, p. 430): "Leontes' sudden jealousy was a little difficult to make convincing in any case, so Shakespeare burkes the question of its motivation altogether, leaving us to assume him simply a moody, constitutionally jealous man." FOAKES (1971, p. 95): "The jealousy of Leontes is presented as a given fact about his nature, something he cannot help rather than a morally blameworthy condition of mind."

Other critics believe that Leontes's jealousy is meant to be inexplicable. HUDSON (1848, 1:322-3, 325): It is "purely self-begotten, and fed by its own surmises. . . . The why, the how, and the whence, do not exist; it is there simply because it is there; has no grounds whatever, and would not be jealousy if it had. . . . [323] Altogether a matter of fantasy and will, groundless in its origin, fanatical in its nature, no facts, oaths, or arguments can at all prevail against it. . . . *[325]* The king is of course tenacious and confident of his opinion in exact proportion as he lacks means whereby to justify it; he substitutes his own suspicions for facts, his own surmises for proof." IDEM (ed. 1852, 4:13-14): Jealousy is so "unprovided for in the general ordering of [Leontes's] character" that it even (p. 14) "takes him by surprise, and finds him totally unprepared; insomuch that he forthwith loses all self-control." MARTIN (1891, pp. 6-7): A "sudden access of madness can alone account for the debasing change in the nature of Leontes. . . . Such inexplicable outbreaks of jealousy . . . do occasionally occur in real life. While they last, the very nature of their victims is transformed, and their imagination, wholesome and cleanly till then, becomes . . . foul. . . . Shakespeare has dealt with Leontes as a man in whom the passion of jealousy is inherent[,] . . . breaking out suddenly with a force that is deaf to reason, and which, stimulated by an imagination tainted to the core, finds evidences of guilt in actions the most innocent. . . . [7] This is the jealousy . . . portrayed in Leontes, — a jealousy without excuse, — cruel, vindictive, and remorseless almost beyond belief."

PARROTT (1949, p. 384): It is "causeless, self-centered and recognized by all others in the action as morbid self-delusion. The reader, like the spectator, is expected to take it as such and not to argue about it." STAUFFER (1949, p. 293): Leontes's jealousy is a degrading, "fearful blight . . . almost without external support of any kind." DORAN (1954, p. 215): "The very suddenness with which Leontes' jealousy begins is a way of revealing . . . that it is a diseased state of mind, without external motivation." Yet it is "the most important motivating element in the dramatic situation [Sh.] chooses to develop. It must be accepted as 'given,' just as are the fairy-tale elements of romantic comedy. . . . There is a difference from these conditions, of course, in that Shakespeare uses with great accuracy all the symptoms of psychopathic jealousy, and so denies us the mood of fairy tale." MARSH (1962; 1980, pp. 128-30): Leontes's jealousy "comes unmotivated, quite unreasonably. . . . *[129]* Little better than a beast himself, [Leontes] sees the world around him as beastly. . . . *[130]* Soon he will see himself as the only honest man in it, with the mission of performing justice, for he is so imprisoned in the self that he believes that what he thinks and wants must be right." HARBAGE (1961, p. 442): Leontes's jealousy must be unmotivated "in view of its function in the play as symbol of mysterious evil"; none of Sh.'s other plays "has a larger proportion of well-disposed characters, and this gives to the malady of Leontes an interesting definition. Evil is treated as an inner growth . . . restricted to a single character, and restricted even in him, so that the overall impression is of the health of human tissue."

BARBER (1964, p. 235): Leontes's "jealousy is a datum, one of the postulates of the play, and Shakespeare is only concerned to convince us that Leontes in fact *is* jealous, not to show us how he became so." HOLBROOK (1964, pp. 136-7): "The whole form and mode of the play implies that we shall not overcome such instability as Leontes's by 'knowing the causes'. . . . Through Leontes' jealousy and envy the poetic drama explores . . . controlling the sexual impulses within the moral pattern of life, and the acceptance of 'the lusts of the flesh' and their decay with age as part of the irrevocable make-[*137*]up of the human being." MILLS (1966, p. 108): Leontes's jealousy is "a mental and emotional aberration without immediate effective cause, requiring no corroboration and impervious to contradictory evidence or testimony." WILLIAMS (1967, p. 16): "The depth to which Leontes sinks in his madness is indicated not only by the way he denies the external creations of nature that sustain nobility through time but also by the way he submits the rule of his soul to 'affection,' thus making possible things not so held, and 'fellowing nothing' [cites 214–18]." SMITH (1972, pp. 101–2): *WT* "is not, like . . . *Pandosto*, in any important way a treatment of jealousy. . . . [*102*] The interest in the play is not focused upon how Leontes was persuaded to entertain the awful and mistaken distrust of his wife and friend; the important thing is its consequences." PETERSON (*Time*, 1973, pp. 165, 168): "Among Shakespeare's victims of jealousy and mistrust, Leontes is unique. . . . [His] affliction is self-generated. Its origins are in hereditary guilt." Leontes (p. 168) "very nearly destroys . . . the values . . . upon which [communal man] has grounded his civilization: love, marriage, friendship, family, the law, justice." GOURLAY (1975, p. 380): Leontes moves rapidly from specific distrust of Hermione to a "general distrust of women's truth. . . . Faith seems to him mere stupidity. . . . He chooses a negative certainty rather than the ambiguity of appearances; then he makes a law of it." HAWKINS (1976, p. 81): Leontes, persuaded "in a lightning flash of insight" that Hermione has been unfaithful with Polixenes, and absolutely convinced of the validity of his knowledge, "does not attempt to judge his own conviction critically. Instead, he concentrates on proving Hermione guilty. . . . He therefore admits every shred of evidence which confirms his theory, and imperiously dismisses all efforts to refute it." FOWLER (1978, p. 37): Leontes commits the sins of "jealousy and of self-righteousness. . . . [Jealousy] seems to figure mainly as a representative sin to be repented. The focus is less on the experience of jealousy itself . . . than on its consequences." WRIGHT (1989, p. 226): Sh.'s own dramatic emphasis "is not on how and when the jealousy comes into being but on the moment of its triumph—the moment when Leontes's rational nature collapses."

Several critics suggest that the period in which Sh. lived offers insights into Leontes's jealousy. TINKLER (1937, p. 354): In *WT*, "the problem, the usual Jacobean one of the breach between Reason and Desire, is given a wide context of related emotions. There is an almost pathological study of the birth and growth of jealousy, regarded as an integral part of adolescent experience and made part of a whole mode of apprehension." CRAIG (1948, p. 332): When Sh. wrote *WT*, "many books were being issued which taught that reason was dethroned by jealousy and other feral passions and that 'unbridled folly was suffused with fury.' Greene had learned this in the university. . . . Shakespeare simply accepted his source. . . . The psychology of the passions known to Shakespeare and his age provided not only for obsession but for the obtrusion of all the evil passions." MAVEETY (1966, p. 266), however: "Why did Shakespeare deviate from his source, making Leontes' jealousy unmotivated? The answer lies in the particular view of life Shakespeare is here presenting. . . . We sometimes suffer through no human or predictable agency, but rather, it would seem, by the will of the gods. Apparently, it was Shakespeare's intention to base the jealousy of Leontes on this . . . possibility." LAWRENCE (1960; 1969, pp. 176–7): Sh. "altered his source in making the king's jealousy break forth abruptly, in the midst of gay and playful conversation, but he has left us in some indecision as to how far these suspicions had already been smouldering beneath the surface. . . . [*177*] Sudden and unjustified suspicions were . . . common in popular story-telling. . . . Greene's novel . . . is set in a framework of romantic commonplaces. Archaic details of the old and widespread Accused Queen motive were occasionally retained by both Shakespeare and by Greene. . . . Sudden and baseless rages are common in romance, and easily became a convention in romantic drama." TAYLER (1964, p. 128): Sh.'s audience, well aware that "the harmony of Eden had been lost to man so that his 'stronger blood' was no longer free of hereditary 'imposition' . . . was better prepared than modern critics for Leontes' sudden and unmotivated jealousy, the towering excess of passion that . . . introduces the chaos and death for which Leontes is finally to do penance." MCFARLAND (1972, p. 129): Leontes's "mysterious rage" expresses the persisting view in Sh.'s era on "the probability of baseness in human relationships. The dual potentiality of man, either to be like animals or like the angels, was often insisted on by Shakespeare's philosophically minded predecessors in the Renaissance." FELPERIN (1972, p. 216): "If the jealousy of Leontes mirrors that passion as it exists in living men, . . . it also comes literally out of the blue—the kind of heaven-sent, or rather hell-sent, madness . . . which . . . conventionally afflict[s] the protagonists of [earlier] dramatic romances. . . . The point is that it is . . . psychologically convincing that Leontes' jealousy is sudden and inexplicable (do we really understand any better than the Elizabethans the *causes* of destructive behavior?)."

Critics try, implying that to understand Leontes's aberrations is to understand Leontes. H. COLERIDGE (1851, 2:148–9): "Though unaccountable, [Leontes's jealousy] is not impossible. . . . How slight a spark may cause explosion in the foul atmosphere of a despot's heart it is hard to say. . . . The grossness of Leontes' imaginations, [*149*] his murderous suggestions, and inaccessibility to reason, remorse, or religion, is naturally consequent on the base passion, say rather the unclean dæmon, that possesses him." And KNIGHT (1947; 1965, p. 96): Leontes's evil is "self-born and unmotivated"; yet commentators vainly search for motives to explain his actions "without realizing that the poet is concerned not with trivialities, but with evil itself, whose cause remains as dark as theology: given a 'sufficient' motive, the thing to be studied vanishes. In Leontes we have a . . . coherent, realistic and compact . . . study of almost demonic possession." MAHOOD (1957, p. 148): Because his audience would not demand it, Sh. would not have to show "logically clear motivation of character" for Leontes; rather they would accept "the seemingly incalculable in human behavior" by attributing it to "demonic possession."

GAUGER (1987, p. 28) alone suggests that Leontes's overwhelming jealousy stems not from a character trait or flaw but from a philosophical attitude wherein normal and normally accepted opposites and contrasts seem suspended, and a course of action is allowed that can only be explained by extreme "indifference" to the dictates of a balanced course of action. Causality becomes unreliable; paradoxes prevail. Great effort is expended to explain Leontes's jealousy, but the "indifference" phenomenon explains the equivocalness of Leontes's attitude and is accepting of its inherent incongruities (in Ger.).

Other critics suggest that Leontes is simply weak and unstable. CLARKE (1863, p. 346): The "abrupt" and "violent antagonisms in character," produced by "casual and slight inducement," nearly always "take place in highly excitable and impulsive natures. . . . [His] every action betrays the weak and unstable man." DOWDEN (1875; 1877, pp. 407–8): Leontes's passion is not "a terrible chaos of soul [but] . . . a gross personal resentment." He does not suffer "sorrowful, judicial, indignation" but rather displays a (p. 408) "hideously grotesque passion" of a kind which BRYANT (1955; 1961, p. 214) calls "undisguised pharisaical pride." GRANVILLE-BARKER (1912; 1974, p. 20): Leontes's jealousy is "a nervous weakness, a mere hysteria. . . . Only in the passion of anger or cruelty, cold or hot, can he be sure of himself at all. Let him relax, and he is, as he says, a feather for each wind that blows [1084]." BROOKE (1913, pp. 258–9): Leontes, "naturally noble . . . is also weak. . . . Violence, it is said, goes with weakness; and the more furious the violence, the greater the weakness. . . . [259] In the end . . . his native jealousy . . . has been worked through. It cannot occur again."

MOWAT (1969, pp. 40–1, 44): Leontes's "character is in keeping with the pettiness of his passion. . . . Shakespeare omits all mention of courage in Leontes, and has him actually [41] fear to take open revenge on Polixenes. . . . Even his method [slow-working poison] is a cowardly one. . . . His one burst of courage, his defiance of the oracle, [is] crushed immediately by the news of his son's death. . . . And the single dramatization of his 'bounteous courtesy' is the scene of his too-persistent urging of Polixenes to delay his departure. . . . Shakespeare leaves us little to admire in Leontes. . . . [44] That his reason was so weak . . . indicates to us a basic defectiveness . . . a basic rottenness in the character." IDEM (1976, pp. 10–20): "Jealousy which does not spring from deep love or passion . . . is more selfish, more nearly related to envy and greed than to love. . . . [11] It is such petty, selfish jealousy that afflicts Leontes. His chief worry is that 'They're here with me already; whisp'ring . . . / 'Sicilia is a so-forth!' [302–3]. His greatest torment is that he is being laughed at [quotes 924–7]." Leontes's (p. 15) "ready acceptance of his common lot with the typical cuckold" might lead us to ask (p. 17) "what kind of pettiness, of self-hatred, must lie in the soul of one who can thus imagine, thus display, himself as an object of scorn? . . . [20] [Leontes] is so distorted away from greatness and nobility that audience identification with him repeatedly breaks down."

SANDERS (1987, pp. 24–5): Leontes has "located and begun to relish the pleasure that [his jealous] self-appointed vexation contains. Yes . . . 'pleasure'. Nobody embarks on a course of gratuitous self-torment without promising himself some perverse satisfactions along the way. . . . [25] The instinct touched is very primitive and very powerful. The sentiments . . . require no explanation at all. They rise from a perennial stratum of the male mind . . . (I think this is the impression conveyed by Leontes' tone of gloomy relish) . . . which seems, utterly incongruously, to have a ring of gratified exultation about it: 'Physic for't there's none' [282] — as if the thing that torments him is also a source of unholy jubilation. 'Nay, there's comfort in't' [278] has an irony beyond the fact that the fellowship of cuckolds would seem to provide scant 'comfort' for poor Leontes. The darker irony is that the comfort he is discovering is real and deep. . . . Jealousy consoles the man who believes himself to be merely its victim." MINCOFF (1992, p. 89): Leontes's "jealous reaction is that of a weakling who needs every outward support to protect his ego. . . . He is, in fact, a rather ignoble figure, though not without some saving features, especially his family affections before his insane jealousy destroys most of them and the evident respect, affection, and loyalty he inspires in those about him."

But MORLEY (1887, p. 10): "The jealousy of Leontes is painted throughout as an insane delusion." SYMONS (in IRVING & MARSHALL, ed. 1890, 7:320): He is "meanly, miserably, degradedly jealous, with a sort of mental alienation or distortion—a disease of the brain like some disease of vision." LEWES (1894, p. 303): Leontes's jealousy "robs him of clearness of understanding, makes him deaf to all pleadings . . . and causes everything to appear to him as false and insincere. The mad visions of his blinded brain alone seem to him true and real." ARMSTRONG (1913; 1969, pp. 61, 116): Sh. may have been interested in "an unusual psychological type . . . a mind insulated from all evidence, running on its own involuted circuit which nothing can break." Leontes becomes (p. 116) "a jealous, insane scoundrel. . . . It is really fortunate for [Hermione's] sake that the crash comes, and she is relieved of the monster until he is chastened and more fit to come near her." LENZ (1986, pp. 94-5): "The sheer irrationality of Leontes' behavior tells us he is mistaken. . . . Shakespeare sets jealousy against a background of long-established mutual amity [quotes 25-7]. The eruption of Leontes' jealousy in the face of 'such affection' shocks us. . . . [95] What surprises us about Leontes' jealousy is that it makes sense, despite its sharp contrast to former friendship and love."

SCOTT (1920, pp. 145, 148): "Although not suffering from a depressive illness as understood in modern terminology, Leontes presents a typical example of the jealous melancholy described by Elizabethan writers" which Sh. makes into a (p. 148) "brilliant exposition of the basis of a mental disease—in this case paranoia. . . . It is useless to object that Shakespeare could not himself have had such precocious knowledge either. It is all there, and what is more astonishing is that so much understanding of morbid psychology has been packed into so few words—and in a poetic metre." CUVELIER (1983, pp. 35-9): Since "unmotivated" does not mean "causeless," Sh.'s audience might find in "contemporary theories regarding mental pathology"—particularly those on melancholy—the clue to Leontes's behavior. "Jealousy was generally defined as a melancholy passion . . . involving both fear and suspicion, so that the underlying humour would be readily identified. Yet in the case of Leontes, Shakespeare takes great pains to display as many signs of it as possible," including Leontes's aggressive monosyllabic language, satirical turn of mind, dismal images, and (p. 36) symbolic references such as his rejection of the oracle, which indicates a "horror of the sun," one of the main symptoms of melancholy. Leontes's (p. 38) "chaotic, cryptic utterance [cites 214-22] . . . [39] and shattered elocution reflect . . . his perception of the outer world. . . . Adust melancholy makes disgusting and horrifying images form in the patient's fancy: thus the vision of a spider in his cup (636–42) appears to Leontes as the embodiment of the venomous *knowledge* he now possesses."

SCHWARTZ (1973, pp. 258–72): Leontes is paranoid. He idealizes "boyhood in the interest of clinging to a paradisal version of pre-Oedipal existence when confronted by the temptation toward sexual contact. . . . [*259*] The maternal nourisher [becomes] a malevolent seductress when Leontes feels deprived of signs of love. . . . [*260*] In his paranoid delusions of betrayal, Leontes acts out the whole range of pathological boundary violations. . . . [*268*] Hermione becomes the object of Leontes' obstinate substitution of projection for perception. . . . [*270*] Psychoanalysis has shown that the spider [636–42] . . . represents the sexually threatening mother, contact with whom signifies incest. On a deeper level, it signifies the horror of maternal engulfment. . . . [*272*] He would sacrifice Hermione, paradoxically, to recreate the image of his sacred ideal, and to reclaim his own repose." IDEM (1975, pp. 198–9): "In the trial scene Leontes' vow to 'recreate' himself derives from his ambivalent desire for [*199*] feminine powers. . . . Shakespeare transforms the fear of loss into socially viable ways of coping with masculine anxieties."

VAN DOREN (1939; 1953, pp. 313–14, 317): "Leontes infects the whole of the first three acts with the angry sore of his obsession. There is no more jealous man in literature"; his jealousy has (p. 314) "a curious way of feeding on itself. . . . The expression of it gives him in some perverse way a horrible pleasure. . . . [*317*] Leontes is an artist of jealousy, an expert in self-hurt." STRONG (1954, p. 202): "Leontes suffers from the form of inferiority complex commonest in Shakespeare, that of readily believing the woman he loves to be unfaithful to him. . . . The picture presented by his obsession is so powerful that it is unchecked by reality. . . . Violent and unreasonable though his behaviour has been, the obsession is . . . a neurosis, not a psychosis." HOLBROOK (1964, p. 165): At the height of his violent rage against his infant daughter and any who seeks to defend her, Leontes is in a "neurotic state of unbalance[,] . . . ineffectual in his disordered reason, impotent in the face of reality." GRENE (1967, pp. 74–5): Leontes's certainty that he has been cuckolded "covers his whole life, as father, husband, king. . . . [*75*] For his obsession to run its course, reality must be challenged. . . . He is bent on warping reality to his will." STEWART (1983, pp. 251, 258), having acted the part of Leontes, believes that the "character (and behaviour) is firmly rooted in reality" and "psychologically coherent to the extent that a modern audience can follow step by step his desperate descent into obsessional behaviour, persecution, cruelty and self-torture. . . . [*258*] The very ambiguity, the increasing sensuality of the scene, establish a context in which Leontes' breakdown is going to occur. The breakdown is sudden, massive, and entirely overwhelming."

Leontes's ego interests critics. HOROWITZ (1965, p. 73): "King Leontes is possessed by a passion that infects his judgement, deals out dooms that are the province of gods, and remains deaf to the voices of human reason. . . . Nothing can alter his outlook. . . . Leontes sets his judgement above that of mere humanity." When Leontes rejects the oracle, he "reaches the ultimate length to which he can go in imposing his own will upon reality and bending it, tyrannically, to the shape of his passions."

BURTON (1970, p. 220): Leontes's jealousy "springs from a sense of insecurity which in turn springs from a guilty sense of unworthiness that justifies its fears by distorting what it sees." BASS (1977, pp. 17-19): To assuage his own ego, Leontes "looks on young Mamillius as the model of himself, before 'corruption'"; Leontes (p. 18) "can see no other self than his own . . . (i.e. no rival for himself become young again)." But when Leontes denies the oracle, (p. 19) "his very image, Mamillius, is stricken dead." BYLES (1979, pp. 81, 84, 90-1): "The relationship between narcissistic dependency or fixation and superego aggression provides the dynamics for intense disillusion in love"—though less intense for Leontes because he has "no ideal view of love. . . . [*84*] Leontes does not suffer from guilt so much as from shame at his failure to perceive Hermione adequately. Shame is far less destructive than guilt. . . . [*90*] Leontes comes to realize he is absolutely mistaken in his suspicions, but . . . this realization does not make him feel worthless. . . . [*91*] Leontes' narcissism sustains him."

CALDER-MARSHALL (1982, p. 248): Quite simply, Leontes "has never grown up. Perhaps his jealousy of Polixenes stems from a childhood envy which he had never got over. . . . It is childish, therefore not totally unsympathetic." LANDE (1986, pp. 57-8): Polixenes's refusal to extend his visit (akin to Hermione's delay in accepting Leontes's marriage proposal) is a "direct assault on [Leontes's] authority and his capacity to impose his way on his world. . . . [*58*] He is outraged when they [Hermione and Polixenes] do not immediately comply with his wishes. . . . He can only wonder if perhaps he is not as great and powerful as he believes himself to be. Doubt is steadily intensifying within him and threatening to overwhelm and destroy what he values most above all else: his sense of himself as king." COHEN (1987, pp. 207, 220-1): Leontes transforms his "sexual agony into an instrument of passionate blame in a king of narcissistic adventure." Through a (p. 220) "self-torturing voyeurism," Leontes provides himself with (p. 221) "a desperately needed motive" for putting into words what he both loves and fears—"the image of [his wife] making love to other men."

Other critics speculate on Leontes's possible homosexuality. STEWART (1949, pp. 35-6): Leontes's jealousy "is derived from his 'own actual unfaithfulness in real life.' . . . Camillo, the text hints to us, has been Leontes's assistant in covert immoralities. . . . An early fixation of his affections upon his friend, long dormant, is reawakened in Leontes—though without being brought to conscious focus—by that friend's actual presence for the first time since their 'twyn'd' [130] boyhood. An unconscious conflict ensues and the issue is behaviour having as its object the violent repudiation of the newly reactivated homosexual component in his character. In other words, Leontes projects upon his wife the desires he has to repudiate in himself. . . . The catastrophic suddenness as well as the obsessional [*36*] force of Leontes's jealousy, stunning alike to his court and to ourselves as we read, is also described by Freud as typical, as is the sufferer's complete loss of all sense of evidence." AUDEN (1961, p. 11): Leontes offers "a classical case of paranoid sexual jealousy due to repressed homosexual feelings." ELLIS (1964, pp. 546-7): "Leontes' behavior is classically projective. . . . For it is Leontes and not Hermione who loves, or has loved, Polixenes. Such guilt demands punishment. . . . [Leontes] desperately needs a victim whose sacrifice will carry away his own sin, and it doesn't matter much who the victim is. . . . [547] His frenzy departs as suddenly as it appeared. Not inexplicably, however. It departs at the shock of hearing of his son's death. But it would seem not merely the shock which brings him to his senses, for now he also has sacrificed his victim. His sin has been carried away, and his sanity returns." NUTTALL (1966, pp. 17–22): "If we supply [Leontes] with the sort of good reason for jealousy some critics seem to want, he instantly ceases to be a villain. . . . [18] We have seen enough to realise that the abruptness of Leontes' emotion, so far from being awkwardly artificial, is really close to the apparent capriciousness of real life. It is only in works of fiction that everyone has a good reason for everything he does. . . . [20] Leontes' strange jealousy *coincides* with the visit of his dearest friend . . . [and] erupts at the emotionally laden moment of parting from this friend. The human intelligence, faced with a coincidence, naturally tries to transform it into a causal relation. . . . Shakespeare has not only given us the correlation but has left a trail of clues as well. These 'clues' take the form of the merest innuendo, and the reader must estimate for himself the weight of inference which they may properly be called upon to bear. The sequence of innuendo works . . . by first stressing the special strength of the attachment between Leontes and Polixenes, and the associating it with sexuality. . . . [22] The theory that [Leontes's] jealousy is a cloak for guilt felt at a childhood love has at least the merit of placing [lines 153–60] in a coherent framework of explanation."

BARBER (1969, p. 65) agrees: Leontes exhibits "projective or paranoid jealousy as a defence against homosexual attraction. . . . The primary motive is the affection of Leontes for Polixenes, whatever name one gives it. The resolution becomes possible because the affection is consummated . . . through Perdita and Florizel"—a variation on ideas advanced by SCHLEGEL in 1808 (see n. 59–60). REID (1970, pp. 271–4): "Mamillius dies because he represents the masculinity in Leontes which is under an absolute eclipse in his delusional jealousy of Polixenes. . . . [273] Mamillius . . . represents—or . . . *is*—Leontes' masculine self. Perdita is Leontes' feminine self. The exaggerated evaluation of Mamillius in the opening scene is the defensive cover for the threatened masculinity of Leontes. The pointed avoidance of mention of the expected second heir is the absolute denial of his feminine self. Only by accepting—not denying—one's feminine impulses is one free to employ [274] one's masculine impulses. . . . The union of Florizel and Perdita is the fulfillment of the intolerable homosexual wish of Leontes. . . . It is resolved and order is reinstated." FIEDLER (1972, pp. 151–2): Leontes's "unacknowledged homosexual desires" for Polixenes are disguised "as nostalgia for the 'innocence' of their childhood"; Polixenes shares this "covert passion" and thus carries on (p. 152) a disguised flirtation with Leontes through his "courtly banter with the Queen." Mark TAYLOR (1982, p. 43): Leontes is "blocked by time from returning to the alliance the two boys once enjoyed. . . . [H]e reacts by imagining the adultery of Polixenes and Hermione . . . a psychologically convincing displacement" of a feeling that appears as jealousy because his friend is enjoying his wife but is, actually, "subconscious jealousy that his wife is enjoying his friend." GARNER (1989, p. 144): Leontes's ugly remarks about women and sex (188, 286, 368, etc.) indicate that "on the surface all of these fantasies express disgust with women, which is provoked by fear and hate; beneath it they may manifest suppressed homosexual feelings of the men who experience and share the fantasies."

LANDE (1986, p. 59) objects: "The overwhelming threat, in the face of which Leontes . . . disintegrates is a sexual one only on the surface. There is nothing within the text to support the claim . . . of an unconscious homosexual conflict." ORGEL (ed. 1996, pp. 24, 26–7, 29) also rejects such readings: STEWART's theory of a "guilty reaction" to an adolescent homosexual love is "rather quaint, and quite anachronistic: there is no evidence that suppressed guilt over adolescent homosexuality was a Renaissance problem. . . . [26] The Jacobean family, like the Jacobean state, is a patriarchy, and Shakespearian drama reflects a deep cultural ambivalence about the place of women in it. . . . [27] Leontes' fears . . . are merely the cultural currency of the age, articulated continually in sermons and pamphlets. . . . [29] Leontes' paranoia . . . has clear cultural co-ordinates. . . . [I]t registers the fears of a patriarchal society about the power of women, exemplified in sexual power."

Finally, critics comment on Leontes's rehabilitation. BURTON (1970, pp. 231–2): "The fact that all the people whom [232] Leontes injured strive hard to make him forget their injuries must be our guarantee that he is worthy of the love of Hermione." CHAMPION (1970, pp. 156, 159–61, 170–1): Only Leontes "is developed on the level of transformation" from the gracious host whose jealousy, "once he becomes suspicious of his wife's fidelity and his friend's integrity, grows through the first half of the play to overwhelming and frightening proportions" to the tyrant whose (p. 159) "mental perturbations have . . . destroyed his ability to rule either himself or his kingdom" to the contrite king who (p. 160) "becomes painfully aware of his folly and stupidity" to the confirmed repentant whose (p. 161) "crowning achievement of his love is articulated by Paulina" as she brings Hermione's alleged statue to life. The (p. 170) "transformed character is what he is not because he has lived through, escaped, and forgotten his past experiences, but because he has been molded and transfigured by them. His past suffering has provided a kind of wisdom by purging his vision and by making him aware of true values, especially of redemptive and forgiving [171] love. . . . [Leontes] cannot recapture totally what his folly has cost him. . . . The consequences have been inescapable, and he faces a future tinged with the waste of past years." ENRIGHT (1970, p. 178): Leontes is "not the nasty little horror that some critics have held him to be; however wrongly he suffers . . . he does suffer. There is no chance that we shall weep over him. . . . [But] the mere idea of Hermione ever being reunited to the Leontes of some interpretations—bitter, foul-minded, impotent, senilely rotten—is utterly repellent. . . . It is true though, and plain enough, that Leontes will have to pay a very high price to regain the Hermione [of the trial scene]." WHEELER (1980, pp. 165–6): "In Leontes, Shakespeare allows the richness of relations grounded in mutual trust to flow back into the life of a character who has fearfully transformed those riches into a nightmare of violent jealousy. . . . [166] Leontes, restored fully to himself in the arms of Hermione, presides over the ending of *The Winter's Tale* with kingly power and autonomy." COLLEY (1983, pp. 43, 45–6, 51–2): Leontes's rage "develops from his moral ignorance. His

deliverance from the consequence of that rage depends upon his painful and prolonged education about the nature of time, change, and sexual maturity." He is driven
to irrationality when he recalls his prepubescent (p. 45) "sexual innocence and the
loss of that innocence when he took Hermione as his wife." In arousing (p. 46) "his
love and his sexual passions," she leads him to "embrace time, mortality and the
promise of death. . . . [51] The knowledge of love, and the awareness of passing
time, that his [52] marriage to Hermione and his life with her should have revealed
to him [does not occur]. . . . It takes him sixteen years to live and to experience his
debt to time and his responsibilities of married love. . . . The quest for what he lost,
however, does not send Leontes on a search for Perdita. His quest does send him into
an extended exploration of his inner self." STOCKHOLDER (1987, p. 193): "Under the
guise of submission to the process of spiritual regeneration, Leontes satisfies his desire
for maternal nurturing. That nurturing, however, retains sexual overtones, and
thereby betrays his association of sexuality with incest, because of the concealed
identification of the now maternal Paulina with Hermione, and it acquires masochistic
dimensions from being placed in a context that fuses it with punishment."

For additional discussions of Leontes and jealousy: HERFORD (ed. 1904, 4:272),
MACKENZIE (1924, p. 431), HEARN (1928, p. 102), CRAIG (1948, p. 332), SIEGEL (1950,
pp. 304–6), GEYER (1955, pp. 188–9), FRYE (1962, p. 243), ELLIS (1964), FRYE (*Perspective*, 1965, pp. 114–15), HOLLAND (1966, pp. 280–2), RABKIN (1967, p. 221),
REID (1970, pp. 266–77), HOFLING (1971), HELLENGA (1976, p. 13), LANGMAN (1976,
p. 199), NAGATA (1977, p. 49), SUHAMY (1984), FUZIER (1984), BARBER & WHEELER
(1986, pp. 329–31), CAVELL (1987, pp. 196, 199), SANDERS (1987, pp. 21–2), STOCK-
HOLDER (1987, p. 185), CANFIELD (1989, pp. 60–1).

MAMILLIUS

The child delights some critics. SWINBURNE (1880; ed. 1925, 11:159–60): "By giving
us our last glimpse of Mamillius" as he laughs and chats with his mother, it is almost
certain that "at the very end [of *WT*] . . . we remember him all the better because
the father whose jealousy killed him and the mother for love of whom he died would
seem to have forgotten the little brave sweet spirit with all its truth of love and tender
sense of shame." BRANDES (1898, 2:348): "Mamillius is one of the gems of the play;
a finer sketch of a gifted, large-hearted child could not be." TERRY (1932, p. 27), who
debuted in the part in 1856 (see p. 802): "It is easy to recognize in Mamillius that
imaginative, philosophic, poetic temperament which in its maturity is so frequently
studied by Shakespeare [e.g., Romeo and Hamlet]." CRUTTWELL (1955, p. 129): "High
birth on one hand, and on the other an inherent superiority which was (or ought to
be) the consequence of high birth" accounts for the "inherent 'nobleness' [913]
which broke the boy Mamillius' heart when he heard of his mother's disgrace."

Others, however, find Sh.'s child creations unsuccessful. KELLETT (1923; 1969,
pp. 81, 86–9): "The children in [Sh.'s] plays are not child-like at all. . . . We notice
in these children the unfailing symptoms of the thorough prig. They are all forward
and pedantic. . . . [86] [Mamillius is] pert as well as shrewd and over-sharp"; he

differs from young Macduff, for example, (p. 87) "in the degree, but not in the kind, of his precocious pertness. . . . [*88*] Amid the impertinences of his little lecture to the waiting-ladies he contrives to show off a good deal of mature observation. . . . It is notable that [Hermione] finds the boy so troublesome that 'tis past enduring' [587]. Even the tale . . . of the man who dwelt by a churchyard is introduced by a cynical and adult-like gibe at 'yond crickets' [626], the women. . . . [*89*] In fact, only the astonishing breadth of Sh's treatment of older people makes us notice the narrowness that marks his treatment of children. . . . His children are colourless . . . and are drawn with vastly less penetration." ENRIGHT (1970, p. 171) concurs: Mamillius is "almost as trying" as Macduff's son.

TINKLER (1937, pp. 346–7): Mamillius is unimpressive "as a personal, tragic figure. . . . It is only when one becomes aware of the immense importance of his rôle for the effect on, the part played in, other people, that he becomes interesting. . . . [*347*] The burden of Scapegoat and Tragic Hero is shifted from Leontes to his son as the latter becomes the concrete symbol of the spiritual health of his father."

PAULINA

GRIFFITH (1775, p. 108) anticipates many critics: Paulina's "strong passions and ungovernable temper" deserve praise and reproof. HUDSON (1848, 1:329–30): Paulina is "perhaps the noblest termagant that we have any portrait of. . . . Furious, hot-tempered, headstrong, and reckless, in the full assurance that her ends are just, she stops not to consider the fit-[*330*]ness of her means; and thus does injury from her very willingness to suffer it. But, though we cannot help regretting her conduct, inasmuch as it tends to hinder where she means to help; neither can we help respecting and honouring her for it, inasmuch as it obviously springs from the noblest impulses. . . . Loud, voluble, violent, and viraginous, with a tongue that seems sharper than a sword, and an eloquence that seems enough to raise a blister, she has, however, too much honour and good sense to use them without good cause, and at the same time too much generous impulsiveness not to use them at all hazards when she has good cause." JAMESON (1889; 1967, pp. 194–5, 197–8): Paulina is "one of the striking beauties of the play[,] . . . strongly drawn from real and common life; a clever, generous, strong-minded, warm-hearted woman, fearless in asserting the truth, firm in her sense of right, enthusiastic in all her affections; quick in thought, resolute in word, and energetic in action" but also (p. 195) "heedless, hot-tempered, impatient, loud, bold, voluble, and turbulent of tongue; regardless of the feelings of those for whom she would sacrifice her life, and injuring from excess of zeal those whom she most wishes to serve. . . . [*197*] While we honour her courage and her affection, we cannot help regretting her violence. . . . [*198*] We can only excuse Paulina by recollecting that it is a part of her purpose to keep alive in the heart of Leontes the remembrance of his queen's perfections, and of his own cruel injustice." JAMESON's observations influenced later critics; for example, CLARK (1936, pp. 76–7) repeats many of them, sometimes verbatim. CLARKE (1863, p. 356): "Paulina is a specimen of those headstrong women who, taking up . . . a cause, allow no minor point to sway or interfere with their course of action. . . . There is another point in the female character that Shakespeare has exemplified with his usual felicity, in the conduct of Paulina. . . . When Leontes . . . is wallowing in the very slough of mean despondency, Paulina cannot forego the gratification of punching him in his maundering distress." The CLARKES (ed. 1865, 1:682, n. 49): "In Paulina the poet has given us a perfect picture of one of those ardent friends whose warmth of temper and want of judgment injure the cause they strive to benefit." SNIDER (1875, p. 89): She is "a courageous, strong-worded woman who is a little too free with her tongue over a penitent wrongdoer"; IDEM (1877, 2:63): "Her husband is Antigonus, who is the boldest of the courtiers in defense of Hermione; yet he has submitted to his wife, who must, therefore, be still bolder than he."

Critical admiration mixed with censure continues. BRANDES (1898, 2:351): "She has more courage than ten men, and possesses that natural eloquence and power of pathos which determined honesty and sound common sense can bestow upon a woman. . . . She is untouched by sentimentality; there is as little of the erotic as there is of repugnance in her attitude towards her husband." BETHELL (1947, p. 60): Paulina has "something of a 'morality' flavour; she symbolises conscience, always at Leontes' right shoulder to prompt him to right conduct. Yet she is a scold, presented as a comic figure, for the conscience in its nagging persistence can be both comic and serious at the same time." SIMPSON (1950, p. 122): "The task of making her at once attractive and convincing is not rendered easier by the fact that she is a matron. . . . [Yet] all who have met the type can vouch for her genuineness. Impulsive alike in admiration of nobleness as in condemnation of meanness, she shows herself a . . . courageous and disinterested [champion] of Hermione. . . . From the moment she hears of the king's conduct to his queen, she makes it her business to reveal to him the injustice of his charge. . . . Never does Paulina waver in her decision and determination to achieve this. . . . Nothing daunts her." NUTTALL (1966, p. 35): In Paulina's "ferocious castigation" (1362–89) of Leontes following his repentance (1335–57), "we must either find Paulina's behaviour grotesquely unnecessary or else find something thin and only half-convincing in Leontes' breast-beating. I think the second alternative is the right one. The king's proposal to 'new-woo my queen, recall the good Camillo' [1341], has too facile a confidence. Nevertheless there is something unpalatable in Paulina's [response]. She is a goblin-figure, a little larger than life. Her ways and speech have something monstrous about them, alternately alarming and somehow enormously good." GRENE (1967, p. 79): Paulina acts bravely and with good intentions—but, of course, does harm. In confronting Leontes with his infant daughter, Paulina "only forces Leontes over the brink to direct action and brings about the exposure of the child." BELLETTE (1978, pp. 68–9): "In many ways she is a counterpart of Camillo—a subject forced into 'disloyalty' yet guardian of the truth and loyal to what the King himself has destroyed. It is true she is often injudicious, in the traditional manner of the outspoken servant. . . . [69] However[,] . . . she comes to Leontes as physician, 'with words as medicinal as true' [942]." BATTENHOUSE (1980, pp. 136–7): Paulina immaturely dares to tonguelash a distraught king, though Sh. later "shows her growing in wisdom and skill." In her (p. 137) "hasty belief" that

Hermione truly has died, her moral sensibilities are so shocked at this seemingly irreparable disaster that her "bitter anger" is released against Leontes; but "once Paulina's sense of mission shifts from denunciation to the aiding of Leontes . . . she manifests arts characteristic of a mature pastor." SANDERS (1987, pp. 51-2): "Critics have contrived to defend, even to admire (in a theoretical kind of way) the spiritual therapist that Paulina now—and rather suddenly!—becomes. . . . But I've found none that actually **likes** what she does to her patient. [*52*] To be so often resuscitating distress . . . smacks rather of sadism."

Some critics find no fault with Paulina at all. INCHBALD (ed. 1808, 3:5): Paulina, "all tenderness united with spirit, has such power over the scenes in which she is engaged for the protection of the new-born child, that, like the queen, she confers honour and interest upon Leontes, merely by his keeping such excellent company." LLOYD (1894, p. 161): She is "a necessity to the play; without the support derived from her constant presence, it would not be intelligible how such a mind as that of Leontes could have the force and freshness of feeling, after sixteen years elapsed, that are required . . . to satisfy our sympathies with the honour of Hermione." MARTIN (1891, pp. 12, 19): "She is a woman of no ordinary sagacity, with a warm heart, a vigorous brain, and an ardent temper. Her love for Hermione has its roots in admiration and reverence for all the good and gracious qualities of which the queen's daily life has given witness. She has been much about her royal mistress, and much esteemed and trusted by her. Leontes, knowing this, obviously anticipates that she will not remain quiet when she hears of the charge he has brought against the queen, and he has thrust her into prison. Accordingly he has given express orders that Paulina is not to be admitted to the prison, and this fresh act of cruelty she learns from the governor only when she arrives there in hope of being of some comfort to her much-wronged mistress." Sh. uses Paulina to deliver (p. 19) "the concentrated judgment of every man and woman in Leontes' kingdom" that Hermione is innocent.

CAZAMIAN (1931; 1965, pp. 293-4): Paulina is "a worthy lady, a genuine creation, true in every feature to the slightly heightened life that drama demands. A courtier's wife, she awes not only her husband, but the king's officers and the royal person; she bears down all resistance—a triumph won by transparent honesty, courage, and the power of a biting tongue. The lively force of her railing is due to a robust hold [*294*] upon the paradoxes of an absurd situation; indignation carries her forward, but shrewd sense guides her to victory. She is the instrument of the kindly fate that soothes, and finally heals, the souls poisoned or crushed by the madness of one selfish man." WILSON (ed. 1931, pp. xxiv, xxvi): She "can hardly be praised too highly. . . . [*xxvi*] We remember [the play] by the full-charactered Paulina, fit companion for any woman, young or old. . . . She [stands] out by her tenacious courage and cunning." PARSONS (1950, p. 228): Paulina stands out as "essentially human, kind, true, loyal, courageous, impetuous, hot-tempered and outspoken. . . . She risks great danger for her love of a friend—without a shred of self-interest." HOLBROOK (1964, pp. 162-4): Paulina is the "embodiment of commonsense maturity and honesty in the court. . . . The several loyalties throughout the play are a subtle presentation of differing human sensibilites and their modes of behaviour in a situation where loyalty is called to act on its own responsibility, even at risk to life itself, so that the frail values of human relationship are given the ultimate test." Paulina represents (p. 163) "a loyalty to the kingdom, and a desire to cure the community." Thus she never ceases to oppose Leontes but instead (p. 164) "insists on the firm and normal reality of sound relationships and governing values, though she knows in this insistence that she faces death from the psychotic dictator. Yet she knows, too, that to insist on the norms is the only way to expose the aberration." HURD (1983, p. 303): Whether Paulina is functioning as the "voice of moral justice," as the skillful stage manager who provides the perspective for our major insights about the play, or, in the last act, as the agent of reconciliation who, "even more than the oracle, makes things work in this play," she is not only a pivotal character but "the most admirable . . . in this, one of Shakespeare's most beautiful plays." Others who unreservedly admire Paulina are: SMEATON (1911, p. 513), HARBAGE (1961, p. 447), HIBBARD (1964, p. 113).

Some criticism focuses on gender. SHERMAN (1902, p. 124): Sh. creates Paulina to temper Hermione's "self-sufficiency and strength" and, by displaying "mannish" behavior herself, "to remove all hint of mannishness" from our perception of Hermione. PYLE (1969, pp. 41, 43): In Sh.'s time "there were exceptional women, from Queen Elizabeth down, and for them allowance had to be made" by the rest of society. Paulina, "of conspicuous goodness," is actually capable of exercising "a man's determination of character . . . in the service of the right." She is (p. 43) "unmannerly only when the king is mad, and to the king's true self . . . a 'loyal servant' and 'obedient counsellor' [965–6], speaking out for his own good." DUSINBERRE (1975, pp. 220–1): Paulina's conscience, like Hermione's innocence, compels speech, but Paulina "bows to femininity with an orator's subtlety, talking incessantly of subjects on which she protests womanly silence [e.g., at 1409–23]"; her eloquence (p. 221) "contrasts with the cowardly silence of Leontes' courtiers." ASP (1978, pp. 147–56) finds in Paulina a likeness of "the Renaissance counterpart of the female *consolatio* figure found in many medieval works. . . . There are striking parallels" between the two "that would explain Paulina's dominance within the action of the play and her unique function vis-à-vis Leontes." For example, the female advisor (p. 150) is "always dominant in the relationship" and seems to possess "part of the divine *numen*, a fact that gives her words authority and a certain infallibility within the limits of her nature. She is usually a solitary figure so that her preeminence is not compromised by . . . conflicting authorities. . . . She rebukes and shames her subject. . . . Then she uses reasoned arguments to prove her points. . . . Finally, she encourages him to persevere in his new wisdom." Having been willingly accepted as Leontes's advisor [1424–6], Paulina leads him (p. 154) through the steps of purgation—guilt, contrition, repentance, confession, and amendment—to a (p. 156) "reunion with the goodness and grace emanating from Hermione." All the ensuing reunions are "symbolic expressions of that union with divine love which is the final end of medieval consolation literature." ENGLAND (1982, p. 75) also suggests that Paulina's "name is not only intentionally Christian but may even suggest her role as a healer in the Pauline tradition." BERGGREN (1980, pp. 29–30): Paulina "seals the image of feminine power in the late plays" by preserving the maternal heroine and perhaps by being "introduced to us as the mother of three girls, sufficient recommendation in a world where boy children die of shock while infant girls survive far [*30*] worse. . . . Paulina seems the most selfless of all Shakespeare's women, ruthless in a cause that offers no personal profit whatsoever." When Leontes calls her a "mankind witch" (982), the adjective "perfectly encapsulates the spirit of [*WT*], which exorcises the violence of masculine jealousy and redeems it through the kind of patience Penelope achieved." DASH (1980, pp. 275–6): Paulina "exhibits a fearlessness and self-confidence that suggest her later role as the scourge of Leontes. . . . [In the jail scene] her brilliance, wit, and sophistication sparkle. Thus introduced, neither as a lady-in-waiting to the Queen nor as a member of Hermione's staff, Paulina functions as an independent, a woman with a staff of her own. . . . [*276*] Although the range of her capacities is still a mystery to us—and will remain so until the play's closing scene—we know that her challenge to the men to 'be second' [930] to them in courage and imaginative action is not empty ranting." The line actually reads "be second to me." CALDER-MARSHALL (1982, p. 246): Paulina "probably talks too much, but she is the only person who confronts Leontes with what he's done and what kind of person he's becoming. . . . Paulina has no tact. She's very much a woman of today, dare one say a feminist in the best sense of the word? She's the sort of friend that everyone would like to have when things are going badly. She's loyal and fights like a tiger. She's the kind of woman who would look after battered wives and give the husband hell if he deserved it, as Leontes does." NOVY (1984, pp. 176–7): "In Paulina's confrontation with Leontes the issue of female subordination is raised and resolved in a way that, while unorthodox, leaves no doubt of Paulina's autonomy [cites 955–9]. Throughout the play she takes on Leontes as an equal, undaunted by his tyranny. When she speaks of herself as 'a foolish woman' [1418], it is plainly only a rhetorical gesture." She (p. 177) restores "Hermione to Leontes' esteem and finally to his presence" and then accepts Leontes's marital arrangements, seemingly designed to "place her back in a patriarchal framework": but of course "she has already demonstrated unambiguously how little marriage subordinates her." NEELY (1985, pp. 199–200): Though she "absorbs the most brutal of the verbal and physical expressions of Leontes' repudiation of Hermione and his daughter . . . [Paulina] believes [*200*] Leontes is salvageable—and worth saving for [Hermione]. . . . Her attacks on Leontes . . . are calculated, judicious, positive."

Though CARRINGTON (1956, p. 25) calls Paulina "an inconsistent and undeveloped character," most critics think otherwise; they apparently feel, however, that she cannot be discussed or judged in a vacuum, so they often look at the roles, traditional and otherwise, that she plays in *WT*. MATTHEWS (1913; 1970, p. 338): Paulina "plays her part, urged by her own individuality"; she never becomes a "mere creature of the story, a puppet pulled to and fro by the playwright to compel the forward movement of the plot." HERFORD (ed. 1916–, p. xxiii): Paulina plays the part of "an earthly providence, intervening in the action at its most critical point to forestall disaster and turn the menacing perils to a happy issue." DAVIES (1939, p. 147): "Paulina is carefully and vigorously drawn, and has the sympathy of the audience from her first appearance. . . . She gets the better of Leontes in a very brisk quarrel [963–

1058] and has a fine exit in the same scene. After the supposed death of Hermione . . . she brings Leontes to his senses in a scene of remarkably eloquent verse
[1362–1423]. . . . Paulina has remarkable vitality and freshness, and has a part of
first-rate importance in the action of the play." CHAMPION (1970, pp. 167–9): "Paulina
serves . . . to provoke laughter (even during Leontes' bitterest moments). . . .
[*168*] [She is] angry and indignant . . . a termagant, infuriated by the masculine
tyrant who dispenses judgment with such preposterous casuistry. The result is a character totally functional in the narrative itself, but also one who, by her loquacity,
provides for the spectator a release from tension in the midst of Leontes' wrath. . . .
[*169*] Shakespeare creates emotional distance [in the final act] by forcing us to observe the emotions through Paulina, as she, like a puppet-master, stages her greatest
scene." SMITH (in EVANS, ed. 1974, p. 1565): Hermione's "dignified patience" requires
Sh. to create a Paulina to resist Leontes's tyranny and defend her mistress' innocence:
"In her later manipulation of affairs toward a happy ending, [Paulina] recalls the
capable women in the problem comedies." ABARTIS (1977, pp. 106–7): Paulina is
Leontes's purge, and her "guilt-inflicting speeches draw off the anger of the audience
from Leontes," whose remorse is so "thorough that it has almost [*107*] become a
disease; finally, Paulina's constant goading makes the audience wish for the complete
absolution of Leontes, for his rejection of that neurotic self-punishment."

She sometimes plays "the good shrew." ENRIGHT (1970, pp. 173, 176): "Paulina
is formidable, more than a bit of a shrew. . . . [*176*] Lest we should conceive of her
as a termagant wholly and solely, Paulina is given, among her plain speaking, a faint
touch of that gentleness and temperate tone which she preserves throughout." HART-
WIG (1970; 1972, pp. 105, 116, 134): Paulina "plays the shrew" to Leontes's tyrant
in the first half of the play, confessor to Leontes's penitent in the last; in the statue
scene (p. 116), "Paulina achieves, with the confident skill of a good stage director,
or a good playwright, the fusion of illusion and reality into joyful truth. . . . [*134*]
Since Antigonus had earlier been a surrogate victim for Camillo, absorbing the blame
and the duty that Leontes would have cast upon Camillo, it is now the best of all
comic conclusions to allow Camillo the opportunity to replace Antigonus. Paulina's
tongue has a new victim and Leontes is free at last." SUMMERS (1984, pp. 30–1):
Paulina is "the choral, fearless truth-teller who denounces abused authority and madness. . . . [*31*] [She descends] from a long line of comic stage shrews who reduce
to absurdity masculine claims to superior authority. Paulina, however, is not simply
the wilful shrew, but the good shrew who happily takes on the duty of stating truth
[see 855 ff.]." WAYNE (1985, p. 182): Paulina is Sh.'s refashioning of the shrew. The
transformation from "unregenerate agent of discord . . . to a regenerative agent for
concord" occurs because Sh. permits her "to upset the marital hierarchy and
. . . create concord through discord." If Paulina "destroys" her own husband and
marriage, that is not as important as what she creates—"a concord that is also marital . . . even familial, and well worth saving." DAVIES (1986, pp. 169–71): "Paulina
is a central and little understood figure . . . who both delivers the child and mediates
between male and female figures. . . . [*170*] Paulina is Hermione's attendant, her shadow, her voice, her devoted follower. Only to the unseeing Leontes is

Paulina a 'mankind witch' [982] though . . . we do see, or rather hear, what he means. . . . [*171*] As 'shrew' [Paulina] invites derision; as the haranguing voice of conscience . . . she claims our respect. . . . In the latter phase of action, she provides the initiate with the means of final enlightenment."

PEARSON (1979, pp. 195–210) offers a dark, but questionable, interpretation: Leontes superimposes "upon the character of Paulina that of the urban witch" who provides (p. 196) "refuge for young ladies of good family whose amorous adventures had led to pregnancy" and preserves their chaste image by disposing of "the evidence against it, often by abandoning the babes on doorsteps. . . . Most frequently, she was old or middle-aged; her functions as bawd, madame and matchmaker were a natural development of youthful prostitution." Leontes reviles Paulina (p. 201) "as a 'mankind witch' and 'a most intelligencing bawd' [982–3]. . . . [*202*] Leontes' acceptance of his single state, except Paulina find him a wife . . . places Paulina in the role of procuress. . . . [*204*] In accepting Paulina's condition—that only she can procure a wife for him—Leontes himself prepares the way for the role she assumes in the final scene . . . [in which] a necromantic conjuring is an archetypal possibility. . . . [*210*] Paulina as urban witch functions as the most sustained example in [*WT*] of mankind's universal propensity to make wrong judgments. By introducing the archetype and building it to a climax in the final scene, only to eliminate it completely, Shakespeare has forced his audience to participate in the misconception" of taking appearance for reality.

ROBERTS (1991, pp. 161, 163): Paulina claims special consideration as the "voice of truth [who] insists on the . . . falsity of Leontes's accusations." Through the sixteen years that follow on Leontes's (p. 163) "fatal rejection of wife and daughter, Paulina . . . has become [his] unquestioned mentor and subjected him to a long process of reeducation."

PERDITA

Perdita is occasionally treated as one of a foursome, along with Marina (*Per.*), Imogen (*Cym.*), and Miranda (*Tmp.*). BRANDES (1898, 2:272): Perdita and the other young women of the romances "suffer grievous wrongs, and are in no case cherished as they deserve; but their charm, purity and nobility of nature triumph over everything. . . . The foulness of life has no power to defile them." WILSON (ed. 1931, p. xxvi): "Perdita stands out—as all the maidens in these later plays stand out—in a simple, almost divine dignity." COOK (1991, pp. 37–8): "To assume that the vulnerable young heroines of Shakespeare's late plays are entering upon courtship, marriage, or sexual activity at the usual age inevitably lessens the sense of wonder and distance the romances should evoke. But even modern audiences need only consider the effect of a twenty-five-year-old Marina or Perdita or Miranda to see the shattering difference that would result. Could a grown woman convincingly preside, like Perdita, as an innocent virginal queen over sheepshearing rites where [*38*] earthy hanky-panky provides half the fun?" WEBSTER (1942; 1955, p. 278) thinks not: "She [Perdita] is sixteen or she is nothing."

In discussing Perdita specifically, critics focus not on her youth but on other estimable qualities that destine her "to remain for ages unrivalled" as a character (DOUCE, 1807, 1:364). FURNIVALL (1877, p. xcii): Perdita is "endowed with all that is pure and holy. . . . The mind delights to linger [on her], and does so with happiness." JAMESON (1889; 1967, pp. 141–4): She possesses a "beautiful combination of the pastoral with the elegant, of simplicity with elevation, of spirit with sweetness. . . . [*142*] The impression of her perfect beauty and airy elegance of demeanour is conveyed in two exquisite passages [cites 1951–9 and 2185–8]. The artless manner in which her innate nobility of soul shines forth through her pastoral disguise is brought before us at once [cites 1975–9]. Her natural loftiness of spirit breaks out where she is menaced and reviled by the king as one whom [*143*] his son has degraded himself by merely looking on. . . . Perdita has another characteristic, which lends to the poetical delicacy of the delineation a certain strength and moral elevation which is peculiarly striking. It is that sense of truth and rectitude, that upright simplicity of mind, which disdain all crooked and indirect [*144*] means, which would not stoop for an instant to dissemblance, and is mingled with a noble confidence in her love and in her lover." CLARK (1936, p. 71) repeats JAMESON's observations. BRYANT (1955; 1961, p. 218): "From the beginning there is more to Perdita than meets the eye. . . . [She] is herself the 'fairy gold' that transforms all who come within her range." MARSH (1962; 1980, p. 143): Perdita's "beauty, her vitality, and her freshness and honesty are at once suggested by the image of Spring with which she is introduced by Florizel [quotes 1799–1800]. She is the bringer of Spring, the renewer of life and . . . she is invested with the freshness and delicate beauty of the daffodils." PYLE (1969, p. 82): "Perdita has that clearness of judgement with which Shakespeare customarily endows his girl-lovers. . . . Shakespeare has an unfailing sense of the fitness of things. . . . The inequality of their rank troubles her, not because she feels herself unworthy of Florizel, but because it must incline the king against their marriage. It is plain that if she had felt herself unworthy her common sense would itself have opposed all thoughts of the match."

SCHANZER (ed. 1969, pp. 26–7): In *Pandosto*, "Fawnia's thoughts, when she finds herself in love with the Prince, . . . dwell mainly on the difference of rank between them. Where for Perdita 'the difference forges dread' [1817] because it threatens the continuance of their relationship, Fawnia sees her love for the Prince as a violation of the order of nature, and therefore likely to have dire consequences. As she is preoccupied with social [*27*] rank, what pleases her most about the projected marriage to Dorastus is the thought of one day becoming queen. . . . We are worlds away from Perdita." PETERSON (*Time*, 1973, pp. 172, 174): Perdita resists Florizel's request that "she enter and enjoy the world of illusion. . . . She may wear the robes of Flora, but she refuses to assume the goddess's identity. Her refusal is initial proof of the innocence and integrity of her love. . . . [*174*] Her refusal to surrender to holiday folly confirms that she is not, as Polixenes fears, an angler for his son's affections." HARDING (1979, p. 59): Perdita has "such qualities as tenderness, sympathy, creativeness, faithful love." Through her, the play "affirms that these qualities are among the possibilities of human nature, and further that they may be united with sexual attraction and life-enhancing freshness. . . . We can take [Sh.] to assert that these qualities . . . are part of the human potential and, in the convention of European culture, to be looked for especially in women." COOK (1980, pp. 54, 58): Perdita's "most single striking quality" is her true innocence, "which is not to be confused with ignorance." Perdita "positively [shines] with goodness. . . . [She is] never prissy, never dull. . . . [*58*] Perdita is a delight. She is loved and loving, she is the queen of the shepherds' feast day, a true and natural princess."

Natural, for some critics, refers primarily to her country upbringing. SMEATON (1911, p. 509): In Perdita, sincerity, sweetness, beauty, and graciousness meet. "Absolutely unsophisticated, because she has always lived face to face with the grand elemental verities of nature, so sincere and guileless, moreover, that she hates false colours in men and women, and false (or forced) hues in flowers," Perdita delights in the "sight of general happiness." STOLL (1937; 1966, p. 102): Perdita is "innocently familiar with the ways of 'great creating nature' [1898], sprightly and humorous, exquisite and tender!" She is also earthy, joyous, girlishly charming, buoyant, resilient, and so forth. MAHOOD (1957, p. 163): "If Perdita is full of grace in every meaning of the word, she owes that upbringing to the two old peasants. Polixenes' praise of the custom of grafting 'a gentler Sien, to the wildest stocke' [1904] is vivid dramatic irony, not only because he is shortly going to repudiate his theory when his son seeks to marry a shepherdess, but because Perdita's upbringing has been just such a fruitful grafting." PAFFORD (ed. 1963, p. lxxviii): She is "peasant, matter-of-fact, and down-to-earth. . . . Perdita has plenty of natural good sense; she is by no means stupid or vacant, for there can be no true charm where there is no understanding vitality in the eyes."

Other critics use the term *natural* in reference to Perdita's intrinsic superiority. ARMSTRONG (1969, p. 67): "Full grown, Perdita, Queen of the feast, her royal origin proclaiming itself even in rural exile, is an intensely attractive figure, partly because of spontaneity and warm generous sensuality." BERKELEY & KARIMIPOUR (1985, pp. 90–3): Perdita, a princess of the best blood raised in low condition, illustrates that "good blood is obviously the essence, the transmitter of human excellence." Perdita's royal blood ensures the retention of (p. 91) "all her wonderful characteristics even in deprivation"; it is further indicated by her beauty, (p. 92) "angelic intelligence," sweet and refined speech, "highly developed sense of tact," (p. 93) lack of condescension to her supposed family, and "disdain" of indecencies. ADAMS (1989, pp. 107–8): "The daughter of royalty, Perdita is instinctively, *naturally*, recognized as superior to her humble adopted environment. By genetic inheritance, presumably, she talks a different dialect than her 'brother'. . . . Though the audience bravely agrees, for the moment, that the sun shines on rich and poor alike, it would not be satisfied if this peerless [*108*] piece of earth married a common shepherd-clown. It will not be satisfied until, recognized socially as an authentic princess, she is united with her 'natural' social equal, an authentic prince" who proves his passion for her by being willing to give up his princedom.

For a few critics, no such distinctions are possible. HUDSON (1848, 1:331–2): Perdita has "native intelligence as distinguished from artificial acquirements, and inborn dignity bursting through all the disadvantages of the humblest station. . . . [*332*] The graces of the princely and the simplicities of the pastoral character seem striving which shall express her loveliest." SCHÜCKING (1922; 1948, p. 246): Perdita is "a child of nature, a king's daughter who has grown up among simple shepherd folk. But she keeps within the limits of realism, and is, moreover, endowed with the whole wealth of personal touches which go to make up a Shakespearean character. She is modest, unassuming, not submissive, however, but independent, full of natural dignity, frank, gay, adroit, sparkling with youthful vivacity, intelligent, with all sorts of carefully cultivated little interests, possessed of that instinctive knowledge of the world which is so truly feminine, profound, sincere, full of genuine feeling and tender reverence, confident and brave. What an intense and exuberant vitality!" COHEN (in GREENBLATT, ed. 1982, p. 130): "Perdita serves . . . [to unite] court with country and upper class with lower" because she is "the product of her innate nobility" but also of sixteen years of life with the Shepherd and the Clown.

Many critics think Perdita's virtues reflect Hermione's part in her. HUDSON (1848, 1:332–3): With "the same delicacy and chastity of honour as her mother, she has less sternness and severity of carriage. . . . [*333*] With her mother's depth, intensity and calmness of feeling, no perturbations can reach her." Nor does he later (ed. 1852, 4: 18–19) see reason to change his mind. HALL (1871, p. 245): "Perdita possesses fully the nature of her mother. She has the same calm dignity, the same repose, the same resignation and power of self-denial. Both mentally and in her physical aspect, she is a true copy of the wronged Hermione." SNIDER (c. 1890, pp. 489–90): "We may see in her conduct, flashes of the supreme maternal characteristic—long-suffering; she is always the possibility of an Hermione. She would be able to endure to the last, were the call made upon her; whenever the flint of trial strikes upon her simple girl-life, sparkles of courage fill the air. . . . She is her mother as a young maiden. . . . With the quiet strength and deep ethical feeling of Hermione, she combines all the warmth and simplicity of youthful love. . . . [*490*] Perdita . . . is thus the connecting link between the two main groups." BROOKE (1905; 1913, p. 274): Perdita has admirable "native intellect. . . . [The] sight of the knot of a difficulty is always clear, and so is her solution of it. This is the mother's intellect in the child. . . . In this handing down of similarity of character, Shakespere is perhaps scientifically and certainly poetically right; and he supports this idea of his throughout the rest of the play. Perdita, with a difference, descends from her mother." TILLYARD (1938; 1962, pp. 46–7): "Other parts of her character are a deep-seated [*47*] strength and ruthless common sense. . . . It is through Perdita's magnificence that we accept as valuable the new life into which the play is made to issue. . . . She is Hermione's true daughter and prolongs in herself those regenerative processes which in her mother have suffered a temporary eclipse." Only WEBSTER (1942; 1955, p. 278) disagrees: The fact that Perdita is the image of her mother is "the least important thing about her. She brings with her a new world, as far from Leontes' Sicily as May from December."

Some critics, tempted to dwell on possible flaws in Perdita, easily find reason not to, leaving the perfect princess intact. INCHBALD (ed. 1808, 3:6): "Quite as improbable as the unprovoked jealousy" of Leontes is that "the gentle, the amiable, the tender Perdita, should be an unconcerned spectator of the doom which menaced her father; and carelessly forsake him in the midst of his calamities." LLOYD (1894, p. 167): The eagerness of the Shepherd and the Clown to avoid Polixenes's wrath by disclaiming responsibility for Perdita "acquits her of ingratitude as well as presumption in moving easily towards the superior rank due to her nature as to her descent. Her own courage and collectedness at once place her in contrast to the bewildered and frightened hinds, and bring her worthily into sympathy with the patience and self-support of her brave mother Hermione." MATTHEWS (1913; 1970, pp. 339–40): "Perdita is more than the story requires. She is one of Shakespeare's most enchanting heroines. She may be lauded by other characters in the play and her beauty may be praised by all who gaze upon it. But she is not dependent for her charm upon any eulogy from others. She speaks for herself; she is what she is . . . an ideal of ineffable maidenhood." Though she (p. 340) falls from grace once, in deserting her supposed father when he is threatened with death, "this is only what one must expect in a dramatic-romance."

POLIXENES

Polixenes does not create much of a critical stir. Occasionally he is treated lightly. WIGSTON ([1884?], p. 13): Polixenes "includes in himself a great element of Time; for he unites through his issue, the circle he unwittingly broke." A few critics nearly dismiss him. SMEATON (1911, p. 508): Polixenes is "altogether a slighter character [than Leontes], one of these amorous, kindly-dispositioned men who can refuse nothing to a woman." CARRINGTON (1956, p. 21): He "does not make so strong an impression as Leontes" even though he is Leontes "in reverse"—getting "worse as Leontes gets better."

Critics see a major flaw in his character when they fix on his behavior at Leontes's court. Mark TAYLOR (1982, pp. 37–8): Polixenes's speech to Hermione about the days before he and Leontes met their wives (141–5) is "ill-mannered and boorish. . . . Polixenes' rudeness in blaming her and his own wife for his and Leontes' fall from grace" is nearly inexcusable, while "the implication that [Polixenes] could have remained sexually indifferent forever had not *his wife* grown into womanhood" is strange and unnatural. Polixenes (p. 38) "reveals a profound fear and loathing of female sexuality, before which he is humanly inadequate." KEETON (1930; 1967, p. 153) "cannot altogether acquit Polixenes of cowardice, for he thinks only of his own skin and does not consider the probable effect of his flight upon Hermione." PYLE (1969, p. 25): "The action of the play depends on [Hermione] being left to face the music alone, and Polixenes must therefore be lowered in our esteem. . . . But in view of his respect and admiration for Hermione we are bound to make excuses for him, and to remind ourselves that in flying for his life he does what we have blamed Leontes for not doing—he takes the advice of the wise Camillo." ENRIGHT (1970, pp. 170–1): That Polixenes and Camillo "should make their escape so expeditiously, leaving Hermione" merely because it is difficult to see how their continued presence would help her at all and Polixenes is in mortal danger in Sicilia, (p. 171) "does not induce us to admire him."

Yet his violent behavior at the sheepshearing is not seen as seriously detrimental to the audience's view of him. LONG (1961, pp. 75–8): Polixenes's anger grows "in opposition to the revelry of the scene. . . . [76] As he watches Florizel and Perdita dancing together [1988–9], Polixenes sees their mutual interest only as light dalliance between a prince and an unusually attractive girl. . . . And when Autolycus sings his first peddler's cry, Polixenes is strengthened in his belief that Florizel is . . . interested in a light love that can be purchased with trinkets [2044–55, 2169–78]. . . . [77] As he observes [the satyrs], time out of mind the symbols of unbridled lust and carnality, Polixenes is struck by another thought. . . . [Perdita] desires [Florizel's] body as well as his money. . . . Now Perdita becomes in his mind a seductress with stark sexual cravings as her motivation and Prince Florizel as her victim. . . . [78] Well might Polixenes turn savagely on her [cites 2265–70]." BONJOUR (1969, pp. 208, 211): "Such misbehaviour as Florizel's [attempted betrothal without Polixenes's approval] is so unexpected on the part of Polixenes that he cannot explain it rationally; in his eyes his son has not only been seduced by Perdita's beauty, but in a way bewitched. Hence the very violence of his attack against that bewitching beauty which is the prime cause of all his troubles." But Polixenes's corresponding threats against Perdita's beauty (p. 211) "remain entirely hypothetical, and we never have the impression that Perdita's death is imminent, or really at stake." WILLIAMSON (1986, p. 151): At the sheepshearing, Polixenes is forced to deal with the problem of the obedience of an adult child, "a special burden to the father who is king because on the child's marriage depends the future of the realm. . . . [Polixenes is] deeply shaken by his son's behavior, both because Florizel casually anticipates his father's death (an oedipal wish for power without rivalry for the mother's love) and because he refuses to consider revealing his match with Perdita to his father."

SHEPHERD AND CLOWN

These two characters are sometimes dismissed succinctly. DOUCE (1807, 1:363): The Clown is "a mere country booby." SCHLEGEL (1808; 1846, p. 397): "Perdita's foster-father and his son are both made simple boors, that we may the more distinctly see how all that ennobles her belongs only to herself." WILLIAMS (1967, p. 7): "The shepherd and his son are what the Elizabethans called 'natural,' that is, mentally incapable of any art."

Other critics are less terse if no more admiring. LLOYD (1894, p. 167): The "unhesitating selfishness of the old man and his son at the approach of danger, though otherwise they are creditable rustics enough, the singleness of their anxiety to save their own skins from royal vengeance, by proving the foundling none of their blood, without any thought of her fate and fortune, belongs to the revulsions that characterize the play." SCHANZER (ed. 1969, pp. 20–1): The Clown, though "a masterpiece of comic portraiture," provides a "contrast between the two generations . . . by no means favourable to the young." The response of father and son to the good fortune that befalls both at the end of the play shows that (p. 21) "the old Shepherd [represents] traditional rustic virtues . . . while his son . . . is shown to be made of a much cheaper metal." NELSON (1973, p. 57): "An element of greed" in the Shepherd is a "dark quality," but it is not sustained enough to produce tragedy and is finally "subsumed by the . . . overpowering activity" of the idealized Perdita.

Some critics admire the old Shepherd. MARSH (1962; 1980, p. 141): The Shepherd takes up the abandoned baby "for pity [1517]" and obviously has what Leontes lacks—"common humanity, a respect for life, and a joy in seeing it perpetuated." BERRY (1965, pp. 96–7)): The old Shepherd's speech about his late wife as hostess of the sheepshearing (1860–67) provides a particularly "penetrative insight into the Shepherd's 'character' . . . his 'humanity' . . . and also something about his history. . . . He sound[s] the golden tradition" of the Bohemian-Arcadia myth when he remembers the (p. 97) "golden past." LINDENBAUM (1972, p. 19): This old man is endowed by Sh. with nearly as much dignity as Perdita herself. BATTENHOUSE (1980, p. 134): The Shepherd's "half-prophetic insight" leads both Shepherd and Clown to take the fardel to Polixenes. In this action, they reflect "St Paul's idea that freedom from the law is possible by sights that transcend human custom," and though they are only dimly aware of a higher mystery, "they travel with a faith that the tokens will reveal it and they are willing to offer Autolycus their gold, and even put the clown in pawn, in pursuit of this hope. . . . By their service of patient good will they prove their own inner gentility." COHEN (in GREENBLATT, ed. 1982, p. 130): "To the extent that [Perdita] sums up the movement of the play, [the Shepherd and the Clown] bear half the meaning of [*WT*]. . . . They assert or practice a series of values that link them to nature and to Perdita, in this way providing a commentary on the court. Finally, their thinking reveals a synthetic [coalescing] impulse that anticipates Perdita's role and that is socially ratified in their elevation to courtiers at the end of the play."

The Winter's Tale *on the Stage*

Performances

Six performances of *WT* in the 17th c. can be identified with certainty. On 15 May 1611 Simon Forman visited the Globe Th. to see *WT* acted by the King's Men (CHAMBERS, 1923, 2:216). Court records attest to a further five performances by the King's Men at the First and Second Banqueting Houses, Whitehall: 5 Nov. 1611, in the presence of King James (4:177); 1612–13, in a season of 14 plays in honor of the marriage of Princess Elizabeth and the Elector Palatine and in the presence of Prince Charles, the Princess, and the Elector (4:180); Easter Tuesday, 7 Apr. 1618, in the presence of King James (CHAMBERS, 1930, 2:346); 18 Jan. 1623/4, in the presence of the Duchess of Richmond (2:347); and 16 Jan. 1633/4 (2:352). CHAMBERS suggests that the inclusion of *WT* in a 1619 MS list of plays drawn up in the Revels Office (see p. 605) may indicate that it was among the plays being "considered for performance at Court," c. 1619–20 (2:346); BENTLEY (1941, 1:95, n. C) calls this suggestion "plausible." On 19 Aug. 1623 Sir Henry Herbert, Master of the Revels, issued a license, which may have been for the performance of 18 Jan. 1623/4 (CHAMBERS, 1930, 1:488, 2:347).

BALDWIN (1927, ch. 9, chart 4) assigns the parts for the play's initial performance: Leontes = Richard Burbadge (or Burbage), Autolycus = John Lowin, Shepherd = Henry Cundall (or Condell), Polixenes = William Ostler, Camillo = John Heminges, Florizel = John Underwood, Clown = Robert Armin, Antigonus = Alexander Cooke, Paulina = John Rice, Hermione = James Sands, Perdita = Richard Robinson, Mamillius = Armin's apprentice. BARTHOLOMEUSZ (1982, pp. 13, 244, n. 11) accepts BALDWIN's assignment of Leontes, but assigns Autolycus to Armin, Hermione "possibly" to John Rice, and Paulina to Robinson.

The only contemporary comments on 17th-c. performances are the entry in Forman's diary and the entry in the court record for 1633–4, which notes that the performance was "likt" (CHAMBERS, 1930, 2:352). BARTHOLOMEUSZ (1982, pp. 12–27 *passim*) conjectures details of early staging and performance (1611–34). He suggests, for example, that in accordance with 379 Polixenes and Hermione actually kiss (p. 18) and that the satyrs would be costumed as were those in Jonson's *Oberon* (p. 16); see also n. 2159 and p. 608.

After the Restoration *WT* was among the 108 Blackfriars plays assigned c. 12 Jan. 1668/9 to Thomas Killigrew's company (NICOLL, 1923, p. 315). SHATTUCK (1965, p. 495) catalogs one promptbook, known as the Padua promptbook (anon., c. 1640), and a preparation copy (1670s) attributed to actor-director Joseph Ashbury, Smock Alley, Dublin. EVANS (1963, 2.1:23) describes the Padua *WT* as "an unfinished cutting of the play, one which could never have reached production." Earlier (1960, 1.1:8–9) he had suggested assigning it to Sir Edward Dering and his group of amateur actors, who performed in the 1620s; subsequently (1967, p. 239), however, he considered "the Dering provenience questionable, though still not impossible" and suggested (p. 242) that the promptbook might have "belonged to some kind of splinter group touring the provinces or abroad shortly before the closing of the theatres in 1642 or during the interregnum." BARTHOLOMEUSZ (1982, p. 14) discusses the Padua promptbook as the first in the traditions "of cutting away the fat" from *WT* yet also "of embellishing it with music cues."

WT and its adaptations, chiefly those by Macnamara Morgan and David Garrick, were performed in London 112 times in the 18th c. In the period 1701–50, *WT* played 14 times in two seasons. Between 1751 and 1800, adaptations dominated; they account for all but two of the 98 performances in 29 seasons. The revivals and adaptations were popular choices for benefits (45 performances), and they were played at the command of their majesties twice and of the Prince of Wales thrice (VAN LENNEP et al., 1960–8, *passim*; SCHNEIDER, 1979). SHATTUCK (1987, 2:120) lists one anonymous, late-18th-c. promptbook, made on Tonson's 1758 ed. of Garrick's alteration.

It is not always possible to determine whose adaptation was performed. For example, the performance at Covent Garden 12 Mar. 1774 has been described both "*as altered* by Garrick" (HOGAN, 1957, 2:682) and as "seem[ing] to be some adaptation of Garrick's *Florizel and Perdita*" (STONE, 1962, 4:1792). DASH (1971) and PEDICORD (1981) speculate about the adapter of versions performed from the late 1750s to the early 1770s, including an abbreviated Garrick version that eliminates Hermione. DASH (p. 154, n. 13) lists performances of versions attributed to more than one adapter.

Before Garrick's version captured the stage, an unadapted *WT*, announced as "Not Acted these Hundred Years," was revived at Goodman's Fields on 15 Jan. 1741 between two parts of a concert; it played 8 times in January and once in April. Manager Henry Giffard, as Leontes, led the cast (SCOUTEN, 1961, 3:847, 881). The next season Covent Garden revived *WT* for a further five performances, the first at the command of the Prince and Princess of Wales (SCOUTEN, 1961, 3:942). The final performance, on 21 Jan. 1742, presages the next chapter in *WT*'s stage history: "A New Grand Ballet call'd the *Rural Assembly*" was presented "with all new habits and other decorations proper to the entertainment" and with an expanded cast: Chasseur, Pastors, Shepherdesses, Nymph of the Plain, Old Herdsman, Cottage Nymph, Two Nymphs of the Vale, and a Sylvan (SCOUTEN, 1961, 3:961). This elaboration of the sheepshearing scene anticipated the adaptations that would dominate the second half of the century.

The first of these was Morgan's popular *Florizel and Perdita; or, The Sheep Shearing*, an afterpiece in two acts with music by Thomas Arne, which played at Covent Garden and Drury Lane for approximately 25 performances in 12 seasons over a span of 44 years, from its premiere, 25 Mar. 1754, to its last performance, 12 May 1798. Morgan's adaptation cuts the Sicilian scenes. He introduces Pan to sing "Shepherds hear the voice of Pan" at the rural feast and a priest to solemnize the marriage of Florizel and Perdita. Writing about the performance at Covent Garden on 24 March 1761, GENEST (1832, 4:626) observes that "this piece seems to have been turned into an Opera to suit the prevailing taste of this theatre." More bluntly, ARCHER (1887, p. 512) describes it as "nothing but the fourth act [of *WT*], torn from its context and 'written up' by a forgotten playwright."

More popular than Morgan's adaptation, Garrick's version in three acts, originally announced as *The Winter's Tale* but also known as *Florizel and Perdita*, played over 60 times in 18 seasons between 1756 and 1795. During its first season it was performed 13 times; during the season of 1779–80, it was the second most popular show in the repertoire, playing 15 times, just three fewer than Sheridan's hit *The School for Scandal*. Garrick based his adaptation on Acts 3, 4, and 5; conflated several gentlemen to create Rogero, taking the name from *WT* 3031; truncated the statue scene; and added speeches (see p. 819). Michael Arne wrote "The Sheep-Shearing Song" for Susanna Cibber, who created Garrick's Perdita. In many productions thereafter, Perdita, another character, or a vocalist performed "Come, come, my good shepherds, our flocks we must shear." William Charles Macready cut the song in 1837 (SHATTUCK, 1965, no. 8).

Garrick's "masterly" (DAVIES, 1808, 1:314) Leontes introduced the business of stepping back when Hermione comes down from the pedestal. Descending from the "temple," Hannah Pritchard's "inimitable" Hermione presented a "countenance

. . . serene and composed" (*Universal Museum*, Feb. 1762). The reference to "the temple" and the engraving based on Robert Edge Pine's portrait of Pritchard in which she wears a cross in 5.3 (see below) associate Hermione for the first time with Christian iconography. Cibber's delightful "grace" (MURPHY, 1801, 1:286) and "neat simplicity in singing" (GENEST, 1832, 4:446) created a Perdita unrivaled until 1845. Margaret Martyr, who had played Mopsa (May 1785), was the first actress to play Florizel as a breeches part.

Less successful were *The Sheep-Shearing; or, Florizel and Perdita*, an adaptation by George Colman the Elder, which was performed in summer seasons at the Haymarket, once in 1777 and twice in 1783, and a revival of Sh.'s unaltered *WT*, "not acted for 30 years," which played twice at Covent Garden, 24 Apr. 1771 and 4 May 1772, for the benefit of Thomas Hull, who prepared the text and first doubled Camillo and Time (STONE, 1962, 4:1543). Adaptations played in such provincial cities as Dublin as early as 1754 (BARTHOLOMEUSZ, 1982, p. 29). The first American performance was at the John St. Th., New York, 1795 (ODELL, 1927, 1:391–2).

Eighteenth-century illustrations reveal details of possible costuming and stage design; portraits and engravings of actresses as Hermione may shed light on the performers' interpretations of the role. John Zoffany painted Elizabeth Farren as Hermione (c. 1780; see HIGHFILL et al., 1978, 5:163). Engravings portray Pritchard as Hermione in 5.3 (1765; see HIGHFILL et al., 1987, 12:178), Elizabeth Hartley as Hermione in 5.3 (GENTLEMAN, 2nd ed., 1775), Isabella Mattocks as Hermione in 717–19 (HULL, in GENTLEMAN, ed. 1779), Richard Yates as Autolycus in 4.3 (GARRICK, ed. 1785), and the discovery of Perdita in 3.3 (Gent, ed. 1773). See also MERCHANT (1959, pp. 208–20).

In the first half of the 19th c., actor-managers gradually restored much of Sh.'s text (see p. 821), attempted historical accuracy in costume and scenic design, and filled out the stage picture in scenes such as 1.1 and 3.2 with numerous silent characters. Kemble, who had included Garrick's adaptation in his first season as manager of Drury Lane (1788) and then dropped the adaptation from the repertoire, produced *WT* at Drury Lane on 25 Mar. 1802 (11 performances) and revived the production at Covent Garden in 1807 (6 performances) and 1811 ("several" performances [SHATTUCK, 1974, 9.3:1; GENEST, 1832, 8:286–97 *passim* lists five performances in 1811–12]). SHATTUCK (1974, 9.3:iii) catalogs five promptbooks for the production, in which Kemble played Leontes and Sarah Siddons Hermione.

Kemble's only uncomplimentary critic, ANON. (1802), complains about the visual confusion caused by the designers, who mixed historical periods in the properties and costumes for the newly restored Sicilian scenes. Kemble's staging of 3.2, which introduced properties emblematic of regal power and more than 40 extras, became the dominant model imitated or modified by 19th-c. actor-managers. By making Leontes and his court the focus of a formal stage picture and by placing Hermione and her three female attendants at the greatest possible distance from Leontes, Kemble intensified the emotional distance between the king and his falsely accused queen. To reinforce visually the shift from the public trial to Leontes's private remorse, Kemble broke 3.2 after Hermione is borne off by the women (1334 approximately) and played the rest of 3.2 as a new scene in Leontes's closet.

Kemble's production influenced Charles Young (Covent Garden, 1819), William Charles Macready (Drury Lane, 1823), John Vandenhoff (Drury Lane, 1834), Samuel Phelps and Amelia Warner (Sadler's Wells, 1845), and Warner (Marylebone Th., 1847). Warner had played Hermione for Macready at Drury Lane and for Phelps at Sadler's Wells, and her *WT* was one of the "most successful productions" of her management of the Marylebone (ODELL, 1931, 6:123). The Theatre Royal Bristol also based its productions of 1819 and 1824 on Kemble's version.

Between 3 Nov. 1823 and 30 May 1843, Macready, who had first played Leontes in Bath in 1815 (POLLOCK, 1875, 1:113), revived *WT* for seven seasons at Drury Lane and three at Covent Garden. In 1837 Macready altered Kemble's staging of 3.2 to make the stage picture less formal and more appropriate to Macready's interpretation of Leontes (see p. 804). In 1837 he also excised Garrick's additions to the text and introduced Helen Faucit, who would become the most acclaimed Hermione since Siddons.

Phelps and Warner's revival, which opened 29 Nov. 1845 for a season of 45 performances, played a total of 137 times in nine seasons at Sadler's Wells, where it closed on 29 Sept. 1862 (ALLEN, 1971, pp. 314-15). Indebted to Kemble's production as modified by Macready in 1837, Phelps was "evidently" the first to give *WT* "a wholly Grecian setting" (BARTHOLOMEUSZ, 1982, p. 65). More significantly, Phelps was the first producer to demonstrate the advantages of staging *WT* in a theater smaller than Covent Garden and Drury Lane. In the more intimate Sadler's Wells Th., actors conveyed more effectively the thoughts and emotions in Sh.'s poetry (pp. 78-9).

The tradition "of substituting a poetry of scenery for the poetry of language" in *WT* (BARTHOLOMEUSZ, 1982, p. 98), which was to dominate the second half of the 19th c., began with Charles Kean at the Princess Th. on 28 Apr. 1856. KEAN (1856, p. ix) claims that the text had "been carefully preserved throughout"; in fact, he omitted 62% of Sh.'s script (WILSON, 1985, p. 2), presented the Sicilian scenes as "*tableaux vivants* of the private and public life of the ancient Greeks" (KEAN, p. vi), and set the Bohemian scenes in "the more barbaric and primitive splendours of . . . Asia Minor" (MERCHANT, 1959, p. 211). A popular success, Kean's production ran for 102 consecutive performances. The cast included Kean as Leontes, Ellen Terry as Mamillius, and Ellen Kean as Hermione.

Kean's *tableaux vivants* included a sumptuous farewell banquet in honor of Polixenes (1.2), at which 36 youths performed a Pyrrhic dance. Kean set 3.2 in the theater at Syracuse and filled the stage with more than 170 extras, including 45 children. Time, last seen in London productions in 1771 carrying his scythe and glass, was transformed into Cronus; Cronus, Luna, the stars, and Phoebus presented an elaborate, three-part allegory of the passage of time. The statue scene opened with a "procession by torchlight" (*Standard*, 1 May 1856) including six principals and more than 100 extras. Kean intensified Garrick's response to the moving statue (see above p. 800): in his more public scene, "As she slowly raises her hand, all shrink backwards" (SHATTUCK, 1965, no. 19).

Kean's influence spread to the provinces, where it was greater than in London, and to the US. "Faint echoes" (BARTHOLOMEUSZ, 1982, p. 185) of the banquet in 1.2

can be discerned as late as 1958 (see below, p. 808). WELLS (1962, p. 78) discusses "two theatrical burlesques [of 1856] both aimed, to some extent, at this production." William Burton's were the first significant productions in the US. His first (Burton's Th., New York, 1851), about which little is known, featured Warner as Hermione. His next (Burton's Th., 1856) achieved a measure of independence from London. Anticipating by two months Kean's restoration of Time, Burton staged him as the traditional figure, carrying a scythe and hour glass. Burton was the first to stage Act 1 before a backdrop of Mt. Etna, which erupted along with Leontes's jealousy. At least one other production (that of the Saxe-Meiningen Co., which performed *WT* in London in 1881) provided a view of Etna to locate the play in Sicilia (BARTHOLOMEUSZ, 1982, p. 115). In 1857, reviving *WT* at the larger New Th., Broadway, Burton retained some elements from 1856 (Mt. Etna and an English setting for the Bohemian scenes, for example), incorporated elements from Kean's production (such as the Pyrrhic dance and the theater at Syracuse), and expanded Kean's allegory of the passage of time by adding such spectacle as a display of the zodiacal signs and the personification of the Four Seasons (Playbill).

Charles and Adelaide Calvert (Prince's Th., Manchester, 1869) borrowed from and adapted Kean's version and introduced spectacle and effects that their successors would in turn borrow from them. Leontes's defiance of the oracle as "meere false-hood" (1322) provoked "a sudden storm, with thunder, &c. — great consternation" (CALVERT, ed. 1869). The Calverts' most important contribution was to extend to the entire 5th act the religious tone that Pritchard had introduced into Garrick's statue scene. Accompanied by an incense-bearing attendant and mourners "singing a hymn in praise of the dead," Leontes offered "oblations of incense and flowers" at "the mausoleum of Hermione and Mamillius," set in "a sacred grove." The Calverts placed 5.3 in "a small temple" and ended the production with a paean, sung by the court. At Booth's, New York, Lawrence Barrett presented in 1871 40 performances of *WT* "derivative" of Kean and the Calverts (BARTHOLOMEUSZ, 1982, p. 111).

In the preface to his 1876 ed. (p. v), Edward SAKER (Alexander Th., Liverpool, 1876), who had been an "exceedingly humourous" Clown in Kean's production (*Times*, 1 May 1856), thanks Ellen Kean, who had lent Kean's promptbook, and Calvert, who had "volunteered suggestions." Saker's revival was "an elaboration of Kean's version, with less text and more spectacle" (JACKSON, 1978, p. 102). To Kean's Bithynia (Bohemia), with its sheep and goats, he introduced "'real trees . . . real water'" (p. 102); to the Calverts' thunderbolt he added a weird lighting effect, "'a pale, steel-blue radiance . . . [of] ghastly but intense light'" at the point from which the thunderbolt had come (p. 103).

In 1878, 22 years after Kean's production, *WT* returned to London with effects borrowed from Kean, Calvert, and Saker. F. B. Chatterton's "magnificent and instructive spectacle" (*Times*, 30 Sept. 1878) at Drury Lane, however, was neither a critical nor a financial success.

The last major production of *WT* of the 19th c., by the American actress Mary Anderson, opened in Nottingham, was transferred to the Lyceum (1887), and toured the US (1888). Although it was unpopular with the critics, it was the longest-running production of the 19th c., including 164 nights in London (BARTHOLOMEUSZ, 1982, pp. 116-17). It influenced the first *WT* at Stratford-upon-Avon (1895; see below) and Viola Allen's production in New York (1904). Forbes-Robertson was Leontes. Anderson's heavily cut text reduced the running time to 2 hours, 8 minutes, and five acts to thirteen scenes. The chief novelty of the production was her decision to play both Hermione and Perdita, roles she was the first to double. Anderson retained the Calverts' storm and Saker's lighting effect; she modified the religious tone the Calverts had introduced into 5.3.

For the first production at Stratford-upon-Avon, Ben Greet borrowed the music composed for Anderson's and staged the shepherds' dance, "as nearly as possible a reproduction" of Anderson's (*Birmingham Daily Post*, 24 Apr. 1895). As had Anderson, Greet excised Kean's spectacle, such as the allegory of the passage of time, and borrowed the storm introduced by Calvert and enhanced by Saker.

Kemble's restoration of the Sicilian scenes opened the way for reinterpretation of Leontes and Hermione. Kemble and Siddons established standards by which their successors would be judged, and introduced business their successors would continue or sometimes modify. The 19th-c. actor was expected to retain Leontes's regal bearing ("the dignity of the King") while revealing his jealousy ("the emotions of the man") (*Daily Advertiser*, 12 May 1807). On the occasion of Kemble's retirement, Hazlitt (*Times*, 25 June 1817, in HOWE, 1930, 5:377) recalled his fine playing of "the growing jealousy of the King, and the exclusive possession which this passion gradually obtains over his mind." Kemble's delivery of 377-89 marked the development of Leontes's conviction of and despair at Hermione's adultery. Leontes's entrance in 2.1 with 17 men shattered the domestic atmosphere; a courtier named Thasius, not one of the anonymous officers or guards, obeyed Leontes's order to remove Mamillius (SHATTUCK, 1965, no. 3); and a chilling annotation directs Leontes to throw "Mamillius over to Thasius" (SHATTUCK, 1965, no. 4).

Although some reviewers in 1823 complained about Macready's giving Leontes an inappropriate stammer, about his rewriting of lines, and about his incomprehensibly rapid delivery, the assessment was predominantly complimentary. In Macready's performance, which gave the king "less of dignity" than Kemble had done, "the incipient jealousy . . . gradually ripening into a conviction of his consort's guilt, and finally terminating in bitter hatred, was traced through all its tortuous ramifications" (*Times*, 4 Nov. 1823). Macready's numerous changes in stage position in 1.2, recorded in James R. Anderson's partbook for Florizel and for Leontes (for whom he was understudy), testify to Macready's restless energy (SHATTUCK, 1965, no. 8). His "energy and fire" (*Times*, 4 Nov. 1823) illuminated, especially, the statue scene, which reviewers applauded unanimously. "His burst of emotion on recovering his long-lost *Hermione* . . . was very finely conceived and executed," observed *The Examiner* (1823). Modifying Garrick's business, Macready retreated from the statue when Paulina said she could awaken it. When the statue seemed to move, "he appeared for a time annihilated; lost in amazement, and love, and joy. But when she descended from the pedestal and moved forward a few paces, the persuasion that she is a thing of life becomes irresistible, and . . . he rushes convulsively into her embraces" (*Morning*

Post, 2 Oct. 1837). Looking back on the statue scene, Helen Faucit, by then Lady Martin, recalled Macready's "passionate joy [that] seemed beyond control" (*Blackwood's Edinburgh Mag.,* 1891).

In contrast with Macready, who made "rapid transitions," Phelps made a "gradual transition from one state of mind to another, with an underlying struggle of emotions" (ALLEN, 1971, p. 178). Phelps's major contribution was to embody COLERIDGE's interpretation of Leontes as a man with "a genuine jealousy of disposition . . . having certain well known and well defined effects and concomitants" (see n. 181-92). Phelps's creation "was not . . . a sympathetic character, and yet it was so convincing on the stage that spectators were held in the grip of the emotions displayed. They felt the climax of the statue scene with a palpable shock" (ALLEN, 1971, pp. 177-8). BARTHOLOMEUSZ (1982, p. 78): "By 1858 . . . Phelps had begun to play Leontes as 'an ancient Greek king,'" accommodating his interpretation to the Grecian design.

Kean, the first actor to establish Leontes's jealousy from the very beginning of 1.2, relied on elaborate visual effects to convey it (BARTHOLOMEUSZ, 1982, p. 87). To mark the transition from "the irascible tyrant" to "the dejected sufferer," Kean fainted when Paulina announced Hermione's death (SHATTUCK, 1965, no. 21).

As had Kean, Henry B. Irving, in the first production of *WT* at Stratford-upon-Avon, portrayed Leontes's jealousy from the moment he stepped on the stage, "a gloomy, restless, and irritable man" who lacked "some degree of dignity" (*Daily Chronicle,* 25 Apr. 1895). At the trial, "when he sat upon the throne of Justice, stern, immovable, pitiless, and powerful, he looked the picture of an imperious tyrant whose sole being was actuated by a revengeful spirit" (*The Sunday Chronicle,* 28 Apr. 1895).

A major challenge to the 19th-c. actress was to portray the lighter side of Hermione. The outstanding tragic actress of her generation, Siddons, was not well suited to "the playful elegance with which Hermione urges Polixenes" (*Times,* 12 Nov. 1807) and conveyed "too much of unbending and freezing dignity" in the scene (*Times,* 29 Nov. 1811). Her performance in the trial scene, in contrast, was praised for "her indignation at the groundless charge" (*Daily Advertiser and Oracle,* 26 Mar. 1802) as well as for "the eloquence of dignified and insulted innocence" with which she defended herself (*Morning Advertiser,* 12 Nov. 1807). Siddons is best remembered for the statue scene, in which she introduced Grecian drapery and pose and signaled that she was alive by suddenly moving her head when Paulina called for music to awaken her (BOADEN, 1825, 2:314).

Helena Faucit, the consummate Victorian Hermione and the most successful of Macready's four Hermiones, was the first actress to win praise for all of Hermione's scenes. She conveyed in 1.2 a "confiding openness of disposition, frank in its spotless purity, and loving her lord so entirely that she loves nothing else but for his sake." When she rose to defend herself in the trial scene, she forgot "all physical weakness in the earnestness of her emotion." As was Macready, Faucit was most celebrated in the statue scene: "she descended from the pedestal, with a slow and gliding motion, and wearing the look of a being consecrated by long years of prayer and sorrow and seclusion" (*The Scotsman,* 3 Mar. 1847, in WILLIAMSON & PERSON, 1991, 15:411).

Faucit's innovative costume for this scene, which she describes in her 1 Nov. 1890 letter to Lord Tennyson (*Blackwood's Edinburgh Mag.*, Jan. 1891, in WILLIAMSON & PERSON, 1991, 15:414-15), dressed Hermione as a living queen, not a marble statue, unlike actresses since Siddons.

Warner introduced to New York (Burton's Th., 1851) her "Victorian interpretation [of Hermione], decorous and subdued" (BARTHOLOMEUSZ, 1982, p. 101). In the trial scene she conveyed "physical weakness and moral power . . . injured innocence and gentlest submission to the hard decrees of fate" (*Albion*, 27 Sept. 1851, in ODELL, 1931, 6:124). Undeterred by her husband's exhaustive historical research, Ellen Kean concealed layers of starched petticoats beneath her Grecian costume (TERRY, 1932, p. 15) and, as Faucit and Warner had done, modeled Hermione on an idealized Victorian heroine.

In her memoirs Mary ANDERSON (1896, p. 244) recalls that she had sought "to keep alive the sympathies of the audience with both Hermione and Perdita from beginning to end." Whereas Kemble, Macready, and Kean had added stage business to establish Leontes's fondness for Mamillius, Anderson added business, such as Hermione's greeting Mamillius with a kiss and Mamillius's attempt to present her with flowers, to call attention to the affection shared by Hermione and her son (SHATTUCK, 1965, no. 28). Anderson also reshaped the text to highlight Hermione's plight and introduced stunning effects in the trial scene. Her Hermione crouched at the altar during the thunderstorm, and with a grand gesture covered her face with her cloak and collapsed at 1329 (*Illustrated London News*, 17 Sept. 1887). The scene closed at 1389, with Paulina moaning over the lifeless body of Hermione until the curtain dropped (SHATTUCK, 1965, no. 28). The London critics, however, were not impressed by Anderson's doubling of the mother and the daughter, which called more attention to the actor than to the roles, or by the unsatisfactory solution to the problem of presenting both characters in 5.3. Anderson simply cut Perdita's lines and introduced a "strange, veiled, speechless figure, who keeps her back to the audience and who is addressed as Perdita" (*Times*, 12 Sept. 1887).

Freed from the visual tradition represented by Kean and seizing the option of playing a full text, 20th-c. directors gradually developed their own traditions. Sicilian scenes were often set in winter, lighting effects frequently signaled the onset of Leontes's jealousy, and visual images—such as Mamillius's nursery toys and the bear—reinforced motifs explored by the production. Seeking a unifying device, some directors introduced characters such as the three gentlemen (5.2) or Time into several scenes; called attention to a phrase, such as "A sad Tale's best for Winter" (618) or "It is requir'd You doe awake your Faith" (3300-1); or created a dominant visual image, such as the change of seasons or the zodiacal signs. Unlike the many directors who contrasted the dominant tones of Sicilia and Bohemia, some, such as Peter Hall (1988) and Adrian Noble (1992), stressed analagous themes and situations. By playing *WT* in repertoire with other late Shn. works, artistic directors at the Royal Shakespeare Company (1969), the Stratford (Ont.) Shakespeare Festival (1986), and the National Theatre (1988) invited audiences to reexamine individual late plays in the broader context of Sh.'s other late plays. By relocating Sicilia to a society outside the typical audience's experience, to a place such as a tribal court in the Arctic Circle (1976), directors seemed to suggest that Leontes's jealousy was alien to the audience's cultural norms. By locating the action near to the historical era or the geographical location of the audience, other directors, such as Terry Hands (1986), sought an immediacy of action for the emotionally charged issues. Several directors, most notably Robin Phillips (1978) and Hall (1988), questioned the reconciliation of Hermione and Leontes. In the second half of the 20th c. in productions such as David Thacker's (Young Vic, 1991), Leontes's private, domestic life overshadowed his public, royal role. As the century wore on, actresses playing Hermione, Paulina, and Perdita had the advantage of working with a fuller text than had their predecessors, whose lines had been reduced. By the end of the 20th c., *WT* was firmly established in the theatrical canon.

Working in the pictorial tradition of 19th-c. productions, Herbert Beerbohm Tree (His Majesty's Th., 1906) staged a heavily cut script and reached "the limits of spectacular realism . . . on the picture-frame stage" (BARTHOLOMEUSZ, 1982, p. 130). Unscripted stage business helped to establish location, such as springtime in Bohemia (4.3): Perdita sang at the cottage window; Florizel listened and threw her a posy; Autolycus awakened, hummed "Will you buy" (2139–44), and washed in the stream; and the Clown entered leading a donkey to drink from the brook (SHATTUCK, 1965, no. 35), which covered so much of the stage that it seems the "merrymakers had chosen a somewhat inconvenient spot for their gambols" (*Tribune*, 3 Sept. 1906). Tree introduced three unifying devices: theme music for Perdita; theme music for interpolated allusions to Apollo as well as at 1312; and additional thunder to mark the stages of Leontes's jealousy (BARTHOLOMEUSZ, 1982, pp. 127, 130). Moreover, he took advantage of a special circumstance affecting his female lead. "Ellen Terry made her theatrical debut as Mamillius in Charles Kean's production of *The Winter's Tale* in 1856. . . . Tree hit upon the idea of having Miss Terry appear again . . . , this time in the role of Hermione. . . . Tree not only secured a star but created an occasion for his production" (SCHMITT, 1970, p. 21).

Six years later Harley Granville-Barker (Savoy Th., 1912) played almost a full text (BARTHOLOMEUSZ, 1982, p. 139) and explored conventions of Renaissance staging. Granville-Barker altered the Savoy stage to create a platform with a discovery space and replaced the elaborate scenery and properties favored by the 19th c. with simple scene changes and minimal properties (KENNEDY, 1993, pp. 71–3). Granville-Barker's staging innovations allowed continuous action and encouraged an "Elizabethan intimacy between actor and audience" (STYAN, 1977, p. 83). KENNEDY (1985, p. 136) ranks the production "as one of the four or five most important Shakespearian productions" of the 20th century. Granville-Barker recognized the structural importance and stage-worthiness of small roles, such as those of the three gentlemen, whose lines had been reduced or reassigned in the 19th c. and whom he successfully restored (p. 133; *Daily Chronicle*, 23 Sept. 1912); Time, who had sometimes been cut and sometimes, as in Kean's production (1856), been part of an allegorical presentation; and the bear, which many 19th-c. productions had cut (see p. 832). The decor was simple: Norman Wilkinson designed two sets—the interior of Leontes's palace and the exterior of the Old Shepherd's cottage—and Albert Rothenstein "painted drop curtains, which provided varying depths of stage, and which were suggestive of time and place but were not scenically realistic." Rothenstein's eclectic costumes placed the play "in the world of fancy, fantasy, and romance" (KENNEDY, 1985, pp. 125, 128). Granville-Barker used traditional English music and authentic English country dances only when Sh. called for music or dance (*Standard*, 21 Sept. 1912). Unlike 19th-c. producers, Granville-Barker directed *WT* "as a human drama concerning ordinary and not semi-heroic creatures" (*Westminster Gazette*, 23 Sept. 1912). For more on this production, see DYMKOWSKI (1986, pp. 39–45).

Directing the first major production after World War II, Anthony Quayle (Stratford-upon-Avon, 1948) owed more to Kean and Tree than to Granville-Barker. Quayle opened his 1.1 during the final moments of a "sumptuous entertainment" (SHATTUCK, 1965, no. 51) and closed the scene with "a Kean-like Bacchanalia of barbaric intensity" (BARTHOLOMEUSZ, 1982, p. 203), played a heavily cut text, and closed with a procession and a song in praise of Apollo. A veteran of the Eastern European front, Quayle gave the Sicilian scenes a contemporary resonance by placing them behind the Iron Curtain and introducing a tyrannical ruler. Motley (Sophia Harris, Margaret F. Harris, and Elizabeth Montgomery) designed a blighted landscape and a dimly lit palace decorated with geometrical displays of spears, a celestial globe, and representations of supernatural creatures. The Bohemian scenes were set in the Cotswolds.

In the early 1950s two productions of *WT* were part of a trend that sought to incorporate Elizabethan staging practices, such as fluid action, into performances of Sh. (VENEZKY, "Productions," 1951, p. 335). At the Comédie Française (1951) a "simple, artistic setting of poles and curtains," rearranged to indicate change of place, kept "the action in continuous flow" (pp. 335, 337). Peter Brook's landmark production (Phoenix Th., 1951) played on Sophie Fedorovitch's set of "modified upper and inner stages," which "assure[d] continuous scenes" (p. 335). Brook was influenced by, but made a number of significant departures from, Granville-Barker. For example, he used direct address "sparingly" (BARTHOLOMEUSZ, 1982, p. 172), cut the text (pp. 170, 178), and read 5.3 as "the truth of the play," not, like Granville-Barker, as a stage effect (TREWIN, 1971, p. 60). Brook's staging of the transition from 3.3 to 4.2 was acclaimed: the highly effective storm on the seacoast of Bohemia turned into a heavy snowstorm, from which Time emerged. As he spoke, the storm abated and gave way to springtime (BARTHOLOMEUZ, 1982, p. 176; see also RYLANDS, 1953, p. 143, and TREWIN, 1951).

On successive days in July 1958, productions in two quite different styles opened at summer festivals in Stratford, Connecticut, co-directed by John Houseman and Jack Landau, and in Stratford, Ontario, directed by Douglas Campbell. Houseman, seeking a style "sufficiently formal to give the characters their fairy-tale quality, yet not so remote from life as to negate the human emotions," chose "ancient semipolitical, semireligious symbols of the Mediterranean tarot card pack" (HOUSEMAN, 1983, p. 140).

Campbell's version, with Tanya Moiseiwitsch's Rubenesque costumes and props (BARTHOLOMEUSZ, 1982, p. 187), included "faint echoes of Charles Kean's celebrated banquet" (p. 185) and other business for which there is no textual basis (p. 188). To unify Acts 1-3 with 4-5, Campbell expanded the role of Time, who opened and closed the production and "read several minor" roles (*Christian Century*, 29 Oct. 1958; see also BARTHOLOMEUSZ, 1982, p. 188).

Peter Wood's production (Stratford-upon-Avon, 1960) compared favorably with Brook's, especially in regard to the strength of the casting of major roles, Wood's attention to minor roles, and Jacques Noel's "uncluttered" stage (*Financial Times*, 31 Aug. 1960). Color—"the red of passion, the purple of repentance, and the gold of celebration"—marked three dominant moods of the production (SPEAIGHT, 1960, p. 452). Presenting the three gentlemen (Ian Richardson, Roy Dotrice, and Peter Jeffery) as "aged scholars," Wood expanded their parts to make them a unifying device; they were tutors to Mamillius and witnesses to Leontes's accusation of Hermione and to her trial; one announced Mamillius's death (BARTHOLOMEUSZ, 1982, pp. 204-5).

Trevor Nunn's production (Stratford-upon-Avon, 1969) was one of the most influential of the late 20th c. Christopher Morley's design, which broke with the tradition represented by the "exquisite pictures" of Wood and Noel, drew instead on the work of Granville-Barker (BARTHOLOMEUSZ, 1982, pp. 210, 212). Morley's designs for the Sicilian scenes introduced one strong visual image, a three-sided white box representing Mamillius's nursery, and two special effects, strobe lights and a rectangular box with mirrored walls. Dominating the sparsely furnished white box, an oversized hobby horse was used as a visual symbol at 368 (promptbook, SCL) and seemed "symbolic both of innocence and lust" (SPEAIGHT, 1969, p. 437). Other nursery toys assumed symbolic values when, for example, in 1.2 Mamillius and Leontes (Barrie Ingham) took turns peering through a kaleidoscope, and at the close of 1.2 Polixenes (Richard Pasco) played with a yo-yo (promptbook). Strobe lights signaled the onset of Leontes's jealousy, arrested the action, and forced the audience to "see the blameless Hermione [Judi Dench] and Polixenes as they appear in the King's feverish dream" (*New York Times*, 17 May 1969). The other special effect, the box, "became a glittering symbol, reflecting light, linking the anguished Leontes, [who appeared within the box as] Time's prisoner, and the cold statue," which was presented within it (BARTHOLOMEUSZ, 1982, p. 213). By setting the Bohemian scenes in rural 1960s England, Nunn attempted, as had Frank Dunlop (Edinburgh, 1966; see also p. 818 below), to make Bohemia meaningful to contemporary audiences. Having cast Judi Dench as Hermione and as Perdita, he solved the technical problem in 5.3 by having Dench and her stand-in make a "mechanical quick-change" after 3238 (BARTHOLOMEUSZ, 1982, p. 220). Anderson had solved the problem by cutting Perdita's lines (see p. 806)

John Barton with Trevor Nunn (Stratford-upon-Avon, 1976) set *WT* within the Arctic Circle. Having created an appropriate set, designer Di Seymour costumed Leontes and his subjects in "Scandinavian furs and folk-woven materials, hot reds and oranges predominating" (WARREN, 1977, p. 173). The drapery featured "strange signs resembling runes and figurative scenes, such as reindeer hunting" (LAROQUE, 1976, p. 91). The design concept did not easily accommodate the trial (3.2), which was staged in "far too tribal and nomadic a court" (DAVID, 1978, p. 224), and "the shearing of sheep [which] was implausible in a landscape where no sheep could have pastured, and the flowers . . . would hardly have bloomed" (SPEAIGHT, 1977, p. 188). The bear and Time were dominant motifs. Bears figured prominently in the decor; the bear (John Nettles) reappeared as Time, in effect "transforming the bear into an allegory of Death and making Antigonus a victim of Time" (LAROQUE, 1976, p. 91); and "the satyrs' dance became a ritual hunt-ballet in which the main dancer was the bear" (BARTHOLOMEUSZ, 1982, p. 222).

Among the productions that set *WT* in a society familiar to late 20th-c. audiences are those by Robin Phillips and Adrian Noble. Seeking an autocratic period within the "historical memory" of their audiences (R. P. KNOWLES, 1985, p. 26), Phillips and his designer, Daphne Dare (Stratford, Ont., 1978), placed Leontes's court in Czarist Russia, 1880, and Bohemia in the Ukraine, 1896 (KNOWLES, 1985, p. 27). The Sicilian scenes revealed an uneasy relationship between Brian Bedford's Leontes, a "superbly repressed autocrat . . . [with] a festering passion," and "Margot Dionne's gracious Hermione, . . . composed yet suggesting pre-existent tensions between herself and Leontes" (BERRY, 1979, pp. 168-9). Phillips's handling of 5.3 was "superb with Hermione at first shrouded in darkness and gradually being illuminated through the lighting of innumerable candles" (*Guardian*, 15 June 1978). Phillips made the reunion of Hermione and Leontes tentative and secondary to the reunion of Hermione and Perdita (BERRY, 1979, p. 169). He cut 3321-2 and the match of Paulina and Camillo. Berry (p. 170) finds the result "a fascinating design: but it is not precisely Shakespeare's."

For the RSC's small-scale tour (UK, 1984; Poland, 1985), Adrian Noble set the Sicilian scenes in the "frock-coated, bemeddaled [sic] world" (*Guardian*, 12 Dec. 1984) of postwar Italy, and Bohemia in "the raucous pop world of . . . Carnaby Street" (*Financial Times*, 22 Oct. 1984). The touring production played in venues ranging from a cattle shed to Lincoln Cathedral; with only limited seating available, most members of the audience were promenaders. Reviewers applauded Noble's achievement. RATCLIFFE (1984): "The apparently spontaneous tumble of players and punters produces confrontations and images which few who see them will quickly forget: Leontes in his anger ([Alun] Armstrong) scatters spectators to one side as he runs up the steps to poison the nursery calm; the messengers from Delphi (William Haden and Graham Turner) stand in light at the top of a sprawl of people, like immigrant survivors on a raft, stunned and humbled by the momentous nature of what they have just seen." At Lincoln Cathedral "Hermione's [trial] was breathtakingly staged, with the innocent queen and jealous king facing each other across half a mile of carpet cordoned off by officious ushers" (*Times*, 27 Oct. 1984).

Two years later on the main stage at Stratford-upon-Avon, design overpowered Terry Hands's production, which "based its reading on the notion that political tyranny reenacts the egotism of a spoilt childhood" (SHRIMPTON, 1987, p. 177). Large polished panels upstage and a glass floor hazily reflected Leontes's nursery-kingdom and, by also reflecting parts of the auditorium, seemed to transform the audience into subjects of the immature king. Hands drew on the productions of his RSC colleagues (Nunn, 1969, and Barton and Nunn, 1976) in, for example, the doubling of Hermione and Perdita (which SHRIMPTON, p. 178, finds "pointless"), the white Regency costumes, the wintry Sicilia, staging Sicilian scenes in a nursery, and introducing the bear as a design motif. But, especially in the use of the nursery and the bear, Hands "paraded his theatrical devices and exaggerated the play's 'theatrical self-consciousness'" (WARREN, 1987, p. 86). Mamillius's nursery floor was covered with an oversized bearskin, with head and flashing eyes; the bearskin was lifted dramatically to devour Antigonus; in Bohemia, Perdita and Florizel rested on it; Mamillius had a white teddy bear; Autolycus entered masquerading as a bear. Hands's 1986 production was rethought and redesigned for London (Barbican Th., 1987), where it emphasized "vanished innocence" (*Guardian*, 16 Oct. 1987).

David William (Stratford, Ont., 1986) made design serve the script rather than compete with it, as Hands had done. Setting Sicilia in an 1830s European court and Bohemia in "a Hardyesque rural community," he focused on the public and private relationships in those societies, not on "period authenticity" (WARREN, 1988, pp. 163, 165–6). William's treatment of Leontes and Paulina was original. By directing Leontes as a weaker person than Polixenes, Hermione, or Paulina, William "suggested a reason for Leontes's sudden explosive insecurity" (WEIL, 1987, p. 234).

With the same company of actors, Peter Hall staged *WT*, *Cym.*, and *Tmp.* (National Th., 1988) on a permanent set evocative of a Jacobean indoor playhouse and in Carolingian costumes (design: Alison Chitty). Hall's reading of *WT* found a dark "emotional unity that binds the two halves of the play together" (*Guardian*, 20 May 1988). The onset of Leontes's (Tim Pigott-Smith's) jealousy altered other characters: "Basil Henson's . . . Camillo discovers his talent for deception. Peter Woodward's boyish Polixenes loses his innocence in a flash . . . . Sally Dexter's radiantly confident Hermione takes on an aloof dignity" (*Times*, 20 May 1988). The "revelry" in Bohemia was "astringent" (*Guardian*, 20 May 1988). WELLS (1990, p. 144): "There was a wolfish menace in Ken Stott's overloud Autolycus, contemptuous of those he fooled; an elaborate, ferocious dance of half-naked, phallus-bedecked satyrs brought before a scared Florizel [Steven Mackintosh] and Perdita [Shirley Henderson] an image of the wilder forces of nature and sexuality, and Polixenes' angry disowning of Florizel visibly paralleled Leontes' rejection of the baby Perdita."

Hall's staging of 5.3 reversed the usual stage picture: Hermione's back was to the audience; Leontes and the court faced Hermione and the audience behind her. When Hermione turned, her face, "lined with hurt as well as age," conveyed "the cost of Leontes' psychotic jealousy" (*Spectator*, 28 May 1988). The reunion of Hermione and Perdita was joyous; the reconciliation of Leontes and Hermione was extremely tentative.

Luc Bondy's production opened in Paris in April 1988 and played at the Avignon Festival in July (LAROQUE, 1988, pp. 97–9). Leontes (Michel Piccoli) and Polixenes (Bernard Ballet) were not matched physically, were approaching 50, and gave a "sinister, hollow ring" to their memories of boyhood (CAMPOS, 1990, pp. 41–2). Three years later Bondy's "magnificent new production" (Berlin, 1991) of Peter Handke's translation contrasted an "orderly" Sicily, its architecture characterized by "harsh angles," with "the dreamy disorder of Bohemia" (*Times*, 3 Jan. 1991). Costumes and set were contemporary. In a variation of the theme struck by Phillips and Hall, 5.3 returned Hermione "to a world irremediably poisoned by the events of 16 years before and to a husband who has lost the capacity to give and receive love" (*Times*, 3 Jan. 1991).

With a company of 14, David Thacker (Young Vic, 1991) staged a small-scale, minimalist production in the round and stripped Leontes of the accoutrements of absolute monarchy. He had "no court, no system of power, no trappings of authority" (*Plays and Players*, Nov. 1991, p. 31). Sheelagh Keegan's sunken circle within a larger circle—a spare, flexible set—provided a visual counterpoint to the embrace of Leontes and Polixenes at the opening and of Hermione and Leontes at the close (*Spectator*, 14 Sept. 1991) and to the "tight family circle" (*Sunday Telegraph*, 22 Sept. 1991).

Théâtre de Complicité, a British touring company whose earliest work was the staging of company-devised plays, selected *WT* for its second text-based production. Complicité incorporated images familiar from recent productions (a desolate, wintry Sicily; Mamillius's nursery toys). Its methods drew enthusiastic reviews, such as Paul Taylor's praise of its enactment of unscripted scenes: "I have never, for example, seen the transition from pastoral Bohemia back to the wintry penitential world of Leontes' Sicilia effected as magically or as arrestingly as here. Holding model galleons aloft, the people making the trip start a progress round the stage. Then, snow starts to fall and, as this is a production where the actors play more than one role, the group of travellers slowly transforms itself, before your very eyes, into the funereal procession that trudges after Leontes in his daily circuits of repentance. It's a haunting, unforgettable sequence" (*Independent*, 4 Apr. 1992; see also *Independent*, 2 Mar. 1994).

Noble set his second production for the RSC (Stratford-upon-Avon, 1992) in "some nonspecific, early-twentieth-century aristocratic world" (SMALLWOOD, 1993, p. 349) and stressed, as Hall had done, an "emotional unity" binding the two halves of the play. Unlike Hall, Noble celebrated an emotional warmth in the reconciliation of Hermione (Samantha Bond) and Leontes (John Nettles) and Polixenes (Paul Jesson) and a communal warmth in the sheepshearing scenes, staged as a village fête reminiscent of Stanley Spencer's Cookham.

With a company of 10, Stéphane Braunschweig (Centre Dramatique National Orléons-Loiret, Edinburgh Festival, 1994) "opt[ed] throughout for minimalist austerity" (*Guardian*, 25 Aug. 1994). He brought out the private, not the public, effects of Leontes's jealousy (*Guardian*) and made "the scenery itself [design: Giorgio Barberio Corsetti] a symbol of the play's often distorted emotional perspectives" (*Financial Times*, 25 Aug. 1994). Hermione appeared in 3.3, remained on stage, and became Time. In 5.3 "the dead Mamillius's tunic hangs in silent reminder of just what has been destroyed, the resurrected queen and her reunited king intone their ostensibly joyous lines in halting monotone: no happy ending, but an intimation that life goes on, at bitter cost" (*Scotsman*, 25 Aug. 1994). Although it was often perceptive and ingenious, reviewers found that the production lacked "imaginative sympathy" (*Sunday Telegraph*, 28 Aug. 1994).

Ingmar Bergman (Royal Dramatic Theatre of Sweden, 1994) staged *WT* as a play within a play. By staging his production on a set that mirrored the shape of the auditorium (design: Lennart Mork) and by placing an audience on stage, Bergman attempted to break down the barrier between stage and auditorium, between actor and audience (TÖRNQVIST, 1995, pp. 83–5). Lighting indicated the stages in Leontes's "inner development. When his jealousy was kindled, the windows were lit deep red. Later, when his love for Hermione had died, or rather lay dormant, a cold winter night with a starry sky and a frosty moon above snow-clad trees could be glimpsed outside the windows" (p. 85). The play and the play within the play had a Christian frame of reference. For example, Bergman set 5.1 in a cloister and made Leontes a flagellant (p. 89). As the statue, Hermione lay on a catafalque (p. 90).

For Method and Madness's small-scale tour (Lyric Th., Hammersmith, 1997) director Mike Alfreds relied on effective doubling by his cast of eight, an uncluttered set, and minimal props, music, and sound effects. The production opened with Mamillius (Fergus O'Donnell) announcing "A sad Tale's best for Winter" (618) as behind him "the actors [were] literally cloaking themselves in the world of the play, dressing each other in simply-draped coloured cloths edged in fur" (*Financial Times*, 16 June 1997).

For the inaugural season of Sh.'s Globe (1997) director David Freeman and designer Tom Phillips, R.A., set *WT* in an African society that worshipped primitive deities. Leontes's (Mark Lewis Jones's) throne and one permanent prop, the "shrine," to which characters made obeisance, were constructed from abandoned tractor tires (aid from the UN?). Freeman introduced black magic, practiced chiefly by Paulina, and made anger, expressed by shouting and eruption into uncivil—and unscripted— behavior, the predominant tone.

In 20th-c. productions of *WT*, especially those in which directors played a fairly full text and collaborated with their designers on a controlling concept, performances are best seen in relation to other aspects of the production. In the case of Leontes, for example, performances by Esmond Knight (Stratford-upon-Avon, 1948) and Jeremy Irons (Stratford-upon-Avon, 1986) were complemented by the stage picture; performances by Barrie Ingham (Stratford-upon-Avon, 1969), Ian McKellen (Stratford-upon-Avon, 1976), Borje Ahlstedt (Sweden, 1994), and others were indebted to the lighting designer; and other performances, such as Colm Feore's (Stratford, Ont., 1986), are best understood in context with, in Feore's case, the decision to play Leontes as weaker than Polixenes, Hermione, and Paulina. In these and other productions, actors had, of course, to decide how best to convey the source and expression of Leontes's jealousy.

Henry Ainley (Savoy Th., 1912) broke with the tradition of making Leontes dignified, noble. Blurring some of Leontes's sentences, Ainley conveyed "the King's fevered, irrational, or . . . neurotic mood and temperament" (*The Nation*, 28 Sept. 1912). Ainley's "displays of physical frenzy," which were "fascinatingly ugly . . . powerful, rather horrible," and his "disagreeable-looking" appearance made it possible to understand why it had taken Lillah McCarthy's Hermione three months to "make up her mind" and why "in the Statue scene she exhibited a comparative coldness" (*Westminster Gazette*, 23 Sept. 1912).

Well suited to the Eastern European design of Quayle's production (Stratford-upon-Avon, 1948), "Esmond Knight's full-voiced and passionate Leontes" (*Birming-ham Evening Despatch*, 5 June 1948) possessed a "mind wholly distorted by his strange obsession" (*Leamington Spa Courier*, 11 June 1948). The tradition of playing Leontes "as a man singled out for destruction by a power outside himself" was continued at, for example, Stratford, Ont. (1958), by Christopher Plummer (BARTHOLO-MEUSZ, 1982, p. 187).

Two performances in Britain set the course for the second half of the century. After John Gielgud's Leontes (Phoenix Th., 1951), TREWIN (15 Sept. 1951) claimed it would no longer be possible to label Leontes "unplayable." Gielgud "appears to have given the jealousy . . . a romantic dignity" (BARTHOLOMEUSZ, 1982, p. 170). He "turned [the] gnarled verse" (TREWIN, 21 July 1951) to "a wild-hurtling music" (TRE-WIN, 1971, p. 60) and wept "romantic tears" (*Times*, 28 June 1951). With Mamillius, Leontes showed "his only touch of warmth and humanity"; at the trial he was "cold cruelty itself, refusing to look at Hermione and betraying emotion only by a slight nervous gesture of the fingers" (VENEZKY, "Productions," 1951, p. 338); "as the king repentant, [he] used all his emotional grandeur in the remembrance of his queen" (TREWIN, 1971, p. 60); Gielgud "retreated" from the moving statue, as had Garrick and Macready (BARTHOLOMEUSZ, 1982, p. 172). In a performance (Stratford-upon-Avon, 1960) that, according to some reviewers, matched the acting standards set by Gielgud, Eric Porter's "self-pitying" Leontes (*Yorkshire Post*, 31 Aug. 1960) was "a sick man, . . . his mind racing with the *tremor cordis* that finds its natural expression in the feverishly disjointed verse" (*Observer*, 4 Sept. 1960).

In Ian McKellen's (Stratford-upon-Avon, 1976) "exquisitely sensitive reading" (DAVID, 1978, p. 223), Leontes "suddenly switche[d] from demonic tyranny . . . to the pathos of a man destroyed by his own sexual fantasies" (*Guardian*, 5 June 1976). In contrast with McKellen's Scandinavian "fairy prince spell-struck" (DAVID, 1978, p. 223), Alun Armstrong's 1950s Sicilian Leontes (RSC tour, 1984) had a "craggy, raw-edged emotional directness" (*Financial Times*, 13 Dec. 1984). RATCLIFFE (1984): "It is terrible to watch Mr Armstrong weep, because he does not look the weeping kind" (*Observer*, 16 Dec. 1984).

Jeremy Irons (Stratford-upon-Avon, 1986) and Paul Shelley, who replaced Irons when the production was transferred to London (Barbican Th., 1987), offered two different interpretations. Irons's Leontes, "a monster of the nursery, a fractious brat whose jealousy expressed itself in tears and tantrums, . . . spoke . . . with infantile exaggeration" (SHRIMPTON, 1987, p. 177) and, seeking laughter, turned *WT* into "a trivial domestic comedy in which adultery was a topic for smutty jokes" (WARREN, 1987, p. 86). Shelley played "a tortured fantasist who both dreams of his wife's adultery and is haunted by a memory of some idyllic, sexless past" (*Guardian*, 16 Oct. 1987).

Tim Pigott-Smith (National Th., 1988) played "the *tremor cordis* . . . and the twinges of his jealousy [as] a physical symptom, recurring later in the action at moments of especial stress" (WELLS, 1990, p. 144). Insecure, Leontes teased and bullied courtiers, sought reassurance from the audience, and allowed Paulina (Eileen Atkins) to scold him and, later, to comfort him.

In Bondy's first production of *WT* (Paris, 1988), Michel Piccoli's middle-aged Leontes "quickly" established an "oddness" in which "everything he says can be dangerous" (CAMPOS, 1990, p. 43). Three years later (Berlin, 1991) the Leontes of Hans Christian Rudolph, whose "jealousy [was] a physical pain burning his heart" (*Times*, 3 Jan. 1991), recalled Pigott-Smith's performance.

Simon McBurney's "brilliant and unnerving" Leontes (Théâtre de Complicité, 1992) "was impossible for the audience comfortably to control and pigeon-hole. Unquestionably a tyrant, this Leontes could be turned by the deaths of his son and queen into a twitching heap with staring eyes, demanding Paulina's tenderness as well as her ferocity, exiting to great shouts of 'sorrows'" (1435; HOLLAND, 1994, p. 171).

At Stratford-upon-Avon in 1992 Leontes's (John Nettles's) jealousy sprang from his misreading of Hermione's innocent sensuousness. "In a series of freezes of the others [in 1.2], he hovered round the fringes of the group, an isolated and furtive figure, peeping and spying and sharing his desperate imaginings with the audience in a dislocated, clipped, staccato delivery, with angry changes of rhythm surging through the lines, a delivery that seemed . . . highly effective in suggesting a mind almost audibly cracking up" (SMALLWOOD, 1993, p. 349).

Especially in the first half of the century, actresses playing Hermione followed in the 19th-c. tradition. Ellen Terry (His Majesty's Th., 1906), who had played Mamillius in Kean's production (1856), distinguished "between [Hermione's] deep, passionate love for Leontes and her frank comradeship for Polixenes" (*Morning Post*, 3 Sept. 1906; see p. 807). When accused of adultery, Terry's Hermione was "heart-broken, and . . . made it seem that she was sorely grieved that [Leontes's] mind was thrown out of balance" (*Daily News*, 3 Sept. 1906). Diana Wynyard (Stratford-upon-Avon, 1948), who with Ena Burrill (Paulina) introduced a civilizing tone to Quayle's barbaric Eastern European Sicilia, evoked reviews similar to those given 19th-c. actresses; she portrayed, for example, "the dignity of a gracious goddess . . . [and] the rich humanity of a wife and mother" (*Stage*, 10 June 1948). Wynyard gave a similar interpretation when she repeated the role in Brook's production (Phoenix Th., 1951).

A number of 20th-c. productions questioned the nature of the reconciliation of Hermione and Leontes. In 5.3 Lillah McCarthy's Hermione (Savoy Th., 1912) "exhibited a comparative coldness. Indeed, Camillo's phrase 'She hangs about his neck' [3322] was hardly realised in the acting" (*Westminster Gazette*, 23 Sept. 1912). Breaking her pose as the statue, Sally Dexter's Hermione (National Th., 1988) "moved forward unsmiling. . . . There was a world of unspoken emotion between husband and wife as, left alone together, they sombrely joined hands again" (WELLS, 1990, p. 144). Productions including Stratford, Ont., 1978; Berlin, 1991; and Edinburgh, 1994, also reunited a dysfunctional couple. (See above, pp. 810, 811, 812.)

In other productions Hermione provided a motive for Leontes's jealousy. Penny Downie (Stratford-upon-Avon, 1986) was an "exceptionally flirtatious and ingratiating" Hermione, and Paul Greenwood's Polixenes "lavished cuddles, back-rubs, and love-lorn gazes upon her" (SHRIMPTON, 1987, p. 178). When the production was transferred (Barbican Th., 1987), Downie's Hermione and Martin Jacobs's Polixenes gave Leontes no cause for jealousy but did, nevertheless, suggest that "had things been different, these two might have loved each other with all the reckless carnal passion of which they are falsely accused" (*Plays and Players*, Feb. 1988, p. 21). Bulle Ogier's Hermione (Paris, 1988) provoked Leontes's jealousy, and at times her "almost exaggeratedly pure" Hermione seemed to be drawn to Ballet's unattractive Polixenes (CAMPOS, 1990, pp. 42–3).

Exploring many aspects of Hermione's character, Judi Dench (Stratford-upon-Avon, 1969) was "a bewitching queen, as rare and precious as the text suggests, with a tart wit which gives way . . . to a sombre strength and dignity" (*Spectator*, 23 May 1969). Many recent depictions have called attention to Hermione's human qualities rather than her regal status. They include Marilyn Taylerson's (Stratford-upon-Avon, 1976), Lynn Farleigh's (RSC tour, 1984), and Samantha Bond's (Stratford-upon-Avon, 1992).

In the 20th c. Paulina has most often been presented as a woman whose admirable strength tempers Leontes. Brook (Phoenix Th., 1951) directed Flora Robson to play her "as a force for sanity in the insane world created by Leontes" (BARTHOLOMEUSZ, 1982, p. 173). Eileen Herlie's (Stratford, Ont., 1958) Paulina was a "fearless woman of moral passion" (*New York Times*, 23 July 1958). Peggy Ashcroft (Stratford-upon-Avon, 1960) "seemed to combine an iron strength of character with mature grace and sweetness" (BARTHOLOMEUSZ, 1982, p. 209). Brenda Bruce (Stratford-upon-Avon, 1969), who portrayed a "practical, witty great lady," was succeeded when the show was transferred (Aldwych Th., 1970) by Elizabeth Spriggs, who "gave Paulina a spiritual dimension" (BARTHOLOMEUSZ, 1982, p. 217). Barbara Leigh-Hunt (Stratford-upon-Avon, 1976) was "triumphantly forceful" (DAVID, 1978, p. 224). Janet Dale's (RSC tour, 1984) "notable Paulina, elegant and beautifully spoken" (*Financial Times*, 22 Oct. 1984) gave a "thrilling denunciation of Leontes" (*Times*, 27 Oct. 1984) but was also "good-hearted" (*Financial Times*, 13 Dec. 1984). Eileen Atkins's (National Th., 1988) strong, compassionate Paulina also guided Leontes's penance. Other treatments departed from the dominant one. The "near-crazed grief" of Susan Wright's (Stratford, Ont., 1986) Paulina after Hermione fainted indicated "that she thought Hermione dead. . . . Moved by his [Leontes's] genuine anguish, she decided then and there to help him" (WARREN, 1988, p. 166). Instead of aiding Leontes, Gemma Jones's (Stratford-upon-Avon, 1992) bossy Paulina, "a county lady . . . forever doing good works and opening bazaars, [who] was far from the moral power the text can reveal" (HOLLAND, 1994, p. 175), seemed to leave Leontes to draw on his own inner resources. At another extreme (Paris, 1988), Leontes and Paulina (Nada Strancar) were "manipulators, falsifiers, showmen, at opposite ends of the play" (CAMPOS, 1990, p. 43).

STAGING THE BEAR AND TIME

The bear, restored by Kemble in 1802, asks two major questions of the director: what effect should the bear create and how should the effect be achieved? On theatrical bears in Sh.'s time, see n. 1500. Nineteenth-century promptbooks and theater reviews yield little information about staging the bear. In the 20th c. bears have been frightening (Stratford-upon-Avon, 1969; *Spectator*, 23 May 1969); "ludicrous" (Chicago, 1994; BRAILOW, 1995, p. 15); humorous (New York, 1985; DEITER, 1985); "pantomime-type" (St. George's Th., 1980; PEARCE, 1981, p. 130; and Young Vic Th., 1981; *Guardian*, 27 Nov. 1981); and even cuddly (Alabama, 1976; KAY, 1977, p. 221). Technical effects have evoked the bear: shadows (Stratford-upon-Avon, 1960; *Illustrated London News*, 17 Sept. 1960); noise and thunder (Young Vic, 1991; *Spectator*, 14 Sept. 1991). Human bears have appeared as an unclear, muffled figure (San Diego, 1963; PROSSER, 1963, p. 447); in running shorts and track shoes (Venice Beach, Calif., 1979; STODDER & WILDS, 1980, p. 267); and in a dancer's practice clothes (Washington, D.C., 1987; TOCCI, 1987, p. 10). The bear has been a symbolic feature (Stratford-upon-Avon, 1986; WARREN, 1987, p. 86), and has been presaged by Mamillius's teddy bear (Stratford-upon-Avon, 1969; promptbook, SCL; and 1986, FUZIER & MAGUIN, 1986, p. 94). Bears have been diverted from Perdita by Antigonus (Oregon, 1984; DESSEN, 1985, pp. 604–5) and by Hermione (Stratford-upon-Avon, 1992; SMALLWOOD, 1993, p. 350). By augmentation of the fur on Leontes's costume, the BBC (1980) linked Leontes with the bear (PEARCE, 1981, p. 98). At Sh.'s Globe Th. (1997) "Hermione, who [had] been hovering in spirit over the abandoned Perdita," drew on claws and became the bear (*Times*, 6 June 1997).

Although some directors treat the Chorus simply or reassign the lines to another character, such as Camillo (Stratford-upon-Avon, 1992; promptbook, SCL), others have used Sh.'s choric figure to explore themes and motifs. At Stratford, Ont., 1958, Campbell, whose production examined the importance of Time to "the repentance of the sinner and the return of the lost," expanded the role of Chorus by introducing Time into some scenes as a silent participant and into other scenes as the speaker of a minor role (*Christian Century*, 29 Oct. 1958, p. 1240). In other productions the role has been expanded either by absorbing other parts, such as Archidamus, gaoler, mariner, and the bear (Birmingham, 1986; COCHRANE, 1987, p. 90) or by introducing Time as a silent witness or participant: Schenectady, N.Y., and Williamstown, Mass., 1981 (LITTLEFIELD, 1982, p. 207); Washington, D.C., 1987 (TOCCI, 1987, p. 9); Boston, 1987 (BIGGS, 1988, p. 20). Time has been an "unsuitably resurrected" Mamillius (New York, 1985; ALTER & LONG, 1985, p. 22); a gardener (Complicité, 1992; *Independent on Sunday*, 5 Apr. 1992); a young cricketer (Chicago, 1994; BRAILOW, 1995, p. 15); and a foreshadowing of Autolycus (Sh.'s Globe Th., 1997), with whom he was doubled. Entering from the Globe's yard, Time (Nicholas Le Prevost), a cider-swilling beggar, engaged the audience and sought help onto the platform. Time has stage-managed dumbshows (Los Angeles, 1981), "spotlighting each character he mentions" (WILDS, 1982, p. 388); has given some of his lines to other members of the company (Method and Madness, 1997); has participated in a masque as "a carnival monster . . . [which] gave birth to the child Mamillius" (Stratford-upon-Avon, 1981; *Times*, 1 July 1981, p. 13); and has appeared "to some extent a baroque allegorical figure, flying on in flapping, fluffy wings" (Stratford-upon-Avon, 1986; WARREN, 1987, p. 86).

SCREEN AND SOUND RECORDINGS

ROTHWELL & MELZER (1990, pp. 313–16) catalog eight versions on film: three abridgements (USA, 1910; Italy, 1913; Germany, 1914); three transmissions by the British Broadcasting Corporation (in 1962, with Leontes = Robert Shaw, Hermione = Rosalie Crutchley, Florizel = Brian Smith, Perdita = Sarah Badel; Frank Dunlop's 1966 production for the Edinburgh Festival, broadcast in 1968, with Leontes = Laurence Harvey, Hermione = Moira Redmond, Paulina = Diana Churchill; and the BBC Shakespeare, broadcast in 1980); two USA productions (scenes from the Berkeley Shakespeare Festival, 1982, and a workshop production at the Lincoln Center Institute, 1985). MCKERNAN AND TERRIS's (1994, pp. 179–82) filmography of the National Film and Television Archive (NFTVA) lists two UK arts shows that feature segments of Hall's 1988 and Noble's 1992 productions.

The National Sound Archive of the British Library holds audio recordings:

1. full text with William Squire as Leontes, Margaretta Scott as Hermione, Michael Bates as Autolycus, and the Marlowe Dramatic Society (Decca Record Co., 1960);

2. full text with John Gielgud as Leontes, Rachel Gurney as Hermione, and Peggy Ashcroft as Paulina (Caedmon, 1961);

3. abridged text, with Eric Portman as Leontes, Diana Wynyard as Hermione, and Wendy Hiller as Paulina (Odhams Books Ltd., 1963);

4. abridged text, with the Folio Theatre Players, dir. Christopher Casson and William Styles (Spoken Arts Inc., New Rochelle, n.d.);

5. 1.2, "Too hot, too hot," [181] with Gielgud (Caedmon, 1979);

6. 2.1 with Ellen Terry, recorded 1911 (Delta Record Co., 1963);

7. 3.2 with Gielgud, Gurney, Ashcroft (1961; HarperCollins, 1996);

8. 3.2 with Eric Porter as Leontes, Elizabeth Sellars as Hermione, and Paul Hardwick as Officer (from Stratford-upon-Avon, 1960, Argo, n.d.);

9. 4.4 (1926–62) with Judi Dench as Perdita and Peter McEnery as Florizel (Argo, [1964]);

10. off-the-air recording with Edith Evans as Paulina, Gurney as Hermione, and Jill Bennett as Perdita (BBC, 25 Mar. 1966);

11. off-the-air recording with Ronald Pickup as Leontes, Hannah Gordon as Hermione, Barbara Jefford as Paulina, and Gielgud as Time (BBC, 14 Oct. 1981);

12. theater performance by RSC (dir. Trevor Nunn, recorded 1971);

13. theater performance by RSC (dir. Terry Hands, recorded 1988);

14. theater performance by National Theatre (dir. Peter Hall, recorded 1988);

15. theater performance by RSC (dir. Adrian Noble, recorded 1993);

16. theater performance by RSC (dir. Gregory Doran, recorded 1999).

Scores of operas, ballets, rock musicals, etc., based on the play are listed by GOOCH & THATCHER (1991, 3:1940–2). Incidental music composed for productions is also listed (3:1908–40).

The Text on the Stage

Productions of *WT*, like those of Sh.'s other plays, reflect tastes, biases, and interpretive ideas of actors, directors, managers, and critics and their times. Susceptible to these fluctuating ideas, the play in some versions has been reshaped quite freely. Alterations have been made by cutting, adding, transposing, and substituting.

THE VERSIONS

This survey analyzes theatrical texts of *WT* in acting versions, typescripts marked as promptbooks, some actors' partbooks, and preparation copies used in production, primarily those listed in SHATTUCK (1965, pp. 495–506), with some additions. Omitted from discussion are incomplete promptbooks and partbooks, some duplicates of versions included in the survey, and versions that were not staged (Shattuck nos. 1– 4, 6, 7, 9, 12, 13, 15–17, 19, 20, 22–27, 29–31, 36–8, 40, 41, 44, 45, 54). Several adaptations are also omitted from consideration: Charles Marsh's (1756), as FURNESS (ed. 1898, p. 413) notes, "is a gallimaufry of the original, and as it was never acted, . . . I think we can dismiss it without lasting regret or more space"; Macnamara Morgan's adaptation (1762) bears little resemblance to Sh.'s play and had no influence on subsequent productions of *WT*; the adaptation by George Colman the Elder (1777) draws as heavily on Garrick as on Sh. By contrast, Garrick's extremely popular abridgment, *Florizel and Perdita*, is given a place in this survey because it influenced subsequent productions. The following are the versions analyzed:

1. Garrick: FLORIZEL and PERDITA. A Dramatic Pastoral, In Three Acts. Alter'd from The WINTER'S TALE of Shakespear By David Garrick. As it is performed at the Theatre Royal in Drury-Lane. London: Printed for J. and R. Tonson, in the *Strand*. 1758. (Cornmarket Press Facsimile, 1969.)
   Presented on 21 Jan. 1756, Garrick's version summarizes the events of Sh.'s Acts 1–3 in opening dialogue between Camillo and a courtier of Bohemia, then continues with the basic events of Acts 4 and 5. The Garrick alterations adopted in subsequent productions occur in the art vs. nature debate, the revels of the sheepshearing, some of Autolycus's scenes, and the statue scene.

2. Bell's Sh.: The Winter's Tale, A Tragedy, by Shakespeare, As Performed at the Theatre-Royal, Covent-Garden: Regulated from the Prompt-Book, With Permission of the Managers, By Mr. Younger, Prompter. An Introduction, and Notes Critical and Illustrative, are added, by the Authors of the Dramatic Censor [GENTLEMAN and DERRICK]. London: Printed for John Bell, near Exeter-Exchange, in the Strand; and C. Etherington, at York, 1773. In vol. 5 of *Bell's Edition of Shakespeare's Plays*. London, 1774. (Cornmarket Press Facsimile, 1969.)
   Adhering closely to the original, Thomas Hull prepared this text for production on 24 Apr. 1771 (ODELL, 1920, 1:381–2), and it was probably the version performed in 1773 at Covent Garden. Though "not a popular success" (BARTHOLOMEUSZ, 1982,

pp. 245-6), it represents an attempt to present nearly the whole play, something not done since 1742 (see *WT on the Stage*, p. 800). GENTLEMAN & DERRICK (p. 151) laud Hull's *"studiously pruned and regulated"* text but argue in footnotes for both retentions and further cuts.

3. Kemble: Shakspear's Winter's Tale, A Play; With Alterations By J. P. Kemble; Now first published, as it is acted by Their Majesties Servants of The Theatre Royal, Drury Lane, Thursday, March 25, 1802. London: Printed by C. Lowndes, No. 66, Drury Lane.

Kemble, preparing to assume the management of Covent Garden, chose *WT* for his final production at Drury Lane where, from the beginning of his tenure, he had "determined to strike a valiant blow . . . for the restoration of great drama, carefully and authentically produced" (BAKER, 1942, p. 124). Kemble cuts several major speeches, subtly alters characterization, and replaces Sh.'s ending with Garrick's statue scene from *Florizel and Perdita*.

4. Inchbald's Sh.: The Winter's Tale; A Play, In Five Acts; By William Shakspeare. As Performed at the Theatre Royal, Drury Lane. Printed Under the Authority of the Managers From the Prompt Book. With Remarks by Mrs. Inchbald. London: Printed for Longman, Hurst, Rees, and Orme, Paternoster Row. [1807]. In *The British Theatre; or A Collection of Plays, Which Are Acted at The Theatres Royal, Drury Lane, Covent Garden and Haymarket. . . . In Twenty-Five Volumes*. Vol. 3. 1808. (Rpt. New York: Hildesheim, 1970.)

Inchbald reprints Kemble's 1802 text, making some minor changes primarily in stage directions and business. This edition provides text for the partbook of Macready's production (no. 7) and the promptbook for Burton's (no. 9).

5. Kemble: Shakespeare's Winter's Tale; A Play; Adapted to the Stage by J. P. Kemble; And Now First Published As It Is Acted at the Theatre Royal In Covent Garden. London: Printed For The Theatre. 1811. (In *The Folger Facsimile Promptbooks*. Series I. Charlottesville, 1974.)

The acting ed. of 1811 offers substantially the same text as the acting ed. of 1802, but when Kemble revived *WT* for "several performances beginning on November 28, 1811 . . . midway in Mrs. Siddons's [Hermione] farewell season" (SHATTUCK, 1974, 9:i), he made some new cuts, additions, and alterations to create the promptbook discussed here. "This promptbook in the Wister Collection . . . is at once a thorough record of the Covent Garden production and Kemble's rehearsal book" for the play he "regarded as of the tragic genre" (p. iii).

6. Cumberland's Sh.: The Winter's Tale: A Play. In Five Acts. By William Shakspeare. Printed from the Acting Copy, With Remarks, Biographical and Critical, By D—G. [George Daniel]. . . . As Now Performed at The Theatres Royal, London. Embellished With A Portrait of Mrs. Bunn, In The Character of Hermione. Engraved on Steel by Mr. Woolnoth, From an Original Drawing by Mr. Wageman. London: John

Cumberland, 2, Cumberland Terrace. In *Cumberland's British Theatre*. Vol. 5. [1830?]

The text of this acting version adheres closely though not completely to Kemble's acting ed. of 1802 (no. 3). This production opened at Drury Lane on 3 Nov. 1823. William Charles Macready starred as Leontes.

7. Macready: A copy of Inchbald's Sh., marked by J[ames] R. Anderson for his role as Florizel and as understudy to Macready's Leontes, dated 2 Oct. 1837. [Shattuck no. 8; Folger Library, WT 2.]

Anderson's partbook, created for Macready's production at Covent Garden, 30 Sept. 1837, illustrates Macready's debt to Kemble through the many virtually identical duplications in Anderson's hand of handwritten prompt markings by Kemble that appear in no. 5. (Another copy of the 1811 acting ed. [Shattuck no. 5; Sh. Centre Library 50.37/1811] has some notations that mention Macready and give the date 22 May 1837. SHATTUCK (1965, pp. 495–6) attributes those earlier 1837 entries to John Willmot, Macready's prompter.) Anderson's partbook is extensively marked and shows the restoration of Sh.'s statue scene in preference to the Garrick alteration.

8. Phelps: A copy of Cumberland's ed. [no. 6, c. 1829–31] marked by Samuel W. Phelps and William C. Williams for Phelps's Sadler's Wells production of 19 Nov. 1845. Later production years are noted on blank front pages: 1846, 1848 to 1851, 1855, 1856, 1858, and 1860 to 1862. [Shattuck no. 10; Folger Library, WT 14.]

In using the Cumberland text, Phelps perpetuates the basic Kemble acting version (no. 3), particularly its handling of the roles of Leontes and Perdita. Phelps follows Macready (no. 7) in restoring some original lines as well as the statue scene.

9. Burton: A copy of Inchbald's Sh. marked by John Moore, stage manager for William Burton, for the New York production at Burton's Theater, Wednesday, 13 Feb. 1856. [Shattuck no. 14; Folger Library, WT 13.]

Moore, whose signature appears across the cover of this copy, "brought from England a transcription of Macready's promptbook: thus Burton had before him a well-worked version upon which to found his own" (SHATTUCK, 1976, p. 114). A playbill (dated for the opening performance of 13 Feb. 1856) inserted in Burton's copy lists H. Jordan in the role of "Time, as Chorus" and announces "New Scenery," including the "Appearance of Time, surrounded by Clouds"; the *New York Daily Tribune* review of 14 Feb. 1856 also notes the restoration of Time, though Folger WT 13 does not show it.

10. Kean: "The Winter's Tale" with manuscript alterations for Charles Kean's revival at The Princess's Theatre on 28 Apr. 1856. [SHATTUCK no. 18; Folger Library WT 7.]

Pages cut from Charles Knight, *The Pictorial Edition of the Works of Shakspere, Comedies* [1841], 2:333–93, and bound in a brown paper cover serve as preparation copy for this production. George Ellis, stage manager, contributes production notes;

J. W. Cole marks cuts and offers marginal comment, sometimes on Kemble's staging. Cuts are substantial, other alterations more sparing. Many of the changes seem to have been influenced by Kemble's texts (nos. 3, 5).

11. Kean: Shakespeare's Play of The Winter's Tale, arranged for representation at The Princess's Theatre, with Historical and Explanatory notes, by Charles Kean. As first performed on Monday, April 28th, 1856. Entered at Stationers' Hall. London: Printed by John K. Chapman and Co., 5, Shoe Lane, and Peterborough Court, Fleet Street. Price One Shilling. To Be Had In The Theatre. (Cornmarket Press Facsimile, 1970.)

This printed acting ed. cuts fewer lines than the preparation copy (no. 10) for the same production. SDs are exceptionally detailed, fleshing out for the reader Kean's conception of a Greek setting and describing his elaborate presentation of Time. *Punch* (17 May 1856) comments that Kean never allows the play to get in the way of spectacle, "the so-called poetry being cut down to the scantiest dimensions, and delivered with the utmost rapidity, and with no intrusive attempt at acting." Some of the alterations to Florizel's part may be attributed to Kean's decision to use an actress in the role. Copious notes follow each act.

12. French's Standard Drama, no. 317: The Winter's Tale. A Play in Five Acts. Written by William Shakspeare. With original casts, costumes, and the whole of the stage business, correctly marked and arranged, by Mr. J. B. Wright, Assistant Manager of the Boston Theatre. Samuel French, New York. [1860?]

Wright offers a "synopsis of scenery and incidents of The Winter's Tale as produced at Burton's Theatre, New York, 1857, under the direction of Mr. W. E. Burton, aided by Mr. John Moore, stage manager" (p. 4). Burton's 1856 production (no. 9) opened in New York a little over two months before Kean achieved a great success in London with his extravagantly staged *WT* (nos. 10 and 11). The next year Burton opened *WT* at his New Theater, Broadway, on 6 April 1857. An advertisement that ran on that day in the *New York Daily Tribune* indicates, as clearly as does the synopsis, that Burton, aware of Kean's success, adopted elements of Kean's spectacle: Greek scenery, a "Pyrrhic Dance, by sixteen Grecian Youths" (Kean had used thirty-six), and a "classical allegory of the Course of Time" (p. 4). The text owes more to Kemble (no. 3) and Burton (no. 9) than to Kean.

13. Calvert: A WINTER'S TALE. By William Shakespere. Arranged for Representation at the Prince's Theatre, Manchester, By Charles Calvert. Entered at Stationers' Hall. Manchester: John Heywood, 141 and 143, Deansgate. [1869.]

Calvert's introduction to this acting edition is dated 1 Sept. 1869. In it he proclaims his debt to his "illustrious predecessors" Macready, Phelps, and Kean, while rejecting the "singular delusion that a Shakesperian play is injured by what is called too much attention to the embellishment of its stage setting" (iv). As one might expect from this declaration, his text harks back to Kemble's (through Macready and Phelps) while the elaborate additions to SDs reflect Kean's production ideas.

14. Anderson: Shakespeare's Winter's Tale As Performed by Miss Mary Anderson and Company. Under the Direction of Mr. Henry E. Abbey. Acting Edition with Illustrations By Edwin John Ellis and Joseph Anderson. New York: Scribner and Welford. 1888.

The preface to Anderson's acting ed. of *WT*, as produced at Palmer's Theater, New York, 14 Nov. 1888, claims fidelity to F as far as possible but argues that the needs of the stage and demands of modern tastes make large excisions unavoidable; in fact, "a literal adhesion to the text as it has been handed down to us would . . . savour of superstition." A number of alterations can be attributed to decisions she had previously made about the text for her 1887 season in London. A major one was the doubling of Hermione and Perdita, which "had not been conspicuously done until it was done by her" (WINTER, 1892, p. 105); indeed KENNEDY (1985, p. 123) credits Anderson with doubling the parts "for the first time in history."

15. Allen: The Viola Allen Acting Version of The Winter's Tale, A Play in Four Acts by William Shakespeare. This version was arranged by Mr. Frank Vernon and presented by Miss Viola Allen and her Company of Players on The Stage of The Knickerbocker Theatre, December 26, 1904. New York: McClure, Phillips & Co., 1905.

Vernon's production notes explain that Allen curtailed her text only after "consulting the opinions of eminent English and American scholars" (p. vii). She alters the sequence of a few scenes and abandons Greek costume and settings in favor of Byzantine ones in an effort to eliminate anachronisms. Vernon admits no indebtedness to Anderson (no. 14), but clearly it exists: Allen doubles Perdita and Hermione and adopts many of Anderson's other changes, including the altered conclusion.

16. Allen: A promptbook made on a copy of Allen's acting ed. (no. 15). [Shattuck no. 32; New York Public Library, Lincoln Center, Theatre Collection: *NCP.330694B.]

Allen's acting ed. differs slightly from Anderson's (no. 14) but further changes in this promptbook eliminate many of those differences, making Anderson and Allen virtually identical.

17. Ames: A copy of a reading ed. (Thomas Crown & Company, 1902) marked by Winthrop Ames and John Corbin for the promptbook of the Ames production that opened in New York on 28 Mar. 1910 at the New Theater [Shattuck no. 42; New York Public Library, Lincoln Center, Theatre Collection: *NCP + .42607B].

Corbin (the stage manager) and Ames both contributed to the final form of the promptbook. Corbin's cuts and other changes often follow Kean (no. 11). Ames's changes, queries, and suggestions are added marginally but are sometimes rejected by Corbin. Additions are usually typed out and pasted in the ed. Corbin notes that he cuts 350 lines, and playing time is 2 hours 54 minutes.

18. Granville-Barker: SHAKESPEARE: THE WINTER'S TALE. With a Producer's Preface by Granville-Barker. London. William Heinemann, [1912].

This book reflects the production that opened at the Savoy Theatre, London, on 21 Sept. 1912. Convinced that every Elizabethan play should be delivered as swiftly and uninterruptedly as possible, Granville-Barker divides the play into two parts. He eliminates act and scene designations from this edition, adds and alters sparingly, and cuts only 20 lines (WELLS, "Modern Stage," 1967, p. 177), making this, according to DYMKOWSKI (1986, p. 44), "probably the first performance in England of a play by Shakespeare that the author could himself have recognized for his own." TREWIN (1964, p. 54) cites an admirer of this version: "It must electrify people to find that a Shakespeare play makes sense when not gutted of vital parts." The play was nonetheless "withdrawn" after six weeks.

19. Woolfe: A copy of Gollancz's Temple ed. (1894) marked for Frank Woolfe's promptbook of the Memorial Theatre production, Stratford-upon-Avon, 11 July 1932. [Shattuck no. 47; Sh. Centre Library 71.21/ 1932W.]

A note (p. 1ᵛ) says that Woolfe prepared his version "using the 1931 prompt book for the [William] Bridges-Adams production" (not available at the Sh. Centre Library). Thus Woolfe presumably subscribed to the Bridges-Adams conception of "'pleasing the real average play-going public' [by doing] . . . 'whatever will most quickly and unobtrusively make the majority of your audience feel at home in the play'" (BARTHOLOMEUSZ, 1982, p. 200)—in this case, primarily cutting.

20. Payne: A copy of the New Eversley Sh. (1935) marked for B. Iden Payne's promptbook of the Memorial Theatre production, Stratford-upon-Avon, 23 Apr. 1937. [Shattuck no. 48; Sh. Centre Library 71.21/1937W.]

Payne creates a subtly altered text by changing single lines and phrases rather than complete speeches or scenes. BARTHOLOMEUSZ notes: "The main lines of interpretation, the cuts in the text, do not appear to have changed much between Stratford and New York [see no. 21]" (p. 202). This version retains the art vs. nature debate in 4.4, however, whereas the New York production does not.

21. Payne: A 1945 typescript marked for B. Iden Payne's promptbook of the Theater Guild production, which opened at the Cort Theater, New York, 15 Jan. 1946. [Shattuck no. 50; *NCP .347022B.]

Not merely a duplicate of no. 20, though they often correspond, this version has many affinities with Kemble, particularly in its cuts, the most obvious of which is of Perdita's debate with Polixenes, as BARTHOLOMEUSZ notes (p. 169).

22. Quayle: A copy of an unidentified Sh. ed. marked for Anthony Quayle's promptbook of the Memorial Theatre production, Stratford-upon-Avon, 4 June 1948. [Shattuck no. 51; Sh. Centre Library 71.21/1948W.]

Quayle adds nothing, alters just once, but cuts about 975 lines. According to stage manager Robert Gaston, Quayle's production on 25 Oct. 1948 ran 2 hours 50 minutes, nearly the same playing time given for the Ames (no. 17) version.

23. Wood: A copy of the Cambridge Pocket Shakespeare (1959) marked for Peter Wood's promptbook of the Memorial Theatre production, Stratford-upon-Avon, 30 Aug. 1960. [Shattuck no. 57; Sh. Centre Library 71.21/1960W.]

Wood's cuts are moderate, his substitutions and alterations sparing. A few changes are independent of other versions; those that are not indicate no reliance on any single earlier text.

24. Nunn: A copy of Kermode's Signet Classic ed. (1963) marked for Trevor Nunn's promptbook of the Royal Sh. Theatre production, Stratford-upon-Avon, 15 May 1969. [Not in Shattuck; Sh. Centre Library 71.21/1969WIN.]

Nunn rearranges lines in the sheepshearing scene and occasionally substitutes synonyms for words that could be unclear to an audience. Like Anderson (no. 14), he doubles Hermione and Perdita, though he "had no idea that the doubling had been done by Mary Anderson at the end of the nineteenth century." Where her production devised a successful, if not critically pleasing, strategy for accommodating both characters on stage in the last scene, Nunn's did not, according to BARTHOLOMEUSZ (p. 219).

25. Barton: A copy of Wilson's New [Cambridge] Ed. (1959) marked for John Barton's promptbook of his and Trevor Nunn's Royal Sh. Theatre production, Stratford-upon-Avon, 1 June 1976. [Not in Shattuck; Sh. Centre Library 71.21/1976W.]

One might expect this text to be a simple replication of Nunn (no. 24), but it is not. Barton, for example, does not double Hermione and Perdita, nor does he rearrange lines in the sheepshearing scene according to Nunn. He makes a number of independent changes.

26. Eyre: A copy of Schanzer's New Penguin ed. (1969) marked for Ronald Eyre's promptbook of the Royal Sh. Theatre production, Stratford-upon-Avon, 25 June 1981. The book was also used in 1982 at both the Theatre Royal, Newcastle, and the Barbican. [Not in Shattuck; Sh. Centre Library 71.21/1981W.]

Eyre cuts and substitutes moderately, reorders lines in the sheepshearing scene (though not according to Nunn), and occasionally replaces words or phrases that could seem obscure to an audience. He does not perpetuate the doubling of Hermione and Perdita. His text reflects no single early version throughout, but he does duplicate Anderson's (no. 14) unusual cut of the Clown's comic description of the deaths of Antigonus and the Mariners.

27. Hands: Schanzer's New Penguin ed. (1969) marked for Terry Hands's promptbook of the Royal Sh. Theatre production, Stratford-upon-Avon, 30 Apr. 1986. [Not in Shattuck; Sh. Centre Library 71.21/1986W.]

Hands cuts, alters, and substitutes sparingly. He revives the doubling of Hermione and Perdita and makes a few independent alterations.

RESHAPING THE TEXT

While Granville-Barker comes close, no production of *WT* fully meets SHAW's (1919; 1961, pp. 267–8) challenge to present any Sh. play in its original version, thereby making "Shakespear, and not the producer, the ultimate authority," since "experience remorselessly proves that Shakespear making a fool of himself is more [*268*] interesting than the judicious producer correcting him." After Garrick's adaptation, structural change begins with the reduction of F's five acts (retained from Bell through Calvert) to four acts in Anderson and Allen (nos. 15 and 16) and two in Granville-Barker and succeeding versions. F's 15 scene divisions are completely eliminated in Granville-Barker. Bell has eight scenes, Quayle eleven, Wood thirteen, Kemble and derivative versions fourteen. Only two scenes (3.1 [1145–72] and 4.1 [1579–1611], "Delphos" and "Time") are ever omitted entirely, and no version omits both. Scenes are transposed, as are smaller units. Verbal substitutions usually occur when diction seems offensive or unclear. Additions are rare. Cutting of blocks of dialogue and thinning (removing words or lines within speeches, presumably to make the text more accessible and more intelligible) are the means most often used to shape the play. Alterations are prompted by everything from the supposed indecency and incoherence of the text to the leading lady's doubling the roles of Hermione and Perdita to the presumption that brevity and speed of action will please the audience.

Most productions of *WT* have some affinity with others, but many are independent artistic efforts and get independent treatment here. Garrick's adaptation of *WT* (*Florizel and Perdita*) is a special case: it is the source of some significant alterations that are cited when other productions adopt them. Since Granville-Barker's version stages nearly the whole text, unless it is specifically mentioned below it reads with F. Kemble (no. 3) is the direct ancestor of Inchbald (no. 4), Kemble (no. 5), Cumberland (no. 6) and, through Inchbald or Cumberland, of Macready (no. 7), Phelps (no. 8), Burton (no. 9), and French (no. 12). Kean (no. 10) is the direct ancestor of Kean (no. 11), and Anderson (no. 14) of Allen (nos. 15, 16). Of the versions from Woolfe (no. 19) to Hands (no. 27), only Payne (no. 20) is directly related to Payne (no. 21). The others are independent versions despite obvious borrowings. In the following discussion, the first text of the groupings above represents all others in that group, and only differences are noted.

CUTS

1.1 The Ritual Exchange of Compliments

Camillo and Archidamus introduce Leontes and Polixenes, touch on their past, and note that the kingdom has a beloved heir. PYLE (1969, p. 11, n. 1) rejects the search in this initial scene for double meanings that allegedly prepare the audience for the estrangement of the two kings (see n. 1), claiming it would be "the extreme of literary as distinct from dramatic interpretation of drama. . . . It would be a poor playwright who would start his play with double meanings before even a single meaning had been imparted." Yet something in this first scene must be troublesome in the staging—perhaps the "atmosphere of excess . . . dotted throughout with ironies" (HARTWIG, 1972, p. 121)—because, as SANDERS (1987, p. 4) remarks, the opening conversation between Archidamus and Camillo "has perplexed directors, and the usual consequence has been that the scene gets cut" liberally by Bell, Payne, and Quayle, all of whom omit mention of Mamillius, and substantially by Kean, Anderson, Ames, Woolfe, Nunn, Barton, Eyre, and Hands. Like Granville-Barker, however, Kemble, Calvert, and Wood decline to cut a single word.

1.2 The Invitation

Polixenes refuses Leontes's request to extend his nine-month stay in Sicilia, agreeing to remain only after Hermione asks him. All versions but French cut the "sneaping winds" (64-5), probably because nothing is lost in the omission, but Polixenes's lines should not be as easy to excise since, as COLERIDGE (1813; 1960, 1:110) notes, "Polixenes' obstinate refusal to Leontes . . . and yet his after-yielding to Hermione . . . is at once perfectly natural . . . and yet so well calculated to set in nascent action the jealousy of Leontes." Yet Payne (no. 21) cuts Polixenes's assurance that no one but Leontes could move him to stay (75-8), and all other versions except Kean (no. 11), Calvert, and Payne (no. 20) cut from three to seven lines of Polixenes's rationale for going. His reflections on the "sinless" childhood he shared with Leontes, and Hermione's speculation about whether the men have "tript" since they met their queens (130-52), is important to some literary critics: PYLE (1969, p. 15), for example, following WILSON (ed. 1931, p. 133), believes that Sh. "intended Leontes to be seen as overhearing Hermione's last words ['Th'offences . . . vs" (149-52)], and . . . misinterpreting them, . . . enough in the shorthand of stage psychology to constitute the seeds of jealousy." Some theatrical producers interpret otherwise. The editors of Bell—believing that "tho' curtailed, this scene of invitation is still too long, quibbling and flat, concerned in terms, on the Queen's side, rather childishly low, than maturely royal"—repair the alleged defect by cutting 134-52, with subsequent versions through Woolfe cutting some of her lines (e.g., 150-2, labeled "a bit broad" by Ames). Perhaps unappreciative of what WHITE (1981, p. 102) calls Hermione's "amply relaxed sensuality of language," Bell, Kemble, Anderson, Payne, Woolfe, and Nunn delete 161-2 ("cram's . . . things"), while Bell and Kean eliminate 164-5 ("You . . . Acre").

1.2 The Onset of Jealousy

As Leontes becomes irrational and obsessed, Bell disposes of thirty lines (192-222) of his inchoate suspicions about Hermione's fidelity and Mamillius's legitimacy, explaining (p. 156): "We have never met with so strange a picture as this exhibited by *Leontes*, who, from what he himself has desired, picks out suspicion; indeed some passages which follow this speech, in the original, show his majesty to be little better than a bedlamite. . . . They are properly omitted." Other productions may also want to save Leontes from being seen this way: Quayle cuts heavily (197-211; 217-22).

Anderson, Woolfe, and Hands cut the pun involving horns (199–200). Kemble, Anderson, Ames, Payne (no. 21), and Wood omit "Affection? thy Intention stabs the Center" (214), probably because the line puzzles but has no particular dramatic impact. In concession to the squeamish, Bell prunes 272–91—"incoherent indecent lines, unfit for both stage and closet" (p. 158)—while Calvert cuts 272–89. In these lines, Leontes voices nasty thoughts about Hermione to his uncomprehending child, and condemns widespread infidelity and one's wife being "sluiced" by one's neighbor. The last reference is cut by Kemble, Anderson, Ames (276–80), Payne (no. 21; 278–82), and Quayle (278–80). Kemble (285–8) and Anderson (283–91) cut more of Leontes's rant ("no Barricado for a belly"), but French does not; Ames calls 283–8 "obscure" and cuts; Payne (no. 20) cuts the same lines, while Payne (no. 21) cuts 283–5 only. Granville-Barker, who spares the rest of the bawdry, cuts as Ames does.

1.2 The Alienation of Camillo

Though he pays tribute to Camillo's past service (324–8), Leontes also charges the courtier with deception, negligence, and cowardice (328–39), charges against which Camillo naturally defends himself (340–58). Taming the exchange considerably, Payne (no. 20) cuts the entire incident (324–58), Anderson nearly all of it (331–55). Eliminating fifteen or more of these discomfortable lines: Kean, Ames, Woolfe, Payne (no. 21), Quayle, Wood, Nunn, Barton, and Eyre. All versions except Woolfe, Quayle, Wood, Nunn, Eyre, and Hands cut the reference to a cuckold's horn (361). Leontes's attendants are offended when Leontes calls Hermione a "Holy-Horse" (see n. 368): Bell, Kean, Woolfe, Payne (no. 21), and Eyre cut it. Continuing to derogate the absent Hermione, Leontes claims the whole court knows that the Queen "puts to" like a flax-wench "[b]efore her troth-plight" (369–70): Bell, Kean, Calvert, Allen, Payne (no. 21), and Woolfe cut the lines. Payne (no. 21) and Nunn are consistent in also cutting Camillo's objection at 371–3 ("I . . . taken"). Perhaps aware of the sexual connotations of "nothing" (382–9), Ames exults in a marginal comment, "This is one of Leontes' big chances." Corbin's vehement "No! No! No!" is written under Ames's note. Corbin prevails and cuts.

1.2 The Defection of Camillo

Dialogue leading up to Camillo's revelation—that Leontes, believing Polixenes has "toucht" Hermione "[f]orbiddenly," wants Polixenes dead (468–530)—merits cutting in some productions. Approximately one-third of the lines are eliminated in Bell, Ames, Payne (no. 20 and no. 21 differ slightly), Barton, and Eyre. Kean (532–5) and Payne (no. 21, 532–46) cut Polixenes's hyperbolic mention of Judas. Ames, marking 534–6 ("Turne . . . shun'd") "obscure" and 539–41 "not coherent," cuts, but when Corbin makes a longer cut (550–62, omitting Camillo's plan of escape, further assurance of his honesty, and a warning not to reveal anything to Leontes), Ames suggests in a marginal comment that "So much cutting makes the Scene too deadly." Apparently not. Cutting goes on in all versions between 534 (the lines immediately following the allusion to the betrayal of Christ) and the end of the scene (582). Bell,

Kemble, Kean, and Payne (no. 21) delete all or most of 568–79, thereby eliminating lines which, in praising Hermione, condemning Leontes's jealousy, and expressing fear for Hermione's safety, sympathetically establish Polixenes's concern for the consequences of his visit.

2.1 Confronting Hermione

Macready, Burton, Phelps, Kean, French, Anderson, and Woolfe cut two relatively innocuous references to Hermione's pregnant bulk (607, 611–12). Calvert cuts the first; Bell, Kemble (nos. 3 and 5), Inchbald, Cumberland, Ames, Quayle, and Hands, the second. Sh.'s metaphoric "Spider in the Cup" speech (636–42) is expendable to Kemble, Kean, Anderson, Payne (no. 21), and Woolfe. Phelps restores the speech, and Allen, in one of her few divergences from Anderson, does not cut it.

Literary critics have sometimes deplored Leontes's crude treatment of Hermione (see Characters, Leontes, p. 780), so perhaps it is not surprising to find stage productions that eliminate instances of it. Bell, Kemble, Kean, Calvert, Anderson, Ames, Woolfe, and Hands cut Leontes's nasty "let . . . thus" (660–2). Perhaps conscious of the sexual connotations of the word *Thing* and the associated charge that Hermione is a "Bed-swaruer, euen as bad as those | That Vulgars giue bold'st Titles," Bell prints Hull's text as cut (686–91, 694–8) but reproduces Sh.'s lines (686–98) in a footnote, explaining: "We think these lines, which we preserve for the reader, should also be spoken" (p. 167), a feeling not shared by Burton, Kean (no. 10), Anderson, Woolfe, Quayle, Barton, Eyre, and Hands, who cut approximately the lines Bell cuts. Payne and Nunn make the first cut (686–91), Kean (no. 11) and Calvert the second.

2.1. Ignoring Good Counsel

After Hermione's dignified exit to prison, the rest of the scene (733–818) is taken up with Leontes's courtiers vigorously defending Hermione and with Leontes just as vigorously rejecting their counsel. Anderson and Allen, who double Hermione and Perdita for their theatrical companies, choose to make Hermione the center of the scene, ending it with her exit by cutting 733–818 (Anderson) and 733–4, and 740–818 (Allen). Other versions do not excise Leontes but perhaps lead the audience toward a sympathetic view of him by cutting some of his stubborn insistence on infallibility, and his courtiers' arguments against it. Kean cuts 738–49, in which Antigonus and a Lord defend Hermione, and Nunn even more of their defense of her in the face of Leontes's anger (738–55). Bell, Calvert, Ames, Woolfe, Payne, and Quayle omit 754–76, in which Antigonus damns Hermione's detractor, mentions gelding his daughters, and agrees with the nameless Lord that he would rather Leontes lacked "credit" in this matter than the rest of the court. All other versions cut about half of these lines. Sh.'s Leontes continues to behave as if "he is now almost a god" (MARSH, 1980, p. 133), claiming that he needs no advice from his courtiers but consults them because of his "natural goodnesse" (777–86). Cutting all or nearly all of these lines are Bell, Kemble, Kean, Woolfe, Quayle, Wood, Nunn, Barton, and Eyre. Bell and Quayle also cut more than half the remaining lines (787–818), in which Leontes continues to berate his courtiers but also admits that he has sent to the Oracle, not because he doubts but because others—"Whose ignorant credulitie, will not | Come vp to th'truth" (810-11)—do.

2.2, 2.3 The Appearance of Paulina

Productions that feature a more sympathetic Leontes than the one Sh. creates, directors who find Paulina as overwhelming as some literary critics do (see Characters, p. 786), or stage versions that center on Hermione may not need—perhaps cannot tolerate—the forceful, outspoken woman who becomes the dominant presence in many scenes. Paulina boldly declares she will tell Leontes how dangerous his behavior is (855-61): Anderson and Kean cut. Emilia says no one but Paulina could do the job (869-81): Anderson, Kean, and Eyre cut the lines; Woolfe, Nunn, Barton, Wood, and Hands omit half or more of them. Paulina's explanation of the baby's status as prisoner, meant to reassure the jailer (888-94), is cut by Bell, Calvert, Anderson, and Quayle. Here, however, Allen makes none of the cuts Anderson does.

When Paulina challenges the courtiers, confronts Leontes with his infant daughter, and insists he acknowledge the child (928-1058), no audience can doubt her lack of self-interest and fearlessness. Anderson, Payne (no. 21), and Nunn cut some of it (937-44), though Allen does not follow Anderson in eliminating 963-8, Paulina's offer to be Leontes's physician and heal him of his evils. Bell, Kean, Ames, Woolfe, Quayle, Wood, Barton, and Eyre cut some of the lines (966-8). Paulina calls Leontes mad for slandering his family with "rotten" opinions: Allen now cuts as Anderson does (981-1014). Ames cuts 983-8, finding the lines "obscure"; Payne (no. 20), Woolfe, and Eyre also cut. All versions except Ames and Nunn omit much of the rest (1004-14). Kemble, Kean, Calvert, and Anderson (but not Allen) cut Leontes's charge that Perdita is the "Issue of *Polixenes*" (1015) and, with Bell, his cruel order to burn mother and child (1016-17). Both Anderson and Allen cut 1020-52. In this segment, Paulina points out how alike Leontes and his child are (1020-30): Phelps and French cut half these lines, diverging from Kemble who, with Kean, Woolfe, and Payne, cuts only a few. Paulina also expresses contempt for Leontes's threats to burn her at the stake and force her from his presence (1040-52): Phelps, Kean, and Quayle cut this passage the most; Kemble, Payne (no. 21), and Wood cut a few lines.

The changes in Paulina's part require further modification of Leontes's role. In Sh.'s text, Leontes continues to behave (1059-1143), Bell notes, with "hare-brained barbarity. . . . He storms, 'tis true, but in a most laughable manner" (pp. 174-5). Little of the behavior here ridiculed survives the cut in Anderson (1062-99). Bell omits Leontes's harsh alternatives (commit the baby to the fire or he will bash its brains out, 1063-71): Payne, Quayle, Wood, Nunn, Barton, and Eyre omit the first threat (1063-6), Kemble, Kean, and Calvert the second (1066-9). In cutting 1090-2, Bell, Kean, and Calvert omit Leontes's twice calling the child a bastard. Leontes further threatens Paulina and Antigonus with death (1102-5) and torture (1113-15): Barton and Eyre cut both threats; Nunn cuts the first only; Bell, Anderson, Payne, and Wood cut the second. The remainder of the scene (1116-43) has Antigonus expressing pity for the child (but nonetheless willing to abandon it as ordered) and the announcement that the messengers have returned with the oracle's response: Wood eliminates nearly all the lines (1121–43). Quayle cuts 1129–35. All other versions except Calvert, Ames, Payne (no. 20), and Nunn thin this segment.

3.1 Delphos

According to Bell's ed. (p. 176), this short scene (1144–72) is "unnecessary [and] justly left out," and Bell, followed by Kean, Calvert, Anderson, Woolfe, and Quayle, omits it. It is blocked for cutting in Burton but is restored, though French cuts the whole scene. Ames and Payne (no. 21) cut lines that establish the scene's locale (1146–9). Nunn cuts 1164–72, while Payne (no. 21), Barton, Hands, and Eyre do some thinning.

3.2 The Trial

This scene contrasts Hermione's rationality with Leontes's obsessiveness. Yet Kemble, Kean, and Anderson (Allen retains about four more lines than Anderson) eliminate Hermione's first rebuttal of the charges, which illustrate Leontes's warped judgment (1235–62). Calvert cuts quite a few of Hermione's lines (1236–48) and omits, as does Bell, a reference to Hermione's "bastard" (1261–2). By cutting a few packed lines (1281–5), Anderson gets rid of the word *strumpet*—but also eliminates Hermione's objections to being called one and to the "immodest hatred" that spurs Leontes to deny her normal childbed privileges. Bell, Kean, and Calvert cut the childbed charge (1281–3). Kean (no. 11), Calvert, and Anderson (but not Allen) cut 1299–1303, Calvert noting that it "must certainly jar unpleasantly on the ear of a student of history to hear Hermione speaking of herself as the daughter of 'the Emperor of Russia'" (preface, p. iii). Phelps diverges from Kemble to cut this phrase only; Kean (no. 10) also cuts it.

In the aftermath of his perverse rejection of the Oracle, Leontes assures Paulina that Hermione will recover from her swoon, admits his sins, assumes that reconciliation will be taken care of easily, accepts Paulina's disdain for his inadequate attempts at repentance, and vows to do daily penance (1334–1435). However, Anderson and Allen shift the focus of attention from Leontes to Hermione; except for retaining part of 1387–9 ("the Queene . . . yet"), Anderson ends the scene at 1333, and Allen differs only slightly in retaining for Paulina part of 1332 ("This newes is mortall to the Queene") and part of 1388 ("The sweet'st, deer'st creature's dead") but otherwise excising Leontes and Paulina as Anderson does. All versions make cuts in this section: Bell, Kean, Calvert, Woolfe, Quayle, and Wood cut half or more of the lines.

3.3 Perdita Abandoned and Rescued

In soliloquy (1457–1500), Antigonus recounts the dream in which Hermione tells him he will not survive the "vngentle businesse" of abandoning Perdita (1476–8). Since Antigonus now declares his belief that Perdita is Polixenes's bastard (1483–8), he must also believe Hermione is an adulteress. STAUFFER (1949, p. 353, n. 44) and NICOLL (1952, p. 169) think this failure of trust and faith inevitably dooms Antigonus; Woolfe and Payne (no. 21) may think so too, since they cut both passages. Woolfe alone follows Bell in omitting the famous SD *"pursued by a Beare"* (1500), an omission that Bell explains this way (p. 105): *"Shakespeare* had here introduced a bear— a most fit actor for pantomimes or puppet-shows; but blushing criticism has excluded the rough Gentleman." Blushing criticism also excludes a few mildly suggestive lines from the rest of the scene (1501–77). The Shepherd touches on young men who do nothing but get wenches with child (1503–5): Phelps, Burton, Kean, Calvert, and Anderson cut. The Shepherd may read "Waiting-Gentlewoman" into the escapade that results in an abandoned baby (1511–17), but the audiences of Phelps, Kean, Calvert, and Anderson do not hear him do it. The Clown's seemingly insensitive description of the deaths of Antigonus and the mariners (1524–54) is the pivotal point of the play for some critics (see "Technique: Structure," p. 748), yet Anderson cuts 1524–54, Eyre 1521–54. Anderson and Quayle also cut a final reference to the bear and Antigonus (1567–77).

4.1 Time

Relying on the conversation between Polixenes and Camillo in 4.2 to establish the passage of time, Kemble, Anderson, and Ames cut Time's soliloquy (1579–1611). Though Burton's promptbook does not indicate the restoration, playbills for his first production make note of it, as does the *New York Daily Tribune* review of 14 Feb. 1856. French also restores the scene and, like Kean (no. 10), Payne (no. 20), Wood, and Hands, cuts no lines at all. Among lines that Calvert omits are the only ones to mention Florizel by name before he appears (1600–2).

4.2 Polixenes and Camillo

Reminiscent of 59–116 (in which Polixenes is dissuaded from leaving Sicilia), this scene (1612–66) shows Polixenes using praise, claims of his own need, and promises of rewards to come in order to delay Camillo's departure from Bohemia and to get him to join in spying on Florizel. Stage versions apparently cannot reconcile the Camillo swayed by Polixenes's blandishments with the Camillo of exceptional integrity and virtue whom literary critics write of (see Characters, p. 768), since each version cuts all or most of the flattery (1623–32). All versions except Bell, Calvert, Ames, and Quayle thin between 1633 and 1666. Specific cuts remove Polixenes's reference to Florizel's neglect of duty (1638–41) and also Camillo's similar reference (1642–6): Kemble and Kean (no. 10) cut both references; Kean (no. 11), Anderson, Woolfe, Payne (no. 21), Eyre, and Hands cut the first; Nunn cuts all of the second, while Anderson, Woolfe, Wood, Nunn, Barton, Eyre, and Hands cut some of Camillo's criticism of the Prince (1644–5). Kean (no. 10) is the only version to boost Polixenes's image slightly by deleting part of his admission (1648–9) that he has set spies on his own son.

4.3 Autolycus and the Clown

Part of Autolycus's vitality lies in the raffish career he sketches for the audience, and though his "sins" are relatively tame, some are cut. Garrick omits the "tumbling in the hay" stanza (1677-80) of Autolycus's entry song, as do Kean and Anderson. Garrick leads in cutting Autolycus's honest admission that fear keeps him from anything more dangerous than petty theft (1696-7). Bell, Kemble, Kean, Calvert, Anderson, and Hands follow. Bell, Kemble, Kean, Calvert, and Anderson cut Autolycus's disregard for "the life to come" (but see n. 1698). Kean and Anderson remove references to Autolycus's association with loose women (1754-5), Anderson to his questionable job history (1759-66). Garrick probably improves clarity by removing 1711-13 (lines which Woolfe and Hands also cut): the Clown's "three-man song-men," "Meanes and Bases," and the lone Puritan who "sings Psalmes to horne-pipes" produce little agreement on meaning (see n. 1711 ff.). Omitting these lines and more are Bell, Calvert, and Payne, who cut 1709-13; Kemble and Kean, 1709-14; and Anderson, 1711-17.

Time-saving seems to motivate other cuts. Kemble, Kean, Anderson, Woolfe, Payne, Wood, Nunn, Barton, and Eyre cut from two to ten lines of the twenty-nine that cover stage business involved in Autolycus's picking the Clown's pocket (1718-46). Sh. has Autolycus repeat that he was once in service to Prince Florizel (1681-2, 1755-6); Calvert cuts the first statement. Nunn cuts the seemingly important lines (1778-90) that bring the sheepshearing—and the possibility of more "profit"—to Autolycus's attention. Autolycus has, however, overheard the Clown talking to himself about the sheepshearing as he enters (1705).

4.4 Florizel and Perdita

When Perdita expresses to him her misgivings about their romance, Florizel refers to the gods' lustful pursuit of lovely female mortals in order to proclaim the virtue of his feelings about Perdita. Kemble and Kean (no. 10) omit all these lines (1820-42); Kean (no. 11), Anderson, and Allen (no. 16) cut most of Florizel's speech (1826-36); Bell omits all of Perdita's contention that Florizel will be forced to break with her (1837-42); Woolfe, Payne (no. 21), Quayle, Wood, Eyre, and Hands cut some lines from each character's dialogue. All versions except Calvert, Allen, Ames, Payne (no. 20), and Quayle save some time by cutting or thinning Florizel's repetitious assurance that he will not desert Perdita (1843-54).

Though Perdita is a princess unaware, several versions emphasize her royalty rather than her ignorance. The Shepherd, noting how his late wife served as mistress of the feast, encourages Perdita to emulate her by welcoming and serving all, singing, dancing, and toasting each guest as she moves from table to table, though she might get as flushed and tipsy as his wife did (1860-7). Kemble (nos. 3 and 5), Cumberland, Kean, Calvert, Anderson, and Woolfe cut most of this description of unregal behavior; Bell, French, and Wood cut the lines suggesting the wife's tipsiness (1865-7).

4.4 Art vs. Nature

The debate between Perdita and Polixenes (1887–1921) is sometimes viewed as the central statement of theme in the play (see Criticism: Themes and Significance, p. 730); it also shapes audience perception of Perdita, for if, as PAFFORD (ed. 1963, p. lxxviii, n. 3) says, "We are nowhere directed to think that Perdita is particularly intelligent," these lines indicate that we are not meant to think her a fool either. Yet as important as the debate seems to be in the reading, several productions omit it. French (differing from Kemble), Calvert, Allen, and Quayle cut exactly as Garrick does (1887–1916). Kemble, Kean, Anderson only, and Payne (no. 21) cut a bit more (1887–1921). Bell cuts 1892–1916. Wood cuts Perdita's distaste for painted flowers and painted women (1912–16). Garrick may have cut to make Perdita suitably deferential and docile for 18th-c. audiences (DASH, 1980, p. 281); even Bell observes (p. 94) that Perdita's "modest humility" is the trait that "recommends the supposed shepherdess exceedingly to [the audience's] favour." Kemble defers only to the "powers of his actors" (BOADEN, 1825, 2:2)—or in this case, a lack of power—in cutting the debate completely. The *Times* review of 26 Mar. 1802 reveals that Kemble's Perdita (Catherine Hicks) is attractive but almost "destitute of sensibility," with a voice so weak that "it is almost impossible to hear her distinctly, even at a short distance from the stage." Instead of "attending to the speeches addressed to her, or the business of the scene . . . [Hicks] was frequently employed in adjusting her dress." In later productions, Kemble could and did change actresses, but he did not change his text, and productions that derive from his, as well as some that do not, deprive Perdita of much of her spirit as well as some wonderful lines. Kemble and Kean (no. 10) further diminish Perdita's stage presence by cutting Florizel's "too large" praise of her, and her response (1947–74); Wood also cuts most of these lines (1947–52, 1959–71). Anderson cuts twenty-eight, Calvert twenty-four lines—mostly from Florizel's dialogue. Cutting more evenhandedly between both characters, Wood deletes eighteen lines, Bell and Payne (no. 21) sixteen lines. Perdita's reference to maidenheads (1929–30) is cut by Kean and Anderson. Perdita's allusion to Proserpina and Dis (1930–2), considered significant (see Themes and Significance, p. 736), is deleted by Garrick, Kemble, and Kean; Anderson (but not Allen) deletes "Bright Phœbus" (1938). Garrick, followed by Kemble, Kean, and Anderson only, cuts a reference to maiden maladies (1938–9).

4.4 Songs and Dances

Though all but Hands omit Perdita's injunction that Autolycus's songs will contain no scurrilous words (2038–9), many versions try to make sure they do not. The servant's ironic assurance that Autolycus's songs are free of bawdry (2016–25) is omitted by Kemble (but not French), Kean, Calvert, and Anderson. Garrick, Bell, and Payne cut "of Dildo's and Fadings" (2019–20). Autolycus enters singing "Lawn as white" (2044–55); the song may not be ribald, but Kean and Anderson cut all but the refrain, Payne cuts nearly as much (2046–53), and all of them omit the questionable "poaking-stickes" (see n. 2052), which Woolfe and Nunn also cut. Anderson and Wood cut the entire ballad of the usurer's wife (possibly bawdy; see n. 2084-2103); Kean and Calvert omit the reference to birth (2085-6) and, followed by Barton and Eyre, cut Autolycus's speech containing a reference to "Midwiues" (2091-3). The "ballad of a Fish" (2097-2103) contains reference to sexual intercourse (see n. 2101-2): Anderson cuts it entirely, while Kemble, Kean, and Calvert cut the two offending lines. Bell and Anderson cut Autolycus's reference to copulation (see n. 2116-17) and the sexual rivalry of the part song, "Two maids wooing a man" (2118-33). Garrick, Kemble, Kean, and Eyre omit Autolycus's lines (2116-17); Phelps, diverging from Kemble, restores them. Though apparently free of anything scurrilous, "Will you buy" (2139-44) is omitted completely by Kean (no. 10), Calvert, Anderson, Nunn, and Hands. Garrick, Bell, Kemble, Anderson, Woolfe, Payne, and Wood cut the description and the dance of the satyrs (2145-64), but French does not.

4.4 The Aborted Betrothal and Its Results

Audience perception of Polixenes is affected as he moves to prevent Florizel and Perdita from a binding betrothal (2165-2285), for while Polixenes might accept the "casual coupling . . . expected from country folk, matrimony with their betters seems out of the question" (COOK, 1991, p. 201), despite his stance to the contrary in the art vs. nature debate. Several stage versions reduce Polixenes's ranting—intentionally or not, the cuts make him more consistent in his views, less violent and repugnant in his behavior—and some of them parallel the change in Polixenes with a reduction in the determination and devotion of the young lovers. Polixenes hints that Florizel missed a chance to buy Perdita's favor when he did not buy any of Autolycus's trinkets (2174-8); Kemble, Kean, Calvert, Anderson, Woolfe, Payne, Quayle, Wood, and Barton cut this suggestion. Florizel repudiates the idea (2181-3), but Kemble, Anderson, Payne, Woolfe, and Barton cut his gallantry. Polixenes, berating "Doricles" for not having his father at the betrothal, seems to grow more agitated each time "Doricles" spurns arguments about a father's rightful place in his son's life (2225-58): Polixenes is considerably more tranquil after Anderson cuts almost all of this section (2231-51), Woolfe more than half (2231-40, 2243-7), Kemble, Kean, and Calvert only a little less (2231-43). Bell, Payne, Barton, and Eyre get rid of all or most of Polixenes's abrasive questions (2233-7). Polixenes threatens Perdita with disfigurement (2269-70) and a generally cruel death (2281-5). Kean may feel one threat is enough, since he cuts Polixenes's vindictive idea of ruining Perdita's beauty (2265-70). Polixenes also threatens to bar Florizel from the succession (2273) and to deny kinship with him (2274-5). Bell, Kemble, Kean, Calvert, Anderson, Woolfe, Payne (no. 21), Barton, and Eyre omit only the latter, with its denial of kinship emphasized by the reference to *Deucalion* (see n. 2275). Quayle omits that reference only (2275).

Bell notes that despite the five pages that Hull "cut out of [this] scene, it is still too long and may be charged with unessential intricacy; what follows [after Polixenes's exit at 2285], to the end of the act [2723], we think might be spared one half, it is harping too much on one string; the ear and taste must both pall" (p. 208). Most succeeding versions spare some, if not half. Florizel voices his commitment to Perdita quite clearly at 2310-12, so the elaboration that begins at 2313 and continues through the hyperbole of 2328-31 is not essential: Kemble and Kean cut 2313-31; Anderson cuts nearly all of this; other versions thin or cut from two to twelve lines. In a terse exchange (2399-2401), Camillo asks if Florizel has "thought on" a place to go, and the Prince replies "Not any yet." Far more wordily, they have already said something like this (2381-98): Bell, Kean, Calvert, Anderson, Payne (no. 21), and Wood cut the whole segment, Woolfe all but one line (2382), Kemble all but three (2392-4); Payne (no. 20), Quayle, Nunn, Barton, Eyre, and Hands cut a number of these lines. The basic story Florizel is to tell Leontes, some questions from Florizel, and a few compliments to Perdita take up forty-eight lines (2423-70), which are sometimes repetitive: cutting large segments of dialogue are Hands (44 lines), Nunn (41), Bell, Anderson, Quayle, and Wood (39 each), Woolfe (37), Calvert (33), Payne (32 lines), Kemble (29), and Kean (27). Cutting less than half are Ames, Barton, and Eyre. Quayle and Payne omit Autolycus's self-satisfied speech about having sold all his trumpery (2472-95); Anderson omits most of it (2472-90). Cutting and thinning by fifteen lines or less are Garrick, Bell, Kemble, Calvert, Kean, Woolfe, Nunn, Barton, Eyre, and Hands. Florizel, Perdita, and Camillo exit (2552) after Autolycus and Florizel exchange clothes, a piece of business that critics find puzzling, if not superfluous (see n. 2511-12). Kemble deletes the exchange, cutting 2496-2519 and 2521-43; all versions except Ames cut some of these lines. With consistency, Kemble also cuts lines that contain a reference to the clothing exchange (2553-60): Woolfe, Wood, Nunn, and Barton also cut them.

Anderson ends the scene at 2552; other versions omit some of the remaining lines (2553-2723), primarily cutting Autolycus at his best (or worst). Garrick is the first to delete Autolycus's stated intent to do Florizel a good turn (2592-3): Bell, Kemble, Kean, Calvert, Payne (no. 21), Quayle, Wood, and Eyre follow. Autolycus's posturing as a courtier before the Shepherd and Clown (2599-2635) is cut heavily by Bell, Kemble, Kean, Woolfe, Payne (no. 21), and Quayle. Wood, Nunn, Barton, and Hands cut this section moderately. Parts of 2605-10 provoke critical concerns (see n. 2607-8). While it seems unlikely that they would bother an audience watching a performance, these are among the few lines that Granville-Barker cuts, following Garrick's cut, as do Calvert, Nunn, and Hands.

Autolycus creates a vivid description of the torments the Clown will suffer (2665-72); Bell cuts this funny (if mean-spirited) display (2668-72). Quayle cuts Autolycus's misleading offer to bring the Shepherd and Clown to the King and into his favor (2675-80), while Calvert, Woolfe, Payne (no. 21), Nunn, Barton, and Eyre omit one or the other of Autolycus's promises. Some redundant information is offered (2688-2705), and Wood saves playing time by cutting all of these lines, while Woolfe, Quayle, Hands, and Nunn cut a dozen or more lines. Bell, Kemble, Kean, Payne, Barton, and Eyre omit about six lines. Only Bell and Kean eliminate Autolycus's reference to urinating on the hedge (2706-7). Autolycus once again says he will try to do Florizel a good turn (2713-23): Calvert, seemingly intent on eliminating any suggestion that Autolycus once served Florizel, cuts these lines. Phelps diverges from

Kemble to cut as Calvert does, and Nunn and Barton follow. Kemble, Kean, and Woolfe cut a bit less (2716–22) but retain the connection between Florizel and Autolycus.

5.1 Leontes and Paulina

To remind the audience of Leontes's situation after the long fourth act, Sh. has him return to the stage expressing regret for his sins and praising his lost queen. Paulina's objections to Leontes's suggested remarriage are couched in dialogue that reminds Leontes, the court, and the audience of Hermione's perfections, Sicilia's losses, and the unfulfilled Oracle (2740–82). Garrick, who opens his adaptation with a summary of these events, and Anderson, who consistently truncates the major roles except those of Hermione and Perdita, cut 2750–82. All other versions cut from eight to twenty-eight of these forty-three lines, perhaps to save time, perhaps to eliminate Leontes's reacting to Paulina's "characteristic bluntness" with "the whimpering of a beaten dog" (PILGRIM, 1983, p. 35).

In speculating that Hermione's "sainted spirit" will haunt him and drive him to murder a new wife (2783–2809), Leontes twice promises unconditionally not to take one (2792 and 2809). Garrick, Quayle, Barton, and Eyre cut the first promise and the emotionally overwrought dialogue that follows it. Anderson cuts the dialogue and the last promise. Kemble, Kean, and Ames retain both promises but cut the intervening dialogue. Bell and Woolfe omit the idea of Hermione's spirit driving Leontes to murder (2797–2800); Calvert and Payne (no. 21) adopt F3's omission at 2798, changing the reading from "just such cause" to "just cause."

Paulina gains remarkable control over Leontes's life (2810–29) by twice getting him to promise never to marry without her consent. Hands, however, eliminates that control entirely, cutting 2810–17 and 2826–9. No other version omits the first promise (2812), but one is enough for Kemble, Kean, Ames, Anderson, Payne (no. 21), Barton, and Eyre, who cut the second (2826). Bell and Hands cut half, and every other version except Ames and Payne (no. 20) cuts all or most, of the irritable exchange between Paulina and a servant who praises Perdita's beauty (2843–64). Paulina next reminds Leontes of Mamillius's death, and he responds with appropriate pain (2867–77): Quayle and Woolfe spare him this.

5.1 The Arrival of Florizel and Perdita

Subsequent stagings prune F's version of the young lovers' arrival at the Sicilian court. Kemble, Kean, and Anderson fail to appreciate the irony of Leontes's telling Florizel, "Your Mother was most true to Wedlock, Prince, | For she did print your Royall Father off, | Conceiuing you" (2879–81); they cut. Lines 2885–2940 contain Leontes's self-pitying laments for his past follies and losses, as well as the "disgraceful improbability" that "Florizel should introduce himself to the court of Sicilia, by speaking arrant falsehoods" (INCHBALD, ed. 1808, 3:6). Bell, Kean, Anderson, Woolfe, Payne (no. 21), Quayle, Barton, and Hands cut two-thirds or more of this segment. Ames cuts a little more than half the lines but echoes Kemble, who cuts a selective half

(2886–93, 2897–2901, 2906–8, 2919–23, 2931–7) that lets Florizel tell as much truth as possible. Nunn eliminates twenty-three various lines of courtly language, Wood and Eyre about fifteen.

Polixenes is made to behave less like the Leontes of Acts 1–3 when Hands deletes nearly all lines revealing that the Shepherd and Clown are also in Sicilia and are still the objects of Polixenes's fury (2950–70). Kemble, Kean, Calvert, Anderson, Woolfe, Payne (no. 21), Quayle, and Nunn also cut any mention of the terror Polixenes causes the two men (2959–69).

Leontes obviously agrees with Polixenes's expectation that Florizel's wife will be of noble birth, since he expresses regret that Florizel has broken with his father in choosing a wife of unsuitable station (2982–6); Anderson, Woolfe, Quayle, and Wood cut the lines, however, giving Leontes a tolerance with which Sh. did not endow him. Kemble, Kean, and Calvert cut Leontes's regret over the break (2983–4); Payne (no. 21), Nunn, Barton, and Eyre cut his regret that Perdita is not well-born (2984–6). All these versions, as well as Kean and Hands, cut the possibly erotic line about Florizel "enjoying" Perdita (2986).

At 1845 ff. and 2340 ff. Florizel vows that his feelings for Perdita will not change or be thwarted: Bell, Anderson, Wood, Nunn, Barton, and Eyre cut a repetition at 2987–90. Quayle alone cuts Leontes's unknowingly incestuous interest in Perdita, Paulina's sharp reminder of Hermione, and Leontes's instant excuse for his interest (2995–3000).

5.2 The Fulfillment of the Oracle's Prophecy

Sh. has the discovery of Perdita's identity and the ensuing joyful reunions revealed in a talky onstage narrative (3010–3120) that Bell (p. 218) labels a flat but acceptable means of maintaining the drama of the statue scene. Bell, in fact, retains all but fifteen of these lines, one of its few cuts—3104–9, also cut by Kean and Hands—ridding the play of *Iulio Romano*, a reference with a long critical history (see n. 3104–5). Woolfe and Anderson, by contrast, apparently find this narration flat and unacceptable: Woolfe cuts the whole sequence; Anderson cuts all but about thirty-five lines (retaining only the information that Perdita and proof of her identity have been found). Garrick omits the mention of the deaths of Antigonus and the mariners, as well as the joy that stimulates Paulina's notable eye movement (3068–84). No one else cuts Antigonus's death, but Burton diverges from Kemble (French does not) to cut the loss of the mariners and Paulina's eye movements, as do Ames, Nunn, and Barton. Quayle, Eyre, and Hands cut only the loss of the mariners. Kean, Calvert, and Payne (no. 21) omit only Paulina's unusual eye movement. Burton makes other cuts that Kemble does not (3023–4, 3037–9, 3042–9, and 3053–67), but in each of these instances, French reads with Kemble.

Bell does cut from 3121 to the end of the scene (3182); Kean follows. Apparently finding no delight in the somewhat repetitive dialogue, they eliminate Autolycus's soliloquy and his subsequent humbling at the hands of the newly ennobled Shepherd and Clown. Cumberland, French, Calvert, and Wood delete the entire soliloquy

(3121–34), Nunn most of it (3122–30, 3133–4). In the remainder of the scene, Garrick and Wood cut 3137–8; Garrick, Payne (no. 21), Nunn, Barton, and Eyre cut 3140–1. In particular, Garrick cuts 3175–80, which has three repetitions of "tall fellow," and in this cut he is followed by Kemble, Kean, Calvert, and Anderson, while Nunn and Barton cut 3178–80.

5.3 The Statue Scene

Payne (no. 21), Nunn, Barton, and Hands omit most of the preliminary courtly ritual (3186–3201), cutting as quickly as possible to Paulina's revelation of the statue (3208). Bell, Kemble, Kean, Calvert, Anderson, Woolfe, Quayle, Nunn, Barton, and Eyre think it better to omit Leontes's tactless exclamation that his queen was not so wrinkled with age as her statue is (3216–18) and, with Wood and Kean (no. 10), the self-recrimination of 3223–5, instances of which are also cut by Garrick, Kemble, Anderson, Payne (no. 21), and Barton (3228–9) and by Anderson and Payne (no. 21) at 3230–1.

Perdita has a mere seven lines in this scene (3234–8, 3287–8), a number that could easily be handled by an understudy. This fact suggests to PARTRIDGE (1982, p. 4) that Sh.'s intention may have been to double the roles of Hermione and Perdita as a way of overcoming the difficulty of casting separately the roles of mother and daughter who must markedly resemble each other. WEBSTER (1942, p. 282) feels that doubling does "great violence to Shakespeare's intention, and [has] nothing to recommend it save the possibility that the audience may want to see one woman star through the whole play instead of two in half the play each." Only four of the versions under consideration double the roles. Of those, Anderson and Allen use here a silent double, cutting 3230–50. Nunn keeps Perdita's first speech only, Hands two lines of it (3237–8). Some of the versions not doubling the roles still find Perdita's lines unimportant enough to cut: Calvert omits both little speeches, Kean the first, Woolfe the second, and Garrick part of the first. The rest of the dialogue preceding the reanimation of Hermione (3239–3305) can be cut to save playing time. All versions except Ames, Payne (no. 20), and Wood omit from two (Garrick) to thirty-five (Payne, no. 21) lines.

Though Simon Forman ignores the statue scene entirely and some critics find it contrived, forced, and flat, others—COGHILL (1958, pp. 39–40), for example—view it as a deeply satisfying, astonishing, magical, and daring piece of theater (see n. 3321–3). In production, however, despite the mere thirty-five lines (3306–40) that Sh. uses to take the audience from the first indication of Hermione's return to her last words in the play (and the only ones she has spoken since 1318), Garrick, Bell, Kemble, Kean, Calvert, Anderson, Payne (no. 21), Quayle, Nunn, and Barton cut from four to fourteen of the lines. Bell omits half of Hermione's short speech (3337–40). Anderson cuts the last twenty-nine lines of the play (3341–3369)—a move that eliminates, among other things, Leontes's making a match for Paulina—and then introduces two lines from another play for the conclusion (see below, p. 849). Payne (no. 21) cuts nearly as much (3244–65), as do Kean, Calvert, and Woolfe (3345–60), who also eliminate the matchmaking (3349–59). Other versions cutting this material include Kemble (who omits 3350–7 and uses alterations and additions to change what he does not cut). French does not follow Kemble or Burton in cutting. Garrick, Quayle, Barton, Wood, Eyre, and Hands all cut a few lines from the end of this scene.

SUBSTITUTIONS, TRANSPOSITIONS, AND ADDITIONS

A few original substitutions occur in stage versions, some affecting plot and characterization but most involving no more than a word or two employed to replace language deemed lewd, archaic, or obscure. Alterations adopted from reading editions are generally not discussed here. An exception is the substitution throughout of "Bithynia" for "Bohemia" in Bell, Kean (no. 11), and Calvert. Kean alone explains his adoption of HANMER's emendation: the oracle of Delphi (Delphos in the original but changed throughout in Kean) points to a period when Syracuse is the equivalent of Athens at "the summit of her political prosperity [and] . . . assuming that the civilization of Athens was reflected by Syracuse, [then] . . . to connect the country known as 'Bohemia' with an age so remote would be impossible" (p. vi).

Additions account for the smallest body of change to the text. Payne (no. 21) adds a short prologue stressing the folk-tale nature of *WT*. Opening SDs in Kean (no. 11), adopted in principle by Calvert, reflect Kean's conception of place (Syracuse) and time (739 B.C.), as well as his desire to keep the entire play free of what he believes to be disrupting anachronisms. Corbin, in preparing Ames's version, opens on — and sets many later scenes in — the "alcove": the "General Notes on Decoration," appended to the prompt copy, explain that he thinks the alcove an authentic feature of the Elizabethan stage within which locality is established at a glance by properties, the main stage being neutral ground from which the idea of locality is absent. Since Corbin believes that much of the early action of *WT* is possible "only when we assume the alcove appears as an apartment, removed from the main stage which thus becomes a sort of anteroom" (p. 1), his handling of the text is guided by his conception of staging.

1.2. The Invitation, etc.

A number of substitutions clarify language: Barton changes "Gest" (98) to "Time," and Eyre follows. Eyre substitutes "to come" for "behind" (125), though both mean the same thing. Cumberland changes "hoxes" (334) to "boxes," but Phelps restores the original reading in his promptbook; Calvert alters to "hoaxes." "Holy-Horse" (368) becomes "hobby-horse" in Kemble, Allen (no. 15), Ames, Granville-Barker, Payne (no. 20), and Barton; Calvert and Allen (no. 16) alter to "wanton." Bell alters "Potion" (417) to "portion." Another group of substitutions eliminates perceived indecencies or provocative language. French avoids sexual connotations by having Hermione instead of "ride's" (164) say "ride in," Calvert "drive us." In Phelps "Cuckolds" (273) becomes "false ones." Anderson, though not Allen, keeps Leontes from degrading Hermione entirely by substituting "My Wife's not honest" for "My Wife's a Holy-Horse, deserues a Name | As ranke as any Flax-Wench, that puts to | Before her troth-plight" (368–70). His distaste for the sullying of his marital "Sheetes" (426) because Polixenes has illicitly "toucht" Hermione (529) is downplayed in Kean, where Leontes's "honour" is tainted because Polixenes "approach'd" the Queen.

2.1 Confronting Hermione

Substitutions are few here. In the teasing that Mamillius endures, Kean changes a lady-in-waiting's already mild "wanton with us" to the innocuous "play with us" (609). Kean's unsubtle foreshadowing changes the "Church-yard" in Mamillius's story (625) into a prophetic "grave-yard." Barton reduces 631–2 ("on . . . ships") to the single word "hence." Quayle uses the "Spider in the Cup" speech (633–42) in place of 900–3 ("It . . . Adultresse"), where it works well but no better than in its original location. Nunn adopts the glosses of KERMODE (ed. 1963), replacing "pinch'd Thing" and "Tricke" (648) with "puppet" and "toy." Anderson substitutes "false" for "an Adultresse" (692), but Allen does not. Kemble adopts MALONE's (ed. 1790) "feodary" for "Federarie" (694): the change can make little difference to an audience, but it does reflect Kemble's friendship with the notable editors of his day (MALONE, REED, and STEEVENS) and his practice of consulting them on the texts. Kemble considered MALONE "his most respected advisor on scholarly points" (BAKER, 1942, p. 212).

2.1 Ignoring Good Counsel

Having cut much of the sensible advice offered to—but ignored by—Leontes, stage versions have little of importance remaining to alter. Kemble makes several transpositions affecting Antigonus's role. He assigns to Antigonus the Lord's speech at 738–40 ("For her [my Lord] | I dare my life lay downe, and will do't . . . the Queene is spotlesse"), thus letting Antigonus ironically foreshadow his own fate. He strengthens Antigonus's resistance to Leontes's folly by assigning him another lord's bold defiance of the king (774–6: "more . . . might"), and in this Kean and Hands follow Kemble. Finally, Kemble moves 784–9 to follow 814, thus ending his scene not with Antigonus's impertinence but with his regret that Leontes has made his accusations so public a matter. French, however, does not transpose.

2.3 Confronting Leontes

The substitutions that occur here generally seek to improve Leontes's image: his "bastard" becomes "brat" at 992 in Kean and Calvert, "creature" at 1085 in Kemble (but not French), Kean, and Calvert, "hateful issue of Polixenes" (in Kemble) and "infant" (in Kean and Calvert) at 1107. Sh. has Leontes say he will "burne" his infant daughter (1086); Kemble has Leontes merely "end" the baby's life. Paulina becomes "loud-tongu'd" rather than "lewd-tongu'd" (1104) in Kean and Anderson only. Perhaps seeking a more logical chronology, Payne (no. 21) rearranges the abandonment of Perdita so that it precedes Hermione's trial. After Leontes's "No: Ile not reare Anothers Issue" (1125–6), the order is: 1437 (to "*Babe*"); 1439–56 ("*Ant. . . . business*"); 1491–3 ("The . . . cannot"); the addition of "Act One, Scene 7"; 1457; 1437–8

("*Enter Sheepeheard, and Clowne.*"); 1459-61 ("thy . . . waking"); 1464-6 ("in . . . lay"); 1467-1577 ("And . . . *Exeunt*"); the addition of "Act One, Scene 8"; 1126 ("*Enter a Seruant*" is altered to "*Leo. R with 3rd & 4th Lords, 2nd Lord enters L. and speaks*"); 1127-41 ("Please. . . . Triall"); 1143 ("*Exeunt*"); 1145 on.

Kean's stage version is alone in changing "Delphos" to "Delphi" at 1130, but to support his transposition of 3.1, Kemble alters 1130-1. Cleomenes and Dion, having returned safely from Delphos, now "are both landed, | Hasting to th' Court" in F; Kemble has them "even now | Entering" the court. Kean and Calvert cut 3.1 but adopt Kemble's change to let the audience know that the Oracle's response will be introduced at the trial.

3.1 Delphos

In Kemble, as noted, 1144-72 follows 897, the scene thus coming between 2.2 and 2.3. This staging elicits a written comment in the margin of Kean (no. 10), where the scene is cut: "I [J. W. Coles] see nothing gained by the alteration." French does not transpose.

3.2 The Trial

During her trial, Hermione details the terrible things that have been done to her. One of them is that her infant daughter has been "Hal'd out to murther" (1280). By transposing 3.2 and 3.3, Anderson shows the baby's abandonment before the audience hears about it from Hermione. Substitutions generally offer an innocuous word for an original that might be deemed offensive: the *body* of Hermione's "first Fruits of my body" (1276) becomes "affection" in Bell, "our marriage" in Kemble (but not French) and Kean, "my marriage" in Anderson (but not Allen). "Strumpet" (1281) becomes "wanton" in Kean, Calvert, and Anderson, though the difference seems negligible. In F, an officer of the court reads the oracle (1313-16); Barton distributes the lines between Dion, Cleomenes, and other courtiers and ladies, appropriately reserving the last two highly dramatic lines (the King "*shall liue without an Heire, if that which is lost, be not found*") for Paulina. Kemble gives her 1317, the cry of multiple lords: "Now blessed be the great *Apollo*"; French does not follow Kemble or Burton in this. By substituting "dead" for the euphemistic "gone" (1327, 1328), Bell and Kemble eliminate the minor suspense that Sh. creates, but this change gives Kemble a chance to let Leontes moan, at the end of 1328, "Oh, oh, oh! — My son! — ."

At least two versions offer additions to SDs that bear directly on the interpretation of the text. At 1185 Calvert has Hermione "brought in on a Lectica [defined by him as "a couch for carrying persons in a lying position, from one place to another"] by her Female Attendants"), a matter of staging that would be incongruous if Calvert neglected to cut Hermione's complaints about her poor treatment in childbirth. Kemble (though not French) unfortunately destroys the power of the original scene, in keeping with the general subduing of Leontes's behavior and, consequently, Paulina's: Kemble presents as nearly private what F presents as public spectacle — Paulina enters at 1358 to confront Leontes with news of Hermione's death and to accuse him of being responsible for it. A line added for Leontes after 1338 — "Break up the court" — clears the stage of trial spectators; Kemble then closes the public setting ("*The Court of Justice*") on Leontes's dismal behavior and distances him from this embarrassing performance by having him discovered in the privacy of "*The King's Closet*," attended by only two courtiers. In this diminished setting, before this attenuated audience, Paulina plays out her weakened role. George Ellis, stage manager for Kean (see no. 10), thinks that "J. Kemble makes what follows [1338] take place in a front scene, probably for the convenience of setting a back scene for the next" scene on the seacoast of Bohemia. J. W. Cole, who marked Kean's promptbook and often commented on Kemble's staging, crosses out Ellis's note.

4.1 Time

Bell admits the necessity of the chorus for transmitting essential information but "cannot much compliment Time on his speech here," preferring instead the lines with which Hull replaces "If . . . may" (1609–11):

> And grant to Time your free indulgence now;
> Time, who doth *all* for you; on whom depend
> Your hopes and fears, your chiefest foe or friend
> As he is us'd; if well, he on his wings,
> Delicious transport to the lover brings,
> Comforts the mourner, sets the captive free,
> And to the Bard gives immortality.
> Think well on this; grant then what Time requires,
> So may Time grant each honest heart's desire.

Kean (no. 11) alters Sh.'s simple SD: "*Enter Time, the Chorus*" (1579) becomes "the gem of the spectacle . . . for which MR. KEAN is in no way indebted to SHAKSPEARE," according to a caustic review in *Punch* (10 May 1856). The acting ed. describes what theatergoers saw: "A classical allegory representing the course of time. Luna in her car, accompanied by the stars (personified), sinking before the approach of Phoebus. Chronos as time, surmounting the globe, describes the events of the sixteen years supposed to have elapsed. Ascent of Phoebus in the Chariot of the Sun." Kean provides the model for the extravagant staging in Burton's production of 1857 (as recorded in French) and in Calvert's of 1869.

4.2 Polixenes's Intervention

A significant reordering of material occurs in Payne (no. 21) with the transposing of 4.2 (1612–66) and 4.3 (1667–1794). The scene with Autolycus separates the exchange at Court, in which Polixenes orders Camillo to accompany him to the Shepherd's cottage to spy on Florizel, and the sheepshearing, at which Polixenes confronts his son. Payne (no. 21) eliminates the separation of Polixenes's scenes, though the dialogue between Florizel and Perdita is kept intact to provide the time for Camillo and Polixenes to enter at 1863 in disguises simple enough to be eliminated in one grand gesture at 2260 (in most versions). Kemble, Kean, Woolfe, and Eyre alter Camillo's statement (1617) about the years of his exile: Kemble, Kean, and Eyre change fifteen to sixteen, Woolfe changes to eighteen. These changes, of course, affect Perdita's age (see n. 1617).

4.4 The Sheepshearing

Garrick inserts a song for Perdita after 1974. Kemble adopts stanzas I, IV, and V, inserting them after 1878. A stage direction in Kemble (no. 5) indicates a song, probably the same one, since succeeding versions also show this Garrick interpolation. Phelps notes that *"This* [song] *is sometimes omitted"*: Macready, Burton, and French do, in fact, omit it; Phelps does not. The song is especially appropriate to a submissive Perdita:

I

Come, come, my good shepherds, our flocks we must shear;
In your holy-day suits, with your lasses appear:
The happiest of folk, are the guiltless and free,
And who are so guiltless, so happy as we?

II

We harbour no passions, by luxury taught;
We practice no arts, with hypocrisy fraught;
What we think in our hearts, you may read in our eyes;
For the roses will bloom, when there's peace in the breast.

III

By mode and caprice are the city dames led,
But we, as the children of nature are bred.
By her hand alone, we are painted and dress'd;
For the roses will bloom, when there's peace in the breast.

IV

That giant, ambition, we never can dread;
Our roofs are too low, for so lofty a head;
Content and sweet chearfulness open our door,
They smile with the simple, and feed with the poor.

V

When love has possess'd us, that love we reveal;
Like the flocks that we feed, are the passions we feel;
So harmless and simple we sport, and we play,
And leave to fine folks to deceive and betray.

A few directors rearrange lines in this scene quite freely, satisfying perceptions of the play that might not be apparent to an audience. Kemble switches 1980–1 ("Good . . . Creame.") to follow Perdita's interpolated song (1878); French lacks the song but moves the line. Burton restores it to F position, as he does Kemble's insertion of "Is . . . maids" (2066) and "Is . . . whispring" (2068–71) at the start of the Clown's speech at 1986. French, however, reads with Kemble. Payne (no. 21) follows Kemble's move of 2013–15 ("I. . . . lamentably") to follow "singing" at 2037. Though the bawdry of "Lawne as white" (2043–55) is uncertain, the possibility of it may contribute to Kemble's replacing this song with "Will you buy" (2139–44), which he then closes with 2072–3, "Come . . . gloues." French substitutes 2072–3 for 2056–60. Kemble earlier follows Garrick in changing "Maiden-heads growing" (1930) to "honours growing"; French retains the F reading; Bell makes it "blushes glowing" and changes "Lusts" (at 1835) to "wishes." Kean puts 1971–4 ("But . . . 'em.") after "The Queene of Curds and Creame" (1981) and replaces the whole of "Will you buy" (2139–44) with the two-line refrain (2054–5) of "Lawne as white," indicating repetition as necessary to cover Autolycus's exit. Payne (no. 21) transposes the Clown's "folow me girles" (2137–8) and Autolycus's "And you shall pay well for 'em" (2138); Wood puts 2136–7 ("Wenches . . . both") after "girles" (2138).

Like Kean, Nunn moves 1971–4, but in this case to follow 2163; he then puts 2161–3 (the Shepherd telling a servant to let the twelve dancing "satyrs" enter) after 2152, the last line of the servant's description of the dance and dancers, though he also moves 2145–52 (in which he inexplicably makes all instances of "they" and "them" into "we") to follow 1981 ("The Queene of Curds and Creame"). He puts the SD of 1988–9 after "'em" (1974); puts "He . . . best" (1995–2000), lines from one of the Shepherd's speeches, into his next speech instead (following "silent," 2003); reduces 2006–11 ("if . . . Tunes") to one line ("There's a pedlar at the gate"); and rearranges Polixenes's threatening speech, moving 2270–6 ("For . . . Court") to follow 2285. After all the rearranging in which Nunn indulges, his resulting text is not an obvious improvement over F, and no succeeding version, including that of his collaborator Barton, adopts these changes.

4.4 The Elopement Plot

When it is not cut, the "clothing crux" (2496–2552; see n. 2511–12) is attacked through alterations, substitutions, and additions. Bell offers a complicated solution that no one else adopts, first changing Camillo's exclamation on seeing Autolycus (2503–4) from "Wee'le . . . aide" to "How chance oft hits the mark, when wisdom fails! | Now, my best lord, if you dare trust your course, | Intirely to my skill—." Camillo has in mind the exchange of the Prince's garments "for the out-side of [Autolycus's] pouertie" (2511), an exchange that presumably helps Florizel look even less like a prince than he already does; but if he is "obscur'd With a Swaines wearing" (1806–7), the exchange does not meet the other necessity—that Florizel's clothes make Autolycus look like a courtier to the Shepherd and Clown (and not stretch credulity by appearing in clothing recognizable as Florizel's). To make the exchange logical, Bell earlier (2312) has Florizel reveal rich clothes under his shepherd's vest, then alters F's "dis-case . . . boot" (2512–15) to read "retire with us to the next covert, change garments with this gentleman, (thou must think there's necessity in it) and tho' the bargain on his side be worst, yet thou shalt have gold to boot." Finally, to emphasize the action and take Perdita into account, Bell substitutes the following for F's 2521–43:

Cam.	There's earnest to prove it. [Gives him a purse.]
	The business dispatched, thou shalt have as much more.
Flor.	I partly guess your drift.
Cam.	You must exchange
	Your costly garment for this rustic's rag.
	You, my sweet lady, take your lover's hat,
	And shepherd's habit, so shall we deceive
	Each prying eye, till we are safe aboard.
Perd.	Alack the shame on't, that a lowly maid
	Should to such peril and unworthy shifts,
	Reduce your greatness!
Flor.	Sweetest Perdita,
	Fear not, but list my words.

Kemble, as we have seen, cuts the clothing exchange but explains Autolycus's costume by substituting for "to . . . extempore" (2553–60)

Well, I am transform'd courtier again—four silken gamesters, who attended the king, and were revelling by themselves, at some distance from the shepherds, have drank so plentifully, that their weak brains are turn'd topsy-turvy—I found one of 'em, retir'd from the rest, sobering himself with sleep under the shade of a hawthorn; I made profit of occasion, and exchang'd garments with him. The pedler's clothes are on his back, and the pack by his side, as empty as his pockets,

and following with most of the rest of his speech (2473–7, 2481–6, 2488–95) as well as 2567–9 from a later speech. Kean, Calvert, Anderson, Ames, Granville-Barker, and Payne (no. 21) deal with the problem by leaving intact Sh.'s "change Garments | with this Gentleman" (2513–14) but directing an exchange of cloaks between Florizel and Autolycus. At 2535–6 Barton has Perdita pick up Autolycus's coat, hat, and fake beard (not mentioned in F until 2596–7), presumably for Florizel to wear. Quayle, Eyre, and Hands also transpose a few phrases and lines but do not create significant changes.

5.2 The Fulfillment of the Oracle

As several critics note, the first reunion (3010 ff.) can be played without Autolycus; Kemble, Kean, and Calvert reassign his lines to various courtiers and have him enter later. Quayle and Barton, by contrast, increase Autolycus's importance by letting him take credit for bringing the Shepherd and Clown to Florizel's ship—not in soliloquy but before the courtiers leave the stage (in Quayle, 3121–30 precedes Autolycus's first line [3010]; in Barton, 3121–8 follows the second [3011]). Payne (no. 21), who names the two gentlemen Cleomenes and Dion, also draws attention to Autolycus at 3035 by directing that Dion "anticipates [Autolycus's] grab for Cleomenes' pocket."

Kemble follows Garrick as the latter creates, with additions and alterations, the Clown's idea that gentlemanly behavior must be corrupt. After the newly made "gentleman" says to Autolycus, "Giue me thy hand" (3164), he complains of finding it empty: "Hast nothing in it?—Am I not a courtier? | —I must be gently consider'd." Autolycus's earlier lines—"Seest thou not the ayre of the Court, in these enfoldings? Hath not my gate in it, the measure of the Court?" (2612-14)—are then inserted into the Clown's speech, while Autolycus replies with the Shepherd's line from 2688, "Here is what gold I have, sir."

Sh. allows the Clown and Shepherd a small triumph over Autolycus that Garrick and Kemble do not, for after the last line of the scene (3182), they let Autolycus exult: "O, sweet sir!; I have brib'd him with his own money." Barton also lets Autolycus best the Clown and Shepherd, adding SDs in which Autolycus steals their purses (3166), takes chains from their pockets (3178), pilfers their handkerchiefs (3180), and removes additional "chains off their backs" (3181).

5.3 The Statue

Only in this scene do additions and alterations change the text as much as cutting does, though not necessarily for the better. Garrick alters 3236-41 ("Lady . . . dry") as follows:

> *Flor.*   Rise not yet;
> I join me in the same religious duty;
> Bow to the shadow of that royal dame,
> Who, dying, gave my *Perdita* to life,
> And plead an equal right to blessing.
>
> *Leon.*   O, Master-piece of art! nature's deceiv'd
> By thy perfection, and at every look
> My penitence is all afloat again.

Kemble, aware of the popularity of Garrick's adaptation, uses Leontes's lines in place of 3236-46 (in which Perdita, Paulina, and Camillo all speak). Burton marks these lines but does not indicate a cut; French reads with Kemble.

At 3258-9, Leontes says, "Let be, let be: | Would I were dead, but that me thinkes alreadie." Perhaps for clarity, Kean (no. 11) adds to the line, "I am but dead, stone looking upon stone" (noting that "this line is introduced from [J.P.] Collier's emendations").

F is quite restrained as the statue "comes to life" (3316-23). Kemble offers this modified but still effusive variation of Garrick's alterations and additions:

> *Leon.* Support me, Heaven!—
> If this be more than visionary bliss,
> My reason cannot hold.—My queen? my wife?—

But speak to me, and turn me wild with transport. —
I cannot hold me longer from those arms.
She is warm, — she lives!
   Per. O Florizel!
   Leon. Her beating heart meets mine, and fluttering owns
Its long-lost half: these tears that choke her voice
Are hot and moist, — it is *Hermione*!

Macready and Phelps cut the interpolation and restore the original reading; Burton marks the interpolation for possible cutting. French follows Kemble's version except for Perdita's interjection.

Following Paulina's line, "Our *Perdita* is found" (3332), Kemble adopts Garrick's addition:

And with her found
A princely husband whose instinct of royalty
From under the low thatch
Where she was bred,
Took his untutor'd queen.

Macready and Phelps cut it from their texts; Burton marks it for cutting; French does not print it. Consistency allows Garrick's alteration of "my daughters head" (3335) to "their princely heads," a change that Kemble adopts but Macready and French reject.

Sh. "makes the reunion of Leontes and Hermione wordless. In that scene he shows his awareness, as a dramatist, of realities which language cannot get at, not even the subtle tool of his own poetry" (EWBANK, 1971, p. 104). Hermione's words (3333–40) are directed solely to her daughter. Garrick is the first to shift the emphasis of the reunion to Hermione and Leontes (with more matter but surely less art). Kemble follows with a modified version:

Leon.   Hark, hark! she speaks —
      O, pipe, through sixteen winters dumb! then deem'd
      Harsh as the raven's throat; now musical
      As nature's song, tun'd to the according spheres!
Herm.   My lord, my king, — there's distance in those names, —
      My husband! —
Leon.   O, my *Hermione*! have I deserv'd
      That tender name? Be witness, holy powers,
      If penitence may cleanse the soul from guilt,
      Leontes' tears have wash'd his crimes away.
      If thanks unfeign'd be all that you require
      Most bounteous gods, for happiness like mine,
      Read in my heart, your mercy's not in vain.
Herm.   No more my best lov'd lord; be all that's past
      Buried in this enfolding, and forgiven.
Leon.   Thou matchless saint! — Thou paragon of virtue!

Perd.	Thus let me bow, and kiss that honour'd hand.
Herm.	Thou, Perdita, my long-lost child, that fill'st
	My measure up of bliss.

Macready and Burton restore the original ending (3349-69); Phelps gets rid of the interpolation and restores most of 3359-64. French dispenses with Leontes's first and Hermione's last speech of Kemble's modification, returning to the F text with Hermione's line at 3333. Garrick's alteration for 3349, "O peace *Paulina*," becomes "No, no Paulina; | Live bless'd with blessing others. — My Polixenes!" Kemble adopts it; Macready and Burton restore F's reading; French reads as Kemble does. Bell does not cut Leontes's matchmaking but alters it away, substituting for 3350-61 ("Thou . . . Brother") the following:

> Thou must partake our bliss. Be a king's gratitude
> A holy charm to witch inquietude,
> From all thy hours to come! my royal brother,
> Join here with me, and my redeem'd *Hermione*,
> O! how those eyes reproach me! pardon, pardon.

Kemble, having cut the matchmaking, is obliged to alter 3358-9 and does so by following Garrick. F has Leontes tell Camillo to "take [Paulina] by the hand: whose worth, and honesty | Is richly noted"; Garrick turns the compliment to Camillo with, "Now pay thy duty here — thy worth, and honesty | Are richly noted." Macready and Burton, but not French, restore the F reading.

After "daughter" at 3365, Garrick keeps Perdita docile and humble with an added speech in which she acknowledges her common upbringing but promises to learn to be a princess; he follows this with cloying reassurance from Florizel. Since Kemble does not adopt all of Garrick's changes in the last act, it is easier to understand why Macready and Burton restore the original reading than it is to forgive Kemble for adapting from Garrick in the first place to produce this:

> *Per.* I am all shame,
> And ignorance itself, how to put on
> This novel garment of gentility;
> And yield a patch'd behaviour,
> That ill becomes this presence. I shall learn,
> I trust I shall, with meekness — but I feel —
> Ah, happy that I do! — a love, a heart,
> Unalter'd to my prince, my Florizel.
>   *Flor.* Be still my queen of *May*, my shepherdess;
> Rule in my heart; my wishes be thy subjects,
> And harmless as thy sheep.

Having left not a line of the original after Hermione's dialogue ends at 3340, Anderson imports the concluding couplet from *AWW* ("All yet seems well if it ends so meet, (*sic*) | The bitter past, more welcome is the sweet") to round off the abrupt ending. Anderson explains ("Preface," n.p.): this couplet offers "a more effective climax than the general conversation with which the 'Winter's Tale' comes to an end"—and a more appropriate one, since "no alien hand . . . was called in to add these closing lines," particularly if the "alien hand" is as obvious as it is execrable in Garrick, Bell, and Kemble.

In Garrick, whose revision is adopted by Kemble but restored by Macready, Leontes's simple directive to Paulina—"Hastily lead away" (3369)—becomes

> —then thank the righteous gods,
> Who, after tossing in a frightful storm
> Guide us to port, and chearful beams display,
> To gild the happy evening of our day.

Bell substitutes for Leontes's brisk and practical concluding lines (3363–9) these obvious utterances:

> *Leo.*   . . . join with us to bless
> These comforts of our age.
> *Pol.*   Deign, gracious heaven,
> To ratify this benediction, given
> By our imperial breath.
> *Leo.*   Stand forth, *Hermione*,
> A shining proof that innocence can bear
> Affliction's sharpest tortures, unimpair'd;
> And from the trial to the wond'ring sight,
> Come forth more pure, more amiably bright.

The Winter's Tale, in its original form, was for years ignored as a theatrical vehicle, but FREY (*Vast Romance*, 1980, p. 166) fairly observes that now, "when we examine the stage and critical histories of *The Winter's Tale*, we see, no doubt, some of the same or similar errors, misconceptions, and stock responses propagating themselves afresh in each age."

In fact, the "errors and misconceptions" of the Morgan and Garrick adaptations, as summarized by DASH (1980, p. 274), describe equally well the "restored" versions of Hull, Kemble, and the other actor-managers who modeled their productions on Kemble's for some fifty years: they "cut out Leontes' passion-wracked passages, his intense spurts of jealousy, and his arrogance. Since characters in drama are defined by their interaction with other characters, the omission of the early scenes affected not only the portrait of Leontes but also those of Hermione and Paulina. . . . Hermione's strength becomes unnecessary if there is no challenge, no contest, for her to face. And Paulina's role as the voice of conscience also loses its meaning. By revising, excising, and emending . . . Garrick [and many subsequent stage versions] substituted weak women for strong, and strong men for weak."

Indeed, the play's resurrection onstage, like Hermione's in the statue scene, has not been achieved without some effort, as the preceding examination shows. "We also see, however, an advancing interest in the wholeness of the play. We may now be coming closer to a respect for the entire artifact. After two centuries of redactions, the full text [of *WT*] flourishes upon our stage" (FREY, *Vast Romance*, 1980, p. 166)— or on most of our stages most of the time. At the very least it seems that the sometimes startling revisions and reshapings that characterize 18th- and 19th-century versions have given way to a circumspect admiration for the Shakespearean text, which still accommodates a wide—if no longer infinite—variety of interpretations.

Music in The Winter's Tale

By Sh.'s time songs and dances in both their popular and their sophisticated guises had become virtually indispensable complements of the spoken drama. Inheritors of many of the artistic traditions of the morality plays and interludes of preceding centuries, the dramatists of the Renaissance inevitably made use of incidental music, and they discovered that songs and even dances could heighten and sometimes transform dramatic situations.

MOORE (1916, pp. 81, 101) notes that Sh. made highly original use of music in his plays, combining a love of odd song-words and song-music with his keen sense of dramatic structure. His stage songs were of three principal kinds: ballads, popular favorites, and dramatic songs written or adapted expressly for his plays. The first two categories indicate Sh.'s familiarity with a vast popular tradition upon which he freely drew to supplement songs of his own composition. LATHROP (1908, pp. 1-2): In Sh.'s plays "snatches and scraps of song . . . [2] are . . . like conversation. . . . A frequent form taken by a trivial contest of wit . . . is the pert application of bits of familiar songs. . . . Popular songs or improvisations to familiar tunes are employed as quips and jeers. . . . Men of vacant minds at ease troll snatches of song. . . . Evans [in *Wiv.*] covers his fear by singing. Men who are exhilarated by drinking sing. . . . Fools . . . and mad persons betray their lightheadedness by irrelevant scraps of melody." Sh. may have read Wager's *The Longer Thou Livest the More Fool Thou Art* (1569), in which Moros sings "the foot of many songs" cited in a long list of incipits (ed. Benbow, ll. 70.2-101), and Sh. could also have seen Beaumont's *The Knight of the Burning Pestle* (1607) in which Old Matthew Merrythought sings almost three dozen fragments of popular songs to give point to his dialogue. In the third category, by contrast, are the song lyrics of Sh.'s own composition, of which NOBLE (1923, p. 12) comments: "It was he who first grasped all the possibilities afforded by song for forwarding the action and who made it a vital part in his dramatic scheme." Still another category, nonvocal music in the spoken drama, is most effectively displayed at the climax of *WT*, when the revivification of Hermione takes place (3306 ff.).

INGRAM (1966, p. 244): "The second half of *The Winter's Tale* is suffused with music as the ceremonies of love and forgiveness and reconciliation are celebrated." PAFFORD (ed. 1963, p. 172): "It is the singing voice in [4.3] and the first part of [4.4] which is the chief musical element" in the play. *WT* includes six songs to be sung by the remarkable Autolycus, four as solo songs to the accompaniment of his plucked string instrument within a 475-line section of Act 4 (1669-2144). Since their exuberant lyrics contain interwoven phrases and refrains drawn largely from popular folk songs and ballads, they may have been sung to popular tunes. By contrast, Autolycus is assigned a more demanding singing part in the sixth (2118-33), which is a striking art song for three solo voices—its lyric most likely Sh.'s creation—to be sung by him in dialogue with Mopsa and Dorcas. While for KNIGHT (1947, pp. 100-1) "Autolycus is a blend of burly comedian and lyrical jester," who is also (p. 101) "a sweet, smooth-voiced rogue," for SMITH (1972, p. 109) he is "more rogue than minstrel, but his merriment is the means by which the winter part of the play is transformed into the spring part." LATHROP (1908, p. 4): "Autolycus . . . through his songs expresses the delights of irresponsible living sweetly and perfectly." Indirectly they summon up to Polixenes no less than to a theater audience several reactions to well-known variations on the subject of amorous trifling. Quoting RYLANDS (1934, p. 112) to the effect that Sh.'s "success [with songs] lies in a fusion of the natural with the artificial," PAFFORD (p. 173) notes that "in these songs there is much more of the natural than of the artificial, much more of the traditional and unaffected singing of 'tavern and field' and much less of 'delicate artifice and charming affectation' than is the case with most of Shakespeare's earlier songs." FRYE (*Perspective*, 1965, pp. 144-5), speaking of *WT*'s pastoral society: "No mysterious music is heard in this world except the ballads of Autolycus, although Autolycus complacently notes the Orpheus-like influence of his songs [quotes 2484-6]. But it is music that awakens Hermione in another area of the [*145*] natural society, the chapel of Paulina."

MELLERS (1965, pp. 136-52) regards the country dances of shepherds and shepherdesses in *WT* no less than the ceremonial courtly dances in the more sophisticated contexts of Sh.'s earlier comedies as representing "human togetherness" (p. 137) through their patterned steps and turns. They thus could be seen as providing an artistic picture of the well-ordered society whose members sustain their existences creatively and harmoniously through their social interchanges. For him (p. 152) "the song speech is the drama of the personal life; the dance music is the communal values of the public life." BRISSENDEN (1981, p. 76): "Dancing is . . . associated with harmony as it had been in the comedies but it is now also related to discord. . . . By this connection with both concord and disorder the dance contributes to the distinctive tone of the play, in which the apparently tragic is transmuted into a state that, while not always of serene and utter joy, nevertheless holds optimistic promise for the future." For Renaissance attitudes to social dancing, see HOWARD (1996, pp. 33-44).

Following the early work of GREENHILL et al. (1884), GOOCH & THATCHER (1991, 3:1908-61) describe the incidental music for *WT*, dating from the late Elizabethan and the early Jacobean periods up to the present, and list the depositories in which a number of these items can be found. There are 490 listed under five main headings, the most comprehensive entitled simply "Incidental Music." Theater directors reviewing the lists of surviving *WT* scores from the 20th c. alone will perhaps be surprised to discover that on rare occasions eminent composers have contributed settings, including Mario Castelnuovo-Tedesco (for a 1935 Vienna production), Darius Milhaud (Paris, 1950), and Aram Khachaturian (Erevan, USSR, 1956). In many instances their settings, surviving sometimes in print, sometimes only in manuscript, are available for examination and presumably for use, though whether they were copyrighted GOOCH & THATCHER do not always say. Among such recognizable names, however, are those of dozens of lesser known music devisers and arrangers whose contributions have often attained remarkable dramatic effectiveness.

The following songs and dances appear in *WT*:

1. "When Daffadils begin to peere" 1669-80 (4.3.1-12)
2. "But shall I go mourne for that" 1683-90 (4.3.15-22)
3. "Iog-on, Iog-on, the foot-path way" 1791-4 (4.3.123-6)
4. A Daunce of Shepheards and Shephearddesses 1988-9 (4.4.165)
5. "Whoop, doe mee no harme good man" 2023-5 (4.4.198-200)
6. "Lawne as white as driuen Snow" 2044-55 (4.4.218-30)
7. "Get you hence, for I must goe" 2118-33 (4.4.297-308)
8. "Will you buy any Tape?" 2139-44 (4.4.315-23)
9. "A Dance of Twelue Satyres" 2164 (4.4.342)
10. Music strikes to awaken Hermione 3306 (5.3.98)

As for the music itself, we provide transcriptions below of settings that could have been heard in Sh.'s own day. SENG (1967, pp. xi-xii) comments on the discovery since 1900 of "a surprising amount of new material. As a result, modern producers and stage directors [*xii*] can now avail themselves of reasonably authentic melodies; and rather than regarding the songs in Shakespeare's play as mere divertissements from the dramatic action, they can begin to regard them as integral parts of the plays." Of the ten songs and dances in *WT*, five (nos. 1, 2, 3, 6, and 8) are solos sung by Autolycus; one (no. 7) is the trio he shares with the girls. Five (nos. 1, 2, 3, 5, and 8) have ditties cast as quatrains whose marked anapestic movement in all but the first spells out an almost inevitable metrical complement for each in 6/4 or 6/8 time. Appended to one of these (no. 6) is the extended burden of a pedlar hawking the feminine adornments he has for sale, but for another (no. 5) only the closing climactic line of its quatrain survives ("Whoop, doe me no harme good man"), reported by the Shepherd's servant as he informs the Clown that the wide range of the prettiest love-songs which Autolycus has in his repertory includes one whose burden makes a maid to answer with this phrase to keep "some stretch-mouth'd Rascall" (2021) at bay. Fortunately the entire tune for the quatrain has survived under the title of its final line, but not with its preceding lines, which may have described an offensive assault. All five were presumably intended to be set to traditional popular broadside ballad tunes, and such tunes are here transcribed as settings to enable listeners no less than performers of today to realize how the nature of a performance of this play in the dramatist's own day could be essentially re-created in our own. (See SABOL, 1982, no. 398 n.)

Complementing these five songs are two relatively extended and sophisticated lyrics (nos. 6 and 7) also sung by Autolycus, and their surviving tunes are apparently original settings by composers of Sh.'s day. The special setting for the first of these two lyrics, demanding no little artistry from the vocalist, is preserved in the printed songs of John Wilson (1595–1677), who late in his career was the learned Doctor of Music at Oxford but who in his younger years was actively engaged in writing music for the stage and even performing it there. The second of these two—"Get you hence"—is a dialogue song, a more complicated type usually scored for two or three singers whose interchanges sometimes verge on the melodramatic. The lyric of this highly dramatic seventh was presumably written by Sh. for this play and its surviving setting probably devised by Robert Johnson, a composer of several stage songs of the period.

WARD (1957) deals with the process of compiling ballad tunes of the late 16th and early 17th centuries for the lyrics mentioned by title in *A Handefull of pleasant delites* (1584). He shows that modern eds. of Sh.'s lyrics for singing must recognize that while several Elizabethan and Jacobean ballad tunes may each at first have been a specifically composed setting for a particular poetic text, many such musical settings were subsequently used by dramatists as well as by performers seeking satisfactory musical frames for other lyrics. When Richard Jones printed the texts of "sundrie new sonets and delectable Histories" in *A Handefull*, he included no music, but the modern editor of that collection, Hyder Rollins, cites the tune that he thinks is needed for an individual lyric's presentation. All *Handefull* tunes that achieved some measure of distinction are examples of such *Gebrauchsmusik* or, as 16th-c. Italians called comparable pieces, *arie per cantar*, "airs for singing," appropriate to any poetry having the requisite meter and stanzaic form. Sh.'s lyrics are here provided with contemporaneous rather than later settings, for even those of the mid-17th c. display a considerable difference in popular music styles from those prevalent in Sh.'s lifetime.

The standard sources of the broadside ballad tunes of Sh.'s day are CHAPPELL (1859), WOOLDRIDGE (1893), and SIMPSON (1966). WARD (1967) amplifies the new material WOOLDRIDGE brought to light. To these collections may be added the facsimiles (1961) of RAVENSCROFT's *Pammelia* (1609), *Deuteromelia* (1609), and *Melismata* (1611), three collections of popular music largely for the theater. Many such familiar tunes would naturally have been in the repertory of Autolycus, who might accompany himself on a lute; although the play does not mention his doing so, the one of his seven songs most recently recovered (no. 7 below) includes a lute accompaniment for its vocal score. All six settings—excluding, of course, "Whoop, doe me no harme good man" (2023–5), a lyric outcry merely mentioned as being in his repertory—doubtless were self-accompanied. Dialogue songs also are often represented in *Melismata*. The piece sung by Autolycus conversing with Dorcas and Mopsa—"Get you hence" (2118–33)—would have prompted a complex special setting, presumably an assignment for a composer for the theater like Robert Johnson or John Wilson.

The three items of nonvocal instrumental music (nos. 4, 9, and 10) are all instrumental dances scored for treble and bassus, pieces which appear in short scores in the first two sections of British Museum Additional MS 10,444, a famous collection of dance music for the English court masque compiled late in the Jacobean period by Sir Nicholas L'Estrange. Virtually all the significant masque dances are transcribed in

SABOL (1982) from this source, together with many of their contemporaneous cognate versions from other sources. The two-part settings for treble and bassus which appear in Add. MS 10,444 are especially useful for performances requiring short score arrangements, such as the dances in *WT*.

Since the tune entitled "The Shepherds' Dance," which appears in Add. MS 10,444 as no. 118, possesses the spirited flavor of a piece that might originally have been used for the dance of the Arcadians in Jonson's *Pan's Anniversary* (1620), it has been suggested by J. P. Cutts and others as the ideal setting for "A Daunce of Shepheards and Shephearddesses" (no. 4) in *WT*. However, a more suitable choice may be the piece entitled "The Maypole" (no. 123), the treble on fol. 37ᵛ and the bassus on fol. 86ᵛ, since, after an extended opening episode featuring an entire group of dancers, its contrasting and constantly shifting strains from duple to triple rhythm and back again more fittingly underscore the contrasting pairs of dancers—a May Lord and a May Lady, a country clown and a country wench, and, leading them, a host and a hostess—and even solo figures are given an opportunity to display aspects of their particular callings. WARD (1986), discussing the widespread use in the contemporary drama of "the national dance of England," the morris, shows a family of musical variants branching from a common "morris tune." "One such branch, possibly the first to establish its independence, is 'Staines Morris'" (p. 303); "The Maypole" belongs to another. To "The Maypole" here are added two short pieces both entitled "Staynes Morris," the first in William Ballet's Lute Book from Trinity College, Dublin (MS D.1.21/1), and the second from PLAYFORD (1651, p. 87). Each of these two, after an opening company dance, may be used for short, separate dances of individual duos. "The Maypole" was originally used for the second antimasque of Francis Beaumont's *Masque of the Inner Temple and Gray's Inn* and then possibly for the dance in the outdoor scene of *The Two Noble Kinsmen* (3.3), each of which features a dramatic episode providing a description of a group of company dancers followed by a series of pairs of participants who essentially serve as counterparts to the various pairs subsequently seen in action in *WT* 4.4. And likewise, no. 150 in Add. MS 10,444, entitled simply "A Masque," also presents musical characteristics especially effective for underscoring the awakening of Hermione in 5.3.

For two of these three nonvocal compositions, suitable settings are available in four and five parts for a company of instruments, chiefly strings. The expense accounts from the Pell Order Book (as recorded in C. H. Herford and P. E. Simpson, eds., *Ben Jonson*, 10:521) for the "Satyrs' Dance" and related music pieces first used in *Oberon* attribute its two-part setting to Robert Johnson and its four-part setting to Thomas Lupo (see SABOL, 1982, nos. 107, 249). The two-part setting for treble and bassus, from British Library Add. MS. 10,444, is included here. While the surviving contemporary five-part setting for "The Maypole" appearing in Wilhelm Brade's *Newe Ausserlesene liebliche Branden* (1617) and not included here expands the simple treble and bassus parts of Add. MS 10,444, it does so needlessly, since the morris dance was often performed outdoors to music traditionally provided simply by a piper and a taborer, and this accompaniment was ordinarily embellished by the tiny bells attached to the costumes as well as to the limbs of the dancers. These jingling bells were frequently tuned to harmonize with each other. Since the third of the items included here from Add. MS 10,444 — the short piece entitled simply "A Masque" to accompany the awakening of Hermione in 5.3 — consists solely of a version for treble and bassus, two additional inner parts have been editorially provided here in the event that for this quieter indoor setting a string quartet could be used to provide a contrast to the music of the preceding outdoor scenes. The whole of the two sections of Add. MS 10,444, consisting of Jacobean masque and antimasque dances, has been transcribed and edited in SABOL (1982).

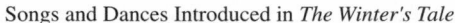

Songs and Dances Introduced in *The Winter's Tale*

1. "When Daffadils begin to peere"
1669-80 (4.3.1-12)

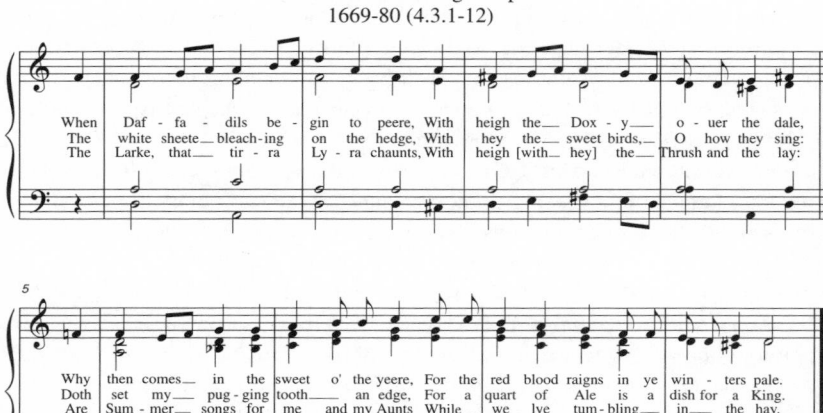

F1 has three stanzas of four lines each, all tetrameter: 4/4/4/4.

Music: RITSON (1813, 3:281-3) gives a tune not printed before and "not obtained without some difficulty." A setting composed by William Boyce around 1759 is reprinted in CAULFIELD (1864?, 2:49). LONG (1961, p. 72) sets the words to "Row well, ye mariners" from Thomas Robinson's *Schoole of Musicke* (1603), which is reprinted in WOOLDRIDGE (1893, 1:127). Considerably smoother than the tune from Robinson is a closely related item entitled "Lusty Gallant," which is reproduced in SIMPSON (1966, pp. 476-8). SIMPSON's presentation is based on sources cited in CHAPPELL (1859, pp. 476-8) and in WOOLDRIDGE (1893, 1:234-6). The latter also cites William Ballet's Lute Book (Trinity College Dublin, MS 408\2) as one of the earliest sources of the tune and notes its use in Nicholas Breton's *The Workes of a Young Wyt* (1577) and in Thomas Nashe's *The Terrors of the Night* (1594). In Thomas Proctor's *A Gorgious Gallery of Gallant Inventions* (1578, sig. D1ᵛ), there is a "propper Dittie" that is also to be sung "to the tune of lusty Gallant." WARD (1968, p. 22) provides a photofacsimile of p. 83 of the second part of Ballet's Lute Book, an early lute setting of "Lusty Gallant," which has been transcribed for keyboard as the first of the items

856

comprising the surviving settings of Autolycus's lyrics. WARD (1967, p. 58) cites additional sources for "Lusty Gallant," including the cantus part of Thomas Ravenscroft's "Round of three Country dances in one" appearing in *Pammelia* (1609, no. 74), whose lyric text begins thus: "Now foote it as I do, Tomboy Tom." VLASTO (1954, p. 234, ex. 13) finds a second source for this round in the library of King's College, Cambridge, MS KC 1.

2. "But shall I go mourne for that"
1683-90 (4.3.15-22)

The original lyric contains 8 lines of alternating tetrameter and trimeter: 4/3/4/3/4/ 3/4/3 (the trimeter lines are indented). GREENHILL et al. (1884, p. 75) record a setting by J. Lampe in 1748, and there is an anon. setting in CAULFIELD (1864?, 2:52). LONG (1961, p. 73) has set the words to a tune entitled "The Noble Shirve" in WOOLDRIDGE (1893, 1:126). A period setting of a ballad tune that aptly accommodates this lyric text is reproduced in SIMPSON (1966, no. 516), "Who List to Lead a Soldier's Life" (see pp. 773– 50). This setting is reproduced here, even though the sources of the tune date largely from the mid-17th c., including every ed. of PLAYFORD from 1651 to c. 1728 and several keyboard settings of that period.

As CHAPPELL (1859, p. 227) observes, "Soldier's Life" is but another version of "Tomorrow is St. Valentine's Day," "one of Ophelia's songs in *Hamlet*." WOOLDRIDGE (1893, 1:303–4) transcribes the version from PLAYFORD (1651) but notes that several ballads dating from the late 16th c. are directed to be sung to this tune, which indeed may have been a different tune from that first used but perhaps still satisfies the metrical pattern of Sh.'s lyric.

3. "Iog-on, Iog-on, the foot-path way"
1791-4 (4.3.123-6)

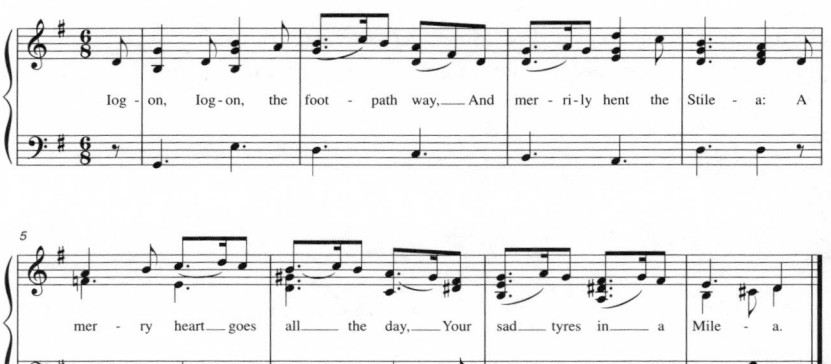

The original tune is preserved in a number of early settings. The lyric, not of Sh.'s composition, under the title "Hanskin," appears in MAITLAND & SQUIRE (1899; 1979, 2:494-500) in a set of variations by Richard Farnaby (c. 1590?). Under the title "Jog on" it appears in every ed. of PLAYFORD from 1651 to 1698. The tune reappears— this time as a song with three stanzas—in *An Antidote Against Melancholy: Made up in Pills* (1661, sigs. L1 - 1ᵛ) and in PLAYFORD's *Catch that Catch Can or The Musical Companion* (1667, sig. M3) in an arrangement by John Hilton for three voices. There are many popular copies of the tune: CHAPPELL (1859, p. 212), ELSON (1901, p. 248), and GIBBON (1930, p. 104), as well as NAYLOR (1931, p. 185), PAFFORD (1959, p. 173), and KINES (1964, p. 27). HARDY (1930, p. 77) gives both the MAITLAND & SQUIRE and the PLAYFORD versions. LONG (1961, p. 74) reprints the Hilton setting as if the three parts were a single melody. The occasional attachment of the names Farnaby or Hilton does not mean that either was the composer. Verses 2 and 3—in *An Antidote* and *Catch that Catch Can*—were not necessarily composed at the same time as verse 1. The Hilton arrangement appears in ORGEL (ed. 1996, p. 277).

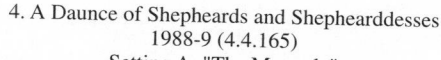

4. A Daunce of Shepheards and Shephearddesses
1988-9 (4.4.165)
Setting A: "The Maypole"

Setting B: "Staynes Morris"
Version 1

Version 2

Music: Because a dance in Jonson's masque *Oberon* may reappear in *WT* (see p. 608), the manuscript in which it is found, Add. MS 10,444, could well be the repository of other contemporary theatrical pieces. Hence, "The Maypole" is transcribed here from it, in treble and bassus parts only, found respectively on fol. 35ᵛ and fol. 85ᵛ. In SABOL (1982), it appears anonymously as item 123. As CUTTS (1954, p. 197) points out, the music may have been used as well for the dance of shepherd boys in Jonson's *Pan's Anniversary* (1620). A five-part version from Wilhelm Brade's *Newes Ausserlesene liebliche Branden* (1617) may be found in SABOL (1982) as item 272. BARTHOLOMEUSZ (1982, p. 15), noting that the Shepherd's Servant remarks to his master that "if you did but heare the Pedler at the doore, you would neuer dance againe after a Tabor and Pipe: no, the Bag-pipe could not moue you" (2006–8), points out that these instruments were used to accompany the morris dance, which was traditionally performed on Whitsunday (see *H5* 2.4.25 [913]). The present festivities are Whitson-Pastorals (1949). Thus two versions of "Staynes Morris" are also included here.

5. "Whoop, doe mee no harme good man"
2023-5 (4.4.198-200)

PAFFORD (ed. 1963, pp. 101-2): "Although no more words of this song have been found, there is a contemporary tune with the name — with 'goodman' as one word — by William Corkine in *Ayres, to Sing and Play to the Lute and Basse Viol*, 1610, fo. 11b. (Because no words are given this is not included in the reprint by E. H. Fellowes [in *The English School of Lutenist Song Writers*. 2nd ser. 1926?].) This version gives the tune with variations. [WOOLDRIDGE (1893, 1:96-7) reproduces the tune alone from Corkine's *Ayres* (1610), and CHAPPELL (pp. 208 and 774) also reproduces and comments on it.] The tune may have been used for a ballad called *Jockey and Jenny*, entered in *Stationers' Register*, 9 Dec. 1615 (iii. 579) (see Rollins, *Analytical Index to the Ballad-Entries*, 1924, p. 112, item 1291), [*102*] which presumably reappears as *Johnny and Jinny* in *Westminster Drollery*, 1672." CHAPPELL (1859, p. 208): "A song with this burden will be found in Fry's *Ancient Poetry*, but it would not be desirable for republication." See n. 2023-4, however, and SABOL (1982, no. 398 n.).

6. "Lawne as white as driuen Snow"
2044-55 (4.4.218-30)

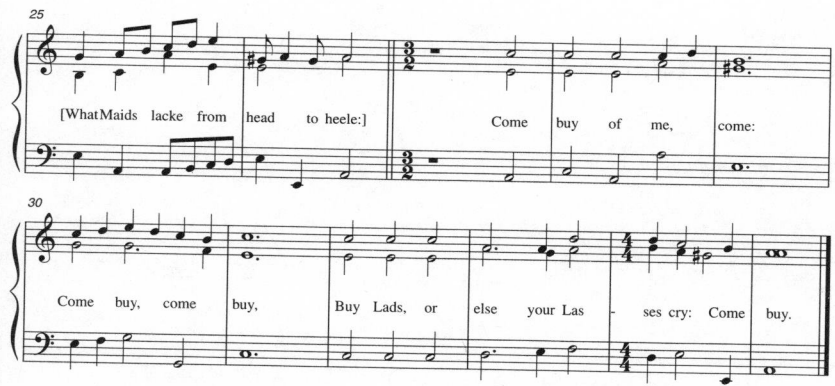

The earliest known setting, for three voices, appears in John Wilson's *Cheerfull Ayres or Ballads* (1660, sigs. L4ᵛ-K1ᵛ). The transcript given here of "Lawne as white" joins together in a compact setting its three voice parts — the Cantus Primus and Secundus with the Bassus supported by a bass viol part. It is set a minor third below that of Wilson's lyric text on the assumption that the melody in middle voice range would best suit most actors assigned the Autolycus role. A lute accompaniment may easily be devised from the three voice parts. Facsimiles of the Cantus Primus appear in FURNESS (ed. 1898, pp. 388-9) and in LONG (1961, pp. 142-3). Reprints of the song or tune are given by VINCENT (1906, pp. 30-1), HARDY (1930, pp. 78-9), GIBBON (1930, p. 121), PAFFORD (1959, p. 174), CUTTS (1959, pp. 128-30), LONG (1961, p. 80), and KINES (1964, pp. 29-31). SENG (1967, p. 240) notes that Wilson's version can hardly have been the original music setting since he was only 15 years old at the time of the song's first performance. NOSWORTHY (1958, p. 65) and CUTTS (1959, p. 129) conjecture that Wilson was merely providing his arrangement of the original tune by an earlier composer. A transcript by Michelle Dulak appears in ORGEL (ed. 1996, pp. 278-9).

7. "Get you hence, for I must goe"
2118-33 (4.4.297-308)

Version 1: a) Lyric text: Folio 1 (1623)
  b) Lyric text and music: Drexel MS 4175, lix

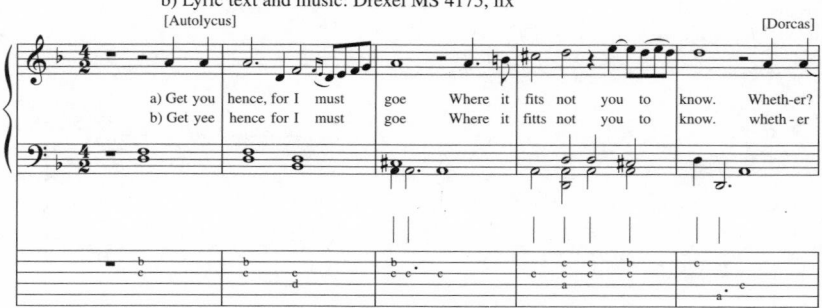

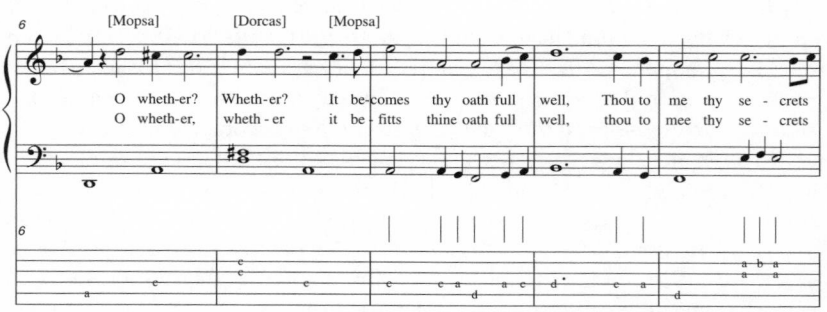

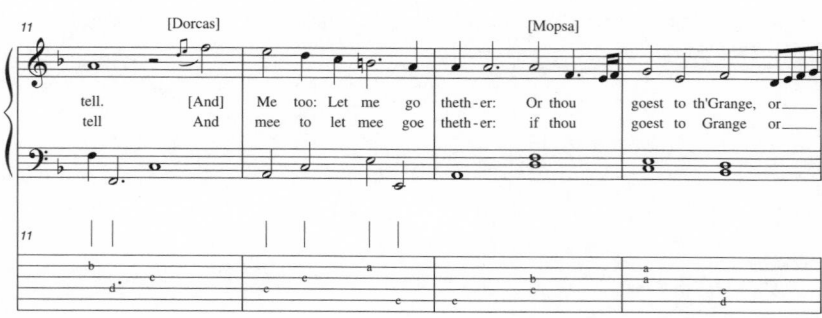

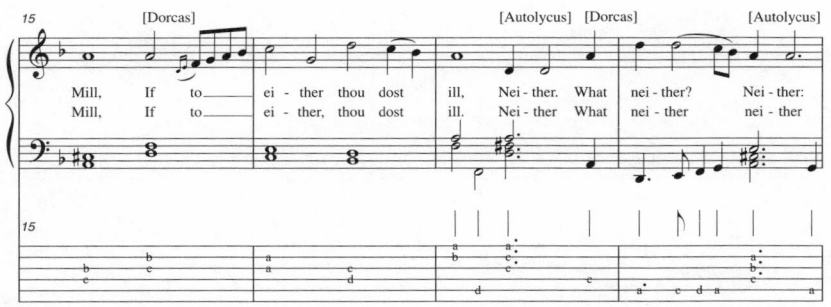

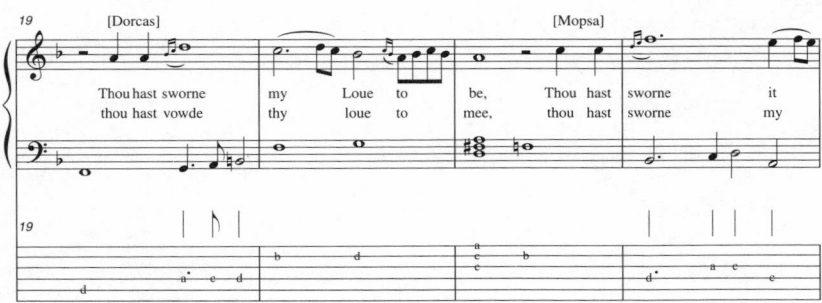

In this dialogue song, which is set to a tune in the play called "Two Maids Wooing a Man" (2110-11), the complexity of scoring has required a setting for alternating voices in rapid interchange far more demanding in ingenuity than that provided by the usual workaday ballad tune. What clearly seems to be the original music, composed probably by Robert Johnson, was discovered by J. P. CUTTS in the New York Public Library MS Drexel 4175, a mid-17th c. MS designated as "Anne Twice Her Booke." Robert Johnson's association with the King's Men is well established, and the two dances listed below as Nos. 9a and 9b, both of which were introduced in *Oberon*, appear to be his work. Words and music for this song are found in CUTTS ("Setting," 1956, and 1959, pp. 17-18). There is a fragmentary version of the same song for three voices in Drexel MS 4041 (fols. 127-9); this second version is also in CUTTS (1959, p. 19). SENG (1967, p. 244)), noting at least six errors in CUTTS's transcripts, points to a more reliable edition by SPINK (1961, pp. 62-3), reprinted in ORGEL (ed. 1996, pp. 279-81), and an edition by LONG (1961, pp. 82-3), who also provides a facsimile of the Drexel 4175 version. The fragmentary version of Drexel 4041 includes a second stanza that may have been part of Autolycus's original song. Autolycus implies that his rendition is incomplete, for he later says: "Wee'l haue this song out anon by our selues" (2134).

JORGENS (1987, vols. 9, 10) reproduces in facsimile the two early 17th-c. settings of this song. Drexel 4175, item lix, is set in D minor with lute accompaniment scored for three alternating voices in successive bass and treble clefs over an unfigured bass enclosing a text of one stanza. In its present transcript, Version 1, the lyric text from Drexel 4175 appears under the lyric from F1. Drexel 4175 reads *vow'de* and *sworne* in 2131 and 2132 where F1 reads *sworne* in both. Drexel 4041, here transcribed as Version 2, is set in C minor, and the twelve tetrameter lines in each of two stanzas are given completely, the second verse following at the close of the first. The last line in each verse, intended to be sung as a part song by the trio, is appropriately spaced, the text for the unlabeled Treble 1 (for Mopsa) being placed over that of similarly unlabeled Treble 2 (for Dorcas), and both over the lyric text for the bass vocalist. For some reason the copyist extends his musical notation only to the middle of measure 17 of the 26 measures comprising the whole dialogue, and the words of the lyric alone continue for the last four lines of the twelve. The placement of the words of the final line of the lyric for each voice part—those for Voices 2 and 3 being immediately beneath those for Voice 1—makes it clear that the original consisted of a duo for Verse 1 and a trio of voices in the last line of Verse 2. Suitable musical notation for the last 10 measures is here supplied editorially, in brackets; it is derived from Version 1 with appropriate adjustment of key and time values. Virtually all dialogue songs conclude with a duo if not a trio, and for the inner voice in the closing measures a suitable part has been supplied here.

8. "Will you buy any Tape?"
2139-44 (4.4.315-23)

The original tune for Autolycus's final song has come to light in relatively recent times. The earliest setting given by GREENHILL et al. (1884, p. 75) seems to be one by William Boyce (1710-79), composed about 1769 and reprinted in LINLEY (1816, 1:29). There is an anonymous setting in CAULFIELD (1864?, 2:58-9) that might conceivably be one of the traditional stage versions which CAULFIELD says he is collecting. If so, his setting may be even earlier than the one by Boyce, but CAULFIELD is not, as SENG (1967, p. xi) points out, a reliable editor. LONG (1961, p. 85) has set the song to a contemporary tune, "Sellenger's Round" (see WOOLDRIDGE, 1893, 1:256-8).

To these popular tunes may be added from Thomas Ravenscroft's *Pammelia* (1609) the setting for item 74, whose general title, "A Round of three Country dances in one," indicates that the whole consists of three dances joined with a Basse or Ground, which can serve each of the three. The Cantus, the Medius, and the Tenor may be performed individually with the Basse or Ground, or presumably together as a piece for "4 *Voc.*" Each of the three has an individual text. That of the Medius part, which has been named "The Cramp," has long been identified and discussed by the principal editors of popular ballad and dance tunes: see CHAPPELL (1859, p. 89), WOOLDRIDGE (1893, 1:143-4), and SIMPSON (1966, pp. 138-9). The sentiments of its lyric text, beginning "[The] crampe is in my purse full sore," are very much like those of Autolycus as he sings of money as "a medler" (2143), and the jaunty tune in 6/4 time serves as a fitting vehicle to express his views. For fuller details see also WARD (1967, p. 35), and for another early appearance Wilhelm Brade, *Newe Ausserlesene liebliche Branden* (Hamburg, 1617). The setting of the *Pammelia* no. 74 Medius part here follows CHAPPELL.

9. A Dance of Twelue Satyres
2164 (4.4.342)

(a) The setting, for treble and bassus, is from British Library Add. MS 10,444, where it is entitled "The Satyrs' Masque" and attributed to Robert Johnson. The present version is reproduced from SABOL (1982, no. 118); ORGEL (ed. 1996, pp. 282–3) reprints it from SABOL (1978, no. 107, pp. 209–10).

(b) A second setting, also entitled "The Satyrs' Masque," for consort in four parts—cantus, altus, tenor, and bassus, with bassus generalis—appears in Thomas Simpson's *Taffel-Consort* (Hamburg, 1621) as item 24, attributed to Robert Johnson. It is transcribed in SABOL (1982) as no. 249. As indicated in n. 2164, BRISSENDEN (1981, p. 92) believes that the appearance here of satyrs, who were identified with disorder and sexual licence, together with (p. 94) "the trickery of Autolycus and the bawdry of the two girls," motivates Polixenes to turn on Florizel and Perdita with "emotional wildness." Autolycus's efforts to sell his wares are hardly trickery, however, and "bawdry" is not the word for the girls' contention over the Clown, which has already been decided in favor of Mopsa. The love triangle is given light-hearted musical expression in the trio sung by Autolycus and the two girls (2118–33), which is followed by Autolycus's exit song, "Will you buy any Tape?" (2139–44). The satyr dance seems unrelated except as another expression of rustic high spirits.

It is also held (see n. 2146) that the music was composed by Robert Johnson for Ben Jonson's masque of *Oberon*, performed at Whitehall on 1 January 1611 as part of the celebration of Prince Henry's investiture as Prince of Wales. Since one "three" of the twelve participants in "The Satyrs' Dance" "hath danc'd before the king" (2159), it is thought they did so as dancers in *Oberon*. These men not only may have trained the footwork of their new fellow dancers but also may have seen to it that Robert Johnson's music was used. The recreation of an episode of a royal theatrical show would no doubt have proved a rare delight for a popular audience, but some critics are skeptical. BULLOUGH (1975, 8:115), for example: "Perhaps some of Jonson's dancers were King's Men, and repeated their antics in Shakespeare's play. There is no proof that Robert Johnson's music for *Oberon* was used again in *The Winter's Tale*."

10. Music strikes to awaken Hermione
3306 (5.3.98)

SANDERS (1987, p. 122): "At this point of exquisite equipoise, he [Sh.] summons his last resource, the metamorphic miracle-worker, music—coactive with what's unreal, it's true, but not in the nightmare fashion of jealous delusion. Only music can make real the unreal in a way that reintegrates it with the creative continuum, awakening, uniting, redeeming. It will be slow, halting, painful—this musical summoning of the numbed soul out of the great frost of matter—but it is the miracle of miracles." The anonymous setting entitled "A Masque" for treble and bassus appears in two voices in British Library Add. MS 10,444, the treble on fol. 43ᵛ and the bassus on fol. 93ʳ. A modern transcript of these two parts appears in SABOL (1982, no. 150). Originally used as a formal dance for an unidentified Jacobean masque, it here serves as accompaniment for a dramatic transformation scene. It consists of three strains; the opening chords of the first two strains, over which are superimposed fermatas followed by brief rapidly moving passages, supply a fitting musical response by a group of performers who have been directly ordered to waken Hermione (3306), and then in the third strain, which suddenly shifts to triple meter, the slow duple rhythm of the closing measures of the first strain suddenly changes to accompany even more positively this wondrous metamorphosis. STERNFELD (1971, pp. 166–7): "The belief that heavenly music rewards the good, punishes the bad, heals the sick, and foretells divine plans to anguished mortals operates. . . . On the stage this heavenly music is usually repre-[*167*]sented by the soft music of strings." PYLE (1969, p. 177): "In the statue scene Shakespeare gained an effect in dramatic terms comparable to that of a transformation scene in a masque, achieving the masque-inventor's object 'to merge spectator and actor in a single mimetic illusion'" (quoting ORGEL [1965, p. 188]).

Further information about the use of music in Sh. may be found in AUDEN (1957), BONTOUX (1936), BRIDGE (1899?), BROOKE (1929), CHAMBERS (1957), CHAMPION (1970), COX (1969), CUTTS ("Rôle," 1956), DRAPER (1985), DUCKLES (1954), EWBANK (1980), FELPERIN (1972), FINNEY (1962), GODDARD (1951), GOOCH & THATCHER (1996), HOLLANDER (1961), HOWARD (1994), KIMMINS (1911), LAMSON (1936), LAWRENCE (1924), MARDER (1950), MOORE (1922), MUIR & SCHOENBAUM (1971), NEILSON & THORNDIKE (1913), NICOLL (1938 and 1958), ORGEL & STRONG (1973), OVERTON (1989), PALMER (1971), ROBINSON (1584; ed. 1924), STERNFELD (1956 and 1962), THORNDIKE (1916), TILLYARD (1938), VAN DOREN (1939), WILLIAMS (1967), and WILSON (1660).

BIBLIOGRAPHY

Abartis, Caesarea. *The Tragicomic Construction of* Cymbeline *and* The Winter's Tale. Salzburg, 1977.

Abbott, E[dwin] A. *A Shakespearian Grammar*. Rev. & enl. 1870. (Rpt. New York: Dover, 1966.)

Abrams, Richard H. "Leontes's Enemy: Madness in *The Winter's Tale*." *Aspects of Fantasy: Selected Essays from the Second International Conference on the Fantastic in Literature and Film.* Ed. William Coyle. Westport, Conn., 1986. Pp. 155-62.

Adams, F. "*Winter's Tale*, [575-6.]" 8 *N&Q* 2 (1892), 444.

———. "*Winter's Tale*, [2279-81.]" 8 *N&Q* 5 (1894), 64.

Adams, Joseph Q. "Greene's *Menaphon* and *The Thracian Wonder*." *MP* 3 (1906), 1-9.

———. *A Life of William Shakespeare*. Boston, 1923.

———, ed. *The Dramatic Records of Sir Henry Herbert*. New Haven, 1917. (Rpt. New York: Blom, 1964.)

Adams, Robert M. *Shakespeare: The Four Romances*. New York, 1989.

Adamson, W. D. "The Calumny Pattern in Shakespeare." *REAL: The Yearbook of Research in English and American Literature* 4 (1986), 35-66.

Adelman, Janet. *The Common Liar: An Essay on* Antony and Cleopatra. Yale Stud. in English 181. New Haven, 1973.

Albright, Evelyn M. *Dramatic Publication in England, 1580-1640*. New York & London, 1927.

Alden, Raymond M. *Shakespeare*. Master Spirits of Lit. New York, 1922. (Rpt. New York: AMS, 1971.)

———. *A Shakespeare Handbook*. New York, 1925. (Rev. & enl. by Oscar James Campbell, 1932.)

Alexander, Marguerite. *A Reader's Guide to Shakespeare and his Contemporaries*. London & New York, 1979.

Alexander, Peter. *Shakespeare*. OUP, 1964.

———. *Shakespeare's Life and Art*. 1938. (Rpt. London: James Nisbet, 1946.)

———. "Shakespeare's Punctuation." *Proceedings of the British Academy* 31 (1945), 61-84.

Alexander, S. "Art and Nature." *BJRL* 11 (1927), 256-72.

Allen, Don C. *The Star-Crossed Renaissance*. Durham, N.C., 1941. (Rpt. New York: Octagon, 1966, 1973.)

Allen, Percy. "Names in *The Winter's Tale*." *TLS*, 18 July 1936, p. 600.

Allen, Shirley S. *Samuel Phelps and Sadler's Wells Theatre*. Middleton, Conn., [1971].

Allison, A[nthony] A. *Robert Greene 1558-1592. A Bibliographical Catalogue . . . to 1640.* 1975.

Almasy, Rudolph. "'Go Together You Precious Winners All': A Reading of Shakespeare's *The Winter's Tale.*" *WVUPP* 27 (1981), 120-7.

Alter, Iska, & William B. Long. "*The Winter's Tale.*" *ShakB* 3 (Nov./Dec. 1985), 21-2.

Amyot, Thomas (1775-1850). Contributor to COL1.

Anders, H[enry R. D.]. Rev. of *The Golden Asse* of Lucius Apuleius . . . with an Introduction by E. B. Osborne. *SJ* 62 (1926), 172-3.

—————. *Shakespeare's Books.* Schriften der Deutschen Shakespeare-Gesellschaft 1. Berlin, 1904. (Rpt. New York: AMS, 1965.)

Anderson, John L. *A Fifteenth Century Cookry Boke.* New York, 1962.

Anderson, Mary. *A Few Memories.* New York, 1896.

Andreas, James R. "'Music Awake Her: Strike Tis Time': Generic Modulation in *The Winter's Tale.*" *TPB* 21 (1984), 24-5.

Andrews, Michael C. "Sidney's *Arcadia* and *The Winter's Tale.*" *SQ* 23 (1972), 200-2.

Anon. Contributor to CAM1.

—————. Contributor to CAM2.

—————. Contributor to DYCE2.

—————. Contributor to HAL.

—————. Contributor to mPER.

—————. Contributor to v1898.

—————. *Amadis of Fraunce, The Treasurie of.* Tr. out of French [by T. Paynell]. [1572?].

—————. Anonymous MS notes in F2 quoted in SING2.

—————. "The Backward Half-Look." *TLS,* 1 Nov. 1957, p. 656.

—————. "English Sculpture in English Literature." *TLS,* 18 July 1929, pp. 565-6.

—————. "Notes and News." *Poet Lore* 3 (1891), 224-5.

—————. "Recent Editions of Shakspeare." *The Edinburgh Review* 81 (1845), 172-202.

—————. Rev. of *The Works of William Shakespeare,* ed. William Aldis Wright, vol. 3. 7 *N&Q* 12 (1891), 160.

—————. "Shakespeare and Natural Phenomena." *TLS,* 13 Feb. 1930, p. 121.

—————. "Shakespeare, and the New Discovery." *Fraser's Mag.* 47 (1853), 245-56.

—————. "Shakespeare's *Winter's Tale.*" *Gent. Mag.* 72 (1802), 231-2.

—————. "Shakespeare Vindicated." *Monthly Mag.* 30 (1 Jan. 1811), 538.

—————. *The Thracian Wonder: A Comical History.* 1599(?). *The Dramatic Works of John Webster.* Ed. William Hazlitt. 4 vols. 1857 4:115-212.

—————. *The Trial of Chivalry.* 1601(?). *Three Centuries of Drama.* Ed. Henry W. Wells. 1895. Pp. 124-41.

Ansari, A. A. "The Mockery of Art in *The Winter's Tale.*" *Aligarh Jour. of English Stud.* 4 (1979), 124-41.

Apperson, G[eorge] L. *English Proverbs and Proverbial Phrases.* 1929.

—————. "Some Shakespearian Names." *Gent. Mag.* 287 (1899), 278-83.

Arber, Edward, ed. *A Transcript of the Registers of the Company of Stationers of London; 1554-1640 A.D.* 5 vols. London & Birmingham, 1875-94. (Rpt. Gloucester, Mass.: Peter Smith, 1967.)

Archer, William. *Play-Making: A Manual of Craftsmanship.* 1912. (Rpt. New York: Dover, 1960.)

—————. "*The Winter's Tale.*" *Nineteenth Century* 22 (1887), 511-21.

Armstrong, Cecil F. *Shakespeare to Shaw.* 1913. (Rpt. New York: AMS, 1969.)

Armstrong, Edward A. *Shakespeare's Imagination: A Study of the Psychology of Association and Inspiration.* 1946. (New ed. Lincoln, Nebr., 1963.)

Armstrong, John H. S. *The Paradise Myth.* OUP, 1969.

Arnold, Paul. "Esotérisme du *Conte d'Hiver.*" *MdF* 318 (1953), 494–512.

Aronson, Alex. *Psyche & Symbol in Shakespeare.* Bloomington, Ind., 1972.

Arrowsmith, W. R. "Notes on Several Misunderstood Words." 1 *N&Q* 7 (1853), 566–8.

Arthos, John. *The Art of Shakespeare.* New York, 1964. (Rpt. Norwood, Pa.: Norwood, 1974.)

——. "Shakespeare and the Ancient World." *Michigan Quarterly Review* 10 (1971), 149–63.

Asp, Caroline. "Shakespeare's Paulina and the *Consolatio* Tradition." *ShakS* 11 (1978), 145–58.

As You Like It [pseud. John Loveday?]. "Original Observations and Conjectures on Shakespear." *Gent. Mag.* 59 (1789), 710–13.

Auden, W[ystan] H. "The Alienated City: Reflections on 'Othello.'" *Encounter* 17 (Aug. 1961), 3–14.

——. "Music in Shakespeare: Its Dramatic Use in His Plays." *Encounter* 9 (Dec. 1957), 31–44. (Rpt. in *The Dyer's Hand and Other Essays,* ed. Auden, New York, 1962, pp. 500–27, and in *Shakespeare Criticism 1935–60,* ed. Anne Ridler, OUP, 1963, pp. 306–28.)

Avery, Emmett L. See *The London Stage 1660–1800.*

Awdeley, John. *The Fraternitye of Vacabondes.* 1575. (*RSTC* 993. 2nd ed. 1575, *RSTC* 994, rpt. in *The Rogues and Vagabonds of Shakspere's Youth,* ed. Edward Viles & F. J. Furnivall, 1869 and 1880.)

Aydelotte, Frank. *Elizabethan Rogues and Vagabonds.* Oxford Historical & Literary Stud. Vol. 1. Oxford, 1913.

Babb, Lawrence. *The Elizabethan Malady.* East Lansing, Mich., 1951.

Bagehot, Walter. "Shakespeare—The Man" (1853). *Literary Studies.* Introd. George Sampson. Vol. 1. N.d. Pp. 112–53.

Bailey, N[athan]. *An Universal Etymological English Dictionary.* 1721. (Rpt. Hildesheim: Olms, 1969.)

Bailey, Samuel. *On the Received Text of Shakespeare's Dramatic Writings and its Improvement.* 2 vols. 1862–6.

Baker, Herschel, ed. *Four Essays on Romance.* Cambridge, Mass., 1971.

——. *John Philip Kemble: The Actor in His Theatre.* Cambridge, Mass., 1942.

Bald, R. C. "'Assembled' Texts." 4 *Library* 12 (1931–2), 243–8.

——. "Shakespeare on the Stage in Restoration Dublin." *PMLA* 56 (1941), 369–78.

Baldwin, T[homas] W. *On Act and Scene Division in the Shakespeare First Folio.* Carbondale & Edwardsville, Ill., 1965.

——. *The Organization and Personnel of the Shakespearean Company.* Princeton, 1927. (Rpt. New York: Russell & Russell, 1961.)

——. *William Shakspere's Petty School.* Urbana, 1943.

——. *William Shakspere's Small Latine & Lesse Greeke.* 2 vols. Urbana, 1944.

Bamber, Linda. *Comic Women, Tragic Men.* Stanford, 1982.

Barber, Cesar L. *Shakespeare's Festive Comedy.* Princeton, 1959.

——. "'Thou that beget'st him that did thee beget': Transformation in 'Pericles' and 'The Winter's Tale.'" *ShS* 22 (1969), 59–67.

——, & Richard P. Wheeler. *The Whole Journey: Shakespeare's Power of Development.* Berkeley, [1986].

Barber, Charles. *The Theme of Honour's Tongue*. Gothenburg Stud. in English 58. Göteborg, 1985.

———. "*The Winter's Tale* and Jacobean Society." *Shakespeare in a Changing World*. Ed. Arnold Kettle. New York, 1964. Pp. 233–52.

[Barclay, James.] *An Examination of Mr. Kenrick's Review of Mr. Johnson's Edition of Shakespeare*. 1766. (Rpt. in *On Johnson's Shakespeare*, Johnsoniana II. New York: Garland, 1975.)

Baret [Barrett], John. *An Alvearie or Quadruple Dictionarie*. 1580.

Barkan, Leonard. *The Gods Made Flesh*. New Haven, 1986.

———. "'Living Sculptures': Ovid, Michelangelo, and *The Winter's Tale*." *ELH* 48 (1981), 639–67.

Barrington, Daines. *Observations on the More Ancient Statutes*. 5th ed. 1796. (1st ed. 1766.)

Barry, H[enry?], Rev. (b. 1781 or 1782). Contributor to COL1.

Bartholomaeus Anglicus. *Batman vppon Bartholome*. 1582.

Bartholomeusz, Dennis. The Winter's Tale *in Performance in England and America 1611–1976*. Cambridge, 1982.

Barton, Anne. "'Enter Mariners, Wet': Realism in Shakespeare's Last Plays." *Realism in European Literature*. Ed. Nicholas Boyle, Martin Swales, & Richard Brinkmann. Cambridge, 1986. Pp. 28–49.

———. "Leontes and the Spider: Language and Speaker in Shakespeare's Last Plays." *Shakespeare's Styles: Essays in Honour of Kenneth Muir*. Ed. Philip Edwards et al. Cambridge, 1980. Pp. 131–50. (Rpt. in *William Shakespeare's* The Winter's Tale, ed. Harold Bloom, New York, 1987.)

———. *The Names of Comedy*. Toronto, 1990.

———. *See* Righter, Anne.

Barton, Dunbar P. *Shakespeare and the Law*. Boston, 1929. (Pub. in England as *Links between Shakespeare and the Law*, 1929; rpt. New York: Blom, 1971.)

Baskerville, Charles R. *The Elizabethan Jig and Related Song Drama*. Chicago, 1929. (Rpt. New York: Dover, 1965.)

Bass, Eben. "*The Winter's Tale*: Great Difference betwixt Bohemia and Sicilia." *MSE* 6 (1977), 15–24.

Bate, Jonathan. *Shakespeare and Ovid*. OUP, 1993.

Bateson, F. W. "How Old Was Leontes?" *Essays and Studies* NS 31 (1978), 65–74.

Bather, F. A. "The Puns of Shakspeare." *Winchester College Shakspere Society. Noctes Shaksperianæ*. Ed. Charles H. Hawkins. Winchester & London, 1887. Pp. 69–91.

[Bathurst, Charles.] *Remarks on the Differences in Shakespeare's Versification in Different Periods of his Life*. 1857.

Battenhouse, Roy. "Theme and Structure in *The Winter's Tale*." *ShS* 33 (1980), 123–38.

Baughan, Denver E. "Shakespeare's Probable Confusion of the Two Romanos." *JEGP* 36 (1937), 35–9.

Baum, Paull F. "The Young Man Betrothed to a Statue." *PMLA* 34 (1919), 523–79.

Bayfield, M[atthew] A. *A Study of Shakespeare's Versification*. Cambridge, 1920. (Rpt. Folcroft, Pa.: Folcroft, 1970.)

Bayne, Ronald. "Religion." *Shakespeare's England*. Ed. Sidney Lee & C[harles] T. Onions. 2 vols. OUP, 1916. 1:48–78.

Baynes, T[homas] S. *Shakespeare Studies*. 1894. (Rpt. New York: AMS, 1972.)

Becket, Andrew. *Shakspeare's Himself Again*. 2 vols. 1815.

Beisly, Sidney. *Shakspere's Garden.* 1864.

Bellette, A. F. "Truth and Utterance in *The Winter's Tale.*" *ShS* 31 (1978), 65-75.

Bentley, Gerald Eades. *The Jacobean and Caroline Stage.* 7 vols. OUP, 1941-68.

————. *Shakespeare and His Theatre.* Lincoln, Nebr., 1964.

————. "Shakespeare and the Blackfriars Theatre." *ShS* 1 (1948), 38-50.

Berek, Peter. "'As We Are Mock'd with Art': From Scorn to Transfiguration." *SEL* 18 (1978), 289-305.

Berger, Thomas L., & William C. Bradford, Jr. *An Index of Characters in English Printed Drama to the Restoration.* Englewood, Col., 1975.

Bergeron, David M. "Hermione's Trial in *The Winter's Tale.*" *EiT* 3 (1984), 3-12.

————. "The Restoration of Hermione in *The Winter's Tale.*" *Shakespeare's Romances Reconsidered.* Ed. Carol McG. Kay & Henry E. Jacobs. Lincoln, Nebr., 1978. Pp. 125-33.

————. *Shakespeare's Romances and the Royal Family.* Lawrence, Kan., 1985.

Berggren, Paula S. "'From a God to a Bull': Shakespeare's Slumming Jove." *CML* 5 (1985), 277-91.

————. "The Woman's Part: Female Sexuality as Power in Shakespeare's Plays." *The Woman's Part.* Ed. Carolyn R. S. Lenz, Gayle Greene, & Carol T. Neely. Urbana, 1980. Pp. 17-34.

Berkeley, David S. *Blood Will Tell in Shakespeare's Plays.* Lubbock, Tex., 1984.

————, & Zahra Karimipour. "Blood-Consciousness as a Theme in *The Winter's Tale.*" *EIRC* 11 (1985), 89-98.

Berkenhout, John. [Thirty-fourth letter to his son.] "Shakespeare." *St. James's Chronicle* No. 4622 (2-4 Dec. 1790), 2.

Bernard, John D. "The Pastoral Vision of *The Winter's Tale.*" *ISJR* 53 (1979), 219-25.

Berry, Francis. *Poets' Grammar.* 1958.

————. *The Shakespeare Inset: Word and Picture.* 1965.

Berry, Ralph. Interview with Sir Peter Hall. *On Directing Shakespeare.* New York, 1977. Pp. 208-16. (2nd ed. 1989.)

————. *Shakespeare and Social Class.* 1988.

————. *The Shakespearean Metaphor.* 1978.

————. *Shakespearean Structures.* 1981.

————. "Stratford Festival Canada." *SQ* 30 (1979), 167-75.

Bertram, Paul B. *White Spaces in Shakespeare.* Cleveland, 1981.

Bethell, S[amuel] L. *Shakespeare & the Popular Dramatic Tradition.* 1944. (Rpt. 1970.)

————. The Winter's Tale: *A Study.* [1947.] (Rpt. Folcroft, Pa.: Folcroft, 1974.)

Bevan, Elinor. "Revenge, Forgiveness, and the Gentleman." *REL* 8, No. 3 (1967), 55-69.

Bevington, David. *Action Is Eloquence.* Cambridge, Mass., 1984.

————. "Shakespeare's Professional Career: Poet and Playwright." *William Shakespeare: His World, His Work, His Influence.* Ed. John F. Andrews. 3 vols. New York, 1985. 2:309-29.

Biggens, Dennis. "'Exit pursued by a Beare': A Problem in *The Winter's Tale.*" *SQ* 13 (1962), 3-13.

Biggs, Murray. "*The Winter's Tale.*" *ShakB* 6 (Mar./Apr. 1988), 19-20.

Birch, William J. *An Inquiry into the Philosophy and Religion of Shakspere.* 1848. (Rpt. New York: AMS, 1972.)

Biswas, D[inesh] C. *Shakespeare in His Own Time.* Delhi, 1979.

————. *Shakespeare's Treatment of His Sources in the Comedies.* Calcutta, 1971.

Black, Ladbroke. *The Love Letters of Henry the Eighth*. 1933.

Blackstone, William (1783–80). Contributor to MAL, v1785.

Blades, William. *Shakspere and Typography*. 1872. (Rpt. New York: AMS, 1971.)

Blake, N[orman] F. *Shakespeare's Language: An Introduction*. 1983.

Bland, D. S. "The Heroine and the Sea: An Aspect of Shakespeare's Last Plays." *EIC* 3 (1953), 39–44.

Blissett, William. "This Wide Gap of Time: *The Winter's Tale*." *ELR* 1 (1971), 52–70.

B[lount], T[homas]. *Glossographia*. 1656. (Rpt. Menston: Scolar, 1969.)

Bluestone, Max. *From Story to Stage: The Dramatic Adaptation of Prose Fiction in the Period of Shakespeare and his Contemporaries*. The Hague & Paris, 1974.

Boaden, James, ed. *Memoirs of the Life of John Philip Kemble, Esq*. 2 vols. 1825.

Boas, Felix. *Der Sturm und das Wintermärchen, zwei Shakespeare'sche Dramen, in ihrer symbolischen Bedeutung*. Stettin, 1882.

Boas, Frederick S. *Shakspere and his Predecessors*. 1896.

Boas, Guy. "Exit Antigonus." *Drama* NS 70 (Autumn 1963), 34–5.

Bolte, Johannes. "Eine holländische Uebersetzung von Shakespeare's Taming of the Shrew vom Jahre 1654." *SJ* 26 (1891), 78–86.

———. "Zur Schlussscene des Wintermärchens." *SJ* 26 (1891), 87–90.

Bonjour, Adrien. "The Final Scene of *The Winter's Tale*." *ES* 33 (1952), 193–208.

———. "Polixenes and the Winter of his Discontent." *ES* 50 (1969), 206–12.

Bontoux, Germaine. *La Chanson en Angleterre au Temps d'Elisabeth*. OUP, 1936.

Boodle, R. W. "The Theory of the Classical and Shakespearian Dramas." *Shakespeariana* 2 (1885), 313–20.

———. "*The Winter's Tale* [744]." *Shakespeariana* 2 (1885), 42, 260–1.

Boose, Lynda E. "The Father and the Bride in Shakespeare." *PMLA* 97 (1982), 325–47.

Booth, Stephen. "Exit, Pursued by a Gentleman Born." *Shakespeare's Art from a Comparative Perspective*. Ed. Wendell M. Aycock. *PCLS* 12 (1981), 51–66.

———. "Speculations on Doubling in Shakespeare's Plays." *Shakespeare: The Theatrical Dimension*. Ed. Philip C. McGuire & David A. Samuelson. New York, 1979. Pp. 103–31.

———, ed. *Shakespeare's Sonnets*. New Haven, 1977.

Borinski, Ludwig. "Shakespeare's Comic Prose." *ShS* 8 (1955), 57–68.

Boutroux, Émile. "L'Art et la Nature, dans Shakespeare et dans Bacon." *A Book of Homage to Shakespeare*. Ed. Israel Gollancz. OUP, 1916. Pp. 383–6.

Bowden, Henry S. *The Religion of Shakespeare. Chiefly from the Writings of the Late Mr. Richard Simpson*. 1899.

Bowers, J. L. "The Romances." *Shakespeare at 400*. Cape Town, 1965. Pp. 42–63.

Bowers, R. H. "Autolycus in 1636." *SQ* 11 (1960), 88–9.

Boyle, R. *Shakespeares Wintermärchen und Sturm*. St. Petersburg, 1885.

Bradbrook, M[uriel] C. "Dramatic Romance as an Open Form in *The Winter's Tale*." *De Shakespeare à T. S. Eliot: Mélanges Offert à Henri Fluchère*. Paris, 1976. Pp. 81–92. (Partly duplicates "Open Form in *The Winter's Tale*," *The Living Monument*, 1976, pp. 206–14.)

———. *Elizabethan Stage Conditions: A Study of Their Place in the Interpretation of Shakespeare's Plays*. Cambridge, 1932. (Rpt. Cambridge: CUP, 1968.)

———. *The Living Monument: Shakespeare and the Theatre of His Time*. Cambridge, 1976.

Bradford, William C. *See* Berger, Thomas L.

Bradley, Henry. "Shakespeare's English." *Shakespeare's England*. Ed. Sidney Lee & C[harles] T. Onions. 2 vols. OUP, 1916. 2:539–74.

Brailow, David S. *"The Winter's Tale." ShakB* 13 (Spring 1995), 14–15.

Brainerd, B. "The Chronology of Shakespeare's Plays: A Statistical Study." *Computers and the Humanities* 14 (1980), 221–30.

Brand, John. *See* Hazlitt, W[illiam] Carew.

Brandes, Georg. *William Shakespeare: A Critical Study.* Tr. William Archer, Mary Morison, & Diana White. 2 vols. 1898. (1st Danish ed. 3 vols. Copenhagen, 1895–6.)

Brereton, J. LeGay. "The Relation of *The Thracian Wonder* to Greene's *Menaphon." MLR* 2 (1907), 34–8.

Bridge, [J.] Frederick. *Shakespearean Music in the Plays and Early Operas.*. 1923. (Rpt. New York: Haskell House, 1965.)

————. *Songs from Shakespeare.* [1899?].

Bridges, Robert [S.]. "On the Influence of the Audience." *The Works of William Shakespeare.* Ed. A. H. Bullen. 10 vols. 1904–7. 10 (1907): 321–34. (Rpt. as *The Influence of the Audience; Considerations Preliminary to the Psychological Analysis of Shakespeare's Characters*, New York, 1926, and as "The Influence of the Audience on Shakespeare's Drama," *Collected Essays Papers &c. of Robert Bridges*, vol. 1, OUP, 1927.)

Briley, John. "Of Stake and Stage." *ShS* 8 (1955), 106–8.

Brink, Bernhard ten. *Five Lectures on Shakespeare.* Tr. Julia Franklin. New York, 1895.

Brissenden, Alan. *Shakespeare and the Dance.* Atlantic Highlands, N.J., 1981.

Brockbank, J. P[hilip]. "Shakespeare and the Fashion of These Times." *ShS* 16 (1963), 30–41.

————. *"The Tempest*: Conventions of Art and Empire." *Later Shakespeare.* Ed. John Russell Brown & Bernard Harris. Stratford-upon-Avon Stud. 8. 1966. Pp. 183–201.

Brook, G[eorge] L. *The Language of Shakespeare.* 1976.

Brooke, C[harles] F. Tucker, ed. *The Shakespeare Songs.* 1929.

Brooke, Stopford A. *On Ten Plays of Shakespeare.* 4th Impression. 1913. (1st impression 1905.)

Brooks, Harold F. (1907–90). Contributor to ARD2.

Brown, John Russell. "Laughter in the Last Plays." *Later Shakespeare.* Stratford-upon-Avon Stud. 8. Ed. John Russell Brown & Bernard Harris. 1966. Pp. 103–25.

————. *Shakespeare and His Comedies.* 2nd ed. 1962. (Rpt. Methuen, 1968. 1st ed. 1957.)

————. *Shakespeare's Plays in Performance.* New York, 1967. (Eng. ed. 1966.)

Brown, Norman O. *Hermes the Thief: The Evolution of a Myth.* Madison, 1947.

Browne, C. Elliot. "Notes on Shakespeare's Names. II." *Athenæum* No. 2544 (29 July 1876), 147–8.

Browne, William (?) S. (b. 1829). Contributor to CAM2.

Bryant, J. A., Jr. "Shakespeare's Allegory: *The Winter's Tale." SR* 63 (1955), 202–22. (Rpt. in *Hippolyta's View*, Lexington, Ky., 1961, pp. 207–25.)

Bryant, Jerry H. *"The Winter's Tale* and the Pastoral Tradition." *SQ* 14 (1963), 387–98.

Bucknill, John C. *The Medical Knowledge of Shakespeare.* 1860. (Rpt. New York: AMS, 1971.)

Buland, Mable. *Presentation of Time in the Elizabethan Drama.* New York, 1912. (Rpt. New York: Haskell House, 1966.)

Bullard, J. E., & W. M. Fox. *"The Winter's Tale." TLS,* 14 Mar. 1952, p. 189.

Bulloch, John. *Studies on the Text of Shakespeare: With Numerous Emendations.* 1878. (Rpt. New York: AMS, 1972.)

B[ullokar], J[ohn]. *An English Expositor.* 1616. (Rpt. Menston: Scolar, 1969.)

Bullough, Geoffrey, ed. *Narrative and Dramatic Sources of Shakespeare.* 8 vols. 1961–75. Vol. 8: *Romances.* 1975.

Bulthaupt, Heinrich. *Shakespeare.* Vol. 2 of *Dramaturgie des Schauspiels.* 4 vols. Old-enburgh, 1903.

Bulwer, John. *Chirologia.* 1644.

Burchfield, Robert. "The Bare Infinitive in *The Winter's Tale.*" *Shakespeare: Text, Language, Criticism.* Ed. Bernhard Fabian & Kurt Tetzeli von Rosador. Hildesheim, 1987.

Burney, Charles. *A General History of Music.* Ed. Frank Mercer. 2 vols. 1935. (Rpt. New York: Dover, 1957. 1st ed. 4 vols. 1776-89.)

Burton, H[arry] M. *Shakespeare and His Plays.* New York, 1958.

Burton, Julie. "Folktale, Romance, and Shakespeare." *Studies in Medieval English Romances: Some New Approaches.* Ed. Derek Brewer. Woodbridge, 1988. Pp. 176-97.

Burton, Philip. *The Sole Voice: Character Portraits from Shakespeare.* New York, 1970.

Burton, Robert. *The Anatomy of Melancholy.* 1628. Ed. Thomas C. Faulkner, Nicholas K. Kiessling, & Rhonda L. Blair. 2 vols. Oxford, 1989-90.

Bush, Geoffrey. *Shakespeare and the Natural Condition.* Cambridge, Mass., 1956.

Byles, Joan M. "*The Winter's Tale, Othello,* and *Troilus and Cressida*: Narcissism and Sexual Betrayal." *AI* 36 (1979), 80-93.

C., A. (poss. Anthony Chamier, 1725-80). Contributor to MAL.

C., P. A. [*sic*]. "A Study of Shakespeare's *Winter's Tale*: Considered in Connection with Greene's *Pandosto* and the *Alkestis* of Euripides." *Poet Lore* 4 (1892), 516-21. (Rpt. with slight revisions as by Charlotte Porter & Helen A. Clarke in *Poet Lore* 14 [1903], 132-7.)

Cairncross, Andrew S. "Compositors E and F of the Shakespeare First Folio." *PBSA* 66 (1972), 369-406.

Caldecott, Harry S. *Spoils: Studies in Shakespeare.* Rev. & enl. ed. N.p., [1891].

Calder-Marshall, Anna. "*The Winter's Tale.*" *Shakespeare in Perspective.* Vol. 1. Ed. Roger Sales. 1982. Pp. 241-9.

Calderwood, James L. *Shakespeare & the Denial of Death.* Amherst, 1987.

Caldwell, Ellen M. "Animating Word and Spectacle in the Masque Scenes of *The Winter's Tale.*" *ISJR* 58 (1984), 281-8.

Camden, Carroll. *The Elizabethan Woman.* Houston, 1952. (Rev. ed. Mamaroneck, N. Y., 1975.)

Campbell, John. *Shakespeare's Legal Acquirements Considered.* 1859.

Campbell, Oscar J. *See* Alden, Raymond M.

Campos, Christophe. "Tales of Two Winters: Shakespeare in London and Paris." *Franco-British Studies* 10 (Autumn 1990), 35-53.

Canfield, J. Douglas. *Word as Bond in English Literature from the Middle Ages to the Restoration.* Philadelphia, 1989.

Capell, Edward. *Notes and Various Readings to Shakespeare.* 3 vols. 1783. (Vol. 1, pt. 1 issued separately 1774. Rpt. 3 vols. New York: Burt Franklin, 1970.)

Caro, J. "Die historischen Elemente in Shakspeare's 'Sturm' und 'Wintermährchen.'" *ESn* 2 (1879), 141-85.

Carrington, Norman T. *Shakespeare: "The Winter's Tale."* Notes on Chosen English Texts Ser. [1956.]

[Carruthers, Miss.] *Flower Lore.* Belfast, 1879. (Rpt. Detroit: Singing Tree, 1972.)

Cartwright, Robert. *New Readings in Shakspere; or, Proposed Emendations of the Text.* 1866.

Castelain, Maurice. "Shakespeare et Ben Jonson." *Revue Germanique* 3 (1907), 21-65, 133-80.

Castrop, Helmut. "Romanze, Tragikomödie und Satyrspiel in *The Winter's Tale.*" *SJH 1987.* Ed. Werner Habicht, Jorg Hasler, & Kurt Tetzeli von Rosador. Bochum, 1987. Pp. 57-77.

Caulfield, John. *A Collection of the Vocal Music in Shakespeare's Plays.* 2 vols. [1864?].

Cavell, Stanley. *Disowning Knowledge in Six Plays of Shakespeare.* Cambridge, 1987.

[Cawdrey, Robert.] *A Table Alphabeticall, Conteyning . . . Hard Vsuall English Wordes.* 1604. (Rpt. Gainesville, Fla.: Scholars' Facsimiles & Reprints, 1966.)

Cazamian, Louis. *The Development of English Humor, Parts I and II.* New York, 1965. (Part I first pub. New York, 1931; rpt. 1951. Part II first pub. Durham, N.C., 1952.)

————. *L'Humour de Shakespeare.* Paris, [1945].

Cercignani, Fausto. *Shakespeare's Works and Elizabethan Pronunciation.* OUP, 1981.

Chalmers, George. *An Apology for the Believers in the Shakspeare-Papers.* 1797. (Rpt. New York: Kelley, 1971.)

————. *A Supplemental Apology for the Believers in the Shakspeare-Papers.* 1799. (Rpt. New York: Kelley, 1971.)

Chambers, E[dmund] K. *The Elizabethan Stage.* 4 vols. OUP, 1923. (Rpt. with corrections 1945, 1951, 1961, & 1974.)

————. *The Medieval Stage.* 2 vols. OUP, 1903.

————. *Shakespeare: A Survey.* 1925. (First pub. in Red Letter Sh., 1904–8.)

————. "Shakespeare." *The Year's Work in English Studies: Vol. VII: 1926.* 1928. Pp. 117–34.

————. *William Shakespeare: A Study of Facts and Problems.* 2 vols. OUP, 1930.

Chambers, H[erbert] A., ed. *A Shakespeare Song Book.* [1957.]

Chambers, R. W. "Some Sequences of Thought in Shakespeare and in the 147 Lines of 'Sir Thomas More.'" *MLR* 26 (1931), 251–80.

Chamier, Antony (1725–80). Contributor to JOHN.

Champion, Larry S. *The Evolution of Shakespeare's Comedy: A Study in Dramatic Perspective.* Cambridge, Mass., 1970.

————. "The Perspective of Comedy in *The Winter's Tale.*" *CE* 32 (1971), 428–47.

Chandler, Frank W. *The Literature of Roguery.* 2 vols. Boston, 1907.

Chappell, W[illiam]. *The Ballad Literature and Popular Music of the Olden Time.* 2 vols. 1859. (First pub. 17 parts, 1855–9. Rpt., introd. F. W. Sternfeld, New York: Dover, 1965.)

————. *A Collection of National English Airs.* 2 vols. 1838–40.

————. *See* Wooldridge, H. Ellis.

Charbonneau-Lassay, Louis. *The Bestiary of Christ.* Tr. D. M. Dooling. New York, 1991.

Charlton, H[enry] B. "Shakespeare's Comedies: The Consummation." *BJRL* 21 (1937), 323–51.

————. *Shakespearian Comedy.* 1938.

Charnock, R. S. "*The Winter's Tale* [755]." 5 *N&Q* 3 (1875), 303–4.

Chedworth, John [4th baron]. *Notes upon Some of the Obscure Passages in Shakespeare's Plays.* 1805.

Chew, Samuel C. "Time and Fortune." *ELH* 6 (1939), 83–113.

————. *The Virtues Reconciled: An Iconographic Study.* Toronto, 1947.

Childress, D. T. "Are Shakespeare's Late Plays Really Romances?" *Shakespeare's Late Plays: Essays in Honor of Charles Crow.* Ed. Richard C. Tobias & Paul G. Zolbrod. Athens, Ohio, 1974. Pp. 44–55.

Chittenden, Fred J., & Patrick M. Synge, eds. *The Royal Horticultural Society Dictionary of Gardening.* 2nd ed. 5 vols. Oxford, 1965–9.

Clapp, Henry A. "Time in Shakespeare's Comedies." *Atlantic Monthly* 55 (1885), 386–403.

Clark, Cumberland. *The Eternal Shakespeare*. 1930.

———. *Shakespeare and Home Life*. 1935.

———. *Shakespeare and Psychology*. 1936.

Clarke, Charles Cowden. *Shakespeare-Characters; Chiefly Those Subordinate*. 1863.

———, & Mary Cowden Clarke. *The Shakespeare Key*. 1879. (Rpt. New York: Ungar, n.d.)

Clarkson, Paul S., & Clyde T. Warren. *The Law of Property in Shakespeare and the Elizabethan Drama*. Rev. ed. New York, 1968. (1st ed. Baltimore, 1942.)

Clemen, Wolfgang. *The Development of Shakespeare's Imagery*. 1951. (1st Ger. ed. Bonn, 1936.)

Clubb, Louise G. "The Tragicomic Bear." *CLS* 9 (1972), 17–30.

Cochrane, Claire. "*The Winter's Tale*." *CahiersE* 32 (Oct. 1987), 90–1.

C[ockeram], H[enry]. *The English Dictionarie*. 1623. (Rpt. Menston: Scolar, 1968.)

Coggins, Gordon. "Greene's *Pandosto*: A 'Ghost' of 1584." 6 *Library* 2 (1980), 448–56.

Coghill, Nevill. "*Macbeth* at the Globe, 1606–1616 (?): Three Questions." *The Triple Bond: Plays, Mainly Shakespearean, in Performance*. Ed. Joseph G. Price. University Park, Pa., 1975. Pp. 223–39.

———. "Six Points of Stage-craft in *The Winter's Tale*." *ShS* 11 (1958), 31–41.

Cohen, Derek. "Patriarchy and Jealousy in *Othello* and *The Winter's Tale*." *MLQ* 48 (1987), 207–23.

Cohen, Walter. "Shakespeare and Calderón in an Age of Transition." *Genre* 15 (1982), 123–37. (Also pub. in *The Power of Forms in the English Renaissance*, ed. Stephen Greenblatt, Norman, Ok., 1982, pp. 123–37.)

Coleridge, Hartley. *Essays and Marginalia*. Ed. Derwent Coleridge. 2 vols. 1851.

Coleridge, Samuel Taylor. *Coleridge's Criticism of Shakespeare*. Ed. R[eginald] A. Foakes. Detroit, 1989.

———. *Coleridge's Shakespearean Criticism*. Ed. Thomas M. Raysor. 2 vols. Rev. ed. London & New York, 1960. (1st ed. 1930.)

———. *Seven Lectures on Shakespeare and Milton*. Introd. J. Payne Collier. 1856.

Coles, E[lisha]. *An English Dictionary*. 1676. (Rpt. Menston: Scolar, 1971.)

Colie, Rosalie L. *Shakespeare's Living Art*. Princeton, 1974.

Colley, Scott. "Leontes' Search for Wisdom in *The Winter's Tale*." *SoAR* 48 (1983), 43–53.

Collier, J[ohn] Payne. *New Particulars Regarding the Works of Shakespeare*. 1836. (Rpt. New York: AMS, 1973.)

———. *Notes and Emendations to the Text of Shakespeare's Plays, from Early Manuscript Corrections in a Copy of the Folio, 1632*. 1852. (Rpt. New York: 1853, rpt. New York: Burt Franklin, 1970. 2nd ed. rev. & enl. 1853.)

———. *Reasons for a New Edition of Shakespeare's Works*. 1841. (2nd, enl., ed. 1842; rpt. New York: AMS, 1973.)

———, ed. *Illustrations of Old English Literature*. 3 vols. 1866. (Rpt. New York: Blom, 1966.)

———, ed. *Shakespeare's Library*, 2 vols. [1843]. (2nd ed. rev. William Carew Hazlitt, 6 vols. 1875.)

Collins, David G. "The Function of Art in Shakespeare's *The Winter's Tale*." *BSUF* 23 (1982), 55–9.

Collins, J[ohn] Churton. "Shakespeare as a Prose Writer." *Gent. Mag.* 249 (1880), 735–47.

Colman, E[rnest] A. M. *The Dramatic Use of Bawdy in Shakespeare*. 1974.

Cook, Ann Jennalie. *Making a Match: Courtship in Shakespeare and his Society*. Princeton, 1991.

Cook, Judith. *Women in Shakespeare*. 1980.

Cook, Phyllis. "William Shakspere, Botanist." *ShAB* 15 (1940), 149–65.

Cooper, Helen. *Pastoral: Medieval into Renaissance*. Ipswich, Eng., 1977.

Cooper, Lane. *The Poetics of Aristotle: Its Meaning and Influence*. Ithaca, N.Y., 1923. (Reissued 1956.)

Cooper, Thomas. *Thesavrvs Lingvae Romanæ & Britannicæ*. 1565. (Rpt. Menston: Scolar, 1969.)

Cornish, James. "'Clamour your Tongues,' [*WT* 2071]." 1 *N&Q* 6 (1852), 312.

Cornwall, Barry. *See* Procter, Bryan Waller.

Corson, Hiram. *An Introduction to the Study of Shakespeare*. Boston, 1889.

————. "Shakespeariana." *The Cornell Rev.* 3 (1876), 281–2.

Cosgrove, Brian. "*The Winter's Tale* and the Limits of Criticism." *Studies: An Irish Quarterly Rev.* 66 (1977), 176–87.

Cotgrave, Randle. *A Dictionarie of the French and English Tongves*. 1611. (Rpt. Menston: Scolar, 1968.)

Cottrell, Beekman W. "*The Winter's Tale*." *"Lovers' Meeting": Discussions of Five Plays by Shakespeare*. Carnegie Ser. in Eng. 8. Pittsburgh, 1964. Pp. 69–82.

Cowling, G[eorge] H. *Music on the Shakespearian Stage*. Cambridge, 1913. (Rpt. New York: Russell & Russell, 1964.)

————. "Shakespeare and the Elizabethan Stage." *A Series of Papers on Shakespeare and the Theatre . . . By Members of the Shakespeare Association*. 1927. Pp. 157–85. (Paper read 29 Oct. 1926.)

Cox, Lee S. "The Role of Autolycus in *The Winter's Tale*." *SEL* 9 (1969), 283–301.

Craig, Hardin. *The Enchanted Glass*. OUP, 1936.

————. *An Interpretation of Shakespeare*. Columbia, Mo., 1948.

————. *Shakespeare: A Historical and Critical Study*. Chicago, 1931.

————. "Shakespeare and Wilson's *Arte of Rhetorique*, an Inquiry into the Criteria for Determining Sources." *SP* 28 (1931), 86–98.

————. *Shakespeare's Revisions*. Baltimore, 1931.

Craik, George L. *The English of Shakespeare*. 1857. (2nd, rev., ed. 1859; 3rd, rev., ed., ed. W. J. Rolfe, Boston & New York, 1867.)

Craik, T[homas] W. (1927–). Contributor to OXF2.

Crane, Milton. *Shakespeare's Prose*. Chicago, 1951.

Creizenach, Wilhelm. *Geschichte des neueren Dramas*. Vierter Band. *Das englische Drama im Zeitalter Shakespeares*. Erster Teil. Halle a. S., 1909. (Eng. tr. Cécile Hugon, rev. Alfred F. Schuster, 1916. This rpt. New York: Haskell House, 1964.)

Croft, John. *Annotations on Plays of Shakespear*. York, 1810.

Crooke, Helkiah. *Mikrokosmographia. A Description of the Body of Man*. 2nd ed. 2 pts. 1631.

Crosby, Joseph (1822–91). Contributor to HUD2.

————. "On a Passage in *The Winter's Tale*." *The American Bibliopolist* (Dec., 1876), pp. 121–2.

————. *One Touch of Shakespeare: Letters of Joseph Crosby to Joseph Parker Norris, 1875–1878*. Ed. John W. Velz & Frances N. Teague. Washington, D.C., 1986.

Crosse, Gordon. "*The Winter's Tale* and *Pericles*." *TLS*, 13 Dec. 1934, p. 895.

Crow, John. "Deadly Sins of Criticism, or, Seven Ways to Get Shakespeare Wrong." *SQ* 9 (1958), 301–6.

Crupi, Charles. "*The Winter's Tale* and *The Thracian Wonder*." *Archiv* 207 (1971), 341–7.

Cruttwell, Patrick. *The Shakespearean Moment and Its Place in the Poetry of the 17th Century*. New York, 1955.

Cunningham, J[ames] V. *Woe or Wonder: The Emotional Effect of Shakespearean Tragedy*. Denver, 1951.

Cunningham, Peter, ed. *Extracts from the Accounts of the Revels at Court, in the Reigns of Queen Elizabeth and King James I.*. Sh. Soc. Pubs. 7. 1842. (Rpt. New York: AMS, 1971.)

Cunnington, C[ecil] Willet, & Phillis Cunnington. *Handbook of English Costume in the Seventeenth Century*. Boston, 1972.

————. *Handbook of English Costume in the Sixteenth Century*. Rev. ed. 1970. (1st ed. 1954.)

Curtis, Harry, Jr. "The Year Growing Ancient: Formal Ambiguity in *The Winter's Tale*." *CLAJ* 23 (1980), 431–7.

Cust, Lionel. "Painting, Sculpture, and Engraving." *Shakespeare's England*. Ed. Sidney Lee & C[harles] T. Onions. 2 vols. OUP, 1916. 2:1–14.

Cutts, John P. "Jacobean Masque and Stage Music." *M&L* 35 (1954), 185–200.

————. *La Musique de Scène de la Troupe de Shakespeare*. Paris, 1959. 2nd ed. rev. 1971.

————. *Rich and Strange: A Study of Shakespeare's Last Plays*. Pullman, Wash., 1968.

————. "Robert Johnson, King's Musician in His Majesty's Public Entertainment." *M&L* 37 (1956), 221–33.

————. "Le Rôle de la Musique dans les Masques de Ben Jonson." *Les Fêtes de la Renaissance*. Journées Internationales D'Études. Paris, 1956. Pp. 285–303.

————. "An Unpublished Contemporary Setting of a Shakespeare Song." *ShS* 9 (1956), 86–9.

Cuvelier, Élaine. "'Perspective' in *The Winter's Tale*." *CahiersE* 23 (Apr. 1983), 35–46.

Dam. *See* Van Dam.

Danby, John F. *Poets on Fortune's Hill*. 1952.

Daniel, Peter A. Contributor to CAM2.

————. *Notes and Conjectural Emendations of Certain Doubtful Passages in Shakespeare's Plays*. 1870. (Rpt. New York: AMS, 1972.)

————. "Time-Analysis of the Plots of Shakspere's Plays." *New Shakspere Society's Transactions 1877–9*. [1879.] Pp. 117–346.

Dash, Irene G. "Bohemia's 'Sea Coast' and the Babe Who Was 'Lost Forever.'" *Literary Onomastics Studies* 3 (1976), 102–8.

————. "Garrick or Colman?" *N&Q* 216 (1971), 152–5.

————. "A Penchant for Perdita on the Eighteenth-Century Stage." *The Woman's Part*. Ed. Carolyn R. S. Lenz, Gayle Greene, & Carol T. Neely. Urbana, 1980. Pp. 271–84.

————. *Wooing, Wedding, and Power: Women in Shakespeare's Plays*. New York, 1981.

David, Richard. *Shakespeare in the Theatre*. Cambridge, 1978.

Davidson, Clifford. "The Iconography of Illusion and Truth in *The Winter's Tale*." *Shakespeare and the Arts*. Ed. Cecile W. Cary & Henry S. Limouze. Washington, D.C., 1982. Pp. 73–91.

Davies, John. "On Some Obscure Words in Shakespeare." 5 *N&Q* 5 (1876), 243–4.

Davies, Stevie. *The Idea of Woman in Renaissance Literature*. Brighton, 1986. (Also pub. as *The Feminine Reclaimed*. Lexington, Ky., 1986.)

Davies, Thomas. *Memoirs of the Life of David Garrick*. 2 vols. 1808. (Rpt. New York: Blom, 1969.)

Davies, W[illiam] Robertson. *Shakespeare's Boy Actors*. 1939. (Rpt. New York: Russell & Russell, 1964.)

Davis, Cushman K. *The Law in Shakespeare*. 2nd ed. St. Paul, Minn., 1884.

Davison, Peter. *Popular Appeal in English Drama to 1850*. 1982.

Day, M[uriel] C., & J[ohn] C. Trewin. *The Shakespeare Memorial Theater*. London & Toronto, 1932.

Dean, John. *Restless Wanderers: Shakespeare and the Pattern of Romance*. Salzburg, 1979.

Deaton, Mary. "Something Shakspere Left Out." *ShAB* 11 (1936), 52–6.

De Bray, Lys. *Fantastic Garlands*. Poole, Dorset, 1982.

Deighton, Kenneth. *The Old Dramatists: Conjectural Readings*. 2nd Ser. Calcutta, 1898.

Deiter, Marjorie. "*The Winter's Tale*." *ShakB* 3 (Jul./Aug. 1985), 9.

Delius, N[icolaus]. "Die Prosa in Shakespeare's Dramen." *SJ* 5 (1870), 227–73.

Dent, Alan. *World of Shakespeare: Animals & Monsters*. New York, 1973.

————. *World of Shakespeare: Plants*. Reading, Berkshire, 1971.

Dent, R[obert] W. *Proverbial Language in English Drama Exclusive of Shakespeare, 1495–1616: An Index*. Berkeley, 1984.

————. *Shakespeare's Proverbial Language*. Berkeley & London, 1981.

Desai, Chintamani N. *Shakespearean Comedy: With a Discussion on Comedy, the Comic and the Sources of Shakespearean Comic Laughter*. Indore City, 1952. (Agra Univ. diss.)

Dessen, Alan C. "Reviewing Shakespeare for the Record." *SQ* 36 (1985), 602–8.

————. *Shakespeare and the Late Moral Plays*. Lincoln, Nebr., 1986.

D'Ewes, Simonds. *The Journals of All the Parliaments During the Reign of Queen Elizabeth*. Rev. and pub. by Paul Bowes. 1682.

Dey, E. Merton. "*The Winter's Tale*, [223–8]," 9 *N&Q* 6 (1900), 4–5; "[2739–40]," 10 *N&Q* 5 (1906), 264; "[252–60]," 10 *N&Q* 7 (1907), 144.

Dobrée, Bonamy. "The Last Plays." *The Living Shakespeare*. Ed. Robert Gittings. 1960. Pp. 140–54. (Rpt. 1962.)

Dobson, E[ric] J. *English Pronunciation 1500–1700*. 2nd ed. 2 vols. OUP, 1968. (1st ed. 1957.)

Dodd, William. *The Beauties of Shakespear*. 2 vols. 1752. (Rpt. New York: Augustus M. Kelley, 1971. 3rd ed. 1780.)

Dodds, M. H. "The Age of Shakespeare's Characters." *N&Q* 177 (1939), 197.

Dodoens, Rembert. *A Niewe Herball, or Historie of Plantes*. Tr. Henry Lyte. 1578. (Corrected and amended ed. 1619.)

Dolan, Frances E. "Taking the Pencil out of God's Hand: Art, Nature, and the Face-Painting Debate in Early Modern England." *PMLA* 108 (1993), 224–39.

Donawerth, Jane. *Shakespeare and the Sixteenth-Century Study of Language*. Urbana, 1984.

Doran, Alban H. G. "Medicine." *Shakespeare's England*. Ed. Sidney Lee & C[harles] T. Onions. 2 vols. OUP, 1916. 1:413–43.

Doran, Madeleine. *Endeavors of Art: A Study of Form in Elizabethan Drama*. Madison, 1954. (Rpt. 1972.)

Douce, Francis. Contributor to v1793 and v1821.

––––––. *Illustrations of Shakspeare, and of Ancient Manners.* 2 vols. 1807.

Dowden, Edward. *Shakspere.* Literature Primers. 1875. (Rpt. New York: American Book Co., 1890.)

––––––. *Shakspere: A Critical Study of His Mind and Art.* 3rd ed. 1877. (Rpt. London: Routledge, 1962. 1st ed. 1875.)

Drake, Nathan. *Shakspeare and His Times.* 2 vols. 1817. (Rpt. New York: Burt Franklin, 1969.)

Draper, John W. *The Humors and Shakespeare's Characters.* Durham, N.C., 1945. (Rpt. New York: AMS, 1970.)

––––––. "Shakespeare's Ladies-in-Waiting." *Neophilologus* 49 (1965), 255–62.

Draper, R[onald] P. "Shakespeare's Pastoral Comedy." *Études Anglaises* 11 (1958), 1–17.

––––––. *"The Winter's Tale": Text and Performance.* 1985.

Drew, Anne Marie. "A Sigh into a Looking Glass. The Trickster in *The Winter's Tale* and *Happy Days.*" *Comparative Literature Studies* 26 (1989), 93–114.

Driver, Tom F. *The Sense of History in Greek and Shakespearean Drama.* New York, 1960.

Dryden, John. "Defence of the Epilogue. Or, *An Essay on the* Dramatique Poetry *of the last Age.*" *The Conquest of Granada.* Part II. 1672. *The Works of John Dryden.* Ed. H. T. Swedenberg et al. 19 vols. 1961–79. 11 (1978):203–18.

Duckles, Vincent. "The 'Curious' Art of John Wilson." *JAMS* 7 (1954), 93–112.

Duffin, Ross W. "An Encore for Shakespeare's Rare Italian Master." *The Elizabethan Review* 2 (1994), 21–5.

Duncan-Jones, E. E. "Hermione in Ovid and Shakespeare." *N&Q* 211 (1966), 138–9.

Dusinberre, Juliet. *Shakespeare and the Nature of Women.* 1975.

Duthie, George I. *Shakespeare.* 1951.

Dutton, Richard. *Mastering the Revels: The Regulation and Censorship of English Renaissance Drama.* Iowa City, 1991.

Dyce, Alexander, *A Few Notes on Shakespeare; with Occasional Remarks on the Emendations of the Manuscript-corrector in Mr. Collier's Copy of the Folio 1632.* 1853. (Rpt. New York: AMS, 1971.)

––––––. *Remarks on Mr. J. P. Collier's and Mr. C. Knight's Editions of Shakespeare.* 1844. (Rpt. New York: AMS, 1972.)

––––––. *Strictures on Mr. Collier's New Edition of Shakespeare, 1858.* 1859. (Rpt. New York: AMS, 1971.)

––––––, ed. *The Dramatic Works of Robert Greene.* 2 vols. 1831.

Dyer, T[homas] F. Thiselton. *The Folk-lore of Plants.* 1889. (Rpt. Detroit: Singing Tree, 1968.)

––––––. *Folk-Lore of Shakespeare.* New York, 1884.

Dyer, William T. Thiselton. "Natural History. II. Plants." *Shakespeare's England.* Ed. Sidney Lee & C[harles] T. Onions. 2 vols. OUP, 1916. 1:500–15.

Dymkowski, Christine. *Harley Granville Barker: A Preface to Modern Shakespeare.* Washington, D.C., 1986.

E., B. *A New Dictionary of the Terms . . . of the Canting Crew.* [1699.]

Eaton, T[hamar] R. *Shakespeare and the Bible.* 1860. (Rpt. New York: AMS, 1972.)

Eccles, Audrey. *Obstetrics and Gynaecology in Tudor and Stuart England.* 1982.

Eccles, Mark. *Shakespeare in Warwickshire.* Madison, 1961.

————. "Sir George Buc, Master of the Revels." *Thomas Lodge and Other Elizabethans.* Ed. Charles J. Sisson. Cambridge, Mass., 1933. Pp. 409–73. (Rpt. New York: Octagon Books, 1966.)

————, ed. *Measure for Measure.* A New Variorum Ed. of Sh. New York, 1980.

EDD. *See* Wright, Joseph

Edwards, Francis. "Topical Allusions in *The Winter's Tale.*" *The Bard* 1 (1975), 28–42.

————. "Topical Allusions in *The Winter's Tale—II.*" *The Bard* 2 (1976), 47–64.

Edwards, Philip. "The Declaration of Love." *Shakespeare's Styles: Essays in Honour of Kenneth Muir.* Ed. Philip Edwards et al. Cambridge, 1980. Pp. 39–50.

————. "'Seeing Is Believing': Action and Narration in *The Old Wives Tale* and *The Winter's Tale.*" *Shakespeare and his Contemporaries: Essays in Comparison.* Ed. E[rnst] A. J. Honigmann. Manchester, 1986. Pp. 79–93.

————. *Shakespeare and the Confines of Art.* 1968.

————. "Shakespeare and the Healing Power of Deceit." *ShS* 31 (1978), 115–25.

————. *Shakespeare: A Writer's Progress.* OUP, 1986.

————. "Shakespeare's Romances: 1900–1957." *ShS* 11 (1958), 1–18.

[Edwards, Thomas.] *A Supplement to Mr. Warburton's Edition of Shakespear. Being the Canons of Criticism, and Glossary.* 1748. (Rpt. New York: AMS, 1972; 2nd ed. 1748; 3rd ed. 1750; 5th ed.: *The Canons of Criticism, and Glossary,* 1753; 6th ed. 1758; 7th ed. 1765, rpt. New York: Augustus Kelley, 1970.)

Egan, Robert. *Drama Within Drama: Shakespeare's Sense of His Art in* King Lear, The Winter's Tale, *and* The Tempest. New York, 1975.

Eggers, Walter F., [Jr.]. "'Bring Forth a Wonder': Presentation in Shakespeare's Romances." *TSLL* 21 (1979), 455–77.

————. "Genre and Affective Distance—The Example of *The Winter's Tale.*" *Genre* 10 (1977), 29–46.

Ellacombe, Henry N. *The Plant-Lore & Garden-Craft of Shakespeare.* 3rd rev. ed. London & New York, 1896. (1st ed. 1878; 2nd ed. 1884, rpt. New York: AMS, 1973.)

[Elliot, M(adeleine) Leigh-Noel.] *Shakespeare's Garden of Girls.* 1885.

Ellis, Alexander J. *On Early English Pronunciation, with Especial Reference to Shakspere and Chaucer.* 5 pts. London & Berlin, 1869–89. Pt. 3. 1871.

Ellis, John. "Rooted Affection: The Genesis of Jealousy in *The Winter's Tale.*" *CE* 25 (1964), 545–7.

Ellis, Oliver C. de C. *Cleopatra in the Tide of Time.* 1947.

Elson, Louis C. *Shakespeare in Music.* Boston, 1901. (Rpt. Freeport, N.Y.: Books for Libraries, 1970.)

Elton, William. "Two Shaksperian Parallels." *ShAB* 22 (1947), 115–16.

Elze, K[arl]. "Noten und Conjecturen zu Shakespeare." *SJ* 11 (1876), 274–300.

————. "Shakespeare's muthmassliche Reisen." *SJ* 8 (1873), 46–91. (Tr. L. Dora Schmitz as "The Supposed Travels of Shakespeare," *Essays on Shakespeare,* [1874], pp. 254–315. *Essays* rpt. Port Washington, N.Y.: Kennikat, 1970.)

Empson, William. "Hunt the Symbol." *Essays on Shakespeare.* Ed. David B. Pirie. Cambridge, 1986. Pp. 231–43. (First pub. 1964.)

————. *The Structure of Complex Words.* 1951. (Rpt. Ann Arbor, 1967.)

Engel, Wilson F., III. "Sculpture and the Art of Memory in Elizabethan and Jacobean Drama." *MLS* 10, No. 2 (1980), 3–9.

England, Eugene. "Cordelia and Paulina, Shakespeare's Healing Dramatists." *Literature & Belief* 2 (1982), 69–82.

Enright, D[ennis] J. *Shakespeare and the Students*. 1970.

Erickson, Peter [B.]. "Adrienne Rich's Re-Vision of Shakespeare." *Women's Re-Visions of Shakespeare*. Ed. Marianne Novy. Urbana & Chicago, 1990. Pp. 183–95. (Rpt. in *Rewriting Shakespeare, Rewriting Ourselves*, ed. Erickson, Berkeley, 1991, pp. 146–66.)

———. "Patriarchal Structures in *The Winter's Tale*." *PMLA* 97 (1982), 819–29. (Rpt. with revisions in Erickson, *Patriarchal Structures in Shakespeare's Drama*, Berkeley, 1985, pp. 148–72.)

Estrin, Barbara L. "The Foundling Plot: Stories in *The Winter's Tale*." *MLS* 7, No. 1 (1977), 27–38.

———. *The Raven and the Lark*. Lewisburg, Pa., 1985.

Ettin, Andrew V. *Literature and the Pastoral*. New Haven, 1984.

Evans, B[enjamin] Ifor. *The Language of Shakespeare's Plays*. Bloomington, Ind., 1952.

———. *A Short History of English Drama*. 2nd ed. Boston, 1965. (1st ed. 1948.)

Evans, Bertrand. *Shakespeare's Comedies*. OUP, 1960.

Evans, G. Blakemore. "New Evidence on the Provenance of the Padua Prompt-Books of Shakespeare's . . . *Winter's Tale*." *SB* 20 (1967), 239–42.

———, ed. *Shakespearean Prompt-Books of the Seventeenth Century* 1.1 (1960), 3–24; 2.1 (1963), 19–29.

Evans, G. L. *See* Lloyd Evans, Gareth.

Everett, Barbara. "'Shakespeare's Investiture Play.'" *TLS*, 22 Jan. 1970, p. 84.

Ewbank, Inga-Stina. "Shakespeare's Poetry." *A New Companion to Shakespeare Studies*. Ed. Kenneth Muir & S. Schoenbaum. Cambridge, 1971. Pp. 99–115.

———. *Shakespeare's Styles: Essays in Honour of Kenneth Muir*. Cambridge, 1980.

———. "The Triumph of Time in *The Winter's Tale*." *REL* 5 (1964), 83–100. (Rpt. in *Shakespeare's Later Comedies: An Anthology of Modern Criticism*, ed. D. J. Palmer, Baltimore, 1971.)

F., W. F. "Shakspeariana." 4 *N&Q* 12 (1873), 284.

Faas, Ekbert. *Tragedy and After: Euripides, Shakespeare, and Goethe*. Kingston, Ont., & Montreal, 1984.

Fabiny, Tibor. "'Veritas Filia Temporis': The Iconography of Time and Truth and Shakespeare." *ALitASH* 26 (1984), 61–98.

Fairchild, Arthur H. R. *Shakespeare and the Arts of Design (Architecture, Sculpture, and Painting)*. Univ. of Missouri Stud. 12. Columbia, Mo., 1937.

Falconer, Alexander F. *Shakespeare and the Sea*. New York, 1964.

Farjeon, Herbert. *The Shakespearean Scene*. [1949.]

Farmer, John S., & W. E. Henley. *Slang and Its Analogues*. 7 vols. 1890–1904. (Rpt. in 1 vol., New York: Arno, 1970.)

Farmer, Richard (1735–97). Contributor to v1773, v1778, and v1793.

Farnham, Willard. *The Shakespearean Grotesque*. OUP, 1971.

Farrell, Kirby. *Play, Death, and Heroism in Shakespeare*. Chapel Hill & London, 1989.

———. "Self-Effacement and Autonomy in Shakespeare." *ShakS* 16 (1983), 75–99.

———. *Shakespeare's Creation*. Amherst, 1975.

Faucit, Helena. *See* Martin, Helena Faucit.

Felix, Minutius. *See* Hardinge, George.

Felperin, Howard. *Beyond Deconstruction: The Uses and Abuses of Literary Theory*. OUP, 1985.

———. *Shakespearean Romance*. Princeton, 1972.

————. "'Tongue-Tied, Our Queen?': The Deconstruction of Presence in *The Winter's Tale*." *Shakespeare and the Question of Theory*. Ed. Patricia Parker & Geoffrey Hartman. New York, 1985. Pp. 3-18. (Rpt. in Felperin, *The Uses of the Canon: Elizabethan Literature and Contemporary Theory*, OUP, 1990, pp. 35-55.)

Felver, Charles S. *Robert Armin, Shakespeare's Fool: A Biographical Essay*. Kent State Univ. Bull. 49, No. 1; Research Ser. 5. Kent, Ohio, 1961.

Fenton, Doris. "The Extra-dramatic Moment in Elizabethan Plays before 1616." Univ. of Penn. diss. 1930.

Fergusson, Francis. *Shakespeare: The Pattern in his Carpet*. New York, 1970. (*WT* material first pub. as introd. to Laurel ed., 1959.)

Fiedler, Leslie A. "The Defense of the Illusion and the Creation of Myth." *EIE 1948*. New York, 1949. Pp. 74-94.

————. *The Stranger in Shakespeare*. New York, 1972. (Rpt. Briarcliff Manor, N.Y., 1973.)

Field, Barron (1786-1846). Contributor to HAL.

————. "Conjectures on Some of the Corrupt or Obscure Passages of Shakespeare." *The Shakespeare Society's Papers* 3 (1847), 131-42.

Finney, Gretchen L. *Musical Backgrounds for English Literature, 1580-1650*. New Brunswick, N.J., [1962].

Firth, C. H. "Ballads and Broadsides." *Shakespeare's England*. Ed. Sidney Lee & C[harles] T. Onions. 2 vols. Oxford, 1916. 2:511-38.

Fischer, Walther. "Shakespeares späte Romanzen." *SJ* 91 (1955), 7-24.

Fisher, Alfred Y. *An Introduction to the Study of Shakespearean Comedy*. Pt.1. Dijon, 1931.

Fisher, Sidney T. *Some Proposed Shakespeare Emendations and Notes*. 3rd ed. Montreal, 15 July 1985. (1st ed. 1984.)

Fitch, John G. "Sense-Pauses and Relative Dating in Seneca, Sophocles and Shakespeare." *American Jour. of Philology* 102 (1981), 289-307.

The Fitzwilliam Virginal Book. *See* Maitland, J. A. Fuller.

Flatter, Richard. "*The Winter's Tale*." *TLS*, 4 Apr. 1952, p. 237.

Fleay, Frederick G. *A Biographical Chronicle of the English Drama 1559-1642*. 2 vols. 1891. (Rpt. New York: Burt Franklin, n.d.)

————. *A Chronicle History of the Life and Work of William Shakespeare: Player, Poet, and Playmaster*. 1886. (Rpt. New York: AMS, 1970.)

————. *A Chronicle History of the London Stage 1559-1642*. 1890. (Rpt. New York: Burt Franklin, n.d.)

————. "On Metrical Tests as Applied to Dramatic Poetry. Pt. I. Shakspere." *New Shakspere Society's Transactions, 1874*. [1874]. Pp. 1-16. (Rpt. in *Shakespeare Manual*, 1876, pp. 121-38, rpt. 1878. Rpt. in *Occasional Papers on Shakespeare: Being the Second Part of Shakespeare the Man and the Book*, ed. C[lement] M. Ingleby, 1881, pp. 50-141.)

Fleissner, Robert F. "What *The Winter's Tale* Unveils: Who Is 'The Best.'" *N&Q* 234 (1989), 336-8.

Florio, John. *Queen Anna's New World of Words, Or Dictionarie of the Italian and English tongues*. 1611. (Rpt. Menston: Scolar, 1968.)

Foakes, R[eginald] A. "Character and Dramatic Technique in *Cymbeline* and *The Winter's Tale*." *Studies in the Arts: Proceedings of the St. Peter's College Literary Society*. Ed. Francis Warner. New York, 1968. Pp. 116-30.

————. *Shakespeare: The Dark Comedies to the Last Plays: From Satire to Celebration.* Charlottesville, 1971.

Fortescue, J. W. "Hunting." *Shakespeare's England.* Ed. Sidney Lee & C[harles] T. Onions. 2 vols. OUP, 1916. 2:334–50.

Foss, George R. *What the Author Meant.* OUP, 1932.

Fothergill, Robert A. "The Perfect Image of Life: Counterfeit Death in the Plays of Shakespeare and His Contemporaries." *UTQ* 52 (1982–3), 155–78.

Fowler, Alastair. "Leontes' Contrition and the Repair of Nature." *E&S* 31 (1978), 36–64.

Franz, Wilhelm. *Die Sprache Shakespeares in Vers und Prosa.* Shakespeare-Grammatik in 4. Auflage. Halle a. S., 1939. (First pub. as *Shakespeare-Grammatik* in 1898–9. 2nd ed., 1909; 3rd ed., 1924; 4th ed. incl. all material from *Orthographie, Lautgebung und Wortbildung in den Werken Shakespeares mit Aussprachproben*, Heidelberg, 1905, and *Shakespeare's Blankvers*, 2. Auflage, Tübingen, 1935.)

Freeburg, Victor O. *Disguise Plots in Elizabethan Drama: A Study in Stage Tradition.* Columbia Univ. Stud. in Eng. and Comp. Lit. New York, 1915. (Rpt. New York: Blom, 1965.)

French, A. L. *Shakespeare and the Critics.* Cambridge, 1972.

Frey, Charles H. *Experiencing Shakespeare.* Columbia, Mo., 1988.

————. "Interpreting *The Winter's Tale.*" *SEL* 18 (1978), 307–29.

————. "Shakespeare's Imperiled and Chastening Daughters of Romance." *SAB* 43 (1978), 125–40. (Rev. in *The Woman's Part*, ed. Carolyn R. S. Lenz, Gayle Greene, & Carol T. Neely, Urbana, 1980, pp. 295–313.)

————. *Shakespeare's Vast Romance: A Study of* The Winter's Tale. Columbia, Mo., 1980.

————. "Tragic Structure in *The Winter's Tale*: The Affective Dimension." *Shakespeare's Romances Reconsidered.* Ed. Carol McG. Kay & Henry E. Jacobs. Lincoln, Nebr., 1978. Pp. 113–24.

Fripp, Edgar I. *Shakespeare, Man and Artist.* 2 vols. OUP, 1938.

————. *Shakespeare Studies, Biographical and Literary.* OUP, 1930. (Rpt. New York: AMS, 1975.)

Fry, John. *Pieces of Ancient Poetry, From Unpublished Manuscripts and Scarce Books.* Bristol, 1814.

Frye, Northrop. *Anatomy of Criticism: Four Essays.* Princeton, 1957.

————. "The Argument of Comedy." *EIE 1948.* New York, 1949. Pp. 58–73.

————. *Fables of Identity.* New York, [1963].

————. *A Natural Perspective: The Development of Shakespearean Comedy and Romance.* New York & London, 1965.

————. "Nature and Nothing." *Essays on Shakespeare.* Ed. Gerald W. Chapman. Princeton, 1965. Pp. 35–58.

————. *Northrop Frye on Shakespeare.* Ed. Robert Sandler. New Haven, 1986.

————. "Recognition in *The Winter's Tale.*" *Essays on Shakespeare and Elizabethan Drama in Honor of Hardin Craig.* Ed. Richard Hosley. Columbia, Mo., 1962. Pp. 235–46. (Rpt. in *Shakespeare's Later Comedies: An Anthology of Modern Criticism,* ed. D. J. Palmer, Baltimore, 1971, and in Frye, *Fables of Identity*, New York, 1963.)

————. "Romance as Masque." *Shakespeare's Romances Reconsidered.* Ed. Carol McG. Kay & Henry E. Jacobs. Lincoln, Nebr., 1978. Pp. 11–39. (Previously pub. in somewhat diff. form in Frye, *Spiritus Mundi*, Bloomington, Ind., 1976.)

————. *The Secular Scripture. A Study in the Structure of Romance.* 1976.

Frye, Roland M. *Shakespeare and Christian Doctrine*. Princeton, 1963.

————. *Shakespeare: The Art of the Dramatist*. 1982. (1st ed. Boston, 1970.)

Fuller Maitland, J. A. *See* Maitland, J. A. Fuller.

Furnivall, Frederick J. "Introduction." *The Leopold Shakspere*. [1877.] Pp. vii–cxxvi.

————. "Scraps." *The New Shakspere Society's Transactions. 1877-9*. [1879.] P. 108.

————. "Scraps." *The New Shakspere Society's Transactions. 1880-6*. [1886.] P. 646.

————. *The Succession of Shakspere's Works*. 1874. (Separate pub. of the introduction to G. G. Gervinus, *Commentaries on Shakspere*, tr. Fanny E. Bunnètt, 1874. Rpt. New York: AMS, 1972.)

————. "Winter's Tale." 5 *N&Q* 10 (1878), 244.

Fuzier, Jean. "Shakespeare et la jalousie: Le Cas de Léontès dans *The Winter's Tale*." *Caliban* 21 (1984), 81–94.

————, & Jean-Marie Maguin. "The RSC 1986 Spring and Summer Season at the Royal Shakespeare Theatre and Swan Theatre, Stratford-upon-Avon." *CahiersE* 30 (Oct. 1986), 93–5.

Gajdusek, R. E. "Death, Incest, and the Triple Bond in the Later Plays of Shakespeare." *AI* 31 (1974), 109–58.

Garber, Marjorie. *Coming of Age in Shakespeare*. New York, 1981.

————. *Dream in Shakespeare*. New Haven, 1974.

————. "'The rest is silence': Ineffability and the 'Unscene' in Shakespeare's Plays." *Ineffability: Naming the Unnamable from Dante to Beckett*. Ed. Peter S. Hawkins et al. New York, 1984. Pp. 35–50.

————. *Shakespeare's Ghost Writers*. New York & London, 1987.

Gardner, C. O. "Three Notes on *The Winter's Tale*." *Theoria* 54 (1980), 61–6.

Gardner, Helen. "The Argument about 'The Ecstasy.'" *Elizabethan and Jacobean Studies Presented to Frank Percy Wilson*. OUP, 1959. Pp. 279–306.

Garner, Bryan A. "Shakespeare's Latinate Neologisms." *ShakS* 15 (1982), 149–70.

Garner, Shirley N. "Male Bonding and the Myth of Women's Deception in Shakespeare's Plays." *Shakespeare's Personality*. Ed. Norman N. Holland, Sidney Homan, & Bernard J. Paris. Berkeley & Los Angeles, 1989. Pp. 135–50.

Garner, Stanton B., Jr. "Time and Presence in *The Winter's Tale*." *MLQ* 46 (1985), 347–67.

Garrett, John, ed. *More Talking of Shakespeare*. London & New York, 1959.

Gasper, Julia, & Carolyn Williams. "The Meaning of the Name 'Hermione.'" *N&Q* 231 (1986), 367.

Gauger, Wilhelm. "Zweierlei Mass in *Measure for Measure*." *Von Shakespeare bis Chomsky: Arbeiten zur Englischen Philologie an der Freien Universität Berlin*. Ed. Elfi Bettinger & Thomas Meier-Fohrbeck. Frankfurt am Main, Bern, & New York, 1987.

[Genest, John.] *Some Account of the English Stage, from the Restoration in 1660 to 1830*. 10 vols. Bath, 1832. (Rpt. New York: Burt Franklin, 1964.)

Genouy, Hector. *L'Élément pastoral dans la Poésie Narrative et le Drame en Angleterre, de 1579 à 1640*. Paris, 1928.

Gentleman, Francis, & Samuel Derrick. "The Winter's Tale, Introduction [and notes]." *Bell's Edition of Shakespeare's Plays*. 8 vols. 1774. 5:151–225.

Gerard, John. *The Herball or Generall Historie of Plantes*. 1597.

Gervinus, G[eorg] G. *Shakespeare Commentaries*. Tr. F[anny] E. Bunnètt. Rev. ed. London & New York, 1877. (Rpt. New York: AMS, 1971. 1st Eng. ed. 2 vols, 1863. 1st Ger. ed. Leipzig, 1849-50.)

Gesner, Carol. *Shakespeare and the Greek Romance: A Study of Origins.* Lexington, Ky., 1970.

Geyer, Horst. *Dichter des Wahnsinns. Eine Untersuchung über die Dichterische Darstellbarkeit Seelischer Ausnahmezustände.* Gottingen, 1955.

Gibbon, John M. *Melody and the Lyric from Chaucer to the Cavaliers.* 1930. (Rpt. New York: Haskell House, 1964.)

Gilbert, Miriam. "'This Wide Gap of Time': Storytelling and Audience Response in the Romances." *Iowa State Jour. of Research* 55 (1979), 235–41.

[Gildon, Charles.] "An Explanation of the Old Words Us'd by *Shakespear* in his Works" and "Remarks on the Plays of Shakespear." In supplementary vol. 7 (1710) added to Nicholas Rowe, ed., *The Works of Shakespear,* 6 vols., 1709, pp. lxviii–lxxii, 257–444. (Rpt. New York: AMS, 1967.)

Giles, Henry. *Human Life in Shakespeare.* Boston & New York, 1887. (1st ed. 1868.)

Girard, René. "Jealousy in *The Winter's Tale.*" *Alphonse Juilland: D'une passion l'autre.* Ed. Brigitte Cazelles & René Girard. Saratoga, Calif., 1987. Pp. 39–62.

Goddard, Harold C. *The Meaning of Shakespeare.* Chicago, 1951.

Gokak, V. K. "The Structure of Daffodils in *The Winter's Tale.*" *Literary Criterion* 6, No. 1 (1963), 137–52.

Golding, Arthur, tr. *Ovid's Metamorphoses.* 1567. Ed. John Frederick Nims. New York, 1965. Ed. W. H. D. Rouse. New York, 1966.

Goldman, Michael. *Shakespeare and the Energies of Drama.* Princeton, 1972.

Gollancz, Israel, ed. *A Book of Homage to Shakespeare.* OUP, 1916.

Gooch, Bryan N. S., & David Thatcher. *A Shakespeare Music Catalogue.* 5 vols. OUP, 1991.

Gosse, Edmund. "The Songs of Shakespeare." *A Book of Homage to Shakespeare.* Ed. Israel Gollancz. OUP, 1916. Pp. 52–5.

Gotch, H. G. "*The Winter's Tale,* [2976]." 9 *N&Q* 5 (1900), 330–1.

Gould, George. *Corrigenda and Explanations of the Text of Shakspere.* Continuation 2. 1887. (1st ed. 1881; new issue [enl. ed.] 1884.)

Gourlay, Patricia S. "'O my most sacred Lady': Female Metaphor in *The Winter's Tale.*" *ELR* 5 (1975), 375–95.

Grantley, Darryll. "*The Winter's Tale* and Early Religious Drama." *CompD* 20 (1986), 17–37.

Granville-Barker, Harley. Preface to *The Winter's Tale: An Acting Edition.* 1912. Pp. iii–x. (Rpt. in *More Prefaces to Shakespeare,* ed. Edward M. Moore, Princeton, 1974, pp. 19–25.)

Gray, Henry D. "Chronology of Shakespeare's Plays." *MLN* 46 (1931), 147–50.

Green, Henry. *Shakespeare and the Emblem Writers.* 1870. (Rpt. New York: Burt Franklin, n.d.)

Green, Kate Richmond, ed. *Interpretations of* A Winter's Tale *and* King Lear. Chicago, 1890. (First pub. as *Interpretation of* A Winter's Tale, The Shakespeare World No. 1, ed. H. Kate Richmond-West, Chicago, 1882.)

Greenblatt, Stephen. *Shakespearean Negotiations: The Circulation of Social Energy in Renaissance England.* Berkeley, 1988.

Greene, Gayle. "Women on Trial in Shakespeare and Webster: The Mettle of <Their> Sex." *Topic* 36 (1982), 5–19.

Greene, Robert. *The Second and last Part of Conny-catching.* 1592. Elizabethan and Jacobean Quartos, ed. G. B. Harrison, 1922. (Rpt. New York: Barnes & Noble, 1966.)

————. *The Thirde and last Part of Conny-catching.* 1592. *A Disputation Between a Hee Conny-catcher, and a Shee Conny-catcher.* 1592. Elizabethan and Jacobean Quartos, ed. G. B. Harrison. 1922. (Rpt. New York: Barnes & Noble, 1966.)

Greenhill, J[ames], W[illiam] A. Harrison, & F[rederick] J. Furnivall, comps. *A List of All the Songs & Passages in Shakspere Which Have Been Set to Music.* Rev. ed. The New Shakspere Soc. Pubs. Ser. 8, No. 3. 1884.

Greenlaw, Edwin. "Shakespeare's Pastorals." *SP* 13 (1916), 122–54.

Greer, Germaine. *Shakespeare.* OUP, 1986.

Greg, W[alter] W. "Another Note." 4 *Library* 12 (1931–2), 248.

————. *A Bibliography of the English Printed Drama to the Restoration.* 4 vols. 1939–59. Vol. 3. 1957. (Rpt. London: The Bibliographical Soc., 1970.)

————. *Dramatic Documents from the Elizabethan Playhouses.* 2 vols. OUP, 1931. (Rpt. OUP, 1969.)

————. *The Editorial Problem in Shakespeare: A Survey of the Foundations of the Text.* 3rd ed. OUP, 1954. (1st ed. 1942.)

————. "An Elizabethan Printer and his Copy." 4 *Library* 4 (1924), 102–18.

————. *Pastoral Poetry & Pastoral Drama.* 1906. (Rpt. New York: Russell & Russell, 1959. First pub. 1905.)

————. "Prompt Copies, Private Transcripts, and the 'Playhouse Scrivener.'" 4 *Library* 6 (1926), 148–56.

————. Review of Evelyn M. Albright, *Dramatic Publication in England, 1580–1640.* *RES* 4 (1928), 91–100.

————. *The Shakespeare First Folio.* OUP, 1955.

————. "Some Notes on Crane's Manuscript of *The Witch*." 4 *Library* 22 (1941–2), 208–22.

————. *Two Elizabethan Stage Abridgements: The Battle of Alcazar & Orlando Furioso.* OUP for The Malone Society, 1922.

Greif, Karen. "'If This were Play'd upon a Stage': Harley Granville Barker's Shakespeare Productions at the Savoy Theatre, 1912–14." *HLB* 28 (1980), 117–45.

Grene, David. *Reality and the Heroic Pattern.* Chicago, 1967.

Grey, Zachary. *Critical, Historical, and Explanatory Notes on Shakespeare.* 2 vols. 1754. (Rpt. New York: AMS, 1973.)

Greyerz, Georg von. *The Reported Scenes in Shakespeare's Plays.* Bern, 1965.

Griffin, William J. "Names in *The Winter's Tale*." *TLS,* 6 June 1936, p. 480.

Griffith, [Elizabeth]. *The Morality of Shakespeare's Drama Illustrated.* 1775. (Rpt. Eighteenth Century Sh. 14. London: Cass, 1971.)

Grillo, Ernesto. *Shakespeare and Italy.* Glasgow, 1949. (Rpt. New York: Haskell House, 1973.)

Grindon, Leo N. *The Shakspere Flora.* Manchester, 1883.

Grindon, Rosa. *Shakespeare & his Plays from a Woman's Point of View.* Manchester, 1930.

Grivelet, Michel. "Métamorphose et la poésie dans *Le Conte d'hiver*, IV, 4, 116–46 [1930–62]." *La Métamorphose dans la poésie baroque française et anglaise: Variations et résurgences.* Ed. Giséle Mathieu-Castellani. Etudes Littéraire Français 7. Tübingen, 1980. Pp. 183–8.

[Grose, Francis.] *A Classical Dictionary of the Vulgar Tongue.* 1785. (Rpt. Menston: Scolar, 1968.)

————. *A Provincial Glossary.* 1787. (Rpt. Menston: Scolar, 1968.)

Grose, Kenneth H., & B. T. Oxley. *Shakespeare*. 1965. (2nd ed. New York, 1969.)

Guazzo, Stefano. *The civile conversation*. . . . Introd. Edward Sullivan. Tudor Translations. Ser. 2. Vols. 7 & 8. 1925.

Guilpin, Edward. *Skialetheia or A Shadowe of Truth, in Certaine Epigrams and Satyres*. [1598.] Ed. D. Allen Carroll. Chapel Hill, 1974.

Guj, Louisa. "*The Winter's Tale* and the Eleusinian Goddesses." *Revista di Letterature Moderne e Comparate* 36 (1983), 5-24.

Gurr, Andrew. "The Bear, the Statue, and Hysteria in *The Winter's Tale*." *SQ* 34 (1983), 420-5.

————. "The Many-Headed Audience." *Essays in Theatre* 1 (1982), 52-62.

————. *The Shakespearean Stage 1574-1642*. 3rd ed. Cambridge, 1992. (1st ed. Cambridge, 1970.)

H., M. "Original Elucidations of *Shakespear*." *Gent. Mag.* 60 (1790), 306-7.

Haas, Virginia J. "Ralph Crane: A Status Report." *AEB* NS 3 (1989), 3-10.

Hale, John K. "The Maturing of Romance in *The Winter's Tale*." *Parergon* 3 (1985), 147-62.

Hale, Matthew. *Pleas of the Crown*. 1678. (Rpt. London: Professional Books, 1972.)

Hales, J[ohn] W. "Shakespeare's Greek Names." *Cornhill Mag.* 33 (1876), 208-16. (Rpt. in *Notes and Essays on Shakespeare*, 1884, pp. 105-19, rpt. New York: AMS, 1973.)

Hall, H[enry] T. *Shaksperean Fly-Leaves and Jottings*. New & enl. ed. 1871. (Rpt. New York: AMS, 1970. 1st ed. 1869.)

Hall, Sir Peter. *See* Berry, Ralph, 1989.

Halliday, F[rank] E. *The Poetry of Shakespeare's Plays*. Cambridge, Mass., 1954.

Halliwell, James O. *A Dictionary of Archaic and Provincial Words*. 2 vols. Brixton Hill, 1852.

————. *The Remarks of M. Karl Simrock on the Plots of Shakespeare's Plays*. Shakespeare Soc. Pubs. 43. 1850. (Rpt. Nendeln, Liechtenstein: Kraus, 1966.)

Hammersmith, James P. "Two Speech Assignments in *The Winter's Tale*, F1 (1623)." *PBSA* 75 (1981), 171-4.

Hankins, John E. *Backgrounds of Shakespeare's Thought*. Hamden, Conn., 1978.

————. "The Pains of the Afterworld: Fire, Wind, and Ice in Milton and Shakespeare." *PMLA* 71 (1956), 482-95.

————. *Shakespeare's Derived Imagery*. Lawrence, Kans., 1953. (Rpt. New York: Octagon Press, 1967.)

Happé, Peter. *Notes on 'The Winter's Tale.'* Shakespeare Workshop Eds. 1969.

Harbage, Alfred. *Annals of English Drama 975-1700*. 2nd ed. rev. S[amuel] Schoenbaum. 1964. (3rd ed. rev. Sylvia S. Wagonheim. 1989.)

————. *Shakespeare and the Rival Traditions*. New York, 1952. (Rpt. New York: Barnes & Noble, 1968.)

————. *William Shakespeare: A Reader's Guide*. New York, 1961.

Harbottle, Cecil. "The Old Corrector on *The Winter's Tale*." 1 *N&Q* 8 (1853), 95-7.

Harding, D. W. "Shakespeare's Final View of Women." *TLS*, 30 Nov. 1979, pp. 59-61.

[Hardinge, George.] *Another Essence of Malone*. 1801.

————. Minutius Felix (pseud.). *The Essence of Malone*. 2nd ed. 1800.

————. "The Winter's Tale." *Miscellaneous Works*. 3 vols. 1818. 3:29-81.

Hardman, C. B. "Theory, Form, and Meaning in Shakespeare's *The Winter's Tale*." *RES* NS 36 (1985), 228-35.

Hardy, Barbara. *Shakespeare's Self-Conscious Art*. F. E. L. Priestley Lecture Ser. Lethbridge, Alberta, 1989.

Hardy, T. Maskell. *The Songs from Shakespeare's Plays*. 2 pts. 1930.

Harman, Thomas. *A Caveat for Common Cursetors*. 1567. (Unauthorized rpt. 1567, ed. Edward Viles & F. J. Furnivall in *The Rogues and Vagabonds of Shakspere's Youth*, Early English Text Soc., 1869, rpt. New Sh. Soc., ser. 6, no. 7, 1880.)

Harp, Richard L. "*The Winter's Tale*: An 'Old Tale' Begetting Wonder." *DR* 58 (1978), 295–308.

Harris, Bernard. "'What's past is prologue': *Cymbeline* and *Henry VIII*." *Later Shakespeare*. Stratford-upon-Avon Stud. 8. Ed. John Russell Brown & Bernard Harris. 1966. Pp. 203–34.

Harris, Frank. *The Man Shakespeare and his Tragic Life Story*. 1909.

———. *The Women of Shakespeare*. 1911.

Harris, [Thomas?]. Contributor to v1803.

Harrison, G[eorge] B. "A Note on *Coriolanus*." *Joseph Quincy Adams Memorial Studies*. Ed. James G. McManaway et al. Washington, D.C., 1948. Pp. 239–52.

———. *Shakespeare*. 1927.

Harrison, Thomas P., Jr. "Aspects of Primitivism in Shakespeare and Spenser." *Studies in English* 20 (1940), 39–71.

Harrison, William. *The Description of England*. Ed. Georges Edelen. Ithaca, N.Y., 1968. (1st ed. 1587.)

Hart, Edward L. "A Mixed Consort: Leontes, Angelo, Helena." *SQ* 15 (1964), 75–83.

Hart, Henry C. "*Winter's Tale* [2279–81]." 8 *N&Q* 7 (1894), 64.

Harting, James E. *The Birds of Shakespeare*. 1871. (Rpt. Chicago: Argonaut, 1965.)

Hartt, Frederick. *Giulio Romano*. 2 vols. New Haven, 1958.

Hartwig, Joan. "Cloten, Autolycus, and Caliban: Bearers of Parodic Burdens." *Shakespeare's Romances Reconsidered*. Ed. Carol McG. Kay & Henry E. Jacobs. Lincoln, Nebr., 1978. Pp. 91–103.

———. "The Tragicomic Perspective of *The Winter's Tale*." *ELH* 37 (1970), 12–36. (Rpt. as "*The Winter's Tale*: 'The Pleasure of That Madness'" in *Shakespeare's Tragicomic Vision*, Baton Rouge, 1972, pp. 104–36.)

Hasler, Jörg. "Romance in the Theater: The Stagecraft of the 'Statue Scene' in *The Winter's Tale*." *Shakespeare, Man of the Theater*. Ed. Kenneth Muir et al. Newark, Del., 1983. Pp. 203–11.

Hassel, R[udolph] Chris, Jr. *Faith and Folly in Shakespeare's Romantic Comedies*. Athens, Ga., 1980.

———. *Renaissance Drama and the English Church Year*. Lincoln, Nebr., 1979.

Hastings, William T. "The Ancestry of Autolycus." *ShAB* 15 (1940), 253.

Hatcher, O. L. "The Sources and Authorship of *The Thracian Wonder*." *MLN* 23 (1908), 16–20.

Hattori, Takakazu. "The Sustaining Function of Realism in *The Winter's Tale*." *Essays on the English Bible and English Literature in Honour of Dr. Tateo Kanda.*. Ed. Toshiki Yamamoto. Tokyo, 1982. Pp. 85–104.

Hawkins, Harriet. *Poetic Freedom and Poetic Truth*. OUP, 1976.

Hazlitt, William. *Characters of Shakespear's Plays*. 1817.

Hazlitt, W[illiam] Carew. *Faiths and Folklore*. Brand's Popular Antiquities of Great Britain. 2 vols. 1905. (1st ed. of Brand's work, 1777.)

———. *Shakespeare's Library: A Collection of the Plays Romances Novels Poems and Histories Employed by Shakespeare in the Composition of His Works*. 2nd ed. rev. 6 vols. 1875. (Rpt. New York: AMS, 1950. 1st ed. 2 vols, 1843. *See* Collier, John Payne.)

Hearn, Lafcadio. *Lectures on Shakespeare*. Tokyo, 1928.

[Heath, Benjamin.] *A Revisal of Shakespear's Text*. 1765. (Micro-card rpt. Louisville, Ky.: Lost Cause Press, 1966.)

Heilbron, J. L. *See* Shumaker, Wayne.

Heilbrun, Carolyn G. *Toward a Recognition of Androgyny*. New York, 1973.

Heims, Neil. "Shakespeare's *The Winter's Tale*." *Expl* 46, No. 4 (1988), 6-7.

Hellenga, Robert R. "The Scandal of *The Winter's Tale*." *ES* 57 (1976), 11-18.

Henderson, [John?] (1747-85). Contributor to v1785.

Henderson, Katherine U., & Barbara F. McManus. *Half Humankind: Contexts and Texts of the Controversy about Women in England, 1540-1640*. Urbana & Chicago, 1985.

Henke, James T. *Courtesans and Cuckolds: A Glossary of Renaissance Dramatic Bawdy (Exclusive of Shakespeare)*. New York & London, 1979.

Henley, Samuel (1740-1815). Contributor to MAL, v1785, v1793.

Henley, W. E. *See* Farmer, John S.

Henn, T[homas] R. *The Living Image: Shakespearean Essays*. 1972.

Herford, C[harles] H. *Shakespeare*. The People's Books 51. [1912.] (Rpt. Philadelphia: R. West, 1978.)

————. "Shakespeare and the Arts." *BJRL* 11 (1927), 273-85.

Herrick, Marvin T. *Italian Comedy in the Renaissance*. Urbana, 1960.

————. *Tragicomedy: Its Origin and Development in Italy, France, and England*. Illinois Stud. in Lang. and Lit. 39. Urbana, 1955.

Hertzberg, W. "Metrisches, Grammatisches, Chronologisches zu Shakespeare's Dramen." *SJ* 13 (1878), 248-66.

Hetherington, Robert J. "Shakespeare after 400 Years." *The Listener* 76 (1966), 812.

Hibbard, G. "Politics in the Romances." *Revue de Philologie, Filolosŝki Pregled*. 1964. Pp. 103-16.

Hieatt, Charles W. "The Function of Structure in *The Winter's Tale*." *YES* 8 (1978), 238-48.

Higgins, John. *The Nomenclator, or Remembrancer of Adrianus Junius*. 1585.

Highfill, Philip H., Jr., ed. *Shakespeare's Craft: Eight Lectures*. Carbondale, Ill., 1982.

————, Kalman A. Burnim, & Edward A. Langhans. *A Biographical Dictionary of Actors . . . in London, 1660-1800*. 16 vols. Carbondale & Edwardsville, Ill., 1973-93.

Hillman, Richard W. "The 'Gillyvors' Exchange in *The Winter's Tale*." *ESC* 5 (1979), 16-23.

Hinman, Charlton. *The Printing and Proof-reading of the First Folio of Shakespeare*. 2 vols. OUP, 1963.

Hirschberg, Julius. "The Valley (*The Winter's Tale*, [1023])." *SJ* 56 (1920), 107.

Hirsh, James E. *The Structure of Shakespearean Scenes*. New Haven & London, 1981.

Hirst, David L. *Tragicomedy*. The Critical Idiom 43. 1984.

Hobson, Alan. *Full Circle: Shakespeare and Moral Development*. London & New York, 1972.

Hoeniger, F. David. "The Meaning of *The Winter's Tale*." *UTQ* 20 (1950), 11-26.

————. *Medicine and Shakespeare in the English Renaissance*. Newark, Del., 1992.

————. "Shakespeare's Romances Since 1958: A Retrospect." *ShS* 29 (1976), 1-10.

Hofling, Charles K. "Notes on Shakespeare's *The Winter's Tale*." *PsyR* 58 (1971), 90-110.

Hogan, Charles B. *Shakespeare in the Theatre 1701-1800: A Record of Performances in London*. 2 vols. OUP, 1952-7.

————. See *The London Stage 1660-1800*.

Holbrook, David. *The Quest for Love.* 1964.

Holbrook, Sibyl C. "Husbands in Shakspere." *ShAB* 20 (1945), 173–90.

Holden, William P. *Anti-Puritan Satire 1572–1642.* New Haven, 1954.

Holdsworth, R. V. "Sexual Allusions in *Love's Labour's Lost, The Merry Wives of Windsor, Othello, The Winter's Tale* and *The Two Noble Kinsmen.*" 33 *N&Q* 3 (1986), 351–3.

Holinshed, Raphael. *Chronicles* [1587]. 6 vols. 1807–8. With contributions by William Harrison. (Rpt. New York: AMS, 1965, 1976. 1st ed. 2 vols, 1577.)

Holland, Joanne F. "The Gods of *The Winter's Tale.*" *PCP* 5 (1970), 34–8.

Holland, Norman N. *Psychoanalysis and Shakespeare.* New York, 1966.

———. *The Shakespearean Imagination.* New York, 1964.

Holland, Peter. "Shakespeare Performances in England, 1992." *ShS* 46 (1994), 159–89.

Hollander, John. *The Untuning of the Sky: Ideas of Music in English Poetry.* Princeton, 1961.

Holme, Randle. *The Academy of Armory.* Chester, 1688. (Rpt. Menston: Scolar, 1972.)

Holmes, Martin. *Shakespeare and His Players.* London & New York, 1972.

———. *Shakespeare's Public, the Touchstone of His Genius.* 1960.

Holt, Charles L. "Notes on the Dramaturgy of *The Winter's Tale.*" *SQ* 20 (1969), 47–51.

Homan, Sidney R. "*The Tempest* and Shakespeare's Last Plays: The Aesthetic Dimensions." *SQ* 24 (1973), 69–76.

Honigmann, E[rnst] A. J. *Myriad-minded Shakespeare.* 1989.

———. "Re-enter the Stage Direction: Shakespeare and Some Contemporaries." *ShS* 29 (1976), 117–25.

———. "Secondary Sources of *The Winter's Tale.*" *PQ* 34 (1955), 27–38.

———. *Shakespeare's Impact on his Contemporaries.* 1982.

———. "Shakespeare's Mingled Yarn and 'Measure for Measure.'" *PBA* 67 (1981), 101–21.

———. *The Stability of Shakespeare's Text.* Lincoln, Nebr., 1965.

Hook, Frank S. "The Manuscript Alterations in the Honeyman First Folio." *PBSA* 53 (1959), 334–8.

Hoppin, James M. *The Reading of Shakespeare.* Boston & New York, 1906.

Horne, Herbert P. "Brief Note upon the Winter's Tale." *Century Guild Hobby Horse,* June 1888. Pp. 109–113.

Horowitz, David. *Shakespeare: An Existential View.* London & New York, 1965.

Horwitz, Eve. "'The Truth of Your Own Seeming'. Women and Language in *The Winter's Tale.*" *Unisa English Studies* 26 (1988), 7–14.

Hosley, Richard. "The Playhouses and the Stage." *A New Companion to Shakespeare Studies.* Ed. Kenneth Muir & S. Schoenbaum. Cambridge, 1971. Pp. 15–34.

———, ed. *Oberon, the Fairy Prince by Ben Jonson. A Book of Masques in Honour of Allardyce Nicoll.* Cambridge, 1967. Pp. 43–70.

Hotine, Kate. "Shakespeare's 'Winter's Tale.'" *ConR* 211 (1967), 46–8.

Hotine, Margaret. "Treason in *The Winter's Tale.*" *N&Q* 228 (1983), 127–30.

Hotson, Leslie. *Shakespeare's Motley.* OUP, 1952.

———. "The Wool-Dealer of Stratford." *The Times,* 22 Nov. 1930, p. 13.

Houseman, John. *Final Dress.* New York, 1983.

Howard, Skiles. "'Ascending the Riche Mount': Performing Hierarchy and Gender in the Henrician Masque." *Rethinking the Henrician Era.*. Ed. Peter C. Herman. Urbana & Chicago, 1994.

———. "Rival Discourses of Dancing in Early Modern England." *SEL* 36 (1996), 31–56.

Howard-Hill, T[revor] H. "The Compositors of Shakespeare's Folio Comedies." *SB* 26 (1973), 61–106.

—————. "Knight, Crane, and the Copy for the Folio *Winter's Tale.*" *N&Q* 211 (1966), 139–40.

—————. *Ralph Crane and Some Shakespeare First Folio Comedies.* Charlottesville, 1972.

—————. "Ralph Crane's Parentheses." *N&Q* 210 (1965), 334–40.

—————. "Shakespeare's Earliest Editor, Ralph Crane." *ShS* 44 (1992), 113–29.

Howe, P[ercival] P., ed. *The Complete Works of William Hazlitt.* 21 vols. [1930–4]. Vol. 5. 1930.

Hoy, Cyrus. "Fathers and Daughters in Shakespeare's Romances." *Shakespeare's Romances Reconsidered.* Ed. Carol McG. Kay & Henry E. Jacobs. Lincoln, Nebr., 1978. Pp. 77–90.

—————. *The Hyacinth Room: An Investigation into the Nature of Comedy, Tragedy, & Tragicomedy.* New York, 1964.

—————. "Jacobean Tragedy and the Mannerist Style." *ShS* 26 (1973), 49–67.

Hudson, Henry N. (1814–86). Contributor to CAM2.

—————. *Lectures on Shakspeare.* 2 vols. New York, 1848. (Rpt. New York: AMS, 1971.)

—————. *Shakespeare: His Life, Art, and Characters.* 2 vols. 4th ed., rev. Boston, 1872. (Rpt. New York: AMS, 1973. 1st ed. 1855.)

Hughes, Merritt Y. "A Classical *vs.* a Social Approach to Shakspere's Autolycus." *ShAB* 15 (1940), 219–26.

Hugo, François-Victor, tr. *Œuvres Complètes de W. Shakespeare.* 18 vols. Paris, 1865–73. Vol. 4, 1868. (1st ed. Paris, 1859–66.)

Hulme, Hilda M. *Explorations in Shakespeare's Language.* 1962.

—————. "The Spoken Language and the Dramatic Text: Some Notes on the Interpretation of Shakespeare's Language." *SQ* 9 (1958), 379–86.

Hunt, Maurice. "Leontes' 'Affection' and Renaissance 'Intention': *Winter's Tale* I.ii.135–46 [211–22]." *UMSE* 4 (1983), 49–55.

—————. *Shakespeare's Romance of the Word.* 1990.

—————. "'Standing in Rich Place': The Importance of Context in *The Winter's Tale.*" *RMR* 38 (1984), 13–33.

—————. "The Three Seasons of Mankind: Age, Nature, and Art in *The Winter's Tale.*" *ISJR* 58 (1984), 299–309.

Hunter, Edwin R. *Shakspere and Common Sense.* Boston, 1954.

Hunter, G[eorge] K. "Elizabethans and Foreigners." *ShS* 17 (1964), 37–52.

—————, ed. *All's Well That Ends Well.* New Arden Sh, 1962.

—————, ed. *The Malcontent.* By John Marston. The Revels Plays. 1975.

Hunter, Joseph. *New Illustrations of the Life, Studies, and Writings of Shakespeare.* 2 vols. 1845. (Rpt. New York: AMS, 1976.)

Hunter, Mark. "Act- and Scene-Division in the Plays of Shakespeare." *RES* 2 (1926), 295–310.

Hunter, Robert G. *Shakespeare and the Comedy of Forgiveness.* New York, 1965.

Huntley, Richard W. *A Glossary of the Cotswold (Gloucestershire) Dialect.* 1868.

Hurd, Myles. "Shakespeare's Paulina: Characterization and Craftsmanship in *The Winter's Tale.*" *CLAJ* 26 (1983), 303–10.

Hurdis, James. *Cursory Remarks upon the Arrangement of the Plays of Shakespear.* 1792.

Hussey, S[tanley] S. *The Literary Language of Shakespeare*. 2nd ed. London & New York, 1992. (1st ed. 1982.)

Ingleby, C[lement] M. "Mr. Collier's 'Notes and Emendations:' Passage in *The Winter's Tale* [1811]." 1 *N&Q* 7 (1853), 378-9.

————. "Shakespeare and Greene's *Diary*." 6 *N&Q* 11 (1885), 410.

————. *Shakespeare Hermeneutics, or The Still Lion*. 1875. (First pub. as "The still Lion. An essay towards the restoration of Shakespeare's text." *SJ* 2 [1867], 196-243; enl. as *The Still Lion*, 1874.)

————. *Shakespeare's Centurie of Prayse*. 2nd ed. Rev. Lucy Toulmin Smith. 1879.

————. *Shakespeare, the Man and the Book*. 2 vols. 1877-81.

Ingleby, Holcombe. "*Winter's Tale* [2279-81]." 8 *N&Q* 7 (1894), 64.

Ingram, John K. "On the 'Weak Endings' of Shakspere." *New Shakspere Society's Transactions 1874*. [1874]. Pp. 442-64. (Rpt. Vaduz: Kraus, 1965.)

Ingram, R. W. "Musical Pauses and the Vision Scene in Shakespeare's Last Plays." *Pacific Coast Studies in Shakespeare*. Ed. Waldo F. McNeir & Thelma N. Greenfield. Eugene, Ore., 1966. Pp. 234-47.

Ioppolo, Grace. *Revising Shakespeare*. Cambridge, Mass., 1991.

Irvine, Theodora. *A Pronouncing Dictionary of Shakespearean Proper Names*. New York, 1945. (1st ed. 1919.)

Isaacs, J[acob]. "Shakespeare." *The Listener* 76 (1966), 895-6.

————. "Shakespeare after 400 Years." *The Listener* 76 (1966), 685-7.

————. "Shakespeare's Earliest Years in the Theatre." *Proceedings of the British Academy* 39 (1953), 119-38.

Iwasaki, Soji. *Nature Triumphant: Approach to* The Winter's Tale. Sophia Univ. Ren. Monographs 10. Tokyo, 1984.

————. "*Veritas Filia Temporis* and Shakespeare."*ELR* 3 (1973), 249-63.

J., H. B. "'Prigging Tooth' or 'Pugging Tooth.'" 1 *N&Q* 7 (1853), 257-8.

Jabez. "'Land-damn.'" 5 *N&Q* 3 (1875), 383-4.

Jackson, Russell. "Shakespeare in Liverpool: Edward Saker's Revivals, 1876-81." *TN* 32 (1978), 100-9.

Jackson, Zachariah. *A Few Concise Examples of Seven Hundred Errors in Shakspeare's Plays*. 1818. (2nd ed., enl., 1818.)

————. *Shakespeare's Genius Justified*. 1819.

Jacobs, Henry E. *See* Kay, Carol McG.

Jacquot, Jean. "The Last Plays and the Masque." *Shakespeare 1971: Proceedings of the World Shakespeare Congress, Vancouver, August 1971*. Ed. Clifford Leech & J. M. R. Margeson. Toronto, 1972. Pp. 156-73.

Jain, S. A. *Shakespeare's Conception of Ideal Womanhood*. Madras, 1948.

James, D[avid] G. *Scepticism and Poetry*. 1937.

Jameson, [Anna B.]. *Shakspeare's Heroines: Characteristics of Women, Moral, Poetical, and Historical*. 2nd ed. 1889. (Rpt. New York: AMS, 1967. First pub. as *Characteristics of Women, Moral, Poetical, and Historical*. 2 vols. 1832; 2nd ed. first pub. 1833.)

Jamieson, Michael. "Shakespeare's Celibate Stage: The Problem of Accommodation to the Boy-Actress in *As You Like It, Antony and Cleopatra*, and *The Winter's Tale*." *Papers Mainly Shakespearian*. Ed. G[eorge] I. Duthie. Aberdeen Univ. Stud. 147. Edinburgh & London, [1964]. Pp. 21-39.

Jarrell, Randall. "Four Shakespeare Plays." *Kipling, Auden & Co*. New York, 1980. Pp. 328-31. (First pub. 1961.)

Jervis, Swynfen. *Dictionary of the Language of Shakespeare.* [Ed. Alexander Dyce.] 1868.
————. *Proposed Emendations of the Text of Shakspeare's Plays.* 1860. (2nd, rev. ed. 1861.)
Jewkes, Wilfred T. *Act Division in Elizabethan and Jacobean Plays.* Hamden, Conn., 1958.
Johnson, Samuel. *A Dictionary of the English Language.* 2 vols. 1755. (Rpt. New York: AMS, 1967. 4th, rev. ed., 2 vols., 1773, rpt. Beirut: Librairie du Liban, 1978.)
————. *Proposals for Printing, by Subscription, The Dramatick Works of William Shakespeare.* 1756. *Johnson on Shakespeare.* Ed. Arthur Sherbo. Vol. 7 of *The Yale Edition of the Works of Samuel Johnson.* New Haven & London, 1968. Pp. 51–8.
Jonas, Maurice. *Shakespeare and the Stage.* 1918. (Rpt. Folcroft, Pa.: Folcroft, 1969.)
Jones, Emrys. *The Origins of Shakespeare.* OUP, 1977.
————. *Scenic Form in Shakespeare.* OUP, 1971.
Jones, Gemma. "Hermione in *The Winter's Tale.*" *Players of Shakespeare: Essays in Shakespearean Performance by Twelve Players with the Royal Shakespeare Company.* Ed. Philip Brockbank. Cambridge, 1985.
Jorgens, Elise B., ed. *English Song 1600–1675.* 12 vols. 1986–9.
Jorgensen, Paul A. *Redeeming Shakespeare's Words.* Berkeley, 1962.
Joseph, Sr. Miriam. *See* Miriam Joseph, Sr.
Josephs, Lois. "Shakespeare and a Coleridgean Synthesis: Cleopatra, Leontes, and Falstaff." *SQ* 18 (1967), 17–21.
Jusserand, J[ean] J. "Ben Jonson's Views on Shakespeare's Art." *The Works of William Shakespeare.* Ed. A. H. Bullen. 10 vols. 1904–7. 10 (1907): 297–319. (Rpt. in Jusserand, *The School for Ambassadors and Other Essays,* 1925, pp. 255–88; rpt. Freeport, N.Y.: Books for Libraries, 1968.)
————. *The English Novel in the Time of Shakespeare.* Tr. Elizabeth Lee. 1890. (New ed. 1966; 1st Fr. ed. 1887.)
————. Introduction to *WT. Works.* Ed. Sidney Lee. 40 vols. New York, 1907–9. 15 (1907): ix–xlv.
————. "*Winter's Tale.*" *The School for Ambassadors and Other Essays.* 1925. Pp. 227–52. (Rpt. Freeport, N.Y.: Books for Libraries, 1968. First pub. 1907.)
Kable, William S. "Compositor B, The Pavier Quartos, and Copy Spellings." *SB* 21 (1968), 131–61.
Kahn, Coppélia. "The Providential Tempest and the Shakespearean Family." *Representing Shakespeare.* Ed. Murray M. Schwartz & Coppélia Kahn. Baltimore, 1980. Pp. 217–43. (Rpt. in *Man's Estate: Masculine Identity in Shakespeare,* Berkeley, 1981, pp. 193–225.)
Kail, Aubrey C. *The Medical Mind of Shakespeare.* Balgowlah, New South Wales, 1986.
Kamachi, Mitsuru. "The Theme of Time in *The Winter's Tale.*" *Albion* (Kyoto Univ.) 25 (1979), 18–38.
————. "What's in a Name?: Hermione and the Hermetic Tradition in *The Winter's Tale.*" *Shakespeare Studies* (Japan) 29 (1991), 21–36.
————. "'Would Her Name Were Grace': A Reconsideration of *The Winter's Tale.*" *Shakespeare Studies* (Japan) 18 (1979–80; 1983), 57–71.
Karimipour, Zahra. *See* Berkeley, David S.
Kastan, David S. "Shakespeare and 'The Way of Womenkind.'" *Daedalus* 111.3 (1982), 115–30.
Kato, Yukio. "On Leontes' Jealousy: 'Plausibility' in *The Winter's Tale.*" *Bulletin of Kyoto Univ. of Education* Ser. A, No. 63 (1983), 117–39.

Kaul, Mythili. "The Old Shepherd's Speech in *The Winter's Tale*." *UCrow* 7 (1987), 96–100.

Kaula, David. "Autolycus' Trumpery." *SEL* 16 (1976), 287–303.

Kay, Carol McG. "Alabama Shakespeare Festival." *SQ* 28 (1977), 220–3.

———, & Henry E. Jacobs, eds. *Shakespeare's Romances Reconsidered*. Lincoln, Nebr., 1978.

Kean, Charles. Preface. *"The Winter's Tale"* . . . *As First Performed on Monday, April 28th, 1856*. [1856.] Pp. v–x. (Rpt. Cornmarket, 1970.)

Keeton, George W. *Shakespeare and His Legal Problems*. 1930. (Rpt. Buffalo: William S. Hein, 1987. Rev. in *Shakespeare's Legal and Political Background*, 1967.)

Keightley, Thomas. "Shakspeare Emendations." 1 *N&Q* 7 (1853), 44–5. Continued in "Shakspeare Criticism," pp. 615–16, and in "Etymologies," 2 *N&Q* 4 (1857), 86–7.

———. *The Shakespeare-Expositor: An Aid to the Perfect Understanding of Shakespeare's Plays*. 1867. (Rpt. New York: AMS, 1973.)

Kellett, E[rnest] E. *Suggestions: Literary Essays*. Cambridge, 1923. (Rpt. Freeport, N.Y.: Books for Libraries, 1969.)

Kellner, Leon. *Restoring Shakespeare: A Critical Analysis of the Misreadings in Shakespeare's Works*. Leipzig & London, 1925. (Rpt. New York: Biblo & Tannen, 1969.)

Kennedy, Dennis. *Granville Barker and the Dream of Theatre*. Cambridge, 1985.

———. *Looking at Shakespeare*. Cambridge, 1993.

Kennedy, Milton B. *The Oration in Shakespeare*. Chapel Hill, 1942.

Kennet. "Shakespeare." *The Listener* 76 (1966), 969.

Kenrick, W[illiam]. *A Review of Doctor Johnson's New Edition of Shakespeare*. 1765. (Rpt. in *On Johnson's Shakespeare*, Johnsoniana II, New York: Garland, 1975.)

Kermode, Frank. *Shakespeare: The Final Plays*. Writers and Their Work 155. 1963.

———, ed. *The Tempest*. By William Shakespeare. Arden Sh. Cambridge, Mass., 1954.

Kernan, Alvin. "The plays and playwrights." *The Revels History of Drama in English*. Ed. J[ohn] Leeds Barroll et al. 8 vols. 1975–83. 3 (1975): 237–474.

K[ersey], J[ohn]. *Dictionarium Anglo-Britannicum*. 1708. (Rpt. Menston: Scolar, 1969.)

———. *A New English Dictionary*. 1702. (Rpt. Menston: Scolar, 1969.)

Kettle, Arnold, ed. *Shakespeare in a Changing World*. New York, 1964.

Kiessling, Nicholas K. *"The Winter's Tale*, II.iii.103–7 [1026–30]. An Allusion to the Hag-Incubus." *SQ* 28 (1977), 93–5.

Kilbourne, Frederick W. *Alterations and Adaptations of Shakespeare*. Boston, 1906. (Rpt. New York: AMS, 1973.)

Kilgour, Henry. "'Land-damn.'" 5 *N&Q* 3 (1875), 384.

Kimmins, Grace T. *Songs from the Plays of William Shakespeare, with Dances*. 1928. (First pub. c. 1911–13.)

Kines, Tom. *Songs from Shakespeare's Plays and Popular Songs of Shakespeare's Time*. New York, 1964.

King, T[homas] J. *Casting Shakespeare's Plays: London Actors and Their Roles, 1590–1642*. Cambridge, 1992.

Kinnear, Benjamin G. *Cruces Shakespearianæ: Difficult Passages in the Works of Shakespeare*. 1883.

———. "The Winter's Tale [744]." *Shakespeariana* 2 (1885), 259–60.

Kirsch, Arthur. *Shakespeare and the Experience of Love*. Cambridge, 1981.

Kitto, H[umphrey] D. F. *Greek Tragedy*. 1939. (Rpt. Garden City, N.Y.: Doubleday, 1954.)

Klein, Julius L. *Geschichte des Drama's*. 13 vols. in 15. Leipzig, 1865–76.

Knight, G[eorge] Wilson. *The Christian Renaissance with . . . New Discussions of Oscar Wilde and the Gospel of Thomas.* 1962. (1st ed. Toronto, 1933.)

————. *The Crown of Life: Essays in Interpretation of Shakespeare's Final Plays.* OUP, 1947. (Rpt. New York, 1966.)

————. *Principles of Shakespearian Production.* London & New York, 1936. (Reissued as *Shakespearian Production,* London & Evanston, Ill., 1964.)

————. *The Shakespearian Tempest.* OUP, 1932. (Rpt. London: Methuen, 1960.)

————. *The Sovereign Flower.* 1958.

Knights, L. C. "'Integration' in *The Winter's Tale.*" *SR* 84 (1976), 595–613. (Rpt. in *William Shakespeare's* The Winter's Tale, ed. Harold Bloom, New York, 1987.)

Knobel, E. B. "Astronomy and Astrology." *Shakespeare's England.* Ed. Sidney Lee & C[harles] T. Onions. 2 vols. OUP, 1916. 1:444–61.

Knowles, Richard. Private contributor.

————, ed. *As You Like It.* A New Variorum Ed. of Sh. New York, 1977.

Knowles, Richard P. "History as Metaphor: Daphne Dare's Late 19th- and Early 20th-Century Settings for Shakespeare at Stratford, Ontario, 1975–1980." *THSt* 5 (1985), 20–40.

————. "'The More Delay'd Delighted': Theophanies in the Last Plays." *ShakS* 15 (1982), 269–80.

Knowlton, Edgar C. "Nature and Shakespeare." *PMLA* 51 (1936), 719–44.

Kökeritz, Helge. *Shakespeare's Names: A Pronouncing Dictionary.* New Haven, 1959.

————. *Shakespeare's Pronunciation.* New Haven, 1953.

Koeppel, Emil. "Ein Vorbild für Shaksperes Statue der Hermione." *Archiv* 97 (1896), 329–32.

Kolbe, F[rederick] C. *Shakespeare's Way: A Psychological Study.* 1930.

Koppel, Richard. "Scenen-Eintheilungen und Orts-Angaben in den Shakespeare'schen Dramen." *SJ* 9 (1874), 269–94.

Kozmian, Stanislaus. "A Winter's Tale." *Athenæum* No. 2506 (6 Nov. 1875), 609.

Kreider, Paul V. *Elizabethan Comic Character Conventions.* Ann Arbor, 1935. (Rpt. New York: Octagon, 1975.)

————. *Repetition in Shakespeare's Plays.* Princeton, 1941. (Rpt. New York: Octagon, 1975.)

Krier, Theresa M. "The Triumph of Time: Paradox in *The Winter's Tale.*" *CentR* 26 (1982), 341–53.

Künstler, Ernst. "Böhmen am Meer." *SJ* 91 (1955), 212–16.

————. "Julio Romano im *Wintermärchen.*" *SJ* 92 (1956), 291–8.

Kuhl, E. P. "*The Winter's Tale.*" *TLS,* 9 May 1952, p. 313.

Lamb, Mary E. "Ovid and *The Winter's Tale.*" *Shakespeare and Dramatic Tradition.* Ed. W. R. Elton & William B. Long. 1989. Pp. 69–87.

Lambrechts, Guy. "Proposed New Readings in Shakespeare: The Comedies." *Homage à Shakespeare: Bull. de la Faculté des Lettres de Strasbourg* 43 (1965), 945–58.

Lamson, Roy, Jr. "English Broadside Ballad Tunes 1500–1700." Harvard diss., 1936.

Lancaster, H. Carrington. "Hermione's Statue." *SP* 29 (1932), 233–8.

Lande, Maydee G. "*The Winter's Tale*: A Question of Motive." *AI* 43 (1986), 51–65.

Lang, Andrew. "The Comedies of Shakespeare. XI.—*The Winter's Tale.*" *Harper's New Monthly Mag.* 88 (1894), 710–20.

Langbaine, Gerard. *An Account of the English Dramatick Poets.* Oxford, 1691. (Rpt. New York: Burt Franklin, 1965.)

Langlin, J. N. "On Shakespeare's Provincialisms." *Shakespeariana* 1 (1883–4), 185–8.

Langman, F. H. "*The Winter's Tale.*" *SoRA* 9 (1976), 195-204.

Langworthy, Charles A. "A Verse-Sentence Analysis of Shakespeare's Plays." *PMLA* 46 (1931), 738-51.

Laroque, François. "Feasts and Festivity in *The Winter's Tale*. A Study of the 'Sheep-shearing Scenes.'" *CahiersE* 6 (Oct. 1974), 8-14.

————. "A New Ovidian Source for the Statue Scene in *The Winter's Tale.*" *N&Q* 229 (1984), 215-17.

————. "Pagan Ritual, Christian Liturgy, and Folk Customs in *The Winter's Tale.*" *CahiersE* 22 (Oct. 1982), 25-33.

————. "*The Winter's Tale.*" *CahiersE* 10 (Oct. 1976), 90-2.

————. "*The Winter's Tale.*" *CahiersE* 34 (Oct. 1988), 97-9.

Lascelles, Mary. "Shakespeare's Pastoral Comedy." *More Talking of Shakespeare*. Ed. John Garrett. London & New York, 1959. Pp. 70-86. (Rpt. in *Notions and Facts: Collected Criticism and Research*, OUP, 1972.)

Latham, Grace. "Some of Shakspere's Metaphors, and His Use of Them in the Comedies." *New Shakspere Society's Transactions 1887-92.* [1892]. Pp. 397-427. (Read 8 Apr. 1892.)

Latham, R. G. "The 'Coast' of Bohemia, in *The Winter's Tale.*" *Athenæum* No. 2594 (14 July 1877), 48-9.

Lathrop, H. B. "Shakespeare's Dramatic Use of Songs." *MLN* 23 (1908), 1-5.

Latimer, Kathleen. "The Communal Action of *The Winter's Tale.*" *The Terrain of Comedy*. Ed. Louise Cowan. Dallas, 1984. Pp. 125-42.

Lavater, Lewes [i.e., Ludwig]. *Of Ghostes and Spirites Walking by Nyght*. Tr. R. H. 1572. Ed. J. Dover Wilson & May Yardley. Oxford, 1929.

Law, Robert Adger. "On Certain Proper Names in Shakespeare." *Studies in English* 30 (1951), 61-5.

————. "On the Dating of Shakespere's Plays." *SAB* 11 (1936), 46-51, 141.

Lawlor, John J. "*Pandosto* and the Nature of Dramatic Romance." *PQ* 41 (1962), 96-113.

Lawrence, W[illiam] J. *Speeding Up Shakespeare*. 1937. (Rpt. New York: Blom, 1968.)

————. "Thomas Ravenscroft's Theatrical Associations." *MLR* 19 (1924), 418-23.

————. *Those Nut-Cracking Elizabethans*. 1935. (Rpt. New York: Haskell House, 1969.)

Lawrence, William W. *Shakespeare's Problem Comedies*. Baltimore, 1969. (1st ed. 1931; rev. ed. 1960.)

Leavis, F. R. "The Criticism of Shakespeare's Late Plays: A Caveat." *Scrutiny* 10 (1942), 337-45. (Rpt. in *The Common Pursuit*, 1952, pp. 173-81.)

Lee, Sidney. "Bearbaiting, Bullbaiting, and Cockfighting." *Shakespeare's England*. Ed. Sidney Lee & C[harles] T. Onions. 2 vols. OUP, 1916. 2:428-36.

————. Introduction. *Shakespeare's Comedies, Histories & Tragedies Being a Reproduction of the First Folio Edition 1623*. OUP, 1902. Pp. xi-xxxv.

Leech, Clifford. "Masking and Unmasking in the Last Plays." *Shakespeare's Romances Reconsidered*. Ed. Carol McG. Kay & Henry E. Jacobs. Lincoln, Nebr., 1978. Pp. 40-59.

————. "Shakespeare's Songs and the Double Response." *The Triple Bond: Plays, Mainly Shakespearean, in Performance*. Ed. Joseph G. Price. University Park, Pa., & London, 1975. Pp. 73-91.

————. *Shakespeare's Tragedies and Other Studies in Seventeenth-Century Drama*. OUP, 1950.

————. "The Structure of the Last Plays." *ShS* 11 (1958), 19-30.

————, & Margeson, J.M.R., eds. *Shakespeare 1971: Proceedings of the World Shakespeare Congress, Vancouver, August 1971*. Toronto, 1972.

Lees, Francis N. "Plutarch and *The Winter's Tale.*" *N&Q* 221 (1976), 161-2.

Legouis, Émile. "Çà et Là." *A Book of Homage to Shakespeare*. Ed. Israel Gollancz. OUP, 1916. Pp. 405-10.

Leimberg, Inge. "'Give me thy hand': Some Notes on the Phrase in Shakespeare's Comedies and Tragedies." *Shakespeare: Text, Language, Criticism*. Ed. Bernhard Fabian & Kurt Tetzeli von Rosador. Hildesheim, 1987. Pp. 118-46.

————. "'The Image of Golden Aphrodite': Some Observations on the Name 'Hermione.'" *SJH*, 1988. Pp. 130-49.

[Lennox, Charlotte R.] *Shakespear Illustrated*. 3 vols. 1753-4. (Rpt. New York: AMS, 1973.)

Lenz, Joseph M. *The Promised End: Romance Closure in the Gawain-poet, Malory, Spenser, and Shakespeare*. New York, 1986.

Lerner, Laurence. "An Essay on Pastoral." *EIC* 20 (1970), 275-97. (Rpt. in *The Uses of Nostalgia: Studies in Pastoral Poetry*, 1972, pp. 275-97.)

Lettsom, William N. (1796-1865). Contributor to DYCE1 and DYCE2.

————. Contributor to William S. Walker 1854 and 1860.

————. "New Readings in Shakespeare." *Blackwood's Edinburgh Mag.* 74 (1853), 181-202, 303-24, 451-74.

————. "The Winter's Tale, [1789]." 1 *N&Q* 7 (1853), 378.

Lever, J. W. "Three Notes on Shakespeare's Plants." *RES* 3 (1952), 117-29.

Levin, Harry. "Shakespeare's Nomenclature." *Essays on Shakespeare*. Ed. Gerald W. Chapman. Princeton, 1965. Pp. 59-90.

Levith, Murray J. *What's in Shakespeare's Names*. Hamden, Conn., 1978.

Lewes, Louis. *The Women of Shakespeare*. Tr. Helen Zimmern. 1894. (1st Ger. ed. 1893.)

Lewis, [John Delaware? (1828-84)]. Contributor to CAM1.

Lievsay, John L. *Stefano Guazzo and the English Renaissance*. Chapel Hill, 1961.

Linden, Stanton J. "Perdita and the Gillyvors: *The Winter's Tale* [1887-1916]." *N&Q* 224 (1979), 140.

Lindenbaum, Peter. *Changing Landscapes: Anti-Pastoral Sentiment in the English Renaissance*. Athens, Ga., 1986.

————. "Time, Sexual Love, and the Uses of Pastoral in *The Winter's Tale*." *MLQ* 33 (1972), 3-22.

Linley, William, ed. *Shakespeare's Dramatic Songs*. 2 vols. 1816.

Linthicum, M[arie] C. *Costume in the Drama of Shakespeare and his Contemporaries*. OUP, 1936.

Lippmann, Edmund O. von. "Shakespeare's Ignorance?" *New Review* 4 (1891), 250-4.

Littledale, H[arold]. "Folklore and Superstitions: Ghosts and Fairies: Witchcraft and Devils." *Shakespeare's England*. Ed. Sidney Lee & C[harles] T. Onions. 2 vols. OUP, 1916. 1:516-46.

————, ed. *The Two Noble Kinsmen*. By William Shakspere & John Fletcher. 2 Pts. Pt. 1. Revised Text and Notes. 1876.

Littlefield, T. H. "Shakespeare in Upstate New York." *SQ* 33 (1982), 207-8.

Litto, Fredric M. "The Coherence of the Oracle of Delphi in *The Winter's Tale*." *EAA* 5-6 (1981-2), 163-71.

Livingston, Mary L. "The Natural Art of *The Winter's Tale*." *MLQ* 30 (1969), 340-55.

Lloyd, Julius (1830-92). Contributor to CAM1.

Lloyd, William W. (1813-93). Contributor to SING2.

————. *Critical Essays on the Plays of Shakespeare*. 1894. (1st ed. 1858; rpt. 1875.)

————. "'Winter's Tale' [575-6]." 8 *N&Q* 1 (1892), 470-1.

Lloyd Evans, Gareth. *The Upstart Crow. An Introduction to Shakespeare's Plays.* Ed. and rev. Barbara Lloyd Evans. 1982.

The London Stage 1660–1800. Ed. William Van Lennep, Emmett L. Avery, Arthur H. Scouten, George W. Stone, & Charles B. Hogan. 5 pts. in 11 vols. Carbondale, Ill., 1960–8. *Index* ed. Ben R. Schneider, Jr. 1979.

Long, John H. *Shakespeare's Use of Music: The Final Comedies.* Gainesville, Fla., 1961.

Lothian, J. M. "Shakespeare's Knowledge of Aretino's Plays." *MLR* 25 (1930), 415–24.

Lounsbury, Thomas R. *Shakespeare as a Dramatic Artist.* New York, 1901.

Lovejoy, Arthur O. *Essays in the History of Ideas.* Baltimore, 1948.

————, & George Boas. *Primitivism and Related Ideas in Antiquity.* Vol. 1 of A Documentary History of Primitivism & Related Ideas. Baltimore, 1935. (Rpt. New York: Octagon, 1965.)

Ludwig, Jay B. "Shakespearean Decorum: An Essay on *The Winter's Tale.*" *Style* 8 (1974), 365–404.

Lüders, Ferdinand. "Prolog und Epilog bei Shakespeare." *SJ* 5 (1870), 274–91.

Lüthi, Max. *Shakespeares Dramen.* Berlin, 1957.

Luserke, Martin. *Pan—Apollon—Prospero.* "Ein Mittsommernachstraum," "Die Winterssage" und "Der Sturm." *Zur Dramaturgie von Shakespeare-Spielen.* Hamburg, 1957.

Lyons, Clifford. "Stage Imagery in Shakespeare's Plays." *Essays on Shakespeare and Elizabethan Drama in Honor of Hardin Craig.* Ed. Richard Hosley. Columbia, Mo., 1962. Pp. 261–74.

MacDonald, George. *Orts.* 1882. (Rpt. as *The Imagination and Other Essays,* Boston, 1883, and, enl., as *A Dish of Orts,* 1908.)

MacDonald, Michael. "Magic, Science, and Folklore." *William Shakespeare: His World, his Work, his Influence.* Ed. John F. Andrews. 3 vols. New York, 1985. 1:175–94.

Macdonald, Susan. "A Conversation in *The Winter's Tale.*" *Graduate English Papers* (Arizona) 6 (1974), 1–2.

Mack, Maynard. "Engagement and Detachment in Shakespeare's Plays." *Essays on Shakespeare and Elizabethan Drama in Honor of Hardin Craig.* Ed. Richard Hosley. Columbia, Mo., 1962. Pp. 275–96.

Mackail, J[ohn] W. *Lectures on Poetry.* OUP, 1911. (Rpt. Freeport, N.Y.: Books for Libraries, 1967.)

Mackay, Charles. *New Light on Some Obscure Words and Phrases in the Works of Shakespeare and his Contemporaries.* 1884.

Mackenzie, Agnes M. *The Women in Shakespeare's Plays.* 1924.

Mackinnon, Lachlan. *Shakespeare the Aesthete: An Exploration of Literary Theory.* Houndmills, 1988.

MacNeice, Louis. "Autolycus." *The Collected Poems of Louis MacNeice.* Ed. E. R. Dodds. New York, 1967.

Macquoid, Percy. "Costume." *Shakespeare's England.* Ed. Sidney Lee & C[harles] T. Onions. 2 vols. OUP, 1916. 2:91–118.

Madden, D[odgson] H. *The Diary of Master William Silence.* 1897.

Magnusson, A. Lynne. "Finding Place for a Faultless Lyric: Verbal Virtuosity in *The Winter's Tale.*" *UCrow* 9 (1989), 96–106.

Mahon, John. "Perdita's Reference to Proserpina in Act IV of *The Winter's Tale.*" *N&Q* 229 (1984), 214–15.

Mahood, M[olly] M. *Bit Parts in Shakespeare's Plays.* Cambridge, 1992.

————. "The Fatal Cleopatra: Shakespeare and the Pun." *EIC* 1 (1951), 193-207.

————. *Shakespeare's Wordplay*. 1957. (Rpt. London: Methuen, 1965.)

Maitland, J. A. Fuller, & W. Barclay Squire, eds. *The Fitzwilliam Virginal Book*. 2 vols. 1899. (Rpt. New York: Dover, 1979.)

Maitra, Sitansu. *Shakespeare's Comic Idea*. Calcutta, 1960.

Male, David A. *"The Winter's Tale."* Shakespeare on Stage. Cambridge, 1984.

Malone, Edmond (1741-1812). Contributor to v1778, v1785, v1793, v1821.

————. "An Attempt to Ascertain the Order in Which the Plays Attributed to Shakspeare Were Written." *The Plays of William Shakspeare*. Ed. Samuel Johnson & George Steevens. 10 vols. 1778. 1:269-346.

————. *A Second Appendix to Mr. Malone's Supplement to the Last Edition of the Plays of Shakspeare*. 1783.

————. *Supplement to the Edition of Shakspeare's Plays Published in 1778*. 2 vols. 1780.

Manning, H. C. *Shakespeare's Speache: Echoes of Elizabethan and Stuart Pronunciation*. Dorchester, 1929.

Manwayring, Henry. *The Sea-mans Dictionary*. 1644. (Rpt. Menston: Scolar, 1972.)

Marcham, Frank. *The King's Office of the Revels 1610-1622*. 1925.

Marder, Louis. "Shakespeare's Musical Background." *MLN* 65 (1950), 501-3.

Markel, Michael H. "Why Hermione Lives But Desdemona Dies: An Approach to Shakespearian Genre Definition." *Publications of the Arkansas Philological Assn.* 4, No. 2 (1978), 50-6.

Marks, Jeannette. *English Pastoral Drama*. 1908.

Marsh, Derick R. C. *The Recurring Miracle: A Study of* Cymbeline *and the Last Plays*. Pietermaritzburg, South Africa, [1962]. (Rpt. Lincoln, Nebr., [1969]. 3rd ed. Sydney, 1980.)

Marshall, Cynthia. "Dualism and the Hope of Reunion in *The Winter's Tale*." *Soundings* 69 (1986), 294-309.

Martin, Helena Faucit. "Shakespeare's Women: . . . Hermione." *Blackwood's Edinburgh Mag.* 149 (1891), 1-37. (Rpt. in *On Some of Shakespeare's Female Characters*, 5th ed., 1893, pp. 337-92, rpt. New York: AMS, 1970.)

Martinet, Marie-Madeleine. "Images de l'Art et Temps Theatral, ou le Seuil de l'Ombre." *Verité et Illusion dans le Theatre au Temps de la Renaissance*. Ed. M. T. Jones-Davies. Paris, 1983. (Translation forbidden.)

————. "*The Winter's Tale* et 'Julio Romano.'" *EA* 28 (1975), 257-68.

Martz, Louis L. "Shakespeare's Humanist Enterprise: *The Winter's Tale*." *English Renaissance Studies Presented to Dame Helen Gardner in Honour of her Seventieth Birthday*. Ed. John Carey. Oxford, 1980. Pp. 114-31.

Marudanayagam, P. "Shakespeare's *The Winter's Tale* [414-23]." *Expl* 41, No. 3 (1983), 18-19.

Marx, Leo. *The Machine in the Garden*. New York, 1964.

Marx, Theodor. "'Land-damn.'" 5 *N&Q* 4 (1875), 102.

Masefield, John. *William Shakespeare*. Home Univ. Libr. of Modern Knowledge. Rev. ed. 1912. (Rpt. Folcroft, Pa: Folcroft Library Eds., 1978. 1st ed. 1911.)

Mason, John Monck (1726-1809). Contributor to MAL.

————. *Comments on the Last Edition of Shakespeare's Plays*. 1785. (Rpt. as pt. 1 of *Comments on the Several Editions of Shakespeare's Plays, Extended to Those of Malone and Steevens*, Dublin: 1807, rpt. New York: AMS, 1937.)

————. *Comments on the Plays of Beaumont and Fletcher with an Appendix Con-*

taining Some Further Observations on Shakespeare, Extended to the Late Editions of Malone and Steevens. 1798. (Appendix rpt. New York: Garland, 1972.)

Masson, David. *Shakespeare Personally*. 1914.

Matchett, William H. "Some Dramatic Techniques in *The Winter's Tale*." *ShS* 22 (1969), 93–107.

Mathew, F[rank]. *An Image of Shakespeare*. 1922. (Rpt. New York: Haskell House, 1972.)

Matthews, [James] Brander. *Shakspere as a Playwright*. 1913. (Rpt. New York: AMS, 1970.)

————. *A Study of the Drama*. New York, 1910.

Maveety, Stanley R. "Hermione, a Dangerous Ornament." *SQ* 14 (1963), 485–6.

————. "What Shakespeare Did With *Pandosto*: An Interpretation of *The Winter's Tale*." *Pacific Coast Studies in Shakespeare*. Ed. Waldo F. McNeir & Thelma N. Greenfield. Eugene, Ore., 1966. Pp. 263–79.

Maxwell, J[ames] C. (1916–76). Contributor to ARD2.

————. "The Ghost from the Grave: A Note on Shakespeare's Apparitions." *DUJ* 48 (1956), 55–9.

————. Rev. of Kenneth Muir, *Shakespeare's Sources. Vol. I: Comedies and Tragedies*. *RES* NS 9 (1958), 314–16.

————, ed. *Cymbeline*. New [Cambridge] Sh. 1960.

McClenthen, F. C. "A Passage in *The Winter's Tale* [575–7]." *Shakespeariana* 5 (1888), 168–9.

McCloskey, John C. "Shakespeare's *The Winter's Tale*, I, ii." *Expl* 23 (1965), no. 40.

McDonald, Russ. "Poetry and Plot in *The Winter's Tale*." *SQ* 36 (1985), 315–29.

McFarland, Thomas. *Shakespeare's Pastoral Comedy*. Chapel Hill, 1972.

McIver, Bruce. "Shakespeare's Miraculous Deception: Transcendence in *The Winter's Tale*." *MSpr* 73 (1979), 341–51.

McKenzie, D. F. "Compositor B's Role in *The Merchant of Venice* Q2 (1619)." *SB* 12 (1959), 75–89.

————. "Stretching a Point: Or, The Case of the Spaced-out Comps." *SB* 37 (1984), 106–21.

McKernan, Luke, & Olwen Terris, eds. *Walking Shadows: Shakespeare in the National Film and Television Archive*. 1994.

McKerrow, Ronald B. *Printers' & Publishers' Devices in England and Scotland 1485–1640*. 1949. (First pub. 1913.)

————. *Prolegomena for the Oxford Shakespeare: A Study in Editorial Method*. OUP, 1939.

McLuskie, Kathleen E. "'The Emperor of Russia was my father': Gender and Theatrical Power." *Images of Shakespeare. Proceedings of the Third Congress of the International Sh. Assn., 1986*. Ed. Werner Habicht et al. Newark, Del., 1988. Pp. 174–87.

McManaway, James G. "Recent Studies in Shakespeare's Chronology." *ShS* 3 (1950), 22–33.

————. "Textual Studies." *ShS* 18 (1965), 186–92.

McManus, Barbara F. *See* Henderson, Katherine U.

McManus, Eva B. "Chastity, Women's 'Otherness' and Patriarchy: Issues in *The Winter's Tale*." *ShN* 38 (1988), 24.

McMurtry, Jo. *Understanding Shakespeare's England*. Hamden, Conn., 1989.

McPeek, James A. S. *The Black Book of Knaves and Unthrifts in Shakespeare and Other Renaissance Authors*. Storrs, Conn., 1969.

Meader, William G. *Courtship in Shakespeare: Its Relation to the Tradition of Courtly Love*. New York, 1954.

Melchiori, Barbara. "Still Harping on My Daughter." *EM* 11 (1960), 59-74.

Meldrum, Ronald M. "Dramatic Intentions in The Winter's Tale." *Humanities Assn. Bull.* 19 (1968), 52-60.

Mellers, Wilfrid. *Harmonious Meeting: A Study of the Relationship between English Music, Poetry and Theatre, c. 1600-1900.* 1965.

Mendilow, Adam A. "Two Notes on Shakespeare." *Studies in the Drama.* Scripta Hierosolymitana 19. Ed. Arieh Sachs. Jerusalem, 1967. Pp. 262-8.

————, & Alice Shalvi. *The World and Art of Shakespeare.* New York, 1967.

Mendl, R[obert] W. S. *Revelation in Shakespeare.* 1964.

Merchant, W[illiam] Moelwyn. *Shakespeare and the Artist.* OUP, 1959.

Merriam, Thomas. "Did Shakespeare Model Camillo in *The Winter's Tale* on Sir Thomas More?" *Moreana* 19, No. 75-6 (Nov. 1982), 91-101.

Mézières, A[lfred]. *Shakespeare, ses œuvres et ses critiques.* Paris, 1882. (1st ed. Paris, 1860.)

Miko, Stephen J. "*Winter's Tale.*" *SEL* 29 (1989), 259-75.

Mills, Barriss. "Motivation in *Othello* and *The Winter's Tale.*" *The Univ. Rev.* 33 (1966), 107-12.

Mills, Laurens J. *One Soul in Bodies Twain: Friendship in Tudor Literature and Stuart Drama.* Bloomington, Ind., 1937.

Milton, John. *The Complete English Poetry of John Milton.* Ed. John T. Shawcross. New York, 1963.

Milward, Peter. *Shakespeare's Religious Background.* 1973.

————. "A Theology of Grace in *The Winter's Tale.*" *Eng. Lang. and Lit.* 2 (1964), 27-50.

Mincoff, Marco. "Plot Construction in Shakespeare." *Annuaire de l'Université de Sofia, Faculté historico-philologique* 34 (1941), 1-51.

————. *Things Supernatural and Causeless.* Newark, Del., 1992.

Minsheu, John. *Ductor in Linguas, The Guide into Tongues.* 1617. (Rpt. Delmar, N.Y.: Scholars' Facsimiles & Rpts., 1978.)

Miriam Joseph, Sr. *Shakespeare's Use of the Arts of Language.* Columbia Univ. Stud. in Eng. & Comp. Lit. 165. New York, 1947.

[Mitford, John.] "Conjectural Emendations on the Text of Shakspere, with Observations on the Notes of the Commentators." *Gent. Mag.* NS 22 (1844), 115-36, 451-72; NS 23 (1845), 115-32, 571-85.

Mönkemeyer, Paul. *Prolegomena zu einer Darstellung der englischen Volksbühne zur Elisabeth- und Stuart-Zeit nach den alten Bühnenanweisungen.* Göttingen, 1905.

Montmorency, J. E. G. de "Shakespeare and Pictorial Art." *ConR* 103 (1913), 737-41.

————. "Shakespeare's Legal Problems." *ConR* 137 (1930), 797-801.

Moore, John R. "Ancestors of Autolycus in the English Moralities and Interludes." *Washington Univ. Stud., Humanistic Ser.* 9 (1922), 157-64.

————. "The Functions of the Songs in Shakespeare's Plays." *Shakespeare Studies by Members of the Department of English of the University of Wisconsin.* Madison, 1916. Pp. 78-102.

————. "The Songs of the Public Theaters in the Time of Shakespeare." *JEGP* 28 (1929), 166-202.

[Morehead, Robert.] *Explanations and Emendations of Some Passages in the Text of Shakespeare and of Beaumont and Fletcher.* Edinburgh, 1814.

Morley, Henry. Introduction. *The Winter's Tale.* Cassell's National Library. [1887.] Pp. 5–14.

Moro, Bernard, & Michèle Willems. "Death and Rebirth in *Macbeth* and *The Winter's Tale.*" *CahiersE* 21 (Apr. 1982), 35–48.

Moulton, Richard G. *The Moral System of Shakespeare.* New York & London, 1903. (Rpt. as *Shakespeare as a Dramatic Thinker,* New York & London, 1907, rpt. Norwood, Pa.: Norwood Eds., 1977.)

————. *Shakespeare as a Dramatic Artist.* 3rd, rev. & enl. ed. OUP, 1893. (1st ed. 1885.)

Mount, C. B. "Sir Philip Sidney and Shakespeare." 8 *N&Q* 3 (1893), 305.

————. "*Winter's Tale* [2279–81]." 8 *N&Q* 4 (1893), 443.

Mowat, Barbara. *The Dramaturgy of Shakespeare's Romances.* Athens, Ga., 1976.

————. "A Tale of Sprights and Goblins." *SQ* 20 (1969), 37–46.

Mueller, Martin. "Hermione's Wrinkles, or Ovid Transformed: An Essay on *The Winter's Tale.*" *CompD* 5 (1971), 226–39.

Muir, Kenneth. "The Conclusion of *The Winter's Tale.*" *The Morality of Art: Essays Presented to G. Wilson Knight.* Ed. D[ouglas] W. Jefferson. New York, 1969. Pp. 87–101.

————. "The Dramatic Function of Anachronism." *Proceedings of the Leeds Philosophical and Literary Soc.* 6, No. 8 (May 1951), 529–33.

————. Introduction: *Shakespeare—The Winter's Tale. A Casebook.* 1968.

————. *Last Periods of Shakespeare, Racine, Ibsen.* Detroit, 1961.

————. *Shakespeare as Collaborator.* 1960.

————. *Shakespeare's Sources. 1: Comedies and Tragedies.* 1957. (Rpt. with new appendices, 1961. Vol. 2 never pub. Rev. as *The Sources of Shakespeare's Plays,* 1977.)

————. "Theophanies in the Last Plays." *Shakespeare's Late Plays: Essays in Honor of Charles Crow.* Ed. Richard C. Tobias & Paul G. Zolbrod. Athens, Ohio, 1974. Pp. 32–43.

————, & S[amuel] Schoenbaum, eds. *A New Companion to Shakespeare Studies.* Cambridge, 1971.

Murphy, Arthur. *Life of David Garrick Esq.* 2 vols. 1801. (Rpt. New York & London: Blom, 1969.)

Murray, Christopher. "Shakespeare at the Abbey." *SQ* 32 (1981), 173–6.

Murry, J[ohn] Middleton. *Shakespeare.* 1936.

Mutschmann, Heinrich, & Karl Wentersdorf. *Shakespeare und der Katholizismus.* Speyerer Studien Reihe 2, Band 2. Speyer, 1950. (Tr. as *Shakespeare and Catholicism,* New York, 1952.)

Naef, Irene. *Die Lieder in Shakespeares Komödien: Gehalt und Funktion.* Berne, 1976.

Nagata, Yoshiko. *Shakespeare's Underthought in the Later Plays.* Sophia Univ. Renaissance Monographs 4. Tokyo, 1977.

Naito, Kenji. "The Innate Wisdom of Perdita." *Poetry and Drama in the Age of Shakespeare: Essays in Honour of Professor Shonosake Ishii's Seventieth Birthday.* Ed. Peter Milward & Tetsuo Anzai. Tokyo, 1982. Pp. 156–66.

Nares, Robert. *A Glossary of Words, Phrases, Names, and Allusions.* Enl. ed. by James O. Halliwell & Thomas Wright. 2 vols. 1876. (1905 ed. rpt. Detroit: Gale Research, 1966. 1st ed. 1822.)

Nathan, Norman. "Leontes' Provocations." *SQ* 19 (1968), 19–24.

Naylor, Edward W. *Shakespeare and Music.* New ed. 1931. (Rpt. New York: Da Capo Press & Blom, 1965. 1st ed. 1896.)

Neely, Carol T. *Broken Nuptials in Shakespeare's Plays*. New Haven & London, 1985.

——. *"The Winter's Tale:* The Triumph of Speech." *SEL* 15 (1975), 321-38.

——. "Women and Issue in *The Winter's Tale*." *PQ* 57 (1978), 181-94.

Neilson, William A., & Ashley H. Thorndike. *The Facts About Shakespeare*. New York, [c. 1913].

Nelson, Thomas A. *Shakespeare's Comic Theory: A Study of Art and Artifice in the Last Plays*. The Hague, 1972 [1973].

Nevo, Ruth. *Shakespeare's Other Language*. New York, 1987.

Newman, Judie. "'Exit, pursued by a bear': *The Winter's Tale*." *N&Q* 233 (1988), 484.

Newton, K. M. *In Defence of Literary Interpretation: Theory and Practice*. Basingstoke, 1986.

Nicholl, Charles. *The Chemical Theatre*. 1980.

Nichols, James. *Notes on Shakespeare*. 2 pts. 1861-2. (2nd ed. 1862.)

Nichols, John. *Illustrations of the Literary History of the Eighteeenth Century*. 8 vols. 1817-58. (Rpt. New York: Kraus-AMS, 1966.)

——. *The Progresses, Processions, and Magnificent Festivities, of King James the First*. 4 vols. 1828. (Rpt. New York: Kraus-AMS, 1969.)

Nichols, Mary P. *"The Winter's Tale*: The Triumph of Comedy Over Tragedy." *IJPP* 9 (1981), 169-90.

Nicholson, Brinsley (1824-92). Contributor to CAM1 and CAM2.

——. "Shakespeare Illustrated by Massinger and Field." 3 *N&Q* 11 (1867), 433-5.

——. "Shakspeariana." 4 *N&Q* 12 (1873), 283-4.

——. "Shakspeariana." 6 *N&Q* 6 (1882), 23.

——. "The Winter's Tale II, i." *Shakespeariana* 1 (1883-4), 124-5.

Nicoll, Allardyce. *A History of Restoration Drama 1600-1700*. Cambridge, 1923. (3rd ed. 1940.)

——. *Shakespeare*. 1952.

——. "Shakespeare and the Court Masque." *SJ* 94 (1958), 51-62.

——. *Stuart Masques and the Renaissance Stage*. New York, 1938.

Noble, Richmond. *Shakespeare's Biblical Knowledge and Use of the Book of Common Prayer*. 1935. (Rpt. New York: Octagon, 1970.)

——. "Shakespeare's Songs and Stage." *A Series of Papers on Shakespeare and the Theatre . . . by Members of the Shakespeare Association*. 1927, Pp. 120-33. (Paper read 17 Feb. 1926.)

——. *Shakespeare's Use of Song With the Text of the Principal Songs*. OUP, 1923. (Rpt. Norwood, Pa.: Norwood, 1977.)

Norvell, Betty G. "Hermione as a Dramatic Figure." *SPWVSRA* 9 (1984), 8-12.

Nosworthy, J. M. "Music and its Function in the Romances of Shakespeare." *ShS* 11 (1958), 60-9.

——. *Shakespeare's Occasional Plays: Their Origin and Transmission*. 1965.

——, ed. *Cymbeline*. Arden Sh. 1955.

Novy, Marianne. *Love's Argument: Gender Relations in Shakespeare*. Chapel Hill, 1984.

Nuttall, A. D. "Two Unassimilable Men." *Shakespearian Comedy*. Stratford-upon-Avon Stud. 14. 1972. Pp. 210-40.

——. *William Shakespeare: The Winter's Tale*. Stud. in Eng. Lit. 26. 1966.

O'Connell, Michael. "The Idolatrous Eye: Iconoclasm, Antitheatricalism, and the Image of the Elizabethan Theater." *ELH* 52 (1985), 279-310.

O'Connor, John J. Amadis de Gaule *and Its Influence on Elizabethan Literature*. New Brunswick, N.J., 1970.

Odell, George C. D. *Annals of the New York Stage*. 15 vols. New York, 1927-49. (Rpt. New York: AMS, 1970.)

———. *Shakespeare from Betterton to Irving*. 2 vols. New York, 1920. (Rpt. New York: Blom, 1963; Dover, 1966; AMS, 1970.)

Okubo, Junichiro. "Romantic Motives in *The Winter's Tale*—From Greene's Romance to Shakespeare." *Kanawaza Daigaku Hobunggakubu Ronshu* 12 (1965), 1-22.

Onions, C[harles] T. "Natural History I. Animals." *Shakespeare's England*. Ed. Sidney Lee & C. T. Onions. 2 vols. OUP, 1916. 1:475-99.

———. *A Shakespeare Glossary*. Enl. and rev. Robert D. Eagleson. OUP, 1986. (1st ed. 1911; 2nd, rev. ed., with addenda, 1953, rpt. 1958.)

Oras, Ants. *Pause Patterns in Elizabethan and Jacobean Drama*. Univ. of Florida Monographs, Humanities, No. 3. Gainesville, 1960.

Ordish, Thomas F. *Shakespeare's London: A Commentary on Shakespeare's Life and Work in London*. 2nd, rev. ed. 1904. (1st ed. 1897.)

Orgel, Stephen. *The Jonsonian Masque*. Cambridge, Mass., 1965.

———. "The Poetics of Incomprehensibility." *SQ* 42 (1991), 431-7.

———, ed. *The Tempest*. Oxford Sh. Oxford, 1987.

———, & Roy Strong. *Inigo Jones: The Theatre of the Stuart Court*. 2 vols. 1973.

Orger, J[ohn] G. *Critical Notes on Shakspere's Comedies*. [1890.]

Ornstein, Robert. "The Ethic of the Imagination: Love and Art in *Antony and Cleopatra*." *Later Shakespeare*. Stratford-upon-Avon Stud. 8. New York, 1967. Pp. 31-46.

———. *Shakespeare's Comedies from Roman Farce to Romantic Mystery*. Newark, Del., 1986.

Ortego, Philip D. "*The Winter's Tale* as a Pastoral Tragicomic Romance." *Rendezvous* 5 (1970), 31-4.

Overton, Bill. *The Winter's Tale*. The Critics Debate. Basingstoke, 1989.

The Oxford English Dictionary. Ed. James A. H. Murray et al. 12 vols. & supplement. OUP, 1933. (Orig. pub. as *A New English Dictionary on Historical Principles*, 10 vols., 1888-1928.)

Oxley, B[rian] T. *See* Grose, Kenneth H.

Pafford, J. H. P. "The Lady and Her Horsekeeper." *N&Q* 211 (1966), 393.

———. "Music, and the Songs in *The Winter's Tale*." *SQ* 10 (1959), 161-75.

———. "Simon Forman's 'Bocke of Plaies.'" *RES* NS 10 (1959), 289-91.

———. "The Unmarried Primrose." *N&Q* 199 (1954), 37.

———. "*The Winter's Tale*: Typographical Peculiarities in the Folio Text." *N&Q* 206 (1961), 172-8.

Palmer, Daryl W. "Entertainment, Hospitality, and Family in *The Winter's Tale*." *ISJR* 59 (1985), 253-61.

Palmer, D[avid] J., ed. *Shakespeare's Later Comedies: An Anthology of Modern Criticism*. Harmondsworth, 1971.

Palmer, E. J. "The Endings of Shakespeare's Plays." *Winchester College Shakspere Society. Noctes Shakespearianæ*. Ed. Charles H. Hawkins. Winchester, 1887. Pp. 265-73.

Panofsky, Erwin. *Studies in Iconology*. OUP, 1939.

Pares, Martin. "Shakespeare." *The Listener* 76 (1966), 775, 930.

Parker, M[arion] D. *The Slave of Life: A Study of Shakespeare and the Idea of Justice*. 1955.

Parkinson, John. *Paradisi in Sole, Paradisus Terrestris, or, A Garden of Flowers*. 1656.

Parrott, T[homas] M. "'God's' or 'gods' in *King Lear*, v.iii.17." *SQ* 4 (1953), 427–32.

——. *Shakespearean Comedy*. OUP, 1949. (Rpt. New York: Russell, 1969.)

——. *William Shakespeare: A Handbook*. New York, 1934.

Parry, Christopher. "What Is Mamillius Doing?: A Consideration of a Shakespearean Stumbling Block." *The Use of English* 30, iii (1979), 56–62.

Parsons, Natalie. "Shakespeare's Ladies: Paulina, in *Winter's Tale*." *Baconiana* 34 (1950), 228–30.

Partridge, A. C. "*The Winter's Tale* in the Theatre: Structure and Interpretation." *UES* 20 (1982), 1–5.

Partridge, Eric. *A Dictionary of Slang and Unconventional English*. 6th, rev. ed. New York, 1967. (1st ed. 1937.)

——. *Shakespeare's Bawdy*. Rev. ed. New York, 1969. (1st ed. 1948.)

Pattison, Bruce. *Music and Poetry of the English Renaissance*. 1948. (Rpt. New York: Da Capo, 1971.)

Paulin, Bernard. "Autolycus, ou l'intégration d'un marginal." *La Marginalité dans la littérature et la pensée anglais*. Centre Aixois de Recherches Anglaises 4. Aix-en-Provence, 1983. Pp. 7–19.

Pearce, G. M. "*The Winter's Tale*." *CahiersE* 19 (Apr. 1981), 129–30.

Pearson, D'Orsay W. "Witchcraft in *The Winter's Tale*: Paulina as 'Alcaheurta y un Poquito Hechizera.' " *ShakS* 12 (1979), 195–213.

Pearson, Lu Emily. *Elizabethans at Home*. Stanford, Calif., 1957.

Peck, Francis. "Explanatory and Critical Notes on Divers Passages of Shakespeare's Plays." *New Memoirs of the Life and Poetical Works of Mr. John Milton*. 1740. Pp. 222–54.

Pedicord, Harry W. "George Colman's Adaptation of Garrick's Promptbook for *Florizel and Perdita*." *ThS* 22 (1981), 185–90.

Percy, Thomas, Bishop (1729–1811). Contributor to v1773.

Perott, Josef de. "Der Geniale Spitzbube bei Feliciano de Silva und Shakespeares Autolycus." *ESn* 41 (1910), 332–3.

Perring, Philip. *Hard Knots in Shakespeare*. 1886. (1st ed. 1885.)

Peter. Letter 27 August. *Gent. Mag.* 58 (1788), 767–8.

Peterson, Douglas L. "Tempest-Tossed Barks and Their Helmsmen in Several of Shakespeare's Plays." *Costerus* 9 (1973), 79–107.

——. *Time, Tide, and Tempest: A Study of Shakespeare's Romances*. San Marino, Calif., 1973.

Pettet, E. C. *Shakespeare and the Romance Tradition*. 1949. (Rpt. London, 1970.)

Peyré, Yves. "*Le Conte d'hiver*: Regards et miroirs." *Caliban* 21 (1984), 141–55.

Phelps, Samuel (1804–78). Contributor to HAL.

P[hillips], E[dward]. *The New World of English Words*. 1658. (Rpt. Menston: Scolar, 1969. 6th ed. rev. John Kersey, 1706.)

Phillips, Owen H. "The Law Relating to Shakespeare." *Law Quarterly Rev.* 80 (1964), 172–202.

——. *Shakespeare and the Lawyers*. 1972.

Pilgrim, Richard. *You Precious Winners All*. Oxford, 1983.

Pilkington, Ace G. "Romance and Fantasy in *The Winter's Tale*." *Encyclia: The Jour. of the Utah Academy of Sciences, Arts, and Letters* 58 (1981), 79–84.

Pitt, Angela. *Shakespeare's Women*. London & Totowa, N.J., 1981.

Platt, Isaac H. "*Winter's Tale* [755]." *New Shakespeareana* 5 (1906), 89.

[Playford, John.] *The English Dancing Master*. 1651. (Rpt. with prefaces by Hugh Mellor and Leslie Bridgewater, 1933. 2nd ed. [*The Dancing Master*] 1652. 10th ed. 1698.)

Pollard, Alfred W. *The Foundations of Shakespeare's Text*. British Academy Annual Shakespeare Lecture. OUP, 1923.

————. *Shakespeare's Fight with the Pirates and the Problems of the Transmission of his Text*. 2nd. ed. rev. Cambridge, 1920. (Rpt. Cambridge, 1967. 1st ed. 1917.)

————. *Shakespeare's Folios and Quartos: A Study in the Bibliography of Shakespeare's Plays, 1594–1685*. 1909. (Rpt. New York: Cooper Square, 1970.)

Pollock, Frederick. *Macready's Reminiscences, and Selections from his Diaries and Letters*. 2 vols. 1875.

Porter, Charlotte. "Old and New Ideas of Womanhood: The Iphigenia and Alkestis Stories." *Poet Lore* 3 (1891), 269–80.

————. *See* C., P. A.

Praz, Mario. *The Flaming Heart*. New York, 1958.

Preston, Dennis R. "Language and the Structure of *The Winter's Tale*." *Kwartalnik Neofilologiczny* 25 (1978), 421–32.

Price, Hereward T. "Mirror-Scenes in Shakespeare." *Joseph Quincy Adams Memorial Studies*. Ed. James G. McManaway et al. Washington, D.C., 1948. Pp. 101–13.

Price, Thomas R. "The Construction of *A Winter's Tale*." *Shakespeariana* 7 (1890), 195–207.

Prior, R[ichard] C. A. *On the Popular Names of British Plants*. 1863.

Procter, Bryan Waller [*pseud.* Barry Cornwall]. "Memoir of an Essay on the Genius of Shakspere." In *The Works of Shakspere*. [Ed. J. Ogden.] 3 vols. 1844. 1:i–xxviii. (First pub. 1843.)

Prosser, Eleanor. "Shakespeare at Ashland and San Diego." *SQ* 14 (1963), 445–54.

Prothero, R. E. "Agriculture and Gardening." *Shakespeare's England*. Ed. Sidney Lee & C[harles] T. Onions. 2 vols. OUP, 1916. 1:346–80.

Proudfoot, G[eorge] R[ichard]. Contributor to OXF2.

————. "Shakespeare and the New Dramatists of the King's Men, 1606–1613." *Later Shakespeare*. Ed. John Russell Brown & Bernard Harris. Stratford-upon-Avon Stud. 8. 1966. Pp. 234–61.

————. "Verbal Reminiscence and the Two-Part Structure of *The Winter's Tale*." *ShS* 29 (1976), 67–78.

Pruvost, René. *Robert Greene et ses Romans (1558–1592)*. Paris, 1938.

Pulc, I. P. "Shakespeare's *The Winter's Tale*, [1926–41]." *Expl* 29 (1971), no. 76.

Purdom, C[harles] B. *What Happens in Shakespeare: A New Interpretation*. 1963.

————. "*The Winter's Tale*." *TLS*, 21 Mar. 1952, p. 205.

Puttenham, George. *The Arte of English Poesie*. 1589. (Rpt. Menston: Scolar, 1968.)

Pye, Henry J. *Comments on the Commentators on Shakespear*. 1807.

Pyle, Fitzroy. The Winter's Tale: *A Commentary on the Structure*. 1969.

Quayle, Anthony. *A Time to Speak*. 1990.

Quennell, Peter. *Shakespeare, the Poet and his Background*. 1963. (Also pub. as *Shakespeare, a Biography*, Cleveland, 1963.)

Quiller-Couch, Arthur. *Notes on Shakespeare's Workmanship*. New York, 1917. (Pub. in London as *Shakespeare's Workmanship*, 1918.)

Quinones, Ricardo J. *The Renaissance Discovery of Time*. Cambridge, Mass., 1972.

————. "Views of Time in Shakespeare." *JHI* 26 (1965), 327–52.

Rabkin, Norman. "The Holy Sinner and the Confidence Man: Illusion in Shakespeare's Romances." *Four Essays on Romance*. Ed. Herschel Baker. Cambridge, Mass., 1971. Pp. 35-53.

————. *Shakespeare and the Common Understanding*. New York, 1967.

————. *Shakespeare and the Problem of Meaning*. Chicago, 1981.

Raleigh, Walter. *Shakespeare*. English Men of Letters. New York, 1907.

Randall, Dale B. J. "A Glimpse of Leontes through an Onomastic Lens." *SJH*, 1988, pp. 123-9.

————. "'This Is the Chase': Or, The Further Pursuit of Shakespeare's Bear." *SJW* 121 (1985), 89-95.

Rank, Otto. *The Incest Theme in Literature and Legend*. Tr. Gregory C. Richter. Baltimore, 1992. (1st Ger. ed. 1912.)

Ranney, R. H. "Shakespeare and Psychical Research." *Religio-Philosophical Jour.*, 30 Dec. 1893, pp. 500-1.

Rashbrook, R. F. "*The Winter's Tale* [2794-6]." *N&Q* 192 (1947), 520-1.

Ratcliffe, Michael. Theatre review. *The Observer*, 7 Oct. 1984.

Ravenscroft, Arthur. "Monstrous to Our Human Reason: The Limits of Knowledge in *The Winter's Tale*." *Seven Studies in English for Dorothy Cavers*. Ed. Gildas Roberts. Capetown, 1971. Pp. 1-19.

Ravenscroft, Thomas. *Pammelia* [1609]. *Deuteromelia* [1609]. *Melismata* [1611]. Ed. MacEdward Leach. Introd. Matthias A. Shaaber. Philadelphia, 1961.

Ray, John. *A Collection of English Words*. 1674. (2nd ed., rev. and enl., 1691, rpt. Menston: Scolar, 1969.)

————. *A Complete Collection of English Proverbs*. 1670. (2nd ed. 1678; 3rd ed. 1737.)

Rayner, M. E. Contributor to ARD2.

Rea, John D. "The Dyer's Hand." *SAB* 7 (1932), 82-7.

Reed, Isaac (1742-1807). Contributor to MAL.

Rees, James. *Shakespeare and the Bible*. Philadelphia, 1876. (Rpt. Folcroft, Pa.: Folcroft Library Eds., 1974.)

Rees, Joan. "Revenge, Retribution, and Reconciliation." *ShS* 24 (1971), 31-5.

Reese, M[ax] M. *Shakespeare: His World & His Work*. Rev. ed. 1980. (1st ed. 1953, rpt. 1958, 1964.)

Reid, Stephen. "*The Winter's Tale*." *AI* 27 (1970), 263-78.

Reinhold, Heinz. "Die metrische Verzahnung als Kriterium für Fragen der Chronologie und Authentizität im Drama Shakespeares." *Archiv* 181 (1942), 83-96.

Reyher, Paul. *Essai sur les idées dans l'œuvre de Shakespeare*. Paris, 1947.

Reynolds, George F. "*Mucedorus*, Most Popular Elizabethan Play?" *Studies in the English Renaissance Drama in Memory of Karl Julius Holzknecht*. Ed. Josephine W. Bennett et al. New York, 1959. Pp. 248-68.

Rhodes, Neil. *Elizabethan Grotesque*. 1980.

Rhodes, R[aymond] Crompton. *Shakespeare's First Folio*. OUP, 1923.

————. *The Stagery of Shakespeare*. Birmingham, 1922.

Richards, David. "Critic's Notebook." *The New York Times*, 25 Feb. 1994, p. C1.

Richardson, Charles (1806-71). Contributor to KNT2.

Richman, David. *Laughter, Pain, and Wonder*. Newark, Del., 1990.

Richmond, Velma B. "Shakespeare's Women." *MQ* 19 (1977-8), 330-42.

Rico, Barbara R. "From 'Speechless Dialect' to 'Prosperous Art.'" *HLQ* 48 (1985), 285-95.

Ridley, M[aurice] R. *Shakespeare's Plays: A Commentary*. New York, 1938. (Rpt. New York: Folcroft, 1969.)

Riemer, A[ndrew] P. *Antic Fables: Patterns of Evasion in Shakespeare's Plays*. Manchester, 1980.

————. "Deception in *The Winter's Tale*." *SSEng* 13 (1987-8), 21-38.

Righter, Anne. *Shakespeare and the Idea of the Play*. 1962. (Rpt. Harmondsworth: Penguin, 1967.)

————. *See* Barton, Anne.

Ringler, William A., Jr. "The Number of Actors in Shakespeare's Early Plays." *The Seventeenth-Century Stage*. Ed. Gerald E. Bentley. Chicago, 1968. Pp. 110-34.

Ristine, F[rank] H. *English Tragicomedy: Its Origin and History*. New York, 1910. (Rpt. New York: Russell & Russell, 1963.)

Ritson, Joseph (1752-1803). Contributor to v1793.

————. *Cursory Criticisms on the Edition of Shakspeare Published by Edmond Malone*. 1792. (Rpt. New York: Augustus M. Kelley, 1970.)

————. *Remarks, Critical and Illustrative, on the Text and Notes of the Last Edition of Shakspeare*. 1783. (Rpt. New York: AMS, 1973.)

————. *A Select Collection of English Songs with Their Original Airs*. 3 Vols. 1813.

Rittenhouse, David. "A Victorian *Winter's Tale*." *QQ* 77 (1970), 41-55.

Roberts, Jeanne A. "Animals as Agents of Revelation: The Horizontalizing of the Chain of Being in Shakespeare's Comedies." *Shakespearean Comedy*. Ed. Maurice Charney. New York, 1980. Pp. 79-96.

————. *The Shakespearean Wild*. Lincoln, Nebr., 1991.

Robertson, J[ohn] M. *The Genuine in Shakespeare*. 1930. (Rpt. New York: Haskell House, 1972.)

Robinson, Clement. *A Handefull of Pleasant Delites*. 1584. (Rpt. Spenser Soc., 1871, rpt. New York: Burt Franklin, 1967. Ed. Hyder E. Rollins, Cambridge, Mass., 1924.)

Robinson, Stuart. *A History of Dyed Textiles*. Cambridge, Mass., 1969.

Rockas, Leo. "'Browzing of Ivy': The Winter's Tale." *Ariel* 6 (1975), 3-16.

Roderick, Richard. "Remarks on Shakespear." *The Canons of Criticism, and Glossary*. By Thomas Edwards. 6th ed. 1758. Pp. 212-38.

Roffe, Alfred [T.]. *An Essay upon the Ghost-Belief of Shakespeare*. 1851.

————. *A Musical Triad from Shakespeare*. 1872.

Rogers, J. D. "Voyages and Exploration: Geography: Maps." *Shakespeare's England*. Ed. Sidney Lee & C[harles] T. Onions. 2 vols. OUP, 1916. 1:170-97.

Rollins, Hyder E., ed. *A Pepysian Garland*. Cambridge, 1922.

Root, Robert K. *Classical Mythology in Shakespeare*. Yale Stud. in Eng. 19. New York, 1903. (Rpt. New York: Gordian, 1965.)

Rose, Mark. *Shakespearean Design*. Cambridge, Mass., 1972.

Rosenmeyer, Thomas G. *The Green Cabinet: Theocritus and the European Pastoral Lyric*. Berkeley & Los Angeles, 1969.

Rothwell, Kenneth S. "The Shakespeare Plays: *Hamlet* and the Five Plays of Season Three." *SQ* 32 (1981), 395-401.

————, & Annabelle H. Melzer. *Shakespeare on Screen: An International Filmography and Videography*. 1990.

Rouse, W[illiam] H. D. *Shakespeare's Ovid Being Arthur Golding's [1567] Translation of the Metamorphoses*. 1904. (Rpt. Carbondale: Southern Ill. Univ. Press, 1961.)

Rowse, A[lfred] L. "Shakespeare and the Prayer Book." *Ritual Murder: Essays on Liturgical Reform*. Ed. Brian Morris. Manchester, 1980. Pp. 47–56.

————. *William Shakespeare: A Biography*. New York & London, 1963.

Rubinstein, Frankie. *A Dictionary of Shakespeare's Sexual Puns and Their Significance*. 1984.

Rundus, Raymond J. "Time and His 'Glass' in *The Winter's Tale*." *SQ* 25 (1974), 123–5.

Rusev, Rusi. "On the Presentation of Bohemia as a Maritime Country in *The Winter's Tale*." *Philologia* (Sofia) 10–11 (1982), 58–61.

Rushton, W[illiam] L. "Gods Have Taken Shapes of Beasts." *N&Q* 219 (1872), 197.

————. *Shakespeare Illustrated by Old Authors*. Two vols. in one. The First Part, 1867. The Second Part, 1868.

————. *Shakespeare's Legal Maxims*. Liverpool, 1907. (Rpt. New York: AMS, 1973.)

————. *Shakespeare's Testamentary Language*. 1869.

Ruskin, John. *Works*. Library Ed. Ed. E. T. Cook & Alexander Wedderburn. 39 vols. 1903–12. (*Modern Painters*, vol. 2, first pub. 1846; "Essays on Political Economy" first pub. in *Fraser's Mag.* 67 [1863], 441–62; *Proserpina*, Pt. 7, first pub. 1882.)

Russell, Patricia. "Romantic Narrative Plays: 1570–1590." *Elizabethan Theatre*. Stratford-upon-Avon Stud. 9. Gen. eds. John Russell Brown & Bernard Harris. 1967. Pp. 107–30.

Rydén, Mats. "Några växtnamm hos Shakespeare och i svenska översättningar [Some Plantnames in Shakespeare and in Swedish Translations]." *Nysvenska Studier* 23 (1973), 173–99.

————. *Shakespearean Plant Names*. Stockholm, 1978.

Rylands, George [H. W.]. *The Ages of Man: Shakespeare's Image of Man and Nature*. London, 1939.

————. "Festival Shakespeare in the West End." *ShS* 6 (1953), 140–6.

————. "Shakespeare the Poet." *A Companion to Shakespeare Studies*. Ed. Harley Granville-Barker & G. B. Harrison. New York & Cambridge, 1934. Pp. 89–115.

————. *Words and Poetry*. Introd. Lytton Strachey. 1928. (Rpt. New York: AMS, 1972.)

Sabie, Francis. *The Fisherman's Tale . . . 1595*. Ed. J[ames] O[rchard] Halliwell. 1867.

Sabol, Andrew J. *Four Hundred Songs and Dances from the Stuart Masque*. Providence, R.I., 1978. (Augmented ed. 1982.)

Saccio, Peter. "The 1975 Season at Stratford, Connecticut." *SQ* 27 (1976), 47–51.

Sachs, Hanns. "The Tempest." *International Jour. of Psycho-Analysis* 4 (1923), 43–88.

Sacks, Elizabeth. *Shakespeare's Images of Pregnancy*. 1980.

Sahel, Pierre. "Le Spectateur de la fin du *Conte d'hiver*." *Actes du Congrès de Poitiers*. Ed. Société des Anglicistes de l'Enseignement Supérieur. Etudes Anglaises 90. Paris, 1984. Pp. 357–68.

Saintsbury, George. *A History of English Prosody*. 2nd ed. 3 vols. 1923. (Rpt. New York: Russell & Russell, 1961. 1st ed. 1908.)

Salgādo, Gāmini. *The Elizabethan Underworld*. 1977.

Salingar, Leo [G.]. *Shakespeare and the Italian Concept of "Art."* Univ. of Warwick Renaissance Drama Newsletter Supp. 3. 1984.

————. *Shakespeare and the Traditions of Comedy*. Cambridge, 1974.

————. "Time and Art in Shakespeare's Romances." *RenD* 9 (1966), 3–36.

Sanders, Kenneth. "Shakespeare's *The Winter's Tale*—and Some Notes on the Analysis of a Present-Day Leontes." *The International Review of Psycho-Analysis* 5 (1978), 175–8.

Sanders, Wilbur. *The Winter's Tale*. Harvester New Critical Introductions to Sh. Brighton, 1987.

Saunders, J. W. "Staging at the Globe, 1599-1613." *SQ* 11 (1960), 401-25. (Rpt. in *The Seventeenth-Century Stage*, ed. G[erald] E. Bentley, Chicago, 1968, pp. 235-66.)

Savage, F[rederick] G. *The Flora & Folk Lore of Shakespeare*. 1923. (Rpt. New York: AMS, 1975.)

Schack, Adolph F. von. *Geschichte der dramatischen Literatur*. 4 vols. Frankfurt am Main, 1854.

Schanzer, Ernest. "Heywood's *Ages* and Shakespeare." *RES* NS 11 (1960), 18-28.

————. "Shakespeare and the Doctrine of the Unity of Time." *ShS* 28 (1975), 57-61.

————. "The Structural Pattern of *The Winter's Tale*." *REL* 5, No. 2 (1964), 72-82. (Rpt. in *Shakespeare: A Casebook, "The Winter's Tale,"* ed. Kenneth Muir, 1968, pp. 87-97.)

Schelling, Felix E. *Elizabethan Drama, 1558-1642*. 2 vols. Boston & New York, 1908. (Rpt. New York: Russell & Russell, 1959.)

————. *English Literature During the Lifetime of Shakespeare*. Rev. ed. New York, 1928. (1st ed. 1910.)

————. *Foreign Influences in Elizabethan Plays*. New York & London, 1923. (Rpt. New York: AMS, 1971.)

Schlegel, August W. von. *Course of Lectures on Dramatic Art and Literature*. Tr. John Black, rev. A. J. W. Morrison. 1846. (Delivered 1808; 1st German ed. 2 vols., 1809-11. 1846 ed. rpt. New York: AMS, 1965.)

Schmidt, Alexander. *Shakespeare-Lexicon*. 2 vols. Berlin, 1874-5. (2nd ed. 1886; 3rd ed., enl. by Gregor Sarrazin, 1902, rpt. New York: Dover, 1971.)

————. "Zur Shakespeare'schen Textkritik. Ein Sendschreiben an den Herausgeber." *SJ* 3 (1868), 341-69.

Schmitt, Anthony B. "Herbert Beerbohm Tree Produces *The Winter's Tale*." *Ohio State Univ. Theatre Collection Bull.* 17 (1970), 20-31.

Schneider, Ben R., Jr. See *The London Stage 1660-1800*.

Scholes, Percy A. "The Purpose behind Shakespeare's Use of Music." *Proceedings of the [Royal] Musical Association* 43 (1916), 1-15.

Schotz, Myra G. "The Great Unwritten Story: Mothers and Daughters in Shakespeare." *The Lost Tradition: Mothers and Daughters in Literature*. Ed. Cathy N. Davidson & E. M. Broner. New York, 1980. Pp. 44-54.

Schücking, Levin L. *Character Problems in Shakespeare's Plays*. 1922. (Rpt. New York: Peter Smith, 1948. 1st Ger. ed. 1919.)

Schwartz, Murray M. "Leontes' Jealousy in *The Winter's Tale*." *AI* 30 (1973), 250-73.

————. "*The Winter's Tale*: Loss and Transformation." *AI* 32 (1975), 145-99.

Scott, Mary A. "*The Book of the Courtyer*: A Possible Source of Benedick and Beatrice." *PMLA* 16 (1901), 475-502.

Scott, Walter. *Guy Mannering*. Edinburgh & London, 1815.

Scott, W[illiam] I. D. *Shakespeare's Melancholics*. 1920.

Scott, William O. "Seasons and Flowers in *The Winter's Tale*." *SQ* 14 (1963), 411-17.

Scouten, Arthur H. See *The London Stage 1660-1800*.

Seager, H[erbert] W. *Natural History in Shakespeare's Time: Being Extracts Illustrative of the Subject As He Knew It*. 1896.

Segar, William. *The Booke of Honor and Armes*. 1590.

Seltzer, Daniel. "The Actors and Staging." *A New Companion to Shakespeare Studies*. Ed. Kenneth Muir & S[amuel] Schoenbaum. Cambridge, 1971. Pp. 35-54.

————. "The Staging of the Last Plays." *Later Shakespeare*. Stratford-upon-Avon Stud. 8. Ed. John Russell Brown & Bernard Harris. 1967. Pp. 127–65.

Semon, Kenneth J. "Fantasy and Wonder in Shakespeare's Last Plays." *SQ* 25 (1974), 89–102.

Seng, Peter J. *The Vocal Songs in the Plays of Shakespeare. A Critical History*. Cambridge, Mass., [1967].

Sen Gupta, S[ubodh] C. *Shakespearian Comedy*. OUP, 1950.

————. *The Whirligig of Time: The Problem of Duration in Shakespeare's Plays*. Calcutta, 1961.

Senior, Dorothy, ed. *Some Old English Worthies*. 1912.

Sewell, Arthur. *Character and Society in Shakespeare*. OUP, 1951.

————. "Place and Time in Shakespeare's Plays." *SP* 42 (1945), 205–24.

Sexton, Joyce H. *The Slandered Woman in Shakespeare*. Victoria, B.C., 1978.

Seymour, E[dward] H. *Remarks Critical, Conjectural, and Explanatory, upon the Plays of Shakspeare*. 2 vols. 1805.

Shalvi, Alice. *See* Mendilow, Adam A.

Sharp, Cecil J., & Herbert C. MacIlwaine. *The Morris Book*. [1911–24].

Sharpe, Henry. "The Prose in Shakspere's Plays, the Rules for Its Use, and the Assistance That It Gives in Understanding the Plays." *New Shakspere Society's Transactions. 1880–6.* [1886.] Pp. 523–60.

Shattuck, Charles H., ed. *John Philip Kemble Promptbooks*. 11 vols. Charlottesville, 1974. Vol. 9: *The Winter's Tale*, 1811.

————. *Shakespeare on the American Stage*. 2 vols. Washington, D.C., 1976, 1987.

————. *The Shakespeare Promptbooks: A Descriptive Catalogue*. Urbana, 1965.

Shaw, [George] B[ernard]. "On Cutting Shakespear." *Fortnightly Rev.* 112 (1919), 215–18.

————. *Shaw on Shakespeare: An Anthology of Bernard Shaw's Writings on the Plays and Productions of Shakespeare*. Ed. Edwin Wilson. New York, 1961.

Shaw, W[illiam] D. *Tennyson's Style*. Ithaca, N.Y., 1976.

Shepherd, Massey H., Jr. *The Oxford American Prayer Book Commentary*. OUP, 1950.

Sheppard, J. T. "Shakespeare's Small Latin." *The Rice Institute Pamphlet* 44 (1957), 70–86.

Sherbo, Arthur, ed. *Johnson on Shakespeare*. 2 vols. Vols. 7 & 8 of The Yale Edition of the Works of Samuel Johnson. New Haven & London, 1968.

Sherman, L[ucius] A. *What is Shakespeare?* New York, 1902. (Rpt. Folcroft, Pa.: Folcroft Library Eds., 1973.)

Shirley, Frances A. *Shakespeare's Use of Off-stage Sounds*. Lincoln, Nebr., 1963.

————. *Swearing and Perjury in Shakespeare's Plays*. 1979.

Shoaf, R. A. "'For There Is Figures in All Things': Joxtology in Shakespeare, Spenser, and Milton." *The Work of Dissimilitude: Essays from the Sixth Citadel Conference on Medieval and Renaissance Literature*. Ed. David G. Allen & Robert A. White. Newark, Del., 1988. Pp. 266–85.

Shrimpton, Nicholas. "Shakespeare Performances in London, Manchester and Stratford-upon-Avon 1985–6." *ShS* 40 (1987), 169–83.

Shroeder, John W. *The Great Folio of 1623: Shakespeare's Plays in the Printing House*. Ann Arbor, 1956.

Shumaker, Wayne, & J. L. Heilbron, eds. *John Dee on Astronomy*. Berkeley, 1978.

Sider, John W. "The Serious Elements of Shakespeare's Comedies." *SQ* 24 (1973), 1–11.

Sidney, Philip. *The Countess of Pembroke's Arcadia*. Ed. Maurice Evans. Harmondsworth, 1977.

Siegel, Paul N. "Leontes a Jealous Tyrant." *RES* NS 1 (1950), 302–7.

Siemon, James E. "'But it appears she lives': Iteration in *The Winter's Tale*." *PMLA* 89 (1974), 10–16.

———. "The Canker Within: Some Observations on the Role of the Villain in Three Shakespearean Comedies." *SQ* 23 (1972), 435–43.

Sieveking, A. Forbes. "Coursing, Fowling, Angling," "Fencing and Duelling," "Games." *Shakespeare's England*. Ed. Sidney Lee & C[harles] T. Onions. 2 vols. OUP, 1916. 2: 367–75, 389–407, 451–83.

Simpson, Claude M. *The British Broadside Ballad and Its Music*. New Brunswick, N.J., 1966.

Simpson, Lucie. *The Secondary Heroes of Shakespeare and Other Essays*. [1950.]

Simpson, Percy. *Shakespearian Punctuation*. OUP, 1911.

———. *Studies in Elizabethan Drama*. OUP, 1955.

Simpson, Robert. *Shakespeare and Medicine*. Edinburgh & London, 1959.

Simrock, Karl. *The Remarks of M. Karl Simrock on the Plots of Shakespeare's Plays*. With Notes and Additions by J. O. Halliwell. 1850. (First pub. as *Die Quellen des Shakspeare in Novellen, Märchen und Sagen*, Berlin, 1831. 2nd ed. Bonn, 1870.)

Sims, James H. "Perdita's 'Flowers o'th' Spring' and 'Vernal Flowers' in *Lycidas*." *SQ* 22 (1971), 87–90.

Singer, Samuel W. *The Text of Shakespeare Vindicated from the Interpolations and Corruptions Advocated by John Payne Collier Esq. in His Notes and Emendations*. 1853.

Singleton, Esther. *The Shakespeare Garden*. 1933. (Rpt. New York: AMS, 1973.)

Sisson, Charles J. *New Readings in Shakespeare*. Shakespeare Problems 8. 2 vols. Cambridge, 1956. (Rpt. 1961; another issue London, 1961.)

Sitwell, Edith. *A Notebook on William Shakespeare*. 1948.

Skeat, Walter W. *A Concise Etymological Dictionary of the English Language*. Oxford, 1882.

———. "'Land-damn.'" 5 *N&Q* 3 (1875), 464.

———. "The Word 'Mort' in Shakspere." *The Academy* 32 (1887), 286.

Skinner, Stephen. *Etymologicon Linguae Anglicanae*. 1671. (Rpt. Hildesheim: Olms, 1970.)

Skottowe, Augustine. *The Life of Shakspeare*. 2 vols. 1824.

Slater, Ann P. *Shakespeare the Director*. Totowa, N.J., 1982.

Sleeth, C. R. "Shakespeare's Counsellors of State." *RAA* 13 (1936), 97–113.

Smallwood, Robert. "Shakespeare at Stratford-upon-Avon, 1992." *SQ* 44 (1993), 343–62.

Smeaton, [William H.] Oliphant. *Shakespeare, His Life and Work*. [1911.]

Smith, Bruce R. "Sermons in Stones: Shakespeare and Renaissance Sculpture." *ShakS* 17 (1985), 1–23.

Smith, C. Alphonso. "The Chief Difference between the First and Second Folios of Shakespeare." *ESn* 30 (1902), 1–20.

Smith, Charles G. *Shakespeare's Proverb Lore: His Use of the* Sententiae *of Leonard Culman and Publilius Syrus*. Cambridge, Mass., 1963.

Smith, C[harles] Roach. *The Rural Life of Shakespeare*. 2nd ed. 1874 [65 +3 pp.]. (1st ed. 1874 [40 pp.].)

Smith, Hallett. "Leontes' *Affectio*." *SQ* 14 (1963), 163–6.

———. "Shakespeare's Romances." *HLQ* 27 (1964), 279–87.

————. *Shakespeare's Romances*. San Marino, Calif., 1972.

————. "The Winter's Tale." *The Riverside Shakespeare*. Ed. G. Blakemore Evans. Boston, 1974. Pp. 1564–8.

Smith, Homer. "Pastoral Influence in the English Drama." *PMLA* 12 (1897), 355–460.

Smith, James. *Shakespearian and Other Essays*. Cambridge, 1974.

Smith, Jonathan. "The Language of Leontes." *SQ* 19 (1968), 317–27.

Smith, Marion B. *Dualities in Shakespeare*. Toronto, 1966.

Smith, Warren D. "Shakespeare's Exit Cues." *JEGP* 61 (1962), 884–96.

————. "Stage Business in Shakespeare's Dialogue." *SQ* 4 (1953), 311–16.

Smith, William (1690–1767). Contributor to Grey 1754.

Snider, D[enton] J. "Shakspeare's *Winter's Tale*." *Jour. of Speculative Philosophy* 9 (1875), 80–98.

————. *The Shakespearian Drama: A Commentary. . . . The Comedies*. St. Louis, [c. 1890].

————. *System of Shakespeare's Dramas*. 2 vols. St. Louis, 1877.

Sochatoff, A. Fred, ed. *"Lovers Meeting": Discussion of Five Plays by Shakespeare*. Carnegie Ser. in Eng. 8. Pittsburgh, 1964. (Rpt. Freeport, N.Y.: Books for Libraries, 1972.)

Soellner, Rolf. *Shakespeare's Patterns of Self-Knowledge*. Columbus, Ohio, 1972.

Somer, John L. "Ralph Crane and 'an olde play called Winter's Tale.'" *Four Studies in Renaissance Drama*. The Emporia State Research Studies 10, No. 4 (1962), 22–8.

Sonnino, Lee A. *A Handbook to Sixteenth-Century Rhetoric*. New York, 1968.

Sorelius, Gunnar. "An Unknown Shakespearian Commonplace Book." 5 *Library* 28 (1973), 294–308.

Sorell, Walter. "Shakespeare and the Dance." *SQ* 8 (1957), 367–84.

Southey, Robert, ed. *Palmerin of England, by Francisco de Moraes*. Tr. Anthony Munday. 4 vols. 1807. (Preface by Southey, 1:vii–xlv.)

Speaight, Robert W. "The 1960 Season at Stratford-upon-Avon." *SQ* 11 (1960), 445–53.

————. "Shakespeare in Britain." *SQ* 20 (1969), 435–41.

————. "Shakespeare in Britain." *SQ* 28 (1977), 184–90.

————. *Shakespeare on the Stage: An Illustrated History of Shakespearian Performance*. 1973.

————. *Shakespeare: The Man and His Achievement*. 1977.

Spedding, James (1808–81). Contributor to CAM1.

Speirs, John. *Medieval English Poetry: The Non-Chaucerian Tradition*. 1957.

Spence, Lewis. *An Encyclopaedia of Occultism*. 1920. (Rpt. Secaucus, N.J.: Citadel, 1960.)

Spence, R. M. "Some of the Obeli of the Globe Edition in *The Winter's Tale*." 7 *N&Q* 9 (1890), 24.

Spencer, Hazelton. *The Art and Life of William Shakespeare*. New York, 1940. (Rpt. New York: Barnes & Noble, 1970.)

Spencer, Terence [J. B.]. "The Artistry of Shakespeare's *The Winter's Tale*." *Eigo Seinen* 116 (1970), 72–7.

————. *Elizabethan Love Stories*. Baltimore, 1968.

————. "Shakespeare and the Noble Woman." *SJH*, 1966, pp. 49–62.

————. "Shakespeare's Isle of Delphos." *MLR* 47 (1952), 199–202.

————. "The Statue of Hermione." *E&S* 30 (1977), 39–49.

Spencer, Theodore. "Appearance and Reality in Shakespeare's Last Plays." *MP* 39 (1942), 265–74.

————. *Shakespeare and the Nature of Man*. New York, 1942.

Spender, Stephen. *"The Winter's Tale." Shakespeare in Perspective.* Ed. Roger Sales. 2 vols. 1982. 1:234–40.

Spens, Janet. *Elizabethan Drama.* 1922.

Spevack, Marvin. *A Complete and Systematic Concordance to the Works of Shakespeare.* 9 vols. Hildesheim, 1968–80.

———. "Satirical Devices in Shakespeare." *Scholastic Midwifery.* Ed. Jan E. Peters & Thomas M. Stein. Tübingen, 1989. Pp. 1–6.

Spink, Ian, ed. *Robert Johnson: Ayres, Songs and Dialogues. The English School of Lutenist Song Writers.* 2nd ser. Vol. 27. 1961.

Spivack, Bernard. *Shakespeare and the Allegory of Evil.* New York, 1958.

Sprague, Arthur Colby. *Shakespeare and the Audience: A Study in the Technique of Exposition.* Cambridge, Mass., 1935. (Rpt. New York: Russell & Russell, 1966.)

———, & J[ohn] C. Trewin. *Shakespeare's Plays Today: Some Customs and Conventions of the Stage.* 1970.

Spurgeon, Caroline F. E. *Shakespeare's Imagery and What It Tells Us.* Cambridge, 1935.

Squire, John. *Shakespeare as a Dramatist.* [1935.]

Squire, W. Barclay. "Music." *Shakespeare's England.* Ed. Sidney Lee & C[harles] T. Onions. 2 vols. OUP, 1916. 2:15–49.

Stapfer, Paul. *Shakespeare and Classical Antiquity.* Tr. Emily J. Carey. 1880. (Rpt. New York: Burt Franklin, 1970. Orig. pub. as *Shakespeare et l'antiquité.* 2 vols. Paris, 1879–80.)

Starnes, D[e Witt] T. "Shakespeare and Apuleius." *PMLA* 60 (1945), 1021–50.

Stauffer, Donald. *Shakespeare's World of Images: The Development of His Moral Ideas.* New York, 1949.

Staunton, Howard. "Unsuspected Corruptions of Shakspeare's Text." *Athenæum* No. 2423. (4 Apr. 1874), 461–2; No. 2435 (27 June 1874), 862–4.

Stearns, Charles W. *Shakespeare's Medical Knowledge.* New York, 1865. (Rpt. New York: AMS, 1973.)

———. *The Shakespeare Treasury of Wisdom and Knowledge.* New York, 1882.

Steevens, George (1736–1800). Contributor to JOHN and to v1803.

Steiner, George. *The Death of Tragedy.* 1961. (Rpt. London: Faber, 1963.)

Sternfeld, F[rederick] W. "Shakespeare and Music." *A New Companion to Shakespeare Studies.* Ed. Kenneth Muir & S[amuel] Schoenbaum. Cambridge, 1971. Pp. 157–67.

———. "Le Symbolisme Musical dans Quelques Pièces de Shakespeare Présentées à la Cour d'Angleterre." *Les Fêtes de la Renaissance.* Études réunies et présenté par Jean Jacquot. Journées Internationales d'Études. Paris, 1956. Pp. 319–33.

———. "Twentieth-Century Studies in Shakespeare's Songs, Sonnets, and Poems." *ShS* 15 (1962), 1–10.

Stewart, Charles D. *Some Textual Difficulties in Shakespeare.* New Haven, 1914.

Stewart, J[ohn] I. M. *Character and Motive in Shakespeare: Some Recent Approaches Examined.* London & New York, 1949.

Stewart, Patrick. "Acting Leontes." *Du Texte à la Scène: Langages du Théâtre.* Société Française Shakespeare Actes du Congrès 1982. Paris, 1983.

Stockholder, Kay. *Dream Works: Lovers and Families in Shakespeare's Plays.* Toronto, 1987.

Stodder, Joseph H., & Lillian Wilds. "Shakespeare in Southern California and Visalia." *SQ* 31 (1980), 254–74.

Stokes, Francis G. *A Dictionary of the Characters and Proper Names . . . in Shakespeare.* 1924.

Stoll, Elmer E. *Shakespeare and Other Masters.* Cambridge, Mass., 1940.

———. *Shakespeare's Young Lovers.* Alexander Lectures, 1935. OUP, 1937. (Rpt. New York: AMS, 1966.)

Stone, George W. See *The London Stage 1660-1800.*

Stone, Lawrence. *The Family, Sex and Marriage in England 1500-1800.* New York, 1977.

Stopes, C[harlotte] C. *Shakespeare's Industry.* 1916.

Stow, John. *Annales, or, A Generall Chronicle of England.* Cont. by Edmund Howes. 1631 (1632). (*Short-Title Catalogue* 23340; 1st ed. 1598.)

Strachey, Lytton. "Shakespeare's Final Period." *Books and Characters, French and English.* New York, 1922. Pp. 49-69. (First pub. *The Independent Rev.* 3, 1906.)

Streitberger, W. R., ed. *Jacobean and Caroline Revels Accounts, 1603-1642.* Malone Soc. Collections XIII. 1986.

Strong, L. A. G. "Shakespeare and the Psychologists." *Talking of Shakespeare.* Ed. John Garrett. New York, 1954. Pp. 187-208.

Strutt, B. Contributor to E. H. Seymour, *Remarks,* 1805.

Strutt, Joseph. *Sports and Pastimes of the People of England.* Ed. William Hone. 1898.

Studing, Richard. "Shakespeare's Bohemia Revisited: A Caveat." *ShakS* 15 (1982), 217-26.

———. "Spectacle and Masque in *The Winter's Tale.*" *EM* 21 (1970), 55-80.

———. "'That Rare Italian Master'—Shakespeare's Julio Romano." *Humanities Assn. Bull.* 23 (1971), 22-6.

Styan, J[ohn] L. *Drama, Stage and Audience.* Cambridge, 1975.

———. *The Dramatic Experience.* Cambridge, 1965.

———. *The Shakespeare Revolution.* Cambridge, 1977.

———. *Shakespeare's Stagecraft.* Cambridge, 1967. (Rpt. 1975 with a new preface dated 1970.)

Sugden, Edward H. *A Topographical Dictionary to the Works of Shakespeare and his Fellow Dramatists.* Manchester, 1925. (Rpt. Hildesheim: Olms, 1969.)

Suhamy, Henri. "Le Psychologisme contre las psychologie: Quelques remarques sur la jalousie de Léontès et de quelques autres." *Caliban* 21 (1984), 191-210.

Sullivan, Edward. See Guazzo, Stefano.

Summers, Joseph H. *Dreams of Love and Power: On Shakespeare's Plays.* OUP, 1984.

Sundelson, David. *Shakespeare's Restorations of the Father.* New Brunswick, N.J., 1983.

Swetnam, Joseph. *The Arraignment of Lewd, Idle, Froward, and Unconstant Women.* 1615. (Modernized excerpts rpt. in Henderson & McManus, 1985, pp. 190-217.)

Swinburne, A[lgernon] Charles. *Shakespeare.* OUP, 1909. (Written 1905.)

———. *A Study of Shakespeare.* 1880. *Complete Works.* Ed. Edmund Gosse & Thomas J. Wise. 20 vols. 1925. 11:1-222.

Swinden, Patrick. *An Introduction to Shakespeare's Comedies.* 1973.

Symmes, Harold S. *Les Débuts de la Critique Dramatique en Angleterre jusqu'a la Mort de Shakespeare.* Paris, 1903.

Symons, Arthur. Notes and Introduction to *WT. The Works of William Shakespeare.* Ed. Henry Irving & Frank A. Marshall. 8 vols. New York, 1888-90. 7:309-89.

———. "The Winter's Tale." *Studies in the Elizabethan Drama.* New York, 1919. Pp. 53-60.

Synge, Patrick M. *See* Chittenden, Fred J.

T., O. "The Seacoast of Bohemia." *The Nation* 78 (1904), 410.

Tannenbaum, Samuel [A.]. *Shaksperian Scraps and Other Elizabethan Fragments.* New York, 1933.

————. "Textual and Other Notes on *The Winter's Tale*." *PQ* 7 (1928), 358-67. (Rev. in *Shaksperian Scraps and Other Elizabethan Fragments*, New York, 1933, pp. 87-117.)

————. "The 'Valley' in 'The Winter's Tale.'" *ShAB* 7 (1932), 192-3.

Tavera, Antoine. "*Le conte d'hiver*: Analogie et inspiration pastorale." *Études et recherches de littérature générale et comparée.* Annales de la Faculté des lettres et sciences humaines de Nice 22 (1974), 19-41.

Tayler, Edward W. *Nature and Art in Renaissance Literature.* New York, 1964.

Taylor [not further identified]. Contributor to CAM2.

Taylor, Gary. *See* Wells, Stanley.

Taylor, George C. "Hermione's Statue Again (Shakspere's Return to Bandello)." *ShAB* 13 (1938), 82-6.

————. "Shakespeare and Milton Again." *SP* 23 (1926), 189-99.

Taylor, John. "The Patience of *The Winter's Tale*." *EIC* 23 (1973), 333-56.

Taylor, Mark. *Shakespeare's Darker Purpose: A Question of Incest.* New York, 1982.

Taylor, Michael. "Innocence in *The Winter's Tale*." *ShakS* 15 (1982), 227-42.

————. "Shakespeare's *The Winter's Tale*: Speaking in the Freedom of Knowledge." *CritQ* 14 (1972), 49-56.

Ten Brink. *See* Brink.

Tennenhouse, Leonard. *Power on Display: The Politics of Shakespeare's Genres.* New York, 1986.

Tennyson, Hallam. *Alfred Lord Tennyson: A Memoir.* 2 vols. in one. New York, 1905. (1st ed. 1897.)

Terris, Olwen. "The BBC Television Shakespeare: Weary, Stale, Flat, and Unprofitable?" *Walking Shadows: Shakespeare in the National Film and Television Archive.* Ed. Luke McKernan & Olwen Terris. 1994. Pp. 219-26.

Terry, Ellen. *Four Lectures on Shakespeare.* Ed. Christopher St. John [pseud. Christabel Marshall]. 1932. (Rpt. New York: Blom, 1969.)

Thaler, Alwin. "Shakspere and the Unhappy Happy Ending." *PMLA* 42 (1927), 736-61.

————. *Shakspere's Silences.* Cambridge, Mass., 1947. (Rpt. Freeport, N.Y.: Books for Libraries, 1970.)

Thatcher, David. "Shakespeare's *The Winter's Tale*." *Expl* 51:1 (1992), 6-9.

————. "*The Winter's Tale*, I.ii.186 [268]." *SN* 59 (1987), 207-8.

Theobald, Lewis. Letters to Warburton; originals in Folger Library. Phillipps MS 8565. Pub. in *Illustrations of the Literary History of the Eighteenth Century.* By John Nichols. 8 vols. 1817-58. 2:204-655. (Rpt. New York: Kraus & AMS, 1966.)

————. *Shakespeare Restored.* 1726. (Rpt. New York: AMS, 1970.)

Theobald, William. *The Classical Element in the Shakespeare Plays.* Ed. R. M. Theobald. 1909.

Thiriold, Charles. "Child = Female Child." 5 *N&Q* 5 (1876), 371.

Thiselton Dyer. *See* Dyer, T[homas].

Thomas, Henry. *Shakespeare and Spain.* The Taylorian Lecture. OUP, 1922.

————. "Shakespeare Emendations." *TLS,* 4 May 1933, p. 312; 27 July 1933, p. 512.

Thomas, P[ercy] G., ed. *Greene's 'Pandosto' or 'Dorastus and Fawnia' Being the Original of Shakespeare's 'Winter's Tale.'* Shakespeare Classics 2. New York, 1907.

Thomas, Thomas. *Dictionarium Linguæ Latinæ et Anglicanæ.* Cambridge, [1587]. (Rpt. Menston: Scholar, 1972.)

Thompson, Elbert N. S. *The Controversy between the Puritans and the Stage.* Yale Stud. in Eng. 20. New Haven, 1903. Pp. 250–3. (Rpt. New York: Russell & Russell, 1966.)

Thompson, Karl F. *Modesty and Cunning: Shakespeare's Use of Literary Tradition.* Ann Arbor, 1971.

Thomson, J[ames] A. K. *Shakespeare and the Classics.* [1952.]

Thorncliffe. "'Land-damn.'" 5 *N&Q* 3 (1875), 464.

Thorndike, Ashley H. *English Comedy.* New York, 1929. (Rpt. New York: Cooper Square, 1965.)

—————. *The Influence of Beaumont and Fletcher on Shakspere.* Worcester, Mass., 1901. (Rpt. New York: Russell & Russell, 1965.)

—————. "Influence of the Court-Masques on the Drama, 1608–15." *PMLA* 15 (1900), 114–20.

—————. "Parentheses in Shakespeare." *ShAB* 9 (1934), 31–7.

—————. *Shakespeare's Theater.* New York, 1916.

—————. *See* Neilson, William A.

Thorne, James P. "The Grammar of Jealousy: A Note on the Character of Leontes." *Edinburgh Studies in English and Scots.* Ed. A. J. Aitken et al. 1971. Pp. 55–65.

Thorne, W[illiam] B. "The Cycle of Sin in Shakespeare's Late Plays." *UCrow* 4 (1982), 86–93.

—————. "'Things Newborn': A Study of the Rebirth Motif in *The Winter's Tale.*" *HAB* 19 (1968), 34–43.

Thorp, Margaret Ferrand. "Shakespeare and the Fine Arts." *PMLA* 46 (1931), 672–93.

Thümmel, Julius. "Ueber Shakespeare's Narren." *SJ* 9 (1874), 87–106.

Tilley, Morris P. *A Dictionary of the Proverbs in England in the Sixteenth and Seventeenth Centuries.* Ann Arbor, 1950.

—————. "Recurrent Types of Confusion in Shakespeare's Clownish Dialogue." *ShAB* 5 (1930), 104–22.

—————. "Some Evidence in Shakespeare of Contemporary Efforts to Refine the Language of the Day." *PMLA* 31 (1916), 65–78.

Tillyard, E[ustace] M. W. "Reality and Fantasy in Elizabethan Literature." *Essays Literary & Educational.* 1962. Pp. 55–70. (First pub. in *Lehrgangsvortraege der Akademie Comburg,* 1956.)

—————. *Shakespeare's Last Plays.* 1962. (1st pub. 1938.)

Tinkler, F. C. "The Winter's Tale." *Scrutiny* 5 (1937), 344–64.

Tobias, Richard C., & Paul G. Zolbrod, eds. *Shakespeare's Late Plays: Essays in Honor of Charles Crow.* Athens, Ohio, 1974.

Tobin, J[ames] J. M. *Shakespeare's Favorite Novel: A Study of* The Golden Asse *as Prime Source.* Lanham, Md., New York, & London, c. 1984.

Tocci, Margaret M. *"The Winter's Tale."* *ShakB* 5 (Mar./Apr. 1987), 9–10.

Törnqvist, Egil. *Between Stage and Screen: Ingmar Bergman Directs.* Amsterdam, 1995.

Toliver, Harold. *Transported Styles in Shakespeare and Milton.* University Park, Pa., 1989.

Tollet, George (1725–79). Contributor to v1778.

Tooke, J[ohn] Horne. *ΕΠΕΑ ΠΤΕΡΟΕΝΤΑ. Or, The Diversions of Purley.* 2nd ed. 2 vols. 1798–1805. (Rpt. Menston: Scolar, 1968. 1st ed. 1786.)

Topsel[l], Edward, & Thomas Muffet. *The History of Four-footed Beasts and Serpents [and] Insects*. 3 vols. continuously paged. 1658. (Rpt. New York: Da Capo, 1967.)

Traub, Valerie. "Jewels, Statues, and Corpses: Containment of Female Erotic Power in Shakespeare's Plays." *ShakS* 20 (1987–8), 215–38.

Traversi, Derek. *An Approach to Shakespeare*. 3rd, rev. & exp. ed. 2 vols. Garden City, N.Y., 1968–9. (1st ed. 1938.)

————. "A Reading of the Pastoral Scene of *The Winter's Tale.*" *The Winter's Tale*. The Laurel Sh. Gen. ed. Francis Fergusson., New York, 1959. Pp. 20–30.

————. *Shakespeare: The Last Phase*. New York, 1955. (1st Eng. ed. 1954. Reissued Stanford Univ. Press, 1965.)

Trewin, J[ohn] C. *Going to Shakespeare*. 1978.

————. *Peter Brook*. 1971.

————. "Raising a Storm." *Illustrated London News*, 21 July 1951, p. 110.

————. *Shakespeare on the English Stage 1900–1964*. 1964.

————. "Town and Country." *Illustrated London News*, 15 Sept. 1951, p. 418.

————. *See* Day, M[uriel] C., and Sprague, Arthur Colby.

Trousdale, Marion. "Style in *The Winter's Tale.*" *CritQ* 18.4 (1976), 25–32.

Turner, Frederick. *Shakespeare and the Nature of Time*. OUP, 1971.

Tyrwhitt, Thomas (1730–86). Contributor to v1773, v1778, v1821.

————. *Observations and Conjectures upon Some Passages of Shakespeare*. Oxford, 1766. (Rpt. New York: AMS, 1974.)

Ulrici, Hermann. *Shakspeare's Dramatic Art*. Tr. from 1st Ger. ed. by A. J. W. M[orrison]. 1846. Tr. from 3rd Ger. ed. by L. Dora Schmitz. 2 vols. 1876. (1st Ger. ed. 1839; 3rd ed. 1868–9.)

Underhill, Arthur. "Law." *Shakespeare's England*. Ed. Sidney Lee & C[harles] T. Onions. 2 vols. OUP, 1916. 1:381–412.

Unwin, George. "Commerce and Coinage." *Shakespeare's England*. Ed. Sidney Lee & C[harles] T. Onions. 2 vols. OUP, 1916. 1:311–45.

Uphaus, Robert W. *Beyond Tragedy*. Lexington, Ky., 1981.

————. "The 'Comic' Mode of *The Winter's Tale.*" *Genre* 3 (1970), 40–54.

Upton, John. *Critical Observations on Shakespeare*. 1746. (2nd ed. 1748. Rpt. New York: AMS, 1973.)

Van Dam, [Bastiaan] A. P., & C. Stoffel. *William Shakespeare, Prosody and Text*. Leyden, 1900.

Van Doren, Mark. *Shakespeare*. 1939. (Rpt. Garden City, N.Y.: Doubleday, 1953.)

Van Laan, Thomas F. *Role-Playing in Shakespeare*. Toronto, 1978.

Van Lennep, William. See *The London Stage 1660–1800*.

Velie, Alan R. *Shakespeare's Repentance Plays: The Search for an Adequate Form*. Rutherford, N.J., 1972.

Velz, John W. *Shakespeare and the Classical Tradition: A Critical Guide to Commentary, 1660–1960*. Minneapolis, 1968.

Venezky, Alice [S.]. "Current Shakespearian Productions in England and France." *SQ* 2 (1951), 335–42.

————. *Pageantry on the Shakespearean Stage*. New York, 1951.

V[erstegan], R[ichard] (i.e., Richard Rowlands). *A Restitution of Decayed Intelligence*. Antwerp, 1605. (Rpt. Ilkley, Yorkshire: Scolar, 1976.)

Vickers, Brian. *The Artistry of Shakespeare's Prose*. 1968.

————. "Shakespeare's Use of Prose." *William Shakespeare: His World, His Work, His Influence.* Ed. John F. Andrews. 3 vols. New York, 1985. 2:389-95.

————. "Shakespeare's Use of Rhetoric." *A New Companion to Shakespeare Studies.* Ed. Kenneth Muir & S[amuel] Schoenbaum. Cambridge, 1971. Pp. 83-98.

Vincent, Charles, ed. *Fifty Shakspere Songs.* Philadelphia, 1906. (Rpt. New York: AMS, 1973.)

Visser, F[redericus] T. *An Historical Syntax of the English Language.* 4 pts. in 3 vols. 3rd impression. Leiden, 1984. (1st ed. 1963-73.)

Viswanathan, S. "Theatricality and Mimesis in *The Winter's Tale*: The Instance of 'taking one by the hand.'" *Shakespeare in India.* Ed. S. Nagarajan & S. Viswanathan OUP, 1987. Pp. 42-52.

Vlasto, Jill. "An Elizabethan Anthology of Rounds." *Musical Quarterly* 40 (1954), 222-34.

Vyvyan, John. *Shakespeare and the Rose of Love.* New York, 1960.

————. *The Shakespearean Ethic.* 1959.

W., C. A. "Shakspeariana." 4 *N&Q* 12 (1873), 363.

Waage, Frederick O. "Be Stone No More: Italian Cinquecento Art and Shakespeare's Last Plays." *Shakespeare: Contemporary Critical Approaches.* Ed. Harry R. Garvin & Michael D. Payne. Lewisburg, Pa., 1980. Pp. 56-87.

Wain, John. *The Living World of Shakespeare: A Playgoer's Guide.* 1964.

Waith, Eugene M. "Shakespeare and the Ceremonies of Romance." *Shakespeare's Craft: Eight Lectures.* Ed. Philip H. Highfill, Jr. Carbondale & Edwardsville, Ill., 1982. Pp. 113-37.

Walker, Alice (1900-). Contributor to ARD2.

Walker, William S. *A Critical Examination of the Text of Shakespeare.* [Ed. William N. Lettsom.] 3 vols. 1860.

————. *Shakespeare's Versification.* Ed. William N. Lettsom. 1854.

Waller, G. F. "Romance and Shakespeare's Philosophy of Time in *The Winter's Tale.*" *Southern Rev.: An Australian Jour. of Literary Studies* 4 (1970), 130-8.

Walpole, Horace. *Historic Doubts on the Life and Reign of King Richard the Third. Works.* 5 vols. 1768. 2:111-220. (Rpt. EP Publishing, 1974.)

Walter, James. *Shakespeare's True Life.* 1890. (2nd ed. 1896.)

Warburton, William (1698-1779). Contributor to THEO1 and to HAN2.

————. *See* Theobald, Lewis.

Ward, Adolphus W. *A History of English Dramatic Literature to the Death of Queen Anne.* 2 vols. 1875. (Rev. ed., 3 vols., 1899.)

Ward, David. "Affection, Intention and Dreams in *The Winter's Tale.*" *MLR* 82 (1987), 545-54.

Ward, John M. "Apropos *The British Broadside Ballad and Its Music.*" *JAMS* 20 (1967), 28-86.

————. "The Lute Books of Trinity College, Dublin II: MS. D.1.21 (the so-called Ballet Lute Book)." *Lute Society Jour.* 10 (1968), 14-32.

————. "The Morris Tune." *JAMS* 39 (1986), 295-331.

————. "Music for *A Handefull of pleasant delites.*" *JAMS* 10 (1957), 151-80.

Warner, Richard. *A Letter to David Garrick, Esq. Concerning a Glossary to . . . Shakespeare.* 1768.

Warren, Clyde T. *See* Clarkson, Paul S.

Warren, Roger. "'Gust' and Poisoned Cups in *The Winter's Tale* and Sonnet 114." *N&Q* 215 (1970), 134-5.

928

————. "Shakespeare at Stratford-upon-Avon, 1986." *SQ* 38 (1987), 82–9.

————. "Shakespeare's Late Plays at Stratford, Ontario." *ShS* 40 (1987), 155–83.

————. *Staging Shakespeare's Late Plays*. Oxford, 1990.

————. "Theory and Practice: Stratford 1976." *ShS* 30 (1977), 169–79.

Warton, Thomas (1728–90). Contributor to JOHN, v1785, MAL.

————, ed. *Poems Upon Several Occasions . . . by John Milton*. 1785.

Watkins, Ronald. *On Producing Shakespeare*. 1950. (Rpt. New York: Blom, 1964.)

Watson, Robert N. *Shakespeare and the Hazards of Ambition*. Cambridge, Mass., 1984.

Watson, Thomas R. "Shakespeare's *Winter's Tale*." *Expl* 40 (1981), 11–13.

Wayne, Valerie. "Refashioning the Shrew." *ShakS* 17 (1985), 159–87.

Wearing, J. P. *The London Stage: 1890–1899*. Metuchen, N. J., 1976; *1900–1909*, 1981; *1910–1919*, 1982; *1920–29*, 1984; *1940–49*, 1991.

Webb, J. Barry. *Shakespeare's Erotic Word Usage*. Hastings, E. Sussex, 1989.

Webster, Margaret. *Shakespeare without Tears*. New York, 1942. (Rev. ed. 1955; rev. as *Shakespeare Today*, 1957.)

Wedgwood, C. V. "The Close of an Epoch." *Shakespeare's World*. Ed. James Sutherland & Joel Hurstfield. New York, 1964. Pp. 174–92.

Wedgwood, H[ensleigh]. "Land-damn [*WT* 755]." 5 *N&Q* 4 (1875), 3.

Weil, Herbert S., Jr. "Shakespeare Festival, Canada 1986." *SQ* 38 (1987), 227–42.

Weinstein, Philip M. "An Interpretation of Pastoral in *The Winter's Tale*." *SQ* 22 (1971), 97–109.

Weinstock, Horst. "Loyal Service in Shakespeare's Mature Plays." *SN* 43 (1971), 446–73.

Weiss, John. *Wit, Humor, and Shakspeare. Twelve Essays*. Boston, 1876.

Wells, Stanley. "Burlesques of Charles Kean's *Winter's Tale*." *TN* 16 (1962), 78–83.

————. "Happy Endings in Shakespeare." *SJH* 102, 1966, pp. 103–23.

————. Perymedes the Blacksmith *and* Pandosto *by Robert Greene: A Critical Edition*. New York & London, 1988.

————. *Shakespeare: A Dramatic Life*. 1994.

————. "Shakespeare and Romance." *Later Shakespeare*. Stratford-upon-Avon Stud. 8. Ed. John Russell Brown & Bernard Harris. 1966. Pp. 48–79.

————. "Shakespeare Performances in England, 1987–8." *ShS* 42 (1990), 129–48.

————. "Shakespeare's Text on the Modern Stage." *SJH* 1967, pp. 175–93.

————, & Gary Taylor. *William Shakespeare: A Textual Companion*. OUP, 1987.

Welsford, Enid. *The Court Masque: A Study in the Relationship Between Poetry & the Revels*. Cambridge, 1927. (Rpt. New York: Russell & Russell, 1962.)

Wendell, Barrett. *William Shakespeare: A Study in Elizabethan Literature*. New York, 1894. (Rpt. New York: AMS, 1971.)

Wentersdorf, Karl. "Shakespearean Chronology and the Metrical Tests." *Shakespeare-Studien: Festschrift für Heinrich Mutschmann*. Ed. Walther Fischer & Karl Wentersdorf. Marburg, 1951. Pp. 161–93.

————. *See* Mutschmann, Heinrich.

Werstine, Paul. Private contributor.

————. "Line Division in Shakespeare's Dramatic Verse: An Editorial Problem." *AEB* 8 (1984), 73–125.

Wexler, Joyce. "A Wife Lost and/or Found." *UCrow* 8 (1988), 106–17.

Whalley, Peter (1722–91). Contributor to v1785, v1793.

————, ed. *The Works of Ben. Jonson*. 7 vols. 1756.

Wheeler, Richard P. "'Since first we were dissevered': Trust and Autonomy in Shake-spearean Tragedy and Romance." *Representing Shakespeare*. Ed. Murray M. Schwartz & Coppélia Kahn. Baltimore, 1980. Pp. 150–169. (Incorporated into "'*Since first we were dissevered*': Trust and Autonomy in Shakespeare's Development," *Shakespeare's Development and the Problem Comedies*, Berkeley, 1981, pp. 154–221.)

Whibley, Charles. "Rogues and Vagabonds." *Shakespeare's England*. Ed. Sidney Lee & C[harles] T. Onions. 2 vols. OUP, 1916. 2:484–510.

Whitaker, Virgil K. *Shakespeare's Use of Learning: An Inquiry into the Growth of his Mind & Art*. San Marino, Calif., 1953.

White, Beatrice. "Claudius and Fortune." *Anglia* 77 (1959), 204–7.

White, Christine. "A Biography of Autolycus." *ShAB* 14 (1939), 158–68.

White, Edward J. *Commentaries on the Law in Shakespeare*. St. Louis, 1911. (2nd ed. 1913.)

White, Richard G. *Shakespeare's Scholar. Being Historical and Critical Studies of his Text . . . with an Examination of Mr. Collier's Folio of 1632*. New York, 1854.

White, R[obert] S. *Shakespeare and the Romance Ending*. Newcastle upon Tyne, 1981. Rev. as "*Let Wonder Seem Familiar": Endings in Shakespeare's Romance Vision*. Atlantic Highlands, N.J., 1985.

White, Thomas Holt (1763–1841). Contributor to v1793.

———. "Remarks on Shakspeare; with Parallel Passages." *Gent. Mag.* 53 (1783), 933–5.

White, Thomas W. *Our English Homer; or, Shakespeare Historically Considered*. 1892.

Whiter, Walter. *A Specimen of a Commentary on Shakspeare*. 1794. (2nd ed. rev. by the author and enl. by Alan Over & Mary Bell, 1967.)

Whiting, Jere B. *Proverbs, Sentences, and Proverbial Phrases From English Writings Mainly Before 1500*. Cambridge, Mass., 1968.

Wickham, Glynne. "Romance and Emblem: A Study in the Dramatic Structure of *The Winter's Tale*." *The Elizabethan Theatre III*. Ed. David Galloway. Hamden, Conn., 1973. Pp. 82–99.

———. "Shakespeare's Investiture Play: The Occasion and the Subject of *The Winter's Tale*." *TLS*, 18 Dec. 1969, p. 1456.

———. "*The Winter's Tale*: A Comedy with Deaths." *Shakespeare's Dramatic Heritage: Collected Studies in Medieval, Tudor, and Shakespearean Drama*. New York, 1969. Pp. 249–65.

Wigston, W[illiam] F. C. *Bacon, Shakespeare, and the Rosicrucians*. 1888.

———. *A New Study of Shakespeare: An Inquiry Into the Connection of the Plays and the Poems, with the Origins of the Classical Drama, and with the Platonic Philosophy, Through the Mysteries*. [1884.]

Wilders, John. "*The Winter's Tale*." *New Prefaces to Shakespeare*. OUP, 1988. Pp. 263–70.

Wiles, David. *Shakespeare's Clown: Actor and Text in the Elizabethan Playhouse*. Cambridge, 1987.

Wilkes, George. *Shakespeare, from an American Point of View; Including an Inquiry as to his Religious Faith, and his Knowledge of Law*. 3rd ed. New York, 1882. (1st ed. London, 1876.)

Willbern, David. "Shakespeare's Nothing." *Representing Shakespeare*. Ed. Murray M. Schwartz & Coppélia Kahn. Baltimore, 1980. Pp. 244–63.

Williams, Frayne. *Mr. Shakespeare of the Globe*. New York, 1941.

Williams, George W. "Exit Pursued by a Quaint Device: The Bear in *The Winter's Tale*." *UCrow* 14 (1995), 1-5.

Williams, Gordon. *A Dictionary of Sexual Language and Imagery in Shakespeare and Stuart Literature*. 3 vols. London & Atlantic Highlands, N.J., 1994.

Williams, John A. *The Natural Work of Art: The Experience of Romance in Shakespeare's* The Winter's Tale. Cambridge, Mass., 1967.

Williamson, Hugh R. *The Day Shakespeare Died*. 1962.

Williamson, Marilyn L. "Doubling, Women's Anger, and Genre." *WS* 9 (1982), 107-19.

———. *The Patriarchy of Shakespeare's Comedies*. Detroit, 1986.

Williamson, Sandra L., & James E. Person, Jr., eds. *Shakespearean Criticism: Excerpts from the Criticism of William Shakespeare's Plays and Poetry, from the First Published Appraisals to Current Evaluations*. 55 vols. Detroit, 1984-2000. 7 (1988): 367-516; 15 (1991): 393-540.

Willis, Susan. *The BBC Shakespeare Plays*. Chapel Hill, 1991.

Willoughby, Edwin E. (1899-1959). Contributor to CAM3.

———. *The Printing of the First Folio of Shakespeare*. OUP for The Bibliographical Society, 1932.

Wilson, Douglas B. "Euripides' *Alcestis* and the Ending of Shakespeare's *The Winter's Tale*." *ISJR* 58 (1984), 345-55.

Wilson, F[rank] P. *Elizabethan and Jacobean*. OUP, 1946. (1st ed. 1945.)

———. "The Jaggards and the First Folio of Shakespeare." *TLS,* 5 Nov. 1925, p. 737.

———. *The Oxford Dictionary of English Proverbs*. 3rd ed. Oxford, 1970.

———. *The Proverbial Wisdom of Shakespeare*. [Cambridge,] 1961.

———. "Ralph Crane, Scrivener to the King's Players." 4 *Library* 7 (1926-7), 194-215.

Wilson, Harold S. "Nature and Art in *Winter's Tale* [1896] ff." *ShAB* 18 (1943), 114-20.

———. "Some Meanings of 'Nature' in Renaissance Literary Theory." *JHI* 2 (1941), 430-48.

Wilson, John. *Cheerfull Ayres or Ballads*. Oxford, 1660.

Wilson, [John] Dover. "The Copy for *The Two Gentlemen of Verona*, 1623." *TGV*. Ed. Sir Arthur Quiller-Couch & John Dover Wilson. Cambridge & New York, 1921. Pp. 77-82.

———. *The Essential Shakespeare: A Biographical Adventure*. 1932. (Rpt. London: Cambridge Univ. Press, 1933, 1937, 1962.)

———. Introduction. *The Winter's Tale*. A Facsimile of the First Folio Text. Boston & New York, 1929.

———. "The Task of Heminge and Condell." *Studies in the First Folio*. OUP, 1924. Pp. 53-77.

Wilson, M. Glen. "Charles Kean's Production of *The Winter's Tale*." *THSt* 5 (1985), 1-15.

Wilson, Thomas. *The Art of Rhetorique*. Ed. Thomas J. Derrick. New York & London, 1982. (1st ed. 1553.)

Wincor, Richard. "Shakespeare's Festival Plays." *SQ* 1 (1950), 219-40.

Winter, William. *Shadows of the Stage*. New York, 1893. (1st ed. New York, 1892.)

Wise, John R. *Shakspere: His Birthplace and its Neighbourhood*. 1861. (Rpt. New York: AMS, 1976.)

Wolff, S. L. *The Greek Romances in Elizabethan Prose Fiction*. New York, 1912. (Rpt. New York: Burt Franklin, 1961.)

Wollenberg, Robert. *Shakespeare: Persönliches aus Welt und Werk. Eine psychologische Studie*. Berlin, 1939.

Wooldridge, H. Ellis, ed. & rev. ed. *Old English Popular Music by William Chappell*. 2 vols. 1893. (Rpt. New York: J. Brussel, c. 1961.)

Wordsworth, Charles. *Shakspeare's Knowledge and Use of the Bible*. 3rd ed. enl. 1880. (Rpt. New York: AMS, 1973. 1st ed. 1864.)

Wright, Ellen F. "'We Are Mock't with Art': Shakespeare's Wintry Tale." *Essays in Literature* (Western Illinois Univ.) 6 (1979), 147-59.

Wright, George T. "Hendiadys and *Hamlet*." *PMLA* 96 (1981), 168-93.

————. "Shakespeare's Poetic Techniques." *William Shakespeare: His World, His Work, His Influence*. Ed. John F. Andrews. 3 vols. New York, 1985. 2:363-87.

Wright, Joseph, ed. *The English Dialect Dictionary*. 6 vols. Oxford, 1898-1905.

Wright, Laurence. "When Does the Tragi-Comic Disruption Start?: *The Winter's Tale* and Leontes' 'Affection.'" *ES* 70 (1989), 225-32.

Wright, Louis B. "Animal Actors on the Elizabethan Stage." *PMLA* 42 (1927), 656-69.

————. "Extraneous Song in Elizabethan Drama after the Advent of Shakespeare." *SP* 24 (1927), 261-74.

X. "Shakspere's Seaboard of Bohemia." *The Nation* 78 (1904), 370-1.

Yardi, M. R. "A Statistical Approach to the Problem of Chronology of Shakespeare's Plays." *Sankhya: The Indian Jour. of Statistics* 7 (1946), 262-8.

Yates, Frances A. *Shakespeare's Last Plays: A New Approach*. 1975.

Young, Bruce. "Ritual as an Instrument of Grace: Parental Blessings in *Richard III, All's Well That Ends Well*, and *The Winter's Tale*." *True Rites and Maimed Rites: Ritual and Anti-Ritual in Shakespeare and his Age*. Ed. Linda Woodbridge & Edward Berry. Urbana, 1992. Pp. 169-200.

Young, David. *The Heart's Forest: A Study of Shakespeare's Pastoral Plays*. New Haven & London, 1972.

Young, George. *An English Prosody on Inductive Lines*. Cambridge, 1928.

Yune, Chung-Un. "'O She's Warm': An Essay on *The Winter's Tale*." *English Language and Literature* (Seoul) No. 48 (1973), 48-65.

Zesmer, David M. *Guide to Shakespeare*. New York, 1976.

Ziegler, Georgianna. "Parents, Daughters, and 'That Rare Italian Master': A New Source for *The Winter's Tale*." *SQ* 36 (1985), 204-12.

INDEX

a, 56-7, 156, 169, 402, 452, 528, 570, 579, 583; a bailiff, 328, 579; a care, 406; a codpiece, 583; a creature, 492; a custom, 338; a far-off guilty, 156; a foolish woman, 256; a good deed, 290; a good nose, 456; a half-moon, 140; a life, 393, 581; a like, 574; a mariner, 260; a mindless, 112; a new ship, 469; a party, 572; a prayer, 561; a reply, 581; a school-boy's top, 156; a so-forth, 571; a very, 280; a waking, 266

Abartis, Caesarea, 45, 75, 273, 308, 391, 532, 724, 739, 767, 791

Abbott, Edwin A., 17, 19, 21, 23, 29-30, 33, 35-6, 38-41, 46-8, 52, 64-5, 71-2, 79, 81-2, 87-8, 93, 95, 97, 99, 101, 104-5, 107, 111-12, 114-19, 121-2, 125-6, 128-31, 133, 135-6, 138, 141, 143, 154-60, 167-9, 175, 177, 179-82, 185, 188, 190, 192, 199, 203-5, 207, 211, 213, 226, 228, 232-3, 235-7, 242, 244-6, 249-50, 252, 254, 256, 266, 268, 270, 280, 289, 293, 296, 299, 301, 304-5, 327, 335, 337, 348, 350, 373-4, 376, 380, 382, 385, 388, 393, 403, 406-9, 412, 415, 417, 419, 424, 431, 433-7, 439-42, 445, 449, 456, 468-71, 473, 475, 479-81, 491, 493, 495-7, 499-500, 504-5, 509, 511, 514, 516-18, 528, 539, 541, 543-4, 551, 561, 563

abide, 327, 579

aboard, 472; aboard the prince, 526

abound in, 158

about, 457

Abraham, 10

Abrams, Richard H., 60, 77, 205, 487, 553

absence, 582; absence that may, 32

abused, 163; abused, and by, 163

Abuses of Players, Act to Restrain, 138, 323-4

accidentals in F1, irregular, doubtful, and emended, 567-9

account, 315

accusation, 225

acknowledge, 416-17

across, 338

acts (=act division), 139, 214-15, 259, 283, 291-2, 295, 302, 309, 318, 476-7, 517, 594, 747-8, 750-2, 824

Adams, F., 420, 573

Adams, Joseph Q., 592, 612, 701, 717, 724

Adams, Robert M., 7, 17, 19, 24, 28-9, 231, 276, 474, 557, 667, 706, 730, 743, 760-1, 769, 794

Adamson, W. D., 45, 738

adders' heads, 394

address, 346

Adelman, Janet, 272, 550

adieu, sir, 455

adjectives, 64, 104, 180, 189, 221, 226, 237, 347, 366, 433, 437, 541; as adverbs, 108; comparative forms of, 62, 419; converted from adverbs, 187, 253; converted from nouns, 71, 185; phrases, transposed, 376; possessives, transposed, 36, 112, 162, 189, 256, 427, 488, 506, 541, 546; superlative forms of, 72; transposed, 348

Adlington, William, 684

admiring, 449, 539

ado, 176

adventure, 39, 209, 425, 498

adverbs, 123, 133, 162, 180, 211, 230, 232, 258, 267, 346, 439, 496, 541, 543; comparative forms of, 98, 327; as compounds, 135; converted from adjectives, 45, 249, 271, 433, 504; converted from nouns, 442, 534, 539; transposed, 79, 117

adultress, 153

advocate, 179, 466

Aeschylus, 752; *Prometheus*, 277

afeard, 423, 427

affairs, 583

affection, 21, 410, 524, 585; affection of nobleness, 513; affects, 416-17

afflict, 545; affliction, 545

afford you cause, 340

affront, 489

after, 382; after that, 437

again in breath, 491

against, 213; against the feast, 391

age, 468; ages, 462, 580

air, 465, 469, 495; aired abroad, 303

Akrigg, G. P. V., 29

Alabama, performances in, 817

A Larum for London, 694

alas, 518

Albright, Evelyn M., 605

Alcinea, 548

only in, 579

onomatopœia, 545

o patience, 540; o peace Paulina, 559; O these, 369

open, 148, 465

opportune to, 431

oppose, 584; oppose against, 483

or, 140, 168, 286, 345, 386, 440, 569, 582; or by, 133; or else, 103; or thou goest, 399

oracle, 238

Oras, Ants, 612-13, 615

ordering, 373; ordering on't, 575

o're, 576; o're-charged, 244; o're-dyed, 70, 570; o're-dyed blacks, 70; ore-shades, 136; oreween, 303; ore-whelm, 578

Oregon, performances in, 817

Orgel, Stephen, 10, 18, 21, 33, 37, 40, 48, 58, 63, 65, 71, 73, 76-8, 86, 89-90, 100, 103, 105, 107, 111, 114-15, 118-20, 122, 127, 129, 132-3, 135, 150, 168, 180, 186, 190-1, 193, 198, 202-5, 207, 209, 213, 226, 229, 246, 258, 271, 279-80, 285, 287, 292, 298-9, 301, 306-7, 321-2, 324, 328, 332, 334, 337, 339, 344, 346-7, 351, 359, 361, 374, 383, 387, 390, 395, 412, 415, 418, 424, 428-9, 432-3, 436, 438-40, 448-50, 457, 459, 471, 473, 481, 485, 498, 504, 509, 511, 557, 562, 607, 725, 729, 784, 858, 863, 867, 871, 873

Orger, John G., 573, 584

Ornstein, Robert, 10, 34, 37, 93, 193, 243, 252, 417, 489, 507, 550, 756, 765

Ortego, Philip D., 244, 734

Ortelius, Abraham, 716

Ortuñez de Calahorra, Diego, 683-4

Orwin, Thomas, 616

Osgood, Charles G., 335

o'th, 351; o'th'cause, 568; o'th' clock, 567

Othello, 4, 8, 10-11, 24, 42, 55, 60, 62, 65, 70, 73, 78, 80, 83, 89-90, 98, 101, 109, 115, 129, 146, 149, 158, 162, 170-1, 183, 224, 231-2, 237, 345, 355, 392-3, 443, 447, 455, 520, 699, 704, 706, 710, 716, 728, 754

Ottocar II, of Bohemia, 262

our, 159, 177, 257, 570, 580; 'our, 444; our ages, 350; our contract celebrated, 503; ours, 169

out, 151, 362, 574; out himself, 490; out of, 68, 491; out of service, 314; outside, 583

over, 354, 454, 572, 580, 583; over-fond, 526; over-kind, 21; over-much, 488

Overbury, Sir Thomas, 146

Overton, Bill, 717, 873

overture, 169

Ovid, 332, 343, 366, 537, 548; *Fasti*, 336, 363; *Heroides*, 8, 342; *Metamorphoses*, 6, 11-12, 267, 342, 363, 365, 383, 396, 419, 523, 553, 694, 696-7

owe, 226

own, 230, 374, 410, 580; owning, 234

Oxford Classical Dictionary, 5, 7

Oxley, B. T., 115, 149, 753

P., W., 522

pace softly, 330

padding, 65

Pafford, J. H. P., 1, 5, 7, 9, 18, 21-3, 29, 32, 36-9, 43, 46, 48, 50-1, 53, 56-8, 62-3, 68, 70, 74, 77, 80, 82-5, 87-90, 92-6, 98, 100-1, 103-5, 107, 109, 114-15, 117-23, 125-6, 128-9, 133-4, 137, 141, 143, 146, 148-50, 152, 157-8, 164-9, 172-5, 180, 183-4, 191, 194, 196, 198-201, 203, 209-11, 213, 216-17, 219-20, 225, 231-2, 236-40, 249, 251, 256, 266, 268-9, 271, 275, 279-82, 284-5, 287-90, 292-4, 296-7, 300-2, 305, 307-8, 311-15, 317-20, 322-3, 325-6, 329, 334, 337-9, 344-5, 348, 355, 357-9, 366-8, 370, 375-9, 381, 383, 385-8, 391, 393-4, 397, 401, 403, 407, 409, 411, 414-15, 418-20, 423-5, 427, 431, 435-6, 439-44, 446-7, 450-1, 453, 455-6, 460-1, 467, 470, 473-4, 480-1, 483-5, 487, 491, 493, 495, 499-500, 503, 505, 511, 514-17, 519, 524, 526-7, 529-31, 535-6, 539, 541, 545, 547, 551, 553, 555, 559, 561, 564, 588, 590, 594, 601, 606, 613-14, 617, 717, 720, 751, 757-8, 764, 770-1, 773, 775, 794, 834, 851-2, 858, 861, 863

pair, 376; paired, 495

Palmer, David J., 873

Palmer, E. J., 564

Palmer's Th., New York, performances in, 823

Panofsky, Erwin, 291-2

pantler, 347

paragon, 498

parasite, 85

parcels, 393

parentheses, 35, 83, 92, 106-7, 114, 129, 154, 168, 170, 193, 225, 299, 304, 385, 435, 483, 485, 542, 563, 603, 753, 756, 758

Pares, Martin, 523

Paris, performances in, 811, 815-16, 853

Parker, Marion D., 159

Parkinson, John, 351, 353, 357

Parrott, Thomas M., 272, 503, 548, 550, 612, 669, 693, 768, 776

Parry, Christopher, 19, 24, 26, 37-8, 44, 51, 55, 59, 66, 71-2, 75, 80-1, 83-4, 86-7, 89-90, 92, 95, 100, 102, 105, 111, 115, 117-18, 120, 125, 129, 142, 144, 149, 152, 158, 160, 165, 169, 172, 178, 181, 187-9, 191, 194, 198, 203-5, 209-10, 215, 217, 221, 230, 246, 248, 251, 255-6, 260, 265, 273, 279, 283, 285, 289, 297, 299, 301, 305, 317, 326, 329, 332, 337, 343, 349, 351, 359, 361, 366-7, 369-70, 375, 378, 383, 385, 391-2, 397, 399, 405, 407, 409, 425, 428, 430, 435, 442, 449, 453, 459-60, 462, 467, 469, 475, 477-8, 480, 485, 489, 491, 494-6, 501, 509, 519, 525-7, 529, 533-5, 537, 540-1, 543, 545, 557-8, 563, 569

Parsons, Natalie, 788

part, 31, 35, 306, 397; part o'th'cause, 185; part performed, 564

963